Passionate Vegetarian

Passionate Vegetarian

by Crescent Dragonwagon

Illustrated by Robbin Gourley

WORKMAN PUBLISHING • NEW YORK

For Ned Shank

February 19, 1956–November 30, 2000

What a feast we had!

Library of Congress Cataloging-in-Publication Data
Dragonwagon, Crescent.
[Passionate Vegetarian]
Passionate Vegetarian.
p. cm.
ISBN 1-56305-711-5 (alk. paper)—ISBN 0-7611-2825-5
1. Vegetarian cookers. 2. Cookery, International. I. Title: Passionate vegetarian. II. Title.
TX837 .D73 2002
641.5'636–dc21 2002072584

Cover and book design by Lisa Hollander with Lori S. Malkin and Sophia Stavropoulos
Cover Photo by Anthony Lowe

Workman books are available at special discounts when purchased in bulk for premiums and sales promotions as well as for fund-raising or educational use. Special editions or book excerpts can also be created to specification.
For details, contact the Special Sales Director at the address below.

Workman Publishing Company, Inc.
708 Broadway
New York, NY 10003-9555
www.workman.com

Printed in the U.S.A.

First printing October 2002
10 9 8 7 6 5 4 3 2 1

Acknowledgments

The "knowledge" in the word "acknowledgment" is evident as I consider how much friends, family members, and colleagues have given this book and me. On every page, in each sentence, recipe and illustration, as well as in navigating the unexpected turns my private life took in the course its writing, I received generous help.

Workman Publishing is the gold standard of the publishing world. Behind every Workman title there really *is* a Peter Workman: singular visionary, genius, and mensch. That a writer can actually call Peter and talk to him is almost unbelievable today; that he actually listens is even more amazing. Thank you, Peter.

Suzanne Rafer edited *Dairy Hollow House Soup & Bread* and *Passionate Vegetarian*. She remains my respected, beloved, and chronically overworked friend: a woman who possesses integrity, vision, kindness, and one hell of a closet. Like Peter, Suzanne is a to-the-bone mensch. Thanks, Suze.

And thanks for choosing irrepressible, smart Jennifer Griffin, to follow the project through to publication. Jen did as good a job of almost driving me around the bend as you did, Suzanne, with equal benefit to the book and just about as good a time had by both of us. Jen, your hard-headedness, clarity, pushing for yet one more rewrite, and willingness to stand and fight when it mattered, are inspirational.

Managing editor Katherine Adzima oversaw the copyediting and proofreading. Without her, there is no way this mega-project, with its ever-tightening deadlines, would have stayed on track. Thanks, Katherine.

Thank you, Lisa Hollander, for bringing your own sensibility and passion to the project, and especially for finding Robbin Gourley's sensual, inviting illustrations. Thanks, too, to supporting designers Sophia Stavropoulos and Lori Malkin, plus Barbara Peragine, Frank Milliron, and Monica McCready, for tireless work.

Workman's publicity and promotion department under the direction of knowledgeable, good-natured, super-competent Jim Eber, is better than ever. Thank you, Jim. I knew I was in good hands from the moment we met. I am grateful not only for your ceaseless work on the book's behalf, but your remembering the human being behind it. I am grateful, too, to your enthusiastic colleague Kate Tyler.

No author could have a better agent than tough-minded, tender-hearted Edite Kroll: funny, deeply caring, feisty, energized, loyal, and so smart. Edite, I am so grateful for our decade-plus partnership. Thank you.

Long may I work with all of you, my esteemed professional collaborators and colleagues.

Thanks of a different order go to recipe-testers Amber Alexander, the late Sylvia Teague, and Robin Gill. Each brought special skills, style, and sensibilities to the kitchen and book. In different phases of *PV,* I see your three sets of competent hands at work. Sylvia, I miss you so much. Robin and Amber, long may you thrive, cook, and live wisely.

Thank you, too, to my "pan-pals," far flung and generous. I am grateful to readers Wendy Newman and Wendy Schatz; my darling friend Wenonah Fay Holl, San Antonio chef Jay McCarthy, New York chef Michael Romano (Union Square Cafe), former Dairy Hollow guest Marilyn Kennedy, Southern cook extraordinaire Ronni Lundy, Thai expert and IACP pal Nancie McDermott, and the ever-inspiring KJ and Clary from Center Street South, all of whom contributed recipes or ideas. Lynn Rosetto Kasper answered questions for me, as did food chemists Shirley Corriher and Harold McGee, Roger Breslin of Real Goods, the staff of the Environmental Working Group, and, locally, Tom Galyen at Hart's, and both the previous and present owners of Ozark Country Market. And God bless Keith Burmylo, of Ermillio's Italian Home Cooking (here in Eureka Springs also) for getting intimate with squeezed roasted garlic at a moment's notice. Thank you.

Thank you, Emily Kaitz and Marilyn Cain, for the lyrics to "Pico de Gallo"; to Joanne Purchany of

West Bend; the Weber Grill team, and Florence Scheffer, of Meyer Corporation, the manufacturers of Circulon pans. Ingredients were supplied by Erich Parker of Asceptic Packaging, American Spoon Foods, Orchards' Harvest Inc. (dried cherries), Frasier Maple Syrup, King Arthur Flour, Phipps Farm, the late chef Gary Hollerman of Indian Harvest, Mary Jo Cheesman of the U.S. Rice Federation, and Mike Davies of Konrikon Rice. Again, thank you.

Thanks also go to those who participated at least once, sometimes many times, in tastings: Sue and Mike Andrews, Jae and Michael Avenoso, Phyllis Becker, Steve Beecham and Gary Egan, Doug Behrends and Sharon Wilcox, Marilyn and Harry Boling, John and Renee Brochu, Jan Brown, Charlisa Cato, Zoe Caywood, David Crough, Stan Dean and Joe Hill, James and the late Susan DeVito, Cynthia and Kirk Dupps, Bill and Irene Douglass, Kathe and Joe Dyer, Chou Chou Yearsley, Susan Francolini, Dee Gabb, Sally Williams-Gorrell, Joe Hammond, Brenda Hammond, Phyllis and Gary Jones, Kyle and Laura Kellams, Barbara Kellogg, David and Roger Pettit, Pat Kriegler and Alice Holt, Hank Krussel, Al and Lynn Larson, Read and Stella Larson, Kathy Lick, Paula Martin, Craig and Patt Milam, John Mitchell and Gwen Bennett, Jason Oury, Lamont and Steve, Pam and Richard Quick, Lisa Reeves, David Reeves, Alexandra Teague, Anthony Sawyer, Ernst and Connie Schrader, Frank Smith, Phyllis Spears, Mary Springer and John Willer, Sharon Spurlin, Ellen Stern, Georgene and Wesley Shank, Susan Storch, Mike and Shelley Sutton, the late Sylvia Teague, Raymond Teague, Leslie Tharp, Edward Thurston III, Chris "Blind Boy" Tompson, Paul Wank, Audrey Zickwolf. If you helped at a tasting and I've left you out of the list, it's probably unintentional (let your conscience tell you if I am kidding or not).

Towards the end of 2000, when I lost my beloved Ned, friends kept me tethered to the earth, and gradually escorted me back to life and this book. I can never thank the following people adequately: Chou Chou; George and Starr; Crow, Cheri White, Debbie Dye, Judi Selle, Sandy Wright, Fred (René) Maese, Bill Worthen, Jane Maas, Susan and Rick Smith, Patti Summerville, Peggy Pott, Ramona MacNeal, Lyn and Al Larson, Suzanne and Scott Tucker, Jane Tucker, J.R., Jack from the Oasis, KJ and Clary, Tori, Kay Kelley Arnold, Grace Gladden, Jim Rule and Anna Cox, David and Helen Jeffrey, Jean Gordon and Walter Clancy, Pam and Richard, David Pettit and Barbara Kellog, Scott and Donna Thompson, Jae and Michael Avenoso, Bill Haymes, Corrinia and Rick Briggs; Lewis Epley, Dave Baker, and the Eureka Springs Rotary; Sharon Parker, Jim Swiggart, Pam Jones, the Ozarks Chorale, Susan Mack, Elizabeth Karmel, and Wayne Petersen.

In a category all his own is Steven Weintz. Thank you, Steven. I appreciate, also, the help of his assistant, Miss Enid Beannie.

I must also mention with deep gratitude William F. Symes.

The love I carry for each of you is individual, particular, tinged with the sharpest sweetness. Your willingness to partake in sorrow, thus solace, overwhelms me. Here, if I have forgotten names, and I feel sure I have, it is simply because I was so out of my mind at the time. Thank you for bringing me back.

Lastly, I thank those who kept the Writers' Colony at Dairy Hollow, Ned's and my last joint dream, alive. The Boards, staff, donors, and writers; the decisive action of many (including my brother, Stephen Zolotow), all combined to assure WCDH's continuance. I am deeply grateful to you brave, generous risktakers. May the vibrancy of the ongoing project itself reward your faith. The poet Wislawa Szymborska describes "the joy of writing" as "revenge of a mortal hand." In cocreating WCDH, I think you helped make possible an institution that transcends personalities, fosters creation, and thus cheats time, and death itself.

I blow a few more late-blooming thank-you kisses in the direction of Connecticut and Vermont. Thank you, Ken Frazier. Thank you, Deborah K.

The support of my mother, Charlotte Zolotow, and her belief in my gift, underlies all that I do and have done, including this book.

Again and forever, thank you, Ned.

Contents

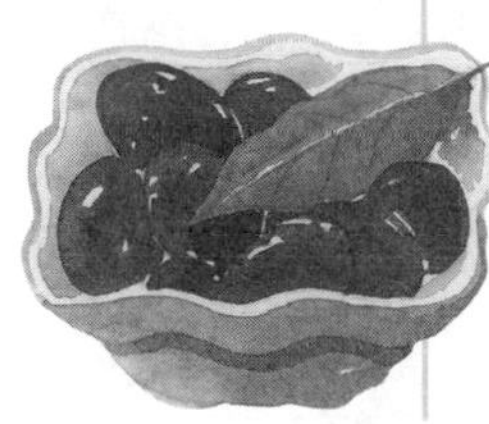

CHAPTER 5

Satisfying Stews

CHAPTER 6

Deep Dish, Savory Cobblers, Gratins & More

CHAPTER 7

Wrapped, Stuffed & Stacked

CHAPTER 8

Great Grains

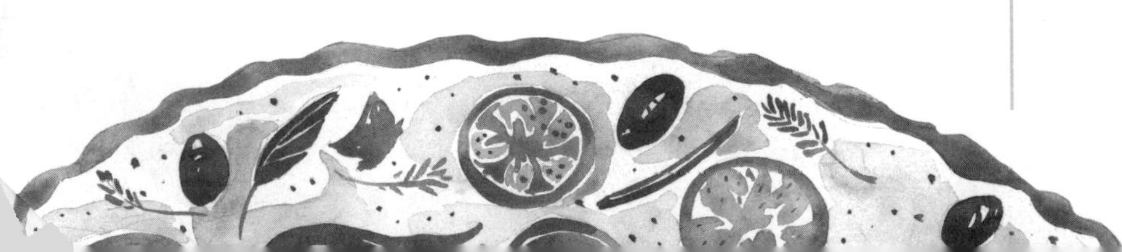

Invitation

There is a feast waiting for you here. Breathe it in.

Even as you cross the porch and approach, the fragrances you inhale as you stand in front of the door welcome you. Even as you raise your hand to knock, you know that here you will be well fed, well loved, well tended, satisfied. You sniff again.

You recognize the scent of something baking (a turnover, a savory mashed potato–topped pot pie, a bubbling casserole, a pizza), something sautéing (onions, mushrooms, carrots), something stewing (a steam of red or white wine, garlic-tinged, a mélange of roux and herbs and stock). And something is grilling, intoxicatingly. (Is it eggplant? Red bell pepper? And in what was it marinated to make its fiery baptism so aromatic?) Some of the fragrances calling you are familiar and comforting: bread just out of the oven, brownies baked earlier in the day. Some are simple, elemental smells—the moist, calming vapor of simmering potatoes; the steam of brown rice, buckwheat, pasta, or polenta. Some aromas are harder to place, but no less captivating. Your senses quiver curiously, in anticipation. Is that . . . chili? Curry? If the latter, is it Indian, Thai, even Jamaican? If Thai, is it a red, green, or yellow curry? Cumin seed, mustard seed, coriander seed are sizzling in oil. Here too are ginger, garlic, peanut oil, sesame—ah, a stir-fry, also sizzling, in a hot, hot wok.

Suddenly, continents shift, and associations. You are inhaling—can it be?—Thanksgiving. The resinous clarity of sage; sweet potatoes baking with brown sugar and butter; simmering cranberries, sharp and sweet. With your nose's intelligence, you can identify and name the cooked-down sweet-fruited harvestlike steam, fall's essence escaping a buttery golden crust: apple pie. And that darkening, deepening cinnamon-clove-nutmeg spiciness: pumpkin pie. And that, the dried fruit, molasses, spice: mincemeat pie, but without the meat.

Welcome to this book, this feast. You have arrived at the right place if you care for sensual, satisfying food. Many of the dishes here are old favorites from countries and cultures the world over. Others, brand new, feature methods of preparation or ingredients perhaps new to you: tofu, tepary beans, tempeh, umeboshi plum paste, kale, collards, cashew butter, broccoli rabe, plantain, arame, seitan, chipotle, tamarind, shiitake and hen-of-the-woods mushrooms. . . .

> *". . . this is food for people who count good eating as one of the important pleasures of life."*

The first thing these recipes share is that they are all sensual and satisfying; the second, all are vegetarian (without meat, fish, or chicken, or products made from them), and some are vegan (free not only of meat, but of eggs and dairy products as well). In most cases, they are more healthful and lower in fat than their mainstream counterparts. Yet this is food for people who count good eating as one of the important pleasures of life.

Must you be a vegetarian to enjoy these foods? Of course not, any more than you have to be Italian to enjoy Italian food.

I assume that if you've found your way to this cookbook, you already eat less meat than perhaps you once did, or no meat at all, or else you wish to move in that direction. Or, you may simply be an adventurous cook and eater, maybe one who has enjoyed recipes from my earlier books, and wants new and delicious sensations. Whatever your point of origin, there is a place set for you at this feast. And because, at a feast, proselytizing is out of place, and I am not an "-ism" type of person anyway, I will not go into great detail on the whys and wherefores of vegetarianism. There are plenty of other books that do, from standpoints that include health, nutrition, environment, and ethics; I've listed some of the best on page 1065 in Thoughtful Vegetarian's Bookshelf.

Enter the Entree

Putting together any meal requires forethought, a well-provisioned kitchen, timing. Much of success comes from balancing: the universal lack of time with convenience, seasonality, budget, the family's varying tastes.

Planning vegetarian meals requires one additional consideration, a rethinking of common assumptions. What makes a main dish main? Why is one collection of dishes known as dinner, and another as breakfast? Do you suffer from the Pork Chop Syndrome? When you think about vegetarian food, do you picture a bland plate with a pile of mashed potatoes, a pile of green beans, and a big blank space where the pork chop belongs?

The Pork Chop Syndrome comes from the outdated idea that meals need a single, focal, main-dish entree, a centerpiece that is usually meat, fowl, or fish. Around it, the other components are organized. Other dishes—starch, a vegetable, maybe a salad—are accompaniments, and get correspondingly less time, money, and thought. They frame the main dish.

The main dishes of such meals are what we might call "centerpiece entrees." If you think about planning meals in this way, vegetarian meal design will naturally flummox you, for although some vegetarian dishes lend themselves to being centerpiece entrees, the majority do not.

One dish that does lend itself to traditional menu planning and is familiar to everyone is the casserole. But a casserole differs from a true centerpiece in that it incorporates what would be side dishes into its substance. Take lasagna: pasta, cheeses, vegetables, sauces, all in one dish. The ingredients are ensemble players, all equally important to the finished dish. Because they combine many components, entrees like casseroles usually have few or no accompaniments; maybe a salad and bread. And anything that combines components in this way can play the role: entree-style soups or stews, some tortes or pies, certain stuffed-vegetable mélanges.

Less well known but very useful for vegetarian menu planning is the component plate. Instead of the meal having a single focus, like a pork chop or a casserole, the meal consists of a number of smaller dishes, usually with one large portion of rice or another starchy grain. Instead of these different elements being precombined, as in a casserole ensemble, the diner picks and chooses, putting together different combinations with each bite. Each of these small dishes is a distinct component of dinner, making an essential contribution to the meal. While rice or another starch is essential, it does not serve as a centerpiece; instead, it's a kind of backdrop for other, more highly flavored, nutritionally dense dishes. Since every bite is different, this is a tremendously interesting, sophisticated way to eat, making possible many interminglings of tastes and textures throughout the meal.

The component plate that will be most familiar to at least some Americans is what, in Indian restaurants, is called the thali, but you may also recognize its counterparts from other parts of the world. True Moroccan couscous, the Greek mezze plate, the Italian antipasti, and the Ethiopian dinner of injeera all fall into this category. Each of these traditional dishes combines a starchy grain with several smaller dishes of vegetables, meats, and condiments. Happily, the component plate can be artfully, deliciously composed of many vegetarian foods of any origin.

Such meals might seem daunting at first, since they are really three, four, or five little dishes rather than one, and most people feel lucky if they steal the time to get one or two reasonably healthful dishes from scratch on the table. But clever stratagems minimize time and complications, and become habitual far more easily than you'd think. For instance, never ever cook a single cup of rice or beans—make a potful; plan on cooking enough vegetables, soup, or casserole to have leftovers. Beans can turn up on salad one day, in a Mexican casserole the next, as the base of a heartwarming soup or stew, and so on. This book is filled with tips for clever, painless ways to simplify meal planning.

I too am a passionate lover of good food. I quit eating meat more than twenty-five years ago, and to me, vegetarian cooking's seeming limitations have always created the opportunity for originality and invention. Deep, dark stews, sauced, styled, and scented as attentively as if they contained beef or lamb, but meatless. Eggplant, cut into fillets, stuffed with spiced chickpea flour, braised in the oven. Roasted carrots transformed into the base for a gingery, garlicky dip. Light, citrus-sparked lemon mousse, as rich on the tongue as forbidden fruit, but without cream or eggs. Abundant, sensual, innovative, generally healthful, good for eater and environment, doors and windows flung wide open to the world—this is the feast that awaits you.

Whys and Hows of This Book

The idea for this book originated years ago with Suzanne Rafer, my beloved editor at Workman Publishing. Suzanne knew what few in the food world did at the time: I was a closet vegetarian, and had been so a good long time. Why closeted? A moment, here, of what the Hollywood folks call "backstory." I have been feeding people, professionally and otherwise but always with joy and enthusiasm, my entire adult life. For eighteen years I owned and ran a country inn and restaurant called Dairy Hollow House with my adored husband, Ned Shank (you'll meet him later in this introduction). It was named after its immediate neighborhood, a bright green valley (in local parlance, a hollow) just outside of the small Ozark Mountain community of Eureka Springs, Arkansas. Dairy Hollow House won praise from publications like *Gourmet, Bon Appétit, The New York Times, Condé Nast Traveler,* and *Southern Living,* and, more important, from the guests Ned and I welcomed to the inn—eleven thousand of them by 1998, when we mailed out our final Moos-Letter. Ned worked brilliantly as the front desk/maitre d'/all-around guy. While he worked his magic up front, I did mine behind the scenes, in the kitchen.

Local foragers showed up at our back door when they had a stash of morels or chanterelles. Local growers knew to call me in the winter, tell me what varieties they were thinking of planting, and ask what else I might like. Guests knew that everything—from the stock in the soup to the sorbets and ice creams—was made from scratch. They also knew that if they were vegetarians, or allergic to green peppers, or diabetic, or lactose-intolerant, they had only to let us know in advance and they would get a meal every bit as glorious as everyone else's.

Because of the inn, the restaurant, and our guests, I continued to *cook* meat, fish, and poultry long, long after I myself last ate any of these. Back in 1979, when we opened, and especially in the South, no serious food person was comfortable confessing such heresy as vegetarianism was then. So, publicly, I kept (uncharacteristically) quiet about it.

Privately, it was another matter. I enthusiastically cooked redolent green curries and plump, stuffed kabocha squashes, chilis of every description. My retinue of rices was not just white and brown, but wild, jasmine, red, forbidden, short, long, arborio—plain, pilau'd, pudding'd, and risotto'd. I once explained to Julia Child, at her request, how I make barbecued tofu. Two of my dishes led to proposals of marriage (never mind that I *was* married). My salads were crisp, green, ever changing. And Suzanne knew that this food was as big, bright, vibrant, varied, abundant, celebratory, and exuberant as the much-praised restaurant cooking I did at Dairy Hollow, if not more so. She knew I refused to see "healthful" and "body-and-soul-satisfyingly delicious" as opposites, and that while fat-conscious, I was not fat phobic. She knew that if I

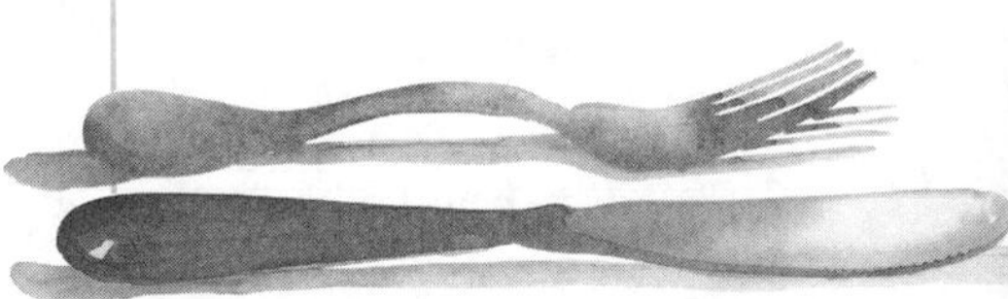

was passionate about food per se, I was a hundred times more so about vegetarian food. And I think she suspected that because I had kept it under wraps for so long, all that pent-up energy would make for an exciting and comprehensive book.

Just how right Suzanne turned out to be has shocked us both. Neither of us had any idea how big this book would be, or that I'd work on it for close to a decade. But to say to a vegetarian who has been a serious working cook for almost thirty years, "Write a vegetarian cookbook," is like saying, "Write *The Joy of Cooking*." I felt a responsibility to bring to the page what I bring to the table: the full spectrum of a deeply satisfying cuisine that explodes the myths of bland-equals-healthful, celebrates less-familiar ingredients (such as soyfoods), and coaxes those who may have sampled them only with reluctance or hesitation, without really understanding their culinary properties and fine points.

I was eager to share not just recipes that really work, but techniques and ingredients as well. These are scattered throughout, in lots of boxes containing extras—lore, fact, nutritional info, details about particular ingredients, anecdotes, "innecdotes," menus. But the book is organized conventionally, by course, from hors d'oeuvres through desserts. Entrees, the biggest question mark for many who are cutting back on meat or eliminating it from their diets, get several chapters, each offering different approaches, and an introduction to meal planning, "Enter the Entree" (page 3), addresses this. Although three chapters deal with entrees per se (Satisfying Stews; Deep Dish: Savory Cobblers, Gratins & More; and Wrapped, Stuffed & Stacked), my style of vegetarian cooking is pretty fluid. You'll find many salads that are entrees in Salads and My Salad Days, many main-dish soups in Soups for Spirit & Sustenance, many appetizers that can easily be scaled up or paired to take center stage in Welcoming Hors d'Oeuvres. And a single choice each from the chapters Great Grains; Vegetable World; and either A Bountiful Bowl of Beans, Celebrating Soyfoods, or Savory Cakes, Burgers & Patties combines to make countless fabulous, ever-changing dinners of the style I call "component." Component meals are meals consisting of many small dishes. And, since many of us are time-pressed and view meatless cooking as time-consuming, I also offer many streamlined options; thus, "Cook Once for Several Meals" tips appear after many recipes, and there's a whole chapter devoted to Quick Fix.

Component meals are meals consisting of many small dishes.

In short, every chapter except those on sauces and desserts has plenty of main-course ideas. No one will go hungry or want for satisfaction here. Regardless of category, this is truly swoon-worthy, knock-your-socks-off, delicious food. Regardless of how much or little meat you eat, I hope you will find dishes here that you'll return to time and again.

Food at its best serves three purposes: to nourish our bodies, give sensual pleasure, and serve as a benign medium of contact—both with our fellow human beings and with the larger world. To me, good vegetarian cooking does all three perfectly. Deeply pleasurable, it celebrates the senses, the seasons, our connections to each other, and our short, uncertain, bittersweet time on this lovely green-gold-and-blue globe on which we spin. The best food erases the line between worldly and spiritual. It is both down-to-earth and transcendental. It is delicious and sensual, sacramental and elemental.

So, again, I invite you to my cooking.

And I invite you to my life, for it is inseparable from my cooking. Cooking and eating are among the most important ways we weave days into lives, celebrating joys and grieving sorrows, consoling, healing, and moving ahead with energy despite the unlooked-for transitions sometimes forced on us. To hunger is to be alive, and to hope.

So, break bread with me. Let me offer you a portion of stew, a tangle of green, garlicky salad, a slice of pie, as we sit together at table, hungering for peace, plenty, meaning, love, hope, and yes, very, very good food.

The Bowl He Brought the Salad In

I met my late, much-loved husband, to whom this book is dedicated, over an apple crisp. This was at a potluck dinner in Little Rock, Arkansas, in 1977. The apple crisp had just come out of the oven; it was still steaming as I, in kitchen mitts, set it down on the table of my friend Starr Mitchell. I looked up and straight into the large blue eyes of Ned Shank, with whom I would share the next twenty-three years. It was about as close to a *Some Enchanted Evening* moment as two people get in this life. But it was earthier: The aromas of cinnamon, apples, buttery oatmeal, and brown sugar made corporeal the immediate connection between us.

Ned was tall and bearded, handsome, intelligent, funny. He'd brought salad in a blue-and-gray pottery bowl. It turned out he'd made the bowl: Ridged rings, still visible and tactile, climbed its side, left by his long, confident fingers, which had coaxed the once-pliable clay up and out as his long legs kicked and turned the pottery wheel. When he later showed me boxes of tureens, plates, vases, and candlesticks he'd made in high school and college, he announced cheerily, "My dowry."

Throwing pottery was one of Ned's countless side-talents. A historic preservationist, he played banjo, fiddle, and harmonica. He was a killer Scrabble player. (We kept a lifetime score, and overall he beat me exactly half the time.) His side-talents were also practical: He'd put himself through college working at a moving company, and viewed packing as an art. He once packed and mailed an antique tea set of paper-thin bone china encrusted with dragons from a hotel room in Portland, Oregon, to Eureka Springs, Arkansas. It arrived without a single broken teacup.

Ned could fix almost anything out of anything—he once made a very elegant light fixture for my mother from a tuna can spray-painted black. He greatly enjoyed washing dishes if left alone ("It's like meditation"). He casually sketched and cartooned all his life, but in his last year started going to life-drawing sessions. There, he finally unleashed his full natural gift: Seemingly driven, he created close to five hundred drawings in the time that turned out to be left to him. His first children's book, *The Sanyasin's First Day,* was published that same last year.

Throughout our marriage, we ate together. Restaurant meals—Thai, Chinese, Indian, Korean, Italian, contemporary American—some at our favorites: breakfast at the Capitol Hotel in Little Rock; lunch at Union Square Cafe in New York; dinner at Restaurant Nora in D.C.; brunch at Café Flora in Seattle; Monday-night chalupas and almost anything the rest of the week at our beloved local Center Street South (where the vegetarian enchilada on the menu is still described as filled with "a Nedley of mixed fresh vegetables"). We once had lunch at a fly-in resort in Alaska—two hours in a four-seat plane with runners instead of wheels, landing on a frozen lake—where we went to teach at the Alaska Bed and Breakfast Association. There was our first-anniversary dinner, at Jacques Cagna, in Paris, about which more later. There were South Indian lunches in Kerala, eaten side by side on the floor, squares of banana leaf in front of us piled high with fat, red-veined kernels of rice surrounded by spoonfuls of half a dozen curries, condiments, sauces, crisp circles of okra. There was the dinner at the hotel restaurant in Mobile, Alabama, when the waiter (boiled-lobster red with sunburn and wearing a white jacket so crisply, painfully starched it crackled audibly when he walked across the dining room) attempted to flambé some strawberries and set the tablecloth on fire.

In addition to dining out, there were adventures in our own restaurant: the many dinners we served others during our inn years. We aided and abetted many proposals of marriage, gave out certain recipes hundreds of times (among them our cornbread, page 451; Roasty-Toasty Potatoes, Carrots, and Onions, page 790; Chocolate Bread Pudding Maurice, page 1059; Iced Herbal Cooler, page 380; Honeyed Browned-Butter Pecan Pie, page 1023; and Ginger Sorbet, page 1045). We served Hillary and Bill Clinton, Betty Friedan, Andy Williams; hosted countless weddings, anniversaries, and birthday parties. After a fiftieth birthday party for a Fayetteville neurosurgeon, the birthday guy (he and his wife were regular guests) clasped my hand and said, "Bonnie and I have traveled all over the world. But the happiest occasions of my whole life have been *right here*."

Our shared history as innkeepers, of being part of so many peoples' lives intimately if evanescently, is bittersweet now, being so wholly vanished. I recall dozens of entertaining inn-incidents. But I do so without my conspirator, to whom I needed only say, "Do you remember when the Bolings were checking out, and Maurice got that sorbet, and . . . ?" for both of us to dissolve in gales of laughter.

At Table

Besides these adventures were the breakfasts, lunches, and dinners Ned and I shared at home. At a potluck following that first one where we met, Ned left the blue-and-gray pottery bowl behind. We'd dated once by that point. A day later, I showed up at his apartment, ostensibly to return the bowl. He invited me in, then invited me to live with him. Being the hard-to-get type, I said no for five days. Then I moved in. A month later he asked me to marry him. I said, "Can I think about it?" He said, "No, you have to tell me now." I said yes. It was one of countless yesses that gave color to our whole marriage.

By the time we met, I had tapered from eating red meat (and plenty of it) to just eating chicken and fish, to just seafood occasionally, to finally eating only foods of plant origin, supplemented with dairy products and occasional eggs. He'd just finished reading Frances Moore Lappé's *Diet for a Small Planet* and was moving in the same direction. It was not a huge conversion experience for us, nor did we ever spend a lot of time talking about it—we'd just found, individually, that we felt better not eating flesh, that we shared environmental and social beliefs relating to food, plus we both loved the tastes and freshness our ever-developing plant-centered diet offered us.

Eating was never utilitarian to us. Rather, eating well—not just healthfully but satisfyingly, sensually, and socially—was a consistent, constantly changing daily pleasure. Our shared dinners at home, and the time we willingly gave them, were also one expression of deep partnership. Sometimes we shared the overall experience: not just the first bite of the apple pie made from the first Arkansas apples of the season, but having driven to the farmer's market in Berryville on the first fall morning cold enough to wear sweaters. Ned sitting on the kitchen step-stool reading aloud to me as I peeled and sliced the fruit, then mixed and rolled the crust he would later scrape remnants of from the bread board as he brought the kitchen back to order again. Meals nourished us and celebrated our connection, not just to each other but to the cycles of life themselves.

All these Ned-and-Crescent meals were vegetarian, for we "were" vegetarian. But we always chafed a little at this identity. This was the way we ate, not what or who we were. That what we ate was less expensive, often less caloric, usually more healthful than we could have gotten eating out was incidental. Our way of eating, the way of eating you'll find here, was not based on deprivation. It was alive, nourishing, singing with flavor; lusty, full-flavored, often exotic—though sometimes it was simple, stripped-down, and comforting, too. Like our marriage, the way we ate was a daily yes—a hundred thousand small daily yesses.

One day Ned went out on his customary and reveled-in three-times-a-week bicycle ride. It turned out not to be to the Conoco station out by the lake—the one where they rent canoes, which he had nicknamed "Canoe-Co." It turned out to be into eternity.

I am still here in noneternity: the world of seasons, of ripening fruit, of bills to be paid, of the cat (does she remember him?) who still wants to go out when she's in and in when she's out, of warm flannel sheets, some of which are newly purchased, and on some of which I slept with him. In the summer—there's been one without him—I still make the iced herbal cooler of which we must have drunk ponds-worth over the years. In the winter—there have been two since he's been gone—I still make hot chocolate, sometimes with dairy milk, sometimes with soy.

What Remains

I am still here, but I am different. For months after Ned's death I barely ate. (How could I taste, let alone digest, when my sweet partner had suddenly, absolutely vanished from the earth, could never close his eyes in ecstasy at something so simple as a perfect baked red yam or a plate of pancakes?) But eventually, I began to eat again, and sometimes take a little pleasure in it. Of course, this marked my slow, reluctant return to life, a life utterly not what I had planned. To eat, despite this, also became a series of yesses. Yes to the work of learning to live almost despite myself, even when faced with irreconcilable loss. Yes to food that nourishes and delights body and soul, honors the fragile planet from which it comes and on which we all dwell, some in peace and plenty, some in discord and hunger. Yes to life on its own inherently high-risk terms, which offers no guarantees.

What we eat is part of the way we are rooted to our very temporary home in the world. Eating well honors life. For me it means honoring Ned and the feast we had together, too.

What I am left with is who I am because of loving, knowing, and losing Ned, who is simultaneously that beautiful twenty-one-year-old boy I fell in love with, and the beautiful forty-four-year-old man with whom the last words I exchanged were "I love you" just before noon on the unseasonably warm late-November day in 2000. What I am left with is the countless adventures we shared together, some of which, in the course of this book, you will also share. What I am left with are two entities we created together, the one recalled, the other (in altered form) going strong.

The first is Dairy Hollow House, our inn. The second, in the site and buildings the inn once occupied, is the Writers' Colony at Dairy Hollow, a nonprofit that offers uninterrupted residency for writers and composers. Meals are also served to the resident writers (yes, they feast on some of the dishes in this book, although the Colony, like the inn, is not vegetar-

ian). The Colony also offers many community-service and educational events, some involving food—like the once-a-month potluck dinner, literary salon, and reading called "Poetluck." Though Ned, its first executive director, is gone, the Colony still flourishes under the guidance of an energetic board and now–executive director Sandy Wright, a friend of ours who served on the board and stepped up to take the position after Ned's death.

I flourish, too—sometimes. Missing does not end, as anyone

who has grieved will tell you. But I have glimpses. I write these words a year and a half after Ned's death. Just as eating well seems to me to honor both Ned and life itself, so does loving. I am . . . dating (horrible word, but fascinating experiences, though not ones I imagined I'd ever revisit). The adventures and meetings continue—none over apple crisps and bowls of potluck salads, but some sweet and all interesting.

But all this is another story. You will just have to wait for it, as I will.

The pottery bowl Ned brought the salad in continues to see service. It's been filled with green salads, spicy bean stews, marinated grain mixtures. It's been heated, lined with blue cotton napkins to hold home-baked rolls or wedges of cornbread. It's contained fresh whole strawberries on the stem, surrounded by smaller bowls of sour cream or tofu crème and brown sugar, for dipping. It's traveled to many potlucks and somehow remained unbroken. That bowl seems to me radiant: It seems to me that it contains not just food and personal history, but the non-negotiable fact that one lover outlasts another, that objects outlast those who make and use them, and that love itself goes on, despite its fragility and our knowledge of this. That bowl is patina'd with meaning. And those rings, left by his long, now-vanished fingers.

I mentioned our first anniversary dinner at Jacques Cagna, in Paris. We were just getting over jet-lag; every street light, as well as the huge circular window of Notre Dame, seemed haloed in a nimbus of light. In memory, the restaurant was warm, its interior a softened rose pink, in an ancient building whose old timbers were still visible. I wore pants and a tunic of burgundy jacquard silk, its color echoed by the kir royales we were drinking. Ned was in a suit. How handsome he was; how young we both were. Everything we laid eyes on seemed flushed, tumescent; every breath a sigh of pleasure. We were surrounded by puffs of delicious aromas as lids were whisked off still-steaming dishes by practiced waiters with the flourish of magicians.

We'd written in advance asking if a vegetarian meal might be prepared for us, and it was, perfectly. Peppery watercress soup. A platter of various vegetable preparations. A timbale. A poached peach blushed with red, trapped in a cage of spun caramel. And then there was the cheese cart.

It was rolled ceremoniously to our table between the salad and dessert courses, by two elegant waiters. The cart, which squeaked slightly, had three shelves. And it was covered with cheeses. Oozing cheeses, firm cheeses, cheeses set on straw, on leaves, on footed platters, blue-veined cheeses, pale creamy cheeses and cheeses of a deeper yellow, cheeses dipped in ash, in grape seed . . . an infinity, a universe, a galaxy of gorgeous French cheeses, all offered to us.

Ned and I later came to view the cheese cart as indicative of a larger truth. It became a story we told together, many times, something like this:

Crescent: So they rolled the cart over. . . .

Ned: But we had just had this incredible three- or four-course meal, and we knew dessert was still coming. . . .

Crescent: And we were so full. So we said no.

Ned: We said no! To the cheese cart! Our one first-anniversary dinner, at Jacques Cagna!

Crescent: The waiters looked at each other. . . .

Ned: . . . with this complete, classic French-waiterly disgust . . .

Crescent: And they more or less turned on their heels and walked away, wheeling the cart.

Ned: It was, "Pah! Zhese vulgar Americains! 'Orrible!"

Crescent: We were full. But we should have said yes anyway.

Ned: Yes. . . . And, you know . . . *(dramatic pause; Ned knew how to tell a story)* that's the only regret of our married life: We should have said "Yes" to the cheese cart.

Present and Future

I began this book in 1994. Ned was very much alive, and his presence pulses still on almost every one of its pages. After some soul-searching, I decided to leave Ned in, in present tense. I loved our life together, and *Passionate Vegetarian* documents bits and pieces of its daily sweetness. Here, life as we lived it remains.

I don't know exactly what prompted me to tell Ned in advance that I planned to dedicate this book to him, long before it came out, instead of just surprise him with the published version, which is the way I've typically dedicated books. But we'd been through some hard times two years earlier that people with any sense might have split up over. Fortunately, we were hard-headed, and possessed something bigger than sense. We came through our difficulties into luminous renewal: a hard-won knowledge that while no life is exempt from pain, we could choose meaning, and joy, and deep connection. That love and life were precarious and without guarantee was shimmeringly clear to both of us by then, and made all the more precious because of this. In that phase I told him; in that phase he thanked me; in that phase we exchanged a glance that contained the entire conversation of our shared time, as many of our glances did by then. Sitting at our old battered maple dining room table, sun streaming in behind us, we both knew we were affirming something larger than gift and receipt.

Ned, wherever you are—this is for you.

My shared story of life with Ned on this earth came to an end neither of us wanted. My story continues into the unknown future. Meals yet to be eaten, countries yet to be visited, unimaginable joys and sorrows. And, in hope and faith, despite grief, perhaps at some point the unforeseen sharing of my life with someone Ned never knew.

Dear readers, fellow sojourners in life, love, and food in a world we inhabit together, I invite you to join me in what has turned out to, in part, commemorate the man who was the great love of the first part of my life. I hope that this book's recipes will please and nourish you, its stories entertain, its information be useful.

May you cook from it and celebrate every bite, every ingredient, and everyone who grew or made every ingredient. May you grow strong and healthy. May you be fortunate enough to break bread with those you love fully, with nothing held back. And may you, when you break bread in solitude, be resilient and self-loving, again with nothing held back.

And may you always, always say "Yes" to the cheese cart.

CHAPTER 2

Welcoming Hors d'Oeuvres

Starters *start.* Like a good inn's front desk or the wafting smell of something delicious as you stand on the lit front porch of a home to which you've been invited to dinner, they're the salutation. They attract, announce, tease just a little, beckon, intimating pleasures to come. Not strictly necessary, they signal conviviality, festivity, express the cook's wish to welcome, and perhaps astonish a little . . . to leave behind the stressful world that lies beyond the hosts' door. In the vegetarian palette, many classic hot starters are both international and easily upgraded to entree status. Boost up the spanakopita portion, or make the stuffed mushroom a portobello instead of a button, and the dish moves from the outskirts of the meal to center plate. The exceptions: many good old intensely cheesy or oil- or butter- or egg-rich starters, most of which have departed altogether.

Here are mostly simple, homey starters, recipes that wouldn't serve as entrees, though they might turn up as part of a component dinner (see page 3). Don't suppose, though, that simple and homey means dull; you'll find some true dazzlers. I call your attention to Oven-Roasted Shiitake Mushrooms with Garlic and Coarse Salt (page 48), a sublime, succulent dish, almost embarrassingly easy to make, and a personal favorite. It is the first hors d'oeuvre that comes to mind when planning almost any menu, a frequent visitor to my component-plate entrees, and something I will make forever.

You'll also find versatile cold hors d'oeuvres, many appropriate for casual entertaining. We'll start with ever-adaptable spreads, dips, pâtés, and "slathers," to use Sheila Lukins's felicitous verb-to-noun descriptor. Many here are considerably lighter and more intriguing than their classic kin, based on vegetable or legume purees instead of eggs, mayo, sour cream, or cream cheese. Fat content in most has been considerably reduced, down to just enough to give finished dishes body and soul. Interesting techniques and spicings intensify flavors so the fat goes unmissed.

But what would a slather be without something of contrasting texture on which *to* slather? Hence, a basket full of crisps and toasts and the like. Most of the made-from-scratch breads and crackers, you'll find in the grains chapter. Here are more quick fixes, like various ways to dress up ready-made tortillas and other simple breads. Canapés and bruschetta crisps that the host has already spread for the guest shine here. Later in the chapter you'll come across crisps of another kind—crudités, a gardenful of fresh, mostly raw vegetables made for dipping. Even if you've made crudités forever, expect some new ideas. You'll also find what wasDairy Hollow House's famous Relish Tray Redefined. It is the American version of those great Italian and Middle Eastern starter platters, antipasti and mezze, which are also here. Any are perfect for great, showy, welcoming abundance with little or no last-minute fuss.

Cheese? It's present, but it is no longer the first thought I have for hors d'oeuvres. The old standbys—brie wrapped in nut-studded puff pastry, and artichoke dip laden with Parmesan, mayonnaise, and olive oil—are gone. Just as many savvy nonvegetarians have moved high-fat meat from the center of the entree to, most of the time, a supporting ingredient, so too do in-the-know ovo-lacto vegetarians use cheese, judiciously, in small amounts. Instead of cheese-plus-pie-crust-plus-cream (as in the quiches of yesteryear), you'll find starters like Fresh Figs with Garlic-Feta Cream (page 38), a sweet-plus-savory beginning where the more densely calorie ingredients pair with fresh fruit.

Starter or Entree?

Vegetarian cooking and eating is fluid when it comes to assigning particular dishes to particular courses (see page 3 on menu planning for further explication). For events where you need lots of substantial starters, such as a stand-up buffet or cocktail party for a number of people, browse this whole book, not just this chapter. Consider miniaturized versions of the many stuffed vegetables in the entree sections, for instance. Consider the marinated vegetable, fruit, and/or grain salads. Look at the stacked casseroles; many of them, baked, cooled to room temperature, then cut into tiny pieces, make fine first courses. Small versions of the dumplings or turnovers or crêpes are also well received. Most of these are substantive enough, though, that you should plan on having small plates and forks available, not just napkins.

Dips, Slathers, & Spreads

Dips, slathers, and spreads are unfussy, informal, and put guests at ease by giving them an activity—reaching out, dipping, applying substance to substance—as they begin to relax and converse. A large platter of crisp vegetables in the middle of the table is not only a communal offering but enticingly decorative. Add a large basket of crisp toasts, a vessel or two or three of a savory spread, pâté, or dip, and you may not need a centerpiece. Such starters offer choice and variety, a range of sensations: Will you spread this pâté on a moistly crisp, pungent radish, a succulent cherry tomato, or a dry, enjoyably crunchy toast? Since starters like this are made in advance and served cold, they are cook-friendly. And the exuberance of the display communicates generosity, saying, "Relax, there's plenty. We're not stingy around here. Pull up a chair. Help yourself. Lots more where that came from."

Morocc'n'roll Oven-Roasted Carrot Spread

I first discovered the surprising goodness of carrots with cumin in a simple, delicious grated salad served at a Moroccan-themed party back in the Dairy Hollow House years, when assorted friends got together each Christmas Eve to celebrate and feast on a different nationality's cuisine, each of us preparing a dish from the chosen country, working out of whatever cookbooks sounded authoritative.

If you're thinking, "Yuck—pureed carrots—baby food," let me just say, "No way." This is a voluptuous but not overly rich spread, with an intense, haunting flavor. You can prepare it up to three days in advance, refrigerate, and bring to room temperature before serving with any cracker, crisp, or crudité. **SERVES 4 TO 6**

VARIATION

MOROCC'N'ROLL OVEN-ROASTED CARROT DIP: ***Turn this spread into a dip by adding ½ to 1 cup liquid: ¼ cup carrot juice and ¼ cup olive oil is ideal, with additional juice or oil as needed. Or, for a tangier, less perfumed, pale-colored version—a bit more conventional but very good—use yogurt or reduced-fat sour cream for the liquid.***

Oil or cooking spray
1 pound (about 6 medium) carrots, unpeeled, stem end left on
1 large red onion, unpeeled, quartered
1 head garlic, unpeeled, cut in half crosswise
2 tablespoons olive oil
1 tablespoon tamari or shoyu soy sauce, plus more to taste
2 teaspoons ground cumin
2 teaspoons paprika
Pinch of cayenne
1 to 4 tablespoons commercial or homemade vegetable stock (see page 139), water, carrot juice, or additional olive oil
Salt and freshly ground black pepper to taste

1 Preheat the oven to 375°F.

2 Oil or spray with cooking spray a baking dish large enough to accommodate all of the vegetables in a single layer.

3 Bring a large pot of water to a boil. Drop the carrots into the boiling water and blanch for 4 minutes for long, skinny carrots; 5 to 6 minutes for fatter ones. Drain well.

4 Place the carrots in the prepared baking dish along with the onion and garlic. Toss the vegetables with 1 tablespoon of the oil, rubbing the oil into the vegetables a bit. Drizzle with the tamari and toss again. Arrange so they're cut-side down.

5 Bake until the carrots are soft—you should be able to pierce them easily with a fork at their thickest point—and quite brown here and there, especially on the edge that has touched the dish. This will take about 40 minutes, longer if the carrots are plump. Let cool.

6 Cut the stem ends from the carrots and remove the papery skin from the onion. Place the carrots and onion in a food processor. Squeeze the garlic cloves out of their skins directly into the food processor, discarding any that are either still hard or deep brown. Add the cumin, paprika, and cayenne, along with the remaining tablespoon of oil, and pulse. (The mixture will still be a little dry and chunky.) Add the stock (or other liquid) a tablespoon at a time. Pulse until smooth; then season to taste with additional tamari, salt, and black pepper.

7 Let the spread mellow, covered and refrigerated, overnight or up to 3 days, so the flavors can blend. Take it out of the refrigerator at least 1 hour before serving to bring to room temperature. Then scoop into a ramekin or serving dish, smoothing the top. Serve with crackers, crudités, or pita chips.

COOK ONCE FOR 2 MEALS The roasting method for carrots described here is essentially that used in Roasty-Toasty Potatoes, Carrots, and Onions (page 790), one of my personal favorites and one of the inn's all-time most popular side dishes. So, the smart money says double the roasted carrot component of this recipe. Serve half the carrots straight from the oven, as part of tonight's dinner. Reserve the rest for this fabulous spread, which can be served tomorrow or the day after.

Roasted Carrot Spread with Fresh Ginger and Curry

The triple blast of heat in this Asian-inspired version of the previous recipe gives it knockout appeal. Fresh ginger, cayenne, and curry roll over the tongue in successive waves of warmth and wide-awake flavor. My old friend Jan Brown was in the kitchen with me the first time I made this. She took a spoonful straight from the food processor, closed her eyes, gave a long, slow, soulful *"Mmmmmmm,"* then opened her eyes wide and began capering around the kitchen: A glee dance known to those who aren't afraid of expressing the goofy joy of recognizing when something—even as small on the scale of life as a spread—is just as right as can be.

Try serving this with some Asian-scented crisps or crackers such as the tamari-glazed rice crackers available in most natural foods stores. For crudités, use snow peas, red pepper strips, and jícama. **SERVES 6**

VARIATION

TRIPLE-BLAST GINGERY ROASTED CARROT DIP: ***See variation notes on the Morocc'n'Roll Oven-Roasted Carrot Spread (page 13). Substitute tomato or orange juice for the carrot juice when thinning.***

- 1 pound (about 6 medium) carrots, unpeeled, stem end left on
- 1 large red onion, unpeeled, quartered
- 1 head garlic, unpeeled, cut in half crosswise
- 2 tablespoons mild vegetable oil, such as corn, peanut, or canola
- 1 tablespoon tamari or shoyu soy sauce, plus more to taste
- 2 tablespoons finely minced peeled ginger
- 2 teaspoons Dairy Hollow House Curry Spice Blend (page 901) or a good commercially made curry powder
- 2 tablespoons honey
- 1 tablespoon toasted sesame oil
- Pinch of cayenne
- 1 to 4 tablespoons commercial or homemade vegetable stock (see page 139) or water
- Salt and freshly ground black pepper to taste
- Minced cilantro (optional)

1. Preheat the oven to 375°F.

2. Oil or spray with cooking spray a baking dish large enough to accommodate all the vegetables in a single layer.

3. Bring a large pot of water to a boil. Drop the carrots into the boiling water and blanch for 4 minutes for long, skinny carrots; 5 to 6 minutes for fatter ones. Drain well.

4 Place the carrots in the prepared baking dish along with the onion and garlic. Toss the vegetables with 1 tablespoon of the oil, rubbing the oil into the vegetables a bit. Drizzle with tamari and toss again. Arrange so they're cut side down.

5 Bake until the carrots are soft—you should be able to pierce them easily with a fork at their thickest point—and quite brown here and there, especially on the edge that has touched the dish. This will take about 40 minutes, longer if the carrots are plump. Let cool.

Ginger

6 As the carrots bake, prepare the spice sauté: Heat the remaining tablespoon of oil over medium heat. Add the ginger and sauté for 2 minutes, then add the curry powder and sauté, stirring constantly, for another 30 seconds. Remove from the heat.

7 When the carrots have finished baking, cut off the stem ends and remove the papery skin from the onion. Place the carrots and onion in a food processor. Squeeze the garlic cloves out of the skins directly into the food processor, discarding any that are either still hard or deep brown. Add the sautéed ginger-curry mixture, along with the honey, sesame oil, and cayenne. Stir in additional tamari to taste. Pulse. The mixture will be a little dry and chunky, so begin adding the liquid, 1 tablespoon at a time. Pulse until smooth and season to taste with salt and black pepper as well as additional soy sauce, if needed.

8 Let the spread mellow, covered and refrigerated, overnight, so the flavors can blend. Remove from the refrigerator at least 1 hour before serving to bring to room temperature. Then scoop into a ramekin or serving dish, smoothing the top. If desired, garnish with minced cilantro. Serve with crackers, crudités, or pita chips.

COOK ONCE FOR 2 MEALS The roasting method for carrots described here is essentially that used in Roasty-Toasty Potatoes, Carrots, and Onions (page 790), an excellent side dish, while the spread itself makes a wonderful soup base that freezes quite well. Thus, this recipe gives you the potential for three great dishes if you triple the roasted carrots. Serve one-third of the roasted carrots straight from the oven as tonight's vegetable. Use the rest of the carrots for a double recipe of this spread, which can be served with crackers and crudités, tomorrow or the day after. Any left over can be used for soup.

To make an outstandingly good Gingered Curry of Carrot and Lentil Soup (the from-scratch version is on page 151), combine one batch of the spread with 4 to 5 cups cooked lentils and enough vegetable stock to make it soupy. Serve with a dab of yogurt, Yogurt Sour Cream (page 910), or Tofu Sour Cream (page 909) and a sprig of cilantro. Accompany with either toasted chapatis for dipping or a scoop of cooked brown basmati rice in the bottom of each bowl.

Spread It Around

For a chunky spread that is just too good to miss, please see the recipe for G'vetch (page 749), a braised Russian-style vegetable stew. It is very thick, can be made ahead, and, when served at room temperature, is quite wonderful piled on a cracker or crisp toast.

Voluptuous Roasted Red Pepper Spread

Invented one October to use the last batch of red and yellow peppers left after an early frost, this late-summer favorite speaks of abundance. Its romantic soft peachy-salmon color, silken texture, and full flavor work well on The Relish Tray Redefined (page 53), Antipasto Platter (page 56), or Middle Eastern Platter (page 59). Serve with crudités, crackers, and/or Parchment Cracker-Bread (page 31), especially the cracked pepper variety.

Where dips are concerned, I'm a little like Goldilocks—cream cheese– or sour cream–based dips are too creamy, bean dips and spreads are often not creamy enough (unless you add a lot of tahini, olive oil, or peanut butter). But this is "just right," thanks to the use of both neufchâtel cheese (a dead ringer for cream cheese, yet with 30 percent less fat) and beans. These point up but do not overwhelm the lustrous, distinctive flavor and texture of roasted red or yellow bell peppers (use them interchangeably as long as they are big, blocky, and firm). The surprise secret ingredient is golden miso (see page 173). Sweet, salty, and rich, it brings everything together. **SERVES 8 TO 12**

3 red bell peppers, roasted (see page 782)
1 yellow bell pepper, roasted (see page 782)
1 large or 2 small cloves garlic, quartered
8 ounces neufchâtel reduced-fat cream cheese
1 can (15 ounces) chickpeas, well drained (reserve liquid for soup stock)
1½ teaspoons golden miso (traditional white miso)
Freshly ground black pepper to taste
Juice of ½ to 1 lime
Minced Italian parsley (optional)

Combine all the ingredients except parsley in a food processor. Pulse until smooth. Scrape the spread into ramekins or a serving bowl. If served immediately, it is a little on the runny side, but if refrigerated for an hour or two it firms up considerably. Garnish with parsley, if desired, and serve.

IN THE PINK

Voluptuous Roasted Red Pepper Spread with Crudités
(SEE PAGE 62)
and Parchment Cracker-Bread
(PAGE 31)

*

Michael Romano's Union Square Cafe Indian Borscht
(PAGE 154)

*

Outrageously Good Pan-Crisped Millet-Vegetable Cakes
(PAGE 825)

*

Sliced pink tomatoes (such as Pink Pea, Pink Grape, or Brandywine Pink) with ribbons of curly purple basil on red-leaf lettuce, with Honeyed Red-Wine Vinaigrette
(PAGE 79)

*

Fresh strawberries and raspberries with a splash of Frangelico over vanilla ice cream or Soy Delicious

VARIATION

VOLUPTUOUS ROASTED RED-FETA SPREAD: ***For a chunkier, heftier spread, in which the salt of feta plays rather nicely off the peppers' sweetness, stir in 8 ounces or so crumbled, well-drained creamy feta before placing the spread in the serving bowl and refrigerating.***

COOK ONCE FOR 3 MEALS Always make more of this than you need. You can serve any remaining spread a night or two later by tossing it with hot fettuccine, sautéed green peppers and onions, cooked fresh baby artichokes or cooked frozen artichoke hearts, and maybe a few tablespoons of vegetable stock if you have some on hand. Add plenty of freshly ground pepper and a handful of minced Italian parsley and you have Voluptuous Pasta Vie en Rose. A few pitted kalamata olives are also good in this pasta, and so are peas—this is one of those recipes with which you can play fast and loose and still end up with something utterly delicious.

Or use it to make *the* most appealing Vie en Rose Grilled Vegetable-Herb Sandwich. Slather the spread along the inside of a crusty baguette split lengthwise, then sprinkle with pitted, coarsely chopped kalamata olives and shredded fresh basil leaves. Finally, layer on slices of garden-fresh tomatoes (golden if you can get them). If you really want to get ambitious/delicious, add rounds of tender grilled eggplant and/or more grilled red pepper.

Hillbilly Hummus

Ozark ingredients intersect Middle Eastern standards: Chickpeas are replaced by black-eyed peas, tahini by peanut butter. The only person who ever guessed that the mystery ingredient was peanut butter was my dear friend and Ozark native Steve Colvin. **SERVES 4 TO 6**

- **2 cups (or one 15-ounce can) cooked, very soft black-eyed peas, drained, at least ½ cup liquid reserved**
- **2 tablespoons natural, unhydrogenated peanut butter, plus more to taste**
- **2 cloves garlic, peeled**
- **½ teaspoon dried sage, or 1 leaf fresh sage, minced**
- **2 teaspoons cider vinegar**
- **Pinch of cayenne, or to taste (optional)**
- **Salt and freshly ground black pepper to taste**

1 In a food processor, combine the black-eyed peas, peanut butter, garlic, sage, vinegar, cayenne, salt, and black pepper. Pulse until smooth. Begin adding the reserved bean liquid, and, if you like, additional peanut butter, and keep pulsing until the consistency is smooth and velvety.

2 Refrigerate overnight, or up to 2 days. Bring to room temperature before serving.

Black-Eyed Pea Pâté

Richer, thicker, slightly more dressed-up than Hillbilly Hummus, this makes a party-sized batch. The ingredients may sound peculiar (brandy and peanut butter?), but they work big-time. One Thanksgiving, with some trepidation, we served this to everyone at the restaurant (carnivores, in previous years, had gotten a classic, deadly-rich chicken- and duck-liver pâté) as part of our Relish Tray Redefined (page 53). The enthusiasm with which it was received meant it retained its Thanksgiving spot on our menu for several years. One might call it "faux gras." Leftovers freeze well. **SERVES 12 TO 15**

3 tablespoons mild vegetable oil, such as corn, canola, or peanut oil
2 large onions, diced
3 carrots, diced
3 bay leaves
3 cloves garlic, minced
4 cups (or two 15-ounce cans) cooked, very soft black-eyed peas, drained, liquid reserved for use in stock
⅓ cup natural, unhydrogenated peanut butter (or ½ cup toasted walnuts or pecans, finely ground)
⅓ cup nutritional yeast (see page 239)
2 to 3 tablespoons cognac or brandy
1 tablespoon tamari or shoyu soy sauce
Salt and freshly ground black pepper to taste
Minced red, green, and yellow bell peppers and 1 sprig Italian parsley

1 Place a 12-inch skillet over medium heat. Add the oil, then the onions, and sauté for 3 minutes. Lower the heat slightly and add the carrots and bay leaves. Sauté, stirring often, until the vegetables are quite soft but not brown, another 6 to 7 minutes. Add the garlic and sauté for 1 minute. Remove and discard the bay leaves.

2 Scrape the mixture into a food processor. Add the black-eyed peas, peanut butter, nutritional yeast, cognac, and tamari and pulse until very smooth. Taste for seasoning and, if necessary, add salt and pepper. Pulse again. Scoop the spread into ramekins and refrigerate overnight to let the flavors blend. Serve at room temperature, garnishing with a confetti of peppers and a sprig of parsley, with lots of crudités and/or crackers on the side.

COOK ONCE FOR 2 MEALS This is such an excellent sandwich spread that if your household contains more than one person who brown-bags lunch regularly, you might want to double the recipe. I love it on good chewy multigrain bread, well toasted, with sliced tomato, paper-thin slices of red onion, and any tender green with personality, like arugula. No mayo or mustard, please.

Mushroom-Lentil Pâté

Too many years ago to count, this was the first vegetarian pâté I invented. Like the previous spread, leftovers make a great sandwich, especially on chewy whole grain bread with fat slices of really juicy summer tomatoes and fresh leaf lettuce. No dressing needed. **SERVES 4 TO 6**

- 2 tablespoons mild vegetable oil, such as corn, canola, or peanut
- 2 tablespoons butter
- 2 large onions, diced
- 1 carrot, diced
- 3 bay leaves
- 3 cloves garlic, minced
- ½ pound regular domestic mushrooms, cleaned and quartered
- ½ pound shiitake mushrooms, stems removed (reserve for stock), cleaned and sliced
- 2 cups cooked, very soft lentils
- ¼ cup almond or cashew butter
- ¼ cup nutritional yeast (see page 239)
- 2 to 3 tablespoons cognac or brandy
- 1 tablespoon tamari or shoyu soy sauce
- Salt and freshly ground black bell pepper to taste
- Minced red, green, and yellow peppers and 1 sprig Italian parsley

1 Place a 12-inch skillet over medium heat. Add the oil and butter; when hot, add the onions and sauté for 3 minutes. Lower the heat slightly. Add the carrot and then the bay leaves. Sauté, stirring often, until the vegetables are quite soft but not brown, another 6 to 7 minutes. Add the garlic and mushrooms and sauté for 8 minutes more. Remove and discard the bay leaves.

2 Scrape the mixture into a food processor. Add the lentils, nut butter, nutritional yeast, cognac, and tamari. Pulse until very smooth. Taste for seasoning and, if necessary, add salt and pepper. Pulse again. Scoop the spread into ramekins and refrigerate overnight to let the flavors blend. Serve at room temperature, garnishing with a confetti of peppers and a parsley sprig, with lots of crudités and crackers.

VARIATION

DOUBLE-MUSHROOM SANDWICH: ***Many people, my brother Stephen among them, love a great big juicy grilled portobello mushroom on a sandwich. To double the mushroom flavor of such a sandwich, grill or sauté a whole portobello cap (see pages 769–70 for some mushroom grilling ideas). Split a baguette—preferably a whole grain, sourdough, crisp-crusted baguette. Drizzle one cut side of the baguette with any juices from the grilled mushroom, and liberally slather the other with Mushroom-Lentil Pâté. Slice the mushroom to make it fit neatly on the bread, and place it on the pâté side. Add leaf lettuce, tomato, and, if you want to really go to town, a little pile of grilled onions. Top with the mushroom-juiced baguette half and feast.***

Austin Hill Country Hummus

Instant dried black or pinto beans are a *great* innovation. They make as-good-as-from-scratch "refried"-style beans in no time, with no hassle and no fat.

The traditional foodways of the Ozark hills mostly came from the Appalachians, moving east to west. The foodways in Texas, Arkansas' due southwest neighbor, by contrast, more often moved from south to north, up from Mexico. You can taste the influence both in the type of beans and the seasonings called for here, compared to the Hillbilly version (page 18).

Austin, in the heart of what Texans call Hill Country, is a hip, agreeable little city, bohemian, slightly urbane, and pleasingly funky due to its university and an eccentric population. Its music scene is in constant ferment, there are lots of good restaurants, lots of good *vegetarian* restaurants, and the biggest natural foods supermarket in the world, Whole Foods Market. Here's a typically "Austin-tacious" (yes, they really do say that down there) recipe. Tahini, while not Texas traditional, is not only delicious but gives it that faintly "old hippie" flavor—very Austin. **SERVES 4 TO 6**

AUSTIN CITY LIMITS

Dos Equis

*

Austin Hill Country Hummus

*

Pamela Jones's Absolutely Incredible Roasted Vegetable Salsa
(PAGE 915)

*

Tortilla chips

*

Lime Soup Yucatán
(PAGE 170)

*

CD's Famed Tofu Broccoli Enchiladas
(PAGE 340)

*

Spanish Millet
(PAGE 548)

*

Coconut Crème Caramel Mousse-Custard
(PAGE 1054)

2 cups dehydrated black bean flakes (the with-salt-only variety)
2 cups boiling water, preferably spring or filtered
2 teaspoons cumin seeds
2 cloves garlic, chopped
1 canned chipotle pepper plus 1 teaspoon of the adobo sauce in which it is canned (or more to taste), or 1 fresh green serrano or 1 fresh green jalapeño chile, seeded
1 tablespoon tahini
1 teaspoon to 2 tablespoons fresh-squeezed lemon juice
Salt to taste
Minced cilantro

1 Place the dehydrated black bean flakes in a small bowl and pour the boiling water over them. Cover and let stand for 5 minutes.

2 Meanwhile, heat the cumin seeds in a dry cast-iron skillet over medium heat. Toast them, shaking the pan constantly, until they brown slightly and give off fragrance, about 3 minutes.

3 Transfer the black beans and their soaking liquid to a food processor. Add the toasted cumin, the garlic, chipotle (or other chile) and adobo sauce, tahini, and lemon juice (start with the lesser amount, taste, and

add until it's just right). Pulse until smooth. Add salt and additional adobo sauce to taste (if you didn't use canned chipotles and thus don't have adobo on hand, and it tastes a little bland to you, use a few drops of Tabasco or your preferred hot sauce to get it up and running). Pulse again.

4 Serve immediately, sprinkled with cilantro, with whole wheat Tortilla Flats (page 30) and crudités on the side. Or, use it in Hill Country Quesadillas (page 52).

Mockamole

Buttery-rich avocados are high in fat but far too luscious to do without. Not that there isn't a time and place for straight avocado, but this recipe extends them perfectly. Who would *believe* that *frozen green peas* could extend avocados so flawlessly, that this isn't just some ersatz, health-foody mix? However, you can't use baby peas or petite pois, as they have too high a proportion of inner flesh to outer skin. So, pureed, the texture doesn't come out right. To me, but for a faint sweetness present and an absent oiliness on the tongue, this is indistinguishable from real "guac" (pronounced "gwok"), as it's affectionately known. Use it as you would use the original. **SERVES 6 TO 8**

1 bag (16 ounces) frozen peas
1 to 2 ripe Hass avocados, peeled and pitted
1 teaspoon salt
Juice of 1 to 3 lemons or limes
1 tomato, diced
½ onion, finely diced
1 to 2 tablespoons minced cilantro (optional)

1 Place the frozen peas in a strainer and run very hot tap water over them until they are thawed and bright green. Transfer to a food processor and pulse until very smooth, pausing from time to time to scrape down the sides of the work bowl. Add one-quarter of 1 avocado, the salt, and the juice of 1 lemon or lime. Process again. Transfer the mixture to a bowl.

2 Coarsely mash in the remaining avocado, leaving the mixture visibly chunky. Stir in the tomato and onion. Taste, and season with additional lemon, maybe salt, too, if you feel it's needed. Last, stir in the cilantro, if using.

3 Serve with Tortilla Flats (page 30), commercial tortilla chips, or as part of any Mexican spread (including the ample array of enchiladas here, pages 340–44), or with Hill Country Quesadillas (page 52).

95 South Main Artichoke Leaves

In spring when the artichoke crop is abundant and cheap, Ned and I go on an artichoke spree. During this brief thistle-frenzy, we sometimes make recipes calling for artichoke bottoms, dropping great piles of trimmed-off leaves, each one delicately bordered with a lip of succulent flesh. These can be spread, lotuslike, in a circle around a dish of dip, as I did to celebrate our dear Eureka Springs Historical Museum's twenty-fifth anniversary. The address—95 South Main. Stop in when you're in town.

The dip is spiked with herbs, horseradish, and garlic, and can be made up to two days in advance; just drain any accumulated water from the dip bowls. The artichokes, too, can and should be cooked in advance, so they have time to chill.

SERVES 10 TO 20 AS PART OF AN HORS D'OEUVRES SPREAD

- 1 package (10½ ounces) silken tofu, preferably reduced fat
- 3 tablespoons Italian parsley leaves
- 1 scallion, white and 2 inches of green, chopped
- 2 to 3 cloves garlic, halved
- 3 tablespoons extra virgin olive oil
- ½ to 1 teaspoon prepared horseradish
- Grated zest and juice from ½ lime
- Salt and freshly ground black pepper to taste
- Cones of leaves broken off from 2 or 3 cooked whole artichokes, separated into individual leaves
- Thin slivers of tomato (optional)
- Thin slivers of Greek olives (optional)
- Thin slivers of roasted red pepper (optional)

1 Combine the tofu, parsley, scallion, garlic, oil, horseradish, and lime zest and juice in a food processor. Pulse until smooth, pausing from time to time to scrape down sides of the work bowl. Taste and, if necessary, add salt and pepper. Don't overdo it; the flavors continue to develop after the dip is made. Transfer to 2 small bowls.

2 Arrange artichoke leaves in rings around the dip bowls on one very large or two medium-large platters. Alternatively, spoon a bit of dip onto the end of each artichoke leaf, then garnish each with a bit of tomato, olive, and/or roasted pepper, if using.

SUMMER'S-LAST-BREATH SUPPER

95 South Main Artichoke Leaves

*

Olivada (PAGE 24)
and Parchment-Cracker Bread (PAGE 31)

*

Potato-Crusted Summertime Skillet-Pie (PAGE 265)

*

Greek-Style Smothered Okra (PAGE 775)

*

Amaretti and Cocoa-Stuffed Peaches (PAGE 989)

*

Fresh melon slices

Eggplant Tapenade with Hijiki

Classic tapenade is like a smooth olivada (see below), but with the addition of anchovies and oil-packed tuna. Here, grilled eggplant substitutes for tuna, adding silken texture and a subtle, wonderful flavor. Hijiki, a seaweed often used in Japanese dishes, gives a hint of the sea, much less assertive than anchovy. Affix a mental Post-it note to remind yourself next time you make grilled eggplant to save two or three good slices to make this. **SERVES 4 TO 6**

1 tablespoon dried hijiki seaweed
3 thick slices eggplant, grilled as in Grilled Eggplant and Zucchini Rolls (page 402), skin removed
1 cup pitted black olives, preferably Greek kalamatas or Italian Alfonsos (but, in a pinch, regular old canned California black olives in brine will do)
2 to 3 cloves garlic, minced
2 tablespoons extra virgin olive oil
1 tablespoon capers, drained (optional but traditional)
Juice of 1 lemon

1. Soak the hijiki in ¼ cup hot water for 5 minutes, until slightly softened. Drain.

2. Combine the eggplant, olives, garlic, oil, capers, and lemon juice, along with the drained hijiki, in a food processor. Pulse-chop until you have a well-mixed but still slightly chunky spread.

3. Serve immediately, or cover and refrigerate for up to 3 days. Bring to room temperature and serve with crackers or toasts.

Olivada

Just reading the ingredients for this Mediterranean spread—black olives, garlic, olive oil, capers, herbs—you know how good it will be. Intense, addictive, versatile, to vegetarian tastes this is far better than the anchovy-dominated classic. **SERVES 3 TO 4**

1 cup pitted black olives, preferably Greek kalamatas or Italian Alfonsos (but, in a pinch, regular old canned California black olives in brine will do)
2 cloves garlic, minced
1 tablespoon capers, drained
2 tablespoons extra virgin olive oil

Combine the olives, garlic, capers, and oil in a food processor. Pulse chop until you have a well-mixed but still slightly chunky spread.

COOK ONCE FOR 4 MEALS You can do an awful lot with olivada, in either version, besides serve it on crackers. You can spread a thin layer of it in sandwiches (heavenly on a crisp baguette with mozzarella, fresh tomato, and arugula). You can cut a pocket in thick eggplant steaks (a technique described fully on page 397), smear the olivada in the middle, with or without cheese, and slowly grill the eggplant. You can stir a bit into many salad dressings. And you can make Pasta Olivada. Toss with cooked angel-hair pasta, adding any bits of this-and-that that capture your fancy: diced fresh or sun-dried tomato, snipped fresh basil leaves, cooked eggplant, sautéed broccoli and winter squash, crumbles of feta or ricotta salata. You can't go wrong here.

VARIATION

SUN-DRIED TOMATO OLIVADA: ***Soak 1 to 2 sun-dried tomatoes in hot water to cover for about 1 hour, or until very soft. Finely chop, and then pulse-chop them with the other ingredients.***

From the Innecdote Files:

New Year's Eve, 1989. We were doing a far more high-falutin' starter than was usual for Dairy Hollow House: beggar's purses of crêpes enfolding a dab of sour cream, knotted with a ribbon of blanched green chive, and topped with a little scoop of fresh American caviar, shiny and black. With it we served the usual caviar fixings: little separate piles of diced hard-cooked egg white and yolk and some minced red onion. And, as each order came in, I'd make up a hot-from-the-griddle yeast-risen buckwheat blini, a small round warm brown sun, one per plate. Neither vegetarian nor low fat, this combo made an elegant plate, and John Mitchell, our waiter, kept returning with reports of guest ecstasy.

Then, John (now the owner of a local antique shop called Mitchell's Folly, and self-described "Dairy Hollow Waiter Demeritus") said he had a couple who described themselves as "semivegetarians." "They were wondering," he said, "if you could do something instead of caviar."

Thrown on my mettle, the old "YES! I can pull it off!" chef's kitchen-adrenaline kicked in. A quick scan of the memory banks: olivada. Couldn't be sure I remembered the name right, let alone the recipe, but how wrong could a chunky, garlicky paste of black olive be? It would be salty and black, vaguely caviarlike. And it could be done in a trice, if we had olives on hand. Which, by chance, we did. Into the processor they went. In hardly thirty seconds, olivada: not at all the same as caviar, yet every bit as showily festive, right down to its appearance and savor.

More guest ecstasy. YES! John and I high-fived.

A Palette of Sour Cream–Style Dips

Here is gathered a rainbow of convivial dips, varying in color and spicing but every one simple, inviting, and distinctive in its flavor. Accompanied by an assortment of vegetable dippers and crackers, toasts, and so on, each batch serves 6 to 8 people, if it's the only hors d'oeuvre. Or, each can serve up to 12 if you're offering several nibbles.

Begin each recipe with 1½ to 2 cups of something creamy . . . your choice as to what. You could use Tofu Sour Cream (page 909, and, in general, my current favorite choice for dips), Yogurt Sour Cream (page 910), commercially made sour half-and-half, reduced- or full-fat sour cream, or Tofu Mayonnaise (page 906).

▲ **DIJON-HERB DIP:** *Add 2 tablespoons Dijon mustard, 2 cloves minced garlic, a minced sprig of fresh basil, a little salt, lots of freshly ground black pepper, and perhaps a squib of extra virgin olive oil. Made with silken tofu–based mayo, this is a perfect dipper for artichoke leaves.*

▲ **PESTO DIP:** *Add 2 to 4 tablespoons pesto, either commercial or homemade. I particularly like Lemon, Basil, and Sun-Dried Tomato Pesto (page 918), as well as the Pesto Santo Tomas (page 920). Stir in 1 to 2 cloves minced garlic and a teaspoon additional olive oil for extra oomph.*

▲ **DIP À LA RUSSE:** *Puree 1 roasted beet, 1 clove garlic, 1 tablespoon fresh dill, 2 teaspoons tamari or shoyu soy sauce along with ¼ cup or so of your total measure 1½ to 2 cups of "something creamy" in a food processor. Stir the pureed mixture into the remaining "something creamy." Add a tablespoon or so of finely minced dill pickle, if you like. Serve with vegetable crudités, and some Pita Bread Toasts (page 30). For a richer version, buzz a tablespoon of tahini into the puree.*

▲ **'50S-STYLE ONION DIP REDUX:** *Add 2 finely diced onions that have been slowly sautéed in 1 tablespoon olive oil until caramelized, 1 clove minced garlic, 1 tablespoon tamari or shoyu soy sauce, ½ teaspoon paprika, and salt and freshly ground black pepper to taste. The classic '50s go-with was potato chips; do an update with thick-cut russet potato chips made by Terra, either the olive oil variety or the salt-and-vinegar type. If you don't eat chips, crudités or crackers are also fine and dandy.*

▲ **LIPTAUER DIP:** *Add 2 minced scallions, ½ minced green bell pepper, 1 teaspoon caraway seeds, 1 teaspoon paprika, a teeny pinch of cayenne, and salt and freshly ground black pepper to taste. This Hungarian-inspired dip is wonderful with cherry tomatoes, fat wedges of red, green, and yellow peppers, and scallion brushes (see page 64).*

▲ **GINGERED JADE SPINACH DIP:** *Puree 2 cups steamed and very well drained fresh spinach with about ¼ cup of the "something creamy," 2 teaspoons finely grated ginger, 2 teaspoons tamari or shoyu soy sauce, 1 teaspoon toasted sesame oil, and 1 teaspoon sugar in a food processor. Transfer to a bowl and stir in the remaining "something creamy." Add 1 can well-drained finely chopped water chestnuts (or, if you can get them and have the patience for it, 10 fresh water chestnuts, peeled and finely chopped—infinitely more delicious). This is lovely served with quickly blanched bright green snow peas,* *carrot and/or celery sticks, cauliflower, and mushroom caps. It makes a stupendous appetizer tray when ringed with Nori Rolls (page 40), served with wasabi paste and pickled ginger (page 43). To really set things off, add some spicy puffed rice-with-vegetable wasabi chips.*

▲ **Garlic-Tahini Dip** *par excellence: Use Tofu Sour Cream as a base, add ½ cup tahini, 3 to 4 quartered cloves garlic, 1 tablespoon tamari or shoyu soy sauce, and 1 to 2 tablespoons apple cider vinegar and buzz smooth in a food processor.*

▲ **Creamy Salsa Verde y Blanca,** *a current favorite that is spicy-hot and unbelievably, addictively tasty: Puree 4 cloves garlic (or, if you happen to have it on hand, 1 heaping teaspoon Roasted Garlic puree [page 899]); 2 serrano chiles, stems removed, seeds included, coarsley chopped; ½ cup cilantro leaves; and ¼ teaspoon salt with your choice of "something creamy" in a food processor.*

Double this: *Use half as a dip, and mix the other half with ½ cup rice milk or soy milk for use as the sauce in Calabacitas Cobbler with Cornmeal Biscuit Crust (page 254).*

▲ **Chipotle-Orange Crème Dip:** *Remove stems from 2 canned chipotle peppers in adobo sauce. Puree the peppers, including their seeds, with 1 tablespoon of the adobo sauce, 1 teaspoon brown sugar, finely grated zest of 1 orange, a pinch of salt and 1 clove garlic with the creamy base of your choice. Stir in a few tablespoons minced cilantro if you like. Serve with Tortilla Flats (page 30) or jícama cut in finger-sized sticks.*

▲ **Forest Mushroom Dip:** *Soak 1 ounce dried porcini mushrooms in boiling dark vegetable stock or commercial mushroom stock, to cover. When mushrooms have softened and liquid is lukewarm, remove porcini, picking out any bits of grit. Transfer porcini to food processor along with the strained soaking liquid and 2 ounces neufchâtel cheese and 1 clove garlic. Meanwhile, slowly saute 1 thinly sliced onion in a little butter, and when golden brown, add 6 to 8 sliced button mushrooms and 6 to 8 sliced shiitake mushroom caps. Saute a moment longer, cover, and let steam about 30 seconds, then add this mixture to ingredients in processor. Buzz until a thick, chunky puree forms. Season well with salt, freshly-ground black pepper, and a bit of grated nutmeg. Stir this into the 1½ cups of "something creamy."*

▲ **Dilled Tofu Spinach Dip:** *Use Tofu Sour Cream as a base, add 1 clove garlic plus 2 teaspoons to 1 tablespoon fresh dill and buzz smooth in a food processor. Stir in ½ box frozen chopped spinach, thawed and squeezed dry, and 1 finely chopped scallion.*

NOTE

Any of thes dips can be dolloped on and tossed with hot pasta to make a creamy, totally quick, sprightly pasta sauce. They're also all excellent on a split, steaming hot baked potato—like jazzed-up sour cream. The tofu versions, hard though it may seem to believe, really do give a satisfying feeling of rich creaminess. They are an enormous boon to those who can't or don't eat dairy products.

Crisps, Croûtes & Crackers

Always tuck several kinds of toasts and crackers in any dip-accompanying basket: It takes no extra effort, and adds much more festivity. Make sure the crackers contrast in shape, texture, and taste.

At Eureka's much-loved Center Street South of the Border, for instance, oblong baskets contain a mixture of just-fried triangular corn tortilla chips and long rectangular strips of crisply fried flour tortillas sprinkled with a delicious chile-spice mixture. Owners Clary and K.J. serve them with a salsa platter: eight (yes, eight!) kinds of salsa and the duo of chips. Now *that's* what I call salsa and chips!

And at the inn's Thanksgiving dinner, along with The Relish Tray Redefined (page 53), the bread plate always sported a hand-sized homemade Parchment Cracker-Bread (page 31), usually made with cracked black pepper, a simple toast, and another cracker, sometimes purchased, sometimes homemade.

Why make a cracker or croûte when you can buy so many perfectly good ones? First, most tastier commercial crackers are higher in fat than homemades; second, homemades—or even one batch of homemade served alongside some good store-boughts—make the bread basket accompanying your dip totally one-of-a-kind. Third, you get tastes, textures and freshness you just can't get out of a box. Fourth, I think guests feel special and fussed-over when they see obviously made-from-scratch crackers or crisp toasts.

In this chapter, you'll find a few quick-fix crisps—those that start from commercially made tortillas or breads, plus the magnificent, don't-miss Parchment Cracker-Bread. For more elaborate breads for toasting, check out Great Grains (Chapter 8), where you'll find several choices.

Homemade Crunchy Toasts

These are nothing more than slices—sometimes cut into triangles or other shapes—of good bread slowly oven-toasted to perfection. The idea is that, by using a low oven temperature and a long baking period, the bread slices are crunchy all the way through but not at all browned. Quite different from warm, brown on the outside, soft and light on the inside, breakfast toast. If kept tightly covered, these toasts will keep for several days. **64 SMALL TOASTS PER LOAF OF BREAD**

1 loaf bread, sliced, crusts removed if desired

1 Preheat the oven to 300°F.

2 Cut each slice of bread into quarters or any other shape. I prefer little triangles. Place wire racks on cookie sheets and arrange the cut bread in a single layer on the racks. This allows hot air to circulate all around the bread, so that you don't have to turn it. (You could put the bread directly on the oven racks but you'd wind up with crumbs on your oven floor.) Lower the heat to 250°F and put the bread in the oven. Bake for 30 minutes. Take one toast out, let it cool briefly, and bite. It must be crisp all the way through but not browned. The type of bread you're using, the thickness of its slices, the accuracy of your oven temperature, and whether your oven has any hot spots—all these affect the time it takes to make a perfect croûte; 40 to 50 minutes is about average at this temperature.

3 Let the toasts cool on their racks. After they have completely cooled, store them in tightly sealed containers. If they have been baked all the way through to complete dryness, some varieties will keep perfectly for as long as 2 to 3 weeks.

Croûtes, Crostini & Kin

▲ **CROÛTES:** *Hard-crusted French- or Italian-type breads, such as baguettes, cut relatively thick and toasted, become croûtes, for floating on soups or stews (as the gratinéed croûte atop classic French onion soup) or placing in the bottom of the bowl. They are sturdy enough to hold up without disintegrating, and to soak up some of the broth yet retain a bit of crunch around the edge. Toasts made from these breads are quite hard and are not really appropriate for serving with spreads.*

▲ **CROSTINI:** *When these same crusty breads are cut thin (say ¼ inch or so) and toasted, they become crostini, Italian for "little crusts." When topped with any one or two of a panoply of good things, they often begin an Italian meal. In Italy, the bread is often grilled over a wood fire, or* abbrustolito, *and called bruschetta.*

Crostini may also be toasted dry in an oven, as I've described above, grilled, pan- or deep-fried, or alternated with cubes of cheese, skewered, and again grilled. Toppings tend to be a little fancier than those that garnish bruschetta; often a chicken liver paste is used, a favorite easily, if nontraditionally duplicated for vegetarians with the black-eyed pea or soft, brown, intensely savory mushroom-lentil pâté on pages 19 and 20. Olivada (page 24) and Eggplant Tapenade with Hijiki (page 24) are also perfect.

▲ **BRUSCHETTA** *are rarely hard-crunchy all the way through and tend to be finished with more simple, rustic toppings: garlic, coarse salt, and olive oil, say, or still-warm-from-the-garden diced tomatoes. If you have a grill, you can easily make bruschetta.*

▲ **AMERICAN-STYLE TOASTS** *call for something less hard. I opt for a good homemade white or light whole-wheat bread, sliced a little more thinly than normal. Use a plain bread—seeds, herbs, large pieces of cracked wheat, and other additions will likely burn or get too hard during the toasting process. Also, you don't want a too-sweet bread.*

Do you leave the crust on? Take the crust off? Crust off is fancier; crust on is rustic, homey, and more "real food" in look. You choose.

NOTE

If you use olive oil, the pitas bake quickly enough so that you can use the sesame seed variety without fear of their burning.

Pita Bread Toasts

Pita crisps up quickly. Although soft pita breads are traditionally served with hummus and other Middle Eastern dips, once toasted, very crunchy and chiplike, they work with almost any dip. You can omit the olive oil, if you like, and bake them at 300°F for 25 to 30 minutes. **MAKES 24 TRIANGLES**

3 whole wheat pita breads, plain or with sesame seeds
2 to 3 teaspoons olive oil, or olive oil in a spray pump

1 Preheat the oven to 350°F.

2 Cut around the edge of a pita bread with a knife, pulling it gently into two circles. Brush or spray the insides of the pita lightly with the oil. Repeat with the rest of the bread. Stack all the circles and cut them into eighths, as if you were cutting them into miniature wedges of pie. Arrange the pita triangles in a single layer on a cookie sheet. Bake for 8 to 12 minutes, until golden. Serve warm, or cool thoroughly and store in a tightly sealed container. Use within a day or two.

VARIATION

CORN TORTILLA FLATS: ***Using corn tortillas, follow this recipe, but cut them into triangular wedges. If serving with the flour tortilla flats, just sprinkle the wedges with salt, no chili powder.***

Tortilla Flats

Another crisped-up ethnic bread, these are zapped with a little sprinkle of chile powder. From Eureka's Center Street South we learned the trick of cutting flour tortillas into long strips, about ¾ inch wide, and dusting with the chili powder. Corn tortillas are cut into triangles and left undusted, creating a little variety both in the mouth and the chip basket. **MAKES 35 FLATS**

6 to 8 flour tortillas, preferably whole wheat
1 tablespoon or so mild vegetable oil, such as corn, canola, or peanut (or use a few spritzes of vegetable oil in a spray bottle)
1 to 2 teaspoons chili powder
½ teaspoon salt

1 Preheat the oven to 400°F.

2 Brush the tortillas lightly with oil. Stack and cut into strips about ¾ inch wide. (Some strips will be short and have rounded edges, since you are cutting across a circle; some will be long.)

3 Lay the wedges down in a single layer on a nonstick or cooking-sprayed baking sheet. Combine the chili powder and salt. Sprinkle with the salt mixture and bake for 8 to 12 minutes, until crisp. Let cool before storing in a tightly sealed container. Before serving, rewarm them for 2 minutes at 350°F.

Firefly Dusk in July

A showy appetizer spread with predominantly Southwestern flavors, yet the Asian and Italian notes that pop in work amazingly well. Most of the work is done in advance; only the Hill Country Quesadillas need be fixed at the last minute, and they can be easily done by the guests themselves on a grill, as long as you have the quesadilla components ready. Cut sprays of wild honeysuckle and place them in loose tangles, unvased, on the table; add small white unscented votive candles and a few white pitchers of field daisies. The lemonade goes in an icy glass pitcher, beaded with condensation; the beer and wine in buckets of ice. Mint juleps are made to order by one of the hosts or a friend who's the designated julep maker.

Roasted Carrot Spread with Fresh Ginger and Curry (PAGE 15)

Pita Bread Toasts (PAGE 30)

Platter of fresh vegetable crudités (SEE PAGE 62)

Jenelle's Tomatoes Rockefeller (PAGE 430)

Hill Country Quesadillas (PAGE 52) **with Arkansalsa** (PAGE 913)

Oven-Roasted Shiitake Mushrooms with Garlic and Coarse Salt (PAGE 48)

Icy Dos Equis, Sauvignon Blanc, mint juleps, or minted lemonade

Parchment Cracker-Bread

I can never thank my darling pan-pal Vicki Caparulo enough for this remarkable and dramatic thin, crisp cracker-bread. Known in Sardinia (its place of origin, Vicki tells me) by the incredibly romantic name of *Carta di Musica* (meaning music paper; that is, the very thin paper on which songs are scored), this bread was always a much-loved part of Dairy Hollow's Thanksgivings, made large and served convivially with The Relish Tray Redefined (page 53). This is the plain recipe, but try all the dressed-up variations. **MAKES 12 APPROXIMATELY 8-INCH CRACKER-BREADS**

1 cup unbleached all-purpose flour, plus about 2 cups additional for dusting
½ cup semolina flour (see page 495)
1 teaspoon salt
½ cup warm water, preferably spring or filtered

1 Preheat the oven for 45 minutes, to 450°F. If you plan to use a baking stone or quarry tiles in the oven, see pizzas (page 269) for details, then cut out and reserve several sheets of heavy parchment paper to fit the baking stone.

2 Combine the flours and salt in a large bowl, and stir in the water a little at a time until a thick, somewhat stiff dough is formed. Turn the dough out onto a floured board and knead gently for a minute or two.

3 Form the dough into a log and divide it into four equal pieces. Cover three pieces with plastic wrap and set aside. Divide the remaining piece into three parts. Let them rest for a moment, to slightly relax the gluten in the flour and make rolling a little easier.

4 On a well-floured board, flour both sides of one of the dough pieces. Roll it out using a heavy rolling pin, working center to top and then center to bottom. Flip the dough over, make a quarter turn,

Flatbread, Round Flavor

This delightful flatbread lends itself to all manner of improvisation and changes. Here are a few. In all cases, don't roll the dough out quite all the way until the toppings are really very firmly pressed into it; you'll need to really bear down with that ol' rolling pin to achieve this.

- **Black Pepper Flat Bread:** *My personal favorite, but then I cannot resist the pleasant irritation of heat or spiciness. Have a dish of ⅓ cup or so coarsely ground black pepper on hand. Before rolling, sprinkle each dough piece liberally with the pepper, then with the flour for rolling it out. When you flip it over the for second side's rolling, repeat. Bake as directed.*
- **Sweet Seed Parchments:** *Have a dish of ⅓ cup or so toasted sesame seeds, poppyseeds, or a combination of the two on hand. Before you sprinkle each dough piece with flour to roll it out, sprinkle liberally with the seeds; when you flip it over for the second side's rolling, repeat. Bake as directed.*
- **Savory Seed Parchments:** *Combine 2 teaspoons each anise, caraway, and dill seeds, plus enough toasted sesame seeds and/or poppyseeds to equal ⅓ cup total. Place the seed mix in a small dish. Before you sprinkle each dough piece with flour to roll it out, sprinkle liberally with the seeds; when you flip it over for the second side's rolling, repeat. Bake as directed.*
- **Savory Seed Parchments Plus:** *Add a little dehydrated minced onion to the seed mixture, and proceed as above.*
- **Herb Parchments:** *Moisten the undivided dough with just a little extra water, and stretch it out a bit. Sprinkle the dough heavily with the herb mixture from Bread Herbs for Dipping (page 904) and knead the herbs into the dough with your fingers until they're evenly distributed. Then proceed as above.*
- **Herb-Parmesan Parchments:** *Again, moisten the undivided dough with just a little extra water, and stretch it out a bit. Sprinkle the dough heavily with the herbs as above, and knead them into the dough along with two or three tablespoons dry, very finely grated Parmesan cheese. Then proceed as above.*

dust it again with flour and roll it out, again working center to top and then center to bottom. Continue flipping and turning, and then flouring and rolling the dough until you have a roundish sheet thin enough to see your hand through it ($^1/_{16}$ inch or less).

5 Repeat this process, cutting each of the original four logs into three pieces, flouring, rolling, and turning. There will be excess flour on the breads. Don't worry about that or the shape; the irregularity of the breads adds to their charm and their obvious made-from-scratchness. As each sheet is rolled, place it on one of the parchment pieces, if using the quarry tile method, or on an ungreased baking sheet. Place only as many sheets as will fit without overlapping (usually 2).

6 As your parchment or sheets fill up, place the parchment on the tiles or stone, or the baking sheet in the oven, and bake the breads for 3 to 4 minutes or until they are bubbled and beginning to brown lightly. Turn each flatbread over with tongs and continue to bake, watching carefully, until the bread is lightly browned on both sides, 2 to 3 minutes more. Transfer immediately to a rack to cool. Repeat with the remaining breads, using a new sheet of paper each time if you're using that method. Once cool, these may be stored for a day or two in an airtight container.

NOTE

There are a couple of secrets to this recipe. Expect to get a little rough and tough with the dough when rolling it out; at that phase, it likes to be beaten up a little.

Although the preparation is essentially simple, it is time-consuming, because you can only bake a couple of breads at a time, and each is flipped over halfway through. But the results are worth every minute!

Crostini & Canapés

Toasts or breads, spread with a savory melange, garnished, and served open-faced are a starter par excellence. They appear everywhere from Nordic smorgasbord tables to the Italian countryside. One step up from providing guests with a do-it-yourself dip or spread, the host prepares the garnished spread on toast ahead of time—but not *too* far ahead or the bread will get soggy. Set up the components early in the day—the spread, the toasts, the garnishes—but don't put them together more than 20 to 30 minutes before serving.

Any of the toasts described (most especially small thin crostini from French or Italian bread) can serve as a base for these. Any of the spreads, like Hillbilly Hummus (page 18), Austin Hill Country Hummus (page 21), Eggplant Tapenade with Hijiki (page 24), Olivada (page 24), or Mushroom-Lentil Pâté (page 20) can top the toasts. So can plain old delicious chopped summer tomatoes mixed with a bit of garlic and a dash of salt or some scissored basil, a smear of Yogurt Cream Cheese (page 910), soft lovely goat cheese, a sliver of good mozzarella, pitted Greek or Italian olives coarsely chopped and tossed with torn-up arugula, or almost any combination you can dream up. The visual trick, when making a platter of these, is to top each with a little sprig or slice of something colorful and appropriate to the topping: a cilantro sprig on the Austin Hill Country Hummus or Morocc'n'-Roll Oven-Roasted Carrot Spread, a basil leaf on tomato or goat cheese plus Eggplant Tapenade or neufchâtel plus Olivada, or a sprig of dill and a sliver of raw onion and cucumber atop a simple spread of Yogurt Cream Cheese (page 910). Some other possible toppings that you should check out are Eggplant-Lentil Caponata (page 390), Cabbage and Greens with Kidney Beans and Caramelized Garlic (page 718), the mushroom filling for Polenta Lasagna (page 374) with a little garlic added and topped with grated Parmesan, and many of the fillings in Wrapped, Stuffed & Stacked (Chapter 7).

NOTE

This Indian mixture is often found inside samosas (deep-fried North Indian turnovers) or inside the South Indian pancakes known as dosha.

Masala Bruschetta

How good this wonderful spiced potato filling is! Enjoy this fusion dish as a light intro to an Indian meal or as an exotic note in a buffet spread. The crisp bread provides great contrast to the spicy but not *too* spicy mixture. I have added non-traditional roasted red pepper, both for its luscious flavor and for its color, beautiful against the yellow turmeric and bright green peas. **MAKES 24 BRUSCHETTA**

- 4 medium-sized potatoes, well-scrubbed
- 2 teaspoons cumin seeds
- 1 tablespoon mild vegetable oil, such as corn, canola, or peanut; or butter, clarified butter, or 1½ teaspoons each butter and oil
- 1 onion, finely minced
- 1 small fresh hot green chile, such as a serrano, finely minced (remove seeds and white membranes if you'd like the finished dish less hot; leave in for heat)
- 1 tablespoon minced peeled ginger
- 2 teaspoons black or brown mustard seeds
- 1 to 2 tablespoons very finely minced cilantro leaves
- 1½ teaspoons salt
- 1 teaspoon ground coriander
- 1 teaspoon Garam Masala (page 902) or curry powder
- ½ teaspoon turmeric
- ⅛ to ¼ teaspoon cayenne
- Juice of ½ lemon
- ¾ cup frozen petite pois
- 1 red bell pepper, charred, skin removed, diced (optional)
- About 24 crisp but not hard Italian or French bread toasts, preferably grilled
- 2 tablespoons Yogurt Sour Cream (page 910) or Tofu Sour Cream (page 909)
- Cilantro leaves

1 Bring 3 cups water to a boil in a small saucepan over medium-high heat. Drop in the potatoes and cook until tender but not mushy, 15 to 20 minutes. Remove from the heat, drain well, and let cool. Peel the potatoes and dice them into ¼-inch cubes. Set aside.

2 As the potatoes cook, toast the cumin seeds in a small, dry iron skillet over medium heat until brown and fragrant, 2 to 3 minutes. Remove the cumin seeds from the heat and set aside.

3 Again, working as the potatoes cook, heat a large nonstick skillet over medium heat. Add the oil (or clarified butter or butter-oil combination) and the onion. Sauté until just starting to color, about 7 minutes. Lower the heat slightly and add the chile, ginger, black or brown mustard seeds, and toasted cumin seed. Cook, stirring often, for 3 to 4 minutes, until the mustard seeds start to pop. Add the minced cilantro, salt, ground coriander, Garam Masala or curry powder, turmeric, cayenne, and about 3 tablespoons water. Stir for a moment or two, then add the diced potatoes and lemon juice. Turn the heat down to low and let the potatoes and spices cook, stirring fairly often but gently, carefully turning the potatoes.

4 Place the frozen petite pois in a strainer and run very hot tap water over them until they are thawed and bright green. Drain well and add them to the potato mixture along with the optional (but so good) roasted red pepper. Stir to combine. Taste; it may need a little more salt or cayenne. This much can be done ahead and the mixture refrigerated. Rewarm before serving.

5 No more than 30 minutes before serving, neatly place about a tablespoon of the warm potato mixture on each toast. Dab about ¼ teaspoon Yogurt Sour Cream on top. Garnish with a cilantro leaf.

DOCK ON THE BAY SUPPER

Terry's Leek Bruschetta

*

The Salad
(PAGE 68)

*

Eternal Soup
(PAGE 142)

*

Lemon Mousse-Custard
(PAGE 1052)

Terry's Leek Bruschetta

My brother Stephen's best friend and bridge tournament cohort is Andy Goodman. Terry, Andy's wife, is a dancer and fine cook—for human beings, cats, and dogs. She owns Dandy Doggie, a small organic dog biscuit bakery, and is the author of *Purrfect Dishes*, a cookbook for cats or, at least, the humans who cook for them. The Goodmans are *serious* food people. On a visit to Andy and Terry, I was served these extraordinarily good, very simple bruschetta.

MAKES 10 TO 12 BRUSCHETTA

1 bunch leeks (3 or 4), roots and all but 1 inch of green removed
1 tablespoon butter
Salt and freshly ground black pepper to taste
10 to 12 small, thin, crisp Croûtes (page 29)
10 to 12 sprigs Italian parsley

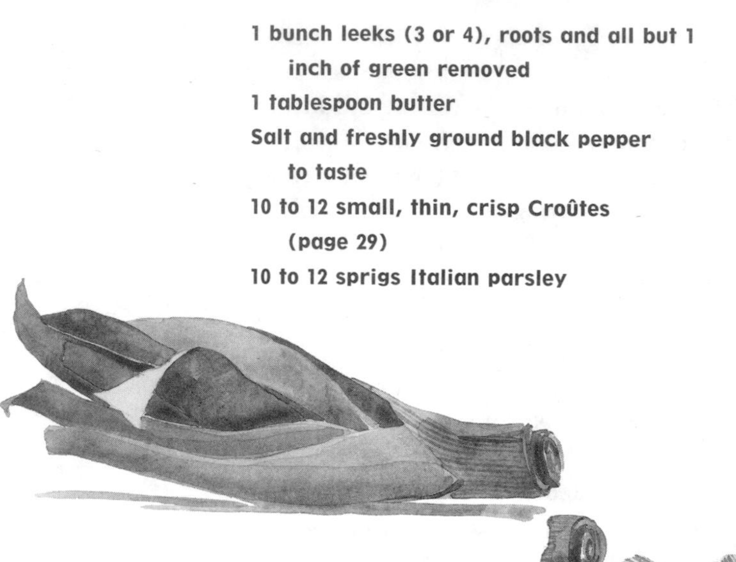

1. Split the leeks lengthwise and rinse very well to remove all dirt and grit. Slice crosswise into ¼- to ⅛-inch half-circles.

2. In one very large, or two smaller non-stick skillets, melt the butter over medium heat. When hot, add the leeks. Cook until just barely wilted, about 4 minutes. Lower the heat and cook very slowly, stirring occasionally, for about 15 minutes, or until the leeks are very soft and limp and partially caramelized. Season with salt and pepper to taste. Pile the leeks atop crisp Croûtes and garnish with sprigs of Italian parsley.

Angel Biscuits with Cheese and Sweet Honey-Tarragon Mustard Butter

NOTE

You can, if you like, substitute rosemary, basil, or thyme for the tarragon—but I think tarragon tastes best.

This is one of those old-fashioned hors d'oeuvres—delicious, eminently nibble-able, irresistible but so high in fat you don't even want to think about it. However, it was so often served at Dairy Hollow wedding receptions (both as given below, and with the addition of a sliver of smoked ham) and was so popularly received that I can't quite bring myself to leave it out. The secret ingredient is the sweet tarragon mustard butter. An herbal hint: If you grow your own herbs, try the plant labeled "Mexican Marigold" or "Texas Tarragon" instead of true tarragon. See the next page for details. **MAKES 24 BISCUITS**

½ recipe dough for feather-light Angel Biscuits (page 514)
1 cup salted butter, softened to room temperature
Leaves from 1 large branch tarragon (or Mexican Marigold, also known as Texas Tarragon, 3 to 4 loosely packed tablespoons leaves)
3 tablespoons smooth Dijon mustard
2 tablespoons honey
Pinch of cayenne
8 to 10 ounces extra-sharp Cheddar cheese, such as sharp Vermont Cheddar, shaved into paper-thin slices
Sprigs of tarragon (or Mexican Marigold)

1 A week to 3 days before you plan to serve these, prepare the biscuit dough. After the dough's refrigerated overnight rest, roll it out and cut out biscuits with a heart-shaped cookie cutter. Immediately after cutting them out, freeze the unbaked biscuits on a baking sheet.

2 Up to a week in advance, make the Sweet Honey-Tarragon Mustard Butter. Either in a food processor or by hand, combine the butter, tarragon, mustard, honey, and cayenne. Beating or buzzing, whip the mixture to a smooth creaminess. Scrape the butter into a small bowl, cover, and refrigerate.

3 Up to 2 hours before serving, bake the biscuits, still frozen, as directed on page 514, Step 4, allowing 1 to 2 minutes more to compensate for having been frozen. Take the mustard butter from the refrigerator so it can warm up to a spreadable but not too soft consistency.

4 Let the baked biscuits cool for 15 to 20 minutes, then split them in half crosswise. Give the bottom half a smear of mustard butter, add a sliver of extra-sharp Cheddar, and cover with the top half. If you like, poke a sprig of tarragon into the center of each biscuit, creating an upright, leaf-plumed floral toothpick. Once assembled, serve as soon as possible—certainly within 1½ hours.

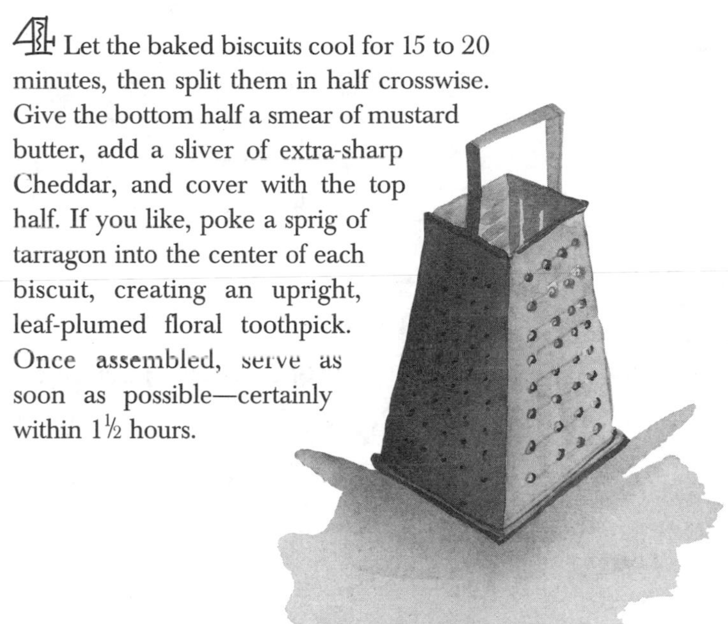

Texas Tarragon Tales

In the last few years an herb called Mexican Marigold, Mexican Mint Marigold, or Texas Tarragon has become widely available at nurseries, but it's still not nearly as common among cooks as it should be. It is a dead ringer for the slightly sweet, haunting, faintly anise-y notes of true tarragon (Artemisia dracunculus, var. sativa), *and far less finicky to grow.* Tagetes lucida, *the botanical name for Texas Tarragon, is much more vigorous than true tarragon, which for me has never grown with much generosity.*

A single Texas/Mexican tarragon plant in a flower pot on a sunny wall yields clouds of leaves—more herb than I can use in a whole summer's worth of tarragon mustard butter, salad dressings, salads, omelettes with herbs, and pastas tossed with vegetables.

My friend Jim Long, herbalist, gardener, and writer, believes that Mexican Mint Marigold is a mild stimulant, like a weak caffeine, when used fresh or steeped dry in hot water like a tea. "I used to use the herb in chicken salad, really good in that!" he e-mailed me in answer to my query about the plant's botanical name. "But I noticed on several occasions that when I served it in the evening, people didn't sleep well that night." But, he adds, "I don't think the keeping-awake thing is likely if the herb is cooked slightly."

NOTES

If the garlic cloves are small, use more. Also, if you double the recipe, there's enough bulk to make it worth doing in a food processor, in which case quarter the garlic cloves; don't put them through a press.

Since the ingredients are few, they must be the best. Taste a fig before you purchase enough for the recipe. Any variety will do as long as the figs are sweet, juicy, intensely flavored, softly yielding but not overripe—anything less than the apogee of figdom will not do.

Fresh Figs with Garlic-Feta Cream

This passionate seasonal combination is my favorite starter, next to the Oven-Roasted Shiitakes, but rarer, since figs are available for such a short time. I look forward to it each late summer/early fall. The way this salty-sweet pairing surprises the mouth gives a frisson of pleasure even more intense than that I recall from the prosciutto and melon of my carnivore days. Elegant simplicity—perfection, and easily made, too. **MAKES 12 TO 15 CANAPÉS**

8 ounces cream cheese, neufchâtel reduced-fat cream cheese, or yogurt cream cheese, softened to room temperature
4 to 5 cloves garlic, peeled and pressed
4 ounces feta cheese, crumbled medium- fine
12 to 15 fresh figs, halved

1 Combine the cream cheese and garlic, beating until smooth. Stir in the feta. Chill. (This can be done up to 3 days in advance.)

2 When ready to serve, allow the cheese mixture to soften to room temperature. Place 3 fig halves on each plate. You may either spread them with the garlic-feta cream, or place a dollop of the cream next to the figs. In either case, this is a transcendent combination.

Crisp Lettuce Tempeh "Spring Rolls"

In 1977, a just-out-of-college Ned and I got together, courtesy of an internship with the National Trust for Historic Preservation that brought him to Little Rock. His job: writing a history of Arkansas' first statehouse, later made famous when

Bill Clinton announced his presidential victory on its steps. Ned's then-boss, Lucy Robinson, brought some traditional lettuce-wrapped pork spring rolls to a potluck dinner held in our little apartment on Arch Street. I was already a vegetarian; Ned was then in the vegetarian-at-home-social-carnivore phase so he (and everyone else) tucked in, brushing the leaves with the hoisin sauce, rolling up the fragrant filling. I looked on, and had another helping of pasta salad. I decided that one of these days I'd do a meatless, just-as-good-if-not-better version of the lettuce rolls. Tempeh gives these meaty heft, hearty flavor, and protein; raw jícama fills in for fresh water chestnuts but is much easier to prepare and find. You may use either regular or smoked tempeh (such as Fakin' Bacon), which must be cooked before you begin. After that, as with almost all Chinese-style recipes, the main work is in chopping and dicing beforehand. **MAKES 15 TO 20 ROLLS**

TEMPEH FILLING

¼ cup "croutakis"—dried, diced shiitake mushrooms (see page 767), or ⅓ cup whole dried shiitakes (see note)
½ cup boiling vegetable stock (see page 139) or water, preferably spring or filtered
¼ head green cabbage, cored, very finely chopped
10 string beans, stems and tails removed, halved lengthwise and very finely diced
3 scallions, white plus 3 inches of green, very finely chopped
1 rib celery or bok choy, very finely diced
1 carrot, very finely diced
1 cup peeled, finely diced jícama (about ¼ pound)
8 ounces regular or smoked tempeh, precooked (see note)

SAUCE

Reserved mushroom soaking water
1 tablespoon plus 1 teaspoon cornstarch
2½ tablespoons tamari or shoyu soy sauce
2½ tablespoons mirin (Japanese rice wine) or sweet sherry
1 tablespoon plus 1 teaspoon brown sugar
Several vigorous grinds of black pepper

STIR-FRY

Thumb-sized piece of fresh ginger, peeled and very finely minced
3 cloves garlic, finely minced
1 tablespoon hoisin sauce
1 teaspoon mild vegetable oil, such as corn, canola, or peanut
1 teaspoon dark toasted sesame oil

FOR SERVING

15 to 20 outer leaves iceberg lettuce
Scallion brushes (optional), for spreading hoisin sauce
Additional hoisin sauce
Thai Crystal (page 923; optional)

1 Place the "croutakis" or whole dried shiitakes in a small, heatproof bowl. Pour the boiling vegetable stock (or water) over them

NOTES

If using whole dried shiitake mushrooms, after they've soaked, inspect them very carefully for grit and bark. Dice finely. The mushroom soaking liquid will also have to be strained through a fine-mesh sieve to remove grit.

TO PRECOOK TEMPEH: ***You have three choices. Simply steam the plain tempeh over boiling water for 10 minutes. Or prepare Basic Oven-Baked Marinated Tempeh (page 641), using garlic as the optional seasoning and rice vinegar as the vinegar. Or use smoked tempeh strips and brown them quickly in a skillet according to the package directions.***

and set aside to soak for at least 30 minutes. Drain the soaked mushrooms, reserving the mushroom soaking liquid. Combine the soaked, drained "croutakis" with the cabbage, string beans, chopped scallions, celery, and carrot in a medium bowl.

2 Set up a mise en place (see page 107), for your stir-fry. First comes the vegetable mixture, next the jícama, in a separate container.

3 Finely dice the tempeh until its consistency is almost a thick, chunky paste. Place the tempeh paste in a small bowl on the "mise" tray also.

4 Prepare the sauce: Combine 3 tablespoons of the reserved mushroom soaking liquid with the cornstarch in a small bowl. Mush smooth, using your fingers, then stir in the mirin (or sherry), tamari, brown sugar, and black pepper. Set this small sauce bowl on your "mise" tray, along with the remaining mushroom liquid. Place the minced ginger and garlic in one bowl, and in another the 1 tablespoon hoisin sauce. Now we're ready to actually start cooking!

5 Combine the vegetable and sesame oils in a wok over medium-high heat. Add the ginger and garlic, which will immediately sputter fragrantly, and stir, counting to 25. Add the chopped vegetables and continue stir-frying for 2 minutes. Add the mushroom soaking liquid and cook for 1 to 3 minutes, until the vegetables are crisp-tender. Add the sauce mixture and cook just until it has thickened to a glossy clarity, 30 seconds, if that. Add the tempeh and stir-fry for a few seconds (at this point it will want to stick; don't worry, just keep stirring as fast as you can). Remove from the heat and stir in the diced jícama and the hoisin sauce. Transfer the filling either to one large bowl (if you're serving buffet-style) or 4 to 6 small plates. Place the separated lettuce leaves around the large bowl of filling or divide the leaves among individual plates.

6 At table, using the scallion brush if desired, diners brush a little hoisin sauce on a lettuce leaf, then scoop a little of the vegetable-tempeh filling into it and curl the leaf around the filling. A tasty extra is a little Thai Crystal for dipping, spooned onto each plate.

VARIATION

THAI-FLAVOR CRISP LETTUCE TEMPEH "SPRING ROLLS": ***When the filling comes off the heat, stir in 2 tablespoons each finely scissored basil, spearmint, and cilantro leaves and 1 to 2 small hot green or red chiles, with seeds, halved and cut into very thin half-rings. Serve with Thai Crystal (page 923).***

Nori Rolls

The seaweed-wrapped Japanese equivalent of spring rolls, Nori Rolls could not be more different in feeling, flavor, or appearance. Folks who live in a metropolitan area can just bound off to the nearest sushi place when overcome with that only-sushi-will-do hankering, but out here in the country we fend for ourselves. We? Yes—it's not just me that gets the occasional nori yen. Far, far from the sea, in a beautiful cabin on the ridge of a mountain overlooking Berryville, Arkansas, at a potluck evening celebrating my friends Ramona and Chuck McNeal's twentieth anniversary, someone brought a tray of these . . . and they didn't last long! So I advise doubling, tripling, or quadrupling this recipe. **MAKES 3 NORI ROLLS**

2 to 4 of the vegetables and condiments prepared for sushi, singly or in combination (see note)
3 sheets nori (also called laver), about 7 by 8 inches
1 recipe Sushi Rice (recipe follows)
About 2 teaspoons dried wasabi (horseradish) powder mixed with 1½ teaspoons water to form a paste
Sweet, Quick-Pickled Sushi Ginger (recipe follows)
Dipping sauce (see page 43)

1 Decide if you want to make one kind of Nori Roll or several, and in what combination. Choose and prepare your vegetables accordingly.

2 Assemble a mise en place tray with the prepared vegetables, nori, Sushi Rice, and other chosen condiments. Also have on hand a bamboo mat (either a traditional bamboo mat for making rolls, or any undyed slatted bamboo placemat) or a clean dish towel, a small bowl of water, and a very sharp knife.

3 Toast the nori, one sheet at a time, by quickly passing it back and forth about 2 to 3 inches directly above a medium-low gas flame. Toast the entire sheet, moving back and forth and top to bottom, until it turns a half-shade paler.

4 Now you're ready to roll. With the mat or dish towel lying in front of you with its short end facing you, position a piece of the toasted nori on it, its short end about ½ inch from the end of the mat or towel. Wet one hand (now you know what the water bowl was for), and scoop up about ½ cup of the prepared rice. Spread the rice about ½ inch thick across the nori, leaving margins of about ½ inch on the short ends, and about 1¼ inches on the long ends. With your finger, make an indentation down the middle of the rice, a trough. Lay a row of vegetable and/or condiment ingredients in the trough. (Remember, if you choose a combination that includes wasabi, to go easy on it—it's nose-explodingly hot; guests can always use additional wasabi when they mix up their own condiments. Go easy on the salty umeboshi plum paste, too.)

5 Using the towel or mat as structural support, begin tightly rolling up the filled nori sheet. You have to be careful to tuck the vegetables into the roll as you get to them so nothing squishes out at the far end. Roll away from you and up along the short end of the roll, moving the length of the nori. The mat or towel stays on top of the roll; you don't want to roll it into the nori. When you're finished, you should have a nice, dark green roll with a spiraled filling that you can just see on either end of the roll.

6 Move the roll to a wooden cutting board. Wet the blade of the very sharp

NOTE

VEGETABLES AND CONDIMENTS FOR NORI ROLLS:

▲ ***1 carrot, peeled, quartered lengthwise, and blanched in boiling water for 1 minute***

▲ ***4 to 6 shiitake mushroom caps sliced into ¼-inch-thick pieces. Combine in a saucepan with 1 tablespoon water, 1 tablespoon tamari or shoyu soy sauce, 2 teaspoons sugar, and 1 teaspoon mirin. Bring to a boil, covered, and cook 30 seconds. Remove from the heat and drain.***

▲ ***½ cucumber, peeled, seeded, and sliced lengthwise into long, thin strips***

▲ ***½ avocado, mashed coarsely***

▲ ***½ pound fresh spinach, stems removed, steamed and well drained***

▲ ***1 red pepper, charred, skinned, seeded, and diced***

▲ ***About 1 tablespoon sesame seeds, toasted***

▲ ***About 2 teaspoons wasabi paste***

▲ ***About ½ teaspoon umeboshi plum paste (see page 118)***

knife with a little of the water, and, using a gentle sawing motion, carefully slice the roll, crosswise, into 6 equal pieces, wiping the blade on a damp towel between each slice. Continue with remaining sheets of nori.

7 Serve on individual plates or on a large platter with the pickled ginger, prepared wasabi paste, dipping sauce, and condiments of your choice.

Sushi Rice

1 cup Japanese short-grain rice, white sticky rice, or 1 cup short-grain sweet brown rice
Water, preferably filtered or spring
2 tablespoons plus 1 teaspoon rice vinegar
1 tablespoon sugar
2 teaspoons mirin (Japanese rice wine) or sherry
½ teaspoon salt

1 In order to get the proper, sticktogethery texture, you will need to either wash the rice (if using white rice) or soak it (if using brown). *For white rice:* Put the rice in a bowl, pour cold water over it, swish it around, and plunge your hands in, gently rubbing the grains of rice to release some of the starch. Drain and repeat until the water is no longer milky with released starch, about 3 washings. Drain the rice in a sieve, and leave it in the sieve placed over a bowl or the sink to catch drips; let drain for about 1 hour. *For brown rice:* Soak the rice in 1⅓ cups water for 6 hours or overnight. Drain well, rinsing a few times.

2 Place either type of rice plus 1¼ cups cold water in a medium-sized heavy pot with a tight-fitting lid. Cover and bring to a boil over medium heat. When the rice begins to steam, turn the heat as low as it can go and cook the rice for 20 minutes (40 minutes for brown). Then, turn the heat as high as it will go and count to 5. Turn off the heat and allow the rice to sit, covered, without lifting the lid, for 15 minutes.

3 Turn the cooked rice out onto a large tray, bowl, or platter (a wooden or at least non-metallic vessel is traditional here). Have a wooden spoon or paddle, chopsticks, or a wide-tined fork ready as well as something for fanning—a pot lid or folded-over newspaper will do; a fan is traditional. Quickly sprinkle the rice vinegar, sugar, mirin or sherry, and salt over the hot rice. Then, fanning with one hand, use the wooden spoon to lift, turn, and mix the seasonings into the rice. Stir and fan, fan and stir, until the rice has cooled to just hotter than lukewarm, 3 to 5 minutes. Let the rice stand until it has reached room temperature. Cover. Do not refrigerate. Use within 2 to 3 hours.

Sweet, Quick-Pickled Sushi Ginger for Nori Rolls

Just like what we know and love from Japanese restaurants, only not so pink—because not so food-colored. **MAKES ABOUT ⅓ CUP**

2 ounces fresh ginger, peeled and sliced paper-thin by hand or in a food processor using the 1-mm slicing blade, to equal about ⅓ cup, lightly packed
⅓ cup white rice vinegar
¼ cup sugar

1 Bring a medium saucepan of water to a boil. Drop in the sliced ginger, let the water return to a boil, count to 3, and drain the ginger. Refresh with cold water, drain again, and pat dry with a towel. Place in a small bowl and set aside.

2 Bring the vinegar and sugar to a boil and boil, stirring constantly, just until sugar dissolves. Remove from the heat and pour over the blanched ginger. Cover and refrigerate for at least 5 hours, preferably overnight.

VARIATIONS

GREAT COMBINATIONS FOR NORI ROLLS:

▲ ***Cucumber strips with wasabi and sesame seeds***

▲ ***Carrot strips with radish sprouts, steamed spinach, and umeboshi plum paste (see page 118)***

▲ ***Carrot strips, avocado, and shiitakes***

▲ ***Avocado, sprouts, and cucumber with wasabi***

▲ ***Spinach, sesame, and shiitakes***

▲ ***Carrot, sesame, red pepper strips, and shiitakes***

Asian Dipping Sauces

The simplest possible dip is just tamari or shoyu soy sauce, poured in a shallow bowl, to which diners can add as much or as little wasabi as they like. Although simple is traditional, you can easily jazz things up, adding savory, sweet, or spicy to the salt of the tamari. Omit the sweet or gingered variations if you're serving the rolls with pickled ginger. Otherwise, try adding any one or two or three of the following to ¼ cup tamari or shoyu soy sauce:

▲ *½ to 1½ teaspoons toasted sesame seeds, on toasted sesame oil, toasted peanut oil, or finely chopped toasted peanuts*

▲ *1 clove garlic, pressed*

▲ *1 scallion, most of the green cut off, cut into the thinnest possible rings*

▲ *1 tablespoon rice vinegar (or, nontraditional but very tasty, fruit vinegar, such as peach or raspberry)*

▲ *1 teaspoon Chile Buzz (page 782) or Thai Crystal (page 923)*

▲ *A few drops Tabasco or similar hot sauce*

▲ *1 teaspoon to 1 tablespoon sugar, brown sugar, honey, or Rapidura*

▲ *½ teaspoon finely grated ginger*

▲ *½ to 1 teaspoon commercially made ginger-garlic paste or Chinese chile paste with garlic*

▲ *1 tablespoon mirin, sherry, or Marsala*

▲ *2 teaspoons to 1½ tablespoons hoisin sauce*

NOTE: *Keep these sauces in the back of your mind, to serve with any hot or cold Asian noodle dish, take-out Chinese dumplings, or stir-fries that seem to need a little oomph.*

Marinated Mixtures & Mélanges

Bathe assorted fresh vegetables (raw or blanched), or perhaps olives, maybe even fruit, in a vinegary, salty or sweet, piquantly seasoned liquid, and you have a superb do-ahead starter. Usually on the salty side, marinated mélanges make a perfect foil to many beverages, alcoholic or non. They are great sit-around, nibble, talk, have another nibble foods. Though many marinated combinations are dripping with oil, just as many others are completely free of it, leaning more toward the brine-y or pickle-y side. The two here are light, falling into the latter category.

Mediterranean Cornucopia of Olives

NOTE

To keep this going indefinitely, just add olives and fresh kumquats to the marinade, making sure that the kumquats stay submerged beneath the level of the brine-oil-vinegar mixture to prevent spoilage. The fresh kumquats will be a brighter orange than those that have been soaking awhile.

The muted tones of many varieties of olives—purple-black, ink-black, gray-black, and gray-green—are stunningly set off by golden orange kumquats: the visual equivalent of the sparking that takes place in the mouth. Hot peppers, spices, and garlic are the flavors strong enough to stand up to the olives. Throw everything together and let it marinate. This is a perfect and beautiful centerpiece for any not-too-formal, stand-up-and-walk-around reception: Try it in your prettiest footed glass bowl—even a punch bowl will do—as part of an hors d'oeuvres assortment.

Plan a trip to your favorite specialty foods store or deli a few days before your party to pick up as many different varieties of olives, sold in bulk, as possible. Large quantities are given, because even if you have some left over after a party the mixture keeps nearly indefinitely in the fridge. Just keep adding olives to the marinade to keep the mix going. Include a variety, some brined, some dry-cured; Greek nafplion,

French picholine, Greek kalamata, black Italian gaetas and Alfonsos, Moroccan green cracked, small semidry salt-cured, imported and domestic—whatever you can find that looks good. Combined, they always harmonize.

If fresh kumquats are out of season or unavailable, substitute 1 or 2 fresh oranges. Wash them well, then cut into chunks (peel and all), seeds picked out with the tip of a knife. **MAKES ABOUT 2½ QUARTS**

- **2 quarts assorted green and black olives, some in brine**
- **½ to 1 pound fresh kumquats, halved and seeded (or 1 to 2 oranges)**
- **6 cloves garlic, peeled and half-smashed with the side of a knife, but left whole (or more to taste)**
- **¼ to ⅓ cup extra virgin olive oil**
- **¼ to ⅓ cup cider vinegar**
- **1 tablespoon dried red chile pepper flakes (or 5 or 6 whole dried red chiles, broken up roughly)**
- **1 tablespoon fennel seeds**
- **1 tablespoon cracked coriander seeds**
- **1 tablespoon coarsely cracked black pepper**
- **4 bay leaves**
- **2 small branches fresh thyme**

Drain the olives, reserving 1½ cups or so of brine. Lightly rinse the brine-cured olives, then combine them with the kumquats and garlic. Add the oil, vinegar, red pepper, fennel and coriander seeds, black pepper, bay leaves, and thyme, along with the reserved brine. Toss to combine. Allow to marinate, preferably in a glass gallon jar, for at least 2 days, giving the jar a shake when you think about it. Serve at room temperature.

Take the A Train

When I lived in the Fort Greene section of Brooklyn, New York, back in 1969, I used to hop the IND subway from Lafayette Street, go two stops to Borough Hall, then walk a block or two over to Atlantic Avenue and Court Street. At that time, there were blocks of small, family-owned Lebanese and other Middle Eastern restaurants, where I feasted on garlicky baba ghanoush and hummus, very oily but succulent stuffed vegetables, and salads studded with salty feta cheese. These meals, which then seemed so exotic, were often given syncopation as I listened to family members sitting at back tables conversing heatedly in Arabic as they snapped green beans or diced onions.

A lifelong fondness for these dishes has remained. Many of these flavors appear in some of the dips here. Pita chips or warmed wedges of noncrisped pita bread are natural choices with any of them. So is a bowl of Mediterranean Cornucopia of Olives and some nice un-fussed-over crudités, like crisp radishes with the greens still on them or whole cherry tomatoes.

Marinated Vegetable Antipasti

Big, bad, bold, bright, beautiful flavors—perfect as is, on a few nice green lettuce leaves, or as part of an Antipasto Platter (see page 56). This is considerably fresher-tasting, tangier, and less oily than the classic versions. If this is too tart for your palate, adjust it by doubling or even tripling the amount of oil, which will create something closer to the classic, though *still* lighter than most original recipes. You can make it for a party a good ten days in advance and it'll still be just right. Keep a jar with everything up to the chickpeas ready-made in the fridge for healthful nibbling and easy enjoyment whenever you want a quick crunch or a spark for salads. **SERVES 8 TO 10**

MARINADE

2¾ cups vegetable stock (see page 139)
¼ cup cider vinegar
3 tablespoons olive oil
2 tablespoons balsamic vinegar
1 tablespoon tomato paste
1 tablespoon brown sugar or honey
1 tablespoon minced fresh basil
1 tablespoon whole coriander seeds
1 teaspoon dried oregano leaves
1 teaspoon salt
½ teaspoon freshly ground black pepper
3 cloves garlic, pressed
3 bay leaves
1 dried red chile pepper
Juice of 1 lemon

VEGETABLES

2 carrots, scrubbed but not peeled, sliced on the diagonal into ⅛-inch ovals
2 ribs celery, cut into 3-inch lengths
¼ pound small whole domestic mushrooms, cleaned, stems cut flush with cap (if large, halve or quarter them)
½ head cauliflower, pulled into florets
1 large onion, cut into ½-inch-thick rounds
1 zucchini, halved lengthwise, then cut into ½-inch slices

TO FINISH (OPTIONAL)

½ bunch scallions, roots and topmost portion of green removed, sliced into ⅛-inch rounds
1 to 2 red bell peppers, charred, peeled (see page 782), cut into strips
1 cup canned chickpeas, well drained
½ to ¾ cup well-drained kalamata olives or Italian oil-cured olives

FINAL ADDITIONS (OPTIONAL)

½ cup Italian parsley leaves, finely minced
1 to 2 tomatoes, preferably garden-ripe, cut into wedges

1 Combine all of the marinade ingredients in a nonreactive saucepan and bring to a boil. Have the remaining ingredients ready, along with a large, slotted skimmer.

2 Drop the carrots into the boiling marinade. Cook for 4 minutes. Scoop out the carrots and place in a large bowl, leaving the marinade boiling. Drop the celery into the marinade and cook for 1½ minutes. Scoop it out and add to the carrots. Drop in the mushrooms and cook for 1 minute. Scoop them out and add to the other cooked vegetables. Follow the same procedure for the cauliflower (2 minutes), the onion slices (1½ minutes), and the zucchini (2 minutes).

3 Fish out and discard the dried chile from the marinade. Pour whatever's left of the marinade over the bowl of vegetables and toss in as many of the optional ingredients as you'd like. (If you're doing this well ahead of time, don't add the optionals until 1 or 2 days before serving.) Refrigerate for at least 3 hours, preferably overnight or longer. Remove the bay leaves and add the parsley and tomato wedges, if desired, just before serving.

Salads as Starters

Here are just a few of the salads in this book that work especially well as first courses. Enlarge them and they could serve as entrees or parts of component plates. Eating meatlessly is very fluid.

- *Salad of Grilled Zucchini with Cilantro Vinaigrette (page 92)*
- *Arugula Salad with Grilled Eggplant and Shiitakes (page 94)*
- *Smashed Radish and Arame Salad (page 81)*
- *"Hot Thai in the Old Town Tonight" Noodle-Tofu Salad (page 119)*
- *Fatoush (page 500)*
- *Beet and Orange Salad with Rainforest Vinaigrette (page 97)*
- *Farmer's Market Salad Plate with Caper Dressing (page 112)*
- *Fresh Artichoke Half with Black-Eyed Pea Salad, and Yogurt Dipping Sauce (page 388)*
- *Southwestern Fatoush (page 501)*
- *Mediterranean Rim Salsa (page 917)*
- *Ronni's New Wave "Killed Lettuce Salad" (page 74)*
- *The Salad (page 68) with feta, olives, and tomatoes*

Hot Starters

Sometimes you need to get a party or meal off to a hot start. If you happen to be hosting a big event, and you have the resources (staff, perhaps hired for the occasion; friends, pressed into service, or reasonably presentable, nonantisocial teenagers), by all means have a few trays circulating around the room. For a hot, somewhat substantial appetizer to pass around, the Angel Biscuits with Cheese and Sweet Honey-Tarragon Mustard Butter (page 36) are always crowd-pleasing, though my very favorite is Oven-Roasted Shiitake Mushrooms with Garlic and Coarse Salt.

If not passing hot starters, you can place them on the buffet table, replenishing periodically; at smaller dinners, whisk in the starter—on individual plates or on a larger, pass-around serving platter—as your guests are sitting down.

"For my own meals I like simplicity above all. I like newness in what I serve. . . . I like leisure. I like a mutual ease."

—**M. F. K. Fisher,** *Serve it Forth*

Oven-Roasted Shiitake Mushrooms with Garlic and Coarse Salt

If you make one hors d'oeuvre out of this cookbook, let it be this one. Six years of making and serving these nearly every night in the restaurant did not dim my enthusiasm for them. One co-chef, Sam "Catfish" Routh, and I used to jive around the kitchen barking like seals when there were a few extra, begging each other for more (I hope the sound did not reach the dining room), while another, Fred Maese, proudly served enormous platters of them, platter after platter, straight from the oven at his fiftieth birthday party.

So straightforward that they are the height of sophistication, these are pure simplicity to make: four ingredients, five if you count the garnish. Using less oil yields mushrooms that are drier, chewier, a little crisp around the edges; the larger amount yields more succulent, moister mushrooms. Both are good beyond good. You'll be making this a bunch, so try it both ways. **SERVES 6 TO 8**

Cooking spray (optional)
1¼ pounds shiitake mushrooms, stems removed (save the stems for stock)
1 to 3 tablespoons olive oil (or use this amount plus a little extra Garlic Oil, page 898, and omit the diced garlic)
1 tablespoon very finely minced or pureed garlic
1½ teaspoons coarse sea salt (if salt is in very large crystals, you may crush it a bit with a mortar and pestle)
Herb sprigs (thyme or rosemary)

1 Preheat the oven to 400°F.

2 Spray a jelly roll pan or a baking sheet with sides with cooking spray, or use a nonstick pan.

3 Toss the mushrooms with the oil, garlic, and salt. Place the shiitakes in a single layer on the prepared pan, caps up or down, it makes no difference. Just make sure that they have room to breathe.

4 Bake, uncovered, for 10 to 12 minutes. Remove the pan from the oven and shake a few times. Some of the mushrooms should be starting to get a little golden on the lighter, underneath-side of the caps. You will probably need to put them back in for a little longer—say, 3 to 5 minutes, maybe more if your oven wasn't really hot when you put them in. You want at least a third of the mushrooms starting to turn a nice golden color on the gill side and getting a little crunchy. If you have used the lesser amount of oil, this will happen more quickly.

5 Serve, warm or at room temperature, garnished, if you wish, with an herb sprig on each one.

COOK ONCE FOR 2 MEALS Make a double recipe of the shiitakes. Serve half and hide the other half away until they are cool, then refrigerate. A night or two or three later, whip them out and slice them. Use them to make a Shiitake Mushroom Pizza with the crust on page 350, with or without cheese and other ingredients. Or try a Shiitake Mushroom Sandwich, much like the one we periodically indulge in at the New Moon Spa, in Eureka's castlelike, landmark Crescent Hotel. It features a big helping of the sautéed (hence moister) version of these mushrooms, lettuce, tomato, wedges of sliced smoked tofu, sprouts, sometimes avocado, sometimes cheese, sometimes a kind of Russian dressing-y spread.

Stuffed Deviled Mushrooms

The usual stuffed mushroom relies on whopping amounts of grated Parmesan cheese and olive oil (in which the diced mushroom stems are usually sautéed) for flavor. Besides having a fraction of the fat, these move beyond the cliché, are quicker to do, and to me are much tastier. Ground raw mushroom stems, rather than sautéed, cut the need for excessive olive oil, yielding a delightfully moist filling with an essence-of-mushroom quality that cheese varieties lack. The tiny bit of Dijon works magic, too. **MAKES 25 STUFFED MUSHROOMS**

25 medium button mushrooms, cleaned
Cooking spray
½ cup soft whole wheat breadcrumbs
3 large basil leaves, finely chopped
1 teaspoon Dijon mustard
1 large clove garlic, quartered
2 teaspoons olive oil
1 large onion, finely chopped
1 tomato, halved, seeded, and grated (skin discarded)
Salt and freshly ground black pepper to taste

1 Preheat the oven to 375°F.

2 Remove the stems from the mushrooms by twisting as if unscrewing stem from cap. Coarsely chop enough stems to equal 1 cup and place in the work bowl of a food processor. Save the remaining stems for another use (such as in stock, page 139). Place the mushrooms, stem side up, in a shallow baking dish sprayed with cooking spray. Bake, uncovered, for 15 minutes.

3 Add the breadcrumbs, basil, mustard, and garlic to the stems in the food processor. Buzz until a smooth paste is formed. Leave the mixture in the work bowl.

4 Heat the olive oil in a nonstick skillet, or one that has been sprayed with cooking spray, over medium heat. Add the onion and sauté until softened and translucent, about 5 minutes. Add the grated tomato and sauté for 2 minutes more. Remove from the heat, and scrape into the food processor. Pulse a few times to combine, but leave some onion-y texture. Season with salt and freshly ground black pepper.

5 Remove the mushrooms from the oven. They should appear slightly shriveled on the bottom, and the cap may have a bit of exuded mushroom juice. Pour any

of this juice into the mixture in the processor and pulse just once or twice. Scoop a heaping teaspoonful of the filling into each mushroom cap. Place the stuffed caps back in the baking dish and bake until the tops color slightly and get a bit crusty, 20 to 25 minutes.

Mushrooms Diablo

This hot, sweet, spicy Dairy Hollow classic has improved since the days of the first Dairy Hollow House cookbook, when we made it with *tons* of butter. In its current incarnation, the fat is much reduced and the liquid reduces down in the oven, concentrating the flavors.

They have the extra advantage of keeping very well, since they include quite a bit of vinegar. Easily done ahead and reheated at the last minute, this dish is perfect for occasions when you'll have your hands full with other last-minute details. **SERVES 4 TO 6 AS A FIRST COURSE, 10 TO 12 AS PART OF AN HORS D'OEUVRES BUFFET**

Cooking spray
1 tablespoon butter
1 large onion, cut vertically into very thin crescents
1 red bell pepper, stemmed, seeded, and finely slivered
1 green bell pepper, stemmed, seeded, and finely slivered
1 yellow bell pepper, stemmed, seeded, and finely slivered
1 pound domestic mushrooms, cleaned and quartered
½ cup red-wine vinegar
¼ cup good hearty red wine
2½ tablespoons Dijon mustard
2½ tablespoons Pickapeppa sauce
1 teaspoon tamari or shoyu soy sauce
¼ cup brown sugar
Salt and freshly ground black pepper to taste
3 tablespoons golden raisins

1 Preheat the oven to 350°F.

2 Spray a large skillet with cooking spray, add the butter, and place over medium-high heat. When butter is melted and quite hot but not brown, add the onion. Sauté until translucent and starting to soften, about 3 minutes. Add the red, green, and yellow peppers and sauté for 3 minutes. Add the mushrooms, turn down the heat to medium-low, and continue to sauté for another 3 minutes.

3 As the mushrooms cook, whisk together the vinegar, red wine, mustard, Pickapeppa, and tamari. When well blended, whisk in the brown sugar and salt and black pepper (you can hardly have too much black pepper in this, so keep grinding).

4 Raise the heat under the skillet. Add the vinegar mixture, along with the raisins. Scrape the mixture into a nonreactive 9-by-14-inch casserole dish and place in the preheated oven. Bake, uncovered, stirring occasionally, until the liquid has reduced to a thick syrupy sauce, 30 to 40 minutes. Serve hot, warm, or at room temperature.

Hill Country Quesadillas

This could be a starter lunch or supper—it's easy and good, unpretentious, and perennially appealing. **MAKES 6 QUESADILLAS**

1 recipe Austin Hill Country Hummus (page 21)
6 whole wheat tortillas
3 ounces grated sharp Cheddar or Monterey Jack cheese
Cooking spray

OPTIONAL BUT WONDERFUL ACCOMPANIMENTS
A good commercial salsa, Arkansalsa (page 913), or Pamela Jones's Absolutely Incredible Roasted Vegetable Salsa (page 915)
Regular or light sour cream or sour half-and-half, Tofu Sour Cream (page 909), or Yogurt Sour Cream (page 910)
Sliced avocado or Mockamole (page 22)

1 Spread one-sixth of the Hill Country Hummus on one half of each tortilla. Divide the cheese among the tortillas and fold shut into half-circles.

2 Heat a nonstick skillet, or one that has been sprayed with cooking spray, over medium-high heat. Place the tortillas in the skillet (you'll probably be able to fit 2 at a time). Cook until starting to brown underneath, about 2 minutes, then flip over to brown the other side. Brown the remaining tortillas.

3 With a pizza cutter or sharp knife, cut the quesadillas into small triangles as if cutting wedges from half a pie. Pass the quesadillas immediately, while still meltingly hot. Have as many of the optionals on the table as possible, so people can add fixin's as they like.

VARIATION

MEDITERRANEAN RIM "QUESADILLAS": ***Fill tortillas with conventional Middle Eastern–Style hummus, commercial or from scratch, along with a teeny sprinkle of feta cheese. Cook as in the recipe, serving with Mediterranean Rim Salsa (page 917), and Olivada (page 24) or Eggplant Tapenade with Hijiki (page 24).***

First-Class, First-Course Nibbling Platters

Three parts of the world—America, Italy, and the Middle East—each have their own translation of the same abundantly welcoming idea: a beautiful, bountiful, heaped-high, nonfussy platter mostly of crisp, fresh, colorful vegetables, with a few pickles and a bowl of a spread, paste, or pâté. Sometimes hard-cooked eggs, pickled or otherwise, and maybe a wedge of cheese is added. Serve with bread or crackers; have it waiting on the dining room table or buffet when your guests arrive, and you've expressed generosity, hospitality, and good-things-to-come without breathing a word.

The Relish Tray Redefined

Over the years this awaited guests who came to the inn's Thanksgiving dinners. It is intentionally old-fashioned—ordinary California black and green pimento-stuffed olives, for instance, as opposed to the more full-flavored Mediterranean olives, and good old carrot and celery sticks. But the pickles were always from scratch, the pâté might be from black-eyed peas or mushrooms (instead of chicken liver) or not pâté at all but Voluptuous Roasted Red Pepper Spread (page 17). The hard-cooked eggs were autumnal yellow and irresistible, having been bathing for a week or more in a vinegary turmeric marinade. Put it all together and you had something unpretentious, pretty, and totally pleasing . . . traditional, but new and fresh. Guests loved it. As Mark Dewitz, once chef at Dairy Hollow House, said, surveying a counter-top of them all made up and ready to be carried to the dining room, "It's like, the relish plate redefined." **QUANTITY VARIABLE**

NOTE

Befitting the celebration of that most American of all holidays, this is a dish designed to be shared, conversed over. A small plate could feed two; a large, four to six. Larger than that gets unwieldy if it's a sit-down dinner; it's too big to pass around and not everyone can reach it seated. However, if you have it set up on a buffet where guests can circulate around it, a Relish Tray Redefined can be enormous. Hence the quantities given are flexible; multiply things out as needed. Do allow at least 2 tablespoons per person; that is, a ¼-cup ramekin for 2 people, a ½-cup container for 4 people, and so on. If using just a few relish plate items, be more generous.

Large, decorative lettuce leaves (romaine or red-leaf) or flat collard green leaves, or chard leaves, washed and dried, 1 for every 2 or 3 people

Small-to-large ramekins of pâté or spread such as Hillbilly Hummus (page 18), Black-Eyed Pea Pâté (page 19), Mushroom-Lentil Pâté (page 20), and so on

Raw vegetables for crudités (see page 62), 2 or 3 of each variety of vegetable per person, well drained and patted dry

Dewitz-Dragonwagon Pickled Eggs, well drained, quartered (allow ½ egg per person) (recipe follows)

Pitted black California olives, 1 to 3 per person

Pimento-stuffed green olives, 1 to 3 per person

1 or 2 sweet relishes, such as Pineapple or Mango Pachadi (page 925), Fresh Ginger and Pear Relish (page 930), or Cora Pinkley Call's Uncooked Ozark Relish (page 929) (allow 1 to 2 heaping teaspoons per variety, per person)

Basket of crackers, toasts, and breads; Parchment Cracker-Bread (page 31) is highly recommended for inclusion here

1 Place the large, decorative leaf or leaves on your plate or platter. Be sure to use a plate large enough to contain all you're going to put on it. The leaves serve as backdrop for all the delicious things you're about to start heaping. Start by placing the ramekin of hummus, black-eyed pea pâté, or whatever spread you've decided on, in the center of the leaf-covered plate. The ramekin should be heavy enough to weight down the leaf and visually anchor the plate.

2 Pile the raw vegetables decoratively around the ramekin, each type grouped together. Keep an eye to color, placing for maximum contrast; orange carrots should be next to pale green celery or bright green scallions, for example, not next to yellow bell pepper strips. Next, add the quartered Dewitz-Dragonwagon Pickled Eggs, little piles of both the black and green olives, and little piles of the salty-tart pickles and sweet relishes. Again, think through the colors. The pickles and olives are more drab then the fresh vegetables so you might want to intersperse them.

3 Place the plate on the serving table with an accompanying basket of crackers, toasts, and breads. As long as the room isn't so warm that it will cause the fresh vegetables to wilt, the tray can go out up to 45 minutes before serving.

Henri Charpentier Wings It

"Give me your biggest platter,' I commanded him and when he brought it I was filled with envy for it was a very old thing more than a yard long and half as wide at the middle. It was a piece of ancient porcelain treasured up in that Alpine village who can say how many generations. The tracery of brown cracks over its gray-whiteness created such a longing of passion in me. . . . But I went to work.

"Diagonally I arranged a row of tomato slices so that it became a strip of scarlet of the platter; then in turn I arranged other stripes of raw cucumber slices, of raw carrot thinner than pepper, Madame hastened, in response to my shoutings, to deliver to me some beets that she had boiled that morning. Sliced, they gave me the magenta stripe my palette needed. The white was made of slices of cold boiled potatoes. . . . I reduced the flesh from a double handful of black ripe olives [into] pungently flavored . . . crumbs and made thin circles of green from the flesh of brine-cured olives. In the geography of that interesting platter these things became mountains. There was also a hill of lettuce.

"Do you not see what I had devised? An assortment of hors d'oeuvres."

—**Henri Charpentier,** *Those Rich and Great Ones, or Life à la Henri*

Dewitz-Dragonwagon Pickled Eggs

My redoubtable editor, Suzanne Rafer, remarked via Post-it note on this recipe in the manuscript, "So, Dragonwagon is puttin' on Dewitz?" Yes, that, and also thanking Mark Dewitz for introducing me to these. Start the eggs at least a week before you need them, two weeks is even better. Believe it or not, due to the vinegar and salt, they'll keep just fine in the refrigerator for several months. A gallon glass jar of the white ovoids, their sides pressed against the glass, the liquid yellow and mysterious, is always one of the warning signs that Thanksgiving is just around the corner here. They're haunting and addictive in their tart, yellow pickliness—I highly recommend doubling the recipe. **MAKES 12 EGGS**

VARIATION

PASSIONATELY EMPURPLED PICKLED EGGS: ***Omit the turmeric. Add to the pickling mixture an additional ½ to 1 cup sugar, honey, or Rapidura. Add 3 beets, baked as described on page 701, and quartered, to the jar with the eggs and the pickling mixture.***

- 2½ cups cider vinegar or distilled white vinegar
- 2½ cups water, preferably spring or filtered
- ½ cup sugar, brown sugar, or Rapidura
- 2 tablespoons turmeric
- 1 tablespoon salt
- 1 tablespoon whole black peppercorns
- 2 teaspoons whole allspice berries
- 3 bay leaves
- 2 cinnamon sticks, broken in half
- 1 slice fresh ginger
- 12 large eggs, preferably organic, hard-cooked
- 24 whole cloves

1 Combine the vinegar, water, sugar, turmeric, salt, peppercorns, allspice, bay leaves, cinnamon sticks, and ginger in a non-reactive pot over medium-high heat. Bring to a boil, then turn the heat down and simmer as you peel the hard-cooked eggs.

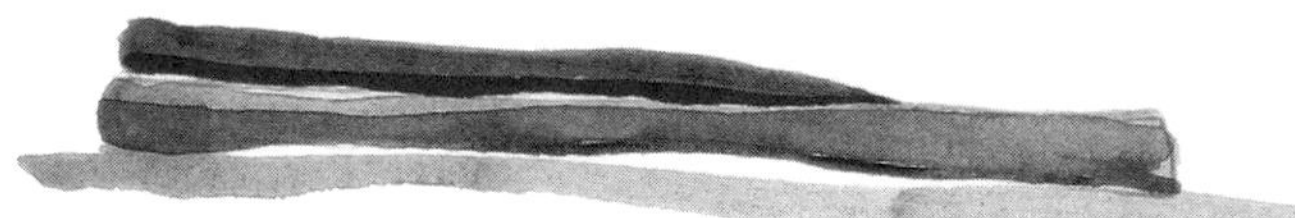

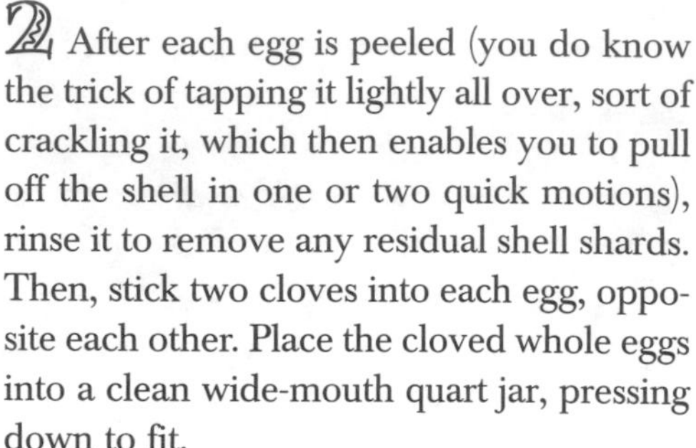

2 After each egg is peeled (you do know the trick of tapping it lightly all over, sort of crackling it, which then enables you to pull off the shell in one or two quick motions), rinse it to remove any residual shell shards. Then, stick two cloves into each egg, opposite each other. Place the cloved whole eggs into a clean wide-mouth quart jar, pressing down to fit.

3 Pour the hot pickling mixture, with all of its spices and the slurry of turmeric from the bottom, over the eggs. The eggs should be covered and there may even be a bit left over; if, however, this is not the case, top off the jar with a little more cider vinegar. Let the eggs cool, uncovered, then cover, tighten the lid, and place in the fridge for at least 1 week. Shake every few days to redistribute the spices, but expect that the eggs won't be evenly yellow, and that there will be a trace of brown around the clove site. Either remove the cloves from the eggs before serving or warn your guests that they're there.

Antipasto Platter

When The Relish Tray Redefined (page 53) goes to Italy, this is what happens. Although classic antipasti usually include many varieties of highly seasoned preserved meat, so abundant are the possible and equally traditional vegetable components that you can put a meatless platter together that is positively overflowing. (You may also, if so inclined, add some the soy-and-seitan-based vegetarian ersatz deli "meats." They vary in quality, and some vegetarians don't enjoy eating anything even pseudo-"meaty" but some of these products are quite tasty.)

Such platters are infinitely variable; almost any vegetable can be grilled and served at room temperature and/or diced and marinated. I love beets, for example, red and/or golden, baked or pressure-cooked (see page 701), dressed with the merest hint of good olive oil, vinegar, salt, and a dab of honey (they do tend to bleed, though, so put them in a separate bowl or ramekin). Another possibility, if not using the Eggplant-Lentil Caponata or the Marinated Vegetable Antipasti with the optional chick-peas, is to drop in a salad of marinated beans or legumes. **QUANTITY VARIABLE**

NOTE

Serve this, in lieu of salad, before almost any pasta or risotto dinner. Or, with enough bread and a hot hors d'oeuvre (maybe the Stuffed Deviled Mushrooms on page 50), it could be dinner.

Large, decorative lettuce leaves (romaine or red-leaf), flat collard green leaves, or chard leaves, washed and dried, 1 for every 2 or 3 people

Small-to-large ramekins of Eggplant-Lentil Caponata (page 390), and/or Marinated Vegetable Antipasti (page 46), or, if pressed for time or trying to pull a rabbit out of a hat for unexpected company, commercial bottled marinated artichoke hearts or red peppers (allow 2 tablespoons per person; that is, a ¼-cup ramekin for 2 people, a ½-cup for 4 people, and so on; if using artichoke hearts, allow 2 per person)

Raw vegetables for crudités (see page 62), 2 to 3 of each variety of vegetable per person, well drained and patted dry—be sure to include fennel

Hard-cooked eggs, peeled and quartered (allow ½ egg per person), or Italian-Style Stuffed Eggs (recipe follows)

Italian black olives, 1 to 3 per person, or a scoop of Mediterranean Cornucopia of Olives (page 44) or Olivada (page 24)

Italian green olives, 1 to 3 per person, or a scoop of Mediterranean Cornucopia of Olives (page 44) or Olivada (page 24)

½-ounce wedges provolone and/or fresh mozzarella, 1 or 2 per person

Grilled zucchini (see page 797), cooled to room temperature, 1 to 2 slices per person, or, if you didn't use the Eggplant-Lentil Caponata, grilled eggplant

Commercially made pickled pepperoncini, 1 per person

Red bell peppers, charred, skinned, and cut into eighths, ¼ pepper per person (see page 782)

Basket of crackers, toasts, and breads; Parchment Cracker-Bread (page 31), is highly recommended for inclusion here, as is a nice long loaf of hard-crusted Italian bread

1 Place the large, decorative leaf or leaves on your plate or platter. Be sure to use a plate large enough to contain all you're going to put on it. The leaves serve as backdrop for all the delicious things you're about to start heaping. Start by placing the ramekin of caponata or antipasti in the center of the leaf-covered plate. The ramekin should be heavy enough to weight down the leaf and visually anchor the plate.

2 Pile the raw vegetables decoratively around the ramekin. Keep an eye to color, placing for maximum contrast; orange carrots should be next to pale green celery or bright green scallions, for example, not

next to yellow bell pepper strips. Next, add the quartered hard-cooked eggs, little piles of both kinds of olives, and the wedges of provolone and/or fresh mozzarella. Lay the grilled zucchini and/or eggplant out, a little pile of the pickled pepperoncini and one of red peppers. Again, think through the colors. The pickles and olives are more drab than the fresh vegetables so you might want to intersperse them.

3 Place on a serving table, with accompanying basket of crackers, toasts, and breads. As long as the room isn't so warm that it will cause the vegetables to wilt, the platter can go out up to 45 minutes before serving.

Italian-Style Stuffed Eggs

You might think that stuffed or deviled eggs would be an endangered menu item by now, what with years of bad press about yolk's cholesterol, plus all that mayo. But put them on a buffet table, and, without fail, you'll see they are one of the first things to vanish. Perhaps it's because they are easily recognized, familiar comfort food, *and* festive. Or it could just be that they're good.

In classic deviled eggs, the yolks are mashed with mayonnaise; in Italian-style, the mayonnaise is very lemony and they are garnished with pickled caper buds and a sweet sprinkle of diced roasted red bell pepper. I prefer to substitute Tofu Mayonnaise.

"Because the egg is such a useful article, it deserves respectful handling."

—America's Cook Book, 1938

MAKES 16 TO 20 STUFFED EGG HALVES

8 to 10 hard-cooked eggs, peeled, rinsed, patted dry, and halved (see peeling trick described in Step 2 of Dewitz-Dragonwagon Pickled Eggs, page 55)
⅓ cup Tofu Mayonnaise (page 906), or ¼ cup commercial mayonnaise
Finely grated rind of 1 large or 2 small lemons
Salt and freshly ground white pepper to taste
Well-drained small capers; finely minced roasted red bell pepper; Italian parsley

Pop the egg yolks out of the whites, and, with a fork, mash them to fluffiness, working in the mayonnaise. Add the lemon rind, salt, and white pepper. Mound the mixture back into the egg whites. Garnish each yolk with a few capers, a bit of red pepper, and a leaf of Italian parsley.

Marvelous Mezze

Long before the phrase "Mediterranean diet" came into common parlance, a cookbook published by the Greek Orthodox Church of Hempstead, Long Island, in 1961, found its way to me in Eureka Springs. As I remember, it arrived circa 1972 via Mrs. Jerald Hanks. Did she give it to me because I had brought some baklava to a potluck? It must have been something like that as, in those days, I used to import filo dough from New York, and my pastries were the talk of the town. Now filo's available right here in Eureka Springs and filo-wrapped tidbits are no longer such an oddity.

At any rate, Mrs. Hanks very kindly sought me out, said, "I thought you would like this," and presented me with The Grecian Gourmet. *Its spiral binding is now crumpled, its pages funky and yellowed with age, for it has been much used. It expanded my Greek cooking horizons far beyond baklava and savory pastries to mezedakia or assorted appetizers. These, I'm told, start many meals in Greece, usually accompanied by a glass of ouzo or wine.*

Small dishes—served not only in Greece, but all around the Mediterranean—have a laid-back quality ideal for entertaining. Most can be done ahead, served warm, cold, or hot, and they're usually healthful. Many are traditionally vegetarian or near-vegetarian, using meat, if at all, only as a minor player, in the line of a condiment or garnish. But even better, such dishes are delicious: honest, unfussed-over, yet extraordinarily varied. Whether Greek-accented, Turkish, Israeli, Lebanese, or Russian, a mezze array offers many samplings and layers of flavors, textures, and colors. As Paula Wolfert, scholar/doyenne of the region's food, says, they're "easy to love."

They're also easy to play with. Once you understand the basic interplay of freshness, tartness, and olive-oil richness binding many of the region's marinated salad-type dishes, you can fool with the seasonings that particularize different regions and individual cooks until you find the blend that pleases you.

Some recipes for mezze you'll find here in hors d'oeuvres, but look also in the chapters on salads, beans, grains, and wrapped and stuffed foods. There are now many good Greek cookbooks available—one of my favorites is The Greek Vegetarian, *by Diane Kochilas—but there weren't in 1972, and there are some family-style recipes I've never seen anywhere else but in* The Grecian Gourmet. *So, Mrs. Hanks, thank you again.*

Middle Eastern Platter

Throughout the Mediterranean, Caucasus, and North Africa, room temperature starter platters reach their penultimate expression. Local variations and possible additions are beyond number, but all express true abundance, pure hospitality.

QUANTITY VARIABLE

NEAR EAST FEAST

Middle Eastern Platter

*

Middle Eastern–Style Pilaf with Noodles and Red Lentils
(PAGE 483)

*

Greek-Style Green Beans
(PAGE 689)

*

Fresh figs

*

Baklava

*

Turkish coffee and mint tea

Large, decorative lettuce leaves (romaine or red-leaf), flat collard green leaves, or chard leaves, washed and dried, 1 for every 2 or 3 people

Small to large ramekins of traditional hummus (commercially made, from any good cookbook, or, in a pinch, the instant variety from the natural foods store, perked up with some extra lemon juice, olive oil, and ground cumin), Hillbilly Hummus (page 18), or baba ghanoush (roasted eggplant dip, from any good Mediterranean cookbook, or commercially made)

Greek or Moroccan black olives, 1 to 3 per person, or, better yet, another large ramekin of Mediterranean Cornucopia of Olives (page 44) or Olivada (page 24)

Salad of Limas, Green Beans, and Chickpeas with Lemon and Parsley (page 103)

Raw vegetables for crudités (see page 62), 2 to 3 of each variety of vegetable per person, well drained and patted dry

Rice-stuffed vine leaves, 1 or 2 per person (use the recipe opposite, or commercially made)

Lemon wedges, 1 for every 2 or 3 people

½-ounce wedges feta cheese, 1 per person, or a ramekin of the Garlic-Feta Cream (page 38)

Commercially made pickled pepperoncini, 1 per person

Red bell peppers, charred, skinned, and cut into eighths, ¼ pepper per person

Beets, baked (see page 701), cooled, peeled, sliced, and marinated with the merest hint of good olive oil, a touch of honey, vinegar, and salt

Basket of crackers and warmed pita breads; Parchment Cracker-Bread (page 31) is highly recommended for inclusion here

1 Place the decorative leaf or leaves on a large plate or platter as back drop for all the delicious things you're about to start heaping. Place the ramekins on the leaves to weight down the leaves and visually anchor the plate.

2 Pile the raw vegetables decoratively around the ramekins. Keep an eye to color, placing for maximum contrast; orange carrots should be next to pale green celery or bright green scallions, for example, not next to yellow bell pepper strips. Next, add a pile of olives and one of marinated beans, then a pile of the stuffed vine leaves with the quartered lemon wedges. Next, the feta wedges (if you decided against Garlic-Feta Cream), and little piles of both pickled pepperoncini and red bell peppers. Again, think through the colors. The pickles and olives are more drab then the fresh vegetables so you might want to intersperse them.

3 Place on a serving table, with accompanying basket of crackers, toasts, and breads. As long as the room isn't so warm that it will cause the vegetables to wilt, the platter can go out up to 45 minutes before serving.

Stuffed Grape Leaves

Every household in Greece, Turkey, Lebanon, and other nearby countries has its own variation on grape leaf filling. Here's mine: with mint, currants, rice, lentils, pine-nuts, and herbs—of which the fresh mint is most vital. At home, I make these with wild grape leaves, which grow all over the hollow. Fresh leaves have a more lemony-fresh flavor than the bottled kind, but the bottled kind, packaged in brine, are fine, too. **MAKES 12 TO 15**

¼ cup pine nuts
1 tablespoon olive oil
Cooking spray
1 large red onion, finely chopped
1 carrot, finely diced
1½ cups cooked short-grain brown rice
½ cup cooked lentils, preferably Pardina or Puy lentils
1 tablespoon tomato paste
¼ cup currants
⅓ cup finely minced fresh parsley
¼ cup finely minced fresh mint or spearmint
1 tablespoon finely minced fresh dill
Salt and freshly ground black pepper to taste
12 to 15 large fresh or bottled grape leaves, prepared for stuffing (see note)
1 cup water, preferably spring or filtered
2 lemons, halved, plus additional lemons, cut lengthwise into quarters

1 Place the pine nuts in a small, dry skillet and toast over medium heat about 3 minutes, or until golden.

2 Heat the olive oil over medium heat in a nonstick skillet, or one that has been sprayed with cooking spray. Add the onion and sauté for 3 minutes. Add the carrot and lower the heat. Continue to sauté slowly, stirring often, about 10 minutes more, or until onion is quite soft. Scrape onion and carrot into a bowl. Set skillet aside, unwashed.

3 Add the rice, lentils, tomato paste, currants, toasted pine nuts, parsley, mint, and dill to the carrot mixture in the bowl. Stir well to combine. Season with salt and pepper to taste. (Bottled grape leaves will need less salt than fresh.)

4 Lay a grape leaf flat on your work surface. Place a rounded teaspoonful of the filling (a little more, if leaves are extra-large) in the middle of the leaf. Fold the sides of the leaf over the filling, then roll the length of the leaf to form a neat little packet. Place, seam-side down, in the reserved skillet. Continue until all grape leaves are stuffed.

5 Pour the water over the leaves in the skillet and bring to a boil. Squeeze in the juice of the 2 lemons, lower heat to the merest simmer, and cover tightly. Let simmer, adding water if necessary, about 40 minutes, or until leaves are tender. Serve warm or at room temperature, offering additional lemon quarters for squeezing over the leaves.

NOTE

Here's how to prepare bottled or fresh grape leaves prior to stuffing: If you are using grape leaves from a jar, remove entire contents, unfurl the leaves from their rolled, cylinder form, and rinse them well before using. With a scissor, snip off the tough stems.

If you can find fresh grape leaves: Select leaves about as big as your palm, choosing those with as few holes in them as possible. Wash the leaves thoroughly. Pat them dry, and, using a scissor, snip off the tough stem. Steam them just until they wilt, about 1 minute, then rinse with cold water and drain well.

Crudités . . .

Crudités, properly pronounced "cru-di-TAYs," has been frequently and deliberately mispronounced by my friend Jan Brown and me since the early days of our association, as "CRUDE-ites." Yet another intentional mispronunciation is offered by this book's editor, Suzanne Rafer: "crude-diddies." Because, let's face it, isn't "crudités" pretty high-falutin' for just cut-up raw vegetables?

Just cut-up raw vegetables—but they are so good, for many reasons, on a buffet table. Though some are tastier than others, as a group they add a light, fresh crispness and variety to a dip or spread offering: They are a boon to those watching calorie or fat intake and, most of all, have a strong visual appeal.

Crudité baskets or platters are now even easier to put together with many of the new precut products available—everything from pared thumb-size baby carrots to broccoli and cauliflower florets. When purchasing prepared vegetables, examine them carefully for freshness, as precut vegetables lose their appeal far more quickly than whole.

I should note that I used to be adamant about preparing crudités at the last minute and not ever soaking them, primarily because so many vitamins are water-soluble. I have changed my thinking on this, however; the vegetables I have suggested soaking are just so much crisper, sweeter, and fresher tasting with an overnight ice water bath, and their prep is so much easier, that I just had to come around.

Remember to save all vegetable trimmings (except those from members of the cabbage family or strong-flavored vegetables, like fennel or radish) for the stock pot.

BROCCOLI: *Broccoli has a certain flavor when raw that I am not wild about, though it does have its partisans. Raw or quick-blanched, though, it's pretty on a platter. To use it raw: Wash well, cut into 1- to 1¼-inch florets (reserving stems for another use), and cover with ice water. Refrigerate overnight. Even better: Bring a huge pot of water to a boil and drop in the prepared florets. Blanch for maybe 20 to 30 seconds or just until the green color intensifies. Immediately drain, and rinse under cold running water to stop the cooking. Dry very well, patting, and refrigerate until serving time.*

CARROTS: *Peel the carrots, cut off stem ends, quarter lengthwise, then halve. Drop into ice water and refrigerate overnight. Drain and pat dry before placing on the serving platter. If you can find organic carrots, do use them, as they are usually noticeably sweeter.*

CAULIFLOWER: *Delicious raw—crisp, mild, and pretty whether snowy white or white mottled with a blush of purple. Core out the tough center and break into bite-size florets. Drop into in ice water and refrigerate overnight. Drain and pat dry before placing on the serving platter.*

CELERY: *Cut the root ends off of a celery bunch and remove the tough outer ribs. Wash the inner ribs well, dividing into individual ribs. Remove most of the leaves (don't forget that stock pot). With a sharp paring knife, cut off the base end of each rib and, if there are any noticeable strings, pull them gently up and off the celery. Then cut the celery ribs once or twice lengthwise and once or twice crosswise into sticks that are of a handy size. Drop into ice water and refrigerate overnight. Drain and pat dry before placing on the serving platter.*

A celery caveat: Classic as it is, celery is one of the ten most heavily sprayed vegetables grown. If I can't purchase certified organic celery, I either forgo it or sub-

. . . More Crudités . . .

stitute trimmed ribs of bok choy cabbage (sometimes called celery cabbage) instead.

CUCUMBER: *I stay away from waxed cucumbers, preferring to go for the fresh summer cukes, crisp and sweet. If the waxed variety is all that is available, peel them; otherwise, leave the peel on. Slice on the diagonal into slices about 3/8 inch thick, drop into ice water, and refrigerate overnight. Drain and pat dry before placing on the serving platter.*

A cuke caveat emptor: Alas, cucumbers also make the ten least wanted list, in terms of heavy pesticide spraying. This, plus the wax, has caused me to drop them from my crudités list unless I can purchase certified organic.

FENNEL: *Delicious and licorice-flavored, sliced fennel is de rigeur on an antipasti plate, where it may be offered grilled and at room temperature, or raw. Cut off the green tops (you may reserve them as a garnish), the tough root at the base, and remove any tough outer layers. This leaves a round form from golf- to tennis ball–size. Halve, and remove the triangular core. Slice across, and you'll have what look like large, pale slices of celery (it's in the same family as celery), in curved C shapes. Drop into ice water and refrigerate overnight. Drain and pat dry before placing on the serving platter.*

GREEN BEANS: *Raw green beans do have their fans, but I am not among them. If you find uniformly thin, unblemished green beans, by all means use them, but only after a quick blanching, about 20 seconds, in boiling water, just long enough to deepen their color and take the fuzz off. Immediately drain, and rinse under cold running water to stop the cooking. Dry very well, patting, and refrigerate until serving time.*

JÍCAMA: *Exquisitely crisp and very sweet, when this rather ugly-looking tuber is cut up, its flesh resembles nothing so much as fresh water chestnuts. Choose jícama (HEE-kah-mah) that are not too large and are still firm and smooth. There's treasure beneath that unprepossessing brown skin. Peel it off and thinly slice the jícama. I'm partial to rectangles of jícama 2 inches by 1 inch and 1/4 to 1/2 inch thick. Drop into ice water and refrigerate overnight. Drain and pat dry before placing on the serving platter.*

MUSHROOMS: *Skip raw mushrooms, of any variety, on a crudité platter, as they contain a phytochemical—an enzyme—that, when raw, is a carcinogen. If you like, steam small whole button mushrooms for about 2 minutes, then soak them in an oil-and-vinegar marinade seasoned with bay leaf, peppercorns, mustard seeds, and salt. Or grill larger mushrooms, such as portobellos (see page 769) then use them, sliced, on the platter.*

PEA PODS: *Choose edible-pod peas, either the flatter snow peas or the more rounded sugar-snaps (the latter are my favorite). Wash them in cold water, break off the stem end if desired (these aren't eaten, but make nice handles for picking them up), and wrap them, with a little water still clinging to them, in paper towels. This is both to dry them and keep them fresh and crisp for storing up to overnight. Don't soak them.*

PEPPERS—RED, YELLOW, AND GREEN BELLS: *The one vegetable for crudités that must, in my view, not be prepped in advance but cut up as close to serving time as possible, as their delightful crispness often turns mushy when they are cut up in advance. Otherwise, they're sugar-sweet, especially the reds and yellows, crisp, and nothing, but nothing, has such color. Cut out the stem end, halve the peppers, remove the seeds, and cut into*

. . . and Still More Crudités

strips or wedges, as you prefer. Gently go over the strips or wedges with a paring knife to remove any residual ribs of white membrane. If you must do them in advance, soak them in ice water, refrigerated, then drain well and pat dry just before serving, discarding any whose edges have gotten soft.

A caveat for peppers, which you'll see repeated throughout this book: As much as I adore them, they, like cukes and celery, are among the ten most heavily sprayed vegetables grown—both the conventionally raised American ones and, even more so, the out-of-season peppers imported from South America. With the deepest regrets—for these are among my favorites, raw or cooked, visually and tastewise—I use only locally grown organic peppers, or those that are certified organic.

RADISHES: *If possible choose small radishes with their green tops still attached. I wash them well, plunk them in ice water, refrigerate for at least a couple of hours or up to a day in advance, drain, and dry well. I serve them with leaves and skinny little root hairs still attached. I think that they're gorgeous on the platter that way, plus they stay crisper.*

Daikon, a Japanese radish that looks like a stout, very straight white carrot, is also wonderful—crisp, mild, considerably less peppery than the red. Slice daikon on the diagonal to make pale ovals about ¼ inch thick. You may soak them in ice water overnight, drain, and pat dry, but I think they are really better if chilled whole and sliced just before using.

SUMMER SQUASH: *I am not a fan of raw summer squash or zukes, though I'm very fond of them sautéed even briefly. If you like them raw, they fare best chilled whole, and cut up just before use. Choose smallish, unblemished summer squash; wash well, remove stem ends, and slice on the diagonal into ovals about ¼ inch thick. Instead of piling them on the platter, overlap them so the colored skin shows, not just the pale interior.*

CHERRY TOMATOES: *Do not refrigerate tomatoes, as they get cottony inside. Rinse well, drain, and pile up on the platter. If you can get a variety—the traditional round red ones, the bright golden yellow, or tiny pear-shaped tomatoes—use them all. (The yellow pear-shaped ones are treasures—sweet and intriguing and wonderful, as sunny-flavored as they look.) I leave the stems on because I like the way they look and they do give you a handle to pick the tomatoes up with.*

SCALLIONS: *Okay, here's the exception to the rule—the one crudité I fuss with (though it still comes out looking like a green onion, not a daisy or something). It's as easy as can be to make a scallion brush, which will look festive and charming and a bit silly on the platter. Choose scallions whose white ends, above the roots, are at least ⅜ inch in diameter. Cut off the roots, removing any of the limp green and the outermost layer of papery skin. Cut off all but the bottom three inches of green, too (save the discards here for your soup bag). Place the trimmed scallion on a cutting board, and, with a sharp paring knife, make a vertical ½- to 1-inch cut through the white part of the scallion, in effect halving the base of the scallion while still leaving the top intact. Rotate the scallion and make a second cut, quartering the scallion base. Repeat with remaining scallions, and put them in a container of ice water. Refrigerate for several hours or overnight. In the morning, voilà! The cut edges have curled up and you have scallion brushes.*

CHAPTER 3

Salads & My Salad Days

Thirty years ago, when I first fell in love with Eureka Springs, it was a wondrous, Brigadoon-feeling small town—but you couldn't get a good green salad here, or even buy the ingredients to make one at home. Then, as now and throughout its history, Eureka Springs's income derived from serving visitors. When I arrived as a teenager, though, the city did not feel like a tourist town. Then it was easily possible to live without a car, managing all necessities on foot. Walking into town from Dairy Hollow, I'd stop at the post office, then work my way down hilly Spring Street. I'd pay local bills in turn, not only dropping off checks but visiting briefly: Paula at SWEPCO, the telephone company lady, soft-spoken and shy. At city hall, a magnificent small-scale courthouse constructed of local stone (an architectural style my preservation-ist husband calls with great satisfaction "Ozark rusticated Italianate") I paid the water bill (which had come in an envelope with the slogan "Eureka Springs—the City That Water Built"), and said "Hey" to Nita, Katherine (whose husband, Joe, was my postman), and whichever city council members happened to be around.

On my way home, I'd shop at Blondie's Market. If I'd forgotten my checkbook, I used the generic one (from the single local bank) that lay on the checkout counter. I'd load my purchases into a backpack or string bag and carry them home or, if I had too much to tote, one of Blondie's delivery boys would get it to Dairy Hollow by late afternoon. It's hard not to feel nostalgia for those days.

But here's what I could count on finding in Blondie's produce aisle: Onions. Potatoes. Carrots. Cabbage. Iceberg lettuce (most of the time). Bananas (most of time). Apples. Scallions (sometimes). Oranges and lemons (usually, but the oranges were never very good). The salads that could be made out of the usual Blondie's pickings were lackluster. When there was fresh broccoli, it was a red-letter day. I'd buy two heads and steam them both. One was for dinner, with butter and lemon (if Blondie's had had lemons that day). The other, cold, was nibbled on over the next couple of days, splashed with a garlicky vinaigrette.

Time passed. Things changed. There were losses and there were gains. A loss: the gentle, personable down-home-ness of Blondie's style of commerce. A gain: the vastly wider options and better quality of ingredients for possible salads.

The SWEPCO office moved out to the highway. Then the phone company. Where Blondie's Market once stood is a crafts shop. We now buy our groceries at Hart's Family Center, the supermarket up on the highway. Hart's seemed staggeringly new and large when it opened. Then, and now, it gave us the world. Fresh ginger, tofu, romaine lettuce, fresh spinach, eggplant, fresh red jalapeño and serrano peppers, artichokes, mangoes, and now even fresh mesclun salad mix. In the summer there's fresh basil and thyme from local growers, maybe local string beans, peppers, tomatoes, Arkansas peaches. The Hart's canned goods aisle has chipotle peppers in adobo sauce, black beans. These ingredients sparkle on the tongue that still remembers the iceberg-scallion-carrot-and-shredded-cabbage boredom of the Blondie's era.

Hart's is our year-round basic. Now there's also a farmer's market in the summer, and Ozark Country Market, an organic food store, and there are many locals who put the "culture" in agriculture. Shiitake mushrooms are grown locally; and I make the best, best salad with them (sizzling-hot mushrooms sautéed, splashed with dressing, the whole poured hot over spinach just enough to wilt it slightly). Mesclun is grown not fifteen miles from here, and organically. Blueberries? Organic too, from half a dozen sources (how sweetly calming it is to pick your own under the summer sun).

Could organic gardeners have thrived when Eureka Springs was still the tiny, sleepy, not-quite ghost town it was when I first met and fell in love with it, when it was the municipal equivalent of Rip Van Winkle just waking up, stretching, yawning, leaning with astonishment into the present day? Probably not. Sophistication, time, globalization—all had to work, as did the nature of change itself. Inevitable, constant. With every gain, losses. With every loss, gains.

You Live Where? Eureka!

Our historic Victorian downtown squirrels its way up and down a steep hill, with a radically right-angled curve in the middle. Historic, yes—but, because of activities like buying groceries and paying phone bills, it was not embalmed or reenacted. The past lived side by side with the present. As for "Victorian," while we have plenty of gingerbread front porches, turrets and cupolas, bow and bay windows, our downtown is something else: commercial Victorian buildings, mostly stone, mostly two and three storys, shops below and apartments above, appealing, individually featured facades (here tile, there a stepped-back entrance with the windows angled just so, here a faded, almost gone but still visible merchant name—someone long dead—painted in gold Gothic letters). Captivating; timeless. It was an enduring enchantment for this former New Yorker: I remember almost taking it in through my pores when I first arrived, this simple pleasure, to walk this safe, sweet, archaic place, running my errands and seeing neighbors.

When Ned and I closed Dairy Hollow House to launch the Writers' Colony, we got countless letters and e-mails mourning the inn's transition:

"But we've spent nine of our last eleven anniversaries with you!" "But Alicia was conceived in the Rose Room!" "But where will we go when we want a really a good salad?" "But Eureka won't be the same without you two running Dairy Hollow House!"

How could I say, and not sound ungrateful, something like, "Well, of *course* it won't be the same! Nothing ever is." So I didn't say anything, but "Thank you," and "I'm glad that Dairy Hollow House meant so much to you." And I *was* glad, and honored. Who would have wanted to pour so much time, energy, and Love into such an endeavor as the inn, and not have it affect others.

I'm still here. Still paying my bills, if no longer on foot. Ned and I are still married, passionately engaged at midlife, having survived, even thrived, despite and throughout the storms of loss and difficulty from which, maturity gradually shows us, no one is exempt. We still feed friends, play Scrabble, walk to town. And we work together on creating the Colony, organizing the details of welcoming writers, their creative time respected and protected, so that they may work where once we housed guests, I hope long after Ned and I are part of Dairy Hollow.

Eureka Springs remains a real town, still. It changes, because change is the currency of life. But at its core Eureka is green and vital, fresh, alive, full of contrast, texture, shades. Like a good salad, the kind for which I can now easily buy the ingredients. So, sometimes, I just stop thinking: I just go on and make myself one.

Green Salads

Almost any meal is greatly improved by the addition of a really good green salad. Nothing makes me quite so happy or tells me quite as much about a restaurant's attention to detail as such a salad. Because there are only so many accurate words to describe salads—fresh, crisp, green, refreshing—descriptions may become tired. But a perfect salad itself is never tired. Learn to make a green salad right, have the proper ingredients on hand, take the time needed (not much, especially in this era of easily available prewashed, prebagged greens), and you'll have a reliable source of pleasure and health throughout your days.

The cardinal rules of green salad making as I understand them are given in the following master recipe.

The Salad

Eating a perfectly made salad is a religious experience. It is life changing, and afterwards, difficult for the converted to resist preaching, especially when confronted with a counterfeit, so common in what passes for salad.

The Salad is the best salad I make. Now, every salad I make is good, but in my secret heart of hearts I believe that they aren't *true* salads. Only The Salad, pristine and straightforward, is the real thing. This is salad as salad was meant to be—the essence of fresh, of green, cool, crisp. It's the innocent lasciviousness of the Garden of Eden, melting, sweetly buttery leaves, combined with those that are peppery and in-your-face, as well as garlic, naked and unashamed.

The only really time-consuming parts of salad making are the washing and thorough drying of the greens. This can be done up to two days ahead of time (the method follows). You may think I am completely crazed on this topic, and I am, because the vast majority of salad mediocrity is caused by not-quite-fresh lettuces that are not-quite-washed and then not-quite-dried. However, you may now skip this step if you purchase good prewashed greens, such as a mesclun or spring mix. If you feel you must wash them again, do so—but dry, dry, dry, thoroughly. And make sure that whatever greens you buy are absolutely fresh and unwilted. **SERVES 4 TO 8**

6 to 8 cups torn, mixed salad greens, a mixture of softer greens (spinach, butterhead) with crisper (romaine) and sweeter, gentler flavored (oakleaf, reddina, butterhead) with more assertive (arugula, watercress, raddichio), or prewashed mesclun or spring mix

1 to 3 tablespoons best-quality extra virgin cold-pressed olive oil

3 to 4 cloves garlic, or more to taste

Salt and freshly ground black pepper to taste

1 lemon, halved

Dash of Pickapeppa sauce, vegetarian Worcestershire, or ½ teaspoon Dijon mustard (optional)

1 Unless you have purchased prebagged, prewashed, ready-to-eat salad greens, begin by washing the greens in cold water. Wash them extremely well; plan to take some time over it. Discard any brown-edged, wilted, or spoiled leaves; pull lettuce heads apart. In a colander, swish the greens in cold water and rinse well several times.

2 Dry the greens. Using either a salad spinner or a clean, dry pillowcase, throw off as much water as possible from the greens via centrifugal force. For the pillowcase method, dump the washed greens into a pillowcase—an old flannel one works well—and step outside. Ignoring how completely goofy you look to any passers-by, get a secure grip, then swing the heck out of it, in large vigorous circles, either over your head like a lasso or in front of your body. The greens will end up at the bottom of the pillowcase, on the opposite end of where you are gripping it, and the water will be largely flung off it. Remove the greens from the spinner or pillowcase and, using paper towels, carefully blot each and every leaf to complete bone-dryness. (When I do this ahead of time, as I used to in the restaurant, I layer the spun greens in a large bowl, with paper towels between the layers, then cover the whole bowl with plastic film into which I poke a hole or two with a tip of a knife so the greens can breathe.)

3 Put 4 to 8 salad plates in the freezer to chill.

4 Assemble a big salad bowl, a garlic press, and a small strainer along with a sharp knife. This, too, can be arranged ahead of time to make your final preparations quick and easy.

5 Just before serving, line up the remaining ingredients, tools, and utensils.

6 Pour the oil into the large salad bowl. Put the garlic through the press, right into the oil in the bowl. Then add the washed,

NOTE

There's a range of 1 to 3 tablespoons oil given. I like a salad with very, very light dressing, almost none. I go for 1 tablespoon; 3 gives you more traditional results; 1 tablespoon per person is the norm, but this is way too much for my taste and I think it overwhelms the greens' delicacy.

dried salad greens. Toss the greens with gentle vigor, until each leaf glistens with a light sheen of oil. Swiftly sprinkle the greens with ½ to 1 teaspoon salt, several enthusiastic grinds of pepper, the juice of half the lemon squeezed directly through a strainer to trap any seeds (if it's an especially large or juicy lemon, don't squeeze out every last drop), and a small shake of the Pickapeppa, Worcestershire, or Dijon.

7 Toss a few more times to distribute the seasonings, then taste. Add more salt, pepper, the juice of the other half of the lemon as needed—probably not more Pickapeppa, though. Taste again, and adjust the seasoning until it's perfect.

8 Quickly get the chilled salad plates from the freezer and divide the impeccably dressed greens among them. Serve immediately. We're talking, right now!

Dressing to Excess

In many of the salad recipes that follow, a dressing recipe is included. In most cases that recipe makes much more than you'll need for a single batch of salad, especially if you dress a salad as lightly as I do. Why, then, the larger quantity? Here are three good reasons:

1. *When making dressing in a processor, which is the quick, painless, easy way to do it, a slightly larger quantity emulsifies much more successfully than a mini-batch.*

2. *Most vinaigrette-type salad dressings keep well for several weeks in the fridge, and having them on hand is a good incentive to eat more salads.*

3. *In addition, most vinaigrette-type dressings allow you to put together marinated vegetable, grain, and other nongreen salads at a minute's notice. See the* Cook Once for Several Meals *that follow most of the larger-quantity dressings.*

Any nonsweet, strongly flavored vinaigrette allows you to pull off the following very neat trick:

Simple Bean Dip or Sauce: *Dump a 16-ounce can of any type of beans into a food processor (I particularly like butter beans, navy beans, or canellini for this) along with 2 tablespoons of your favorite on-hand garlicky-herbal vinaigrette (Sharp Classic Vinaigrette with a Bite, page 72, is perfect for this). Buzz until smooth. Add salt and pepper to taste. Use as a dip for artichoke leaves or other crudités, as a spread for bread, or heat quickly and serve as an impromptu sauce for grains or pasta.*

You can also make a delicious, creamy, simple dip or sauce the exact same way, substituting one 12.3-ounce box firm reduced-fat silken tofu for the can of beans. A delicious mix—lower in carbohydrates and overall calories than the bean version.

Salad of Local Greens and Basil Vinaigrette

If your greens are good but less perfect than those The Salad demands, or you are entertaining and just can't hack the last-minute fuss The Salad requires, make this, one of my favorite alternatives. It's a basil-scented, vinaigrette-dressed classic tossed salad. This is a salad that you might be served at a really good restaurant (though probably with too much dressing). The dressing recipe makes way more than you'll need for one batch of salad because, like most of the vinaigrettes here, it's an irresistible starting point for "Cook Once for Several Meals" ideas. Not only does it keep well, but you can use it to marinate just about any leftover cooked vegetable or to make a potato, broccoli, cauliflower, or whatever salad that will do you proud. You can also toss it with well-drained cooked beans and some diced tomatoes.

The Parmesan isn't necessary but it's awfully good. **SERVES 4 TO 6**

NOTE

OTHER OPTIONAL AND EXCELLENT ADDITIONS TO SCATTER ON TOP: ***any cooked or raw vegetable or condiment, diced baked beets (page 701) or strips of roasted red or yellow pepper (page 782), diced garden tomatoes, a few kalamata olives, or paper-thin slices of raw fennel or artichoke heart.***

6 to 8 cups mixed salad greens, washed and dried (see page 69, Steps 1 and 2)
1 cup very thinly sliced red or green cabbage (optional)
2 to 3 tablespoons Sharp Classic Vinaigrette with a Bite (recipe follows), or Four-Star Fresh Basil-Lemon Dressing with Tofu-Tomato Cream (recipe follows)
1 lemon, halved (optional)
Salt and freshly ground black pepper to taste (optional)
¼ cup freshly grated Parmesan cheese, or more to taste (optional)

1 Put salad plates into the freezer to chill.

2 Place the salad greens, and cabbage, if using, in a large bowl. Drizzle the dressing over the greens, starting with the lesser amount. Toss like the dickens. Taste a leaf. In order to get by with the minimum amount of dressing and the maximum amount of flavor, you may need to add a little lemon juice. Squeeze it through a strainer to catch the seeds and add some salt and pepper. Try this first, then, if it's still not to your liking, add a little more dressing. Toss again.

3 Add the Parmesan. Toss. Remove the chilled plates from the freezer and divide the salad among them. If you like, garnish with any vegetables, and serve immediately.

Sharp Classic Vinaigrette with a Bite

This easy dressing from the first *Dairy Hollow House Cookbook* is a workhorse. Always a star, but never a prima donna. It is classic for a good reason: It has countless uses. The only thing non-classic is the shocking amount of garlic and mustard. They are the teeth in its bite. The marinated vegetable and bean salads on pages 86 and 108 also use this sterling dressing. **MAKES ABOUT 1¾ CUPS**

½ cup cider vinegar
¼ cup good grainy Dijon mustard
4 to 6 cloves garlic, peeled
½ teaspoon salt
5 to 6 solid grinds black pepper
1 to 3 good-sized leaves fresh basil
1 cup extra virgin cold-pressed olive oil

Combine the vinegar, mustard, garlic, salt, and pepper in a food processor. Start the machine and, with the motor running, gradually drizzle in the oil.

Vinaigrette Variations

For sure you'll Cook Once for Several Meals *with this wonderful basic dressing on hand.*

TRY A HEIGHT-OF-SUMMER TOMATO SALAD *by cutting as many dense, garden-fresh tomatoes into chunks as you can get your hands on. Toss 4 to 6 cups tomatoes with ¼ cup or so dressing and add a little extra salt and pepper and maybe some minced basil and/or parsley. Don't refrigerate it; eat it immediately, at room temperature.*

CORN, RADISH, AND PARSLEY SALAD *is another straight-from-the-garden spectacular: Use one of the super-sweet corn varieties and cut the kernels straight off the cob—use 6 to 8—you should end up with about 4 cups corn. Taste a kernel; if tender and sweet, not starchy, you can and should use it raw. If not, steam the cut kernels for 3 minutes. In either case, toss the corn with a cup or so of sliced, well-washed radishes, ½ cup finely minced parsley, and 2 to 3 tablespoons dressing. Taste and add salt and freshly ground black pepper, and maybe a little more dressing. Arrange a bed of greens on each plate, lay slices of big, dense tomatoes on top, then pile on a scoop of the corn mixture. So good!*

CORN, RADISH, AND CILANTRO SALAD *For this divine Southwestern version just substitute cilantro for parsley.*

Four-Star Fresh Basil-Lemon Dressing with Tofu-Tomato Cream

In its original very creamy incarnation, this new favorite dressing came from the Del Bar Restaurant, Lake Delton, Wisconsin. With just a little tinkering—the Del Bar's canned tomatoes became fresh, vinegar became lemon juice, mayo became tofu, the seasonings got turned up—an already delicious dressing got lighter, brighter, and more contemporary.

Toss a tablespoon or two with any green leafy salad, maybe with some purple onion and nice long strips of finely julienned carrot; put a couple of beet slices on the plate; carry it out to the patio with a piece of toast for a summer lunch. Use the dressing as a dip, or spread it on a sandwich instead of mayo (on a feta cheese and tomato sandwich—dynamite). Dress a pasta salad or marinate leftover cooked vegetables in it. **MAKES ABOUT 2 CUPS**

½ cup coarsely chopped Italian parsley leaves
About 5 ounces (½ package) silken tofu, medium or firm
¼ cup diced tomato (1 to 2 fresh tomatoes, peeled, seeded, and chopped)
¼ cup fresh-squeezed lemon juice
2 tablespoons coarsely chopped fresh basil leaves
1 tablespoon Dijon mustard
1 teaspoon salt
2 cloves garlic, roughly chopped
1½ teaspoons sugar
Grated rind of 1 lemon
Freshly ground black pepper to taste
Dash of Tabasco or similar hot sauce
½ cup extra virgin olive oil

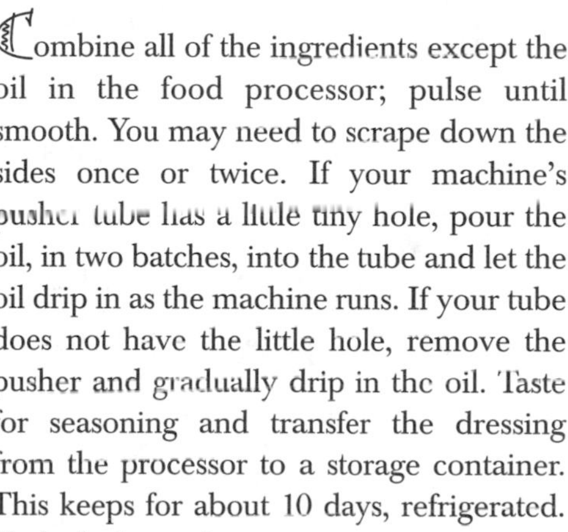

Combine all of the ingredients except the oil in the food processor; pulse until smooth. You may need to scrape down the sides once or twice. If your machine's pusher tube has a little tiny hole, pour the oil, in two batches, into the tube and let the oil drip in as the machine runs. If your tube does not have the little hole, remove the pusher and gradually drip in the oil. Taste for seasoning and transfer the dressing from the processor to a storage container. This keeps for about 10 days, refrigerated. Shake before using.

Ronni's New Wave "Killed Lettuce Salad"

Warning: This is addictive. The old-time Ozarks version of wilted lettuce salad—hot dressing poured on the greens wilts or "kills" them slightly—used fresh dandelion greens and other tonic spring gatherings. My "pan pal" in Louisville, Kentucky, Ronni Lundy, a storyteller, cookbook writer, journalist, and fine cook, says in *Shuck Beans, Stack Cakes, and Honest Fried Chicken* that killed lettuce "may sound strange, perhaps unappetizing. But to those of us who grew up eating it, killed lettuce stirs deep dark cravings in the heart." Ronni shares her killed lettuce passion with Lenore Crenshaw, a Monticello, Kentucky, native, who grew up on the same Southern fare Ronni did but quit eating meat about twenty years ago. The two friends attempted to collaborate on "approximating that rich bacon taste" without all the bacon fat. Improbably, tamari or shoyu soy sauce, toasted sesame oil, umeboshi plum vinegar (see page 118), and gomashio (see ingredients) did the trick. I took things a step further with the addition of Ned's Marsala-Marinated Portobello Grill. The resulting hybrid will knock your socks off. It is a perfect-beyond-perfect early springtime supper—especially with Ronni's Skillet-Sizzled Kentucky Buttermilk Cornbread (see page 452.) **SERVES 2 AS AN ENTREE (WITH CORNBREAD), 4 AS A SIDE**

"You get a bowl of killed lettuce and a hot piece of cornbread and a glass of cold milk and you've got you a dinner."

—singer **Brenda Lee**

Ingredients for 1 recipe Ned's Marsala-Marinated Portobello Grill (page 770)
1 large, crisp head romaine lettuce, any brown outer leaves removed, brown base removed
1 to 3 scallions, greens removed, white parts split down the middle and slivered
1 lemon, halved
1 tablespoon umeboshi plum vinegar
1 teaspoon tamari or shoyu soy sauce
3 tablespoons light (untoasted) sesame oil, or olive oil
1 tablespoon dark (toasted) sesame oil
2 teaspoons gomashio (toasted, half-ground sesame seeds mixed with sea salt, available in natural foods stores)

1 Prepare Ned's Marsala-Marinated Portobello Grill to the point where the mushrooms are marinating.

2 About 10 minutes before you wish to serve the salad, grill the mushrooms as described on page 771, Step 2.

3 As the mushrooms grill, slice (yes, slice with a knife) the romaine lettuce, crosswise, into thin shreds. Place the shreds in a large bowl and toss with the slivered scallions.

4 After the mushrooms have been turned and are grilling on their second side, whisk together the juice of ½ the lemon with the umeboshi plum vinegar and the tamari or shoyu soy sauce. Pour the mixture over the lettuce and scallion mixture and toss well.

5 Combine the oils and set aside.

6 Remove the mushrooms from the grill pan and set them aside. Immediately pour the oil mixture into the hot grill pan and quickly heat it until almost smoking. Pour the hot oil over the lettuce, tossing well with a wooden spoon and fork. Taste, adding the juice of the second lemon half if you think it necessary. Immediately divide the salad among serving plates, sprinkle each portion with a little gomashio, and arrange the grilled portobellos over the top.

VARIATION

SPEED DEMON KILLED LETTUCE SALAD WITH MUSHROOMS: ***Invented when I was visiting someone without a grill pan, this variation substitutes Annie's Shiitake Mushroom Vinaigrette for the dressing and marinade ingredients, and prewashed mesclun for the shredded romaine. You'll need the scallions; cooking spray; approximately ¾ pound assorted mushrooms, sliced (I mix shiitakes, portobellos, and whatever other varieties I can find); and the dressing. Put the mesclun and scallions in a large bowl. Sauté the mushrooms in a cooking-sprayed nonstick pan over high heat just until they soften. Quickly pour 3 to 4 tablespoons dressing over them. Immediately, with the dressing and mushrooms sizzling, pour over the mesclun, toss, and serve.***

Salad of Tender Greens with Sweet-Peppery Blackberry Vinaigrette

An extraordinarily good late spring–early summer salad, depending on when the blackberries come in. I look forward to the brief time of the year when

everything called for in this recipe is in season. Serve it at a very special dinner in early July—you'll wow yourself in the kitchen and your guests in the dining room.

This salad is all beautiful, extravagant contrast, of texture, taste, color. Tender salad greens, in a palette of pale greens, vie with soft, sensual, dead-dark blackberries and the amazing sparkle of edible flowers (bright yellow or orange nasturtium blossoms) along with the golden-brown crunch of almonds and crisp cubes of tempeh. Of all the ingredients, the berries hold the key: Blackberries, a very Arkansas fruit, are extremely tart, with a wonderful, faint undernote of bitter that points up both the tart and the sweet.

Make the Sweet-Peppery Blackberry Vinaigrette, as well as the optional Crisp Tempeh Cubes, before you start the salad. **SERVES 4 TO 6 AS A FIRST-COURSE OR SIDE SALAD, SERVES 2 TO 4 AS AN ENTREE**

VARIATION

Toss extra blackberry dressing with cantaloupe, strawberries, honeydew, and seedless green grapes for an unforgettable Blackberried Fruit Salad. Garnish with a few whole blackberries, fresh mint, and, if desired, a sprinkling of toasted almonds. Or, process any extra in a food processor with a package of silken tofu for a slightly sweet mayo to toss with squares of steamed tempeh, diced fresh fruit, and scallions for a Fruited Tempeh Salad with Blackberry Mayo. Sounds improbable but is delicious, like a Ladies-Who-Lunch chicken salad without the chicken.

6 to 8 cups tender mixed salad greens, washed and dried (see page 69, Steps 1 and 2)
About ¼ cup Sweet-Peppery Blackberry Vinaigrette (recipe follows), or to taste
1 cup fresh, whole, unbruised blackberries, rinsed and set gently on a paper towel to dry
½ cup raw almonds, coarsely chopped and lightly toasted
Unsprayed edible flowers, 6 to 8 perfect blossoms (nasturtiums or pansies)
6 to 12 long garlic chives
Crisp Tempeh Cubes (optional; recipe follows)

1 Chill 6 to 8 salad plates in the freezer.

2 Toss the salad greens in a large salad bowl with the Sweet-Peppery Blackberry Vinaigrette, tossing until the leaves are very, very lightly coated. Divide the dressed greens among the chilled plates. Then, scatter a few of the blackberries over each salad, along with some toasted almonds. Top the salads with an edible flower, and slide a long garlic chive (or two) into each one, placing so it sticks out a bit from the plate but is anchored by the greens. Finally, divide the room-temperature Crisp Tempeh Cubes among the salads and serve immediately. Pass additional dressing at the table.

Sweet-Peppery Blackberry Vinaigrette

Simply delicious, this melds sweet, spicy, hot, tart, and even a tiny hint of bitterness. Just gorgeous flavors. This dressing tends to separate, so shake it up well before you use it.

⅓ cup blackberry vinegar or juice drained from frozen blackberries (see note)
¼ teaspoon salt
1 teaspoon freshly ground black pepper, or more to taste
1 cup almond oil, if available, or peanut oil if not
1 to 2 tablespoons honey

Place the blackberry vinegar or juice in a food processor along with the salt and pepper. Turn the machine on, and with the motor running, drizzle in the almond oil through the hole in the pusher tube. When it has emulsified, remove the pusher tube, and, with the motor running, drizzle the first tablespoon of honey directly into the dressing. Stop the machine and taste. If you'd like it a bit sweeter, add the second tablespoon of honey, again with the machine running.

Crisp Tempeh Cubes

2 tablespoons blackberry vinegar or unsweetened blackberry juice (see note)
2 teaspoons tamari or shoyu soy sauce
2 teaspoons honey
1 teaspoon Pickapeppa sauce
1 package (8 ounces) tempeh, cut into ½-inch cubes
2 tablespoons nutritional yeast (see page 239)
¼ cup crisp breadcrumbs or cracker crumbs
1 teaspoon almond oil
Cooking spray (optional)

1 Combine the blackberry vinegar or juice, tamari or shoyu soy sauce, honey, and Pickapeppa in a small nonreactive bowl. Stir well to blend. Add the diced tempeh. Refrigerate for at least 1 hour, or as long as overnight.

2 About 1½ hours before you'll be fixing the salad, preheat the oven to 400°F.

3 Remove the cubed marinated tempeh from the refrigerator and bring to room temperature. Lift it from any residual marinade.

4 Combine the nutritional yeast and breadcrumbs with the almond oil in a small bowl. Shake the tempeh in this mixture and place the coated tempeh on a nonstick baking sheet or one that has been sprayed with cooking spray. Bake the tempeh cubes until one side is getting brown, 15 to 20 minutes; turn and bake for an additional 10 to 15 minutes. The cubes should be lightly browned, somewhat crisp on the outside, and tender within. Let cool to room temperature and scatter atop finished salad as directed in main recipe.

COOK ONCE FOR 2 MEALS Double the marinade, and, in addition to the cubed tempeh, marinate a second 8-ounce cake of tempeh, cut in half. Breadcrumb and bake it, too, and use it the next day as part of a Tempeh, Golden Tomato, and Arugula Sandwich, on a nice baguette or even plain whole wheat toast. Dress with a little mustard, an herby or sharp vinaigrette, or Tofu Mayonnaise (page 906).

NOTE

If you can get blackberry vinegar, do so. If not, or if you'd like a more vibrantly flavored and colored dressing, use the following trick: Buy a bag of unsweetened frozen blackberries. Let them thaw. Drain off ⅓ cup of the blackberry juice, straining out any seeds. (Use the thawed blackberries in muffins, a cobbler, or a crisp.)

VARIATIONS

For a totally different but equally wonderful sensation, try this salad mixture with my beloved Four-Star Fresh Basil-Lemon Dressing with Tofu-Tomato Cream (page 73), or with Curried Vinaigrette (see Fresh Curried Beets, page 702)—knockouts.

A heartier salad, with little bits of crispness, is Roasted Sweet Potato and Apple Salad with Honeyed Red-Wine Vinaigrette: Simply substitute a large, peeled sweet potato or yam for the butternut squash. This was Ned's suggestion, and an excellent one. Easily make an entree with the addition of the Crisp Tempeh Cubes on the previous page.

Roasted Butternut Squash and Apple Salad on a Bed of Bitter Greens

Inspired by the Vibrant Pumpkin Salad in Vikki Leng's *Earthly Delights,* a gorgeous vegetarian cookbook originally published in Vikki's native Australia, where she is known as "Vikki the Vego," this glowing fall salad uses butternut squash instead of pumpkin, has my own take on the dressing, and is served on a bed of lettuce and cabbage.

Peeling and dicing the squash (*dicing* is not exactly an accurate word, by the way, because due to the squash's curves, some of the pieces will be triangular, not square) is the only time-consuming part of the recipe. Even the dressing, though its list of ingredients might seem lengthy, goes together one-two-three. You can also prepare the squash ahead of time, as long as you warm it to room temperature before serving.

SERVES 4 TO 6

1 large butternut squash, about 1 pound, halved, seeded, and peeled
Cooking spray (optional)
2 teaspoons tamari or shoyu soy sauce
1 teaspoon olive oil
About 1½ teaspoons honey
Honeyed Red-Wine Vinaigrette (recipe follows)
8 to 10 cups assorted salad greens, half mild (oakleaf, romaine, and/or Boston lettuces) and half bitter or pungent (arugula, watercress, curly endive), well washed and dried (see page 69, Steps 1 and 2)
1 to 2 cups very thinly sliced green cabbage
½ cup cilantro leaves, chopped medium-fine
1 sweet, crisp apple, such as Gala, peel on, diced into ⅓-inch pieces
2 to 3 tablespoons toasted sesame seeds, or chopped, toasted pecans, toasted pumpkin seeds, or—best yet—tamari-roasted pumpkin seeds (optional)

1 Preheat the oven to 400°F.

2 Place 4 to 6 salad plates in the freezer to chill.

3 Cut the peeled squash into ½-inch dice. Place the cut-up butternut squash on a large nonstick baking sheet or one that has been sprayed with cooking spray. Toss the squash with the soy sauce and oil and bake until the squash pieces are lightly browned, slightly shriveled-looking and semicrisp on the outside and barely tender all the way through, 20 to 30 minutes. The squash should definitely keep its shape. Remove the squash from the oven, keeping the oven on. Immediately drizzle a little honey over the squash, toss, and return to the oven. Bake for 5 to 10 minutes more, until the squash is all browned. Remove from the oven and let cool to room temperature.

4 As the squash bakes, make the vinaigrette (recipe follows). Up to this point the recipe can be done in advance.

5 When ready to serve, toss the salad greens and cabbage with 2 tablespoons of dressing. Toss in the roasted squash (warmed slightly if desired), cilantro, and apple. Taste; add more dressing if needed. Divide the salad among the chilled plates and top each with a scattering of the toasted nuts or sesame seeds, if desired. Serve *immediately;* it doesn't wait once it's been tossed. Pass additional vinaigrette at the table.

COOK ONCE FOR 2 MEALS Try doubling the amount of roasted butternut squash and serve the first half as a side vegetable. It won't hurt to keep the second half for tomorrow or the day after when you can whip it out to star in this salad.

Honeyed Red-Wine Vinaigrette

A basic, slightly sweet vinaigrette, versatile and mighty tasty. **MAKES ABOUT 1⅔ CUPS**

⅓ cup red wine vinegar
1 teaspoon tamari or shoyu soy sauce
3 to 4 cloves garlic
Juice of ½ lemon
¼ teaspoon salt
5 to 6 solid grinds black pepper
⅔ cup extra virgin olive oil
2 to 3 tablespoons honey, or, for vegans, sugar or Rapidura

Combine the vinegar, tamari, garlic, lemon juice, salt, and pepper in a food processor. Start the machine buzzing, and gradually, through the hole in the pusher-tube, drizzle in the oil. Remove pusher-tube, and, with the motor running, drizzle in the 2 tablespoons honey. Stop the machine. Taste, and if you feel the dressing should be sweeter, add the remaining tablespoon of honey.

VARIATIONS

This recipe makes way more dressing than you need. Here are other things you can do with it:

Check out the Tempeh "San Francisco Chicken Salad–Style" (page 647), for which this faintly rosy dressing is essential.

And another: Make Crunch Salad, marinating a pleasingly loud mixture of julienned carrot, celery, and jícama with finely shredded cabbage.

And another: For Springtime Soba and Asparagus Salad, combine cooked, cold soba (buckwheat) noodles with steamed or stir-fried angle-cut asparagus (cooked just until tender) with a drizzle of this dressing and a tiny bit of minced ginger. Top with a sprinkle of toasted sesame seeds. If you like, add some diced prepared Asian-style tofu (such as that made by White Wave), and you've got a very fine cold meal.

Vegetable Salads

Let us move from green and green with a garnish to a number of salads where a single vegetable holds primary sway. These are usually quite simple to put together, good to remember on the days when you see a particularly luscious-looking pile of, say, bright pink juicily fresh-looking radishes at the market, or notice that the same brand of organic carrots you liked so much last week is on sale this week.

Minted Beet Salad with a Touch of Vanilla

Beet aficionados that we are, Ned and I couldn't *believe* that Joyce Goldstein, at her glorious now-no-more San Francisco restaurant Square One, had come up with an outstanding, improbable way to glaze beets that we'd never even thought of and that we couldn't even guess what it was. Delicious, elusive . . . sweet, but not fruity—almost floral, but not rose water; was it cinnamon? Nutmeg? It was Ned who cried, "Vanilla!" so loudly triumphant that the folks at the next table turned and momentarily gazed our way. We immediately began using the occasional hit of vanilla on our hot beets. From there to here: a chilled marinated beet salad with vanilla and vinegar, zipped right along by a lot of fresh, minced spearmint. I have been asked for this recipe *a lot*. You don't serve this on greens, but scoop it onto your plate, ideally as part of a buffet. It holds well, can and should be prepared in advance, and is really, really easy to make. **SERVES 6 TO 8 AS A SALAD, OR 10 TO 12 AS PART OF A BUFFET**

VARIATION

Shred the cleaned beet greens and steam until tender; toss with the beets and dressing as in the recipe. This is particularly good with Four-Star Fresh Basil-Lemon Dressing with Tofu-Tomato Cream (page 73) substituted for the vanilla-mint treatment described here.

¼ cup hazelnut or walnut oil (if unavailable, use any mild vegetable oil, such as corn, canola, or peanut; do not use olive oil here)
3 tablespoons vinegar, preferably raspberry or blueberry (but a good balsamic also works here, surprisingly)
3 tablespoons honey
¾ teaspoon pure vanilla extract
Salt and freshly ground black pepper to taste
5 to 8 beets, baked, peeled, chilled (see page 701); quartered if large, halved if medium, left whole if very tiny
About ⅓ cup finely minced spearmint leaves

Whisk together the oil, vinegar, honey, vanilla, salt, and pepper. Add the beets and toss well. Add the spearmint and toss again. Chill it well, and taste again for seasonings just before serving.

AUGUST ASIAN INFUSION

Smashed Radish and Arame Salad

*

"Hot Thai in the Old Town Tonight" Noodle-Tofu Salad
(PAGE 119)

*

Nori Rolls
(PAGE 40)

*

Crisp Lettuce Tempeh "Spring Rolls"
(PAGE 38)

*

Spicy Eggplant with Buckwheat Ramen Noodles
(PAGE 121)

*

Ginger-pear sorbet

Smashed Radish and Arame Salad

Light, refreshing, with almost no oil, this salad is delightfully Asian in flavor, easily put together, and pretty as can be, threaded with thin dark strands of arame. The arame, a preshredded seaweed (if you're unfamiliar with seaweeds—and perhaps put off by the very idea of eating them—be sure to see "Have We Been Introduced Yet?" on page 82 for information), mild and black, very pleasingly contrasts with orange carrots and white and fuschia radishes. Smashing the radishes enables them to soak up more of the dressing, besides making each bite variable in shape and more interesting to eat. This recipe combines two versions of the traditional Chinese method of smashing radishes for salad, one in *Oriental Vegetarian Cooking,* by Gail Duff, and the other in the old *Thousand Recipe Chinese Cookbook,* by Gloria Bley Miller. **SERVES 4**

Non-Chickens of the Sea

HAVE WE BEEN INTRODUCED YET?

Arame and hijiki are seaweeds, used in Japanese cooking (as are many other seaweeds, or sea vegetables as the macrobiotic folks call them). I happen to like the taste, texture, and especially the appearance of these two—like fine black threads or ribbons, contrasting nicely with almost anything you'd put them with. Both arame and hijiki are from a large-leafed algae. When purchased, the leaves have already been parboiled, shredded into the fine strands, and dried. Both are rich and full of sea-flavor; hijiki is a little stronger. Both require a brief presoaking before being added to dishes and will swell when soaked. Arame will double or triple, hijiki quadruple or pentuple (there's probably a real word for "grow to five times its original size" but I like this one, don't you?), post soaking. They have a nice texture, too; soft yet with an agreeable resiliency that gives an almost crunchy chewiness. Packaged, arame and hijiki keep in your cupboard indefinitely and are nice to have in your culinary repertoire.

Another seaweed that vegetarians, in particular, will like in their pantries: agar, the meat-free equivalent of gelatin. (It's important and particular enough in its usage and demands that I've gone into detail on it on page 127.)

Seaweeds grow and are harvested from all the world's oceans, from off the coasts of Japan and Korea to the Atlantic off Ireland, Scotland, and Wales; even Maine and Canada. They are extraordinarily high in many minerals and they add the taste and smell of the sea, plus their own individual flavors and highly interesting textures, to many dishes.

If you've ever been to a Japanese restaurant, you've probably enjoyed rice-plus-something rolled in a black-green sheet of nori. Nori's another seaweed, and is actually cultivated underwater, on bamboo-framed nets. After harvest, it is washed, chopped, pressed into sheets on bamboo mats, and dried (see the recipe for Nori Rolls on page 40 to learn how to make these for yourself).

You've probably also had soup made with dashi, which is the light base stock for many Japanese soups. Dashi's key ingredient is kombu, another seaweed, also large-leafed, in the kelp family. Kombu is not eaten per se; it serves, rather, as a flavor enhancer, because it is packed with glutamic acid—the natural, unprocessed kin of refined monosodium glutamate. Kombu, which comes packaged in large strips, not fine threads, is also frequently cooked with beans, as it's said to speed up their cooking time as well as render them more digestible and flavorful (it dissolves into the beans, slowly, adding a subtle pleasant creaminess). Kombu, like other kelps, is also one of the richest sources of natural iodine.

If you're thinking, "Ugh," about all this, you may not realize that you've been eating seaweeds all your life—even if you've never been to a sushi bar. Irish moss, a seaweed that grows guess where, is the plant from which the common additive carageenan is refined. Every American has eaten carageenan (and those who are label readers may have wondered about it), for it's used as a neutral-flavored stabilizer, thickener, emulsifier, and gelling agent in many commercially made ice creams, salad dressings, puddings, dips, spreads, and the like. In these processed foods, it usually substitutes for something good or real—better by far, I think, to eat one's seaweed as seaweed up front, not as faked texture.

1 bag radishes (16 ounces), heads and tails removed
1 carrot, grated
1 tablespoon white or brown rice vinegar
1 tablespoon umeboshi plum vinegar (see page 118)
1 tablespoon tamari or shoyu soy sauce
2 teaspoons brown or turbinado sugar, or Rapidura (see page 959)
3 tablespoons dried arame seaweed (see opposite)
1 teaspoon toasted sesame oil
Salt and freshly ground black pepper to taste
1 tablespoon sesame seeds, toasted (optional)

1 Smash the radishes by placing them, one at a time, on a cutting board. Lay the flat side of a broad knife or cleaver across each radish, and, pressing down with a quick explosive movement, smash the radish, partially squashing it. If the radishes are very large, you might need to whack them with a mallet or even the bottom of a pot. Place the smashed radishes in a small nonreactive bowl along with the grated carrots, vinegars, tamari, and sugar. Let stand, covered and refrigerated, for 2 to 3 hours.

2 Fifteen minutes or so before serving, place the arame in a glass measuring cup or small bowl and pour 1 cup water, preferably spring or filtered, over it. Soak until softened, 5 to 10 minutes. Drain the arame well and then toss it with the smashed radishes, adding the sesame oil. Season with salt and pepper to taste. Serve, sprinkling each portion with toasted sesame seeds, if using.

"Write about a radish
Too many people write about the moon.
The night is black
The stars are small and high
The clock unwinds its ever-ticking tune
Hills gleam dimly
Distant nighthawks cry.
A radish rises in the waiting sky."

—**Karla Kuskin,** "Radish,"
from *Dogs and Dragons, Trees and Dreams*

Moroccan Carrot Salad

This combines the faintly exotic North African seasonings, about which people tend to be love-'em-or-hate-'em, with the comfortingly familiar grated carrots. The carrots are blanched briefly before being grated; this leaves plenty of texture but the raw edge is taken off. This is my version of an early Paula Wolfert recipe from *Couscous and Other Good Food from Morocco.* **SERVES 4 TO 6**

1 to 1½ pounds carrots
3 large cloves garlic
2 to 3 tablespoons extra virgin olive oil
1 tablespoon ground cumin
1 tablespoon paprika
½ teaspoon salt, or to taste
Dash of cinnamon (optional)
Dash of cayenne (optional)
1 lemon, halved
1 teaspoon honey (measured into the same spoon as the one you did the olive oil in, so the honey will glide out)
¼ cup finely minced cilantro
¼ cup finely minced Italian parsley

1 Bring a large pot of water to a boil over high heat. Drop in the carrots and blanch for 3 minutes. Drain the carrots well and blast them with cold water until they're cool. Dry. If the peel seems tough, remove it; otherwise, leave it on. Grate the carrots (doing so in a food processor is a good move from the standpoint of knuckle preservation).

2 Place the grated carrots in a bowl and, with a garlic press, squeeze the garlic over the top. Then, drizzle in the olive oil (start with just a tablespoon) and sprinkle on the cumin, paprika, salt, and cinnamon and cayenne, if using. Squeeze half the lemon through a sieve onto the salad, then stir in the honey. Taste. You may want to add the second tablespoon of oil (or even more oil—though Wolfert doesn't specify amounts I am quite sure the Moroccans use way more oil than this) or squeeze in the second lemon half, or add more salt. On the other hand, if you're going to chill the salad—a good idea, as the flavors will blend, develop, and heighten—you might want to wait and do your final taste-testing after it comes out of the fridge.

3 In any case, just before serving, toss in the minced cilantro and parsley.

VARIATIONS

CARROTS À LA JAN BROWN: ***Cut the carrots into plump circles, using a wavy crinkly-edged cutter, substitute a little minced dill for the parsley and cilantro, and add a tablespoon of freshly toasted sesame seeds.***

CARROTS SARAH LEAH: ***Use just a tablespoon of olive oil, omit the lemon, and use 1 tablespoon balsamic vinegar and 2 or 3 tablespoons red wine vinegar. This approach is the brainchild of Sarah Leah Chase, author of the*** **Nantucket Open-House Cookbook.**

When serving this salad on a buffet, rather than grating, slice the raw carrots into fat circles or ovals, and blanch them until crisp-tender. These circles are easier to pick up.

If you cook and grate the carrots as described, then toss them with a little Four-Star Fresh Basil-Lemon Dressing with Tofu-Tomato Cream (page 73), you will have a salad entirely different, but still pleasing.

Cora Pinkley Call's Ozark "Sour Cream" Salad

Cora Pinkley Call, a now-deceased Ozark herbalist, Eureka Springs resident, and writer, was a keeper of local folk-customs. Her *From My Ozark Cupboard* is one of the few cookbooks that doesn't condescend to the people in this part of the world. Perhaps because she was a native Ozarkian, she resisted the hillbilly stereotype with a vengeance and was quite testy about others who gave in to it. "You will perhaps find more 'individualists' living life the way they want to in the Ozarks than elsewhere," she wrote in 1950 (words still true today), ". . . the Ozark folk live well and happily within the 400-mile boundary of the enchanting hills *regardless of what the fourth-rate journalists and mediocre novelists have to say about them*" (emphasis mine). One of her relatives, June Westphal, is a local historian.

Though Cora doesn't say, I imagine this salad was an early spring treat in the old days—made with the last of the wintered-over-in-the-root-cellar cabbage and the first spring cream and eggs. (You didn't know? Cows do not naturally produce milk year round; hens do not naturally lay year round; spring is when they get enthusiastic and really can't help themselves. Soooo much milk and cream! Eggs galore!)

SERVES 6 TO 8

VARIATION

I have defatted the recipe somewhat by substituting Yogurt Sour Cream for real sour cream, although this might be one case where you'd enjoy using whole milk yogurt.

Instead of Yogurt Sour Cream, you could also use commercially made "light" sour cream, sour half-and-half (not fat-free, however), or Tofu Sour Cream (page 909).

½ head green cabbage, finely shredded
3 hard-boiled eggs, preferably organic, peeled and halved
1 cup Yogurt Sour Cream (page 910)
¾ teaspoon sugar
½ teaspoon salt
1 tablespoon vinegar, preferably tarragon
Freshly ground black pepper to taste

1 Place the cabbage in a large bowl.

2 Separate the hard-cooked egg yolks and whites. Dice the whites, and add to the cabbage.

3 Place the yolks in a food processor with the Yogurt Sour Cream, sugar, salt, vinegar, and pepper. Buzz the yolk mixture until smooth, stopping several times to scrape the bowl. Pour the dressing over the cabbage and toss well.

VARIATION

A handful of sliced fresh radishes tossed in at the last moment adds a pleasing, crunchy freshness, as will cherry tomatoes, stemmed, washed, and left whole. In the summer, you might even find local golden cherry tomatoes, perhaps the little pear-shaped varieties called "sun-drops"—sweet and delicious as can be. Toss in some drained, sliced pimento-stuffed green olives (the so-called salad olives, which are bunged up a bit, are perfect for this; cheaper and a time saver: no slicing) to create a sort of antipasto; a little diced mozzarella will do the same.

Winter Vegetable Salad with Chickpeas

Treat this recipe as idea, not gospel: very loosey-goosey. In its essentials, it is both basic and classic. If you have some dressing on hand, it is just a matter of steaming or blanching vegetables. You can be quite improvisational about which ones you use and you can even use leftovers from last night's dinner; then, marinate them. Although some vegetables, notably broccoli and green beans, will lose their full vividness after a bath in the marinade, they will taste just great. Add thick slices of good homemade bread and perhaps some cheese passed at the table, and you've got a meal. Add cooked pasta and a little extra dressing, and you have an excellent pasta salad. Remember, though, the trick to a really good salad—virtually any kind—is always underdressing it. **SERVES 4 TO 6**

4 to 6 cups any combination of several of the following vegetables, steamed or blanched separately until barely crisp-tender: thickly sliced carrots, green beans in ¾-inch length, cauliflower florets, broccoli florets, julienned peeled broccoli stems, small whole button mushrooms (they are steamed just long enough to take the rawness out), thickly sliced peeled parsnip

1 red onion or 1 bunch scallions, roots removed, finely diced

1 can (15 ounces) chickpeas, well drained (save the liquid for soup stock)

½ cup finely minced Italian parsley (optional)

¼ to ½ cup Sharp Classic Vinaigrette with a Bite (page 72) or Four-Star Fresh Basil-Lemon Dressing with Tofu-Tomato Cream (page 73)

Salt and freshly ground black pepper to taste

Combine the vegetables, onion or scallions, chickpeas, parsley, if using, and the vinaigrette. Toss well, then season with salt and pepper. Marinate, refrigerated, for at least 1 hour, preferably overnight (don't be dismayed when the broccoli loses its bright green color; it happens). Season again. Add more dressing if you really feel you need to. That's it!

First-Course and Composed Salads

A bit fussier and a lot prettier, most of the following salads combine elements of several vegetables, or sometimes vegetables and fruit, grilled or marinated or otherwise given special treatment, then served in or on a bed of greens. These aren't the salads you'll turn to day in and day out, but you'll love them once in a while as part of a special dinner or, if served in larger portions, perhaps as dinner in their own right. Some of the earlier salads, like the Salad of Tender Greens with Sweet-Peppery Blackberry Vinaigrette (page 75) or the Roasted Butternut Squash and Apple Salad on a Bed of Bitter Greens (page 78), with Honeyed Red-Wine Vinaigrette (page 79), could also have gone in this section as well, so do cruise back and look them over, too.

Celery Root Salad Vinaigrette in Artichoke Half

Celery root is a homely root in the celery family, and oh! is it a treat. It's crunchy, but not stringy. Under its unsightly tap-rooted brown skin (which must be peeled with a knife) it's pure white. Here, we usually see it only in the spring, late March, early April—just when the market is flooded with new-harvest artichokes, also. Their timing inspired this combination, a lovely first-course salad for a special dinner you'd like to linger over. Don't be alarmed when you see the amount of vinaigrette called for; only 1 tablespoon actually goes into the salad, the rest is set on the table in individual dishes for those who care to use it as an artichoke-leaf dip. **SERVES 8**

NOTE

Be sure and check out the celery root soup on page 156.

1 medium celery root, washed, peeled, and shredded
⅓ to ½ cup Sharp Classic Vinaigrette with a Bite (page 72) or Four-Star Fresh Basil-Lemon Dressing with Tofu-Tomato Cream (page 73)
4 fresh artichokes, steamed to tenderness, halved, choke removed (see page 387), chilled
Salt and freshly ground black pepper to taste
Chopped Italian parsley, wedges of lemon, sliced tomatoes (optional)

1 Combine the shredded celery root with 2 teaspoons to 1 tablespoon of the vinaigrette and toss well. Marinate, refrigerated, for up to 8 hours.

2 At serving time, place the artichoke halves on 8 first-course plates, hollow side up.

3 Taste the celery root and, if needed, add salt and pepper. Divide it among the artichokes, placing a small scoop in each hollow.

4 Shake the remaining vinaigrette and divide it among 8 small serving dishes, which should be placed on the table.

5 Decorate each plate with any or all of the optional garnishes and serve. The celery root salad is eaten with a fork and the artichoke leaves by hand, with each diner dipping the artichoke, leaf by leaf, into the vinaigrette, if so desired.

VARIATIONS

CELERY ROOT AND CARROT SALAD IN MISO-MUSTARD DRESSING: *Omit the artichoke and use two medium peeled and shredded celery roots. Separately, shred 3 carrots. Place each shredded vegetable in a separate bowl. Make Tofu Mayonnaise (page 906), but omit the salt, increase the mustard to 2 tablespoons, and add 2 teaspoons white or golden miso. Toss the celery root and carrots, each in their respective bowls, with 1 to 2 tablespoons of the Miso-Mustard Dressing. Marinate, chilled, for at least 1 hour or up to 8. Serve one scoop of each shredded vegetable on greens.*

CELERY ROOT–POTATO SALAD: *Combine cooked, diced potatoes with an equal amount of shredded celery root, a little raw minced onion, and Tofu Mayo (page 906). Add salt, lots of freshly ground black pepper, maybe a diced hard-cooked egg or two. The comfort of potato salad but with fewer calories.*

Cascabel Salad of Grilled and Raw Vegetables

Two secrets make this alluring salad what it is. One is Jay McCarthy's complex, subtle yet in-your-face, hot-sweet-spicy dressing—great stuff; and the other is the grilled sweet potatoes. I particularly love it as an accompaniment to a burger of Simple Grilled Portobellos (page 769). **SERVES 4 TO 6**

2 large sweet potatoes, peeled and cut lengthwise into long discs about ¼ inch thick
½ pound shiitake mushrooms, stems removed
¼ pound fresh snow peas, stems removed
Juice of 1 lemon
1½ tablespoons tamari or shoyu soy sauce
1 tablespoon olive oil
1 bunch scallions, white and ⅔ of green, minced
1 red bell pepper, cut vertically into ¼-inch strips
2 tablespoons Jay McCarthy's Cascabel Dressing (recipe follows)
1 tablespoon honey
1 head fresh, crisp romaine lettuce, shredded
¼ head red cabbage, shredded

1 Preheat the grill.

2 Combine the sweet potatoes, shiitake caps, and snow peas in the lemon juice, half of the tamari or shoyu soy sauce, and the oil. Toss well.

3 Place the sweet potato slices on the grill and cook, turning once, until grill-marked and tender but not mushy, 4 to 6 minutes on each side. Place the snow peas and shiitakes in a vegetable or fish grilling cage, and grill them for 2 to 3 minutes on each side.

4 Combine the scallions, red bell pepper, dressing, honey, and the rest of the tamari in a bowl.

5 When the vegetables come off the grill, add the snow peas and mushroom caps to the scallion-pepper mixture.

6 When they are cool enough to handle, cut the sweet potato slices into long strips and add them to the dressed vegetables. Toss together and marinate, preferably overnight.

7 Toss the shredded romaine and red cabbage together and serve the marinated vegetable salad on top.

Jay McCarthy's Cascabel Dressing

Jay McCarthy, a peripatetic, passionate, high-energy Texas chef and general crazy-man (I like that in a person), combines the Southwestern flavors of his present home with the Caribbean notes of his Jamaican childhood, with Asian riffs as called for by inclination or inspiration. Jay's ability in combining and contrasting is magical—textures and flavors, exotics paired with everyday ingredients, Jamaican allspice here, cactus there. Yet he always stops short of too much or fussed-over. This dressing, of dizzying intensity and carefully orchestrated flavors, is so good

VARIATION

SIMPLIFIED VARIATION (JAY-APPROVED): ***Substitute Tabasco for sriracha, and A-1 Steak Sauce for tamarind.***

you will have to restrain yourself from applying it as a facial.

Remember, you'll need Roasted Garlic puree (page 899) and tamarind paste (see below) before you start. The former requires advance prep time, the latter doesn't—but unless you have tamarind sitting around your kitchen, it might take a trip to the local Indian or Asian market or a well-stocked supermarket. If you can't deal with finding exotica, see the simplified variation. **MAKES ABOUT ¾ CUP**

1 tablespoon Roasted Garlic puree (page 899)
1 tablespoon honey
1 tablespoon smooth Dijon mustard
1 tablespoon tamari or shoyu soy sauce
1 tablespoon seedless extracted tamarind paste (see below)
1 tablespoon fresh-squeezed lemon juice
1½ teaspoons sriracha (bright red, very thick chile pepper puree, sold in Asian markets)
1½ teaspoons chili powder
1 tablespoon toasted sesame oil
3 tablespoons olive oil

Combine all of the ingredients except the oils in a blender or food processor and buzz until thick and smooth. With the motor running, first drip in the sesame oil and then the olive oil.

Meet Tamarind

HAVE WE BEEN INTRODUCED YET?

Long, locustlike pods with brown papery skin hang from the tall trees that shade much of the hotter parts of India, Asia, and North Africa. These are tamarind trees. Under the skin is a seed-filled dark-brown pulp with the soft, sticky texture and color of a date. It looks dubious, but its flavor is like nothing else—tart as lemon juice but with a faint, not-too-sweet fruitiness. It's used in Worcestershire and A-1 sauce, as a finishing note in many curries and chutneys (such as Avial, the South Indian stew on page 195), and, because of its tartness, makes a most refreshing drink when sweetened and mixed with water and poured over ice—something like a brown lemonade.

Dried tamarind, which does not require refrigeration and retains its sticky datelike texture, is sold in packages at Asian food stores, and it keeps indefinitely. The package may say "seedless"; it's a fib. No matter—it's still easy to use.

To make seedless extracted tamarind paste, pull off a hunk of the sticky tamarind—2 or 3 tablespoons—and place it in a bowl with an equal amount of warm water. Let stand for 5 minutes, then sort of smush it with your fingers a little. By this point, it should be mostly melted into a thinnish, soft, dark brown paste. Pour the tamarind-water paste through a strainer (to catch the seeds) into a clean container. Discard the seedy residue in the strainer and use the thin seedless extracted tamarind paste in any recipe calling for it. The operation is much simpler and quicker than it sounds. Even though you'll use tamarind paste only once in a while, it keeps well, so why not keep it on hand?

Cora Pinkley Call's Ozark-Style Stuffed Tomato Salad

Another from Cora, who gives only the vaguest of directions. She hollows out her tomatoes for stuffing just as I do when making a cooked or main-dish filling. For salads like this, though, I prefer cutting straight down through the center of the tomato three times, almost but not quite to the bottom, leaving an attachment from which you can open out the tomato into six flower-like petals. You then plunk the tomato onto a nice bed of greens, scoop your favorite cold filling into the middle, and sit yourself down to lunch. Needless to say, this '50s commonplace luncheonette counter and tearoom specialty (usually, then, filled with tuna salad or cottage cheese) gets *really* good only with vine-ripened, height-of-summer tomatoes and local organic peppers and cukes. Sometimes vegetable salad filling mixtures similar to this are called "Farmer's Chop Suey." **SERVES 4 TO 6**

VARIATIONS

Two easy low-fat vegan variations: Omit the hard-boiled egg, replacing it with 6 ounces firm reduced-fat tofu, crumbled, or 1 cup canned chickpeas, well drained and coarsely mashed. If you feel like really tweaking this dish, you could use 2 tablespoons Jay McCarthy's Cascabel Dressing (page 89) in the vegetable marinade and add diced Thai-style or savory baked tofu to the mix.

4 or 5 radishes, scrubbed, halved, and sliced paper-thin
3 scallions, trimmed, white and 3 inches of green finely diced
1 green bell pepper, cut into ¼-inch dice
1 red or yellow bell pepper, cut into ¼-inch dice
1 rib celery, halved or cut into thirds lengthwise, then diced finely, or 1 rib bok choy, diced
1 cucumber, peeled, seeded, and cut into ¼-inch dice
1 cup very thinly shredded cabbage
2 hard-boiled eggs, diced (or see the vegan variations)
2 tablespoons Sharp Classic Vinaigrette with a Bite (page 72), Four-Star Fresh Basil-Lemon Dressing with Tofu-Tomato Cream (page 73), Cilantro Vinaigrette (page 94), or any other nonsweet dressing
Salt and freshly ground black pepper to taste
8 to 15 good fresh, large lettuce leaves, well washed and thoroughly dried (red-leaf is nice here)
4 to 6 large, garden-ripe tomatoes, sliced 3 times vertically from stem end to not quite through base, making 6 attached segments

1 Combine all the diced vegetables—radishes, scallions, bell peppers, celery, and cucumber—with the cabbage and hard-boiled eggs (or vegan alternatives). Toss with the dressing, then season with salt and pepper. This may be done up to 1 day in advance.

2 On chilled salad plates, arrange 1 to 3 large leaves of lettuce. Place a tomato in the center of each plate, then pull the tomatoes open a bit to create a blossom effect. Divide the marinated vegetable mixture among the opened tomatoes, scooping it into the center of each one. Serve at once.

VARIATION

GOOD AS IT IS, SALAD OF GRILLED ZUCCHINI ***begs to be tinkered with. In winter, simplify it by eliminating the corn and tomato. You can add slices of seductively delicious ripe avocado, or give it crunch with a sprinkle of vegetarian bacon bits.***

As for go-withs, what about good old corn-bread? Or corn chips (baked or fried, depending on your taste and fat-intake preference)? What about quesadillas made with Austin Hill Country Hummus (page 21)? What about using it as a first course, preceding CD's Famed Tofu Broccoli Enchiladas (page 340)? Consider Brazilian Rice (page 473), Chilaquiles (pages 376–78) or Enchiladas Very Verde (page 340). In fact, the possibilities and alternatives are endless.

Salad of Grilled Zucchini with Cilantro Vinaigrette

When I had dinner at the White House—What, bragging? Me? Are you kidding?—this was more or less the salad that was served, except the dressing was tossed with the greens before the grilled corn was added, and it was a creamy dressing (for the same effect, blend about 5 ounces reduced-fat silken tofu into the dressing recipe . . . although something tells me they probably didn't use tofu at the White House). Nonetheless, it was delicious there and it is here.

SERVES 6 TO 8

- 2 ears corn, husks and silks removed
- 4 to 6 medium-small zucchini, stem ends removed, sliced horizontally into long flattish pieces, each the length of the whole zucchini and roughly ⅓ inch thick
- 1 to 2 tablespoons olive oil
- Cilantro Vinaigrette (recipe follows)
- 6 to 8 cups mixed fresh salad greens, such as romaine, oakleaf, red-leaf, and limestone lettuce, plus fresh spinach
- 2 large tomatoes, peeled, seeded, and chopped

1 Preheat the grill to high.

2 Place the husked corn directly on the grill. Grill the corn, turning occasionally with tongs, until it is lightly browned in parts, and the yellow is slightly intensified and has lost its raw look, about 18 minutes.

3 Brush the zucchini slices lightly with the oil and place them directly on the grill. Grill the zucchini, turning once or twice, until they are quite tender, 4 to 6 minutes on each side.

4 As the vegetables are done, remove them from the grill. Drizzle 1 to 2 tablespoons of the vinaigrette over the zucchini slices while they are still warm, toss, and refrigerate until nearly ready to serve. Let the corn sit until cool enough to handle. Slice off the kernels (you may reserve the cobs for stock if you wish) and refrigerate. If desired, chill salad plates in the freezer.

5 About 30 minutes before serving time, remove the zucchini and marinade from the refrigerator and let come to room temperature.

6 When ready to serve, divide the salad greens among chilled salad plates. Sprinkle each pile of greens with some grilled corn kernels. Lift zukes from their vinaigrette bath, shaking or scraping off as much marinade as possible. Lay the slices over the corn-sprinkled greens. Transfer the vinaigrette, including any remaining from the cuke marinade, to a serving vessel for use at the table. Top the salad with the diced tomato. Serve at once, passing the remaining vinaigrette at the table.

COOK ONCE FOR 2 MEALS Make a full meal of this by adding cooked black or pinto beans that, after being well drained, have been marinated in a little of the Cilantro Vinaigrette. You can also add a little grated sharp Cheddar or jack cheese.

A Real Tomato Never Chills Out

Never, ever refrigerate a tomato! *And when you go to market, try to select tomatoes that have never been refrigerated. Once a tomato has been deeply chilled, its texture changes forever, going from fleshy and juicy to cottony, and it will lose much of its heady, distinctive tomato scent. This is one reason why a perfectly ripe tomato, straight from the vine, sun-warmed, eaten out in the garden, is such a sublime, essence-of-tomato, pure summer experience.*

Store tomatoes on a kitchen counter. To ensure even ripening and to prevent rotting, the tomatoes should be in a row, not piled atop each other in a basket (except for brief periods of time). If you must refrigerate a cut-open half-eaten tomato, bring it back to room temperature before eating it—but it's a poor second best.

While we're on the subject of tomatoes: This vegetable (well, technically and botanically, tomatoes are a fruit, but never mind) is rich in a natural phytochemical called lycopene, which, like the sulfur compounds in cabbage-family vegetables, has been shown to have a protective effect against cancer. As if any of us needed another reason to enjoy tomatoes!

Cilantro Vinaigrette

So good it'll make your toes curl the first time you taste it.
MAKES ABOUT 1¾ CUP

4 cloves garlic, minced
2½ cups cilantro leaves
1 cup Italian parsley leaves
½ cup fresh-squeezed lemon juice
¼ cup diced tomato
1½ teaspoon salt
1 teaspoon sugar
Plenty of freshly ground black pepper
Dash Tabasco or similar hot sauce
1 cup olive oil

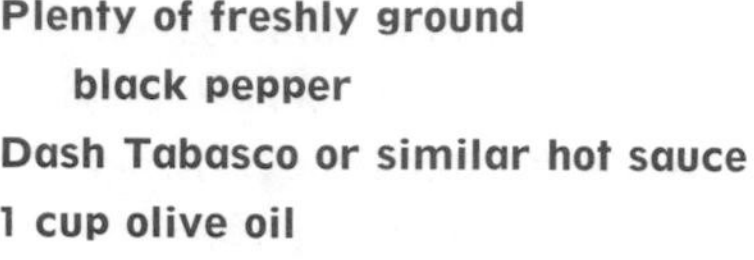

Combine all of the ingredients except the oil in a food processor; buzz until smooth. You may need to scrape the processor sides down once or twice. If your machine's pusher tube has a tiny hole, pour the oil into the tube in two batches and let it drip in as the machine runs. Otherwise, remove the pusher and gradually drip in the oil. Taste for seasoning and transfer the dressing to a refrigerator storage container.

VARIATIONS

For a slightly more assertive Southwestern flavor, add 1 teaspoon toasted cumin seeds to the mixture before processing.

Here's CD'S NEW FAVE HONEYED-JALAPEÑO CILANTRO VINAIGRETTE:
Omit the parsley, tomato, and sugar. Substitute vinegar—preferably peach vinegar, but cider will do—for the lemon juice. Add ⅓ cup honey with the vinegar as well as 1 jalapeño pepper (seeded or not, depends on how hot you like it). Drip in the olive oil as described. It's wonderful over diced honeydew with a little minced red onion and cubes of ripe but not overripe avocado. Or try it over simple greens with tomato and scallions. My friends Chou Chou and Steve Weintz even spoon it over enchiladas like a sauce.

Arugula Salad with Grilled Eggplant and Shiitakes

Another irresistibly appealing use of the cilantro dressing in a salad of an entirely different character, due to the pleasing bite of arugula paired with the creamy, almost-sweet eggplant and meaty shiitakes. Although I've now run into grilled eggplant with cilantro on hip menus across the country, it's always seemed to me the quintessential "California cuisine" dish. This is because I first had the combination almost twenty years ago at John Downey's eponymous, excellent chef-run restaurant in Santa Barbara. **SERVES 6 TO 8**

8 to 10 medium, or 6 to 8 large, fresh shiitake mushroom caps, stems removed (save for soup stock)

1 large or 2 small eggplants, stem ends removed, sliced horizontally into long flattish pieces, each the length of the whole eggplant and roughly ⅓ inch thick

1 to 2 tablespoons olive oil

Cilantro Vinaigrette (opposite page), or CD's New Fave Honeyed-Jalapeño Cilantro Vinaigrette variation

6 to 8 cups very fresh arugula leaves, well washed and very well dried (handle them tenderly; they're fragile and bruise easily)

1 Preheat the grill to high.

2 Lightly brush the shiitake caps and eggplant slices with the oil. Place them directly on the preheated grill. Grill the shiitakes for 6 to 8 minutes and the eggplant for 8 to 12 minutes, turning once with tongs about halfway through. The mushrooms should be slightly softened and a little "grill-y" and the eggplant lightly browned and very tender inside.

3 Remove the vegetables from the grill. Drizzle about 2 tablespoons of the Cilantro Vinaigrette over the vegetables while they are still warm, toss well to combine, and refrigerate until nearly ready to serve.

4 About 30 minutes before serving time, remove the vegetables from the refrigerator and let them come to room temperature. Slice each eggplant oval into three or four long vertical strips and cut the shiitakes into slices. When ready to serve, divide the arugula among chilled salad plates. Place equal portions of eggplant on top of each serving of greens. Top with a portion of shiitakes. Pass the remaining vinaigrette at the table.

VARIATION

This salad is excellent with the shiitakes and eggplant still warm or hot from the grill, tossed with the cilantro dressing and served on the cold greens.

Pineapple-Jícama Salad with Purple Cabbage and Baby Spinach

This lovely combo is almost like a large-chunked fruited salsa, except the jícama makes it delectably crisp and it's not very spicy. Perfect as part of a Mexican-inspired dinner or brunch, it's a trip to the farmer's market in a bowl. Feel free to play with the proportions and even the selected fruits and vegetables. **SERVES 4 TO 6**

VARIATIONS

SWEET-SAVORY TROPICAL FRUIT AND JÍCAMA SALAD: ***Omit the banana and mango; add 1 to 2 diced tomatoes, preferably red-ripe garden tomatoes, and a cup or so of canned or bottled nonmarinated (water-packed) hearts of palm, sliced across the grain.***

TROPICAL FRUIT AND JÍCAMA SALAD WITH A KICK: ***Just add one each of finely diced red and green chiles to the recipe, along with 2 tablespoons each minced fresh mint and fresh basil. Add ¼ cup cilantro leaves, 2 tablespoons raw sugar, 1 to 2 tablespoons tamari or shoyu soy sauce, the grated rind of 1 lemon or lime, and the juice of same. A real kick!***

1½ to 2 cups peeled, diced jícama, in ½-inch cubes
1 small red onion, halved and sliced paper-thin
1 ripe fresh mango, pit removed, peeled and all nonfibrous parts cut into ½-inch dice (or whatever shapes you can manage; mango is a bit soft for precise dice)
1 banana, ripe but not soft, peeled, halved lengthwise, and sliced into half-circles
½ fresh, juicy pineapple, core and skin removed, diced into ½-inch squares
Handful or so of cherry tomatoes, tiny yellow pear-shaped variety if available
Cilantro Vinaigrette (page 94; the Southwestern-y variation with toasted cumin is good here)
¼ head purple cabbage, shredded or thinly sliced as for coleslaw
8 to 10 ounces fresh prewashed baby spinach leaves (if not using the prewashed variety, buy a pound and wash the leaves very well—bulk spinach is often sandy—remove coarse stems, and dry the leaves thoroughly)

1 Combine the jícama, onion, mango, banana, pineapple, and yellow cherry tomatoes in a bowl. Toss lightly with a few tablespoons of the Cilantro Vinaigrette. You may serve it immediately or let it marinate for up to 2 hours (longer, and the banana will get too soft). If you want to make the salad ahead, add banana at the last minute.

2 When ready to serve, divide the slivered purple cabbage among 6 to 8 salad plates, topping this bed with a smaller mound of bright green baby spinach (be sure you can still see the purple peeking out beneath it, though). Top each portion with a scoop of the jícama salad and serve.

Corner of Celery Root and Jícama

Although the registration card of DHH guest Elizabeth Price read "Muskogee, Oklahoma," she is not a Muskogee native. In fact, Elizabeth has lived in California, Texas, and Missouri, among other places, and her food tastes are thus broader than might be easily satisfied at the local Johnson Foods Store, which though limited in some regards, can certainly not be faulted on the friendly helpfulness of its staff. This point was brought home to her, she told us, when she asked a clerk at the supermarket, "Where's jícama?" "Just a minute, I'll go ask," replied the clerk. Who returned with a second clerk. Who asked Elizabeth, "Now, hon, what was the name of that street you were looking for?"

Beet and Orange Salad with Rainforest Vinaigrette

Because both beets and fruits are rich in sugar and intensely colored, they often pair together happily. The dressing's fruity notes come from the fresh mango, papaya vinegar, and—I know it sounds weird but trust me—banana. A few soulful tender greens, the beets themselves sparked by sliced orange and onion, cilantro to tweak things a bit, and there you have it. **SERVES 4 TO 6**

VINAIGRETTE

- 1 fresh mango, peeled, pitted, and diced
- ¼ cup vinegar, preferably papaya or peach (the Spectrum brand, available in most natural foods stores, is excellent, but use cider vinegar if you can't find it)
- 3 tablespoons honey
- 2 tablespoons raw cashews
- 1 tablespoon mild vegetable oil such as corn, canola, or peanut (almond oil, if you have it, is also excellent here)
- 1 teaspoon finely minced, peeled, fresh ginger
- 1 teaspoon tamari or shoyu soy sauce
- Juice of ½ lemon or lime
- Pinch cayenne
- Salt and freshly ground black pepper to taste
- 1 small banana, ripe but not soft

SALAD

- 8 to 12 large red-leaf lettuce leaves, well washed and dried
- 4 to 6 medium-large beets, baked (page 701), then chilled, peeled, and sliced into rounds about ⅓ inch thick
- 3 oranges, peeled, thinly sliced, and seeded
- 1 large red onion, halved stem to root, then sliced paper-thin
- ½ pound mesclun or other baby salad green mix
- 1 to 2 tablespoons additional raw cashews, toasted and finely chopped (optional)
- 2 to 4 tablespoons cilantro leaves (optional)

1 Chill 4 to 6 medium-large salad plates.

2 Combine half of the mango with the vinegar, honey, raw cashews, oil, ginger, tamari, lemon or lime juice, cayenne, and salt and pepper to taste in a food processor. Buzz to smoothness and taste; you may want to add more of some or all of the ingredients. Stir in the remaining mango. You can do this a couple of days ahead of time. If so, reserve the banana, with the peel on, until you are almost ready to serve the salad. Then, peel

NOTE

A little advance planning is required. Early in the day, or a day or two before you plan on serving the salad, bake and chill the beets and do the processor phase of the vinaigrette. You can finish putting everything together an hour or two before serving or even at the last minute, if you wish.

VARIATION

For a smaller presentation, more suitable as a side salad for 6 to 8 than this first-course arrangement, dice the oranges and beets into ½-inch pieces, and the onion into ¼-inch dice. Tear up all the greens, tossing well with about one-quarter of the dressing. Pile the greens on small chilled salad plates, and divide the beet, orange, and onion mixture among them. Drizzle with dressing and sprinkle with the cashews and cilantro, if desired.

and dice it into tiny (⅓-inch) cubes. Stir the cubes into the dressing.

3 When ready to serve, remove the chilled plates from the refrigerator. Arrange a couple of the red-leaf lettuce leaves on one side of each plate. Lay down a beet slice on the lettuce leaves, overlap it with an orange slice, then another beet slice, then a half-circle of red onion. Repeat, dividing these overlapping explosions of color among each plate.

4 Fill in the blank spot remaining on the plate with the mesclun mix. When ready to serve, drizzle the dressing lightly over each plate and sprinkle with the optional toasted cashew pieces and cilantro leaves.

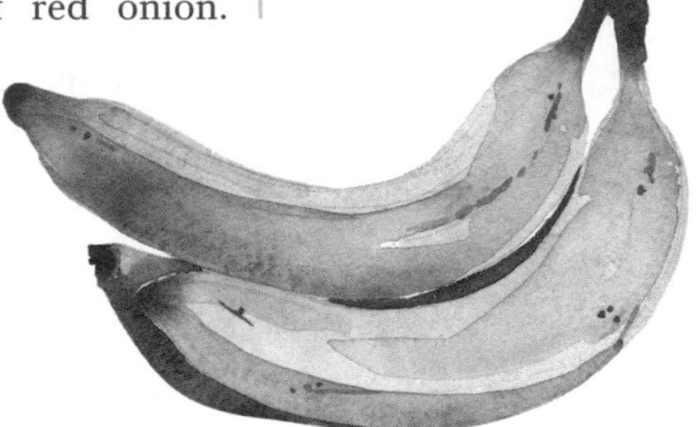

Orange, Grapefruit, and Avocado Salad with Jerusalem Artichokes

This is another salad where fresh fruit is served on greens, and it's very good. It also contains a dressing that is sweet and low in fat, which really works here. This salad is an excellent choice for January, February—those gray months when we crave color for both the eye and mouth. It calls for a reduced-fat dressing, which works primarily because it's quite sweet—but work it does, in a big way. To add even more color, toss in some pomegranate seeds; both delicious and festive. **SERVES 6 TO 8**

1 bag (10 ounces) prewashed spinach, or 1 pound fresh spinach, thoroughly washed and dried, long stems removed (preferably the curly, crumpled-leaf variety)
½ small red onion, peeled and thinly sliced
¼ head red cabbage, thinly sliced as for coleslaw
New Wave Poppyseed Dressing (recipe follows)
1 pound fresh Jerusalem artichokes, very well scrubbed but not peeled, thinly sliced or julienned
2 navel oranges, peeled and sectioned, seeds removed
1 ruby red grapefruit, peeled and sectioned
1 ripe avocado, peeled and pitted

1 Tear any large spinach leaves into bite-size pieces. Place the spinach in a large salad bowl, along with the onion and red cabbage. Just before ready to serve, drizzle in ¼ cup of the New Wave Poppyseed Dressing and toss to coat.

2 Place the Jerusalem artichokes in a small bowl and drizzle them with 1 to 2 tablespoons of the dressing, tossing to coat.

3 Arrange a large mound of the Jerusalem artichokes on top of the big bowl of dressed salad. Place pieces of the oranges, grapefruit, and avocado in a decorative pattern on top of the greens and around the Jerusalem artichokes. Pass the remaining New Wave Poppyseed Dressing at the table. Alternatively, you can arrange 6 to 8 individual salad plates in the same fashion.

New Wave Poppyseed Dressing

Our version of this Texas classic is slightly less sweet than the original, making it more dimensional in flavor than cloying. It's slightly spicier, and, with a thickened vegetable stock replacing some of the oil initially called for, much reduced in fat. While you don't strictly *have* to use the umeboshi plum vinegar, it adds something quite special. Also offered is a three-seed variation with still a little more kick.

This makes a fairly large batch, but, because of the vinegar, it will keep in your fridge for a month quite nicely. **MAKES ABOUT 2 CUPS**

1 cup plus 2 tablespoons vegetable stock (see page 139)
2 tablespoons cornstarch
¼ onion, peeled and quartered
⅓ cup cider vinegar
2 tablespoons umeboshi plum vinegar (see page 118)
¼ cup sugar
1½ teaspoons dry mustard
1 teaspoon salt
½ cup mild vegetable oil such as corn, canola, or peanut
½ cup honey, warmed before measuring to thin it slightly
¼ cup poppyseeds

1 Bring 1 cup of the stock to a boil. Dissolve the cornstarch in the remaining 2 tablespoons stock and whisk the mixture into the boiling stock. As soon as the stock thickens and becomes clear, which should

VARIATIONS

SPICY THREE-SEED DRESSING: ***Measure 1 teaspoon celery seeds into a ¼-cup measure. Add 1 tablespoon toasted sesame seeds and top off with poppyseeds to make a full ¼ cup. To intensify the toasty sesame flavor, substitute 1 tablespoon toasted sesame oil for 1 tablespoon of the vegetable oil. I sometimes add a teaspoon of sweet Hungarian paprika and a pinch of cayenne to this version too.***

GINGERED THREE-SEED DRESSING: ***Make the above with a tablespoon or so of peeled, minced fresh ginger and a good dash of tamari or shoyu soy sauce (cut back salt accordingly). Use it to marinate steamed green beans, serving them on a bed of greens with some sliced red onions on top.***

Helen Corbitt's Poppyseed Trail

Arkansas being adjacent to Texas, and Eureka Springs' population including many, many ex-Dallas residents, one can sometimes trace in our local cuisine a certain provenance. Lots of Tex-Mex dishes appear on Eureka tables, as

have dozens of Texas sheet cakes, a mega-chocolate cake with super-sweet gooey pecan-studded icing that over the years has probably added, in toto, a frightening amount of local avoirdupois. But one of the most interesting ties I noticed, coming from the East Coast to the Ozarks, was the Helen Corbitt one. I noticed it because every single Eurekan/Texan friend of mine, without exception, no matter what other cookbooks might or might not be there, always had the same two: Helen Corbitt's Cookbook *(1957) and* Helen Corbitt Cooks for Company *(1974). Invariably the covers were torn, the pages speckled, the volumes obviously well loved and repeatedly used.*

Corbitt—she's deceased now—was the doyenne of upper-crust Texas cuisine for many years. She directed catering at the Houston Country Club; at the venerable Driskill Hotel in Austin; and at the Greenhouse, a Texan spa (since her recipes are not remotely what we could call "light," and since she was not a small woman, I imagine this was a stretch for her). Finally, she arrived at the post most identify her with to this day: food, beverage, and catering director at Neiman Marcus, where she designed menus for every soigné Dallas charity ball and occasion for years.

It's easy to see the appeal of her books, especially when you add the elite allure of Neiman's. Her recipes were mainstream enough to appeal to almost any eater, yet had some little flourish: Her noodle casserole, for example, is the dressed-to-the-nines version of the generic cream-of-mushroom soup hotdish, noodles bound with a creamy custard, but Helen added whole sautéed mushrooms, Burgundy, and sour cream. You could feel upper crust, but still eat pretty much what you'd grown up on—probably especially appealing for any riche *who were feeling a little too* nouveau. *"Hamburgers need a touch, too," she wrote—and served hers on split, toasted buns, which were broiled with a thin slice of onion and Roquefort cheese.*

But the single recipe she is most identified with is a very, very sweet poppyseed dressing. "Rumors extend hither and yon that I created it," she wrote, somewhat self-aggrandizingly. "I hasten to deny this; but I did popularize it when I realized that on the best grapefruit in the world (Texas grapefruit) it was the most delectable dressing imaginable. Today there is hardly a restaurant or home in Texas that does not have some kind of poppyseed dressing." True. I initially found it very surprising: awfully sweet on a green salad, even if there were some citrus fruit sections or grapes thrown in. But it grew on me. My lightened-up version of Helen Corbitt's Poppyseed Dressing appears on *page 99.*

be almost immediately, remove the mixture from the heat, transfer to a small bowl, and refrigerate until cool.

2 Place the onion in a food processor, along with the cider and umeboshi plum vinegars, sugar, dry mustard, and salt. Turn the machine on, and, with the motor running, drizzle in the oil and honey. When the oil and honey have been incorporated, transfer the mixture to a bowl. Whisk in the poppyseeds and the chilled thickened vegetable stock. Taste for seasonings; you might find that you need a little more salt or dry mustard.

COOK ONCE FOR 2 MEALS Toss just a little New Wave Poppyseed Dressing into any fruit salad. Or use it as a dip, placing it in a ramekin or small bowl in the center of a large platter of cut-up fresh fruit, skewers provided.

New Wave Poppyseed Coleslaw

I just mentioned how well the dressing keeps. Having a jar of it in your refrigerator means you can make this delicious, eminently simple salad, perfect with anything spicy, at the drop of a hat. If the dressing is on hand, and you buy one of those bags of precut, shredded cabbage et al. for slaw, this is virtually an instant salad.

NOTE

Nice with a veggie burger of some kind and some oven-baked potato fries.

1 bag (16 ounces) prepared fresh-cut slaw mix (unseasoned shredded green and purple cabbage and grated carrots)
¼ cup New Wave Poppyseed Dressing (page 99), basic or any variation
1 crisp, red apple, skin on, washed and diced

Combine all of the ingredients, tossing well, and serve. You may pass additional dressing at the table, if you like.

Sliced Avocado and Mango on Tender Greens

Here color and flavor contrast—pale green, mild buttery avocado, bright golden sweet mango—plays against similar textures. You end up with a striped half—is it an avocado half, or a mango half?—in the gay colors of a tropical beach umbrella. Several dressing options are given; whichever you choose, go very, very easy in your drizzling—you want to spark up the flavors not drown them. I think the Curried Vinaigrette is the best, but you can't go wrong with any of the suggestions.

SERVES 4

4 medium-large, whole, perfect, tender lettuce leaves, such as Boston lettuce

3 to 4 cups torn tender assorted lettuce leaves or mesclun

1 avocado, perfectly ripe, peeled, halved, and pitted

1 mango, perfectly ripe, cut vertically, parallel to the wide side of the pit, then peeled (giving you two large slices, curved on one side, flat on the other, as well as some residual mango still on the short uncut sides of the pit)

2 to 4 tablespoons one of the following dressings: Curried Vinaigrette (see Fresh Curried Beets, page 702), Sweet-Peppery Blackberry Vinaigrette (page 76), Honeyed Red-Wine Vinaigrette (page 79), or Cilantro Vinaigrette (page 94)

3 to 4 scallions, minced

Freshly ground black pepper (set your peppermill to a coarse grind, if possible)

1 Place salad plates in the freezer to chill. Remove them a few minutes before you're ready to serve and place a whole lettuce leaf in the center of each. Top with the torn lettuce or mesclun mix.

2 Working across the avocado halves the short way, cut each half into crosswise slices about ¼ inch thick. Do the same with the mango halves.

3 Reassemble a striped "mangocado" on each plate by carefully laying down a piece of avocado, then a piece of mango, then avocado, moving up sizewise. What you want is a construction roughly the size and shape of a pit-side-down avocado half or mango half, but striped in green and yellow. The green stripes will most likely be a little taller than the yellow, but the whole thing should look captivating, pleasing, a little goofy but delicious.

4 Carefully drizzle just the merest little bit of dressing over each "mangocado" half. If you put the dressing in a squeeze bottle, you'll be able to control your drizzle admirably. Top with a sprinkling of scallion and a bit of coarsely ground black pepper.

Bean & Legume Salads

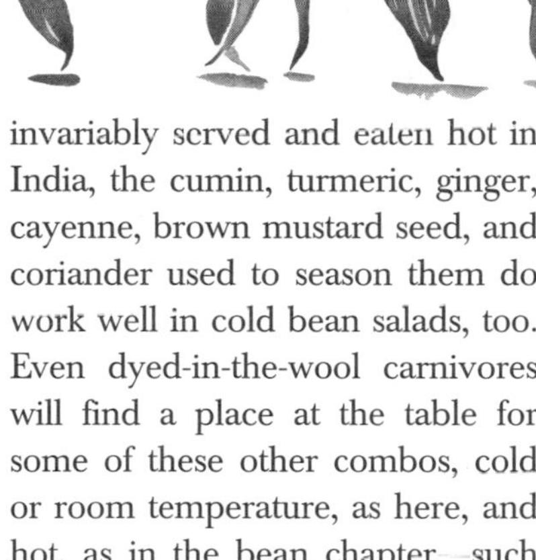

That beans are inexpensive, protein- and fiber-packed, and satisfying when fixed right, is indisputable. Equally true is the fact that without attention, they are bland, blah, and boring. Seasoning is all, in legume-land.

That land is found the world over. While in America, and especially in the South, we've most often relied on a hunk of fatback or other salted or smoked pork for bean seasoning, other cultures have other ideas. From the vegetarian standpoint, those ideas are not only "other" but better, and they work just as well in bean salads eaten cold or at room temperature as in hot bean dishes. The Middle Eastern flavors of garlic, lemon, parsley, and spices along with a hearty splash of olive oil work so very well with beans that it's no wonder marinated bean dishes are popular throughout this part of the world, as well as throughout the Mediterranean. Though beans are almost invariably served and eaten hot in India, the cumin, turmeric, ginger, cayenne, brown mustard seed, and coriander used to season them do work well in cold bean salads, too. Even dyed-in-the-wool carnivores will find a place at the table for some of these other combos, cold or room temperature, as here, and hot, as in the bean chapter—such dishes are not just good for you, but just plain *good*.

Salad of Limas, Green Beans, and Chickpeas with Lemon and Parsley

Here's a three-bean salad that's literally a world away from the conventional salad bar–style syrupy three-bean salads. This one, filled with Mediterranean notes, is buoyantly clear-flavored. It's come a long way since its

SALONIKA SOJOURN

Salad of Limas, Green Beans, and Chickpeas with Lemon and Parsley

*

Platter of sliced feta

*

Crusty rustic bread

*

Olive oil

*

Bread Herbs for Dipping
(PAGE 904)

*

Fresh figs; fresh grapes

starting point, Bean Salad, Politiko Style, from my beloved, weather-beaten *Grecian Gourmet Cookbook*. That bean salad was delicious, but even to my prefat-conscious taste, too oil-heavy. It also called only for white beans; for my money, a little boring and none too pretty. Still, Bean Salad, Politiko-style got me started. I commenced to tinker, going for more color, more flavor, less oil, beginning the journey to the salad below. **SERVES 8 TO 10 AS A STARTER OR COMPONENT; 6 TO 8 AS AN ENTREE**

½ pound green beans, stem ends snipped, sliced into 2-inch pieces
1 package (10 ounces) frozen baby lima beans, thawed (or the equivalent, if you are fortunate enough to find them, of fresh, raw limas)
2 carrots, well scrubbed, sliced into diagonal circles
1 can (15 ounces; 1¾ cups cooked) chickpeas, well drained
2 ribs celery, diced
½ large red onion, sliced in half and then crosswise, pulled into paper-thin slices
Salt and freshly ground black pepper to taste
1 to 2 lemons, halved
⅓ to ½ cup finely chopped Italian parsley
1 to 3 tablespoons extra virgin olive oil

1 Bring 1½ inches water to a boil in a pot over medium heat. Place a steaming basket over the boiling water and add the green beans. Cover and steam until the beans are still crisp-tender with a little bite, but have lost all rawness ("just long enough to take the fuzz off them," as an old friend used to say). If the beans are slim and tender, this should be 3 to 4 minutes; fatter beans, which are no less delicious in this salad, can take 10 to 12 minutes. Remove the steamer from the pot, reserving the steaming water. Rinse the green beans under cold water, drain well, and transfer to a bowl.

2 Repeat the same process with the limas over the same water, steaming for about 10 minutes. Once they're cooked, rinsed with cold water, and drained, combine with the green beans.

3 Repeat the same process with the carrots, again using the same steaming water, steaming for 1 minute. Rinse, drain, and add to the beans in the bowl.

4 Leaving the cover off of the steaming pot, remove the steamer, and raise the heat to a hard boil. Cook to reduce the steaming liquid to 1 tablespoon or less, 6 to 8 minutes. Watch closely so you don't scorch the liquid.

5 While the steaming liquid is reducing, add the chickpeas, celery, and red onion to

the bean mixture, along with salt and pepper to taste (be sure to add enough salt; beans require it to come up to full flavor). Squeeze the first lemon into the salad through a strainer (to catch seeds); if it's not very juicy, squeeze in the juice of the second lemon. Stir in the minced parsley and the oil (much, much more oil is traditional in these sorts of salads than is called for here, but I don't feel that it is necessary for a full-flavored, pleasing salad). Add the reduced steaming liquid and stir to blend.

6 Refrigerate for at least 2 hours; overnight is better. Before serving, bring to room temperature, taste, and, if necessary, reseason. (If you didn't already use it, you might need that second lemon now.) Serve as a first-course salad as part of a Middle Eastern–style feast of small dishes, or as one element in a component dinner.

Marinated Black-Eyed Peas with Greens Italia

Here's what happens when you take classic Southern ingredients (black-eyed peas and greens), marinate and spice them in the Venetian manner (olive oil, garlic, vinegar, loads of fresh herbs, including the surprise hits of mint and sage), and add a vegetarian twist (a bit of arame seaweed to give the salty oceanic tang supplied by anchovies in the original). Serve it, with good crusty bread, as a first course, or, in the dog days of summer, let it be a major player on a component plate that also includes fresh tomatoes, grilled eggplant, grilled zucchini, and maybe a slice of ricotta salata along with some great bread. **SERVES 6 TO 8 AS A SUBSTANTIAL FIRST COURSE, 4 TO 6 AS AN ENTREE**

NOTE

If all of the fresh herbs called for are not available, you can either omit those unavailable, or substitute one-third to one-half as much dried herb as fresh.

This salad must sit overnight in the refrigerator for the flavors to develop fully. Take it out long enough before serving for the beans to come up to room temperature and taste again to correct the seasonings.

BEANS

2 cups black-eyed peas
Water, preferably filtered or spring
2 carrots
2 ribs celery
1 onion, quartered, skin on
1 whole head garlic

GREENS

3 tablespoons olive oil
½ red onion, finely minced
1 large bunch collards, kale, turnip greens, chard, or beet greens, well washed, tough stems removed, and sliced across the grain into 1½-inch-wide strips (this is about 1¼ pounds; you may also use a combination of any or all of these greens)
10 cloves garlic, chopped
¾ cup vegetable stock (see page 139)
1 to 2 tablespoons arame seaweed (see page 82)

HERBS AND SEASONINGS

¼ cup Italian parsley, chopped medium-fine
3 tablespoons fresh basil, chopped medium-fine
2 tablespoons fresh mint, chopped medium-fine
1 tablespoon fresh sage, chopped medium-fine
1 tablespoon fresh thyme leaves, chopped medium-fine
1 tablespoon fresh oregano leaves, chopped medium-fine
1½ to 2 tablespoons balsamic vinegar or red wine vinegar
Salt and freshly ground black pepper to taste

Sprigs of fresh basil and Italian parsley (optional)
Cruets of olive oil and red wine vinegar

1 Pick over and rinse the black-eyed peas and place them in a medium-large pot with water to cover. Add the carrots, celery, onion, and garlic and bring to a boil. Turn the heat down to a simmer and let the beans cook, half-covered, until done but not mushy, 1 to 1½ hours. (Timing can vary a little depending on the age of the beans.) Let cool for a few minutes, then drain very well, reserving the bean liquid for another use such as stock. Pick out and discard the carrots, celery, and onion. Pick out and reserve the garlic.

2 Heat 2 tablespoons of the oil in a large, deep skillet over medium heat. Add the onion and sauté until just starting to become translucent, about 2 minutes. Add the greens and continue sautéing until greens are starting to get limp, 3 to 7 minutes (the timing will vary according to the type of greens).

3 Lower the heat slightly and add the garlic and the remaining tablespoon of oil. Sauté, slowly, just until the garlic is fragrant and starting to turn golden; do not allow it to brown. Add the vegetable stock and arame and bring to a boil. Add the well-drained beans and cook, stirring gently so as not to smash the beans, until good and hot. Remove the mixture from the heat and immediately stir in all of the herbs and the balsamic vinegar.

4 Squeeze the reserved head of cooled garlic so that most of the soft flesh inside will squoosh out (you don't have to do it clove by clove). Gently stir this soft garlic paste into the beans. Add salt (you'll need plenty of it) and lots of pepper. Let cool to room temperature, then cover and refrigerate overnight. Remove the beans

from the refrigerator an hour or so before serving to allow dish to come to room temperature. Check the seasoning; you may well need more salt, pepper, oil, and/or vinegar. Serve, at room temperature, garnished with sprigs of fresh basil and/or parsley. Pass cruets of olive oil and red wine vinegar at the table.

Mise en Place

Mise en place (pronounced MEEZ-ahn-plahs) is both a French cooking term and a method. Affectionately abbreviated throughout this book as simply "mise," it means "put in place." It is the arrangement of all of your prepared ingredients in bowls on the counter or on a tray so that they are ready to go.

When you first consider it, doing a mise appears compulsive or overly fussy. It can look like creating unnecessary work for yourself. Nothing could be further from the truth; it not only creates less work, but it promotes the pleasure and ease of doing that work. Mise en place is the key to well-organized cooking with absolute minimal stress, no matter how inexperienced or experienced you are in the kitchen. It's especially essential if the recipe is complex or new to you, or if you've got a lot going on at one time. Never again will you discover that you don't have an ingredient, or wonder whether you've added it or not. If you find yourself feeling frantic while you cook (and can't imagine why anyone would find cooking fun or relaxing), if you find your kitchen wholly and depressingly trashed every time by the time you've finished a recipe, mise will transform your life.

Begin a mise by reading the recipe all the way through before you actually start cooking. This gives you a theoretical grasp of the processes, as well as of all the ingredients on hand and any that aren't. If you need to get something from the supermarket or make a substitution, you'll know before you've started—no surprises and accompanying mania midstream. If thawed frozen raspberries are called for, you'll know to take them out of the freezer ahead of time. If butter is required in that state described as "softened to room temperature," well, you'll do that in timely fashion too.

Now you move on to ingredients that, unlike the examples given above, don't take much or any forethought. You assemble the raw materials for the recipe, ingredient by ingredient, taking out any tools you might need. You measure and prep each, placing it in its own little bowl or container or zip-top bag on a tray, before you start cooking. As you go along, each larger source-container gets put away. Does every cook need to do a mise each and every time? No, not for very simple recipes, especially if you are an experienced cook. But there are three categories of dishes for which mise is essential. These are:

- ▲ *baked goods (because they rely on chemical processes—the interaction between leavening agents and flours—and if you leave something out or add it at the wrong time, it's not always possible to compensate)*

- ▲ *stir-fries (because once the heat is on under the wok or skillet, everything moves very, very fast, and you need to be attentive; you can't be chopping ingredients and sautéing at the same moment), and*

- ▲ *dishes with a lot of ingredients (most curries are pretty simple to put together, but they rely on almost layered systems of spicing—perhaps six or eight or ten different spices, whole or ground or both, which may be called for at different times).*

It is astonishing how much smoother and more deeply pleasurable this simple activity makes cooking. You will discover, as you do it, that you are not just getting your ingredients in place, but yourself, too.

Ebony and Ivory

To paraphrase, "Ebony and Ivory / live together on perfect chicory . . ." Black beans and white; lovely. Done with canned beans and with some Sharp Classic Vinaigrette on hand, it's quick as can be. The flavors are fresh, simple, and direct but the onion and garlicky dressing give the beans a kick, while the celery and red pepper play off their smoothness. To keep the colors distinct and not muddy, put this together at the last moment. **SERVES 4 TO 6**

VARIATIONS

Make a meal of this by adding a little grated sharp Cheddar or jack cheese; give it Southwestern heat with a finely diced fresh serrano chile or two and a good sprinkle of minced cilantro, plus a drizzle of juice from the canned chipotle you used in the dressing. Speaking of which; if you don't have the Sharp Classic Vinaigrette on hand, you can get by with a few tablespoons oil and vinegar and a little pressed garlic in each bowl of beans. Or try the salad with any of the variations of Cilantro Vinaigrette (page 94).

1 can (15 ounces) black beans
1 can (15 ounces) white beans (navy beans)
¼ cup Sharp Classic Vinaigrette with a Bite (page 72)
2 ribs celery, diced
2 red bell peppers, charred, peeled, seeded, and diced (page 782)
½ large red onion, finely minced
Salt and freshly ground black pepper to taste
6 to 8 cups washed salad greens, including some bitter greens like chicory

1 Open both cans of beans. Keeping them separate, drain each can of beans, reserving the liquid for stock. Again keeping them separate, place the beans in a colander and rinse very well. Place each type of bean into a small bowl.

2 Add half of the vinaigrette to each bowl of beans. Toss well and refrigerate.

3 At serving time, place the beans in one bowl. Combine the celery, bell peppers, and onion with the beans and toss well. Season with salt and pepper to taste. Serve the salad scooped onto the salad greens.

Grain & Pasta Salads

If you're looking for pleasing and unusual ways to start incorporating the whole-grain cereals that countless nutritionists and health advocates recommend, look no further. You will quickly see why whole grains have a place far beyond the breakfast bowl or simple side dish. Hearty, solid, full-flavored, these next salads might round out a light meal, but are perfectly capable of being a meal in themselves, and at least one marinated rice, potato, or pasta salad is pretty much de rigeur on most buffets or at potlucks. Although they may be served with an underpinning of greens and cooked vegetables or herbs in them, their heart, soul, and substance lies in their comforting carbohydrates. The trick, as with all salads, is not to overdress them, so their true goodness can come through.

Remember, if you make these salads ahead of time (and the convenience of being able to do so is one of their pleasures), taste and re-season them before serving them. Sometimes seasonings meld just perfectly during a refrigerator sojourn; at other times, they just fade away.

Rice and grains are always good for strategic cooking. Any time you cook pasta, grains, or potatoes, always remember there are dozens of salad possibilities. Have the starch of your choice hot for dinner one night, then make the leftovers the base for a salad the next day or the day after.

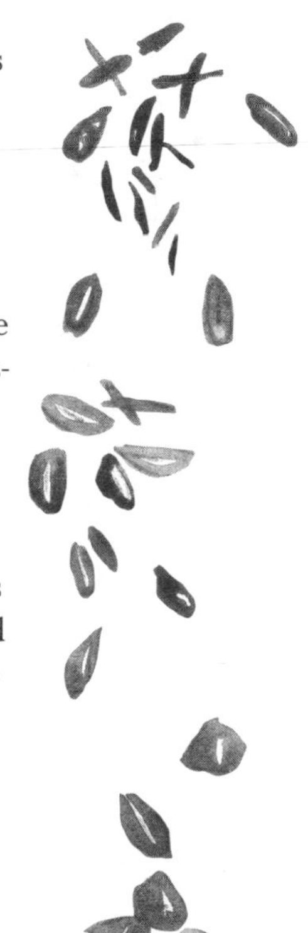

Three-Grain Salad with Dried Cranberries and Grapefruit

Improbable, refreshing, I like the way tart notes play off gentle heat, sweetness, and herbs, and soothing grain mitigates all. It's like a Christmas stocking—there are little surprises in every bite. And speaking of Christmas, it's a perfect choice for wintertime, both hearty and refreshing, at a time when there's not much that's fresh and juicy around. If your taste runs to mild, use charred sweet bell peppers; to me, however, the poblanos, with their faint heartbeat of sweet, chocolatey heat, are excellent here.

This salad's origins—from which I've digressed to fit my own personal quirks of taste—are in one of the niftiest mail-order catalogs for grain and bean eaters, that of Indian Harvest, a Minnesota-based company that's carried all manner of beautifully spotted heirloom beans, esoteric grains, and grain-bean medleys for over two decades. The recipe that inspired me, Cabernet Craisin Salad ("Cabernet" alluding not to wine, but to the name of one of their grain medleys), appeared in their catalog. It was developed by the late chef Gary Holleman, an unpretentious and kind man, who used to refer to himself as "the bean and rice guy." **SERVES 4**

VARIATION

MAIN DISH THREE-GRAIN SALAD: ***To create a main dish, add either 6 ounces crumbled feta cheese or 8 ounces diced savory baked tofu or smoked tofu (such as that made by Tree of Life), plus an optional ¼ cup toasted walnut pieces or pine nuts. Serve on a great big bed of washed, well-dried, very fresh leaf spinach.***

I have also occasionally substituted balsamic for the red wine vinegar, and New Wave Poppyseed Dressing (page 99) for the vinegar, oil, and seasonings.

1 ruby-red grapefruit, peeled
4½ cups cooked Indian Harvest Cabernet Medley (or any homemade grain medley, such as brown rice, barley, and wheat berries), cooled
2 poblano chiles, or sweet red bell pepper, charred, peeled, seeded, and diced (see page 782)
¼ cup minced Italian parsley
¼ red onion, minced
1 rib celery, diced
2 to 4 tablespoons dried unsweetened cranberries
⅓ cup cranberry juice
¼ cup red wine vinegar
2 tablespoons extra virgin olive oil
2 teaspoons Rapidura or brown sugar
1½ teaspoons fresh rosemary leaves
1 teaspoon salt, plus more to taste
Freshly ground black pepper to taste

1 Working over a strainer that's set into a bowl, section the grapefruit with a small sharp paring knife, removing all fiber and seeds. The object here is to end up with small grapefruit chunks for the salad, and to catch enough juice in the bowl for the dressing.

2 Combine the grapefruit pieces with the grain medley, chiles, parsley, onion, celery, and cranberries, tossing well.

3 Combine the grapefruit juice with the cranberry juice, vinegar, oil, Rapidura, rosemary, and salt and pepper in a small jar, mixing well. Pour a tablespoon or two over the salad and toss to coat. Pass the remaining dressing at the table.

Grain Dreams

Though I have specified particular grains in these salads, any single grain or combination of grains you have on hand will work just fine. Although I usually make my own combos, those from the bean-and-grain mail-order company Indian Harvest are delicious and downright inspiring. I order from them periodically not only because they are so good but because I love to get stuff by mail.

If you want to get the Indian Harvest catalog, call them at 1-800-346-7032.

Parky's Pepper Mill Pasta Salad à l'Italia

John and Marge Parkhurst, retirees who live here in Eureka, publish an entertaining, always interesting one-page monthly cooking newsletter—*The Pepper Mill,* by "stamp-scription"—just for friends, in which a nonvegetarian version of this recipe appeared. John writes the text, Marge illustrates and occasionally adds handwritten editorial comments like "A LUSCIOUS SALAD!" which appeared next to this. This is a pasta salad with a difference—several differences, actually—the first one being that it does not use butterfly, corkscrew, or other standard-issue pasta salad pastas, but rather the tiny trompe l'oeil rice-shaped pasta known as riso, orzo, or sometimes melon-seed. Like regular pasta, you cook these in lots of boiling salted water till barely done, then rinse under cool water.

VARIATION

Try this with real rice, especially short-grain brown rice, sometimes.

SERVES 4 OR 5 AS AN ENTREE

1 lemon
¼ cup Tofu Mayonnaise (page 906) or conventional or reduced-fat natural foods store–style mayonnaise
2 to 3 tablespoons extra virgin olive oil
1 tablespoon red-wine or balsamic vinegar
1 tablespoon capers, with their liquid
2 teaspoons finely minced fresh tarragon or Mexican Marigold, a.k.a. Texas Tarragon (see page 37)
6 to 8 threads saffron
1 teaspoon dried oregano leaves
½ pound dry riso or orzo or melon-seed pasta, cooked and drained according to package directions, chilled
15 to 20 kalamata or oil-cured black olives
3 Roma or plum tomatoes, diced
1 red pepper, charred, peeled, seeded, and diced (see page 782)
½ cucumber, preferably unwaxed and unpeeled (peel if waxed), halved lengthwise, seeds scraped out, then halved again and sliced crosswise into ¼-inch pieces
1 rib celery, diced
2 to 3 tablespoons finely minced Italian parsley
Salt and freshly ground black pepper to taste
Whole romaine leaves, washed, dried, and chilled, for serving
3 ounces smoked provolone cheese or smoked tofu, diced; freshly grated Parmesan; toasted pine nuts; parsley and mint sprigs (optional)

VARIATION

Since this is another one of those great all-embracing dishes that take happily to all manner of additions, consider tossing in any or all of the following: 2 diced scallions, a tablespoon of any pesto, a few well-drained, coarsely chopped marinated artichoke hearts. Consider an extra garnish or two: vegetarian bacon bits, crumbles of Gorgonzola, crisp herbed croutons, or fresh basil sprigs.

1 Finely grate the rind of the lemon and set aside. Halve the lemon. Combine the juice from half of the lemon with half of the lemon rind, the mayo, oil, vinegar, capers, tarragon, and saffron. Rub the oregano between your palms into the dressing. Whisk well, holding back the remaining lemon rind and juice.

2 Pour the dressing over the chilled pasta and toss to coat. Add the olives, tomatoes, roasted red pepper, cucumber, celery, parsley, and salt and pepper and toss again. Refrigerate for at least 1 hour, preferably overnight.

3 When ready to serve, taste again (chilling dulls the flavors). Add additional salt and pepper, and maybe that remaining lemon rind and juice. Toss again and serve, on romaine leaves, each portion sprinkled with any or all of the optional garnishes.

COOK ONCE FOR 2 MEALS Parky points out that "if you cooked up a whole one-pound box of riso and used half for the salad, you have the other half left over. Use it in making another Italian favorite, FRITTATA." Parky's Pasta Frittata is on page 891, in Quick Fix (Chapter 13).

Farmer's Market Salad Plate with Caper Dressing

This is a beautiful dish that is a full-meal salad plate, combining sprightly flavors, appealing colors, and textural contrast. One salad dressing, zippity-do-dah'd with the salty, vinegary, spicy/vegetal tang of capers, is used to marinate three components—a cooked grain, a cooked bean, and a cooked vegetable. Pile the whole thing on a bed of lettuce leaves, add a tomato cut into eighths, and you have one grand meal that will see you nicely through the doggiest of the dog-days. You don't even need bread to accompany it. I know the amounts are large, but you will be happy to have this in your fridge to eat your way through and share with friends. You may serve it with feta, but it stands up quite well without, too. **SERVES 8 TO 10**

BEAN SALAD

3½ to 4 cups cooked or canned assorted beans, well drained

½ bunch scallions, roots and any dried-out green ends removed, white and fresh green parts sliced

GRAIN SALAD

4½ cups any cooked, nonsticky whole grain or a combination of grains (I've made this with spelt, and also with a combination of long-grain brown and wild rices; there are few grains it wouldn't be good with)

1 carrot, scrubbed, diced

1 rib celery, diced

1 yellow or red bell pepper, diced (optional)

VEGETABLE SALAD

1 pound fresh green beans, tipped and tailed, blanched in boiling water until crisp-tender, then immediately drained and shocked with cold water and ice

½ cup loosely packed basil leaves, chopped

TO FINISH

Caper Dressing/Marinade (recipe follows)

Salt and freshly ground black pepper to taste

Large red-leaf and butter lettuce leaves, washed and very well dried

Fresh tomatoes, cut into wedges

Feta cheese (optional)

1 Place ingredients for the bean salad in one bowl, for the grain salad in a second, and for the vegetable salad in a third.

2 Pour one-third of the Caper Dressing over each of the three salads; toss well. Season each salad with salt and pepper to taste. Refrigerate each of the salads (I like to place them in zippered plastic bags; it saves room in the fridge, and they are easily transported to picnics). Marinate for at least 4 hours, preferably 1 to 2 days.

3 To serve, place a bed of lettuce leaves on each plate. Top with one scoop of each of the three salads, a few wedges of tomato, and an optional slice or two of feta.

NOTE

Several types of beans, in contrasting colors, really do add to this. My ideal choice is a combination of Giant Peruvian lima beans (from Phipps; www.phippscountry.com) borlotti beans, and Tongues of Fire, all cooked separately to maintain their individual colors. But well-drained canned black beans, kidneys, and chickpeas would also do just fine.

Caper Dressing/ Marinade

¼ cup extra virgin olive oil

¼ cup red wine vinegar

1½ tablespoons grainy Dijon mustard

1 tablespoon Pickapeppa sauce

3 cloves garlic

Juice of 1 lemon

¼ to ⅓ cup bottled capers, rinsed

Place all of the ingredients except the capers in a food processor and buzz until the garlic is pulverized. Add the capers and pulse/chop, just until the capers are finely minced but not smooth.

Wild Rice, Pasta, and Roasted Asparagus Salad

What could say "spring" more cogently? Add some strips of baked savory or Asian-style tofu and/or add some stir-fried edible-pod peas for a main-dish meal. The dressing's very low in oil, too. **SERVES 4 TO 6**

1 pound asparagus, cut diagonally into ¾-inch pieces
3 carrots, scrubbed, and sliced diagonally into ¼-inch ovals
1 teaspoon mild vegetable oil such as corn, canola, or peanut
1 tablespoon tamari
Cooking spray (optional)
1 bunch scallions (about 8 medium), sliced ¼ inch thick
2 cups cooked wild rice
12 ounces butterfly pasta, cooked al dente
Sweet Sesame-Ginger Dressing (recipe follows)
¼ cup coarsely chopped cilantro (optional)
2 to 4 tablespoons toasted sesame seeds (optional)

1 Preheat the oven to 450°F.

2 Toss together the sliced asparagus, carrots, and oil. Add the tamari and toss again. Place the vegetables in a nonstick baking dish large enough to leave air space

About These Pasta Salads

Pasta salad is a staple of my kitchen. I love the Winter Vegetable Salad with Chickpeas (page 86), and the pasta salad variation. And the Inn's house pasta salad, which is in Dairy Hollow House Soup & Bread Cookbook, *on page 384, is always a winner. These are standards with flavorings you might expect. The pasta salads here, however, are different. With their ginger notes, they have a decidedly Asian bent. Most people don't think of ginger as a natural mate for pasta, but once you pair ginger with garlic, sesame oil, or peanut butter, it's practically crying out for a bowl of pasta.*

around them or one that has been sprayed with cooking spray. Bake until the vegetables begin to brown but are still fairly crisp, 10 to 12 minutes. Add the scallions, shaking the pan very well, and bake for another 5 minutes. Remove from the heat and turn the oven-roasted vegetables out into a bowl.

3 Add the cooked wild rice and butterfly pasta, and toss very well. Add 2 to 3 tablespoons of the dressing, toss well, and taste. Add more dressing if you like. Refrigerate until serving time. Just before serving, add the cilantro and toasted sesame seeds, if using, and toss one more time.

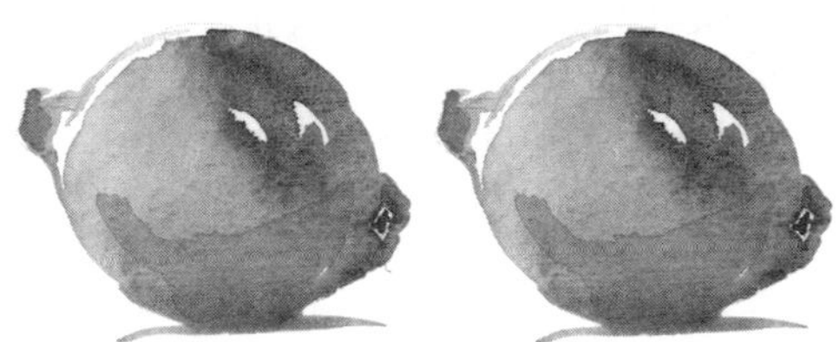

Sweet Sesame-Ginger Dressing

3 tablespoons fresh-squeezed lemon juice
2 tablespoons honey
1 tablespoon mirin (Japanese rice wine)
2½ teaspoons tamari or shoyu soy sauce
2 teaspoons to 1 tablespoon very finely minced peeled fresh ginger, fibers removed prior to mincing
1 teaspoon Asian-style toasted sesame oil
Pinch of cayenne
5 to 6 solid grinds black pepper

Combine the lemon juice, honey, mirin, tamari or shoyu soy sauce, ginger, sesame oil, cayenne, salt, and black pepper in a small jar.

NOTE

Unlike many of the other dressings in this chapter, this will not emulsify, because it's so low in fat. But as a splash for the rice and pasta, it works quite well.

Quinoa, Corn, and Buckwheat Noodle Salad

Quinoa (pronounced KEEN-wah; see page 564) is a charming South American grain that cooks up into little stars. Its flavor, though in no way its texture, reminds me of corn. So I combined the two of them—along with curly buckwheat ramen noodles, for contrast—in a cold salad. I dressed it lightly with sesame and a lot of fresh ginger, but, just for a change, no garlic and no sweetener.

GINGERLY "REORIENTING" TO SPRING

Quasi-Vietnamese Spring Rolls
(PAGE 314)

*

Steamed pea pods and baby carrots, with Gingered Jade Spinach Dip
(PAGE 27)

*

Quinoa, Corn, and Buckwheat Noodle Salad

*

Green or jasmine tea (hot or iced)

*

Vanilla ice cream with crystallized ginger and toasted almonds, or Ginger Sorbet
(PAGE 1045)

Because this dressing doesn't keep well, and is so specific to this salad, it's the exception to the leftover rule. Quantity-wise, there's just enough to do one batch of the salad. **SERVES 4 TO 6**

- 3 cups cooked quinoa (if you're unfamiliar with this ingredient, please see "Keenly Quinoa" on page 564 for basic information, including how and how much to cook for this yield)
- Kernels cut from 4 ears sweet corn
- 1 package buckwheat ramen noodles, noodle clusters broken into quarters, then cooked according to package directions, miso seasoning packet discarded or saved for another use (note: do not overcook the noodles; cook for the minimum suggested cooking time)
- 3 scallions, minced (optional)
- 3 tablespoons finely minced Italian parsley (optional)
- Sesame-Ginger Dressing (recipe follows)

Combine the quinoa, corn, noodles, scallions, and parsley. Toss well. Add the Sesame-Ginger Dressing and toss again. Serve immediately, or refrigerate and serve up to 2 days later.

Sesame-Ginger Dressing

- 2 tablespoons tamari or shoyu soy sauce
- 1 to 2 tablespoons fresh-squeezed lemon juice
- 1 tablespoon mild-flavored vegetable oil such as corn, canola, or peanut
- 1 tablespoon toasted sesame oil
- 1 tablespoon tahini
- 1 tablespoon very finely minced peeled fresh ginger, fibers removed prior to mincing

Combine all of the ingredients in a small bowl and whisk the dickens out of them with a fork.

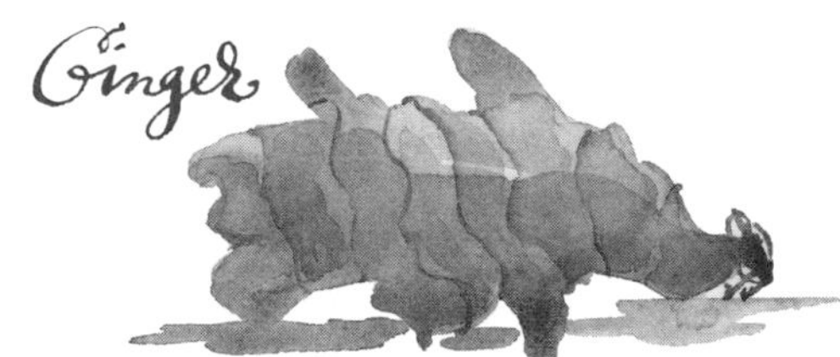

Gingered Salad with Cilantro, Tofu, and Hominy

Corn, also used with ginger in the previous salad, takes another form in hominy (see page 440 to meet this fascinating and ancient incarnation of maize). This is a main-dish salad, invented improvisationally. We happened to have these particular ingredients sitting around in the fridge and cupboard one August day, and the delicious, surprising main-dish salad that resulted has remained a favorite ever since. Expect a wonderful mélange of flavors (a little spicy, a tiny bit sweet, somewhat Thai) and textures (very crisp, very soft, and somewhere in between).

SERVES 4 TO 6

One can (14½ ounces) white hominy, well drained
2½ cups mung bean sprouts
½ cup cilantro leaves, scissored into medium pieces
1 bunch scallions, sliced into thin rounds
1 large, red-ripe summer tomato, diced
2 teaspoons Thai Crystal (see page 923) or Thai-style chile-garlic sauce
1 head romaine lettuce, washed, dried, torn into bite-size pieces
¼ head iceberg lettuce, slivered
1 package (8 ounces) savory baked tofu, diced
Sesame-Ginger-Miso Dressing (recipe follows)

1. Combine the hominy, bean sprouts, cilantro, scallions, tomato, and Thai Crystal and marinate, refrigerated, for 1 to 4 hours.

2. Just before serving, combine the lettuces. Place a bed of mixed lettuce on each serving plate, or line a large serving bowl with the lettuces. Divide the hominy salad among the plates or place it in the center of the serving bowl. Top with the diced tofu. Pass the Sesame-Ginger-Miso Dressing at the table.

Sesame-Ginger-Miso Dressing

Just a few changes between this and the previous dressing, but what a difference! **MAKES ABOUT ¾ CUP**

2 tablespoons mild-flavored vegetable oil such as corn, canola, or peanut
2 tablespoons tamari or shoyu soy sauce
2 tablespoons umeboshi plum vinegar
1 tablespoon toasted sesame oil
1 tablespoon dark miso
1 tablespoon honey
2 teaspoons very finely minced fresh ginger
Pinch of cayenne
Several vigorous grinds of black pepper

Combine all of the ingredients in a small bowl and whisk the dickens out of them with a fork.

VARIATION

This salad—improvisational, after all, from birth—is very agreeable to further variation. Try a sliced avocado across the top or a tablespoon of toasted sesame seeds. And add a grated carrot to the marinated hominy base.

Meet Umeboshi: Plum Delicious

HAVE WE BEEN INTRODUCED YET?

Macrobiotics, a dietary system based on balancing the acid and alkaline (yin and yang), is too restrictive for my kind of eating, though I know people who thrive on it and seemingly don't mind its culinary restraints. Whatever one may think of that way of eating, however, there's no doubt that it's introduced some intriguing ingredients into the American diet. Thanks to its practitioners, such exotica as seaweeds (see page 82) and umeboshi plum condiments in several forms, are widely available in natural foods stores.

Part Asian folk medicine, part seasoning, part condiment, umeboshi (pronounced ooh-may-BOW-shee) are small plums native to Japan, Taiwan, and China. Still primarily grown in these countries, more recently the trees have been imported to parts of the Pacific Northwest and are now being grown here. Umeboshi are picked green and pickled with salt and shiso leaves (also called beefsteak or perilla leaves). Some of the small-scale American growers are also processing the plums now, part of the heartening movement of present-day rediscoverers of past culinary craft—the artisanal "boutique farmers," tofu or seitan makers, natural-rise bakers, micro-brewers, and so on who give all of us who cook and seek out quality ingredients much hope.

There are many reputed health benefits of umeboshi—it's been considered a general tonic, purifier, and longevity promoter, even a hangover cure—for four thousand years in China. In sixteenth-century Japan, they were said to be essential in the Samurai diet and the secret of Samurai strength and stamina. But the culinary reasons these small pinkish plums are prized is beyond question. They contain three of the four layers of taste we perceive: they are tart (or sour), salty, and bitter (in other words, every taste except sweet). When you first eat one, it's intense enough that you might not like the flavor—but, like eating hot and spicy dishes, you will soon crave it.

Because of this sour-salty-bitter matrix, umeboshi, used as seasoning in many dishes, plays over the tongue and provides just the right piquant, balancing note in a variety of ways. Added judiciously, the taste of umeboshi is often hard to identify as such; it's more the effect the plums give. You won't taste such dishes and say, "Oh, umeboshi . . . "; it's more like, "Mmmm, what makes this so good?" Tofu Sour Cream (page 909) is one almost unbelievable example.

Available in several forms, umeboshi keep indefinitely and are well worth keeping on hand. You can buy whole salted plums (usually with pits), or a very concentrated, forthright puree of umeboshi. Lastly, there's umeboshi vinegar—not a true vinegar but an extremely tart, salty liquid that is drained from the pickled umeboshi plums and their usual sidekick, flavorful shiso leaves. The closest analogy with which most Americans might be familiar is sauerkraut juice, but that underrates it. Umeboshi vinegar is a great seasoning and condiment; utterly addictive. I splash it not only on a variety of cooked vegetables, but on grains—even and especially a nice hot mixed-grain breakfast porridge. Sounds strange, I know, but it tastes just right to me some mornings.

"Hot Thai in the Old Town Tonight" Noodle-Tofu Salad

I adore Thai flavors: those take-the-top-off-the-roof-of-your-mouth circles of vibrant, bright chiles, the mitigating, interesting greenness of basil, mint, and cilantro; a little sweetness here, some unctuous too-high-in-fat-to-really-be-prudent coconut milk there, wise ginger, gentle tofu, tricolor curries, the crunch of peanuts.

This salad is my tribute to these tastes. I am grateful to Steven Raichlen's Cambodian Salad in *High-Flavor, Low-Fat Vegetarian Cooking* for the garlic-frying tip as well as for some of the directions this recipe has taken. **SERVES 4 TO 6 AS AN ENTREE, 8 TO 10 AS AN ACCOMPANIMENT**

About 6 ounces transparent bean-thread noodles
¼ cup mild vegetable oil such as, corn, canola, or peanut
6 cloves garlic, halved, any visibly green interior stem removed, thinly sliced across the grain
3 cups mung bean sprouts
3 to 4 assorted sweet bell peppers; ideally, 1 each red, yellow, and green, plus 1 Hungarian Wax or Sweet Banana pepper, cored, seeded, white interior fiber removed, cut into thin slivers
3 carrots, scrubbed, coarsely grated into large shreds (use the medium or large shredding disc on a food processor) or hand-cut into fine julienne
2 fresh tomatoes, cut into wedges
1 bunch scallions, white and 1 inch of the green parts, cut into ¼-inch slices
½ head iceberg lettuce, cored and sliced thickly
1 cup thinly sliced red cabbage
⅔ cup loosely packed basil leaves, sliced into ¼-inch strips
⅔ cup loosely packed mint leaves, chopped
⅔ cup cilantro leaves
1 package (8 ounces) savory baked tofu, each cake cut in half horizontally, then into strips about ⅜ inch by 1½ inches
Thai Splash Dressing (recipe follows)
1 to 3 fresh jalapeño or serrano chiles, sliced into paper-thin circles (leave the seeds in for heat, or wuss out and remove them if you want things milder)
3 to 4 tablespoons finely chopped roasted peanuts
1 hard-cooked egg, very finely minced (optional)

1. Soak the noodles in very hot tap water in a large bowl for about 10 minutes.

2. Heat the oil in a wok. When very hot, drop in the sliced garlic and cook until slightly golden-colored—20 seconds or so, max. Scoop out the garlic with a slotted spoon. Set the garlic aside to drain on a paper towel, blotting to remove excess oil. Save most of the garlic oil, refrigerated, for use in another dish; reserve 2 teaspoons of the oil for this dish.

3. Bring a medium pot of water to a boil. Drain the soaked noodles—which should be pliable by now—and cut them into 4-inch lengths with a kitchen shears. Place the noodles in the boiling water and cook until tender, about 1½ minutes. Drain through a colander. Rinse well with cold running water and, when cool to the touch and fully drained, toss the noodles with the reserved 2 teaspoons garlic oil. Refrigerate until ready to use.

4. Bring a fresh pot of water to a boil. Put the bean sprouts in a colander and pour the boiling water over them to quick-blanch the sprouts. Run cold water over the sprouts and then drain very thoroughly. Refrigerate until ready to use.

5. When just about ready to serve, combine the bean sprouts and noodles in a large bowl. Add the sweet pepper slivers, carrots, tomatoes, scallions, lettuce, red cabbage, basil, mint, cilantro, and strips of tofu and toss everything together thoroughly.

6. When ready to serve, add the Thai Splash Dressing, sliced chiles, and the reserved fried garlic. Toss to combine. Garnish with peanuts and the egg, if using, and serve immediately.

Care for Seconds?

In the old pre-Internet Dairy Hollow House days, I gave the inn's 800 number in my cookbooks, so that if you ran into a problem or had a question or comment, you could just give a buzz. But now, of course, there's an easier way. It's www.dragonwagon.com, *the constantly updated online, ongoing, and on-target extension of my life and my books. What with new vegetarian options—from rediscovered heirloom vegetables to brand-new second-generation soyfoods—coming to market weekly, plus my own and various pan-pals' constant fooling around in the kitchen and consequent development of new recipes, plus on-the-road discoveries of both new vegetarian restaurants and fabulous meatless options starting to be available in non-vegetarian restaurants . . . plus my own pleasure in interacting with readers . . . plus profiles of some of the growers, chefs, authors, and culinary friends you've met in passing in this book . . . plus details of when and where I'll be teaching cooking and/or writing—I hope you'll come visit there soon and often, not just for second helpings but thirds, fourths, and more.*

Thai Splash Dressing

⅓ cup fresh-squeezed lime juice
2 to 3 tablespoons tamari or shoyu soy sauce
1 to 2 tablespoons brown sugar
1 teaspoon toasted sesame oil
Finely grated rind of 2 limes
1 to 2 cloves garlic, pressed
Salt and plenty of freshly ground pepper to taste

Combine all of the ingredients. Taste; it should be distinctly salty, sweet, and sour. Feel free to play with the ingredients until it's just right.

Spicy Eggplant with Buckwheat Ramen Noodles

Can you stand one more gingery salad? You can if it's this one! Fresh ginger teams up with garlic, cayenne, and cilantro for smashing results. However, the eggplant wins Best Supporting Actor because without it, the others would not look nearly so good. It undergoes a transformation of texture—from spongy to silken—as it is cooked. Remarkably friendly to a thousand flavors, eggplant lends its amiability the world over, to dips and spreads (like the countless variations of Middle Eastern baba ghanoush), spreads-with-a-texture appetizers (like Italian caponata), and main courses without number. Grilling it until the skin chars gives eggplant a special smoky quality that's hard to beat.

The eggplant sauce, without the pasta, can be used as a spread or dip. **SERVES 8 AS A SUBSTANTIAL FIRST COURSE, 4 AS AN ENTREE**

EGGPLANT SAUCE

- 2 medium-large eggplants, skin on, pricked with a fork a few times
- 2 cloves garlic, chopped
- 2 tablespoons finely minced fresh ginger
- 2 tablespoons mirin (Japanese rice wine) or sherry
- 1 to 2 tablespoons rice wine vinegar
- 1 to 2 tablespoons tamari or shoyu soy sauce
- 1 tablespoon brown sugar
- 1 tablespoon natural, unhydrogenated roasted peanut butter
- 1 teaspoon toasted sesame oil
- Pinch of cayenne

PASTA

- 2 packages (6 ounces) buckwheat or brown rice ramen noodles, seasoning packages discarded or saved for another use
- 1 teaspoon toasted sesame oil
- 1 cucumber, peeled, halved, seeded, cut diagonally into ⅓-inch slices

GARNISH

- 2 scallions, green part included, minced
- ¼ cup cilantro leaves, chopped
- 2 teaspoons toasted sesame seeds (optional)

1 Either grill the whole eggplants over a medium flame, turning often with

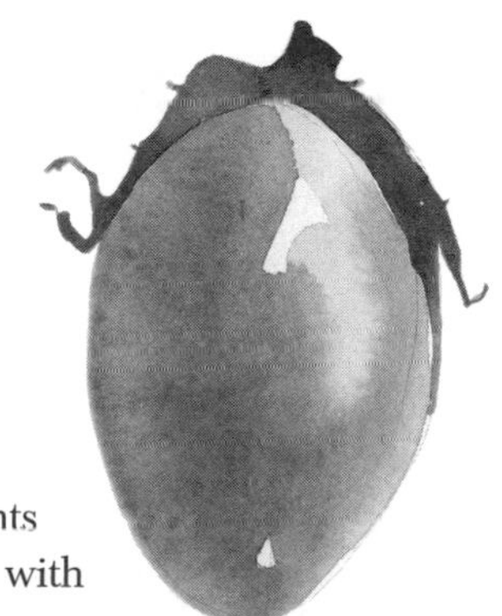

tongs, until the skin is black and charred, or cut them in half lengthwise and bake them, cut side down, on a nonstick or well-oiled baking dish at 375°F. Grilling should take 20 to 25 minutes; baking 45 minutes to 1 hour. In either case, the eggplants are done when the inner flesh is soft and oozing liquid and they have collapsed slightly. Remove from the heat and allow to cool.

2 When cool enough to handle, either scrape off the grilled, black shards of skin that remain on the grilled eggplants or scoop the innards out of the baked eggplants, discarding the skins. Place about one-third of the eggplant flesh in a food processor; pull the remaining eggplant into long stringy pieces, then coarsely chop and place in a bowl.

3 To the eggplant in the food processor, add the garlic, ginger, mirin, vinegar, tamari, brown sugar, peanut butter, toasted sesame oil, and cayenne. (On ingredients where I've given ranges, start with the lesser amounts; eggplant sizes vary as much as individual tastes.) Buzz the mixture until smooth; taste, and start playing with the seasonings until it's just as you like it, remembering that you want a highly seasoned paste since it will be diluted by both the chopped eggplant and the pasta. Also, the flavors will develop somewhat as it sits.

4 Transfer the eggplant puree to the bowl with the chopped eggplant and stir well. Refrigerate for a couple of hours to let the flavors blend. Bring to room temperature and taste for seasonings before you finish the dish.

5 Just before serving, cook the ramen in boiling water according to the package directions, omitting the seasoning. Drain well in a colander and run cold water over the noodles until cool. Shake dry and turn out into a bowl. Toss with the teaspoon of toasted sesame oil and the cucumber slices. Spoon the room-temperature eggplant sauce over the pasta (if the eggplant seems congealed, stir it up well first). Sprinkle with the minced scallion, cilantro leaves, and the toasted sesame seeds, if using.

COOK ONCE FOR 2 MEALS Double the eggplant component and serve half with the pasta. Place the other half in a ramekin and serve it (bringing it to room temperature first) asa dip or spread as part of supper later in the week.

Potato Salads

From all that exotica to back home, down home—for what could be more all-American than potato salad? Here are three variations that push the envelope just a little. The first is a reduced-fat, tofu-mayonnaise'd version of the classic we all knew and (once) loved, a recipe that in its original draft (in the first *Dairy Hollow House Cookbook)* was perfected by Jan Brown's mama. It has plenty of surprises in it—olives, pickles—but is mainstream enough to attend the Baptist Sunday School Picnic in Utica, Mississippi (Hattie Mae Cox, I write that just for you). The second is also an updated, reduced-fat version of an inn classic that appeared in my first cookbook, a somewhat French potato salad, in which the potatoes cook in a rich broth that then becomes part of the final dressing. Number three puts in its first public appearance here, but newcomer though it may be, there's nothing shy and retiring about it. It is hot, hot, hot, contains both sweet and white potatoes, and is utterly addictive.

Mama Murray's Classic Kansas Potato Salad, Take Two

Mama Murray was Jan Brown's mother, Jan being one of my favorite culinary and general pals, as well as my collaborator on cookbook number one, as well as an extraordinary quilter, and a guidance counselor. You, unfortunately, are not as lucky as we are, because you don't have her in your life and your kids' school as we do . . . so console yourself with her great family potato salad; it's classic with a twist.

Along with the pickled eggs in the starter section, this is one of the few times in the whole year when hard-cooked eggs make it into something I eat. You can certainly leave them out. But what would a classic American potato salad really be without eggs? Besides, look at all the fat grams/calories you're saving by using tofu mayo instead of the real deal. **SERVES 6 TO 8**

VARIATION

For a simpler potato salad that is absolutely addictive, omit olives, pickles, and brine, and add 1 peeled, shredded celery root (celeriac). Lately, I make this just about every time I run into celery root at the market.

8 to 10 medium potatoes, scrubbed but not peeled
1 teaspoon salt, plus more to taste
1 cup Tofu Mayonnaise (page 906)
3 tablespoons prepared yellow mustard (you could use Dijon . . . but in keeping with the down-home sensibilities here, you might want to go for something unfancy like French's)
1 tablespoon celery seed
1 cup thinly grated kosher-style sour garlic dill pickles
1 cup finely sliced pimento-stuffed green olives
1 tablespoon brine from the green olive jar
1 teaspoon paprika
4 hard-cooked large eggs, peeled and chopped (optional)
Freshly ground black pepper to taste

1 Drop the potatoes, with 1 teaspoon salt, into a medium pot of rapidly boiling water. Cook until tender, 20 to 30 minutes.

2 As the potatoes cook, whisk together the Tofu Mayonnaise, mustard, and celery seed in a large mixing bowl. Stir in the grated dill pickles, the sliced green olives, brine, and paprika.

3 When the potatoes are done, turn them out into a colander (reserve potato-cooking water for use in stock, or baking bread), and place under cold running water until cool enough to handle. Peel and chop into salad-sized pieces. Stir the potatoes into the Tofu Mayo mixture, along with the hard-cooked eggs, if using, and season with salt and pepper to taste (you probably won't need much salt, as the potatoes cooked in salted water, plus there's salt in the mustard, pickles, olives, and brine).

Nouveau'Zarks Baby Potato Salad

How pleased I felt the first time I thought to boil potatoes for potato salad in stock! It's a good trick. In this recipe redo from cookbook number one, plain yogurt substitutes for heavy cream. However, for taste reasons and since you use so little of it, I recommend that the yogurt be full-fat . . . preferably Brown Cow brand from the natural foods store. But, naturally, you can go with fat free if you like. If you can get the little tiny marble-sized potatoes for this, so much the better. **SERVES 4 TO 6**

1¾ cups good vegetable stock, preferably Golden Stock or Oven-Roasted Vegetable Stock (pages 140–41) or one of the decent canned ones
1 teaspoon Pickapeppa sauce
¼ teaspoon salt, plus more to taste
1½ pounds small new potatoes, preferably red-skinned and no bigger than a ping-pong ball, well scrubbed but not peeled
6 scallions, minced
⅓ cup plain yogurt, preferably full-fat
3 tablespoons grainy, country-style Dijon mustard
3 tablespoons good hearty red wine, such as a Beaujolais
1 tablespoon extra virgin olive oil
Plenty of freshly ground black pepper to taste

1. In a medium saucepan, preferably a nonstick one with a good tight-fitting lid, combine the stock, Pickapeppa, and ¼ teaspoon salt. Bring to a boil. Drop in the potatoes and cook, tightly covered, over medium heat until tender but not mushy, 15 to 20 minutes (if you have very tiny potatoes, the cooking time might be even briefer). The stock will not cover the potatoes completely, which is why you need the tight lid; the trapped steam will also serve as a cooking medium.

2. When the potatoes are done, lift them from their bath of stock, reserving both the stock and the potatoes. As soon as the potatoes are cool enough to handle, halve them (if they are tiny) or quarter or slice them thickly (if they are larger), and transfer to a medium nonreactive bowl. Add the scallions, yogurt, mustard, wine, oil, and 1 tablespoon of the reserved cooking liquid (save the rest for your stock pot). Season to taste with salt and plenty of pepper and marinate, refrigerated, for several hours or overnight.

VARIATIONS

A truly great Variation is GREEK POTATO SALAD: Add, to the above recipe, 1 to 2 pressed cloves garlic, 2 to 3 ounces coarsely crumbled feta cheese, 8 to 10 black pitted and halved kalamata olives, and 2 red peppers, charred, peeled, seeded, and cut into long strips. You may also add a few tablespoons minced fresh parsley and basil or oregano.

Simpler, but also very pleasing, is PESTO POTATO SALAD: Add 1 or 2 tablespoons prepared pesto to the salad.

Southwestern-Style Three-Potato Salad

Potato salad reinvented, this is hot, just a tiny bit sweet, robust, and absolutely addictive—even to people who say, at first bite, "Oh, no, too hot for me." The heat plays off the creaminess of the tofu-based (and relatively low-fat) dressing oh

CINCO DE MAYO BUFFET

Pitchers of lemonade

*

Tub of iced Dos Equis, alcohol-free beers, and ginger beers

*

Chips (baked or fried) with Pamela Jones's Absolutely Incredible Roasted Vegetable Salsa
(PAGE 915)

*

Southwestern-Style Three-Potato Salad

*

Chilaquiles Windflower
(PAGE 376)

*

Warmed whole wheat tortillas

*

Calabacitas
(PAGE 801)

*

Portobello and Shiitake Mushroom Fajitas
(PAGE 346)

*

Bittersweet Chocolate Torte Ibarra
(PAGE 1004)

so nicely. You may never go back to mayonnaise-y potato salads again. One of my beloved Eureka recipe testers, artist and pal Mary Springer, so enjoyed this at a tasting that she brought it to a church potluck. It enjoyed talk-of-the-town status for some time after that. **SERVES 6 TO 8**

1 large sweet potato
2 pounds small red-skinned or yellow-skinned potatoes, or Yukon Golds
1 pound small purple potatoes
1 tablespoon cumin seeds
1 Serrano chile, stem removed, seeds and fiber also removed if you want it less hot, finely diced
1 poblano chile, charred, peeled, seeds removed, diced
¼ to ½ red onion, finely diced (to equal about ⅓ cup)

CHIPOTLE-TOFU MAYO
1 box (10½ ounces) silken tofu
1 to 2 cloves garlic, peeled and quartered
2 tablespoons extra virgin olive oil
2 tablespoons fresh-squeezed lime juice
1 tablespoon adobo sauce from canned chipotle peppers in adobo
1 teaspoon salt
Freshly ground black pepper

Handful of cherry tomatoes, halved
3 tablespoons finely minced parsley
3 tablespoons finely minced cilantro

1 Preheat the oven to 375°F.

2 Prick the sweet potato with a fork, place on a sheet of foil, and wrap it up tightly. Bake until tender, about 1 hour. Let cool and peel.

3 In separate pots of boiling salted water, cook the whole red-skinned (or yellow-skinned) potatoes or Yukon Golds, as well as the purple potatoes. Cook until tender but not mushy, about 15 minutes. Drain well, but do not peel; keep warm until ready to put into the mayo mixture.

4 In a small, dry skillet, toast the cumin seeds over medium heat, stirring almost constantly, until the seeds darken slightly and become fragrant, about 3 minutes. Turn the seeds out into a large bowl and add the Serrano, poblano, and onion.

5 Combine the tofu, garlic, oil, lime juice, adobo sauce, and salt in a food processor. Buzz until smooth, pausing to scrape down the bowl. Stir the mixture into the cumin seeds and peppers. While the potatoes are still warm, slice them, skin on, and add them directly into the mayo mixture. Grind plenty of fresh pepper over the salad and toss well to combine. Add the sweet potato and tomatoes and very gently toss again. Taste for seasonings. Sprinkle with the parsley and cilantro and serve. You can also refrigerate and serve several hours later. (If you do refrigerate and you feel that too much of the dressing has been absorbed, at serving time drizzle another tablespoon or so of olive oil over the salad and toss.)

Jelled Salads

One of my early cooking mentors, a then-hippie named Michael Starbow who had once catered professionally, gave me two pieces of advice when cooking for large groups of people: "People always love anything with melted cheese over it and they love Jell-O salad. No matter what they claim individually, put 'em in a group and put out a jello salad or anything with cheese melted over it—those will be the first dishes to go." Even then I found it idiosyncratic, but I listened, and, having cooked for many a potluck dinner, and worked what was called "the line" (meaning the buffet line) of a large Southern resort hotel, I guaran-damn-tee you, Michael was right.

But not for vegetarians—or so I thought—since gelatin is made from calves' hooves. Then I learned about agar, and still later, Hain, one of the larger natural food manufacturers, came up with packaged SuperFruits Naturally Flavored Dessert Mixes, a vegetarian, natural foods equivalent of gelatin; it sets up not with agar but another jelling agent called carageen and is sweetened with dehydrated cane juice instead of white sugar (though it's still, like mainstream gelatins, a little sweet for my taste). All the flavorings and colorings are natural.

Agar and carageen are both seaweeds, virtually flavorless, used, like gelatin is, to transform edible liquids to solids. I've only seen carageen in the Hain's mix (it's also added to countless other foodstuffs as a stabilizer); agar is the only readily available vegetarian equivalent of unflavored gelatin. Called "kantan" in China and Japan, it can be used in every way unflavored gelatin is. Or so I heard—because virtually every natural foods and vegetarian cookbook I read would say virtually the same durn thing: "Agar can substitute for gelatin. It comes in three forms: bars (which must be torn into small pieces first), flakes, or powders. Use less powder than you would flakes or bars. Just play with it in your kitchen until you get the proportions right." This vagueness became the source of much "agar-vation," especially as the agar in the flakes and torn-up bars gave inconsistent results, usually lumps of jellied substance floating in unjellied liquid. I was ready to throw in the towel.

But when my beloved Wenonah Fay Holl sent me a recipe for tomato aspic, I knew I had to give it another shot. If a recipe is from Wenonah Fay, it is no ordinary aspic. I got determined all over again to figure out the agar method and formula. And I finally nailed it . . . with the help of a packet of agar *powder*—not flakes, not bars—bought in San Francisco, which gave directions for use in English, Chinese, and what looks to be Cambodian or Vietnamese. I have since found the powder more easily, but never with as simple, clear directions. (Wenonah Fay's aspic was worth all this. It's just delicious. See page 129.)

The trick to making agar work is, as you might have guessed, not to mess around with bars or flakes but to use this powder. It's far easier to measure than the lighter-than-air flakes, it dissolves like a dream, and you can use some basic proportions and one method to achieve predictable results. Hallelujah!

To my surprise, an agar molded salad turned out to be better by far than a gelatin-molded one. Although agar sets up firmly, and cuts with a nice edge, it has in the mouth a more yielding texture; definitely jelled, but without that obnoxious rubberiness. It also has a structural component that is just great: It can be reboiled, to become liquid and then solid a second time, even a third time. This is really handy if you want to embark on a layered creation of one sort or another.

Here are the basic agar proportions and method, plus some tips for molding and unmolding salads.

Basic Proportions: 1 tablespoon agar powder to 3 cups liquid. If you are adding watery ingredients or want a slightly firmer set, cut the liquid back slightly (my recipes will indicate how much).

Basic Method: Combine agar and cold liquid, whisking well. Pour into a saucepan, preferably a nonreactive one. Bring to a full boil over medium heat, stirring constantly. Remove from the heat and slowly pour into a lightly oiled pan or mold or one that has been sprayed with cooking spray. Like gelatin, it will thicken as it cools. Allow at least 3 hours for the agar to set firmly, more if the mold is a large one.

The Spell of Jell

Jelled salads may seem fussy at first, but once you get the hang of them, you might also get cravings. There are just a few tips of the trade to know before you get started:

Be wary of pineapple: *Just as with conventional gelatin, you cannot use raw pineapple, which contains an enzyme that will eat the gel, causing it to stay liquid. If you want to use fresh pineapple, dice it and cook it first (you might as well used canned, since you're losing the fresh appeal by cooking it). Another anti-agar agent in jelled salads, according to Meredith McCarthy, a well-known vegan cook, in her book* Fresh from a Vegetarian Kitchen, *is umeboshi plum vinegar.*

Wet hands help out in unmolding: *When it comes time to unmold your salad, wet your hands lightly; it will make the mold slip more easily when your hands come in contact with it. Too, if you're unmolding directly onto a plate (without a bed of lettuce underneath), make sure the plate is a little wet. That way if the mold doesn't come out dead center on the plate, you can move it around till it's positioned just right. (This is a tip for the compulsive. I myself think that anyone who would notice an unmolded salad isn't dead-center and would, even inwardly, carp about this, doesn't deserve to be your friend. Besides, what are garnishes for?)*

Oil the mold: *Always remember, oil your mold or spray it with cooking spray. (And count your blessings, back in the not-so-fabulous '50s they used to oil 'em with mayonnaise.)*

Proportions for large molds: *Because the larger the mold, the more delicate it is structurally, you will probably want to use a slightly larger proportion of agar to liquid whenever you do a mold larger than 1 quart: Instead of 1 tablespoon agar to 3 cups liquid, try 1 tablespoon agar to 2¾ cups liquid.*

Some fruits sink and some float: *Sinkers are canned apricots, peaches, pears, or cherries; whole strawberries; fresh orange sections; and most grapes. Floaters are fresh apple, peach, pear, or banana pieces; raspberries; some small grapes; sliced strawberries; and blueberries. To make a pattern, pour some of the agar'd liquid into the mold and let it start to congeal or even half set, lay in the fruit, vegetables, or what have you in the pattern, and then pour some more of the starting-to-thicken liquid over the pattern. Repeat in layers if desired.*

Wenonah Fay Holl's "Aspics of Love" Salad

There is something so "ladies who lunch" about tomato aspic, isn't there? But that doesn't detract from the charm of this cool, jelled tomato salad of Wenonah Fay's (for more about her and her delicious peanut soup see page 146). It's lemony, and has such a refreshing balance between tart, tangy, and sweet that it is quite irresistible. Wenonah Fay's original called for lemon Jell-O, for which I've substituted fresh lemon juice and rind, sugar, and agar. The simplest of dressings—yogurt and good salty feta, with a bit of pepper—sets it off to a T. But if you avoid dairy products, try Tofu Sour Cream (page 909) or one of the dips on pages 26–27 as a dressing. **SERVES 4 TO 6**

Cooking spray
3 lemons
30 ounces (2 cans) stewed tomatoes, very well drained, both juice and pulp reserved
Water, preferably spring or filtered
¾ cup sugar
2 tablespoons agar powder (not flakes or bars)
Salad greens such as flat-leaf spinach
Simple Yogurt-Feta Dressing (recipe follows)

1 Lightly spray 1 large or 8 small molds with cooking spray. Set aside.

2 Grate the rind of the lemons. Set rind aside; cut lemons in half and juice them, removing and discarding the seeds. Combine the lemon juice and the juice drained from the stewed tomatoes in a glass measuring cup. Add enough water to make 5½ cups liquid total. Transfer to a nonreactive bowl.

3 Whisk the sugar and agar into the liquid. Let stand for 3 minutes to dissolve the agar. Transfer the mixture to a nonreactive pot and bring to a full boil over high heat, whisking like the dickens. Immediately turn the heat down to a simmer and cook, at a bare simmer, for 2 minutes. Stir in the drained stewed tomatoes and the reserved

lemon rind and immediately turn the mixture out into the prepared mold(s). Refrigerate until firmly set, about 3 hours.

4 Arrange the salad greens among 4 plates and unmold 1 aspic onto each plate. Alternatively, arrange the greens on a platter and unmold the larger aspic onto it. Pass the dressing at the table.

Simple Yogurt-Feta Dressing

1 cup plain yogurt (if desired, for a creamier texture, use 1½ cups yogurt and drain it, as for Yogurt Sour Cream, page 910, for 2 hours)

2 ounces feta cheese, finely crumbled

⅛ teaspoon salt (optional)

Freshly ground black pepper to taste—a lot

Combine the yogurt, feta, salt, and pepper in a small serving bowl. Serve at once, or cover and refrigerate until serving time.

Carrot-Orange Crown Salad

At a slumber party when I was maybe nine, somebody's mother made a salad of grated carrot in a little fresh orange juice. I loved it so much that I promptly went on a two-week-or-so, day-in day-out grated-carrot-in-fresh-orange-juice jag. I thought of the flavors again recently when I wanted to create something bright and jelled. So here they are, recaptured. The result is refreshing, cheerful, and vivid—and you can make it even more vivid by substituting blood oranges for the regular oranges. If you want the crown effect, set it up in a fancy ring mold or bundt pan sprayed with cooking spray. Like all jelled salads, it is, to me, a little '50s, but nonetheless, as one dinner guest remarked, "I could eat a lot of this." **SERVES 4 TO 6**

2 lemons
4 oranges
About 3 cups carrot juice
1 tablespoon agar powder (not flakes or bars)
3 tablespoons honey or sugar
3 carrots, grated
Orange twists, carrot curls, and fresh mint (optional)

1 Lightly spray a mold with cooking spray. Set aside.

2 Grate the rind of 1 lemon, and the rind of half of 1 orange. Set aside. Juice both lemons as well as the orange whose rind you just grated. Pour the juices into a 1-quart measuring cup, and add sufficient carrot juice to equal 3 cups plus 2 tablespoons liquid. Whisk in the agar powder and let stand for 5 minutes.

3 Peel, section, and dice the 3 remaining oranges in pieces small enough to hit with a fork, but large enough to be distinct. Set aside.

4 Combine the agar-juice mixture with the honey or sugar in a medium saucepan over medium heat. Bring to a boil, stirring constantly, and boil for a few seconds. Remove from the heat and let cool until the mixture starts to thicken, 15 to 20 minutes, then stir in the reserved rinds, orange sections, and grated carrots. Immediately turn out into the prepared mold. Refrigerate, covered, until set, 1 to 2 hours. Serve, garnished, if desired, with an orange twist, a curl of carrot, and a sprig of fresh mint.

Sticky Situations

There is little I hate worse than food sticking onto the bottom of a pot, giving the whole dish a slightly burnt flavor—unless it is food cooked with an excessive amount of oil, which I dislike just about as intensely. Unfortunately, the latter is commonly used to prevent the former. But there is a way around this conundrum.

Here is the short-form on why, over and over and over in this book, I suggest you treat dutch ovens, skillets, and sauté pans, et al., with cooking spray as a preliminary part of almost every recipe.

What is cooking spray? Essentially, oil that is in a form of dispenser other than a conventional bottle, so that it may be pumped or sprayed, rather than poured. Thus, the thinnest sheen of the oil can coat the cooking vessel (or occasionally, a food itself), rather than a small lake's worth being required.

There are plastic pump bottles which you, yourself, may fill with the oil of your choice. I, myself, prefer the less environmentally sound but more effective already-filled aerosol cans of olive or canola oil, for I feel you get a lighter, more even, quick coat of spray with them than with the pumps. But I am careful about what I use in a spray. Spectrum brand canola or olive oil sprays are excellent; plain (original) Pam is good (it's canola oil plus lecithin, which is a component of soybeans). Avoid like the plague anything "butter flavored"—it can taint a whole dish with its fakeness. This includes Butter-flavored Pam and other supermarket equivalents, as well as a spray called Vegelene.

After spraying, it's optional to add a soupçon of additional oil or butter for flavor (genuine, real-food flavor), if desired. I usually do this, as you'll see in the recipes that follow—but this bit of oil is not needed functionally to prevent sticking.

Jelled Fruit Salads à la Hain

As mentioned in the introduction to this section, Hain now makes an all-natural vegetarian gelatin, which I believe is widely available. It comes in four flavors: strawberry, orange, raspberry, and cherry. The texture is that of a slightly less bouncy Jell-O; the convenience factor is great, and, assuming you add some fresh fruit and/or Tofu Crème to it to jazz it up, it's good—at least for the times when you get those retro-hankerings, or want something quick and easy. Kids love gelatin (and so do many adults, though most won't admit it. Like their '50s predecessors, it's a toss-up as to whether these are salads or desserts. I hate to admit it, but I have sometimes polished off leftovers of these for breakfast.

Wait a minute, I can hear you saying, "Tofu Crème? How did that get in there?" Well, remember that those Fab '50s salads often had a layer of a cream cheese concoction in the middle, or a layer of whipped cream folded into the Jell-O mix, or were frosted in a sweetened mayonnaise-y dressing, or served with a straight pour of heavy cream. If you go for these sorts of salads, most likely you'll agree that the creaminess was a nice counterpoint in texture, color, and taste to the jelled part. Okay: Tofu Crème is the healthier, up-to-date version of that layer—and guess what: No kidding, it is really good. As in jelled salads of yore, you can fold it in as a layer, or serve it alongside.

Tofu Crème

The lowfat, vegan, delicious, and quick answer to Cool Whip. Less fluffy, creamier, and very, very tasty atop a jelled salad. **MAKES ENOUGH FOR 5 SERVINGS (1 BATCH) OF JELLED FRUIT SALAD**

1 box (12.3 ounces) reduced-fat silken tofu (firm or extra firm)
1 to 3 tablespoons brown sugar, honey, Rapidura, or maple syrup, or your chosen sweetener (see page 959)
1 tablespoon raw (not roasted) cashew butter
1 teaspoon pure vanilla extract (or ½ teaspoon vanilla and a drop of almond extract)

Combine all of the ingredients in a food processor and buzz until very, very smooth, stopping a few times to scrape down the bowl. If using as a topping, transfer crème to a small container and refrigerate. If using it as a layer, leave it in the food processor and use as directed in the recipes that follow or as you need it.

Strawberry, Raspberry, or Cherry Jelled Fruit with a Tofu Crème Layer

I just love these, layered in glass parfait glasses. They could be salad or dessert. They are definitely retro and a little low-brow but never have I fed them to anyone who didn't love them. **SERVES 5**

- **1½ cups boiling water, preferably spring or filtered**
- **1 box (3 ounces) Hain SuperFruit Naturally Flavored Dessert Mix (strawberry, raspberry, or cherry)**
- **1 recipe Tofu Crème (opposite page), still in food processor**
- **1½ cups frozen, no-sugar-added strawberries, raspberries, or black cherries**
- **Additional fresh fruit and mint sprigs (optional)**

1 Have ready five 1-cup serving dishes, preferably glass, so you can see the colors and layers of the finished dessert. (Or, use custard cups, lightly coated with cooking spray, and reverse the salad out onto a plate at serving time.)

2 Measure the boiling water into a 4-cup Pyrex glass measuring cup. Add the Hain's and whisk like crazy, until the mix has dissolved (it will be clumpier initially than regular gelatin, but it will dissolve; just keep whisking).

3 Scoop out ¼ to ⅓ cup of the dissolved Hain's. Buzz it into the Tofu Crème.

4 Stir the still-frozen fruit into the dissolved Hain's. Almost immediately, it will start to set up. Spoon about half of the mixture into the prepared cups, then spoon the Tofu Crème over that, and top with the remaining Hain's mixture. Cover, refrigerate until cold (at least 1½ hours), and serve—in the cup, reversed out, and garnished or not as you prefer.

VARIATION

In the summertime, fresh or frozen peach slices, tossed with a little lemon juice, and a few pitted fresh cherries are nice in the cherry Hain's. Use a drop of almond extract in the Tofu Crème with this.

Triple-Citrus Jelled Salad

Nice in winter, when citrus is often the only really good fruit available at the market. The colors are as sunshiny as the tart-sweet flavors. This works very well for brunch. **SERVES 5**

1 ruby-red grapefruit
1 large navel orange
2 lemons
Boiling water, preferably spring or filtered
1 box (3 ounces) Hain SuperFruit Naturally Orange Flavored Dessert Mix
Tofu Crème (page 132; optional)
Additional fresh sliced orange (optional)

1 Have ready five 1-cup serving dishes, preferably glass, so you can see the colors and layers of the finished dessert. (Or, use custard cups, lightly coated with cooking spray, and reverse the salad out onto a plate at serving time.)

2 Peel and section the grapefruit, removing as much of the white pith and tough membrane as possible. Work over a strainer set in a bowl, so you can catch any juice and trap the seeds. Discard the white stuff and separately reserve caught juice and grapefruit sections. Do the same to the orange.

3 Pour the grapefruit and orange juices into a 4-cup Pyrex glass measuring cup.

4 Grate the lemon rind, and stir it into the Tofu Crème, if using. Refrigerate the crème. Juice the lemons through a sieve, discarding seeds, right into the Pyrex cup and add boiling water to the juices to equal 1½ cups total. Add the Hain's and whisk like crazy, until the mix has dissolved (it will be clumpier initially than regular gelatin, but it will dissolve: just keep whisking).

5 Let cool slightly, then stir in the orange and grapefruit pieces. Divide the mixture among the prepared cups and chill for at least 1 hour. Serve with the lemon-zested Tofu Crème on the side, if using.

Soups for Spirit & Sustenance

The last cookbook I wrote was about soup. Two-hundred-plus different varieties of soup later—soup stocks, soup lore, soup legend; bean soup, American soup, Indian soup, Chinese, French, Italian soup—years of my life, sometimes three meals a day devoted to soup—and I can say honestly, I still love soup. That I still make it for lunch almost daily, still come up with new soups, still admire its infinite, economical adaptability. To congenially take in whatever's on hand yet still turn out delicious and full of sustaining comfort—what other course but soup so truly claims this talent?

For vegetarians, or those who find themselves incorporating more meatless dishes into their diets, there are further reasons for soup loving. Soups have a special affinity for ingredients at the heart and soul of vegetarian cooking: beans, vegetables, whole grains. Think minestrone, think heady mushroom-and-barley, thick split pea, spicy lentil. Potages like these are as satisfying as they are healthful, and when a person cuts back on or cuts out meat, they are often among the first happy main-course discoveries. This chapter offers some recent personal favorites and other perennial standards, ranging from starters to entrees, simple to fairly highfalutin', but all certain to please.

Think minestrone, think heady mushroom and barley, thick split pea, spicy lentil.

New Stock Options

I write in *Dairy Hollow House Soup & Bread,* "stock is that flavorful liquid in which meat, fowl, or vegetables have been cooked, and to which they have given their essence." It's still true. We are concerned here only with vegetable-based stocks, but the "essence" part remains fundamental, as does the importance of these intensely flavorful liquids. Stock's long and helpful reach extends far beyond the soup pot, though, especially for vegetarians. Good stock is vital to stews, casseroles, sauces, and gravies. It is good stock that most often rings flavorful changes on those old workhorses of meatless cuisine, beans and grains, commonly cooked in plain water. It is good stock that underpins the glossy, piquant, sweet or hot sauces that transform tofu, tempeh, and seitan from plain basics to genuinely satisfying dishes that speak cogently of abundance, not deprivation or blandness for the sake of health.

What follows are my newest versions of the tried-and-true favorite stock recipes. All these stocks are quite full-bodied and concentrated in flavor; you can use them as-is for sauces, but for some soups you may prefer to dilute them slightly. If you are pressed for time, you'll discover that you still have good stock options (see the note on page 141); the new aseptically packaged broths in a box, introduced in the late '90s, offer a quick and easy alternative that is 90 percent as good as homemade to the cook.

But whether you buy it or make it, it's important to take a little time to understand what stock is, the part water plays in it, how it's used, and why good stock is essential in the vegetarian kitchen. Then we'll move on to general information about stock and stock-making.

Liquid Assets for Vegetarians

When preparing most of the stocks that follow, drop ingredients into *cold* salted water, bring to a boil, then turn down the heat and simmer the heck out of them. This method creates flavorful stock because the initially cold water and salt draw out the vegetables' flavor and color. All that is left of the vegetables by the end of cooking time is tasteless fiber, ready only for the compost bin: The flavor is all in the stock—what I call *primary* stock. Primary stock is the make-or-break ingredient not only in soups but in stews, sauces, bean dishes, risotti, and many casserole-type entrees.

The smart cook will, however, also end up with occasional jars of what I call *secondary* stock—in most cases, very mild-flavored vegetable cooking water. Blanching, a technique opposite to the one described above, locks color and flavor into the vegetable, as opposed to surrendering it to the liquid. A vegetable is blanched by dropping it into rapidly boiling unsalted water, allowing it to cook briefly, speedily draining, and rinsing with very cold water. The drained water from the blanching or cooking—secondary stock—can often be reused. It makes a nice base for a primary stock; just use it instead of plain water. Or cook dried beans in it and nudge the bean flavor up a notch. Potato cooking water, which is slightly thickened from the cooked-out potato starch, is wonderful used in breads instead of plain water (yeast dotes on potato water) and works nicely in some soups. So does carrot blanching water, or green bean blanching water, or sweet potato cooking water. Note that blanching water from the cabbage family (broccoli, cauliflower, Brussels sprouts, turnips) is the exception to the rule. These vegetables leave behind the characteristic "overcooked cabbage" smell.

The Water Principle

Your vegetable stock may be from an assortment of raw or roasted vegetables, from the stems of shiitake mushrooms, or from miso, a fermented Japanese bean paste (see page 173). But the main ingredient for each is the same, and it's one that is, or ought to be, tasteless. It's water.

Not very long ago, you skirted wacko ness in public opinion if you distrusted the safety of the water coming out of your tap or disliked its taste. That has changed. Groundwater, and in some cases the underlying water tables, are widely polluted with bacteria like E. coli *as well as heavy metals like barium and arsenic, and runoff from fertilizers and pesticides. To supply cities with safe drinking water, virtually all American communities treat water with a mélange of chemicals, including chlorine and chloramine. Then there's the problem of the pipes themselves: in older cities they are often made of lead, which leaches into the water. All of these factors, in my mind, add up to water of questionable safety and definitely inferior taste.*

I used to suggest spring or bottled water for cooking and drinking; but this isn't really practical or economical for anything except maybe drinking water, and bottled water is sometimes a scam—just regular municipal tap water in a sharp bottle. (Read labels; see if the company cites a particular spring and notes "bottled at the source.") Besides, even if your bottled water is pure, anything that requires more than a cup or two, such as cooking pasta, makes bottled water out of the question. These days I suggest (and use) a water filter. Purchase the best you can afford; see what it's guaranteed to filter out, and how often you should change the filter. The over-the-sink models are easily installed; some even come with a green light to indicate water purity, which changes to yellow when it's time to replace the filter (about once a year).

Adding Oomph, or Flavor Boosters

If a stock you've made tastes insipid or bland, or if you have some leftover vegetable cooking water on hand with but a ghost of flavor and you want to amp it up, here are a few last-minute tricks to turn dull to delectable. These are the sort of rabbit-from-hat tricks good cooks know and use almost unconsciously, leaving just-starting-out cooks to wonder what went wrong.

The first step is always tasting. Take a spoonful, put it into your mouth, roll it around on your tongue. Think with your brain, mouth, and memory. What does it need? Heat, body, saltiness? Would a touch of sweet or sour do it, would something aromatic help? With each addition, pause and taste. Start conservatively, especially with salty additions. Try adding:

- ▲ A vegetable bouillon cube or a teaspoon of vegetable broth powder or a bit of Marmite (smoked nutritional yeast concentrate; sounds horrid, but sometimes does the trick)
- ▲ 1 teaspoon to 1 tablespoon tomato paste or sun-dried tomato paste
- ▲ 1 tablespoon or more good brandy, cognac, sherry, or marsala
- ▲ 1 teaspoon to 1 tablespoon honey, brown sugar, Rapidura, or rice syrup (see page 959), barley-malt syrup (see page 960), or thawed frozen apple juice concentrate
- ▲ 1 teaspoon to 1 tablespoon miso
- ▲ 1 large piece of kombu seaweed: drop it into the finished stock, let it sit for 10 to 20 minutes, then remove
- ▲ 1 teaspoon to 1 tablespoon Pickapeppa sauce
- ▲ ¼ to 1 teaspoon dark molasses
- ▲ 1 teaspoon to 1 tablespoon Garlic Oil (page 898) or Roasted Garlic puree (see page 899)
- ▲ 1 teaspoon to 1 tablespoon pesto, either commercially made or homemade (see page 918)
- ▲ A little tamari or shoyu soy sauce
- ▲ 1 tablespoon to ¼ cup nutritional yeast (see page 239), whisked in (you'll think it won't blend, but it will; you'll think it won't taste good, but it does)
- ▲ Good ol' salt, preferably sea salt, and freshly ground black pepper
- ▲ Your favorite seasoning blend; or try Dragon Salt (page 900)
- ▲ A few drops of lemon juice or vinegar (go easy)
- ▲ ½ teaspoon to 2 teaspoons umeboshi plum paste (see page 118)
- ▲ Freshly grated nutmeg (often an addition to mushroom or onion soups, or anything creamy; works with brandy or sherry, too)
- ▲ A tiny fleck of cinnamon and/or ground cloves (good with chili or in spicy potages; can work miracles with tomato-based soups or sauces)
- ▲ Juice of 1 orange and maybe a bit of grated zest, too (magic with sweet potatoes, butternut squash)

As you play with these and get more comfortable, the secrets of kitchen alchemy begin to reveal themselves to you. Certain combinations bounce off ingredients better than others; you may need a couple to bring a particular stock or recipe up to snuff. Tomato paste, cognac, and honey—a bit of each—work wonders on many vegetable-based dishes, not just stocks and soups. Lemon juice and black pepper season any number of dishes to a turn. Bean soups and other bean dishes usually need more salt than other recipes, but sometimes a bit of lemon juice or vinegar moderates them perfectly.

The Great Ice Cube Tip

Short on freezer space but want good homemade stock on hand? Prepare any good vegetable stock, and after it has been strained, return it to the rinsed stockpot. Raise the heat, bringing it to a hard boil, and cook until it has evaporated to half its original volume. Cool to room temperature, then pour into an ice cube tray and freeze. When the cubes are frozen, pop them out of the tray and store them in a sturdy zippered freezer bag.

Each cube equals about ¼ cup concentrated stock. Use as is as a flavor booster or dilute with an equal part filtered or spring water, wine, or vegetable cooking water.

Cubism also works for coconut milk. Coconut milk, even the canned, no-sugar-added reduced-fat variety, is quite extraordinarily high in saturated fat. It is also (a) a vegetarian product, (b) irreplaceable in certain recipes, (c) quick to spoil, even in the refrigerator, and (d) pricey. However, many of the dishes in which coconut milk is irreplaceable work well with just a little *coconut milk (as chefs know, a tiny bit of cream or butter makes all the difference in the world). So, next time something you're making calls for just a bit of coconut milk, open the can, pour out what you need, pour the remainder into ice cube trays, freeze the cubes, pop them out, and bag them.*

Basic Found Vegetable Stock

Make a careful stock from scratch or use Imagine Foods, Kitchen Basics, or Pacific Foods Vegetable or Mushroom Broths (page 141) when you need a stock with an absolutely predictable flavor. Most of the time you can be loosey-goosey and make this simple stock from vegetable odds and ends, feeling a certain self-congratulatory pleasure at your thriftiness and environmental-soundness. This stock's character changes, depending on what scraps dominate, but it's almost always good if you follow the basic guidelines. Despite its malleability, a found vegetable stock is rarely incompatible with a dish. If it is too mild at the end, jazz it up with a little tamari or shoyu soy sauce or a spoonful of whisked-in miso.

Start accumulating ingredients over a few days to one week in a sturdy plastic bag in the fridge. **QUANTITY VARIABLE**

About 8 to 10 cups assorted vegetable trimmings (carrot, onion, string bean, peas, celery, bell pepper, squash, tomato, mushroom, leek; anything but trimmings of cruciferous vegetables).
1 whole head of garlic, papery skin on, cut in half across the middle (to expose each garlic clove)
1 onion, quartered, unpeeled
Water, to cover, preferably spring or filtered
About 1 to 1½ teaspoons salt per quart water

1 Bring all the ingredients to a boil in a large stockpot, preferably enameled or stainless steel. Turn the heat down to low, and let simmer gently, uncovered, for 1 hour or so.

2 Cool to lukewarm, then strain. Use immediately or store in the fridge or freezer.

Golden Stock

1 large onion, unpeeled, quartered
1 large carrot, quartered
1 large sweet potato, quartered
1 large white potato, quartered
1 whole head garlic, papery skin on, cut in half across the middle
3 ribs celery with leaves, each cut in half
6 cups water, preferably spring or filtered
1 to 2 teaspoons salt
Small pinches of dried oregano, basil, sage, and rosemary, to taste (optional)
½ cup nutritional yeast (see page 239)
1 tablespoon light (white or golden) miso

1 In a soup pot, combine all the ingredients except the nutritional yeast and the miso. Bring to a boil, then turn down the heat to medium-low and let simmer until all the vegetables are quite soft, about 1 hour. Let cool, then strain, discarding the solids.

2 Whisk the nutritional yeast and miso into the lukewarm stock. Taste for seasoning; you may need a touch more miso. Use immediately, or cool to room temperature, then refrigerate or freeze.

MAKES ABOUT 5 CUPS

Dark Stock

2 large onions, unpeeled, quartered
1 large carrot, quartered
2 large white potatoes, quartered
1 whole head garlic, papery skin on, cut in half across the middle
3 ribs celery with leaves, each cut in half
6 cups water, preferably spring or filtered
1 tablespoon tamari or shoyu soy sauce
Small pinches of dried oregano, basil, sage, and rosemary, to taste (optional)
¼ cup nutritional yeast (see page 239)
1 tablespoon dark miso

1 In a soup pot, combine all the ingredients except the nutritional yeast and the miso. Bring to a boil, then turn down the heat to medium-low and let simmer gently, uncovered, until all the vegetables are quite soft, about 1 hour. Let cool, then strain, discarding the solids.

2 Whisk the nutritional yeast and miso into the lukewarm stock. Taste for seasoning; you may need a touch more miso. Use immediately, or cool to room temperature, then refrigerate or freeze.

MAKES ABOUT 5 CUPS

Hearty Stock

2 large onions, unpeeled, quartered
1 large carrot, quartered
2 large white potatoes, quartered
1 whole head garlic, papery skin on, cut in half across the middle
3 ribs celery with leaves, each cut in half
¾ cup lentils
6 cups water, preferably spring or filtered
1 to 2 tablespoons tamari or shoyu soy sauce
Small pinches of dried oregano, basil, sage, and rosemary, to taste (optional)
¼ cup nutritional yeast (see page 239)
1 to 2 tablespoons dark miso
2 tablespoons butter or mild vegetable oil

1 In a soup pot, combine all the ingredients except the nutritional yeast, the miso, and the butter or oil. Bring to a boil, then turn down the heat to medium-low and let simmer, uncovered, until all the vegetables and lentils are quite soft, about 1 hour. Let cool, then strain, discarding the solids.

2 Whisk the nutritional yeast and 1 tablespoon of the miso into the lukewarm stock. Taste for seasoning; you may need more miso. Use immediately, or cool to room temperature, then refrigerate or freeze.

MAKES ABOUT 5 CUPS

Oven-Roasted Vegetable Stock

Cooking spray
3 onions, unpeeled, quartered
3 large carrots, halved
8 ribs celery with leaves, each cut in half
2 whole heads garlic, papery skin on, cut in half across the middle (to expose each garlic clove)
3 tablespoons mild vegetable oil
¼ cup tamari or shoyu soy sauce
6 cups room temperature water, preferably spring or filtered
2 bay leaves
2 sprigs fresh parsley
Salt to taste
1 teaspoon whole peppercorns

1 Preheat the oven to 350°F. Spray an 11-by-13-inch baking pan with cooking spray.

2 Place the onions, carrots, celery, and garlic in the pan. Drizzle with the oil and pour over the soy sauce, tossing the vegetables to coat. Bake until the vegetables are deeply browned, almost burnt-looking, about 1 hour.

3 Transfer the vegetables to a large heavy soup pot. Add 4 cups of the water and the remaining ingredients.

4 Pour the remaining 2 cups water into the baking pan and, using the blade of a spatula, scrape up all those wonderful, browned, carmelized bits on the botton. Add this to the soup pot.

5 Bring the water to a boil, then turn down the heat and simmer, partially covered, 30 minutes. Cool slightly and strain, discarding the solids. Use immediately, or cool to room temperature, then refrigerate or freeze.

MAKES ABOUT 5 CUPS

NOTE

QUICK STOCK OPTIONS

I still make homemade stocks. They are always superior to anything that comes out of a can, cube, or packet, with two possible exceptions: the stocks from Imagine Foods, Kitchen Basics, and Pacific Foods.

The Natural Vegetable Broths and Mushroom Broths from these companies were almost as good as homemade and come in 32-ounce aseptically-packaged boxes. They will always have a place in my cupboard.

Eternal Soup

Beany, vegetable-y, thick and nourishing, this slow-cooking, delicious, simple soup takes virtually zero prep time. Why, then, is it eternal? Because this is for people who have no time. You put the stuff in and leave it, replenishing speedily the next day and the next. One caveat: You must have a slow-cooker or Crockpot. Were you and friends to eat the whole pot's worth, this recipe would serve four to six, but then you would be losing its eternal, add-on quality.

Eternal Soup began at Moonshine Cottage, my writing studio, where renovation had reached that stage where it also seemed eternal. I went two years without a full kitchen, I was stoveless, sinkless, hungry for lunch, tired of sandwiches. In this environment, necessity and crankiness gave rise to Eternal Soup. Occasionally I fed it to a carpenter or two, but mostly it was for my own solace and nourishment. Its simmering fragrance comforted me through working on a book under deadline from within a state of decor best described as Late London Blitz. As I stepped over boards and belt sanders, bypassed sheetrock and paint buckets, to get to my soup (tightly covered against the showers of sawdust), I managed to have faith that Moonshine Cottage, and my book, would both be done in my lifetime. And so they have been.

Soup & Bread readers will recognize Eternal Soup as a stripped-down ongoing version of The Soup, its character as ever-changing, its presence as constant. In winter months, it is rarely permitted to get all the way empty without being replenished. The instant beans called for are one of the great finds of the decade for time-pressed vegetarians or semivegetarians.

SERVES 4 TO 6

Eternal Variations

Something as simple as Eternal Soup is meant to be fooled with indefinitely. Beside the instant dried beans at the natural foods store, you will find dried instant lentil chili, pea soup, and so on. A 5½-ounce box of any of these can be used instead of the dried bean flakes or can be added to the pot as you go along. Despite being a make-it-from-scratch person, these instant preservative free legume-based dried soups are excellent products, beans and their kin dehydrate far more successfully than vegetables. Also, instead of or in addition to the bean flakes, add a can or two of any cooked beans, liquid included. Or use the dehydrated beans the first day—they create a rather lush base—and the second day, add a can of chickpeas.

And what of the vegetables? For the frozen mix, I often choose the variety called gumbo, which includes corn, red and green peppers, and okra, but Mediterranean mixtures, with red pepper, pole beans, and zucchini, are nice too. Frozen green beans are also good. Frozen spinach makes the soup a little muddy.

There is no law that states you cannot mix frozen and fresh vegetables if you want to give a little snap to Eternal Soup. One day I brought with me two stalks of celery, two organic carrots, and one lone leek, all already washed and chopped. I threw them all in with the previous day's leavings, adding, I think, tomato juice. This was about 9 A.M. *By noon the soup was wonderful. Eternal Soup welcomes, really, just about any fresh vegetable you care to add, though excessive turnip or cabbage-family members might dominate the flavor. Summer squashes break down quickly into nearly indistinguishable pieces, but are tasty. Raw potato is good but thickens the soup; still, adding one small potato (or sweet potato) to the pot might be the way to go. Butternut and similar hard orange squashes, once peeled, are excellent additions; besides being beta-carotene-rich they hold their shape awhile, then melt down pleasantly. I have also added leftover stir-fries; Eternal Soup prefers simple stir-fries of vegetables in garlic and olive oil or soy sauce.*

Neophyte cooks, I urge you to be bold with this. Leap in. The recipe might sound uncomfortably vague, but you can't go wrong here.

3 cups dehydrated black bean or pinto bean flakes (see page 594)
2 cups homemade vegetable stock or Imagine Natural Vegetable Broth
1 bag (16 ounces) frozen vegetables, either a mixture or a single vegetable, or 3 to 4 cups virtually any assortment of fresh, raw cut-up vegetables
½ to 1 cup "something tomatoey," could be tomato puree, good-quality bottled salsa (as hot or mild as desired), canned diced tomatoes with green chiles, spicy or regular tomato or mixed vegetable juice, or leftover spaghetti sauce
Boiling water, preferably spring or filtered, to cover
Salt and freshly ground black pepper to taste

ADDITIONS (OPTIONAL)
Parmesan cheese
Hot sauce
Chopped cilantro or parsley
Yogurt Sour Cream (page 910), or Tofu Sour Cream (page 909)

1 Plug in a slow cooker. Pour in the dehydrated bean flakes, stock, vegetables, and tomato product of choice. Turn the heat to high. Add boiling water (in my pre-stove days at Moonshine I used a plug-in tea kettle) as needed until the pot is nearly full. Stir well a few times. Cover.

2 Let simmer for 1 to 2 hours, or until you can smell its fragrance or until you start getting hungry. Turn the heat to low if you feel some ingredients might be getting overcooked.

3 When ready to eat, season with salt and pepper, ladle out the soup, and add whichever of the optional additions or whatever else appeals to you. Serve with toast, crackers, or a scoop of cooked pasta or grain in the bottom of each bowl.

4 After lunch is over, unplug the slow cooker. Let the soup cool to room temperature, then cover and place the entire pot in the fridge for tomorrow. Next day, add more liquid and/or more beans and vegetables—any of the first four ingredients listed above—stir, reheat slowly (allowing any fresh ingredients to cook through), and eat—with a canny sense of satisfaction.

Roasted Red Pepper Soup with a Cilantro-Jalapeño Swirl

On a scale of one to ten this recipe gets a ten. Smooth, voluptuous, creamy (yet without a drop of cream), this mildly sweet, faintly smoky vegan soup of sunset hue is elegant and intriguing. Its texture is from pureed white beans, its character from charred red bell peppers, and depths are added by miso. The recipe assumes you have the red peppers charred and peeled. If you don't, simply make charring them the first step, burning them on one or two burners while you begin the sauté on another.

The bright green Cilantro-Jalapeño Swirl is optional, but the color on the red soup makes it even more exciting, and adds a kick I love. You can cheat and use a few drops of Tabasco's Jalapeño Sauce. The bright green of a tropical parrot (thanks, alas, to added food color), it too will add kick, show-off style, and vividness. But believe me, no one will complain if you serve this plain or with a parsley sprig. **SERVES 4 TO 6**

1 teaspoon to 2 tablespoons olive oil
Cooking spray
1 large onion, chopped
2 bay leaves
4 cloves garlic, minced
4 cups cooked or canned navy beans, well drained
5 red peppers, charred, steamed, and peeled (see page 782)
4 cups vegetable stock, commercial or homemade (see pages 139–41)
1 teaspoon honey
Juice of 1 to 2 lemons
3 tablespoons white, golden, or mellow miso (see page 173)
Salt and freshly ground black pepper to taste
Cilantro-Jalapeño Swirl (recipe follows) or Tabasco's Jalapeño Sauce
Cilantro leaves (optional)
Sour cream, Yogurt Sour Cream (page 910), or Tofu Mayonaise (page 906) (optional)

1 Add the amount of oil you prefer to a nonstick skillet or one that has been sprayed with cooking spray.

Heat the skillet over medium heat and add the onion and bay leaves. Sauté them together for 4 minutes, or until the onion is starting to wilt. Lower the heat as low it will go and add the garlic. Cook for another 6 to 8 minutes, stirring often, or until the garlic is tender but not browned. Remove the bay leaves and scrape the sauté into a food processor.

2 Add the beans, red peppers, about ¾ cup of the stock, and the honey to the processor mixture. Buzz until very smooth. Meanwhile, heat the remaining vegetable stock on the stove in a medium saucepan. Add the processed mixture to the hot stock and heat together. Bring to a simmer, then turn the heat down very low.

3 Squeeze the juice of 1 of the lemons into the miso along with a few tablespoons of the hot soup. Stir to dissolve the miso, then stir this mixture into the pot of hot soup. Heat through. Taste and add salt and pepper. Add the juice of the second lemon if you feel it's needed (you might also want to add a touch more honey).

4 Serve hot, with 1 teaspoon of the Cilantro-Jalapeño Swirl stirred on top of it, or use one of the optional garnishes.

Cilantro-Jalapeño Swirl

1 cup loosely packed cilantro leaves
½ teaspoon salt
3 fresh jalapeño chiles, stems and some or all of the seeds and ribs removed
Juice of 1 lemon
2 to 3 tablespoons vegetable stock (see page 139)

HONEYSUCKLE SUPPER IN JULY

Pita Bread Toasts
(PAGE 30)
with Dilled Tofu-Spinach Dip
(PAGE 27)

*

Roasted Red Pepper Soup with a Cilantro-Jalapeño Swirl
(PREVIOUS PAGE)

*

Ronni's New Wave "Killed Lettuce Salad"
(PAGE 74)

*

Ned's Marsala-Marinated Portobello Grill
(PAGE 770)

*

Biscuits

*

Fresh corn done on the grill, Greek-Style Smothered Okra
(PAGE 775)

*

Blueberry Crisp
(PAGE 977)

Combine all of the ingredients in a food processor or blender and buzz, scraping down the sides of the bowl a couple of times, until fairly smooth. Drizzle 1 teaspoon of the finished mixture on top of each cup of soup and stir lightly.

COOK ONCE FOR 2 MEALS Do you have just a bit of this wonderful soup left? Make a Roasted Red Pepper Salad Dressing: Measure the amount you have left into a jar with a tight-fitting lid. Add twice as much olive oil and an equal amount of freshly squeezed lemon juice and shake the jar like the dickens. Taste and add a bit of honey or sugar, if you like, and a little salt and freshly ground pepper. Add a little more leftover soup to this mix—1 cup, to be precise—and make the best possible sauce for Pumpkin and Bean Lasagna with Caramelized Garlic (page 367). In fact, why not just double the recipe?

Wenonah Fay's Chilled No-Middle-Ground Peanut Soup

A weaver and fabric artist now in her eighties, Wenonah Fay Holl is compact, tiny as a twig, with beautiful posture and bright, clear hazel eyes that almost give off a crackle. We know her and knew her late husband, Gordon, because they were close friends of Louis and Elsie Freund, whom readers of previous Dairy Hollow cookbooks may remember. We consider knowing Gordon and Wenonah Fay one of the countless gifts Louis and Elsie bestowed on us. When she sent me the recipe Wenonah Fay noted, "I am a peanut butter freak, so this is a summertime constant. Now, Crescent, it has a different taste, and only special people like it. And it seems to be one of those things about which there is no middle ground. You either like it or you don't."

I'm in the "like it" column: Totally improbable ingredients add up to something hauntingly delicious. If there are leftovers I'll have them for breakfast with toast, and think myself well fed indeed. No, it's not low fat, but neither is it gratuitously high fat—the fat in the peanut butter is both unsaturated and really crucial for flavor and texture. **MAKES 4 TO 6 SMALL SERVINGS**

NOTE

A note to those with mixed feelings about raw onion: The recipe offers a range. Use a quarter of the onion, and the taste will be subtler; with the entire onion, you get that warming, piquant, whole onion flush. Both are good.

2 cups apple juice
¼ to 1 medium yellow onion, quartered
1 rib celery, chopped
1 teaspoon curry powder
½ teaspoon dried ginger
1 clove garlic, peeled
½ cup low-fat or fat-free yogurt
½ cup smooth peanut butter, preferably natural (unhydrogenated, no sugar added)
1 to 3 tablespoons fresh-squeezed lemon juice
Grated nutmeg (optional)

Combine all the ingredients in a blender or food processor and process thoroughly, to liquefy. Transfer to the refrigerator and chill for at least 3 hours, or overnight. Serve in chilled cups, with a dusting of freshly grated nutmeg, if desired.

Instant Soups: Best in Show

Instant soups are convenient: portable, quick, and a godsend for vegetarians on the road. Pack some for when you know you'll be in a vegetarian-friendly environment; then, all you'll need is hot water for something fast and nourishing. But tastewise, instant soups are all over the map.

Here's how to select a good one:

▲ *Be a diligent label reader. For health and taste reasons, avoid products with monosodium glutamate, gums and preservatives; and watch out for added oils or fats.*

▲ *Shop at the natural foods store. You are more likely to find such products there than at the supermarket, unless your market has a large natural foods section. Brands I have used and recommend include some varieties of Taste Adventure, Fantastic Foods, and Nile Spice.*

▲ *Know what works tastewise, as well as what doesn't, in instant soups.*

WHAT WORKS: *The most successful instant soups are built around dried, cooked legume flakes, such as split pea, black bean, kidney bean, lentil, and navy bean soups, as well as various chilis. The label will describe the featured legume as precooked. These legume soups are flat-out good. Instant miso soups such as Miso Cup (which comes in a foil envelope) are also pleasant, though one-dimensional (try the Miso Cup variety with dried tofu and scallions).*

WHAT SORT OF WORKS: *Dried vegetables, while no match for fresh, fall within the acceptable range. Seasonings should read something like "herbs, garlic, and spices." Instant couscous in soup is tolerable, but just barely.*

WHAT DOESN'T WORK: *Dried tomato soup tastes fake, even when it's technically not. Instant rice has an unappealing crumbly texture. "Cream of" soups don't taste remotely creamy, frequently smell off, and are prone to leaving unappealing clots of powdered milk in the bottom of the cup. Now you know.*

African Groundnut Soup

This soup—served hot, rich as sin, of African provenance—has skipped in and out of my life for almost (good God!) thirty years.

Most peanut-based dishes are loosely of African provenance, since these legumes (technically not nuts at all) are native to Africa and were brought to the Americas with slaves. They grow underground, hence "groundnuts," and are used in dishes all over Africa. There are Sudanese lamb and peanut butter soups; chicken with a tomato–peanut butter sauce on the Ivory Coast. But the flavors and combinations translate easily to vegetarian dishes. Although peanuts and peanut butter seem astonishingly high in fat, remember that the fat is unsaturated and healthful. Plus, it comes packaged in the peanut itself, with lots of high-quality protein. Fat content or no, this soup's incredible ease and utter deliciousness will seduce you, especially given how few ingredients it has. Since its rich heartiness seems right for winter eating, when okra is rarely in season, I use frozen Gumbo Mix, which contains okra as well as corn, celery, and red peppers. **SERVES 8 TO 10**

2 quarts water, preferably spring or filtered, or mild vegetable stock
1¼ cups smooth peanut butter, preferably natural (unhydrogenated, no sugar added)
1 can (6 ounces) tomato paste
2 bay leaves
1 teaspoon paprika
3 to 4 tablespoons tamari or shoyu soy sauce
8 ounces (about ½ package) frozen Vegetable Gumbo Mix
Freshly ground black pepper to taste
Minced Italian parsley (optional)

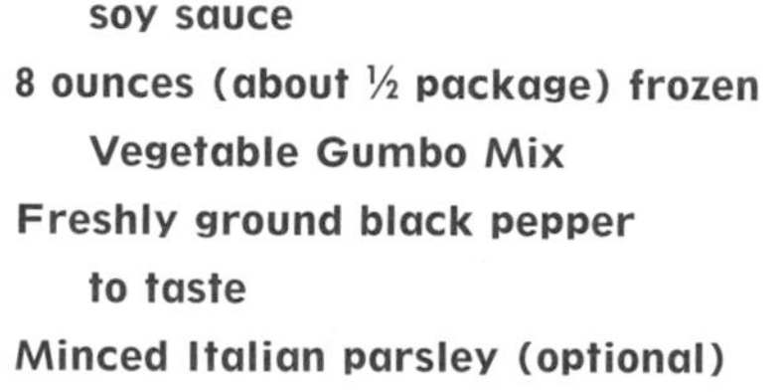

1 Bring 2 cups of the water to a boil. Place the peanut butter in a large, heatproof bowl and pour the boiling water over it, whisking to smooth the peanut butter into the water. Whisk in the tomato paste.

2 Combine this mixture with the remaining water, the paprika, and tamari in a large soup pot. Bring to a boil, then turn the heat down to a simmer. Cook over low heat for about 20 minutes, giving it a stir once in a while.

3 Add the frozen vegetables and cook for another 10 minutes. Add pepper and

perhaps more tamari; proceed cautiously, adding it a tablespoon at a time until you've hit it just right. Garnish with minced parsley, if desired, and serve hot, at once.

COOK ONCE FOR 2 MEALS Rich as this is, it makes an excellent sauce. Double the liquid component in steps 1 and 2. Reserve half, refrigerated, while making soup from the other half. Then, a day or two or three later, heat the refrigerated peanut butter mixture and serve it over some commercially prepared oven-baked or savory tofu, on top of a nice bed of white and wild rice, with a simple green vegetable—broccoli, green beans—on the side.

Hungarian Potato and Sweet Potato Soup

In 1995, Ned and I were addressing the Pacific Northwest Bed and Breakfast Innkeepers Guild Conference in Portland, Oregon. One night, we dined at the Old Wives Tale, a casual vegetarian restaurant. We swooned over their paprika-pinked, dill-enhanced, rich-as-Croesus Hungarian mushroom soup, a house specialty for some two decades. It's truly wonderful, but so cream-dense you almost feel guilty looking at it (not *so* guilty, however, that you can refrain from consuming it—at least, we couldn't). I didn't even ask for the recipe—you know, "don't ask, don't tell" that much cream. But I couldn't wait to get home to my kitchen to try to re-create it, de-creamified, with the flavors and intense deliciousness intact. The original mushrooms got transmuted to potatoes and sweet potatoes, cream was omitted and replaced with a dab of neufchâtel, and *voilà*!

Soothing, truly luscious. This reborn soup is excellent with very lightly buttered sourdough toast and the good, garlicky The Salad (page 68). It doesn't lend itself too well to nondairy substitutions. However, if you're a diehard nondairy eater, try it with soy milk and soy cream cheese. This variation, which I served once to a lactose-intolerant friend, sent her into shivers of pleasure. **SERVES 4 TO 6**

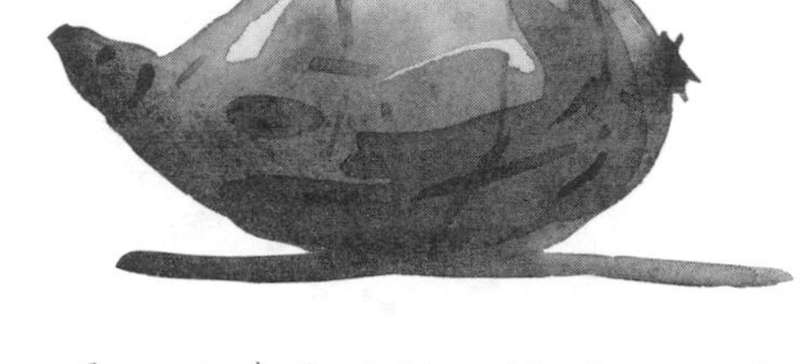

- **7 cups vegetable stock (see page 139)**
- **3 fist-size potatoes, preferably Yukon Gold, peeled and chopped**
- **2 medium sweet potatoes or 1 large yam, peeled and chopped**
- **1½ teaspoons vegetable oil (optional)**
- **1½ teaspoons olive oil (optional)**
- **1 large leek, roots removed, split, well washed, and chopped**
- **1½ tablespoons Hungarian sweet paprika**
- **1 cup low-fat milk**
- **1 tablespoon dried dillweed**
- **¼ teaspoon tamari or shoyu soy sauce**
- **Freshly ground black pepper, and plenty of it**
- **Salt to taste**
- **2 to 3 ounces neufchâtel reduced-fat cream cheese, cut into small pieces**
- **Minced parsley or fresh dill (optional)**

1 Bring 6 cups of the stock to a boil in a large soup pot. Drop in the potatoes and sweet potatoes and reduce the heat to a medium simmer. Half-cover and let the potatoes cook until tender, about 15 minutes.

2 Meanwhile, heat the oil and butter in a conventional skillet (omit the oil and butter if using a nonstick skillet sprayed with cooking spray). Add the leek and toss it around, stir-frying, until it is limp and slightly browned, about 5 minutes (a little longer and over slightly lower heat in the no-oil version). Sprinkle with the paprika and stir-fry for another 1 to 2 minutes, stirring. Add the remaining 1 cup stock and stir to deglaze.

3 Add this mixture to the simmering potatoes and stock. Add the milk, dill, tamari, pepper, and salt. (Since it takes a while for the full dill flavor to emerge, if you are serving the soup right away, you might want to add more dill; if it will sit for an hour, or be reheated the next day, this amount is adequate.)

4 Lower the heat under the soup and add the pieces of cheese. Stir like crazy to break up the cheese so it melts into the soup. Taste for seasoning. Garnish with parsley or dill and serve hot.

COOK ONCE FOR 2 MEALS Leftovers are memorable on pasta, just as-is or with sautéed red bell pepper dice thrown in. Serve with a crisp, bitter green salad (with arugula or escarole) and there you are. Just a smidgen of the leftover soup also makes a dreamy omelet filling.

Gingered Curry of Carrot Soup with Bell Peppers

Fireworks in a bowl, bright and bold. A smooth, burnished puree is highly seasoned, and it saturates the palate with layers of flavor that wash over the tongue, one after the other. Rich yet without a drop of cream, the velvety texture contrasts nicely with the bite of fresh ginger and curry. A bowlful is easily turned into a full meal: Just serve it with a scoop of any hearty grain-and-bean-based salad on a plate of arugula and spinach and good crusty bread.

You want this to be decidedly spicy, so don't be shy about using the upper amount of curry. You also want it decidedly sweet. If the carrots are very sweet naturally (nibble one raw), use less honey; if not, add more. **SERVES 6 TO 8**

VARIATION

CHILLED GINGERED CURRY OF CARROTS WITH BELL PEPPERS: ***Omit the butter and use 2 tablespoons vegetable oil. Add an extra teaspoon or so of fresh ginger and cut the vegetable stock back to 9 cups. When the puree is done, let it cool to room temperature and whisk in 3 cups low-fat cultured buttermilk or yogurt. This soup is thinner in consistency and lighter in color than the hot soup and extremely refreshing.***

Cooking spray
1 tablespoon mild vegetable oil, such as corn, canola, or peanut
1 tablespoon butter
1 large onion, chopped
1 tablespoon peeled and diced fresh ginger, any tough strings removed
1 pound carrots, stem ends removed, peeled only if the skin is very tough, and chopped
1 large yellow bell pepper, chopped
1 large red bell pepper, chopped
2 to 3 tablespoons curry powder, preferably homemade (see page 901)
10 cups well flavored vegetable stock (see page 139)
2 tablespoons to ¼ cup honey, or to taste
Salt to taste
Minced cilantro (optional)
Diced yellow bell pepper (optional)
Seeded and very finely diced fresh jalapeño chile (optional)

1 Heat the butter and oil in a large nonstick soup pot, or one that has been sprayed with cooking spray. Add the onion and ginger and sauté over medium heat until starting to soften, 3 to 4 minutes. Add the carrots and yellow and red bell peppers and stir-fry for another 5 minutes.

2 Add the curry powder and cook, stirring, for another minute, or until the curry is browned slightly and is trying to stick to the pot (don't let it). Pour the stock over the vegetables, bring to a

boil, turn down the heat to a simmer, cover, and cook for about 15 minutes, or until the carrots are just tender. Remove from the heat. Add the honey and whisk it in. Let cool slightly.

3 Strain the soup, reserving both the liquid and the solids. Transfer the solids to a food processor and buzz until smooth, adding just enough liquid so the machine runs smoothly. You will have to do this in two batches.

4 Recombine the vegetable puree with the liquid. Reheat, garnish with the minced cilantro, pepper, and chile, and serve, hot, in heated cups.

COOK ONCE FOR 2 MEALS Use leftovers as a brightly flavored sauce for a mixture of steamed or stir-fried broccoli, mushrooms, and tofu. Serve over steamed white or brown rice, with or without Western-Style Blueberry Chutney (page 927). Really, this makes a delightful sauce for almost any vegetable mix; diced cooked potatoes and peas added to it are also memorable.

Wendy's Pumpkin-Apple Soup with Curry and Coconut Milk

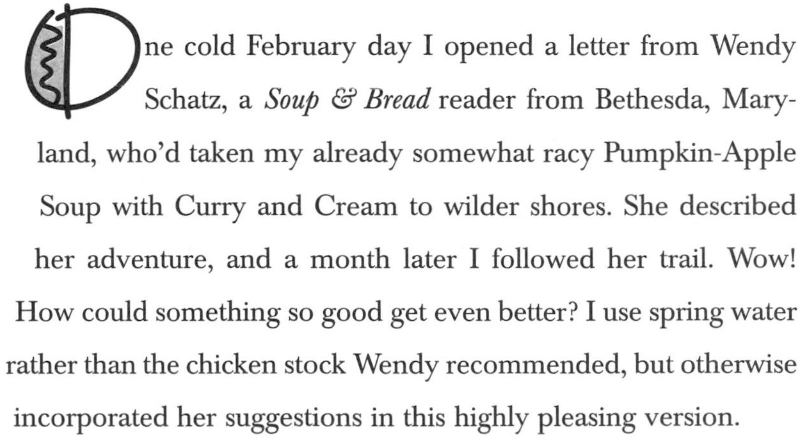

One cold February day I opened a letter from Wendy Schatz, a *Soup & Bread* reader from Bethesda, Maryland, who'd taken my already somewhat racy Pumpkin-Apple Soup with Curry and Cream to wilder shores. She described her adventure, and a month later I followed her trail. Wow! How could something so good get even better? I use spring water rather than the chicken stock Wendy recommended, but otherwise incorporated her suggestions in this highly pleasing version.

Wendy serves this with naan, Indian flatbread. It's an excellent choice, and it is available in many markets. Try garlic naan—even better. Or simply heat whole wheat tortillas, giving them as generous a slather of heavily garlicked butter or oil as your conscience permits. **SERVES 6 TO 8 AS A STARTER**

1 small to medium sweet eating-pumpkin, seeds and strings removed and reserved, cut into 4-inch chunks
3 crisp, well-flavored apples, such as Granny Smiths, Staymans, Macouns, or Winesaps, unpeeled, cores and stems removed and reserved, diced

PUMPKIN-APPLE STOCK

Seeds and strings from pumpkin
Cores and stems from apples
2 heads garlic, skins left on, whole
1 large onion, unpeeled, quartered
1 large potato, unpeeled, quartered
Zest of 1 lemon
2 carrots, halved
3 whole cloves
1 stick cinnamon
5 whole peppercorns
3 whole allspice
6 cups water, preferably spring or filtered

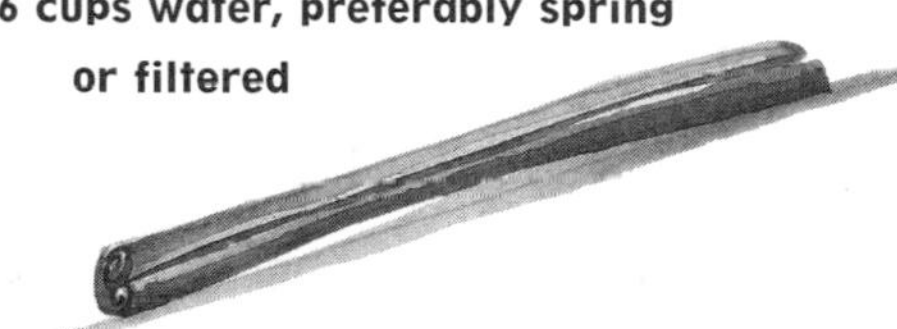

APPLE ONION SAUTÉ

2 teaspoons butter
2 teaspoons mild vegetable oil, such as corn, canola, or peanut
1 large onion, diced
2 teaspoons finely diced fresh ginger
1 tablespoon curry powder, best-quality commercial or homemade (page 901)

ASSEMBLING AND GARNISHING

½ cup frozen apple juice concentrate, thawed
1 cup canned unsweetened coconut milk, preferably reduced-fat
Toasted unsweetened shredded coconut

1 Combine all the stock ingredients in a large soup pot and bring to a boil. Turn the heat down to low and simmer, covered, for 45 minutes. Cool. Strain, discarding the solids.

2 Meanwhile, steam or pressure-cook the pumpkin until tender.

3 Heat the butter and oil in a nonstick 10-inch skillet over medium heat. Add the onion and sauté until somewhat softened, about 3 minutes. Add the ginger and sauté for 1 minute more, then add two-thirds of the diced apples and sauté for another 2 minutes, stirring often. Sprinkle with curry powder and, stirring often, cook for 1 to 2 minutes more, or until very aromatic.

4 Remove from the heat. Scrape half of this mixture into a food processor along with the cooked pumpkin.

5 Place the remaining onion mixture in a large soup pot. Add ¼ cup of the pumpkin-apple stock to the skillet to deglaze, and scrape the pan contents into the soup pot. Add 3 cups more stock. Bring to a boil, turn

down the heat, and simmer for 10 minutes, stirring occasionally.

6 Add the apple juice concentrate to the food processor and buzz until the mixture is smooth. Add this to the soup pot, along with the coconut milk. Do not permit the soup to boil.

7 Serve garnished with the remaining diced apples and a bit of toasted coconut. Swoon. Say, "Thank you, Wendy!"

Michael Romano's Union Square Cafe Indian Borscht

Michael Romano is chef and co-owner, with the equally charming Danny Meyer, of New York's Union Square Cafe. This recipe, an adaptation of one that appeared in the Union Square Cafe's spring 1997 newsletter, represents perfectly the kind of fusion that Michael loves—Indian spicings paired with base notes from other cuisines—and that he later brought to another of Danny Meyer's ventures, Tabla. I'd enjoyed this vibrant, fiery-hot soup at the restaurant on a previous visit, and was *thrilled* to see it in the newsletter. This may be my current very favorite soup, and speaking as a soup diva, that's saying a lot. It is not for the fainthearted. It's incendiary—almost detonates in your mouth. Yet just retyping this recipe makes me hunger for it. That's why I have left the rather enormous quantities (it freezes like a dream).

Turn the heat down by using fewer chiles or by substituting ¾ cup canned unsweetened coconut milk for the tomatoes. The coconut milk idea is Michael's, but I think the soup is even better without this touch of unctuousness. **SERVES 12**

4 medium beets, well-scrubbed, roots trimmed
3 tablespoons mild vegetable oil, such as corn, canola, or peanut
3 onions, sliced
3 jalapeño chiles, seeded or not as you prefer, diced
3 tablespoons peeled and finely minced fresh ginger
1 tablespoon cumin seeds, toasted for 3 minutes in a dry skillet and ground, or 2 teaspoons ground cumin
1 teaspoon ground turmeric
1 teaspoon ground coriander
¾ teaspoon freshly ground very hot dried Thai (bird) chiles, or 1 teaspoon crushed red pepper
¼ cup white or brown basmati rice, well rinsed and drained
1 to 2 teaspoons salt, or to taste
Freshly ground black pepper, to taste (Michael recommends ¼ teaspoon)
3 quarts vegetable stock (see page 139)
1 to 2 tablespoons honey
1 cup canned diced tomatoes in juice
¾ teaspoon Garam Masala (page 902)
Yogurt, sour cream, sour half-and-half (light sour cream), or Tofu Sour Cream (page 909) (optional)
Fresh cilantro leaves (optional)

1 Preheat the oven to 350°F. Wrap the beets individually in foil and bake until tender but not mushy, 60 to 70 minutes. Let cool to where you can handle them, then slip off the skins, cut into ¼-inch slices, and pulse/chop in a food processor to a fine but not pureed consistency.

2 Heat the oil in a very large soup pot over medium heat and add the onions. Sauté until the onions are wilted and translucent but not browned, about 15 minutes. Add the jalapeños and ginger and continue to sauté for another 5 minutes. Add the cumin, turmeric, coriander, and dried chiles and sauté for another 8 minutes (the air will become a bit—cough! cough!—a bit—cough!—pungent).

3 Add the rice and stir well to coat with spices and oil. Add the salt, pepper, stock, 1 tablespoon of the honey, and the tomatoes. Bring to a boil, then turn down the heat to the merest simmer and cook until the rice is very tender, 20 to 25 minutes for white basmati and 45 to 50 for brown. Remove from the heat and let cool slightly.

4 Strain the soup, reserving both the liquid and the solids. Working in batches, puree the solids in a food processor, adding only as much liquid as needed per batch to make a smooth, thick puree. Return the puree to the soup pot with the reserved liquid and beets.

5 Heat through. Add the Garam Masala and taste, adding salt, pepper, and perhaps more honey. Serve with a dollop of yogurt and sprinkle with cilantro, if desired.

VARIATION

CASHEW-CREAMED CELERY ROOT SOUP: ***Vegans should substitute margarine or olive oil for the butter. Substitute a low-fat, but not fat-free, unflavored soy milk for the milk. When the vegetables are done, place 2 to 3 tablespoons raw (untoasted) cashew butter in a heatproof bowl. Ladle in a good scoop of the hot soup (as brothy a ladleful as possible) and whisk it to soften the cashew butter. Stir the mixture back into the pot, heat through, and serve, garnished with a little minced garlic chives or parsley.***

Peppery Pedregon Potato–Celery Root Soup

If you don't know celery root, also called celeriac, you should. Peeling the knobby root takes persistence, and the root looks so unprepossessing you'll be dubious. But if you persevere, you'll be rewarded with a flavor and texture unlike anything else. This soup is simple, subtle, heartwarming, superlative for colder-than-it-ought-to-be, almost-spring nights. Ned always greets celery root soup with major enthusiasm.

This is a vegetarian version of Cynthia Pedregon's Celeriac Soup, as served in the Peach Tree Tea Room, Fredericksburg, Texas. I've used vegetable stock instead of chicken, added celery seeds, and rung other changes, but the basic idea, including the large and all-important amount of freshly-ground black pepper, is Cynthia's.

Although I give the lower-fat dairy version, many who've tasted both think the vegan variation, at left, with a bit of cashew butter, is even better.

I serve it texture-y. If you prefer it pureed, well, that's what your food processor is standing there looking hopeful for. **SERVES 4**

Cooking spray
2 teaspoons butter
½ large onion, finely diced
4 cloves garlic, chopped
¼ teaspoon celery seed
1 celery root, peeled and diced into ½-inch cubes
2 medium potatoes, well scrubbed (peeled or not, as you prefer), diced into ½-inch cubes
5 cups Golden Stock (page 140) or good-quality commercial vegetable stock
¾ to 1 teaspoon freshly ground black pepper
Salt to taste
1 cup evaporated skim milk
1 tablespoon cornstarch
Plain yogurt, Yogurt Sour Cream (page 910), reduced-fat sour cream, or Tofu Sour Cream (page 909) (optional)
Minced fresh garlic chives or parsley (optional)

1 Heat the butter in a nonstick soup pot or one that has been sprayed with cooking

spray. When the butter melts, add the onion, garlic, and celery seed and gently sauté over low-medium heat for about 5 minutes, or until the onion has started to soften.

2 Add the celery root and potatoes, stock, 3/4 teaspoon pepper, and a little salt. Bring to a boil, turn down the heat to a simmer, and cook, half covered, until the potatoes and celery root are very tender, 30 to 40 minutes. Add all but 2 tablespoons of the evaporated skim milk, stir well, and heat through again.

3 Smush the cornstarch into the remaining 2 tablespoons evaporated milk. When the soup is very hot, scoop a ladleful into the cornstarch mixture, stir, then add the mixture back into the pot. It should immediately thicken, just a bit. Remove from the heat and taste for seasonings.

4 Serve hot, lightly dolloped, if you like, with yogurt and sprinkled with garlic chives.

The Good Root

As vegetables go, celery root is ugly—a knobbly, gnarled brown root. The ugliness is only skin deep, however; it has a great, delicious crispness and a deep but pleasant celery taste—with no strings attached. It used to be rare in American markets, but these days it's easy to find.

The French are smart enough to appreciate this good root; but then, they shred it and absolutely coat it in a (to me) distasteful amount of sauce, which masks its delicacy. Try it, instead, in a soup that really lets its goodness shine through. Or shred the peeled root and toss with a mustardy homemade Tofu Mayonnaise (page 906).

Summer's End Potato-Mushroom Chowder with Basil-Tomato Finish

The last of summer's basil finds a good home here. This is perfect for the kind of late August or early September night when, though the day has been hot and the garden is overflowing, you first sense, more than feel, that tiny chilly hint of approaching autumn.

Rich, hearty, no added fat, and almost no fuss, this pot of deliciousness will leave you with only the food processor, a knife, and a soup pot to clean. If you wish,

substitute chopped broccoli (including peeled stems) for the greens. A good vegetable stock is essential. Serve with a big green salad, dressed with tangy, mustardy dressing, and good crusty bread. This is easily made vegan; just use Tofu Sour Cream (page 909) in the finish. **SERVES 4 TO 6**

SUMMER'S END SOUP SUPPER

Green salad with late-summer tomatoes, red onion, and Sesame-Ginger-Miso Dressing (PAGE 117)

*

Sourdough whole wheat toast

*

Summer's End Potato-Mushroom Chowder with Basil-Tomato Finish

*

Sliced August peaches with early fall raspberries, brown sugar, and a splash of Frangelico

Cooking spray
1 large onion, diced
1½ cups sliced mushrooms
3 carrots, scrubbed, grated or finely chopped
1½ quarts vegetable stock (see page 139)
2 large red-skinned potatoes, scrubbed, peel left on, halved and thinly sliced
1½ to 2 cups lightly packed chopped chard, kale, turnip, or collard greens
3 cloves garlic, peeled
1 red-ripe garden tomato, unpeeled, quartered
½ cup Yogurt Sour Cream (page 910), sour half-and-half (light sour cream), or Tofu Sour Cream (page 909)
½ to ¾ cup fresh basil leaves
1½ tablespoons cornstarch
Salt and freshly ground pepper to taste

1 Heat a large nonstick soup pot or one that has been sprayed with cooking spray. Add the onion and sauté over medium-high heat until the onion softens, 6 to 7 minutes. (If you've used cooking spray, the onion will grow a little brown around the edges.) Add the mushrooms and sauté for another 3 minutes. Add the carrots and sauté for 2 minutes more.

2 Add the stock and bring to a boil. Drop in the potatoes, lower the heat to a simmer, cover, and cook for 10 minutes. Uncover and drop in the greens. Cook, uncovered, for another 10 minutes, stirring often.

3 Meanwhile, combine the garlic, tomato, Yogurt Sour Cream, basil, and cornstarch in a food processor. Buzz until quite smooth, scraping the sides of the work bowl a time or two.

4 When the soup's cooking time is complete, raise the heat to get the soup extremely hot, then turn down low and stir the garlic-basil-cornstarch mixture into the hot soup. Cook just long enough for the soup to heat the basil mixture through and to thicken ever so slightly, which should happen almost instantly. Taste to make sure there's no taste of raw cornstarch (cook a little longer if there is) and season with salt (a little) and pepper (a lot).

Russian-Style Potato-Mushroom Chowder with a Dill-Tomato Finish

Ned and I liked the previous soup so much that we took it a step further, adding more, and more intensely flavored, mushrooms. Mushrooms and potatoes are an earthy combination, much loved by the Russians, as are such staple foods as dill, sour cream, and cabbage. This soup combines all of them, with exceptional results. Again, you would hardly believe such hearty deliciousness is low fat and simple, but it is. It's more wintry than the previous soup, and, like it, can easily be made vegan. **SERVES 4 TO 6**

1½ quarts vegetable stock (see page 139)
2 ounces dried mushrooms, such as porcini
Cooking spray
1 large onion, diced
1½ cups sliced button mushrooms
1½ cups sliced shiitake mushrooms
3 carrots, scrubbed, grated or finely chopped
2 large red-skinned potatoes, scrubbed, peel left on, halved and thinly sliced
1½ to 2 cups lightly packed chopped cabbage or Savoy cabbage
3 cloves garlic, peeled
1 garden tomato, unpeeled, quartered, or ¼ cup canned diced tomato
½ cup Yogurt Sour Cream (page 910), sour half-and-half (light sour cream), or Tofu Sour Cream (page 909)
About ½ cup fresh dill leaves, chopped
1½ tablespoons cornstarch
Salt and freshly ground black pepper to taste

1 Bring ½ cup of the vegetable stock to a boil in a small saucepan, reserving the rest for use later in the recipe. Place the dried mushrooms in a small heatproof bowl, and pour the boiling stock over them. Set aside, covered, to soak for 30 minutes.

2 Heat a large nonstick soup pot or one that has been sprayed with cooking spray. Add the onion and sauté over medium-high heat until the onion softens, 6 to 7 minutes. (If you've used cooking spray, the onion will grow a little brown around the edges.) Add the button mushrooms and shiitakes and sauté for another 3 minutes. Add the carrots and sauté for 2 minutes more.

3 Add the reserved stock and bring to a boil. Drop in the potatoes, lower the heat to a simmer, cover, and cook for 10 minutes. Meanwhile, drain the soaked mushrooms carefully through a fine-mesh strainer (or one lined with cheesecloth or a coffee filter), straining the flavorful soaking liquid right into the soup. Pick through the rehydrated mushrooms, removing any little bits of woodsy material you find, and chop the mushrooms medium fine. Add them to the simmering soup too, along with the chopped cabbage. Cook, uncovered, for another 10 minutes, stirring often.

4 Meanwhile, combine the garlic, tomato, Yogurt Sour Cream, dill, and cornstarch in a food processor. Buzz until quite smooth, scraping the sides of the work bowl a time or two.

5 When the soup's cooking time is complete, raise the heat to get the soup extremely hot, then turn down low and stir the garlic-dill-cornstarch mixture into the hot soup. Cook just long enough for the soup to heat the dill mixture through and to thicken ever so slightly, which should happen almost instantly. Taste to make sure there's no taste of raw cornstarch (cook a little longer if there is) and season with salt (a little) and pepper (a lot).

COOK ONCE FOR 2 MEALS This soup thickens as it cools. If you make a double batch and stir in an additional cup of sour half-and-half (light sour cream) and perhaps some extra sautéed mushrooms, you have a dreamy, stroganoff-like sauce for pasta or grains or vegetables and tofu—not light, but quite luscious.

Charlotte's Pantry Sweet Potato Soup

I convinced my octogenarian mother that she'd love having a food processor, but only by promising to come and teach her how to use it. So, one April day, we had Cuisinart Class, one teacher, one student. We buzzed, sliced, and pureed for hours. We put blades on and took them off, attached spindles and twisted bowls, "left to right, until you hear the click." Right off the bat we whizzed up some Olivada (page 24), as well as a batch of delicious chilled Lunar Gazpacho (page 175). But in disregard for our carefully laid plans, it was cold and overcast; except for the narcissus in bloom under the kousa dogwood in her backyard, it might have been November. Obviously, we needed hot soup. We also needed quick and easy. A speedy visual cruise through her kitchen yielded ingredients for this astonishingly satisfying, quick-fix full-meal soup (although the only thing Cuisinart-worthy was slicing onions). Make it as is, but, more important, use it as inspiration for your own pantry cruise. You may substitute vegetable stock for the water-plus-cube we used, and the results are even better. **SERVES 4 TO 6**

1 teaspoon olive oil
Cooking spray
½ onion, sliced
1 can (15 ounces) kidney beans
1 can (15 ounces) chickpeas
2 bay leaves
1 can (8-ounces) tomato sauce
2½ cups water, preferably spring or filtered
1 vegetarian bouillon cube
1 sweet potato, peeled and cut into ½-inch dice
Salt and freshly ground black pepper
Minced parsley (optional)

1 Heat the oil in a medium-large nonstick soup pot or one that has been sprayed with cooking spray. Add the onion and sauté quickly, over high heat, until the edges start to brown, about 4 minutes. Lower the heat and add both kinds of beans plus their liquid, the bay leaves, tomato sauce, and water. Bring to a boil, then turn down to a simmer.

2 Drop in the bouillon cube and sweet potato, stirring well. Cover the soup and cook, at a slow simmer, for about 25 minutes, or until the sweet potato is cooked through. Correct the seasonings with salt and pepper. Serve, hot, in cups, with a little minced parsley, if desired.

"P'oatage" of Asparagus, White Wine, and Lemon

At one time, one of my very favorite soups was the Asparagus-Cheese Soup with White Wine, which appears in both *Dairy Hollow House Cookbook* and *Soup & Bread*. It's a fine soup, but rich, and after a while, if one is a fairly low-fat eater, the pleasures of cream begin to pale—not for health reasons but because your palate changes and the way cream feels in your mouth is suddenly not so wonderful.

This soup has a creamy texture, but without that too-rich feeling a high-fat soup can leave in your mouth. Although this is sparked with lemon rind and white wine, the asparagus comes through loud and clear, lightly, brightly singing its springtime refrain unmuted. Though I still served the other soup at the restaurant occasionally, this is where my own springtime cravings lead me. Its secret is . . . oatmeal. I know how improbable it sounds. But cooked in the stock, then pureed in the food processor with the asparagus stalks, it creates a smoothed-out amalgamation that is as pleasing as can be. After experiencing its delights, I have developed several other "p'oatages." **MAKES 4 TO 6 GENEROUS SERVINGS**

6 cups vegetable stock (see page 139)
2 pounds fresh asparagus, tough ends broken off, stems peeled if you want the finished soup super-smooth
1⅓ cups uncooked oatmeal (rolled oats)
Finely grated zest of 2 large lemons
3 tablespoons nutritional yeast (see page 239)
2 cups white wine
Salt to taste

1 Bring 3 cups of the stock to a boil in a nonstick soup pot and drop in the asparagus. Cook until tender, about 4 minutes. Remove the asparagus from the stock. Let the asparagus cool slightly on a cutting board.

2 Meanwhile, add the oatmeal to the stock in the soup pot. Bring to a boil, turn down to a simmer, and cover. Cook, covered, for 20 minutes.

3 As the oatmeal cooks, stack the asparagus and cut off the tips, reserving them. Slice the stalks. Place the asparagus stalks in a food processor with the lemon zest and nutritional yeast.

4 When the oatmeal-stock mixture has cooked, add it, too, to the food processor and buzz until smooth. Return this thick puree to the soup pot. Add the wine and the remaining stock. Bring to a boil, turn down to a simmer, and cook, stirring often, for about 20 minutes. Taste, adding salt until it's to your liking.

5 Serve, garnished with the reserved asparagus tips.

Golden Days of Summer Corn Soup

One hot, late-summer Saturday in the days when we did dinners nightly at the inn, I wandered into the walk-in cooler in search of inspiration for that night's second soup choice. Something light, refreshing, uncomplicated-tasting was in order. A box of vivid yellow peppers, a heap of fresh corn on the cob, plenty of sweet local carrots—I'd struck gold. Could the fact that I'd picked a large bouquet of the earliest plumes of goldenrod, only that morning, have influenced me?

That evening, a young vegetarian from Kansas City dined with us and was passionate in her compliments on the soup. How was it made, she asked me, swooning and swaying in her seat with half-closed eyes. "It's the essence of the best, sweet corn I ever ate in my whole life—and I love sweet corn." Here is the recipe I gave her, which I dedicate to anyone equally corn loving.

This is vegan. Please note that most of the vegetables here are coarsely cut, because they will be pureed. **SERVES 4 TO 6**

Cooking spray
1 tablespoon vegetable oil
1½ large onions, peeled and cut into eighths
4 large carrots, unpeeled, quartered lengthwise and then halved
2 large golden-yellow peppers, seeded and cut into eighths
1 tomato, cut into eighths
1 tablespoon tamari or shoyu soy sauce
5 to 6 cups water, preferably spring or filtered
5 to 7 ears fresh corn, husks and silks removed
1 to 2 tablespoons honey, sugar, or Rapidura
Salt to taste
Contrasting-color edible flowers, such as maroon-red nasturtiums (optional)

1 Put a large pot of water on to boil for cooking the corn. Meanwhile, add the oil to a second large, nonstick soup pot, or one that has been sprayed with cooking spray. Add the oil, and place over medium-high heat.

2 Add the onions to the oil and sauté for about 5 minutes, or until starting to brown and stick a little, but not soften. Stir fairly

often, because the heat is high. Add the carrots and sauté for another 5 minutes, then add the peppers. Sauté for 3 more minutes, then add the tomato and tamari. Sauté, stirring constantly, for 1 more minute (the mixture will very much want to stick following the tamari addition). You want it to get quite brown. Pour 5 cups of the water over the vegetables. Bring to a boil, turn down to a simmer, cover, and cook until the carrots are tender enough to pierce easily with a fork, 10 to 15 minutes.

3 Meanwhile, add the corn to the pot of boiling water. Cook until barely done, 3 to 4 minutes. Drain well and rinse with cold water. Cut the corn kernels off the cobs.

4 When the carrots are tender, drain the vegetables, reserving their cooking water. Puree all the vegetables, including half of the corn, in a food processor, using as much of the cooking water as necessary to make a smooth puree. Add the honey. Combine the pureed vegetables with the whole-kernel corn, adding the additional cup of water if it seems too thick to you. Season with salt. Reheat and serve, garnished with edible flowers, if desired.

Tofu Cream of Fresh Herbs and New Potato Soup

Can tofu "pass" as cream to your average nonvegetarian eater? I am no fan of culinary dissembling, nor was it really fair to use inn guests as guinea pigs. But, knowing the frisson of horror that the general population (still) feels at the very word *tofu,* I did dissemble, briefly, in the interest of discovering if the following fresh, lively-tasting creamless wonder was as good as I thought.

So one day, at the staff menu-meeting, I described this soup to waitresses Carolyn and Susan simply as Cream of Fresh Herbs and New Potatoes. On sampling, both were rapturous. Off to the dining room they went, enthusiastically describing the evening's soup to the guests. I scanned the cups as they came back—empty. When I made the round of the tables I asked, "Did you have the Cream of Fresh Herbs and New Potatoes Soup? What did you think? I'm testing it for my new cookbook. Should it be included?" Everyone said, "Oh, *yes!*" A few added, "How long will we have to wait for the recipe?" Only then did I confess the secret ingredient. Tasting is believing: No one gagged or made a face. One gentleman said, "Oh, good, now I like it even more." **SERVES 8 TO 10**

2 quarts vegetable stock (see page 139)
¼ cup converted rice
1½ tablespoons mild vegetable oil, such as corn, canola, or peanut
1 large onion, finely chopped
1 pound new potatoes, scrubbed, peel left on, cut into small dice
2 tablespoons minced fresh basil, preferably cinnamon or Thai basil
1 tablespoon minced fresh dill
1 teaspoon minced fresh rosemary
1 teaspoon thyme leaves, preferably lemon thyme
1 cup finely minced Italian parsley
2 to 3 tablespoons tamari or shoyu soy sauce
2 packages (10½ ounces each) firm silken tofu
2 tablespoons nutritional yeast (see page 239)
1 teaspoon umeboshi plum paste
Salt and freshly ground black pepper to taste

1 Combine 2 cups of the stock with the rice and bring to a boil. Turn down to a simmer and let simmer, half-covered, for 25 to 30 minutes, or until very soft and overdone. Drain the rice, reserving both stock and rice.

2 Heat the oil in a large soup pot. Add the onion and let cook, stirring occasionally, until quite limp and starting to brown, about 8 minutes. Add the potatoes, reserved rice-cooking stock, and the remaining stock. Bring to a boil, lower the heat to a simmer, and cook for about 20 minutes.

3 Combine the basil, dill, rosemary, thyme, and parsley. Set aside about 2 tablespoons of the herbs for a garnish and add the remainder to the soup, along with the tamari, adding more or less to taste—much depends on how flavorful or salty the stock itself is. Continue cooking for about 5 minutes.

4 Combine the reserved cooked rice, tofu, nutritional yeast, and umeboshi plum paste in a food processor. Buzz until very smooth and thick with no distinguishable lumps of tofu or grains of rice. This may take as long as 3 minutes, and you may have to stop the processor, scrape the sides, and pulse now and then.

5 Using a whisk vigorously, combine the tofu-rice cream with the hot soup. Add salt and pepper to taste; the soup may require quite a bit of both. Simmer for another 5 to 10 minutes and then serve, hot, sprinkled with the reserved fresh herbs.

WRITERS' COLONY BOARD SUPPER IN SEPTEMBER

Wild Rice, Lentil, and Mushroom Soup

*

Roasted Butternut Squash and Apple Salad, on a Bed of Bitter Greens (PAGE 78) with Honeyed Red-Wine Vinaigrette (PAGE 79)

*

Ronni's Skillet-Sizzled Kentucky Buttermilk Cornbread (PAGE 452)

*

Stuffed Ginger–Black Pepper Baked Pears (PAGE 994)

Wild Rice, Lentil, and Mushroom Soup

A hearty, full-flavored wintertime soup, eminently pleasurable, this started its life as a nonvegetarian soup, incorporating the post-Thanksgiving turkey gravy and the post-Christmas goose gravy. But it is simply too good to have only twice a year, or leave solely to the province of meat-eaters. Although robust, it is rich and elegant; small cups are a fine starter on a cold night when the snow is blowing, while large bowls are satisfying as an entree served with salad and bread. The wine is excellent in this, but not strictly necessary. Incidentally, it is vegan. **SERVES 4 TO 6**

1 teaspoon to 1 tablespoon olive oil
Cooking spray
1 onion, diced
1 carrot, diced
1 rib celery, diced
2 bay leaves
1 small handful shiitake mushrooms, cleaned, stems removed, diced
3 cups vegetable stock, preferably shiitake mushroom stock (see page 141)
4 cups Chicken-Style Gravy (page 949)
½ cup hearty red wine, such as a Burgundy (optional)
1 cup cooked lentils
1 cup cooked wild rice
3 large fresh tomatoes, diced, or 1 cup canned diced tomatoes
Minced Italian parsley (optional)

1 Heat the oil in a large nonstick soup pot, or one that has been sprayed with cooking spray, over medium heat. Add the onion and cook for 4 minutes, or until it begins to soften. Add the carrot, celery, bay leaves, and shiitakes and continue to sauté, stirring often, for another 5 minutes. Add the stock and bring to a boil. Turn down the heat and simmer for 10 minutes.

2 Stir in the gravy, the wine, if using, the cooked lentils, cooked wild rice, and the tomatoes. Heat through and simmer, over very low heat, for about 10 minutes more. Serve piping hot, with a little parsley, if desired.

Wendy Newman's British Isles Pear and Parsnip Soup

The letter (with an Old Saybrook, Connecticut, postmark) began, "Dear Crescent Dragonwagon. My husband and I are in the U.S. whilst he is doing some research here. We are both from England. On a recent trip home I came across the enclosed recipe for pear and parsnip soup which has now become a family favourite. Having read in your *Soup & Bread* that you didn't have a parsnip soup recipe, I thought I would share this one with you. Parsnips are used a lot in Britain, especially roasted. . . . Some people also cut them into strips and fry them to eat like chips (french fries!)."

This is what I adore about being a cookbook writer—perfect strangers become "pan pals" and send you kind letters, sometimes with recipes, like this terrific soup. Anyone who thinks "healthful" and "good" are mutually exclusive has not tried this creamless potage par excellence, which you could serve with utter confidence if Julia Child came to supper at your house. Parsnips look like white carrots, with a flavor that's a cross between carrots and parsley, quite sweet. If you don't know them, take a parsnip to lunch today! Don't miss the Parsnip-Barley Burgers (page 831), either.

This delectable, smooth soup is sweet but savory, and it will have your guests begging "More, more!" I substituted vegetable stock for the chicken Ms. Newman suggested, but otherwise the recipe is unchanged. Because its color is unprepossessing, you do need the garnish. Peppery watercress is the perfect foil to the slight sweetness, but arugula would do, or a scatter of minced parsley. **SERVES 4**

3 ripe pears, peeled, cored, and chopped
3 to 4 medium parsnips, peeled and chopped
6½ cups vegetable stock (see page 139)
Salt and freshly ground black pepper to taste
Watercress sprigs

1 Combine the pears, parsnips, and 2½ cups of the stock in a medium soup pot over medium heat. Bring to a boil, turn down the heat to a simmer, and let cook, partially covered, until the parsnip pieces are tender, about 15 minutes.

2 Drain, reserving both the liquid and the solids. Puree the solids, with just a little of the reserved stock, in a food processor or blender until smooth. You could put it through a food mill or sieve if you want it extra smooth and are willing to fuss; sometimes parsnips have a woody core. But this probably won't be necessary.

3 Return the p\ureed mixture and reserved stock to the soup pot, along with the remainder of the stock. Season to taste with salt and pepper and simmer for 15 minutes. Serve hot, with a watercress sprig floating on top of each cup.

Gingered Mushroom, Sweet Potato, and Wild Rice Soup

East meets West in a fusion that is poetic yet stalwart. Sweet plays off salty; a few slightly crunchy vegetables balance the soft, heavy graininess of the wild rice. Even the staunchest carnivore wouldn't miss the meat.

This soup was invented as a way to use the robust, dark, salty, gingery stock in which commercially made seitan is usually packed. Too strong to stand alone, too assertively gingery to use in many dishes, and very salty, this stock is nonetheless so good and flavorful it seems a shame to throw it out. Here, its character remains, tamed by the addition of milder stock. The trick is getting the balance right: Too much seitan stock will make the soup too salty; not enough will make it blah. The precise amount of stock a seitan package contains will vary; most 8-ounce boxes of seitan are packed in about 2½ cups. For these reasons, recipe quantities are inexact. The important thing is to taste the measured seitan stock and combine it with the milder stock in proportions that fit your liking.

The precise chop size of the vegetables is important; it means you get a taste of each component comfortably on the spoon with every bite. You can do the base stock, rice, and sweet potato early in the day, but do your stir-fry at the last minute.

SERVES 4 TO 6

About 2½ cups ginger-tamari-kombu stock from purchased seitan (see above)
About 5 cups any mild, unsalty vegetable stock (see page 139)
½ cup wild rice, well rinsed
1 large or 2 small sweet potatoes, peeled and diced into ½-inch cubes
Cooking spray
1 teaspoon toasted sesame oil
1 large onion, chopped
1 red bell pepper, chopped
½ pound shiitake mushrooms, stems removed, sliced
1 handful small, fresh spinach leaves, preferably a crumpled-leaf variety
1 tablespoon mirin (sweet rice wine; available in the Asian foods section of most large supermarkets)
1 tablespoon cornstarch
6 scallions, roots removed, white parts plus 3 inches of green sliced

1 Taste the two stocks and combine them in proportions that work both for your taste and the character of your seitan stock. (When we make this using the stock from White Wave seitan, we use 2½ cups of seitan stock to 5 cups mild vegetable stock.) You want to end up with 7 to 8 cups of a savory well-flavored mixture—not too salty or gingery, but enough.

2 Bring the stock to a boil in a medium-large soup pot or Dutch oven. Add the wild rice, turn down the heat to a simmer, and cook, partially covered, for 40 minutes. Add the sweet potatoes. Keep simmering, partially covered, for another 10 minutes. (The soup can be done in advance up to this point.)

3 Meanwhile, but no more than 10 minutes before you are ready to serve, place a nonstick wok or skillet, or one that has been sprayed with cooking spray, over medium heat and add the sesame oil. Add the onion and stir-fry for about 4 minutes, or until beginning to soften. Add the red pepper and stir-fry for 1 minute more. Add the shiitake mushrooms and stir-fry for about 3 minutes, or until the mushrooms soften slightly.

Spinach

4 Taste the sweet potatoes and wild rice. If they're done, and you're just about ready to serve the soup, proceed. Add the mushroom-pepper sauté to the soup. Get out 6 to 8 soup bowls and put a few spinach leaves in each one. Bring soup up to a boil.

5 Combine the mirin and cornstarch in a small bowl, mushing to a paste with a few

drops of water, using your fingers to smooth out all lumps. Ladle in a little of the hot soup and whisk to combine it with the cornstarch mixture, then stir the contents of the bowl into the boiling soup and stir a few times. It should thicken just a bit and grow slightly glossy almost immediately. Stir in the scallions.

6 Immediately remove from the heat and ladle over the spinach leaves in the soup bowls. Serve.

Lime Soup Yucatán

Here is my vegetarian version of the lovely, citrus-y *sopa de lima* from the Yucatán. This lime-scented soup, offered in a chicken version in many Latin American cookbooks, is one of the few soups served hot that can truly be called refreshing. It is light, piquant, pleasing.

An excellent starter, it could be made a main-course soup by adding a handful of cooked pasta or rice to each bowl, a poached egg, or a little diced firm tofu.

SERVES 4 TO 6

2 quarts vegetable stock (see page 139)
1 head garlic, cloves peeled and coarsely chopped
3 to 6 whole cloves
1 teaspoon dried sage leaves
2 cups peeled and diced butternut squash (1½-inch pieces)
½ cup fresh-squeezed lime juice
2 teaspoons olive oil
Cooking spray
1 large onion, diced
2 to 4 serrano or other hot green chiles, diced (remove seeds and ribs for a milder soup; leave them in for heat)
½ cup canned diced tomatoes in tomato puree
4 corn tortillas, stacked and cut in half, then into ½-inch strips
½ cup cilantro leaves
Salt, freshly ground black pepper, and Dragon Salt (page 900)
1 lime, thinly sliced, seeds removed but peel left on

1 Preheat the oven to 350°F. Combine the stock, half of the garlic, the whole cloves, sage, squash, and lime juice and bring to a boil in a large soup pot. Turn down the heat and simmer gently for 20 minutes. Scoop out the whole cloves with a slotted spoon and discard them.

2 Meanwhile, heat the oil in a nonstick skillet, or one that has been sprayed with cooking spray, over medium heat. Add the onion and sauté until softened and translucent, about 5 minutes. Add the chiles and remaining garlic and sauté for another 1 to 2 minutes. Swirl in a ladleful of the hot broth to deglaze the pan and pour the whole shebang back into the soup pot, along with the tomatoes.

3 Place the tortilla strips on a baking sheet and bake for 3 to 5 minutes, or until crisp. Put a few strips in each soup serving bowl.

4 Stir the cilantro into the soup and season to taste with salt, pepper, and Dragon Salt. Ladle the finished soup over the prepared soup bowls and serve at once, hot, with a slice of lime floating on top of the soup.

Soba Noodles in Broth with Vegetables

This, a light supper of soulful buckwheat noodles in savory, aromatic broth, is the Japanese equivalent of chicken soup with noodles. It's a wintertime favorite of one of my longtime friends, musician Bill Haymes, who enjoys a bowl of it at Benkay, a Japanese restaurant in Nashville, Tennessee.

In Japan it's sometimes made with chicken stock, but much more often with dashi, a mild, near-instant stock made with kombu seaweed and dried bonito flakes—fish. However, according to William Shurtleff and Akiko Aoyagi, the authors of *The Book of Tofu*, *The Book of Miso,* and *The Book of Tempeh,* several vegetarian versions are served in Buddhist monasteries and restaurants. In the version below, you can use either regular vegetable stock, or Shiitake-Kombu Dashi, the recipe for which follows.

Note that the cooking method for soba is somewhat different than for traditional wheat noodles, because buckwheat's makeup is far lower in gluten (wheat protein).

SERVES 4 TO 6 AS AN ENTREE; 8 TO 10 AS A STARTER

VARIATION

SIMPLE SOBA NOODLES IN SEITAN-VEGETABLE STOCK BROTH:

If you eat seitan (see page 232) regularly, you probably have on hand the stock in which the seitan is packed. This is generally nothing more than an intensely salty soy-kombu-ginger broth. You can use it to make an excellent quickie version of soba soup: Simply substitute it for part of the vegetable stock, omit the soy sauce and ginger, and cut the amount of miso in half. Specifically, for the 8 cups of vegetable stock called for, substitute 2 or 3 cups of the seitan stock, and make up the difference with veggie stock.

VARIATION

NOT-SUCH-A-BIG-PRODUCTION NOODLED JAPANESE BROTH FOR ONE: ***This is a quickie I make when I crave something light, nourishing, lowish in calories and fat but with a little protein kick. Heat 2 to 3 cups Imagine Natural Vegetable Broth to a boil with 2 teaspoons to 1 tablespoon tamari or shoyu soy sauce and a teaspoon of prepared fresh ginger paste (in the produce section at many markets). When it comes to a boil, add ½ bundle (about ¾ ounce dry) very thin, fine cellophane noodles, also called bean threads, 1 or 2 sliced mushrooms, and 1 carrot, sliced on an angle into very thin ovals. Drop in 3 ounces diced firm fresh tofu (I like Tree of Life brand Smoked Garlic-Lemon Tofu here). Simmer until the noodles are transparent, maybe 3 minutes. Meanwhile, dice a scallion into a large soup bowl. Pour the hot soup over the scallion and enjoy.***

8 ounces soba (Japanese buckwheat noodles)
12 cups (3 quarts) Shiitake-Kombu Dashi (recipe follows) or vegetable stock (see page 139)
2 to 3 cloves garlic, minced
1½ tablespoons peeled and finely chopped fresh ginger
½ pound shiitake mushrooms, stems removed and reserved for the dashi recipe below, caps sliced
2 carrots, peeled, scored by cutting out 3 to 4 tiny lengthwise triangular wedges, and sliced crosswise to make flower-shaped slices
3 tablespoons mirin or sweet sherry
2 tablespoons plus 1 teaspoon tamari or shoyu soy sauce
1 teaspoon to 1 tablespoon rice vinegar (optional)
½ teaspoon sugar
2 tablespoons miso (dark or red is traditional, but I prefer golden, traditional white miso; see next page)
4 ounces firm tofu, not silken, cut into ½-inch cubes
About 16 spinach leaves, preferably a crumpled-leaf variety, well washed, stems removed
4 scallions, roots and outer leaves removed, thinly sliced
½ cup grated daikon radish

1 Bring a large pot of water to a full boil. Drop in the soba and stir. When the water returns to a boil, add ½ cup cold water. Let return to a boil a second time and repeat the cold water treatment. You may need to do it once more. Cook until the noodles are just barely tender, 5 to 7 minutes. Drain well and rinse thoroughly with cold water, combing your fingers through the noodles to separate them.

2 Meanwhile, combine the dashi, garlic, and ginger in another pot and bring to a boil. Reduce the heat to medium-low and add the shiitakes. Cover and simmer for 6 minutes. Add the carrot and simmer for 2 minutes more. Add the mirin, tamari, vinegar, if using, and sugar.

3 Place the miso in a small heatproof bowl. Ladle a spoonful of the hot soup over it and whisk to dissolve the miso. Pour the dissolved miso into the large pot. Add the tofu, simmer for 1 minute, and remove from the heat.

4 Get out soup bowls, divide the noodles among the bowls, and place a few leaves of spinach in each one. Ladle the soup over noodles and spinach, being sure everyone gets broth, shiitakes, carrots, and tofu. Sprinkle each portion with the scallions and grated radish and serve at once, hot.

Shiitake-Kombu Dashi

MAKES 3 QUARTS

Stems from ½ pound fresh shiitake mushrooms
3 quarts plus ½ cup water, preferably spring or filtered
½ teaspoon salt
3 strips kombu seaweed (see page 82), each about 3 inches wide by 7 inches long, wiped lightly with a damp cloth but not rinsed

1 Bring the shiitake stems and water to a boil with salt, then turn down the heat to a simmer and cook for 40 minutes. Strain through cheesecloth or a coffee filter, discarding the stems. Allow the stock to cool to room temperature.

2 Add the kombu to the cooled stock and bring to a boil. *Immediately* turn off the heat and remove the kombu.

Meet Miso

HAVE WE BEEN INTRODUCED YET?

If you've ever had bean soup at a Japanese restaurant, you've tasted miso. It's a soft, salty, highly concentrated seasoning paste, traditionally made from soybeans, salt, a grain (such as rice or barley), and a fermenting agent. It's readily available in natural foods stores and, sometimes, in the natural foods section of supermarkets.

Although miso is exotic to many Americans, it has been used for thousands of years in Asian countries and is a standard item in Japanese kitchens, where it's often used as we use bouillon cubes: Add boiling water, stir, and you have a full-flavored, distinctive broth. According to William Shurtleff and Akiko Aoyagi, who wrote The Book of Miso, *more than 70 percent of the Japanese begin the day with a cup of miso soup instead of coffee.*

But miso's horizons extend further. Though commonly used solo as a broth base, it's even better when added to other stocks, which tames the miso's individual personality, and gives the stock body, richness, and finish without tasting miso-ish. Further excellent miso uses: in salad dressings, dips (see Voluptuous Roasted Red Pepper Spread, page 17), soups, sauces, and stews. In Japan, miso forms the base for savory toppings, part condiment, part sauce, used to snap up bland but toothsome tofu, and many other dishes. These toppings, in which miso is cooked with water or stock, sugar, seasonings, often sake or mirin, and sometimes other ingredients (like seafood, nuts, or vegetables), are available commercially or easily made at home.

There are dozens of misos, all savory, some sweet and savory. Each has an individual flavor, as wines from different years and hillsides do. In a pinch you can use misos interchangeably, as you might substitute Gruyère for Cheddar, but getting to know and use different misos enriches your culinary repertoire.

In general, longer-aged misos have a darker color and stronger, heartier, saltier flavor. They do not require refrigeration and keep indefinitely. These are the types you'll recognize as having that "Japanese restaurant soup" taste. All of the following are dark types: mugi, *a barley miso;* kome *and* genmai, *rice misos;* soba, *a buckwheat miso; and* hatcho, *probably the most widely available, is from pure soybeans. I am merely skimming the surface; but there are dozens of dark miso varieties.*

Younger misos are lighter in color (beige, golden, ivory white) and taste. They have a delicate, appealing sweetness and need to be refrigerated. They're generally sold as "sweet miso," "mellow miso," "mellow white miso," or "traditional white miso" (I think of them as golden).

When it comes to fresh misos, I prefer the taste of the light young misos to that of the older, dark ones; however, I use both and always have a tub of at least one of each kind. To approximate the difference between the two main types in very loose culinary equivalencies, you could say the dark misos are "beefy," while the light are more "chicken-y." Not a perfect analogy, but one to get you started tasting misos.

Lemony-Herbed Vichysquashz

After a creamy, chilled fish and potato soup called Fishysoisse in *Dairy Hollow House Soup & Bread,* could this be far behind? Piquantly refreshing, very lemony, this is just the ticket when your garden (or your neighbor's) overflows with yellow crookneck squashes. Unlike traditional vichyssoise, this is creamless, though it does contain potatoes. Its origination point, from which it has strayed but owes allegiance, is the Chilled Zucchini Soup with Leeks and Herbs from *The Perennial Political Palate,* the third of the cookbooks written by the women of the Bloodroot Collective. **SERVES 4 TO 6**

Cooking spray
1 tablespoon olive oil
2 large onions, coarsely chopped
3 cloves garlic, coarsely chopped
⅔ to 1 cup loosely packed assorted fresh herbs, according to availability and your liking, preferably including some lemony herbs, stripped of any woody stems, chopped if necessary
1 quart water, preferably spring or filtered
1 to 2 stems lemon grass, bulb end plus 4 inches of green, bulb pounded to release flavor
2 potatoes, peeled and chopped
2 to 3 lemons
4 to 5 cups chopped yellow squash (about 7 small to medium golden crooknecks)
2 tablespoons tamari or shoyu soy sauce
½ teaspoon salt
Freshly ground black pepper to taste
Sprigs of fresh herbs (optional)
Thinly sliced half-circles of lemon (optional)
Sour cream or reduced-fat sour cream (optional)

An Herbal Note

The Bloodroot directions say, "Collect garden herbs: We like ½ cup fresh basil, 2 tablespoons summer savory stripped off the hard stems, and 1 tablespoon thyme leaves similarly stripped." They use fresh mint as the garnish. I try to use a few of the so-called lemon herbs along with the more conventional selections. Here's what I've had the pleasure of snipping: 2 leaves fresh sage; a generous sprig of Mexican Marigold, also called Texas Tarragon or False Tarragon (see page 37); about 1 tablespoon lemon thyme leaves; about ⅔ cup loosely packed lemon basil; and a leaf or two of lemon verbena.

1 Heat the oil in a nonstick soup pot or deep skillet, or one that has been sprayed with cooking spray. Add the onions and garlic and sauté over high heat until they start to brown, about 5 minutes. Add the herbs and sauté for 1 minute more. Add the water, lemon grass, and potatoes. Bring to a boil, turn down the heat to a simmer, and cook for 15 minutes, or until the potatoes are soft but not falling apart.

2 Grate enough zest from 2 of the lemons to equal 2 teaspoons. Cut the 2 lemons in half, reserving the third lemon, and juice them through a strainer to catch the seeds. Set the juice aside. Add the zest to the simmering soup. Add the squash, tamari, salt, and pepper. Bring to a boil, turn down the heat to a simmer, and cover. Simmer for 8 minutes, or until the squash is tender but not falling apart.

3 Place a strainer over a bowl and strain the soup, reserving both the liquid and the solids. Remove and discard the lemon grass stalks. Puree the solids, in batches, in a food processor, then recombine with the liquid. Whisk in the lemon juice. Chill the soup well.

4 Taste the chilled soup, adding additional lemon juice, salt, or tamari as needed.

5 Serve, very cold, preferably in chilled cups. You may garnish with little sprigs of any of the herbs you used as well as a thin half-circle of lemon. Some might enjoy a spoonful of sour cream or reduced-fat sour cream as well.

Lunar Gazpacho

As cool and delicate as the pale green wings of a luna moth under a wash of moonlight, this white gazpacho is cool and lovely. Its yogurt base combines Middle Eastern notes with those of almond-based Spanish gazpachos. But what makes it is this Dairy Hollow twist, invented on a sweltering day to make chilled soup even cooler: pureed green grapes. "What is it about your cucumber soup with mint?" asked Steve Ritchie, co-owner of Rock Cottage Inn and esteemed local colleague, when he came to dine—a little mournfully—on one of the

DOG-DAYS LADIES' LUNCHEON ON THE STONE PATIO AT MOONSHINE COTTAGE

Shandygaffs
(PAGE 30)

*

Wenonah Fay Holl's "Aspics of Love" Salad
(PAGE 129)

*

Lunar Gazpacho

*

Pita Bread Toasts
(PAGE 30)

*

Fresh raspberries spooned over lemon sorbet

last nights before we closed the restaurant for nightly service. "We just had cucumber-mint soup, but it wasn't this good." I told him: grapes, and now I'm telling you. A jar in the refrigerator will hold you in good stead on too-hot-to-cook days. **SERVES 4 AS A STARTER**

- 1 cup vegetable stock (see page 139)
- 2 cucumbers, peeled and seeded if seeds are tough
- ⅓ cup loosely packed fresh mint leaves
- ¾ pound green grapes
- 2 cups plain yogurt, nonfat or not, as you prefer
- 8 to 10 raw whole almonds
- Several grinds of fresh black pepper
- ½ teaspoon salt
- Additional mint sprigs (optional)

1 Place the stock in a food processor. Halve the cucumbers and add them with the mint. Reserve ⅔ cup of the grapes and add the rest to the food processor. Add 1 cup of the yogurt, the almonds, pepper, and salt. Buzz this mixture to near-smoothness and turn out into a glass bowl.

2 Quarter the reserved grapes. Stir them and the reserved 1 cup yogurt into the soup in the bowl. Chill well. Serve in chilled cups, preferably pale green ones, with a garnish of fresh mint, if desired.

Citrus-Buttermilk Soup with Minted Fruit Salsa

Totally refreshing, not overly sweet, this dish is a perfect icy blast for hot summer days, and its pale pastel shades dotted with bits of vibrant-hued salsa make it a great choice for summer entertaining. Don't skimp on the serranos for the fruit salsa, and please leave seeds and fiber in for heat; they are what takes this across the border, from smoothie or dessert to, definitely and deliciously, soup. Other than buzzing the frozen bananas in at the end (this gives a perfect iciness and mellow, mild thickening), everything can be done in advance. **SERVES 4 TO 6**

6 oranges
Juice of ½ lemon
3 tablespoons sugar, honey, or maple syrup
2 to 3 cups perfectly ripe, flavorful strawberries, stems removed, or an equal amount of cut-up full-flavored ripe cantaloupe
Dash salt
2 cups buttermilk
1 red bell pepper, seeded and diced
2 green serrano chiles, very finely minced, keeping seeds and ribs for heat
2 tablespoons finely minced fresh mint
2 very ripe bananas, peeled, then frozen solid
Sprigs of fresh mint (optional)

1 Grate the rind of 1 orange and set it aside. Carefully section, then dice, the bald orange and 1 of the other oranges into ¼- to ½-inch dice and set aside. Juice the remaining 4 oranges.

2 In a blender or food processor, combine the orange juice and rind, lemon juice, sugar or honey, half of the strawberries or cantaloupe, and salt. Buzz until smooth, pour into a pitcher, swirl in the buttermilk, and chill well.

3 Halve the remaining strawberries, then slice crosswise to make small half-circles, or cut up the remaining cantaloupe into small dice. Toss the strawberries or cantaloupe with the diced orange, diced red pepper, serranos, and mint. Refrigerate this salsa separately from the soup.

4 Place soup dishes, preferably shallow rather than open ones, stemmed glasses, or glass cups in the freezer to chill.

5 Just before serving, pour about 1 cup of the chilled soup into a blender or processor. Add the frozen bananas and buzz and pulse until the banana is completely smooth and the mixture has thickened a bit. Add a little more chilled soup as needed to buzz smoothly. Return this banana'd batch to the rest, and stir to combine.

6 To serve, place a generous scoop of salsa in the middle of each soup dish. Pour chilled soup around the salsa, garnish with a mint sprig, and serve at once. (Alternatively, simply stir the salsa into the soup just before serving.)

Bouillabean Soup with Rouille and Crisp Garlic Croûtes

Our Freshwater Fish Soup Provençal, served often in the restaurant, was always joyously received by guests. I felt it behooved me to make a vegetarian version: beans whole and pureed in a tomato sauce with intriguing notes of herbs and citrus. They are what makes the soup so good, adding an elusive piquant, delicious note. **SERVES 6 TO 8 AS A MAIN DISH**

1½ cups navy beans, soaked overnight in 1 quart water, preferably spring or filtered

MEDITERRANEAN SOUP BASE

2 tablespoons olive oil
1 large onion, chopped
2 carrots, chopped
2 ribs celery, with leaves, chopped
8 to 10 cloves garlic, chopped
1¾ cups diced fresh or canned tomatoes in juice (14-ounce can)
Grated rind of ½ orange
1½ teaspoons dried basil
Tiny pinch of cayenne
Large pinch of saffron
½ teaspoon dried thyme
1 quart vegetable stock (see page 139)
1 to 2 tablespoons tomato paste
1 cup dry white wine
2 teaspoons honey, sugar, or Rapidura

BEAN–WHITE WINE STOCK

2 cups bean cooking liquid
1½ cups dry white wine
Juice of 1 lemon
3 whole cloves
3 bay leaves
1 large onion, unpeeled, quartered
1 head garlic, unpeeled, halved crosswise
2 teaspoons salt
1 teaspoon fennel seeds
1 tablespoon black peppercorns

THE FINISH

½ pound green beans, ends snipped, cut into 1- to 2-inch lengths
1 can (15 ounces) chickpeas, drained
1 bag (8 ounces) frozen artichoke hearts (optional)
About ½ cup well-drained kalamata olives, pitted but left in large chunks if possible
Salt and lots of freshly ground black pepper to taste

GARNISH

2 or 3 Croûtes (page 29) per serving
About ¾ cup freshly grated Parmesan cheese
Enlightened Red Pepper–Garlic Rouille (recipe follows)
About ¾ cup minced fresh Italian parsley

1 Drain the beans well, discarding the soaking water, and place the beans in a medium-large pot with 1 quart water. Bring to a boil, turn down the heat to a low simmer, cover, and cook until the beans are tender but not falling apart, about 1½ hours. Let the beans cool, then drain them again, this time saving the liquid. Set the beans, as well as their liquid, aside.

2 As the beans cook, make the tomato base: Heat the oil in a large pot over medium heat. Add the onion and sauté, stirring, until it starts to color, about 7 minutes. Add the carrots, celery, and garlic and cook, stirring, for another 10 minutes. Add the tomatoes, orange rind, basil, cayenne, saffron, thyme, vegetable stock, tomato paste, wine, and honey. Bring to a boil, then turn down

the heat to a simmer. Cook, half covered, for about 40 minutes.

3 Meanwhile, in a separate pot, combine the bean cooking liquid, wine, lemon juice, cloves, bay leaves, onion, garlic, salt, fennel seeds, and peppercorns. Let this, too, simmer for about 40 minutes. Let cool slightly, then strain, discarding the solids. Add the liquid to the tomato base.

4 To finish the Bouillabean, drop the green beans into the simmering tomato–bean stock mixture. Cover the pot and simmer for 15 minutes. Add the chickpeas, artichoke hearts, if using, and olives and simmer for 10 minutes. Measure out 1 cup of the cooked beans for use in the rouille and set aside. Add the remainder to the simmering mixture. Taste and season with salt and pepper. (Around this time you should make your rouille.)

5 When ready to serve the soup, place the croûtes on a baking sheet and sprinkle the Parmesan over them. Run them under the broiler until the Parmesan melts. Place 1 cheese-topped croûte in the bottom of each bowl. Top with a generous spoonful of rouille, then ladle the soup over. Top with a second cheesed croute, a smaller spoonful of rouille, and a good sprinkle of parsley. Serve, immediately, to fanfare, with extra Parmesan and rouille passed at table.

Enlightened Red Pepper–Garlic Rouille

Although a combination of three dried herbs is called for here, when fresh sweet basil is available, it is astronomically good with ½ cup lightly packed fresh basil leaves used instead.

In this litigious age, no cookbook writer would ever, ever dare recommend the use of raw eggs, which are sometimes contaminated with salmonella—although almost all of us (cookbook writers, that is, and plenty of other people) will confess to eating them from time to time with no ill effects. Consider yourself informed, then, and make your own choice. The rouille is good without the egg yolks, just less rich and not traditional—but what about Bouillabean is exactly traditional anyway?

8 to 10 large cloves garlic, peeled
1 teaspoon salt
½ teaspoon dried thyme
½ teaspoon dried basil
½ teaspoon dried rosemary
¼ cup soft breadcrumbs
3 tablespoons of the soup liquid
1 to 2 egg yolks (optional; see note above)
2 red peppers, charred, peeled, seeds and ribs removed, coarsely chopped
⅛ teaspoon cayenne
Reserved 1 cup cooked beans
¼ cup olive oil

Combine all the ingredients in a food processor and buzz, pausing to scrape down the sides several times, until you have achieved a thick, almost pastelike sauce.

VARIATION

JANUARY OUT-OF-THE-CUPBOARD LIMA BEAN AND SUN-DRIED TOMATO SOUP WITH CABBAGE:

The slight sweetness and crunch of cabbage are delicious added to this soup. Simply slice ¼ to ½ head of green or Savoy cabbage into thin ribbons, steam just until wilted, and add to the soup a few minutes before serving.

January Out-of-the-Cupboard Lima Bean and Sun-Dried Tomato Soup

Necessity mothered this vigorous cold-weather soup one January evening when Ned and I returned home, not having been in situ for a couple of weeks. What with being happy to be back, boxes of interesting mail to go through, frigid temperatures outside, and two cats who, despite having been cared for in our absence, were very glad to see us, we were not motivated to go shopping. Scrabbling around the kitchen, we found half a bag of sun-drieds (as one of our noun-izing chefs used to call them), a package of dried limas, two shriveled carrots, two onions starting to go soft. From these unpromising beginnings came about this rich, wonderful soup. It's even better the next day, and gratifyingly low fat, so eat two bowls, and remember it when next you get snowed in. **SERVES 6 TO 8 AS A MAIN COURSE**

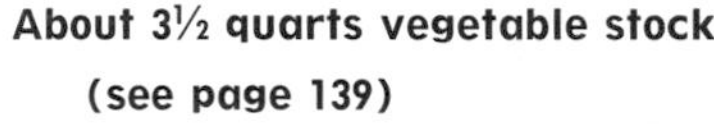

About 3½ quarts vegetable stock (see page 139)
10 sun-dried tomatoes (not packed in olive oil)
2½ cups (1 pound) dried large lima beans, washed and picked over, soaked or speed-soaked (see page 594)
1 teaspoon to 1 tablespoon olive oil
Cooking spray
2 large onions, chopped
2 carrots, chopped
6 large cloves garlic, chopped
Salt and plenty of freshly ground black pepper
1 teaspoon hot sauce
Minced Italian parsley or cilantro (optional)

1 Bring the stock to a boil. Place the sun-dried tomatoes in a small bowl and ladle enough hot stock over them to cover them. Set aside to rehydrate for at least 2 hours.

2 Drain the beans, discarding the soaking liquid. Add the remaining stock to the

limas. Bring back to a boil, lower the heat to a simmer, and cook over low-medium heat for 1 to 1½ hours, until softened.

3 Toward the end of this period, heat the oil in a nonstick skillet, or one that has been sprayed with cooking spray, over medium heat. Add the onions and sauté for 3 minutes, or until starting to become translucent. Add the carrots and half of the garlic and sauté for another 2 minutes.

4 While sautéing the vegetables, scoop out half the cooked limas with a little of their cooking liquid and place them in a food processor. Add the rehydrated sun-dried tomatoes, reserving their soaking liquid. Add the reserved garlic. Process the limas, garlic, and tomatoes together, forming a thick puree.

5 Scrape the sautéed vegetables into the pot of cooked limas and their cooking liquid, along with the sun-dried tomato liquid, and lima-tomato puree. Stir well, add salt to taste, plenty of pepper, and the hot sauce. Simmer, half covered, over extremely low heat for 30 minutes. Serve hot, garnished with minced parsley or cilantro.

COOK ONCE FOR 2 MEALS You might be able to imagine how good a sauce the leftovers, which thicken slightly, would make for pasta, and you're right. The sauce, particularly excellent in the cabbage variation, is just great spooned over fettuccine, then lashed with freshly ground pepper and just-grated Parmesan cheese. Lovely. Crisp bread, crisp salad, and you've got it.

Pumpkin-Tomato Bisque

An inn favorite, slightly revised from the version that appeared in *Soup & Bread,* this soup is lush, sensual, velvety, and easily made. What more could you ask of a potage? How about this: no cream and very little added fat. Besides being swooningly delicious, the bisque also has a wholesome wallop of the intensely orange beta-carotene–rich squashes, and it can be prepared ahead and frozen. When I prepared this on *Good Morning America,* Charlie Gibson ate one bowl on camera and another two off. Pretty much everyone who tastes it is equally enthusiastic.

The pumpkin can be replaced in whole or part by butternut squash or any other sweet hard squash or by sweet potatoes or yams, or a combination of all these.

SERVES 6 TO 8

- 2 teaspoons to 2 tablespoons mild vegetable oil or butter
- Cooking spray (optional)
- 1 large onion, chopped
- 4 cups Golden Stock (page 140)
- 4 cups fresh or canned pumpkin or butternut squash puree
- 1 can whole tomatoes with their juices, pulse/chopped medium fine but not pureed in a processor
- 1 tablespoon maple syrup
- Salt and freshly ground black pepper to taste
- Minced Italian parsley

1 Heat the oil or butter in a nonstick soup pot, or one that has been sprayed with cooking spray, over medium heat. (Omit the cooking spray if using the larger amount of oil or butter.) Add the onion, and sauté until softened, about 5 minutes.

2 Add the stock and heat through. Add the pumpkin, whisking in. Heat again. Add the tomatoes and maple syrup and heat through. Season to taste with salt and pepper.

3 Serve hot, garnished with parsley.

Satisfying Stews

Home food, good food, usually simple (but sometimes sophisticated), stews are slow-cooking mixtures, ingredients plus liquid plus seasoning fusing together in one pot. Stews differ from soups in that the ingredients are usually in larger, chunkier pieces, the proportion of liquid to solid is reduced, and what liquid there is may well be thickened.

But like soups, they scent the house with fragrant, savory steams that breathe welcome.

Stew has been part of humankind since time out of mind. It has hung in iron pots over ancient open fires since the days when humans first crafted iron; it has been sealed in clay pots and buried in coals; it has simmered on stoves in tiny city apartment kitchens, it's been speeded up in pressured times with pressure cookers, or cooked patiently in crockpots, ingredients bubbling as they meld into redolently fragrant, deeply comforting, welcome tenderness. A good stew satisfies.

I have divided these stews, some original, some traditional, some vegetarian versions of traditional favorites from the world over, into three sections. First are Hot Pots: Chilies, Curries & Other Spicy Stews—seductively exotic fragrances of Bangkok and Bombay and the Yucatán. Next, Homey, Hearty Stews. These are the vegetarian equivalent of stews you might have grown up with, not spicy but full of deeply savory, darkly robust flavors and textures and as reminiscent of your own hearth as the hot pots are of faraway places. Both of these varieties are perfect for the long, gray, wintry days; they scent the entire house as they cook, then warm the eaters right down to the bone.

The third category, vegetable-based ragoûts, are called Plenteous Potages. Lighter than the other stews, their central ingredients are vegetables themselves, though sometimes in conjunction with legumes or grains. Many of these I refer to as ragoûts, which has come to refer to thick, well-seasoned stews, usually meat-based. However, the word's origin is French, *gouter,* to taste; therefore, a ragoût is a dish that literally causes you to retaste, restimulating the appetite.

So get out your pot (a 4- to 6-quart Dutch oven or other heavy soup pot will do nicely here). I prefer enamel-clad cast-iron soup pots to others, though a heavy nonstick Dutch oven also has its place in stew-world. Dice the onions. Let your hands smell like garlic. Call some friends. Set the table, with the yellow napkins. Chill the wine, the beer, the cider, or all three. For making a stew warms the cook as well, and that warmth is meant, like stew, to be shared.

Hot Pots:
Chilies, Curries & Other Spicy Stews

You'll see that a lot of these sit-up-and-take-notice stews employ legumes: Stews and legumes are made for each other. First off, stew is a natural medium for the dried bean, which regains plump succulence through a slow-cooking bath in hot liquid. And second, the bean's somewhat bland flavor undergoes a startling, wondrous metamorphosis when attentively seasoned: Garlic, any one (or more) of the panoply of hot peppers, each with its own subtle undernotes, and perhaps ginger, cumin, turmeric—all of these bring out the best in a bean. The origins might be Pakistani, Tex-Mex, or Brazilian, but combine major spicing and beans and you can be sure that there is good eating ahead.

The recipes that follow call for beans in various forms—canned, dried, precooked, and dehydrated. However, if you decide to try a stew that calls for a cup or two of dried beans but you didn't start cooking the beans early enough in the day (and don't have a pressure cooker, which makes short work of bean cooking), simply substitute canned beans. You will obviously have to make some adjustments in timing and the amount of liquid; however, a little kitchen time and experimentation will show you exactly how interchangeable beans can be. And it's handy to know, should you wish to pull a switch, that:

- ▲ 1 cup of dried beans equals 2 to 2¼ cups cooked; and
- ▲ one 16-ounce can of beans also equals 2 cups.

Another bean-interchangeability note: Although I love to use and play with the so-called heritage beans (see page 617) and frequently call for them, bean varieties can usually stand in for one another without much problem. Though their colors, shapes, sizes, and cooking times vary considerably and their tastes more subtly, all beans have in common a comforting innocent starchiness. So don't worry too much about using kidney beans if the recipe calls for black, cooked if it calls for canned, canned if it calls for dried. Use what you have and adapt.

One other point in the make-it-work-for-you line: Although I've given stove-top directions, in many cases, after the usual initial sauté, the whole thing can be transferred to a crockpot for slow, carefree, don't-worry-about-us, we'll-be-here-waiting-for-you-when-you-get-back cooking.

Serve your stew with cornbread or crusty European bread, or thick slices of a nice multigrain, toasted, or over a cooked grain; add a salad, and you're there.

Chilies

As defined here, chilies are bean-based stews whose primary flavoring notes are Southwestern or south of the border. This is not the standard definition given by culinary researchers, who lay claim—with historical good reason—to "chili" as simplified, stripped-down, chuckwagon cowboy food (no tomatoes, no beans, just meat and spicy seasonings), originating when Anglo cowboys, ranchers, and settlers came in contact with the chile peppers and vibrant seasonings of the American Southwest. Chili was thus one of the first American "fusion foods." After all, consider that chili powder (made of powdered chile peppers, cumin, garlic, oregano, usually salt, sometimes allspice), the seasoning mix that is the gold standard for any "bowl of red" was invented by a German immigrant to Texas (see page 200)! Beef, and pork, too, were imports—no more native to America than chili powder, or, for that matter, cowboys.

My definition of chili is more free-wheeling. If untraditional, its roots are ancient. My kind of chilies predate cowboy chilies; they rely on ingredients that *were* native to the New World. Tomatoes, pumpkins, corn, squashes, potatoes, peppers of all kinds, occasionally even unsweetened chocolate, but especially chile peppers, with their palette of heat and color and their delicate undernotes that simmer beneath the burn. And while the soybean was known in China, the lentil and split-pea in India, the black-eyed pea in Africa and Asia, the chickpea (or garbanzo bean) and the fava in the Middle East and some parts of Europe, America was the birthplace of an overflowing cornucopia of beans: kidney beans and black beans, navy beans and cranberry beans, lima beans and runner beans, brown tepary beans, white tepary beans—even fresh green beans! (The latter are, after all, nothing more than the immature pod of the kidney bean.)

The chilies here are highly seasoned stews to which all, or at least some, of these native American foodstuffs are integral. Some may not be what's traditionally called "chili," but don't hold that against them. Their roots go deep in the American soil, and they are more healthful, more nourishing, and every bit as delicious as—though mostly quite different from—your basic, straight-up bowl of Texas Red. Have a bite, and feel *your* roots sink down deeper into the earth on which you stand.

For more about the physiological effects chilies have on us, please see the box below. If you find hot food addictive, you'll be especially interested, because you may be right.

One last important note: All chilies tend to blossom in flavor a day or two after they're made, so not only *can* they be done ahead, they really *should* be. Virtually all of them, except the white chili (page 189), can be frozen for up to three months.

Hot Stuff: The Mind-Altering Chile

What is it about the flavors of the Indian subcontinent, Mexico and Central America, and Thailand that are so peculiarly addictive? Although we think of all these cuisines as hot, and indeed they often are, their effect, in hot climates, is to cool the body, because they induce sweat—"gustatory sweat" as a study done in the '50s put it. But this does not explain why, in the temperate United States, hot, spicy flavors have become so very pleasing to contemporary palates.

Eating the chiles that are so frequently part of Indian and most other hot-climate cuisines may have a physiologically addictive component. Chile-heads know this experientially, but there's proof. As Wall Street Journal *reporter Amal Naj explains in* Peppers, a Hot Pursuit, *when we eat capsicum, the chemical in chile peppers that causes the sensation of heat, nerve endings in tongue and mouth respond by immediately, urgently messengering the burning sensations to the brain, in catastrophic terms. These neurotransmitters have no way of knowing that the chile, whatever sensation it causes, does not do real harm, so, says Naj, "in a panic they carry the worst possible message: 'Fire! Fire!'" On receiving this message, the brain automatically begins attempting to flush out the offending substance, producing the symptoms we hot-food lovers know so well. "[T]he heart beats faster, the mouth salivates, the nose sniffles . . . the head and face break out in a torrential sweat."*

But why on earth should we like such sensations? Because, says Naj, in response to this perceived danger and pain, the body produces its own natural painkiller, endorphin. "Endorphin produces the same effect as a shot of morphine," continues Naj, "[I]t causes a high. . . . [T]aking a bite of the pepper is like giving oneself a mild dose of painkiller. . . . As the pepper eater takes another bite—since pepper doesn't desensitize the tongue, although the threshold for tolerance is raised—another burst of pain is perceived by the brain and it spurs it to release more endorphin. The continued release builds into a rush. In effect, when we go for the habaneros or serranos, we are drugging ourselves, with narcotics from our own homemade, self-manufactured pharmacopoeia." He concludes, "The endorphin theory also explains why the pepper eater has a tendency to eat hotter and hotter peppers till he can't stand it anymore: it's the craving for more and more endorphin."

Brown Tepary Bean, Seitan, and Ancho Chile Stew with Poblano-Citrus Salsa

The flavors and colors of this chunky stew are buoyantly cheering: hot but not searing, complex with sweet undernotes and a beautiful golden-brown color. Brown tepary beans and large cubes of potato, butternut squash, and seitan make it hearty, an almost-but-not-quite-traditional chili. A sprightly fruit salsa cuts the richness and heat marvelously. **SERVES 6 TO 8, ACCOMPANIED BY A COOKED GRAIN OR BREAD AND SALAD**

1½ cups brown tepary beans, black-eyed peas, azuki beans, or small red beans
8 to 9 cups water, preferably spring or filtered
2 ancho chiles (dried poblanos)
1 teaspoon cumin seeds
2 teaspoons olive oil
Cooking spray
1 large onion, chopped
1 rib celery, chopped
4 cloves garlic, sliced
1 teaspoon paprika
Pinch of cayenne
Tiny pinch of cinnamon
2 large potatoes, skin left on, cut into 1-inch chunks
1 medium butternut squash, peeled and diced
1 package (8 ounces) traditionally seasoned seitan, drained and cut into 1-inch chunks (see page 232)
1 tablespoon tomato paste
1¼ teaspoons salt
Freshly ground black pepper to taste
2 teaspoons Rapidura, honey, or molasses
Cooked brown rice, barley, or other grain, or corn tortillas, or any cornbread
Poblano-Citrus Salsa (recipe follows)

1 Rinse and pick over the beans and place them in a heatproof bowl.

2 Bring 2 cups of the water to a boil, pour it over the tepary beans (if using black-eyed peas, azuki beans, or small red beans, skip the presoaking), and soak for 1 hour. Drain well and rinse.

3 Place the beans and the chiles along with 4 cups of the remaining water in a nonstick

pressure cooker or a conventional stew pot, or one that has been sprayed with cooking spray. Cook until tender, 20 to 25 minutes under pressure or 1½ hours conventionally.

4 Toast the cumin seeds in a small, heavy skillet, dry, over medium heat, stirring frequently until they darken and grow fragrant, about 3 minutes. (Toasting the cumin seeds is optional, but it does deepen the flavor. If you choose to leave 'em untoasted, just add them in the next step.)

5 Heat the oil in a nonstick skillet, or one that has been sprayed with cooking spray, over medium heat. Add the onion and sauté until it is starting to wilt, about 4 minutes. Add the celery and continue sautéing for 2 minutes longer. Add the garlic and sauté for an additional minute. Add the paprika, cayenne, and cinnamon along with the cumin. Scrape into the bean pot and bring to a boil. Stir in the potatoes, butternut squash, seitan, tomato paste, salt, a healthy amount of black pepper, and finally the Rapidura. If the mixture seems to have too high a percentage of solids to liquids to be truly stew-like, add all or part of the remaining water. Lower the heat to a simmer and cook, half-covered, stirring occasionally, until the potatoes are done, about 25 minutes. Serve hot, accompanied by or scooped over rice, barley, or the starch of choice, with Poblano-Citrus Salsa passed at the table.

COOK ONCE FOR 2 MEALS Leftovers of this or any other chili or spicy bean stew can be used to fill Tamale Pie (page 449) or Cornbread Pie à la Hippie (page 451). The other marvelous chili redo for not all, but most, chilies is this: Use it as a topping for a baked sweet (not white) potato. A perfect match with this chili, even right down to the citrus salsa!

Very Teparies . . .

Brown tepary beans, a fascinating legume, are heirloom beans available by mail from Indian Harvest (800-346-7032). The folks there refer to them as "a desert survivor," because teparies are able to grow under extremely arid conditions. Slightly wrinkled, caramel-brown, and smallish, they're cultivated by the Pima Indians along Arizona's Gila River, where the only water all year long comes in the spring floods. Starchy like all mature beans, with a texture reminiscent of black-eyed peas, teparies possess a faint undernote of sweet, chestnutlike flavor.

Remember that beans are usually used interchangeably, as long as you adjust the cooking time. If you don't want to order "teps," substitute the more readily available black-eyed, azuki, or small red beans, none of which requires presoaking.

Poblano-Citrus Salsa

I know that the idea of citrus on beans is a bit of a stretch, but it is so fresh tasting that one bite will make you a convert. Four cups might seem like a large amount, but because the salsa's not very spicy, you'll eat more than usual.

Cut all of the ingredients into an equally small dice, about ¼ inch, except for the serrano, which should be very finely minced. **MAKES 4 CUPS**

- **2 poblano chiles, charred until black, skinned, stems removed, and diced (seeds and membranes removed for mildness or left in for extra heat)**
- **2 oranges, peeled, sectioned, seeded, and diced**
- **2 serrano chiles, minced (seeds and membrane removed for mildness or left in for extra heat)**
- **1 red onion, diced**
- **1 fresh grapefruit, peeled, sectioned, seeded and diced**
- **½ teaspoons salt**
- **2 to 3 tablespoons finely chopped cilantro (optional)**

Toss all of the ingredients together in a medium bowl. Cover and refrigerate until serving time. (Although the salsa will keep overnight, it is best eaten within a few hours of being made.)

COOK ONCE FOR 2 MEALS This is from my "pan-pal" and friend Susan Mack of Atlanta, who adored this whole stew recipe but really fell for the citrus salsa: Add diced avocado and jícama to leftover (or planned-over) salsa and you have a wonderfully refreshing salad.

White Chili with Eggplant, Poblanos, and Posole

Of all the chilies here, this is a contender for the position of my current, don't-miss favorite. Its finished hue is more peachy-salmon than white, its bite mild but definitely there. Moderated by gentle creaminess, the warming trend is subtle and gradual, beginning in the mouth but suffusing the whole being. Serve with a good white-cornmeal cornbread—try Ronni's Skillet-Sizzled Kentucky Buttermilk Cornbread (page 452). Although the cheese is optional, the small amount of Monterey Jack that's stirred in is essential in bringing the flavors together. However, if you're making this ahead of time don't add the cheese until the next-day reheat. **SERVES 8 TO 10**

VARIATIONS

VEGAN WHITE CHILI: *Substitute your favorite nondairy Monterey Jack- or Cheddar-style cheese and stir in 2 to 3 tablespoons soy-based natural "creamer" (such as White Wave's Silk Soymilk Creamer).*

Less pretty but awfully popular with the man of our house is **BROWN CHILI:** *Omit the eggplant; omit the cheese; add an 8-ounce package commercially made spicy ready-ground tofu with the hominy.*

- 2½ cups white beans, such as navy, white tepary, Great Northern, or pea beans
- 7 to 8 cups vegetable stock (see page 139)
- 2 bay leaves
- Cooking spray
- 1 tablespoon olive oil
- 2 large onions, chopped
- 10 cloves garlic, 6 chopped, 4 whole
- 3 poblano chiles, seeds and membranes removed (or left in for extra heat), chopped
- 1 or 2 serrano chiles, seeds and membranes removed (or left in for extra heat), chopped
- 2 teaspoons ground cumin
- 2 teaspoons dried oregano
- Salt and freshly ground black pepper to taste
- 1 can (10 ounces) tomatoes and green chiles (such as Ro*Tel)
- 1 tablespoon tomato paste
- 1 can (10 ounces) white hominy (posole) very well drained (see page 440)
- 1 large eggplant, peeled and cut into 1-inch cubes, debittered if need be (see page 742)
- 1 cup (4 ounces) grated Monterey Jack cheese
- To accompany: chopped cilantro, pickled jalapeños, toasted whole wheat tortillas, diced tomatoes, assorted salsas

1 Rinse, pick over, soak or quick-soak, and drain the beans (see page 594). Place the beans, enough stock to cover them by 1 inch, and the bay leaves, in a nonstick pressure cooker or stew pot, or one that has been sprayed with cooking spray. Cook until tender, 18 to 25 minutes under pressure or 1 to 1½ hours conventionally.

2 Heat the oil in a nonstick skillet, or one that has been sprayed with cooking spray, over medium heat. Add the onions and sauté until softened, about 5 minutes. Add the chopped garlic, poblanos, and serranos and sauté for an additional 2 minutes. Add the cumin and oregano and sauté for 1 minute more.

Kiss and Ro*Tel

*To understand this, you have to understand Ro*Tel. Ro*Tel is a brand of tomatoes, green chiles, salt, and the ever-elusive label ingredient, "spice." It originated in the 1940s in Elsa, a small Texas farming community in the Rio Grande Valley, and is an "original, secret old family recipe," as the can says. That family was—of course—the Rotelles, farmers who, in their quest to expand the marketing of their produce, came up with several different products. But the tomato and green chile mixture was the one that hit. Though the Rotelles long ago sold out to American Home Foods, and the product is now canned in Vacaville, California, Ro*Tel lives on. American Home Foods sells about 38 million cans of it annually.*

*Ro*Tel is really much more than canned tomatoes and green chile. It is an institution. It is a way of life. It is motherhood and apple pie. No grocery store or supermarket in Texas and certain other parts of the Southwest and Mid-South would dare be without it. To those who are indoctrinated into or grew up eating it, the very sight of the 10-ounce white cans sitting next to the ordinary tomatoes, the name "Ro*Tel" in caps, in black, on a yellow box, with the little star in the middle a bright red, and the tomato and three green chiles sitting by the white bowl, is reassuring. As the label used to say, but alas, no longer does, "It'll Jump Start Yer Heart."*

3 When the beans are meltingly tender but not falling apart, scrape the sautéed mixture into the bean pot. Fish out and discard the bay leaves. Deglaze the pan with a little vegetable stock and then pour the deglazing liquid into the bean pot. Raise the heat and bring to a boil, then lower the heat to a simmer, adding salt and black pepper to taste.

4 Remove 3 or 4 ladlesful of the fully softened beans from the pot and place them in a food processor along with the canned tomatoes and green chiles (use all the liquid, too), tomato paste, and whole garlic cloves. Puree. Set aside.

5 Add the hominy and eggplant to the beans and simmer, half-covered, stirring occasionally, until the eggplant is almost tender, 7 to 10 minutes. Add the pureed mixture and cook, stirring occasionally, at a very low simmer, for another 5 to 6 minutes. Taste and, if necessary, correct the seasonings.

6 Just before serving, stir in half of the grated cheese. Serve, at once, passing the remaining cheese and, if desired, an array of the suggested accompaniments: cilantro, pickled jalapeños, tortillas, tomatoes, and salsas—if possible a bevy of varieties.

COOK ONCE FOR 2 MEALS Leftovers of this or any other chili or spicy bean stew can be used to fill Tamale Pie (page 449) or Cornbread Pie à la Hippie (page 451). In addition, you can make a luscious calorics-be-damned Creamy, White Chili Bean Chowder from leftovers. Make a classic thin white sauce, allowing 1 cup sauce for every cup of leftover chili. Dilute further with vegetable stock or additional white sauce until soupy. Add salt, pepper, and canned green chiles to taste.

CD's Neo-Traditional Red Chili

Last, but definitely not least, here is the vegetarian equivalent of a basic traditional red chili. If you count the with-meat precursor, I've been making it for thirty-seven years. I got the hang of it as a sixteen-year-old New Yorker blessed with three close West Texas friends who provided my initiation into Tex-Mex, among many other things. Genie taught me her mama's chili: no beans, beefy, but fired-up with true chili's seasonings, consistency, and feel. This is what I worked to recapture when I quit eating meat six years later. I still think of Genie every time I make chili.

SHADES OF HALLOWEEN

Roasted Red Pepper Soup with a Cilantro-Jalapeño Swirl
(PAGE 144)

*

Baked sweet potato topped with Kachina's Chili
(SEE BOX, OPPOSITE)
or CD's Chili Mole
(SEE BOX, OPPOSITE)

*

The Salad
(PAGE 68)
with sliced avocado

*

Dessert Nachos
(PAGE 1034)

I made this with pinto beans for years, until my friend Kachina introduced me to black bean chili. Actually, as you'll see from the list of variations that follow, friends have lit my chili path all the way along, each with a unique and captivating twist. No matter which variation you choose, please don't be put off by the length of the ingredient list: It's primarily spices and herbs. **SERVES 8 TO 10 GENEROUSLY, WITH FIXIN'S AND CORNBREAD**

1 pound pinto beans, picked over and well washed
Water, preferably spring or filtered, for soaking
2 bay leaves
1 ancho chile
1 jalapeño chile
Freshly ground black pepper to taste
Cooking spray
2½ to 3 quarts any well-flavored vegetable stock (see page 139) or spring or filtered water plus 2 vegetable bouillon cubes
1 to 4 tablespoons olive oil
2 large onions, chopped
2 to 3 green bell peppers, stemmed, seeded, and chopped
1 tablespoon cumin seeds
1 tablespoon hot chili powder
2 teaspoons ground cumin
2 teaspoons ground coriander
2 teaspoons sweet Hungarian paprika
½ teaspoon dried oregano
Pinch of cayenne pepper, or to taste
3 cloves garlic, pressed or minced
1 can (16 ounces) chopped tomatoes in juice
¼ cup tomato paste
1 to 2 tablespoons Pickapeppa sauce
1½ teaspoons tamari or shoyu soy sauce
Salt to taste
1 to 3 teaspoons honey or Rapidura
1 package (10 ounces) spicy-style ready-ground tofu
Chili fixin's: grated sharp Cheddar or Monterey Jack cheese, diced raw onion, pickled jalapeños, sour cream, Yogurt Sour Cream (page 910) or Tofu Sour Cream (page 909), chopped cilantro, Tabasco sauce

1 Prepare the beans by either the presoak or quick-soak method (see page 594).

2 Drain and rinse the beans well. Place the beans, the bay leaves, ancho, jalapeño, and lots and lots of black pepper in a nonstick stew pot, or one that has been sprayed with cooking spray. Add enough stock to cover them by 1½ inches and place over medium heat. Bring to a boil, then turn the heat down to a simmer. Simmer, covered, until the beans are nearly tender, 1½ to 2 hours.

3 When the beans are almost ready, heat the oil in a skillet over medium heat. One tablespoon of oil will suffice in a nonstick; otherwise, use the larger amount. Add the onions and sauté until they start to soften, 3 to 4 minutes. Stir in the bell peppers and sauté for another 2 minutes, then add the cumin seeds, chili powder, ground cumin, coriander, paprika, oregano, and cayenne and cook, stirring constantly, for 2 minutes. Add the garlic and sauté for 30 seconds. Remove from the heat. Scrape into the

simmering beans. Deglaze the pan with a little bit of the bean cooking liquid, and then pour the deglazing liquid back into the beans.

4 Add the tomatoes, tomato paste, Pickapeppa, tamari, salt—it will take quite a bit—and the honey or Rapidura. Lastly, stir in the ground tofu. Simmer, partially covered, until the seasonings are well blended, about 30 minutes.

5 Just before serving, pick out the bay leaves as well as the stems from the ancho and jalapeño chiles. Mash a couple of ladlesful of the beans against the sides of the pot to slightly thicken the chili. Serve, hot, either right away or (even better) the next day, with any or all of the fixings for people to doctor their own bowl of red.

COOK ONCE FOR 2 MEALS Leftovers of this or any other chili or spicy bean stew can be used to fill Tamale Pie (page 449) or Cornbread Pie à la Hippie (page 451). A curious-but-so-good chili redo, not for all but for most chilis, is to use leftover chili as a topping for a baked sweet (not white) potato. Any red chili with black beans is the best sweet potato topping. Not only is the taste perfection, but the colors—wow!

Chili for Me

Chili with TVP: *TVP—dried textured vegetable protein made from soy, and very inexpensive—is something I got into the habit of using in chili years ago. To use it: Omit the ground spicy tofu. Soak 1⅓ cups TVP in 1 cup boiling water for 15 minutes, then add 2 teaspoons salt and ½ teaspoon freshly ground black pepper. Add the seasoned TVP to the skillet when you add the spices. Cook, stirring, and finish as directed.*

Kachina's Chili: *Substitute black beans for pintos.*

Charlotte's Chili: *Serve the chili—any of the above chilies—over cooked elbow macaroni.*

Chou Chou's Chili: *My friend Chou Chou is the only person I know to put cinnamon—⅛ to ¼ teaspoon per batch—in her chili. Cinnamon's not traditional to chili, but it is used in classic Mexican mole sauces and gives an exotic, hard-to-place sweetness that's awfully nice. Add the cinnamon with the spices.*

CD's Chili Mole: *This superb variation has an indefinable, rich, elusive taste. Use black beans, and add, with the spices, ⅛ teaspoon cinnamon, ⅛ teaspoon anise seeds, and a teeny-tiny pinch of ground cloves. In addition, add ¼ cup raisins or currants with the stock and 1 ounce chopped unsweetened chocolate, 2 tablespoons peanut butter, and 1 tablespoon tahini with the tomatoes.*

Mary Davies's Pressure-Cooked Inverness Chili Mole: *Mary was for many years a fellow innkeeper, at Ten Inverness Way, in Inverness, California, and is now an Episcopal priest. Start by sautéing the onions and peppers in the pressure cooker, then add spices, beans (dry, unsoaked; pintos are Mary's bean of choice), and liquid. Her chiles of choice are pickled jalapeños, not dried anchos. Add a 3-inch cinnamon stick, omit anise seeds but use the same amount (⅛ teaspoon) of grated nutmeg. No peanut butter, no tahini, and—this is pretty interesting—no tomatoes (the beans are cooked, instead, in plenty of water or vegetable stock). Cook the chili under pressure for 20 minutes, release the pressure, open the pot, and stir in 1 ounce chopped semisweet chocolate and 1 bunch fresh cilantro, chopped. Serve asap.*

Curries: How to Get Curried Away

In *From My Heart: Cuisines of Mexico Remembered and Reimagined,* Mexican restaurateur Zarela Martinez recalls her mother preparing a succulent Indian curry for friends, including Suqui, "a lovely, very dramatic woman whose gestures and voice at all times were high theater." When she "outdid herself in constantly telling Mother how absolutely delicious every bite was," writes Martinez, "Father finally looked up and said, 'Suqui, don't get curried away!'"

Well, when you eat a good one, it's *easy* to get curried away. People do it not only in India, but also, as Martinez explains, in Mexico and many other parts of the world.

The word *curry* derives from the Tamil word *kari,* meaning "sauce." But colloquially, it means any spicy dish originating on the Indian subcontinent, where not only Indian languages and dialects, but also dress, foodways, and arts change from state to state. While this multiplicity makes endless bureaucratic complications, it also makes the culture rich and vibrant—nowhere more so than in its food. Curries have a thousand faces, from gentle to fearsome.

You may already know that curry powder is not made from the curry plant but is an extravagant blend of spices—at least 5, up to as many as 25 of them. It is characteristically yellow from turmeric root, with a mild to fiery level of heat from chiles. The holy trinity of a curry blend is *always* turmeric, cumin, and ground coriander seeds (the seeds of the same plant whose fresh leaves are called cilantro). But with this trinity there is a panoply of extra saints and gods and goddesses—ground chile, asafoetida, cinnamon, cloves, fenugreek, black pepper, and countless others—all of whom populate curry heaven.

Curry powder as we know it is not used in India; rather, it's Anglicized shorthand for the elaborate, subtle, complex, and interesting spicings done there. In India, a different spice mixture, a masala particular to the unique ingredients of a specific curry, is mixed up dish by dish. In addition to the dry spices selected, Indian cooks often use "wet" aromatics (ginger, garlic, and fresh chiles, usually pounded to a paste). They then fry both the wet and dry seasonings in a little oil or clarified butter before adding them to the dish, the fried spice mixture being known, in some parts of India, as a *bhagar.* On top of that, quite often a second round of spices and aromatics is fried and added at the last, just when the dish is finished cooking. This last-minute addition is called (depending on where you are in the country) a *taraka.* Add to this the further variables of regional specialties. Bengali food is totally different from Kerala cooking; Gujerati dishes bear little similarity to Goan or Hyderabati. You can see how diverse things might become.

You can also see how, out of very simple, very plain, largely vegetarian ingredients, radically different flavors are achieved from the same basic foodstuffs. Besides spicings (not necessarily hot, either—many curries are quite mild, and some are even sweet), there are also traditional ways of precisely slicing and chopping ingredients for particular dishes for further variations of texture, appearance, and taste. Also, most people in India—except the poorest of the poor—have cooks. Labor is readily available and cheap, but appliances, sometimes even utensils, are rarer. Hence one of the challenges in adapting Indian recipes for American usage is making them less labor-intensive, balancing the elaborate seasonings of individual masalas that make Indian food glorious with the American penchant for I-want-it-quick-I-want-it-simple-and-I-want-it-now.

Curry's varieties compounded as the inhabitants of the Indian subcontinent traveled. When Indians moved slightly to the East—to Singapore, Malayasia, Thailand—their beloved ingredients and methods crossbred with those of the locals, as well as with those of other immigrants. Green curries, red curries, masaman curries developed, as well as Asian stir-fries finished with a little curry spicing. All these are now considered, rightfully, great local dishes in their own right. And when Indians went to Jamaica as indentured servants in the mid-1800s, they influenced West Indian cuisine as well: Curried goat has long been one of Jamaica's two most famous dishes (rice and peas, page 618, being the other), and foods ranging from "patties" (turnovers with a meat-and-potato or vegetable stuffing, page 348) to "rundown" (a stew, which follows on page 206) are curried. East Indians also worked in Africa, and curry flavors find their way here and there into the foods, such as a ground beef and custard casserole called *babbotee*, of that continent as well.

Lastly, while the British might have ruled India, culinarily India ruled the British. Few signs of the bland English dishes remain in vast Mother India, whereas the British took home with them many curry dishes, as well as the sweet pickled conserves known as chutneys. England today has hundreds of Indian restaurants, while India has, to my knowledge, not a single English eatery.

Why is that? Although there may be a physiological component, we get "curried away," I think, for sensual reasons. In their huge variety, curries are so *good*—interesting, complex in the way they start with one taste on the tongue and then burst into another, and another, from peppery to sweet to hot—all in one mouthful. Once you have been initiated into their infinite variety—for curry is not one dish, but a thousand—they become part of your life, and you'll feel periodic, irresistible cravings.

Avial

Avial is a hodge-podge-y, spicy vegetable stew from the South Indian province of Kerala. Always made from whatever's at market that day, Avial, served daily, changes daily—a homey, unfancy dish, served with rice at the two-in-the-afternoon main meal. Small portions of various other curries and pickles (two or three on a normal day, eight to ten at a festival or wedding feast) also accompany it.

But though its ingredients change, the basics are simple: Vegetables, cut in characteristic, precise rectangular strips 2 to 3 inches long and ¼ to ½ inch wide, are cooked in a turmeric-tinged, spicy hot broth, and finished with coconut. Don't seed the green chiles if you want lots of heat. **SERVES 4 TO 6**

VARIATION

Even within South India, avial varies widely from state to state and home to home. Some versions add a cup of yogurt to the coconut mixture; some use lemon juice instead of tamarind. The yogurt is tasty and adds protein, but bear in mind that if reheated, the yogurt will curdle.

- 2 to 3 cups water, preferably spring or filtered
- 1 teaspoon salt
- 2 large potatoes, peeled and cut into strips about the shape and width of your finger
- 2 large sweet potatoes, peeled and cut into strips about the shape and width of your finger
- 1 eggplant, unpeeled, cut into strips about the shape and width of your finger
- 2 cups green beans, stems removed, cut crosswise into ½-inch pieces
- 1½ teaspoons turmeric
- Pinch of cayenne
- Grated meat of 1 fresh coconut, or 1 cup dried shredded unsweetened coconut
- 1 to 3 fresh green chiles, such as serranos, stems removed, halved
- ½ teaspoon dry-roasted cumin seeds
- 2 tablespoons prepared seedless extracted tamarind paste (see page 90)

1. Bring 1 cup of the water and the salt to a boil in a large, nonstick pot. Drop in the potatoes, sweet potatoes, eggplant, and green beans and return to a boil. Lower the heat to a simmer and cook, half-covered, stirring occasionally, until the vegetables are tender but not falling apart, about 25 minutes. Stir in the turmeric and cayenne and check for liquid. There should be some, but not a lot of water; you may need to add an additional ½ cup or so.

2. Combine the fresh coconut with the chiles, cumin seeds, and tamarind paste in a food processor. (If using dry coconut, heat 1 cup of the remaining water, and place it in the food processor along with the chiles, cumin seeds, tamarind paste, and the dried coconut.) Buzz, pulse-chopping and scraping down the sides of the work bowl, to make a fine grind. Do not puree.

3. Remove the vegetable stew from the heat and stir in the coconut-tamarind mixture. Taste and, if necessary, adjust the seasoning with salt. Serve piping hot or lukewarm.

Avid Avial Eaters

In addition to referring to this stew, the word avial *literally means "mixture" or "miscellaneous" in the South Indian tongue of Malayalam. This language is spoken in Kerala, which in turn translates as "Land of the coconut trees," a perfect description of this rural, easy-going state which borders the juncture of the Arabian Sea and the Indian Ocean. As you might expect, like most Kerala dishes, avial contains coconut.*

The word has one more meaning. Put together an outfit that mixes and matches just a little too much, and Keralites will say it's "avial"—and this is not *a compliment.*

Curried Eggplant–Sweet Potato Soup-Stew

Unlike Avial, this is not a from-the-source curry, but an invented one. It's true, though, to the flavors of North Indian cooking. If you've not experienced curry before, this might be a good place to start. I am so fond of the seductive potage of the same name from *Dairy Hollow House Soup & Bread,* and I have gotten so many enthusiastic comments from readers, that I could not resist including this updated main-dish version here. I make it with evaporated skim milk or plain soy milk at home; I used to use half-and-half at the inn's dining room. All are equally delicious, the first two more healthful and the third richer and more voluptuous. **SERVES 4 AS AN ENTREE**

Cooking spray
1 large eggplant, peeled and sliced into ¼-inch rounds
6 cups Golden Stock (page 140)
¼ cup long-grain converted white rice
2 small or 1 large sweet potato, peeled and cut into 1-inch chunks
2 fist-sized potatoes, unpeeled, cut into ½-inch chunks
1 tablespoon butter, or mild vegetable oil, such as corn, canola, or peanut; or half butter and half oil
1 large onion, finely chopped
1 Granny Smith apple, peeled, cored, and finely chopped
1 ripe tomato, chopped
1 tablespoon tamari or shoyu soy sauce, or to taste
2 teaspoons honey, sugar, or Rapidura, or to taste
1 to 1½ tablespoons best-quality curry powder
Pinch of cayenne
1½ cups evaporated skim milk (or, for a special occasion, half-and-half)
Diced red bell pepper
Cilantro leaves

1 Preheat the oven to 400°F.

2 Spray a baking sheet with cooking spray and place the eggplant slices on it in a single layer. Cover tightly with foil and bake until very tender, about 30 minutes. Remove the foil and let cool. Divide the eggplant in half and coarsely chop one half and set aside. Set the eggplant slices aside.

3 Combine 5 cups of the stock with the rice in a large, heavy nonstick soup

pot, or one that has been sprayed with cooking spray, over medium heat. Bring to a boil, then lower the heat to medium-low and simmer, covered, until the rice is tender, about 25 minutes. Strain and reserve the stock, transferring the rice to a food processor.

4 Return the stock to the pot and bring to a boil over medium heat. Drop in the sweet potatoes and potatoes. Return to a boil, then lower the heat to a simmer. Simmer, half-covered, as you proceed with the recipe. Melt the butter in a large nonstick skillet, or one that has been sprayed with cooking spray, over medium heat. Add the onion and sauté until it starts to soften, about 3 minutes. Add the apple and sauté for 1 minute. Stir in the tomato, tamari, honey, curry powder, and cayenne. Increase the heat to medium-high and cook, stirring constantly, until most of the liquid has evaporated. Stir in the remaining cup of stock and cook, stirring frequently, for 1 minute more. Scrape this mixture into the food processor.

5 Add half of the baked eggplant to the processor and buzz to a thick puree. Stir the puree into the simmering potato-stock mixture. Stir in the reserved chopped eggplant. Season with salt and pepper, then stir in the evaporated skim milk. Cook, at a bare simmer, uncovered, for 15 minutes. Serve hot, with red bell pepper and cilantro sprinkled on top.

VARIATIONS

CURRIED EGGPLANT SOUP-STEW WITH PEAS: ***Three minutes before serving, stir in 1 cup thawed frozen peas for a nice green polka-dot effect.***

VEGAN VERSION: ***Omit evaporated milk. Use soy milk or make and use homemade cashew milk. Cashew milk is made by pouring 2 cups boiling water over ½ cup cashews. Let stand for 1 hour; then, buzz smooth in the food processor, straining off and discarding any remaining solids.***

Katherine's Paneer in Tomato Masala

An excellent company-worthy curry. Though it's very hot, the cubes of homemade cheese soothe the fire, so that even those who don't usually care for spicy foods are very, very happy with it. You may think you know this dish from the much-loved Indian-American restaurant version, *mattar paneer* (paneer with peas in a creamy sauce), but this is much lighter and fresher-tasting.

This dish, typically more North than South Indian, was taught to me by Katherine Lindsay, an American who has lived in South India for many years, where she is the librarian at the Shri Atmananda Memorial School. The addition of green beans is not traditional, but is Katherine's own delicious touch.

Paneer is a soft, homemade fresh cheese. Rarely available commercially, it is a full-fat cheese, tender, with some of the "squeak" of cottage cheese. Easily made and firm enough to dice when prepared properly, it is generally dusted with flour and fried before being added to the finished dish. If the idea of making cheese is too much for you, or if you're vegan, just use firm traditional water-packed tofu, cut into cubes, instead. **SERVES 4**

MASALA MIXTURE

1 tablespoon coriander seeds
1 scant teaspoon cumin seeds
1 scant teaspoon poppyseeds
½ teaspoon whole black peppercorns
Seeds of 2 cardamom pods
2 cloves
¾-inch stick cinnamon

AROMATICS

2 cloves garlic, pressed
¼ to ½ teaspoon peeled, finely minced ginger

SAUCE BASE

6 small tomatoes, quartered
¼ cup water, preferably spring or filtered
2 teaspoons sugar
½ teaspoon salt
Pinch of ground red chile or cayenne (substitute paprika for a milder dish)

TO FINISH

Cooking spray
2 teaspoons vegetable oil
1 large onion, diced
4 green chiles, such as serranos, diced (seeds and membranes removed for mildness or left in for extra heat)
½ to ⅔ pound green beans (about a double handful), washed, stemmed, and sliced into ¼-inch pieces
Paneer (available at Indian markets), cut into ½-inch dice, or 1 package firm conventional tofu, preferably reduced fat, drained for 15 minutes and diced

1 Using a mortar and pestle or an electric spice grinder, grind the coriander, cumin, poppyseeds, peppercorns, cardamom seeds, cloves, and cinnamon stick to a fine powder. Set aside.

2 Mash the garlic and ginger to a fine paste, using a mortar and pestle. Set aside.

3 Combine the tomatoes, water, sugar, salt, and ground red chile in a food processor and buzz to a smooth sauce. Set aside.

4 Put the masala, the garlic-ginger paste, and the sauce on a mise en place tray (see page 107), along with the remaining ingredients. Heat the oil in a small wok that has been sprayed with cooking spray, over medium-high heat. Add the onion and stir-fry for 2 to 3 minutes. Add the green chiles and stir-fry for another minute. Add the ginger-garlic paste along with the masala mixture and stir-fry for 30 seconds. Pour in the tomato mixture and add the green beans. Cover and cook for 5 minutes. Add the paneer or tofu cubes, partially cover, and cook for an additional 10 minutes. Serve hot, over rice.

NOTES

The traditional fried paneer for this dish is made by heating ¼ cup oil in the wok before sautéeing the onions. Shake the diced paneer in a little flour, to coat lightly. When the oil is hot but not smoking, add the paneer and fry, turning once, until golden, about 30 seconds per side. Place the paneer on a paper towel to drain. Lower the heat to medium and, using the oil remaining in the wok, complete the dish.

I usually serve this over rice, alongside a dollop of plain yogurt and a salad of cucumber and tomato.

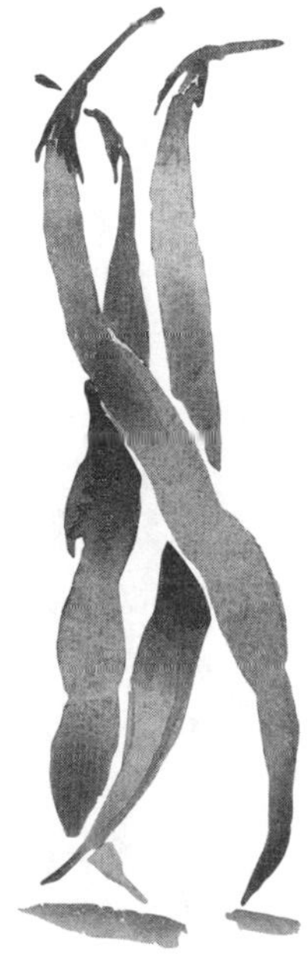

NOTE

Eggplant can be two-faced: tender and mild or bitter. For more on how to up the odds on choosing a nonbitter eggplant, please see page 742. If you goof, nibble a bit of a diced eggplant. If it's at all bitter, place it in a bowl of lightly salted water to cover for 15 minutes, keeping the eggplant submerged by placing a plate on top. Drain well before using.

Thai Green Curry of Eggplant, Chickpeas, and Green Beans

I love the sweet, searingly hot havoc Thai green curries wreak, but I rarely order them in restaurants. This is because most Thai restaurants use a splash of the traditional fish sauce *(nam pla),* a salty flavoring sauce similar to soy sauce but derived from fish. Traditional Thai dishes also use full-fat coconut milk, canned and unsweetened. Reduced-fat coconut milk, also canned, is the real thing and just as good. Remember, however, even reduced-fat coconut milks pack a wallop of saturated fat. Coconut milk, especially this much, should be considered the vegan equivalent of heavy cream—a once-in-a-while indulgence.

A recipe for homemade green curry paste follows. While it is superb, you can also take advantage of the good premade curry pastes, such as my favorites from Taste of Thai.

All Thai curries work with any cooked rice, but plain steamed jasmine rice is traditional and perfect. **SERVES 6 TO 8, WITH RICE OR NOODLES**

The Chili-Curry Connection

Proof of the global culinary net woven by human hungers can be found in Christopher Columbus's search for trade routes east for spices. One juxtaposition is the Anglicized curry powder used in Indian cooking and chili powder, that blend of dried chile, cumin, oregano, salt, pepper, and sometimes dehydrated garlic, ubiquitous in many Tex-Mex–style dishes. According to Ann Wilder, of Vann's Spices, there is "what amounts to a fable, with many variations," that chili powder was invented as a substitute for curry powder, using seasonings available in the New World. Culinary historian Elizabeth Rozin gives definitive explication. "It was a German," she says. "His name was Willie Gebhardt, and he lived in New Braunfels, Texas. His 'chili' powder, invented in the late 1880s, helped popularize the taste we know today as chili. Gebhardt's Chili Powder, the brand he began manufacturing commercially in 1902, is still one of the most popular."

3½ cups reduced-fat unsweetened coconut milk
Cooking spray
¼ cup Green Curry Paste (recipe follows)
1 medium eggplant, cut into 1-inch dice
1 pound green beans, washed and stemmed, cut into 2-inch pieces
1 cup canned or cooked chickpeas, well drained
2 tablespoons tamari or shoyu soy sauce
1 tablespoon dark brown sugar
2 teaspoons grated lime rind
½ cup loosely packed basil leaves
¼ to ½ teaspoon salt (optional)
Diced fresh red bell pepper, or rings of fresh hot red pepper
Cooked jasmine rice (page 467)
Thai Condiment Tray (see below; optional)

1 Heat the coconut milk in a medium-large nonstick saucepan or small Dutch oven or one that has been sprayed with cooking spray over medium-high heat. Bring to a gentle boil and simmer, stirring occasionally, for 5 minutes. Add the curry paste, whisking it into the coconut milk, and continue cooking for 2 more minutes.

2 Add the eggplant, green beans, chickpeas, tamari, brown sugar, and grated lime rind. Bring to a gentle boil and cook, stirring occasionally, for 8 to 10 minutes. When the eggplant is barely tender and the green beans remain crisp-tender, add half of the basil leaves and stir to wilt. Taste and adjust seasonings, adding the optional salt, if necessary, as well as perhaps a little more sugar, curry paste, or tamari.

3 Turn out into a serving bowl and sprinkle with the remaining basil and the red pepper. Serve at once, with plain steamed rice, with the Thai Condiment Tray, placed on the table, if desired.

Thai Condiment Tray

No doubt you've seen this on Thai restaurant tables—a tray full of little dishes of lots of good things with which to amend your food. As my pan-pal Nancie McDermott writes in *Real Thai,* "Doctoring one's plate . . . is serious business for Thai diners, who have strong ideas about how much *kreung broong,* or seasonings, to add. . . . Thais first add two tablespoons of this and a bit of that, tossing everything together until it suits their tastes." Although the fish-based *nam pla* is part of the traditional condiment tray, tamari or shoyu soy sauce can easily be substituted.

So, just put out a tray with as many of the following as you can manage, each in its own little dish:

- Tamari or shoyu soy sauce
- Coarse-grained sugar, such as turbinado
- Finely chopped roaste peanuts
- Wedges of fresh lime
- Dry red chiles
- Chile vinegar sauce or pickled chiles
- Thai Crystal (page 923)
- Coarsely chopped cilantro leaves

NOTE

Cilantro (also known as coriander or Chinese parsley) is a Mediterranean native. You'll find it throughout the near and far East, in Thai and Indian cooking, and in the Americas, in all manner of Southwestern, Mexican, and Central American cuisines. For all the popularity this would seem to indicate, cilantro is—at least to American tastes—a real love-it-or-hate-it flavor. Some salivate with pleasure and pile large leafy hills of it onto any vaguely compatible dishes. Others deplore its flavor and now near-ubiquity. Julia Child is said to be no cilantro fan. And one Arkansas writer and social activist, the late Diane Blair, so deplored its burgeoning popularity that she once wrote a letter to the editor at the Arkansas Times, begging readers to cease and desist cilantro-ing dishes brought to communal meals like parties or pot lucks.

Green Curry Paste

Although you can buy ready-made green curry pastes that are quite good and turn the creation of Thai curry into a matter of a minutes, fresh from scratch is not only much better but also fun to do once in a while. This one is adapted from Nancie McDermott, but uses fermented black bean paste, available at Asian markets or in the Asian food section of some supermarkets, instead of shrimp paste. The recipe makes enough for 4 full batches of the Thai green curry; stirring in a tablespoon or two takes any stir-fry from ordinary to tingling. I love having green curry paste on hand; however, once ground, the flavors do begin to erode. The best way I've found to keep the flavor sacrosanct is to scrape the mixture, in ¼-cup portions, into small zippered freezer bags, place these in a large-sized zippered bag, and then in a second one, and freeze for 3 to 4 months. The reason for all this double-triple bagging is to ensure your frozen raspberries won't taste startlingly of coriander and garlic.

Lemon grass, essential to this recipe, is available at Asian markets and is easily grown in the home garden. It even does well throughout the winter in a sunny window. It's a sturdy, tough herb that really does look like a grass, not herby at all, with a delicious lemony-floral taste and bouquet. It makes a soothing tea, also. If you can't find fresh, skip the recipe: Dried lemon grass is haylike, entirely lacking the perfume of the fresh. **MAKES ABOUT 2 CUPS**

2 tablespoons coriander seeds
2 teaspoons cumin seeds
10 whole black peppercorns
6 stalks fresh lemon grass, including white bulbous base, well washed
1 cup coarsely chopped fresh cilantro, including washed roots and stems if possible
1 cup coarsely chopped serrano or jalapeño chiles
⅓ cup coarsely chopped garlic
2 tablespoons peeled, finely chopped ginger
2 teaspoons finely grated lime rind
2 teaspoons fermented black beans, or fermented black bean and garlic sauce
2 teaspoons salt
¼ red onion, coarsely chopped

1 Dry-roast the coriander and cumin seeds in a small, heavy skillet over medium heat until browned and fragrant, 3 to 5 minutes, shaking the skillet often or stirring to prevent burning. Place the roasted spices in a mortar along with the peppercorns and, using the pestle, crush to a fine powder. Set aside.

2 Cut away the grassy tops of the lemon grass stalks as well as any tough root section, leaving a 3-inch-long piece with a

clean, smooth, flat base at the root end. Remove and discard the tough outer leaves. Thinly slice the lemon grass crosswise.

3 Place the cilantro, chiles, garlic, ginger, lime rind, beans, salt, and onion in a food processor along with the crushed spices and lemon grass. Buzz, pausing several times to scrape down the sides of the processor. You may need to add just a little water to achieve the requisite consistency, which is thick enough to be mounded in a spoon with all of the ingredients chopped to a barely textured puree.

Mild Tempeh Curry with Cauliflower, Corn, and Spinach

A gentle, satisfying, slightly sweet yellow curry that is very gentle indeed if you seed the chiles. It's not traditional, but takes flavor notes from both Indian and Thai curries pleasingly. If you're new to curry-world, this is an excellent introduction. The sauce is rather thin; if you'd like it a bit thicker, simply draw off a bit of the liquid, dissolve a teaspoon or two of cornstarch in it, and whisk it back into the hot, finished curry. **SERVES 6 TO 8**

Cooking spray
1 package (6 ounces) smoked tempeh (such as Lightlife Smoky Tempeh Strips)
1½ teaspoons mild vegetable oil
1 onion, chopped
6 cloves garlic, minced
1 to 2 serrano chiles, diced (seeds and membranes removed for mildness or left in for extra heat)
2 teaspoons peeled, minced ginger
1½ teaspoons to 1 tablespoon curry powder
Dash of ground cloves
Pinch of cinnamon
2 large tomatoes, chopped
1 head cauliflower, pulled into large florets
½ teaspoon salt
1¾ cups vegetable stock (see page 139)
⅓ cup raisins or currants
Kernels cut from 2 ears corn (or 1 cup frozen corn kernels)
1 package (10 ounces) prewashed fresh spinach, coarsely chopped
½ cup reduced-fat unsweetened coconut milk
1 to 2 tablespoons honey, brown sugar, or Rapidura
Minced cilantro and mint

1 Heat a nonstick skillet, or one that has been sprayed with cooking spray, over

VARIATION

Instead of the commercially made smoked tempeh, substitute 6 to 8 ounces of any marinated and baked tempeh (see Basic Oven-Baked Marinated Tempeh, page 641).

medium heat until extremely hot but not smoking. Add the tempeh strips and brown lightly, about 3 minutes on each side. Remove the tempeh from the skillet and allow to cool. Dice the tempeh into 1¾-inch-long pieces. Set aside.

2 If necessary, re-spray the skillet, then add the oil. Place over medium heat, and when the oil is hot, add the onion. Sauté until the onion starts to soften, about 4 minutes. Add the garlic, serranos, and ginger and sauté for 2 minutes. Add the curry powder, cloves, and cinnamon and cook, stirring, for 1 minute more.

3 Add the tomatoes and cauliflower. Stir well to coat with the spices. Add the salt and cover. Steam for 3 minutes. Lift the cover and add the vegetable stock and raisins or currants. Re-cover, lower the heat slightly, and simmer for 20 minutes.

4 Stir in the corn, spinach, coconut milk, and honey. Cook, covered, until the spinach wilts, about 3 minutes. Add the tempeh and stir to combine. Serve hot, over rice, garnished with a generous sprinkle of minced cilantro and mint.

Thai-Style Tomato-Tofu Soup-Stew

Hot, luscious, delectable. Best in the summer with heavy, red-ripe tomatoes but works quite well with straight-out-of-the-can tomatoes on cold winter days. If you imagine the unctuous velvety soothe of a good homemade tomato soup with the kick of Thai spices you'll have something of the idea. The infused stock can be made in advance. For an extra measure of flavor, when using fresh tomatoes, char them (on a grill or in a hot skillet) until portions of the skin begin to blacken and peel back. Let cool and remove the skin.

Serve over any simply cooked rice, such as Thai jasmine rice. **SERVES 4, WITH RICE**

INFUSED STOCK

5 cups Golden Stock (page 140), or any flavorful vegetable stock
1 tablespoon tamari or shoyu soy sauce
2 teaspoons coriander seeds
4 stalks fresh lemon grass, bruised and cut into 1½-inch pieces
Two ¼-inch-thick slices ginger

SOUP-STEW

1 teaspoon mild vegetable oil, such as corn, canola, or peanut
Cooking spray
½ red onion, minced
1 bunch scallions, white and 2 inches of green, chopped
5 to 7 cloves garlic, minced
2 to 4 serrano chiles (seeds and membranes removed for mildness or left in for extra heat)
1½ teaspoons peeled finely minced ginger
4 to 6 fresh, dead-ripe tomatoes, charred if desired, peeled, and diced, to equal 3 cups diced; or one 28-ounce can diced tomatoes with their juice
1 can (14 ounces) reduced-fat unsweetened coconut milk
2 tablespoons tamari or shoyu soy sauce
2 tablespoons cornstarch
1 tablespoon Rapidura or brown sugar
¼ head napa cabbage, cut into thin ribbons
1 package (8 ounces) savory baked tofu, sliced into ¼-inch-wide strips
Salt and freshly ground black pepper to taste
Cooked rice, preferably Thai jasmine rice (page 467)
Chopped cilantro and/or Thai basil
Sriracha or other hot sauce

1 Combine the stock, tamari, coriander seeds, lemon grass, and slices of ginger in a medium pot over medium-high heat and bring to a boil. Lower the heat and simmer, half-covered, for 40 minutes. Remove from the heat and let infuse for 1 hour. If you don't have the time, just proceed with the recipe.

2 Heat the oil in a large nonstick soup pot, or one that has been sprayed with cooking spray, over medium-high heat. Add the onion and sear until brown at the edges, 4 to 5 minutes. Lower the heat to medium and add the scallions. Sauté until the scallions wilt, about 3 minutes. Slightly lower the heat and add the garlic, serranos, and minced ginger. Sauté for another 3 minutes.

3 Add the tomatoes and bring to a boil. Pour the Thai-infused stock through a strainer, directly into the tomato mixture. Lower the heat to a simmer and stir in the coconut milk. Simmer as you do the next steps.

4 Combine the tamari, cornstarch, and Rapidura in a small dish or measuring cup, smushing the cornstarch in with your fingertips.

5 Drop the cabbage into the simmering soup-stew. Cook until wilted, but still a little crisp, 2 to 3 minutes. Stir in the tofu. Ladle out a little of the hot liquid and whisk it into the cornstarch mixture. When well blended, dump the mixture into the stew, stirring to beat the band. The soup-stew should immediately thicken and get a glossy look. Taste for seasoning and, if necessary, add salt and pepper to taste. Remove from the heat and serve at once, in deep bowls, over a big spoonful of rice, garnished with cilantro and/or Thai basil. Pass the sriracha at the table.

NOTE

According to my Jamaican-American culinary pan pal, San Antonio chef Jay McCarthy, a rundown is a dish that's been reduced by slow cooking. "The term comes from the Jamaican description of the process," write Jay and his collaborator, Robb Walsh, in Traveling Jamaica with Knife, Fork, and Spoon. *"You cook it till it 'run-down.'" In their book, Jay and Robb describe a vegetarian rundown served at Peppers Garden-of-Eating, "a delightful open-air . . . 'Rasta'raunt above the beach at Fairy Hill," run by a Rastafarian named Sister Fire. This recipe—Robb and Jay's written interpretation of Sister Fire's—has taken a few turns in my hands. Jay and Robb call for half a Scotch bonnet chile, searingly hot, squatty little round peppers: If you can find them, or their kin, the habanero, go for it—but any fresh hot chile will do.*

West Indian Rundown

This last curry is from Jamaica. The fat content has been reduced considerably but the results are outrageously good. The seitan is optional; it certainly makes the rundown higher in protein and more "meaty," but it's good without, too. Or substitute an equivalent amount of diced savory baked tofu. Allspice and fresh thyme, characteristic Jamaican seasonings, set this curry apart from all others. **SERVES 4 TO 6**

2 teaspoons mild vegetable oil, such as corn, canola, or peanut
Cooking spray
1 onion, cut vertically into crescents
3 cloves garlic, chopped
½ bunch scallions, roots trimmed, white and 2 inches of green chopped into ½-inch pieces
1½ teaspoons curry powder
1 can (14 ounces) reduced-fat unsweetened coconut milk
2 cups vegetable stock (see page 139), plus additional as needed (or the "additional" can be water, preferably spring or filtered)
4 to 6 ounces traditional-style dark seitan, rinsed and diced into ½-inch cubes (optional)
3 carrots, scrubbed, and sliced into ½-inch rounds
1 large potato, skin on, cut into slices about ¼ inch thick
½ butternut or acorn squash, peeled, seeded, and chopped into 1½-inch pieces
5 allspice berries
2 large sprigs thyme
1 to 2 fresh green or red chiles, chopped
½ juicy, red-ripe fresh tomato, diced
Cooked rice or any grain

1. Heat the oil in a nonstick soup pot, or one that has been sprayed with cooking spray, over medium heat. Add the onion and sauté until it starts to soften, about 3 minutes. Add the garlic, scallions, and curry powder and sauté for another 1 to 2 minutes.

2. Add the coconut milk and vegetable stock. Raise the heat and bring to a boil. Immediately lower the heat to a simmer. Drop in the seitan, carrots, potato, butternut or acorn squash, allspice, and thyme. Half-cover and simmer, stirring occasionally, until the vegetables are tender, 20 to 25 minutes, adding water or stock as needed to prevent burning and to maintain a nice, thick, stewlike consistency.

3. Add the chiles and tomato and simmer for an additional 10 minutes. Before serving, either remove the whole allspice berries or warn your guests that they're there. Serve hot, over cooked rice or any cooked grain.

Other Spicy Stews

Here are five more spicy stews. Neither chilies nor curries, from mild to major in heat, and distinctly seasoned.

The first is the infamous, wondrous, nothing-else-even-comes-close Gumbo Zeb, from Louisiana, love-child of Spanish, French, African, and Native American cooking, probably the most popular soup back in Dairy Hollow House days. It never fails to seduce.

The second is posole-bean soup-stew, which has many of the Southwestern seasonings we all know and love, combined with vegetables and hominy.

The third, from Africa, is palaver stew, whose hot, rich sauce is traditionally made with peanut butter.

The fourth, Hainanese Tofu and Seitan in Ginger Brown-Bean Sauce, hails from the South China seas, where a similar preparation is used for chicken.

And the fifth is the snappy Steven's Spicy Black Bean Soysage Stew, which brings us back to the New World. It was invented on the spot when I was short on time and long on affection for a friend I was visiting. He'd had one of those days, in a big way, and went off to a one-hour meeting. Inside of that hour I had the satisfaction of shopping and fixing the stew plus salad and garlic bread, so he could walk into a fragrant kitchen, one inhalation of which said, "There, there, it will be all right."

Gumbo Zeb

In gumbo making, assembling your readied ingredients beforehand is a must. Measure out your spices, wash and chop your vegetables and greens, lay out the ingredients for each mixture on its own tray before you begin any actual recipe directions. There'll be a lot going on, you'll have your hands full; you cannot possibly assemble the ingredients as you go. This recipe will leave you with a fantastic base for soups and stews. When finished, dilute it with any savory liquid or stock to taste. Freeze the remainder for up to four months. **MAKES 2 TO 3 QUARTS**

VARIATION

If in the ingredients list I miss any greens you have frozen from last year's garden, or if you chance to find some green exotics at the local supermarket, by all means add them. Also, if the only fresh green you can find is cabbage, go ahead and drop 10-ounce boxes of frozen greens, as many of the varieties mentioned as you can find, into the boiling stock mixture.

ROUX

½ cup mild vegetable oil, such as corn, canola, or peanut
½ cup unbleached all-purpose flour

VEGETABLE SAUTÉ

4 tablespoons (¼ cup) butter
1 large onion, chopped
1 green bell pepper, stemmed, seeded, and chopped
½ bunch celery with leaves, chopped
½ large bunch (4 to 5 large) scallions, chopped

SEASONING PUREE

4 cloves garlic, peeled
2 tablespoons Pickapeppa sauce
2 tablespoons tomato paste
2½ teaspoons Tabasco
1 teaspoon dried basil
1 teaspoon dried oregano
1 teaspoon dried thyme
½ teaspoon paprika
¼ teaspoon cayenne
¼ teaspoon ground allspice
¼ teaspoon ground cloves
3 to 4 good grinds of fresh black pepper
1 can (8 ounces) whole tomatoes, drained, coarsely chopped, the juice and tomatoes reserved separately
½ bunch Italian parsley, leaves and stems, rinsed and coarsely chopped

STOCK AND GREENS

Cooking spray
3 cups any well-flavored vegetable stock (see page 139)
One cup tomato juice or V8 vegetable juice
½ teaspoon salt
2 bay leaves
3 bunches assorted greens, (choose from mustard greens, spinach, turnip greens, beet tops, collard greens, kale, and swiss chard) very well washed and cut into thin ribbons

TO SERVE

Hot cooked white rice; any cooked, sliced, or crumbled soysage

1 Make the roux with the oil and flour: Pour the oil into a large skillet or pot. Turn the heat to medium and immediately whisk in the flour. Stir frequently as the roux changes color from white to yellow to fairly brown. While the roux cooks, proceed with the other steps, but be sure to keep an eye on it, stirring very frequently. Warning—this is a long, slow process requiring attention.

2 Prepare the vegetable sauté: In a heavy cast-iron skillet, melt the butter over medium heat. Add the onion and sauté until softened, 5 to 6 minutes. Add the bell pepper and celery; lower the heat slightly and continue sautéing for another 10 minutes. (Don't forget that roux—keep stirring it while the vegetables sauté.) Add the scallions and sauté until limp, about 5 minutes more.

3 Meanwhile, between the sautéing and the roux-stirring, you will have time to prepare the seasoning purée (trust me, you will). Place all the ingredients for the seasoning purée except the tomatoes and parsley in a food processor. (Pause to stir both roux and vegetable sauté.) Buzz the purée ingredients until the garlic is finely chopped.

4 Check the roux again (has it started to brown?), then add the tomatoes and

parsley to the food processor. Chop coarsely.

5 Pause to take note of where you are, and go stir the roux and vegetable sauté. (By now you have three mixtures: the roux, the sautéed vegetables, and the spicy, chunky, paste in the food processor.) So far, so good. When the vegetables have softened, remove from the heat and set them aside. Keep working on the roux until it has reached a nice toasty brown. It may be ready now, or it may take a little longer.

6 Now prepare the stock and greens into which the other three mixtures will eventually go. Spray a large soup pot with cooking spray. In it, bring to a boil the stock and 1 cup of the tomato juice. Add the salt and bay leaves. Drop in the fresh greens. Bring back to a boil, then turn down the heat to medium-low and simmer, covered, for about 30 minutes.

7 Stir the roux. By now it should be dark caramel brown, but if it isn't, continue to cook it, stirring. When the roux has browned, remove it from the heat and let it cool for a few minutes. Drain off any excess oil that has separated out, but be sure to leave every bit of the browned flour. Vigorously whisk in the 1 cup tomato juice. It will be smooth and thick, a pale orange paste.

8 When the greens have finished their 30-minute simmer, remove them from the heat. To the stock pot, add the roux mixture, the vegetable sauté, and the seasoning puree. Give a taste and adjust the seasoning, set the pot back on the stove, and let simmer over the lowest possible heat, covered, for 15 minutes. Stir often.

9 Remove from the heat and let cool to room temperature. That's it—you've got your concentrated gumbo base, enough, when made into soup, to feed 5 to 10 hearty eaters. It freezes well, so for smaller batches of Gumbo Zeb, use part now, and freeze the rest in small portions.

10 Completing the Gumbo Zeb: Now dilute the base with any savory liquid or stock to taste. Equal parts base and stock make a delicious soup, but if you like a particularly fragrant, spicy gumbo, you might use 60 percent base to 40 percent savory liquid. Add any soysage, sautéed, sliced, and served in the bowl with a mound of cooked rice.

Toux Doux a Roux

What turns good soup into a glorious gumbo? Simple: roux. There's nothing much to roux (pronounced like the last syllable of "kangaroo") on the face of it—mere flour and oil, cooked and stirred together until brown. Roux serves to thicken and flavor the gumbo.

1. *Into a skillet, pour 1 part mild oil—not olive oil. Turn the heat to medium and whisk in 1 equivalent part unbleached all-purpose flour. Note the color—a pale parchment-cream with a barely yellow tinge.*
2. *As the roux colors, keep whisking. It will become a light brown first, then will darken. My own preferred roux coloration is deep brown, just a shade or so past caramel. Preparing your roux ought to take at least 45 minutes; 1¼ hours is preferable. It cannot be hurried.*

A roux can be made ahead of time and refrigerated. I have never kept a browned roux longer than two or three days before using it, but since there's nothing in it that would spoil, I imagine it would keep well for a couple of weeks. But why would you want to wait that long for gumbo?

If you doux the roux ahead of time, reheat it gently before using.

Posole-Bean Soup-Stew with New World Vegetables

This is more or less a thicker, less tomato-y version of the delicious *sopa* made by our own Clary Perez at Center Street South of the Border, here in Eureka Springs. She serves it in the colder months, only on Saturdays and Sundays, so this is how we fake it when we get a yen at other times. I add a few more vegetables and beans to make it more of a main dish. This makes an enormous batch; just the thing to bring to a potluck, or prepare ahead when you know you need something easy, and your family (or weekend guests, perhaps) will be in need of something sustaining in the coming days. **SERVES 8 TO 10, WITH TORTILLAS**

1 tablespoon olive oil
Cooking spray
1 large onion, diced
2 serrano chiles, finely diced (seeds and membranes removed for mildness or left in for exra heat)
2 ribs celery, diced
4 cups vegetable stock, homemade (see page 139) or commercial
1 can (28 ounces) diced tomatoes in juice
½ pound green beans, stemmed and cut into 1-inch lengths
2 carrots, scrubbed, sliced into ¼-inch rounds
2 large potatoes, unpeeled, cut into ¾-inch dice
1 butternut squash, peeled, cut into ¾-inch dice
1 can (16 ounces) hominy, rinsed and drained
1 zucchini, quartered lengthwise and sliced into ½-inch pieces
1¼ cup cooked pinto beans or black-eyed peas, or one 15-ounce can, well drained
1 teaspoon salt
1 teaspoon sugar, honey, or Rapidura
¼ teaspoon ground allspice
Freshly ground black pepper to taste
Baked or fried corn chips (optional)
Grated Cheddar cheese, dairy or soy (optional)

1 Heat the oil in a nonstick Dutch oven, or one that has been sprayed with cooking spray, over medium heat. Add the onion and sauté until softened and translucent, about 5 minutes. Add the chiles and celery and sauté for another minute.

2 Pour the stock over the sauté, along with the juice from the canned tomatoes, reserving the tomatoes. Bring the mixture to a boil. Add the green beans, carrots, potatoes, and butternut squash. Cover and

bring to a simmer. Lower the heat and simmer until the vegetables are very tender, 30 minutes.

3 Uncover and add the hominy, zucchini, pinto beans, salt, sugar, allspice, and black pepper. Simmer for another 10 minutes, and taste for seasonings.

4 Serve very hot, with the optional corn chips pointing up out of the soup like sharks' fins and a good sprinkle of Cheddar melting on top, if using. Steamed or grilled tortillas make the perfect accompaniment.

Groundnut and Greens Palaver with Black-Eyes

My good old *Cookbook of the United Nations,* published in 1970, provided some of my earliest awakenings to international cooking. A remarkable number of those recipes from African countries contain peanuts or peanut butter: in sauces and stews, from Ghana, Gambia, the Ivory Coast. One stew—spicy, with spinach, beans, and meat or chicken, was called "palaver," the kind of word one would find in an Evelyn Waugh novel. How appropriate, I thought, understanding it to mean casual conversation, sit-around storytelling—just what you'd be likely to do over a good pot of stew. I wasn't entirely wrong. According to the *Dictionary of Word Origins,* by John Ayto, it "originated as a piece of naval slang picked up by English sailors in Africa. There they came across Portuguese traders negotiating with the local inhabitants, a process known in Portuguese as *palavra,* 'speech' (a descendent of Latin *parabola,* source of English *parable).* They took the Portuguese word over as *palaver,* applying it first to 'negotiations' and then by extension to 'idle chatter.'"

But consider this, from *The African-American Kitchen: Cooking from Our Heritage,* by Angela Shelf Medearis: "My first experience with African food was when a friend

VARIATIONS

For a more-true-to-the-original "MEATY" PALAVER, add 8 ounces commercially made, traditionally seasoned seitan, rinsed and cut into 1-inch squares, along with the black-eyed peas.

A KENYAN KUNDE PALAVER: ***I learned this from*** **The World in Your Kitchen,** ***by Troth Wells. Just sauté the onion until soft, then add 6 chopped fresh tomatoes, 2 cups partially mashed cooked black-eyed peas, and the peanut butter dissolved in hot water. Season to taste with salt and freshly ground pepper. Heat through; that's it.***

NOTE

"ORATURE"

Kenyan novelist Ngudi wa Thiong'o came up with the word "orature" to describe the complex literature of African storytelling, which is created in spoken, rather than written, language. Griots—revered, trained storytellers—enthrall, entertain, and educate their audiences throughout the continent to this day. The audience is part of a griot's performance, which is part memorized and part invented, styled for the spot, with listeners responding in the local language equivalents of "Amen!" or "Tell it!" or "Go on, don't stop." More than what we think of as storytelling, orature combines elements of music, dance, and theater. It is a still living, collective part of life throughout a continent whose traditions remain primarily oral to this day.

from Ghana lived with my family. Having graciously offered to prepare a traditional African dinner, she served us a tomato-based stew called palaver (also known as palava in different regions) which contained small portions of beef and spinach served over rice. It had a wonderful aroma, and we couldn't wait to try it. She warned us it was hot; we thought it would be like the Mexican dishes we're accustomed to from living in Texas, and assured her we were used to eating spicy foods. Several glasses of cold water later, we realized we were wrong! It was one of the hottest dishes any of us had ever attempted to eat. I found out later that the word *palaver,* which originated in West Africa, means 'trouble.' "

So, is palaver conversation or trouble? Or, to the Africans, did conversation with English or Portuguese automatically mean trouble? Perhaps, here in melting-pot America, we'll mix meanings into this rich, hot stew. It melds traditional African versions, ingredients the slaves brought over, and my own ways of making initially omnivorous dishes meatless. The result is a stew to be reckoned with . . . and have conversation over. Even if we come to the table hungry and weighted with our troubles, let us—through discourse, and good spicy nourishment—leave satisfied, burdens lifted. Now *that's* palaver. **SERVES 6 TO 8**

6 cups water, preferably spring or filtered
1 teaspoon mild vegetable oil, such as corn, canola, or peanut
Cooking spray
1 large onion, chopped
1 serrano chile, diced (seeds and membranes removed for mildness or left in for extra heat)
1 teaspoon curry powder
¼ to 1 teaspoon cayenne
8 to 10 gratings of fresh nutmeg
1 can (10 ounces) tomatoes and green chiles
1 large sweet potato, peeled and cut into 1-inch dice
1 cup smooth peanut butter (natural, unhydrogenated, no sugar added)
2 tablespoons tomato paste
About 2 tablespoons tamari or shoyu soy sauce, plus more to taste
1 pound spinach, very well washed, chopped (or one 10-ounce package prewashed spinach)
½ pound mustard greens, well washed, chopped
½ cup sliced fresh okra
3 cups cooked black-eyed peas
Salt and freshly ground black pepper
Minced Italian parsley (optional)

1 Put the water on to boil.

2 Heat the vegetable oil in a large nonstick soup pot, or one that has been sprayed with cooking spray, over medium heat. Add the onion and sauté until starting to soften, about 4 minutes. Add the serrano, curry powder, cayenne, and nutmeg and sauté for another minute, stirring constantly. Add 4 cups of the boiling water, along with the canned tomatoes with green chile and the sweet potato. Bring to a boil, then lower the heat to a simmer. Simmer, half-covered, for 15 minutes.

3 Place the peanut butter in a large, heatproof bowl. Add the remaining boiling water, whisking constantly to blend. When blended, whisk in the tomato paste. Set aside.

4 Add the 2 tablespoons of tamari, spinach, mustard greens, and okra to the simmering palaver. Cover and cook for 10 minutes.

5 Lift the lid and, stirring carefully, add the peanut butter mixture. Keep stirring; it will take a few minutes to smooth out. When smooth, add the black-eyed peas and cook for a few minutes to heat through. Season with salt and pepper to taste, and serve immediately, with or over rice or other grains. If desired, garnish with minced parsley. It can also be made a day or two ahead of time and reheated (gently, stirring often, so that the peanut butter doesn't scorch).

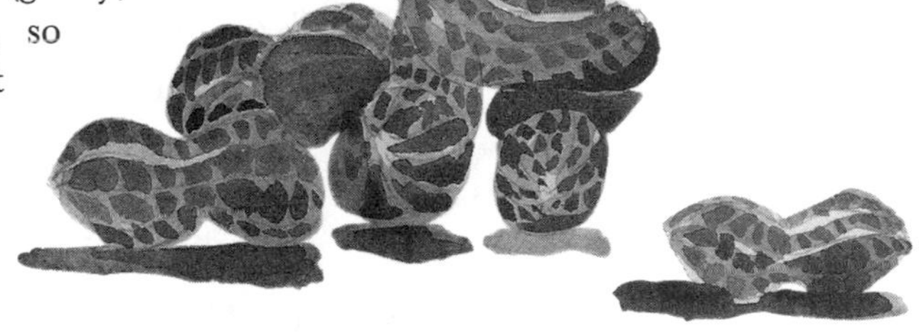

African Gifts to American Tables

Peanuts are something of an anomaly. Biologically, they are a legume (a bean) not a nut, yet their fat and flavor content is much more nut- than beanlike. And while most beans grow in pods, from branches, peanuts grow underground (hence "groundnuts"), each plant sending out a network of roots and nuts, in their characteristic soft, figure-8–shaped, nobbly brown shells.

Peanut butter is thought of as an almost archetypally American food. I have friends who bring jars of peanut butter with them when they travel abroad, either as personal comfort food or as a house gift to foreign friends, who view it as an exotic imported luxury. Yet the peanut's origins are African, and it is in Africa that many of its most interesting and delicious uses are found.

The story of this not-so-American American food is one of survival. Even enslaved, unwilling, and coerced, the bound-over Africans did what all American immigrants did—contributed, changed, and influenced that stew that is the American melting pot, bringing with them their traditional foodstuffs and cooking methods, where they mingled with the other ingredients and traditions. Ethiopian slaves brought okra. The black-eyed pea, though native to Asia, was brought to America by way of Africa and African slaves; the sesame seed, and its oil, dating back to Assyrian times, were also brought over by the slaves. Lastly, slaves brought the peanut . . . a gift that was to become even more American than apple pie.

Hainanese Tofu and Seitan in Ginger Brown-Bean Sauce

This is a vegetarian redo of a chicken stew that hails from Hainan Island, in the Gulf of Tonkin, off China's southern coast. It's traditionally served over rice cooked in the super-rich stock left over from cooking the chicken. Accompanied by additional chicken stock and a lively, aromatic seasoning sauce built off fermented brown bean sauce (*dao jiow,* available at Asian markets), it is, to me, the Southeast Asian equivalent of arroz con pollo, the Spanish rice-and-chicken dish.

The starting point for this recipe is in Nancie McDermott's *Real Thai.* I came across it long after I'd quit eating meat, fish, or chicken, and I wondered: Could a dish in which chicken was so essential be vegetarianized? Yes! My adaptation uses both tofu and seitan, is improbably rich and pleasing, and delights all who've tasted it. Its only drawback is that it is very brown—but the monochromatic palette is overcome with a scattering of brightly colored garnishes.

As with the chicken original, the stock is all-important. Make sure you use a flavorful one. Serve with rice, of course, and a slightly sweet Asian fusion salad, such as Pineapple-Jícama Salad with Purple Cabbage and Baby Spinach (page 95), and Cilantro Vinaigrette (page 94). Serve sorbet for dessert, and you've had a very nice meal indeed.

Please note that several ingredients are used twice. You'll save yourself aggravation if you prepare them at the same time. Sliced ginger goes into the stock, minced ginger into the condiment sauce; finely chopped garlic into the condiment sauce, coarsely chopped into the rice. **SERVES 6**

STOCK

3 quarts Golden Stock (page 140), Dark Stock (page 140), or any brown flavorful vegetable stock, commercial or homemade
Stems from ½ pound shiitake mushrooms, caps reserved for stew
4 stalks lemon grass, bruised and cut into 1½-inch pieces
Two ¼-inch-thick slices ginger
2 tablespoons tamari or shoyu soy sauce
1 tablespoon coriander seeds
10 stems cilantro, preferably with washed roots still attached

STEW

8 ounces firm conventional tofu, preferably reduced fat, drained, rinsed, and cut into ½-inch chunks
8 ounces commercially made "traditional-style" seitan, well drained and rinsed, cut into ½-inch chunks
Reserved caps from ½ pound shiitake mushrooms, halved or quartered if larger than 1¼ inches

CONDIMENT SAUCE

2 to 3 serrano chiles, finely minced (seeds and membranes removed for mildness or left in for extra heat)
⅓ cup fermented brown bean sauce (dao jiow), available from Asian markets
3 tablespoons white vinegar
1½ tablespoons tamari or shoyu soy sauce
1½ tablespoons peeled, finely minced ginger
1 tablespoon sugar or Rapidura
1½ teaspoons finely chopped garlic

RICE

3 cups Thai jasmine rice
1 tablespoon coarsely chopped garlic
3 cups reserved vegetable stock

GARNISH

Remaining reserved vegetable stock
5 to 6 scallions, roots removed, white part and 3 inches of green thinly sliced
2 to 3 small cucumbers, peeled and sliced crosswise on the diagonal into ⅛-inch pieces
1 red bell pepper, finely diced
½ cup chopped cilantro

1 Combine the stock, mushroom stems, lemon grass, sliced ginger, 2 tablespoons tamari, and coriander seeds in a medium pot over high heat. Bring to a boil, then lower the heat to a simmer and cook, half-covered, for 20 minutes. Add the cilantro stems and simmer for another 20 minutes. Remove from the heat and infuse for another hour or so, if you've got the time. Strain.

2 Return the strained stock to medium-high heat and bring to a boil. Immediately lower the heat to a simmer. Add the tofu, seitan, and shiitake caps and poach for 10 minutes. Using a slotted spoon, lift the tofu, seitan, and mushrooms from the stock. Set aside on a mise en place tray. Reserve the stock.

3 Make the condiment sauce by combining the chiles, brown bean sauce, vinegar, tamari, ginger, sugar, and garlic in a small bowl. Set aside on the mise en place tray, along with the ingredients for the rice and garnish.

4 Place the rice in a colander and rinse several times in cold water until the water runs clear. Place the rice in a pot with a tight-fitting lid. Add the garlic and 3 cups of the reserved stock. Place over high heat and bring to a hard boil, stirring occasionally.

NOTE

FRESH GINGER LEMONADE

If you are as fond of the flavors of ginger and lemon as I am, then Fresh Ginger Lemonade will thrill you. Squeezing all those lemons is a bit of a hassle, but I bet you'll wind up making this half a dozen times each summer anyway—nothing else is so refreshing in hot weather. In a saucepan, combine 1½ cups water, preferably spring or filtered, 1½ cups sugar, and about ¼ cup fresh, coarsely chopped ginger. Bring this to a boil, stir until sugar dissolves, and let steep, covered but unrefrigerated, overnight. Next day, scoop out the sugar-poached ginger with a little syrup and buzz it into a fine puree in a food processor or blender. Transfer puree and remaining syrup to a 2½-quart pitcher. Add the freshly squeezed juice of 10 to 12 lemons, for a total of about 1¾ cups juice. Add 3 cups additional water, stir well, and fill the pitcher and serving glasses with ice, to dilute. Serves 4 to 6.

Boil until the surface of the rice is barely exposed, 3 to 5 minutes. Stir the rice once more, turn the heat down as low as it can go, cover, and cook for 25 minutes. Turn off the heat and let the rice stand undisturbed for 15 minutes. Lift the lid and stir to fluff the grains and separate them just a bit (it will be sticky, though, and intentionally so; that's the deal with properly cooked Asian-style rices).

5 Heat the remaining reserved stock. Place a mound of rice in each serving bowl. Top with the poached tofu, seitan, and mushrooms. Scatter the scallions, cucumbers, red pepper, and cilantro on top. Ladle some hot stock around the rice (so the rice is an island sticking up out of the stock). Pass the condiment sauce at the table, for diners to mix in as desired.

Steven's Spicy Black Bean Soysage Stew

Sparked with commercial canned tomatoes and green chiles, brightened with orange sweet potato, enriched with canned black beans, this tastes and smells as if had been cooking all day. Yet, inside of 30 minutes, it can warm a house with its gentle aromas. It has a very carnivorous feel to it, thanks to the soysage—I use Lightlife's Gimme Lean Sausage-Style, which is primarily made of soy and wheat proteins and seasonings. You could substitute any cooked, browned vegetarian sausage patties or used sautéed crumbled Soyrizo, a highly seasoned soysage based on the traditional flavors of the Mexican and Spanish pork sausage known as chorizo. All these new-generation soyfoods can be found in the refrigerated or frozen foods sections of most natural foods emporiums.

If your nonstick skillet is large and high-sided, you can do the whole thing in one pot. **SERVES 4 TO 6**

7 ounces Lightlife Gimme Lean Sausage-Style soysage, thawed
Cooking spray
2 teaspoons olive oil
1 medium onion, sliced vertically into thin crescents
2½ cups vegetable stock (see page 139)
1 large sweet potato, peeled and cut into ½-inch dice
1 can (15 ounces) black beans
1 can (14½ ounces) diced tomatoes with green chiles
2 tablespoons cornstarch
Salt and freshly ground black pepper to taste
Cooked rice or other grain, or toasted bread, to serve with the stew

1 Form soysage into 6 to 8 patties.

2 Spray a nonstick skillet with cooking spray and place it over medium-high heat. When hot, add the patties, cooking until just browned, 3 to 4 minutes per side. Remove the patties from the skillet and set aside.

3 Add the oil to the hot skillet along with the onion. Sauté until the onion softens slightly, about 3 minutes. Then, if the skillet's large enough and high-sided, add the vegetable stock and sweet potato. (If the skillet is the more usual 8 to 10 inches in diameter with 1½-inch-high sides, transfer the onions to a soup pot that has been sprayed with cooking spray and then add the stock and sweet potato.) Bring to a boil, then lower the heat to a simmer. Loosely cover and cook until the sweet potato is tender, 12 to 15 minutes.

4 Drain 3 to 4 tablespoons of liquid from either the beans or the tomatoes with green chiles, reserving it in a small dish. Add the beans and tomatoes to the pot. Return the stew to a gentle boil.

5 Using your fingers, smush the cornstarch into the reserved liquid, to make a thin slurry. Stirring constantly, mix into the stew, which should thicken almost immediately. Add salt and pepper to taste.

6 Serve the stew in large bowls, ladled over rice, if desired, and a soysage patty or two. Serve steaming hot.

SOLACE SUPPER

Mesclun salad with scallions, diced avocado, and fresh corn with Cilantro Vinaigrette
(PAGE 94)

*

Steven's Spicy Black Bean Soysage Stew with rice

*

Vanilla ice cream or Soy Delicious with sliced strawberries, fresh raspberries, and The Very Best Hot Fudge Sauce
(PAGE 1063)

Homey, Hearty Stews

If, as we have seen, the hotter the climate, the spicier the food, does the reverse hold true? Could we expect that the colder the climate, the more tame its seasonings?

Evidently we could. Compare the seasonings of a *blanquette de veau* or Irish stew with those of avial or rundown. When's the last time you ran into a hot pepper in a British, Swedish, or Norwegian recipe, or in an Anglican or Lutheran church cookbook? Case closed.

But "tame" need not mean plain, bland, or boring—just not spicy-hot. The stews of cold climes may be redolent of herbs and garlic, spiked with red or white wine, studded with dried or fresh mushrooms, enriched with tomato sauce or even fruit (fresh, dried, or juice), or given the piquant interplay of sweet-sour. Vegetables, grains, and beans—the workhorses of vegetarian cuisine—almost always play roles. Consider the full-flavored stews and casseroles of France and the colder parts of the Mediterranean. Consider the taste of a really good Irish stew; or the Russian use of dill, cabbage, beets, sour cream, mushrooms; or the slow-cooked Jewish stews and pot roasts, hearty cholents and sweet tzimmeses.

But, you may say, such pots of goodness are usually given flavor and texture, by meat. True, but that is nothing more than a challenge for any good vegetarian cook. You may not believe me until you try, but some of the ingredients that sound strangest to mainstream eaters—nutritional yeast, miso, seitan—are the very things that, with other carefully chosen ingredients and good techniques, make vegetarian stews so good.

Deep December Ragoût of Seitan, Shiitakes, and Winter Vegetables

NOTE

I make this dish in a heavy-gauge, nonstick Dutch oven. If you use a conventional cast-iron or enamel-clad one, spray the heck out of it with cooking spray before you start, and expect to stir the dish considerably more often than I suggest here to prevent sticking.

I swooned the first time I made this. What makes it exceptional? It's hearty, deeply flavorful, lapped in a rich, glossy, savory sauce, spiked with red wine—serious wintertime satisfaction in a bowl. It's the entree Ned chose one year for his February birthday dinner. It is everything you want from a stew, from the seductive aroma with which it warms the house as it simmers, to its robust, filling substance and big, distinct ("manly," we might have said in prefeminist days) chunks of potato and other vegetables. Dried shiitakes absorb the ragoût; garlic (and no wimpy amount of it, either) is used almost as a vegetable in its own right. And, though it seems impossible that something so stalwart should be low fat, low fat it is. See the menu on the next page for serving ideas. **SERVES 4 TO 6**

Cooking spray
1 tablespoon olive oil
1 large onion, cut vertically into thin slivers
¼ cup unbleached white all-purpose flour
3½ cups vegetable stock (see page 139)
¼ cup nutritional yeast (see page 239)
¼ cup tamari or shoyu soy sauce
1 cup hearty, full-bodied, tannic red wine such as Cabernet, Barolo, or Barbaresco
1 cup canned diced tomato in tomato puree
1 tablespoon umeboshi plum vinegar (see page 118)
1 tablespoon honey
¼ teaspoon Dragon Salt (page 900)
A major grinding of black pepper—½ to 1 teaspoon or so
8 to 10 cloves garlic, quartered or thickly sliced
6 to 8 dried shiitake mushrooms, broken roughly into quarters
1 package (8 ounces) "traditional-style" dark seitan, well drained, diced into beef-stew-size squares, 1 to 1½ inches
4 small potatoes, scrubbed, peel on, cut into large pieces
2 carrots, scrubbed, peel on, sliced crosswise into ½-inch rounds
1 parsnip, halved lengthwise, sliced crosswise into ½-inch pieces
2 cups green beans, stemmed and sliced into 2- to 3-inch pieces
1 zucchini, halved lengthwise and sliced crosswise into ½-inch pieces
Minced Italian parsley (optional)

1 If using a conventional Dutch oven, spray it with cooking spray, but you will have better results with a nonstick one. Heat the oil in the Dutch oven over medium-high heat. Add the onion and sauté until it starts to brown but is still a little crisp, about 6 minutes.

2 Sprinkle the onion with the flour and, lowering the heat to medium, continue to sauté for 4 minutes. Add about ½ cup of the stock, stirring to blend it into the flour. When the liquid is free of any flour lumps, add a little more stock. When it is well incorporated, add the remaining stock, stirring. Add the nutritional yeast, stirring as the flakes dissolve. Add the tamari, wine, tomatoes, umeboshi plum vinegar, honey, Dragon Salt, and pepper. Stir in the garlic and bring the mixture to a boil. Immediately lower the heat to a simmer.

3 Drop in the shiitakes along with the seitan, potatoes, carrots, parsnip, and green beans. Lower the heat slightly. Cover and cook, stirring every so often, at a bare simmer until the potatoes are nearly done, about 35 minutes. Uncover and add the zucchini. Cover and cook until the vegetables are tender but still holding their shape, 10 to 15 minutes. Serve hot, with a sprinkle of parsley, if desired.

VARIATIONS

TEMPEH'D DEEP DECEMBER RAGOÛT OF SHIITAKES AND WINTER VEGETABLES: ***Omit the seitan. Prepare one batch of Basic Oven-Baked Marinated Tempeh (page 641), using red wine vinegar, black pepper, and honey in the marinade, and cut it into squares. Stir the baked tempeh pieces into the stew along with the zucchini.***

DEEP DECEMBER RAGOÛT OF SHIITAKES AND WINTER VEGETABLES WITH CHICKPEAS: ***Omit the seitan. Drain a 15-ounce can of chickpeas, reserving both the liquid and the beans. Use the bean liquid as part of the vegetable stock called for in the main recipe. Add the beans when you add the zucchini.***

DEEP-DECEMBER DINING

Salad of Local Greens and Basil Vinaigrette, with Parmesan
(PAGE 71)

*

Deep December Ragoût of Seitan, Shiitakes, and Winter Vegetables
(PREVIOUS PAGE)
served over Basic Mashed Potatoes
(PAGE 788)

*

Crusty multi-grain bread with Better
(PAGE 905)

*

Baked Sugarplum Apples with Lightened-Up Pastry Cream and Almonds
(PAGE 970)
or Honeyed Cranberry-Burgundy Poached Pears
(PAGE 993)

Cholent

This cholent, in most ways traditional and thick with all of the customary grains and beans, offers seitan instead of beef, and has slightly revved-up seasonings. It is a definitive comfort food, savory and good, sustaining. Dark stock is awfully important here; the Oven-Roasted Vegetable Stock is perfect. Of course, this means planning ahead, and turns the stew into a big deal. You can simplify matters and still end up with a delicious stew using a good commercial vegetable stock: There's one final choice to make between oven and Crockpot methods, equally long and slow, as for many good things. Any of the aseptically packaged organic mushroom broths will do nicely.

Serve with challah bread and a well-dressed (vinegary-mustardy-garlicky) crisp green salad. **SERVES 6 TO 8**

½ cup dry lima beans, picked over and well rinsed
½ cup dry white beans, picked over and well rinsed
1 tablespoon olive oil
Cooking spray
2 large onions, chopped
2 ribs celery, chopped
2 carrots, chopped
2 or 3 parsnips, scrubbed, peeled, and chopped
3 cloves garlic, sliced
2 bay leaves
1½ teaspoons paprika
¼ to ½ teaspoon peeled, minced ginger
4 to 5 cups Oven-Roasted Vegetable Stock (page 141), or other flavorful stock
1 cup tomato sauce, commercial or homemade
½ cup barley
⅓ cup lentils
5 or 6 small whole new potatoes, well scrubbed
About ½ pound green beans, stems and tips removed, cut into 1½-inch lengths
1 package (8 ounces) commercially prepared "traditional-style" seitan, well rinsed and cut into 1-inch chunks
½ teaspoon freshly ground black pepper
¼ to ½ teaspoon salt

1 Soak the beans (see directions on page 594).

2 When the beans are finished soaking, if you plan to bake your cholent in the oven, preheat it to 350°F.

3 Heat the oil in a large, oven-to-table casserole or Dutch oven that has been

Sabbath Suppers

According to Jewish religious law, lighting or extinguishing a fire on the Sabbath (Friday night, all day Saturday) is forbidden; yet it's considered a mitzvah *(holy act), to eat a hot midday meal on Saturday. What to do? The precursor of a slow cooker, a hot fire, was started in the home or village baker's oven before the Sabbath; then, on Sabbath Eve, a tightly lidded pot of cholent, a hearty, whole-meal-in-a-pot stew, was placed in the still-hot oven. As the fire gradually died down, the stew cooked slowly and deliciously, simmering leisurely all night long and staying hot into the next day. Many who grew up in observant Ashkenazic families (that is, Jews of Eastern European origin) say that waking to the warm, savory fragrance of cholent in the oven is one of the aromas most defining and evocative of their childhoods.*

Since the Polish and Russian shtetls, or small villages to which Ashkenazic Jews were confined, were usually very poor, this dish was largely vegetarian in its original form—two or three types of dried beans, a grain (sometimes barley, sometimes buckwheat kasha), potatoes, and a few other vegetables. If there was meat, it would most likely be just a small chunk, even for a special Sabbath-day meal. However, as Jews grew more affluent, the percentage of meat in the cholent grew. Nowadays, a 2- to 2½-pound brisket or chuck roast is not uncommon. Not uncommon, but also not needed, as this recipe succulently proves.

sprayed with cooking spray over medium heat. Add the onions and sauté until they have started to soften, 4 to 5 minutes. Add the celery, carrots, and parsnips and sauté for 3 minutes more. Add the garlic, bay leaves, paprika, and ginger and sauté for an additional minute. Pour in the stock and bring to a boil.

4 Add the soaked beans along with the tomato sauce, barley, lentils, potatoes, green beans, diced seitan, pepper, and salt. There should be enough liquid to cover all of the ingredients, with 1 to 2 inches of headroom left at the top of the pot, as the beans and barley will both swell. Add additional stock or water if needed. Bring the mixture back to a boil. Stir well and lower the heat to a simmer. Tightly cover the pot.

5 To oven-bake the cholent, turn the preheated oven down to 200°F. Transfer the stew into the oven, and bake for 7 to 12 hours or overnight (20 hours is traditional). To cook the cholent in a Crockpot, transfer it to a large Crockpot set on low and cook, covered, for the same length of time.

At the end of the cooking, check and, if necessary, adjust the seasonings. Serve hot in soup bowls.

VARIATION

If you don't have stock on hand, fake it with the following: Combine ⅓ cup seitan stock with 2 cups mushroom stock and an additional ⅔ cup wine. Since the seitan stock is quite gingery and salty, omit the ginger and salt from the recipe, tasting for saltiness after the dish is done.

Tzimmes

In Yiddish, to make a fuss or big deal over a small matter is to make a tzimmes; a messy, confused, mixed-up state of affairs. But the word also refers to a glorious, surprising one-pot stew that combines dried fruits and big chunks of vegetables. Traditionally, it's made two ways: as a meatless side dish, or as a main dish, a slab of brisket simmering in the midst of the fruits and vegetables, growing more piquant and sweet-savory during a long, slow cooking.

This vegetarian version, in which seitan replaces the beef, is a main dish. Despite its name, it is in no way a big deal to make. You brown the onion and aromatics, add everything else, and let it all simmer away. A last-minute thickening finishes the dish. The results are voluptuous.

Because beef provides the main nonsweet note in the traditional version, and infuses the sweet components with flavor, meat tzimmes usually calls for water as the liquid, maybe with just a little orange juice, and sometimes a very sweet wine. When using seitan instead of beef, good stock is essential to get the savory note.

SERVES 4 TO 6

1 tablespoon olive oil
Cooking spray
1 large onion, chopped
3 cloves garlic, sliced
1½ teaspoon peeled, minced ginger
3 cups Oven-Roasted Vegetable Stock (page 141) or aseptically packaged mushroom stock
Grated rind and juice of 1 orange
½ cup low-tannin, fruity red wine, such as Beaujolais or Côtes du Rhône Villages
¼ cup brown sugar or Rapidura
¼ teaspoon ground cinnamon, preferably Saigon
10 large pitted prunes, halved
10 dried apricots, halved
2 large sweet potatoes, peeled and cut into 1-inch chunks
1 large white potato, peeled and cut into 1-inch chunks
1 Braeburn or other firm, tart apple, peeled and cut into ½-inch chunks
1 package (8 ounces) commercially made "traditional style" seitan, drained and rinsed, cut into 1-inch squares
2 tablespoons cornstarch
Salt and freshly ground black pepper to taste

1. Heat the oil in a large nonstick pot, or one that has been sprayed with cooking spray, over medium heat. Add the onion and sauté until it has softened, about 4 minutes. Add garlic and ginger, and sauté for an additional minute. Add the stock, orange rind and juice, wine, brown sugar, and cinnamon. Bring to a boil and drop in the prunes, apricots, sweet potatoes, white potato, and apple. Lower the heat to a simmer and cook, half covered, until the vegetables and dried fruits are very tender, about 40 minutes.

2. With a ladle, scoop out ¼ cup of the cooking liquid. Place it in a small bowl and set it aside to cool.

3. Add the seitan to the stew and cook, stirring occasionally, still half-covered, over very low heat, for another 20 minutes.

4. When just about ready to serve, raise the heat to a boil. Smush the cornstarch into the reserved ¼ cup of the cooking liquid. When the stew is boiling, stir in the cornstarch mixture. The stew should immediately thicken and get a clear gloss. Season with salt and pepper. Serve hot.

Mélange of Braised Winter Vegetables with Savory Tofu

A one-pot supper packed with good things, the outline for this inspired combination came from Cynthia Pedregon's Braised Cabbage in *The Peach Tree Family Cookbook*. With all due respect to Cynthia, she undersells the goodness of this dish by calling it merely "braised cabbage." It's a skillet's worth of garden bounty, more than the sum of its parts. The vegetables steam in their own juices with the help of the balsamic and tamari. Those nested on the bottom get kind of caramelized and sweet-sour and then are carefully stirred in to flavor the whole. All of the vegeta-

VARIATION

MÉLANGE OF BRAISED WINTER VEGETABLES WITH SOYSAGE: ***In the late '90s, progressive natural foods companies began coming up with many delicious and pleasing varieties of nonmeat sausage. Two of my personal favorites are Boca Burgers Breakfast Patties and Lightlife Lean Italian Links. Use either of these to ring a change on this braise: Omit the tofu, and cook 4 to 6 nonmeat sausage patties or links separately, according to package directions. Cool slightly, cut into large but forkable chunks, and stir into the mélange just before serving.***

bles, except the red pepper, are those we commonly associate with winter, although they are now mostly available year round. Humble, unassuming, and homey, this has enough flair that you'll come back to it time and again.

To make it as we do at our house, you'll need a deep, nonstick skillet with a tight-fitting lid. The one I use has a 9-inch bottom and is 3 inches deep; just perfect for this dish.

This is less liquidy than the rest of the stews in this chapter—it has almost a stir-fry feel rather than that of a stew. Yet its slow cooking puts it squarely in the stew category. Serve with brown rice, buckwheat noodles, or quinoa for a simple, very good supper. **SERVES 4**

- 1 tablespoon olive oil
- 4 large cloves garlic, peeled and sliced
- 1 small onion, sliced vertically into thin crescents
- ½ head green cabbage, thinly sliced
- 1 sweet potato, peeled and cut into ½-inch cubes
- 1 small turnip, sliced into ¼-inch rounds
- 1 red bell pepper, sliced
- 1 medium acorn squash, unpeeled, stem end removed, seeded, cut into ¼-inch rings
- 3 tablespoons balsamic vinegar
- 1½ tablespoons tamari or shoyu soy sauce
- 1 tablespoon honey or maple syrup
- 1 package (8 ounces) savory baked tofu, diced into ½-inch cubes
- Salt and freshly ground black pepper to taste

1 Heat the oil and garlic in a large, deep nonstick skillet with a tight-fitting lid, over medium-low heat. Cook very slowly until the garlic is somewhat tender and golden but not browned, 1 to 2 minutes. Add the onion and cook until it begins to become translucent, about 3 minutes.

2 Layer the cabbage, then the sweet potato, turnip, red pepper, and squash over the onion. Drizzle the balsamic vinegar, tamari, and honey into the skillet. Scatter the tofu over the top. Cover very tightly and cook until the vegetables are tender, 25 to 30 minutes, without stirring or lifting the lid.

3 Lift the lid, and gently, gently fold the soft, browned, caramelized onions and cabbage strands up and through the other vegetables, being careful not to break them up. Season with salt and pepper. Serve immediately, over brown rice or other grains; this stands up nicely to assertive buckwheat.

Tuscan Bean and Vegetable Stew

Home cooking from Tuscany, this thick, fragrant potage of beans (whole and pureed, dried and fresh), herbs, vegetables, and pasta is served over crisped Italian bread. Astute readers of the first Dairy Hollow House cookbook will see its roots in the Tuscany Bean Soup recipe there. While the soup could serve as a full meal, this is far more decisively so, due to a thicker texture, extra vegetables, and the use of both pasta and bread. The optional Parmesan's great. Serve with The Salad (page 68), and you have dinner, peasant food fit for royalty. **SERVES 8 TO 10**

BEANS

2 cups white beans, such as navy or Great Northern, picked over, rinsed, soaked overnight in water (preferably spring or filtered) to cover, then drained and rinsed well
6 cups water, preferably spring or filtered
2 red onions, chopped
3 cloves garlic, peeled and sliced
2 sprigs Italian parsley, coarsely chopped
2 large ribs celery, with leaves, coarsely chopped
2 tablespoons chopped basil

SAVORY SAUTÉ

2 tablespoons olive oil
Cooking spray
1 red onion, chopped
2 zucchini, stem ends removed, cut into 1-inch cubes
3 large tomatoes, preferably garden ripe, with skin
1 teaspoon fresh thyme leaves
2 teaspoons honey
Salt and freshly ground black pepper to taste

VEGETABLES FOR STEW

3 large potatoes, well scrubbed, peel on, cut into 1-inch chunks
½ pound green beans, stems and tips removed, sliced crosswise into 1-inch pieces
3 cups Golden Stock (page 140), or other mild but flavorful vegetable stock
1 small head savoy cabbage, cored, sliced into thin ribbons
1 small bunch green Swiss chard, washed, center rib removed, cut once lengthwise then crosswise into ribbons

TO FINISH THE STEW

Salt and freshly ground black pepper to taste
8 to 10 crisp Croûtes (page 29)
8 ounces (about 4 cups cooked) elbow macaroni, cooked al dente

GARNISH

¼ red onion, finely minced
Italian parsley, finely chopped
Freshly grated Parmesan cheese
Tamari or shoyu soy sauce
Olive oil, in a cruet, to pass at the table

NOTES

This goes together a bit more fussily than most of the stews in this chapter. There are several components, all of which get combined at the last. Most of the parts can be done ahead and the whole simply put together when ready to eat.

Please note that red onions are called for in three places in the recipe; 1¾ red onions, coarsely chopped, go into the bean pot, another one, finely chopped, goes into the savory sauté, and the reserved quarter, also finely chopped, is used for garnish. You'll make things easier for yourself if you chop all the onions at one time.

1 Start the bean pot: Place the soaked beans and the 6 cups water in a large soup pot over medium-high heat. Add the onions, garlic, parsley, celery, and basil and bring to a boil. Immediately lower the heat to a simmer, and simmer, half-covered, stirring occasionally, until the beans are softened but still retain their shape, 1 hour and 15 minutes to 2 hours (depending on the age of the beans).

2 About 15 minutes before the beans are ready, begin the sauté: Heat the oil in a large, nonstick skillet, or one that has been sprayed with cooking spray, over medium heat. Add the onion and sauté until it has softened, about 4 minutes. Add the zucchini, and sauté for another 3 minutes.

3 Puree the tomatoes and thyme in a food processor until smooth (don't wash the food processor just yet; you'll be using it again shortly). Add the tomato puree to the sauté, along with the honey and salt and pepper to taste. Simmer for 5 to 10 minutes. Remove from the heat and set aside.

4 Back at the bean pot, scoop out about half of the beans, leaving as much liquid as possible in the pot. Allow the scooped-out beans to cool for a few moments. Add the potatoes, green beans, stock, and the sauté mixture to the simmering beans in the pot. Stir well, raise the heat, and bring to a boil. Lower the heat to a simmer, cover, and simmer until the potatoes begin to soften, 15 to 20 minutes.

5 Puree the scooped-out beans in the food processor, working in batches if necessary. Set aside.

6 Set a vegetable steamer over boiling water in a large saucepan with a tight-fitting lid. Add the cabbage to the steamer, cover, and steam for 4 minutes. Lift the lid and add the chard. Replace the cover and steam until both cabbage and chard are limp but not overcooked, another 2 to 4 minutes. Remove from the heat and set aside.

7 When the potatoes in the main bean pot are tender, finish the stew: Stir the bean puree into the simmering pot. Season amply with salt and pepper to taste. It will require lots of both, but will reward you by suddenly blossoming into full flavor. Add the steamed cabbage-chard combo, raise the heat slightly, and, stirring often, simmer for 5 more minutes

8 Warm soup bowls slightly. Place a croûte in the bottom of each warmed bowl. If you intend to eat the entire pot of stew right away, stir the cooked pasta into it. Otherwise, divide the pasta among the soup bowls. Ladle hot soup over the bread and pasta in each bowl. Sprinkle with onion, parsley, grated Parmesan cheese, and tamari. Also pass these garnishes, along with some olive oil in a cruet, at the table.

Gingered East-West Three-Bean and Vegetable Stew

What if you cooked a pot of beans not with the old familiars of the Western bean pot, but instead with the ginger-garlic-miso-sesame flavors of the East? What if you used distinctly Western vegetables—tomatoes, sweet potatoes, celery root? I always like to travel where my "what ifs" take me, and this simple stew's final destination proves that there is something new under the sun with beans, beyond the expected chili/curry/garlic-plus-herbs variations. A perfect warm-up to pleasure a chilly, wet day in early spring, it has both late-winter and early-spring vegetables in it, and is a tonic celebration of both. If celery root's unavailable, substitute 2 ribs celery, finely minced. **SERVES 6 TO 8, WITH GRAIN OR PASTA**

SOMETHING NEW UNDER THE (LATE-WINTER) SUN

The spring's first asparagus, steamed, on a bed of local greens, drizzled with Sharp Classic Vinaigrette with a Bite
(PAGE 72)

*

Gingered East-West Three-Bean and Vegetable Stew, over a mix of barley and kamut
(SEE PAGE 227)

*

Italian Carmelized Oranges
(SEE PAGE 987)

- 2 cups Jeanne Ramu's Three-Bean Mix (page 381), or any one of the following beans: azuki, mung, or black-eyed peas
- About 6 cups water, preferably spring or filtered
- 2 large sweet potatoes, peeled and cut into ¾-inch cubes
- 1 celery root, peeled and cut into ½-inch cubes
- ¼ pound shiitake mushrooms, stems removed (reserve for stock pot), caps thickly sliced or quartered
- 2 teaspoons toasted sesame oil
- Cooking spray
- 1 red onion, sliced vertically into thin crescents
- 2 tablespoons peeled, finely minced ginger
- ½ pound asparagus, cut diagonally into ½-inch slices
- 1 tablespoon finely chopped garlic (about 6 cloves)
- 2 tablespoons white or golden miso, preferably chickpea miso
- 2½ tablespoons honey or Rapidura
- ½ cup canned crushed tomatoes in juice
- 1 tablespoon tamari or shoyu soy sauce, or to taste
- 1 teaspoon salt, or to taste
- ½ teaspoon freshly ground black pepper, or to taste
- Cooked whole grain pasta, such as buckwheat soba, or any cooked grain
- Minced Italian parsley or cilantro

1. Pick over and rinse the beans. Place in a large pot along with the water. Bring to a boil over medium-high heat. Lower the heat to a simmer and cook, half-covered, until almost tender, about 40 minutes.

2 Uncover and add the sweet potato, celery root, and shiitakes. Cover and cook until the sweet potato is almost tender, another 10 to 12 minutes.

3 While the beans are cooking, heat the oil in a nonstick skillet, or one that has been sprayed with cooking spray, over medium heat. Add the onion and sauté until it becomes limp and translucent, about 5 minutes. Add the ginger, then the asparagus, and sauté for another 2 minutes. Add the garlic and sauté for an additional minute.

4 Place the miso and honey in a heatproof measuring cup. Ladle out about ½ cup liquid from the simmering beans, and whisk it into the miso until the miso dissolves. Add the tomatoes, then add the mixture to the onions and asparagus and cook for 2 minutes. Remove from the heat and set aside.

5 When the beans and vegetables are tender, pour the miso mixture into the pot. Stir well, and add the tamari, salt, and pepper, to taste. Turn the heat off and let the stew stand on the hot burner for 10 to 30 minutes to allow the flavors to blend. Reheat if necessary, to serve, hot, over your choice of pasta or grain, garnished with parsley or cilantro, if desired.

Proceeding Gingerly

Many supermarkets now carry a bottled, ready-to-use paste of fresh ginger, as well as one combining pastes of fresh garlic and fresh ginger. You can usually find them near the produce section or in the Asian foods aisle. A jar or two of such a paste in your fridge drastically speeds up preparing any ginger-studded dish at home, whether a stir-fry or this stew, shaving perhaps 10 minutes off a recipe's prep and clean-up time. These pastes taste like the real thing, because they are: They've got maybe 85 percent of the flavor wallop of the equivalent prepared from scratch. Use them in a recipe in equal measure to the fresh.

When I say "fresh" I mean that these pastes, which must be refrigerated after opening, are made from fresh ginger rhizomes or garlic cloves and do not include taste-changing but not unhealthful preservatives like salt or vinegar. Alas, they do contain potassium sorbate, a more questionable (to me) preservative, but not one that alters flavor. They also contain a smidgen of soy oil.

Although I am a fairly fanatic from-scratch cook, I am happy to keep a bottle of ginger paste in my refrigerator door for those we-want-to-eat-NOW moments—or when I'm out of fresh ginger.

Veggie Sauerbraten

Since the German word *sauerbraten* translates to "sour beef," a veggie version would seem to be an oxymoron. But just you wait—this seitan-centered version is a dead ringer for the real long-marinated sweet-sour pot roast of beef in a delicious thickened gravy. When I was a child the sight of the beef floating in its mysterious spice-filled marinade for several days in the fridge, followed by the tantalizing aroma as it finally simmered, was a sight and scent I associated with December—my mother often made it for family holiday dinners. When my friend Steven Weintz rhapsodized about the sauerbraten his mother used to make, pining for a vegetarian version, which he considered impossible, I was delighted to rise to the challenge. "Yes, but with sweet and sour cabbage, and potato pancakes?" he prompted. Sure enough, the classic accompaniments I grew up with too. See the sweet and sour red cabbage on page 720, and use any recipe for potato pancakes or latkes, or even use a good, frozen ready-made potato pancake. You can also serve potato dumplings or mashed potatoes with this.

There are two secret ingredients that give this dish its special tang. The first is ginger, in two forms: a bit of dried ginger and (surprise!) some crumbled gingersnap cookies stirred in at the end. The second is juniper berries, which traditionally flavor gin. **SERVES 6 TO 8**

3 packages (24 ounces total) traditionally seasoned seitan (see page 232), drained, rinsed, and left in large chunks

MARINADE

1 cup dry red wine
1 cup red wine vinegar
1½ medium onions, sliced into rings
1¼ teaspoons black peppercorns
1 scant tablespoon juniper berries
3 bay leaves, broken in half

SAUTÉ

2 tablespoons mild vegetable oil, such as corn, canola, or peanut
1 large onion, chopped
2 carrots, scrubbed and chopped
2 ribs celery, washed and chopped

TO FINISH THE DISH

2 tablespoons unbleached white all-purpose flour
Pinch of powdered ginger
1½ cups vegetable stock (see page 139)
½ cup finely crumbled gingersnap cookies
1 tablespoon brown sugar or Rapidura
Salt and freshly ground black pepper to taste
To serve with the dish: Braised Red Cabbage (page 720), and potatoes—boiled and mashed (see page 788), as dumplings, or as pancakes

1 Place the seitan in a large, glass, heat-proof bowl. Set aside.

2 Combine the red wine, vinegar, sliced onions, peppercorns, and juniper berries in a medium nonreactive pot over high heat. Bring to a boil. Lower the heat and simmer for 5 minutes. Remove from the heat and let cool slightly. Pour the marinade over the seitan. Cover the bowl and refrigerate.

VARIATION

Try adding 1 to 1½ teaspoons caraway seeds to the marinade.

Marinate the seitan for 1 to 3 days, turning the pieces occasionally.

3 When you're ready to prepare the sauerbraten, remove the seitan from the marinade, picking out and discarding any of the whole spices that cling to it. Dice the seitan into 1-inch cubes and set aside. Strain the marinade, reserving the liquid and discarding the solids.

4 Heat the oil in a large, heavy, nonreactive soup pot, preferably nonstick, over medium-high heat. Add the chopped onion, and sauté for 3 minutes. Lower the heat slightly and add the carrots and celery. Continue sautéing until the vegetables are all quite soft, 10 to 12 minutes.

5 To finish the dish, sprinkle the flour and ginger over the sautéed vegetables. Cook, stirring frequently, until the flour colors a bit, 3 to 4 minutes. Gradually stir in the reserved marinade along with the stock, scraping up any little browned bits as you go along and smoothing the flour into the liquid. Raise the heat and bring to a boil. Immediately lower the heat to a simmer and cook, covered, for 10 minutes. Stir in the gingersnaps and brown sugar. When well blended, add the seitan and simmer for another 10 minutes. Taste and, if necessary, add salt and pepper to taste.

6 Serve hot, preferably with Sweet and Sour Cabbage and a potato dish.

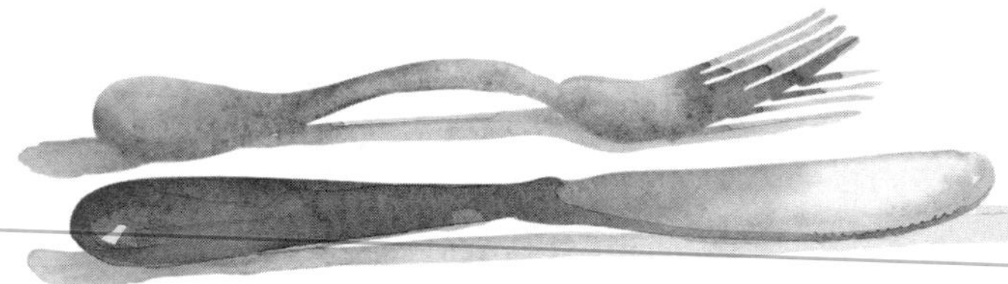

Seitan Gulyas

Gulyas, often Americanized as goulash, is a rich paprika-infused Hungarian stew: earthy, spicy, hearty, yet, when properly made, also hauntingly delicate. In its original incarnation, it's usually made with slowly braised beef, but sometimes pork or veal stand in, along with a mixture of vegetables and usually a soupçon of caraway seed. Sour cream almost always plays a part, sometimes dolloped atop the finished stew, more often stirred into the sauce, which is usually served over an amenable and comforting starch, most often buttered noodles or dumplings. But it's the paprika, red and rich, that is gulyas' distinctive eternal verity. Try to find Hungarian paprika for the dish; it is both redder and more full-flavored.

VARIATIONS

VEGAN VARIATIONS: ***This will still be delicious with the Yogurt Sour Cream omitted and oil substituted for Better. Or, for a creamy vegan version, stir the tablespoon of flour into ½ cup Tofu Sour Cream (page 909) instead of sour cream and cook, stirring, over low heat until the mixture thickens.***

I get a hankering for this good dish once every year or two. Seitan, such a perfect stand-in for beef in nearly any braised stew-type dish, is a dead ringer when the dish is attentively made and well seasoned. I've had people actually dispute me on my gulyas, insisting that it can't, absolutely cannot, be vegetarian. But it is. **SERVES 4**

NOTE

Berry's, an exquisite Hungarian restaurant in Westchester, New York, where my family occasionally dined when I was growing up, spoiled me for anything less than the very best gulyas.

An enchanted place, it was located in a small, warm house, with dark interior walls; you entered through an anteroom where a small, elegantly turned-out pastry case stood, and the fragrant, wafting sigh of cinnamon, hazelnuts, yeast bread, apples, and cherries exhaled from an unseen oven, alternating with a deeper aroma, that of sautéing onion and simmering stew. A crisp maitre d' led you to an intimate dining room, where your own white-clothed table waited. The murmur of muted conversation, well-dressed people leaning over their own tables, courtly, accented servers bringing delicious, slightly exotic dishes—all wove a kind of enchantment that, though long gone, I can never dismiss or forget.

1 tablespoon Better (page 905)
Cooking spray
2 medium onions, finely chopped
2 pale green Italian frying peppers (also sometimes called Hungarian wax peppers or sweet banana peppers), or 1 green bell pepper, seeded and diced
½ pound domestic mushrooms, wiped and sliced
2 cloves garlic, pressed
2 tablespoons sweet Hungarian paprika
⅛ to ¼ teaspoon hot Hungarian paprika or cayenne
½ teaspoon caraway seeds
1 large fresh tomato, peeled, seeded, and chopped
1 package (8 ounces) "traditional-style" dark seitan in broth, drained, rinsed, and diced into 1-inch chunks
1 cup vegetable stock (see page 139)
½ cup sour cream, sour half-and-half, or Yogurt Sour Cream (page 910)
1 tablespoon unbleached white all-purpose flour
Salt and freshly ground black pepper to taste
Minced Italian parsley or dill (optional)
About 4 cups hot cooked noodles, rice, bulghur, potatoes, dumplings, or other neutral starch for serving

1 Heat the Better in a large nonstick Dutch oven, or one that has been sprayed with cooking spray, over medium heat. Add the onions and lower the heat. Cook, stirring often, until the onions are very soft, but not browned, 10 to 12 minutes. Add the peppers and mushrooms. Raise the heat slightly and cook, stirring, for another 5 minutes. Add the garlic, paprikas, and caraway seeds and cook, stirring, for 1 minute. Add the tomato and stir for 1 minute. Add the seitan and vegetable stock. Stir well and bring to a boil. Cover and lower the heat to a low simmer. Simmer for about 40 minutes.

2 Combine the sour cream with the flour in a small bowl. Ladle out a little of the hot gulyas sauce and whisk it into the sour cream mixture. Whisk the sour cream mixture back into the gulyas pot and cook, over extremely low heat, until the sauce thickens very slightly, about 3 minutes. Taste and, if necessary, add salt and pepper (be especially generous with the latter). Do not allow the mixture to boil. Serve, very hot, with a garnish of parsley or dill, over noodles, rice, or other bland starch.

Meet Seitan

HAVE WE BEEN INTRODUCED YET?

Seitan (pronounced "SAY-tan") is, like tempeh and tofu, one of those foodstuffs as traditional to the cuisines and cooking in the countries of its origin as it is foreign in America. However, unlike tempeh and tofu, once you acquire and use your first package of seitan, there is no learning curve. Almost everyone loves it, first bite.

Seitan is wheat protein, what you get if you remove the starch and fiber from wheat. Another name for it is gluten, which bakers know as one of the essential structural factors in making yeast-raised bread. While in bread-baking you "develop" the gluten by the process known as kneading, seitan is made by rinsing higher-protein wheat flours until only a spongy ball remains. At this point it is raw and unappealing. But when chunks are poached in savory liquid, then cut up and added to a stew or gulyas, they are truly a dead ringer for beef; in particular, a cooked-to-tender stew-beef cut. Use it appropriately, and if you don't want to, you don't need to say a word about the dish being vegetarian, as no one would dream that it was. Seitan has been used to make the vegetarian "parallel universe" to such dishes as sauerbrauten, corned beef, beef pot pie, ad infinitum. Truly, if you can do it with stew beef or slow-cooked beef, you can very likely, with just a bit of recipe-tweaking, do it with seitan.

Ready-made seitan is also extremely convenient. It is easily available in several varieties and "cuts" from natural foods stores and Asian markets, and many mainstream supermarkets are starting to carry it as well. However, it's interesting to make seitan from scratch at least a time or two, and you can also find boxed seitan "mix" (really just high-gluten flour or pure dry gluten, sometimes called "vital wheat gluten") at natural foods stores. Directions come with the mixes.

Before you go deep into seitaning, here's one important caveat: Seitan is not a whole food. It is made up of part of the wheat grain—its protein—and as such it is as fractionated and inherently unbalanced as white flour, bran, or wheat germ. Since one of my core beliefs is that foods should be eaten as whole as possible as often as possible, seitan—easy and appealing though it is—should be an occasional choice, not a several-times-a-week, or daily, vegetarian mainstay (unlike, say, beans or soyfoods).

If you do get enamored of seitan and want to explore its further horizons, check out the cookbooks Eco-Cuisine *and* Friendly Foods, *by Ron Pickarski, a former Franciscan friar who frequently uses seitan in his delicious, if fairly elaborate, recipes. Another simpler but quite comprehensive seitan cookbook is* Simply Heavenly!, *a vegan offering written by Abbot George Burke of the Holy Protection Orthodox Monastery.* Simply Heavenly! *also gives great detail on making seitan from scratch and flavoring it in various ways to make "UnChicken," "UnPork," "UnShrimp," and so on. It also contains various nondairy "cheezes" and "kreems." Although this kind of terminology is very, very, very "unpleezing" to me as a serious cook, the basic info is useful and good.*

Virtually all seitan is sold (sometimes as "wheat gluten" or "wheat meat") in a portion of the liquid or broth in which it was poached. Unlike the water in which tofu is sold, which is serves only as a medium to store the tofu and keep it fresh, the seitan broths are usually quite strongly flavored and very salty and can be eaten. When I use seitan broth, though, I dilute it with a lot of vegetable stock or filtered water. And I don't usually use this resulting stock in the same dish as the seitan—to my taste, it's too much.

Following are some of the ready-to-serve varieties of seitan currently available:

TRADITIONAL-STYLE DARK-COOKED SEITAN: *This seitan, probably the most widely available, is poached in a very strongly flavored dark, gingery-salty tamari broth. Use the broth with caution; it tends to dominate. The seitan itself is delicious, and the one I most often call for in my recipes. It is dark in color and comes in irregular-size chunks, which you then dice or slice as needed. Some is sold fresh, in the refrigerator case; some is processed and put up in jars, and is shelf stable. There are many regional seitan brands, most often available in jars, and one national, White Wave. White Wave seitan comes in rectangular plastic tubs, like tofu.*

Dark-cooked seitan is good smothered in gravy with all the dominant, assertive flavors that might typically be enjoyed with beef: tomatoes, mushrooms, red wine, vinegars, and the like.

"CHICKEN"-STYLE SEITAN *is poached in a lighter broth and is a golden color. It, too, comes packed in liquid, and is also available in the refrigerator section or on the shelf. Although intended as a chicken substitute, to me it doesn't work because its chewy-hearty texture is very beeflike. Frankly, I don't much care for it; I always use tofu or tempeh if I want to replicate poultry. About the one place I think it might really fly (so to speak) would be in a nonchicken pot pie.*

SEITAN FAJITA STRIPS: *These are light-colored strips of preseasoned seitan, more "chicken"-ish than beefy. Unlike other seitans, the strips are somewhat uniform and vacuum-packed, so there's no poaching liquid. They can be found in the refrigerator case. The strips are, of course, designed to be used in lieu of steak or chicken strips in fajitas. I've tried them—but I much prefer Portobello and Shiitake Mushroom Fajitas (page 346) over the seitan.*

SEITAN STEAK-OUT IN WHITE WINE AND GARLIC: *The newest entry in the seitan universe, it is poached in a much less salty version of the traditional dark-cooked broth, resulting in a lighter, more delicious broth, seasoned with wine and garlic, excellent used in sauces.*

Seitan is also a frequent player in many soy-based meat parallels, like various types of soysages. In the ingredients list it is almost always referred to as "wheat gluten."

To start you on your seitan journey, here are some of the recipes in which it's used in this book: Deep December Ragoût of Seitan, Shiitakes, and Winter Vegetables (page 218), Tofu-Seitan "Meatballs" (page 836), Hainanese Tofu and Seitan in Ginger Brown-Bean Sauce (page 214), Brown Tepary Bean, Seitan and Ancho Chili Stew with Poblano-Citrus Salsa (page 187), West Indian Rundown (page 206), Seitan Sancocho (page 237), Veggie Sauerbraten (page 228), Tzimmes (page 222), Seitan Gulyas (page 230).

Seitan Smothered in Brown Gravy, Shiitake Mushrooms, and Onions

NOTE

You must have dark brown roux (page 209) on hand to make this recipe.

A deep, dark, wintery stew, which will soothe body and soul on a gray and gusty day. Even the smell is comforting. Although you could add potatoes, I prefer serving this with a nice neutral starch (noodles, rice, bulghur, potatoes, dumplings, bread). Another option is to add peeled, diced butternut squash to the mix. **SERVES 4**

- 1 tablespoon butter, preferably clarified (or, for vegans, soy margarine or mild vegetable oil such as corn, canola, or peanut)
- Cooking spray
- 2 medium onions, sliced vertically into thin crescents
- ½ pound shiitake mushrooms, stemmed and sliced
- 3 cloves garlic, pressed
- 3 bay leaves
- 1 package (8 ounces) seitan in broth, drained, rinsed, and diced into 1-inch chunks
- 1½ cups vegetable stock (see page 139)
- ½ cup hearty red wine
- 2 tablespoons dark brown roux (page 209)
- 2 tablespoons dark miso
- 1 teaspoon brown sugar
- Salt and plenty of freshly ground black pepper to taste
- Minced parsley, and confetti of finely diced red and yellow bell peppers (optional)

1 Heat the butter in a large nonstick Dutch oven, or one that has been sprayed with cooking spray, over medium heat. Add the onions and lower the heat. Cook, stirring often, until the onions are very soft, but not browned, 10 to 12 minutes. Add the mushrooms, raise the heat slightly, and cook, stirring, for another 5 minutes. Add garlic and bay leaves and cook, stirring, for an additional minute. Add the seitan and stock. Stir well and bring to a boil, then cover and lower the heat to a bare simmer. Simmer 35 to 40 minutes.

2 In a small bowl, whisk together the wine, Dark Brown Roux, 1 tablespoon of the miso, and brown sugar. At the end of the simmering time, ladle out a little of the simmering liquid and stir it into the wine mixture. Whisk the wine mixture into the simmering pot. Cook over extremely low heat until the sauce thickens slightly, another few minutes. Adjust the seasoning with salt and lots of freshly ground pepper. You may wish to add the additional tablespoon of miso now, also. Do not allow the mixture to boil. Serve very hot, with a garnish of minced parsley and/or diced red and yellow peppers, if desired.

Sliced Brisket of Seitan, Jewish-Style

A delicious classic, this is based on a well-flavored Jewish-style pot roast of beef brisket. The gravy is divine, and a dead ringer for the real thing. Serve it with the optional Horseradish Tofu Sour Cream (since it is nondairy, and the pot roast is nonmeat, even the kosher can enjoy it) and either boiled potatoes or potato latkes. This has been scarfed up more quickly than you could spin a dreidl at Barbara Harmony's annual Hanukkah potluck (where we have been known to sing a rousing "Oy, Come Ozark Jewry / Though you're far and few-ry," to the tune of "Oh Come All Ye Faithful.")

Please note that the carrots and parsnips get a quick precooking before use. This is to tenderize them slightly, and can be done by steaming (4 minutes), blanching (3 minutes in fiercely boiling water), or pressure-cooking (place on a steamer tray in the cooker, raise the heat to full pressure, immediately turn off the heat, release pressure, and open cooker). **SERVES 6 TO 8**

SEITAN "BRISKET"

Cooking spray
4 medium onions, peeled and sliced vertically into thin crescents
4 carrots, scrubbed, trimmed, sliced crosswise into 1-inch chunks, blanched (see note above)
4 ribs celery, rinsed and chopped
2 parsnips, scrubbed, trimmed, sliced crosswise into ¾-inch chunks, blanched (see note above)
1 tablespoon tamari or shoyu soy sauce
1½ to 2 pounds commercial traditional-style seitan, drained and sliced

GRAVY

3¼ cups vegetable stock (see page 139), the more flavorful the better
¾ cup fruity red wine, such as Beaujolais
3 tablespoons brown sugar or Rapidura
Lots of freshly ground black pepper to taste
3 tablespoons butter or mild vegetable oil
¼ cup unbleached white all-purpose flour
4 cloves garlic, finely minced
Salt to taste

GLAZE

3 tablespoons red wine
2 tablespoons brown sugar or Rapidura
1½ tablespoons dark miso

Horseradish Tofu Sour Cream (optional; recipe follows)

1 Preheat the oven to 375°F.

2 Spray a large (8 by 12 inches or up to 8 by 14 inches), heavy baking dish with cooking spray. Add the onions and place in the oven. Roast for 40 minutes. Remove the dish from the oven and add the carrots, celery, parsnips, and tamari, shaking the dish to distribute. Return to the oven and roast, uncovered, for another 30 minutes.

3 Remove the dish from the oven and place the sliced seitan on top of the roasted vegetables. Combine the stock, ¾ cup wine, and 3 tablespoons brown sugar and pour the liquid over the seitan and vegetables. Grind plenty of black pepper over the top. Cover tightly with foil and return to the oven. Bake for 50 minutes.

4 Remove the pan from the oven. Uncover and ladle off as much of the hot cooking broth as you can into a large measuring cup (don't worry about getting every last drop).

5 Heat the butter in a large skillet over medium heat. Whisk in the flour and cook, whisking constantly, for 3 minutes. Gradually whisk in the reserved cooking broth. Cook, whisking constantly, until smooth and thick, 2 or 3 minutes. Stir in half of the garlic.

6 Scrape every last bit of the sauce back into the seitan, stirring well to blend (it will thicken any broth remaining in the pan). Taste for salt, and, if needed, add a little.

7 Raise the oven temperature to broil. Prepare the glaze by whisking the red wine, brown sugar, miso, and remaining garlic together. Brush, spoon, or drizzle over the sauced seitan (there will just be a little, not enough to cover the whole thing). Return to the oven and broil, uncovered, until bubbling hot and deeply browned, 5 to 10 minutes. Serve hot, dolloped with Horseradish Tofu Sour Cream, if desired.

Tisket-a-Brisket

There are numerous ways to play with this succulent seitan dish. Here are a few.

SEITAN BRISKET, JEWISH-STYLE, WITH POTATOES AND CABBAGE: *A fabulous one-dish supper. Add half a dozen small to medium steamed unpeeled russet potatoes, halved or quartered, when you add the thickened gravy. Also add half a green cabbage, cut into wedges and steamed until not quite tender.*

TZIMMES SEITAN BRISKET, JEWISH-STYLE: *Just delish, this takes the dish from savory to sweet. Add a dozen pitted prunes, halved, to the roasted vegetables at the same time you add the broth-wine mix and bake as directed. While the dish bakes, peel and slice 3 to 4 large sweet potatoes, and steam them until just barely tender. Scatter the sweet potatoes over the seitan, then pour in the gravy, stir, and continue as directed in the basic recipe.*

Horseradish Tofu Sour Cream

- 1 box (12.3 ounces) reduced-fat silken tofu
- 1 tablespoon umeboshi plum paste (see page 118)
- 1 to 2 tablespoons commercially prepared creamy-style horseradish, or to taste
- Salt and freshly ground black pepper to taste
- 2 teaspoons mild vegetable oil, such as corn, canola, or peanut (optional)
- 1 tablespoon minced Italian parsley

Combine the tofu, umeboshi plum paste, and 1 tablespoon of the horseradish in a food processor. Buzz until smooth, pausing to scrape down the sides of the work bowl. Season with salt and pepper and add the remaining horseradish, if desired. Transfer to a serving bowl and sprinkle with the parsley.

Seitan Sancocho

So common is sancocho throughout the Caribbean, Columbia, and the Dominican Republic that the verb *sancochar* means "to stew." Some versions are made with all beef, pork, or chicken; some combine meats and add lamb; some are built around fish and seafood. What they all have in common is a thinnish but full-flavored brothy sauce. Ned's Aunt Mitzi Gavidia, who spent much of her life in El Salvador, says that the Salvadoran version is always seasoned with bay leaf and oregano and contains carrots, potatoes, tomato, and onion. This is more Caribbean, containing plantain and taro. It is inspired by a nonvegetarian sancocho in Stephen Raichlen's *Healthy Latin Cooking.* **SERVES 4 TO 6**

TOFU-SEITAN MARINADE

16 ounces reduced-fat firm traditional-style tofu, drained and cut into 1-inch cubes
8 ounces savory-style seitan, drained, rinsed, and cut into 1-inch cubes
6 tablespoons fresh-squeezed lime juice
2 tablespoons fresh-squeezed orange juice
6 cloves garlic, pressed
3 bay leaves

BROWNING THE STEW

½ cup whole wheat flour
½ cup unbleached white all-purpose flour
1 teaspoon paprika
Several grinds of black pepper
2 tablespoons olive oil
Cooking spray

FINISHING THE STEW

1 tablespoon butter or Better (page 905)
1 large onion, chopped
1 bunch scallions, roots removed, all the white and 4 inches of green chopped
5 cloves garlic, sliced
2 to 3 jalapeño peppers (seeds and membranes removed for mildness or left in for extra heat), minced, or ½ habanero or Scotch bonnet chile (seeds and membrane removed or left in) minced
1 green bell pepper, cored and seeded, chopped
8 cups vegetable stock (see page 139)
2 green plaintains, peeled and cut into ¾-inch slices
1 small butternut squash, peeled and cut into 1-inch cubes
1 cup peeled, cubed taro (dasheen)
1 cup peeled, cubed yucca
½ cup minced Italian parsley
½ cup minced cilantro
3 bay leaves
1 tablespoon red wine vinegar, plus more to taste
Salt and freshly ground black pepper to taste
4 to 6 cups cooked white or brown rice (see page 461)

1 Combine the tofu and seitan in a glass baking dish. Whisk the lime and orange juices together. Add the garlic and bay leaves. Pour over the tofu and seitan and toss to combine. Marinate, refrigerated, for 1 to 2 hours.

2 Lift the tofu and seitan from the marinade, reserving any residual liquid. Combine the flours with the paprika and pepper in a large plastic bag. Add the tofu and seitan and shake well to coat. One piece at a time, remove the tofu and seitan from the bag and shake off the excess flour.

3 Heat the olive oil in a large Dutch oven that has been sprayed with cooking spray, over medium heat. Add the floured tofu and seitan and brown slowly, allowing one side to cook for 4 to 5 minutes, then gently turn and brown the other sides. Remove chunks as they are browned, and let drain on a paper towel. When all of the pieces have been browned, set aside.

4 Add the butter to the oil remaining in the Dutch oven, over medium heat. When melted, add the onion and sauté until slightly softened, about 5 minutes. Then add the scallions, garlic, jalapeños, and bell pepper. Sauté for 5 minutes, then add the stock. Raise the heat and bring to a boil. Add the plaintains, squash, taro, and yucca and lower the heat to a simmer. Stir in half the parsley and cilantro, as well as the bay leaves from the marinade plus any liquid left. Simmer, half-covered, until the starchy vegetables are tender and the squash has almost disintegrated, 15 to 20 minutes.

5 Add the browned tofu and seitan to the stew, stirring it in gently. Add 1 tablespoon of the vinegar, and salt and pepper to taste. You want a well flavored savory liquid with plenty of bite to it, so add more vinegar if desired. Stir in the remaining parsley and cilantro and serve over steaming hot rice in big bowls.

Meet Nutritional Yeast

HAVE WE BEEN INTRODUCED YET?

In the mid-sixties, a subculture of nutritionally aware cooks and eaters began to use brewer's yeast—a non-leavening yeast that is one of the single largest natural sources of the B-vitamin complex, and quite high in protein to boot—as a health supplement. You were supposed to sprinkle the brownish powder on breakfast cereal or into smoothies. There was one problem: It tasted dreadful—bitter, and dominating whatever you put it into.

The food chemists stepped in, and, starting with the super-nutritious brewer's strains, they began to experiment with them, cultivating them on different foodstuffs. Bingo! They arrived on a molasses-fed yeast, developed for direct human consumption. This was given the unfortunate name of nutritional yeast, which disguises the fact that it is truly tasty. It is a genuinely useful ingredient worthy of a place on any serious cook's shelf.

Nutritional yeast is golden in color, and comes in small nonuniform flakes that dissolve easily when whisked into liquid. Its taste is savory, not sweet; it should be used in things like sauces, broths and stocks, and stews, never something sweet like a smoothie. It is widely available in bulk at natural foods stores. Sometimes it is labeled Good-Tasting Nutritional Yeast, and it is good-tasting; its flavor is reminiscent of a dry, finely grated Parmesan cheese.

Store nutritional yeast at room temperature in a jar with a tightly fitting lid for up to 2 or 3 months.

Plenteous Potages

Milder than the chilies or curries that opened this chapter, lighter than the mostly European-derived stews that followed, these stews are built around vegetables. When legumes and grains put in an appearance, they do so only as supporting players. Instead, tubers, growing secretly beneath the earth, and green-stuffs of all sorts from above it, play leading roles, usually in combination.

These dishes will nourish and please you some spring evening with a bit of chill to it still, or on an early fall day edged with the winter ahead—and they will help you cope when your garden hits the too-much-of-everything-all-at-once phase.

Besides their own juices and broths, vegetable mélanges do well with wine- or tomato-based sauces, light fresh-tasting gravies, or—my favorite—the cutting zing of fresh lemon. Some are traditional: Most people are familiar with ratatouille and succotash, though perhaps not the particular take on either given here. But many of these offerings are originals—inspired by a trip to the farmer's market, the lighter way many of us eat now, and my own understanding of what vegetables offer nutritionally as well as sensually. Sometimes, something more capricious inspires a new way of putting things together: a mood, a browse through a foreign cookbook—and there's that sudden, dawning moment of "what if . . ." in which so much creative endeavor begins.

Artichoke and Lima Bean Ragoût in Lemon-Garlic Sauce

This is one of my favorite vegetable stews, perfect for spring, when (in good years) artichokes are plentiful and inexpensive. Here, they team up with some of the usual suspects—garlic, white wine, a lot of lemon—as well as buttery-starchy lima beans and baby carrots. The combination is highly flavorful, tonic, bracingly lemony, different flavors in each bite. You may be reminded of the Greek soup and sauce, *avgolemono,* but there's nary an egg in sight.

Delightful with a good hunk of sourdough toast (the kind with a crust so crisp it tears up the roof of your mouth), it's also outstanding over pasta or quinoa and is also excellent done ahead and reheated. It will keep for up to a week in the fridge just fine, due to the preservative effects of the lemon juice, and is special enough to be served to company.

If you are fortunate enough to spy fresh lima beans—in season for only a few precious weeks toward the end of the summer, and usually only available at larger farmer's markets—jump on them, as we say down here, like a cat on a june-bug. They are astonishingly good; inherently buttery, sweet and unstarchy, a bit chestnutlike in flavor. The work in shucking them (removing bean from pod) is as nothing compared to the deliciousness of the fresh bean. **SERVES 6 TO 8**

1 teaspoon olive oil
Cooking spray
1 onion, chopped
1 rib celery, minced
1 tablespoon finely chopped garlic (about 5 to 6 cloves)
3¾ cups any mild vegetable stock (see page 139)
½ cup dry white wine
2 teaspoons tomato paste
8 ounces ready-to-cook baby carrots (or 3 regular carrots, scrubbed and cut into 1-inch lengths)
2 large potatoes, peeled and cut into ¾- to 1-inch dice
Salt and freshly ground black pepper to taste
1 package (16 ounces) frozen baby lima beans (or, if you are able to get them, 2 pounds fresh lima beans, shelled, to equal 2 cups after shelling)
2 lemons
1 teaspoon butter
1 tablespoon unbleached white all-purpose flour
6 large whole artichokes, cooked and cooled, hearts and bottoms only (see page 387), or two 10-ounce packages frozen artichoke hearts, quartered
½ cup finely minced Italian parsley

1 Heat ½ teaspoon of the oil in a nonstick soup pot, or one that has been sprayed with cooking spray, over medium heat. Add the onion and sauté just until it starts to soften, about 4 minutes. Lower the heat slightly, and add the celery and 2 teaspoons of the garlic, and continue sautéing for another 2 minutes.

Add two cups of the vegetable stock along with the wine and tomato paste. Raise the heat to a boil and drop in the carrots and potatoes. Lower the heat to a simmer. Add salt and pepper to taste. Simmer, half-covered, until the potatoes are almost tender, about 15 minutes. Add the frozen baby lima beans, stir well, and simmer for another 10 minutes.

VARIATION

ARTICHOKE AND EDAMAME RAGOÛT IN LEMON-GARLIC SAUCE: ***Edamame, delicious slightly sweet green soybeans (see page 626), are now widely available frozen. Substitute 2 cups shelled frozen edamame for the limas to make a wonderful variation on this ragoût.***

2 Grate the rind of the lemons, then halve the lemons and squeeze out their juice, discarding the seeds.

3 Heat the remaining oil along with the butter in a nonstick skillet, or one that has been sprayed with cooking spray, over medium heat. Whisk in the flour and cook for 2 minutes, then slowly whisk in the remaining 1¾ cup stock and 1 teaspoon garlic along with the lemon juice and rind. Cook, whisking constantly, for 1 minute. Immediately scrape the sauce into the simmering vegetables.

4 Add the artichoke pieces, stir well, and cook until just heated through. Add half of the minced parsley. Taste and, if necessary, correct the seasoning. Serve hot, with the remaining parsley sprinkled over the top.

COOK ONCE FOR 2 MEALS Make twice the amount. Because of the lemon juice, it keeps exceptionally well in the fridge; 6 days, a week, no problem. First, serve it hot—either as straight stew or over pasta, with a sprinkling of Parmesan. Then, a few days later, serve it at room temperature, as a Mediterranean-style salad, with extra olive oil for drizzling. A hunk of good bread and a wedge of feta or ricotta salata, a bowl of green salad, and you have a superlative lazy summer luncheon. Artichoke is notoriously tough to pair with wine, but you might try it with a nicely acidic, crisp white wine—like a Chablis or other cool-climate Chardonnay—and remember what it feels like to kick back.

As the Crow Dines

I was once making a triple batch of this artichoke soup-stew. Though I usually save the pulled-off leaves to nibble on later, I had such a bundle left that I instead took them out to the backyard compost bin, inadvertent neighborhood cafe to the local wildlife. As I walked over to the bin, I wondered idly what the possums and raccoons, who ecstatically gnaw down discarded corn cobs, would make of the stickery-pointed inedible leaves, with only their thin, succulent, edible tipping. I couldn't imagine they'd have come across much artichoke detritus in the Ozarks.

The next day I glanced out the kitchen window and saw not a possum or raccoon, but a large, handsome, shiny black crow, perched on the limestone retaining wall near the compost bin. It had removed a large cone of inner leaves from the bin. Using one claw to hold the pointy end of the leaves down securely against the top of the rock wall, the crow leaned forward, and, with beak wide open, bit down on the fleshy edge and made a distinct, whole-headed, scraping-off motion. It paused, head tipped to one side, thoughtful, looking for all the world as if considering: "Hmmm, interesting . . . what would this be good with? Sauce Remolade, perhaps? Drawn butter?" Then, leaving the spent leaves untidily on the wall, it flew back into the compost bin, dug around for a few more leaves, and performed an encore. The crow was so entertaining I didn't even mind picking up after it.

Ragoût of Shiitake Mushrooms, Black-Eyed Peas, and Southern Greens

The vast majority of the dishes in this book are those I've made at home, for myself and Ned and friends, over my twenty-plus years as a vegetarian. What follows, however, is something we also used to serve at the inn's restaurant. Deservedly popular, it combines succulent locally grown shiitake mushrooms with cooked black-eyed peas and blanched fresh greens in an Italian-style tomato sauce, which is then ladled over creamy sunlight-bright yellow corn grits. It's everything you want in a dish—strong, vital, clear, delicious, full of large flavors—but also healthful, and very pretty on the plate. It has an unfussed-over, straightforward appeal, ample with a generous spirit.

This is a full-bodied dish. It holds up just fine to any good, tannic, equally full-bodied red wine—a Cabernet, a northern Rhone, a Barolo. **SERVES 4 TO 6**

NOTE

You'll need one batch of Basic Wintertime Italian Tomato Sauce (page 931) to make this. If making it expressly for this dish, season with 4 to 6 cloves garlic, and omit the dried herbs and use 2 tablespoons minced basil and ½ teaspoon finely chopped fresh rosemary needles instead. If, however, you already have some on hand, use it as is. You can also substitute your favorite commercially made pasta sauce.

1 tablespoon olive oil
½ pound shiitake mushrooms, cleaned, tough part of stems removed, coarsely sliced or halved
3 to 4 cloves garlic, pressed
3½ cups (1 batch) Basic Wintertime Italian Tomato Sauce (page 931), or good commercial tomato sauce
2 cups cooked black-eyed peas (see page 592), or well-drained canned black-eyes
Salt and freshly ground black pepper to taste
Honey, if necessary
1 bunch hearty greens (kale, turnip, mustard, or chard), washed, sliced as thinly as possible
Polenta (pages 441–46), with ½ cup grated Parmesan stirred in, hot and ready to serve
Freshly shaved Parmesan

1 Heat the oil in a large nonstick skillet or one that has been sprayed with cooking spray over medium heat. Add the shiitakes and sauté until they start

FROM THE INN DAYS

Voluptuous Roasted Red Pepper Spread
(PAGE 17)
Parchment Cracker-Bread
(PAGE 31)
and Crudités
(PAGE 62)

*

The Salad
(PAGE 68)
Pumpkin-Tomato Bisque with bread
(PAGE 181), **or Michael Romano's Union Square Cafe Indian Borscht**
(PAGE 154)

*

Ragoût of Shiitake Mushrooms, Black-Eyed Peas, and Southern Greens
(PREVIOUS PAGE)

*

Roasty-Toasty Potatoes, Carrots, and Onions
(PAGE 790)
Greek-Style Green Beans
(PAGE 689)

*

Chocolate Bread Pudding Maurice
(PAGE 1059)

to soften, about 3 minutes. Stir in the garlic and sauté until the mushrooms start to stick, another few minutes. Remove from the heat.

2 Combine the tomato sauce and black-eyed peas with the shiitakes. Return to very low heat and cook, stirring occasionally, for 20 to 25 minutes. Season with salt and pepper to taste. If the tomatoes aren't sweet, add a drop of honey.

3 Bring a large pot of water to a hard boil. Drop in the greens and blanch just until the color brightens and the greens get limp, about 45 seconds. The blanching process is very quick, but timing varies, depending on the tenderness of the greens and the thickness of the pieces; chard is done almost instantly, collard greens in 40 to 60 seconds. Drain well (save the blanching water to go into stock, if you like). Quickly pour cold water over the greens to stop the cooking.

Stir about one-quarter of the blanched greens into the hot ragoût, reserving the remainder.

4 If possible, warm or heat dinner plates.

5 Place a big ladleful of polenta with Parmesan in the center of each serving plate, with the middle slightly hollowed to make a nest for a good-sized spoonful of the ragoût. Top the ragoût with a little tangle of the reserved blanched greens, and lay a few slices of shaved Parmesan along the edges of the plate.

French-Style Springtime Vegetable Stew

Take an early spring morning, still a little cold, at the town square on market day, the day as well as the season so new that the local farmers are just setting up. This is the warming bowl you might make the evening after such an excursion. Asparagus, tiny new potatoes, and carrots—all the vegetables that say "rites of spring" are in it. And the sauce! Exquisite; you won't believe, when you read the ingredients, that it can be so good. **SERVES 6 TO 8**

Cooking spray
1 tablespoon olive oil
1 large onion, sliced vertically into thin slivers
12 to 15 small, whole button mushrooms, cleaned, stems cut flush with caps, stems chopped, caps reserved
2 ribs celery, chopped
¼ cup unbleached white all-purpose flour
3½ cups Golden Stock (page 140), or other light, mild but flavorful vegetable stock
3 tablespoons nutritional yeast (see page 239)
8 to 10 cloves garlic, peeled, quartered or thickly sliced
1 cup fruity, slightly sweet white wine, such as a Chenin Blanc, Riesling, or Gewürztraminer
¼ cup canned diced tomatoes in tomato puree
1 tablespoon tamari or shoyu soy sauce
2 teaspoons umeboshi plum vinegar (see page 118)
1½ teaspoons honey
¼ teaspoon salt
A good grinding of black pepper—½ to 1 teaspoon or so
12 to 15 very small new potatoes, preferably no larger than the size of pecans in the shell, scrubbed, peel on, left whole (use more if you can get the very tiny potatoes; fewer if you must use larger ones)
6 ounces fresh ready-to-eat baby carrots, or 2 regular carrots, scrubbed, sliced into ½-inch rounds
1 teaspoon butter
1 pound fresh asparagus, bottoms chopped off, sliced on the diagonal into 1-inch lengths
3 scallions, sliced into ¼-inch rounds
½ pound sugar-snap peas, strings removed
¼ pound fresh shiitake mushrooms, stems removed, caps sliced into ¼-inch strips
8 ounces savory baked tofu, diced
Minced Italian parsley (optional)

1 If using a conventional Dutch oven, spray it thoroughly with cooking spray, but you'll have better results using nonstick.

2 Heat the oil in the Dutch oven over medium-high heat. Add the onion and sauté until it starts to soften, 4 to 5 minutes. Add the chopped button mushroom stems and celery and sauté for 2 minutes longer. Sprinkle the onions and celery with the flour. Lower the heat to medium and continue to cook for 4 minutes. Add about ½ cup of the stock, stirring to make a smooth blend. When the liquid is free of any flour lumps, stir in a little more stock. When blended, add the remaining stock, stirring. Add the nutritional yeast, stirring to dissolve. Add the garlic, wine, tomatoes, tamari, umeboshi plum vinegar, honey, salt, and pepper. Bring the mixture to a boil, then immediately lower the heat to a simmer.

3 Drop in the potatoes, carrots, and button mushroom caps. Lower the heat slightly, cover, and barely simmer, stirring every so often, until the potatoes are nearly done, about 20 minutes.

4 Just before the ragoût is ready, place a large nonstick skillet, or one that has been sprayed with cooking spray, over medium-high heat. Add the butter. When melted, add the asparagus, scallions, sugar-snap peas, and shiitake mushroom strips and stir-fry for 3 minutes—just long enough to sear everything without really cooking it through. Remove from the heat and set aside.

VARIATIONS

The skinny little green beans, sometimes called haricots, are delicious in this stew; stem them, cut into 1½-inch lengths, and drop into the stew when the potatoes have cooked about 15 minutes. Even better, if you can get them, are fresh peas; add 1 to 1½ cups worth, fresh from the pod, with the tofu.

5 Add the tofu into the simmering stew. Stir well. Cover and cook for 4 minutes. Uncover and scrape in the stir-fried mixture. Stir well, put the lid back on, and cook until the potatoes and carrots are tender, and the asparagus and peas still have a little springtime crunch. Serve immediately with a liberal sprinkle of parsley, if desired.

COOK ONCE FOR 2 MEALS This stew makes a savory cobbler that is perfection; reheat leftovers (or make a double batch in the first place), turn out into a baking dish that has been sprayed with cooking spray and top with any of the savory biscuit doughs. Bake, at 400°F, until the biscuits are golden and the stew is bubbling hot.

Braise à la Chinoise

NOTE

It pushes the envelope to call this stew rather than stir-fry, because it cooks so quickly—no more than 10 or 12 minutes. But it's far softer than a typical stir-fry and just feels and tastes more stewlike. The star anise is essential.

A stew of an entirely different nature, this is a reinterpretation of the traditional sweet-salty-aromatic Chinese home-cooking method known as "red-cooking." Dark soy sauce gives the characteristic rich reddish color as well as the salty note, which is backed up by light soy sauce and a bit of salt. The sweet element comes from sherry or sweet rice wine (mirin) and sugar, with a bit of additional sweetness from fragrant star anise (or sometimes five-spice powder, in which star anise is predominant). Any ingredient that is both firm-textured and absorbent can be red-cooked. In this case, I have used tofu, with a variety of vegetables. **SERVES 4 AS PART OF A CHINESE MEAL**

1 tablespoon mild vegetable oil, such as corn, canola, or peanut
Cooking spray
1 tablespoon peeled, finely minced ginger
1 piece star anise
1 teaspoon finely minced garlic
½ head firm white or napa cabbage, cored and sliced
1 pound haricots verts (very thin green beans), stem ends removed (or regular green beans, stemmed, cut sharply on the angle into 1-inch pieces)
¼ pound shiitake mushrooms, stems removed, sliced into strips
1 large red-ripe tomato, peeled and diced
¼ cup Golden Stock (page 140)
2 tablespoons mirin (Japanese rice wine) or sherry
2 tablespoons tamari or shoyu soy sauce
2 teaspoons sugar
1 teaspoon white or golden miso, such as chickpea-rice miso (see page 173)
8 ounces savory baked tofu or Thai-style tofu, cut into ¼-inch strips

1 Heat the oil in a large nonstick pot, or one that has been sprayed with cooking spray, over medium-high heat. Add the ginger and star anise. Begin stirring, and after 30 seconds, lower the heat to medium. Still stirring, add the garlic, and almost immediately, as it becomes fragrant, add the cabbage, green beans, and shiitakes. Stir-fry for another minute, turning so that all of the ingredients get caressed by the ginger-garlic mixture.

2 Add the tomato, stock, mirin, tamari, sugar, and miso, stirring well. Lower the heat to a simmer. Cover the pot and simmer for 5 minutes. Lift the lid, and give a quick stir. Cover and simmer for another 4 minutes.

3 Stir again, and add the tofu. Again, cover and simmer for an additional minute. The vegetables should be cooked a bit more than is usual for Chinese food, yet retain the tiniest bit of crunch here and there. Remove the star anise and serve immediately, in deep bowls over rice.

Creole-Spiced Southern-Style Ragoût over Cheddar Cheese Corn Grits

This is another vegetarian dish that we served in the restaurant, usually in the summertime. It combines the best of several enduring favorites. The roux from my beloved Gumbo Zeb and many of its seasonings are here, somewhat tamed. Lima beans and fresh tomatoes, a lovely combination that appears in several of the stews in this section, are also here. Served over plain rice, the stew is rich and appealing. It can be done ahead and reheated very successfully. **SERVES 6 TO 8**

1 tablespoon mild vegetable oil, such as corn, canola, or peanut
Cooking spray
1 large onion, finely chopped
3 ribs celery, finely chopped
1 green bell pepper, finely chopped
1 bunch scallions, roots and dry stems removed, finely chopped
1 tablespoon finely chopped garlic
3 cups (5 to 6) coarsely chopped fresh tomatoes
1 bag (16 ounces) frozen lima beans (or, if you are able to get them, 2 pounds fresh lima beans, shelled, to equal 2 cups)
1 tablespoon Pickapeppa sauce
2 teaspoons sugar
½ teaspoon dried thyme
½ teaspoon dried basil
½ teaspoon dried oregano
½ teaspoon freshly ground black pepper
Dash of cayenne
Dash of ground cloves
¼ tablespoon dark roux (page 209)
½ cup vegetable stock (see page 139), or water, preferably spring or filtered
¼ cup red wine
Salt to taste
Corn Grits made with cheddar cheese (follow the Parmesan and Cayenne variation, substituting Cheddar for Parmesan, page 445), or cooked rice, hot, for serving
Minced Italian parsley

1 Heat the oil in a large nonstick pot, or one that has been well sprayed with cooking spray, over medium heat. Add the onion, followed by the celery, then the green pepper, garlic, and finally the scallions, stir-frying for 2 minutes between each addition. Add the tomatoes and then the lima beans. Stir in the Pickapeppa, sugar, thyme, basil, oregano, pepper, cayenne, and cloves. Bring to a boil, then lower the heat to a simmer. Cook, over very low heat, for about 15 minutes.

2 Combine the dark roux with the stock and wine, smoothing together with a whisk or in a food processor. Add the roux mixture to the ragoût, stirring to blend. Simmer for another 5 minutes and season to taste. Remove from the heat and serve over grits or rice, sprinkling with minced parsley.

COOK ONCE FOR 2 MEALS Thin down leftovers with diced tomatoes in juice or puree, heat, and use as a filling for Cornbread Pie à la Hippie (page 451). Stew leftovers are also scrumptious spooned over mashed potatoes.

New World Succotash Stew

Forget the pallid frozen succotash mixtures of your youth. This is redolent with all summer's best, full-flavored and interesting, yet each ingredient clearly tasting like itself. While I'm passionate about fresh limas, their season is brief; if you can't get them, the frozen are fine as long as everything else is fresh. For a little more delicacy, leeks step in instead of onions, but if you're leekless, a sliced onion will do as well. But it's the herbs that really give this dish perfume and poetry.

Perhaps you may know that succotash takes its name from the Narraganset Indian word *msickquatash,* which some authorities claim means "fragments" and others, "whole, boiled kernels of corn." Either makes sense. It pleases me that many of these ingredients are New World natives: the potatoes, corn, tomatoes, butternut squash, and, of course, the limas (named for Lima, Peru, where it was found as early as 1500). You eat an ancient bowl when you dine on this.

This makes a fun, light, pleasing summer supper served with Ronni's Skillet-Sizzled Kentucky Buttermilk Cornbread (page 452), and The Salad (page 68). **SERVES 6 TO 8**

1 tablespoon butter, or, for vegans, margarine or mild vegetable oil
Cooking spray
2 leeks, roots and all but 1 inch of green removed, split lengthwise, washed extremely well, and sliced
1 tablespoon tamari or shoyu soy sauce
2 tablespoons unbleached white all-purpose flour
1¼ cups Golden Stock (page 140), or other mild but flavorful vegetable stock
2 medium-sized potatoes, peeled and diced into ½-inch cubes
1 small butternut squash, peeled and diced into ½-inch cubes
2 cups fresh, dead-ripe summer tomatoes, peeled if you find the skin objectionable, and chopped (about 3 medium tomatoes; if you must, substitute the equivalent of diced canned tomatoes in juice)
1 bag (16 ounces) frozen lima beans (or, if you are able to get them, 2 pounds fresh lima beans, shelled, to equal 2 cups)
Kernels from 4 to 6 ears corn (about 3½ cups)
1 teaspoon honey
⅓ cup finely chopped Italian parsley
⅓ cup finely chopped cilantro
⅓ cup finely chopped basil
Salt and freshly ground black pepper to taste

1 Heat the butter in a nonstick pot, or one that has been sprayed with cooking spray, over medium-high heat. Add the leeks and sauté until they start to soften, 4 to 5 minutes. Add the tamari and sauté for 1 minute longer.

2 Sprinkle the leeks with the flour, then lower the heat slightly and cook, stirring, for 2 minutes. Gradually add the stock, whisking to smooth it into the flour. When the liquid is free of any flour lumps, add the potatoes, butternut squash, and the tomatoes. Cover and simmer gently for 10 minutes.

3 Lift the lid and add the limas, corn, and honey. Cover and simmer until the potatoes and limas are done, another 10 to 15 minutes. Remove from the heat and add the parsley, cilantro, and basil. Stir well and season to taste with salt and pepper. Serve hot. (If you prepare the stew ahead of time, don't add the herbs until after it has been reheated.)

COOK ONCE FOR 2 MEALS This makes a lot, so you might not even need to double it in order to have the pleasure of "déjà food" from it. Leftovers are delicious cold, scattered over a bed of spinach, for a substantial and summery salad. You don't really need to, but you could drizzle a little Basil Vinaigrette (page 71) over the spinach if you like. I have also rolled up last night's stew in a warmed whole wheat tortilla with a little grated smoked provolone.

CHAPTER 6

Deep Dish Savory Cobblers, Gratins & More

Eating or preparing certain foods can be like crossing your own threshold after a party: serene comfort after excitement, diversion, and giddiness. Conversation, champagne, and the necklace from the safety deposit box may sparkle at a black-tie affair, but isn't the most sublime moment when you come home? You exhale that breath you didn't know you'd been holding in, slide out of your social self (along with your dressy shoes), and, if you're lucky, enjoy a postmortem with someone you love. Many of the most comforting foods we eat are deep-dish. This chapter is devoted to them.

It's true that the scent of bread baking and of onions sautéing or soup simmering will always elicit "Mmmmmmms." But the fragrance of a savory casserole or pot pie at midbake ranks right up there in terms of pure pleasure. There's synergy—radiant heat plus the multiple ingredients of most deep-dishes in an especially tantalizing commingled waft.

Dishes like these usually feed a small crowd; they're not the quick-fix items of the unattached, like the omelet or grilled cheese sandwich. Ideal for gatherings of kin or friends, when everyone is around the table, they're meant to be eaten with enthusiasm and happiness, amid good conversation. These are dishes for which families clamor, the ones that neighbors ask you to bring to potlucks. Most such foods cure, at least temporarily, a broken heart, offering solace in a too-much, too-fast world.

And that, at certain times, is intoxication enough.

Cobblers & Shepherd's Pies

These deep-dish main courses are, to many, the gold standard of home comfort food, a cross between a pie and a casserole. They are hearty, heart-warming dishes that, for the most part, you can *only* find at home. Not only are such casseroles too uncomplicated for most eateries, their method of preparation is not compatible with restaurant service. Such dishes are best eaten soon after they come out of the oven; they don't wait well, nor do they reheat well (perhaps because many of them were originally invented to use up leftovers, and so the fillings may already be on round two). Nor, being scooped out of their baking dish, do they lend themselves to attractive plating-up.

It's different, though, when the whole casserole is served, as it is at home. Then you really want to tuck in, especially around the edges, where the crust or topping may be exceptionally golden and crisp. In this chapter you'll find vegetarian versions of the shepherd's pie—where a dark, savory filling is topped with snowy mashed potatoes (or sunset-orange sweet potatoes)—and the cobbler, packed to overflowing with good things hidden beneath a golden-brown crust of homemade biscuits, as well as a few adventuresome variations of both.

Dishing on Deep-Dish: How-To's and Hints

The general principle of savory deep-dish pies is this: A filling with the consistency of stew, either made from scratch for the dish or composed of leftovers (perhaps intentional déjà food), is heated and placed in a well-oiled 2- to 2½-inch-deep casserole. It is then topped with a breadlike or starchy topping—cornbread batter, biscuits, mashed white or sweet potatoes, filo dough, or short-crust pastry—and the whole thing is baked until the top is crusty and golden brown. Here are some hints for a successful deep-dish pie:

- ▲ Always make sure your filling is good and hot before you lay down the top crust. This helps prevent the underside of the crust from getting mushy, even if the crust is mashed potatoes and not pastry, and especially if the top crust is biscuit dough or cornbread batter.

- ▲ The best proportions for these pies are about two or three to one, that is, about two-thirds to three-fourths of the depth should be filling and the remainder should be topping or crust. Too little filling and the crust will be sodden and dominant.

- ▲ Almost any soup, stew, or bean dish can make a good filling, with a few exceptions. Curry flavors don't work too well in most cases, and, to my taste, creamy potages are not as good as those that are tomato- or broth-based. Also, if the soup or stew or bean dish has a heavy starch element, it won't do (mushroom soup as a base, yes; mushroom-barley soup, no). But you can hardly go wrong with a chili. And most stews—even those with a few potatoes—work fine. So does any soup thick with vegetables and tomatoes.

- ▲ If you don't have enough filling, thin out what you have with equal parts vegetable stock and canned, diced, or stewed tomatoes (assuming, of course, that the flavors of these additions will work with the original filling). Adjust the seasoning as needed.

- ▲ If you have Basic Wintertime Italian Tomato Sauce (page 931) on hand, you've got a head start on a great filling. To 2½ cups of sauce, add 1 to 2 cups of any cooked beans, well drained, and/or 1 to 2 cups of any cooked vegetable or vegetable mix, cut into bite-size pieces.
  Green beans are exceptionally good here, and so are large cubes of barely steamed eggplant. You could also use any unsauced frozen vegetable combo, such as gumbo mix, which is corn, okra, and red peppers. Combine these ingredients, cover with bread or potato topping, and bake.

- ▲ Two of the easiest toppings for a leftover-based deep-dish pie are mashed potatoes and mashed sweet potatoes. If even this is too much work, make up some instant potatoes. Barbara's Bakery, a natural foods store brand, makes some that are preservative free.

- ▲ For a breadlike crust, try cornbread crust, biscuit crust, or filo pastry topping.

CORNBREAD CRUST: Preheat the oven to 400°F. Make any cornbread recipe (see pages 451–52), but use ⅓ cup extra milk or buttermilk. Although eggs will make a richer, moister crust, you can omit them from any recipe and just add extra buttermilk until you've reached proper batter consistency, that is, thick but pourable. If it's too thick, add more buttermilk (or the vegan equivalent—unflavored soy milk with a little lemon juice), then pour the cornbread batter over the heated stew mixture in the casserole, pop the whole thing into the oven, and bake until crusty and golden, 35 to 45 minutes.

BISCUIT CRUST: Preheat the oven to 425°F. Make either Classic Biscuits, Reduced-Fat but Still Really Good (page 511) or any of the variations that follow it (the Cornmeal Biscuits are exceptional here). Place the biscuits on top of the heated filling in the casserole. Put into the oven and bake until crusty, 15 to 20 minutes.

FILO PASTRY: See the notes on filo on page 311.

Calabacitas Cobbler with Cornmeal Biscuit Crust

Calabacitas is Spanish for diced, sautéed squash with just a hint of spice. It's an agreeable combo that virtually reinvents summer squash or zucchini. Finished calabacitas flaunt their versatility as everything from a side dish to a crépe filling to an ingredient in a layered casserole. Here, they're served up in a vegan "cream" sauce accented with green chile and cilantro, and topped with cornmeal biscuits. If you prefer a noncreamy sauce, try Tomatillo Salsa Verde (page 944) or New Mexico–Style Green Chile Sauce (page 942). **SERVES 6 TO 8**

About 3 cups leftover calabacitas (see page 801)
Salsa Verde y Blanca with Tofu (recipe follows)
Cooking spray
8 Cornmeal Biscuits (page 513)

1 Preheat the oven to 425°F.

2 Combine the calabacitas and salsa in a nonstick saucepan, or one that has been sprayed with cooking spray, over low-medium heat and heat together slowly, stirring often. As the mixture heats, prepare the Classic Biscuits, cornmeal variation up to Step 4.

3 Spray eight 1-cup ramekins or an 8-inch square glass baking dish with cooking spray. Transfer the heated calabacitas mixture into the prepared ramekins or baking dish.

4 Top each ramekin with an unbaked biscuit, cut to shape, or arrange the biscuit dough over the top of the baking dish and immediately pop into the oven. Bake for 12 to 15 minutes, or until the biscuits are brown and the calabacitas mixture is fragrant and bubbling hot. Any extra biscuits can be baked alongside the cobbler on a baking sheet that has been sprayed with cooking spray.

Salsa Verde y Blanca with Tofu

While working on a different recipe for this book—Wanda's Soft Corn Crêpe-Tortillas with Calabacitas (page 338)—I discovered at the last minute that a vegetarian guest had a lactose allergy and couldn't eat the Salsa Poblano Blanca y

Verde (page 947) I had prepared. I threw stuff in the Cuisinart at the eleventh hour, and it was at least as good as, maybe better than, the Salsa Poblano. If you want a milder sauce, you can use one serrano, seeding and deveining it. But if you don't like cilantro, choose another recipe; the cilantro is indispensble here. **MAKES ABOUT 1¾ CUPS**

- **1 (10½ ounce) box soft reduced-fat silken tofu**
- **2 serrano chiles, stems removed, seeds included, coarsely chopped**
- **½ cup cilantro leaves**
- **1 teaspoon salt**
- **4 cloves garlic, quartered, or 1 heaping teaspoon Roasted Garlic puree (page 899)**
- **½ cup unflavored nondairy milk, such as soy, oat, or rice**

Combine all the ingredients except the nondairy milk in a food processor. Pulse, pausing to scrape the sides, then buzz to make a chunky puree. Add the milk and buzz a few more times. Use in the recipe above or reheat gently and serve anywhere you'd enjoy a spicy-creamy cilantro-y sauce: in an omelet, over pasta, and so on.

Curried Lentil-Potato Cobbler with Pumpkin and Tomatoes and Filo Top Crust

In this cobbler, pumpkin and tomato melt into the classic Indian combination of lentils, potatoes, and spices with major attitude. The result is rich yet elusive. The crisp filo top—from an entirely different culture—provides contrast, elegance, and interest. The dish is best hot from the oven. A dollop of whole milk yogurt is a good accompaniment and a good crisp mixed green salad with a squeeze of fresh lemon instead of vinegar starts the meal perfectly. **SERVES 4 TO 6**

FILLING

2 cups lentils, washed and picked over
6 cups water, preferably spring or filtered
1 bay leaf
2 teaspoons butter, mild vegetable oil, such as corn, canola, or peanut, or a combination
1 onion, chopped
1 tablespoon peeled and minced ginger
2 cloves garlic, minced
1 tablespoon black or brown (not yellow) mustard seeds
1½ teaspoons cumin seeds
1½ teaspoons ground coriander
1½ teaspoons ground turmeric
Pinch of cayenne
Dash of cinnamon
Dash of ground cloves
Salt and freshly ground black pepper to taste
3 to 4 fist-size potatoes, scrubbed and cut into ½-inch cubes

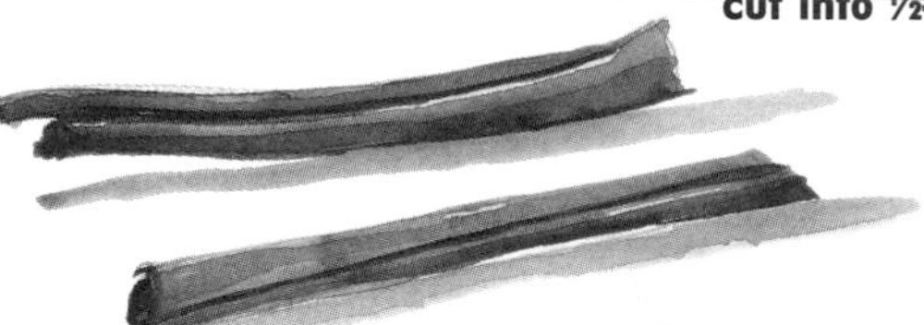

PUMPKIN-TOMATO GRAVY

1 (14-ounce) can tomatoes and green chiles
1½ cups mashed pumpkin or butternut squash, fresh or canned
1 tablespoon maple syrup or honey
1½ cups vegetable stock, commercial or homemade (see page 139)
Cooking spray

TOP CRUST

4 sheets frozen filo dough, thawed
2 to 3 tablespoons melted butter or half butter and half mild vegetable oil, such as corn, canola, or peanut

1 Combine the lentils, water, and bay leaf in a large soup pot and bring to a boil. Turn down the heat to low and cook, covered, for 40 minutes.

2 As the lentils cook, heat the butter and/or oil in a large skillet over medium heat. When it's hot, add the onion and sauté until it starts to soften, about 3 minutes. Add the ginger, garlic, and all the spices and cook, stirring constantly, for about 3 minutes more, or until mustard seeds begin to pop.

3 Lift the lid on the lentils, stir in the spice mixture, and drop in the potatoes. Stir well and cook, half-covered, at a low simmer for 20 to 30 minutes more, until the lentils are soft and the potatoes just barely soft. Remove the bay leaf. Season with salt and lots of pepper.

4 As the potatoes and lentils cook, combine the tomatoes, pumpkin, and maple syrup in a food processor and buzz until smooth. When the potatoes are just barely tender, stir in the pumpkin mixture and the stock and heat through. When quite hot, remove from the heat. Cover and set aside.

5 Preheat the oven to 400°F.

6 Spray a 15-by-10-by-2½-inch casserole with cooking spray. Turn the hot lentil mixture into it. Lay 1 sheet of filo dough over the filling, brush with one-third of the butter, and fold in any overhanging edges. Repeat with the remaining filo and butter. With a very sharp knife, score the filo into large squares, trying not to cut into the filling.

7 Bake until the filo is crisp and brown, 35 to 45 minutes. Remove from the oven and serve hot.

Jazzman's Pie

This shepherd's pie has a groove thing going: a substantial seitan filling that's hot and spicy with the tongue-curling burn of Cajun/Creole spices, topped with sweet potatoes. Though I've given a from-scratch recipe below, you can easily make the pie from planned-for leftovers—just sauce the diced seitan with a little diluted Gumbo Zeb (page 207) for the filling; use mashed leftover baked sweet potatoes with the flavorings listed below for topping. **SERVES 8 TO 10**

SWEET-POTATO TOPPING

6 large yams or sweet potatoes, scrubbed
1 teaspoon to 1 tablespoon butter (optional)
Salt to taste
¼ cup brown sugar
3 tablespoons unsalted roasted peanuts, finely chopped

CREOLE VEGETABLE SAUTÉ

1 tablespoon mild vegetable oil, such as corn, canola, or peanut
1 large onion, chopped
1 green bell pepper, stemmed, seeded, and chopped
3 ribs celery with leaves, chopped
8 to 10 large scallions, chopped

SEASONING PASTE

1 (16-ounce) can whole tomatoes
4 cloves garlic, peeled
1 tablespoon Pickapeppa sauce
3 tablespoons dark Roux (page 207)
2 tablespoons tomato paste
½ to 1 teaspoon Tabasco or similar hot sauce
½ teaspoon dried basil
½ teaspoon dried oregano
½ teaspoon dried thyme
1 teaspoon paprika
Dash of cayenne, or more to taste
Dash of ground allspice
Dash of ground cloves
1 to 2 tablespoons finely chopped Italian parsley
6 to 8 grinds of black pepper
1 teaspoon salt

ASSEMBLY

2 bay leaves
3 cups vegetable stock (see page 139)
1 (8-ounce) box traditional-style or dark seitan (see page 232), drained, rinsed, and cut into ¾-inch chunks
Cooking spray

1 Preheat the oven to 350°F.

2 Prick the yams with a fork, wrap in foil, and bake until very tender, about 40 minutes. Remove from the oven and unwrap the foil so the yams can cool. Set the other topping ingredients aside.

3 Heat the oil in the largest skillet you have. Sauté the onion until it begins to soften, about 4 minutes. Add the green bell

All, all, all that Jazz

Jazzman's Pie is fondly dedicated to Chris "Blind Boy White" Thomson, who, though white, is not blind. He is Eureka's own "trolley jazzman." What, you might ask, is that? Well, our annual Eureka Springs Jazz Festival (held in September) always kicks off with Chris, in Blind Boy persona, clinging onto the back of one of the open trolleys that traverse Eureka, trombone-ing his heart out. I hear him clear across Dairy Hollow. The windows are usually open that time of year—warm days, cool nights, brilliant blue almost-fall skies—and I know another Jazz Festival is starting. Each year I am amazed that another twelve months have fled, that the Jazz Festival is here, and that Ned and I and Blind Boy and so many other locals I love and cherish (even some I respect as adversaries) are still alive and well to enjoy it. As we move from youth through middle age into that time when we start to become well aware that any song, lovely, strong, riffing across the hollow, might be the last we hear or play, that song becomes all the sweeter. And in that moment, with those notes echoing across to me as I look out into the still-green hollow, I say another goodbye to those who have gone. Sykes. Kelly. Eagle. Jeanette. Lester. Steve. Virginia. Ruth. We loved you. We think, we hope, we believe, you knew that.

pepper and celery and sauté for another 2 minutes. Add the scallions and sauté for 1 minute more, then lower the heat and place a lid on the skillet, allowing the vegetables to steam while you complete the next step.

4 Drain the can of tomatoes, reserving the juice. Place the tomatoes in a food processor with the garlic, Pickapeppa, roux, tomato paste, Tabasco, basil, oregano, thyme, paprika, cayenne, allspice, cloves, and parsley. Process briefly.

5 Add the reserved tomato juice, bay leaves, and vegetable stock to the vegetables in the skillet. Heat through. Add the seitan and let heat for 3 minutes more. Stir in the seasoning paste from the processor and cook for 4 to 5 minutes more, or until heated through. Taste and adjust the seasonings.

6 Peel the sweet potatoes and place in a mixing bowl. Using a fixed or hand-held electric mixer, whip the sweet potatoes with as much butter as pleases you, salt, and 2 tablespoons of the brown sugar.

7 Place the tomato-seitan mixture in a nonstick 4-quart baking dish or 2 smaller nonstick dishes, or ones that have been sprayed with cooking spray. Dollop with the sweet potatoes, spreading to cover the filling completely. Bake for 40 to 50 minutes, or until warm and bubbly. Remove from the oven and sprinkle with the remaining brown sugar and the peanuts.

8 Turn on the broiler. Place the dish under the broiler and broil, watching closely, until browned and very hot, 2 to 5 minutes. Serve immediately.

Nouveau Iowa Potato–Black Bean Pie

For years Ned rhapsodized about a casserole his mother used to make, with mashed potatoes, canned black bean soup, and browned hamburger. I was afraid Georgene wouldn't be able to remember it—I reckoned it had likely been something seat-of-the-pants to use up leftovers quickly and economically—but she did. She recalled she'd been making a casserole from a recipe she thinks she probably found in a magazine. The original called for canned condensed tomato soup. She didn't have any on hand, but she did have canned black bean soup . . . thus a Shank family legend was born. This started as my attempt to recapture Ned's memory of that casserole. It became something spicier on the way. If you're thinking "Black beans and potatoes? Too starchy," remember how good black beans and tortillas are. **SERVES 6 TO 8**

MASHED POTATO TOPPING

3 pounds (about 9 medium) potatoes, preferably Yukon Gold or Yellow Finn, peeled and cut into 1-inch pieces
Salt to taste
1 tablespoon butter or vegetable margarine
½ to ⅔ cup low-fat dairy or nondairy milk, warmed, or as needed
Freshly ground black pepper to taste

BLACK BEANS AND "HAMBURGER"

3 cups dehydrated black bean flakes, containing only salt and beans
3 cups boiling water, preferably spring or filtered
1 teaspoon olive oil
Cooking spray
1 onion, diced
2 to 3 ribs celery, diced
6 cloves garlic, chopped
1 (10-ounce) box commercially made spicy-style ready-ground tofu, such as Garden of Eatin's
1 (10-ounce) can diced tomatoes or tomatoes and green chiles
1 tablespoon Pickapeppa sauce

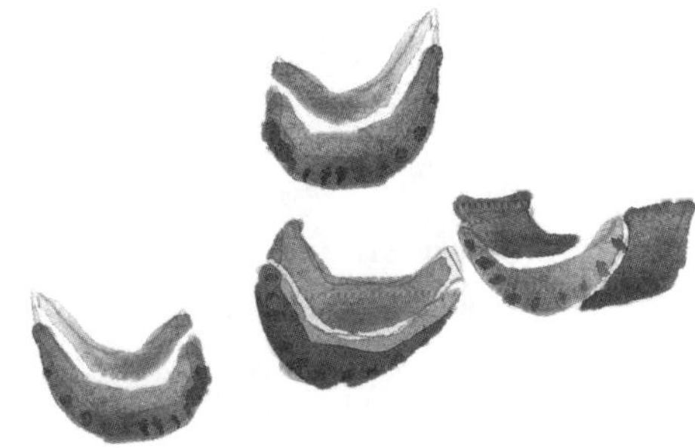

HEARTLAND FEAST

Cora Pinkley Call's Ozark-Style Stuffed Tomato Salad
(PAGE 91)

*

Golden Days of Summer Corn Soup
(PAGE 163)

*

Noveau-Iowa Potato–Black Bean Pie

*

Green Beans Moutarde with Grilled Red Peppers
(PAGE 692)

*

Cherry-Peach Crisp
(PAGE 980)

1 Preheat the oven to 400°F.

2 Ease the potatoes into boiling salted water, and cook for 20 to 25 minutes, until quite tender. Drain, reserving the potato water. Mash the potatoes together with the butter, warmed milk, salt as needed, and pepper. Keep mashing, adding milk or some of the reserved potato-cooking water as needed, until the potatoes are nice and fluffy.

3 As the potatoes cook, prepare the beans: Place the bean flakes in a heatproof bowl and pour the boiling water over them. Stir well, cover, and let sit.

4 Prepare the "burgers": Pour the oil into a nonstick skillet, or one that has been sprayed with cooking spray, and heat over medium heat. Add the onion and sauté for about 4 minutes, or until softened. Add the celery and continue to sauté for 2 minutes more. Add the garlic, lower the heat slightly, and sauté for 1 minute more. Add the ground tofu, tomatoes, and Pickapeppa. Raise the heat under the skillet to bring the mixture to a boil.

5 Combine the tomato mixture with the beans, stirring well to mix everything together.

6 Place the bean-tomato mixture in an 11½-by-9½-by-2-inch casserole or baking dish that has been sprayed with cooking spray. Spoon the mashed potatoes over the filling, spreading it evenly with the back of a spoon.

7 Bake for 25 to 30 minutes, until the potatoes have appealing golden-brown peaks on them (if you don't see any sign of these, you may wish to place the dish under the broiler for the last few minutes). Serve immediately.

Black Bean Bonanza

A good basic deserves as many variations as the Goldberg. Here are just a few:

- *To make this dish even quicker, use leftover mashed potatoes or preservative-free instant mashed potatoes.*
- *To top this dish with cheese, sprinkle with 2 to 4 ounces (½ to 1 cup) grated sharp Cheddar, dairy or nondairy as you prefer, in the last 10 minutes of baking.*
- *To make Sherried Nouveau Iowa Potato–Black Bean Pie (which, it turns out, is closer to what Georgene did), use plain canned tomatoes (not canned tomatoes and green chiles) and add ½ cup dry sherry to the black bean mixture.*
- *Hot Stuff Potato–Black Bean Pie: Substitute either 1¼ cups Chou Chou's "Yer Cheating Heart" Salsa (page 914) or any good commercially made green or red hot enchilada sauce for the tomatoes and green chiles. Top with a sprinkle of minced fire-roasted jalapeños and grated dairy or non dairy cheese (as above). Serve it with a good solid sprinkle of finely minced fresh cilantro, with additional salsa, grated cheese, and reduced-fat sour cream passed at the table.*

Pies

A stuffed and wrapped pastry is tightly budded, its filling enclosed and hidden. By contrast, a pie, open-faced, is in full bloom.

Time was, the standard offering for vegetarians was quiche. This savory custard pie was served so often (and often in such mediocre form) that it became something of a "quiché." Now, classic quiche can be exquisitely good, but it is *always* high in saturated fat, due to its egg-custard filling and shortening-rich crust. Plus, it excludes those who do not eat eggs or dairy products. But the universe of savory pies extends far beyond quiche. Consider using alternative crusts (many with more reasonable fat contents than shortening crust) and fill them with a garden-full of bright flavors and interesting vegetable combinations.

Deep-Dish New World Vegetable Tart in a Crisp Crumb Crust

A two-tone tart with a savory crumb crust and a filling of Southwestern-seasoned New World vegetables—pepper, summer squash, corn, and tomato—hidden under a creamy-custardy (but vegan) topping of butternut squash and silken tofu makes a lovely, pleasing dish, perfect for late summer or early fall. The crust is crumbly; be prepared for it to fall apart more than a conventional crust. No matter, the combo is still sensational.

If you don't have a deep-dish pie pan, make this in a 9-inch square baking dish with 2- to 2½-inch sides. There is too much filling here for a conventional shallow pie pan. **SERVES 6 TO 8**

CRISP CRUMB CRUST

Cooking spray
¾ cup fine crisp breadcrumbs
½ cup crushed Nutri-Grain or other no-sugar-added corn- or wheat flakes, or whole-grain lowfat cracker crumbs, made from crackers such as Ak-Maks
½ teaspoon salt
1 tablespoon butter, melted, or 1 tablespoon mild vegetable oil, such as corn, canola, or peanut
2 tablespoons water, preferably spring or filtered

TOFU-SQUASH TOPPING

1 (10½ ounce) box silken firm or extra-firm tofu, preferably reduced fat
¾ cup pureed butternut squash, acorn squash, or pumpkin (page 805), or canned unsweetened pumpkin puree or frozen mashed squash
1 tablespoon honey
1 teaspoon cornstarch
Salt and freshly ground black pepper to taste
A few gratings of nutmeg
Pinch of cayenne

VEGETABLE FILLING

Salt
2 medium zucchini, grated
3 ears fresh corn, husks and silk removed
1 teaspoon to 1 tablespoon butter, melted, or 1 teaspoon to 1 tablespoon mild vegetable oil, such as corn, canola, or peanut
1 onion
1 poblano chile, diced (optional)
2 teaspoons cumin seeds
3 to 4 cloves garlic, finely chopped
1 tomato, diced
¼ cup vegetable stock (page 139) or water
2 tablespoons cornstarch
3 tablespoons chopped Italian parsley

1 Preheat the oven to 450°F. Spray a 9-by-2-inch deep-dish pie pan with oil or cooking spray, or use a nonstick pan.

2 Combine all the remaining crust ingredients and press into the prepared pan. Bake for 7 to 10 minutes, until slightly colored and a bit firmed up. Remove from the oven and set aside. Lower the oven temperature to 375°F.

3 As the crust bakes, make the topping: Combine the tofu, squash puree, honey, cornstarch, salt and pepper, nutmeg, and cayenne in a food processor and buzz until smooth. Set aside.

4 To make the filling, salt the grated zucchini lightly, toss well, and place in a colander set over a bowl to drain the excess liquid. Set aside. Cut the kernels from the corn and set aside. Heat the butter or vegetable oil over medium heat in a skillet. Add the onion and sauté for about 4 minutes, or until it begins to soften. Add the poblano, if using, and cumin seeds and stir-fry for 2 to 3 minutes more, then lower the heat and add the garlic. Cook for 1 minute more, being careful to avoid browning the garlic. Press the zucchini against the sides of the colander, trying to extract as much liquid as possible; discard the liquid. Add the zucchini and tomato to the skillet and

cook, stirring, for 4 to 5 minutes, until most of the juice has evaporated. Add 2 tablespoons of the stock to the skillet and stir to scrape up any bits stuck to the bottom. Dissolve the cornstarch in the remaining stock and add to the skillet along with the parsley and corn. Remove from the heat. Season to taste with salt and pepper.

5 Spread the zucchini-corn filling in the bottom of the prebaked crust. Spread the tofu-squash topping over that. Bake for 35 to 40 minutes, until the topping is a deep golden brown. Let sit for 15 minutes, then slice into wedges and serve.

Spinach and Wheat Berry Tofu Quiche in a Hashed Brown Potato Crust

Here is a pie with a savor somewhat similar to, and certainly the equal of, a dairy-rich classic quiche—yet it is made without eggs, cheese, or cream. Nutritional yeast (see page 239) provides a hint of cheese flavor. If you like, you may sprinkle several tablespoons of grated Parmesan or sharp Cheddar cheese over the top in the last 10 minutes of baking. While I myself am of the real-cheese-or-nothing school, some lactose-intolerant or vegan friends enjoy a grating of one of the many available soy (or nut- or rice-based) cheeses on the market. But you don't really need cheese of any kind for this good, hearty dish. Enjoy the leftovers cold or warmed for breakfast. **SERVES 6 TO 8**

10- to 12-inch Hashed Brown Potato Crust (recipe follows)

FILLING

2 (10-ounce) packages spinach or 2 pounds fresh spinach, trimmed
1 teaspoon to 1 tablespoon butter, melted, or 1 teaspoon to 1 tablespoon mild vegetable oil, such as corn, canola, or peanut
1 medium onion, chopped
10 to 12 fresh mushrooms, cleaned and sliced
2 cloves garlic, diced
1 (10½-ounce) box silken firm or extra-firm tofu, preferably reduced fat
1 tablespoon cornstarch

A few gratings of nutmeg
3 tablespoons nutritional yeast
1 tablespoon golden miso (traditional sweet white miso) (see page 173)
2 cloves garlic, peeled and left whole
Salt and freshly ground black pepper to taste
½ to 1 cup cooked wheat berries (see page 498)

1 Prepare the crust as directed in the recipe following, partially baking it.

2 Preheat the oven to 375°F.

3 Steam the spinach over boiling water, covered, until wilted, about 3 minutes. Set aside until cool, then coarsely chop. Set aside.

4 Heat the butter or vegetable oil, if using, over medium heat in a skillet. Add the onion and sauté for about 6 minutes, or until limp. Add the mushrooms and the diced garlic and sauté for 5 minutes more. Set aside.

5 Combine the tofu, cornstarch, nutmeg, nutritional yeast, miso, peeled whole garlic, salt, and lots of freshly ground pepper in a food processor and buzz until smooth. Add about 1 packed tablespoon of the chopped spinach to the tofu mixture and process again. Turn the mixture out into a bowl. Stir in the remaining chopped spinach, along with the wheat berries. When the mushrooms and onions have finished sautéing, add about one-third of them and stir until well mixed.

6 Spread the tofu-spinach filling in the partially baked crust. Scatter the remaining sautéed mushrooms over the top, pressing them in lightly. If desired, lay out the mushroom slices in a concentric circular pattern. Bake for 40 to 50 minutes, or until browned on top and set. Remove from the oven and let sit for 15 minutes, then slice into wedges and serve.

Hashed Brown Potato Crust

5 medium russet potatoes, scrubbed
⅓ teaspoon salt
Plenty of freshly ground black pepper
1½ tablespoons mild vegetable oil, such as corn, canola, or peanut

1 Preheat the oven to 450°F.

2 Grate the potatoes in a food processor or by hand. Immediately turn them out

into a bowl of cold water and swish them around in it. Let the potatoes soak for 8 to 10 minutes, then drain them very well. Turn them out onto a dish towel and pat them dry. Put the potatoes in a bowl and toss with the salt and pepper.

3 Heat the oil over medium-high heat in a 10- to 12-inch iron skillet. (Do not use a nonstick skillet here.) Carefully swirl the pan, so the oil coats the sides as well as the bottom of the skillet. With the oil quite hot, sprinkle the grated potato over the skillet as evenly as possible. Cook for 1 minute, then reduce the heat to very low, cover the skillet, and let the potatoes steam, without stirring, for about 5 minutes. At this point they should be translucent on top and lightly browned underneath. Remove from the heat and with the back of a spoon, press the potatoes evenly over the sides and bottom of the skillet, forming a crust.

4 For a partially baked crust, one that you will bake further, bake for 10 minutes, remove, and fill, then bake as directed in the recipe. For a fully prebaked crust, which is used in the Potato-Crusted Summertime Skillet Pie (below), lower the heat to 350°F and bake for 30 to 35 minutes, or until it is golden brown and crusty, top and bottom.

Potato-Crusted Summertime Skillet Pie

Essentially a garlicky, wine-sauced stir-fry piled into a potato crust, this pie smells intoxicating as it bakes. It is festive enough for a party or simple enough for an at-home dinner. The crust will be crisp only for the first hour or so out of the oven, but if you have leftovers, don't worry: Even with a soft crust, even cold out of the fridge the next day, slices of this pie are awfully good. **SERVES 4 TO 6 AS AN ENTREE, 6 TO 8 AS A COMPONENT**

2 teaspoons butter
2 teaspoons olive oil
4 medium zucchini or 2 zucchini and 2 yellow squash, quartered lengthwise, then sliced into ¼-inch-wide quarter-circles
1 bunch Swiss chard (about ¾ pound), stems removed and finely diced, leaves finely slivered
2 tablespoons tamari or shoyu soy sauce
1 large tomato, diced
½ teaspoon sugar
1 tablespoon finely chopped garlic
1 cup dry white wine
2 tablespoons cornstarch
Salt and freshly ground black pepper to taste
10- to 12-inch-thick Hashed Brown Potato Crust (previous page), fully prebaked
2 ounces grated Cheddar, Parmesan, or Jarlsberg cheese, or a combination (about ½ cup)
½ cup soft breadcrumbs
2 tablespoons minced Italian parsley

1 Preheat the oven to 375°F.

2 Heat the butter and oil together over medium heat in a skillet or wok. Add the zucchini and sauté it, tossing it around with a wooden spoon for about 30 seconds. Cover and let steam for 30 seconds more, then remove the lid. Stir-fry, uncovered, for 2 to 3 minutes more, then add the chard and continue stir-frying for 3 to 5 minutes, or until zucchini begins to lose its raw look and the chard leaves have wilted.

3 Add the tamari, tomato, and sugar and raise the heat to high, stirring, to evaporate the tomato liquid. Cook until there is no visible liquid, then turn the mixture out into a bowl. Stir in the garlic.

4 With the heat turned off, pour all but 3 tablespoons of the wine into the skillet and scrape up any bits stuck to the bottom. Dissolve the cornstarch in the remaining wine, smushing with your fingers. Bring the wine in the skillet to a boil, whisk in the cornstarch-wine mixture, and cook until thickened and clear (this should happen almost instantly). Add the thickened wine to the vegetables in the bowl and season with salt and pepper.

5 Turn the vegetable mixture into the prebaked potato crust. Combine the cheese and breadcrumbs and sprinkle over the top. Bake for 35 minutes, or until the top is crusted and golden brown.

6 Remove from the oven and let stand for 10 minutes. Sprinkle with parsley and serve.

Zwiebel Kuchen (German Onion Tart)

This Old World tart is a somewhat fat-reduced version of a fondly remembered onion tart Ned and I enjoyed at a now-defunct Atlanta restaurant called Theda's. A slightly zingy custard held piles of sautéed onion in a yeast crust sprinkled with poppyseeds. When Theda's closed, re-creating this tart became something of a mission for me. I learned it was a traditional German Zwiebel Kuchen, or onion tart. German recipes usually call for a short crust or puff pastry, and sour cream in the custard. The customary seeds are caraway, but, like the Theda's chef, I feel poppyseeds are an improvement because they don't overpower the delectably sweet, slow-sautéed onions.

This can do duty as a substantial starter or an entree (with a salad and maybe a light soup); it can be served hot or at room temperature, at a buffet. I've also included a soy-rich vegan variation. See which you prefer.

Don't use a nonstick skillet for this; you want the onions to caramelize nicely.

SERVES 4 TO 6

Yeasted Pastry Crust with Poppyseeds (recipe follows), prebaked

FILLING

- **1 tablespoon butter**
- **3 large onions, sliced paper thin, or 2 large onions, sliced, and 2 leeks, cleaned and sliced**
- **⅔ cup buttermilk**
- **1¼ cups regular yogurt or yogurt sour cream, or reduced-fat sour cream**
- **1 teaspoon salt**
- **A few gratings of nutmeg**
- **2 large eggs, beaten**
- **1 tablespoon unbleached all-purpose flour**

1. Melt the butter over medium heat in a heavy skillet. Add the onions and saute them, very slowly, stirring often, for 20 to 35 minutes, or until onions are limp and lightly brown. They will shrink dramatically in volume.

2. In a medium bowl whisk together the buttermilk, yogurt, salt, nutmeg, eggs, and flour. Stir in the sautéed onion and turn

VARIATION

VEGAN ZWIEBEL KUCHEN

Sauté onion as directed but substitute vegetable margarine or a mild vegetable oil for the butter. Omit the buttermilk, yogurt, and eggs from filling. Instead, combine the following in a food processor: ⅔ cup plain unsweetened soy milk; 1 (12.3-ounce) package silken tofu, preferably reduced fat; 2 teaspoons raw cashew butter (optional, but tasty in tofu-based custards—it adds richness); 1 teaspoon umeboshi plum paste (optional, but umeboshi's salty-sour, faintly bitter notes make the transition from sour cream to tofu believable); and 1 to 1½ teaspoons salt. Add a few gratings of nutmeg, and buzz until smooth. Then buzz in 3 tablespoons cornstarch or arrowroot, omitting the flour. Stir in the sautéed onions and fill the crust (made with vegetable margarine rather than butter) as directed.

the mixture out into the prebaked crust, spreading evenly.

3 Bake at 325°F (your oven will already be at this temperature if you just baked the crust) for 40 to 50 minutes, or until the filling has set and the top is golden brown. Remove from the oven and let stand for a few minutes, then cut and serve.

Yeasted Pastry Crust with Poppyseeds

- ⅓ cup warm water, preferably spring or filtered
- 1 teaspoon active dry yeast
- ½ teaspoon sugar
- ½ cup unbleached all-purpose flour, plus a little extra for rolling out the dough
- 2 tablespoons semolina flour, or 2 tablespoons unbleached all-purpose flour
- ¼ cup whole wheat flour
- ½ teaspoon salt
- 2 tablespoons butter or vegetable margarine, cold, cut into 6 pieces
- About 2 tablespoons poppyseeds

1 Pour the water into a small bowl or 2-cup measuring cup and sprinkle the yeast and sugar over it. Stir well with a fork and set aside to proof for 10 to 12 minutes, or until foamy.

2 Put the all-purpose, semolina, and whole wheat flours, salt, and butter in a food processor. Pulse about 15 times to cut the butter into the flour and combine all the ingredients.

3 When the yeast is bubbly, turn on the processor and, with the machine running, pour in the yeast-water mixture and buzz until a ball of dough forms. Touch the dough. It should be somewhat sticky but not wet. If it is wet, add another 2 tablespoons flour. If it seems dry, add warm water, a teaspoon at a time, until the desired consistency is reached. Process to knead for 20 or 30 seconds more, or until the dough has smoothed out.

4 Place a bit of extra flour in a medium bowl and turn the dough out into it. Rotate the dough a few times so that it is covered with flour, and let the dough rise, covered, in a warm place, until doubled in bulk, 1 to 1½ hours.

5 Preheat the oven to 475°F.

6 Punch down the dough and let it relax for 10 minutes. Sprinkle the poppyseeds and a little additional flour over a bread board. Form the dough into a flattened disc and roll the dough out over the seeds and flour, sprinkling additional poppyseeds on top of the dough. Roll out the dough, pressing the seeds into it, into an oblong, then press it into an 8- to 10-inch pie pan, pressing it up the edges.

7 Prebake the crust for 10 minutes, then remove from the oven. If it's puffed up in any spots, press down to release the air. Lower the oven temperature to 325°F. Fill the tart with the filling and continue as directed.

Pizza

From deep-dish pies, it is only a short distance to pizza, the ultimate open-crust pie. Pizzas are beautifully given to improvisation, and easily made.

Although the time-pressured can resort to faking homemade pizza with a premade crust (I like Boboli), a pita bread, or a tortilla, I almost always make crust from scratch, with an under-10-minute food processor technique, Quick Yeasted Pizza Dough, Processor-Style (page 350), the original version of which, as far as I know, was developed by cookbook writer Abby Mandel. Although virtually instant to make—and though it freezes well unbaked—do be sure to allow an hour's rising time for just-made dough and a slow, overnight refrigerated thaw and rise for frozen dough.

The recipe yields about 1 pound of dough, enough for 4 small pizzas (about 6 inches), 2 medium pizzas (about 12 inches), or 1 large (about 15 inches). I always use part whole wheat flour and occasionally I'll substitute 2 to 3 tablespoons semolina flour for an equal amount of all-purpose flour, for a slightly toothier crust.

After the dough has risen, been punched down, and relaxed, as per the recipe, form it into 1 large, 2 medium, or 4 small flattened discs. Sprinkle your work surface and each ball of dough lightly with flour, and, working with the heel of one hand while turning the dough with the other in the time-honored pizza-making motion, flatten and enlarge the dough out into a circle, then flip it over and work the other side, stretching it ever thinner and pinching/crimping together any holes that may appear. The ultimate size depends on whether you're inclined toward crisp and thin or thicker and breadier.

After you've got the dough shaped, it's ready to be put on a grill (if you're grill-baking it), or on a cornmeal-sprinkled pan (if you're oven-baking it), or placed on a cornmeal-sprinkled baking sheet (from which you can slide it off if you're baking it directly on the oven rack). At this point, we need to digress and discuss these different baking options, for pizza is essentially a simple dish—a bread dough with just about anything savory on it—and its goodness depends in equal measure on the amicability of the filling ingredients and the baking technique.

Pizzas and Heat

To get a perfect pizza, its ingredients done, its cheese (if you are using cheese) properly melted, and, most of all, its crust crisp, not soggy, specialized heat is required. In effect, you need two kinds of heat, though they both radiate from one source.

The first kind of heat is the surrounding or ambient heat (the hot air of the oven or covered grill). The second is intense but diffuse heat from *beneath* the pizza. This is why pizzeria pizzas are slid off the long wooden spatula, called a peel, directly onto the hot cast-iron floor of the pizza oven. The cast iron gives the pizza that blast from beneath, yet diffuses heat sufficiently so the pizza does not burn in spots, as it would on the floor of a typical oven, where the oven jets would create hot spots. The challenge of ultimate home pizza baking is to simulate a pizza oven, tricking the home oven into providing diffuse but strong heat underneath.

Oven-Baked Pizza

To get good results baking pizza in the oven:

- Set the oven rack at its lowest position.
- Use a pizza screen—a round pizza-shaped disk of heavy-gauge wire mesh or perforated aluminum. Pizza screens need a serious coat of cooking spray or olive oil to keep the dough from sticking.
- Use a heavy, cast-iron pizza pan and place it directly on the oven floor. While you don't get the immediate blast of heat from below, you do get the heat diffusion and quite good results. (These pans are also pretty to serve from, making this casual food a bit more elegant.)
- Line your oven floor with firebrick, available at any lumberyard, hardware store, or do-it-yourself home emporium. Measure the interior dimensions of your oven, and buy enough firebrick to cover it, leaving a 1- to 2-inch gap around all four edges for air circulation. Lay the firebrick on the oven floor and preheat it well before sliding the pizza onto it. The firebrick diffuses the heat so you can bake your pizza directly on it (if you don't have a wooden peel, you can slide it on and off using a cornmeal-sprinkled cookie sheet). You can also bake it in a pizza screen placed directly on the firebrick.

  This sounds like a huge hassle, but if you are a pizza or bread lover, it's worth it. In fact, the oven modification can take place in less time than it takes to describe it.

  If you prefer, use ½-inch-thick unglazed quarry tiles, available at most ceramic tiles stores, instead of firebrick; these heat more quickly than firebrick, but are much more prone to breakage. Again, be sure to leave a margin around the oven floor edges uncovered.

  Here's the beauty of the firebrick method, besides its being low-tech, simple, and inexpensive: You just leave the firebrick in the oven. It doesn't change the baking times on any other dishes, and if you like crisp-crusted, European-style breads, they too can be baked directly on the firebrick.

  Don't use just any old variety of brick—it must specifically be sold as firebrick.
- With all these tricks, it's important that you bake the pizza in an extremely hot oven, 500°F, for as long as directed in the recipe. Make sure your oven is hot by preheating it well in advance, 30 minutes to an hour, depending on how quickly your oven reaches 500°F.

Excellent results can also be had by grilling pizzas; the heat, of course, originates beneath the pizza.

Grill-Baked Pizzas

I was just starting to fool with grilling pizzas when I ran into two articles on the subject in the same month, one in *Fine Cooking* by Southwestern food maven W. Park Kerr and one by Patsy Jamieson in *Eating Well*. I have benefited from the advice of both these experts, and I thank them for their insights. Grill-baking is not right for every pizza, but, like the girl with the curl in the middle of her forehead, when it's good it's very, very good. Here are the times when you'll want to grill-bake pizzas:

- ▲ When you're making a fairly simple, not heaped-up pizza, one with only two or three toppings.
- ▲ When it's summertime and you don't want to heat up the house.
- ▲ When you want to make several small pizzas, perhaps customizing them individually for guests at a patio get-together.
- ▲ If you can't amend your oven suitably with any of the methods described above.

Here's how to grill-bake a pizza. On a preheated grill, grill just the unfilled pizza dough, uncovered, over very high heat for about 1 minute, by which time the dough will be grill-marked and slightly puffed as well as rigid enough on its underside to flip, using tongs. Flip it over onto the cooler area of the grill and spread on your simple toppings (remember, no heaped-up toppings on grill-baked pizzas). Cover the grill, and cook until the toppings are hot and the cheese, if using, is melted. Serve at once.

How you do this varies according to whether your grill is charcoal or gas, and, if gas, how many burners it has.

GAS GRILLS: The easiest one to use is a large-surfaced grill with three burners, which is what I have, and so I write from personal experience in this description. I draw on the *Eating Well* folks' directions for the others.

- ▲ Preheat all three burners, keeping the grill covered, until very hot, then turn off the middle burner, leaving the other two on high. Place 2 or 3 pizza dough rounds down the middle of the grill and cook, uncovered, for 1 minute. Immediately after you've laid them down, lower the temperature of the two lit burners to medium. When the rounds have had their single minute, flip them over, using tongs, apply toppings, cover the grill, and continue cooking as directed, until the toppings are done.
- ▲ Using a two-burner gas grill, preheat with one burner turned to high, the other unlit. Cook the first side of the dough on the hot side, flip, then move them to the cooler, unlit side.
- ▲ Using a one-burner gas grill, preheat on high, cook the dough on the first side on high, then turn down the heat to low and cook the second side.

CHARCOAL GRILLS: In just half the grill, build a medium-hot fire. This is most easily done by dividing the grill in half using two firebricks placed end to end in the middle and building the fire on one side. Grill the first side of the dough on the heated part of the grill, the second side on the unheated part of the grill.

Pizza Pizzazz: Toppings

- *A smear of basil pesto, homemade or commercially prepared, topped with thin slices of fresh tomato (yellow tomatoes, if possible), and a sprinkling of freshly grated Parmesan cheese. Bake in the oven or grill until the Parmesan melts.*

- *A smear of basil pesto or Olivada (page 24), topped with strips of charred, seeded red and/or yellow bell peppers and a sprinkling of freshly grated Parmesan cheese. Bake in the oven or grill until the Parmesan melts.*

- *Either of the pizzas above but with a light scattering of crumbled feta or chèvre beneath the tomatoes or peppers.*

- *A scattering of sliced Oven-Roasted Shiitake Mushrooms with Garlic and Coarse Salt (page 48), topped with a sprinkling of freshly grated Parmesan. Bake in the oven or grill until the Parmesan melts. If you like, barely moisten the dough with a good tomato sauce beneath the shiitakes.*

- *A brush of Garlic Oil (page 898), a scattering of crumbled feta or chèvre, a scattering of fresh spinach or chard that has been steamed until just wilted and well drained, topped with a sprinkling of freshly grated Parmesan cheese. Bake in the oven or grill until the Parmesan melts.*

- *A smear of any salsa, such as Pamela Jones's Absolutely Incredible Roasted Vegetable Salsa (page 915) or Tomatillo Salsa Verde (page 944); a polka-dotting of rehydrated pinto or black beans (see page 594), a sprinkle of pickled or fresh sliced rounds of jalapeño chile, and a light sprinkle of grated Monterey Jack cheese.*

- *A spread of Pesto Santo Tomas (page 920) with a sprinkle of Monterey Jack cheese.*

- *A quick slather of any hummus, topped with a scatter of minced kalamata olives and charred, seeded, and diced red and/or yellow peppers.*

- *A swoosh of "Macro Red" Sauce (page 936), topped with a sprinkle of crumbled reduced-fat fresh tofu and spoonfuls of fresh spinach or chard that has been steamed until just barely wilted and well drained, and finished with a sprinkle of toasted sesame seeds or gomashio.*

- *Pizza alla Mary: A huge tangle of onions very slowly sauteed in olive oil until caramelized and sweetened with a pinch of brown sugar. Sprinkle with crumbled Gorgonzola. Mary Springer wows me every time with this combo.*

NOTE: To vegans or the lactose intolerant: There are plenty of toppings in this list that omit cheese altogether. There are also numerous soy cheeses on the market that loosely mimic mozzarella, Monterey Jack, Cheddar cheese, and so on. While I personally still don't care much for the taste of soy cheese, soy technology has improved in recent years, and they are a lot tastier than they used to be, and a joy for those who don't eat cheese but still long for it.

In the same category are the newly ubiquitous vegetarian "pepperoni slices." You can now find them in the deli case or with the fresh produce in almost every American supermarket. Generally made from a mixture of soy and wheat gluten and seasoned like the real meat versions, these are not at all bad.

CD's Favorite Greek Pizza

This is my favorite pizza. Once I brought several enormous Greek pizzas to the annual Eureka Springs Women's Party. How good those warm Mediterranean flavors seemed to me deep in December, and how they perfumed the car as I drove through the cold, dark night to the large convivial ballroom where the event is held. Well, those pizzas were history long before I quit dancing and headed home.

Fresh chopped dill can be substituted for the oregano and basil. And a cup or so of Basic Wintertime Italian Tomato Sauce (page 931), or the Greek variation thereof, can be substituted for the fresh tomatoes. I might grill zucchini or eggplant pieces and put them on too, along with some charred, seeded, and sliced peppers. I might paint a layer of pesto at the base of this stack, too. Travel in any of these directions and you can hardly go wrong. This is one of those heaped-high pizzas, so don't attempt it on the grill, and don't try for dignity or neatness while eating it. **SERVES 4**

1 recipe Quick Yeasted Pizza Dough, Processor-Style (page 350)
1 tablespoon olive oil
1½ tablespoons very finely minced garlic
2 large tomatoes, sliced
1 (10-ounce) package frozen artichoke hearts, cooked and halved or cut into thirds
10 to 15 kalamata olives, pitted and halved or cut into quarters
1 medium red onion, slivered
4 ounces feta cheese, crumbled
2 to 3 teaspoons dried oregano
1 teaspoon dried basil
3 ounces Parmesan cheese, freshly grated (about ¾ cup)
Freshly ground black pepper to taste
Crushed red pepper to taste (optional)

1 Preheat the oven to 500°F. Roll out the pizza dough into a circle or circles.

2 Brush the dough rounds with half of the oil and sprinkle with half of the garlic. Lay down the tomatoes next, tucking pieces of artichoke, olive, and onion in among them, and sprinkle with the feta.

3 Combine the oregano and basil and, rubbing the herbs between your palms to crush them slightly, sprinkle over the feta. Top with the Parmesan, the

remaining garlic, and a drizzle of oil. Grind a little black pepper and sprinkle some crushed red pepper over the top, if desired.

4 Bake for 12 to 18 minutes, or until the crust is golden brown. Let cool a moment or two, then cut and serve.

Asian Pizza with Asparagus and Eggplant

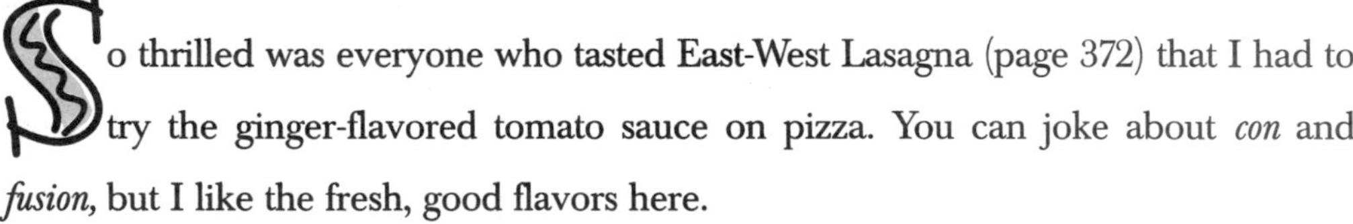

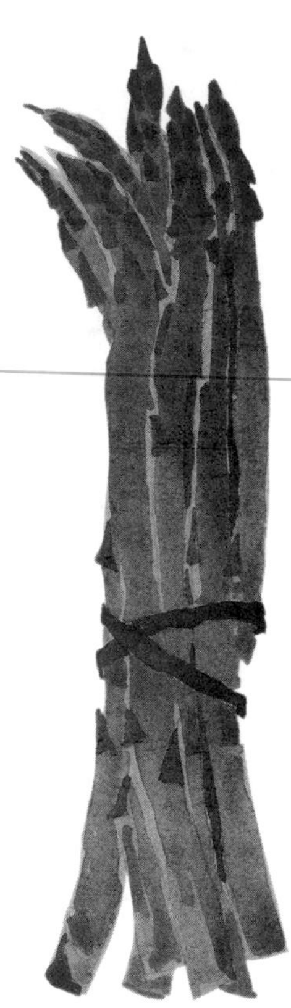

So thrilled was everyone who tasted East-West Lasagna (page 372) that I had to try the ginger-flavored tomato sauce on pizza. You can joke about *con* and *fusion*, but I like the fresh, good flavors here.

The tofu can be frozen and thawed before crumbling for an extra-chewy texture, or you can use half fresh tofu and half commercially prepared oven-baked tofu, Thai-style or savory, diced. **SERVES 4**

1 pound fresh asparagus, tough ends snapped off
1 recipe Quick Yeasted Pizza Dough, Processor-Style (page 350)
1 to 1½ cups Asian Red Sauce (page 934)
8 ounces reduced-fat fresh tofu, crumbled
2 eggplants, grilled (see page 749)
2 scallions, finely minced
Chopped cilantro leaves (optional)

1 Bring a large pot of water to a full boil and drop in the asparagus. Blanch for 3 minutes, or longer if the stalks are stout, or until bright green and tender-crisp. Drain, refresh in cold water, drain again, and cut the stalks at an angle into ½-inch slices. Set aside.

2 Preheat the oven to 500°F or preheat the grill. Roll out the pizza dough into a circle or circles. Set aside.

3 If you're cooking the pizzas on a grill, grill the first side now; then, after the pizza has been flipped, continue with the recipe. Spread the dough with a coating of tomato sauce, sprinkle with the tofu and asparagus, and top with the eggplants. Sprinkle with the scallions.

4 Bake for 10 to 12 minutes, or until the crust is golden brown, or grill, with the second side up, covered, for about 5 minutes.

5 Just before serving, sprinkle with the cilantro, if using.

Savory Puddings, Gratins & Timbales

Puddings and their kin are comfort foods, not in the hearty, warming way of stews, but with something of the nursery mood—safe, soothing, very "Now, now, don't worry." Puddings, timbales, even crisp-crusted gratins possess an inherent, gratifying mildness of texture. Although in flavor these dishes can vibrate with garlic and herbs (as in the famed gratins of Provence) or zing with Southwestern spicings, and although in presentation they can be soignée, at heart they are gently down-home.

Puddings, gratins, and timbales are all related, having in common ingredients (usually including one starch—bread, perhaps, or rice or potatoes), which are bound and cooked together (usually in the oven, though some precook on the stove). As the dish cooks, the binding thickens the relatively loose or liquid raw ingredients into a soothing whole, firm enough to be scooped out, sliced, or perhaps unmolded. Bindings are sometimes custardlike, such as eggs and milk, working their timeless magic. But the transmutation can also take place by way of the potato (or other carb). As it cooks, starch is released into the liquid, causing it to thicken and firm up, as in scalloped potatoes. A binder like cornstarch or arrowroot can do the same trick, and when combined with creamy blended tofu the resulting texture is similar to that of an egg-milk custard (useful for vegans or those watching their egg intake). Each recipe that follows uses one of the three varieties of binder and occasionally offers a variation with a different kind. But once you get familiar with the genre, you can switch them around to meet your own particular tastes, with good results. That being said, a few of the puddings, kugels and soufflés most obviously, really have to be dairy- and egg-heavy and that's all there is to it. Accept their nature or choose a different recipe.

What's the difference between a pudding, a gratin, and a timbale? Gratins are baked in larger, shallower pans, puddings in deeper ones, and timbales in individual-servings.

Gratins, because they leave more surface exposed to the heat of the oven, generally sport a stately crust, with appealing crispness, and a moist interior. Their diverse textures, and the fact that they often contain cheese, makes them good candidates for entrees.

The dimensions of a pudding ensures that it will be much moister and perhaps more tender,

Bain-Marie

In some of these recipes, you'll see that baking in a bain-marie, or hot-water bath, is suggested. For a bain-marie, the filled timbale dish or dishes are placed in a larger baking pan, one with sides, and, once the whole kit-and-kaboodle is in the oven, hot water is poured into the larger dish. The water thus surrounds the smaller filled dishes as they bake. The hot water insulates the dishes, ensuring that the heat and the baking process are even. This means that the outer edge of an egg-bound timbale gets done at the same time as its center. This evenness of cooking makes for a markedly more delicate, smoother texture. Is it necessary? No. Even egg-bound dishes done without it can be delicious (I have a few such here), but they will always be firmer in texture than those that have been bain-marie'd.

with little or no crust. Its texture will be denser and heavier; it's less dimensional and usually not composed in layers. Puddings are substantial components in a meal but rarely stand alone, as gratins can.

Timbales, the fanciest of the three, are somewhere between the gratins and puddings. They are usually firmer, and can be reversed out of their molds. They usually have one dominant flavor ingredient, making them best served as components. However, you can give them—or puddings, for that matter—center stage by serving them with a sauce or composing them of two or three flavors and colors.

Gratins

To make a gratin, you need a gratin dish or two. You probably already own something that will do just fine.

To get the desired crusty top, the dish must be shallow, with straight-up-and-down sides no more than 1½ inches high. And the dish must be made of glass, glazed ceramic, or enamel-coated iron. While glass is cheapest and what you're likeliest to have on hand, and glazed ceramic is most attractive in a rustic sort of way, my favorite gratin dishes are enamel-clad iron. They wear like, well, iron, are really lovely, and, if you wind up carting things from place to place or serving things at buffets, you will love the way they keep foods warm.

VARIATION

Arrange a scattering of steamed, just barely limp fresh spinach over the tomatoes. This is very good.

Mediterranean Gratin of Tomatoes, Potatoes, Feta, and Olives

Inspired by a side-dish gratin in Richard Olney's *Provence the Beautiful,* this summery dish could serve as a light main course or a hearty component. Serve it with a salad some July evening, or as an accompaniment for a simply baked winter squash, and you'll be pleased. The olives and feta can be omitted if you'd like it lighter both in taste and fat content.

SERVES 4 TO 6

Cooking spray
4 to 5 medium potatoes (about 1½ pounds), scrubbed or peeled if desired
1 to 2 tablespoons olive oil
2 large onions, diced
4 fresh tomatoes, preferably garden-ripe, sliced ¼ inch thick
Salt and freshly ground black pepper to taste
2 to 3 teaspoons fresh thyme leaves
½ cup pitted and halved kalamata olives
⅔ cup coarsely crumbled feta cheese
½ to ⅔ cup Breadcrumb Topping Provençal (recipe follows), using crisp crumbs

1 Preheat the oven to 375°F. Spray a medium-large gratin or baking dish with cooking spray.

2 Bring a medium saucepan of water to a boil, drop in the potatoes, turn down the heat slightly, and cook until the potatoes are half done, about 15 minutes. Drain and slice into ¼-inch rounds while still hot.

3 As potatoes cook, heat about one-third of the oil over medium heat in a skillet. Add the onions, lower the heat, and cook, stirring occasionally, for about 20 minutes, or until the onions are so soft they're droopy and starting to brown.

4 Arrange half of the tomatoes in the gratin dish. Sprinkle them with salt (remembering that both the feta and the olives are salty), plenty of pepper, and the thyme. Scatter about one-third of the onions over the tomatoes and top with half the cooked potato slices, still warm. Scatter with half of the olives and feta and another round of seasoning. Repeat the layering with the tomatoes, seasonings, onions, potatoes, olives, feta, seasonings. Top with the final third of the onions.

5 Sprinkle with the breadcrumb topping, patting it gently over the gratin. Drizzle the remaining oil over the crumbs.

6 Bake until the crumbs are golden brown, 40 to 45 minutes. Serve hot or at room temperature.

Breadcrumb Topping Provençal

A thrifty way to use up ends of bread, this is so simple it hardly seems necessary to have a recipe for it. You will use this seasoned bread crumb topping often if you keep it on hand, in a ziptop bag in the fridge or freezer—so do. And be ready for crunch. I like to make a batch of both soft and crisp crumbs to keep at the ready. But if using soft crumbs where crisp are called for, bake a little longer or raise the oven temperature a little; if using crisp where soft are called for, add them a little later in the baking than the recipe suggests.

Start with bread, either crisp, such as Croûtes (page 29), or soft. Ideally, the bread is a good, slightly soured, part–whole grain European loaf, not too heavy. You do not want a loaf with too dominant a flavor (that is, not a rye with caraway or a pumpernickel). But a decent white bread is not bad. At the restaurant we used to use a combination of buttermilk bread and rosemary foccacia (both recipes are in *Dairy Hollow House Soup & Bread).* Please note that this breadcrumb mixture keeps in the fridge for about 1 week, or in the freezer for 3 or 4 months. **MAKES 3 CUPS TOPPING**

About ⅓ loaf leftover bread to yield 3 cups crumbs, crisp or soft
3 to 5 cloves garlic, pressed
1 tablespoon olive oil
1 tablespoon Italian parsley leaves (optional)
1 tablespoon basil leaves (optional)

1 Tear the bread into large pieces and place them in food processor. Pulse to make fine crumbs. Measure the crumbs for the recipe. You'll probably need about 3 cups.

2 Combine the crumbs, garlic, oil, parsley, if using, and basil, if using, in the food processor and pulse, then run the machine until fine crumbs are formed and the garlic and herbs are finely chopped.

Crumb Ideas: Soft and Crisp

Soft Ideas

- *Use the breadcrumbs when you need a crisp topping for any casserole or stuffed vegetable that will be baking longer than 40 minutes.*
- *Use instead of plain breadcrumbs in little savory cakes, patties, and stuffings.*
- *Use as the basis for a simple stuffed vegetable filling: Combine the breadcrumbs with leftover steamed vegetables, pureed or finely chopped, maybe an egg and some cheese, a sautéed onion if you like, maybe the innards of the vegetable you're stuffing. Place in the vegetable case and bake at 350 to 375°F until hot and crusty.*
- *Stir a small handful of the breadcrumbs into any sautéed vegetable mélange and moisten with a little leftover sauce or soup for a dandy, substantial omelet or crêpe filling.*

Crisp Ideas

- *Toss with cooked noodles.*
- *Toss with cooked dumplings.*
- *Sprinkle over steamed carrots or cauliflower.*
- *Use to coat tofu or tempeh for oven baking* *(see page 641)*
- *Use to top almost any casserole or stuffed vegetable that will bake for 40 minutes or less, which will add a nice crunch on top.*

Creamy American-Style Scalloped Pesto Potatoes

Here's a too-good-to-be-true story. When we tested two variations of this herb-scented version of the scalloped potatoes that many Americans who came of age in the 1950s will recall, the nondairy, reduced-fat, vegan variation (made with homemade pesto without Parmesan) was preferred by every single person tasting it, including several dyed-in-the-wool meat-and-potatoes types. Remember, if you're fixing it for vegans, though: Most commercial pestos contain Parmesan cheese.

Precooking the potatoes in plain soy milk on the stovetop before baking them is the trick to the dish's luscious creaminess. It might seem a little fussy the first time you do it, but after you do, no other scalloped potato will seem truly there.

By taking advantage of ready-made pestos that are now almost universally available, this version is somewhat simplified. If you make your own pesto (Lemon, Basil, and Sun-Dried Tomato Pesto, page 918, is good here), so much the better.

To me the gratin is best suited as a component, but a fairly major one. Try it with a light soup to start and a steamed green and/or orange vegetable alongside. **SERVES 4 TO 6 AS A SIDE DISH**

Cooking spray
6 medium russet potatoes (about 1½ pounds), well scrubbed or peeled, thinly sliced
2 cups unflavored soy milk, such as plain Soy Silk
Salt and freshly ground black pepper to taste
1 large onion, thinly sliced
⅓ to ½ cup basil pesto, commercial or homemade, or to taste
½ cup Golden Stock (page 140) or any mild but flavorful stock, or additional soy milk
Breadcrumb Topping Provençal (page 277)

1 Preheat the oven to 375°F. Spray a 1½- to 2-quart gratin dish with cooking spray and set aside. Rinse the potatoes and shake off as much excess moisture as possible.

2 Spray your largest, deepest skillet with cooking spray. Add the potatoes and soy milk. Bring to a boil, then lower the heat to a simmer. Cook until the potatoes are almost tender, and most of the milk has been absorbed (what milk remains will be very thick and creamy). Depending on how thin you sliced your potatoes, this should take 15 to 20 minutes. Remove the potatoes from the stove and season with salt and pepper—don't stint on the latter. In a separate bowl, toss the onion with the pesto.

3 Layer half the potatoes (along with any remaining soy milk still clinging to them), the onions, and then the remaining potatoes in the prepared dish. Pour the stock or additional soy milk over the vegetables, and top with the breadcrumb topping. Cover tightly, first with waxed paper, then with foil, and bake for 20 minutes.

4 Uncover the dish and bake for 20 to 30 minutes more, by which time the potatoes should be very tender, the sauce almost completely absorbed, and the crumb topping nicely crisped.

and there's more . . .

Scalloped Herb-Garlic Potatoes: *Combine 2 tablespoons Roasted Garlic puree (page 899), 3 cloves raw garlic, a small handful each of minced basil and parsley, and a few teaspoons fresh thyme leaves. Use this instead of the pesto in the basic recipe. You may also do this with no herbs at all.*

Scalloped Potatoes Au Gratin: *Use either the basic recipe or the herb-garlic variation above, but add a layer of grated sharp Cheddar cheese on top of the onions before baking and, 15 minutes into the second baking, top with additional grated Cheddar. Another way to go is with grated Parmesan cheese, again on top of the onions and midway through the second baking.*

Born (Again) to Be Wild Reincarnated Scalloped Potatoes with Chipotle Chiles: *Toss the onion with 1 tablespoon minced canned chipotle pepper in adobo and 3 cloves pressed garlic; use cilantro pesto.*

Scalloped Potatoes with Wild Mushrooms: *An earthy, glorious fall favorite for cold rainy days, spring or fall. Omit the pesto and onions. Sauté about a pound total of as many varieties of mushrooms as you can get: shiitakes, maitakes, morels, oyster mushrooms, chanterelles. Use either butter or a little olive oil for sautéing. Raise the heat and stir if the mushrooms seem to be exuding too much juice—you want any mushroom liquid virtually boiled away, until only a light clinging syrup sheens the mushrooms. Press 3 cloves garlic into the mushrooms when they come off the heat, and season lightly with salt and pepper. Sandwich the mushrooms between layers of the milk-bathed potatoes, and proceed as directed.*

Sorrel-Scented Kugel-Gratin of Greens, Potatoes, and Zucchini

Simple, satisfying, filling, yet mild and light, a cross between a kugel and a gratin. The potatoes are grated, not sliced, and given interest by sorrel, the tart, lemony leaf that's somewhere between a green and an herb. Don't be afraid to use too much sorrel; its tartness is moderated by the other ingredients, and by cooking.

This makes a pleasing addition to any component meal and, although unorthodox when served instead of a grain underneath a ladleful of stew, it is nonetheless delicious. Some say it is even better reheated the next day, crisped slowly in a nonstick skillet. **SERVES 4 TO 6**

VARIATION

Quickie, no-grating-or-chopping version: Substitute a 10-ounce package of frozen chopped spinach, thawed, drained, and squeezed dry, for the kale. Use 5 to 6 cups frozen grated potatoes instead of fresh, and omit the zucchini altogether. Use a teaspoon of dried basil, oregano, or thyme, or a combination of all three, instead of the sorrel. Bake as directed.

3 to 4 medium russet potatoes (about 1¼ pounds), well scrubbed
2 to 3 medium zucchini, stem ends removed
Salt
1 large bunch kale (about 1 to 1¼ pounds), well washed, coarse stems removed
Cooking spray
2 teaspoons olive oil
1 large onion, diced
2 large eggs, beaten
½ cup low-fat milk, oat, soy, or rice milk, or evaporated skim milk
1 to 2 large bunches sorrel (about 1 pound), stems removed, leaves stacked, rolled up tightly, and thinly sliced
3 cloves garlic, minced
Freshly ground black pepper to taste
A few gratings of nutmeg
½ cup freshly grated Parmesan cheese (optional)

1 Grate the potatoes in a food processor or by hand. Immediately dump the grated potatoes into a bowl of cold water and let soak. Grate the zucchini. Sprinkle the grated zucchini with about ½ teaspoon salt, then place it in a colander, pressing slightly as you do so. Place the colander in the sink or on a plate where the water it will exude can drip. Let the zucchini and potatoes stand like this for 20 to 30 minutes, as you complete the recipe.

2 Preheat the oven to 375°F.

3 Bring a medium pot of water to a boil. Drop in the kale, let the water return to a boil, then drain the kale. Refresh the blanched kale in cold water, let drain, and chop. Place in a medium bowl. Spray a 3-quart gratin or baking dish with cooking spray.

4 Heat 1 teaspoon of the oil over medium heat in a skillet. Add the onion, lower the heat, and sauté, stirring, for 7 to 10 minutes, until the onion is limp and starting to color around the edges.

5 Meanwhile, drain the potatoes and blot somewhat dry with a paper towel. Add to the bowl containing the blanched kale. Press down further on the zucchini, squeezing it as dry as possible. Add it, too, to the bowl, along with the eggs, milk, sorrel, and garlic. Stir in the sautéed onions.

6 Season the mixture with a little additional salt, plenty of pepper, and nutmeg. Stir in 1 tablespoon of the Parmesan. Mix very well.

7 Turn the mixture into the prepared dish and cover with the remaining Parmesan, then drizzle with the remaining 1 teaspoon oil.

8 Lower the oven temperature to 350°F and bake the gratin for 45 to 50 minutes, until set and golden brown. Serve hot from the oven, or reheat the next day.

Creamy Gratin of Exotic Mushrooms and Potatoes

Another potato-based gratin? Yes, and this one—creamy, stuffed with fresh and dried exotic mushrooms—is one of my favorites. It is different from any of the preceding, even the mushroom variation of the scalloped potatoes given earlier (page 280), because added to the classic potato and mushroom combination (if a combination can be both earthy and ethereal, potatoes and mushrooms are) is an enigmatic ingredient, mustard, which is tantalizing. **SERVES 4 TO 6**

¼ cup boiling water, vegetable stock, or low-fat milk
½ ounce dried mushrooms, such as shiitake, porcini, or oyster
2 pounds potatoes, preferably Yukon Gold or fingerling, well scrubbed, sliced into ½-inch rounds
Cooking spray

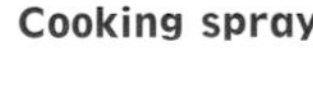

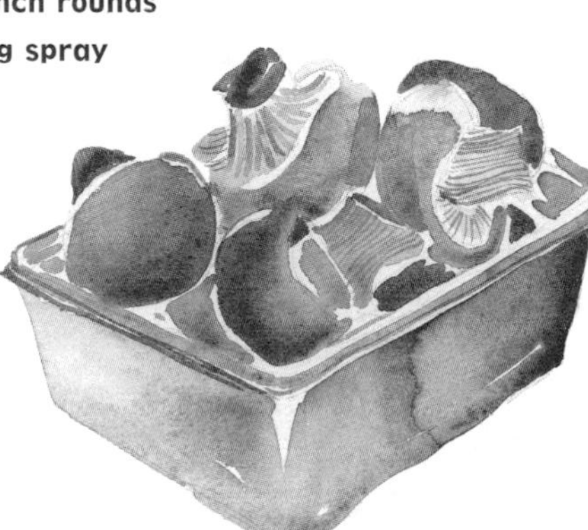

1 tablespoon butter, Better (page 905), olive oil, or a combination
½ large onion, chopped
½ pound assorted fresh mushrooms, such as morels, shiitake, boletus, portobellos, or cremini, cleaned, tough stems removed, coarsely chopped
2½ cups low-fat milk
1 tablespoon plus 1 teaspoon cornstarch
2 ounces neufchâtel reduced-fat cream cheese, softened to room temperature
1½ teaspoons prepared Dijon mustard
2 cloves garlic, pressed
Pinch of freshly grated nutmeg
Salt and freshly ground black pepper to taste

1 Preheat the oven to 350°F.

2 In a heatproof bowl, pour the boiling stock or water over the dried mushrooms and set aside to steep.

3 Bring a medium-large pot of water to a boil, and drop in the potatoes. Let blanch for 3 minutes, drain, and run cold water over them.

4 Heat a large nonstick skillet, or one that has been sprayed with cooking spray, and add the oil and butter. Add the onion and cook over medium heat, stirring often, for 3 to 5 minutes, or until translucent. Add the fresh mushrooms and stir-fry for 4 minutes more. Lower the heat, cover the pan, and steam the mushrooms briefly, 1 to 2 minutes, or until they soften slightly but before they begin exuding much juice. Combine with the potatoes.

5 Strain the dried mushrooms through a coffee filter, reserving the soaking liquid. Pick through the mushrooms carefully to remove any grit and give them a quick rinse just to be sure there's no other dirt hidden. Coarsely chop any large pieces of soaked mushroom, then add the rehydrated mushroom pieces to the potato-mushroom mixture.

6 Place the milk in a small saucepan over medium heat. Dissolve the cornstarch in the reserved mushroom soaking liquid. When the milk is hot, whisk in the cornstarch mixture. When the milk thickens, remove from the heat and whisk in the neufchâtel along with the mustard, garlic, nutmeg, salt, and plenty of pepper. Combine the cooked potato and mushroom mixture with this sauce and taste again for seasonings.

7 Spray an 8-inch baking dish with cooking spray. Spoon in the potato mixture. Cover the dish with aluminum foil and bake for 35 minutes, or until hot and bubbly and the potatoes are soft. Remove from the oven. Preheat the broiler.

8 Broil until bubbly and golden, 5 to 10 minutes. Serve at once, hot from the oven.

VARIATION

VEGAN VARIATION: ***Substitute plain, unflavored soy milk for dairy milk and soy cream cheese for dairy creamy cheese.***

Spinach or Zucchini Featherbeds with Mustard and Lemon

Strata fit loosely into the gratin family. Bread stands in for potatoes, and an egg-and-cheese custard is poured over them, making a savory, eggy pudding. For many of our inn years, our Featherbed Eggs, done with cornbread and baked in

NOTE

Marion Cunningham coined the term "featherbeds" for a recipe in her excellent breakfast book. I find the term irresistible and have adopted it.

individual ramekins, were one of the most popular breakfast entrees. Most inns serve some variation of the dish, as do most hosts given to entertaining at brunch, since these dishes have the eminently endearing virtue of being fix-it-ahead-of-time, bake-it-at-serving-time dishes.

Here, barely cooked green vegetables are added, and lemon, dry mustard, and nutmeg give a frisson of pleased surprise. While you can use this as a breakfast or brunch dish, it's equally good for lunch or supper, as is, with tomato sauce over it, or as part of a vegetable dinner. For brunch, try it with Roasty-Toasty Potatoes (page 790), some commercially made vegetarian soysage, and melon slices heaped high with strawberries, grapes, and pineapple.

Eggs and cheese are inherent to featherbeds' success. This recipe can't be made vegan. **SERVES 6**

- **1½ lemons**
- **2 cups barely cooked zucchini or fresh spinach, very well drained and chopped**
- **1 cup (3 to 4 ounces) grated Jarlsberg or Swiss cheese**
- **¼ medium red onion, finely minced**
- **4 large eggs**
- **2 cups low-fat milk, or part evaporated skim milk and half-and-half**
- **Salt and freshly ground black pepper**
- **½ to 1 teaspoon Tabasco or similar hot sauce to taste**
- **½ teaspoon dry mustard**
- **2 or 3 gratings of nutmeg**
- **Cooking spray**
- **8 slices whole wheat bread, preferably slightly stale, torn into large crumbs**

1. Grate 1 teaspoon of zest from the lemon and place it in a medium bowl. Add the zucchini and toss well. Halve and juice the lemon, squeezing it over the zucchini through a strainer to catch any seeds. Toss the zucchini again.

2. Add ⅔ cup of the cheese and the onion to the zucchini and toss one more time. Set aside.

3. Combine and beat together the eggs, milk, salt, pepper, Tabasco, dry mustard, and nutmeg. Set aside.

4. Spray a 9-inch square baking dish or six 1-cup ramekins with cooking spray. Scatter about half of the breadcrumbs in the pan or ramekins. Ladle or pour about one-third of the egg-milk mixture over the

bread, then pat the zucchini-cheese mixture over that. Top with the remaining bread, and pour the remaining milk-egg mixture over all. Sprinkle the remaining cheese on top. Cover and refrigerate at least 4 hours, or overnight.

5 Preheat the oven to 350°F. Uncover the featherbeds and bake until nice and golden, 40 to 50 minutes for one whole dish, 25 to 30 minutes for the ramekins. I like the strata best served hot from the oven, but it's pretty agreeable about waiting and not bad served warm, making it a nice choice for a buffet.

Featherbeds Galore . . .

Rich Featherbeds: *Soften 4 ounces neufchâtel reduced-fat cream cheese, and add it by the spoonful to the casserole or to each ramekin, adding a decadent creamy surprise to the middle of each portion. Excellent.*

Featherbeds Rancheros: *Omit the green vegetable, lemon, lemon zest, and mustard. Instead, place 2 sliced tomatoes over the bread, and use Monterey Jack or Cheddar instead of Jarlsberg cheese. Top the tomatoes with the chopped onion, the cheese, and 2 to 3 tablespoons chopped roasted green chiles, either out of a can or fresh charred, peeled, and diced poblanos. If you like, substitute 6 wheat or corn tortillas, torn, for the bread. Add a pinch of chile powder to the egg mixture. Naturally, you'd want to serve this with some good refried black beans, salsa, a mug of good Mexican-style hot chocolate with cinnamon, and grilled pineapple for dessert.*

Wild Mushroom Featherbeds: *Use 1 tablespoon Dijon mustard; substitute grated Parmesan cheese for half the Jarlsberg cheese. Instead of the green vegetables, use a mushroom sauté: In a nonstick skillet or one sprayed with cooking spray, using as little butter or olive oil as possible, sauté ½ pound or so assorted mushrooms. As they soften, add about 4 cloves minced or pressed garlic. Drain the mushrooms, reserving any juices and adding them to the egg mixture along with a bit of fresh thyme and a drop of Pickapeppa sauce. Go extra-heavy on the black pepper. You can use the bread as is, or dab a bit of softened neufchâtel cheese here and there, as in the rich featherbeds variation. You might also like using some fresh spinach in combination with the mushrooms.*

Cornbread Featherbeds: *Replace the bread with crumbled leftover cornbread. This was the Dairy Hollow official featherbed bread of choice.*

Extra-Creamy Featherbed Eggs: *Use reduced-fat sour cream cheese to replace one-third of the milk. This gives the finished dish a slightly softer, more custardlike texture, and a richness in the mouth that is pretty irresistible. Try this with the wild mushroom version above.*

Gratin of Fresh Fennel and Artichokes with Feta

None of these flavors is a shrinking violet, but they all put aside their aggressions to work together nicely here. The underlying sweetness of the fennel and artichokes plays off the salty feta. This is definitely haute. **SERVES 4 TO 6 AS A SIDE DISH, 3 TO 4 AS AN ENTREE**

- 1 (10-ounce) package frozen plain artichoke hearts
- 1 tablespoon olive oil or Better (page 905)
- 1 large onion, chopped
- 1 large or 2 medium bulbs fennel, tough outer layers removed and root end sliced off, green tops trimmed off with a few fronds reserved for garnish, halved vertically then sliced crosswise into ⅓-inch slices
- ½ teaspoon fennel seeds
- 2 cups low-fat milk, evaporated skim milk, or plain Soy Silk
- 1 tablespoon plus 1 teaspoon cornstarch
- ¼ cup vegetable stock
- 2 ounces neufchâtel reduced-fat cream cheese, softened, or vegan cream cheese
- 2 cloves garlic, pressed
- Salt and freshly ground black pepper to taste
- Grated zest of 1 lemon
- Cooking spray
- 3 to 4 ounces feta cheese, crumbled

1 Steam the artichoke hearts over boiling water, covered, until not quite tender, about 4 minutes.

2 Heat a large pan over medium heat. Add the oil, then the onion, and cook, stirring often, for 3 to 5 minutes, or until translucent. Add the fennel and fennel seeds and stir-fry for 4 minutes more.

3 Lower the heat, cover the pan, and steam the fennel and onions together, stirring occasionally, for 6 to 8 minutes, or until the fennel softens slightly but still has a tiny bit of crunch. Remove from the heat and combine with the artichoke hearts. Preheat the broiler.

4 As the fennel steams, put the milk over medium heat in a small saucepan. In a measuring cup, dissolve the cornstarch in the vegetable stock. When the milk is hot, whisk in the cornstarch mixture. When the milk thickens, remove from the heat and whisk in the neufchâtel cheese along with the garlic, salt, and plenty of pepper. Combine the cooked vegetable mixture with this sauce and taste again for seasonings. (Go a little easy on the salt, because you haven't yet added the feta, which is quite salty, but don't stint on pepper.) Add the lemon zest.

5 Spray 4 to 6 individual ramekins (number depends on both the size of your

VARIATIONS

CRUNCHY-TOPPED GRATIN OF FENNEL AND ARTICHOKES: *Instead of, or in addition to feta, sprinkle the ramekins with soft Breadcrumb Topping Provençal (page 277).*

GRATIN OF FRESH FENNEL AND FRESH ARTICHOKES: *Boil or steam 3 large fresh artichokes, as described on page 387. Reserving the leaves for another use, discard the choke and cut the hearts, bottoms, and any tender portions of stem into chunks, substituting them for the frozen hearts. You do not need to steam these, since they're already cooked.*

VEGAN GRATIN OF FRESH FENNEL AND ARTICHOKES: *Substitute plain, unflavored soy milk for skim milk and use soy cream cheese instead of neufchâtel. Skip the feta altogether, or top with your favorite vegan cheese; a soy Parmesan-type works nicely here.*

ramekins and the size of the fennel pieces you're working with) with cooking spray. Divide the mixture among them and sprinkle the crumbled feta cheese on top of each.

6 Broil the ramekins until they are bubbly and the feta cheese is golden, 5 to 10 minutes. Serve at once, garnished with the reserved fennel fronds.

COOK ONCE FOR 2 MEALS Make twice the amount of the gratin recipe at left. Two or three days after you've had it in ramekins, reincarnate it as Artichoke-and Fennel-Stuffed Potatoes Twice-Baked with Feta. Just bake 4 large potatoes until tender, split them, scoop out the potato flesh, and mash chunkily. Stir the potato into the fennel-artichoke-sauce mix and pile back into the potato halves. Sprinkle the feta over the stuffed potatoes and broil until golden. Serve immediately, with a salad and maybe a simple tomato soup to start.

Eastern European Casserole of Sauerkraut, Cabbage, Apples, and Noodles

Here is the first of several improbably delicious noodle dishes in this chapter. I love these flavors together. It may be genetic, since I am of Russian-Polish extraction. This casserole is drier, less dense or puddinglike than most here. Try a creamy mushroom soup to start.

Use a natural foods store brand of sauerkraut for this, preferably organic, naturally fermented kraut from a jar or lead-free can (do not use ordinary canned sauerkraut, which tastes metallic and unpleasant). Vegans should select egg-free pasta, but the broad noodle shape is traditional for this dish. **SERVES 4 TO 6**

1 tablespoon butter, preferably clarified, or margarine for vegans
1 medium onion, halved and thinly sliced
2 not-too-tart apples, such as Golden Delicious, peeled, cored, and diced
½ small cabbage, washed, cored, and sliced into thin strips
1 teaspoon paprika or 1 tablespoon poppyseeds (optional)
Cooking spray
1½ cups sauerkraut, well drained
½ cup applesauce, no sugar added
1 (8-ounce) package broad egg noodles
Salt and freshly ground black pepper to taste
½ to ⅔ cup crisp breadcrumbs (optional)

1 Heat the butter over medium heat in a skillet. Add the onion and sauté for 4 minutes, or until it is starting to wilt. As you do this, bring a separate pot of water to a boil.

2 Add the apples to the onions and continue sautéing for 3 minutes more, or until the apples begin to soften and color. Add the cabbage strips, raise the heat slightly, and stir-fry for 3 minutes more. Lower the heat and cover the skillet, allowing the cabbage to steam for 5 to 6 minutes, or until limp. Lift the lid, and if any liquid has accumulated raise the heat again to evaporate it. Add the paprika, if using, and remove from the heat. Transfer to a deep ovenproof casserole that has been sprayed with cooking spray. Add the sauerkraut and applesauce, stirring to combine. Preheat the oven to 400°F.

3 Cook the noodles in boiling water according to the package directions until done, but just barely—definitely not overdone. Drain the noodles, rinsing with cold water, and toss them with the cabbage and sauerkraut mixture, adding plenty of salt and pepper. Smooth out the top of the mixture. Cover tightly, first with waxed paper, then with foil, and bake for 25 minutes.

4 Remove the casserole from the oven, uncover, and sprinkle with the breadcrumbs. Raise the heat to 425°F and bake until everything is nice and hot and the breadcrumbs are golden brown and crunchy, 15 to 20 minutes. Serve hot from the oven.

Deadpan Humor

Although heavy nonstick skillets or enamel-clad iron skillets have their place in the kitchen (in mine, anyway), first place belongs to good old-fashioned black, seasoned, cast-iron skillets. I like their look, feel, weight. And some dishes, like cornbread, I would never, never make in anything but. I even used them back in the inn's restaurant, although they are not standard in most commercial kitchens.

Now, back in those days, we had a cook, Sam, for a while. His background had been assisting in one of those "continental" restaurants, where the beef is wellington'd and the side vegetables are blanched, then finished with a whole lot *of butter. This was of course done in a lightweight, curve-sided sauté pan. Sam was thus in the habit of doing the classic backwards-forwards wrist-action, no-spatula-or-spoon sauté tossing motion.*

While Sam was game and eager to learn how we did things at Dairy Hollow House, he was also a little skeptical, especially about our ways with vegetables. The idea that vegetables were more than an afterthought there to add a little color on the plate was hard for him initially. But he went along with it, then got intrigued. Ditto the idea that there were seasonings for vegetables beyond loads of butter and maybe a splash of lemon. That some vegetables should be very slowly cooked while others got nothing more than the quickest of sizzles was also a stretch, but not too big a one, because of his slow-cooking Southern background.

But Sam still pined for the lightweight, curve-sided sauté pans. "I can't do a good sauté!" he'd whine—and I do mean whine. And not just once, but daily. "And these skillets are too heavvvy."

I looked at him—maybe 6 foot 2, maybe 250 pounds, rather rotund and strong as an ox. "But Sam," I said sternly, "those skillets represent Dairy Hollow's employee fitness program."

Vegan French-Style Gratin of Butternut Squash

Winter squash puddings and gratins are not uncommon in the American South, but they're usually on the sweet side, like the butternut squash timbale on page 294. This one leans toward savory, in a South-of-France manner. With grilled eggplant, a salad to start, and some good bread, you have a delightful supper. Add a glass of Chenin Blanc, some purchased sorbet, crisp cookies, and fresh raspberries for dessert, and you've got a light, sophisticated meal. **SERVES 4 TO 6**

Cooking spray
2 teaspoons to 1 tablespoon olive oil
2 leeks, roots and all but 2 inches of green removed, slit down the middle, very well washed, and sliced
3 cloves garlic, chopped
1 large butternut squash, peeled, seeded, and cut into chunks
3 tablespoons water, preferably spring or filtered
5 ounces firm silken tofu, preferably reduced-fat
1½ tablespoons cornstarch
¼ cup plain soy or rice milk
1 teaspoon Rapidura, brown sugar, or honey
Salt and freshly ground black pepper to taste
Freshly grated nutmeg to taste
½ cup soft breadcrumbs

1 Preheat the oven to 375°F. Spray a medium gratin or casserole dish with cooking spray.

2 Place half of the oil in a skillet. Add the leeks and sauté leeks over medium heat, stirring often, until limp, about 10 minutes. Add the squash and water, stir well, and cook, uncovered, stirring often, for 5 minutes more. Lower the heat, add the garlic, stir well, and cover the skillet. Let cook for 20 minutes more, or until the squash is very, very soft. Mash it slightly with the back of a spoon.

3 Place the tofu, cornstarch, soy milk, and Rapidura in a food processor and buzz until smooth.

4 Turn the tofu mixture out into a bowl. Stir in the squash mixture. Season to taste with salt, pepper, and nutmeg. Scrape the mixture into the prepared gratin dish and sprinkle with the breadcrumbs. Drizzle the remaining oil over the top and bake until golden brown, crusty, and firm, 25 to 35 minutes. Let cool slightly and serve.

Savory Puddings

Solid, homey, comforting. Go back for seconds, all's right in the world. These heavier dishes, usually built around a single dominant vegetable, are baked in slightly deeper containers to get their characteristic moist, dense, tender texture, and they have little or no crust. However, none of this is written in stone. If you want a pudding a little drier, bake it in a shallower dish. If you want it a little less homey, bake it in timbale dishes, rather than one large casserole. If you want to serve a pudding as the central part of dinner, add a sauce.

VARIATION

VEGAN VARIATION: ***Use rice or soy milk instead of the dairy milk. Omit the egg. Blend 2 ounces silken tofu into the rice milk mixture until smooth. Add the corn, then pulse/chop until smooth. Extra sweetener (1 or 2 teaspoons) is good here.***

Deviled Corn and Tomato Pudding

In the South, corn puddings and tomato puddings, both a little sweet, are much loved. Here the two are combined, with heart-of-summer results. This pudding is best with fresh corn cut from the cob, but still tasty with frozen corn. For added richness, use half sour cream, reduced-fat sour cream, or yogurt sour cream to replace half of the milk. **SERVES 4 TO 6**

- Cooking spray
- 3¾ cups fresh corn kernels, cut from 7 to 8 ears corn; or frozen corn, thawed
- ¾ cup low-fat milk, evaporated skim milk, or plain soy or rice milk
- ¼ cup cornstarch
- 2 large eggs
- 2 teaspoons Rapidura, brown sugar, or honey
- Salt and freshly ground black pepper to taste
- 1 tablespoon butter or vegetable margarine
- 1 large onion, chopped
- 1 large tomato, diced
- 2 to 3 large leaves basil, finely chopped

1 Preheat the oven to 350°F. Spray 4 to 6 8-ounce timbales with cooking spray.

2 Combine the corn, milk, cornstarch, eggs, sugar, salt, and pepper in a food processor and buzz to a textured puree. Transfer to a medium bowl and set aside.

3 Heat the butter over medium-high heat in a large skillet. Add the onion and sauté for 4 minutes. Add the tomato, raise the heat, and cook until most of the liquid has evaporated, 1 to 3 minutes. Remove from the heat. Stir in the basil.

4 Divide the tomato mixture among the ramekins. Top with the corn mixture. Place the filled timbales in a large pan, place in the oven, and pour hot water into the large pan, around the timbales.

5 Bake for 40 to 50 minutes, or until golden and firmed up. Let stand for 5 minutes, then serve.

Melissa's Spinach Casserole

My friend, writer Melissa Bloch, puts together a quick-as-a-wink, very cheese-filled spinach casserole, with which she's been pleasing family and friends for years. It's a perfect player on a component plate, a much-loved side dish. Try it with piroshkis filled with Mushroom Filling à la Eva (page 354). **SERVES 4**

Cooking spray
2 large eggs
⅓ cup unbleached all-purpose flour
1½ cup low-fat cottage cheese
1 (10-ounce) package frozen chopped spinach, thawed and very well drained
½ to 1 cup (2 to 4 ounces) grated sharp Cheddar cheese
½ to 1 cup (2 to 4 ounces) grated mozzarella cheese
¼ teaspoon salt

1 Preheat the oven to 350°F. Spray a deep-sided 2½- to 3-quart baking dish or casserole with cooking spray.

2 In a medium bowl, combine all the other ingredients, stirring well. Turn the mixture out into the prepared baking dish. Bake, uncovered, for 1 hour, until slightly crusty on top. Let cool for a minute or two and serve, still very hot. If you'd like it more tender, bake it in a bain-marie (see page 275).

COOK ONCE FOR 2 MEALS Prepare double the amount of this recipe. Serve half hot; let the other half cool and then refrigerate overnight. The pudding will become quite firm and can be used as a sandwich filling; this, and slices of nice ripe tomato on a multigrain toast, make a filling and nutritious lunch.

Southern Tomato Pudding

I can't even remember who first taught me this. I know I never ever ate anything remotely like this pudding in the North but have run into it at countless Southern potlucks, partly because it's good lukewarm. It's perfect as part of a component vegetable-based dinner. It's definitely supposed to be on the sweet side.

For extra richness, butter the toasted whole wheat bread before cubing it.

SERVES 4 TO 6

1 tablespoon butter
1 large onion, chopped
3 cloves
2½ cups peeled and chopped fresh tomatoes or diced canned tomatoes
1 tablespoon cornstarch or 2 teaspoons arrowroot
2 tablespoons brown sugar or Rapidura
Salt to taste
About ¼ teaspoon freshly ground black pepper, or more to taste
4 to 5 slices whole wheat bread, toasted and cut into 1-inch cubes
Cooking spray

1 Preheat the oven to 375°F.

2 Place 1 teaspoon of the butter over medium heat in a skillet. Add the onion and the cloves and sauté, stirring often, for about 6 minutes, or until the onions are soft, translucent, and just on the edge of browning. Remove and discard the cloves.

3 Spoon out about ¼ cup of the tomato juices and place in a small bowl. Dissolve the cornstarch in the tomato juices and set aside.

4 Add the rest of the tomatoes to the onions in the skillet. Add the brown sugar, salt, and pepper to the tomatoes, and bring to a boil. Stir in the tomato-cornstarch slurry; the mixture should thicken almost immediately. Remove from the heat.

5 Spray a deep-sided 1½- to 2-quart-capacity casserole with cooking spray. Scoop about half of the tomatoes in and top with half of the bread cubes. Scoop in the remainder of the tomatoes and top with the rest of the bread, pressing the bread in a bit to encourage it to soak up the tomato liquid. Dot the top layer of bread with the remaining 2 teaspoons butter.

6 Bake for 20 to 25 minutes, or until bubbling hot and the top is slightly darkened. Serve as soon as possible, preferably piping hot.

Comforting Cabbage-Apple Kugel

Kugels are Jewish puddings, solid, curative, much loved. They play a major role in Ashkenazi cuisine, with its origins in eastern Europe and western Russia, where the winters are long and access to fresh vegetables and fruit other than those that keep (onions, potatoes, cabbage, carrots, apples) was limited to the very brief summertime. Add to this the strictures of kosher, and you can see how this whole artful subset of dishes developed: Kugels added variety to those few vegetables available all winter, many were dairy free so they could be served with or without meat, and their slow baking worked with available fuel. There are both main-dish and dessert kugels, but given the notorious Jewish sweet tooth, even those intended as accompaniments to entrées, like this appealing cabbage kugel, are on the sweet side. The cabbage, slowly cooked, almost caramelizes. Two excellent, minor changes can also be made: Add ¾ teaspoon cinnamon and/or ½ cup toasted chopped walnuts or almonds. With or without, this is a pleasing dish.

Vegans and the lactose intolerant will be pleased to see that this can be dairy free if oil or vegetable margarine is substituted for the butter. Potato starch adds a nice delicacy. (Just so you don't leave this seemingly obscure ingredient languishing on your shelf, note that potato starch is called for in the Neo-Classic Crêpes, page 332, and in Parsnip-Barley Burgers, page 831.)

This recipe is adapted from Jennie Grossinger's *The Art of Jewish Cooking*. **SERVES 4 TO 6**

Cooking spray
1 to 2 tablespoons butter or Better (page 905)
5 cups finely shredded cabbage or half of a 1-pound bag shredded cabbage
1 apple, peeled and finely diced
3 tablespoons honey, brown sugar, or Rapidura
1 teaspoon salt
1½ cups cubed, toasted whole wheat bread (about 3 slices)
1½ cups water, preferably spring or filtered
¼ cup potato starch
3 large eggs, separated
¼ cup raisins

1 Preheat the oven to 350°F. Spray a 2-quart casserole with cooking spray.

2 Spray a large skillet (not nonstick) with cooking spray and heat the butter in it over medium heat. When the butter has melted, lower the heat slightly and add the cabbage. Cook, stirring often, over low-medium heat for about 20 minutes. Add the apple and cook for 5 minutes more. Sprinkle with 1 tablespoon of the sweetener and the salt, raise the heat very slightly, and cook for 10 minutes more, or until soft and slightly browned. Remove from the heat and let cool slightly.

3 As the cabbage cooks, place the bread cubes in a heatproof bowl. Bring the water to a boil and pour it over the bread. Let stand until cool enough to handle, then squeeze the bread dry, discarding the water.

4 Mash the soaked bread together with the potato starch, then mash in the egg yolks. Stir in the cooled cabbage, the remaining sweetener, and the raisins.

5 Beat the egg whites until stiff and fold them into the cabbage-bread mixture. Spoon into the prepared casserole and bake for 40 minutes, or until set. Serve immediately.

Timbale of Butternut Squash Pudding with Caramelized Onions

Traditional timbales were egg-rich and cream-heavy; with butternut squash puddings sweet and confectionlike. This is neither. Its only sweetness comes from the squash itself, the caramelized onion, and a touch of brown sugar and honey, which is zippity-do-dah'd with curry. This is definitely main-course fare, not dessert. Though similar to the Vegan French-Style Gratin of Butternut Squash (page 289), it's spicier, not crumb-topped, and not vegan. Take your pick; you can't go wrong with either. **SERVES 6 TO 8**

1 large or 2 medium butternut squash, poked with a fork or knife in a couple of places
Cooking spray or oil
1 tablespoon olive oil
2 onions, very thinly sliced
3 cloves garlic, finely diced
2 teaspoons tamari or shoyu soy sauce
1 to 2 teaspoons Thai-style red curry paste (available in the Asian food section of your local supermarket or natural foods market, or at any Asian grocery)
3 tablespoons cornstarch
1 large egg
¼ teaspoon salt
1 tablespoon honey
1 tablespoon brown sugar
¼ cup evaporated skim milk or rice, oat, or soy milk
Freshly ground black pepper

1 Preheat the oven to 350°F.

2 Bake the squash on a nonstick baking sheet, or one that has been sprayed with cooking spray, for 40 minutes to 1 hour, or until tender. Remove from the oven and allow to cool.

3 While the squash bakes, heat the olive oil over medium heat in a nonstick skillet. Add the onions and stir-fry for 6 to 7 minutes, or until limp and starting to color. Reduce the heat to very low and add the garlic. Cover the pan and let the garlic and onions steam together for 4 minutes, then add the tamari and curry paste, and cook, watching closely and stirring constantly, for 2 minutes more, or until deeply golden but not at all burned and with most of the tamari evaporated. Scrape this mixture into a small bowl.

4 Split each squash in half and scrape out the seeds. Scrape the flesh out into a bowl and discard the peel. Transfer the flesh to a food processor and add the cornstarch, egg, salt, honey, brown sugar, milk, and pepper.

5 Combine the squash mixture with the caramelized onions and garlic. Stir well. Taste for seasonings, disregarding the floury taste, which is from the cornstarch and will bake out.

6 Spray 6 to 8 small ramekins with cooking spray and fill with the squash mixture. Place the ramekins in a baking dish and fill the baking dish with very hot or boiling water. Carefully slide the baking dish into the oven. Bake for 40 minutes, or until well set and slightly browned; the tops will be a little dark and cracked. Remove the timbales from the oven and from their water bath. Let cool for 10 to 20 minutes. Run a knife blade around the edge of the timbales, smack them once on the counter, and turn them upside down out onto a serving plate. (Or you may serve them in the ramekins, if you prefer.) Serve immediately.

Dairy Hollow House Summer Squash Pudding

I was quite vain about the side-vegetable plates we sent out with our entrees during the years we had the restaurant. It was not unusual in the summer for each plate to have six or seven fresh vegetables, all prepared differently, with just a bite or two of each, as a nod to traditional Southern vegetable cookery (summertime dinners in much of the South used to be bowl upon bowl of various vegetable preparations—ever changing and straight out of the garden—passed around family style, with a skillet of cornbread).

One frequent visitor to our Dairy Hollow vegetable plates was some form of pudding or timbale, frequently of summer squash. Many people are convinced they don't like summer squash, which is, admittedly, bland. But slightly reinvented, it can be swooningly good. I confess I've made these hundreds of times, each time a little differently, and I never, ever measured—until I wrote this book.

The yield given is approximate. The 6 to 8 serving range means generous-sized portions, but if you're using just a small square on a plate with other things, you could easily count on doubling the number of servings. Unless it's a buffet, in which case people will come back for seconds. **SERVES 6 TO 8**

Cooking spray
3 small to medium yellow summer squash, stem ends trimmed off, halved lengthwise
4 ounces neufchâtel reduced-fat cream cheese, softened
3 large eggs
3 tablespoons cornstarch
½ cup low-fat milk, buttermilk, yogurt, light sour cream, oat or rice milk, or half-and-half or heavy cream
1 teaspoon Pickapeppa sauce
1 teaspoon salt
Freshly ground black pepper to taste
Seasonings (see variations at left)

VARIATIONS

Here are some of the dozens of ways I've fooled with this concept over the years:

- ***Use less vegetable puree and more milk or cream, or half-and-half, or buttermilk.***
- ***Stir in well-drained, cooked and chopped greens of any kind, and either leave the dish as is or sprinkle with a little grated Cheddar cheese toward the end of the cooking period.***
- ***Add 2 tablespoons honey, a dash of cinnamon, and a couple gratings of nutmeg.***
- ***Add a dash of cayenne and 1 teaspoon turmeric plus 1 teaspoon finely minced fresh ginger and 1 tablespoon honey.***
- ***Stir in the kernels cut from 2 or 3 ears of corn and 1 tablespoon or so chopped roasted green chiles, either fresh or canned. Stop there or add ½ cup grated sharp Cheddar or Monterey Jack cheese.***
- ***Add a few tablespoons prepared pesto.***

1 Preheat the oven to 375°F. Spray a conventional 9-inch square baking dish or 6 to 8 ramekins with cooking spray, or use nonstick.

2 Bring a large pot of water to a boil. Drop in the halved yellow squash, and cook for 3 to 5 minutes, or until slightly softened. Drain well and transfer the squash to a food processor. Buzz to a not-quite-smooth puree and measure out 3 cups puree, saving any left for another use (such as in almost any vegetable soup).

3 Place all ingredients except the puree in the food processor and buzz until smooth and well combined. Add puree and buzz again. Taste and season.

4 Pour the pudding mixture into the prepared pan or ramekins. Place the pan or ramekins in a larger pan, and pour in hot water to surround them. Place the pan in the oven and bake for 40 minutes to 1 hour, until the pudding is firm and browned and does not stick to your finger when you touch the surface. Serve in the ramekins, or reverse the puddings out onto serving plates, or cut into squares and serve from the pan.

Broccoli Sformato

Italian vegetable pudding is called *sformato,* meaning "unmolded," because it is traditionally baked in a loaf pan (or sometimes a ring mold), then reversed out onto a serving platter. This maneuver can be tricky, as the texture is creamy, but is more easily accomplished if the mixture is baked in two small pans rather than one large. To prevent the off flavors that sometimes come when eggs interact with metal pans, use glass, ceramic, or enamel-clad pans or terrines, if you have them; if not, try two square Corningware casseroles instead. Or just bake the mixture in individual timbales or custard cups.

Sformati are usually bound with eggs and a bit of béchamel sauce, so they are not light, although I have cut the eggs way back from the typical six (cornstarch makes the difference here). I've also cut back on the butter, leaving just enough for flavor. I messed around some with a vegan version but was not satisfied. It's egg and dairy here, or nothing.

To make a sformato a main dish, serve with a sprightly, noncreamy sauce: tomato or roasted pepper for example. Otherwise, use it as a component. **SERVES 6 TO 8**

VEGETABLE PUREE BASE

2 to 2½ pounds broccoli, divided into florets, stems peeled and chopped
⅓ cup cornstarch or arrowroot
2 large eggs, beaten

BINDING SAUCE

1 tablespoon butter, Better (page 905), olive oil, or a combination
Cooking spray
2 tablespoons unbleached all-purpose flour
1¼ cups low-fat milk, warmed
½ teaspoon salt
Freshly ground black pepper to taste
Several gratings of nutmeg
2 tablespoons nutritional yeast
2 ounces freshly grated Parmesan cheese (½ cup)

PAN PREPARATION

Cooking spray
⅓ cup crisp breadcrumbs

FOR SERVING (OPTIONAL)

Basic Wintertime Italian Tomato Sauce (page 931), "Macro Red" Sauce (page 936), or Greek-Style Tomato Sauce with Lentils (page 932)

1 Preheat the oven to 375°F.

2 Drop the broccoli into a large pot of boiling water and blanch for 3 to 4 minutes, or until the broccoli is just barely tender but still bright green. Immediately drain the broccoli, pouring cold water over it to stop the cooking. Shake off as much water as possible. Transfer the broccoli to a food processor and add the cornstarch and eggs. Pausing a few times to scrape down the sides of the work bowl, buzz the broccoli to a puree. Transfer the mixture to a bowl.

3 Heat the butter, Better, and/or olive oil together over medium-low heat in a nonstick skillet, or one that has been sprayed

Sformarto Forms

Classic Rich Sformato: *Omit the cornstarch and use 6 eggs in the broccoli puree. Use 1½ tablespoons each butter and olive oil, 3 tablespoons flour, full-fat milk in the sauce, and use 4 ounces grated Parmesan cheese (1 cup) instead of 2 ounces (½ cup).*

Other Vegetable Sformati: *Using this as a base recipe, you can easily and deliciously venture into other Sformato terrain: Replace the broccoli with cauliflower, barely cooked spinach or other greens, mushrooms, or asparagus, for instance.*

Spring Sformati with Mirepoix: *Over medium heat, in a skillet that has been sprayed with cooking spray, heat an additional tablespoon of the same butter or oil used in the other part of the recipe. In it sauté 1 medium onion, finely diced, for 4 minutes. Add 1 medium carrot, finely diced, and 2 medium ribs of celery, also finely diced. Sauté about 4 more minutes, or until vegetables are softened, then add the remaining butter, Better, or oil and the flour, preparing the sauce in the same skillet. Replace the broccoli with about 1½ pounds sugar-snap peas (round, edible-pod peas), stems removed. Blanch them, puree them (saving a few whole for a garnish), and continue with the recipe, using the sauteed-vegetable seasoned sauce. Serve, sauced, with a whole sugar snap garnishing each portion.*

with cooking spray. Stir in the flour, and cook, stirring, for about 2 minutes, or until beginning to color. Gradually whisk in the warmed milk, then add the salt, plenty of pepper, and nutmeg. Heat, stirring, until the mixture thickens, then stir in the nutritional yeast and Parmesan. Remove from the heat and stir into the broccoli mixture.

4 Spray 2 small loaf pans very well with cooking spray and add the breadcrumbs. Shake the pans so the crumbs adhere to the sides and bottom of the pan, then turn out the excess crumbs. Divide the broccoli mixture between the pans. Place the pans in a larger pan of hot water and bake for about 45 minutes, or until firm.

5 Carefully remove the sformati from the oven, let stand at room temperature for at least 15 to 20 minutes, then run a knife around the edge of one loaf pan, turn it upside down onto a warmed platter, rap the bottom of the pan sharply a few times, and lo and behold, out should pop your sformato. (If it doesn't, however, don't worry; it will still taste good, and you can serve individual portions of it or mask the torn-up part with the sauce, if you're using one.) Repeat with the second pan.

6 Serve, with or without sauce. If sauced, serve as a whole loaf with the sauce ladled over it, as individual sauced portions, or with the sauce passed at table.

Amma's Stove-top Bread Masala Pudding

Amma is the extraordinarily beautiful matriarch of the extended family with whom I stay in South India, my spiritual home. She could not get over the fact that not only did I want a recipe for bread masala—the South Indian equivalent of made-on-the-stove-top dressing—but that I wanted to write it down. Not only that, I seriously intended to measure each ingredient and had even brought specially marked cups and spoons to do it! Her large, dark eyes overflowed with mirth as I sat beside her, cutting and chopping and interrupting her as she was about to toss something in by saying, "Wait!" and thrusting forward my cup or spoon while making notes. Far too gentle to actually say "Crazy American," she nonetheless seemed to be thinking it, amused and affectionate, as she worked in her unbleached white Kerala-style cotton sari with its colored border, her dark, waved long hair, ribboned with gray, flowing down to mid-back, her movements unhurried and practiced. Every so often one of the servants wandered in and there would be an exchange in Malayalam, of which I'd catch the words "bread masala" and "cookbook." Much laughter.

Look for this recipe all you want in Indian cookbooks or restaurants, but you won't find it. A simple, inexpensive dish, pleasing for supper served with a salad, it is home cooking—from a different home, in a different part of the world—at its best.

SERVES 4 TO 6

2 tablespoons mild vegetable oil, such as corn, canola, or peanut
2 large red onions, finely diced
2 teaspoons black or brown mustard seeds
1 dried red chile, broken up into small- to medium-size pieces
2½ cups diced red-ripe tomatoes
2 teaspoons ground coriander
½ teaspoon freshly ground black pepper
4 to 5 cups cubed good-quality bread, preferably firm white or light whole wheat sandwich bread, crust left on
Salt to taste
Chopped cilantro

1 Heat the oil over medium-high heat in a small wok or heavy skillet. Add the onions and stir-fry for 1 minute. Add the mustard seeds and chile and cook for 2 to 3 minutes more, or until the onion is slightly softened and starting to color a bit around the edges. Lower the heat slightly.

2 Add the tomatoes, coriander, and black pepper. Stir for a few seconds, then add the bread cubes. Cook over medium heat, stirring constantly, until the bread has softened and moistened slightly, absorbing the tomato liquid, and the spices are well distributed, 2 to 3 minutes. The bread should be softened but not soggy. Add salt and serve, hot or warm, sprinkled with a little cilantro.

Polenta, Parmesan, and Roasted Garlic Pudding

The Italian cousin of Southern spoon bread, this dish cannot be made vegan as such—though a good polenta with plenty of roasted garlic stirred in, without the cheese, is certainly possible. Plain or sauced, this polenta is very, very satisfying. **SERVES 4 TO 6**

2½ cups water, preferably spring or filtered
¾ teaspoon salt
1 cup coarse, stone-ground yellow cornmeal
1 teaspoon butter (optional)
2 cups low-fat milk
3 large eggs, beaten
¾ cup freshly grated Parmesan cheese
½ cup Roasted Garlic puree (see page 899)
1 or 2 gratings of nutmeg
Freshly ground black pepper to taste

FOR SERVING (OPTIONAL)
Basic Wintertime Italian Tomato Sauce (page 931), Creole-Style Tomato Sauce (page 932), Tomatillo Salsa Verde (page 944), Chile Buzz (page 902), Jan Hazard's Rich Roasted Vegetable Sauce (page 938), or sautéed peppers and Lightlife Italian Links

1 Bring the water and salt to a boil in a nonstick medium saucepan. Gradually stir in the cornmeal in a steady stream, pouring with one hand while whisking like mad with the other. Boil, stirring constantly, for 1 minute. Suspend the pot in the top of a larger pot of simmering water, making an impromptu double boiler. Cover the smaller pot, and let the cornmeal cook, stirring occasionally, in the double boiler for 30 minutes. Add the butter, if using, to the cornmeal.

2 Preheat the oven to 375°F.

3 Combine the milk and eggs, whisking well, in a large bowl. When the cornmeal

Try these, too

Southwestern-Spiced Polenta: *Add 3 charred, peeled, and roasted poblanos to the custard and substitute grated Monterey Jack for Parmesan. Serve with Cupboard Enchilada Sauce (page 935) or Pamela Jones's Absolutely Incredible Roasted Vegetable Salsa (page 915), and a nice dollop of rehydrated instant black beans.*

Savory Oatmeal Pudding: *So accustomed are we to equating oatmeal with breakfast that this sounds bizarre, but I promise you, it's delish. Substitute ¾ cup oatmeal for the cornmeal. Use only 1 cup water. Place the dry oatmeal in a heatproof bowl. Bring the water to a boil with the salt, and pour over the oatmeal. Let stand for 15 minutes. Preheat the oven and proceed as directed from Step 3 on, using oatmeal mixture instead of cornmeal.*

comes off the heat, beat 1 ladleful of the hot cornmeal mixture into the egg-milk mixture, whisking well. Gradually add the remaining hot cornmeal, half of the Parmesan, the roasted garlic, nutmeg, and black pepper, whisking well.

4 Spray a shallow 1½-quart or 10-by-6-inch baking dish with cooking spray. Turn the pudding into it, and sprinkle with the remaining Parmesan. Place the baking dish in a larger baking dish and pour in boiling water to surround the baking dish with the pudding. Carefully place both dishes in the oven. Bake for 50 to 60 minutes, or until the top is slightly browned and the custard is set around the edges but is still just a bit soft at the center. Let cool slightly and serve warm.

Gingered Apricot-Orange Noodle Kugel with Tofu

Some consider potato kugel the best of all Jewish-style puddings (see page 280). But to me, the slightly sweet noodle kugels are tastier. Here is one of my favorites. It is dairy free, but not vegan—the essence of kugel depends on an egg binder. Bright-tasting, sweet, intensely sparked by dried apricots, this not-quite-dessert pudding makes a most comforting supper on its own or a splendid component. Crumbled tofu takes the place of dry-curd cottage cheese, for which, in the finished dish, it's virtually a dead ringer. The idea, which will delight those who need a dairy-free dish, comes from Gloria Kaufer Greene's *The Jewish Holiday Cookbook.* **SERVES 4 TO 6**

"The proof was in the pudding, but the pudding was ruled inadmissible as evidence."

—Caption on New Yorker cartoon
(attorney leaving courthouse and addressing the media),
Michael Maslin, March 1997

Kinds of Kugels

Kugels like this virtually beg you to vary them. Apple juice can substitute for orange, and carrot juice makes an unconventional kugel. Vanilla soy milk can replace fruit juice for a creamy nondairy kugel. Cinnamon can step in for, or in addition to, the ginger and nutmeg. Peeled, finely diced apple, raisins, even diced prunes all have their afficionados—try them instead of, or with, the apricots. You can omit the tofu. You can add an extra egg or omit one. A bit of cinnamon and sugar added to the breadcrumb topping is not unknown. Melted butter or vegetable margarine can replace the oil. As with the cabbage kugel recipe on page 293, slivered blanched almonds, or sometimes other nuts, are frequently added to this kugel.

Apricot Dessert Kugel: *Increase the orange juice to 1¾ cups, use ¼ cup plus 1 tablespoon sweetener, and add 1 teaspoon cinnamon and 1 tablespoon sugar or brown sugar to the crumb topping.*

1 (8-ounce) package wide egg noodles
Salt
2 teaspoons mild vegetable oil
3 tablespoons fine soft breadcrumbs
3 tablespoons cornflake crumbs or other cereal-flake crumbs
3 large eggs, or 1 whole egg and 2 egg whites
2 tablespoons to ¼ cup sugar, brown sugar, honey, or Rapidura
1½ cups freshly squeezed orange juice
½ teaspoon peeled and minced ginger
A few gratings of nutmeg (optional)
½ cup dried apricots, diced
8 ounces conventional firm tofu, preferably reduced fat, crumbled
Cooking spray

1 Preheat the oven to 350°F.

2 Cook the noodles in boiling salted water according to the package directions, undercooking them very slightly so they are still a tiny bit firm. Drain the noodles well and toss with 1 teaspoon of the oil. Set aside in a large bowl.

3 As the noodles cook, toss together in a small bowl or saucer the breadcrumbs, cornflake crumbs, and the remaining 1 teaspoon of oil. Set aside.

4 In a medium bowl, beat together the eggs and sugar, then add the orange juice, ginger, nutmeg, and ¼ teaspoon salt. Toss over the noodles and add the apricots and tofu. Stir and toss well to combine.

5 Spray an 8-inch square baking dish with cooking spray and add the noodle mixture. Cover tightly and bake for about 40 minutes. Uncover, and sprinkle with the crumb mixture. Bake for 12 to 15 minutes more, or until the kugel is set and the crumbs have crisped up slightly. Serve hot.

Timbales

The uptown cousins of the downtown puddings and the midtown gratins, timbales are the most dressed-up of this genre of dishes. Consider them as a party entree—they have an elegant look, yet are individual portion–sized, making for a neat presentation. I call your attention to this first one, which Ned placed on his personal list of Dishes Most Likely to Be on the Menu if We Ever Do a Dinner at the James Beard House.

An ideal feature of a component plate, timbales look most adorable and bake most evenly when done in ramekins. However, if you have custard cups or ovenproof espresso cups, these can also be used. As a last resort use a cake pan or baking dish and serve the timbale in either wedges or squares.

Mushroom, Wild Rice, and Lentil Timbale-Cake

How can a dish that's so unbelievably rich tasting, one so dense with flavor, a pull-out-all-the-stops centerpiece, perfect for your most soignée occasion, be nearly fat free? How, too, can it be all this and so easy to make (if you have cooked wild rice and lentils on hand) that you could do it for a family dinner as well? Please promise me you won't miss this.

A cake, essentially of ground raw mushrooms bound with breadcrumbs, cornstarch, and eggs, is baked in individual ramekins (you could use a glass or ceramic quiche pan, if you wanted). Cooked lentils, pureed, add protein, flavor, and heft; wild rice adds crunch and distinctive flavor; and the seasonings intensify but do not overpower the mushrooms. After baking, the cakes are reversed out, and a sauce is spooned over them on the plate. **SERVES 6 TO 8**

1 pound domestic mushrooms, cleaned
1¾ cups soft whole wheat breadcrumbs
2 large eggs
1 cup cooked lentils
6 large leaves basil, chopped
3 needles rosemary, finely chopped
2 teaspoons Dijon mustard
3 large cloves garlic, quartered
2 tablespoons cornstarch
2 teaspoons olive oil
1 large onion, finely chopped
2 fresh tomatoes, halved, seeded, and grated, skins discarded
1 cup cooked wild rice
Salt and freshly ground black pepper
Cooking spray or oil
Mushroom-Miso-Mustard Gravy (page 952)

1 Preheat the oven to 350°F.

2 Twist out the mushroom stems. Cut off and discard any tough portion at the base of the stems and coarsely chop the stems. Measure the chopped stems and add enough coarsely chopped mushroom caps to equal 2½ cups. Place the chopped stems and caps in a food processor. (Slice the remaining caps and use them for the mushroom gravy.)

3 Add the breadcrumbs, eggs, lentils, basil, rosemary, mustard, garlic, and cornstarch to the food processor. Buzz until a smooth paste is formed, stopping a few times to scrape down the sides of the work bowl. Leave the mixture in the work bowl. The mixture will be the consistency of split pea soup.

4 Heat the olive oil over medium heat in a skillet. Add the onion and sauté for 5 minutes, or until softened and translucent. Add the grated tomatoes and sauté for 2 minutes more. Remove from the heat and scrape the sauté into the mixture in the food processor. Pulse a few times to combine but leave some chunky texture. Turn the mixture out into a bowl and stir in the wild rice. Season to taste with salt and freshly ground black pepper.

5 Oil 6 to 8 ramekins, or a 10-inch ovenproof skillet or round cake pan, or spray with cooking spray. Spoon in the mushroom-lentil mixture, spreading it evenly and smoothing the top. Set in a larger pan, pour hot water into the larger pan, and place in the oven. Bake, uncovered, until firmed up in the middle (press lightly with your fingertip to test) and dark and crusty on top, about 45 minutes for ramekins or 55 to 60 minutes for a cake pan.

6 Let cool in the ramekins or pan for 10 minutes, then run a knife around the edge and carefully reverse out onto individual plates (if you used ramekins), or a serving plate (if you made one big one). Serve hot, cut into slices, with Mushroom-Miso-Mustard Gravy ladled over the top. Of course you will want a good grain or grain pilaf, or a nice pile of mashed potatoes, to accompany this.

Timbales of Cauliflower Pudding with Creamed Spinach Sauce

White islands of creamy cauliflower with a dark green sauce, also a bit creamy. The best garnish is a confetti-like scattering of tiny dice of yellow and red bell pepper. If, as Mark Twain said, cauliflower is nothing but cabbage with a college education, this version has completed its doctoral. This recipe is inspired by one from *The New German Cookbook*, by Jean Anderson and Hedy Wurz, though there are plenty of French notes. This is remarkably rich tasting, though it has much less fat than the original. **SERVES 6 TO 8**

Cooking spray
1 head cauliflower, broken into florets
¼ lemon, cut lengthwise
1 large egg
3 tablespoons cornstarch
2 ounces neufchâtel reduced-fat cream cheese
1 cup low-fat milk, or rice or soy milk
½ teaspoon salt
Freshly ground black pepper to taste
Freshly grated nutmeg to taste
Creamed Spinach Sauce (recipe follows)

1 Preheat the oven to 350°F. Spray six 1-cup timbale dishes with cooking spray.

2 Bring a large pot of water to a boil and drop in the cauliflower and lemon. Blanch until the cauliflower is crisp-tender, 6 to 8 minutes. Drain well, discard the lemon, and refresh with cold water.

3 Pulse/chop the cauliflower in a food processor. Remove half to a bowl. Puree the remaining cauliflower with the egg, cornstarch, neufchâtel, milk, salt, pepper, and nutmeg. Turn out into the timbale dishes. Place in a roasting pan or baking dish and pour hot water around the timbales.

4 Bake for 40 to 50 minutes, until the puddings are firm and just starting to color. Carefully remove from the oven and let cool for 5 minutes. Run a knife around the edge of each and reverse onto a serving plate. Serve piping hot, with the Creamed Spinach Sauce attractively spooned around it.

Creamed Spinach Sauce

MAKES ABOUT 2 CUPS

1 teaspoon to 1 tablespoon butter
Cooking spray
3 scallions, roots removed, white and 2 inches of green parts sliced
2 tablespoons unbleached all-purpose flour
1¾ cups Golden Stock (page 140) or other mild flavorful stock, homemade or canned
1 (10-ounce) bag spinach, washed, stemmed, and chopped
2 ounces neufchâtel reduced-fat cream cheese, softened
¼ cup slightly sweet white wine, such as Riesling
Leaves from 4 large sprigs Italian parsley, coarsely chopped
Salt and freshly ground black pepper to taste
Freshly grated nutmeg to taste

1 Melt the butter over medium heat in a nonstick skillet or one that has been sprayed with cooking spray. Add the scallions and sauté for 2 minutes. Sprinkle with flour and cook, stirring, for 2 to 3 minutes more. Gradually stir in the stock, whisking to smooth it out. When it thickens, add the spinach. Lower the heat and cover. Let barely simmer for 3 minutes.

2 As the sauce simmers, combine the neufchâtel, wine, parsley, salt, pepper, and nutmeg in a food processor. Pulse/chop, scrape down the sides of the work bowl, then buzz to make a smooth puree.

3 Ladle a little sauce into the processor and buzz again, then add all the processor contents to the sauce on the stove, whisking. Serve the sauce, hot, around the cauliflower custards.

Cleora's Eggplant Soufflé

Once I was a soufflé-makin' fool, fixing all manner of soufflés, maybe (can it be?) two or even three times a month. But, like most people who've moved in a meatless direction, egg-intense days are behind me. This and the occasional chocolate dessert soufflé are virtually the only ones that have stayed at my table. It is simply so unusual and good—a moist soufflé in which eggplant's subtlety is played up, not lost, with a kick of cayenne and sharp Cheddar. It's a sensibility that is both country and sophisticated. I made it at the restaurant four or five times a year as part of our side vegetable plates, and it always garnered raves. To me, it's party food: rich, indulgent, a little fancy, all those things that a good once-in-a-while, go-right-ahead dining experience should be.

This recipe is adapted from one by the late Cleora Butler, a fabled caterer in the Tulsa area. A book of her recipes and memoirs, entitled *Cleora's Kitchen* was published in 1985; food writer Ellen Fly edited it. The book is divided by decades, so you can see when which dishes were popular at parties—remembering that Tulsa was an oil town, and there were fabulously wealthy folks entertaining, yet it was also middle America, so things couldn't be too far-out. This was listed as a 1930s recipe. I have omitted the cup of chopped pecans and scaled back on the cheese and butter. Still, it is mighty rich. **SERVES 4 TO 6 AS AN ENTREE, 6 TO 8 AS A COMPONENT**

2 cups water, preferably spring or filtered
2 teaspoons vinegar
2 large eggplants, peeled and cubed
1 tablespoon butter
Cooking spray
2 tablespoons unbleached all-purpose flour
1 cup low-fat milk or evaporated skim milk
¼ teaspoon salt
¾ cup fine, soft whole wheat breadcrumbs
3 large eggs, separated
1 green bell pepper, stemmed, ribs and seeds removed, finely minced
4 ounces extra-sharp Cheddar cheese, grated (1 cup)
½ teaspoon freshly ground black pepper
¼ teaspoon cayenne

1 Bring the water and vinegar to a boil in a medium saucepan and drop in the eggplant. Cover and simmer for 25 minutes. Drain well.

2 Preheat the oven to 350°F.

3 Melt the butter over medium heat in a nonstick skillet or one that has been sprayed with cooking spray. Whisk in the flour and cook for 2 minutes. Gradually whisk in the milk, stirring until the sauce is thick and smooth. Remove the sauce from the heat and add the salt.

4 Combine the eggplant with the sauce, breadcrumbs, egg yolks, green bell pepper, and half of the cheddar. Stir in the black pepper and cayenne.

5 Beat the egg whites until stiff, then fold them into the eggplant mixture.

6 Spray a 2-quart casserole or soufflé dish or 4 to 6 individual ramekins with cooking spray. Spoon in the eggplant mixture and bake until done, 45 minutes for a single large dish, 35 for smaller ones.

Wrapped, Stuffed & Stacked

Plumped-up pastries and pierogies; luscious layered lasagne; excellent enchiladas; divine dumplings; voluptuous, voluminous vegetables, sensually stuffed—these are among the dishes you'll find in this overflowingly abundant chaper. Here are the classic meatless center-of-the-plate entrees that generally perform their magic by combining the elements of protein (beans, cheese, tofu, tempeh, sometimes nuts), carbohydrate (noodles and doughs of all kinds, cooked grains, breads, tortillas), and vegetables (as themselves or transfigured into sauces). These generous and easy-to-love dishes are universally enjoyed, a great and welcoming starting place for introducing plant-based foods to the formerly carnivorous, so put on your apron, preheat your oven, sharpen your knife, and let's wrap and stack.

Stuffed & Wrapped Pastries & Pastas

Savory fillings wrapped in pastry are served with pride throughout the world. A bite, eyes closed, tells you where you are. Crunchy black mustard seeds, cumin, green chile, potatoes?—India: samosa. Raisins, green olives, cumin, cilantro?—South America: empanada. Whether samosa or empanada, dumpling or spring roll, baked, boiled, or fried, most stuffed pastries are time consuming to make. But they're so good, so enthusiastically appreciated, that they're worth knowing how to make, even if only occasionally.

I've pulled together some general ideas, and then recipes that demonstrate various wrappings. You'll be able to mix and match fillings and wrappings to your heart's content; read, and then get into the kitchen and make my shortcuts work for you.

Wrappers for the Too-Busy

USE A READY-MADE TORTILLA: This is the number one, easy-fix, relatively fat-sparing idea that has caught on like a house afire in recent years.

Here's my take on tortilla wraps: Warm a whole wheat tortilla in a dry skillet just enough to make it pliable. Spread a generous amount of the filling of your choice over half of the surface. Fold the unfilled half over the filling. Bake (on a cookie sheet sprayed with cooking spray) at 400°F, until browned, about 10 minutes, or place in a nonstick skillet, or one sprayed with cooking spray, over medium heat and fry until lightly browned, about 5 minutes; turn and fry the remaining side until lightly browned, about 5 more minutes. You can also brush the exterior of the filled tortilla with a little flavored oil (see Jamaican Curried Vegetable Patties, page 348).

This method gives you a half-round stuffed pastry. If its edges are oozy because the filling has not been perfectly sealed, or if a spinach-ricotta calzone mixture or a dense mushroom piroshki filling are not traditionally wrapped in tortillas, so what? The results are tasty, fast, relatively light—appealing all around.

USE A RICE-PAPER WRAPPER: For details on these versatile, simple, fat-free wrappers, see the Quasi-Vietnamese Spring Rolls recipe on page 314. Here are the basics: Soak the wrapper for about 30 seconds; fill it, roll it up, and eat it—no cooking. That's it! However, because rice-paper–wrapped rolls are served cold or at room temperature, and are not cooked after being filled, the filling should be composed of ingredients that are intentionally raw or precooked, and particularly appetizing chilled or at room temperature.

USE A FOOD PROCESSOR TO MAKE YEAST-LEAVENED DOUGHS: Not instant, but it is fast! And the results—a pliable yeast dough that can easily be rolled out, cut up and stuffed, then sealed and baked—are beguiling. Yeast pastries are healthful, can be low fat (mine are), and send delicious aromas throughout the house while baking.

COOK ONCE FOR SEVERAL MEALS BY USING YOUR FREEZER: For example, make a large batch of yeast-leavened pastry dough, and, after punching it down, divide and freeze (the recipe will give you specific directions). Or take it further: Make a batch, or batches, of filled pastries and freeze them on a wire rack (this allows air to circulate around them so that they freeze more quickly) the second you've finished filling them. Once frozen solid, transfer them to a zippered freezer bag, and store, airtight and labeled, in the freezer. Bake or boil, without thawing, as needed, directly from the freezer to the oven. (Allow a few extra minutes for the cooking time.) Conventional crêpes also freeze like a dream. Again, none of this is instant, but a peaceful afternoon's meditative dumpling- or turnover- or tamale-making is pleasurable, and ultimately time saving.

One shortcut method I cannot recommend—yet—is using commercial ready-to-bake refrigerator roll dough. These cardboard tubes out of which the dough seems to pop and puff are frequently high in fat, preservative-laden, and made from refined, bromated flours. But I bet that in the next few years good refrigerator or freezer doughs, with whole-grain flours, reasonable fat content, and no preservatives, will become commercially available.

Wrappings for the Fat-Conscious

KNOW YOUR FAT CONTENTS: Tortillas, my yeast doughs, vegan crepes, rice-paper wrappers, and noodle-y doughs are all *low fat.* They have either negligible fat grams or up to no more than 2 or 3 per serving.

Filo, crêpes, and biscuit dough wrappers are traditionally *high fat,* but are easily revised to low-to-medium fat, bringing the fat content down to 4 to 8 grams per serving.

Any short-crust or pie-crust dough containing ¼ cup (or more) butter, cream cheese, oil, or shortening per cup of flour and any pastry that's deep-fat fried are *high fat* and no getting around it. Number of fat grams per serving: You don't want to know. Habitual choices should be lower fat. Save the high-fats for occasional indulgence.

Ready-Made Wraps

The easiest pastry wrappings are the premade varieties. I've already mentioned tortillas and rice-paper wrappers. There are also other options, filo dough and both Asian and Western pasta doughs. Depending on where you live, you may find them refrigerated or frozen, in supermarkets and most Asian foods stores.

FILO DOUGH: Filo, the delicate, layered buttery Greek dough most of us first encounter in baklava or spanakopita, is often very greasy and/or soggy. It's easy to forget how good it is when done right and how easy it is to do right. Filo, when conventionally prepared, is not the most healthful breadstuff, which puts it right into the "limited use" category. First, it's made of white, not whole-grain, flour (though I bet we'll see a whole-grain variety offered commercially in the next few years); second, that white flour has been bleached (see page 497). And while filo is itself fat-free, it needs butter or a combination of butter and olive oil, not only for the crisp texture, but to taste good.

I began fooling around with filo to see how little fat I could use and still create a pleasurable crunch. A little fat, as long as it's the real thing, makes all the difference in the world. If you allow a mere 1½ teaspoons butter, or butter–olive oil mix, per sheet of filo dough, as opposed to the who's-counting-but-probably-several-tablespoons per sheet that is traditionally brushed on, you will have great results that are pretty modest in terms of total fat content. Yet another fat-sparing trick: Bake the filo separately. Stack and butter the sheets—just a few—right on a baking sheet, then score into serving pieces. Bake as directed. Then, serve the crisp pastry under, on top of, or beside a little pile of filling. You get a greater percentage of filling to pastry with a lesser percentage of fat. What could be wrong with that? You can also use filo as a top crust only, as in Curried Lentil and Potato Cobbler with Pumpkin and Tomato in Filo Crust (page 255) or Deep-Dish Apple Strudel, (page 968).

Okay. So you've figured out which filo-crusted or wrapped recipe you want to make, and you've chosen a fat-sparing technique. You've purchased filo—most likely in the frozen foods section of your supermarket—in the typical 1-pound box and placed it in your freezer. One box is usually sufficient for any recipe, as it contains 25 to 30 tissue paper–thin pastry sheets, each about 12 by 18 inches, which come stacked, then rolled up with a sheet of waxed paper.

Three days or so before you plan to use it, remove the package of filo from the freezer and let it thaw in the fridge. Two hours before ready to use, take it from the fridge, removing it from the box but leaving it in its plastic bag. Let the filo come to room temperature. Before you're ready to get to work, organize all of your ingredients, including the prepared filling and the melted butter (or butter–olive oil mix). You'll also need the pan or baking sheet called for in the recipe; a pastry brush; a clean work surface (such as a large cutting board or counter); a sheet of waxed paper; a spoon; and a clean, damp, but not wet, kitchen towel. For some recipes, you'll also need a

Innecdote: Fry the Friendly Skies

I eat something deep-fried when I go out to a restaurant maybe once every two years, and I never, ever deep-fat fry at home. But when we had the restaurant, I'd very occasionally succumb to the temptation.

One evening at the restaurant, thanks to a bumper crop of pears passed on to me by then–kitchen manager Audrey's daughter, I had some delicious sweet-spicy pear conserve on hand. I wanted the perfect thing to serve with it for an hors d'oeuvre, and I remembered one of Jan's irresistible recipes from The Dairy Hollow House Cookbook, *written in the pre–fat-conscious days: Walnut Wings. These were simply wonton wrappers stuffed with a walnut half and a dab of ricotta cheese, deep-fried. I hadn't made them in ages, but remembering how good they were, and knowing how perfect they'd be with the pear conserve, I thought, "Oh, go on and fry something just this once." I did, and they came out perfectly.*

Ned came in, saw them, and lit up at this reappearance of a much-loved, much-missed old friend. "Oh!" he said. "Are those—?"

I nodded.

"We earn our wings each day," he said cheerily.

I replied, "We love to fry, and it shows."

sharp knife for scoring the dough into serving-size pieces. Preheat the oven. I mention all this because once you open that airtight plastic bag, you need to work quickly and with focus. Filo is so thin that once exposed to air it dries out, losing its pliable texture and becoming brittle and impossible to work with. This can happen literally in the time it takes to answer the phone.

Lay the sheet of waxed paper on the counter. Open the plastic bag, and pull out the tube of filo sheets. Unroll and place the entire stack on the waxed paper. Immediately cover with the damp towel. Pull back the towel and carefully remove one sheet of filo, placing it on the clean work surface. As fast as you can, recover the stacked filo with the damp towel. Drizzle the filo sheet with about 1½ teaspoons of the melted butter, or butter–olive oil mix, and quickly brush it on with the pastry brush. The whole sheet will not be covered, but do your best to scoot it around. Then, quickly add another sheet, and repeat the drizzle/brush number. Continue making as many filo layers as the recipe directs. (Some desserts that use filo will also have you sprinkle each sheet with crushed nuts or crumbs.) Get the completed recipe into the oven or freezer ASAP after assembly.

One of those why-don't-they-tell-you notes: Sometimes when you go to pull off your top filo sheet, it adheres to the remaining sheets along one edge. Usually when this occurs, all of the sheets are stuck at that edge, like paper on a notepad. If this occurs, take a sharp knife and cut off the sticking edge so you can pull the sheets apart, hassle free.

Attend to any unused filo immediately: Reroll as tightly as possible, and either slide the roll back into its plastic bag and seal the opening with plastic wrap, or tightly wrap the whole thing in plastic wrap. Then, back into its box and into the freezer it goes.

ASIAN READY-MADE PASTA DOUGHS: When you add the variety of wrappers used to make dumplings, egg rolls, and spring rolls throughout Asia to the number of transliterated names by which they're known in America, it is easy to become bewildered. Have no fear. Although what I'm about to say will be an anathema to serious Chinese cooking cognoscenti, commercial Asian pasta doughs are generally similar. They are all based on bleached white wheat flour, water, and salt. They are all "raw" doughs, in that the cook is supposed to boil, steam, or fry them.

What, then, distinguishes these doughs from one another? They may have fresh or dried eggs added, or preservatives, or not. They may come in 3¼-to 3½-inch rounds or squares or 7- to 8- inch squares. Their thinness will range from 1/32 inch to 1/16 inch. And the national origins vary; for Filipino cooking, you might see lumpia skins, which differ from spring roll skins only by being thinner, and could be used interchangeably with all other Asian wrappers. In fact, almost all Asian doughs can be used interchangeably.

WESTERN READY-MADE PASTA DOUGHS: Western ready-made pasta doughs use those same three ingredients—flour, water, salt—to make a dizzying number of pasta shapes, dried and fresh. Some of these come stuffed, such as fresh tortellini or ravioli. Some you can stuff yourself, large shells from dry pastas, mezzalunas from fresh. Some are colored, not with synthetics, but with vegetable extracts like tomato, spinach, beet, or, perhaps, squid ink. Most of these add more color than flavor, but in recent years seasoned pastas, both fresh and dried, have become available. Of those I've tasted, dried wild mushroom pastas, "Cajun" or spicy pastas, and lemon pastas all have true flavors.

How do the Western doughs differ from the Eastern? Primarily in shape and thickness—the Eastern are much, much thinner. But like the Captain's Lady and Rosie O'Grady, they are sisters under the skin.

NOTE

At Vietnamese and Thai restaurants across the country, I've had spring rolls made with many different kinds of noodles. The thin noodles made from bean flour called bean thread noodles are among my favorites. Readily available from Asian markets, they are now also available in many supermarkets. They're white when raw, transparent when cooked. Sometimes they come in a snarled-up nest, sometimes straight as spaghetti in a box, and usually they have several names on the box. The package I'm looking at now says BEAN FLOUR NOODLE, JAPANESE STYLE ALIMENTARY PASTE, H'U TI EU DAI, NOUILLES DE FARINE EN HARICOT VERT, and a name in Japanese characters. Cooking bean thread noodles is ridiculously easy. Soak them in a bowl of hot water for 10 minutes, then drop into boiling water for 1 to 2 minutes, drain, and rinse well under cold running water.

Quasi-Vietnamese Spring Rolls

Here is a basic recipe using my favorite Asian ready-made dough, delicious, quick, idiot-proof rice-paper wrappers. These are not the heavy, deep-fried egg rolls that burn your fingers and leave grease on napkins, but delicate, lunar, translucent white cylinders. Slice the spring roll open, and there lies a poetic layered spiral of lettuce, tofu, herbs, maybe a few other vegetables, a sprinkle of sesame seeds or chopped toasted peanuts. A dipping sauce of fiery garlic Thai Crystal sets off the filling's mild, fresh simplicity with dazzling fireworks.

A trip to an Asian foods store (or possibly the supermarket's Asian food aisle) is necessary to purchase rice-paper wrappers. They come packaged in cellophane, in rounds about the size, color, and dimension of flour tortillas, often with labeling in Asian characters only. Check the ingredients if you have any doubt about what you are purchasing; just rice flour, salt, and water should be listed.

This basic recipe is based on one from my friend Nancie McDermott's *Real Thai.*

MAKES ABOUT 24; SERVES 6 TO 8 AS AN ENTREE

10 leaves crisp romaine lettuce, cut crosswise into ¼-inch slices
3 scallions, roots removed, white plus 3 inches of green finely minced
Leaves from 1 bunch fresh mint (about ¾ cup leaves)
Leaves from ½ bunch fresh cilantro (about 1 loosely packed cup leaves)
Leaves from ½ bunch Thai basil (about 1 loosely packed cup leaves)
2 carrots, coarsely shredded or julienned
1 package (8 ounces) commercially made Thai-style tofu, cut lengthwise into ¼-inch-wide strips
12 ounces (½ package) Vietnamese rice-paper wrapper sheets
3 ounces very thin dried bean thread noodles, cooked (see note; optional)
¼ cup chopped, toasted unsalted peanuts (optional)
Warm water, preferably spring or filtered
Vietnamese Restaurant-Style Dipping Sauce (page 781), or Thai Crystal (page 923)
Salad greens or lettuce leaves

1 Combine the romaine, scallions, mint, cilantro, and basil in a medium bowl. Toss to combine thoroughly. Place on a mise en place tray (see page 107).

2 Place the carrots, tofu, wrappers, noodles, and peanuts on the tray. In addition, you'll need a plastic cutting board (plastic works better than wood for rolling) or a clean, flat work space for spring-roll rolling, a plate on which to place the finished spring rolls, and a round pie pan or dish filled with warm water.

3 Place a wrapper into the warm water, and press it down so that it's fully submerged, holding it down for 20 to 25 seconds. Gently lift from the water and place the now-pliable wrapper on your work surface. (It's okay if it's a bit softer at the edges and still a bit firm in the middle; it'll soften as you work.) Let sit for another 20 or 30 seconds.

4 You are now going to layer a heaped-up line of fillings across the round wrapper, one filling on top of another, in a line parallel to the counter edge. Starting about a third of the way up from the bottom edge of the wrapper (that is, the edge closest to you), lay out a thin row of the cooked noodles ("a small tangle of noodles," says

Four Seasons in a Roll

These rolls are too good to limit to one season. As the year turns, parade the best ingredients and flavors of each period through the center of these lovely transparent cylinders.

Spring Rolls with Tempeh: *To make a knock-your-socks-off spring roll, prepare one recipe Basic Oven-Baked Marinated Tempeh (page 641), but cut the tempeh lengthwise into six ½-inch-thick strips before marinating in a mixture of 3 cloves garlic, pressed; 2 teaspoons grated peeled ginger; 1 teaspoon honey; 1 teaspoon toasted sesame oil; ½ teaspoon Tabasco or sriracha; ¼ teaspoon ground coriander. Use the marinated baked tempeh instead of the tofu.*

Winter Rolls: *Replace the bean thread noodles with cooked thin buckwheat (soba) noodles. Replace romaine lettuce with very finely shredded napa cabbage and a bit of grated carrot. Replace tofu with the Basic Oven-Baked Marinated Tempeh as described above. Replace peanuts with 2 tablespoons toasted sesame seeds. Add 1 small sweet potato, which has been peeled, julienned, tossed with 1 teaspoon each vegetable oil and tamari, spread on a nonstick baking sheet, and baked for 10 minutes at 400°F.*

Summer Rolls: *Substitute 1 cup cooked, well-drained black-eyed peas for the tofu or tempeh. Use bean thread noodles. Substitute 1 tomato, peeled, seeded, and diced, for the carrot. Add 1 cup finely shredded sweet basil to the mint and cilantro. Mix a few leaves of spinach with the romaine. Add 1 raw sweet red bell pepper, cut into slivers about 1½ inches long and ¼ inch wide, as well as the kernels from one ear of fresh corn. These are just delicious.*

Fall Rolls: *Use tempeh, as described above. Use thin whole wheat or spinach spaghetti instead of bean thread noodles. Use red bell pepper, as for Summer Rolls, and basil, mint, and cilantro. Use a little very finely shredded kale mixed in with the romaine. Add a little peeled, finely julienned daikon radish. If you have some of Cora Pinkley Call's Uncooked Ozark Relish (page 929) on hand, a little of that, well drained, is a delicious addition and turns these into Ozark Rolls.*

Nancie, poetically), then heap on it a row of the lettuce-herb mixture, a row of carrots, and then strips of tofu and an optional (but excellent) sprinkle of toasted peanuts.

5 Fold the wrapper edge nearest to you up and over the filling, then tuck it under firmly, compressing the filling down tightly. "When you've completely enclosed the filling in one good turn," instructs Nancie, "fold in the right and left sides tightly. . . . Now roll it up and press the seam to close."

6 Set the finished roll on the plate, seam side down. Continue making spring rolls with the remaining wrappers. Serve, with rolls sliced in half or in thirds, with individual bowls of either of the dipping sauces and a garnish of lettuce leaves.

Vietnamese Restaurant-Style Dipping Sauce

Combine 2 parts hoisin sauce with 1 part sriracha and place the mixture in small bowls. Sprinkle with chopped roasted peanuts and serve. Or serve with Light Savory Dipping Sauce (page 318) or Thai Crystal (page 293).

Pot Stickers

Pot stickers, filled half-moon dumplings, are standard in many Chinese and natural foods restaurants; here in the Ozarks, they're as exotic as can be. We make 'em ourselves or do without. They may be steamed, or fry-steamed. The former is simpler, lower in fat, and delicious; the latter is even tastier, but more time consuming, and higher in fat.

This vegetarian adaptation draws from two sources, both of which offer the traditional pork-filled variety: *The Whole World Cookbook,* and Eileen Yin-Fei Lo's *The Dim Sum Dumpling Book.* Tempeh replaces pork, jícama replaces canned water chestnuts. While canned water chestnuts have a nice crunch, after you've had the pure, stunning sweetness of fresh, they seem like a travesty. If you live where you can get fresh water chestnuts, and are diligent enough to peel them, substitute them for the much easier and still very good jícama.

The leftover gyoza skins will, if tightly wrapped, keep very well frozen. Wrap in plastic wrap, then place in a zippered bag and freeze. **MAKES 35 TO 40**

6 to 8 large leaves bok choy
4 ounces minced Basic Oven-Baked Marinated Tempeh (page 641)
2 scallions, minced
¾ cup peeled, finely diced jícama
2 tablespoons cornstarch
2½ teaspoons sugar, honey, or Rapidura
2 teaspoons peeled, finely minced ginger or commercially made fresh ginger paste (see page 228)
2 teaspoons hoisin sauce
½ teaspoon salt
35 to 40 (about ¾ package) 3- to 3½-inch gyoza wrappers, preferably the type made without egg (but with-egg will do if that's all you've got)
½ teaspoon toasted sesame oil
Cooking spray, if steaming
2 tablespoons peanut oil, if fry-steaming
Cold water, preferably spring or filtered
Light Savory Dipping Sauce (recipe follows)

1 Bring a large pot of water to a boil over high heat.

2 Remove the center rib from the bok choy leaves and dice it into ½-inch squares. Stack the leaves, halve them, stack again, and dice the stack into ½-inch squares. Drop the stem pieces into the boiling water and cook for 1 minute; add the leaves, stir, and cook for 1 minute more. Drain immediately, rinsing with cold water to stop the cooking. Drain extremely well, then blot dry with a paper towel.

3 Combine the blanched bok choy with the tempeh, scallions, jícama, cornstarch, sugar, ginger, hoisin sauce, and salt, mixing well. Let the filling stand, uncovered, to blend flavors, 30 to 40 minutes.

4 Set the wrappers on your work counter, covering with a slightly damp clean kitchen towel. Have a saucer with a little water nearby, as well as the filling and a plate on which to place the finished pot stickers.

5 Spread about 1 slightly rounded teaspoon of the filling down the center of a round wrapper, going not quite to the edge. Dip your finger into the water and moisten the outer edge of the wrapper, then fold it

VARIATION

To fry-steam, heat 1 tablespoon peanut oil in a nonstick skillet over medium-high heat. When very hot, add as many dumplings as you can fit in neat rows, without overlapping (they may, however, touch lightly). Cook for exactly 3 minutes, then pour in ½ cup cold water, lower the heat to medium, and cook until all the water has evaporated, 2 to 3 minutes. Repeat with any remaining pot stickers. Serve while they're still so hot they'll burn your fingers, again with Light Savory Dipping Sauce.

Dim Sum

One of the things that I've missed since becoming a vegetarian is the pleasure of seeking a dim sum restaurant in the Chinatown of any metropolitan area I was visiting. Dim sum are the myriad Chinese dumplings, of every possible shape, texture, and filling. The eccentric satisfaction of these eateries—pointing at crimped or pleated dumplings or balls, or cute little savories, without knowing quite what you are eating, and washing it all down with tea—is not possible for one who eschews meat. Alas, virtually all restaurant dim sum contain meat, unless you can find an all-vegetarian Buddhist Chinese restaurant.

In self-defense, I've taken a do-it-yourself approach, vegetarianizing classic dumplings but using ready-made wrappers. Chinese dumpling-making is a fairly major undertaking—not hard, but time consuming. So I usually join forces with a friend for a wrap-and-rap get-together.

over, making a half-moon, sealing the filling in. Pleat the edge as you seal, then pinch the pleats to firm the edge. Repeat until the filling or the wrappers or both (if you're lucky!) are used up.

6 If steaming, spray an open metal steamer basket, pizza screen (my friend Sylvia Teague's method), or an Asian-style steaming basket with cooking spray. Lay the finished pot stickers in the prepared steamer, taking care that the pot stickers are not touching one another. It is important to allow a little space between dumplings, as they will expand during steaming.

7 Place an inch or two of water in a large pot or wok, bring to a boil over high heat, and place the pot sticker–covered steamer in it, making sure that the water does not touch the steamer. Lower the heat to medium, cover tightly, and steam until the pot stickers are cooked through, about 15 minutes. Repeat steaming as needed to cook any remaining pot stickers. Serve immediately, with Light Savory Dipping Sauce. (For an alternative steaming method, see the recipe for Mushroom Shui-mai, which follows.)

Light Savory Dipping Sauce

In addition to being de rigueur for all manner of Asian dumplings, this sauce is an excellent marinade for tofu. It is also very good sprinkled over stir-fried vegetables to be served over pasta or rice. The vinegar makes it keep indefinitely, so why not double or triple the batch?

2 to 3 cloves garlic, minced
⅓ cup tamari or shoyu soy sauce
⅓ cup rice vinegar
1 teaspoon sugar
½ teaspoon minced peeled ginger
½ teaspoon toasted sesame oil
½ teaspoon sriracha or other hot sauce (optional)

Combine all of the ingredients. Place on the table in small bowls so that each guest has his own private dipping stash. If making a large batch, cover and refrigerate.

Mushroom Shui-mai

Shui-mai, sometimes spelled *sui mai*, are comely little dumplings, resembling a small drawstring bag partially opened to reveal the filling. Traditionally they are made with pork and shrimp, but my version is meat free and intensely mushroomy. Decorate them with a few green peas and a cilantro leaf peeping out of the open part of the purse. **MAKES 25 TO 30**

FILLING

6 ounces shiitake mushrooms, stems removed, quartered
4 ounces traditional-style seitan, well rinsed and coarsely diced
4 ounces button mushrooms, wiped and quartered
3 tablespoons cornstarch
1 tablespoon mirin (Japanese rice wine) or sherry
1½ teaspoons sugar or Rapidura
1 teaspoon tamari or shoyu soy sauce
½ teaspoon toasted sesame oil
½ teaspoon salt
3 scallions, roots removed, white and 4 inches of green finely diced
⅓ cup fresh snow peas or sugar-snap peas, diced
⅓ cup finely diced jícama

WRAPPERS

About 30 (½ package) 3- to 3½-inch gyoza wrappers
Cooking spray

GARNISH

Shelled peas, fresh or frozen
Cilantro leaves
Light Savory Dipping Sauce (opposite)

1 In a food processor, combine the shiitakes, seitan, button mushrooms, cornstarch, mirin, sugar, tamari, sesame oil, and salt. Buzz to a paste, pausing from time to time to scrape down the sides. Scrape the mixture into a bowl and stir in the scallions, snow peas, and jícama. Let stand to blend flavors, about 30 minutes.

2 Set the wrappers on your work counter, covering with a slightly damp clean kitchen towel. Have the filling handy, and a few plates that have been sprayed with cooking spray on which to place the finished dumplings.

3 Place 2 teaspoons to 1 tablespoon of the filling mixture smack dab in the middle of a round wrapper. Draw the edges up around but not over the filling on all sides, pinching in a little, moistening the upper edge, by moistening your thumb and forefinger into water as you pinchand pleating the edges (see what I meant about the drawstring bag effect?). Flatten the bottom a bit, so that the dumplings can stand upright. Please note that you should see a good little bit of the filling—an inch or so. Repeat until filling or wrappers or both (if you're lucky!) are used up.

4 Press 3 peas into the top of the exposed filling. Steam the dumplings as directed in Pot Stickers (page 316), or right on the plate. This works if you don't have a metal steamer, but do have a pot, wok, or Dutch oven large enough to accommodate the dumpling plate with at least 1 inch of space between the edge of the plate and the pot, through which the steam can rise. Place an upside-down heatproof bowl or empty can in the bottom of the pot to act as a pedestal for the dumpling plate. Pour in water to a depth of about 2 inches or whatever's adequate so that the bowl or can will project slightly above the water level. Set the dumpling-filled plate on top of the bowl or can. Cover the pot and bring the water to a boil over high heat. Steam, tightly covered, until the filling's hot and the wrapper is soft, 15 to 20 minutes.

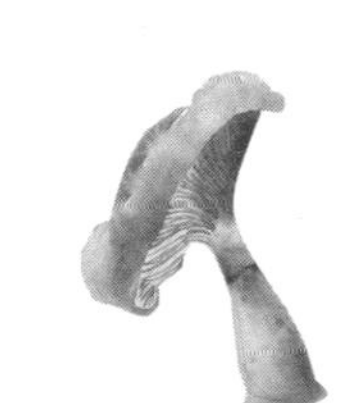

5 Remove the shui-mai from the steamer and poke a cilantro leaf onto the top of each one. Serve hot, with dipping sauce.

Mandu

Another vegetarianized Asian dumpling. Kinship with the two previous recipes is obvious, but the shaping and filling are Korean in origin. Three- to four-inch square wonton wrappers work perfectly as wraps. Kimchee—Korean spicy cabbage and vegetable pickle—gives it kick. Kimchee can be made at home (page 928) or purchased, but if you do buy it, check the label: Sometimes fish sauce (like soy sauce, but made from fermented fish) is added.

Mandu can be steamed or boiled. For a delicate, less watery texture, I suggest steaming (see directions in the previous two recipes). Here, I've given the boiling method. It's nominally easier, and makes them more noodle-y, but you may lose a few to splitting. Both ways are good. **MAKES ABOUT 55; SERVES 6 AS AN ENTREE**

4 scallions, roots removed, all of white and 3 inches of green, thinly sliced
1 to 3 cloves garlic, pressed (use more or less depending on the garlickiness of the kimchee)
4 ounces (½ package) savory baked tofu, very finely diced
1 cup drained kimchee, commercial or homemade (page 928) lightly rinsed, drained, blotted dry, and chopped medium-fine
1 tablespoon cornstarch
1 tablespoon toasted sesame seeds
1½ teaspoons minced peeled ginger
1 teaspoon sugar
Salt and freshly ground black pepper to taste
About 55 (1 package) 3- to 4-inch square wonton wrappers
Light Savory Dipping Sauce (page 318)

1 Combine the scallions, garlic, tofu, kimchee, cornstarch, sesame seeds, ginger, and sugar, tossing to blend well. Season with salt and pepper, tasting to get the filling just right ("just right" should be just a tad salty, since the noodle wrapping is bland). Set aside, uncovered, at room temperature, for 10 to 20 minutes, to allow the flavors to meld together.

2 Set the wonton wrappers on your work counter and cover with a slightly damp clean kitchen towel. Place the filling, a saucer of water, and a plate on which to place the finished dumplings nearby.

3 Mound about 1 slightly rounded teaspoon of filling in the center of a wrapper. Moisten the edges of the wrapper and fold the parallel edges together to form a rectangle with a lump in the middle. Press gently around the lump of filling, sealing it

in the middle of the dough. Repeat with the remaining wrappers and filling, until you run out of one or the other (or, if the dumpling gods are smiling, both at the same time).

4. If steaming the dumplings, see the two previous recipes for directions. If boiling them, bring a large pot (the largest pot you have, or perhaps two smaller ones) of water to a boil over high heat. When it's furiously boiling, lower the heat to a medium boil, and gently drop in some of the mandu. Don't crowd the pot and don't let the water stop boiling for longer than a few seconds. Cook until the mandu float to the top, about 1 minute. Skim them out with a slotted spoon and immediately drain in a colander. Serve as soon as possible with the sauce.

Kasha Kreplach

This is a cross-cultural dumpling if there ever was one: Wonton sheets wrap a vegetarian version of a classic Russian-Jewish filling.

Kasha is a cereal that you may know better as buckwheat groats. To my mind, it is delicious, with a distinctive, hearty flavor, earthy, grainy, and fragrant. If, however, you are not a kasha fan, see the end of the recipe for other ideas on possible fillings. These have a nice, simple fold—triangular, no pleating or tucking. But you can easily use circular gyoza wrappers and make a half-moon shape also. For an eminently satisfying winter meal, serve these, lightly, lightly buttered and tossed with crisp breadcrumbs and finely minced parsley, with a bowl of thick borscht. I've given a few suggested sauces—untraditional, but they dress up the dish, and smooth out the woodsy-nuttiness of the kasha.

The classic cooking method, and my preference, is boiling. It's also possible to brush them with a tiny bit of oil and bake quickly, until golden and a little crisp. See which you like; this recipe makes enough to experiment. **MAKES ABOUT 60**

FILLING

- 1 cup dry kasha, toasted and cooked (see page 536)
- 2 teaspoons butter, or, for vegans, vegetable margarine
- Cooking spray
- 1 onion, finely chopped
- 6 to 8 button mushrooms, wiped and finely chopped
- ½ cup ready-ground tofu
- Salt and plenty of freshly ground black pepper

FOR WRAPPING

- 1 package (about 60) 3- to 4-inch square wonton wrappers, or round gyoza wrappers

TO SERVE

Any of, or several of, these options: butter or vegetable margarine, plain yogurt or Yogurt Sour Cream (page 910), reduced-fat sour cream, crisp breadcrumbs, chopped Italian parsley, Sauce Soubise (page 946), Vegan Sesame Velouté (page 950), or Mushroom-Miso-Mustard Gravy (page 952)

1 While the kasha is cooking, prepare the filling: Melt the butter in a nonstick skillet, or one that has been sprayed with cooking spray, over medium heat. When it stops sizzling, add the onion and sauté until it starts to soften and become translucent, 4 to 5 minutes. Add the mushrooms and cook, stirring constantly, for another 5 minutes. Remove from the heat and scrape into a large bowl. Add the ready-ground tofu and cooked kasha. Toss well and set aside to cool to room temperature.

2 When cool, season with salt and pepper to taste. Set aside, uncovered, to let the flavors blend, 30 to 40 minutes.

Kreplach Creativity

Consider this recipe just a starting point. Any cooked grain—about 2 cups, maybe leftovers from last night's supper—could sub for the kasha. And what if you were to add garlic to the sautéed onion, or finely diced carrot and celery in addition to, or instead of, the mushrooms? And consider using shiitake instead of button mushrooms, or adding a finely minced sun-dried tomato. You could use half a cup of mashed beans instead of the ground tofu, or add a little fresh dill, basil, rosemary, sage, or Italian parsley. Or skip the grain altogether, and use 2 cups leftover mashed potatoes instead. (The latter would be very much like pierogi, the Polish boiled dumpling that is kin to the Russian piroshki.)

Still more possibilities: Fill with leftover black beans and serve with salsa. Or use finely chopped leftover spinach, with or without a little Parmesan and/or ricotta—and then sauce with a puree made from a compatible leftover soup; pumpkin-tomato (page 181), let's say. Or use some mashed leftover split peas, mixed with sautéed onion and garlic, and sauce with leftover curried ginger-carrot soup.

3 Set the wonton wrappers on your work counter, covered with a slightly damp clean kitchen towel. Set the filling, a saucer of water, and a plate on which to place the finished dumplings nearby.

4 Mound about 1 slightly rounded teaspoon of the filling into the center of a wrapper. Moisten the edges of the wrapper with some of the water and fold the opposite corners together, to form a neat little unfancy triangle. Press edges together to seal well. Repeat with remaining wrappers and filling, until you run out of one or the other (or, just maybe, both at the same time).

5 To boil the kreplach: Bring a large pot (the largest you have, or perhaps two smaller ones) of water to a boil over high heat. When it's furiously boiling, gently drop in some of the kreplach. Don't crowd the pot and don't let the water stop boiling for longer than a few seconds. Cook until the kreplach float to the top, about 3 minutes. Immediately skim out of the water with a slotted spoon and drain in a colander. Serve as soon as possible, tossed with one of the sauces or any two or three of the other options.

*

To bake the kreplach: Preheat the oven to 450°F. Brush one side of the kreplach with the tiniest possible bit of mild vegetable oil and lay them out, oiled side up, on a baking sheet sprayed with cooking spray. Bake for 5 minutes, flip over, and bake for 3 minutes on the second side. Serve as for boiled.

Miss Kay's Occhi di Lupo

This recipe is a sentimental journey for me. (Please see page 325 for the full story of these labor-intensive, stuffed rigatoni.) This is an ovo-lacto vegetarian version of that remembered dish. For the cottage cheese, you must—repeat, *must*—use cottage cheese with a good, fresh flavor, not the artificial, additive-laden type common in supermarkets. Most natural foods stores carry good cottage cheese. Miss Kay used full-fat, large-curd cottage cheese, but if you find a tasty low-fat small-curd, go right ahead and use it. **SERVES 4 TO 6**

VARIATION

SAVE-YOUR-SANITY STUFFED SHELLS OCCHI DI LUPO–STYLE: ***Follow the recipe, but stuff filling into 8 ounces of not-quite-cooked large pasta seashells. Proceed as directed. Needless to say, this is much less time consuming.***

- Cooking spray
- 16 ounces rigatoni
- 1 tablespoon olive oil
- 1 medium onion, very finely minced
- 1 box (10 ounces) regular or garlic ready-ground tofu, thawed
- 8 ounces fine-quality cottage cheese, drained of any liquid that can be poured off
- Salt and plenty of freshly ground black pepper
- 1 large egg
- 1 recipe Basic Wintertime Italian Tomato Sauce (page 931), made with half the amount of herbs, and pureed after it is made, or good commercial pasta sauce
- 3 to 6 ounces grated mozzarella cheese (optional)
- 1 ounce grated Parmesan cheese (optional)

1 Spray a nonreactive 8-by-11-inch baking dish with cooking spray. Set aside.

2 Partially cook the rigatoni in boiling water, just until slightly softened but not done. You want it very al dente, with a definite crisp core. Tender noodles will be too flip-floppy to stuff. Drain well, rinsing under cold running water.

3 Heat the oil over medium heat in a nonstick skillet or one that has been sprayed with cooking spray. Add the onion and sauté over medium heat until quite soft, about 7 minutes. Scrape the onion into a bowl. Stir in the ready-ground tofu and cottage cheese. Season with salt and pepper. Stir in the egg.

4 Sit yourself down with the bowl of partially cooked rigatoni, the filling, and the baking dish. Using a fingertip and working from both ends, generously stuff each rigatoni with the filling, then lay it in the pan. Continue until you have one full bottom layer. Begin a second layer, placing the stuffed rigatoni crosswise over the bottom layer. Continue to layer. When all of the rigatoni are stuffed and lined up in the pan, you can either bake them right away or store, covered and refrigerated, for up to 2 days.

5 An hour and a half before serving time, preheat the oven to 375°F.

6 Spoon the sauce over the stuffed rigatoni. Tightly cover the dish with foil and bake, covered, for 40 minutes (50 if the dish has come directly from the fridge). Uncover, sprinkle with the two cheeses, if using, and bake until the tomato sauce is bubbling hot and the cheese has melted and browned, another 10 to 15 minutes. Serve hot from the oven.

Nonreactive?

If you've ever added walnuts to a big ol' cast-iron skillet full of stir-fry, and watched the nuts turn dark purple, you have witnessed reactivity: chemical reactions that occur when certain ingredients (notably acidic foods and eggs as well as walnuts) interact with nonanodized aluminum, unlined copper, or cast iron that has not been properly seasoned. This interaction can not only discolor the foods, but can give them a metallic taste. Nonreactive vessels—those made of stainless steel, glass, glazed pottery, anodized aluminum, enamel-clad cast iron, or properly seasoned cast iron, or which are coated in an unscratched nonstick surface—do not cause such reactions. Nonreactive cookware is generally specified in recipes for long-cooking dishes that use tomatoes, vinegar, or lemon juice.

Occhi di Lupo and Miss Kay

My beloved Miss Kay and I found each other. I was a child, and she was even then elderly, a retired teacher. I spent countless afternoons with her and her grown-up niece Gertrude, in their rambly, quiet home around the corner, where our Elm Place became her Fraser Place, in Hastings-on-Hudson, New York.

Miss Kay grew raspberry bushes and sweet corn. There was a huge evergreen tree on her property, under the sweeping lower branches of which was a cavelike hiding place, thick with pine needles. On the top floor of her house was a tiny, busy sewing room, two sewing machines, countless scraps and stacks of folded cloth. An upright piano, a mah-jongg set, a black cat named Mehitabel, an old, old beagle named Hunter (for whom Miss Kay and Gertrude provided homemade dogfood)—all were endlessly fascinating.

The heart of their home was the kitchen, entered directly through Miss Kay's back door. It was a small, cluttered room, white walls and linoleum both yellowing with age, table stacked with Gourmet, Time, *and* National Geographic*—even as a child I knew it was untidy. The range had an oven with a window in it, unlike ours at home—deeply interesting; you could watch things as they baked and transformed. There was a long narrow pantry next to the kitchen, a large dark formal dining room, in which dinner was eaten in the winter. But in the summer, we carried trays through the living room and out the French doors to the terrace.*

Miss Kay was a thoughtful and serious cook, adventurous for her time. She ate raw sliced pear and blue cheese on salads, which were never made with iceberg lettuce, always romaine. She also ate sliced pears for dessert, with a drizzle of heavy cream, accompanied by Pepperidge Farm Bordeaux cookies—a simple combination I still remember as sublime. She made lemon granita, icy lemon sorbet, which she served with her own fresh raspberries. She made her own orange sponge cake, with freshly squeezed orange juice, and a dense fudgy loaf cake. At least once a week, she and Gertrude ate babotie, which was a South African dish of ground beef in a curried custard.

Miss Kay had no children; I, no nearby grandparents. So we adopted each other, and for the five years I went off to summer camp, the last evening before departure, Miss Kay would fix a dinner of all my favorite dishes, which I would help make. Both my parents were also invited (they were not invited to eat there at any other time, to my recollection, though I went constantly). It being summer, we ate on the terrace.

The anchor of the meal was always the same: occhi di lupo for the entree, fresh raspberries over vanilla ice cream and homemade meringues for dessert.

Occhi di lupo was truly a labor of love, not that I understood this fully then, nor did I know that the dish's name in Italian meant "eyes of the wolf." I have never seen the recipe even described anywhere, nor do I have a clue where Gertrude and Miss Kay unearthed it. A filling of ground beef and cottage cheese was stuffed into rigatoni. That's right, rigatoni—the small tubular noodles slightly larger than ziti. One by one, rigatoni by rigatoni. You'd have to come at the noodle from both ends in order to get it filled properly, delicately wedging the filling in with a pinky, but not too much or too hard or the rigatoni would split. Once stuffed, they were lined up like soldiers in neat rows in a baking dish, a good tomato sauce poured over them, covered, and baked. Serve them with love to feed memory.

She Stuffs Pasta Shells...

If you are new to stuffings, start with purchased Western-style pasta, then move on to made-at-home crêpes—neutral, sturdy, shaped starches ready for a savory filling. The fillings can be used interchangeably, but note that crêpes are larger than pasta, so the ingredients in the filling can be cut into larger pieces, whereas they must be minced more finely for pasta.

After filling, place the stuffed pasta in an oiled baking dish or one sprayed with cooking spray. Spoon a little of a compatible sauce over them and bake until hot—usually starting covered, then removing the cover at the end to brown the topping.

Here are some basic fillings with sauces and crisp toppings that are compatible. Any of these would work with shells, manicotti, or any of the crêpe varieties offered on page 328.

- *Mashed cooked pumpkin, butternut squash, or sweet potato tossed with a little garlic, salt, pepper, Parmesan if you like, and some chopped cooked kale or chard, with Basic Wintertime Italian Tomato Sauce (page 931), or Sauce Soubise (page 946), topped with Breadcrumb Topping Provençal (page 277).*
- *Broccoli-mushroom filling from Crêpes Mornay (page 329), with Sauce Soubise (page 946), Chicken-Style Gravy (page 949), or Vegan Velouté (page 950) topped with Breadcrumb Topping Provençal (page 277).*
- *Crumbled fresh tofu tossed with cooked spinach, salt, pepper, a little nutmeg, and plenty of crushed garlic, with Basic Wintertime Italian Tomato Sauce (page 931), topped with Ned's Frizzled Shiitakes (page 771). Or try the classic version: with fresh ricotta instead of tofu, and a generous sprinkle of Parmesan added.*
- *Beans and greens (see the Beans-and-Greens Enchiladas, page 342) with Salsa Poblano Blanca y Verde (page 947). You could top this with a handful of crushed corn chips, or crisp breadcrumbs seasoned with a little chile powder.*
- *Carrots sautéed with a bit of curry powder and a touch of honey, with fresh corn cut off the cob and a few crumbled veggieburgers with Sauce Mongole (page 933) or Vegan Velouté (page 950), and Breadcrumb Topping Provençal (page 277).*
- *Swiss Chard with Raisins, Olives, and Onions (page 759), with Basic Wintertime Italian Tomato Sauce (page 931).*
- *Cooked lentils, tossed with cooked greens and crumbled feta, with Greek-Style Tomato Sauce with Lentils (page 932), and Breadcrumb Topping Provençal, (page 277). A little diced roasted or grilled eggplant would be quite good in this filling too.*

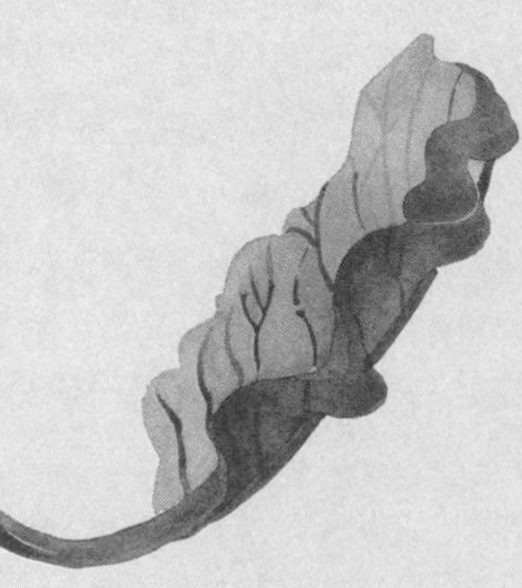

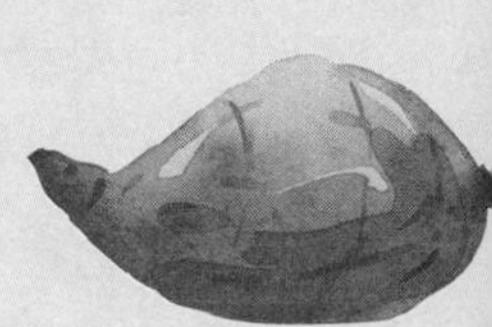

Crêpes

The most delicate and aristocratic of pancakes, crêpes work hard for their sovereignty. They can be starter, entree, dessert, or breakfast, depending on the filling. Classic crêpes are egg-rich; it is largely egg protein that gives them their tensile strength. I used them for many years as part of the inn's breakfast repertoire (broccoli-mushroom crêpes with cheese, gratinéed with garlicky crumbs, were a fave) and at dinner (apples or pears quick-sautéed with butter, rum, brown sugar, a little custard or pudding, topped with whipped cream and walnut praline).

But few eat that way anymore. Crêpes are "light" only in feel. For this reason, and for feeding vegan friends, I had long been on the lookout for an egg-free crêpe that truly duplicated the flavor and texture of the real thing—thin, flavorful, mild, malleable, and pretty. I was starting to despair of actually finding a substitute that met these criteria, though I tried many. The closest were Indian dosai (pronounced "dosha"), in which rice and lentils are soaked separately overnight, ground, and combined into a batter, then fermented . . . too much effort for most of us.

But the dosai hinted that legume protein could mimic the property that eggs give to classic crêpes. This is why, though highly dubious, I tried the crêpe recipe in *The Perennial Political Palate,* the third in the trio of fine vegetarian cookbooks from Bloodroot, a feminist, collective-run restaurant and bookstore in Bridgeport, Connecticut. Bloodroot's crêpes used potato starch, chickpea flour, and unbleached white flour. How could such a bizarre combination possibly mimic the beloved French crêpe? Wouldn't it be floury, or beany? Thick, heavy? Well, I am here to tell you that these vegan crêpes have a mouthfeel and flavor so close to the classic that, but for a minor difference in shade and browning pattern, they could be identical twins. They are glorious! They are everything the old classic crêpes were and less—less fat (none), less cholesterol (none), less expensive. This is why I call them neo-classic. Use them for any course, any time of day, for cheese blintzes or Mushrooms Strogonoff, or plain with lemon juice and powdered sugar, or in a crêpe torte, or any of a thousand ways.

The batter keeps very well too; we've made it, and eaten our way down over a 2-week period, and it stayed perfectly fresh tasting.

Classic Crêpes

I've included classic crêpes for sentimental and historical value; an old love, one I value and think of fondly, even as I've moved on. I also put them in because crêpes, though dated, will never go completely out fashion: They are simply too useful. **MAKES 15 TO 18 5-TO-6-INCH CRÊPES**

3 large eggs
1 cup milk
1 cup unbleached white all-purpose flour
1 tablespoon butter, melted and cooled
¼ teaspoon salt
A bit of softened butter or any mild vegetable oil or cooking spray

1 Combine the eggs, milk, flour, butter, and salt in a blender, food processor, or in a large bowl. Buzz or whisk by hand until the batter is smooth. Allow the batter to rest for at least 1 hour, or cover and refrigerate overnight (or up to 4 days).

2 When ready to make the crêpes, heat a nonstick or a well-seasoned conventional crêpe pan over medium heat. Allow the pan to get good and warm, then give it a quick, light swipe with a paper towel on which you've put a dab of butter or a little oil (you could also use a light coat of cooking spray). You don't technically have to grease a nonstick pan, but you do get a nice crunchy edge to your crêpe if you do. Although the classic crêpe pan is 6 inches in diameter, you can use a larger pan. Just use the specified amount of batter to make 6-inch crêpes in it.

3 As the pan heats, check the crêpe batter, which should be the consistency of heavy cream. If it has set for more than a couple of hours, you might need an extra

The Home Crêperie

There are many "flours" in this garden of crêpes. Sooner or later you'll wind up trying them all, and I bet every variation will please and surprise you as well as those lucky enough to feast at your table.

Buckwheat Crêpes: *For a distinctively flavored crêpe, substitute buckwheat flour for half of the unbleached white flour.*

Whole Wheat Crêpes: *For a grainy, light crêpe, substitute whole wheat pastry flour for ¾ of the unbleached white. Delicious.*

Cornstarch Crêpes: *I discovered when cooking for my dear friend and mentor, Louis Freund, who had a gluten allergy, that the tenderest crêpe is made from cornstarch. Substitute an equal amount of cornstarch for the flour. Cornstarch crêpes do not freeze well.*

Fresh Corn Crêpes: *When we had the restaurant we used these along with Wanda's Soft Corn Crêpe-Tortillas (page 338) in our Mexican-y vegetarian plates. Cut the kernels from 2 ears fresh sweet corn. Pulse-chop the kernels in a food processor with a couple of tablespoons of Classic Crêpe batter until a grainy but evenly textured paste has formed. Combine the corn paste with the remaining crêpe batter. You'll probably need an extra tablespoon or two of milk to get the heavy cream consistency.*

Crêpes for Cheese Blintzes: *Add an extra egg and a heaping teaspoon of sugar to the Classic Crêpes recipe. Cook on one side only.*

Dessert Crêpes: *You can use any crêpe recipe for desserts; add 1 teaspoon vanilla, and/or a bit of cinnamon or nutmeg along with 1 teaspoon sugar to the batter for a touch of sweet and spiciness.*

tablespoon or two of milk to thin it. Pour 2 to 2½ tablespoons of the crêpe batter into the hot pan. Immediately tilt the pan to distribute the batter, swirling to make a very thin covering on the bottom of the pan. You should have a perfectly round crêpe about ⅛ inch thick. If the crêpe is thicker, it's a clue to add a little more milk to the batter.

4 Cook the crêpe for 30 seconds to 1 minute (subsequent crêpes will cook more quickly than the first few). It will be ready to flip when the top surface has a dulled appearance, and, when you lift a corner of the crêpe, the bottom is a nicely mottled golden brown. Flip. Cook until just slightly browned, about 20 seconds (the second side never browns quite as attractively as the first; it looks spottier—in most recipes, this second side is used inside, while the prettier side remains in the public eye).

5 As they are cooked, lay the warm crêpes on a cake rack to cool for a minute or two. Once cooled, the finished crêpes can be stacked with a piece of waxed or parchment paper between them. To store the crêpes, tightly wrap stacks of no more than 10 in plastic wrap, label and date, and freeze for up to 2 months.

Crêpes Mornay with Broccoli and Mushrooms

A much-loved basic, this recipe shows why crêpes have earned their reputation for versatility and deliciousness. It's a classic crêpe in a classic manner. Onions plus almost any two or three vegetables that contrast in color and texture make a good filling. Avoid more than 3 vegetables; it tends to make the stir-fry soggy and without much character.

Like most dishes having several elements (filling, sauce, crêpes, and topping), this is a breeze *if* you've prepped most of the components in advance, tedious if you haven't. **MAKES 15 TO 18 STUFFED CRÊPES; SERVES 4 TO 6**

1 recipe cooked Classic (or buckwheat, whole wheat, or cornstarch) Crêpes (page 327), unwrapped and thawed if frozen

FILLING

2 teaspoons butter, or mild vegetable oil, such as corn, canola, or peanut (or a combination of butter and oil)

Cooking spray

1 medium onion, cut vertically into thin slivers

2 carrots, scrubbed (peeled or not), sliced diagonally into ⅛-inch-thick ovals

2½ cups broccoli florets

Handful of very small whole button mushrooms, wiped clean, or sliced mushrooms, tough stems removed

1 teaspoon tamari or shoyu soy sauce

1 to 2 tablespoons water, preferably spring or filtered, white wine, or vegetable stock (see page 139)

1 to 2 cups Mornay Sauce (page 946), warmed

Salt and freshly ground black pepper to taste

TOPPING

2 to 3 ounces grated cheese, whatever type used in making the mornay (optional)

¼ cup Breadcrumb Topping Provençal (page 277)

1 Preheat the oven to 350°F.

2 Wrap the stacked, cooled crêpes in a sheet of foil. Place on a small baking sheet in the oven to warm until just pliable, about 10 minutes. Remove from the oven, leaving them wrapped, and keep warm. The back of the stove-top with the oven on will usually serve as a warmer.

3 Heat the butter in a nonstick pan, or one that has been sprayed with cooking spray, over medium-high heat. Add the onion and sauté until just starting to soften, about 4 minutes. Lower the heat to medium and add the carrots. Sauté for 1 minute. Add the broccoli and sauté for 1 additional minute. Stir in the mushrooms and tamari, stirring for 30 seconds.

4 Add the water and immediately cover tightly. Steam until the vegetables soften slightly (but remain quite crisp), about 3 minutes.

5 Stir in about ½ cup of the mornay sauce. Taste and season with salt and pepper to taste.

6 Spray a nonstick or conventional oven-to-table 8½-by-11-inch serving dish, or a number of individual gratin dishes, with cooking spray.

7 Place the crêpes, a plate on which to roll them, the remainder of the sauce, and the breadcrumb topping on the counter.

Breakfast at Dairy Hollow

"And best of all, a bountiful breakfast in a basket is delivered right to your door each morning!" No matter how many times I heard the nighttime message on the Dairy Hollow House answering machine, which Ned rerecorded throughout our inn years every couple of months to reflect the change in the seasons and upcoming special events, I never failed to be tickled by the enthusiasm he put into his voice on that particular sentence. It's because the man just flat loves breakfast.

Here is how our crêpes—which typically guests might get for breakfast on the third or fourth morning of a sojourn—stayed nice and warm in their basket. After the crêpes were filled and rolled, they were tucked into a 6-inch iron skillet. We always used to send two crêpes per person, plus an extra "for the room" (kind of like an extra spoonful of tea "for the pot"). They'd be amply sauced, covered with crumbs, and put in a very hot oven. When they came out (timed to be just before breakfast, and the last thing in the basket, which would already have had fresh fruit and fruit juice, bread or muffins or rolls of some kind, meat or a vegetarian alternative like grilled marinated tempeh, butter, inn-made jellies, cream for the coffee our guests made in their own in-room coffee machine), we'd cover the skillet tightly with foil. Then we'd wrap on the little padded Velcro handle-wrappers that former inn dairymaid/waitress Carolyn Morgan cleverly designed and made for us, which kept our guests from burning themselves on the skillet when they took it out.

You see, that's the trick with keeping dishes of this sort hot—use a dish that holds the heat. While Pyrex, glazed pottery, or aluminum baking dishes look pretty, they lose heat far more quickly than a good old cast-iron skillet or a heavy-duty enamel-clad cast-iron baker. If you want food to stay toasty, choose the latter two. You might think, oh, well, I'm *not going to be carrying breakfast crêpes in a basket across the hollow, and you'd no doubt be right (neither am I, any more, come to think of it). But what about carrying a casserole to a potluck dinner? Or even setting it out on the table at a buffet so guests can dip from it? You want it to stay warm long enough for everyone to be served, and even go back for seconds.*

8 Place a crêpe, pretty-side down, on the rolling plate, and spoon a line of filling down the middle. Fold over both sides of the crêpe to cover the filling and place, seam side down, in the prepared baking dish. Continue filling crêpes until all of the crêpes and the filling have been used. Tuck any extra filling on either end of the crêpes in the pan.

9 Ladle a line of sauce down the center of the crêpes. If you still have sauce, you may also do a little on both ends of the crêpes. If using the cheese, sprinkle it over the crêpes as well as in the spaces where there's no sauce. Sprinkle the breadcrumb topping over the crêpes; I usually place it down the middle, over the line of sauce.

10 Place the dish (or dishes) in the oven and bake until the crumbs are browned and the sauce is bubbly, 10 to 12 minutes. Serve hot from the pan, as soon as possible.

Neo-Classic Crêpes

This recipe looks long because I've gone into great detail, in part to overcome any skepticism from seasoned cooks. I guarantee you, it's a great one.

MAKES 26 TO 32 6-INCH CRÊPES

- 2 tablespoons potato starch
- 2¼ to 2½ cups water, preferably spring or filtered
- 1 tablespoon mild vegetable oil, such as corn, canola, or peanut
- 1 teaspoon salt
- 2 cups unbleached white all-purpose flour
- ½ cup chickpea flour (see below)
- Cooking spray or oil

1 Place the potato starch, with about ½ cup of the water, in a food processor. Add the vegetable oil and salt. Process to a thin liquid, pausing to scrape down the sides of the bowl. Add the unbleached white and chickpea flours. Gradually add the remaining water, starting with 2 cups, pausing when needed to scrape down the sides. When the mixture is very smooth, pour it into a bowl. Whisk in as much of the remaining water as needed to bring the batter to the consistency of thin cream. Use immediately or cover and refrigerate for up to 1 week. (If you do allow the batter to rest for any length of time, it will smell "beany," but all beaniness will disappear once the batter is cooked.)

2 Heat a nonstick 6-inch crêpe pan, or one that has been sprayed with cooking spray, over medium heat. You can also give the skillet a quick swipe with an oil-soaked paper towel (cooking spray and oil are optional with nonstick pans; however, you'll get a

VARIATION

Please see the variations for Classic Crêpes, page 329. They all work with the Neo-Classic Crêpes, but remember, you're making substitutions only for the unbleached white flour; leave the potato starch and chickpea flour proportions as they are. For Neo-Classic Crêpes to be used for Tofu-Filled "Cheese" Blintzes (see page 336), use the largest amount of water called for in the recipe, plus 3 to 4 tablespoons extra.

Meet Chickpea Flour

HAVE WE BEEN INTRODUCED YET?

Long used in a variety of ways in some parts of India, where it's called besan, and in Provence, where it goes into a flat, thick griddle bread called socca, chickpea flour is a surprisingly versatile addition to the thoughtful and well-equipped vegetarian kitchen. It is made from ground, toasted chickpeas, and has a mild bean/pea flavor that can dominate or fade, depending on how it is used. It is a must in the Neo-Classic Crêpes. You can even use it to make an almost instant hummus, by making a paste of the flour by adding water and cooking for a few minutes, then removing from the heat and adding tahini, lemon juice, and other seasonings. A precise recipe for the hummus described above may be found on the box of the brand of the flour we prefer, Arrowhead Mills Toasted Garbanzo Flour, which also happens to be a certified organic product. A 10-ounce box is available at any good natural foods store.

pleasant, slightly crisp edge if you use either one). Make sure the pan is really hot—a drop of water sprinkled on the pan should sizzle and evaporate in a few seconds. When very hot, pour in 2 to 2½ tablespoons of the batter, tilting the pan to twirl the batter so it thins out and covers the bottom of the crêpe pan. As the crêpe cooks, the top surface will quickly go from a pale ivory color and wet appearance to a dull-looking deeper beige color moving from the outer edges to the inner core. Cook until browned on the underneath and the edges begin to curl up, 1 to 3 minutes (subsequent crêpes will cook a little more quickly than the first few). Flip and cook the second side until nicely browned, 30 seconds to 1 minute (the second side never browns quite as attractively as the first; in most recipes, this second side is used inside, while the prettier side remains in the public eye).

3 As they are cooked, lay the warm crêpes on a cake rack to cool for a minute or two. Once cooled, the finished crêpes can be stacked with a piece of waxed or parchment paper between them. To store the crêpes, tightly wrap stacks of no more than 10 in plastic wrap, label and date, and freeze for up 2 months.

COOK ONCE FOR 5 MEALS One batch of this crêpe batter fits nicely in a quart jar and keeps perfectly, refrigerated, for at least a week. Just shake before using. You might fill these crêpes with sautéed vegetables. A couple of nights later, you might sauté bananas with brown sugar and cinnamon and roll them inside crêpes. Brunch? Use the crêpes to make blintzes (page 335). Another dinner? Roll leftover black beans in them, and spoon on salsa or enchilada sauce, with or without grated cheese. Or how about crêpe tartlets, perfect as an appetizer or buffet-table item? Spray ramekins or muffin tins with cooking spray and line them with crêpes. Fill, maybe with an eggy quiche-type mixture, leftover cooked vegetables, and a bit of cheese and bake, at 350°F or so, until the filling sets.

Vegan Crêpes Velouté with Broccoli and Mushrooms

This is how the recipe for the classic, very rich Crêpes Mornay with Broccoli and Mushrooms (page 329) transforms when it is lightened up, made vegan and more healthful. Is it as delicious? You bet! I'd even give this one the edge.

MAKES 12 TO 15 STUFFED CRÊPES; SERVES 4 TO 6

VARIATION

These are delicious, and become even heartier, with the addition of some diced savory baked tofu. Or try replacing the velouté with a Sauce Soubise (page 946).

12 to 15 cooked Neo-Classic Crêpes (page 322), thawed if frozen

FILLING

2 teaspoons vegetable margarine or mild vegetable oil, such as corn, canola, or peanut (or a combination)

Cooking spray

1 medium onion, cut vertically into thin slivers

2 carrots, scrubbed (peeled or not), sliced diagonally into ⅛-inch-thick ovals

2½ cups small broccoli florets

Handful of very small whole button mushrooms, wiped clean, or sliced if large, and, tough base removed

1 teaspoon tamari or shoyu soy sauce

1 to 2 tablespoons water, preferably spring or filtered, or Golden Stock (page 140)

1 to 2 cups Vegan Velouté (page 950), warmed

Salt and freshly ground black pepper to taste

TOPPING

¼ cup Breadcrumb Topping Provençal with crisp crumbs (page 277)

1 Preheat the oven to 350°F.

2 Wrap the stacked cooked crêpes in a sheet of foil. Place on a small baking sheet in the oven to warm until pliable, about 10 minutes. Remove from the oven, leaving them wrapped, and keep them warm. The back of the stove-top with the oven on will usually serve as a warmer.

3 Heat the margarine in a nonstick skillet, or one that has been sprayed with cooking spray, over medium-high heat. Add the onion and sauté until just starting to soften, about 4 minutes. Lower the heat to medium and add the carrots. Sauté for 1 minute. Add the broccoli and sauté for an additional minute. Stir in the mushrooms and tamari, stirring for 30 seconds.

4 Add the water or stock and immediately cover tightly. Steam until the vegetables soften slightly but remain crisp, about 3 minutes.

5 Stir in about ½ cup of the velouté sauce. Taste and season with salt and pepper.

6 Spray a nonstick or conventional oven-to-table 8½-by-11-inch serving dish, or a number of individual gratin dishes, with cooking spray. Place the crêpes, a plate on which to roll them, the remainder of the sauce, and the breadcrumb topping on the counter.

7 Place a crêpe, pretty side down, on the rolling plate, and spoon a line of filling down the middle. Fold over both sides of the crêpe to cover the filling and place, seam side down, in the prepared baking dish. Continue filling until all of the crêpes and the filling have been used up. Tuck any extra filling in either end of the filled crêpes in their pan.

8 Ladle a line of sauce down the center of the crêpes. If you like, and you have it on hand, you may also put a little on both ends of the crêpes. Sprinkle the breadcrumb topping over the crêpes; I usually place it down the middle, over the line of sauce.

9 Place the dish or dishes in the oven and bake until the crumbs are browned and sauce is bubbly, 10 to 12 minutes. Serve hot, straight from the dish.

Cheese Blintzes Several Ways

Blintzes are comfort food par excellence. They are simply crêpes plumply stuffed with a soft, pale cheese filling reminiscent of cheesecake, then browned until slightly crispy. I love them so much that I will happily eat good frozen ready-made ones—but how much better they are from scratch! This holds true whether they are browned in lots of butter (rich, good, but perhaps too greasy for today's tastes), just a bit of butter in a nonstick skillet (best, to my taste), or baked (lighter and very tasty, easier, far less rich). And it is true whether they are made with egg-rich crêpes or the vegan Neo-Classic Crêpes. It is true whether they are served with jam, powdered sugar, or warm, lightly thickened, slightly sweetened strawberries or blueberries. (No matter which or what, some fruity accompaniment is de rigueur.) It is even true whether they are made with dairy cheese or a tofu filling.

Blintzes are, of course, a Jewish dish. Underlying their inherent goodness is the fact that they are in accord (if properly made and not served with meat) with kosher dietary laws. The vegan version is pareve.

Classic Cheese Blintzes

Some believe that the filling should be straight cheese; others believe in some sweetening, or a hint of spice or citrus. Your call, though I wouldn't advise using all of the flavorings, just one or two at the max.

For even distribution of filling, I've suggested laying out all of the crêpes and filling them at once, and then, one at a time, rolling up the whole batch. But if you're short on space or time, get a production line going: Cook the crêpes in one pan and fill, roll, and brown the filled crêpes in a second pan while you continue to make crêpes. It's much quicker than the standard method, but I suspect it's a bit nerve-wracking for all but the experienced blintz maker. **MAKES ABOUT 15**

Cooking spray
1 recipe cooked Classic Crêpes for cheese blintzes (page 327)
2 tablespoons softened butter
2 tablespoons mild vegetable oil, such as corn, canola, or peanut, if pan-browning the blintzes

FILLING

1 package (8 ounces) neufchâtel reduced-fat cream cheese
3 packages (24 ounces total) farmer cheese (see note, opposite page)
1 large egg
1 to 4 tablespoons sugar or honey, or to taste (optional)
1 teaspoon grated lemon zest (optional)
A little freshly grated nutmeg (optional)
A tiny bit of cinnamon (optional)
A drop of pure vanilla extract (optional)

TO ACCOMPANY

Any or all of the following: yogurt or sour cream, powdered sugar, applesauce or apple butter, warmed jam, slightly sweetened, slightly thickened strawberries, raspberries, cherries, or blueberries

1 Decide whether you are going to bake or sauté the blintzes. If baking them, preheat the oven to 400°F. If sautéing, spray an 8-inch skillet with cooking spray.

2 Place the crêpes, butter, and oil on a mise en place tray (see page 107) and set aside while you make the filling.

Tofu-Filled "Cheese" Blintzes

These are remarkably good and vegan. I season the filling in tofu blintzes more assertively than I do for cheese blintzes. Make sure you have plenty of raspberry or blueberry sauce. Follow the Classic Cheese Blintzes recipe for the method, but with these changes:

1. *Use Neo-Classic Crêpes for cheese blintzes (page 332) instead of the Classic Crêpes.*

2. *For browning in the pan, omit the butter, use all oil, or half oil and half vegetable margarine.*

3. *When the Neo-Classic Crêpes come out of the pan, place them, uncooked side down, on a rack (not waxed paper, a tray, or a plate, as they will stick).*

4. *For filling, blend the following in a processor: 1 package (10½ ounces) firm reduced-fat silken tofu, 2 to 3 tablespoons cashew or almond butter, ¼ cup brown sugar, 1 teaspoon vanilla, several gratings of whole nutmeg, ¼ teaspoon cinnamon. Transfer the mixture to a bowl and add 1 pound of well-drained reduced-fat, conventional water-packed tofu, broken into crumbles.*

5. *Fill, roll, and brown (sautéing or baking) the blintzes just as you would conventional ones. If you are doing them stove-top and if you have a crêpe or two that breaks open to reveal a bit of the filling, working quickly, dip out a spoonful of the crêpe batter and drip it over the crack to reseal it. Immediately place the blintz, with the spot you just resealed face-down, into the pan, and cook according to directions.*

HALF-AND-HALF CHEESE BLINTZES: *If you are not a vegan, but just starting to fool around with soy foods, and are looking for a place to start incorporating them into your diet, this might be the place, especially if you and your family are already blintz lovers. Go ahead and use the neufchâtel and egg in the filling, but instead of the farmer cheese, use the well-drained 1-pound package of reduced-fat conventional water-packed tofu, crumbled. This is virtually identical.*

3 Combine the cheeses with the egg, sugar, spices, and vanilla in the food processor. Buzz until smooth, pausing from time to time to scrape down the sides. Taste, adjusting the sweetness and spice if desired.

4 If space permits, lay out all of the crêpes, uncooked side down and side by side, on the counter or on a large waxed paper–covered tray. Spoon a heaping tablespoon of filling into the center of each crêpe, shaping it into a vaguely lozenge-shaped rectangle. You should have an equal portion of filling in each crêpe.

5 Enclose the filling by folding in the sides of the crêpe about one-third of the way in on each side, leaving only a small portion of filling visible. Roll the bottom flap of crêpe over this to completely cover the filling, then fold in the top flap. You should now have a neat little pillow of crêpe enclosing the filling. Lay the blintzes out near the stove or oven, seam side down.

6 If baking the blintzes, place them, seam side down, on a cookie sheet (preferably a double-insulated one) sprayed with cooking spray. Spritz them lightly with cooking spray, or the merest brush of softened butter. Bake until browned, about 15 minutes.

7 If pan-browning, heat a nonstick skillet over medium to medium-high heat. Add about ½ teaspoon each of butter and oil. When the oil is hot, add the blintzes, seam side down, and sauté, working in batches and adding additional butter and oil as needed. Once the bottom is browned, turn each blintz once. If the oil is nice and hot when the blintzes go into the pan, 2½ to 3 minutes per side should do it.

8 Serve, hot from oven or skillet, with your choice of accompaniments.

NOTE

A CHEESE NOTE:

Farmer cheese is a mild, delicious cottage cheese that has been very well drained to give it a firmer texture. It's readily available in most metropolitan areas, but you may have trouble finding it in smaller towns. If that's the case, use cottage cheese or ricotta cheese, but drain it in a fine-mesh sieve lined with paper towels for an hour or two.

Wanda's Soft Corn Crêpe-Tortillas

An old favorite, this is a recipe that Jan Brown, my angelic collaborator on *The Dairy Hollow House Cookbook,* got from an old friend of hers, painter Wanda Ross. These are lower in fat than Classic Crêpes though nominally higher than Neo-Classic Crêpes, and not vegan. They have all the delicacy of a crêpe combined with the distinctive taste of a corn tortilla, and are perfect with Mexican-, South American–, or Southwestern-accented fillings. **MAKES 12 TO 15 5 TO 6-INCH CRÊPES**

1 large egg
1 cup low-fat milk
½ cup masa harina (see opposite)
1 heaping tablespoon unbleached white all-purpose flour
½ teaspoon salt
Cooking spray, oil, or butter

Combine the egg and milk with the masa, flour, and salt in a food processor and buzz until well blended. Transfer to a bowl and let stand for 1 hour. Use immediately, or cover and refrigerate for up to 5 days. Cook as for Classic Crêpes (page 327) in a nonstick crêpe pan, or one that has been lightly sprayed with cooking spray or coated with oil or butter.

Wanda's Soft Corn Crêpe-Tortillas with Calabacitas

VARIATION

Wanda's Soft Corn Crêpe-Tortillas are also highly recommended stuffed with piccadillo filling (from the first two steps in Empanadas, page 359), topped with a little of Pamela Jones's Absolutely Incredible Roasted Vegetable Salsa (page 915).

Calabacitas is a south-of-the-border, bursting-with-flavor cousin of succotash. It is a mixed vegetable sauté that always contains finely diced summer squash, usually fresh corn kernels, and a bit of whatever else the garden or market has to offer. Unpretentious but lively, it really takes off when wrapped in tender masa crêpes and topped with salsa. **MAKES 12 TO 15 STUFFED CRÊPES; SERVES ABOUT 6**

1 recipe cooked Wanda's Soft Corn Crêpe-Tortillas (previous page)
1 to 2 cups Salsa Poblano Blanca y Verde (page 947), warmed
3 to 4 cups prepared Calabacitas (page 801), warmed, preferably the variation with butternut squash and zucchini
Salt and freshly ground black pepper to taste
¼ cup Breadcrumb Topping Provençal (page 277), with crisp crumbs (optional)
Long sprigs of cilantro (optional)
Pamela Jones's Absolutely Incredible Roasted Vegetable Salsa (page 915), Arkansalsa (page 913), or your favorite commercially made salsa

1 Preheat the oven to 350°F.

Meet Masa Harina

HAVE WE BEEN INTRODUCED YET?

Masa harina is a variety of corn flour used in many Mexican and South American recipes. If you dip your finger into a bag of it and taste it, you will instantly recognize the flavor as that of corn tortillas.

What makes masa harina different from regular old cornmeal? First, it's more finely ground; second, the corn has been processed with lime, an ancient and remarkable treatment that, among many other things, gives the masa its distinctive taste.

You can purchase masa harina at Hispanic grocery stores or in the Mexican foods section of many supermarkets. Organic masa harina is sometimes available at natural foods markets. It's worth keeping on hand for Wanda's Soft Corn Crêpe-Tortillas alone.

2 Wrap the stacked cooked crêpes in a sheet of foil. Place them in the oven to warm until pliable, about 10 minutes. Remove, leaving them wrapped, and keep warm. The back of the stove-top with the oven on will usually serve as a warmer.

3 Stir about ½ cup of the heated salsa into the warmed Calabacitas. Taste and, if necessary, season with salt and pepper.

4 Spray a nonstick or conventional oven-to-table 8½-by-11-inch serving dish, or a number of individual gratin dishes, with cooking spray. Place the crêpes, a plate on which to roll them, the remainder of the sauce, and the breadcrumb topping on the counter.

5 Place a crêpe, pretty side down, on the rolling plate, and spoon a line of filling down the middle. Fold over both ends of the crêpe and place, seam-side down, in the prepared baking dish. Continue filling until all of the crêpes and filling have been used up. Tuck any extra filling in either end of the filled crêpes in their pan.

6 Ladle a line of sauce down the center of the crêpes. If you like, and you have it on hand, you may also put a little on both ends of the crêpes. Finally, sprinkle the breadcrumb topping over the crêpes; I usually place it down the middle, over the line of sauce.

7 Place the dish (or dishes) in the oven and bake until the crumbs are browned and sauce is bubbly, 10 to 12 minutes. Serve hot from the pan, garnished with sprigs of cilantro and salsa on the side.

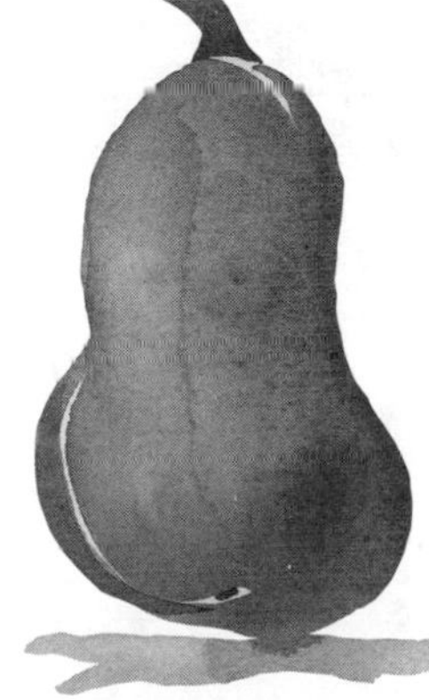

VARIATION

ENCHILADAS VERY VERDE: ***Prepare the enchiladas as in the recipe, adding some thawed, well-drained chopped frozen spinach (or better yet, lightly steamed fresh spinach) with the broccoli. Make Tomatillo Salsa Verde (page 944) and use that instead of Cupboard Enchilada Sauce. The Tomatillo Salsa Verde is every bit as easy to make as the Cupboard, but you do have to have fresh tomatillos—they're readily available these days, but not the kind of thing you probably have sitting in your fridge.***

CD's Famed Tofu-Broccoli Enchiladas

Like most wrapped-and-stuffed dishes, the infinite number of variations that can be deliciously rung on enchiladas makes them widely popular. But unlike many other stuffed dishes, they are easy, easy, easy because many of the components are available ready-made. They're fast, too: I have been known to throw on a pot of Brazilian Rice (page 475), jump into this recipe, tear up a little lettuce, and have dinner on the table in less than half an hour. It's almost unfair that such ease results in such delicious food.

This recipe was born some years ago when Ned and I had a desperate yen for Mexican food, our beloved Center Street South of the Border was closed, and we wanted to eat *right away*. Well, we were eating, and eating well, within 25 minutes. The ingredients are all pretty much out-of-the-cupboard stuff, except the broccoli, which we happened to have. The explanation may sound elaborate, but make them once and they're an absolute no-brainer. So good, so fast, and reasonably healthy, too.

It's simple to turn this recipe into a vegan meal—omit the neufchâtel in the filling and don't put cheese on top—but to me, the combo (especially the neufchâtel in the filling) really takes the dish to its deserved heights. It's better than straight vegan, but also better than straight cheese (this same trick is employed in Half-and-Half Cheese Blintzes, page 336). If you want, at the end add a dollop of sour cream (tofu, yogurt, reduced fat, or the real thing). And, of course, you can always drag out the avocado, pico de gallo, or Arkansalsa (page 913).

Last but not least—more labor-intensive but stratospherically good—bake these with Pamela Jones's Absolutely Incredible Roasted Vegetable Salsa (page 915). **MAKES 6 TO 8 ENCHILADAS; SERVES 3 OR 4**

1 package (16 ounces) firm, fresh (not silken) water-packed tofu, preferably reduced fat
2 to 3 ounces neufchâtel reduced-fat cream cheese or regular cream cheese
2 cloves garlic, peeled and quartered
1½ to 2½ teaspoons top-quality chili powder, preferably New Mexico–style
1 teaspoon salt, or to taste
½ large onion, cut into 4 pieces
2 to 3 cups cooked, coarsely diced broccoli
Cooking spray
Six to eight 8-inch flour tortillas, preferably whole wheat (or eight to ten 6-inch white, yellow, or blue corn tortillas)
Tomatillo Salsa Verde (page 944) or Cupboard Enchilada Sauce (page 935)
3 to 4 ounces grated sharp Cheddar or jack cheese (optional)

1 Preheat the oven to 400°F.

2 Place half of the tofu in a food processor. Coarsely crumble the other half into a bowl and set aside.

3 To the food processor, add the neufchâtel, garlic, chili powder, and salt. Buzz until smooth, pausing several times to scrape down the sides of the work bowl. Add the onion and pulse-chop a few times. Add the broccoli and pulse-chop just a couple of times more. What you're aiming for is a thick, smooth mixture (the seasoned tofu-neufchâtel part) in which nice texture-y chunks of raw onion and cooked broccoli are distinct. Turn the mixture out into the bowl with the crumbled tofu, and stir well to combine. (Now is the time to rinse out your food processor work bowl, reassemble it, and put together the Cupboard Enchilada Sauce in a matter of maybe 1 minute.)

4 Spray a 10-by-13-inch baking dish with cooking spray. Place the filling and a stack of tortillas nearby.

5 Heat a nonstick skillet, or one that has been sprayed with cooking spray, over medium heat. Place a tortilla in the pan and warm just enough to soften it, about 45 seconds. Flip and warm the other side. Pull

Louis's Lemons

At the end of countless harmonious meals shared during almost sixty-one years of marriage, my friends and mentors, artists Louis and Elsie Freund, had one disagreement. Louis was likely to grab for a wedge of lemon—if there happened to be one around—and suck on it at the end of a meal. It's a habit his wife, Elsie, could never understand. She found it appalling—horrible. "Oooh," she said, hunching her shoulders and shivering slightly. "It just gives me the all-overs."

"Mmm!" Louis used to say enthusiastically, teeth sunk deep against the rind, shaking his head in satisfaction and momentarily giving the impression of a bright, solid-yellow smile, then casting the spent rind on the plate. "Why, it's like an exclamation point at the end of the meal!"

"Here, Louis," Elsie would say, with a resigned sigh, unable to deny him this pleasure. She'd pick up the untouched lemon wedge on her plate. "Take mine."

After a life in which the only real sour appeared to be those after-dinner lemons, Louis died on the night of winter solstice, 1999, at age ninety-four. Elsie left the world at age eighty-six, in 2000—in the small hours of the summer solstice.

it out of the skillet and warm another tortilla. As the second tortilla heats, slap about one-sixth of the filling down the middle of the first warm tortilla, roll it, and place, seam side down, in the prepared baking dish. Flip your in-skillet tortilla, and repeat the whole process. Keep going until all of the enchiladas are filled and the dish is full.

6 Pour the sauce of your choice over the enchiladas. Cover with waxed paper, then with foil, and bake until hot, 15 to 20 minutes. Remove the foil and waxed paper and sprinkle the top with the optional cheese. Raise the oven temperature to 450°F and bake until the cheese is melted and bubbly, 5 to 10 minutes. Serve hot.

Beans-and-Greens Enchiladas

Definitely not traditional. Definitely wonderful. This is a straight-out-of-what-you-have-on-hand filling that might become a family staple. It's a quickie, and so healthful it might serve as a poster dish for the Food Pyramid. **MAKES 6 TO 8 ENCHILADAS; SERVES 4 TO 6**

2 cups dehydrated pinto bean flakes seasoned with sea salt
2 cups boiling water, preferably spring or filtered
Cooking spray
¼ head savoy cabbage, coarsely shredded
1 pound fresh spinach, well washed
1 jalapeño chili, stem removed, thinly sliced
1 teaspoon chile powder
Six to eight 8-inch flour tortillas, preferably whole wheat
Tomatillo Salsa Verde (page 944), Cupboard Enchilada Sauce (page 935), or Pamela Jones's Absolutely Incredible Roasted Vegetable Salsa (page 915)
Grated sharp Cheddar or jack cheese (optional)

1 Preheat the oven to 400°F.

2 Place the dehydrated bean flakes in a heatproof bowl, pour the boiling water over them, and cover. Let stand for 5 minutes.

3 Spray a skillet with cooking spray. Place over medium-high heat and add the cabbage. Sauté until it browns slightly at the edges and starts to wilt, 5 to 7 minutes. Toss in the spinach. Lower the heat and cover the skillet. Let steam until the spinach wilts, 1 to 2 minutes. Remove from the heat.

4 Add the sautéed greens to the rehydrated beans, along with the jalapeño and

chili powder. Spray a 10-by-13-inch baking dish with cooking spray. Place the beans-and-greens filling and a stack of tortillas nearby.

5 Heat a nonstick skillet, or one that has been sprayed with cooking spray, over medium heat. Place a tortilla in the hot skillet and warm just enough to soften it, about 45 seconds. Flip and warm the other side. Pull it out of the skillet and warm another tortilla. As the second tortilla heats, quickly slap about one-sixth of the filling down the middle of the first warm tortilla, roll it, and place, seam side down, in the prepared baking dish. Flip your in-skillet tortilla, and repeat the whole process. Keep going until all the enchiladas are filled and the baking dish is full.

6 Pour the sauce of your choice over the enchiladas. Cover with waxed paper, then with foil. Bake until hot, 15 to 20 minutes. Remove the foil and waxed paper and sprinkle the top with the cheese, if using. Raise the heat to 450°F and bake until the cheese is melted and bubbly, 5 to 10 minutes. Serve hot.

Black Bean Enchiladas with Pamela Jones's Absolutely Incredible Roasted Vegetable Salsa

This filling is so simple. Similar to Beans-and-Greens Enchiladas but black beans replace the pintos, and corn tortillas, not wheat, serve as the wrapping. The corn tortillas slightly, deliciously disintegrate in the baking.

Now, about that sauce: Make it a day or two before you make the enchiladas, as it's the sauce that sets these enchiladas transcendently apart, and it takes some time. The recipe makes considerably more salsa than you'll need, but, trust me, this will not be a problem. **MAKES 8 ENCHILADAS; SERVES 4 TO 6**

Eight 6-inch yellow corn tortillas
2 cups dehydrated black bean flakes seasoned with sea salt, such as Taste Adventure
2 cups boiling water, preferably spring or filtered
1½ cups (about ¼ recipe) Pamela Jones's Absolutely Incredible Roasted Vegetable Salsa (page 915)
Grated sharp Cheddar or jack cheese (optional)
Cooking spray

1 Preheat the oven to 400°F.

2 Sprinkle each tortilla lightly with a few drops of water. Stack them and then wrap tightly in foil. Place in the oven to warm and soften, about 10 minutes.

3 As the tortillas warm, place the dehydrated black bean flakes in a heatproof bowl and pour the boiling water over them. Cover and let them stand for 5 minutes.

4 Line up the warm tortillas, the rehydrated beans, the salsa, and, if using, the grated cheese on the counter. Spray an 8-by-11-inch baking dish with cooking spray.

5 You guessed it: enchilada production time. Unwrap the warm tortillas. Place about one-eighth (about 3 tablespoons) of the black bean filling down the middle of the first warm tortilla, roll it, and place, seam side down, in the prepared baking dish. Repeat until all of the enchiladas are filled and the dish is full.

6 Pour the salsa over the enchiladas. Cover with waxed paper, then with foil. Bake until hot, 15 to 20 minutes. Remove the foil and waxed paper and sprinkle the top with the optional cheese. Raise the oven temperature to 450°F and bake until the cheese is melted and bubbly, 5 to 10 minutes. Serve hot.

Center Street–Style Potato-Posole "Nedchiladas" with Tomatillo Salsa Verde

This is my interpretation of a filling developed for Ned by our own much-loved Clary Perez at Center Street South, here in Eureka. Ned had just learned that he was "dys-lactic" (his word for lactose intolerant) and he was particularly unhappy at having to forgo Clary's cheese enchiladas. When you read the recipe—potatoes and posole and tortilla—you might think, "Too starchy," but the combo rocks. **MAKES 6 TO 8 NEDCHILADAS**

2 teaspoons to 1 tablespoon olive oil
1 onion, diced
2 poblano chiles, seeded and diced
¼ teaspoon ground cumin
5 to 6 cloves garlic, minced
2 potatoes, scrubbed and cut into ¼-inch dice
3 tablespoons water, preferably spring or filtered
1 cup drained, canned white posole
Salt and freshly ground black pepper to taste
Tomatillo Salsa Verde (page 944)
Six to eight 6-inch corn tortillas, warmed

1 Preheat the oven to 350°F.

2 Heat the oil in a nonstick saucepan, or one that has been sprayed with cooking spray, over medium-high heat. Add the onion and sauté until just starting to soften, about 4 minutes. Lower the heat to medium and add the poblanos. Sauté for an additional 2 minutes. Add the cumin and cook, stirring constantly, for another minute. Stir in the garlic and sauté for 30 seconds. Add the potatoes and water and place a tight-fitting lid on the pan. Raise the heat slightly and steam until the potatoes are almost cooked and most or all of the water has evaporated, about 10 minutes. Stir in the drained posole and cook until just heated through. Taste and adjust the seasoning with salt and pepper. Remove from the heat.

3 Now it's enchilada-making time. Spray a 10-by-13-inch baking dish with cooking spray. Place the potato-posole filling, the sauce, and the warm tortillas nearby. Spray a skillet with cooking spray, place a tortilla in the skillet, and warm just enough to soften it, maybe 45 seconds. Flip and warm the other side. Pull it out of the skillet and warm another tortilla. As the second tortilla heats, quickly slap about one-sixth of the filling down the middle of the first warm tortilla, roll it, and place, seam side down, in the prepared baking dish. Flip your in-skillet tortilla, and repeat the whole process. Keep going until all of the enchiladas are filled and the dish is full.

4 Pour the Tomatillo Salsa Verde over the enchiladas. Cover with waxed paper, then with foil. Bake until hot, 15 to 20 minutes. Remove the foil and waxed paper. Raise the heat to 450°F and bake for another 5 to 10 minutes. Serve hot.

VARIATION

I often add a 10-ounce box of frozen ready-ground tofu to the filling. It is very tasty, and adds a nice chewy texture. Plus it creates a higher-protein filling. This will also make enough filling for an additional 2 to 4 tortillas. A little chopped, cooked broccoli is another nice addition, as are sliced steamed green beans.

NOTE

This fajita was one of the first recipes developed by Fred (René) Maese, first chef of the writers' colony.

The Writers' Colony at Dairy Hollow (WCDH) is a nonprofit Ned and I cofounded in 1998 that offers uninterrupted residency time for writers and composers. There are only about 40 such havens in America, most on either coast, and I am proud that we started one of them right here in our gorgeous, quirky Ozarks. And I am even prouder of our Board and executive director, Sandy Wright. They ceaselessly continue using their time, resources, and creative energy to bring in many more companies, foundations, and individuals who help support it. The Colony also includes the only studio-suite in the world with facilities specifically dedicated to culinary writers: a dream of a kitchen beautifully fitted out by KitchenAid and Weber Grill. (Our first culinary writer resident exclaimed, "It's like Disney World for cooks!")

Portobello and Shiitake Mushroom Fajitas

Oh, how we used to love to eat at the Blue Mesa in Little Rock—especially the mushroom fajitas. The Blue Mesa is no more, but here is my rendition of the wonderful dish Mark Abernathy used to serve us.

The word *fajita,* as you may know, literally refers to a cut of steak, but has come to mean a stuff-it-yourself, nonbaked enchilada, filled with a sizzling-from-the-grill mixture and garnished with salsas, guacamole, or other zesty condiments.

SERVES 4 TO 6

MUSHROOMS

- 3 cloves garlic, pressed
- 2 to 4 jalapeño chiles, stems removed, seeds and membrane removed or left in for exta heat, minced
- Juice of 2 limes
- 2 tablespoons tamari or shoyu soy sauce
- 1 tablespoon brown sugar
- 8 ounces portobello mushrooms, sliced
- 8 ounces shiitake mushrooms, stems removed (reserve for soup stock), sliced
- Several ambitious grinds of black pepper
- 2 teaspoons olive oil

VEGETABLE SAUTÉ

- 1 tablespoon olive oil
- Cooking spray
- 1 large onion, peeled, sliced vertically into thin crescents
- 1 green bell pepper, seeds and membrane removed, cut into thin slices

FAJITA FIXINGS, AS DESIRED

- Four to six 8-inch flour tortillas, steamed, or grilled lightly
- Mockamole (page 22), guacamole, or sliced avocado
- Yogurt Sour Cream (page 910), Tofu Sour Cream (page 909), sour half-and-half, or full-fat sour cream
- Grated sharp Cheddar or jack cheese
- Arkansalsa (page 913), Pamela Jones's Absolutely Incredible Roasted Vegetable Salsa (page 915), or commercially made salsa
- Shredded lettuce, preferably romaine
- Sliced tomato

1 Combine the garlic, jalapeños, lime juice, tamari, and brown sugar in a glass or nonreactive bowl. When well blended, drop in the portobello and shiitake mushrooms. Toss well, then do some strong pepper-grinding over the mixture. Add the 2 teaspoons olive oil and toss again. Set aside to marinate for at least 1 hour. (Up to 8

hours is fine, covered and refrigerated. An hour or two before serving, remove the mushrooms from the refrigerator and allow to come to room temperature.)

2 Heat 1 tablespoon of the olive oil in a large nonstick skillet, or one that has been sprayed with cooking spray, over medium-high heat. When very hot, add the onion. It should sizzle when added. Stir-fry over medium-high heat until translucent and starting to brown, about 5 minutes. Lower the heat and cook, stirring occasionally, until nearly caramelized, about 15 minutes. Raise the heat back to medium, and add the green bell pepper. Cook, stirring frequently, for another 10 minutes.

3 Preheat the oven to 450°F.

4 Spray a jelly roll pan, cast-iron pizza pan, ovenproof platter, or a baking dish without very high sides with cooking spray. (Ideally, you want a pan suitable to present from the oven to the table, and one large enough to allow air to circulate around the mushrooms.) Place the pan in the preheated oven for 10 minutes.

5 Carefully remove the pan from the oven. Scatter the marinated mushroom mixture over the pan, and return it to the oven. Bake until the mushrooms are slightly softened and a little dried-out looking, 10 to 15 minutes. If there is any marinade left in the bowl, add it to the sautéed onion-pepper mixture, raising the heat to quickly reduce the moisture.

6 Meanwhile, set the table and lay out all of the fajita fixings you've chosen. The only "must" is a stack of warm tortillas. However, the more you add, the more festive the proceedings will be.

7 Remove the mushrooms from the oven. Raise the heat to broil. Toss the sautéed onion-pepper mixture with the mushrooms and place the mixture under the broiler. Broil until sizzling hot, 3 to 5 minutes. Serve, at once, with each diner folding a little of the sizzling mushroom-onion-pepper mixture into a tortilla, along with any of the garnishes on the table. Needless to say, this is a meal to serve friends—and one requiring copious quantities of paper napkins.

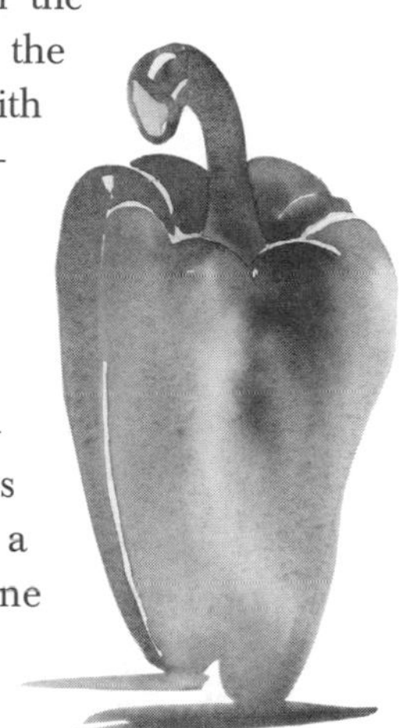

An Especially Winning Fajita

Fred (René) Maese, my good friend, fellow lover of mushrooms and Southwestern flavors, has done a wicked version of these, using Newman's Own Vinaigrette as part of the marinade. Having won the Newman's Own Recipe Contest in the Food Professionals category once a few years earlier (Zona Rosa Chilaquiles, page 377), I felt sure Fred had a winner. I leaned on him pretty heavily to enter the contest. He did, also including a second product—Newman's Own Salsa—to serve with the fajitas. He won! Not only that, but since one of the rules of the Newman's Own contest is that all prize money must be donated to a nonprofit organization, the Writer's Colony at Dairy Hollow—his chosen charity—also won. Thanks, Fred!

WELCOME TO THE ISLANDS

Shandygaffs
(OPPOSITE)

*

Jamaican Curried Vegetable Patties in Tortilla Wraps

*

Jamaica Rice and "Peas," Veronica-Style
(PAGE 618)

*

Oven-Roasted Jerk Eggplant
(PAGE 743)

*

Pineapple-Coconut Mousse Custard
(PAGE 1053)

Jamaican Curried Vegetable Patties in Tortilla Wraps

Why are these "patties" not in the savory cakes chapter? Because in Jamaica a patty is a turnover. And, why are they tacked onto the end of the enchiladas segment? Because this very satisfying recipe demonstrates how nicely a tortilla can replace the usual high-fat shortcrust wrapping. Folded over, tortillas make the classic half-circle patty shape (though the edges are not fork-crimped, and indeed, do not completely enclose the plump filling). Since the traditional patty pastry has a bit of ground annatto, turmeric, curry, or paprika in the dough to give the patties a hint of color, I have added these spices to just the merest squidge of butter to brush on the outside of the tortilla. I use white flour tortillas to better show off the color, but you can substitute whole wheat. Traditional or not, these are delicious. Enjoy them with Oven-Roasted Jerk Eggplant (page 743). This recipe is adapted from Jay McCarthy and Robb Walsh's *Traveling Jamaica with Knife, Fork, and Spoon.* **MAKES 12 PATTIES**

FILLING

- 3 medium potatoes, scrubbed
- 4 carrots, diced
- 1 zucchini or yellow squash, cut into ½-inch dice
- 1 bunch scallions, roots removed, all of the white and about 3 inches of green coarsely chopped
- 3 cloves garlic, quartered
- 2 serrano chiles, stems and seeds removed
- 2 cups fresh, soft breadcrumbs
- 1 teaspoon dried thyme
- 1 tablespoon mild vegetable oil, such as corn, canola, or peanut
- Cooking spray
- 1 large onion, diced
- 1 tablespoon finely minced ginger
- 1 teaspoon curry powder (see page 901)
- ½ to 1 teaspoon salt

QUASI-PASTRY FOR PATTIES

- Twelve 6-inch white flour tortillas
- 1 tablespoon melted butter
- ½ teaspoon paprika
- ¼ teaspoon turmeric

1 Place 3 cups water in a saucepan over medium-high heat. Bring to a boil. Add the

potatoes and cook until almost but not quite tender, 15 to 20 minutes. Add the carrots and zucchini and return to a boil. Boil for an additional 4 minutes. Remove from the heat and drain well (reserve cooking water for use in stock, if desired). Let sit until cool enough to handle.

2 Peel the potatoes and cut them into ¼-inch cubes. Return to the pan with the carrots and zucchini and set aside.

3 Combine the scallions, garlic, serranos, soft breadcrumbs, and thyme in a food processor. Pulse-chop several times, scraping down the sides of the work bowl, then buzz to make a thick paste. (You may need to add 1 to 2 tablespoons water to make a paste; if you kept it, you could use the cooking water from the vegetables.) Set aside.

4 Heat the oil over medium heat in a large nonstick skillet or one that has been sprayed with cooking spray. Add the onion and sauté until beginning to soften, about 4 minutes. Add the ginger and stir-fry for 2 minutes. Add the curry powder and stir-fry for 1 minute. Add the scallion paste and season with the salt. Lower the heat and cook for 3 more minutes, turning the mixture over and over with a spoon. Remove from the heat and gently combine with the reserved vegetables. Set aside. (This part can be done in advance.)

5 About 50 minutes before you plan to serve the patties, preheat the oven to 400°F.

6 Make sure that the flour tortillas and the patty filling are at room temperature. Combine the melted butter, paprika, and turmeric in a small bowl. Have a pastry

NOTE

SHANDYGAFFS

This is a refreshing summer beverage that is a classic with Caribbean food and works well with Tex-Mex, too. Mix equal parts very cold ginger beer (I like Reed's) and beer (Red Stripe in my house). Serve in chilled glasses.

East India in the West Indies

What is curry, an Indian spice mixture, doing in Jamaica, halfway around the world?

When adventuresome Europeans sailed off to India after spices in the 1400s and 1500s, they made as many great finds as they created problems. One of the more minor problems was nomenclature. We now have Indians (who live in India), Indians (who are Native Americans), West Indians (who live in the Caribbean), and East Indians (who are Indians born in India, or whose ancestors were born in India, but who now live somewhere in North American and distinguish themselves thus from the West Indians). The whole thing reaches Marx Brothers proportions of confusion when one considers that East Indians came to the West Indies starting in the late 1880s with the British—as indentured servants.

But the melting pot of cuisine, at least, can always be counted on to reflect and synthesize cross-cultural confusions interestingly. And so it is that curry, of several different types, became part and parcel of Jamaican cooking. Veronica, the beloved housekeeper with whom I got to spend a few growing-up years (whose story, as I knew it, is told on page 618) used to sigh at the mere memory of curry goat. Another much loved Jamaican curry dish is these "patties"—usually filled with spicy meat and potatoes, though sometimes just vegetables. I have to wonder: Is the patty itself the result of more cross-cultural fusion? Is it a reborn version of the British Cornish pasty, a considerably blander meat-potato shortcrust pie, or did it derive directly from the Indian samosa?

brush, dinner plate, and a baking sheet, lightly sprayed with cooking spray, at hand.

7 Now you're going into patty production, which moves much more quickly and easily than describing it. Heat a nonstick skillet over medium heat and briefly warm a tortilla, flipping it over once to make it just hot enough to be pliable. Place the tortilla on the dinner plate and throw another tortilla into the skillet. As the second tortilla warms, put a large scoop of filling on half the tortilla on the dinner plate, folding the other half of the tortilla up and over the filling. This gives you a half-circle filled tortilla, looking something like a turnover, except the filling is showing at the edge. Transfer the filled tortilla to the baking sheet. Remove the second tortilla from the skillet to the dinner plate for filling, and throw another tortilla into the skillet to warm. Repeat until you've warmed and filled all of the tortillas.

8 When all the tortillas have been filled, lightly brush each one with a little of the butter-spice mix. Place the baking sheet in the oven and bake for 20 minutes. Remove the pan from the oven, flip the patties over, and, if you have any of the spice-butter mix left, brush the other side of the patties with it. Return to the oven and bake for another 15 to 20 minutes. Serve hot, if possible, just out of the oven.

Quick Yeasted Pizza Dough, Processor-Style

This dough is traditionally used to wrap Italian calzones and Russian piroshki, but can be used to wrap just about any filling or it can be flattened out for pizza. Piroshki dough usually has a great deal more shortening, which makes it much richer, flakier, and high in fat. Any Russian or Jewish cookbook will have the traditional recipe, if a rich pastry is what you crave. However, these are healthier, easier, and quite delicious.

Because the dough is made in the food processor, the work-time involved is as quick as it gets in yeasted breadstuffs—almost instant to mix up (6 to 8 minutes max), it still has to rise on its own sweet time, 45 minutes to 1 hour. While the dough is rising, you have time to make the filling. **MAKES ENOUGH DOUGH FOR 14 TO 16 SMALL PIROSHKI OR 6 TO 8 LARGE CALZONES**

⅞ cup lukewarm water, preferably spring or filtered (this is 1 cup minus 2 tablespoons)
2 teaspoons active dry yeast
1 teaspoon sugar, Rapidura, or honey
1¼ cups unbleached white all-purpose flour, plus a bit
1 cup whole wheat flour, preferably stone-ground
½ teaspoon salt
1½ teaspoons olive oil or softened butter or other fat, as dictated by the chosen filling recipe

1 Combine the water, yeast, and sugar in a 2-cup glass measuring cup. Stir well with a fork; then let stand in a warm place until foamy, about 10 minutes.

NOTE

Directions and ideas on how to use the dough and fillings are in the box below. For the how-to's of using this versatile dough as a pizza crust, see page 269.

Pastry Procedures

BY HAND: *If you don't have a food processor, proceed as follows. Place the warm water and sweetener in a large bowl, and sprinkle the yeast over it. When the liquid foams, add the oil and salt. Stir in the flours, kneading the last in as the dough gets too stiff to stir. Turn out onto a flour-dusted surface, and knead until smooth and elastic, 6 to 8 minutes. Let rise as directed above.*

SHINY-TOPPED PASTRIES: *Remove from the oven about 5 minutes before they're done, and brush with eggwash—1 whole egg beaten with 1 teaspoon water.*

PESTO DOUGH: *Especially good for calzone or Mediterranean-style fillings, this makes use of commercially prepared pesto, which is usually very oily. If you use homemade, you'll need to add extra oil. Cut back the water by one tablespoon and substitute 3 tablespoons of prepared pesto for the oil.*

MODERATELY RICH RUSSIAN-STYLE PASTRY: *As I mentioned, most recipes for piroshki call for a superrich shortcrust pastry made with major amounts of butter and cream cheese. To get something of the same texture in yeasted dough, omit the water and add 3/4 cup warm buttermilk (ignore the curdled look of the heated buttermilk). For the fat, use 1 tablespoon cold butter, cut into 6 pieces, plus 3 tablespoons neufchâtel cheese, also cut into pieces, incorporating the fat into the flours in the processor. Then, proceed as directed.*

SOUTHWESTERN-STYLE YEASTED PASTRY: *Use butter, not oil; add 1 1/2 teaspoons New Mexico-style ground red chile (not chili powder, but straight, ground New Mexico chiles) to the dough. Try this with a simple filling of rehydrated instant black or pinto beans seasoned with a little chipotle or Pesto Santo Tomas (page 920).*

ASIAN YEASTED PASTRY: *Substitute 1 tablespoon toasted sesame oil for the olive oil or butter. This pastry is good with a filling of minced or crumbled tofu, steamed tempeh, or rehydrated TVP combined with some minced scallions, diced water chestnuts, and diced blanched bok choy or snow peas, with just enough hoisin sauce to hold the mixture together.*

TO FREEZE THE DOUGH: *After the dough is mixed, instead of letting it rise, place it in ziptop freezer bags, labeled and dated, and toss it into the freezer. It must be used within two weeks of freezing. The night before you plan to use the frozen dough, remove it from the freezer and transfer it from the ziptop bag to a medium-large bowl. Tightly cover the bowl with plastic wrap, and let thaw, refrigerated, overnight or for 8 to 10 hours. Refrigerator thawing is essential for even defrosting—room temperature causes uneven rising (risen on the outside, icy at the core). When ready to bake, remove the dough from the refrigerator, knead a couple of times (even though the dough will seem a little soggy) and let rise for an hour before rolling and filling.*

2 Combine the flours and salt with the olive oil in the work bowl of a food processor equipped with a metal blade, and pulse 5 or 6 times to combine.

3 When the yeast mixture is foamy, turn on the processor, and, with the motor running, pour in the liquid. The dough will combine, then begin whapping and thawacking around the work bowl to form a large ball. This happens fairly quickly—within 10 to 15 seconds. Since moisture contents of flours vary, if the dough is too wet and does not begin thawacking around but stays soft and sticky when you touch it, add unbleached flour, a tablespoonful at a time, until it behaves. Using this same recipe, I have sometimes had to add no flour at all and at others as much as 6 tablespoons. It is also remotely conceivable that you might need to go the other way. If the dough seems powdery and doesn't come together, drizzle in warm water, a teaspoonful at a time, until the dough masses together. Turn the dough out of the processor into an oiled bowl. Cover and let rise in a warm place until doubled in bulk, 50 to 65 minutes.

4 Preheat the oven to 450°F.

5 Punch down the dough and let it rest for 3 to 5 minutes. Roll out and fill as directed in the chosen filling recipe. Bake filled pastries, unless otherwise directed in the recipe, until golden brown, about 20 minutes.

Potato-Leek Piroshki

Heartening, peasanty potato, leek, and cabbage are made audacious by a healthy scoop of roasted garlic, a bit of sauerkraut, some fresh dill (a favorite Russian herb), and a good dollop of Dijon mustard. The pastry envelope is light, but no shrinking violet; perfect for the potato-cabbage mixture. The sauerkraut must be of excellent quality. Try a natural foods store brand, kraut from the deli, or some packed in jars or plastic bags at the supermarket; avoid canned, which often has an unpleasant metallic taste. If you don't care for the sauerkraut, just use some extra cabbage. **MAKES 16 MEDIUM-LARGE STUFFED PASTRIES**

NOTE

Start making the filling as the pastry dough rises.

2 large potatoes (about 1½ pounds) scrubbed, cut into eighths
Cooking spray
1 teaspoon butter (optional)
2 large leeks, all white and 1 inch of green, split lengthwise, well washed, sliced crosswise into ¼-inch-thick pieces
⅛ head cabbage, thinly sliced
½ cup sauerkraut, well drained, coarsely chopped
1½ to 2½ tablespoons Dijon mustard
1 to 2 tablespoons Roasted Garlic puree (see page 899)
1 to 2 tablespoons minced fresh dill
1 to 2 tablespoons vegetable stock (see page 139), beer, or white wine
Salt and freshly ground black pepper to taste
1 batch Quick Yeasted Pizza Dough, Processor-Style (see page 350)
1 large egg, beaten (optional)
Poppyseeds or coarse salt (optional)

1 Preheat the oven to 450°F.

2 Bring a small pot of water to a boil over medium heat. Add the potatoes and cook, uncovered, until tender enough to mash, 15 to 20 minutes. Drain well, reserving the water for stock, if desired, and set aside.

3 While the potatoes are cooking, heat a nonstick skillet, or one that has been sprayed with cooking spray, over medium heat. Add the butter, if using. Add the leeks and cook, stirring constantly, until they soften, about 5 minutes. Add the cabbage and sauté for another 3 minutes.

4 Combine the sauerkraut, mustard, roasted garlic, and dill in a medium bowl. Stir in the sautéed cabbage mixture.

5 Return the skillet to medium heat, add the stock, and deglaze the skillet. Pour the deglazing liquid into the bowl.

6 Add the warm potatoes to the cabbage mixture and mash and stir to combine, leaving some texture to the potatoes. Taste the filling, and add salt and pepper to taste. Set aside.

7 By now the dough should be just about doubled. Punch down and let stand for 2 to 5 minutes. Divide into 16 even walnut-in-the-shell-sized balls. Pat each ball out and, one at a time, roll out into very, very thin 6-inch rounds on a floured board.

8 Scoop about ⅓ cup of the cabbage-potato mixture onto each dough circle, patting it out to form a half-circle covering half of the dough round, leaving about ¼ inch of bare dough around the edge. Fold the uncovered side over the filling and pinch the edges together. Crimp and pleat to make a tight seal. (Don't worry in the least about how neat the crimping looks. I like it sort of funky and homemade looking, myself.)

9 Place the finished piroshki on a nonstick baking sheet. (They can also be frozen at this point: Bake, frozen, within 2 weeks, adding 5 to 8 minutes to the baking time.) Bake for 20 minutes. Check to see if

the top is just starting to color and the underneath is a bit deeper golden. If not, continue baking until color is achieved. If using the egg and seeds, remove the piroshki from the oven. Brush with the beaten egg and then sprinkle with the poppyseeds. Return to the oven and bake until the egg wash is quite golden, 3 to 5 minutes. Remove from the oven and serve immediately (but no one will complain about a rewarmed one the next day).

COOK ONCE FOR 2 MEALS The potato filling mixture gives you a jump-start on several meals. I suggest you triple it. One-third fills the piroshki, which, don't forget, can be frozen for later use. Use the second part as the base for Potato-Leek Soup, gently heating the filling while you separately heat 4 cups low-fat milk or soy milk and 2 to 3 cups vegetable stock. Thicken the milk-stock mixture with a scant 3 tablespoons cornstarch dissolved in a little additional stock. Stir in the warm potato-leek filling—mmm. Third, make a Warm Potato Salad—this could be the dish you serve the evening you make the filling. Drizzle a tablespoon or two of olive oil over the final batch of the warm filling, then a couple of tablespoons of cider or balsamic vinegar. Serve as is, or add a few warm, diced hard-cooked eggs or some drained canned chickpeas, mounded on crisp lettuce leaves and surrounded with thickly sliced garden tomatoes.

Mushroom Filling à la Eva for Piroshki

This filling is thick, rich, luscious, and luxurious, full of woodsy, earthy mushroom flavors made high-toned by a whisper of cognac and a caress of creamy neufchâtel. Should you have any extra, serve it on pasta, stuff it into crêpes, spoon it over toast, or thin it down with a little thickened whole milk and white wine and use as a sauce. We used to serve the latter as a hot starter at Thanksgiving, spooned over flaky short-crust pastry leaves (literally—we use a leaf-shaped cookie cutter). **MAKES ENOUGH FILLING FOR 16 LARGE PASTRIES**

2 tablespoons butter
2 tablespoons unbleached white all-purpose flour
Cooking spray
1 onion, very thinly sliced
1 pound shiitake mushrooms, stems removed (save them for stock), picked over to remove bark, sliced
1 pound domestic mushrooms, stems left on, sliced
1 tablespoon Garlic Oil (page 898)
4 ounces neufchâtel reduced-fat cream cheese, softened to room temperature
2 tablespoons cognac
Salt and freshly ground black pepper to taste
Freshly grated nutmeg to taste
1 teaspoon tamari or shoyu sauce, or to taste

1 Place 1 tablespoon of the butter in a small bowl along with the flour. Let stand at room temperature to soften.

2 Heat a large skillet sprayed with cooking spray over medium heat. Add the remaining 1 tablespoon butter. When melted, add the onion, lowering the heat to medium-low. Sauté very slowly until the onion is brown and very limp, about 10 minutes. Add the mushrooms, raising the heat, and stirring until the mushrooms soften.

3 Beat the flour and butter mixture until smooth and set aside.

4 To the mushrooms, add the Garlic Oil and sauté for 2 minutes. Add the butter-flour mixture and cook, stirring frequently, until thickened, about 3 minutes.

5 Combine the softened neufchâtel and the cognac in small bowl, and beat together. When well blended, stir into the mushrooms and season with salt, freshly ground black pepper, and nutmeg to taste. You can hardly have too much pepper here—keep grinding. Taste and, if desired, add tamari to taste. Cool before using as a filling for turnovers.

Eva Sochorova's Piroshki

Asking my Nashville friend Melissa Bloch about the tiny, exquisite mushroom piroshki she'd served me once when Ned and I were visiting led me to her friend, artist and Russian ex-pat Eva Sochorova, who lives in a window-filled house made brighter by her papier-mâché and found-object animals. There, sipping herb tea and nibbling apple cake, I asked Eva to tell me her piroshki secrets. But knowing my purpose, she had already written out this recollection:

"I first ate these some thirty years ago at Madame Schweitzer's, an old Russian émigré who read Pushkin's Eugene Onegin *with me in Russian. Once a week I would visit Madame Schweitzer in her tiny, five-hundred-some-year-old house somewhere not far from the Black Forest, a house with ceilings so low you had to stoop and windows so small that hardly any light entered.*

"There, every Thursday afternoon, while reading together and sighing over Tatyana's unrequited love, Old Russia came to life again. Then she'd move the plate of piroshki toward me, saying, 'Kushay, golubushka, kushay!' (Eat, my little dove, eat!)."

Broccoli-Tofu (or Ricotta) Calzones

This filling can and should be prepared while the calzone dough rises. It can be made with ricotta, instead of tofu, using the mozzarella or provolone, or it can be vegan with tofu and soy mozzarella. Either version, with a salad, can be dinner. To me, you can't put too much homemade pesto in this, but if you're using commercial pesto, be aware that it can be very oil-rich. **MAKES 6 LARGE CALZONES**

Cooking spray
1 tablespoon olive oil
1 large onion, chopped
6 cloves garlic, peeled and chopped (about 1 tablespoon)
1 package firm conventional tofu, preferably reduced fat, or 2 cups ricotta
2 to 3 ounces neufchâtel reduced-fat cream cheese, or regular cream cheese (optional)
2 to 4 ounces grated provolone, mozzarella, or Parmesan cheese, or a bit of each, or the equivalent soy mozzarella and parmesan
2 to 4 cups broccoli, cooked al dente (must not be overcooked), well drained, chopped
½ teaspoon salt, or to taste
½ teaspoon dried thyme (or 1½ teaspoons fresh)
½ teaspoon dried basil (or 1½ teaspoons fresh)
½ teaspoon dried oregano (or 1½ teaspoons fresh)
Freshly ground black pepper to taste
Prepared pesto to taste (optional)
1 recipe yeasted Pastry Crust with Poppyseeds (page 268)
1 large egg, beaten together with about 2 teaspoons water (optional)
Sesame seeds or poppyseeds (optional)

1 Preheat the oven to 450°F.

2 Heat the oil in a nonstick pan or one that has been sprayed with cooking spray over medium heat. Add the onion and cook, stirring, until softened, about 5 minutes. Lower the heat as far as it will go. After the pan has cooled slightly, add the garlic and continue sautéing for another 10 minutes.

3 Place half of the tofu (or ricotta) in a food processor. Coarsely crumble the other half into a bowl and set aside.

4 To the food processor, add the neufchâtel, provolone, and about one-third of the cooked broccoli, the salt, herbs, pepper and, if using, the pesto. Buzz until smooth, pausing several times to scrape down the sides of the work bowl.

5 Scrape the processor mixture into the bowl with the crumbled tofu (or ricotta). Add the onion and garlic mixture and stir to blend. What you're aiming for is a thick, smooth mixture in which texture-y chunks of broccoli are distinct. Taste and, if necessary, adjust the salt, pepper, and herbs.

6 By now the dough should be just about doubled. Punch down, and let stand for 2 to 5 minutes. Divide into 6 even balls, the size of large eggs. Pat each ball out and, one at a time, roll out rounds about ⅛ to ¼ inch thick and 8 to 10 inches in diameter on a floured board.

7 Scoop about 1 cup of the filling onto each dough circle, patting it out to form a half-circle covering half of the dough round, leaving about ¼ inch of bare dough around the edge. Fold the uncovered side over the filling and pinch the edges together. Crimp and pleat to make a tight seal. (Neatness does not count. I think a funky, homemade look works just fine.)

8 Place the finished calzones on a nonstick baking sheet or one that has been sprayed with cooking spray. (They can also be frozen at this point: Bake, frozen, within 2 weeks, adding 5 to 8 minutes to the baking time.)

9 Bake for 20 minutes. Check to see if the top is just starting to color and the underneath is golden. If not, continue baking until color is acheived. If using the egg wash and seeds, remove the pan from the oven. Brush with the beaten egg and then sprinkle with the seeds. Bake until the egg wash is quite golden, 3 to 5 minutes more. Remove from the oven and serve immediately (but no one will complain about a rewarmed one the next day).

NOTE

Serve hot, slashed open, with Basic Wintertime Italian Tomato Sauce (page 931), or any other tasty pasta sauce, ladled over the top.

Somewhat Sicilian Calzones

Several recipes in this book use an intriguing Sicilian way with hearty greens—that is, the addition of a little dried fruit. And many other recipes make use of that classic combo, beans and greens. This recipe takes notes from both approaches, and adds a dash of good old use-what's-in-the-cupboard. It all began with an enormous bag of fresh kale. The use of both sun-dried tomatoes and raisins is especially pleasing, as some of the chewy-textured bits are sweet and others savory, making every bite a surprise. Make the filling while the calzone dough rises.

MAKES 6 LARGE CALZONES

NOTE

Serve hot, slashed open, with Basic Wintertime Italian Tomato Sauce (page 931) ladled over the top.

1 cup dehydrated pinto beans (seasoned only with salt)
¾ cup boiling water, preferably spring or filtered
1 teaspoon olive oil
Cooking spray
1 large onion, chopped
6 cloves garlic, peeled and diced (about 1 tablespoon)
3 to 4 cups chopped blanched kale (this is 1 very large bunch, well washed with tough ribs and stems removed), well drained
3 to 4 tablespoons raisins
2 to 3 tablespoons diced sun-dried tomatoes (not oil-packed)
Salt and freshly ground black pepper to taste
1 recipe Yeasted Pastry Crust with Poppyseeds (page 268)
1 large egg, beaten together with about 2 teaspoons water (optional)
Sesame seeds or poppy seeds (optional)

1 Preheat the oven to 450°F.

2 Place the dehydrated bean flakes in a medium heatproof bowl. Pour the boiling water over them, stirring well. Set aside.

3 Heat the oil in a nonstick skillet, or one that has been sprayed with cooking spray, over medium heat. Add the onion and cook, stirring, until softened, about 5 minutes. Lower the heat as far as it will go. After the pan has cooled slightly, add the garlic and continue sautéing for another 10 minutes. Scrape into the rehydrated bean flakes. Add the well-drained kale, raisins, sun-dried tomatoes, and salt and pepper to taste. Set aside.

4 By now the dough should be doubled. Punch down and let stand for 2 to 5 minutes. Divide into 6 even balls about the size of a large egg. Pat each ball out and, one at a time, roll out into rounds ¼ to ⅛ inch thick and 8 to 10 inches in diameter on a floured board.

5 Scoop about 1 cup of the filling onto each dough circle, patting it out to form a half-circle covering half of the dough round, leaving about ¼ inch of bare dough on the edges. Fold the uncovered side over the filling and pinch the edges together. Crimp and pleat to make a tight seal. Place the finished calzones on a nonstick baking sheet or one that has been sprayed with cooking spray. (They can also be frozen at this point: Bake, frozen, within 1 month, adding 5 to 8 minutes to the baking time.)

6 Bake for 20 minutes. Check to see if the top is just starting to color, and the underneath is a bit deeper gold. If not, continue baking until color is acheived. If using the egg wash and seeds, remove the pan from the oven. Brush with the beaten egg, then sprinkle with the seeds. Return to the oven and bake until the egg wash is quite golden, 3 to 5 minutes. Remove from the oven and serve hot (but no one will complain about a rewarmed one the next day).

Kale

Empanadas

Empanadas are the Latin American piroshki: a rich short crust surrounding local flavors. The classic empanada filling is an aromatic, piquant mixture called picadillo, which I first discovered in the '60s. Many years later, in developing a South American–influenced vegetarian tasting plate for our restaurant, I reconfigured it meatlessly. At the restaurant, we served picadillo wrapped in filo, but it's equally good and a little closer to the real thing when wrapped in yeasted pastry dough. Try either, or use tortillas, as in the Jamaican Curried Vegetable Patties in Tortilla Wraps (page 348). Make the filling while the pastry dough is rising.

NOTE

Picadillo is also an exceptional stuffing for vegetables. Or wrap it in a tortilla or crêpe. It's also good accompanied by almost any starch you can think of.

MAKES 6 LARGE, 8 MEDIUM, OR 12 SMALL EMPANADAS

2 teaspoons to 2 tablespoons olive oil
Cooking spray
1 large onion, chopped
1½ fresh jalapeño or other green chiles, finely chopped (seeds and membranes removed or left in for extra heat)
2 teaspoons cumin seeds
1 package (8 ounces) tempeh, diced into ¼-inch pieces, or 1 package (10 ounces) spicy style ready-ground tofu, thawed
4 to 5 cloves garlic, pressed
2 small cooked potatoes, peel on, diced into ¼-inch pieces
1 large tomato, finely chopped (peel and seeds are fine here)
½ cup sliced pimento-stuffed olives
⅓ cup raisins
2 tablespoons minced Italian parsley
2 tablespoons minced cilantro
Salt and freshly ground black pepper to taste
1 recipe Yeasted Pastry Crust with Poppyseeds (page 268)

1 Heat the oil in a nonstick skillet, or one that has been sprayed with cooking spray, over medium-high heat. Add the onion and sauté until it is aromatic and starting to become translucent, about 3 minutes. Lower the heat slightly, add the jalapeños and cumin, and sauté for another 2 minutes.

2 Lower the heat a bit more and add the tempeh and garlic. Cook, stirring near-constantly, for 2 minutes. Add the potatoes, tomato, olives, raisins, parsley, and cilantro. Season to taste with salt (remember, the olives are salty) and quite a bit of pepper. Cook, stirring constantly, until the picadillo mixture is quite dry, about 4 minutes.

3 Punch down the pastry dough and roll, fill with the picadillo, fold, crimp, and bake as for calzones (see page 357, Steps 8 and 9).

Layered Dishes

A stacked dish might seem far removed from a wrapped one, but layered casseroles are stuffed pastries or pasta deshabillé; unfussy, voluptuously overflowing—a tasty filling panned, instead of wrapped, with pasta or whatever. An enlivening sauce is added, and the whole is baked, creating a class of dishes that are hearty, satisfying, and universally loved. There are French versions (some gratins), Mexican (chilaquiles), and Jewish (though most kugels are baked puddings, some are multilayered enough to pertain here) among others. But the royalty of stacked and layered casserole dishes is undoubtedly the Italian lasagna.

Lasagna (in Italian, with an "a" it's singular, with an "e" it's plural) is often the token vegetarian dish on otherwise nonvegetarian restaurant menus. It is most likely the one thing the family cook knows how to make when the kids come home announcing they've become vegetarian. Traditionally dripping with cheese, most lasagne can hardly be called light, nor are they likely to have major appeal to those who've eaten meatlessly for a lot of years. But most everyone is happy to see them once in a while. And for transitional or semivegetarians—or vegetarians cooking for nons—lasagna can combine comfortable, familiar, and loved with meatless.

The alpha and omega of lasagnadom is what most of us probably think of as the real thing: sheets of pasta, red sauce, creamy ricotta filling, grated cheese, maybe a little spinach or mushrooms thrown in. If the dish seems dated, it may be a while since you've had a really good one, with an artfully seasoned sauce, the pasta not overdone, enough but not excessive cheese, and fresh—not having sat around in a steam table or take-out case too long. Give it another try.

But there's a whole alphabet between alpha and omega. Italian lasagna can be white-sauced, or lemon-sauced; can be filled with a whole gardenful of vegetables, either in addition to or (imagine!) instead of cheese; can feature sliced cooked polenta instead of pasta. And from this general everything-stacked-in-one-pan idea we'll move far afield, geographically and imaginatively.

Dorothy's Lasagna

NOTE

Despite what Dorothy told me, if you use the smaller amount of cheese no one is going to notice or complain.

This is my take on the classic lasagna that Dorothy Gentille Fields, my mother's wry-witted neighbor and good friend, used to bring us a couple of times a year as I was growing up. It has a homemade tomato sauce seasoned with garlic, basil, oregano—and a soupçon of anise seeds (which give the distinctive flavor of the sweet

Italian sausage Dorothy used to add). It has a ricotta filling, plus Parmesan, plus mozzarella. It is safe to say that this is not a light dish.

I once asked Dorothy what made her lasagna so good: "Enough cheese to sink a battleship," she said. I have scaled back the amount of cheese considerably. Although I've called for 3 ounces of each of the firm cheeses, you can go down to as little as 1 ounce or up to as much as 5, and still have a delicious lasagna. **MAKES ONE 10-BY-12-INCH LASAGNA; SERVES 8 TO 10**

12 ounces ricotta
3 cloves garlic, pressed
2 to 3 tablespoons finely minced Italian parsley
A couple of gratings of nutmeg
Salt and freshly ground black pepper to taste
2 large eggs, beaten
1 pound dry lasagna noodles
Cooking spray
1 recipe Red Sauce Fiori (page 932)
3 ounces (¾ cup) shredded Parmesan
3 ounces (¾ cup) shredded mozzarella
3 ounces (¾ cup) shredded provolone
1 to 3 cups vegetables (optional; see variations)

1 Combine the ricotta, garlic, parsley, nutmeg, and salt and pepper in a medium bowl. Add the eggs and stir well to combine. Set aside.

2 Bring a large pot of salted water to a good fast boil over high heat. Add the lasagna noodles and boil, stirring every now and then, until the noodles are pliable but not cooked—almost but not quite to the al dente stage; they would be decidedly hard at the center if you bit one. This should take 6 to 9 minutes, but do check on them. Drain the noodles well, and rinse under cold running water.

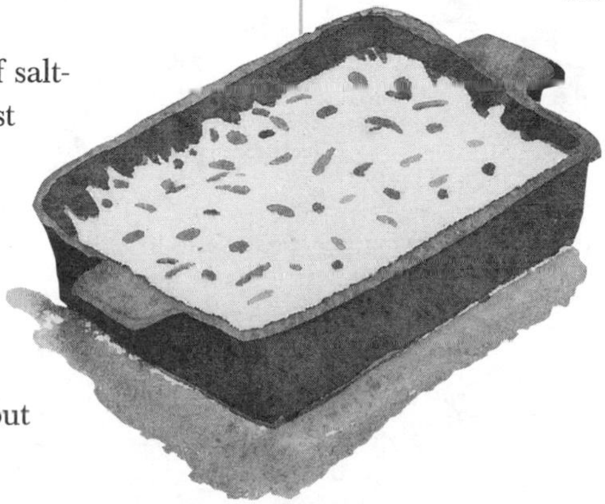

3 If you plan on cooking the lasagna immediately, preheat the oven to 350°F.

4 Spray a 10-by-12-inch baking dish (or two smaller ones) with cooking spray.

5 Assemble the ricotta filling, noodles, sauce, cheeses, and vegetables, if using, on the counter. Layer the ingredients into the prepared baking dish(es) as follows: a little sauce, a layer of pasta, about half the ricotta filling dolloped out then loosely spread (this is not a neat or precise process), a sprinkle of the Parmesan, mozzarella, and provolone cheeses, then more sauce, repeat, using everything except about ⅔ cup of the cheeses. End with a layer of pasta, then sauce.

6 Cover the lasagna tightly. (If baking in a metal pan with no lid, cover it first with waxed paper, then aluminum foil, to prevent the foil from being in direct contact with the dish; if using a glass or enamel-clad baker, waxed paper is not needed.) Bake for 55 minutes, then uncover and sprinkle with the reserved cheese. Raise the oven temperature to 375°F and bake until the lasagna is bubbling hot and the cheese is nice and melty, another 15 to 25 minutes. Remove from the oven and let stand for 10 minutes or so before cutting. (If freezing for later use, see page 370.)

Six Luscious Lasagne

Dorothy's Lasagna Florentine: *Add 1 package (10 ounces) frozen chopped spinach, thawed, well drained, and squeezed dry, to the ricotta, along with 3 or 4 chopped scallions. Proceed as directed.*

Dorothy's "Sausage" Lasagna: *Sauté, according to the package directions, 8 Lightlife Lean Italian Links (one 11.2-ounce package). Cool slightly, and slice the links into good-sized chunks. Sprinkle a layer on top of the first layer of pasta. These excellent sausages are seasoned with anise, just like the real thing, so you may wish to eliminate or cut back on the anise in the sauce.*

Alternatively, for more of a Bolognese sauce effect, stir 1 package (10 ounces) thawed ready-ground tofu into the sauce.

Dorothy's Mushroom or Broccoli Lasagna: *Add a layer of sautéed sliced mushrooms (domestic, shiitake, or a combination) or broccoli florets after that first layer of ricotta. The mushrooms should be sautéed until tender, with any juice reduced to a glaze. The broccoli, however, should not be tender; it should be seared and quite crisp.*

Dorothy's Zucchini or Eggplant Lasagna: *Add a layer of grilled or lightly blanched zucchini or eggplant slices over the first ricotta layer. If you blanch the vegetables, be sure they are well drained, and that any moisture is blotted off with a paper towel.*

Here is **Dorothy's Vegan Lasagna** *for the lactose-intolerant. It nails the flavor, texture, and appearance of the ricotta layer pretty precisely, and it's plenty tasty with the nice wide noodles and good red sauce. You even get a slight Parmesan-ishness with the nutritional yeast. Here's how to do it:*

Substitute 8 ounces crumbled firm conventional tofu for the ricotta in the filling. If you eat eggs, include them in the filling; if not, substitute 2 tablespoons cornstarch or arrowroot. Omit the Parmesan, mozzarella, and provolone. You can either substitute the soy-cheese versions of these if you like them, or sprinkle each pasta layer with about 1 tablespoon nutritional yeast (see page 239).

Really, Really Quick Dorothy's Lasagna: *I can't believe I'm recommending this, but I have to say, given the quality of products now around, it's not bad at all. Substitute fresh uncooked pasta sheets for the cooked pasta; substitute any good commercial red sauce for the Red Sauce Fiori (but add 1/2 teaspoon anise seeds). This means that the only thing you have do before assembling is mix up the ricotta filling. Proceed as directed in the main recipe.*

Grilled Eggplant Lasagna with Lentils and Feta

This is basically a classic vegetarian lasagna, but with all those wonderful Greek/Mediterranean flavors we've come to know and love. Pasta, a Greek-influenced tomato sauce thick with lentils, a bit of feta instead of mozzarella, a creamy béchamel sauce, and grilled eggplant make this both familiar and interesting. I have now cut way, way down on the amount of cheese and fat I used when I first developed the recipe, but there's enough to make a very full-flavored dish. Serve with a good garlicky salad, one with lots of bitter greens; add some crisp-crusted bread and a simple fruit dessert for a heartily satisfying meal. Add coffee and biscotti, maybe a sorbet, and you could serve it to company. **MAKES ONE 10-BY-12-INCH LASAGNA; SERVES 8 TO 10**

NOTE

A gas grill makes grilling a simple, no-big-deal affair. But if you don't have a grill, or have only a charcoal type that you don't feel like messing with, you can use your broiler or grill the slices stove-top by oiling them and grilling in a ridged non-stick pan.

GRILLED EGGPLANT

- 2 medium-large eggplants, peeled and cut, crosswise, into ½-inch slices, soaked in salt water for 30 minutes
- 2 teaspoons to 1 tablespoon olive oil

PARMESAN BÉCHAMEL SAUCE

- 1 tablespoon butter, melted
- 1 tablespoon unbleached white all-purpose flour
- 2 cups low-fat milk, warmed
- 3 tablespoons cornstarch
- ½ cup evaporated skim milk
- ½ to 1 cup (2 to 4 ounces) freshly grated Parmesan cheese
- 2 ounces neufchâtel reduced-fat cream cheese, at room temperature
- ½ to 1 teaspoon freshly grated nutmeg
- Salt and freshly ground black pepper to taste

TO ASSEMBLE

- 1 box (8 ounces) lasagna noodles
- 1 recipe Greek-Style Tomato Sauce with Lentils (page 932)
- 4 ounces crumbled feta cheese
- Cooking spray (optional)
- ½ to ⅔ cup Breadcrumb Topping Provençal (page 277), using soft breadcrumbs

1 Heat a gas grill to hot, then lower the flame to medium.

2 Drain the soaked eggplant. Pat the slices dry and brush lightly with as little oil as possible. Place the eggplant slices on the grill, with grill cover down, and grill over indirect heat until medium-tender and grill-marked on one side, 8 to 10 minutes. Using tongs, turn the eggplant so the other side

VARIATION

Working with these same basic ingredients, you can make a very delicious Greek Eggplant Pastitsio. This famed Greek casserole, usually done with lamb, is topped with a custardy Greek-style macaroni and cheese, a bit simpler to put together since it's in two layers, not 4 to 6.

When the eggplant comes off the grill, cut it into ½- to 1-inch cubes, stir it into the tomato sauce and just spoon it into a prepared baking dish. When the béchamel is ready, whisk in 2 beaten eggs along with the cheese, then fold 8 ounces of cooked-to-al-dente elbow macaroni into it. You will omit lasagna noodles and crumbs. Spoon the macaroni mixture over the tomato-eggplant-lentil layer. Bake uncovered at 350°F, until the topping is golden and firm, about 1 hour.

can grill for the same length of time. Remove the eggplant from the grill and set aside.

3 As the eggplant grills, prepare the Parmesan béchamel sauce: Stir the melted butter into the flour in a nonstick pan over medium heat. Cook for 1 minute, stirring. Whisk in the warm milk, a little at a time, to make a thin sauce. Lower the heat and cook until thickened, 3 or 4 minutes.

4 Using your fingers, mush the cornstarch into the evaporated skim milk to make a thick paste. Raise the heat under the milk sauce and cook, stirring constantly, until bubbles form around the edge. Add the cornstarch paste and cook, stirring constantly, until the sauce thickens. This should happen immediately. Remove from the heat.

5 Stir the Parmesan and neufchâtel cheeses into the sauce, whisking to smooth. Season with nutmeg and salt and pepper to taste. Use plenty of pepper, but go easy on the salt, since the feta's quite salty. Set aside.

6 Bring a large pot of salted water to a vigorous boil. Drop the lasagna noodles into the water and boil, stirring every now and then, until the noodles are pliable but not cooked—almost but not quite to the al dente stage; they would be decidedly hard at the center if you bit one. This should take 6 to 9 minutes, but do check on them. Drain the noodles well, and rinse under cold running water.

7 If you plan to bake the lasagna immediately, preheat the oven to 375°F.

8 Assemble the Greek-Style Tomato Sauce with Lentils, the Parmesan béchamel sauce, grilled eggplant, crumbled feta cheese, lasagna noodles, and breadcrumb topping on the counter. In a 10-by-12-inch nonstick baking dish or one that has been sprayed with cooking spray, layer the ingredients as follows: a little swirl of the tomato sauce, a layer of pasta, a layer of eggplant, a sprinkling of feta, then pasta, then béchamel. Repeat, ending with either sauce. Top with the breadcrumb topping.

9 Cover the lasagna tightly. (If baking in a metal pan with no lid, cover it first with waxed paper, then foil, to prevent the foil from being in direct contact with the dish; if using a glass or enamel-clad baker, waxed paper is not needed.) Bake for 40 minutes, then uncover and bake until the crumbs are crisped and the lasagna is bubbling hot, 15 to 25 minutes. Let stand at room temperature for 10 minutes or so before cutting. (If freezing for later use, see page 370.)

Fresh Artichoke-Eggplant Lasagna with Lemon Sauce

This vegan lasagna is filled with Greek notes and fresh, light flavors that bloom pleasingly on the palate. The creamy layer typically supplied by ricotta is here supplied by . . . hah! I bet you thought I was going to say mashed tofu, didn't you? Nope—a smooth and unctuous mashed bean mixture, close kin to hummus, with a custardlike texture.

Because of the acidity of the lemon juice, please use a nonreactive baking dish: An enamel-clad Le Creuset, a glass Pyrex, or a Circulon baker would all do admirably. Avoid aluminum or nonclad cast-iron bakers: Ingredients may discolor and develop off flavors. **SERVES 8 TO 10**

VEGETABLE FILLING

- 1 eggplant, skin left on, cut into ½-inch cubes
- 1 teaspoon to 1 tablespoon olive oil
- Cooking spray (optional)
- 1 large red onion, chopped
- 2 carrots, diced
- 4 to 6 artichokes, boiled or steamed as described on page 387, hearts only
- 1 cup any good commercially made tomato sauce, or Basic Wintertime Italian Tomato Sauce (page 931)
- Salt and freshly ground black pepper to taste

CHICKPEA FILLING

- 2 cans (30 ounces total) chickpeas, drained, liquid reserved
- 3 cloves garlic, halved (or 1 tablespoon Roasted Garlic puree; page 899)
- 2 tablespoons cornstarch
- About ⅓ cup Italian parsley leaves

FOR ASSEMBLY

- 1 box (8 ounces) dry lasagna noodles
- 1 recipe Simpler Lemon Sauce à la Grecque (page 941), revised as described at the end of that variation
- 1 cup Breadcrumb Topping Provençal (page 277)

1 Steam the eggplant, covered, in a steamer basket set over boiling water, until barely tender, about 6 minutes. Remove from the heat, drain, and set aside to cool.

2 Heat the oil in a large nonstick skillet, or one that has been sprayed with cooking spray, over medium heat. Add the onion and sauté until translucent, about 4 minutes.

Add the carrots and sauté for another 3 minutes. Lower the heat slightly, cover the skillet, and steam the carrots and onions for 5 minutes. Remove from the heat.

3 Combine the cooked, drained eggplant with the onion-carrot mixture and the artichokes and tomato sauce. Tossing well to combine, season with salt and pepper to taste and set aside.

4 Combine the drained chickpeas, garlic, and cornstarch in a food processor and buzz until smooth. The texture will be a bit pasty at this point. Add the drained liquid as needed to achieve a creamy but not wet consistency, a spreadable puree; about ⅓ to ½ cup liquid will be needed. Add the parsley and pulse chop, pausing a few times to scrape down the sides, until the leaves are finely chopped and well distributed but not pureed. Set aside.

5 When you're ready to assemble the lasagna, preheat the oven to 375°F.

6 Cook the lasagna noodles to the al dente stage, as described in the package directions or on page 361.

7 Warm the lemon sauce in a small saucepan over low heat.

8 Spoon a few tablespoons of the lemon sauce into an 8-by-12-by-2½-inch nonreactive nonstick baking dish or a nonreactive dish that has been sprayed with cooking spray. Cover with a layer of noodles. Top the noodles with a layer of the vegetable filling, using about half of the filling,

The Art of the Choke

Because artichokes are one of my favorite vegetables, we served them from time to time at the inn, but not often—their provenance could hardly be less Ozark. (I told, in Dairy Hollow House Soup and Bread, *the story of Ned surveying a pan of steamed artichokes and asking E. Rae Smith, one of our assistants some years back, whether she'd gotten out all the stickery parts, and her reply: "Of course. All that's left is the art.")*

My mother served hot artichokes at the first lunch Ned sat down to with her at her home, back when we were engaged. He looked at the artichoke, looked at the dish of melted butter, looked at her, said, "Oh, well," and proceeded to pour the entire dish over the whole artichoke. More recently, I walked into the twentieth-anniversary party for the Eureka Springs Historical Museum carrying two platters of artichoke leaves (cold) arranged around a little bowl of dip, and as his first move, the president of the financial institution where I used to bank cheerfully popped a whole leaf into his mouth. "No, no, John!" I said, alarmed. "Just the tip!" showing him with a leaf the scrape-the-tip-off-with-your-teeth maneuver. "Well, all right," he said, agreeably, "but what do I do with this?" waving the rest of the hastily retrieved leaf. Good point. Always have a spare bowl for the spent leaves.

and pressing it evenly over the noodles. Top with another layer of noodles, then a layer using all of the bean filling. Top the bean filling with the remaining vegetable filling. Cover with a final layer of noodles. Spoon the remaining sauce over the noodles. Cover tightly with foil.

9 Bake until piping hot all the way through, 50 to 60 minutes. Uncover and sprinkle on the breadcrumb topping. Raise the oven temperature to 500°F and bake until the crumbs are crisp and browned, 7 to 10 minutes. Let stand for 10 minutes before serving.

Pumpkin and Bean Lasagna with Caramelized Garlic

Do you love to cook and to feed others? Do you love hearty, peasant-y tastes that are at the same time just a bit cutting-edge? Then invite a bunch of people you care for over for this wondrous, wholly satisfying lasagna, bursting with the flavors and colors of autumn. Shop at the nearest farmer's market in the morning. Then spend a peaceful afternoon cooking, knowing that your home will be filled with garlic scents and warmth.

I just love this particular lasagna, and so has anyone I've ever fed it to—even people who swear they hate cabbage, squash, and kidney beans. The flavors are magic together. As for sauces: All options work here. My favorite is probably the roasted red pepper, but since it adds more time to the preparation, I only use it if I've made the soup recently and have some on hand (of course, when I do make the soup, I always make extra to set aside for this very purpose). Plain ol' tomato sauce is excellent here, and, if you buy a good ready-made, the

SATURDAY NIGHT WITH FRIENDS, THE FIRST RAINY NIGHT OF FALL

The Salad
(PAGE 68),
made with arugula and bitter greens

*

Pumpkin and Bean Lasagna with Caramelized Garlic
(PREVIOUS PAGE)

*

Steamed green beans with lemon

*

Platter of biscotti, bittersweet chocolates, and dried pineapple

*

Bowl of polished, crisp fall apples

*

Espresso, cappuccino, decaf

easiest. Sauce Soubise is stunning tastewise, giving voluptuous dimension to the dish. Macro-Red is gorgeous visually, slightly sweet; also very good. **SERVES 8 TO 10**

CARAMELIZED GARLIC

3 tablespoons olive oil
Cooking spray (optional)
20 cloves garlic, halved, any green part in the middle removed, cut into ¼-inch dice

PUMPKIN–KIDNEY BEAN FILLING

1 (2-pound) pie-pumpkin or butternut squash, peeled, seeded, and cut into ½- to 1-inch pieces
2 cups cooked or canned kidney beans, well drained

RICOTTA-CABBAGE FILLING

½ green cabbage, sliced into ribbons
3 large eggs
1 container (15-ounces) ricotta, preferably reduced fat
1½ cups milk
2 ounces neufchâtel reduced-fat cream cheese
A few gratings of nutmeg
Salt and freshly ground black pepper to taste

FOR ASSEMBLY

8 ounces whole wheat lasagna noodles, cooked until not quite al dente, as described in earlier lasagna recipes
1 to 1½ cups your choice of any of the following: a good commercial tomato sauce, Sauce Soubise (page 946), Basic Wintertime Italian Tomato Sauce (page 931), "Macro-Red" Sauce (page 936), or leftover Roasted Red Pepper Soup with a Cilantro-Jalapeño Swirl (page 144; omitting the swirl)
1 cup freshly grated Parmesan cheese (4 ounces)

1 Heat the oil in a 10-inch nonstick skillet, or one that has been sprayed with cooking spray, over the lowest possible heat. Add the garlic and cook slowly, stirring frequently, until pale gold on all sides, about 8 minutes. Do not let it get any darker than gold or it will be bitter. Using a slotted spoon, lift the garlic from the skillet, leaving behind as much oil as possible. Spread the caramelized garlic on a plate and set aside.

2 Raise the heat under the skillet to medium. Add the cut-up pumpkin or butternut squash, and stir-fry until slightly softened, about 5 minutes. Add 1 tablespoon water, and pop a tight-fitting lid on the skillet, lowering the heat slightly. Cook, lifting the lid and stirring every so often, perhaps adding a few additional teaspoons of water, until the pumpkin is just about tender, about 10 minutes for pumpkin, 18 to 20 for butternut squash. (It should be slightly firm at the center, soft at the edges, and still hold its shape.) Remove from the heat and transfer to a bowl. Squash a couple of times with the back of a wooden spoon so the pumpkin is partially mashed, but still quite textured, and toss in the kidney beans. Stir to combine and set aside.

3 Set up a steamer over simmering water. Add the cabbage, cover, and steam until just wilted, 1 to 2 minutes. Drain well, blotting dry. Set the steamed cabbage aside in a medium bowl.

4 Combine the eggs, ricotta, milk, neufchâtel, and nutmeg in a food processor. Buzz until smooth, pausing to scrape down the sides of the bowl. Add salt to taste and lots of pepper and buzz again. Pour over the cabbage and stir well to combine.

5 If you plan on baking the lasagna right away, preheat the oven to 350°F.

6 Assemble the cooked noodles, the sauce, the squash-bean and ricotta-cabbage fillings, and the caramelized garlic on the counter.

7 In an 8-by-12-by-2½-inch nonstick baking dish, or one that has been sprayed with cooking spray, layer the ingredients as follows: Swirl about 3 tablespoons of the sauce in the bottom of the dish. Line with a layer of lasagna noodles. Scatter half of the pumpkin filling over the noodles, and then sprinkle with half of the caramelized garlic. Spoon the ricotta-cabbage filling over the garlic. Add another layer of pasta, half the Parmesan, and then all of the remaining pumpkin filling. Sprinkle the pumpkin with the remaining caramelized garlic. Cover with a layer of pasta, then the remaining sauce. You will have some Parmesan left.

8 Tightly cover the lasagna. Bake, covered, until heated through and medium-firm when pressed with a fork, about 60 minutes. Uncover and sprinkle with the remaining Parmesan. Return to the oven and bake for another 15 minutes. Remove from the oven and let stand for 10 minutes before cutting.

VARIATION

VEGAN VARIATION:
Omit the eggs, milk, ricotta, and neufchâtel from the ricotta filling. Substitute ¼ cup cornstarch or arrowroot buzzed with 1 cup unflavored rice or soy milk, 1 pound medium-firm tofu (preferably reduced fat), 1 tablespoon olive oil, and 1 tablespoon tahini or 2 tablespoons tofu cream cheese. Omit the Parmesan, or use rice or soy Parmesan-style cheese instead.

"You would have liked the general store. It smelled like the inside of some foreign spice cake. That was from the barrels of fresh and dried fruit, the bins of tea and the scarlet coffee grinder flecked with dark brown dust, the hanging strings of dried figs and onions, glass jars of glazed fruit . . . strong smells of distant places."

—**Jan Adkins,** *A Storm without Rain*

Stack the Deck: Lasagna Strategy

Lasagna is what used to be called a one-dish meal. But it's only one dish at completion; until then it's actually three or four: sauce, fillings, and starch. Preparation is time consuming, and takes attentiveness, which is why, for those new to the kitchen, lasagna making is nerve wracking.

To simplify matters, make lasagna strategically, in parts. Make the sauce one day (many of the sauces freeze very well); prep the fillings (grate cheeses, or perhaps cook beans or blanch or dice vegetables) another. Finish putting the fillings together yet another day. In some cases (like polenta lasagna) the starch, as well, can be cooked in advance, but in some others (like pasta lasagna) it should be cooked the day of assembling.

The assembly day can be the day the finished lasagna will be baked and served or the day that it is frozen for baking at a later date (at which time it will seem totally simple, easy, and no sweat—there is a lasagna-making amnesia akin to the one mothers have about labor).

Freezing Lasagna

There are a couple of different ways to go in when having frozen lasagna. The first is simple. Freeze the assembled lasagna, in its pan, and then put it directly into a preheated oven (temperature specified in the individual recipe). Bake, covered, for the amount of time specified in the recipe plus an additional 20 to 25 minutes. Uncover and finish baking as directed in the specified recipe.

The second freezer-to-table method is for those who don't want or need a great big lasagna. Preheat the oven to 350°F. Prebake the lasagna (if crumb topping is called for, leaves it off crumbs), covering it first with waxed paper, then with foil. Bake for 30 minutes.

Remove the lasagna from the oven and let cool to room temperature. Refrigerate overnight.

The next day, cut into rectangular portion-size slices. Lift each slice carefully onto a piece of plastic wrap. Sprinkle with breadcrumb topping, if called for, and wrap tightly.

Label, date, and freeze each piece. separately (I know that you think labeling and dating is fussy; I know you think you'll remember what you froze when, but trust me, you won't. I learned to be religious about labeling and dating in my restaurant days, where it is a health department requirement, and I happily continue the practice at home.)

When you've got a hankering for lasagna and are ready to eat your stashed frozen treasure, unwrap a piece or pieces of the frozen lasagna. Place the frozen lasagna in a baking dish (sprayed with cooking spray) just large enough to hold it comfortably, or wrap it tightly in a piece of heavy-gauge foil that has been sprayed with cooking spray. Bake at 350°F for 40 minutes. Uncover and bake until well browned, another 15 minutes.

Foiled Again—Not!

A couple of last general lasagna-making observations, concerning the "one dish" in which the lasagna bakes. Most lasagne go through an initial covered baking, followed by a final uncovered baking. With what do you cover the pan? Well, assuming your baking dish does not have a cover of its own, aluminum foil would seem to be the logical choice, but there's one little problem: Foil and foods, especially acid foods such as tomatoes, often interact badly, the tomatoes eating little holes in the foil and the foil leaving little speckles of aluminum on the tomatoes.

For years I assumed that this was strictly because of the foods' acidity, but my colleagues Shirley Corriher and Harold McGee, food chemists and culinary Sherlock Holmeses, tell me that this is not exactly so. Aluminum foil has a relatively unstable molecular charge. It dissolves into tomatoes only when the pan is of a different metal, like stainless steel or cast iron—the reaction is between the two metals of differing compositions, with the food caught in between becoming tainted. While acid or salty foods speed the reaction, they do not cause it per se, as you can see by putting a slice of tomato on a piece of foil and wrapping it up.

The problem of aluminum-acid reaction can be solved in several different ways:

1 *Use a baking dish or pan that is nonmetal (glass, ceramic, or, best of all—because it holds the heat so nicely—an enameled cast-iron pan).*

2 *Use a baking dish or pan of the same metal: aluminum (less satisfactory, because aluminum cookware tends to be cheap and, if scratched, can leach aluminum into the food, thereby defeating the purpose).*

3 *Place an insulating layer, such as a sheet of waxed paper, between the food and the foil, to prevent contact.*

Now, about pan sizes: Although I have specified pan sizes exactly, don't be afraid of going up or down according to what you have on hand. A larger pan means a thinner lasagna, a smaller means a thicker one—a slight adjustment to the cooking time and you'll be fine.

Making a Meal of It

What makes lasagna a meal? Start with the simplest and mostly lightly dressed of salads, preferably with contrasty greens—some bittery and peppery, some sweet and tender. You couldn't do better than The Salad (page 68), perhaps tossed with some olives and a handful of cooked, chilled fresh green beans tossed in along with a few tablespoons of minced parsley. Or serve an antipasto (page 56) if you don't want to fuss at the last minute. To accompany, bread, good and crusty, slightly warmed (a whole wheat baguette's ideal). If you like, go for broke and slather slices with garlic butter.

The conclusion for such a substantial meal? Fresh fruit; either Compote of Poached Bananas and Star Fruit with Dried Cherries (page 965) or Italian Caramelized Oranges (page 987) or Oranges in Bay-Leaf Syrup (page 985) or just simple wedges of melon, with a scoop of sorbet. The most classic and delectable finish of all is no doubt in-season fresh strawberries drizzled with real, aged, imported balsamic vinegar. The latter is costly, and worth every penny: indefinably and distinctly perfumed, sweet, tart, mellow. If you use the cheap varieties, you simply won't get why this combination is so irresistibly heady, and so passionately loved by Italians (and lovers of all things Italian).

WOK ON THE WILD SIDE

Miso soup

*

East-West Lasagna

*

Ginger Sorbet
(PAGE 1045)
with sliced kiwi and fresh raspberries

*

Jasmine tea

East-West Lasagna

The tomato sauce is gingered, the pasta is rice-paper wrappers, and the fillings—grilled sweet potatoes, tofu, a stir-fry—all are stacked in layers on each serving plate. Yet, it is as recognizably lasagna as it is visually stunning. My friend Chou Chou looked up after her first bite and said, "*This* is a fifty-dollar entree. If I ordered this in a metropolitan restaurant and had to pay fifty dollars for it, I would feel I got my money's worth." Having traveled in India with Chou Chou and seen her haggle over a few rupees (a rupee is worth about 8 cents), I took this as a high compliment. And before you say, "*Asian* lasagna?" remember that Italy didn't even *have* pasta until Marco Polo brought it home.

Making it is a fairly big deal. Some of the components must be done at the last minute, and since it's assembled on the dinner plates you must work quickly to keep everything warm. Before you start assembling, be sure you have plates and all of the components laid out on a good-sized counter. The first time I made this, I thought, as I was putting it together, "Never again, too much trouble." Then, a few minutes later, I tasted it, almost swooned in pleasure—and fixed it again within a month. **MAKES 8 INDIVIDUAL PORTIONS**

1 tablespoon mild vegetable oil, preferably peanut
4 tablespoons tamari or shoyu soy sauce
2 large sweet potatoes, peeled and sliced lengthwise into ½-inch-thick ovals, to yield about 10 to 12 ovals
1 teaspoon toasted sesame oil
1 teaspoon cornstarch
¼ cup vegetable stock (page 139)
3-inch piece lemon grass, pounded
2 tablespoons sherry
1½ tablespoons finely minced peeled ginger
1½ tablespoons finely minced garlic
1 tablespoon fermented black beans
1 tablespoon Sriracha or similar Asian-style chile sauce
2 teaspoons brown sugar, honey, or Rapidura
½ pound snow peas or sugar-snap peas, stems and strings removed
½ onion, cut vertically into thin crescents
1 wedge red cabbage, thinly sliced (⅛ small red cabbage)

FOR ASSEMBLY

16 rice-paper wrappers (see page 311)

1 recipe Asian Red Sauce (page 934)

1 package (8-ounces) Thai-style baked tofu, each piece sliced horizontally into 8 thin slices and then crosswise into 16 thin rectangles, or 1 recipe Basic Oven-Baked Marinated Tempeh (page 641), cut into rectangles

¼ cup chopped cilantro

3 scallions, chopped

2 to 3 tablespoons finely chopped roasted peanuts

1 Preheat the grill to hot, then lower the heat to medium.

2 Combine 1 teaspoon of the oil with 2 teaspoons of the tamari, whisking well with a fork. Using a pastry brush, lightly coat the sweet potato slices with the mixture. Place the sweet potatoes on the grill, over indirect heat, until tender but not mushy, about 8 minutes on each side. Remove from the heat and set aside on a mise en place tray (see page 107).

3 Combine the remainder of the vegetable oil with the sesame oil in a small dish and place on the "mise" tray.

4 Place the cornstarch in a small bowl. Add 1 tablespoon of the stock and smush the cornstarch into it to dissolve. Stir in the remaining stock and set aside on the "mise" tray.

5 Combine the remainder of the tamari with the lemon grass, sherry, ginger, garlic, black beans, sriracha, and sugar in a small bowl. This is the stir-fry sauce seasoning mix. Place it on the "mise" tray.

6 Place the snow peas, onion, cabbage, wrappers, tomato sauce, tofu, cilantro, scallions, and peanuts on the "mise" tray. Have a bowl of very hot water ready. The next few steps are all done more or less simultaneously, so be ready to run.

7 Heat the tomato sauce in a saucepan over medium-low heat.

8 Lay out a warm dinner plate for each person you'll be serving.

9 Heat the vegetable oil–sesame oil mixture in a wok over very high heat. When sizzling hot, toss in the snow peas, onion, and cabbage. Cook, stirring like the dickens, until the vegetables are a little seared but still pretty crisp, about 2 minutes. Drizzle in about three-quarters of the seasoning mix and continue stir-frying over high heat, until crisp-tender, about 3 more minutes. Stir the cornstarch mixture and stir it into the wok. The sauce should thicken immediately. Remove from the heat and stir in remaining stir-fry seasoning.

Mountain Tomatoes

"The tomatoes were scarlet to such a degree as to make an artistic soul like Henri writhe with sheer delight. Don't ask me why mountain tomatoes should be so vivid. Possibly it is the unobstructed kissing of their skins by the ultra-violet rays of the sun. Certainly the big peppers of that hillside garden were varnished with such a green pigment as I do believe is not to be seen in our lower and heavier atmosphere."

—Henri Charpentier,
Those Rich and Great Ones, or Life à la Henri

10 Working quickly, using one wrapper at a time, dip the wrapper into the hot water until pliable, about 30 seconds. Transfer to a cutting board to dry for a few seconds. (It helps to have a team mate at this point; one can stir-fry and dip the wrappers, the other assemble.)

11 One at a time, assemble a lasagna on each plate: Place a soaked wrapper on a plate. Stack a grilled sweet potato and a slice of tofu on one side of the wrapper. Fold the wrapper over to make a half-circle. Drizzle about 1 tablespoon of the tomato sauce over the top. Place a second wrapper so that the half to be filled overlaps the first, and so that it will fold over in the opposite direction: Where you had a closed edge on the underneath you now have a curved open edge. Place a large scoop of stir-fried vegetables on the part of the wrapper laying on top of the filled wrapper and fold the overhanging side over the top. Drizzle about 1 tablespoon of the tomato sauce on top. Drizzle about 1 tablespoon of the sauce around the plate, and sprinkle the plate with cilantro and scallions and peanuts. Repeat, working quickly (it does in fact go more rapidly than it takes to describe doing it), until all of the lasagna has been made. Serve at once.

Polenta Lasagna with Mushrooms Béchamel

Golden squares of polenta are meltingly soft but crisped on top under the broiler in this hearty casserole. A great, not-too-fancy company dish, it works well on a buffet. Start with a good garlicky salad.

The commercially available tubes of cooked polenta (available in almost every supermarket and natural foods store) make the creation of this dish extremely simple.

SERVES 6 TO 8

Cooking spray or oil
½ large onion, sliced
½ pound shiitake mushrooms, stems removed, sliced thick
¼ pound button mushrooms, sliced
¾ cup plus 2 tablespoons low-fat milk
2 tablespoons cornstarch
2 ounces neufchâtel reduced-fat cream cheese, softened to room temperature
¼ cup white wine
Salt, freshly ground black pepper, and freshly grated nutmeg to taste
3½ cups Basic Wintertime Italian Tomato Sauce (page 931), or any vegetarian tomato sauce
1 recipe polenta, made with finely ground cornmeal, "set up" (pages 441–46) and sliced into 2-by-3-inch rectangles, about ⅜ inch thick (or 1 tube of plain or pesto-flavored commercially made polenta)
¼ to ¾ cup (1 to 3 ounces) freshly grated Parmesan cheese (optional)

1 Preheat the oven to 375°F.

2 Lightly oil (or spray with cooking spray) a 9½-by-13½-inch baking dish. Set aside.

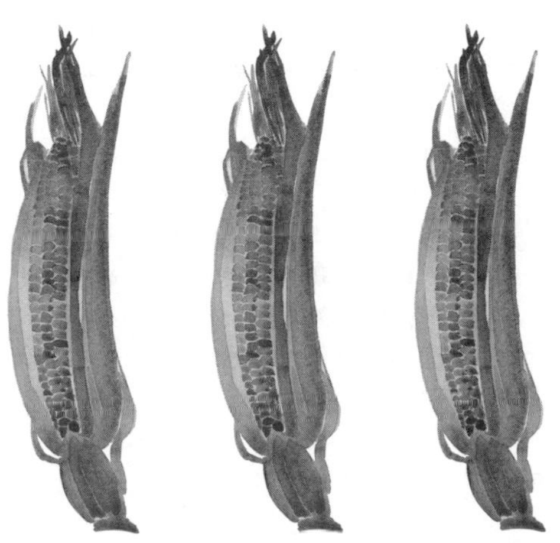

3 Heat a large nonstick skillet or wok, or one that has been sprayed with cooking spray, over high heat. Add the onion and stir-fry until almost translucent and beginning to soften, about 3 minutes. Add the mushrooms and continue to stir-fry until the onion starts to get limp, 3 to 4 minutes. Add ¾ cup of the milk and bring to a simmer.

4 Dissolve the cornstarch in the remaining 2 tablespoons milk. When the mushroom mixture is simmering, stir in the cornstarch mixture. It will almost immediately become very thick and pasty. Stir in the neufchâtel and then the wine. When well blended, remove from the heat. Season to taste with salt, pepper, and nutmeg.

5 Spread a few tablespoons of the tomato sauce in the prepared baking dish. Scatter a sparse layer of polenta slices over the sauce, about one-quarter of the polenta. The polenta doesn't have to completely cover the bottom of the dish, just be evenly spaced. Lightly dust the polenta with the Parmesan, if using. Ladle the mushroom mixture over the cheese. Layer on another quarter of the polenta, and again dust with cheese. Spread the remainder of the tomato sauce over this second layer of polenta. Top with a final layer of polenta.

6 Place in the preheated oven and bake until bubbling hot, 35 to 45 minutes. If desired, sprinkle the top with additional Parmesan and place the dish under the broiler for a few seconds. Remove from the oven and lightly tent with foil to keep warm. Allow the lasagna to rest for 15 minutes before cutting. (This helps it set so it can be cut into nice tidy pieces.)

VARIATIONS

POLENTA LASAGNA WITH MUSHROOMS: VEGAN VARIATION:
This is a case when omitting the dairy does the vegan trick. Do the mushroom-onion sauté, perhaps slightly amping up the amount of mushrooms. When they are almost done, sprinkle with the wine, raise the heat to evaporate the liquid, season, and you've got the filling. If you wish to make it richer, dollop with a rounded teaspoonful of commercially made tofu cream cheese. Scatter the mushrooms and optional tofu cream cheese over the polenta as in the basic recipe. Omit the Parmesan dustings, or substitute soy Parmesan-style cheese.

CASSEROLE OF GRATINÉED POLENTA WITH SAUCE SOUBISE AND WILD MUSHROOMS:
If red sauces are a bit boring, try this dish with Sauce Soubise (page 946). This will turn it into a mighty rich once-in-a-while dish, luscious and swoon-some.

Chilaquiles Windflower

Claudia Ryan, one of the innkeepers of the Windflower in Great Barrington, Massachusetts, learned through an innkeeping newsletter that I was at work on a vegetarian cookbook, and hospitably sent me this recipe. She calls it Mexican Lasagna. "It's a relatively simple casserole," she explained in a letter, "vegetarian and gluten-free, which I developed after I was diagnosed as gluten intolerant. Even my kids enjoy it. It can be easily doubled to make one for the freezer. The black olives add a little fillip, and the use of three different varieties of canned beans make it as interesting as it is speedily put-together." Thanks, Claudia.

I have slightly reduced the amount of cheese Claudia called for. The recipe calls for a *lot* of chili powder, so be sure you love the taste of your brand. And if you don't like heat, be certain that it's not too incendiary. **SERVES 6 TO 8**

2 cans (30 ounces total) chickpeas, drained (if desired, reserve the liquid for use in soup stock)
1 can (19 ounces) black beans, drained (if desired, reserve the liquid for use in soup stock)
1 can (15 ounces) red kidney beans, drained (if desired, reserve the liquid for use in soup stock)
1 can (29 ounces) peeled Italian tomatoes, cut up
1 can (6 ounces) pitted black olives (regular old unfancy California olives), drained and cut into thirds
Cooking spray
½ cup salsa, medium or hot, to taste, commercial or homemade (Pamela Jones's Absolutely Incredible Roasted Vegetable Salsa page 915, is quite good here)
¼ cup chili powder, preferably wheat free
1 package (10 ounces) corn tortillas
8 ounces grated cheese (see note)

1. Preheat the oven to 350°F.

Chilaquiles

These are the Mexican equivalent of lasagna, with all of lasagna's heart-and-soul appeal plus a zap of south-of-the-border piquancy. Tortillas, preferably slightly stale, step in for pasta. Jan and I offered a version in the Dairy Hollow House Cookbook *called Ark-Mex Lasagna. (One restaurant in town has since adopted the phrase, calling their offerings "Ark-Mex Cuisine.") Here are some of my more recent faves. I must brag and mention that in 1997 I won the Newman's Own recipe contest, in the professional category, with my Chilaquiles Zona Rosa, opposite.*

2 Combine all of the beans with the tomatoes (including the tomato juice) and olives in a deep nonstick skillet, or one that has been sprayed with cooking spray, over medium-high heat. Stir in the salsa and chili powder. Bring to a boil. Stir well and lower the heat to a slow simmer. Cook, stirring occasionally, until the flavors have blended and the sauce has cooked down a bit, about 30 minutes.

3 Cover the bottom of an 11¾-by-7½-inch nonstick baking dish, or one that has been sprayed with cooking spray, with tortillas, halving or quartering a couple to fill in any blank spots. Ladle not quite half of the bean mixture over the tortillas, then top with almost half of the cheese. Repeat the layering two times, finishing with a scant layer of a bean-tomato mixture and cheese.

4 Bake, uncovered, until the casserole is heated through and cheese is nicely melted and bubbly, about 30 minutes.

NOTE

Claudia calls for mozzarella and uses twice as much; I prefer the reduced amount but I use a very sharp Cheddar or jack.

Chilaquiles Zona Rosa

In 1997, I entered and, much to my own astonishment, won (in the Food Professionals category) the Newman's Own recipe contest, with this simplified version of chilaquiles. The prize: a free trip to New York, a stay at the Waldorf, and lunch at the Rainbow Room with Paul Newman, Joanne Woodward, the other winners and their guests, and scads of media folks, plus $10,000 to give to my favorite charities.

There is every reason to buy the Newman's Own stuff. The products are good, some quite good, and the intent is even better: 100 percent of the after-tax profits are donated to charity.

Here is the award-winner, simple and very pleasing, proof that "shameless exploitation in pursuit of the common good" as the Newman's folks say, can be very tasty indeed. **SERVES 6 TO 8**

12 corn tortillas
Cooking spray
2 jars (23 ounces total) Newman's Own Medium Salsa
2 packages (16 ounces total) neufchâtel reduced-fat cream cheese, at room temperature
2 large eggs
2 tablespoons cornstarch
About 2 small zucchini, cut crosswise into ¼-inch rounds to yield 2 cups, or 2 cups sliced string beans
1¼ cups fresh corn kernels
1 cup (4 ounces) shredded sharp Cheddar or Monterey Jack cheese

1 Tear or cut the tortillas into quarters. Place the tortilla pieces on a jelly-roll pan. Let stand, uncovered, for at least 1 hour or overnight.

2 Lightly coat a 9-by-13-inch glass or enamel-clad baking dish with cooking spray. Spread ½ cup of the Newman's Own Salsa over the bottom and scatter one-third of the tortilla pieces over the salsa.

3 Place 1 cup of the remaining salsa in a food processor with the neufchâtel, eggs, and cornstarch. Buzz until well combined, pausing from time to time to scrape down the sides. Set aside. In a separate bowl, combine the zucchini (or beans) with the fresh corn. Set aside.

4 Preheat the oven to 350°F.

5 Spoon half of the egg mixture over the tortillas in the dish (it will not cover them completely). Scatter the vegetables over the filling, spreading them out with the back of a spoon. Drizzle another ½ cup salsa over the top. Make another layer using one-third of the tortillas. Cover with remaining cheese mixture, and top with remaining tortillas, then pour the remaining salsa over the top. Cover tightly with aluminum foil and bake for 40 minutes.

6 Uncover; sprinkle with the shredded cheese. Raise the oven temperature to 375°F and bake until the cheese is melted and browned, 10 to 12 minutes. Let stand for 10 minutes, then slice and serve.

CINCO DE MAYO ON THE MOONSHINE PATIO

Freshly squeezed orange juice / mango margaritas

*

Iced wedges of cantaloupe, watermelon, and papaya with lime

*

Chilaquiles Verde Pinto Beans and Potatoes (PAGE 378), with scrambled eggs

*

Roasty-Toasty Potatoes (PAGE 790)

*

Grilled soysage brushed with melted jalapeño jelly

*

Cinnamon rolls

*

Coffee / Mexican hot chocolate

Chilaquiles Verde with Pinto Beans and Potatoes

The heartiness of potatoes, beans, and corn tortillas combined with the delicacy of verde sauce and fresh greens, plus some irresistible cheese, makes a satisfying dish to which you will return time and again. You'll particularly find that this is a great brunch dish. **SERVES 8 TO 10**

1 package (10 ounces) corn tortillas, preferably stale
3 to 4 fist-sized red-skinned potatoes
Cooking spray (optional)
1 teaspoon to 1 tablespoon olive oil
1 large onion, diced
2 poblano chiles, seeds and membranes removed, diced
1½ teaspoons cumin seeds
3 cloves garlic, chopped
2 teaspoons paprika
Pinch of cayenne
1 small bunch fresh greens (such as chard, kale, mustard, turnip or collard greens, or fresh spinach), washed, tough stems removed, and sliced
Salt and freshly ground black pepper
3 cups dehydrated pinto bean flakes
2¼ cups boiling water, preferably spring or filtered
1 recipe Tomatillo Salsa Verde (page 944)
1 to 2 cups (4 to 8 ounces) grated sharp Cheddar cheese (optional)
Sour cream, reduced-fat sour cream, Yogurt Sour Cream, or Tofu Sour Cream (optional)
Chopped cilantro (optional)
Arkansalsa (page 913; optional)

1 Preheat the oven to 350°F.

2 Place the tortillas on a rack in the preheated oven and toast for about 10 minutes. Remove from the oven and break into large chunks. Set aside.

3 Bring a pot of water to a simmer over medium-high heat. Drop the whole potatoes in and simmer until just becoming tender, about 12 minutes. Drain well and cut into ½-inch dice, leaving the peel on. Set aside.

4 Heat the oil over medium heat in a large nonstick skillet or one that has been sprayed with cooking spray. Add the onion and sauté until it is almost translucent, about 4 minutes. Add the poblano and cumin seeds and sauté for another 3 minutes. Add the garlic, paprika, and cayenne and sauté for 1 minute more. Add the potatoes and cook, stirring, for another minute. Pop a tight-fitting lid on the skillet, lower the heat slightly, and steam for 3 minutes. Uncover and add the greens. Replace the lid and steam until the greens are limp, 1 to 3 minutes. Season with salt, pepper, and possibly additional cayenne to taste. Set aside.

5 Place the dehydrated bean flakes in a medium heatproof bowl and pour the boiling water over them. Stir a couple of times, cover, and let stand for 5 minutes. Uncover and stir again.

6 As the bean flakes rehydrate, begin assembling the chilaquiles: Drizzle about ¼ cup of the Tomatillo Salsa Verde over the bottom of an 11¾-by-7½-inch nonstick baking dish, or one that has been sprayed with cooking spray. Scatter about one third of the tortillas over the sauce. Top with the vegetable mixture. Scatter another one-third of the tortillas over the vegetables, along with a few tablespoons of the tomatillo sauce and half of the cheese, if using. Spoon on the beans and, using a knife, do the best you can to spread them evenly over the cheese (they are thick and hard to spread). Finish with a layer of the remaining tortillas and all of the remaining salsa. Cover tightly with waxed paper, then with foil. Bake until the casserole is bubbling hot, 25 to 35 minutes. Uncover and sprinkle with the remaining cheese. Raise

VARIATIONS

Variations on this dish are numberless. If you have some soysage on hand, grill it, chop or crumble it, and add a layer. A layer of Dairy Hollow House Summer Squash Pudding (page 296) is also a nice addition (pour it over the vegetable filling). You can substitute corn chips for the tortillas; tasty, but it amps the fat up considerably. Vegans can simply omit the cheese and have a perfectly acceptable dish. If you don't like tomatillos, which are what make the verde sauce verde, try Cupboard Enchilada Sauce (page 935). Another good once-in-a-while brunch dish: Use half the amount of rehydrated beans and add a layer of fluffy scrambled eggs.

the oven temperature to 450°F and bake until the cheese is melted and brown, 10 to 15 minutes. Remove from the oven and let stand for a few minutes to set before cutting. Serve hot, with any or all the optional garnishes on the side.

Jeanne's "Ramu-Fabu" Three-Bean and Ricotta Casserole

A homey comfort-food layered casserole: nothing fancy, exotic, or spicy, just hearty, easily improvised, and mild. But its plainness is deceptive—you think, "Well, this is good but not *that* good," but then find yourself rummaging in the refrigerator next morning scouting for leftovers. It's from seamstress Jeanne Ramu, who put together the Dairy Hollow tablecloths, dust ruffles, curtains, and even wall paddings with flair and fine attention to detail. **SERVES 6 TO 8**

Iced Herbal Cooler

This recipe was so constantly requested by Dairy Hollow guests back in the inn days that we actually reproduced it on a postcard. As red as the throat of a sunlit ruby-throated hummingbird, deeply refreshing, and easy as can be to make, a mason jar of Iced Herbal Cooler waited in each guest room's fridge in the hotter months of the year, a welcoming way for arriving guests to rehydrate. It's the perfect blend of sweet and tart, caffeine-free, and has carried over to the Writers' Colony, where it is the official beverage at Poetluck and many other events.

1 quart water, preferably spring or filtered, boiling; 8 Celestial Seasonings brand Red Zinger tea bags

1 large (12-ounce) container frozen unsweetened apple juice, thawed

1 quart water, preferably spring or filtered, cold

1 orange, halved

1 lemon, halved (optional)

FOR SERVING: orange, lime, and lemon slices; fresh spearmint sprigs; ice

Pour boiling water over tea bags and allow to steep at room temperature until cool. Lift out the tea bags and squeeze them, to get every drop of flavor out. Pour this extra-strong herbal tea into a pitcher with at least a 2¾-quart capacity. Add the apple juice concentrate and cold water. Stir well. Juice the halved orange directly into the pitcher. Taste; if you'd like it a bit more tart, add the juice of the lemon, too. Serve over ice in tall glasses, with a slice each of orange, lime, and lemon, plus a sprig of spearmint, in each glass.

Cooking spray
2 cups part-skim ricotta
1 large egg
Salt and freshly ground black pepper to taste
Freshly grated nutmeg to taste
1 box (10 ounces) frozen peas
2 teaspoons olive oil
1 onion, cut vertically into slivers
3 cloves garlic, pressed
1½ cups sliced button mushrooms
3 cups cooked brown rice, preferably brown basmati
3 cups cooked (1½ cups dry) Jeanne Ramu's Three-Bean Mix (recipe follows)
1 cup bean cooking liquor
1 cup Breadcrumb Topping Provençal (page 277), using soft crumbs

1 Preheat the oven to 350°F.

2 Spray a deep 10-by-12-inch casserole with cooking spray. Set aside.

3 Combine the ricotta and egg with salt, pepper, and nutmeg to taste in a small bowl. Beat with a fork until well blended and set aside.

4 Pour the frozen peas into a strainer, and place under very hot running tap water until barely thawed but still bright green. Drain well and pat dry. Set aside.

5 Heat the oil in a nonstick skillet, or one that has been sprayed with cooking spray, over medium heat. Add the onion and sauté until starting to become translucent, about 3 minutes. Add the garlic and the mushrooms and stir-fry for 3 minutes. Add the peas to the mushroom mixture and stir to combine. Remove from the heat and set aside.

6 Press the rice into the bottom of the prepared casserole. Spread the cooked beans over the rice, then make a layer of the ricotta mixture. Spread the vegetable mixture over the ricotta. Cover tightly with foil. Bake for 40 minutes. Uncover and raise the oven temperature to 450°F. Sprinkle the breadcrumb topping over the top of the casserole. Return to the oven and bake until golden brown and crunchy, 10 to 15 minutes.

VARIATIONS

Substitute any of the following for the mushroom-pea mixture: 2 to 3 cups of your favorite tomato sauce or other vegetable sauce, such as "Macro Red" Sauce (page 936); 1 bag (16 ounces) frozen corn, broccoli, or red pepper mix; 2 to 3 cups blanched or leftover broccoli, cauliflower, butternut squash, or, in fact, any vegetable you particularly like.

DAIRY-FREE LAYERED THREE-BEAN CASSEROLE: ***Combine 1 package (16 ounces) fresh firm conventional tofu with egg and seasonings in place of the ricotta. For a vegan version, replace the egg with 2 tablespoons cornstarch, diluted in a little water and mashed into the tofu.***

Jeanne Ramu's Three-Bean Mix

Jeanne does not presoak the beans, and it's not neccesary. However, as with all beans, the presoak-and-discard-soaking-water technique does help draw off those troublesome gas-producing compounds.

Azuki beans
Black-eyed peas
Mung beans

Purchase an equal portion of each of the three beans. Combine and store them, preferably in a glass jar, where you can admire their beautiful contrasting shapes and colors. The bean mix keeps well and is very versatile, so you can make up a large quantity at a time; 1⅓ cups of each bean type yields, when combined, a quart jar full. When you want to cook the beans, pour out as much as needed, presoak or quick-soak the beans as you prefer, and cook according to the basic directions given on pages 597-98.

NOTE

RICOTTA SORTA-SALATA: ***Ricotta salata is a pleasing, mild cheese, firm enough to slice, pure white, amiable, with a bit more salty bite to it than creamy fresh ricotta. It's not easy to find in northwest Arkansas, so I occasionally fake it with my Ricotta Sorta-Salata, made by creaming together 1 cup part-skim ricotta, 2 ounces feta cheese, and 1 ounce neufchâtel reduced-fat cream cheese in the food processor. Not authentic, but it does the trick.***

Eggplant Gratin with Ricotta Custard and Parmesan

The traditional version of this Provençal dish is thick with heavy cream, *and* olive oil, *and* Parmesan cheese, *and* eggs. I have "enlightened" it not only for nutritional sanity but because to my taste eggplant is much, much more delicious when its precooking does not take place in a bath of olive (or any other) oil.

Remember, you must have prepared tomato sauce and the eggplants on hand before you start. For all that, it's fairly straightforward: Cooked eggplant slices topped with torn basil line a gratin dish or casserole, are topped first with tomato sauce, then with a light custard, finished with Parmesan cheese and nice herby breadcrumbs, and baked. **SERVES 4 AS AN ENTREE, 6 AS A SIDE DISH**

Cooking spray
2 medium-large eggplants, thinly sliced and soaked in salt water for 15 minutes
½ cup stale but not crisp-dry breadcrumbs
2 cloves garlic
2 tablespoons chopped Italian parsley
1 teaspoon olive oil
3 ounces neufchâtel reduced-fat cream cheese, softened
1 large egg
2 teaspoons cornstarch or arrowroot
½ cup evaporated skim milk
Several gratings of fresh nutmeg
Salt and freshly ground black pepper to taste
¼ pound ricotta salata, crumbled (see note)
8 to 10 fresh basil leaves
1½ cups Basic Wintertime Italian Tomato Sauce (page 931)
2 ounces (about ½ cup) freshly grated Parmesan cheese

1 Preheat the oven to 375°F.

2 Spray a jelly-roll pan and a medium gratin dish or casserole with cooking spray. Set aside.

3 Rinse the salt water off the eggplant slices under cold running water. Pat dry. Lay the eggplant out on the prepared jelly-roll pan. Cover the pan tightly with foil and bake until softened, about 15 minutes. Remove from the oven and set aside.

4 Combine the breadcrumbs with the garlic, parsley, and oil in a food processor. Buzz, pulsing as needed, until the garlic and parsley are finely minced. Transfer the crumb mixture to a small bowl and set aside.

5 Without washing the food processor, make the binding custard: Combine the neufchâtel, egg, cornstarch, and 2 tablespoons of the evaporated skim milk in the food processor. Pulse until the mixture is fairly smooth, pausing from time to time to scrape down the sides. With the motor running, pour in the remaining evaporated skim milk. Season to taste with nutmeg, salt, and pepper. Add the crumbled ricotta salata and pulse to just combine. Do not puree, as you want chunks of ricotta salata remaining in the mixture.

6 Line the bottom of the prepared gratin dish with about half of the eggplant. Tear up the basil and scatter it over the eggplant. Top with the tomato sauce. Add another layer of eggplant, then pour the binding custard over it. Sprinkle the Parmesan over the custard, then cover with the breadcrumb mixture. Bake until the crumbs are golden brown and crisp, about 30 minutes.

Tempeh and Mushroom Stuffed Scalloped Potatoes

Layers of the old-fashioned American side dish of creamy potatoes embrace a satisfying filling of tomato-sauced tempeh and mushrooms, taking this ideal-for-a-potluck dish to a lasagna-esque main course. While a majority of those who know and love tempeh have probably cut back on dairy products (or cut them out altogether), the creamy deliciousness of the cheeses and milk have a nice compatability with tempeh, as well as with mushrooms and potatoes.

SAFE-FROM-THE-SLEET FEBRUARY DINNER

Avial
(PAGE 195)

*

The Salad
(PAGE 68)

*

Tempeh and Mushroom Stuffed Scalloped Potatoes

*

Compote of Poached Bananas and Star Fruit with Dried Cherries
(PAGE 965)

I find that scalloped potatoes really need a modest lashing of heavy cream to reach the sublime state, but one can use considerably less than the standard and have a dish that will still appeal to the die-hard scalloped potato lover. **SERVES 8 TO 10**

- **2 cups evaporated skim milk, or whole milk**
- **½ cup heavy cream**
- **1 clove garlic, sliced**
- **1 bay leaf**
- **Salt and freshly ground black pepper to taste**
- **2 packages (16 ounces total) tempeh, cut into ½-inch cubes**
- **1 to 2 teaspoons butter or olive oil**
- **Cooking spray**
- **5 cups sliced button or cremini mushrooms**
- **3 cups Basic Wintertime Italian Tomato Sauce (page 931), or any good bottled tomato sauce**
- **3 ounces neufchâtel reduced-fat cream cheese**
- **1 tablespoon cornstarch**
- **1 cup shredded mozzarella or Cheddar**
- **¼ cup freshly grated Parmesan cheese**
- **2 pounds russet potatoes, peeled and cut crosswise into ⅛-inch-thick slices**

1 Preheat the oven to 350°F.

2 Combine the evaporated skim milk, cream, garlic, bay leaf, 1⅛ teaspoons salt, and pepper to taste in a small saucepan over medium heat. Bring to a simmer. Immediately remove from the heat and let stand for 10 minutes.

3 Place the tempeh cubes in a steaming basket over boiling water. Steam for 8 minutes.

4 Melt the butter in a nonstick skillet, or one that has been sprayed with cooking spray, over medium heat. Add the mushrooms and sauté until the mushrooms are limp, about 5 minutes. Add the tomato sauce and cook for 1 minute. Remove from the heat and stir in the steamed tempeh. Add salt and pepper to taste. Set aside.

5 Remove and discard the bay leaf from the milk mixture. Transfer about one-third of the milk mixture to a food processor. Add the neufchâtel and cornstarch and buzz until smooth. Set aside.

6 Combine the mozzarella and Parmesan in a small bowl and set aside.

7 Spray a 3-quart baking dish, about 3 inches deep, with cooking spray. Pat the potato slices with a paper towel to absorb excess moisture. Place half of the potatoes, slightly overlapping, in the prepared baking dish. Pour half of the milk mixture over the potatoes and sprinkle with half of the cheese mixture. Spoon the tempeh-mushroom filling over the cheeses. Top with the remaining potato slices, overlapping slightly. Pour the last of the milk over the top. Cover the baking dish with a piece of waxed paper, then with foil.

8 Bake for 30 minutes. Remove the casserole from the oven and uncover. Sprinkle the potatoes with the remaining cheese mixture. Return to the oven and bake until the potatoes are tender and the cheese is a deep, crusty golden brown, 30 to 40 minutes.

Stuffed Vegetables

Captivatingly plump, self-contained stuffed vegetables have infinite variety. Two or three kinds, perched on a plate, make a charming gift-wrapped offering, but even a single stuffed vegetable is interesting, each bite containing the pleasing contradictions of vegetable carrying-case and cargo. Given most stuffings' amiable ability to use up little bits of this and that, it's no wonder that stuffed vegetables are found worldwide.

They abound throughout the Mediterranean. Italy's offerings are wonderful; in the Middle East everything from artichokes to zucchini, olives to grape leaves, are stuffed. Greece has its dolmades, Turkey its dolma. In Israel, stuffed vegetables are a distinct category of dishes called *memuleh,* meaning "filled." Occasionally, these regional stuffings contain meat, but even when they do, it's usually a minor ingredient, which makes the classics easy to revise. Traveling east, garlicky, basil-touched, bread-crumb-based stuffings give over to rice, fragrant with dill and olive oil, sometimes with nuts, dried or fresh fruits, sometimes with a little cheese, often feta. Journeying further east, we see these same ingredients in many guises throughout Russia, with fillings joined by mushrooms, again dill, and often potatoes. In Georgian Russia, the stuffings are a world unto themselves, rich with walnuts and the surprising kick of coriander combined with other green herbs. In India, though stuffed vegetables are not an everyday fixture as in so many other countries, the occasional stuffed vegetable, portly and redolent of coriander, chile, ginger, and countless of the other flavor-deities from India's spice pantheon, does put in an appearance.

In contrast, what American stuffed vegetables come to mind? Only two: "twice-baked potato" and that '50s fixture, boiled-to-within-an-inch-of-its-life green bell pepper with a beef-rice filling. Today's vegetarian table boasts many inventive vegetable stuffings. A few come to mind: corn pudding, tomato pudding, greens puddings, spoonbread, jazzed-up succotashes, mashed potato combos, creamed spinach and other greens, various beans and refried bean concoctions, as well as the Southwestern stir-fry of diced squash known as calabacitas. And there's stuffing itself—you know, the kind that, south of the Mason-Dixon line, becomes "dressing": that bready mixture that goes into the cavity of the turkey on Thanksgiving. These fantastical, uniquely American mixtures of bread, onion, stock, melted butter, herbs, and perhaps diced fresh and dried fruit can fill all kinds of things, on all kinds of occasions (for Thanksgiving, at our house, *always* a pumpkin; see page 428).

The most commonly stuffed vegetables are bell peppers; their almost-empty cavities make them a natural. And there are more interesting pepper-frontiers beyond bells: poblanos, long, triangulated, an almost-black green, wondrous in their chocolate-y sweet-hotness; sassy, seriously hot jalapeños; pale yellow banana peppers. While a garlicky stuffed mushroom is a fixture on many old-fashioned Italian restaurant menus (as is, less often, a similarly stuffed artichoke), stuffed mushrooms have wider shores: portobellos and large shiitakes stuffed with lighter fillings are new and fresh today. Tomatoes, innards scooped out, are another old fave that can be updated. The small cavity in most winter squashes can be enlarged for stuffing; the soft row of seeds in the center of yellow summer squash or zucchini can be removed. An eggplant, potato or sweet potato, a chayote (also known as a mirliton) can, with a little hollowing-out, be stuffable. And then there are the large edible leaves, which come out like little gift-wrapped packages when stuffed, plump and rotund. Cabbage leaves, red-veined chard leaves, grape leaves, or lettuce leaves can all be stuffed.

So consider the alphabetical parade of stuffed vegetable recipes that follows as just a starting point. Look throughout this chapter and indeed the whole book for cross-references; frequently, especially in recipe variations, you'll find suggestions for particular stir-fries or timbales or medleys or grain mixes or purees that also work well as stuffings.

Stuffed Artichokes

My friend, traveler (and travel agent) extraordinaire, Fred Poe, said in the *Arkansas Times,* "The artichoke is a strange vegetable. After we think we have consumed it, there seems to be more of it than when we began." True, but the point is not those great stacks of leftover discarded leaves but the part you *do* eat.

> *"[Her] mother died at a suitable age without pain, lifting the leaf of a stuffed artichoke to her lips, saying, Delicious!"* —**Ellen Douglass,** *Can't Quit You, Baby*

Artichokes are from the thistle family. You see the family resemblance in the inedible (inedible meaning rough and fibrous, not poisonous) stickery cluster of hairy fiber and sharp-pointed immature leaves, usually with a faint purple cast, which cling in the core of the artichoke, protecting the heart. Buried deep within the leaves, this "choke" must be removed. But there is an up side to the hassle: When this fortress called the choke has been removed, a cavity is created in which stuffing may be placed, to noble effect.

The ideal point and method for choke removal depends on the recipe. For some recipes, such as those where the artichoke is to be braised whole, the choke must be excised when the artichoke is intact and raw. This is time consuming and tedious and I rarely do it. It's slightly easier to remove the choke when the raw artichoke is halved or quartered; but again, time consuming. There is only one recipe I am willing to do this for: Fresh Slow-Baked Artichoke Quarters with Minted Crumbs (page 681), and directions for removing the choke are given there. However, choke-removal is simplicity itself when the artichoke is cooked.

Choose compact, plump, evenly green artichokes (or green with a blush of reddish purple), firm but not dried out, with few or no brown spots on the outer leaves. Avoid those whose outer leaves appear shriveled or dried into an exaggerated curl.

Here are several artichoke cooking and preparation plans.

COOKING ARTICHOKES: When preparing cooked artichokes for stuffing, allow one half per person if doing a horizontal stuff, one whole artichoke if doing a vertical stuff.

Trim the stem from each artichoke by cutting flat against the globe. Reserve the stems for cooking alongside the artichokes, regardless of the cooking method you select. The stems can be peeled, then either incorporated into the stuffing, or just nibbled as a cook's treat.

Many people go further than I do when trimming artichokes. Using a pair of sturdy kitchen shears or a knife, many cooks lop off the top inch or so of large artichokes, then they snip off the sharp portion of the tips of the remaining leaves. This seems to me needlessly fussy, so I rarely do it. The artichokes may now be boiled, steamed, or pressure-cooked.

▲ *Boiling* is predictable and easy, but the finished artichoke is often a bit sodden. Bring a large pot of water to a boil over high heat. Drop in the trimmed artichokes and return the water to a hard boil. Lower the heat to medium and simmer until tender, 40 to 50 minutes for very large artichokes, 30 to 40 minutes for medium, and 15 to 20 for those that are very small. You should keep the artichokes submerged in the boiling water, either by fitting them into the pot so that they hold each other in place or by placing a cover slightly smaller than the pot into the pot to keep the artichokes submerged.

▲ *Steaming* yields a better texture, but it does require attention, as you need to keep checking to make sure that the water hasn't boiled away. Place 1 to 2 inches of water into a large pot with a tight fitting lid, and place a fully opened metal steamer into the pot so that it sits just above the water. Fit whole artichokes tightly together and upright on the steamer rack. Bring the water to a boil and cover tightly. Steam the artichokes until done; the timing is about the same as for boiling. Remember to check frequently and add boiling water as needed to prevent burning.

▲ *Pressure-cooking,* to my mind, yields the best artichoke, and certainly the quickest. Place the trimmed artichokes on the rack that comes with the cooker, add ½ cup or so of water, and tighten the lid. Bring up the pressure and cook under pressure for 6 to 9 minutes, depending on the size of the artichokes. Using the pressure-release valve, quick-release the steam.

To tell if they're done—this goes for artichokes cooked by any method—tug at a leaf. It should come off with just a slight pull. It should not fall off. If it does, the artichoke is overcooked—still usable, but softer than desirable.

COOKED ARTICHOKES FOR HORIZONTAL STUFFING: Begin with cooked artichokes that are cool enough to handle (it's fine to run cold water over them). Cut each artichoke lengthwise in half. This will yield two halves, each of which must have the choke removed. Using a spoon tip and a paring knife, plus your fingers, pull out the soft inner leaves at the core. There will be some pale green spiny leaves, usually some with a purplish tinge, and then a brushy, fibrous core, growing right out of the heart. Carefully scoop and pull all of this out, leaving as much of the meaty heart as possible. This leaves you with two artichoke halves, each of which has a nice cavity.

COOKED ARTICHOKES FOR VERTICAL STUFFING: This is a trickier maneuver but the first part is fun. Hold the whole cooked artichoke upright, under rapidly running cold water. The force will open the artichoke partway, like a blooming flower. Further push the leaves out and reach into the center with a spoon, paring knife, or your fingers, and remove the inedible parts from the center. It's more challenging to surgically remove all of the chokey bits in this manner, but it can be done. This leaves a whole artichoke with a central cavity that can be stuffed and served standing upright on the plate.

COOKED ARTICHOKES FOR THE HEART AND BOTTOM: When you need slices of cooked artichoke for omelettes, gratins, and the like, simply pull off all of the cooked leaves, in one motion, bending them off in one cone-shaped clump to reveal the choke. Go after it with a spoon or your fingertips. And there you have it: a cup-shaped artichoke heart or bottom.

HOW TO EAT AN ARTICHOKE SERVED WITH DIPPING SAUCE: Tear off the leaves, one at a time. Grasping each at its pointed tip, dip the base end, which will be edged by a small strip of pale meaty flesh, into the sauce. Place the dipped end of the leaf in your mouth, between your teeth. Bite down, but not through, the leaf, and scrape off the tiny bit of succulent artichoke meat. Discard the remaining teeth-scraped leaf. Eventually, all the leaves will be gone and you'll have reached the heart. Grasping it whole with your fingers, you will have to remove the soft leaves and choke to ready the meat. Cut the heart into small bits and dip the meat into the dipping sauce.

To eat a stuffed artichoke, using a fork, eat the filling from the center first, alternating with one or two leaves from the outside of the globe. After the filling's gone, eat the leaf tips as described above. Then, once again, finish with the grand heart.

Fresh Artichoke Half with Black-Eyed Pea Salad and Yogurt Dipping Sauce

This cold stuffed artichoke—a light entree for a sweltering night, a more substantial starter for a light entree—consists of two small cold dishes that can be prepared in advance. And be sure to prep the artichokes at least the day before you put the finished dish together. For this reason, it is a great party dish. The Black-Eyed Pea Salad and Yogurt Dipping Sauce are good in and of themselves, but become extra special when teamed with artichoke. The salad is lightly dressed with vinaigrette; if desired, you can serve extra oil and vinegar, lemon juice, or your favorite vinaigrette on the side.

The final stuffing and plating can take place a couple of hours before serving. Then, the only last-minute deal is the garnish: a breeze, especially considering how attractive the artichokes are on the plate. This is lovely served with warm, crisp garlic toast. **SERVES 8**

VARIATION

VEGAN VARIATION: ***Don't use hard-cooked egg in the salad. Make a tofu-based sauce by buzzing 2 packages (10½ ounces each) silken tofu with 2 tablespoons olive oil and the mustard in the processor.***

BLACK-EYED PEA SALAD

2½ cups cooked black-eyed peas (fresh or canned), well drained
2 cloves garlic, pressed
¼ red onion, sliced paper-thin
2 teaspoons finely chopped fresh dill
2 teaspoons to 2 tablespoons good, fruity extra virgin olive oil
Juice of ½ to 1 lemon
¼ teaspoon sugar
Salt and lots of freshly ground black pepper to taste
1 hard-cooked egg, finely minced (optional)

YOGURT DIPPING SAUCE

2 cups plain yogurt, or low-fat (not fat-free) sour cream
¼ cup coarse Dijon mustard
½ cup coarsely scissored fresh dill
Fresh dill sprigs

TO FINISH

4 artichokes, cooked and halved for horizontal stuffing (see page 387)
Any or all of the following: confetti of red, yellow, and green bell peppers; finely minced Italian parsley;
2 lemons, quartered lengthwise

1 A day or two before putting the dish together, prepare the Black-Eyed Pea Salad: Combine the black-eyed peas with the garlic, onion, and dill in a nonreactive bowl. Stir in the oil and lemon juice. Season with the sugar and salt and pepper to taste. If using, stir in the egg. Cover and set aside to marinate, refrigerated, for at least 8 hours or up to 3 days. Before using, taste and, if necessary, season with additional dill, lemon juice, oil, salt, and/or pepper.

2 At least 8 hours (or up to 2 days) before using, prepare the Yogurt Dipping Sauce: Combine the yogurt and mustard in a small bowl. Stir in the dill. Cover and refrigerate until ready to use. A few hours before serving, divide the dip among eight 2-ounce ramekins or glass dishes; even teacups. Garnish each with a fresh dill sprig; cover with plastic wrap and refrigerate.

3 No more than 4 hours before serving, mound the artichoke halves with the Black-Eyed Pea Salad. When ready to serve, place on chilled plates and scatter the bell

. . . on Garnishing

"I have carved carrots, beets, potatoes, parsnips, and other root vegetables in shapes like flowers. Now what was the trouble with all that? The patrons were made too much aware that the food had been handled. After all the food is to be eaten. But there was a further difficulty and that was in the time element."

—Henri Charpentier,
Those Rich and Great Ones, or Life à la Henri

pepper and/or parsley around the edge of each plate. Place a lemon wedge and a ramekin of dip on each plate.

COOK ONCE FOR 2 MEALS Make twice the recipe for Black-Eyed Pea Salad. Divide it in half and add a diced tomato, chopped scallions, a diced roasted red bell pepper, and a good double-handful of cooked green beans to one half. Season to taste and serve as a main-dish salad with a skillet of hot cornbread.

Artichoke Stuffed with Eggplant-Lentil Caponata

A hot stuffed, gratinéed artichoke half filled with luscious savory caponata under the crisp crumbs—oh my! Caponata is a slightly sweet vegetable dish of Italian origin, rich with tender-cooked eggplant, tomatoes, sometimes zucchini—really whatever is at hand in the garden and kitchen.

Lentils make the caponata more main dish than relish. Inn guests used to love this dish as part of various vegetarian entree plates. Allow half an artichoke per person if you are also offering a salad and bread or a grain dish. **MAKES 8 STUFFED ARTICHOKE HALVES; SERVES 4 AS AN ENTREE**

4 large artichokes, cooked and halved for horizontal stuffing (see page 387)
Cooking spray (optional)
About ½ recipe Eggplant-Lentil Caponata (recipe follows)
⅔ cup fresh soft breadcrumbs
3 cloves garlic, pressed
1 teaspoon olive oil

1 Preheat the oven to 375°F.

2 Lay the artichoke halves, cut side up, in a nonstick baking dish, or one that has been sprayed with cooking spray, large enough to easily accommodate them. Generously mound the caponata into each cavity.

3 Combine the breadcrumbs with the garlic and oil. Press the crumb mixture onto the caponata to completely cover.

Bake until the crumbs are brown and the artichokes are heated through, 35 to 40 minutes.

Eggplant-Lentil Caponata

Caponata is traditionally used as a warm vegetable side dish, at room temperature as a spread on bread, as a relish, or as a first course. It is a bit more relishlike than its French or Russian cousins, ratatouille or G'vetch (page 749); the vegetables are cut smaller and cooked to almost a puree, and there's a definite sweet-sour tang, as well as the occasional addition of olives or capers or both. Typically made with enough olive oil to float an armada, here it's lightened considerably. **MAKES ABOUT 4 CUPS**

1 cup lentils
2½ cups vegetable stock (see page 139)
2 bay leaves
½ cup raisins
1 tablespoon olive oil
Cooking spray (optional)
1 eggplant, sliced, soaked in salt water for 30 minutes, drained, and cut into ¼-inch dice (I like to leave the skin on; you may peel it if you prefer)
1 zucchini, quartered lengthwise, seeded, then cut crosswise into ¼-inch slices
1 to 2 cups Basic Wintertime Italian Tomato Sauce (page 931), or fine-quality commercially made tomato sauce
2 tablespoons honey
1 tablespoon red-wine or balsamic vinegar
2 tablespoons finely chopped fresh basil
Salt and freshly ground black pepper to taste

1. Place the lentils in a medium saucepan. Add the stock and bay leaves and place over medium-high heat. Bring to a simmer and lower the heat. Simmer until the lentils are almost tender, about 30 minutes. Add the raisins and cook until the lentils are tender but not mushy, about 10 more minutes. You may need to add a little more liquid or you may have to drain off excess liquid. You want a fairly dry mixture.

2. Heat the oil in a large nonstick skillet, or one that has been sprayed with cooking spray, over medium heat. Add the eggplant and zucchini and lower the heat. Sauté for 10 minutes, then cover, occasionally lifting the lid to stir, until tender, 5 to 6 minutes.

3. Add the tomato sauce, honey, and vinegar. Stir in the basil. Add the drained lentil mixture. Cook until heated through, about 3 minutes. Taste and, if necessary, add salt and pepper. You're aiming for something a bit "relishy"—like a sweet-sour ratatouille, so you may need some extra honey and/or vinegar. Use immediately or transfer to a nonreactive container. Cover and refrigerate for up to 1 week.

COOK ONCE FOR 2 MEALS This caponata keeps, refrigerated, for 1 week, or frozen for several months. Although this is a large batch, why not double it, portion it into zippered freezer bags, and freeze? In addition to artichoke-stuffing, it can be used to stuff other vegetables. It can fill crêpes, tortillas, or omelets; top a plate of fettucine or mashed potatoes; cap a pizza.

These Leaves Are Made for Stuffing: Cabbage

Resign yourself to the fact that with this stuffed cabbage style you will only use the big outer leaves, which will leave a small, inner ball of slightly cooked cabbage to be stir-fried later (see also the piroshki filling on page 352). Understand also that because the cabbage and its leaves are in and out of boiling water several times, the process is a little messy. There ought to be a simpler way to do this, but I haven't found it.

Bring a large pot of water to a boil over high heat. Have a pair of tongs and a skimmer (if you have one) ready. Carefully cut off any of the big, semi-unfurled outer leaves that are barely attached to the main head. Drop the leaves, a few at a time, into the boiling water and, as soon as they wilt (30 seconds or so), remove them with the tongs, setting them on paper towels to dry.

As you work your way into the cabbage, you will quickly come to leaves that are more definitively attached to and curled around the head. Though they usually cannot be removed without tearing, they are still large enough for stuffing. Score these leaves at their base, where they join the cabbage, carefully curl them back from the top, as much as they will yield without tearing. Then, place the whole cabbage on a skimmer and gently lower it into the boiling water. Cook for 40 to 50 seconds, then lift the cabbage out of the water with the skimmer or tongs. Let cool briefly and, using a sharp knife, cut off two or three of the now-pliable outer leaves along the base, where you scored them. Repeat until you get the requisite number of leaves. Drain the cabbage leaves on paper towels. Expect a few tears and ragged edges but don't worry about 'em.

Middle European–Style Stuffed Cabbage-Leaf Rolls

The faintly sweet-sour, dill-accented flavor that is characteristic of many middle European dishes has always held great appeal to me. The sweet, in this case, comes from raisins, a touch of honey, and slightly caramelized onion; the sour from tomatoes and yogurt or low-fat sour cream. I used to make the filling with full-fat sour cream and ground beef but I've used these substitutions for some years now with very pleasing results. This is a hearty, wintry, comforting dish. Add thick slices of grainy sourdough rye toast, a lightly dressed green salad with grated fresh beets, and perhaps an intensely orange vegetable such as baked acorn squash or sweet potato.

SERVES 4 OR 5

18 to 22 blanched cabbage leaves for stuffing (see previous page)

STUFFING

1 teaspoon vegetable oil
Cooking spray
1 large onion, chopped
1 clove garlic, pressed
1½ cups cooked (or one 15.8-ounce can) Great Northern beans, well drained
1 slice whole wheat bread
2½ cups cooked brown rice, preferably brown basmati
⅓ cup raisins
¼ cup coarsely chopped toasted walnuts
2 tablespoons fresh minced dill, or 2½ teaspoons dry dill weed
Salt and freshly ground black pepper to taste

TOPPING/SAUCE

2 teaspoons cornstarch dissolved in 2 teaspoons water
1 cup chopped fresh or canned tomatoes with juice
1 tablespoon honey
½ cup Yogurt Sour Cream (page 910), or reduced-fat sour cream
Fresh dill sprigs (optional)

1 Heat the oil in a large nonstick skillet, or one that has been sprayed with cooking spray, over medium heat. Add the onion and cook, stirring, until it is translucent and just barely starting to brown on the edges, 8 to 10 minutes. Remove the skillet from the heat and stir in the garlic. Let cool slightly.

2 Combine ½ cup of the beans and the slice of bread in a blender. Pulse to make a thick paste. Scrape into the sautéed onions and garlic. Add the brown rice, raisins, walnuts, dill, and the remaining beans. Add salt and pepper to taste. Toss well. Taste and, if necessary, adjust the seasonings.

3 Preheat the oven to 375°F.

4 Place the bean stuffing and the blanched cabbage leaves on a counter or other work surface, along with a nonstick 8-inch square baking dish or one that has been sprayed with cooking spray.

5 Lay a large leaf out on the work surface. Trim out the lower portion of the tough, hard center vein that is present in most of the larger leaves, and pull the cut edges up on top of each other to make a somewhat rough and ragged leaf circle. Spoon 2 to 3 tablespoons of the filling about ½ inch from the stem end of the leaf, and mound it into a stubby cigar shape. Fold the leaf edges over the filling, then fold the top over and gently roll the leaf up over the filling to make a fairly neat packet. Don't worry if it looks a little funky, tries to fall apart, or if you can see a bit of the filling through a tear in the leaf. Just tuck it into the dish, seam side down. Continue trim-

ming, filling, and rolling until all the leaves are stuffed. When you come to the smaller leaves, slightly overlap a couple to make one bigger leaf and proceed as above. Reserve one leaf and cut it into pieces as needed to patch any tears or holes. You may have some stuffing left over.

6 Divide the cornstarch mixture in half. Add half to the chopped tomatoes, along with the honey. Add the other half to the Yogurt Sour Cream. Spoon the tomato mixture here and there over the stuffed cabbage rolls. Spoon the Yogurt Sour Cream mixture onto the cabbage, covering the spots left untouched by the tomatoes. Cover and bake for 20 minutes. Uncover and bake until the Yogurt Sour Cream has browned slightly, the tomatoes have thickened, and the dish is piping, bubbling hot, 35 to 40 minutes. Serve at once, with a fresh dill sprig on top of each roll, if desired. If you have extra filling, warm it and serve a little scoop beside the cabbage rolls, or save to use as a pilaf over the next day or two.

These Leaves Are Made for Stuffing: Chard

Chard is like two vegetables in one. While the lower part of the center rib is tough, it's easily removed, and, when diced, can become part of a chard filling or served as a vegetable in its own right.

With a sharp knife, make a skinny upside-down V-shaped cut starting from the base of each washed chard leaf along either side of the rib and extending up about 3 inches. Unless the leaves are exceptionally large, this will remove the tough part of the ribs. If using the cut out ribs in the stuffing, cut them into ¼-inch dice. The diced ribs may be sautéed or blanched with the leaves, as follows.

Bring a large pot of water to a vigorous boil. Drop in the leaves and, if desired, the diced stems. As soon as the leaves brighten in color and soften, less than a minute, drain quickly and rinse.

To use the leaves for stuffing, slightly overlap the bottom of each leaf along the space where you removed the rib. This gives you a more or less long, oval-shaped leaf. Mound ¼ to ⅓ cup filling into a lozenge shape on top of the overlapped part. Fold the long side of the leaves in and over the filling, then roll up to make a fairly neat packet. Place the stuffed chard leaves in a baking dish that has been sprayed with cooking spray and proceed as the specific recipe directs.

CD's Favorite Luscious Stuffed Chard Packets

Among stuffed green leaves, these are my favorites. With its showy veining and slightly crumpled texture, chard is visually alluring as well as easy to work with—much easier than cabbage or grape leaves. When very fresh, chard (particularly red chard, with vibrant contrasting hues of crimson stalk and dark green leaf) almost jumps with life and vitality. I always think of the Dylan Thomas lines "The force that through the green fuse drives the flower / Drives my green age . . . "

In this recipe, chard's faint lemony tang is accented by additional lemon. A few sweet notes in the filling, which rather resembles a warm tabbouleh, appealingly play off this tartness. No sauce is needed; a simple scatter of tomatoes with a splash of olive oil makes a delicious finish to a dish that is both simple and hedonistic.

You may well have a little stuffing left. Save it to eat cold for lunch. **MAKES 12 TO 16 ROLLS; SERVES 4 TO 6**

MY GREEN AGE

Iced Herbal Cooler
(PAGE 380)

*

Mediterranean Cornucopia of Olives
(PAGE 44)

*

Carrots Vichy
(PAGE 731)

*

Crusty bread with extra virgin olive oil and Bread Herbs for Dipping
(PAGE 904)

*

CD's Favorite Luscious Stuffed Chard Pockets

*

Lemon-Glazed Tofu "Teasecake"
(PAGE 1009)

1 tablespoon olive oil
Cooking spray
1 large onion, chopped medium fine
2 carrots, diced
12 to 16 blanched red or green chard leaves, for stuffing (see previous page), stems diced and reserved
4 to 6 cloves garlic, chopped medium fine
1 lemon
3 tomatoes, 1 peeled, seeded, and diced, the other 2 cut into eighths
2½ cups cooked bulghur (coarse cracked wheat)
⅔ cup minced Italian parsley
⅓ cup minced spearmint (optional but delicious; however, if you're not sure about this, you can use less)
⅓ cup raisins or currants
⅔ cup crumbled feta cheese
Salt and freshly ground black pepper to taste

1 Preheat the oven to 350°F.

2 Heat 1 teaspoon of the oil in a large, deep nonstick skillet, or one that has been sprayed with cooking spray, over medium heat. Add the onion and sauté until it starts to get limp, 4 minutes. Add the carrots and chard stems. Raise the heat slightly and sauté for about 3 minutes. Lower the heat to very low and add the garlic. Sauté for an additional minute. Scrape the mixture into a large bowl.

VARIATION

VEGAN STUFFED CHARD PACKETS À LA GREQUE ***are easily made. Omit the feta, and substitute ⅔ cup ready-ground tofu. Both of the Cook Once for 2 Meals options also work for this vegan version.***

3 Grate the lemon rind, and add 1 teaspoon to the vegetable mixture. Juice the lemon through a strainer into the vegetable mixture. Stir to blend.

4 Add the diced tomato, bulghur, parsley, spearmint, raisins, and feta. Toss together to blend. Taste and season with salt and lots of pepper.

5 Spray a 10-by-15-inch nonreactive glass or enamel baking dish with cooking spray.

6 Stuff the chard leaves as directed on page 394 and place them, seam side down, in the prepared baking dish. Tuck a tomato wedge between each chard packet and its neighbor. Drizzle the remaining oil over the top.

7 Cover the casserole tightly with foil. Bake for 45 minutes. Uncover and bake until bubbling, 10 to 15 minutes. Serve hot, warm, or at room temperature, with a little of the pan sauce spooned over each packet.

COOK ONCE FOR 2 MEALS Double the filling; double the blanched chard leaves. Use half of each to make the stuffed leaves. With the remaining, make Greek-Style Chard Calzones: Chop the remaining chard leaves and squeeze out any excess liquid (save it for the stock pot, if desired). Combine the chopped chard with the bulghur mixture and use it to fill a batch of Quick Yeasted Pizza Dough, Processor-Style (page 350), filling and baking as directed. Or use the half of the filling to make a main-dish tabbouleh, adding, perhaps, a little extra olive oil and lemon juice, a couple of diced raw tomatoes and scallions, and maybe a handful of kalamata olives. Serve cold or at room temperature.

Stuffed Eggplants

In America, the curvaceous eggplant is often breaded, deep-fried, tomato-sauced, blanketed under cheese, or grilled—a positive step—only to be drowned in excess vinaigrette. Little then remains of the vegetable's essential delicacy. Perhaps if we called it *aubergine,* as much of the rest of the world does, we would love and respect it more.

There is great variety in potential eggplant stuffings and even in the ways the vegetable can be cut to accommodate whatever deliciousness is in store for it.

TO PREPARE EGGPLANT FOR STUFFING: Eggplant is usually halved lengthwise and scooped out for stuffing. A small, delicate Japanese eggplant makes a portion size suitable for part of a component dinner; medium make a fine centerpiece entree; the large do likewise but present a huge serving. You can't really cut a cooked large stuffed eggplant in two, so the larger "aubergines" really don't lend themselves to stuffing.

Halve an eggplant lengthwise, right through the stem end, leaving a piece of the stem intact on each half. Cut off a tiny sliver and taste to see if there's any hint of bitterness. If there is, drop the eggplant halves into a large bowl of salted water (about ½ teaspoon salt to every quart of water), and weight them down with a heavy plate or skillet so they stay submerged. Let them soak for about 20 minutes.

Remove the eggplants from the salt water, rinse, and drain well. Pat dry.

Scoop out most but not all of the flesh, using a sharp knife to make the basic cuts and a spoon to dig (if you have one, a serrated-edge grapefruit spoon works well). You want to end up with a ½-inch-thick eggplant shell, which will provide a sturdy baking container. Almost immediately, the inner flesh will start to brown; don't worry, all will be fine in the finished dish. Usually the scooped-out eggplant flesh is used in the recipe.

Proceed as directed in the specific recipe.

To prepare pocketed slices of eggplant ("eggplant fillets") for stuffing: Essentially, with 5 cuts, you are going to create two large pocketed "fillets" per eggplant. This is one of those kitchen processes that is done in a flash, but sounds inordinately complex when put into words.

Here's how you do it:

1 Cut one: Slice off the stem end of the eggplant, as close to the stem as possible. This leaves you an oval-shaped eggplant with a squared-off top.

2 Cuts two and three: Vertically slice down from the stem end to the bottom, on the very edge of one side of the eggplant. The removed slice will be oval in outline, very thin at the top where the eggplant curves in, fatter in the middle where it curves out, and scooping in a bit at the base. Repeat this cut on the other side. Discard these two slices. This will leave an eggplant with two pale ivory flat sides (sometimes these cut sides will be tinged with green, and sometimes speckled with very visible brown seeds), and two slightly smaller curved sides that still have their purpley-black skin. It's squared off on top, where you removed the stem, but rounded on the bottom. This is the shape you want.

3 Cut four: Vertically slice the trimmed eggplant into equal halves straight down the middle, creating two fat slices, with large pale surface and curved edges with skin.

4 Cut five: Cut the fat slices in half parallel to the cutting board, as the though you are creating a pocket in a pita. Start your cut on the round end and top ½ inch short of the squared stem end, so that the slices will remain connected. Repeat with the second eggplant slice and proceed as directed in the specific recipe.

To prepare eggplant to be stuffed sandwich-style: Carefully cut the stem off of the eggplant. Slice, crosswise, into ¼- to ⅓-inch thick rounds. Try to keep the slices in order, since each slice will only fit perfectly with the one next to it.

To prepare eggplant for eggplant rolls: Using large eggplants, remove the stems and slice lengthwise into six to eight ¼-inch-thick ovals. You will also get 2 small, thin pieces with skin from each side. Proceed as directed in the specific recipe.

DINNER FOR THE ANNUAL *CASABLANCA* WATCHING

Morocc'n'Roll Oven-Roasted Carrot Spread (PAGE 13) with Pita Bread Toasts (PAGE 30)

*

Raw vegetable basket of cut-up carrots and celery sticks, whole white and red radishes, and cherry tomatoes

*

Mediterranean Cornucopia of Olives (PAGE 44)

*

Stuffed Eggplant Halves with Zhoug, Spinach, and Barley and Morocc'n' Roll Seven-Vegetable Seven-Spice Tagine with Couscous (PAGE 398)

*

Feta cheese and fresh figs

*

Medjool dates stuffed with almonds

Stuffed Eggplant Halves with Zhoug, Spinach, and Barley

An unusual, not-for-everybody eggplant dish of Yemenite origin, this will please the more adventurous eater and the long-time vegetarian.

Please note that, yes, the onion is raw when it goes into the filling, and the scooped-out eggplant pulp is baked rather than sautéed before it goes into the filling. This is because sautéed eggplant is a notorious oil-hog; its spongy texture just soaks it up. Baking also dries out the eggplant a bit, allowing for more distinct pieces, which keeps the filling from getting soggy. Speaking of which, barley or cooked whole-grain wheat is used because they both maintain their shape and texture better than rice.

For the ready-ground tofu, Tree of Life Ready Ground Tofu, Hot and Spicy has the perfect texture and a cumin seasoning that's just right for this recipe. **SERVES 4**

- 2 medium eggplants, halved and prepared for stuffing (see page 396), flesh coarsely chopped and reserved
- 1 tablespoon olive oil
- 1 large onion, chopped
- 1 package (10-ounces) frozen chopped spinach, thawed and well drained, or 1 cup chopped cooked fresh spinach (about 1 pound raw)
- 5 ounces spicy-style ready-ground tofu
- 2 cloves garlic, pressed
- 1 large egg, beaten (or 1 teaspoon cornstarch dissolved in 2 teaspoons water)
- 1½ cups cooked barley (about ⅓ cup raw, if you are cooking it from scratch for this recipe)
- 2 tablespoons tomato paste
- 3 tablespoons Zhoug (page 919), plus additional to serve at the table
- Salt and freshly ground black pepper to taste
- Cooking spray
- 1 large tomato, cored and thinly sliced
- ½ cup crisp breadcrumbs
- 2 teaspoons cornstarch
- 2 tablespoons water, preferably spring or filtered

1. Preheat the oven to 375°F.

2. Place a steamer basket in a medium pot over boiling water. Add 2 eggplant shells

and steam, covered, until slightly softened, about 5 minutes. Steam and cool the remaining 2 shells. Keep the steamer going, and steam the chopped eggplant flesh until quite soft, about 8 minutes. Remove the flesh from the steamer and set aside to cool. When cool, mash slightly. Set aside both the eggplant shells and the mashed eggplant.

3 Heat the oil in a skillet over medium heat. Add the onion and sauté until translucent, soft, and starting to brown at the edges, about 6 minutes. Lower the heat and add the spinach, tofu, garlic, and beaten egg (or cornstarch mixture). Stir for 1 minute, then remove from the heat. Stir in the barley and tomato paste, along with the mashed eggplant. Add the 2 tablespoons of the Zhoug and season with salt and pepper to taste.

4 Lightly spray a glass or enamel-clad cast-iron baking dish large enough to hold the 4 eggplant shells with cooking spray. Set aside.

5 Generously mound the filling into the reserved eggplant shells. Place a slice or two of tomato on top of each filled eggplant. Place the filled eggplant shells in the prepared dish. Cover with foil and bake until the eggplant is tender when you poke it with a fork, 30 to 40 minutes.

6 Toss the breadcrumbs with 1 tablespoon of the Zhoug. Set aside.

7 Remove the eggplant from the oven. Uncover and press the breadcrumb mixture onto the top of each eggplant. Raise the oven temperature to 400°F. Return the eggplant to the oven and bake until the crumbs are golden, 10 to 15 minutes. Remove from the oven.

8 Place the stuffed eggplants on a serving platter or on individual plates.

9 Transfer the juices that have accumulated in the baking dish to a small saucepan over high heat. Mash the cornstarch into the water and, when the pan juices are boiling, whisk in the dissolved cornstarch. The liquid will immediately thicken and turn clear. Either pour into a sauceboat and pass at the table, or ladle a little over each eggplant half. Serve hot, passing additional Zhoug at the table, if desired, along with any extra sauce.

Zhoug

Zhoug is a kind of Yemenite crossbreed of pesto and salsa—a thick, take-the-top-of-your-head-off fiery paste of chiles, garlic, and cilantro. To those of us who are Zhoug fans, a jar of it in the refrigerator is money in the bank (indeed, Zhoug has comforted me when there was little money in the bank). The Zhoug loses some zing in the baking, so pass more at the table.

Grilled Eggplant and Zucchini Rollatini, Sicilian-Style, with Tempeh-Provolone Stuffing

VARIATION

VEGAN VARIATION: ***Omit the provolone. You may replace it with soy provolone or add an extra 3 ounces of tempeh and, if you like, an extra tablespoon of pine nuts.***

Elegant, party-worthy, this is a dish that everyone loves. Many different types of rollatini are served throughout Italy. Each is seasoned a bit differently, but in all, slices of cooked eggplant wrap a savory stuffing. Sicilian versions are especially savory: Surprising culinary tradewinds blow from North Africa to Greece over this large island off the tip of the Italian boot—hence the nuts and dried fruit in the stuffing.

In this version, grated tempeh replaces the typical prosciutto or beef. It's an excellent, mainstream kind of meal, ideal for occasions where you want a vegetarian dish that will please all comers, but don't want to call attention to its meatlessness. The addition of a classic Italian red sauce and cheese make the flavors familiar; the filling, faintly exotic but irresistibly good, has a hearty, "meaty" texture. **MAKES 12 TO 16 SMALLISH ROLLS; SERVES 4 TO 6**

2 large eggplants, stems removed, sliced lengthwise into six to eight ¼-inch-thick ovals, plus 2 small, thin pieces with skin the sides

6 zucchini, stems removed, sliced lengthwise, into three to four ⅓-inch-thick ovals, plus 2 small, thin pieces with skin from the sides

2 tablespoons olive oil

2⅓ cups Basic Wintertime Italian Tomato Sauce (page 931), or any good commercially made tomato sauce

1 cup crisp breadcrumbs

2 ounces diced provolone cheese, plus 3 ounces thinly sliced then cut into long strips

4 ounces tempeh, grated

4 to 6 cloves garlic, pressed
3 tablespoons raisins
3 tablespoons finely minced Italian parsley
3 tablespoons finely minced basil
2 tablespoons chopped toasted pine nuts, walnuts, or almonds
Salt and lots of freshly ground pepper to taste
Cooking spray
Sprigs of Italian parsley or basil (optional)

1 Preheat the grill to hot, then turn down to medium.

2 Brush both sides of the eggplant and zucchini slices except the thin pieces that have outer skin on one side with the oil. Brush the thin pieces on the flesh side only. Place the oiled vegetable slices on the preheated grill over indirect or low-medium heat. Grill, turning once halfway through, until the vegetables are somewhat softened and grill-marked, but not completely cooked, 10 to 15 minutes. Grill the thin pieces on the flesh side only. Remove the vegetables from the grill. Finely dice the thin pieces and place them in a medium bowl. Set the remaining slices aside.

3 To the diced vegetables, add ⅓ cup of the tomato sauce and ¾ cup of the breadcrumbs and the diced provolone cheese. Stir to combine. Add the tempeh, garlic, raisins, parsley, basil, and pine nuts. Season with salt and pepper to taste. Using your hands, toss the mixture together well. Set the stuffing aside.

4 Preheat the oven to 375°F. If not using nonstick, lightly spray a 9-by-11-inch baking dish with cooking spray. Set the eggplant and zucchini slices, the stuffing, the remaining sauce and crumbs, and the cheese strips on the counter.

5 Lay a slice of grilled eggplant out flat on a clean work surface, perpendicular to the edge of the counter. Lengthwise, lay 2 or 3 strips of zucchini over the eggplant (depending on how many pieces of zucchini and eggplant you have; this, in turn, depends on both the size of the vegetables you purchased and how thinly they were sliced). Spoon 2 to 3 tablespoons of the stuffing across the center of the zucchini. Mold the stuffing into a lozenge-shaped mound. Carefully fold both ends of the eggplant and zucchini up and over the stuffing, draping to overlap the ends. Place the rolls, seam side down, in the prepared baking dish. Continue layering, filling, and rolling until all of the eggplant and zucchini slides are used up.

6 Cover the baking dish tightly with foil (if using a metal pan, cover first with a piece of waxed paper). Bake until heated

SEPTEMBER IN SICILY

The Salad
(PAGE 68)

*

Marinated Black-Eyed Peas with Greens Italia
(PAGE 105)

*

Grilled Eggplant and Zucchini Rollatini, Sicilian-Style, with Tempeh-Provolone Stuffing

*

Crusty, rustic Italian bread

*

Lemon sorbet, amaretti cookies, Chocolate-Orange Biscotti
(PAGE 1034)

through, 15 to 20 minutes. Uncover, then pour the remaining tomato sauce over the rolls. Top with the cheese strips and then sprinkle with the remaining breadcrumbs. Return the pan to the oven, uncovered, and bake until the rolls are very hot and the cheese is nice and melty, another 8 to 10 minutes. Remove from the oven and let stand for 2 minutes so that the filling firms up just a bit. Serve hot, garnished with sprigs of parsley or basil, if desired.

Grilled Eggplant and Zucchini Rolls Stuffed with Spinach and Dilled Feta Cream

Although this recipe starts like the Sicilian-style, it ends up with a Greek-accented spinach–feta cheese filling, redolent with dill. It's rich, but far less so than you'd suspect from its creaminess. Serve with rice, barley, or orzo. The eggplant and zucchini slices can be grilled, the filling can be prepared and the rollatini made ahead of time; then all you have to do is sauce, crumb, and bake when ready to serve. **MAKES 12 TO 16 SMALLISH ROLLS; SERVES 4 TO 6**

- 2 large eggplants, stems removed, sliced lengthwise into six to eight ¼-inch-thick ovals, plus 2 small, thin pieces with skin from the sides
- 6 zucchini, stems removed, sliced lengthwise into three to four ¼-inch-thick ovals, plus 2 small pieces with skin from the sides
- 2 tablespoons olive oil
- 8 ounces neufchâtel reduced-fat cream cheese, softened
- 4 to 6 whole cloves garlic, peeled
- 1 large egg
- 2⅓ cups Greek-Style Tomato Sauce with Lentils (page 932)
- 1 cup crisp breadcrumbs

- 4 ounces feta cheese, crumbled
- 1 box (10 ounces) frozen chopped spinach, thawed, well drained
- 3 tablespoons finely minced Italian parsley
- 2 tablespoons finely minced dill
- Salt and lots of freshly ground black pepper to taste
- Cooking spray (optional)
- 2 to 4 tablespoons freshly grated Parmesan cheese
- Sprigs of Italian parsley or dill (optional)

1 Preheat the grill to hot, then turn down to medium.

2 Brush both sides of the eggplant and zucchini slices except the thin pieces that have outer skin on one side with the oil. Brush the thin pieces on the flesh side only. Place the oiled vegetable slices on the preheated grill. Grill, turning once halfway through, until the vegetables are somewhat soft and grill-marked, but not completely cooked, 10 to 15 minutes. Grill the thin pieces on the flesh side only. Remove the vegetables from grill. Finely dice the thin pieces and place them in a medium bowl. Set the remaining slices aside.

3 Combine the neufchâtel with the garlic and egg in a food processor. Buzz until the garlic is finely minced. Scrape into the diced vegetables. Add 1 tablespoon of the tomato sauce and ¾ cup of the breadcrumbs. Stir in the feta, spinach, parsley, and dill, stirring until well blended. Season with salt and pepper to taste. Cover and refrigerate the stuffing for at least 1 hour to firm up slightly.

4 Preheat the oven to 375°F.

5 If not using nonstick, spray a 9-by-11-inch baking dish with cooking spray. Set the reserved eggplant and zucchini slices, the stuffing, the remaining sauce and crumbs, and the Parmesan on a counter.

6 Lay a slice of grilled eggplant out flat on a clean work surface, perpendicular to the edge of the counter. Lengthwise, lay 2 or 3 strips of zucchini over the eggplant (depending on how many pieces of zucchini and eggplant you have; this, in turn, depends on both the size of the vegetables you purchased, and how thinly they were sliced). Spoon 2 to 3 tablespoons of the stuffing across the center of the zucchini. Mold the stuffing into a lozenge-shaped mound. Carefully fold both ends of the eggplant and zucchini up and over the stuffing, draping to overlap the ends. Place the rolls, seam side down, in the prepared baking dish. Continue layering, filling, and rolling until all of the eggplant and zucchini slices are used up.

7 Cover the baking dish tightly with foil (if using a metal pan, cover first with a piece of waxed paper). Bake until heated through, 15 to 20 minutes. Uncover, then pour the remaining tomato sauce over the

GREEK GARDENS

Antipasto Platter
(PAGE 56)

*

Grilled Eggplant and Zucchini Rolls Stuffed with Spinach and Dilled Feta Cream

*

Steamed barley
(SEE PAGE 529)

*

Greek Style Green Beans
(PAGE 689)

*

Baklava

*

Mint tea

rolls. Sprinkle with the Parmesan and then finish with the remaining breadcrumbs. Return the pan to the oven, uncovered, and bake until the rolls are very hot and the crumbs browned, another 8 to 10 minutes. Remove from the oven and let stand for 2 minutes so that the filling firms up just a bit. Serve hot, garnished with sprigs of parsley or dill, if desired.

Stuffed "Fillet" of Eggplant Casablanca with Honeyed Port Wine–Orange Glaze

Eggplant slices with pockets are marinated in the same wonderful quasi-Moroccan concoction I used on what we called Game Hens Casablanca at the inn's restaurant—port wine, orange, honey, plenty of garlic, bay leaves, loads of spices: delicious on mild eggplant. A fascinating stuffing, sweet, salty, and savory, adds to the pleasure. The stuffed eggplants are grilled on one side, baked to melting tenderness, then served with the beautiful glossy deep brown sauce of the marinade. It's labor-intensive, but worth it—elegant, exotic, a definite centerpiece for adventurous eaters who cook for the pleasure of it. **SERVES 6**

3 large eggplants, cut into 6 pocketed "fillets" (see page 397)

MARINADE/SAUCE BASE

10 cloves garlic, pressed
4 bay leaves, broken in half
½ cup tawny port
3 tablespoons balsamic vinegar
1½ tablespoons paprika
1 tablespoon ground cumin
1½ teaspoons freshly ground black pepper
¼ cup honey
1 teaspoon salt
2 oranges, cut in half crosswise, seeds removed, sliced into very thin wheels, then cut into quarters
1 tablespoon tamari or shoyu soy sauce
Pinch of cayenne

STUFFING

4 ounces tempeh
3 cloves garlic, pressed
1 bunch scallions, roots removed, finely chopped
6 medjool dates, pitted and chopped
1 cup green pimento-stuffed olives, quartered
¼ cup chopped cilantro leaves
Juice and finely grated rind of 1 lemon
¼ teaspoon salt
Freshly ground black pepper to taste
Cooking spray
2 tablespoons olive oil

TO FINISH SAUCE

1 tablespoon brown sugar
1 teaspoon umeboshi plum vinegar (see page 118)
2 teaspoons cornstarch
1 tablespoon liquid (cooled-down strained marinade, water, or additional port)

1 Place the eggplant fillets in a deep dish of salted water, weighing them down so they stay submerged. Soak for 20 to 30 minutes to draw out any bitterness. Drain well. Rinse and pat dry.

2 As the eggplant soaks, prepare the marinade: Place the garlic, bay leaves, port, balsamic vinegar, paprika, cumin, and pepper in a food processor. Buzz, pureeing the garlic. With the motor running, carefully drizzle in the honey, processing to incorporate. Add the salt. Stop the machine and add the orange pieces, reserving a couple quarter-slices. Add the tamari and cayenne. Pulse/chop a few times. You just want to cut up the oranges a bit. Transfer the marinade to a nonreactive storage dish large enough to accommodate all of the eggplant fillets.

3 Place the eggplant fillets in the marinade. Open each fillet and rub a little of the marinade into the pocket. Cover and marinate, refrigerated, for at least 2 hours, but preferably overnight, turning once or twice.

4 Combine the tempeh and garlic in a bowl. Add the scallions, dates, olives, and cilantro and toss to combine. Add the lemon rind and juice. Mince the reserved orange and add it to the bowl. Season with the salt and pepper to taste and stir again.

5 Preheat the oven to 375°F.

6 Lift the eggplant fillets from the marinade, reserving the marinade.

7 Divide the stuffing into 6 portions. Carefully place a portion into the pocket of each fillet. Press partially closed.

8 Lightly spray a 9-by-11-inch baking dish with cooking spray. Set aside.

9 Using 1 teaspoon of the oil for each fillet, lightly rub both sides of the fillets with oil.

10 Preheat the grill or a ridged stovetop grill pan. Place the eggplant fillets flat side down on the hot grill or ridged pan and sear until well marked. (You can skip this step if you do not have a grill or a grill pan.) Remove the stuffed eggplant and place them, grill-mark side up, in the prepared baking dish. (If you haven't grilled them, just put them in as is.)

11 Tightly cover the baking dish with foil and bake until the eggplant is quite tender, 35 to 45 minutes. Uncover and bake for 10 minutes.

INFUSION OF INDIA

Gingered Curry of Carrot Soup with Bell Peppers
(PAGE 151)

*

Dal
(PAGE 609)

*

Stuffed Eggplant "Fillets," Gujerati-Style

*

Brown basmati rice
(PAGE 463)

*

Sliced garden-fresh tomatoes and cucumbers

*

Plain yogurt

*

Western-Style Blueberry Chutney
(PAGE 927)

*

Sliced banana, fresh pineapple and mango, cubed and sprinkled with rosewater

12 As the eggplant bakes, bring the reserved marinade to a hard boil over high heat. Lower the heat to a simmer and simmer until the liquid is reduced by about one-fourth, about 5 minutes. When the eggplant has baked uncovered for 10 minutes, brush it with the reduced marinade. Bake, uncovered, until meltingly tender and golden brown on top, another 15 minutes.

13 Strain any remaining marinade through a fine sieve into a small saucepan. Add the brown sugar and umeboshi plum vinegar and bring to a boil over high heat. Dissolve the cornstarch in 1 tablespoon liquid, and then whisk the cornstarch mixture into the hot marinade. You should immeditaely have a clear thick sauce. Pour into a serving bowl.

14 Serve the hot eggplant fillets with couscous, or any other grains, with the sauce passed at the table.

Stuffed Eggplant "Fillets," Gujerati-Style

In this intriguing dish, mild eggplant is suffused, inside and out, with lemony tart, hot and spicy flavors, potent and pungent—*so* good. Meltingly tender, this is a *great* Indian home-cooking dish, one you are unlikely ever to encounter in a restaurant. Anyone who loves Indian flavors will love this dish.

Gujeratis—those from the north Indian state of Gujerat—are very fond of besan, or chickpea flour, which has a distinctive rich, buttery taste. It is used both as a savory flour (little fried balls of seasoned chickpea flour are a common teatime savory) and a seasoning ingredient. Chickpea flour is available in Indian markets as well as in some Asian markets and natural foods stores. My friend Asha Nanavides, Gujerati on her father's side, fed me a fascinating stir-fry of green peppers with spiced chickpea flour that inspired this recipe. Only part of the stuffing is actually used in the eggplant—the rest forms the thin, piquant sauce, fabulous over rice (try brown or white basmati).

SERVES 6

2 large eggplants, cut into 6 pocketed "fillets" (see page 397)
2 tablespoons mild vegetable oil
3 cloves garlic, pressed
¾ cup chickpea flour
1 teaspoon finely minced peeled ginger
¾ teaspoon salt
½ teaspoon ground cumin
½ teaspoon ground coriander
¼ teaspoon ground cayenne
Cooking spray
2 teaspoons black or brown mustard seeds
1 large onion, finely diced
1 large green bell pepper, seeds and membrane removed, finely diced
½ teaspoon turmeric
1½ cups water, preferably spring or filtered
Juice of 1 large lemon
1 teaspoon salt

1 Place the eggplant fillets in a deep dish of salted water, weighing them down so they stay submerged. Soak for 20 to 30 minutes to draw out any bitterness. Drain well. Rinse and pat dry.

2 Place 1 tablespoon of the oil in a medium bowl. Stir in the garlic, chickpea flour, ginger, ¾ teaspoon salt, the cumin, coriander, and cayenne and toss well. Don't worry; it will be very floury.

3 Place about 1 tablespoon of the chickpea flour mixture into the pocket of each fillet and press the eggplant partially closed. Set aside.

4 Preheat the oven to 375°F.

5 Spray a 9-by-11-inch baking dish with cooking spray. Set aside.

6 Heat 1 teaspoon of the remaining oil in a large nonstick saucepan over medium heat. Add the mustard seeds and cook, stirring, until they start to pop, 3 to 4 minutes. Add the onion and sauté for 4 minutes. Add the bell pepper and turmeric and sauté for another 2 minutes. Transfer the mixture to the prepared baking dish.

7 Use the remaining oil to lightly brush one side of each of the eggplant fillets.

8 Place 2 or 3 of the stuffed fillets—to comfortably fit—in the bottom of the saucepan and cook in any residual oil and spices until lightly browned, about 5 minutes. Place, cooked side up, over the vegetables in the baking dish. Sprinkle with a bit of the chickpea flour mixture. Continue cooking until all of the fillets have been browned on one side, placed in the baking dish, and sprinkled with the chickpea flour mixture.

9 Combine the water, lemon juice, and 1 teaspoon salt and pour it into the saucepan over high heat. Cook, stirring constantly, to deglaze the pan. Pour the hot liquid over the eggplant fillets.

10 Tightly cover the baking dish with foil. Bake for 45 minutes. Serve hot, with rice.

Masala Stuffed Eggplant

If you like the North Indian flavors in samosas, you'll like this spiced potato–stuffed eggplant. Large and showy, they serve well as an unusual centerpiece for an Indian meal. Serve with Western-Style Blueberry Chutney (page 927) or any other chutney, a dollop of plain yogurt, and brown basmati rice.

The eggplant cooks to melting softness, giving a richness belied by the dish's low fat content. This does make scooping them out of the baking dish tricky. I use two serving spoons to carefully lift the eggplants. **SERVES 4 TO 6**

3 medium potatoes, well scrubbed, quartered (peel on or off as you prefer)
2 medium or 3 small eggplants, halved and prepared for stuffing (see page 396), flesh coarsely chopped
1 tablespoon cumin seeds
Cooking spray
2 teaspoons to 1 tablespoon mild vegetable oil, such as corn, canola, or peanut; or clarified butter; or 1½ teaspoons each butter and oil
1 onion, finely minced
1 small fresh hot green chile, such as a serrano, finely minced (remove seeds and membranes or leave in for extra heat)
1 tablespoon minced peeled ginger
1 tablespoon black or brown mustard seeds
3 tablespoons very finely chopped cilantro leaves
2 teaspoons Garam Masala (page 902) or curry powder
1½ teaspoons salt
1 teaspoon ground coriander
½ teaspoon turmeric
Pinch of cayenne
Juice of ½ lemon
1 tablespoon honey
1 tablespoon tomato paste
1 cup cooked chickpeas (or canned), well-drained, slightly mashed (I use canned and crush them lightly in my hand while adding them)
Cilantro leaves

1 Preheat the oven to 400°F.

2 Bring 3 cups water to a boil in a small saucepan over medium-high heat. Drop in the potatoes and cook for 15 minutes. Add the chopped eggplant, cover, and cook for an additional 3 minutes. Uncover and continue cooking until the potatoes are tender but not mushy and the eggplant is quite soft but not falling apart, about 5 minutes more. Remove from the heat. Drain well, reserving ¼ cup of the cooking liquid. Let cool.

3 Mash the potatoes and eggplants together until well combined but with some texture. Set aside.

4 Place the cumin seeds in a large, dry

iron skillet over medium heat. Toast until brown and fragrant, 2 to 3 minutes. Remove the cumin to a small bowl and set aside.

5 Let the skillet cool slightly, then spray it very well with cooking spray. Place over medium heat and add the oil. Add the onion and sauté until just starting to color, about 7 minutes. Lower the heat slightly and add the chile, ginger, and mustard seeds, along with the toasted cumin. Cook, stirring often, until the mustard seeds start to pop, 3 to 4 minutes. Add the cilantro, Garam Masala or curry powder, salt, coriander, turmeric, and cayenne, along with the reserved cooking liquid. Stir, then add the potato-eggplant mixture, lemon juice, honey, and tomato paste. Lower the heat and cook, gently stirring fairly often, carefully turning the potatoes over in the pan. Add the chickpeas and stir to combine. Taste; you may want a little more salt or cayenne. Remove from the heat.

6 Spray a 13-inch-by-9-inch baking dish with cooking spray.

7 Stuff each eggplant shell with an equal portion of the potato mixture. Place the stuffed eggplant in the prepared baking dish. Cover tightly with foil and bake for 45 minutes. Remove from the oven and serve with a nice shower of cilantro leaves on top.

Stuffed Mushrooms

The cavity left when the stem is removed from a mushroom cap naturally suggests stuffing. I've placed the stuffed mushroom recipes in the hors d'oeuvres chapter, but Stuffed Deviled Mushrooms (page 50), are also excellent as a main course, or part of a main course. In this case, opt for larger mushrooms, or portobellos, and bake a few minutes longer.

Here are a few other mushroom-stuffing ideas:

- ▲ The removed stem, unless it is woody, can be diced, sautéed, and added to almost anything—breadcrumbs, pureed beans, sautéed onions and garlic, mashed potatoes, drained and chopped cooked greens—to make a tasty stuffing.
- ▲ Mushrooms can be deliciously stuffed with the mixture for Twice-Grilled Eggplant Cakes (page 840) and baked at 375°F until the mushrooms are soft and the filling firm and slightly crunchy on top, 35 to 45 minutes.
- ▲ A simple, quick, and scrumptious (if high-fat) stuffing for a large cap is a dab of neufchâtel (preferably with some garlic beaten in), a good slice of roasted pepper (out of a jar if you're in a hurry), a wedge of marinated artichoke heart (most of the marinade shaken off), and, topping it all, a bit of smoked provolone. Throw the caps into a hot oven, bake until the cheese melts, and serve it up, gooey, hot, and irresistible.

Stuffed Peppers

Stuffed peppers, the first stuffed vegetable most Americans meet, have come a long way from the original green-boiled-to-gray-green hue, standing upright, filled with meat and rice, baked with too-sweet tomato sauce. Today's versions are more healthful, more ethnically inspired, prettier.

For one thing, we now have a rainbow of peppers to stuff: blocky sweet peppers, hot plump green-black jalapeños, in-between heart-shaped sweet-hot poblanos, and pale green elf's cap–shaped anaheims are just a few.

Pepper fillings run the gamut from mild to wild, unpretentious to elegant, hot to soothing—anything you like will work, I guarantee. In addition to the recipe here, consider any of the following:

- ▲ Deviled Corn and Tomato Pudding (page 290) in a red pepper half (add a little diced sautéed ancho chile or grated Cheddar if you like).
- ▲ Vegan French-Style Gratin of Butternut Squash (page 289) in a red pepper half.
- ▲ Timbales of Cauliflower Pudding (page 306) in a red pepper half, with the accompanying Creamed Spinach Sauce served on the plate.
- ▲ Southern Tomato Pudding (page 292) in a yellow or green pepper half.

TO PREPARE BELL PEPPERS FOR STUFFING: I never cut off the top and scoop down into the pepper, making a single, upright, tall, deep vessel. For me, this gives a too high percentage of filling to pepper. And, because so little filling-surface is exposed to the oven heat, the interior is too soggy for me.

I cut large green, red, yellow, or purple sweet bell peppers in half vertically, right down the middle through the stem. In addition to solving the sog-problem, this cut makes a pretty presentation and also yields two servings from a single pepper (although if you're using the pepper as a centerpiece instead of a component, you might consider both halves to be one serving). I leave the little curl of a stem, because, although not edible, it adds interest to the finished dish. Trim off any white membrane and remove the seeds and any miniature internal peppers that are sometimes present with a paring knife.

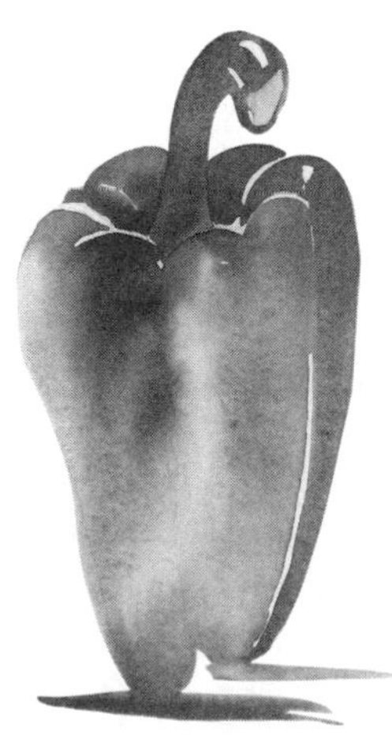

Spray a skillet with cooking spray and then add 2 to 3 tablespoons olive oil to lightly pool in the bottom of the skillet. Place over high heat until quite hot. Add the peppers, cut sides down, to the skillet. There will be great sizzling and carrying-on—ignore it. Let the peppers sear for 3 to 4 minutes, then, using long-handled tongs, flip the peppers over and sear for another 3 to 4 minutes. You want to cook the peppers only slightly—just enough to soften the raw taste and brown them in spots. Remove the skillet from the heat.

Remove the peppers from the oil. Immediately drain on paper towels, wiping to remove any traces of oil. If any oil remains in the skillet, allow it to cool, and then pour it into a small container with a lid. You'll notice the oil has taken on both the color and fragrance of the peppers. Use this Sweet Pepper Oil in pepper fillings, where it adds an extra boost of flavor, or hoard it, refrigerated, for a nice note in any stir-fry that contains bell peppers, or as an aromatic addition to salad dressings.

Tomato-Rice Timbale in a Green Pepper Carriage

This is a firm, velvety-smooth, reddish pink mixture, somewhere between custard and pudding, polka-dotted with rice, and baked in dark green pepper halves. Credit for the idea of putting it in the peppers goes to the inn's former gardener, Jason Oury. The timbale tastes far richer than it actually is, which makes it suitable as a side dish for somewhat soigné occasions. **MAKES 6 STUFFED PEPPER HALVES**

NOTE

Even though the pepper halves aren't put into service until the end of the recipe, make sure you've prepared them before you begin making the timbale.

2 teaspoons olive oil, preferably Sweet Pepper Oil (see opposite page), left over from preparing the peppers for stuffing
Cooking spray
1 large onion, finely diced
3 whole cloves
2 pounds tomatoes (about 8 medium tomatoes), cut in half, seeded, and grated
1½ tablespoons brown sugar
1 tablespoon tomato paste
1 large egg
¼ cup evaporated skim milk
3 tablespoons (about 1½ ounces) neufchâtel reduced-fat cream cheese
1½ tablespoons cornstarch
¼ teaspoon salt, or to taste
Freshly ground black pepper to taste
3 tablespoons finely chopped fresh spearmint or basil
½ cup cooked brown or white rice
6 green bell pepper halves, prepared for stuffing (see opposite page)

1 Preheat the oven to 350°F.

2 Heat the oil in a nonstick skillet, or one that has been sprayed with cooking spray, over medium heat. Add the onion and cloves and sauté until the onions are limp and just barely taking on color, 6 to 7 minutes. Scoop out as much of the sautéed onions as you can and set them aside, leaving the cloves in the skillet. Add the tomatoes, brown sugar, and tomato paste to the skillet and place over medium heat. Cook until thickened, 10 to 20 minutes. Remove from the heat and let rest for a minute or two.

3 While the tomatoes are cooking, place the egg, evaporated skim milk, neufchâtel, cornstarch, salt, and black pepper to taste in a food processor. Process until smooth.

4 Remove and discard the cloves from the tomatoes. Add the tomato mixture to the food processor and buzz, stopping to scrape down the bowl a few times until blended. Add the spearmint (or basil), along with the reserved onion and pulse chop a few times just to combine. Do not puree. Taste for seasonings (ignore the floury taste, which is from the cornstarch and will bake out). You may need to add a touch more brown sugar if too acid tasting,

or a little more spearmint or basil. Stir in the cooked rice.

5 Spray a 13-by-9-inch baking dish with cooking spray. Divide the tomato mixture among the green pepper halves. Place the stuffed peppers in the prepared baking dish. Cover tightly with foil and bake for 25 minutes. Uncover and bake until well set and slightly browned, 15 to 20 minutes. The tops will be a little dark and cracked, and the filling should be quite firm to the touch.

COOK ONCE FOR 2 MEALS Double the filling. Bake half in a small nonstick baking dish. Serve hot or cold, cut into squares, or use as a filling for any of the crêpes, beginning on page 327.

Red Bell Peppers Stuffed with Green Chile, Corn, and Hominy

NOTE

Even though the pepper halves aren't put into service until the end of the recipe, do be sure to prepare them before you begin the stuffing. Also note that the peppers are not baked after they're stuffed.

One evening, at about 6:45, back in the days when we served dinner nightly at the inn at 7:00, two women arrived who wanted a vegetarian meal. But only when they had begun their meal did they explain they were *vegan* vegetarian. That made the night's vegetarian entree, a creamy mushroom lasagna, unsuitable for them. I tore around the kitchen pretty ding-danged fast to come up with a main course. As they ate their hors d'oeuvres, salad, soup, and sorbet, I put together three stuffed vegetables in about 25 minutes, all while getting courses out to the other diners.

I'd made the zucchini boat and stuffed mushroom I chose to serve them on other occasions, but the third was brand new, seat-of-the-pants: a stuffed red pepper half, with a pleasing Southwesterly wallop—an invention strictly mothered by necessity. Still, it was amazingly good. **MAKES 6 TO 8 STUFFED PEPPER HALVES**

2 teaspoons Sweet Pepper Oil left over from preparing the peppers for stuffing (see page 410)
1 onion, diced
½ teaspoon cumin seeds
2 cups corn kernels, fresh or frozen
1 clove garlic, pressed
½ cup cooked white hominy (or canned), well drained
1 tablespoon canned, diced green chile
2 tablespoons vegetable stock (see page 139), or water, preferably spring or filtered
1 teaspoon cornstarch
Salt and freshly ground black pepper to taste
3 large or 4 medium red bell peppers, prepared for stuffing (see page 410)

1 Heat the Sweet Pepper Oil in a nonstick skillet, or one that has been sprayed with cooking spray, over medium heat. Add the onion and sauté until it starts to give off an aroma, about 2 minutes. Add the cumin seeds and sauté until the onion is beginning to soften and the seeds are fragrant, 2 to 4 minutes. Add the corn and sauté for an additional 3 minutes. Add the garlic, hominy, green chile, and 1 tablespoon of the vegetable stock and stir to combine.

2 Dissolve the cornstarch in the remaining tablespoon of stock and immediately stir into the skillet. The filling will quickly thicken just enough to stick together somewhat. Season with salt and pepper to taste.

3 Pile the mixture into the pepper halves and serve.

COOK ONCE FOR 2 MEALS Double the filling and use half as a basis for Fresh Corn Shortcakes: Simply fold it into 2 to 3 cups Vegan Velouté (page 950), a classic white or cheese sauce, Salsa Poblano Blanca y Verde (page 947), or the lovely Southwestern-Style Tomato Gravy (page 433). Serve it over split, toasted biscuits or cornbread with a nice garlicky salad for a great supper.

VARIATION

Omit the canned chiles, and add 1 finely minced fresh serrano, ancho, or jalapeño chile after the onion has cooked for about 3 minutes.

Stuffing Poblano Peppers

Poblanos don't offer a nice big cavity just dying to be stuffed. What they do offer is marvelous flavor—sweet, hot, with an undernote of chocolate—and an almost majestic color, a green so dark it's nearly black. Their cavity is small and triangular; stuffing them is more like filling a small flat purse than a cup. Still, they are not to be missed.

TO PREPARE POBLANOS FOR STUFFING: *Place them on a very hot grill or under a preheated broiler until the skin blisters slightly and is black in spots, about 5 minutes per side. Place in a paper bag or in a bowl with a towel over it, and steam until cool enough to handle. Peel off most of the skin and lay the chiles out flat on a cutting board. Carefully cut a single lengthwise slit down one side of each poblano, leaving the stem attached. The slit should travel, zipperlike, from just under the poblano stem almost to its end point. Reach in and delicately scrape out any seeds and membrane that can easily be removed, being careful not to puncture the chile. Stuff as directed in the specific recipe.*

Poblanos Stuffed with Veggie Chorizo, Black Beans, and Corn

Another lovely Southwestern-style stuffed pepper, the luscious poblano is filled with a mixture of chorizo-style spiced vegetarian soysage, black beans, and corn. Delish. Try it with Brazilian Rice (page 473) or the Pilaf of Oats with Ginger and Jalapeño (page 563), add a salad, maybe the Salad of Grilled Zucchini with Cilantro Vinagrette (page 92), and you've got a sterling meal. This also makes a great brunch dish with scrambled eggs or scrambled tofu. Remember to prepare the poblanos for stuffing before you make the filling. **MAKES 8 STUFFED POBLANOS; SERVES 4 AS AN ENTREE**

VEGGIE CHORIZO

1 package (8-ounces) vegetarian soysage patties, baked according to package directions for 5 minutes, patties halved
4 cloves garlic, peeled
¼ onion, coarsely chopped
1 tablespoon cider vinegar
1½ teaspoons chili powder
1½ teaspoons ground cumin
½ teaspoon coarsely ground black pepper
Pinch of cayenne, or to taste

BLACK BEANS AND CORN

Cooking spray
1 tablespoon corn or canola oil
¾ onion, chopped
¼ teaspoon cumin seeds
1 can (15 ounces) black beans, drained and well rinsed
1 cup corn kernels, fresh or frozen
2 tablespoons water, preferably spring or filtered
1½ tablespoons tomato paste
1 teaspoon sauce from canned chipotles in adobo sauce
½ teaspoon dried oregano leaves
Salt and freshly ground black pepper to taste
8 poblano chiles, prepared for stuffing (see page 410)
Sour cream or reduced-fat sour cream or Yogurt Sour Cream (page 910) or Tofu Sour Cream (page 909) for garnish
Cilantro sprigs

1 Preheat the oven to 400°F. Combine the soysage patties with the garlic, ¼ onion, the vinegar, chili powder, ground cumin, pepper, and cayenne in a food processor

and pulse chop to make a thick, chunky paste. Scrape the mixture into a bowl and set aside.

2 Spray a 12-inch skillet with cooking spray. Place the skillet over medium-high heat and add the oil. When hot, add the ¾ onion and sauté until the onion softens, about 5 minutes. Add the cumin seeds and sauté for another 2 minutes. Stir in the beans, corn, water, tomato paste, adobo sauce, and oregano. Raise the heat to high and cook, stirring, until all of the ingredients are hot and starting to stick to the pan, 3 to 4 minutes. Scrape into the soysage mixture and stir to combine. Taste, adding salt and pepper if necessary.

3 Spray a 13-by-9-inch baking dish with cooking spray. Set aside.

4 Carefully stuff an equal portion of the mixture into each of the prepared poblanos, gently opening them at the slit and mounding the stuffing over it. Gently place the chiles into the prepared baking dish and bake until good and hot, 6 to 8 minutes.

5 Place 2 chiles on each serving plate and top with a dab of sour cream and a sprig of cilantro. Serve hot.

Stuffed Summer Squashes

Members of the Cucurbitae, or squash, family are well known to gardeners as the most aggressive tenants of the garden. No one who plants an entire package of zucchini seeds *ever* does so again. But however rambunctiously fecund squashes may be, they are always welcome in the kitchen. Many types are ideal for stuffing.

Summer squashes have tender skin easily pierced with a fingernail, and the flesh is creamy white. Yellow squash, zucchini, and charming pattypan (rounded squash with a sweetly scalloped edge, like a cross between a flower and a flying saucer) are the squashes of summer. They are very mild in flavor but taste marvelous with a little perking up. A savory stuffing is one admirable way to do this.

Although it's tempting to use great big Moby-squash for stuffing, the small- to medium-sized ones have a better flavor; the large can be virtually tasteless.

GAD-ZUKES! TO PREPARE ZUCCHINI (OR OTHER LONG SUMMER SQUASH) FOR STUFFING: Halve the squash lengthwise, right through the stem end, leaving a piece of stem, if still attached, intact on each half. Drop the squash into boiling water and blanch for 1 minute, less if they're on the small side. Drain well and rinse under cold running water. Pat dry. (Occasionally, if a stuffed squash is to bake for a long time, I don't bother blanching it all, but simply proceed with it raw.)

Using a melon baller or spoon tip, scoop out most but not all of the flesh, which is quite soft and will easily come out. You want to end up with a ⅓-inch-thick squash shell, which will provide a sturdy container for stuffing.

Proceed as directed in the specific recipe. Usually the scooped-out flesh is used in the recipe.

Pattypans are prepared in much the same way, except you slice them equatorially, through their middles (or, if they are very thin, about ¼ to ½ inch down from the stem, just above their middles, but still crosswise). Blanch or not as you prefer, and scoop out the flesh, leaving a sturdy ¾-inch-thick shell for stuffing. The cavity will be circular rather than boat-shaped. Other summer squashes that work well for stuffing when halved crosswise are the new *round* varieties of zucchini, such as Ronde de Nice or Gourmet Globe. They are best used when slightly smaller than a tennis ball. Again, blanch and scoop, leaving a ¾-inch shell.

"Gardener's Solution" Stuffed Zucchini

This recipe offers something easy and delicious to do with the ever- and over-abundant zucchini (or yellow squash). It's nice served with Roasty-Toasty Potatoes, Carrots, and Onions (page 790), or a stir-fry of vegetables with pasta. You can also dress it up with a spoonful of tomato sauce. Good but not racy, it's a fairly classic vegetable stuffing—garlicky, Parmesan'd breadcrumbs—used throughout Italy. You could make it vegan by omitting the Parmesan, but because the ingredients are so simple, it is a little plain without it. **MAKES 8 STUFFED HALVES; SERVES 4 TO 8**

1 teaspoon to 1 tablespoon olive oil
1 large onion, minced
4 medium zucchini (or yellow squash), prepared for stuffing (see previous page), flesh chopped
3 cloves garlic, pressed
1 small tomato, diced
3 to 4 tablespoons shredded basil
1 cup breadcrumbs
½ cup freshly grated Parmesan cheese
Salt and freshly ground black pepper to taste
Cooking spray

1 Preheat the oven to 350°F.

2 Heat the oil in large nonstick skillet over medium heat. Add the onion and sauté until starting to soften, about 4 minutes. Add the chopped zucchini flesh and stir-fry for 2 minutes. Add the garlic, tomato, and basil. Stir for a minute. Add the breadcrumbs and remove from the heat. Stir in the Parmesan and season with salt and pepper. Stir well.

3 Spray a 9-inch square baking dish with cooking spray.

4 Pile an equal portion of the mixture into the prepared squash halves, patting it firmly in place. Place the stuffed squash in the prepared baking dish. Cover the pan with foil and bake for 20 minutes. Uncover and bake until the crumbs are browned and slightly crunchy, 10 to 15 minutes. Remove from the oven and serve hot or at room temperature.

COOK ONCE FOR 2 MEALS Take a look at the recipe for Jenelle's Tomatoes Rockefeller (page 430), which seems similar but is just different enough to make the start of an awfully nice trio-of-stuffed-vegetables plate (add a red pepper half stuffed with corn pudding to round things out). Double the onion and garlic, sauté, then divide it in half. Use half as the base for this recipe, half for Jenelle's Tomatoes Rockefeller, and proceed in two skillets (since many of the ingredients are the same, you'll limit the stuff you have to pull out and put away).

Both the tomatoes and this are good hot, warm, or at room temperature—very pleasing leftovers to find stashed in the fridge.

VARIATIONS

Add ¼ cup chopped olives, preferably Greek, to the filling. Leave it as is or go a step further and make Stuffed Zucchini, Greek-Style: Substitute dill for basil, cut Parmesan cheese down to ¼ cup, and add ¼ cup finely crumbled feta cheese.

Stuffed Zucchini à la Turque, with Bulghur, Tempeh, and Gaziantep Spices

Vegetarians who love good food and are serious cookbook readers often find themselves filled with frustration and lust as they read about fascinating-sounding, intriguingly spiced dishes that contain meat. Paula Wolfert's passionate writing and hunt for authenticity do this to me, but sometimes she leads me into the kitchen to start developing meatless versions of her ethnic recipes. Her Zucchinis Stuffed with Bulgur, Tomatoes, and Hot Pepper, for instance, in *The Cooking of the Eastern Mediterranean*—well, I had stuffed many a zucchini, but never with *two* sauces (one hot, and lemon-spiked, and one cold, a kind of yogurt raita), and never seasoned with the totally beguiling mixture of spices she described. But what to do about the 5 to 6 ounces of lamb her recipe called for? This is what I did. **SERVES 6 TO 8**

VARIATION

VEGAN VARIATION:* *Substitute Tofu Sour Cream (page 909) for the Yogurt Sour Cream in the sauce.

YOGURT SAUCE

2 cups Yogurt Sour Cream (page 910)
1 to 2 cloves garlic, pressed
½ teaspoon salt

ZUCCHINI

12 to 16 small, tender zucchini, about 6 inches long, prepared for stuffing (see page 415), flesh reserved
Salt
Cooking spray
2 teaspoons olive oil
1 medium onion, finely chopped
1 package (8-ounces) tempeh, finely minced
1 large tomato, peeled, seeded, and diced
1 cup coarse-grain bulghur (cracked wheat)
3 small fresh green chiles, most of the seeds removed, finely minced
⅓ cup boiling vegetable stock (see page 139)
2 tablespoons tomato paste
1½ teaspoons Turkish Spice Mixture, (recipe follows)
Freshly ground black pepper

PAN SAUCE

½ teaspoon sugar
Salt and freshly ground black pepper to taste
3 cups hot vegetable stock (see page 139)
1 tablespoon cornstarch
2 lemons
Fresh mint (optional)

1 Combine the Yogurt Sour Cream with the garlic and ½ teaspoon salt in a small bowl. Cover and refrigerate for at least 6 hours so that the yogurt can absorb the garlic flavor.

2 Rub the cut sides of the zucchini with salt and let stand for 1 hour.

3 Finely chop enough of the reserved zucchini flesh to equal 1 cup. Set aside.

4 Spray a large skillet with cooking spray. Add the oil and place over medium heat. Add the onion and sauté until it has softened slightly and is translucent, about 4 minutes. Add the zucchini flesh and stir-fry until it begins to soften, 2 to 3 minutes. Add the tempeh and cook, stirring often, for 5 more minutes. Add the tomato, stir to heat through, and remove from the heat.

5 Add the bulghur to the tempeh mixture. Add the green chiles, ⅓ cup boiling stock, the tomato paste, and Turkish Spice Mixture. Season to taste with salt and pepper, adding a bit more than you think you need. Let the filling rest for 15 minutes.

6 Preheat the oven to 350°F. Spray 2 large baking dishes with cooking spray. Set aside.

7 When the filling is cool enough to handle, knead it for a few moments to blend thoroughly.

8 Drain the zucchini boats of any liquid and pat dry. Loosely stuff with the bulghur-tempeh mixture. Place the zucchini in the prepared baking dishes, tucking them close together but not right on top of each other.

9 Whisk the sugar and salt and pepper into the 3 cups hot vegetable stock. Pour the liquid around the zucchini. Cover tightly, either with lids or foil (if using foil and a metal baking dish, first cover with a layer of waxed paper to prevent any chemical reaction from occurring). Bake for 40 to 45 minutes.

10 Remove the dishes from the oven and let rest for 15 minutes before uncovering. Uncover and drain off and reserve the pan juices in a small saucepan. Add the juice of ½ to 1 of the lemons to the pan juices. Cut the remaining lemon into wedges. Mix the cornstarch with just enough of this liquid to form a smooth paste.

11 Bring the pan juices to a boil over high heat. Whisk in the cornstarch paste, and, as soon as the sauce is thick and clear, remove from the heat.

12 Place the zucchini on a serving platter. Pour the pan juices over the zucchini and serve warm with the chilled yogurt sauce on the side. If desired, add a sprig of mint to the yogurt sauce. Garnish the platter with lemon wedges.

Turkish Spice Mixture

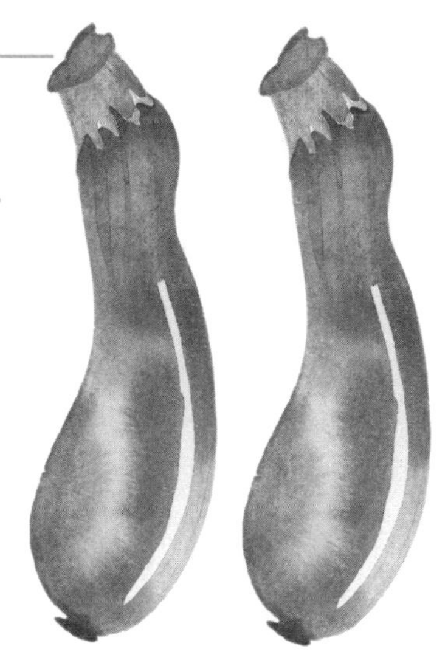

1 bay leaf, broken up
1 tablespoon dried summer savory
2 teaspoons freshly ground black pepper
1 teaspoon ground cinnamon
1 teaspoon freshly grated nutmeg
1 teaspoon dried mint (use plain peppermint, or spearmint tea)
1 teaspoon ground cumin
¼ teaspoon ground allspice

Combine all ingredients. Store at room temperature in a closed jar, for up to 3 months.

Stuffed Summer Suns: Pattypans Baked with Ricotta-Corn Filling

A mild, slightly sweet, summery filling, bound with egg and ricotta and packed with the garden's bounty, is just right for pattypans or round zucchini. Dress them up with a few tablespoons of any fresh herb you like, or some pesto, or garlic, or take it in a completely different direction by adding a few diced green chiles. You can also top the stuffed squash with grated cheese. This is exquisite, and not a little haute, when accompanied by Roasted Red Pepper Sauce with Fresh Pineapple Mint (page 940). **SERVES 4 TO 6**

1 teaspoon to 1 tablespoon olive oil
1 large onion, chopped
Four to six 4-inch pattypan squashes or slightly-smaller-than-tennis-ball-sized round zucchini, prepared for stuffing (see page 415), flesh chopped and reserved
1½ cups part-skim ricotta
1 large egg
1 teaspoon sugar or honey
1 fresh tomato, peeled, seeded, and diced
Kernels from 2 or 3 ears of fresh sweet corn, raw
Salt and freshly ground black pepper to taste
Cooking spray

1 Preheat the oven to 400°F.

2 Heat the oil in a large nonstick skillet over medium heat. Add the onion and sauté until has softened slightly and is

Here Come the Suns

COOK ONCE FOR 2 OR 3 MEALS: *Double the filling recipe. Use one half for the squash stuffing and the other a day or two later, adding some pesto or minced basil to stuff manicotti tubes. Top with any good tomato sauce (see page 931) and maybe a little Parmesan. Or add a jot of chili powder and some minced jalapeño, serrano, or chipotle, roll up in tortillas, top with the salsa of your choice, and bake as for Enchiladas (see page 340).*

MAKE CORN RICOTTA DUMPLINGS, *invented one day when I had more filling than squashes, and truly 1-2-3 when you have leftover ricotta mix. They are quite close relatives to what the Italians call* ravioli nuda, *or nude ravioli (meaning filling, unclothed by pasta). Put a large pot of salted water on to boil. Combine ¾ cup unbleached white flour or, better yet, semolina, with 1 teaspoon baking powder and ½ teaspoon salt. Stir this into about 1½ to 1⅔ cups of the ricotta-egg-corn mixture, along with any liquid it may have released, 2 tablespoons minced Italian parsley (optional), and ¼ cup grated Parmesan cheese. You want a firm mixture, almost like a dough, neither dry nor sticky; one you can easily shape into balls. If you need to, add a little extra ricotta, flour, or Parmesan. Shape into 1- to 1¼-inch balls. You'll end up with about 24 of them. Gently drop into the boiling water. They will sink to the bottom, only to rise again after 40 to 60 seconds; they will be done in 4 to 5 minutes. Taste one to be sure there is no raw flour taste. If there is, let cook for a minute longer. Carefully scoop the dumplings from the water using a slotted spoon. They can serve as either a starter or main dish. Serve simply buttered, perhaps with a pressed clove of garlic and some toasty breadcrumbs for crunch, or gratinée quickly under a broiler with olive oil, garlic, and Parmesan. You can also serve them with any assertive vegetable sauce or perch them in a bundle atop a thick soup.*

translucent, about 4 minutes. Add the chopped squash flesh, and stir-fry until it begins to lose its raw look, 2 to 3 minutes. Remove from the heat.

3 Place the ricotta in a medium bowl. Add the egg and sugar, beating well. Stir in the tomato and corn, along with the onion-squash mixture. Add salt and pepper to taste, stirring well. Divide this mixture equally among the squash shells. (There may be extra filling.)

4 Spray a large nonstick baking dish with cooking spray. Place the stuffed squash in the prepared dish. Cover and place in the preheated oven. Bake for 15 minutes. Uncover and bake until the filling is slightly browned and firm, 15 to 20 minutes.

Stuffed Mirlitons, Creole-Style

Vegetable stuffing takes a turn south here, to the humid, seductive, decadent, lovely city of New Orleans. There, chayote, or mirliton—a summer squash widely used in the Caribbean—is frequently served stuffed. Also called vegetable pear, it has one giant seed in the middle, which is removed, leaving a dandy cavity for stuffing.

This vegetarian version is inspired by the recipe in Leon Soniat's *La Bouche Creole*. It uses vegetarian soysage, several brands of which are now widely available. You may omit the egg, but it does make the filling hold together nicely. I like a combo of butter and olive oil here, but you may use one or the other. **MAKES 8 STUFFED HALVES; SERVES 4 TO 8**

LOUISIANA LULLABY

Mushrooms Diablo
(PAGE 51)

*

The Salad
(PAGE 68)
made with
chicory and arugula

*

Stuffed Mirlitons
Creole-Style
(PAGE 421)

*

Basic Garlic-Braised
Broccoli Rabe
(PAGE 711)

*

Alice Medrich's
Chocolate-Pecan-
Bourbon Cake
(PAGE 1005)

4 mirlitons
About 6 ounces vegetarian soysage, cooked according to package directions and coarsely crumbled
1 cup cooked rice, preferably long-grain brown rice
½ cup freshly grated Parmesan cheese (optional, but good)
Cooking spray
2 teaspoons butter
1 teaspoon olive oil
1 large onion, diced
4 scallions, roots and wilted part of green removed, sliced
½ green bell pepper, diced
3 cloves garlic, pressed
1 large egg, beaten (optional)
1 cup Breadcrumb Topping Provençal (page 277)
3 to 4 tablespoons shredded basil
Salt and freshly ground black pepper to taste
½ teaspoon Tabasco or similar hot sauce
1 recipe Creole-Style Tomato Sauce (page 932)
Minced Italian parsley (optional)

1 Bring a large pot of water to a boil over medium-high heat. Ease the whole mirlitons into the boiling water and boil until barely fork-tender, 25 to 30 minutes, but start checking them at 10 minutes. (You can also steam or pressure-cook them.) Drain well and rinse under cold running water. Pat dry. Cut each in half lengthwise. Remove and discard the seed. Gently scoop out most of the pulp, leaving behind a ¼- to ½-inch-thick shell. Set aside. Chop the flesh and set aside.

2 Preheat the oven to 375°F.

3 Combine the soysage, rice, and Parmesan in a bowl. Set aside.

4 Spray a large skillet with cooking spray and place over medium heat. Add the butter and oil; when hot, add the onion and sauté until starting to soften, about 4 minutes. Add the scallions and green pepper. Lower the heat slightly and sauté until the vegetables are quite soft, 8 to 10 minutes. Add the chopped mirliton flesh and cook for another 10 minutes. Add the garlic and sauté for an additional minute. Remove from the heat and let cool slightly. When cool, stir into the soysage mixture, along with the egg and ½ cup of the breadcrumb topping. Stir well. Add the basil, salt and pepper to taste, and the Tabasco. (How much basil, salt, and pepper you'll need is determined by how well seasoned the soysage is, and your own preference.)

5 Spray an 11-by-17-inch nonreactive baking dish with cooking spray. Set aside.

6 Pile the filling into the mirliton halves, patting the filling in firmly. Place the stuffed mirlitons in the prepared baking dish. Spoon the Creole sauce around and over them. Cover and bake until very hot, about 35 minutes. Uncover, sprinkle with the remaining ½ cup breadcrumb topping. Raise the oven temperature to 400°F. Return the pan to the oven and bake, uncovered, until the tops are browned and slightly crunchy, another 10 minutes. Remove from the oven and serve with a sprinkle of minced parsley, if desired.

Stuffed Winter Squash

While summer squash are tender of skin, winter squash are hard (the better to keep through the long, long winter, my dear). While the flesh of summer squash is pale and somewhat watery, that of the winter squashes is a pale-to-bright orange-yellow, sweet, starchy, and very rich in beta-carotene. And while summer squashes come in few shapes, the winters include pumpkins, both huge and miniature; warty, orange-and-green mottled turbans; small golden and green acorns; cream, green, and orange striped cylindrical delicatas; blue-green hubbards; pale beige butternuts; ad infinitum. They say, collectively, "fall," "abundance," and "stuff me."

To prepare an acorn squash for stuffing, slice a ½-inch "top hat" from the stem end of each squash, or, if the squash are too large for individual servings, cut each in half. In either case, acorn squash are hard-shelled little things; it takes some work to cut through them, unless you have a razor-sharp cleaver and are willing to whack fearlessly. I like to retain the top hat and prepare it alongside the squash, resting it decoratively against it when serving. You can discard it or add it to

your bag of stuff for stock (see page 139). If the acorn squash have a flattened bottom that will allow them to stand upright, no more slicing is needed; if they have a small tip at the bottom, remove a very thin slice, no more than is required to give a level bottom. Next, scoop the inner seeds and stringy pulp from the cavity that remains in the squash.

Miniature pumpkins (if not shellacked for table decorations) are wonderfully sweet, and also come equipped with a neat cavity for stuffing, from which you only have to remove the seeds. Same goes for the delicious sweet dumpling squashes. Delicatas, another very sweet winter squash, are blimp-shaped, resembling zucchini with a harder shell, beautifully striped in golden, green, and buff. Slit them lengthwise and scoop out the seeds and stringy fibers.

Although I love the flavor of butternut squash and use them often, I don't think they're at their best stuffed. Their shape doesn't work naturally, as the shapes of so many other vegetables do. There's little natural cavity, they want to roll on a baking sheet, and they're an awkward size.

The medium-sized pumpkins, preferably the buff-colored ones (sweeter by far than the bright orange ones), on the other hand, are the perfect vehicle for the Thanksgiving-style stuffing on page 428. Cut off and reserve a lid, as you would preparatory to carving a jack-o'-lantern. Scoop out all of the seeds and fibers. Put an inch or two of water in a large pot. Place the pumpkin, cut side down, in the water, cap wedged in near it. Bring to a boil over high heat. Cover tightly and steam for 10 to 15 minutes to precook slightly. Remove the pot from the heat and let cool. When cool, remove from the pot. Since the pumpkin will be eaten with the stuffing, I like to season the inside with salt, pepper, a little tamari, Pickapeppa, and brown sugar, rubbing this into the exposed interior flesh after steaming.

Stuffed Acorn Squash with Shiitakes and Late-Summer Vegetables

Hard-shelled, green ribbed acorn squashes make convenient individual serving cases for stuffing, with their contrasting, slightly sweet orange flesh. They are often teamed with a sweet stuffing or drizzle of honey or maple syrup, but I prefer a savory filling such as this, essentially a gratinéed stir-fry of early fall's bounty. Feel free to add any fresh or dried herbs you like to the breadcrumb topping. Try serving this with a scoop of Lemon-Basil Rice Pilaf with White Wine (page 478). **SERVES 4**

4 small-to-medium or 2 large acorn squash, prepared for stuffing (see previous page)
1 teaspoon honey
1 teaspoon Pickapeppa sauce
1 teaspoon paprika
Salt and freshly ground black pepper to taste
Cooking spray
1 large onion, thinly sliced
4 ounces shiitake mushrooms, stems removed, caps cut into ¼-inch-thick strips
3 cloves garlic, pressed
1 small zucchini, quartered lengthwise, then cut crosswise into ½-inch-thick slices
1 large tomato, chopped
2 teaspoons tamari or shoyu soy sauce
½ cup grated Parmesan cheese (optional)
½ cup fine crisp breadcrumbs
1 tablespoon minced Italian parsley
1 teaspoon olive oil

1 Scrape out a little of the softened squash flesh (much will still be firm and not want to come out, which is fine, because you want a nice sturdy shell for stuffing). Dice the scraped-out squash flesh and set aside.

2 Combine the honey, Pickapeppa, and paprika and rub both the interior of the squash and the cut edge of the top hats lightly in the mixture. Season with salt and pepper to taste.

3 Preheat the oven to 375°F.

4 Heat a large nonstick skillet that has been sprayed with cooking spray, over medium heat. Add the onion and sauté until it is limp and translucent, about 5 minutes. Add the shiitakes. Lower the heat slightly and sauté until they, too, start to get limp, 1 to 2 minutes. Add 1 clove garlic, the

zucchini, tomato, and tamari. Raise the heat and cook, stirring constantly, until the zucchini is no longer raw and the tomato has almost melted into the mixture. Add the reserved squash flesh. Season with salt and lots of pepper. If using, stir in the Parmesan, along with ¼ cup of the breadcrumbs. Remove from the heat and set aside.

5 Spray a 9-inch square baking dish with cooking spray. Set aside.

6 Combine the remaining breadcrumbs with the remaining 2 cloves garlic, the parsley, and oil. Set aside. Mound an equal portion of the filling into each of the 4 squashes. Top with the breadcrumb mixture. Place the stuffed squashes and their lids in the prepared baking dish. Bake until the topping is nice and brown, 20 to 25 minutes. Serve immediately, with the top hat propped up next to each little squash.

VARIATION

To fancy this up a little, add ¼ cup minced pitted kalamata olives and/or a thin layer of grated sharp Cheddar cheese beneath the crumb topping.

Sweet Surprises Stuffed Delicata Squash

Tender and sweet—you want this in a lover's gaze, but hey, it's not bad in a squash, either. These are very autumnal, and have been enthusiastically received by all. Delicatas, striped like a beach umbrella, are very festive, too. This same stuffing is also divine in acorn squash, godivas, kabotas, or miniature pumpkins.

MAKES 10 STUFFED HALVES

5 delicata squash, halved lengthwise, seeds scraped out
2 teaspoons mild vegetable oil, such as corn, canola, or peanut
Cooking spray
1 onion, diced
2 apples, preferably a sweet variety such as Golden Delicious, unpeeled, diced
3 tablespoons frozen apple juice concentrate, thawed
1 tablespoon tamari or shoyu soy sauce
½ cup raisins
½ cup raw cashews, toasted at 350°F for 15 minutes
1 teaspoon paprika
½ cup fine cornflake crumbs
Salt and freshly ground black pepper to taste

1 Steam the squash over boiling water for 4 minutes, then place them in a colander to cool.

2 Heat the oil in a nonstick skillet, or one that has been sprayed with cooking spray, over medium heat. Add the onion and sauté until limp and starting to color, about 7 minutes. Add the apples and continue sautéing for another 3 minutes. Drizzle the apple juice concentrate and tamari over the onions and apples and cook until most of the liquid has evaporated, about 5 minutes. Remove the pan from the heat and set aside.

3 Preheat the oven to 400°F.

4 Scoop about half of the softened flesh from the squashes, leaving a ¼-inch-thick shell for stuffing. Chop the scooped-out flesh—it will be very soft—and stir it into the onion-apple mixture, along with the raisins and cashews. Add the paprika, cornflake crumbs, and salt and pepper to taste. Stir to combine, then place an equal portion into each of the 8 squash halves.

5 If not using a nonstick, spray a 13-by-9-inch baking dish with cooking spray.

6 Place the stuffed squashes in the prepared dish; they can be wedged against each other, but should remain in a single layer. Cover the pan tightly with foil, and bake for 45 minutes. Uncover and bake for an additional 15 minutes. Serve hot.

Susie Pryor's "Perfectly Delicious" Stuffed Acorn Squash

This recipe is from the late mother of our much-loved, recently retired, Arkansas senator, David Pryor. By all accounts Susie Pryor embodied what are to me the best of what I consider "Arkansas" qualities—neighborliness, the love of a good laugh or story, hard work, wry irreverence with deep, private reverence.

Her family remembers that whenever Susie bit into something she particularly liked, she would say, "That is *perfectly* delicious." This—another sweet squash stuffed with an almost-smooth mash rather than a chunky mixture—is exactly that. If you have a pressure cooker, the carrots and turnips can be quickly pressured instead of boiled—4 minutes at pressure should do it. **SERVES 4**

Cooking spray
4 small-to-medium or 2 medium-large acorn squash, prepared for stuffing (see page 423)
Salt
Water, preferably spring or filtered
2 carrots, chopped
2 small turnips, chopped (or better yet, if you can get it, rutabaga, an orange-y, slightly sweet turnip; you want to end up with 1½ to 2 cups chopped turnip or rutabaga)
1 tablespoon butter
1 tablespoon brown sugar
½ teaspoon ground cinnamon
A few gratings of nutmeg
1 cup peeled, finely diced apple

1 Preheat the oven to 350°F.

2 If not using nonstick, spray a 13-by-9-inch baking dish with cooking spray.

3 Place the squash, cut side down, in the prepared baking dish. Cover tightly with foil and bake for 30 minutes. Uncover and check if the squash are very tender. If not, turn the squash right side up, re-cover, and bake for another 20 minutes or so. Remove from the oven and carefully scoop out most of the squash flesh, keeping the outer shell intact. Place the flesh in a mixing bowl. Set both the squash halves and the flesh aside. Do not turn the oven off.

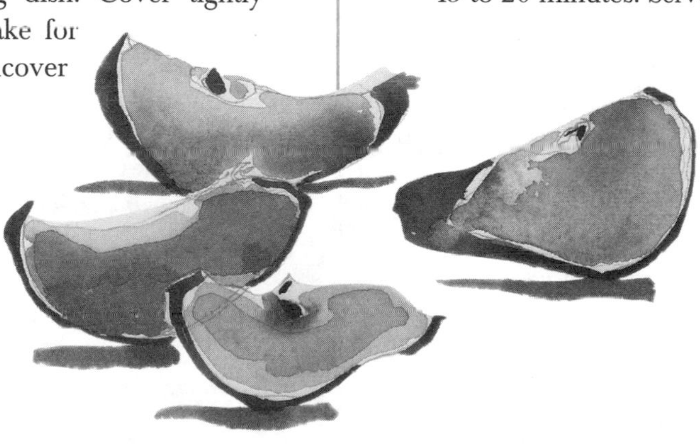

4 As the squash cooks, bring a medium pot of salted water to a boil over high heat. Add the carrots and turnips. Simmer until tender, 15 to 20 minutes. Drain (reserve the water for use in stock, if desired). Add the vegetables to the squash flesh.

5 Using an electric mixer, whip the three cooked vegetables together with the butter, brown sugar, cinnamon, nutmeg, and salt to taste. Stir in the apples. Divide the stuffing equally among the squash shells. Return the stuffed shells to the baking dish.

6 Bake, uncovered, until heated through, 15 to 20 minutes. Serve hot.

VARIATION

Stuffings were made to be played with. Try this updated version of George Washington Carver's Cornbread and Peanut Stuffing—yes, the father of the peanut was also a recipe developer, and his stuffing is good in any sweet winter squash. Either omit the dried fruit and apple juice, or substitute 1 cup each dark and golden raisins for the apricots and prunes (Carver didn't use fruit, but I like it). Substitute a double batch of crumbled cornbread (try Ronni's Skillet-Sizzled Kentucky Buttermilk Cornbread, page 452) for the bread. Use 1 tablespoon butter melted with 2 tablespoons peanut butter and 2 tablespoons roasted peanut oil. Fold in the finely grated rind of 1 to 2 lemons, and 1 cup chopped roasted skinless peanuts.

Neo-Classical Thanksgiving Dressing with Apricots and Prunes, Stuffed in a Whole Pumpkin

This is my favorite Thanksgiving stuffing—in fact, this is my *only* Thanksgiving stuffing. I've made it for at least twentyfive years, and it's always pleased me, friends, family, and inn guests. To my taste, it wouldn't be right with margarine or oil, just butter. But *probably* it wouldn't be bad with less fat or a different one. I make the vegetarian version with vegetable stock, for use in a pumpkin; when I cooked at the inn, where the majority of the guests were meat eaters, I also did a batch with turkey stock.

I dedicate this recipe to the memory of Sondra Krecker, a friend from my earliest years in Eureka Springs. Every Thanksgiving as I make it I hear her telling me again, earnestly, "You have to toast it dry, bone dry, hard dry." You'll need to do a lot of tossing and tasting to get the seasonings just right. Stuffing can be made ahead of time, but don't stuff it into the pumpkin until you're ready to bake it. **MAKES 1 MEDIUM-LARGE STUFFED PUMPKIN**

1 cup dried apricots
1 cup dried pitted prunes
1 cup apple juice
1 loaf good-quality commercially made presliced whole wheat bread
1 large onion, diced
1 to 2 stalks leafy celery, diced (leaves included)
1½ teaspoons to 1 tablespoon dried leaf (not ground) sage
¼ cup butter, melted
Vegetable stock (see page 139) as needed
Tamari or shoyu soy sauce to taste
A small amount of dried leaf basil and oregano to taste (optional)
Salt and freshly ground black pepper to taste
Cooking spray (optional)
1 medium-large pumpkin, preferably one of the buff-colored pumpkins, prepared for stuffing (see page 423)

1 Place the apricots and prunes in a small, heatproof bowl. Place the apple juice in a small saucepan over high heat and bring to a boil. Immediately pour the juice over the dried fruit. Let stand for at least 2 hours, but overnight or a day or two in advance is fine. Drain the dried fruit, reserving both the fruit and the soaking liquid. Coarsely chop the fruit and set aside.

2 Preheat the oven to 375°F, then turn down to 200°F.

3 Set a wire rack on a baking sheet and place a single layer of bread slices on the rack. Place in the preheated oven and bake, slowly, turning once, until the bread is hard, crunchy, and dry all the way through, but not browned. This is a fairly slow process—it might take 45 to 60 minutes, but set the timer at 20-minute intervals to remind you to check. You will either need to do 2 sheets' worth of bread (in which case, reverse their positions in the oven halfway through), or repeat the toasting again until all bread is prepared. Remove the dry bread from the oven and let cool.

4 Coarsely crumble the bread into a large bowl. Add the onion and leafy celery and toss to combine. Measure the sage (starting with the smaller amount) into your hands and rub the leaves back and forth in your palms until they crumble (this releases the volatile essential oils). Add the sage to the bread mixture. Pour the melted butter over the mixture and toss well to combine. Add the soaked dried fruit and toss again. The dressing should still be dry. Begin adding the liquid, a combination of vegetable stock and the reserved fruit soaking liquid. Use more stock than juice, and use just enough to moisten the dressing without making it soggy. Keep tossing, adding stock as needed. Add tamari, starting with about 1 tablespoon. Taste for salt and add it and plenty of pepper to taste. More sage, maybe? This is also the point at which you can add a little dried basil and oregano, too, if you like. The stuffing can be prepared up to this point and stored, covered and refrigerated, overnight.

5 On the day you plan to stuff the pumpkin, preheat the oven to 375°F.

6 If not using nonstick, spray a baking dish large enough to accommodate the pumpkin with cooking spray.

7 Stuff the dressing into the cavity of the prepared pumpkin, topping with the pumpkin's cap. Place the stuffed pumpkin in the prepared baking dish. Place in the preheated oven and bake until the pumpkin is slightly brown and looks a bit collapsed in on itself, or, as Ned says, like a plump European duchess, about 40 minutes. Serve whole, at the table.

"I cain't grow punkins on my land. I tried once, but the vines did so well they filled up the valley plumb level with the ridge tops so it looked like prairie, and the cows couldn't get down to the creek."

—Ozarks farming anecdote, related by **Donald R. Holliday,** in "What Is Work For?" *OzarksWatch,* 1996

Stuffed Tomatoes

If you have not stuffed a tomato, or eaten a good stuffed tomato, you don't know what you're missing. The texture of the tomato's interior is unique among the vegetable carriers. While the outer skin is firm enough to hold things together, the interior is moist, soft, and flavorful. It blends slightly, melding with the filling and adding another layer of savor when cooked.

TO PREPARE A TOMATO FOR STUFFING: Cut a slice off the stem end of the tomato, then reach in with a melon baller, serrated grapefruit spoon, or regular spoon, and scoop out the pulp—that is, the seeds, the juice, and the rays of membrane that radiate out from the center of the tomato. Reserve the tomato pulp—sometimes it's used in the stuffing, or it can be added to tomato sauce or soup. What you're left with is the outer skin and the layer of flesh next to it—anywhere from ⅛ to ⅓ inch thick, depending on the variety and the season.

Turn the hollowed tomatoes upside down on a plate to drain (if you're doing quite a few, set them on a rack that has been placed over a tray; you'll be amazed at how much juice they exude). Let drain for 15 to 20 minutes. Turn upright, and *lightly* season the interior with the salt and pepper. Stuff as directed in a specific recipe.

Before we get into recipes, I'd like to point out that the filling in the recipe for Red Bell Peppers Stuffed with Green Chile, Corn, and Hominy (page 412), is superb in tomatoes. After the tomatoes are stuffed, top with a bit of grated sharp Cheddar cheese (optional), then with some Breadcrumb Topping Provençal (page 277), and give them a quick bake in a nice hot oven— just long enough to melt the cheese and crisply brown the breadcrumbs.

Jenelle's Tomatoes Rockefeller

Spinach-stuffed tomatoes, with bread crumbs, one egg, Parmesan, a few herbs—who would believe that something so simple would meld into such an astonishingly good combo? The filling firms up pleasantly and becomes a bit crisped on top, and the tomato flesh does its meld-with-the-stuffing trick. If you've got the patience for it, you can also stuff small cherry tomatoes, for a sterling appetizer. This is one even dyed-in-the-wool carnivores will enjoy. **SERVES 4 TO 6**

1 teaspoon to 1 tablespoon butter
1 small onion, diced
4 cloves garlic, pressed
⅔ cup soft, fine whole wheat breadcrumbs
1 teaspoon dried oregano
½ teaspoon dried sweet basil
Pinch of dried rosemary
1 box (10-ounces) frozen chopped spinach, thawed and well drained (save the liquid for stock, if desired)
1 large egg, beaten
¼ cup freshly grated Parmesan cheese
Salt and freshly ground black pepper to taste
Cooking spray
4 to 6 tomatoes, prepared for stuffing (see opposite)

1 Preheat the oven to 400°F.

2 Melt the butter in a nonstick skillet over medium heat. Add the onion and sauté until softened, translucent, limp, and just starting to brown around the edges, about 6 minutes. Add the garlic and sauté for 2 minutes. Stir in the breadcrumbs, oregano, basil, and rosemary. When combined, stir in the spinach. Stir well and remove from the heat. Stir in the egg and Parmesan. Season with salt and pepper to taste. Set aside to cool slightly.

3 If not using nonstick, spray a baking sheet with cooking spray.

4 When the mixture is cool enough to handle, stuff it into the prepared tomato shells. Stuff rather firmly, and mound the filling over the tops of the tomatoes. Place the tomatoes on the prepared baking sheet.

5 Bake until the tops are slightly browned and crunchy, about 20 minutes. Serve hot or at room temperature.

Tomatoes Stuffed with Cornbread Dressing and Gravy

Given all the little squibs of leftover cornbread we used to have around the kitchen in our restaurant days, we were always coming up with ideas for this particular "déjà food." This one's especially delightful. If you don't have leftover cornbread, this recipe is a great excuse to make some fresh. The best choice is a nonsweet cornbread, like Ronni's Skillet-Sizzled Kentucky Buttermilk Cornbread (page 452). If you are making cornbread expressly for this recipe, omit the egg and just add ¼ cup extra buttermilk; you don't need that extra richness here.

Once baked in the tomato, the cornbread dressing is crusty on top, moist and soft inside, meant to be eaten so each bite has both stuffing and tomato. Southwestern flavors are perfect with cornbread, and the gravy is *such* a treat. If you are lukewarm about hot-hot spices, substitute ¼ cup chopped roasted green chiles (canned or fresh) for the chipotle.

MAKES 8 MEDIUM-SIZE STUFFED TOMATOES

Cooking spray
8 medium tomatoes, prepared for stuffing (see page 430), seeds and pulp reserved and chopped
2 to 3 cups leftover cornbread, crumbled and lightly toasted (see cornbread recipes on pages 451–52; this amount is just under ½ recipe)
Kernels from 2 ears fresh corn (optional)
½ canned chipotle pepper in adobo sauce, minced finely, with about 1 teaspoon of the sauce
1 large egg, beaten
¼ onion, finely chopped
½ cup instant dehydrated black bean mix
¼ cup cilantro leaves
1 teaspoon toasted cumin seeds
Salt and freshly ground black pepper
Southwestern-Style Tomato Gravy (optional but primo; recipe follows)

1 Preheat the oven to 375°F.

2 If not using nonstick , spray a 13-by-9-inch baking dish with cooking spray.

3 Combine about 2 cups of the tomato seeds and pulp with the cornbread. Add the corn, chipotle pepper and sauce, the beaten egg, onion, dehydrated black beans, cilantro, cumin, and salt and pepper to taste. Mash everything together well, preferably with your hands. The stuffing mixture should be moist but not soggy or crumbly. If it's too wet, add a little more cornbread; if too dry, add a few tablespoons of additional tomato pulp.

Canny Tomato Man

"The distinction of being the most colorful individual associated with the tomato industry in the Ozarks undoubtedly belonged to Frank Mease of Reeds Spring (Missouri), who at one time owned seven canneries. This entrepreneur, who grew wealthy through his agricultural enterprises, also wrote stories for health food magazines and, to show off his good health, would, when he was past eighty, stand on his head atop a straight-back chair in the bed of a pick-up truck—while his son drove him through town."

—Robert McGill, *"Red Gold–Ozark Tomatoes,"* in *OzarksWatch*, 1996

4 Scoop equal portions of the filling into each tomato shell, mounding high. Place the stuffed tomatoes on the prepared baking dish. Cover tightly with foil and bake for 25 minutes; uncover and continue baking until golden and crusty, 10 to 15 minutes. They are awfully good as is, but if you are one of those people whose soul cries out for gravy—or even if you're not—you will find that the one below puts these tomatoes positively over the top. Make it while the tomatoes bake.

5 Spoon and place a pool of the Southwestern-Style Tomato Gravy onto each plate, a plump stuffed tomato into each pool. Serve, perhaps with a salad before and a nice green vegetable accompanying (say, stir-fried green beans).

And Two More . . .

Tomatoes Stuffed with Crusty Country-Style Cornbread Dressing *are just one more delicious way to play the summer song of corn and tomatoes. Again, it's best with nonsweet cornbread. Follow the basic recipe above, but omit the cumin, cilantro, chipotle, and dried black beans. Instead, stir in 1 stalk celery, finely chopped; ½ cup coarsely chopped water chestnuts; and 1 to 1½ teaspoons leaf sage, crumbled between your fingers. When the cornbread mixture is combined, toss in 4 to 6 ounces of any crisply sautéed and coarsely crumbled vegetarian soysage. Bake as directed. If you'd like gravy, omit the chili powder from the recipe above.*

Tomatoes Stuffed with George Washington Carver–Style Cornbread and Peanut Stuffing. *Omit chiptole and sauce, cilantro, cumin, and dehydrated black beans from the cornbread dressing. Puree 2 tablespoons nonhydrogenated roasted peanut butter into the tomato pulp before blending with the cornbread. Then with the corn, onions, etc., stir in ⅓ cup finely chopped unsalted roasted peanuts. Serve with Carver-Style Sweet-Tart Tomato Gravy.*

Southwestern-Style Tomato Gravy

4 cups flavorful vegetable stock (see page 139)
Leftover tomato seeds and pulp
2 teaspoons butter
Cooking spray (optional)
2 teaspoons unbleached white all-purpose flour
½ teaspoon chili powder
2 tablespoons nutritional yeast (see page 239)
1 teaspoon tomato paste
Salt and freshly ground black pepper to taste

1 Place the vegetable stock and tomato seeds and pulp in a medium saucepan over medium heat. Cook for 10 minutes. Remove from the heat and, if you want your gravy smooth, strain; if you don't mind it with tomato pieces, simply proceed.

2 Melt the butter in a nonstick skillet, or one that has been sprayed with cooking spray, over medium heat. Whisk in the flour and chili powder. Cook, stirring, for a couple of minutes, then gradually whisk in the hot stock mixture. Add the nutritional yeast, tomato paste, and salt and pepper to taste. Cook for 3 minutes, then taste for seasonings. (If it's not thick enough to please you, blend a little cornstarch with water and whisk it into the hot gravy.)

VARIATION

CARVER-STYLE SWEET-TART TOMATO GRAVY

Omit the chili powder and add 2 teaspoons Rapidura or sugar, 2 teaspoons lemon juice, and a little grated lemon rind.

Parmesan-Crusted Zucchini Pudding in Tomato Cases

VARIATION

VEGAN VARIATION: ***Use soy or oat milk instead of dairy milk, commercially available tofu cream cheese instead of neufchâtel, and Parmesan-style soy cheese instead of dairy Parmesan.***

This is very similar to the "Gardener's Solution" Stuffed Zucchini (page 416), but slightly more interesting and richer, with the zuke transformed into a pudding and stuffed into a tomato. A great use of summer produce. **MAKES 6 STUFFED TOMATOES**

Cooking spray
4 medium zucchini, thickly sliced, blanched
2 ounces neufchâtel reduced-fat cream cheese (optional)
1 large egg
1 clove garlic, pressed
1 cup evaporated skim milk
¾ cup crisp breadcrumbs
⅓ cup freshly grated Parmesan cheese
1 tablespoon cornstarch
Salt and freshly ground black pepper to taste
6 tomatoes for stuffing (see page 430)

1 Preheat the oven to 375°F.

2 If not using nonstick, spray a baking dish large enough to hold the tomato cases side by side, with cooking spray.

3 Place the blanched zucchini in the food processor, and pulse/chop. Add the neufchâtel cheese, egg, garlic, evaporated skim milk, breadcrumbs, Parmesan, and cornstarch and buzz until a chunky puree is formed. Add salt and pepper to taste. Spoon the puree into the tomato cases.

4 Bake until the tops are lightly browned and slightly puffed, 20 to 25 minutes. Serve hot.

Great Grains

Recorded history, civilization, and in a sense time itself, began when we first planted our bright, revolving globe with the seed-bearing fruits of the edible grasses. Architecture, government, community, commerce, trade, notions of ownership and property, written language (hence literature, as well as accounting and record keeping)—all these were born when humankind began to participate in the cycle of the harvest.

Until humans learned to domesticate the cereals, we were sojourners, traveling from place to place in search of food to gather or hunt. When, some fifteen thousand years ago, we began to plant, tend, harvest, and plant again, the crops themselves charged us to stay in one place. Thereby, our relationship to all nature, and to our fellows, changed forever. We ourselves became rooted. Particular places became "home."

And home became ever homier as we discovered the many ways in which grains can be enjoyed. Wheat is consumed as bread, beer, bulghur, and biscotti; as pasta and pastry; as couscous, cake, and cookies. Corn becomes tortillas, polenta, hominy, hoecake, spoonbread, sweet syrup, breakfast flakes; we even drink it, as whisky. Rice—paella in Spain, risotto in Italy, pilaf, pilau, and perlu throughout the Middle East—is also, in Japan, saki or rice wine, sushi, rice vinegar. In many lands, rice becomes a sweet, comforting dessert pudding; in some, especially America, it's puffed to crispness for the breakfast bowl. Mostly, it is left plain and pure, sometimes sticky, sometimes fluffy. In India, rice is heart and soul of a thousand meals. Ground, it becomes *dosha* and *iddli,* and feeding "first rice" to an infant is celebrated as a joyous family event. Even in America, where wheaten foodstuffs are prevalent and corn our native grain, we still throw rice at weddings, a blessing of prosperity, fruitfulness, abundant continuity, and freedom from hunger for the new couple.

Despite brief flurries of opinion to the contrary, most Americans know that grains sustain us, as they have sustained humanity for millennia. Nothing fills us so satisfyingly; nothing packs so substantial a nutritional wallop; nothing is so basic, or so comforting, as a plate of polenta or pasta, a wedge of cornbread.

For all their variety, we really use whole or cracked grains only three ways. Most often, we serve them as a *basic:* a nutritious component, a plain starch, as a mound of rice, say, with curry or gravy. Then too, they can be a *gussied-up basic:* slightly seasoned, cooked in broth, juice, or wine, with a simple addition or two, but still essentially a component, not a centerpiece. Pilafs are in this category. Last, there are what I call *main grains*—those preparations that are the focus of the plate. Think risotti, many grits and polenta preparations, and the similar category I introduce here as "ri-sort-ofs"—savory porridges of grains other than rice.

Please note that most grains are interchangeable and easily combined. Cooked cracked wheat can substitute for cooked rice in a rice salad; a seasoning paste stirred into amaranth can adorn cooked wheat kernels instead; rye pilaf can become rye-barley pilaf. The important thing is to eat grains as often as possible: for the sensual pleasure it brings; for dinnertime variety; for the individual nutritional profiles of different grains; for the adventure; and, not least, because grains are incredibly economical.

We are now about to walk, grain by grain, through the vast and amber fields. To navigate this huge acreage, I've divided this

Grain Learning Curve

Whole grains are delicious when prepared attentively (though they may be an acquired taste to those who have only had the refined ones). And there is no reason one can't enjoy both refined and whole grains. For example, I genuinely love brown rice, especially "texmati" (more on this later), brown sushi rice, and both long- and short-grain brown rice. I also enjoy good ol' Uncle Ben's Converted and Thai jasmine, both of which are white rices. Arborio, the fat Italian rice used for making risotto, is delicious in white and brown forms. But instant white rice does nothing for me, and brown basmati doesn't do much either. You just have to play around a little and decide for yourself.

chapter into two sections. The first, old friends, covers the three grains most widely eaten throughout the world: corn, wheat, and rice. The second, new friends, visits many less common grains, which you may know slightly (buckwheat, millet), or may not have experienced yet (spelt, quinoa, amaranth). In both sections, I'll give you basic preparations, a gussied-up version or two, and a main grain. Before we get to the specific grains, here's some general information that will be helpful.

Strategies for Incorporating Whole Grains into Your Diet

Yes, many whole grains are, on the face of it, time-consuming to cook. But there are quick, easy ways to include grains in your diet if you strategize a little. Undoubtedly, most of us eat our grains more often as pasta or bread (usually made from refined flour) than in whole form. But these products, while fine now and again, simply don't offer us the nutrients, fiber, and micronutrients whole grains deliver so deliciously.

I discuss in Quick Fix (Chapter 13) some methods of working around the long cooking times of certain grains and beans. Basically, to make grain cooking timely and convenient:

- always cook more than you need for a single meal;
- get yourself a pressure cooker and use it;
- get friendly with the quicker-cooking whole grains (millet, quinoa) as well as the quicker-cooking forms of slow-cooking grains (flaked barley or wheat).

Why Whole Grains Are Worth It

What is meant by "whole grain"? All grains contain a nucleus known as the germ, which is the heart of the grain, for it is this part that would germinate if the grain were planted. I liken the germ of a grain to the yolk of an egg. The germ is one of the most nutritious parts of the grain, rich in vitamin E, the B-vitamins, and a number of minerals, and higher in both fat and protein than some of the other parts of the grain.

But just as an egg requires more than yolk to become a chick, so the germ of a grain needs more than germ to become a plant. Hence each grain includes other components: endosperm, bran, and hull. The endosperm is the largest part of the grain. It is made up mostly of starch, with some protein also supplied to nourish the germ. The bran surrounds the endosperm, an interior protective layer. The outermost, indigestible layer, further protecting germ and endosperm, is the hull. (One reason wheat and rye are so popular is that, unlike barley, rice, and oats, their grains grow "naked"—there is no hard hull to coax the tender grain out of.) Returning to the egg analogy, the yolk is the germ, fed by the white—the endosperm. The thin protective membrane you see when you peel a hard-cooked egg would be the bran, and the shell would be the inedible hull.

When we refine grains, as when we make white flour from whole wheat, or white rice from brown, we generally process out everything except the starchy endosperm. Hence, instead of "whole" grains, we get weakened, partial ones. Even when flours are "enriched" with versions of some of what was removed, they still lack the nutrients of their natural form, the micronutrients (some, perhaps, still unknown to us), and the fiber removed with the bran.

General Tips on Cooking Grains

All grains must be cooked in some form of liquid. The amount of liquid and the cooking time vary from grain to grain and are affected somewhat by the age of the grain (last year's crop will take longer to cook than this year's). But there are four general principles to understand, regardless of the grain.

One is that using a pressure cooker will cut cooking time by about two-thirds. Two is that adding grain to liquid that is already boiling tends to leave the grains separate and distinct, whereas soaking the grain before cooking it, or adding it to cold liquid, tends to yield a stickier end product. The boiling liquid in effect "sears" the outside of the grain, keeping the starch within; the cold water allows it to release gradually, like flour thickening a sauce. Neither end product is better or worse; they're just different.

Three is that, in general, you don't want to stir grains while cooking, which releases starch prematurely and prevents the even steaming that most grains require. When you see little holes in your finished pot of rice, that's where the steam came up. Again, there are exceptions; risotto is creamy and has its own self-made sauce *because* it is stirred. Four is that if you end up with leftover liquid—this sometimes happens when you're cooking barley or whole wheat kernels, which tend to vary in the amount of water they require to cook—do not throw it out. It will be a little viscous from the starch, but it's packed with nutrition. You can either drink it—it's bland but incredibly soothing (in South India they deliberately cook rice this way as a home remedy for upset stomach; it's called *ganyee*)—or use it in bread baking or in stock.

Pastas, which are made from the flour of ground grains (and not just wheat, although the variety of wheat called durum or semolina is by far the most common base for pasta), belong here too. Though many pasta recipes are scattered throughout this book, I have put something about the preparation of various nonwheat pastas—corn, quinoa, rice, buckwheat, and so on—in those grains' sections. Now, be advised: If you grew up on conventional, durum wheat–based spaghetti, you'll probably expect something called pasta to taste and feel a particular way in your mouth. You might be surprised when you experience, say, slippery, assertively flavored buckwheat soba noodles for the first time. But the second or third time—wow! These more exotic pastas are not just for those who are allergic to wheat; they are genuine and distinct culinary escapades, small and delicious adventures with which to enrich your table and your life.

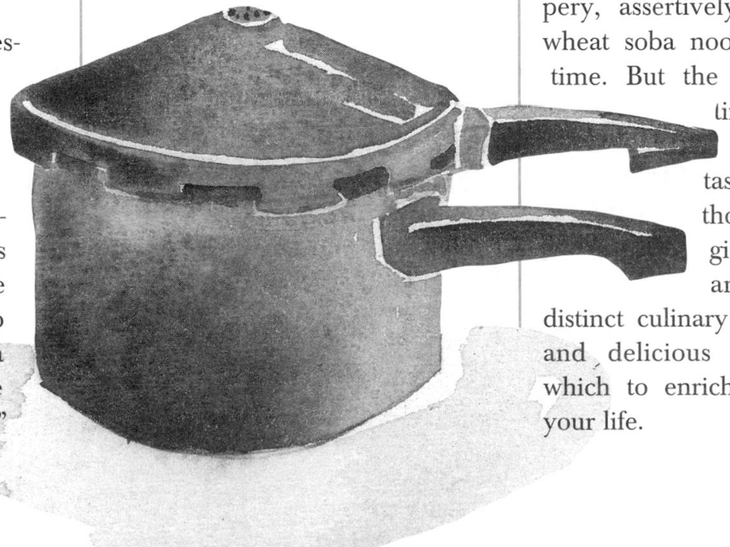

Cornucopia

Although it is not the only grain native to the Americas, corn was by far the most widely used, both when this vast region belonged to its indigenous inhabitants and after Europeans arrived. The Incas and Aztecs first domesticated corn from a wild grain, gradually rendering it, through their agricultural practices, the only grain that cannot breed by itself. What could be a clearer statement of the unique intimacy between humankind and the grain the Arawak Indians called *mahiz,* than that it requires human assistance to reproduce?

Many of our most beloved corn preparations today date back to the earliest ways with the grain. We still eat corn on the cob and tortillas. Popcorn is perhaps the most ancient of the ways we consume maize now. In *The Story of Corn,* Betty Fussell writes about the 1948 exploration of an archeological site in Catron County, New Mexico, where prehistoric corn kernels were uncovered. Later, a few of these were dropped into hot oil—and, lo and behold, after thousands of years, they popped.

Corn began a world-changing voyage with Columbus's return to Europe. The grain was intensely exotic to him and other early explorers—not only its taste and the ways it could be prepared, but its very form. Corn was easily and quickly grown, and astonishingly abundant in yield (where a single grain of wheat yielded thirty to one hundred harvested grains, a single grain of corn returned seven hundred to eight hundred kernels). The early explorers introduced this provocative foodstuff to the rest of the world, which quickly took it up. Within a single generation, corn was grown throughout southern Europe; within two, throughout much of the Western world.

By the time the Jamestown settlers arrived in 1607, and certainly by the time of the pilgrims' first Thanksgiving dinner in 1621 (to which native guests are said to have brought popcorn, in a deerskin pouch), corn was still exotic to most Northern Europeans. So the settlers spurned it, planting instead the seeds of their familiar wheat, barley, and rye. When these old crops failed in the new land, corn—which the American Indians taught the settlers how to prepare, store, and cultivate—enabled the pilgrims and the Jamestown settlers to survive. Indeed, Plymouth Colony governor William Bradford said, "And sure it was God's good providence that we found this corne, for else we know not how we should have done."

From necessity grew affection, then preference. As the colonists' children and grandchildren, born on New World soil, grew up on corn and foods made from it (like cornbread), these foods came to say "home" to many Americans. Inevitably, corn preparations were among America's first "fusion foods": created, as all such dishes are, when cultures collide and mingle. Indian pudding, the sweet, dense dessert still popular in New England, of slow-cooked, molasses-sweetened cornmeal, with milk, eggs, dried fruits, and spices, is just one example.

Besides being uniquely American, corn is unique in the ages, stages, and forms in which we eat it. We eat it fresh, as a vegetable (see page 736); and feed its stalks to farm animals. Dried, we eat it whole or ground; we make it into bread (see page 451) or mush/polenta/grits (see next page); and transform it into hominy and masa harina. We sauté with corn oil; sweeten with corn syrup (see Honeyed Browned Butter Pecan Pie, page 1023). Diverse, larger than life, American from root to tassel, and sustaining us year round, corn is the essence of generous abundance.

Corn in All Its Forms

Sweet corn is the summer vegetable we all know and love. Most corn products like cornmeal and grits are made not from sweet corn, but from starchy field corn. Here are the various forms in which you are likely to meet corn as a grain.

Hominy: Also called *posole,* is whole dried kernels of corn that have been boiled with an alkali agent (traditionally lye or lime), rinsed, and then boiled into a tender mush. A stew that contains hominy may also be called a hominy or *posole.*

Although it's possible to buy dried hominy and cook it yourself, it is more readily available cooked and in the can—not at the natural foods store, but in the supermarket. Sometimes it's with the Latin American foods (in which case it's usually labeled *posole*); other times you'll find it with the canned vegetables. Lest you think that something out of a can is bound to have lost out in the translation, let me assure you that this is not the case. Canned hominy is simply cooked hominy, much as canned beans are simply cooked beans—it's not a case where the whole character of the food is lost in the canning process. Occasionally you'll find hominy canned in various sauces or stews; avoid those. What you want is the plain white or yellow kind. I prefer white.

I use hominy a lot, so you'll find several recipes using it throughout this book, including White Chili with Eggplant, Poblanos, and Posole (page 189); Posole-Bean Soup-Stew with New World Vegetables (page 210); Gingered Salad with Cilantro, Tofu, and Hominy (page 116); and Center Street–Style Potato-Posole "Nedchiladas" with Tomatillo Salsa Verde (page 344).

Hominy Grits: Hominy that has been coarsely ground.

> *"It was part of the Texas ritual. We're rich as son-of-a-bitch stew but look how homely we are, just as plain-folksy as Grandpappy back in 1836. We know about champagne and caviar but we talk hog and hominy."*
>
> —**Edna Ferber,** *Giant*

Cornmeal: Ground corn kernels. Stone-ground whole-grain cornmeal (sometimes called "water-ground," because the grinding stones are often powered by water) is the most flavorful and nutritious cornmeal you can buy. Because it still contains its oily germ, it has a short shelf life. Use freshly ground cornmeal within two or three weeks (it lasts a little longer in cold weather) or refrigerate it.

Cornstarch: A highly refined floury powder, cornstarch is primarily used to thicken sauces when a quick, no-fat-necessary thickener is needed, and a glossy, shiny texture and appearance is desired (most American Chinese restaurants thicken sauces with cornstarch). Some people are also fond of it for thickening fruit in pie fillings. Definitely not a whole-food

The Gritty Truth

Ah, grits, the subject of a thousand regional chauvinisms! How sad it is that when you call this oft-maligned cornmeal mush by its Italian name, polenta, it becomes romantic, hip, $15- to $40-a-plate restaurant fare. Just remember that a grit by any other name is still a grit.

product, it still has its uses in small quantities: as a quick fix in sauces, and also in baking certain cookies and cakes—both for the unique texture it imparts to certain recipes, and in adapting baked goods for the gluten- or wheat-intolerant.

Grits, or corn grits, are cornmeal or the mush made from it. Whereas hominy grits are made from corn kernels processed with an alkaline substance, corn grits are made from unprocessed kernels.

Polenta: The Italian word for cornmeal or the mush made from it.

Masa Harina: Corn that has been boiled with an alkali agent and then ground into a very fine flour. Masa harina is used to make tortillas and to thicken some sauces (some chilies are traditionally masa-thickened). Masa has a distinctive, easily recognizable taste, grainy but not sweet, and quite different from regular cornmeal. Dry masa keeps better than stone-ground sweet cornmeal and its processing allows it to be more finely ground, floury rather than granular like cornmeal.

Basic Polenta, Grits & Mushes

Good old cornmeal, cooked in water or another liquid, makes a kind of substantial, sustaining porridge. A simple food, it's eaten as a neutral grain under any piquant sauce or spiced foodstuff; combined with seasonings and dressed up a bit; eaten as a breakfast cereal with milk and maple sugar; or sliced and browned in little cakes. It's as good and unpretentious as its names: mush (if you're a Yankee) or, as a coarser grind, grits (if you're a Southerner).

I prefer to make my own grits at home from freshly stone-ground cornmeal, but sometimes for convenience I buy commercially prepared salami-shaped tubes of cooked yellow cornmeal, "polenta," from the local supermarket. They keep on the shelf indefinitely and are very, very good. It's well worth having a couple of tubes on your shelf for when a last-minute polenta urge strikes. It's perfect for making firm, sliceable polenta or grits cakes, as a crostini base, for slicing and sautéeing, or in lasagne-type casseroles in lieu of pasta.

But most times I want polenta as soft comfort food, made by slow-cooking coarse stone-ground cornmeal in water. Nothing is better under a spicy stew, especially one rich with dark mushrooms. And sometimes, nothing is better, period. What follows are several methods of this essentially simple process of slow-cooking cornmeal in water.

Double-Boiler Method for Polenta, Grits, or Mush

Precise proportions and directions for making polenta are difficult to give. First off, the more coarsely ground the cornmeal, the more water it will absorb and the longer it will take to cook. Second, in certain recipes you'll want it to cook thicker

To Set up Grits/Polenta

When a properly cooked cornmeal product is chilled, it sets up, or solidifies, enough to be sliced. The slices can be cut in an infinite variety of shapes and thicknesses, and cooked a second time for an outer crispness.

The possible toppings are infinite, and various flavorings and ingredients can be added to the cooked cornmeal before it sets. Polenta slices can serve as a base for hors d'oeuvres or any savory topping, from a simple poached egg to something fancy. They can replace noodles, as in the lasagna recipes on pages 360 to 375. Another option: Line a baking dish or other container with the thick-cooked polenta, spreading it up the sides of the dish, and chill to make a kind of crust. Then fill it as for Tamale Pie (page 449), and bake it.

Make sure the polenta has cooked long enough—you need a finished product that is quite thick. You may either decrease the liquid called for by about 3 tablespoons per cup of cornmeal or grits, or, for even better results, use the same amount of liquid, and cook the meal longer. You want cooked meal that is almost too thick to stir, and has begun to pull or peel away from the sides of the pot. Spoon this thick-cooked polenta into almost any kind of oiled flat pan you like, spreading it out to make a thinnish layer, perhaps ¼ to ¾ inch thick, depending on the size of the pan. Smooth the top of the polenta with a spatula, cover with plastic wrap, and refrigerate until quite solid, a couple of hours at least. What you will end up with is a firm cake of solid polenta, the size and shape of the pan. Turn the set-up mush out of the pan, and slice.

Thinner polenta squares become crunchy on the outside. This makes them perfect as the base for hors d'oeuvres (see crostini below). Thicker shapes will have a creamy inside and a crunchy outside, and are very nice with things like grilled vegetables that have some crunch of their own.

To Make Broiled "Crostini": *Preheat the broiler. Working with thin, set-up polenta, cut the chilled cornmeal cake into diamonds or squares, triangles or rectangles—even circles, using a biscuit cutter, if you like (that will leave you some scraps, but you could use them in any baked polenta lasagne). Place the shapes on an oiled or sprayed baking sheet, give them an optional very light brush or spray of olive oil (this adds flavor and aids in browning), and place them directly beneath the broiler. Broil until the top surface is golden-brown and crusty, 3 to 4 minutes; watch closely. Now, you may serve them browned on one side only, or remove the pan from the broiler, flip the shapes (moment of truth: did you cook the cornmeal long enough so that they hold together during the flipping process?), repeat the optional light brush of oil, and broil for another 3 to 4 minutes to brown the other side. Serve the crostini hot, with any of the canapé toppings listed in Welcoming Hors d'Oeuvres (Chapter 2).*

To Make Baked "Crostini": *Preheat the oven to 375°F. Cut the shapes as above, place on an oiled baking sheet, and brush with optional oil. Bake until the crostini are thoroughly heated, crusty, and starting to color on top, 5 to 7 minutes; watch closely. Again, you may serve them browned on just one side or both; if you choose the latter, flip the shapes, repeat the optional light brush of oil, and bake for another 5 to 7 minutes.*

(as when you're planning to refrigerate it so it can "set up" to a sliceable solid) than if you're serving it wet and unformed, straight from the pot to a waiting bowl.

Butter or olive oil is always optional, always delicious. Although water is the most widely used cooking liquid for polenta, almost anything can be used for variety or richness. All or part spring water or dairy, rice, or soy milk; all or part vegetable stock; perhaps all or part fruit juice (for a sweet dish or hot cereal; apple juice–cooked polenta, with a little almond butter stirred in afterward, is a great favorite with some children I know). Be aware, though, that cornmeal cooked with anything but water—especially milk—does not keep as well.

Assuming you are serving some kind of savory topping with the polenta, allow 1 cup cornmeal for 4 servings. **SERVES 4 AS A SIDE DISH**

Cooking spray
3 to 4 cups liquid (see above for choices, step 1 for proportions)
1 to 2 teaspoons salt, or to taste
1 cup fine, medium, or coarse stone-ground cornmeal, yellow or white, or coarse corn grits
1 teaspoon to 1 tablespoon butter or olive oil (optional)

1 Fill the bottom of a double boiler with water to a depth of 1 to 2 inches, and bring to a boil. Estimate the amount of cooking liquid needed: If using very coarsely ground corn grits, allow 4½ cups liquid to 1 cup grits; for fine- or medium-fine–ground cornmeal, allow 3½ cups liquid to 1 cup meal.

2 Spray the top pot of the double boiler with cooking spray and add the cooking liquid and salt. Place the pot directly on the heat to bring the liquid to a boil.

3 Pour the cornmeal or grits in with one hand in a slow, steady stream, and whisk like the dickens with the other. Immediately transfer this pot to the top of the double boiler, add the butter or oil, if using, and cover with a tight-fitting lid.

4 Let cook, covered, with the water in the bottom pot boiling gently, for 30 minutes to 1¾ hours, depending on the grind of the meal and desired thickness of the finished product (figure about 65 minutes for fine-ground and 1¾ hours for coarse, if you want a firm end result). Give the cooking cereal a stir every 10 to 15 minutes, then increase to every 10 minutes for the last half hour of cooking. Check the base of the double boiler occasionally, and refill the water, which will otherwise boil away.

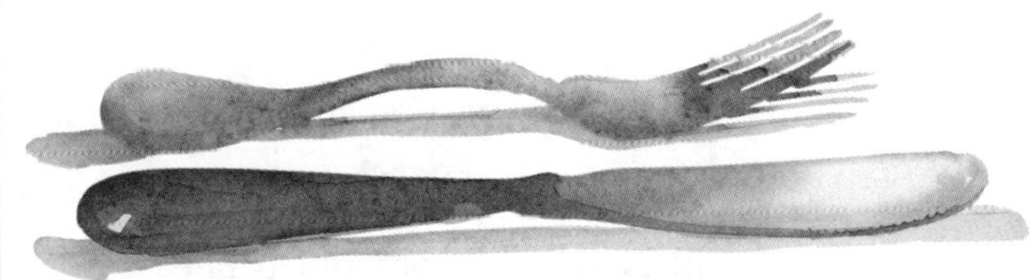

Crockpot Method for Polenta, Grits, or Mush

You say you don't like to stir that much? The possibility of the double boiler boiling dry makes you nervous? All right, here comes easy. Is there a catch? Well, the polenta has to cook for 6 to 9 hours; yes, you read that right. And, given the size of a standard slow cooker, you'll have to make a double batch (8 servings, rather than 4). Of course, that's no drawback. Cook it soft and fluffy for Sunday; let the rest chill and eat it as little cakes or in a casserole during the week. **SERVES 8 AS A SIDE DISH**

Cooking spray
7 to 8 cups boiling liquid (see previous page)
1½ to 2½ teaspoons salt, or to taste
2 cups cornmeal, preferably stone-ground, coarse or fine
1 teaspoon to 1 tablespoon butter or olive oil (optional)

1 Spray the inside of a slow cooker well with cooking spray. Turn the heat to high.

2 Add the liquid, salt, and cornmeal and stir well. Cover and leave on high for 1 hour, then lift the lid, stir well, and turn the heat to low.

3 Continue cooking, stirring very occasionally (once an hour or so, if you happen to think of it), until tender and very thick, 6 to 9 hours. Serve hot, as is, or chill and "set up" for later use.

Oven-Baked Method for Polenta, Grits, or Mush

Food writer Paula Wolfert says this stir-free method of cooking polenta changed her life. She discovered it on the back of a package of Golden Pheasant polenta, and Ed Fleming of Golden Pheasant told her it was an old Tuscan peasant recipe.

Grits, Gussied Up

CREAMY COARSE-GROUND YELLOW CORN GRITS WITH PARMESAN AND CAYENNE: *I almost never use heavy cream at home, but I used to in my restaurant, and indeed most restaurant polentas are finished with a lashing of cream. This was a favorite at Dairy Hollow, especially with Ragoût of Shiitake Mushrooms, Black-Eyed Peas and Southern Greens (page 243). Use coarse-ground yellow corn grits, cooked in salted water using a 1:4 ratio (see page 443, Step 1) for 1 hour to 1 hour and 15 minutes. When very thick but still stirrable, stir in 1/8 to 1/2 teaspoon ground cayenne, 1/4 cup heavy cream, and 1/2 cup freshly shredded Parmesan cheese. Grind in black pepper, too, if you like it. Serve immediately, or keep warm, covered, over hot but not boiling water in a double boiler. Yummy, as most cheese-plus-corn-plus-cream concoctions are.*

POLENTA GORGONZOLA DA VITTORIO: *A trip to New York, to me, used to mean a call to tiny Da Vittorio on 20th Street, for dinner reservations. Now, this impossibly good Italian restaurant is gone, but my interpretation of their much-loved polenta lives on. It is only as good as the gorgonzola you use. Choose either the sharp (naturale) or the less-aged sweet (dolce); I prefer the sweet. Use fine- or medium-fine–ground yellow corn grits, cooked in salted water using a 1:3½ ratio (see page 443, Step 1) for about 1 hour. When very thick but still stirrable, stir in 1/3 cup heavy cream and 1/2 cup crumbled gorgonzola. Grind in some black pepper, too, if you like it. Transfer to a shallow gratin dish or individual gratin dishes and sprinkle with additional crumbled gorgonzola. Run the dish quickly under a broiler until the cheese melts but just barely starts to color, and serve immediately. The perfect accompaniment: a garlicky sauté of bitter Italian greens, like broccoli rabe. Or try Cabbage and Greens with Kidney Beans and Caramelized Garlic (page 718).*

PUMPKIN-PARMESAN POLENTA: *Another simply wonderful variation. I usually use cornmeal rather than grits here, in the 1:3 proportion (see page 443, Step 1), with spring water as the liquid. Peel and seed either 1/2 small pie pumpkin or 1 small butternut or kabocha squash (the latter is especially good here). Dice the pumpkin or squash into 1/2-inch cubes. After you stir the cornmeal into the water, add the cubes, raw, and let them cook with the cornmeal. By the time the cornmeal is done, the squash or pumpkin is very tender and has almost melted into it. Remove from the heat and stir in 1/2 to 3/4 cup freshly shredded Parmesan, and 1/4 cup Yogurt Sour Cream (page 910), or commercial sour half-and-half or reduced-fat sour cream. Again optional, but good, is plenty of freshly ground black pepper, plus a tiny bit of cayenne. This is good beyond reason when served with a garlicky sauté of wild and exotic mushrooms in a nice brown sauce with a base of Oven-Roasted Vegetable Stock (page 141).*

GRATIN OF PUMPKIN-PARMESAN POLENTA: *Oil or spray a 9½-by-13½inch baking dish. Prepare the preceding recipe, but stir in only half the Parmesan and do not add the Yogurt Sour Cream at all. Turn the cooked grits out into a baking dish and allow it to "set up" (see page 442). About 50 minutes before serving, preheat the oven to 375°F. Turn the polenta out of its pan and cut into squares, rectangles, or triangles. Place the polenta pieces on an oiled or sprayed baking sheet, 1 inch apart. Brush each piece very lightly with olive oil. Bake for 35 to 45 minutes, or until the tops are dry and crusty. Raise the oven heat to broil. Sprinkle the tops of the pieces with the remaining Parmesan, run the baking dish under the broiler until the cheese melts, and serve proudly with a tomato or mushroom sauce, pumpkin-tomato sauce, or a dab of Yogurt Sour Cream.*

VEGAN PUMPKIN POLENTA: *Follow the recipe above, but use vegetable stock to replace half the water as the cooking liquid. Omit both the Parmesan and the Yogurt Sour Cream; instead, use a nice dollop of Tofu Sour Cream (page 909), or pumpkin-tomato sauce or a mushroom sauce.*

She wrote about it with something close to rapture in the March 1999 issue of *Fine Cooking*. It works deliciously, and I think you will love it as much as I do.

As Paula writes, it does require a "leap of faith," because for at least half the baking time the water and meal separate, but they reunite roughly 25 minutes into the baking. **SERVES 4 AS A SIDE DISH**

Cooking spray
3½ to 6 cups liquid (see page 443)
1½ to 2½ teaspoons salt, or to taste
1 cup cornmeal, preferably stone-ground, coarse or fine
1 teaspoon to 1 tablespoon butter or olive oil (optional)

1 Preheat the oven to 350°F.

2 Generously spray a 3-quart skillet with cooking spray. A nonstick skillet is much preferred, but make sure it is heat-safe to 350°F; it probably said this on the tag you threw out.

3 Add all the ingredients and stir well. The mixture will separate, with the meal sinking to the bottom. Don't worry. Just put the pan in the oven, uncovered, and forget about it. Don't give it a second thought until 40 minutes are up. At this point, stir the polenta, and bake for another 10 minutes.

4 Remove the pan from the oven and let it sit at room temperature for 5 minutes. Serve the polenta soft, as is, or chill and "set up."

Grilled Cake of Green Chile, Corn, and Grits

I love to make this as part of a component plate, with cooked beans (I usually use black-eyed peas, black beans, or pintos in a spicy tomato sauce) and good gutsy mixed greens—collard plus turnip and kale, say. Add a sweet-sour relish, like Cora Pinkley Coll's (page 929), and you have an abundant South-by-Southwest platter—very pleasing. Or go straight Southwest by serving it with

New Mexico–Style Green Chile Sauce (page 942), or with any one of the chilies (pages 187 to 193). **SERVES 4 TO 6 AS PART OF A COMPONENT DINNER**

- **1 recipe polenta, grits, or mush, cooked (just to the point where a spoon will stand up in it) by any method, preferably using coarse-ground cornmeal or yellow stone-ground grits**
- **3 ears fresh corn, shucked**
- **¼ to ½ cup finely diced charred, peeled, seeded poblanos, or canned green chiles, mildly hot**
- **About 1 tablespoon olive oil**
- **About 1 tablespoon corn oil**
- **1 teaspoon tamari or shoyu soy sauce**

1 Prepare the polenta, grits, or mush as directed. As it cooks, steam the corn for 3 minutes (if the corn is very fresh and tender, you need not presteam it). Cut the kernels off the cob. Place the kernels in a food processor and chop coarsely with 5 or 6 quick pulse/chops to make a chunky puree.

2 When the polenta has cooked to the point where a spoon will stand up in it, add the fresh corn, and cook for 5 to 10 minutes more, stirring a few times, until the mixture is extremely thick.

3 Remove the mixture from heat and stir in the green chiles.

4 Spread the mixture about ½ inch thick in a jelly-roll pan. Let cool, cover with plastic wrap, and refrigerate at least overnight.

5 When ready to serve, preheat the grill or broiler. Cut the chilled polenta into squares or rectangles about 2½ inches long. Combine the oils and tamari in a small bowl and brush the shapes with this mixture. Grill until golden brown and marked, turning once after 5 to 7 minutes and browning the other side. Serve immediately.

Cornmeal-Oatmeal Blueberry Bread

Save this for fresh blueberry time. This is a perfect, not-too-sweet bread, great for tea, breakfast, maybe even dessert. Cornmeal gives a pleasant, toothy crunch, lemon a subtle accent; the blueberries are little explosions of color and flavor in the pale golden loaf. Its texture is light, firm, reminiscent of poundcake, yet it's very low in fat. In the inn days, guests were likely to find this in their breakfast basket in June and July. Now, resident writers at The Writers' Colony at Dairy Hollow enjoy it, sometimes for dessert, with a little vanilla ice cream. For another sweet with a cornmeal crunch, try Neo-Zialetti Ozark-Style Cornmeal Cookies with Lemon and Raisins (page 1038). **MAKES 1 LARGE OR 3 SMALL LOAVES**

Cooking spray
1½ cup unbleached white flour
¼ teaspoon baking soda
1 teaspoon baking powder
⅓ cup stone-ground yellow cornmeal
¾ cup sugar
½ teaspoon salt
3 tablespoons mild oil, such as corn, canola, or peanut
2 large eggs
½ cup plus 2 tablespoons buttermilk
Finely grated rind of 1 lemon
1 cup blueberries, washed and picked over
2 to 4 tablespoons walnuts, toasted and chopped (optional)
¼ cup rolled oats (regular cooking oatmeal, not instant)

1 Preheat the oven to 350°F. If not using nonstick, coat 1 (8-by-4-inch) or 3 (5-by-2-inch) loaf pans with cooking spray.

2 Sift the flour, baking powder, and soda together into a large bowl. Add the cornmeal, sugar, and salt, and stir to combine.

3 In a second bowl, beat together the oil, eggs, buttermilk, and lemon rind until well combined.

4 Combine the blueberries, walnuts, if using, and rolled oats in a third bowl, and sprinkle 1 tablespoon of the flour-cornmeal mixture over them. Gently stir to combine.

5 Quickly stir the egg mixture into the flour-cornmeal mixture, using as few strokes as possible. Gently stir in the blueberry mixture. The batter should be stiff.

6 Spoon the batter into the prepared pan(s). Bake 45 to 55 minutes (for 1 large pan) or 35 to 40 (for 3 small pans). Check ⅔ of the way through the baking period; if the loaves are browning excessively, tent them loosely with foil.

7 Let the baked bread(s) cool 10 minutes in the pan, then run a knife around the edge of the pan, and turn the loaves out onto a rack.

Tamale Pie

In the lovely coming-of-age novel *Cress Delahanty,* by Jessamyn West, which I read when I had barely come of age myself, Cress's Californian mother makes tamale pie. It is described as a homey, family dish, but to me, born and bred in New York, it seemed most exotic. When I moved away from home and began to cook for myself, Tamale Pie was one of my first attempts. I found it delicious—yes, a little exotic, but reminiscent of the cheese-topped casseroles I'd grown up on. Homey and so good.

Tamale Pie's origins are Tex-Mex or Cal-Mex: They're a clear example of hybrid border cuisine. I like this best made with a fine-grain cornmeal, but coarse works just as well. The protein can be supplied by either ready-ground tofu or cooked beans; both are delicious. Green chile sauce can substitute for the red, and it can be vegan or not. Serve a big slice of this with a green salad, Cilantro Vinaigrette (page 94), and sliced avocado. If you felt ambitious, you could make Brazilian Rice (page 473), or steamed tortillas, or start with a bracing bowl of Lime Soup Yucatán (page 170).

SERVES 8

Cooking spray
A double batch of polenta, grits, or mush, cooked until medium-firm by any method (pages 441–46), using 2 teaspoons to 2 tablespoons olive oil
1 tablespoon olive oil
1 large onion, chopped
2 cloves garlic, chopped
1 teaspoon ground cumin
2 tablespoons unbleached white all-purpose flour
1 cup vegetable stock (see page 139)
1¼ cups Basic Wintertime Italian Tomato Sauce (page 931) or good commercial tomato sauce
1¼ cups Chou Chou's Simple "Yer Cheating Heart" Salsa (page 914) or good hot commercial salsa
2 to 3 fresh jalapeño peppers, seeds and membranes removed, chopped
1 package (10 ounces) spicy style ready-ground tofu, thawed, or 2 to 2½ cups cooked pinto or black beans
½ cup sliced black olives
½ cup raisins
¼ teaspoon dried oregano
Salt and freshly ground black pepper to taste
1 to 1½ cups (4 to 6 ounces) grated jack or Cheddar cheese, or nondairy cheese equivalent

1 Into a nonstick 9½-by-13½-inch dish, or one that has been sprayed with cooking spray, spoon the hot cooked cornmeal and let cool a few moments. With a broad knife or spatula, spread the warm cornmeal mixture evenly on the bottom of the pan, and work it up the sides to make a kind of crust. Set aside to cool while you make the filling.

2 Preheat the oven to 350°F.

3 Place the oil in a nonstick skillet, or one that has been sprayed with cooking spray, over medium-high heat. When hot, add the onion and sauté for 3 minutes, until it is starting to become translucent. Add the garlic, lower the heat, and sauté for another minute, stirring often, until the garlic is very lightly browned. Add the cumin and flour and cook, stirring constantly, for 2 minutes, until the mixture starts to brown.

4 Whisk in the stock and tomato sauce, then add the jalapeños, tofu or beans, olives, raisins, and oregano. Season to taste with salt (remember, the olives are salty) and quite a bit of pepper. Cook, stirring, until the mixture is thick and richly aromatic, about 10 minutes. Remove from the heat.

5 Spoon the pie filling into the polenta-lined baking dish. Top with the cheese, if using dairy cheese. Cover the dish and bake for 30 minutes. If using nondairy cheese, sprinkle it on at this point. Uncover and continue baking for another 15 minutes, or until the cheese is melted and bubbly. Remove from the oven, let stand for 5 minutes, and serve hot.

Hot Today, Chile Tamale

Green Chile Tamale Pie: *Divine, and sinus-clearing. Use 2½ to 3 cups New Mexico–Style Green Chile Sauce (page 942) instead of tomato sauce.*

Tamale Cobbler: *Instead of lining the baking dish with polenta, simply spoon the filling right into the dish. Top with slices of commercially prepared polenta, either plain or with cilantro, and sprinkle the cheese over that.*

Red Chile Tamale Pie: *First, toast 6 to 8 whole, dried New Mexico red chiles as follows. Remove their stems. Break them open and scrape out the seeds, then tear the chiles into large pieces. Heat a dry cast-iron skillet. When it's hot, add the chile pieces, skin side down, and press each with a spatula for a few seconds. Turn, press again, and immediately remove from the heat. You want them toasted—their color just starting to change—not burnt (and they burn in a heartbeat if you don't stay on it). Transfer the toasted chiles to a heatproof bowl, and pour 1½ cups boiling water over them. Let stand for 10 minutes, or until soft, then puree them in a food processor. Use this red chile puree instead of all or part of the tomato sauce. Quite wonderful.*

Dairy Hollow House Skillet-Sizzled Buttermilk Cornbread

The cornbread we served at the inn, this is the first Southern food I ever learned to fix. It's the recipe we used in the inn's very first *Moos Letter*, and it has been in many, many magazines and newspapers. Not infrequently am I introduced to people who say, "You're Crescent Dragonwagon? Love your cornbread!" (Oh, what a nice way to be part of peoples' lives! It's not really my cornbread, it's Viola's—but that's another story.) If you find the amount of butter truly unconscionable, you can cut it back to a tablespoon and it'll still be very good. Yellow cornmeal is used up here in the Ozarks. In the Deep South, and to the east, white cornmeal is more frequently the choice. Of course, whichever one you first encountered is the right one. **SERVES 8**

1 cup stone-ground yellow cornmeal
1 cup unbleached white all-purpose flour
1 tablespoon baking powder
¼ teaspoon salt
¼ teaspoon baking soda
1 to 3 tablespoons sugar
1¼ cups buttermilk (or 1 cup plain yogurt mixed with ¼ cup water)
1 large egg
¼ cup mild vegetable oil, such as corn, canola, or peanut
2 to 4 tablespoons butter

1 Preheat the oven to 375°F. Make sure your oven is accurate, too; it really needs to be up to temperature to get perfect results.

2 In a large bowl, combine the cornmeal, flour, baking powder, salt, baking soda, and sugar. (If the baking powder or

Cornbreads

To me, cornbread is the ultimate use of cornmeal. Someday I may just write a whole book on this quintessentially American food and its thousand variations. It is the Southern staff of life, daily bread, the taste of home, and part of every celebration. I used to say, when we had the restaurant, that it was "the sun around which the other planets of the menu revolve," and indeed it was so, served at every dinner, and our most frequently requested recipe. Make a good cornbread, and you will be welcome anywhere.

soda appears at all lumpy, sift it in.) Stir well to combine.

3 In a small bowl, whisk together the buttermilk, egg, and oil.

4 Place a 9- to 10¼-inch skillet over medium heat (our skillets are 10¼ inches; this size is called a Number 7), add the butter, and heat until the butter melts and is sizzling seriously. Tilt the skillet to coat the sides.

5 As the butter's melting, quickly pour the wet ingredients into the dry and, using a wooden spoon, stir the wet and dry together with as few strokes as possible—only as many as are needed to combine the two. Don't beat it; don't smooth it out. Scrape the batter into the hot, buttery skillet—if you've gotten it hot enough it will sizzle as it goes in—and pop it in the oven immediately.

6 Bake until golden brown on top, 25 to 30 minutes. Cut into wedges and serve hot.

Ronni's Skillet-Sizzled Kentucky Buttermilk Cornbread

My pan-pal Ronni Lundy, a native of Corbin, Kentucky, who has lived in Louisville for many years, writes about Southern food with grace, wit, authority, and kindness. This is the simple, stripped-down, decidedly not sweetened, all-cornmeal cornbread she grew up on: true Appalachian and Deep South cornbread. It is made with stone-ground white cornmeal. It's austere, a little dry, but utterly addictive. Besides being just great with a summer dinner of as many different vegetable dishes as you can cook up out of the garden or a trip to the farmer's market, its undistracted simplicity makes it a perfect base, when dried out a little, for stuffing. **SERVES 8**

4 tablespoons butter
2 cups stone-ground white cornmeal
½ teaspoon baking powder
¼ teaspoon salt
½ teaspoon baking soda
1½ cups buttermilk (or 1 cup plain yogurt mixed with ¼ cup water)
1 large egg
Cooking spray

1 Preheat the oven to 450°F. Make sure your oven is accurate, too; it really needs to be up to temperature to get perfect results.

2 Place the butter in a 9- to 10¼-inch cast-iron skillet. Put the skillet in the oven while it preheats.

3 In a large bowl, combine the cornmeal, baking powder, salt, and baking soda. (If the baking powder or soda appears at all lumpy, sift it in.) Stir well to combine.

4 In a small bowl, whisk together the buttermilk and egg.

5 Quickly pour the wet ingredients into the dry and, using a wooden spoon, stir the wet and dry together with as few strokes as possible—only as many as are needed to combine the two. Don't beat it; don't smooth it out.

6 Remove the hot skillet from the oven. By now the butter should be melted and sizzling seriously. Using hotpads, tilt the pan to coat the sides of the skillet.

7 Scrape the batter into the hot, buttery skillet—if you've gotten it hot enough it will sizzle as it goes in—and pop it in the oven immediately.

8 Bake until golden brown on top, 20 to 25 minutes. Cut into wedges and serve hot.

Corn Pasta

Corn makes an especially lovely pasta—a shade or two more yellow than the best imported semolina wheat pasta. Several brands are available at your local natural foods store; I prefer Westbrae. The best "cut" is generally angel hair, which allows for the quickest cooking (essential, given that corn lacks gluten; this ensures the pasta will be done but not falling apart). Although the Westbrae box suggests a 10-minute cooking in boiling water, I've found that 6 minutes does it. The cooking water gets cloudy and the piece you taste for doneness may seem a bit soggy with starch, but when you drain and rinse the pasta, it firms up and the outer starchiness disappears.

Corn pasta's texture differs from that of its wheaten kin. It is more tender (not "mushy"; just less chewy, more fragile in the mouth). The corn flavor is slight, but it's there. I enjoy the change in texture for variety, and I like having something on hand that I can feed to those allergic to gluten or wheat.

Because of the relative delicacy of corn pasta, avoid heavier sauces. A squidge of butter or browned butter, freshly ground black pepper, and a sprinkle of salt and grated Parmesan is great. But very pleasing is sautéed fresh corn, cut off the cob and tossed with cooked corn pasta, along with garlic, olive oil, a few ribbons of fresh basil, and a dead-ripe, diced, raw summer tomato or two (try one golden and one red tomato for stunning visuals). Serve with a good green salad.

Chicos

Dried, unprocessed sweet corn is just what you'd think: sweet corn dried partially on the cob, kernels then removed and dehydrated. Drying concentrates the corn's sweetness and gives a pleasantly chewy texture—much the same transition in taste and texture that fresh fruit undergoes when it is dried. Available whole or cracked into large nubbins, it is rehydrated for use in cooking, and generally finds its way into stews, soups, and puddings. It has several regional names and passionate followings. It's called chicos in the Southwest.

The chicos Zoe Caywood sells at War Eagle Mills and by mail (call 501-789-5343) are grown for her organically at the Nambe Pueblo reservation, north of Santa Fe, New Mexico. Yet this same product, oddly, is also beloved by the Pennsylvania Dutch. One Pennsylvania company, John Cope's Food Products, markets it as "Toasted Dried Sweet Corn." Again, you can order it by mail (call 717-367-5142).

To cook chicos/toasted sweet corn, start by soaking the dried corn. You can soak it by pouring 3 parts boiling water, preferably spring or filtered, over 1 part dried corn, and letting it sit for 1 to 2 hours at room temperature, or even overnight (unless the weather is warm, in which case any soaking longer than an hour should take place under refrigeration). Add the soaked corn and residual soaking water to any hearty soup or stew, and let it simmer at least 30 minutes. Zoe says she uses chicos as she was taught by the Nambe Pueblos—just drop a handful in with simmering beans. The Pennsylvania Dutch preparations run more to creamy stewed corn and corn puddings.

NOTE

Although this cooks very speedily in a pressure cooker, you still need to factor in soaking overnight. I am grateful to Lorna Sass for introducing me to the time-saving pressure-cooker method for beans and chicos, and similar dishes. Her Red Beans and Chicos, in Recipes from an Ecological Kitchen, is close kin to this preparation.

Simple Pot of Chicos and Nightfall Beans

Nightfall beans may be my favorite bean variety, visually at least. A mysterious blue gray, they are irregularly and beautifully speckled with a haze of black. A few reddish-orange beans also find their way into a package. I buy mine from Indian Harvest, a great mail-order source (see page 110). When I don't have any nightfalls on hand for this dish I use pintos. Dried chipotles add a smoky, campfire flavor; a little heat, but not as much as you'd think if you've only eaten the fiery canned chipotles in adobo. Chipotles are jalapeños ripened to redness, then smoked. Anchos, another option here, are dried poblano peppers, not smoked; they have a unique, rich sweetness. **SERVES 4 TO 6 WITH A GRAIN ACCOMPANIMENT**

1½ cups nightfall beans, picked over and rinsed
Cooking spray
¾ cup chicos or dried corn
3 cups water, preferably spring or filtered
1 small dried chipotle pepper, or 1 large ancho pepper
4 to 6 cloves garlic, peeled and sliced
1½ teaspoons salt, or to taste

1 Soak the beans overnight in ample spring or filtered water, covering the beans by a depth of 1 to 2 inches, in a large bowl. Spray the pot of the pressure cooker with cooking spray, add the chicos to it, and cover with the 3 cups water. Let the chicos soak overnight.

2 Next morning, drain the beans, rinse them well, and add them to the chicos and soaking water in the pressure-cooker pot. Add the dried chipotle or ancho, and the garlic.

3 Close the pressure-cooker lid and bring to high pressure. Adjust the heat to maintain high pressure, and cook for 10 to 12 minutes. Turn off the heat and allow pressure to come down naturally for 10 minutes. Quick-release any residual pressure, then open the cooker. Add the salt.

4 Serve hot, in bowls.

NOTE

This is a soothing, simple dish, great with any grain, especially millet, or a good cornbread. I have been known to eat it for breakfast. No kidding. You can fancy it up with a dab of sour cream (or Tofu Sour Cream, page 909, or sour half-and-half) or salsa, or a handful of minced fresh cilantro—but there's something awfully pleasing about it plain.

Potluck Posole

Use this as part of a component dinner, or serve it with Brazilian Rice (page 473) and some reconstituted dehydrated black bean flakes (see page 594). It's as quick as can be, and very, very good. Use a natural foods store brand of reduced-fat sour cream, such as Horizon, which isn't all gunked up with additives, or, for vegans, use commercial or homemade Tofu Sour Cream (page 909). If you don't mind a bit more fat, use sour half-and-half. And if you want to make it astoundingly good, char, peel, seed, and dice a couple of fresh poblano peppers instead of using canned green chiles. There goes the "quick and easy," but it's wonderful. Even with its almost-instant-fix status, this is nothing to sneeze at. **SERVES 4 TO 6**

Cooking spray
2 cans (32 ounces total) white hominy, drained
4 ounces (½ cup) grated Cheddar cheese, the sharpest you can find
1 tablespoon finely diced onion
1 cup natural foods store brand reduced-fat sour cream, or sour half-and-half
1 can (4 ounces) diced green chiles
Breadcrumb Topping Provençal (page 277) made with soft crumbs

1. Preheat the oven to 350°F.

2. Spray a 1½- to 2-quart ovenproof casserole with cooking spray.

3. In a large bowl, combine all the ingredients except the breadcrumb topping, stirring to distribute well.

4. Turn the mixture out into the casserole, top with the crumbs, and bake for about 40 minutes, or until bubbling hot, crisp, and golden of crumb.

Popcorn

This is the quintessential, original, all-American snack food—quick, delicious, quite healthful as long as you don't drown it in melted butter, and infinitely variable.

Corn pops when the water within the kernel is exposed to heat, creating internal steam, which, in turn, causes the kernel to burst open, exposing its frilled, fluffy white insides. Blue and multicolored popcorns are beautiful in the jar, but pop open to a creamy interior. The internal water is essential to the popping process, which is why old or dried-out popcorn is difficult to pop. Store an opened jar of popcorn in the fridge. And here's a great tip from Betty Fussell, author of Crazy for Corn: *"If you've got a longtime opened jar of popcorn in the cupboard, add a tablespoon of water to the jar, shake it, and give the kernels a day to absorb the water." Then pop.*

Popping corn is simplicity itself. Get out your skillet, cast iron if you want a good one-armed upper-body workout, nonstick if you want to make things a little easier. Have a lid that fits the skillet handy, as well as two potholders.

Heat the skillet over medium heat. When it's heated (but not very, very hot), add a single layer of corn kernels; ⅓ to ½ cup in a 12-inch skillet is about right (this will yield about 4 cups popped corn). Cover the skillet, leaving the lid open just a bit. Why? This allows the steam released from the corn to hightail it after popping the kernel, whereas if it's trapped in the pan, it'll make the corn a bit soggy rather than crisp.

As soon as you hear the kernels begin to bombard the lid, begin shaking the pan back and forth to prevent scorching the already-popped kernels. Do this fairly gently, because the lid is partly ajar. Continue until that sudden moment of silence—ah, all the corn has popped.

Here are six things you can do with popped popcorn (in addition to the obvious: butter—just a squidge—and salt).

- *Add a splash of tamari or shoyu soy sauce, a tiny bit of butter, nutritional yeast (see page 239), and Parmesan cheese.*
- *Add 3 or 4 cloves garlic, pressed, to 1 to 2 tablespoons softened butter, mash together, then toss with the hot popcorn and a few shakes of salt.*
- *Season to taste with a spice mixture made as follows: equal parts good curry powder, Old Bay seasoning, and nutritional yeast, and a pinch of ground cayenne pepper.*
- *Season to taste with Dragon Salt (page 900).*
- *Use it as a soup garnish; it's particularly good on tomato soups (so good I like to keep a dish at hand, and keep sprinkling as I eat my way down in the bowl).*

Very Ricely, Thank You

It's truer of rice than of Cleopatra: "Time cannot wither, nor custom stale, her infinite variety." Rice, at about 83,000 varieties strong, is still around.

Rice is the third most widely grown grain on the planet. More wheat and corn are cultivated, but more rice is actually eaten, and eaten as itself (not made into other products) than are kernels of any other grain. Rice is the very heartbeat of life to most of our planet's people—it's the staple food of two-thirds the world's population today. In China people greet each other not with "How are you today?" but "Have you had your rice today?"

Rice is native to Asia, probably China or India, where it has been cultivated for thousands of years. From there it spread across the continent into the Middle East and Europe. In time, Turks, Greeks, and Northern Italians incorporated it into their cuisines.

Rice got off to a bumpy start in the New World. It is believed to have first crossed the Atlantic on slave ships shortly after Columbus's arrival, but it didn't really take hold until the late seventeenth century, in South Carolina. By around the time of the American Revolution, according to cookbook author and historian Sri Owen, nearly thirty-thousand tons of rice a year was being exported from Charleston. "Carolina Gold" made the new colony's fortune as rice was shipped all over the world. Rice cultivation spread south along the low-lying coastal areas to Georgia, and still further south. But the Civil War and the end of slavery, new varieties of rice, and new machines to harvest it contributed to the decline of the rice industry in America. After a series of hurricanes in 1910, the ravaged southeastern rice fields were finally abandoned. Other than single-farm "boutique" rice operations—one each (that I know of) in South Carolina and Florida—rice is no longer commercially grown along the southeast coast.

But foodways die slowly. Rice, explains author John Martin Taylor in *Hoppin' John's Lowcountry Cooking*, "shaped the culture in the Lowcountry for more than two hundred years [and] is so deeply a part of the local kitchen that it appears at the Lowcountry table for very nearly every meal, even though we are now two generations removed from its last cultivation here."

Where is rice grown today? The United States is the world's largest producer, and Arkansas, I am proud to say, is the number-one producing state, followed by California, Louisiana, Texas, Missisippi, and Missouri—all states with regions that meet rice's peculiar horticultural requirements for hot, humid weather and abundant standing water; as they say, "A rice farmer's feet are always wet." Similar conditions prevail in China and Japan, where rice is also grown in large amounts (both these countries also import rice from the United States now) and in Thailand, famous for its aromatic jasmine rice (although the variety actually originated in the Philippines and has also been grown in the United States since 1989).

In North India and Pakistan, different climatic conditions support another aromatic rice, the legendary basmati, a plant characteristically 5 to 6 feet in height, which thrives in cooler temperatures. One would think, then, that it would be perfectly suited for the Great Plains states. Not so: It's too windy, and the wind snaps the grain-laden rice stalks. Hence, all true basmati is imported—although, according to Mary Jo Cheesman at the U.S. Rice Federation, there is now a basmati grown in America, "true in the sense that it's the same genetically," that is bred for shorter stature. Several other aromatic rices cultivatable in the United States, such as texmati (grown in Texas, of course, by a company called Rice Tec), and Louisiana's "popcorn" and "wild pecan" rices (so named because their aromas and flavors are said to be reminiscent of these foods), have also been developed.

All rice is either long, medium, or short grain. This classification is not just based on the size and shape of the grain, but the composition of the carbohydrate of which each type of grain is made up. In general, long-grain rice, in which the quill-shaped kernels are 4 times longer than they are wide, cooks into grains that are fairly firm, dry, and separate from each other. Medium-grain rices (2 to 3 times longer than they are wide) yield a moister cooked product, somewhat sticky. Short-grain rice kernels are almost round, and quite moist after cooking, with plump grains that stick to each other.

Whether long, medium, or short grain, almost all rices are available as refined white rice or as more nutrient-rich unrefined brown. But that's just the beginning. There are dozens of rice subgroups. There are the aromatics, which are mostly long-grain rices (but jasmine, for example, is an aromatic that looks like a long grain when raw, and cooks up like a medium grain). There are the arborio and arborio-type rices, which are medium grain, but a distinct subgroup of medium grain, again with distinct textures and cooking properties. Then there are, in effect, entirely new categories of rice created by further processing. These are the instant or parboiled rices (Uncle Ben's has trademarked its special method of parboiling as "Converted").

What do all these rices have in common? Much, nutritionally speaking. Whole-grain brown rices, whether short, medium, or long grain, are processed only enough to remove the inedible outer hull. What remains is, besides delicious, a package of nutritional goodness typical of a whole grain: plenty of B-vitamins, some vitamin E, some protein, phosphorus, potassium, and fiber. But when the rice's bran and germ are removed by that insidious process known as milling, the fiber, vitamin E, and B-vitamins are removed too. What's left in the white kernel of rice? Starch. Then, some brands "enrich" the rice, adding back in three of the stolen B-vitamins, plus iron.

Converted or parboiled rice is a nutritional middle ground. The rice is soaked, steam-pressured, then dried before bran and hull are removed, a process that drives about 85 percent of the grain's protein and 70 percent of the B-vitamins into the kernel. Though such rice is not as nutritious as whole-grain brown, having lost protein and vitamins, as well as the fiber, it is considerably more nutritious than regular old unenriched white, and somewhat more "natural" in the composition of its nutrients than enriched white. Moreover, the processing firms the starch within the grain, giving the cooked rice the distinct-grain fluffiness that many Americans prefer. This process also increases the grain's ability to hold its shape for a period of time. Even if reheated or sitting on a steam table, the rice grains remain straight and true and firm, instead of splitting and curling back on themselves (called "butterflying").

Other rice products, some familiar and some exotic to Americans, include cream of rice cereal, puffed rice cereal, rice cakes (those thick round crackers that some people adore and others think are like Styrofoam), mochi (rice paste), whole-grain or white rice flour (which makes the best waffles), saki, and both Eastern- and Western-style rice noodles. These offer great possibilities to adventurous eaters.

The answer to "What's the best variety of rice to choose?" depends on personal taste, and how you plan to use the rice in a given meal. What's the best way to cook rice, then? Again, it depends on the variety you picked. Confused? Take your shoes off; stand up; stretch. Come with me for a stroll through the paddy; we'll get our feet wet together.

Rice University

To Wash or Not to Wash

Some recipes—mine as well as others—suggest rinsing, or even washing certain rices before cooking, while other recipes skip this step. Some recipes also call for soaking the rice before cooking, for starting it in cold water and bringing it to a boil, or for dropping it into already boiling water. Why? Because each type of rice has its own requirements, and each country in which it is a staple has its own idea of what constitutes perfectly cooked rice.

In general, Asians wash rice before cooking it. Virtually all rice eaten in Japan, Korea, China, middle- and upper-class India, and Thailand is white, refined rice. It's been through a milling process, which leaves it coated with a dusty and powdery starch. The rinsing removes this, resulting in a product that is cleaner and free of any grittiness. Also, in the case of rices that are intended to be eaten with chopsticks, the desirable texture is moist, the grains sticking to one another. Rinsing enhances this quality, because the starch in the rice begins to dissolve right away.

Oddly, the opposite effect occurs when white basmati rice is rinsed and soaked, because of the differences in the starch structure of this particular long-grain rice. Basmati swells only lengthwise as it cooks, and not around its circumference, so a rinse and a soak keep it from splitting open as it cooks, ensuring distinct, nonsticky individual grains.

I don't recommend that you rinse American white rice. Because it is enriched after being refined, rinsing strips rice of some of its vitamins. Brown rice, being an unrefined product, is best given a quick rinse. Because each kernel is still discrete in its brown coat of bran—the hard coat that makes it take a while to cook to tenderness—a quick rinse will not start the starch-releasing process, and thus will not make the rice any stickier.

To Salt or Not to Salt

Salt is another variable: Some rice recipes call for it, some don't. But the reasoning here is fairly simple. When you are including the rice in almost any Asian meal, omit the salt, as the rice will likely be paired with soy sauce. If the rice is more of a main grain—a risotto, a paella, a pilaf—salt is in order.

Some authors suggest that certain varieties of rice not be salted until after they've finished cooking, because it allegedly slows cooking. I tested this, and can tell you that it's not true. If you're adding salt, add it at the start of the cooking so the salt can dissolve into the water and be absorbed evenly into each grain.

Green Kernels and Husks

When you buy brown rice, particularly in bulk, you may notice that some of the grains have a slightly green cast. This is natural—all the grains of rice on a plant do not mature fully at precisely the same time. The greenish grains are entirely edible, and have the same nutritional value and flavor as the fully brown ones. You may also notice a few grains of deeper brown, with a pointy edge at one end. These are grains that escaped husking, and still have the inedible part of the bran coat on them. Remove such grains before cooking.

A Tight-Fitting Lid

One of the tricks of perfect rice cookery is to use only the minimum amount of water called for and to cover the pot very tightly so none of the steam escapes. The rice is then cooked in part by the trapped steam, which makes for a noticeably lighter, fluffier grain. (The exception to this rule is when you want a risotto, deliberately and deliciously sodden.)

Therefore, make sure your pot has a tight-fitting lid. If it doesn't, wrap foil tightly around the edges of the pot, then cover with the lid.

How to Withstand Pressure

Judicious use of a pressure cooker will save you much time in rice preparation, but you might have to play around with proportions to get exactly the texture you want.

I prefer rice that is a bit on the firm side, slightly chewy and distinct, rather than moist. But when using a pressure cooker, you can't know how wet or dry your rice is until after it is cooked and the lid is unlocked, and then it would seem too late to do anything about it. It's not; read on. It can be disconcerting to find the rice cooked through yet bubbling in water like a thick soup, or with no water at all and on the soggy side of al dente. With this in mind, here's how you can tweak the pressure-cooker proportions I give below:

- For moister rice in the pressure cooker, add an additional 2 to 3 tablespoons water for every 1 cup dry rice before cooking. I doubt you will want it dryer than the proportions I've given here, since I err toward dry, but if you work with Lorna Sass's book *Cooking under Pressure,* for instance (and you should), and you find her dishes too moist, you might try the opposite—substract 1 to 3 tablespoons water per 1 cup dry rice.
- If the rice is a little too wet after cooking, place the pot back on the stove on the lowest heat possible, and cook, uncovered (without pressure), without stirring, for a few minutes longer, keeping a close eye on it, until all liquid has evaporated.
- If the rice is very wet but cooked through, scoop out the cooked rice with a slotted spoon. Or, pour off most of the water (reserving it for soups), relock the lid, bring it back to high pressure, cook for 3 to 5 minutes at high pressure, then let the pressure come down naturally for 10 minutes.
- If the rice is dry and done but on the firm side, moisten it by adding 2 tablespoons water per 1 cup of the original measure of dry rice. Relock the lid, bring it back to high pressure, cook for 1 minute at high pressure, then let the pressure come down naturally for 10 minutes.

Now, one other essential for pressure-cooking rice. For the best-textured rice, never cook less than 2 cups dry rice in a pressure cooker.

Rice Cookers

Some people adore electric rice cookers. I don't have one, and I don't have room on my counter for another appliance—but if I ate rice on a daily basis, I might consider it. The cookers "understand" when all the water's been absorbed, and they turn themselves off, ensuring a perfect product.

To Keep Rice Fresh

The milling of rice was begun to prevent rancidity, spoilage, and insect invasion. White rice will keep almost indefinitely in a tightly closed jar; brown rice, because of the oils in the bran, will most likely taste "off" after two or three months, maybe less in warm weather. If you buy brown rice in bulk, do so at a store with high turnover. And if you keep brown rice much longer than two months, refrigerate it.

To Reheat Rice

The best way to quickly reheat any cooked rice is in a large, nonstick skillet with a tight-fitting lid. Add about 2 tablespoons water, preferably spring or filtered, per 1 cup cooked rice. Turn heat to medium, cover, and reheat for 3 to 5 minutes. Lift the lid to let any residual water evaporate, and voilà.

Innecdote

The empty box of Uncle Ben's Converted fell on the floor. Ned and I both had our hands full, so he—in the inexplicable fashion of the testosteroned—vigorously kicked it in the direction of the wastebasket. I gave him the dubious-but-amused, corner-of-the-eye look common to my sex in such circumstances.

By way of clarification, he said, with a deadpan nod, "Rice hockey."

A Rice Primer

Long grain or short? Brown, white, red, or black? Instant or slow? Cooked under pressure or conventionally? Whatever your preference—or if you don't know enough to have a preference—you will find out all about it here.

Long-Grain Rices

Long-grain rices have long, slender kernels, four times longer than they are wide. Cooked long grains have distinctly separate kernels, and tend toward light and fluffy. It is the most popular of the three rice-grain sizes here.

Mainstream, Easily Found Long-Grain Rices

Long-Grain Brown Rice:

What It Is: A long-grain rice from which only the inedible outer hull has been removed, leaving the entire edible part. This is a whole-grain product. Widely available organic.

What It's Like: Pleasantly grainy flavor, most often described as "nutty," and a toothsome, noticeable texture. It's gentle, yet spirited, and savory. "Fluffy" and distinct grains.

Where to Find It: Supermarkets, natural foods stores (try the organic long-grain brown).

How to Cook It Conventionally: Bring 2¼ cups water–preferably spring or filtered, to a boil with salt to taste. Stir in 1 cup well-rinsed long-grain brown rice. Return to a boil, stir once, turn down the heat to very low, and cover the pot. Barely simmer for 50 minutes; remove from the heat and let stand, covered, another 5 to 10 minutes. Fluff. This yields 3 to 3½ cups.

How to Pressure-Cook It: In a pressure cooker pot, bring to a boil 3⅓ cups water, preferably spring or filtered (add an extra 2 tablespoons to ¼ cup for softer rice). Add salt to taste. As you wait for the water to boil, heat a Flame Tamer (see page 535) on a separate burner. When the water boils, stir in 2 cups rinsed long-grain brown rice. Return to a boil, lock the lid, and bring to high pressure. Move the pot to the heated Flame Tamer. Adjust the heat to maintain high pressure. Cook under high pressure for 27 minutes. Remove from the heat and let the pressure release naturally for 10 minutes. Unlock the lid. Let stand for 1 to 2 minutes more. Fluff. This yields about 5 cups.

Note: While it is possible to pressure-cook brown rice without a Flame Tamer, the results will be stickier, and the rice in direct contact with the pot bottom is liable to stick, and perhaps burn.

How to Use It: Cooked brown rice is a great ingredient to have on hand in the fridge. Reheat in pilafs. Use as a base for a Rice à la Hippie (page 474) or Smokin' Rice (page 472), or reheat it in milk as a breakfast cereal. Leftover brown rice, if brought to room temperature, is also good as a salad; try a heap of it on a pile of good greens with diced savory tofu, diced tomato, and a splash of sesame oil. Or toss with herbs, garlic, olive oil, perhaps some diced kalamatas and a little crumbled feta, or soaked and slivered sun-dried tomatoes. Again, serve it piled on a big plate of salad greens.

Grain Go-Withs: Long-grain brown rice shares approximate cooking time with rye, wehani, or black japonica rice, wheat or kamut or spelt, or black barley; any of these can be cooked jointly with it for a tasty, simple whole-grain pilaf.

Quick ("Instant") Brown Rice:

What It Is: Long-grain brown rice, precooked and dried for very quick cooking.

What It's Like: It has the softish inside-out texture of instant rices—to me objectionable—but it is a whole-grain product, fast, and superior to instant white rice. It is quite fluffy (there's that word again).

How to Cook It Conventionally: Bring 1 cup water, preferably spring or filtered, to a boil with ½ teaspoon salt. Stir in 1 cup instant brown rice. Return to a boil, lower the heat to low, and cover the pot. Simmer for 5 minutes; remove from the heat and let stand, covered, another 5 minutes. Fluff. This yields 1⅓ cups.

Note: If you buy instant brown rice in a box, please follow the directions given there; different companies process their instants in different ways.

How to Pressure-Cook It: Not applicable.

How to Use It: Anytime you need rice in a hurry, it can step in. If unexpected company drops in or a finished grain recipe tastes too highly seasoned, use it to extend an existing dish.

Where to Find It: Both supermarket and natural foods store brands are available. It's also an ingredient of many convenience-food instant soup-in-a-cups.

Special Notes: Because of the way the processing that allows this rice to be "instant" bulks up the dried rice, the yield per cup of dry rice is rather small—which means it's comparatively expensive.

Parboiled, or Converted, Rice:

What It Is: A long-grain rice that is pressure-steamed (or parboiled) before milling. This drives the majority of the nutrients into the heart of the rice. The rice is then milled, which removes the hull (and fiber), leaving the rice white.

What It's Like: If I'm going to eat white rice, this is one of my favorites, and I'm partial to Uncle Ben's. A good American-style parboiled rice cooks up with every grain fluffy and distinct. Its mild, completely neutral bland flavor and desirable texture makes it perfect for many highly seasoned rice dishes. It's not satisfactory for salads; the grains harden when chilled.

Where to Find It: Supermarkets.

How to Cook It Conventionally: Bring to a boil 2¼ cups water, preferably spring or filtered, with ½ teaspoon salt. Stir in 1 cup converted rice. Return to a boil, then lower the heat to low and cover the pot. Let simmer for 20 minutes; remove from the heat and let stand, covered, another 5 minutes. Fluff. This yields 4 cups.

How to Pressure-Cook It: Not applicable; you might just as well do it conventionally, and the results taste better.

How to Use It: Plain, with any good stir-fry, stew, or sauce; jazzed up with a little grated ginger and a teaspoon of peanut butter and a tablespoon of chopped toasted peanuts stirred in at the end, or with a little butter and minced parsley; in Lemon-Basil Rice Pilaf with White Wine (page 478), Middle Eastern–Style Pilaf with Noodles and Red Lentils (page 483), or Eggplant Rice Audrey (page 484).

Grain Go-Withs: Toasted millet cooks up nicely with converted rice.

Enriched Long-Grain White Rice:

What It Is: Hulled, refined long-grain rice, stripped of vitamins and fiber, then "enriched" by the re-addition of some of the former in synthetic form.

What It's Like: Like all nonaromatic white rices, the rice is lacking in flavor; treat it as a pleasing starch and serve with a spicy sauce or gumbo. If you cook this rice the Lowcountry way, ignoring the package directions, you'll avoid the mush and find it quite pleasing for a white rice. With this method, grains are distinct and a bit firm, almost-but-not-quite al dente.

Where to Find It: Supermarkets.

How to Cook It Conventionally: Do it the way Verta Mae Grosvenor suggests in her book *Vibration Cooking.* Combine and bring to a boil 2 cups cold water, preferably spring or filtered, and ½ teaspoon salt. Stir in 1 cup enriched long-grain white rice. Stir once or twice, turn the heat to low, and cover the pot tightly. Let it just barely simmer for "exactly 13 minutes." Remove from the heat and let stand, covered, another 12 minutes before serving. Fluff. This yields about 3½ cups.

How to Pressure-Cook It: Again, not applicable.

How to Use It: Assuming long-

Ginger

grain white appeals to you, in any spiced pilaf dish. Since my pilaf recipes usually call for converted white rice, decrease my liquid amounts by ¼ cup per 1 cup dry rice, if substituting enriched long-grain rice. Please note: This rice should be eaten pretty much straight out of the pot. It does not reheat well, and it very definitely does not "hold" over hot water.

Grain Go-Withs: Toasted kasha (buckwheat) cooks up just about perfectly side by side with enriched long-grain rice.

Instant White Rice

What It Is: Milled rice that has been processed so as to be "cooked" after a 5-minute-or-so soak in boiling water.

What It's Like: Bland, starchy, with the objectionable nibbled, soft consistency of all instant rices.

Where to Find It: Supermarket.

How to Cook It Conventionally: Follow the package directions.

How to Use It: Don't.

Special Notes: Why use this rice? At the very least, use instant brown.

MORE-EXOTIC LONG-GRAIN RICES—*AROMATICS*

Brown Basmati Rice:

What It Is: An unrefined aromatic long-grain brown rice. Organic is readily available.

What It's Like: This is a delicious rice; one of my two favorite browns. The characteristic aroma is less marked in brown than white basmati (to my taste, this is a plus), and the kernels are quite fluffy and distinct, not too sticky. It has a lightness that is pleasing. One highly distinctive basmati characteristic is that when it swells during cooking, it only swells lengthwise, not in diameter.

Where to Find It: Natural foods stores, Indian groceries, some supermarkets, most specialty markets or gourmet foods stores.

How to Cook It Conventionally: Bring 2½ cups water, preferably spring or filtered, to a boil with ½ teaspoon salt. Stir in 1 cup well-rinsed brown basmati rice. Return to a boil, stir once, then turn down the heat to very low and cover the pot. Barely simmer for 50 minutes; remove from the heat and let stand, covered, another 5 minutes. Fluff. This yields 3 to 3½ cups.

How to Pressure-Cook It: In a pressure-cooker pot, bring to a boil 3¼ cups water, preferably spring or filtered (add an extra 2 tablespoons to ¼ cup if you want softer rice), and ½ teaspoon salt. As you wait for the water to boil, heat a Flame Tamer (see page 535) on a separate burner. Stir 2 cups rinsed brown basmati rice into the boiling water. Return to a boil, lock the lid, and bring to high pressure. Move the pot to the heated Flame Tamer. Adjust the heat to maintain high pressure. Cook under high pressure for 27 minutes. Remove from the heat and let the pressure release naturally for 10 minutes. Unlock the lid. Let stand for 1 or 2 minutes more. Fluff. This yields about 5 cups.

How to Use It: Although I generally do not like to cook brown rices with seasonings, preferring to use them as a plain bed for other savory foods to rest on, brown basmati is the one brown I'd consider for a pilaf or paella; it's light enough in flavor and texture that its own fragrance and personality don't overshadow added seasonings. It's less sticky than the other browns too. And try it in Smokin' Rice (page 472)—rice with attitude!

Grain Go-Withs: See long-grain brown rice suggestions (page 461).

Special Notes: Brown basmati leftovers are an excellent breakfast cereal when reheated in milk, oat milk, fruit juice, or even water, and doctored with a bit of almond butter and a splash of maple syrup.

White Basmati Rice:

What It Is: A refined, non-enriched long-grain white rice with a distinctive aroma. Grown in the mountain keeps of Pakistan and North India, it is considered the premier rice of India, and one of the great rices of the world. In India, it's what you get at hotels and upper-class private homes; in America and in Britain, it's what you get at most Indian restaurants. The kernels have a tendency to break apart or split during cooking. Serious rinsing beforehand helps prevent this and also, by removing surface starch, makes the finished kernels more distinct.

What It's Like: Though pure white and fragrant, and with long, thin, quill-like grains that stand apart nicely when cooked, I have to tell the truth—I am not that wowed by white basmati. That said, white basmati is many people's favorite rice.

Where to Find It: Natural foods stores, Indian groceries, some supermarkets, most specialty markets or gourmet foods stores.

How to Cook It Conventionally, Method 1: Rinse 1 cup white basmati rice several times in running water. Bring 1¾ cups fresh water, preferably spring or filtered, to a boil with salt to taste. Stir in the rinsed white basmati and return to a boil. Stir once more, then lower the heat to a simmer, cover tightly, and cook for 20 minutes. Remove from the heat; let stand, still covered, for 10 minutes, and then serve. I prefer this method, which yields a slightly firmer rice, to the one that follows.

Method 2: This is the traditional Indian method of cooking white basmati. It is time-consuming, though simple, and you almost certainly throw out with the soaking water most of whatever nutrients might remain in the refined grain. But this is how you get the true Indian restaurant texture so prized by many people. I learned the basic method from *Madhur Jaffrey's World of the East Vegetarian Cooking,* although she adds another step by sautéing the rice before the final cooking water is added. She says, however, that this step is optional.

Rinse 1 cup white basmati rice several times in running water, preferably spring or filtered. Place the rinsed rice in a bowl, pour 2½ cups water over it, and let soak for 30 minutes. Pour the soaked rice into a strainer. Rinse again, and drain very well, letting it rest in the strainer set over a bowl for about 10 minutes.

Combine the soaked rice with 1¼ cups water and bring to a boil with an optional ¼ to ½ teaspoon salt. Stir once more, then lower the heat to a simmer, cover tightly, and cook for 20 minutes. Remove from the heat and let stand, still covered, for 10 minutes. Serve.

How to Pressure-Cook It: In a pressure-cooker pot, bring to a boil 3 cups minus 1 tablespoon water, preferably spring or filtered, plus salt to taste. Stir in 2 cups rinsed white basmati rice. Return to a boil, lock the lid, and bring to high pressure. Adjust the heat to maintain high pressure. Cook under high pressure for 3 minutes. Remove from the heat and let the pressure release naturally for 7 minutes. Unlock the lid. Let stand for 1 to 2 minutes. Fluff. This yields about 5½ cups. (If you find this a bit too moist for your taste, decrease the water by 2 tablespoons the next time you make it.)

How to Use It: White basmati, plain or simply spiced, is the classic accompaniment to Indian curries (see the curries on pages 195 to 199). Simple spicings only involve cooking one or several of the following whole spices with the rice: a cinnamon stick, 4 or 5 cardamom pods, a few cloves, a couple star anise, or a little aniseed (the last a Lorna Sass suggestion). All except the last should be removed before serving the rice. Slightly more elaborate Indian-style pilafs could include a handful of frozen peas and/or a few toasted raw cashews and some raisins, thrown in at the last. Also, this is the rice used in Katherine's Ghee Rice with Cashews and Melting Onions (page 485).

Brown Texmati Rice:

What It Is: A United States-grown brown basmati-type rice; a cross combining some genetic elements of Indian basmati with those friendly to the Texas rice-growing environment.

What It's Like: A slightly milder version of the brown basmati.

Where to Find It: Natural foods stores, some specialty or gourmet markets.

How to Cook It: See brown basmati for conventional and pressure cooking directions.

How to Use It: See notes on brown basmati, page 463.

White Texmati and Kasmati Rice:

What It Is: These U.S.-grown white basmati-type rices are very similar crosses, combining some genetic elements of Indian basmati with those friendly to the American rice-growing environment.

What It's Like: Very similar to Indian-grown white basmati, just slightly less fragrant. However, unlike Indian and Pakistani basmatis, they do not need to be washed or rinsed before cooking. (This is due to differences in the milling process, which leaves American-grown basmati-type rices without the surface starch of Asian.)

Where to Find It: Gourmet foods stores or specialty markets, maybe natural foods stores and supermarkets.

How to Cook It Conventionally: In a saucepan, combine 1 cup texmati/kasmati white rice with 1¾ cups water, preferably spring or filtered. Let soak for 20 to 30 minutes, then add an optional ¼ to ½ teaspoon salt and bring to a boil. Stir once, then lower the heat and cover tightly. Let simmer for 15 minutes, then remove from the heat and let stand, covered, another 10 minutes. Makes about 3 cups.

How to Pressure-Cook It: In a pressure cooker, bring to a boil 3 cups minus 1 tablespoon water, preferably spring or filtered, and salt to taste. Stir in 2 cups white kasmati rice. Return to a boil, lock the lid, and bring to high pressure. Adjust the heat to maintain high pressure. Cook under high pressure for 3 minutes. Remove from the heat and let the pressure release naturally for 7 minutes. Unlock the lid and let stand for 1 to 2 minutes. Fluff. This yields about 5½ cups. (If you find this a bit too moist for your taste, decrease the water by 2 tablespoons the next time you make it.)

How to Use It: See notes on white basmati, page 463.

Medium-Grain Rices

As you might expect, medium-grain rices tread a middle path. They are shorter than long-grain, longer than short-grain, and combine some of the qualities of both when cooked. That is, the grains are still distinct, individual, and somewhat fluffy, but stick to each other more like short-grains do. And the browns have the slightly sweet flavor characteristic of short-grains.

Medium-Grain Brown Rice:

What It Is: A medium-grain rice from which only the inedible outer hull has been removed, leaving the entire edible part. This is a whole-grain product, and widely available organic.

What It's Like: Delicious, pleasing, and slightly sweeter than long-grain, it has the characteristic chewiness and nuttiness of brown rice.

Where to Find It: Natural foods stores.

How to Cook It Conventionally: Bring 2 cups water, preferably spring or filtered, to a boil, with salt to taste. Stir in 1 cup well-rinsed medium-grain brown rice. Return to a boil and stir once, then turn down the heat to very low and cover the pot. Simmer for 50 minutes; remove from the heat and let stand, covered, another 5 minutes. Fluff. This yields about 3 cups.

How to Pressure-Cook It: In a pressure-cooker pot, bring to a boil 3⅓ cups water, preferably spring or filtered, plus salt to taste. As you wait for the water to boil, heat a Flame Tamer (see page 535) on a separate burner. Stir 2 cups rinsed medium-grain brown rice into the cooker. Return to a boil, lock the lid, and bring to high pressure. Move the pot to the heated Flame Tamer. Adjust the heat to maintain high pressure. Cook under high pressure for 27 minutes. Remove from the heat and let the pressure release naturally for 10 minutes. Unlock the lid and let stand for 1 to 2 minutes. Fluff. This yields about 5½ cups.

How to Use It: Because medium-grain brown rice is always stickier than long, it's especially welcome in stuffings or veggie burgers, in puddings (sweet or savory), and in some casseroles. I also enjoy it under stir-fries and the like, although not so much under wetter, stewier dishes, since it is moist in itself.

Grain Go-Withs: See the suggestions under long-grain brown rice (page 461) for ideas about grains to partner with medium-grain brown rice for cooking.

Medium-Grain White Rice:

What It Is: A refined medium-grain rice, from which the inedible outer hull as well as the bran has been removed. It is usually then re-enriched with added vitamins. Medium-grain white rice, grown today in California, is descended from either Japanese or Indian varieties; the white rice you get in most American Japanese restaurants is medium-grain.

What It's Like: Delicious, pleasing, and slightly sweeter than long-grain, it is soft and sticky.

Where to Find It: Supermarkets, Asian markets.

How to Cook It Conventionally, American-style: Bring 1¾ cups water, preferably spring or filtered, to a boil with salt to taste. Stir in 1 cup medium-grain white rice, unrinsed. Return to a boil and stir once, then turn down the heat to very low and cover the pot. Simmer for 15 minutes; remove from the heat and let stand, covered, another 5 minutes. Fluff. This yields about 3 cups.

Japanese-style: This requires rinsing the rice first, which means bye-bye vitamins. Still, this makes the delicious, sticky mound of rice you get at Japanese restaurants. Place 1 cup medium-grain white rice in a bowl and rinse thoroughly by covering with cold water, preferably spring or filtered, and swishing and rubbing the grains between your hands. Pour off the water and repeat 2 or 3 more times, or until the water is clear and unclouded. Turn the rice out into a sieve and drain well, for 20 to 30 minutes. Combine the washed rice with 1 cup plus 2 tablespoons spring or filtered water. Bring to a fast boil, uncovered, then pop a lid on the pot and turn the heat to medium-low. Cook, covered, for 5 minutes. Drop the heat still lower—virtually as low as you can get the flame—and cook, still covered, for another 10 minutes. Remove from the heat, still covered. Let stand for 10 minutes. Serve.

How to Pressure-Cook It: Not applicable.

How to Use It: With Japanese dishes or any other Asian-influenced dishes. Because of its stickiness, it's especially welcome in stuffings or veggie burgers, in puddings (sweet or savory), and in some casseroles. It's not appropriate under wetter, stewier dishes, since it is moist in itself.

Grain Go-Withs: See the suggestions under long-grain brown rice (page 461) for ideas about grains to partner with medium-grain white rice for cooking.

Black Japonica Rice:

What It Is: A grain some classify as medium and some as short, this beautifully shiny, unusual rice is, yes, black, and Japanese in origin, as you might expect from its name. Most black Japonica in this country is organic. It is usually grown as a "field blend" with a mahogany-colored medium-grain rice, the two harvested and cooked together for a subtle range of colors.

What It's Like: Black Japonica's flavor is both nutty and vegetal, and it has a pleasing chewy texture. To me, it's reminiscent of wild rice in aroma and flavor.

Where to Find It: Natural foods stores, some Asian food stores, and some supermarkets or gourmet stores.

How to Cook It Conventionally: Combine 2 cups water, preferably spring or filtered, with 1 cup black Japonica rice and salt to taste and bring to a hard boil. Lower the heat to a simmer, cover tightly, and cook for 50 minutes. Remove from the heat, still covered, and allow the rice to sit for 10 minutes. Serve. This yields 4½ to 5 cups.

How to Pressure-Cook It: In a pressure cooker, combine 2 cups black Japonica rice with 3 cups water, preferably spring or filtered, and salt to taste. Bring to a boil. As you wait for the water to boil, heat a Flame Tamer (see page 535) on a separate burner. Lock the lid on the cooker, adjust the heat to maintain high pressure, move the pot to the heated Flame Tamer, and cook for 17 minutes. Turn off the heat and let the pressure release naturally for 10 minutes. Unlock the lid, but do not remove. Let rice sit for another 5 minutes before serving.

How to Use It: Because it's so flavorful on its own, it's very nice with just a tiny nubbin of butter, a splash of tamari, and a bit of Parmesan or nutritional yeast. A small amount of cooked Japonica is also delicious folded into pancakes (such as Ethereal Buttermilk-Oatmeal Pancakes, page 558; cut back the oatmeal a little) and served either with sweet or savory accompaniments. It is traditionally used in a hot Thai rice pudding with a coconut milk base, a rendering that never did much for me. I prefer it in combination with other, less assertive grains, where its color and chewy texture are shown to good advantage: hot, in pilafs, and cold or at room temperature in a variety of grain-based salads.

Grain Go-Withs: Try cooking 1 part long-grain brown rice or brown basmati with ¼ part black Japonica and ¼ part spelt or kamut.

Jasmine Rice:

What It Is: One of the aromatics, it's a naturally fragrant (hence its poetic, if inaccurate, name), medium- to long-grain variety of white rice.

What It's Like: Of all the aromatic rices, it is the fragrance of jasmine rice that appeals most to me—much more than basmati—and it's one of the few white rices I really like, despite its nutritional wants. It is a rice that's deliberately cooked on the moist side, the better to soak up those delectable, often juicy Thai sauces, but not quite to the stickiness of Japanese or Chinese rice that allows them to be picked up with chopsticks. I learned the precise method for cooking it from Nancie McDermott's *Real Thai,* and think of her with thanks every time I prepare it.

Where to Find It: Supermarkets, maybe natural foods stores, and Asian foods stores.

How to Cook It Conventionally: Rinse and drain 2 cups jasmine rice several times in cold water. This rinsing not only removes any surface dust on imported rice, but also aids in achieving the desired degree of stickiness. Place the well-drained rice in a heavy pot with 3 cups cold water, preferably spring or filtered. Quickly, uncovered and over high heat, bring to a hard, fierce boil. Stir once or twice, reduce the heat to very low, and cover tightly. Cook for 20 minutes without lifting the lid. Take the still-covered pot from the heat and let stand, undisturbed, for 10 minutes. Remove the cover and fluff the rice with a fork. Serve warm. This yields 3 to 3½ cups.

How to Pressure-Cook It: Rinse and drain 2 cups jasmine rice several times in cold water. Place the well-drained rice in a pressure cooker with 2½ cups cold water, preferably spring or filtered. Quickly, uncovered and over high heat, bring to a hard, fierce boil. Stir once or twice and lock the lid. Adjust the heat to maintain high pressure. Cook for 6 minutes. Take the pot from the heat and let stand undisturbed for 10 minutes to let pressure release naturally. Unlock the lid but leave covered, letting stand for 2 minutes more. Then fluff the rice with a fork. Serve warm.

How to Use It: A natural with any spicy Thai dish, especially one with a coconut milk–based sauce, but it does well with any curry or exuberant stew. And if I have a fresh pineapple on hand and it's grilling weather, I always make enough jasmine rice for dinner so that I can enjoy Entree Salad of Jasmine Rice, Grilled Fresh Pineapple, and Peas (page 480) the next day.

Fit to Be Thai'd

"When I say that a recipe serves a certain number of people, I am expecting that you will be serving it with one or more other dishes, as well as with lots of rice. Thais eat rice, and the other stuff goes with it: entree *or* main dish *in Thai is in fact a phrase,* gahp kao, *which literally means 'with rice.' They love variety in their food as well as in life, and, rather than doubling a recipe, they prefer small amounts from a wide variety of dishes."*

—**Nancie McDermott,** *Real Thai*

Grain Go-Withs: 2 parts jasmine rice work nicely with ½ part millet or cracked wheat, or ¼ part each. After the jasmine has been rinsed, bring it to a boil with additional water in proportion to the other grains, then stir in the other grains and cook as directed for jasmine.

Short-Grain Rices

These plump little grains are almost round. They are quite moist and stick together when cooked.

Short-Grain Brown Rice:

What It Is: A short whole-grain brown rice widely available organically. Many of the kernels have a pale green cast to them, which makes no difference at all in the finished taste and cooking time.

What It's Like: A sticky, but markedly sweet brown rice, short-grain rice is delicious—for years it was my favorite, until I discovered brown basmati (it's now a tie). It is moist and chewy-substantial, not light and fluffy.

Where to Find It: Natural foods stores, possibly specialty or gourmet stores. (Most supermarket brown rice is long-grain.)

How to Cook It and Use It: For conventional and pressure-cooking directions, see those for medium-grain brown rice (page 465). For uses, see suggestions, including grain go-withs, for medium-grain brown rice and long-grain brown rice.

Arborio (and Arborio-Type) Rice:

What It Is: An Italian short-grain rice, shorter than American varieties and almost round. Arborio and its kin (Vialone, Carnaroli, and Baldo) have a magical consistency when cooked by one of two methods (a time-honored but highly labor-intensive one, or a newfangled one, the soul of simplicity and ease). These methods, and these rices, create that sublime dish risotto. All Italian risotti are made from white (refined) rice; however, here in America Arborios are available in both white and brown varieties.

What It's Like: The kernels release their starch, creating a smooth, creamy sauce, neither heavy nor overly firm nor pasty. The kernels themselves remain firm-tender, not soft-mushy—the equivalent of pasta al dente.

Where to Find It: Brown and white, at natural foods stores. White, at some supermarkets. The imported white is also available at specialty and gourmet markets.

How to Cook It: Please see the risotto section (pages 486 to 492) for cooking details.

Sushi Rice:

What It Is: This Japanese-style short-grain white rice is traditionally seasoned and used as a base for sushi and to make nori rolls (maki).

What It's Like: This is a slightly sweet, very sticky rice. Its stickiness is what helps hold the rolls together and makes rolling them a breeze.

Where to Find It: Natural foods stores, Asian foods stores.

How to Cook It: See the recipe for Nori Rolls (page 40).

Sweet Rice (Glutinous Rice):

What It Is: A very short-grain, almost round rice with a very high starch content, sweet or glutinous rice is rarely cooked at home in America. Instead, it mostly goes into rice products, such as mochi (see opposite page) and amasake (see page 471). It's available in both brown and white.

What It's Like: Sweet and starchy. Virtually the only home use you might make of it, outside of the forms listed above, would be in a rice pudding.

Where to Find It: Natural foods stores, Asian foods stores.

How to Cook It Conventionally: In a nonstick saucepan, combine 1½ cups water, preferably spring or filtered, with 1 cup sweet brown rice (it's generally not salted, but if you want to salt it, feel free). Bring to a boil, stir, then turn down to a simmer and cover tightly. Cook for 35 to 40 minutes. Let stand for 10 minutes before using. This yields about 4 cups.

How to Pressure-Cook It: Combine 2 cups sweet brown rice with 2 cups cold water, preferably spring or filtered, in a pressure cooker. Quickly, over high heat, bring to a hard, fierce boil, uncovered. Stir once or twice and lock the lid. Adjust the heat to maintain high pressure. Cook for 10 minutes. Take the pot from the heat and let stand undisturbed for 10 minutes to let the pressure release naturally. Unlock the lid but leave covered, letting stand for 2 minutes longer.

How to Use It: In any rice pudding calling for cooked rice.

Rice Products

Rice-Paper Wrappers: One of my personal favorites. They can be purchased at any Asian market and many supermarkets.

Rice Noodles (or Rice Sticks), Dried, Eastern-Style: Some are thin, some are wide; all are dried noodles of a translucent white, made from refined white rice flour. All are incredibly easy to fix, and very satisfying. Called mai fun by the Chinese, who prefer the vermicelli-thin or thinner (even threadlike) noodles and who usually fry them, they are also wonderful simply soaked and sautéed, and fast, too. Just soak the noodles in hot water until pliable—2 to 6 minutes depending on the width and thickness of the noodles. Add them in the last 2 minutes of cooking to any kind of stir-fry with a sauce, and they're done. They have a lighter, fresher feeling than wheat noodles, a pleasant slipperiness in the mouth, a translucency that is oh so appealing, and that good old noodle satisfaction. Thai and Vietnamese rice noodles are thicker than Chinese, at fettucine width or wider. Find these noodles at an Asian market, perhaps in the Asian foods section of your supermarket, perhaps at the natural foods store. Stay away from the noodles that come with prepackaged seasoning mixes; these are nearly always harsh and chemical in taste. Trust me, you'll do better concocting your own seasonings.

Rice Noodles, Fresh, Eastern-Style: If you are lucky enough to live in a metropolitan area with a large Asian population, you just may be able to find fresh rice noodles, and boy are they good. (If you eat restaurant Thai food, you'll know these as the fat, wide, irregularly shaped noodles called larb or lard on the menu.) Sturdy, chewy, substantial, these are among my favorite pastas. The noodles come uncut, a creamy-white sheet of rice-flour noodle dough, which has already been cooked by steam. After this, the sheets are lightly oiled, folded, and placed in small rectangular packages. When ready to use, cut them into ½-inch-wide strips, and separate. Since they're already cooked, they need only be dropped in boiling water for a few seconds to reheat, or just add them at the last minute to your stir-fry pan, again just long enough to heat.

Fresh rice noodles keep for about 1 week at home, refrigerated. If the noodles become dried out or

brittle (usually a result of using part of a package and not resealing it tightly), just run a little hot water over them and they'll resuscitate instantly.

Rice Pasta, Western-Style: This is pasta made from rice flour instead of wheat. Intended to be as similar to regular wheat pasta as possible, this product is designed primarily for those with a wheat allergy. To me, the Asian rice noodles are much more satisfying than these. Because rice flour lacks gluten, its "tooth" is markedly different from wheaten pastas; even when cooked perfectly, it doesn't have the bouncy, slight resistance that good, properly cooked wheat-based pasta does. However, these are not bad, especially when well sauced. Find them at the natural foods store. (Note that rice pasta aficionados say that Pastariso is the best brand.)

Mochi is one of the stranger and more interesting rice incarnations. Pronounced MOO-chee, it's a traditional Japanese food made of steamed, mashed sweet (glutinous) rice. Orthodox mochi contains just

Quick-Fix Rice Dishes

It's hard to go wrong with any of these simple fixes. Not only can you use them with virtually any variety of rice except the very sticky ones, they're good ideas to jazz up almost any grain or grain combo in this book. They call for already cooked rice.

Nut-Buttered Rice: *Stir in 1 tablespoon peanut, almond, or sesame butter at the end of cooking. If you like, add a second tablespoon of the corresponding nut, toasted and chopped, or toasted seeds. Pistachios are nice with almond or sesame butter, too.*

Rice with Green Herbs: *Stir in a double handful of chopped fresh basil, Italian parsley, cilantro, or scallions, or a combination of several of these.*

Rice Asiana: *Combine the two previous suggestions, plus a teaspoon or two of commercial garlic-ginger paste and a few squares of diced savory baked tofu.*

Pilaf Noel: *Just pour a cup or so of frozen peas into a strainer, run hot water over them, and add them to the cooked grain(s), along with 1 roasted red bell pepper (see page 782), peeled, seeded, and diced (or a little canned red pepper or pimento, if you must). Fluff to combine, and serve.*

rice and water and is inherently bland, like pasta, potatoes, or polenta, but new-age entrepreneurs have expanded the range, adding various flavors—vanilla, almond, cinnamon-raisin, sesame-date—some more successful than others. The sweet ones are best for waffled mochi—more on that in a second. There's also a savory sesame-garlic mochi, which is quite wonderful, as is the plain, when used as mochi cream puffs.

Plain or otherwise, the pounded rice is dried and then cut into large, thick squares. At this point it is very, very firm. It is in this form that the consumer buys it, in vacuum-packed bags, at the natural foods store or Asian market.

The texture of mochi is somewhat reminiscent of cream puffs or popovers, for, as it bakes, the mochi puffs up dramatically, getting golden brown and crisp on the outside, with a soft, moist, melty, chewy interior. To make mochi cream puffs or popovers, which of course contain no cream, preheat the oven to 450°F, cut the mochi into cubes 1 to 2 inches square. Use the larger size if you plan on using them as a breakfast pastry, the smaller if you want them as a starter. Bake on a cooking-sprayed baking sheet for 8 to 10 minutes. They'll puff up and get golden brown on top, at which point they're ready.

For breakfast, split mochi puffs open and try a bit of butter, nut butter, neufchâtel, ricotta and jam, applesauce, or apple butter inside—yum. But mochi really comes into its own when used in the plain or savory-seasoned variety, cut into smaller squares—1 to 1½ inches—and baked. Split the puffs, post-puffing, and fill with any savory filling you like—sautéed vegetables or ratatouille or a not-too-juicy mushroom ragoût or lentil stew—and serve as a starter. If I were catering a vegan wedding, or one where the food needed to be wheat-free, I'd serve these in a New York minute.

The same is true of waffled mochi. To make it, heat a nonstick waffle iron, or one that has been sprayed with cooking spray, until the indicator reads "Bake." Cut a 4-by-4-inch square (about one-quarter of the typical 12½-ounce mochi package), open the waffle iron, place mochi in it, and shut—it won't quite close all the way initially, but after about 1½ minutes the mochi will have spread out on its own, and the lid can be closed fully. Let the mochi bake in the waffle iron for 9 to 10 minutes, and serve hot from the iron. Yes, it puffs up and forms a waffle! Looks like a waffle—but it tastes like waffled mochi. Crisp on the outside with all the lovely little waffley holes, gooey on the inside, good but perplexingly different the first time you eat it, because it resembles something it isn't. The mochi texture, at first bizarre, grows addictive. Try it a few times, and you'll fall in love with it.

Cream of Rice Cereal: Coarse to finely ground particles of rice make a time-honored, soothing breakfast cereal. You might remember the cream of rice of your childhood, which was probably the type made from white rice. Now you can get whole-grain cream of rice at the natural foods store. There are instant, cook-in-a-cup cream of rices, and they're okay but not remotely as good as the from-scratch version. Cook such cereals according to the package directions (since this is a ground whole grain, it has much more of a tendency toward spoilage or insect infestation than does either unground whole brown rice or cream of-rice cereal made from white rice, so don't buy it in bulk—buy it in vacuum-packed packages). There is one proviso with package directions, however: All hot cereals taste best with longer, slower cooking, which package directions won't tell you because they know the general public wants quick, instant, warp-speed results. But if you've got the time, once the cereal has been added to the boiling water (or other liquid), switch the pot to a Flame Tamer (see page 535) and cook for twice as long over very low heat, stirring occasionally. Let stand for 5 minutes, then eat. No, this is not an old cook's tale. According to Margaret Wittenberg, author of *Good Food,* "The flavor of cereals is enhanced with longer cooking [because] the heat converts the starches to dextrins and sugars." Enjoy cream of rice with any of the recommendations under oatmeal (see page 557).

Frozen Rice Mixes: Available in supermarkets in a white rice variety, or at natural foods stores in whole grains, these are bags of frozen rice combined with vegetables. In the natural foods variation, done to perfection by Cascadian Farms, everything you need for a quick supper—brown rice, maybe mixed with other grains, seasonings, vegetables, and beans—is included. Their Cajun mix is especially good.

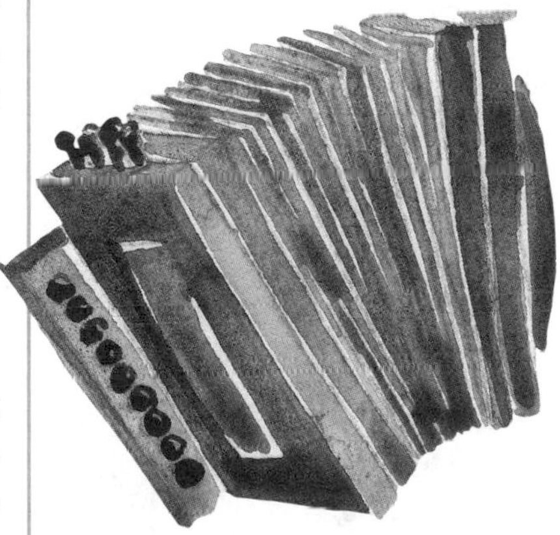

Packaged Rice Mixes: Again, both supermarkets and natural foods stores offer these mixes, which you've seen, and maybe used, a zillion times. They usually include rice, dehydrated vegetables, maybe dehydrated beans, and a seasoning packet. In general, these are high in salt and have a harsh, artificial taste, especially the supermarket brands. Read the fine print, especially if you're vegan: Many of them contain dehydrated chicken or beef broth, or dairy whey. I occasionally use them, but I throw out the seasoning packet. The exceptions to the rule are some of the natural foods brands: The Fantastic Foods mixes are usually good, as are the Casbah.

Amasake (pronounced a-mah-SAH-key)—traditional in Japan—is a very sweet, thick rice beverage, made with cultured sweet brown rice. The culture, called koji, transforms the rice starch into the sugars maltose and glucose. Although low in fat, it is very rich-tasting and quite caloric; the most widely available brands have about the thickness of a custard sauce, although you'll also find thinner or thicker varieties. Many flavors are available—vanilla, chocolate, mocha, or (my favorite) almond.

I use it, occasionally, as is, as a kind of instant crème anglaise for fresh sliced fruit, or to serve with a fruit crisp, especially when cooking for vegans or those allergic to dairy. It can also be "set up" as a thicker custard, using agar (see page 127) and cornstarch; used as the liquid element in smoothies (no need to sweeten the smoothie); or drunk as is, as a kind of milkshake. Some people also recommend it as a sports drink, since it's low fat, high carb, and cultured (hence easily digested). The Japanese serve plain amasake warmed, with a bit of freshly grated ginger as a garnish; some people dilute it and use it instead of milk in baking or in coffee or tea. (If you do, you'll need to cut back on sweetener.) Although nominally an acquired taste—really more an aquired idea—amasake is something you won't use daily, but will be glad to have in your repertoire.

Rice Milk: One of the grain "milks" vegans and the lactose-intolerant rely on, it's a white fluid that is somewhat milky, but also somewhat bland. Even so, until oat milk and refrigerated soy milks came along, it was the most successful low-fat substitute, but I now use it only if cooking for someone who is also allergic to oats or soy.

Smokin' Rice

Where there's smoke there's fire, and in this case, both—from smoked chipotle peppers in adobo sauce, very hot but truly lovely. I adore this recipe, but then I am not faint-hearted about hot food. With smoky chipotle heat underlined by the smokiness of vegetarian "bacon" bits baked in the dish for flavor then sprinkled atop it for texture, this definitely kisses bland goodbye. Since it relies on cooked rice and is reheated in the oven, it's an ideal do-ahead. Like so many rice dishes, it's excellent with beans or a beany stew, or any of the sweet squashes. **SERVES 4**

2 teaspoons olive oil
Cooking spray
1 large onion, chopped
1 carrot, diced
2½ cups cooked brown rice, preferably brown basmati
¼ canned chipotle pepper in adobo sauce, or more to taste, finely minced
1 teaspoon adobo sauce (from the canned chipotle)
¼ cup vegetarian "bacon" bits
¼ cup dried unsweetened cranberries or raisins
¼ teaspoon dried thyme
⅛ teaspoon ground cinnamon
Salt and freshly ground black pepper to taste

1 Preheat the oven to 375°F.

2 Heat the oil over medium heat in a nonstick skillet or one that has been sprayed with cooking spray. Add the onion and sauté until almost translucent, about 3 minutes. Add the carrot and sauté until slightly softened, 5 minutes longer, stirring often. Remove from the heat.

3 Scrape the sautéed vegetables into a bowl. Add the rice, chipotle, adobo, 2 tablespoons of the vegetarian "bacon" bits, and the dried cranberries or raisins. Toss well. Season with the thyme, cinnamon, and salt and pepper, then toss again. If the rice seems at all dry, add a tablespoon or so of water.

4 Place the rice in a nonstick casserole dish or one that has been sprayed with cooking spray. Cover tightly with foil or a lid. Bake until heated through, 25 to 30 minutes. Uncover, toss with the remaining vegetarian "bacon" bits, and serve at once.

Menu

DES COLORES: A SOUTH AMERICAN–INFLUENCED TASTING PLATE

Black Bean Feijoada
(PAGE 602)

*

Brazilian Rice

*

Brazilian Salsa
(PAGE 914)

*

Tempeh Picadillo Filling
(PAGE 359, STEPS 1 AND 2)
in a yellow or red bell pepper half
(SEE PAGE 410)

*

Pineapple Coconut Mousse-Custard
(PAGE 1053)

Brazilian Rice

Spanish rice, Mexican rice—there are lots of variations of this south-of-the-border, tomato-tinged rice. But to me, having served it with vegetarian feijoada on a South American tasting plate, it's Brazilian. **SERVES 4**

2 teaspoons olive oil
Cooking spray
1 small onion, diced
1 clove garlic, pressed
4 tomatoes, peeled, seeded, and finely chopped to yield 1 cup
1 vegetable bouillon cube, such as Morga (optional)
2 tablespoons cider vinegar
½ teaspoon salt (cut to a pinch if using a salted bouillon cube)
½ teaspoon freshly ground black pepper
1¾ cups water, preferably spring or filtered
1 cup long-grain brown rice, such as brown basmati
1 tablespoon finely chopped cilantro leaves

1 Heat the oil in a nonstick pot or one that has been sprayed with cooking spray. Add the onion and sauté for about 3 minutes, or until it starts giving off an aroma. Add the garlic and sauté for another minute. Add the tomatoes, vegetable bouillon cube, vinegar, salt, pepper, and water.

2 Bring to a serious boil. Add the rice, stir once, and turn down the heat to a low simmer. Cover very tightly and cook for 50 to 55 minutes. Turn off the heat, let the rice stand, uncovered, for 5 minutes, and fluff, adding cilantro.

Rice à la Hippie

When I was sixteen, I spent an exuberant, educational year living with eight other people in a Brooklyn brownstone on a quiet, tree-lined street. The year was 1969. We ate a lot of brown rice.

Hippie or alternative cuisine was unsophisticated and high in fat (nuts, cheeses, oils, and butters were staples). But in it lay the roots of the current wave of natural foods, vegetarian, and light or health-conscious ways of eating, as well as the acceptance of ethnic cuisines and their fusions into American. Even with the wisdom of middle age, I cannot quite be embarrassed for the enthusiastic, innocent teenager I was, senses trembling and nose twitching, like a young puppy, full of new hopes for an old world.

Ronnie, one of my compadres, made this glorious rice, often out of leftovers. I still enjoy it, and am always surprised at how good it still tastes to me. Caraway is indispensable here. The fat has been cut way down—the huge cubes of cheese we used to stir in, shocking! But I'm still alive, and so are you. With noses still twitching now and again. **SERVES 6 TO 8**

Basil

Cooking spray
2 teaspoons to 1 tablespoon mild vegetable oil, such as corn, canola, or peanut
1 large onion, sliced vertically into thin crescents
1 large green bell pepper, stemmed, seeded, and sliced vertically into strips
1 carrot, diced
5 or 6 mushrooms, sliced
1 rib celery, diced
4½ cups cooked brown rice, preferably short-grain, preferably leftover and cold from the fridge
2 tablespoons raisins, preferably golden
1½ teaspoons caraway seed
½ teaspoon dried basil
¼ teaspoon dried rosemary
¼ teaspoon dried oregano
¼ teaspoon celery seed
¼ teaspoon dried thyme
2 tablespoons minced dried apricots
2 tablespoons pecans or raw cashews, chopped (optional)
2 to 4 ounces cheese, cut into ¼-inch cubes (I use a combination of Muenster, Cheddar, and mozzarella)

1 In a large nonstick skillet, or one that has been sprayed with cooking spray, heat the oil over medium heat. Add the onion and sauté for 3 minutes. Add the bell pepper and carrot. Sauté for another 3 minutes. Add the mushrooms and celery and sauté for 4 minutes more.

2 Gradually stir in the rice, folding the vegetables into it. Lower the heat and add the raisins, caraway, basil, rosemary, oregano, celery seed, thyme, apricots and nuts, if using. Stir gently, folding the ingredients together but trying to avoid crushing the rice too much. Pop a cover on the skillet and let all the contents steam together over low heat until warmed through, 6 to 8 minutes. (You can add a little water for the rice to steam in if needed.)

3 When the rice is quite hot, stir in the cheese and cook just until the cubes start to melt. Remove from the heat and serve immediately. The cheese should be melty, but still be in discrete bites.

Brown Basmati Rice Pilaf with Southern Greens, Garlic, and Caramelized Onions

I generally cook my brown rice plain, and steam a pile of greens on the side. Or I steam, then sauté the greens with seasonings, then throw in some cooked brown rice at the end. Occasionally I want a more finished all-in-one dish, though, and here it is, soothing and gentle of flavor. Serve with a lentil stew or any flavorful, chunky sauce. **SERVES 4 TO 6**

2½ cups water, preferably spring or filtered
1¼ cups brown basmati rice
1 teaspoon salt
Cooking spray
1 tablespoon olive oil
1 teaspoon butter
2 large onions, very thinly sliced
1 teaspoon crushed garlic, homemade Garlic Oil (page 898), or commercial garlic paste
1 pound Southern greens (kale, collard, turnip, chard, mustard, etc., preferably a mixture), tough stems removed
1 lemon, halved

DECEMBER DINNER FOR TWO AMID THE LISTS AND WRAPPING PAPER

Spice-Market Mélange of Chickpeas and Cauliflower
(PAGE 616)

*

Brown Basmati Rice Pilaf with Southern greens, Garlic, and Caramelized Onions

*

New Wave Poppyseed Coleslaw
(PAGE 101)

*

Christmas cookies from the neighbors

1 Bring the water to a boil in a large saucepan. Add the brown basmati rice and the salt. Stir well. Let the liquid return to a boil, then turn down the heat to very low, cover the pot tightly, and let cook gently for 40 minutes.

2 Meanwhile, in a large nonstick skillet, or one that has been sprayed with cooking spray, heat the oil and butter over medium-low heat. Add the onions, and toss around in the oil and butter until they are coated and starting to soften, then turn the heat to medium-low and cover the skillet. Cook for 25 to 30 minutes, or until the onions are meltingly soft, lifting the lid every few minutes to stir the onions around, and then covering again. Toward the end of this period, uncover, raise the heat to medium, and, stirring constantly, cook until the onions are a sticky, golden-brown mass. Stir in the garlic and cook 30 seconds more.

3 Stack the greens and cut across the grain into very thin slices, using a sharp knife. At the 40-minute point, check the rice. Most, but not all of the water should be absorbed, and the rice should be fairly tender; it may need another 5 minutes to reach this point. When it's done, lift the lid and drop in the greens, pushing the lid down if you need to (the greens will seem like a huge mound, but will immediately wilt down). Let the rice cook for another few minutes, until all the water is absorbed.

4 Remove the rice from the heat and uncover. Let the rice and greens stand for 3 to 4 minutes to dissipate the steam, then toss lightly with a fork to combine. Squeeze the lemon halves over the rice and greens. Turn out onto a serving platter and top with the carmelized onions, or mound onto individual plates and divide the onions over the top of each portion.

Oven-Baked Three-Grain Casserole with Sun-Dried Tomatoes and Vegetables

Simple but with flair, this dish is plain enough to serve as a foil for a spicy bean concoction or stew, but easily revised as main-dish fare (see variations). Barley, brown rice, and whole-grain wheat give a pleasing range of textures. Don't forget to soak the wheat and barley the night before.

In my view, this dish is at its best done ahead and held over to the next day, when it can be formed into little cakes to be sautéed in a nonstick skillet. Like risotto cakes, you get a crisp, golden-brown exterior and a creamily melting interior, full of flavor. For this reason, I like to use a short-grain brown rice, which yields a more cohesive finished dish. If you want a fluffier version, substitute a brown basmati or other brown long grain. **SERVES 4 TO 6**

½ cup whole-grain wheat or kamut or spelt, soaked overnight in water (preferably spring or filtered) to cover
½ cup barley, soaked overnight in water (preferably spring or filtered) to cover
5 or 6 sun-dried tomato halves, diced
Cooking spray
2 carrots, scrubbed, quartered lengthwise, and cut into ½-inch dice
1 small onion, chopped
4 ounces mushrooms, quartered
1 cup frozen whole-kernel corn (or kernels cut from 2 to 3 ears fresh corn)
1 cup short-grain brown rice
¼ cup finely minced Italian parsley
1½ teaspoons salt
1 teaspoon Dragon Salt (page 900)
1¼ quarts vegetable stock (see page 139), boiling (or salted water, spring or filtered, if you prefer a more straightforward grainy flavor)

1 In the morning, drain the soaked wheat and barley (reserve the soaking water for use in stock or in another recipe). Place the sun-dried tomatoes in a small heatproof dish and pour boiling water over them. Let stand for 5 minutes, then drain them. Chop the rehydrated tomatoes and set aside.

2 Preheat oven to 350°F. Spray a 2- to 3-quart casserole dish with cooking spray.

3 Place the soaked wheat in the casserole dish, along with the rehydrated chopped tomatoes, the carrots, onion, mushrooms, corn, barley, brown rice, and parsley. Stir/toss a few times to combine everything. Drop the salt and Dragon Salt into the boiling stock or water, and pour the stock over the grain-vegetable mixture in the casserole.

4 Immediately cover the casserole tightly and put it in the oven. Bake for 65 minutes, remove from the oven, and check to make sure the grains are cooked through and all the liquid is absorbed. (It is very likely that the grains will be done, but if not, add an extra cup of boiling water or stock, cover again, and bake for another 30 minutes.) Let the casserole stand for 15 minutes after removal from oven, then fluff with a fork. Serve hot.

COOK ONCE FOR 2 MEALS Double the recipe. First time out, serve it as is, with a spicy stew, chili, bean dish, or sauce. The second time, make it the main attraction by adding the pesto in the variation, reheating with a cup of any cooked beans stirred in, and perhaps melting a little Cheddar or Monterey Jack over the top. This also makes a fine stuffing for an eggplant or zucchini half, or a scooped-out tomato or acorn squash.

VARIATIONS

Stir in ¼ to ½ cup basil pesto when fluffing after cooking for a delicious, more assertively flavored dish, or add 1 tablespoon butter for a richer one. Or, substitute half an eggplant, finely diced, for the mushrooms.

Lemon-Basil Rice Pilaf with White Wine

VARIATION

Sometimes fresh basil isn't available, but this dish is too good to let that stop you. Instead, try ½ cup minced Italian parsley.

The bright, clear flavor of fresh lemon makes this side dish sparkle, while fresh basil and white wine lend it a distinctive yet delicate flavor. An ideal accompaniment to a surprising range of dishes: those sauced with something sweet-sour or fruity, or with the onion, garlic, and tomato flavors of the Mediterranean, or almost any bean dish or nonstarchy stuffed vegetables, even with curries. Truly a recipe you'll return to time and again, this is a keeper on all counts. And don't miss the Cook Once for 2 Meals suggestion.

Whole-grain rices, with their more dominant toasty-nutty flavors and fragrances, do not work for this; the very plainness of white rice allows the lemon to shine.

SERVES 4 TO 6 GENEROUSLY

2 lemons
About 2⅔ cups vegetable stock (see page 139), or water
¾ cup dry white wine
1 teaspoon salt
1½ cups converted or parboiled rice
½ cup finely slivered fresh basil

1 Grate the rind of the lemons, then juice them and pour the juice into a measuring cup. Add sufficient stock to the lemon juice to equal 3 cups (you may also use water plus a vegetable bouillon cube, such as Morga, if you like).

2 In a medium pot, bring the lemon juice mixture to a boil with the lemon rind, wine, and salt. Stir in the rice, lower the heat to a simmer, cover, and cook for 20 minutes, or until all the liquid has evaporated.

3 Remove from the heat. Add the basil and toss quickly with a fork, so that the hot rice wilts the basil. Cover and let stand for a minute or two. Serve.

COOK ONCE FOR 2 MEALS This refreshing lemon-rice combo is one step away from a salad. Why not double the recipe, eat half tonight, hot, with something savory, and save the rest for a superb main-dish Whole-Garden Lemon-Rice Pilaf? This is a sort of warm rice salad. Reheat the leftover rice in a nonstick skillet with 1 tablespoon water, covering to steam the rice. When hot, toss with the following: 1 tablespoon olive oil, a good solid grinding of black pepper, 1 or 2 diced garden-ripe tomatoes (better yet, 1 yellow and 1 red tomato), 1 cup or so well-drained canned chickpeas, and 1 small diced cucumber. Scoop the salad, warm, onto a nice bed of greens—the perfect summer lunch.

Sweet Rice Pilaf with Citrus, Cinnamon, and Apple

The perfect foil for a spicy curry, or a tart or lemony dish, this was invented on a cold, iced-in, closed-for-the-season January night. It got late, suddenly. We were hungry, suddenly. The water for pasta had been put to boil, when—horrors!—no pasta! And, it turned out, not much else. A scavenge through cupboard and pantry yielded a scruffy-looking orange, a past-its-prime apple. . . . But together with my favorite white rice (and pressure-cooked for speed), they were remarkably good. Try this with Mother-of-Invention Quick Quasi-Thai Stew (page 894), also invented from the cupboard that January night. **SERVES 4**

Cooking spray
2 teaspoons mild vegetable oil, such as corn, canola, or peanut
1 large onion, diced
1 cup converted long-grain rice, such as Uncle Ben's
1 orange, rind grated and pulp reserved
1 sweet, not-too-firm apple, such as Red or Golden Delicious, peeled, cored, and diced
1 stick cinnamon, 3 inches long, broken in half
1 teaspoon salt
2¼ cups boiling water, preferably spring or filtered
2 to 3 tablespoons diced pitted dates
4 whole cloves
1 teaspoon tamari or shoyu soy sauce (optional)

1 In a medium nonstick saucepan, or one that has been sprayed with cooking spray, heat the oil over medium-high heat. Add the onion and sauté, stirring, until the onion is lightly browned, about 6 minutes. Add the rice and stir for another minute, then

add the orange rind, apple, cinnamon stick, salt, boiling water, and dates. Bring to a boil, stir well, drop in the cloves, cover tightly, and cook for about 20 minutes, or until tender.

2 Uncover, and let stand for 5 minutes. With a spoon, pick out the cloves (they should be sitting right on top; this is why you added them after stirring) and the pieces of cinnamon stick. Squeeze the orange over the rice (through a strainer, to catch the seeds). Stir well. Taste and season with soy sauce, if desired.

To Prepare in a Pressure Cooker: Reduce the boiling water used to 2 cups. In a pressure cooker that has been sprayed with cooking spray, follow the directions in step 1 through the addition of the cloves. Then, lock the lid, bring to high pressure, and reduce the heat until high pressure is maintained but not exceeded. Set a kitchen timer for 5 minutes. When the timer goes off, turn off the heat. Release pressure, open pressure cooker, and proceed with step 2.

Entree Salad of Jasmine Rice, Grilled Fresh Pineapple, and Peas

There are so many different ways of cooking rice, each method exploiting certain qualities of the particular rice, but you never quite get over feeling that the one you grew up with is the best. A girl, the daughter of diplomats, who was a bunkmate of mine at summer camp in New England lived most of the year in Thailand. I have a vivid memory of her throwing down her fork one day and remarking with disgust, "I can't eat rice like this, I just can't. At home we call this dishwater rice."

No one could call the jasmine rice in this splendid and refreshing salad dishwater rice. This whole-meal salad is perfectly suited for a lunch for company out on the patio, on a hot, lazy July weekend. To prevent small vegetables, such as pea pods, from falling through the grill bars, place them on one of the sheet pans with small holes in them that are sold with barbecue equipment. **SERVES 4 TO 6**

DRESSING/GRILL SAUCE

4 cloves garlic
2 tablespoons tamari or shoyu soy sauce
1 tablespoon toasted sesame oil
1 tablespoon mild vegetable oil, such as corn, canola, or peanut
1 tablespoon fresh-squeezed lemon juice
1 tablespoon honey

SALAD

½ fresh pineapple, peeled, core removed, and cut into rings
¼ pound pea pods, stems removed
4 cups cooked jasmine rice, cooled
½ crisp apple, such as Granny Smith, finely chopped, or Asian apple-pear
⅓ to ⅔ cup finely chopped fresh basil, mint, or cilantro (or a combination of all three)
1 tablespoon finely chopped crystallized ginger
8 ounces commercially prepared Thai-style baked tofu, such as White Wave, cut into ½-inch cube
¼ cup peanuts, toasted and coarsely chopped (optional)

1 Preheat the grill to hot. Combine all the dressing ingredients, stirring together vigorously with a fork.

2 Lower the grill heat to medium. Brush a little of the dressing on both sides of each slice of pineapple, and toss the pea pods with about 1 tablespoon of the dressing. Place the pineapple on the grill long enough to sear, 3 to 5 minutes. Place the pea pods on a grilling sheet and place it on the grill for about 2 minutes.

3 Turn the pineapple using a pair of tongs, and grill on the other side. Flip the pea pods on the sheet and grill on the other side. Remove the pineapple from the grill when grill-marked on both sides. Remove pea pods when slightly soft. Let the pineapple and peas cool. Dice the pineapple into pieces about ½ inch square and set aside.

4 Toss the rice with the remaining dressing, working it through your hands lightly to mix thoroughly. Add the cooled pineapple and pea pods, the apple, basil, mint, and/or cilantro, and crystallized ginger. Toss again, and let the flavors get to know one another, refrigerated, for at least 2 hours, but preferably overnight.

5 Next day, check for seasonings (you may well need salt or additional tamari). Toss in the tofu. Top with peanuts, if desired, and serve at room temperature.

Indian Restaurant–Style Saffron Rice Pilaf

The building where my mother, Charlotte Zolotow, started her long career as a children's book writer and editor was at 49 East 33rd Street in New York City. This was the site of the old Harper Brothers Building, and she was a secretary. It was 1938, and she made ten dollars a week. By the mid-1960s, the company was Harper & Row, she had long since become an editor, and she was the mother of a teenage daughter who loved exotic food. Every so often I'd meet her for dinner, and we'd walk to a now-defunct Indian restaurant, the name of which I've forgotten. I have not forgotten, though, the brilliant yellow and orange saffron-infused rice. What made it unique was that the color varied from grain to grain: Some grains were vivid red-orange, some the more conventional saffron yellow. Even then I wondered how it was done, little imagining that I would someday travel to India and learn to cook many of these foods at their source. I never did run into this two-tone rice, though—not in India or in any Indian restaurant elsewhere. I am sure now that they simply made two pots of rice, one orange and one yellow, and tossed them together after cooking.

Mine is one-toned and not nearly so bright, but its flavors are vivid, and so is the satisfaction of eating it. You need to use white rice to get the color. Basmati's traditional, but I don't much care for it, so I use Uncle Ben's. Optional apricots add additional gold. **SERVES 4**

¾ teaspoon saffron threads
4½ cups Golden Stock (page 140)
1 tablespoon butter, or, better yet, clarified butter (see page 486)
Cooking spray
1 small onion, chopped
1½ cups parboiled or converted white rice
¾ teaspoon salt
About 2 ounces dried apricot halves (⅓ to ½ cup), diced or cut into quarters, or to taste (optional)

1 In a small, dry skillet over medium-low heat, toast the saffron, stirring often or

VARIATIONS

MUSLIM-STYLE SWEET PILAF: ***Sauté a broken cinnamon stick, 4 cardamom pods, and 4 cloves with the onion before adding the rice. Add the stock, the grated rind and juice of 1 orange, and 2 tablespoons sugar or honey. At the end, you can toss in 2 to 4 tablespoons toasted nuts—pistachios are best, but freshly toasted almonds or cashews are also good.***

MAIN-DISH SWEET PILAF: ***After cooking toss in some diced savory baked tofu or Thai-style baked tofu or Basic Oven-Baked Marinated Tempeh (page 641) or well-drained canned chickpeas. Not traditional, but extremely pleasant, is to substitute finely chopped sun-dried tomatoes for the apricots. I sometimes toss green peas in at the end.***

shaking the pan, until it darkens slightly, 3 to 5 minutes. For maximum color, crush the toasted saffron in a mortar and pestle. Place the toasted saffron in a small heat-proof bowl. Bring ½ cup of the stock to a boil in a small saucepan and pour it over the saffron. Let soak for at least 3 hours, or overnight, refrigerated.

2 About 40 minutes before you wish to serve the rice, heat the butter in a medium-large nonstick saucepan or one that has been sprayed with cooking spray. Add the onion and sauté over medium-low heat for about 10 minutes, or until softened. Add the rice and cook, stirring, for about 2 minutes.

3 Pour in the remaining stock, and bring to a boil, adding the salt, soaked saffron and soaking stock, and apricots. Stir a couple of times, lower the heat, and cover tightly. Cook until the stock is absorbed, about 18 minutes.

4 Let the rice sit, undisturbed, for 10 minutes. Then lift the lid and fluff with a fork. Serve hot.

COOK ONCE FOR 2 MEALS Either version of this leftover rice pilaf is the basis for a delicious Sweet Rice Salad, so double the recipe. Eat part of it hot tonight; tomorrow or the next day, bring the cold rice to room temperature and toss in a diced tomato, a diced fresh pineapple half, 3 or 4 diced scallions, and 1 can (15 ounces) chickpeas or kidney beans, well drained (or 2 cups of any cooked beans you have on hand). A little minced Italian parsley or cilantro couldn't hurt, either. Splash with a little vinegar—fruit vinegars are nice here—and, if you like, a bit of olive oil. Serve the salad on lettuce, with a glass of iced jasmine tea.

Middle Eastern–Style Pilaf with Noodles and Red Lentils

This is my favorite simple pilaf. Such dishes of white rice with sautéed noodles are served throughout Greece and the eastern Mediterranean. They are deliberately on the plain side, but with visual and textural interest. This version does the traditional version one better, however, because it also includes tiny, quick-cooking red lentils. The lentils don't interfere with the pleasing simplicity of flavor, but they do

NOTE

Pilafs like this one cannot be made with brown rice, because in the time it takes for the brown rice to cook, the noodles are mush.

make the dish more substantial, making it the perfect accompaniment for any mixed-vegetable dish like ratatouille, G'vetch (page 749), an asparagus-mushroom-carrot stir-fry, or a platter of stuffed vegetables. **SERVES 6 TO 8**

4 cups water, preferably spring or filtered
½ cup tiny red split lentils (do not substitute)
Cooking spray
2 to 4 teaspoons butter
2 to 4 teaspoons olive oil
¾ cup fine, dry pasta such as vermicelli, angel hair, or fidelli, snapped into 1-inch pieces
1½ cups parboiled or converted rice
1¼ teaspoon salt
Freshly ground black pepper

1 Bring the water to a boil in a medium pot and add the lentils. Turn the heat down to medium and simmer the lentils, uncovered, for 5 minutes. Turn off the heat and allow the lentils to soak in their cooking water for 45 minutes.

2 In a large, deep nonstick skillet, or one that has been sprayed with cooking spray, heat the butter and oil until the butter melts. Add the broken pasta and cook, stirring constantly, until the pasta is starting to turn golden brown, about 3 minutes. As you're doing this, turn on the heat under the lentils and bring them back to a boil.

3 When the pasta is golden brown, add the rice and sauté it, too, stirring constantly, until it becomes shiny and translucent. This will take about 1 minute. Then, all at once, pour in the boiling lentils and their cooking liquid, along with the salt. Give a good stir, and let the whole thing boil furiously for 1 minute.

4 Turn down the heat to very low, cover, and simmer gently for 18 minutes, then turn off the heat and let the dish rest, covered, for another 10 minutes.

5 Season to taste with pepper and serve.

Eggplant Rice Audrey

This is an incredibly savory rice dish, rich with Parmesan and moist eggplant, exuberantly flavored by garlic, tomato, and fresh basil, which we made up out of leftovers for a staff dinner after a very busy night at the restaurant. It was at this time that Audrey, some twenty years older than me and a hard-working ball of energy, would at last sit down with a cup of coffee and confess, "My dogs are talking to me." Since Audrey is fond of both eggplant and rice, I named it in her honor. You can substitute tender leftover grilled eggplant, diced, for the baked. **SERVES 4 TO 6**

- 1 teaspoon olive oil
- Cooking spray
- 1 large onion, diced
- 1 tomato, peeled, seeded, and diced
- 1 teaspoon tomato paste
- 3 cloves garlic, minced or pressed
- ⅓ cup minced basil (about 3 large sprigs)
- 1 cup oven-baked eggplant slices, chopped
- 3 cups cooked rice, preferably a combination of brown basmati, wild, and any good long- or medium-grain white
- ½ cup freshly grated Parmesan cheese
- Salt and freshly ground black pepper to taste

1. Heat the oil in a large, deep nonstick skillet or one that has been sprayed with cooking spray. Add the onion and sauté over medium heat for about 3 minutes, or until starting to soften.

2. Add the tomato and tomato paste, garlic, basil, eggplant, and rice. Stir very well, lower the heat slightly, and cover tightly. Steam for about 3 minutes, or until good and hot. Lift the lid and sprinkle with the Parmesan. Season to taste with salt and pepper and serve at once.

Katherine's Ghee Rice with Cashews and Melting Onions

This is a traditional rice dish, as made in Indian home kitchens. Although it's a North Indian dish, it was given to me by my friend Katherine, who has lived in South India for many years. It's intoxicatingly fragrant as it cooks, and delicious with any curry. **SERVES 4 TO 6**

NOTE

Ghee can be purchased at Indian groceries, or you can make clarified butter, which is very similar. Slowly melt butter until the white solids separate to the bottom of the pan, leaving the clear butter fat on top. Pour off the clear liquid (discard the solids) and store the clarified butter in the refrigerator for up to 6 months.

- 3 cloves garlic, pressed
- 1 teaspoon minced peeled ginger
- 3 tablespoons ghee or clarified butter (see note)
- 2 tablespoons to ¼ cup raw cashews, halved
- 1 large red onion, very thinly sliced
- 1 cup white basmati rice, rinsed twice in running water
- 2 cups water, preferably spring or filtered
- 1 teaspoon salt
- 1 tablespoon minced cilantro leaves (optional)

1 Combine the garlic and ginger in a mortar or mini-processor, and mash together to pulverize. Set aside.

2 Heat the ghee over medium heat in a small wok. Add the cashews and stir-fry until the nuts color slightly. Remove the nuts with a slotted spoon and set aside. Add the onion and stir-fry for 8 to 10 minutes, or until deep golden and limp. Remove the onion from the ghee using the slotted spoon and set aside.

3 Add the rice to the ghee, along with the ginger-garlic paste. Lower the heat slightly and toast the rice, stirring constantly, for about 3 minutes, or until glossy. Add the water and salt to the rice, bring to a boil, and cover. Cook for 10 to 12 minutes, or until the rice is tender. Serve the rice mounded on a flat platter, sprinkled with a garnish of the toasted cashews and fried onions, which should have crisp edges but a melting inner texture, and the cilantro, if using.

Risotto (How Not to Go Stir Crazy)

When it comes to risotto there is bad news, and really, really good news. The bad news: Classic risotto preparation is labor-intensive, calling for sautéing the rice, then adding the savory liquid in ½-cup increments, stirring all the while. This means that, although this delicious dish is eminently guest-worthy, it's virtually impossible to prepare when you have guests if you have any desire to be with them, and of course, forget about fixing it on a busy family-dinner night. Many restaurants partially cook it, then finish it quickly at the last, but this yields an inferior risotto, one markedly less creamy and without the perfect kernel texture that is the whole point of risotto.

The really good news? There is an easy, splendid method of making risotto start to finish in 10 minutes, and it is every bit as good as the traditional way. It takes a little longer when using brown Arborio rice, but it's still fast and nearly stir-free. How? Use a pressure cooker.

It turns out that, actually, this is not news. The Italians have long used pressure cookers in the creation of risotto, though this was a deeply held secret until a 1979 book, *The New Italian Cooking,* by Franco and Margaret Romagnoli, was published. Lorna Sass, who popularized the method in *Great Vegetarian Cooking under Pressure,* says, "More than any other dish, it's the creation of a 5-minute risotto that catapults the pressure cooker into the 1990s kitchen." And I say, if convenience has not already convinced you to buy a pressure cooker, please let the promise of these exquisite and easy risottos do it. Taste one, and not only will you never go back to the stir-crazy method, you'll fall in love with the magic that pressure cookers can perform. This is the only method I use, and the only method I give here.

Here is the basic pressure-cooker risotto method, followed by a number of variations and elaborations.

Basic Pressure-Cooker Risotto

This is your basic risotto, but for all its simplicity, it is a heady, seductive dish. Made with white Arborio rice, it takes but 5 minutes under pressure, and yields a dish with some of the soothing, gentle-but-not-mushy texture of perfect pasta. Made with the brown organic Arborio, it takes 20 minutes, and yields a dish with the classic creamy sauce, with rice kernels that are a bit more assertively flavored and firm. Both are wonderful. **SERVES 4 TO 6**

Cooking spray
1 teaspoon to 1 tablespoon butter
1 teaspoon to 1 tablespoon olive oil
1 small onion, finely chopped
2 cups white or brown Arborio rice
½ cup dry white wine, at room temperature
4½ cups vegetable stock, preferably homemade (see page 139), warmed
¼ to ½ cup freshly grated Parmesan cheese (optional)
Salt and freshly ground black pepper to taste

1 Spray a pressure-cooker pot with cooking spray. Over medium heat, melt the butter and oil together in the cooker. Add the onion and sauté, stirring, until it has softened slightly but is not browned, about 3 minutes.

2 Add the rice and cook, stirring, for about 1 minute, until the grains are shiny and glossed lightly with oil. Raise the heat slightly and stir in the wine. Stir until the wine is mostly absorbed (much less than 1 minute for white rice, and 1½ to 2 minutes for brown).

3 Pour in all but ½ cup of the heated stock and turn the heat to high. Lock the lid

VARIATIONS

▲ ***Sauté a diced carrot and/or a diced rib of celery with the onion.***

▲ ***Scatter loads of minced Italian parsley over the finished risotto, and stir in.***

▲ ***Add ½ to 1 teaspoon crushed saffron threads to the warm broth. This makes your basic Risotto à la Milanese.***

▲ ***Once the lid is released, stir in a handful of any diced, cooked vegetables, either freshly steamed or sautéed, or leftover (if not overcooked). Broccoli, or sautéed broccoli rabe and garlic, are wonderful; so is tender-crisp zucchini with garlic and a bit of tomato; so is G'vetch (page 749) or Greek-Style Green Beans (page 689) or Greek-Style Smothered Okra (page 775).***

Fine Points of Risotto

▲ *Never rinse the rice before cooking; you want to retain any residual surface starch, which cooks into the water to give the desired creamy-sauce effect.*

▲ *Things move quickly when pressure cooking risotto. Make sure your mise en place (see page 107) is complete before you start. If cooking for company, do your "mise" early in the day.*

▲ *Become familiar with your cooker's method for quick-release of steam. On my Duromatic, you simply press the valve down using the side of a knife or spoon end; stand back, unalarmed at the big hiss and steam, and there you are. Other machines require transferring the cooker to the sink and running cold water over it.*

▲ *Almost all classic Italian risotti are enriched at the end with a little (or a lot) of freshly grated Parmesan. This certainly adds to the dish, playing up the sauce's creaminess and making a richer risotto. But I have to say, for all you vegans and lactose-intolerant folks out there, a cheeseless risotto made by this method is not half bad, due to the inherent creaminess of the sauce. However, if you like, make up for the absence of the cheese with a last-minute dose of nutritional yeast, a bit of umeboshi plum paste (see page 118), or a splash of balsamic vinegar. Use homemade stock, if possible—it's richer and tastier by far, and use all olive oil in the sauté portion.*

▲ *In its way, a risotto is as evanescent as a soufflé. To experience it at perfect creaminess, before its sauce thickens too much, dish it up within 1 or 2 minutes of its completion.*

▲ *On the other hand, never worry about leftover risotto. Yes, it thickens—making it perfect for little risotto cakes, which can be sautéed in a nonstick skillet with no additional oil. I look forward to leftover risotto simply to have risotto cakes for breakfast!*

in place and bring the pressure to high over high heat. Once the pressure is reached, cook for 5 minutes if using white Arborio, or 19 if using brown.

4 When done, release the pressure. Unlock the lid and stir in the remaining broth and the cheese, if using. Season with salt and plenty of pepper and serve at once.

Spring Risotto of Artichoke, Lemon, Garlic, and Mint

For this recipe, you'll need to cook the artichokes ahead of time. Also note that I call for scissoring, rather than chopping the chives; snipping is much easier and crushes the chives less. **SERVES 4 TO 6**

Cooking spray
1 teaspoon to 1 tablespoon butter
1 teaspoon to 1 tablespoon olive oil
1 small red onion, finely chopped
2 tablespoons chopped garlic
2 cups white or brown Arborio rice
½ cup dry white wine, at room temperature
4½ cups vegetable stock, preferably homemade (see page 139), warmed
1 lemon, half the rind grated, the pulp halved and juiced
¼ to ½ cup freshly grated Parmesan cheese (optional; see suggestions for vegans, in box, opposite)
2 tablespoons finely snipped chives
4 artichokes, hearts and stems only, cooked and thickly sliced (for cooking directions, see page 387)
⅔ cup finely chopped mint leaves
Salt and freshly ground black pepper to taste

1. Spray a pressure-cooker pot with cooking spray. Over medium heat, melt the butter and oil together in the cooker. Add the onion and sauté, stirring, until it has softened slightly but is not browned, about 3 minutes. Add the garlic and cook, stirring, for 30 seconds more.

2. Add the rice and cook, stirring, for about 1 minute, until the grains are shiny and glossed lightly with oil. Raise the heat slightly and stir in the wine. Stir until the wine is mostly absorbed (much less than 1 minute for white rice, and 1½ to 2 minutes for brown).

3. Pour in all but ½ cup of the heated stock. Add the lemon rind and juice, and turn the heat to high. Lock the lid in place and bring the pressure to high over high heat. Once the pressure is reached, cook 5 minutes if using white Arborio, or 19 if using brown.

4. When time is up, release the pressure. Unlock the lid. Stir in the remaining broth and the cheese, if using. Stir in the artichokes, mint, and chives. Season to taste with salt and plenty of pepper. Serve at once.

Risotto with Green Beans, Garlic, and Sage

Although most of us consider sage a fall flavor because of its association with Thanksgiving dressing, in fact it grows throughout the summer. Here, it positively perfumes this simple, delicious risotto.

If you have skinny, tender green beans, try this with white Arborio; if you have older, tougher ones, use brown Arborio. **SERVES 4 TO 6**

Cooking spray
1 teaspoon to 1 tablespoon butter
1 teaspoon to 1 tablespoon olive oil
1 small onion, finely chopped
1½ tablespoons chopped garlic (about 6 large cloves)
2 cups white or brown Arborio rice
½ cup dry white wine, at room temperature
½ pound green beans, stemmed, sliced crosswise into ¼-inch pieces
4½ cups vegetable stock, preferably homemade (see page 139), warmed
1 tablespoon finely scissored fresh sage
¼ to ½ cup freshly grated Parmesan cheese (optional; see suggestions for vegans, box page 488)
Salt and freshly ground black pepper to taste

1 Spray a pressure-cooker pot with cooking spray. Over medium heat, melt the butter and oil together in the cooker. Add the onion and sauté, stirring, until it has softened slightly but is not browned, about 3 minutes. Add the garlic and cook, stirring, for 30 seconds more.

2 Add the rice and cook, stirring, for about 1 minute until the grains are shiny and glossed lightly with oil. Raise the heat slightly and stir in the wine. Stir until the wine is mostly absorbed (much less than 1 minute for white rice, and 1½ to 2 minutes for brown). Add the green beans and stir a few times.

3 Pour in all but ½ cup of the heated stock and turn the heat to high. Lock the lid in place and bring the pressure to high over high heat. Once the pressure is reached, cook for 5 minutes if using white Arborio, or 19 if using brown.

4 When time is up, release the pressure. Unlock the lid. Stir in the remaining stock, the sage, and cheese, if using, and season to taste with salt and plenty of pepper. Serve at once.

Risotto with Green Herbs and Baby Limas

Madhur Jaffrey's *World-of-the-East Vegetarian Cooking* contains so many good recipes it's hard to know where to start. One is for a "scrumptious, meal-in-itself rice dish, fragrant with the aroma of fresh herbs," which she says she first had at the Tavooz Restaurant in New York. The original dish is Iranian, started on top of the stove and finished in the oven, the rice soaked overnight, then drained and washed several times for a fluffy and dazzling—and time-consuming—result. My version of that recipe takes the flavorings, transmutes them to an easily done pressure-cooked risotto, and lowers the fat. No cheese is added, and you can easily use all olive oil to make this a vegan dish if you like. Don't skimp on the herbs; they are not overpowering, and the hot rice cooks them down instantly. **SERVES 6**

Cooking spray
1 teaspoon to 1 tablespoon butter
1 teaspoon to 1 tablespoon olive oil
1 small onion, finely chopped
1½ tablespoons chopped garlic (about 6 large cloves)
2 cups white Arborio rice
½ cup dry white wine, at room temperature
1 package (10 ounces) frozen lima beans
5½ cups vegetable stock, preferably homemade (see page 139), warmed
½ cup finely chopped Italian parsley
½ cup finely chopped cilantro
½ cup finely chopped dill
½ cup finely chopped scallion greens
Salt and freshly ground black pepper to taste

1 Spray a pressure-cooker pot with cooking spray. Over medium heat, melt the butter and oil together in the cooker. Add onion and sauté, stirring, until it has softened slightly but is not browned, about 3 minutes. Add the garlic and cook, stirring, for 30 seconds more.

2 Add the rice and cook, stirring, for about 1 minute, until the grains are shiny and glossed lightly with oil. Raise the heat slightly and stir in the wine. Stir until the wine is mostly absorbed (much less than 1 minute). Add the limas, breaking the frozen block up as you add it.

3 Pour in all but ½ cup of the heated stock and turn the heat to high. Lock the lid in place and bring the pressure to high over high heat. Once the pressure is reached, cook for 5 minutes.

4 When time is up, release the pressure. Unlock the lid. Stir in the remaining stock and all the green herbs and season to taste with salt and plenty of pepper. Serve at once.

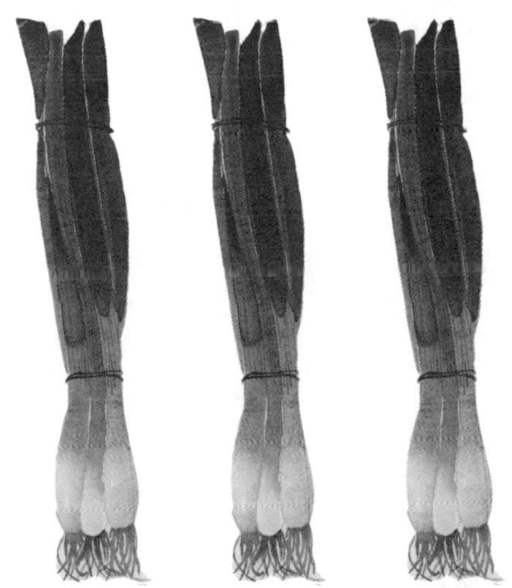

VARIATION

RISOTTO WITH GREEN HERBS AND FRESH BLACK-EYED PEAS: ***To make this using brown Arborio, substitute brown rice for the white, and 10 ounces fresh, raw, black-eyed peas for the limas. The time under pressue should be 19 minutes instead of 5.***

Risotto Russo

A wintertime risotto, as restorative in cold weather as the artichoke variation is in spring. I am a beet lover—and so must you be to appreciate this dish, as intensely colored as it is flavored. The red comes not only from the beet, but also from red wine. For a beautiful supper, make sure you've got some radicchio or red cabbage slivered into the crisp green salad you serve first. **SERVES 6**

Cooking spray
1 teaspoon to 1 tablespoon butter
1 teaspoon to 1 tablespoon olive oil
1 small red onion, finely chopped
2 tablespoons chopped garlic
2 cups white or brown Arborio rice
½ cup dry red wine, at room temperature
4½ cups vegetable stock, preferably homemade (see page 139), warmed
2 small raw beets, trimmed and grated
1½ teaspoons honey or Rapidura
¼ to ½ cup freshly grated Parmesan cheese (optional)
Salt and freshly ground black pepper to taste

"What's the matter with Mary Jane? She won't eat her supper, she hasn't a pain and it's lovely rice pudding for dinner again! . . ."

—**A. A. Milne,** *When We Were Very Young*

1 Spray a pressure-cooker pot with cooking spray. Over medium heat, melt the butter and oil together in the cooker. Add the onion and sauté, stirring, until it has softened slightly but is not browned, about 3 minutes. Add the garlic and cook, stirring, 30 seconds more.

2 Add the rice and cook, stirring, for about 1 minute, until the grains are shiny and glossed lightly with oil. Raise the heat slightly and stir in the wine. Stir until the wine is mostly absorbed (much less than 1 minute for white rice, and 1½ to 2 minutes for brown).

3 Pour in all but ½ cup of the heated stock. Add the grated beets and honey and turn the heat to high. Lock the lid in place and bring to high pressure over high heat. Once the pressure is reached, cook for 5 minutes if using white Arborio, or 19 if using brown.

4 When time is up, release the pressure. Unlock the lid. Stir in the remaining broth and the cheese, if using. Season to taste with salt and plenty of pepper and serve at once.

Wondrous Wheat

Wheat, the most widely grown grain in the world, is the one Americans consume most. We eat wheat as bread, as spaghetti, as couscous. It thickens our sauces, gives substance to our cakes and crackers, fills our breakfast bowls (when we eat our Wheaties). It makes our muffins. It's the crust pizzazzing our pizzas, the way of our waffles, the puff of our pitas.

But if you were to put a kernel of wheat in your palm and stand on the busiest street corner in New York or any other great city in the world, and ask each passerby "What is this?" few would be able to identify the small rice-shaped red-brown grain. We love wheat, but we do not know it. We love it pulverized as flour, and the products made from flour, not as kernel. And, as with almost every other grain, we love it partial, not entire.

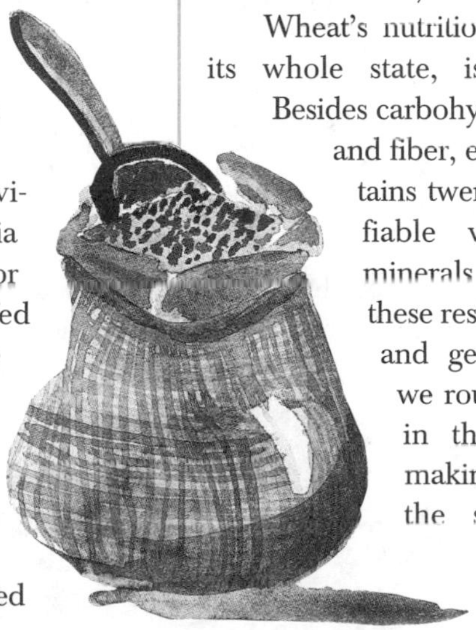

Archaeological evidence in southest Asia indicates that wheat, or its precursors, has fed humankind there since 15,000 B.C. A different strain was cultivated in Egypt as long ago as 4,000 B.C., making that variety, which the ancient Egyptians called kamut, a mere two thousand years younger than barley in its long service to human beings.

Initially, wheat, like most other grains, was eaten, after its inedible outer husk was removed, as a whole or cracked grain that was roasted and then cooked in water. However, once it began to be ground to flour, wheat quickly replaced barley as a grain for making breadstuffs; wheat's unique qualities, in particular the elastic structure of its protein and its high percentage of gluten, make it by far the most easy-to-use bread-grain. (Oddly, wheat is also one of the most common human allergens—or perhaps not so oddly, according to some hypotheses that the more frequently you eat a food, the more prone you are to developing an intolerance to it.)

Wheat's nutritional profile, in its whole state, is impressive: Besides carbohydrate, protein, and fiber, each grain contains twenty-two identifiable vitamins and minerals. Almost all of these reside in the bran and germ, the parts we routinely discard in the process of making white flour, the sad story of "refinement" that takes place time and again as we look at the grains. Refinement followed its predictable course; the whole and nutritionally rich grains of wheat were ground, and then, for the elite who could afford the more expensive product, "bolted," or sieved, to remove the good brown bran and germ. What was left was only the whiter, but nutritionally bereft, starch.

All white flour is "aged" before being bagged and sold; this procedure makes its protein stronger in structure, which in turn makes for baked goods that rise high. In the natural aging process, the white flour, which naturally has a pale yellow color, similar to that of conventional pasta, is warehoused for one to two months. During this warehousing period, it grows paler naturally, moving from yellow to creamy white due to exposure to oxygen.

Obviously, this delay adds expense to the process of flour manufacture. Hence the use, in modern times, of chemicals, notably chlorine dioxide, to speed the aging process, allowing the changes in the protein structure to come about in minutes instead of weeks, and bleaching the flour to pure white. Bleaching destroys what small amounts of vitamin E remain in the flour; moreover, the chemical used is a suspected carcinogen. Although the FDA classifies the amount of chlorine dioxide left in the bleached flour as safe, I very much prefer to avoid bleached flour when I can.

There is another story to be told about wheat's long march into the present. Contemporary wheat is the result of countless hybridizations and crosses over the years—adjustments made both scientifically, by man, and by the plant itself—to adapt it to particular climatic conditions, to increase yield. In the course of these adaptations, wheat has become vastly more complex genetically. Kamut, the wheat the ancient Egyptians ate, has twenty-eight chromosomes; our common contemporary varieties have forty-two. A similar genetic profile marks spelt, or farro, an old European wheat. Now here's the fascinating part: Although kamut and spelt do contain gluten, the component of wheat that is often considered the primary allergen, many people who are allergic to wheat can eat kamut, spelt, and the products made from them. (This is not true for all, alas; check with your doctor or naturopath if you have a serious wheat allergy, but if it's mild, experiment with small quantities on your own.)

Like all grains, wheat's parts are several: bran (the fibrous outer coat of the wheat, the layer remaining after the outer husk has been removed), germ (the storehouse of most of the vitamins), and the endosperm at the center (which contains both the carbohydrate and the gluten, or protein).

Often, with wheat, the bran and germ are stripped away during the process of refining and made into separate products for human consumption (in most other refined grain products, the parts removed are sold as animal feed), each sold at a higher price than that of the whole-grain wheat. We eat wheat's bran in muffins, and packagers cram it into breakfast cereals in various extruded and often sugared forms, the better to fiberize you. Wheat's germ—very popular as a "health food" in the early '70s—is sold in either supermarket or natural foods store varieties. Supermarket wheat germ is toasted to a deep golden brown (and loses some nutritional value but gains in texture). Natural foods market wheat germ (sometimes called raw wheat germ) is tiny flecks of pale gold, and must be refrigerated or it grows rancid astonishingly quickly. Really fresh raw wheat germ has a sweet, pleasing flavor but slightly mushy texture. (Taste and sniff either variety of wheat germ; if there is any trace of bitterness, it is rancid.) And the wheat's starchy endosperm? That's what we use to make white flour.

Gluten is the most complex of wheat's components, but here is a simplified explanation. Gluten is a protein that, when "activated" by the addition of water and the action of kneading, forms long, elastic strands. These strands are the reason wheat is the best choice for the type of bread most people prefer, for they create the delicate structure caused by the bubbles of carbon dioxide given off as the yeast cells multiply. Although gluten is found in some of the other grains as well (rye, barley, and oats all have some), it is far more abundant in wheat, especially in the varieties known as hard or very hard wheat (see opposite).

Gluten is of special interest to vegetarians, for, when rinsed of all wheat starch, formed into a wet mass, and poached in savory liquid, it becomes seitan (pronounced SAY-tan)—among the "meatiest"-textured meat alternatives. Seitan is described in detail, with recipes, on pages 230 to 239.

Intriguing though it is, magical though its properties are, gluten is still a partial food when isolated from the other wheat components. You can guess what I'm going to say next. It's fine to eat white-flour products (bread or conventional pastas, wheat bran, wheat germ, seitan) from time to time, and certainly dozens of our best-loved, most easily accessible meatless products have a base of refined flour—but as always, whenever possible, wise eating dictates that we move toward the whole rather than the partial.

You'll do better eating a bowl of hot cracked wheat, which contains all the elements in a grain of wheat, than a bowl of corporate conglomeration cereal, put together by the folks in the lab at Great Big Giant United Universal Milling Co.

Varieties of Wheat

The main factor that distinguishes between varieties of wheat is the hardness of the kernels. Hardness indicates a wheat's protein content; the higher the protein, the harder the kernel. Kernel hardness also dictates for what purpose the grain (or the flour made from it) is best used.

Very Hard Wheat, sometimes called durum wheat, is a distinct wheat species, *Triticum durum,* and is the hardest wheat grown. It is so high in protein (and correspondingly low in starch) that it makes too rigid a dough for bread making—gluten must have some starch along with it to give the pliability needed for successful dough formation. However, it is perfect for pasta making. Most dried pastas, with their distinctive yellow color, are made from durum wheat, or, more accurately, from the gritty yellow flour known as semolina, which is made from the heart of the durum wheat kernel.

Hard Wheat, usually grown in the winter and hence sometimes called winter wheat, is a member of the species *Triticum aestivum,* and is the most widely grown wheat in America. Why? Because its protein content makes flour made from it perfect for bread making, and we love our breads in America. Hard wheat flour, especially hard whole wheat flour, has a distinct grittiness when you touch it.

Soft Wheats, also *Triticum aestivum,* are higher in carbohydrate (starch) and far lower in protein than either the hard or durum wheat. When ground into cake flour or pastry flour, soft wheats comprise the basis for tender baked goods: pie crusts, cakes, pastries. Rub a bit of soft wheat flour between your fingers, and you will notice that its texture is powdery and soft.

Kamut is an ancient Egyptian grain with a brand-new life in modern America. A hard wheat closely related to durum wheat, kamut's resurrection began rather romantically almost fifty years ago, when the son of a Montana wheat farmer was given some unusually shaped large grains of wheat by a friend who'd gotten them in Egypt. The farmer planted them as a curiosity, exhibiting them as a novelty grain at county fairs and the like as "King Tut's Wheat." In 1977, another Montana father-son team, wheat farmers Bob and Mack Quinn, began working with the grain, cultivating and improving it over a ten-year period. Finally, they began marketing the long-grain wheat under the brand name Kamut.

Whole-grain Kamut has an uneven, bumpy, plump elongated kernel, whose length is even more pronounced after cooking. Its color is more of a buff than a reddish brown. Nearly everyone who tries kamut raves about it; cooked, it has the classic whole-grain nuttiness. It has a little of the pleasing bouncy "pop" that cooked whole-grain wheat and rye have, but is quite tender, and its flavor and aroma are often described as buttery, with a trace of sweetness like that of oats. But its familial relationship to durum wheat comes across—its flour cannot be used successfully in cakes and breads because it is so high in tough glutens. Try it instead in crackers and flat breads.

Spelt (or Farro): I first read about this ancient form of wheat in the early 1980s. I was having an expansive springtime dinner party, Italian, and somewhere, browsing through Italian cookbooks, I came across a recipe for Pastiera Napoletana, an elaborate, unusual Easter tart. It had a sweet Italian-style pastry crust, and a ricotta cheesecake filling that was studded with dried fruits and—here's the kicker—grains of farro. The farro, or wheat, was simmered in milk until tender before being folded into the voluptuous Easter confection. Farro's kernels resemble those of kamut, but are shorter and more rounded. Its flavor and texture are similar, though slightly stickier: delicious, mild, with that pleasing bouncy pop. Spelt or farro and kamut can be used interchangeably.

Unlike kamut, which is a trademarked grain variety, spelts and farros vary. The European imports appear to me to be the equivalent of a soft wheat; lighter in color, quicker to cook to tenderness. American varieties seem more like a hard wheat; reddish brown, taking longer to cook, and firmer even when done.

Wheat Forms

Whole-Grain Wheat is simply whole, unground kernels. The kernels are sometimes called wheat berries, though they do not resemble berries botanically or in any other way. Cooked, they have a remarkably pleasing texture, a sort of bouncy, chewy pop in the mouth. The flavor of whole-grain wheat is nutty, grainy, substantive. It can be cooked conventionally, either with or without an overnight soak (though soaking it considerably speeds up its cooking time) or much more quickly and very successfully in a pressure cooker. Wheat's distinctive texture makes any of these wheat family members quite wonderful in a mixed grain dish, tossed with cooked rice, say, or a mix of rice and barley.

It can also be sprouted, and sprouted wheat is a wonderful thing—astonishingly sweet, pleasantly chewy. Use sprouted wheat on salads or grind it to a coarse paste in a food processor and add it to your favorite whole-grain bread dough.

Cracked Wheat is just what you might expect—whole-grain wheat that has been cracked into large, irregular grits. This results in a quicker cooking time. Cracked wheat is delicious, grainy and full-bodied and shaggy of texture—it makes the best tabbouleh and is very tasty warm, with just a dab of olive oil or a bit of butter, and any of the usual suspects: a squeeze of garlic or a dusting of Parmesan, a scatter of fresh minced parsley, a splash of tamari, or a sprinkle of toasted nuts.

Bulghur wheat is made from wheat kernels that are cooked by steam, then hulled, dried, and cracked to a consistency that ranges from fine to coarse. It tastes a bit less grainy then cracked wheat. Because it has been precooked, the very fine bulghurs need only a brief soak in room-temperature water to tenderize them (this is the wheat form used in instant tabbouleh mixes, such as the excellent one made by Fantastic Foods). Medium- or coarse-grind bulghurs may require, respectively, a soak in boiling water, or even a brief cooking to be fully tender. (If your bulghur does not tenderize quickly, it was probably cracked wheat, an uncooked product, mislabled as bulghur. Not your fault—just add a little more water and cook a little longer.)

Pasta is made from durum wheat flour and water, sometimes with eggs added. Dried vegetable powders used to give pasta color but not much flavor, but these days some of the specialty brands have colored varieties that really do pack a taste wallop—lemon-basil, Cajun, Thai, or (my favorite) really mushroomy wild mushroom pastas. Though pastas come in a zillion different fun-to-eat shapes, they're basically the same—the one big distinction being fresh (more tender) versus dried (chewier, with more tooth).

Couscous is, for all intents and purposes, a pasta—it's made of semolina flour and water, partially cooked, dried, and formed into tiny pebbles. This shape has given rise to the widespread belief that it is a grain. Most vegetarians adore couscous because it can be prepared virtually instantly, and you'll find several recipes exploiting it thus in Quick-Fix (Chapter 13). However, couscous is heavenly when prepared the non–quick-fix way, a relatively easy but time-consuming process involving several steps of soaking, steaming, fluffing, and so on. You'll find that recipe, and the great stew that goes with it, on page 506. A new arrival on the couscous scene are larger couscous grades, like Israeli and Maftoul. These are showing up more and more and are more like pasta in consistency than grain.

Wheat Flour is, of course, finely ground wheat, and there are dozens of types if you really start breaking it down. Within this vast panoply, there are a few you should know. You should know, as well, for what purpose you intend to use the flour. While "all-purpose" yields acceptable products, you'll do much better with specific flours for specific dishes. Here's a sampling of the wheat flours you are most likely to come into contact with, or need (or knead), as well as the uses for which they are best suited.

Bread Flour, made from hard wheat, may be bleached or unbleached, white or whole wheat, organic or not; its protein content, 12.5 to 13.5 percent, gives the sturdy structure by which breads rise.

Cake or Pastry Flour, made from soft wheat, may be white or whole wheat, bleached or unbleached, organic or not. The difference is the protein content, 7.5 to 9.5 percent, which gives the delicate, tender, crumbly texture we seek in pie crusts, biscuits, and the like. Whole wheat pastry flour, by the way, is simply wonderful; you get that tenderness, but with a bit of substance and flavor.

Pasta Flour is flour made from semolina, which comes from the extremely hard durum wheat. Its protein content is about that of bread flour, 12.3 to 13 percent or so, but remember that the particular variety of wheat contributes to texture—in this case, not suitable for bread making.

Depending on its protein content, **white flour** will be labeled as bread, pastry, or all-purpose flour. It is refined, may be bleached or unbleached, organic or not, and may be made from hard or soft wheat. When I use white flour, I usually use an organic unbleached as my standard flour. But organic or not, remember that by virtue of being refined, white flour has just 7 percent of the fiber of whole wheat, and it has lost between 70 and 80 percent of those twenty-two minerals and vitamins. All-purpose flour, refined and usually bleached, is a mixture of hard and soft flours. It is jack-of-all-trades, master of none, but with a protein content of about 10.5, it is serviceable enough to make satisfactory breads or cakes, to thicken sauces, or use for biscuits or crusts. Do not use all-purpose where semolina flour is called for; otherwise, substitution is fine. When most American recipes call for "1 cup flour," they mean 1 cup white all-purpose flour. Do not substitute bread flour in recipes calling for all purpose flour.

Whole Wheat Flour is a whole-grain product. Like all whole grains or whole-grain products, it is more nutritious than its denuded relative, as well as more flavorful; it also spoils more quickly, so don't buy more than you'll use in a month or two unless you can keep it refrigerated or frozen. These flours may be organic or not; they may be stone-ground or not. My choice is organic, stone-ground, very fresh whole wheat flour. You can substitute all-purpose whole wheat for all-purpose white in breads, or go half and half if you're not sure; your products will be heavier. Even better, use whole wheat bread flour, with its higher protein content for better rising. This same strategy works on cakes, though again, all or part whole wheat pastry flour is even better—delicious and, to me, de rigueur for the very best in pie crusts. For crust making, use it to replace up to half the white flour called for in your favorite crust recipe. If you're really good with crusts, try replacing the full amount (it is more crumbly to work with). Whole wheat bread and pastry flour come with the same provisos as to nutritive value, spoilage, and flavor as regular whole wheat flour (see above).

Gluten Flour is made from a combination of higher protein white flour and vital wheat gluten, the pure protein of the wheat (for more about gluten, see page 494); thus it is not a whole-grain food. Gluten flour is used primarily in making seitan (see page 232) but bakers using low-gluten whole grains will add a tablespoon or two to a hearty bread dough to help the dough rise higher.

NOTE

These grains are not standarized; you might end up with a little extra cooking water at the end, which can be drained and reserved for another use, or you might need to add a little more. Keep an eye on things.

Basic Wheat, Kamut, or Spelt, Stove-Top Method

Whole-grain wheat, kamut, and spelt share with whole-grain barley and rye kernels the distinction of being among the slowest-to-cook grains. Cooking them under pressure is the speediest method (see opposite page), but if you don't mind waiting or are cooking a day ahead, this stove-top way works perfectly well. **MAKES ABOUT 3 CUPS; SERVES 4 TO 6 AS A COMPONENT**

Cooking spray
2½ cups water, preferably spring or filtered
¾ teaspoon salt
1 cup whole hulled wheat, kamut, or spelt

1 Spray a heavy-bottomed pot with cooking spray. Add the water and salt and bring to a boil over high heat.

2 Meanwhile, place the wheat, kamut, or spelt in a sieve and rinse well.

3 When the water in the pot is boiling hard, add the rinsed grain and let the water return to a hard boil. Turn down the heat as low as you can (if your burners won't turn down very low without blowing out, you may wish to use a Flame Tamer over the burner, see page 535) and cook for 1 hour and 15 minutes.

4 Test for doneness. If all the liquid is absorbed, and the individual grains are fairly fluffy and have a good tender-chewy texture, they are done. If not, you may need to cook up to 15 minutes longer, adding water accordingly. When done, allow the pot to sit for 10 minutes undisturbed; serve, or use in other dishes.

A Time Saver

Quicker to cook, fuel-saving, and time-saving, this method requires planning ahead. Soak 1 cup wheat, kamut, or spelt in 1 cup water overnight. Next day, cook as above, but use only 1½ cups water. After 30 to 40 minutes, the grains will be tender though still a bit chewy, with some liquid remaining—the perfect hot-cereal breakfast consistency. At 40 to 50 minutes, the grains are done—perfect for mixed-grain pilafs, salads, what-have-you.

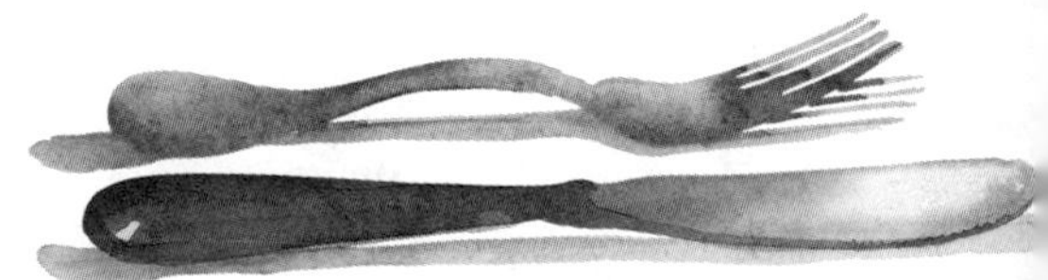

Basic Wheat, Kamut, or Spelt, Pressure-Cooker Method

Follow this method for a grain that has the perfect balance of tenderness and chewiness. In my opinion most cooking authorities advocate too high a proportion of water to wheat, kamut, or spelt. With a Flame Tamer, though, you can use less water and not risk the grain sticking to the bottom of the pot. But again, please note that these grains are not standarized. You might end up with a little extra cooking water at the end, which can be drained and reserved for another use, or you might need to add a little more water, relock the lid, raise then maintain the pressure, and cook for 15 minutes longer than the time given.

These grains have a tendency to foam; the oil keeps the foam down. **MAKES ABOUT 3 CUPS; SERVES 4 TO 6 AS A COMPONENT**

Cooking spray
2⅓ cups water, preferably spring or filtered
¾ teaspoon salt
1 cup whole hulled wheat, kamut, or spelt
1 teaspoon mild vegetable oil, such as corn, canola, or peanut

1 Spray a pressure-cooker pot with cooking spray. Add the water and salt to the cooker and bring to a boil over high heat.

2 Meanwhile, place the wheat, kamut, or spelt in a sieve and rinse well. When the water in the pot is boiling hard, add the rinsed grain and oil. Let it return to a hard boil.

3 Lock the lid down and bring to high pressure, then lift the pot from direct heat, slide a Flame Tamer (see page 535) over the burner, and immediately set the pressure cooker back down on it. Adjust the heat until the pressure is steady halfway between medium and high; cook for 40 minutes.

4 When done, allow the pot to sit for 10 minutes to naturally release the pressure. Unlock the lid and serve, or use in other dishes.

Slow-Cooked Trio of Wild and Brown Basmati Rices and Wheat Berries

Remember to start the wheat berries soaking the night before. This simple combo is very pleasing: hot, as a component, or cold, as the base for any nice grain salad you can dream up. **SERVES 4 TO 6**

½ cup wheat berries
4¼ cups water, preferably spring or filtered
1 teaspoon salt
½ cup brown basmati rice
½ cup wild rice, rinsed well

1 In a small bowl, soak the wheat berries in 1 cup water for at least 8 hours, or overnight. (If you forgot, cover with boiling water and soak for 2 hours.) Drain well.

2 In a medium-large saucepan, bring 3¼ cups of the water to a boil. Add the salt and the soaked wheat berries, turn down the heat to a low simmer, and cook, covered, for 10 minutes. Add the brown basmati and wild rices. Cover and cook for another 40 to 50 minutes, or until all the water has been absorbed and the grains are tender but not mushy. Let stand, covered, for 10 minutes, then fluff and serve.

Fatoush

This is one of those timeless Middle Eastern first courses, sparkling fresh, made in many countries, regions, and villages, each with its own little twist on the basic theme. If you're a tabbouleh fan, you'll recognize with pleasure certain elements of this salad: fresh lemon zinging off olive oil, crunchy diced cucumber vying with soft tomato, the twin green resonance of parsley and fresh mint, a pleasant starchiness balancing all this vegetation. But look! Here's Zhoug, the hot, garlicky, cilantro-filled Yemenite-style pesto described on page 399. And the form of wheat used is toasted, torn-up pieces of whole wheat pita bread, not cracked wheat or bulghur. I've added a local twirl of more color (yellow as well as red tomatoes, and deep purple-brown diced bell peppers—previously roasted, if you like). A bowl of this is perfect summer fare to keep in the fridge to nibble on, or to serve when you're making a dinner otherwise off the grill, or to bring to a potluck. **SERVES 4 TO 6**

VARIATION

Try this with a couple of slices of any rustic, toothsome French or Italian bread instead of the pita, dry-toasted as for Croûtes (page 29).

1½ cups finely chopped red tomatoes
1½ cups finely chopped yellow tomatoes
1 large onion, finely chopped
1 large or 2 small cucumbers, peeled if waxed, seeds scooped out if they are tough, finely chopped
1 "chocolate" bell pepper (the purple-black kind), raw or roasted (see page 782), finely diced
Juice of 2 lemons (about ⅓ cup)
1 to 3 tablespoons extra virgin olive oil, to taste
1 tablespoon Zhoug (page 919)
1 cup mint or spearmint leaves, finely chopped
½ cup Italian parsley leaves, finely chopped
2 whole wheat pitas, preferably with sesame seeds, toasted until dry but not overly brown, broken into small pieces
Salt and freshly ground black pepper to taste
Romaine or other large lettuce leaves (optional)

Combine all the ingredients except the bread and lettuce leaves. Chill well, covered, for at least 2 hours. Up to 30 minutes before serving, add the bread and toss well. Taste again for seasoning after the salad has chilled; you may well need extra salt or lemon or more Zhoug. Serve scooped onto the lettuce leaves, if using.

Southwestern Fatoush

This is a delightful Southwestern-style variation on a Middle Eastern theme. The Zhoug in the previous recipe vanishes; tortillas replace pita. Jícama, which replaces cucumber, gives crunchiness and a touch of sweetness, as does raw corn cut off the cob. As with the above, it's a great summertime in-fridge or potluck dish. **SERVES 4 TO 6**

- 1 teaspoon cumin seeds
- 2 cups finely chopped tomatoes
- 1 large onion, finely chopped
- 1 cup peeled, finely diced jícama
- Kernels from 2 ears sweet corn
- 1 poblano pepper, roasted (see page 782) and finely diced
- Juice of 2 lemons (about ⅓ cup)
- 1 tablespoon mild vegetable oil, such as corn, canola or peanut
- 1 to 2 fresh jalapeño peppers, minced (leave seeds and membranes in for heat, which I always think is desirable; remove if you think otherwise)
- ½ cup finely chopped Italian parsley
- ½ cup finely chopped cilantro
- 2 cloves garlic, pressed
- 2 whole wheat tortillas, lightly toasted on the grill or in the broiler, torn into small pieces
- Salt and freshly ground black pepper to taste
- Tabasco or similar hot sauce (optional)
- Romaine or other large lettuce leaves (optional)

1 Toast the cumin seeds, stirring constantly, in a small, dry skillet over medium heat, until they brown slightly and become fragrant, 3 to 4 minutes. Remove from the heat and immediately pour out of the hot skillet into a bowl to prevent further cooking.

2 Combine all the ingredients except the lettuce leaves with the toasted cumin seeds. Chill well, covered, for at least 2 hours. Taste again for seasoning after the salad has chilled; you may well need extra salt or lemon and you may wish to add a drop or two of Tabasco if the jalapeños aren't coming through as much as you'd like 'em to. Serve, scooped onto the lettuce leaves, if using.

Mediterranean Spelt Salad with Capers, Olives, and Feta

The spelt, by virtue of being cooked with turmeric, takes on a subtle golden cast. This is a great summer salad; take it along on a picnic or serve it with vegetables hot off the grill. This is a generous recipe. **SERVES 6 TO 8**

1 cup spelt or kamut
1 tablespoon turmeric
2½ cups water, preferably spring or filtered
½ cup sliced, pitted kalamata or other Greek olives
1 red or green bell pepper, charred, peeled, and diced
1 tablespoon capers, well drained and rinsed
1 tablespoon extra virgin olive oil, or more to taste
2 tablespoons fresh-squeezed lemon juice, or more to taste
6 ounces feta cheese, cut into ½-inch cubes
¼ cup finely chopped Italian parsley
Salt and freshly ground black pepper to taste
1 pint cherry tomatoes, rinsed, stems removed, halved if very large

1 Combine the spelt or kamut, turmeric, and water and cook by conventional method or in a pressure cooker using the basic method on page 499. Allow the grain to stand for 10 minutes after cooking, then drain off any excess liquid.

2 Turn the grain out into a medium-large bowl. Add the olives, pepper, capers, oil, lemon juice, feta, and parsley, tossing well. Cover and refrigerate for at least 4 hours, or up to 3 days in advance.

3 Just before serving, taste and season with salt and pepper as needed. Toss in the cherry tomatoes and serve.

Kamut-Calypso One-Pot

With the word *calypso* you'd expect Caribbean flavors—but no, this savory all-in-one, very simple pressure-cooked meal takes its name from the beautifully spotted, white-and-cranberry-red calypso bean, not the island music. You could certainly substitute a more readily available bean, such as pintos or kidneys, if you like. Mild and pleasing, the dish's seasonings are very nominally Italian, but it is sparked with all-American corn kernels.

"One-pots" are like stove-top casseroles. Thicker than a soup, or even a stew, they are all-inclusive. With protein (beans), starch (kamut and corn), green vegetables (kale) and orange (sweet potato or squash) included, this is truly a homey supper in itself, although you could add toast or garlic toast if you felt ambitious. Letting it sit a bit will not only thicken the dish, but also deepen the flavors. **SERVES 4 TO 6**

VARIATION

CONVENTIONAL STOVE-TOP METHOD: ***Simmer soaked, drained beans and kamut in 4 cups stock or water, covered, until the beans are tender and the kamut is done but still a little chewy, 1½ to 2 hours. Add the bouillon cube, if using, tomatoes, kale, and sweet potatoes. Stir well, and cook for another 30 to 40 minutes over low heat, stirring occasionally, until the sweet potato is very soft. You may need to add additional stock. Stir in the corn and seasonings.***

1 cup red calypso beans
2 to 5 cups water, preferably spring or filtered
¼ cup kamut
3 cups vegetable stock (see page 139) or additional water plus a vegetable bouillon cube
1 can (10 ounces) crushed tomatoes with roasted garlic (I recommend the Hunt's "Fresh Cuts" brand)
1 bunch kale, sliced crosswise into ½-inch strips (3 to 4 cups)
1 sweet potato, peeled and chopped into ¼-inch pieces (or ½ kabocha squash, peeled, seeded, and chopped (1 to 1½ cups)
1 cup corn kernels, either frozen or cut off the cob
Salt, freshly ground black pepper, and tamari or shoyu soy sauce to taste

1 Quick-soak the beans by placing them in a medium bowl and pouring boiling water over them to cover them amply. Let stand for 1 hour, then drain in a colander, rinsing well.

2 Place the beans in a pressure cooker with the kamut and 3 cups stock, or 3 cups water. Lock the lid down and bring to a boil. Cook at high pressure for 35 minutes. Turn off the heat and allow the pressure to come down naturally.

3 Unlock the lid and add the bouillon cube, if using, the tomatoes, kale, and sweet potatoes. Relock the lid and bring back to high pressure, cooking for 5 minutes more. Release the pressure. Unlock the lid.

4 Stir in the corn (even if frozen, it will instantly thaw and cook perfectly in the hot mixture). Season to taste with salt, pepper, and soy sauce. Serve hot.

Two-Grain Abracadabra Pilaf

In 1994, while exploring an online cooking forum, I came across a detailed description of a white basmati rice dish made by Abra Bennett, who called it "Mystery Rice" and said she invented it but thinks that "it must come from a mystery country that beams out recipes to cooks in need." The combination of flavors sounded wildly intriguing and turned out to be hauntingly good. Here's what it developed into in my kitchen. **SERVES 4 TO 6**

⅔ cup kamut or whole-grain wheat
3 cups water, preferably spring or filtered
1 teaspoon salt
1 cup brown basmati rice
1 tablespoon mild vegetable oil, such as corn, canola, or peanut
3 to 6 cloves garlic, chopped
¼ cup finely minced Italian parsley
¼ cup dry white wine
3 tablespoons unsalted pistachios, preferably freshly shelled from undyed nuts, chopped
3 large pieces crystallized ginger, finely chopped (about 2 tablespoons)
¼ cup finely diced dried apricots, or golden raisins

1 Combine the kamut or wheat and the water in a medium-large saucepan. Add the salt and bring to a boil. Turn down heat to a low simmer and cook, covered, for 25 minutes. Add the brown basmati rice to the simmering kamut or wheat. Cover and cook for another 40 to 50 minutes, or until all water has been absorbed and the grains are tender but not mushy. Let stand, covered, as you prepare the rest of the dish.

2 In a nonstick skillet, or one that has been sprayed with cooking spray, heat the oil over medium heat. Add the garlic and turn down the heat to low, slowly sautéing the garlic for about 4 minutes. Stir in the parsley, add the wine, and bring to a boil. Let it boil furiously for a few minutes, until there is only a tablespoon or two of wine left. Turn the heat down to low.

3 Add the rice-wheat mixture, stirring gently to combine. Cover and steam gently—still over low heat—for about 10 minutes, or until heated through. Lift the lid at the end and raise the heat slightly if you need to evaporate any liquid. Add the pistachios, ginger, and apricots, stir to combine, and serve.

"[My mother's kitchen] was a kind of holy place from which she ministered lavishly to her family via stove and sink and cupboards and flour bins. There were rag rugs on the floor; usually wild white daisies or goldenrod stuck in a milk bottle, or garden flowers (her favorite bunch was of snow-on-the-mountains and small deep red dahlias); and almost always a rolling pin or flour sifter or earthenware mixing bowl was in sight."

—**Edward Harris Heth,** *The Wonderful World of Cooking*

Pasta & Couscous

Essentially a shaped, usually dried dough of wheat flour and water, noodles and pasta and couscous give one of the world's staple grains an infinity of further uses. You'll find pasta recipes throughout this book; there are many in Quick Fix (Chapter 13), and in Wrapped, Stuffed & Stacked (Chapter 7); they also find their way into salads, hors d'oeuvres, soups, and side dishes. So we will focus here on classic couscous. Again, this idiosyncratic foodstuff, so grainlike in appearance and texture, is not a grain, but a tiny pasta.

Quick-cooking pasta is a standby for many vegetarians, and I have several recipes here that use couscous in this manner. But couscous is an entirely different experience when prepared as it is in Morocco and throughout North Africa. It's a hassle, and a big deal; not difficult but time-consuming, a process of many steps. But the results are wholly worth it: fluffy, marvelous, almost as light as air; truly wondrous when served with one or another tagine (or spicy stew), which traditionally accompanies it. If all you've ever tasted is the instant variety, prepare for a revelation.

Seven-Vegetable Seven-Spice Tagine with Couscous

Exotic spice-market flavors make this stew, served over mountains of fluffy steamed couscous, one of those dishes I get an occasional hankering for, ever since enjoying its nonvegetarian kin in Paris at an Algerian restaurant years ago. This version has notes from that remembered one, plus there's a pleasant hot-spiciness borrowed from Tunisia, and good magic from Fez where, food writer Paula Wolfert says, the number seven is lucky. I have tinkered with this to make it vegetarian, but it is influenced by Wolfert's recipe in *Couscous and Other Good Foods from Morocco.*

Steaming the couscous is a bit of a production, but the results are truly sublime.

SERVES 8 TO 10

MOROCCAN BOUQUET GARNI

2 sticks cinnamon
3 allspice berries
1 slice fresh ginger
3 stems fresh cilantro
1 to 2 fresh hot green chiles, split, seeds left in (optional)
3 stems fresh Italian parsley

TAGINE

2 teaspoons olive oil
Cooking spray
1 teaspoon butter
1 large onion, coarsely chopped
1½ teaspoons turmeric
2 teaspoons cumin seeds
2 teaspoons freshly ground black pepper
3 cloves garlic, pressed
1 can (20 ounces) chickpeas, drained (reserve liquid)
1 cup canned crushed tomatoes, with juice
2 quarts vegetable stock, commercial or homemade (see page 139)
¼ teaspoon saffron threads, pounded to a powder with a mortar and pestle
2½ teaspoons salt
1 large sweet potato, peeled and cut into 1-inch cubes
¾ cup (loosely packed) raisins
3 carrots, cut into 2-inch lengths
½ pound green beans, stems removed, cut into 2-inch pieces
1 zucchini, quartered lenthwise and cut into 2-inch pieces
2 green bell peppers, stems, seeds, and fiber removed, cut into large strips
4 cups couscous, preferably steamed (or use instant, if you must)
Harissa Sauce (recipe follows)

1 Before you begin the tagine, start the couscous. Put the couscous in a large, fine-mesh sieve. Turn on the cold water tap and let the water run over it for about 5 minutes, or until the couscous is saturated. Transfer the wet couscous to a large bowl, and let it sit for about 5 minutes. It will swell as it absorbs the water.

2 Rig up a makeshift *couscoussière* (unless you happen to have a real one). You'll need a large, deep pot into which a colander will fit tightly, for in that colander, above boiling water, the couscous is going to steam. Here's how you fake it. Having assured the colander fits into the pot, fill the pot part way with a good deal of boiling water. Get some cheesecloth, or strips of clean towel, dampen it slightly, and make a sort of collar around the outer perimeter of the colander, then wedge the colander into the larger pot, above the boiling water. You want the steam rising from the boiling water below (not touching) the colander, to rise only through the colander's holes, not around the sides, which necessitates a tight fit and nonblockage of the holes. (I promise you will be rewarded ten times over for all this fussiness.)

3 Spray the inside of the colander lightly with cooking spray. With the water in the pot boiling hard, transfer the dampened couscous into the colander, and cover the pot tightly. Let the couscous steam for about 25 minutes. Go ahead and set the timer.

4 As the couscous undergoes this first steaming, begin the tagine.

5 Tie all the ingredients for the Moroccan bouquet garni in a bit of cheesecloth, knotting it with a piece of string. Set aside.

6 Heat the oil and butter in a large, deep, nonstick skillet, Dutch oven, or wok. Add the onion and, over medium-high heat, stir-fry for about 3 minutes, or until slightly translucent. Lower the heat to medium-low. Add the turmeric, cumin, and black pepper and sauté for another 3 minutes, stirring almost continuously. Add the garlic and stir-fry for 1 minute.

7 Place the chickpeas in a small bowl and set aside. Add their liquid to the skillet, along with the tomatoes, stock, saffron, salt, and bouquet garni. Bring to a boil.

8 When your couscous timer goes off, stop what you are doing. Remove the colander from its pot and dump the couscous into a large, oblong baking dish, spreading it out with a kind of fluffing, tossing motion with a large fork. Let cool a few minutes. Then, sprinkle the couscous with the salt and pour an additional 1½ cups of cold, filtered water over it. Toss and fluff again with the fork. Then, spray your hands with the oil, reach in and gently work the couscous with your hands to break up and separate any clots of grain. Let the couscous stand and air dry for a few minutes while you finish the tagine.

9 Ladle out enough of the boiling tagine liquid to fill the bottom of the pot in which you gave the couscous its initial steaming, and set heat to maintain a boil. Transfer the fluffed couscous back into the colander; collar the colander again with cheesecloth; reinsert it into the pot over the boiling tagine liquid, and cover tightly. This second steaming lasts about 20 minutes. The couscous will grow lighter in color and fluffier, and it will take on flavor from the steaming liquid. Again, set the timer.

10 Take the reserved chickpeas, and, one by one, pop them out of their skins (this is optional, but does give a melting smoothness to the beans). Drop the chickpeas into the boiling tagine mixture, then add the sweet potato and raisins. Lower heat and simmer for 5 minutes, then add the carrots, green beans, zucchini, and bell peppers. Let it all simmer together for about 40 minutes, or until all the vegetables are quite tender. Remove the bouquet garni.

11 When the couscous timer goes off, transfer the couscous, piping hot, into a large, wide, fairly deep serving bowl. Fluff it one more time with a fork, and drizzle a little of the tagine broth over it. Cover to keep it warm, and to let it absorb just a bit more liquid. Let stand 10 minutes, or until the tagine is done. Serve the tagine very hot, with the couscous and harissa sauce.

Harissa Sauce

1 cup strained liquid from the stew above
1 teaspoon Classic Harissa (page 921)
Juice of 1 lemon
½ teaspoon ground cumin
½ teaspoon ground coriander seeds
1 to 2 teaspoons olive oil
Minced cilantro and Italian parsley to taste

Combine all the ingredients in a saucepan, and heat well. Pour into a serving bowl and pass with the couscous and tagine.

Sweet Potato and Noodled Couscous Stir-Fry

Here we have an utterly captivating take on that old vegetarian standby, stir-fried vegetables teamed with a grain. Mixing several grains together adds interest as well as internationalism; here's couscous from the Middle East squiggled with brown rice ramen noodles from Japan, and cubes of golden sweet potato from Africa. Then, with the use of five vegetables in the stir-fry (including delectable shiitakes and the somewhat unusual-in-this-context purple cabbage), as well as a slightly heat-spiked, robustly Asian-style soy-ginger-garlic sauce, the dish grows exponentially more pleasing. Top it all off with a garnish of scallion, cilantro, and toasted sesame (Asian again) and roasted red pepper (Mediterranean). A fusion dish for sure, but not a con-fusion one; everything comes together happily. You could take it still further: Add diced firm tofu and an onion slivered into thin crescents to the stir-fry, for example, or substitute asparagus for the broccoli. **SERVES 4 TO 6**

1 large head broccoli, stem peeled and julienned, florets separated into smallish trees
¼ pound fresh green beans, stems removed, cut into 3-inch lengths
2½ cups water, preferably spring or filtered
1 package (3.1 ounces) brown rice ramen noodles, broken into four pieces, seasoning packet discarded
1 tablespoon toasted sesame oil

STIR-FRY SAUCE
¼ cup tamari or shoyu soy sauce
3 tablespoons rice vinegar
1 tablespoon umeboshi plum vinegar (see page 118)
2 thumb-sized pieces ginger, peeled and finely minced (to yield 1½ tablespoons)
5 to 6 cloves garlic, peeled and finely minced (to yield 1½ tablespoons)
1 teaspoon brown sugar
3 to 6 drops Tabasco or similar hot sauce

QUICK-COOKED SWEET POTATO COUSCOUS
2¼ cups vegetable stock (see page 139)
Salt to taste
1 small or ½ large sweet potato, peeled and diced into ½-inch cubes
1 cup couscous

VEGETABLE STIR-FRY

- Cooking spray
- 2 teaspoons mild vegetable oil, such as corn, canola, or peanut
- 8 to 10 medium shiitake mushrooms, stems removed and saved for another use, sliced
- ½ pound snow peas, trimmed
- ⅛ head cored red cabbage, thinly sliced

GARNISH

- ½ cup cilantro leaves, coarsely chopped
- 3 scallions, sliced
- 1 red bell pepper, charred, seeded, peeled, and diced
- 1 to 2 teaspoons toasted sesame seeds (optional)

1 Bring a medium pot of water to a boil and drop in the broccoli and green beans. Blanch for 2 minutes, then drain, rinse under cold water, and set aside. In the same pot, bring the 2½ cups water to a boil and drop in the noodles. Cook for about 2 minutes, or until barely tender, then drain well and rinse thoroughly with cold water. Toss the noodles with 1 teaspoon of the sesame oil, and set them aside with the broccoli and beans on a mise en place tray (see page 107).

2 Prepare the stir-fry sauce by combining the remainder of the sesame oil with all of the sauce ingredients (soy sauce, vinegars, minced ginger and garlic, brown sugar, and Tabasco). Set this aside too.

3 Prepare the sweet potato couscous: Bring the stock to a boil in a medium saucepan, adding salt to taste. Drop in the sweet potato, cover tightly, and cook for about 10 minutes, or until the sweet potato is tender but not mushy. Stir in the couscous, cover the pot, and return to a boil. Immediately turn off the heat. Let the couscous stand, covered, while you finish the recipe (which, if you have your "mise" set up like I told you, will be about 10 minutes).

4 Make the stir-fry: In a nonstick skillet or wok, or one that has been sprayed with cooking-spray, heat the vegetable oil over high heat. Add the blanched broccoli florets and stems, the green beans, shiitakes, snow peas, and red cabbage and sauté, stirring pretty constantly, for about 2 minutes, or until the vegetables are a little seared but still crisp. Drizzle in about half the stir-fry sauce and continue cooking over high heat, tossing continually, for 3 more minutes, or until all is crisp-tender. Remove from the heat and stir in the remaining sauce.

5 Lift the lid from the sweet potato–couscous mixture and fluff with a fork. Stir in the noodles and fluff again.

6 Mound the couscous mixture either in the center of one large platter, or on individual serving plates. Ring the stir-fry around the couscous, spooning any extra sauce over the couscous. Sprinkle with the cilantro, scallions, red bell pepper, and toasted sesame seeds. Serve at once.

Wheaten Breads

If it seems a long stride from an Asian pasta recipe to a loaf of bread, well, there you have wheat's wonder and versatility. Most Americans enjoy wheat (whole grain or not) in the form of bread. And if it is our staff of life, on which we lean, the wood of which that staff is made is wheat.

Bread, especially yeast-risen, is magical and mysterious, and homemade breads—even quick breads—seem to express to those who eat them a particular feeling of being cared for. There is a split second of bread-baking fragrance, a steam that is inhaled and exhaled almost involuntarily, that exudes fundamental well-being to those who breathe it in. Without a word, this fragrance says, "Be at peace, happy, and nourished. All is well."

Our sweet old troubled world continues its daily revolution. Still the sun rises and sets, still the bread rises and is punched down, the yeasts come to life, multiply, and die. In the small, predictable, miraculous drama of their little lives is both nourishment and succor. I think we brush against this larger truth—we may not think we do, or realize that we do—but still, just for a moment, we know: Although lives (and all else) may change or end, life itself continues, effulgent, pure, and unbowed. This is our daily bread.

Quick Breads

Breads leavened with baking soda or powder are called "quick." And quick they are, in comparison to those made with slow-to-rise yeast. Many of our best-loved American breads—cornbreads, biscuits, muffins, even pancakes—fall into this category. So do sweet breads, often almost cakelike confections, served at breakfast, sometimes in lieu of dessert, and, in gentler times, at tea.

You will find many quick breads scattered throughout this book, but here are a few that seemed to me especially "wheaty." You'll find the biscuits that follow have far less fat than usual, but are still amazingly good hot from the oven. Another amazement lies in the Irish Soda Bread (page 516); so very good, so speedily made—I am always surprised by the fact that it is just not in the repertoire of many American home bakers. Now, banana bread is—most of us who bake have a much-loved recipe for it. But I do believe you will find the Spice Islands Banana-Date-Walnut Bread here (page 517) exceptional.

All of these fill the home with that inimitable sweet baking scent—if not quite as seductive as yeast-raised breads, it will nonetheless gladden, and quicken, the heart.

Classic Biscuits, Reduced-Fat but Still Really Good

Remember the limbo, "How low can you go?" Well, as it turns out in the case of the fat in these biscuits, pretty durn low—it's decreased as much as

75 percent from the traditional recipe. Yes, but are they good? They're great! These are light, flavorful, still pleasantly flaky, and thoroughly enjoyable. I think they're more enjoyable, actually, because you can have more of them, guilt-free, than you can the classic.

As always, a light hand is everything when it comes to biscuit making. Here, the dough is a bit stickier; if you've made conventional biscuits, you'll be dubious. But trust me, bake them anyway, and you too will be ecstatic and amazed. And yes, you do have to use either butter or vegetable shortening to get a flaky biscuit; oil alone just doesn't cut it. **MAKES ABOUT 12 GOOD-SIZED BISCUITS**

2 cups unbleached white all-purpose flour (plus a bit to flour the rolling surface)
2½ teaspoons baking powder
½ teaspoon baking soda
1 teaspoon salt
1 tablespoon chilled butter, or better yet, chilled Browned Butter (page 1024)
1 tablespoon mild vegetable oil, such as corn, canola, or peanut
¾ to 1 cup buttermilk
Cooking spray

1. Preheat the oven to 425°F, and make sure it's up to temperature.

2. Sift the flour, baking powder, baking soda, and salt into a medium bowl. Cut the butter or Browned Butter into chunks and scatter over the flour mixture. Drizzle in the oil and quickly cut the fats into the flour with two knives or a pastry cutter.

3. Add ¾ cup of the buttermilk and stir just until the mixture forms a ball (if too crumbly, add just a bit more buttermilk), and turn the dough out onto a floured surface. Knead 4 or 5 times—just enough to firm up the dough. Do not over-knead! The secret of a biscuit, even a reduced-fat one, is to handle it gently . . . tenderly . . . lovingly.

4. With floured hands, pat the dough into a rectangle about ½ inch thick. The top will be sticky. Then, either use a sharp knife to cut straight down through the dough to form squares, or punch straight down through the dough with a biscuit-cutter, without twisting. I usually use a knife—less handling, no wastage, no temptation to reroll and reroll the scraps, on into tough-biscuit eternity. Place the biscuits on a nonstick baking sheet or one that has been sprayed with cooking-spray. Bake immediately for 10 to 12 minutes, until light golden.

A Basket of Biscuits

Vegan Biscuits: *Substitute vegetable margarine or vegetable shortening for the butter. Omit the buttermilk; instead, place 1 tablespoon vinegar or lemon juice in the bottom of your liquid measuring cup, and add enough plain soy, rice, or almond milk to equal ¾ cup. This formula will work in all the variations that follow, except the cheese biscuits, which are inherently nonvegan.*

Whole Wheat Biscuits: *Substitute an equal part whole wheat pastry flour for the unbleached white flour, and you'll have an enchanting biscuit, light and delicate, but with pleasing whole-graininess.*

Cornmeal Biscuits: *Substitute ¼ cup stone-ground yellow cornmeal for an equal part of the unbleached flour or whole wheat pastry flour, and proceed. These are a great biscuit; the grainy crunch of the cornmeal adds a whole new level of pleasure to them. Add a little sugar to these and you've got a great cobbler topping.*

Oatmeal Biscuits: *Pulse, then buzz, 1 cup oatmeal in a food processor until it's reduced to a powdery flour (there will still be some largeish particles). Substitute ¼ cup of this oat flour for ¼ cup of the unbleached white flour: Sift in what you can, then add the particles unsifted.*

Multigrain Biscuits: *Instead of 2 cups unbleached, use ¾ cup unbleached, ½ cup whole wheat pastry flour, and ¼ cup each stone-ground cornmeal and oat flour, made as described for Oatmeal Biscuits.*

Drop Biscuits *can be made from the basic recipe, or any of the variations, and they are ridiculously simple. Just add ¼ cup extra buttermilk and simply stir (no rolling, patting, kneading) and drop the dough by rounded tablespoonful onto a nonstick baking sheet or one that has been sprayed with cooking spray. This means biscuits with one bowl, no cutting board, no rolling pin. What are you waiting for?*

Cinnamon Raisin Drop Biscuits: *To the basic drop biscuit dough, add 2 tablespoons sugar, ½ teaspoon ground cinnamon, and substitute part cream for the buttermilk if you prefer a rich dough. When dough has not quite come together, add ⅓ cup raisins. Bake as directed. Let the drop biscuits cool a few minutes, then drizzle with an icing made of sifted confectioner's sugar thinned to a dribbly texture with a drop of vanilla and a little milk.*

Cheese Biscuits: *Add ¼ teaspoon cayenne to the flour mixture. Cut in ½ cup finely grated Cheddar cheese along with the butter and oil. These are excellent with anything tomato-y, such as stew or soup.*

Pesto-Parmesan Biscuits: *Always much loved in the restaurant (R.I.P.). Cut ½ cup freshly grated Parmesan cheese into the flour along with the butter and oil. Stir 1 to 2 tablespoons pesto in with the buttermilk.*

Herb Biscuits: *Combine 2 tablespoons finely chopped Italian parsley with 2 teaspoons to 2 tablespoons other fresh minced herbs: chives, garlic chives, sage, rosemary, basil, thyme, oregano, a single herb or in combination. Dill is also good, but is best as a solo player. (And dill biscuits are delicious with split pea soup.) The stronger the herb, the less you'll need; rosemary and sage, for instance, tend to dominate the delicate ones, so use just a bit if including them in a blend.*

Rich Shortcake Biscuits: *These can be split and filled with sweetened fruit and a drizzle of Ricotta Crème (page 1061) or Tofu-Cashew Crème (page 1062), or used as topping for various fruit cobblers. Start with either the basic recipe, the whole wheat, or the cornmeal biscuit. Add 2 tablespoons sugar to the dry mix, and instead of the buttermilk use 1 cup minus 1 tablespoon Yogurt Sour Cream (page 910) or commercially made sour half-and-half. Depending on the recipe, you may also wish to add a teaspoon of pure vanilla extract, or a little ground cinnamon or grated nutmeg.*

NOTE

Ned and I first enjoyed Angel Biscuits at an inn called the Randolph House in Bryson City, North Carolina, where they were made tiny—not much bigger than a quarter. Ruth, the innkeeper/cook, gave us the recipe. Hers used self-rising flour; we've substituted unbleached.

Angel Biscuits

An often-requested, very special, very Southern biscuit—light, flavorful, high-rising, meltingly flaky. It is one of the few baked goods I use white shortening in, but nothing works better. A high percentage of shortening, plus buttermilk, plus a triple leavening of yeast *and* baking powder *and* baking soda, is what give these their sublime qualities. While most biscuits are made without yeast, these Angels depend upon it. The yeast rise is what gives them their extra-lightness. The triple sifting is essential, too. If you are in a rush, stick to Classic Biscuits (page 511).

These biscuits are sublime topped with cheese and Sweet Honey-Tarragon Mustard Butter (page 36) and served at, say, a wedding brunch. **MAKES 24 LARGE OR 54 SMALL BISCUITS**

1½ teaspoons dry yeast
¼ cup warm water, preferably spring or filtered
1 tablespoon honey
2½ cups sifted unbleached white flour
2 tablespoons sugar
1½ teaspoons baking powder
½ teaspoon baking soda
¼ teaspoon salt
⅓ cup vegetable shortening
1 cup buttermilk
Cooking spray

1 Dissolve the yeast in the warm water. Add the honey and let the mixture sit until frothy.

2 In a large bowl, sift together three times the flour, sugar, baking powder, baking soda, and salt. Using two knives, quickly cut the shortening into the mixture until it resembles coarse cornmeal. Quickly stir in the yeast mixture and the buttermilk. Stir just until the batter comes together—don't overmix. Turn the dough out of the bowl onto a lightly floured surface.

3 Knead the dough lightly, gently, quickly—30 seconds at most—and then place it in a cooking-sprayed bowl. Cover the bowl with plastic wrap and refrigerate for at least 1 hour or as long as 3 or 4 days.

4 When ready to bake, preheat the oven to 400°F. Remove the dough from the refrigerator and roll it out on a very lightly floured board to a ½-inch thickness. With a knife or a round cutter, cut out biscuits and place them on a nonstick baking sheet, or one that has been sprayed with cooking spray, about ½ inch apart. Bake the little angels until golden—about 12 minutes. Serve hot, with plenty of butter and jam.

Whole Wheat Butterhorns

I've been making these rich, eggy, buttery crescent rolls for special occasions for many years, and they were also often a part of the inn's overflowing bread basket. Leftovers are fabulous in Chocolate Bread Pudding Maurice (page 1059).

MAKES ABOUT 2 DOZEN ROLLS

1 tablespoon dry yeast
1¼ cups milk, scalded then cooled to lukewarm
½ cup honey
¼ cup melted butter, plus extra butter, unmelted
1½ teaspoons salt
3 large eggs, at room temperature
2 tablespoons nutritional yeast
5 to 6 cups whole wheat flour
1 large egg yolk
1 tablespoon milk or water
Cooking spray

1 Put the yeast in a large mixing bowl and add the milk, honey, melted butter, and salt.

2 When the mixture becomes good and frothy, beat in the eggs and nutritional yeast. Add the flour a little bit at a time, stirring to combine, until the dough starts to form a ball.

3 Turn the dough out onto a lightly floured surface and knead it until it is smooth and elastic. Place the dough in a cooking-sprayed bowl and cover loosely with plastic wrap. Let the dough rise for 1 hour to 1 hour and 20 minutes. When the dough has doubled in size, punch it down, re-cover it, and let it rise again. When it has doubled in size—45 to 55 minutes—punch it down a second time.

4 Divide the dough into two balls and roll each into a circle ¼ inch thick. Dot the surfaces of the circles with the remaining butter. Cut each circle into 12 pie-shaped wedges and roll each edge up, starting from the wide end. If you tilt the edges in a bit, you will end up with crescent-shaped butterhorns.

5 Preheat the oven to 400°F. Place the butterhorns on nonstick baking sheets, or ones that have been sprayed with cooking spray, and let them rise a third time, 12 to 15 minutes, or until doubled in volume.

6 When the butterhorns have doubled in size, bake them for 40 minutes.

7 In a small bowl, make a glaze by combining the egg yolk and milk or water and mixing well.

8 After 40 minutes, remove the butterhorns from the oven and brush them with the glaze. Return them to the oven for another 5 to 10 minutes, or until golden and crusty. Serve hot.

Irish Soda Bread

In the inn days, it wouldn't, couldn't, be a Dairy Hollow breakfast on St. Patrick's day without this easily made, classic, savory-with-a-touch-of-sweet bread in the breakfast basket. It made its appearance periodically in the evening's breadbasket too. I've always wondered why it isn't more widely known among American home bakers. Even if you find the idea of caraway seeds weird in a somewhat sweet bread, try them; they're fabulous here.

This is pretty much classic soda bread, with a few tricks—a touch of cinnamon, part whole wheat flour—up its sleeve. **MAKES 1 MEDIUM-LARGE ROUND LOAF**

1 cup unbleached white all-purpose flour
1 cup whole wheat flour (plus a bit for flouring the board)
2 teaspoons baking soda
2 teaspoons baking powder
½ teaspoon salt
¼ cup sugar, plus a little extra
Large pinch of ground cinnamon
4 tablespoons butter, slightly softened
1 cup plus 2 to 4 tablespoons buttermilk
½ cup currants or raisins
1 tablespoon caraway seeds

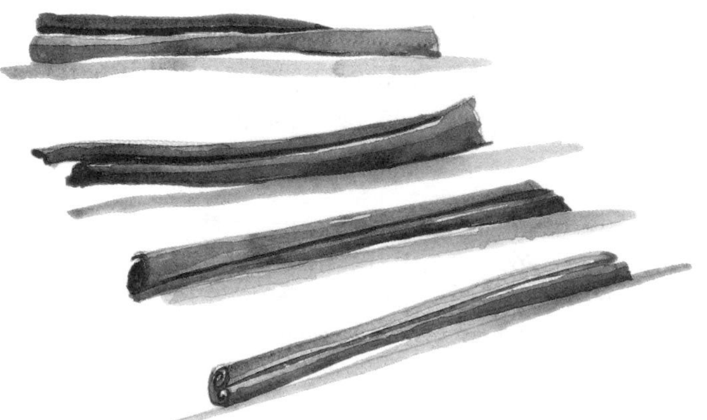

1 Preheat the oven to 375°F.

2 In a large bowl, combine the white and whole wheat flours, baking soda, baking powder, salt, ¼ cup sugar, and the cinnamon. Cut in the butter, using two knives or a pastry cutter, until it's in bits about the size of a lentil. Stir in 1 cup plus 2 tablespoons buttermilk, the currants or raisins, and the caraway, mixing until the dough moistens and just comes together, adding the extra 2 tablespoons of buttermilk if you need to.

3 Swiftly shape the dough into a ball, turn it out onto a lightly floured surface, and knead lightly for 1 minute or less. Place the dough on an ungreased baking sheet and pat it out to form a round, flattened loaf. Using a sharp, floured knife, cut a large X in the top, about 1½ inches in depth. Sprinkle with a bit of sugar, and bake for 35 to 40 minutes. Let cool for 5 to 10 minutes, then serve.

Spice Islands Banana-Date-Walnut Bread

As a child I did not like bananas, in that emphatic and unchanging manner in which children can dislike a food and drive their elders crazy. My father would go slightly bonkers on hearing me order, with the hauteur a seven- or eight-year-old can muster, "A banana split without bananas, please."

But my then–best friend Karen's mother's banana bread changed my mind. And while bananas will probably never make my most favored fruit list, ever since I tasted that bread, bananas and I have been on cordial terms.

The recipe that follows incorporates the flavors I remember from Mrs. Staats's bread. These spices, with dates, bananas, and walnuts, just hum with each other beautifully. It is also low fat and egg-free, although you'd never know it from its richness. **MAKES 1 LARGE LOAF OR 3 SMALL LOAVES**

Cooking spray
2 cups unbleached white all-purpose flour or whole wheat pastry flour (plus a bit extra for the pans)
Grated rind and juice of 1 lemon
3 extremely ripe, black-speckled bananas
¼ cup mild vegetable oil, such as corn, canola, or peanut
½ cup brown sugar or Rapidura
3 tablespoons buttermilk or plain unflavored yogurt (or, for vegans, plain soy yogurt)
½ teaspoon salt
½ teaspoon baking powder
½ teaspoon baking soda
6 to 8 vigorous gratings fresh nutmeg
½ teaspoon ground cinnamon, preferably Saigon
½ to 1 cup pitted, chopped dates
3 tablespoons toasted, chopped walnuts

1 Preheat the oven to 375°F. Select a pan or pans: either 1 large, 6-by-3-inch loaf pan or 3 small, 5-by-2-inch loaf pans. If they aren't nonstick, spray the pans thoroughly with cooking spray, then dust with a little flour, knocking out any excess.

2 Place the lemon rind in a food processor along with the bananas. Pour the lemon juice over the bananas. Add the oil, brown sugar, and buttermilk and buzz to a smooth puree. Set aside.

3 In a medium-large bowl, combine the flour, salt, baking powder, baking soda (if these ingredients are at all lumpy, sift them in), nutmeg, and cinnamon. Set aside.

4 Combine the dates and nuts in a small bowl. Remove 1 tablespoon of the flour mixture and sprinkle it over the dates. Toss well to coat.

5 Pour the banana mixture into the flour mixture and stir to thoroughly combine, but don't overbeat. Stir in the dates and nuts, and turn the stiff batter out into the prepared pans. Cook for 40 to 50 minutes for the large pan, 30 to 40 for the mediums, and 25 to 35 for the smalls. Let cool in the pans for 10 minutes, then turn out onto a wire rack to cool.

Steamed Brown Boston Mountains Bread

No eggs—no oil, butter, or vegetable shortening either. What, then, makes this traditional New England bread so moist and tender, so very rich? If you gaze at the ingredients, there doesn't seem to be much to it. Could it be the raisins or dates that hold the secret, or perhaps the dark molasses? Wrong. While these add homespun allure, the main trick lies in the method: steaming. The moist steam-heat simply gives an incredible texture, intense and solid without being heavy. As you may already know, steamed brown bread is traditionally served with baked beans (see the recipe on page 600)—a combination that makes culinary and nutritional good sense. The batter is truly 1-2-3-easy to put together; only the steaming seems daunting.

Traditional Boston brown bread uses a cup each of rye and whole wheat flour, and cornmeal plus ¾ cup dark molasses. Here, though, close to the Boston Mountains (the most panoramic range of the Arkansas Ozarks, west of us here), I don't always have rye flour on hand (I purchase it only if I'm going to make rye bread), so I usually just use cornmeal and whole wheat, and believe me, it's plenty good. I also like to mellow the twang of the molasses with a little honey. **MAKES 15 SLICES**

Beautiful Steamer: Steamed Bread

How do you steam a bread? The batter is placed into greased pudding molds (Oh! You say you don't happen to have a pudding mold? Then how about an aluminum can or two?). These cans are then set atop a heatproof trivet (No trivet either? Then how about some canning jar rings, or some lightly wadded foil?) inside a pot. The pot must be large enough so that even with the trivet and cans/molds in place, the pot's lid or cover will still fit tightly. The trivet or other heatproof equivalent serves only to elevate the cans/molds, preventing direct contact with the bottom of the pot.

The filled cans/molds are half submerged in simmering water, the pot covered to trap the steam, and the whole is cooked atop the stove . . . for great results that can only be achieved this way.

Strange and troublesome though this method sounds to those of us who bake at the flip of an oven dial, it's not difficult. It was used in colonial times throughout America; it still "bakes" the breads and sweets of many parts of the world where an oven is not a routine part of most kitchens. The moistness that you get in breads or puddings cooked thus is unparalleled; reason enough to have the method in your repertoire.

The batter for this recipe fills one 2-pound coffee can, three 20-ounce cans, four 15-ounce cans, or five 12-ounce cans.

Cooking spray
1 cup stone-ground cornmeal (plus a bit extra for dusting the cans/molds)
2 cups whole wheat flour
1½ teaspoons baking powder
½ teaspoon baking soda
1 teaspoon salt
1 cup raisins, or diced pitted dates
2 cups buttermilk, yogurt, soy yogurt, or soy milk with 2 teaspoons vinegar added
½ cup blackstrap molasses, warmed to flow more easily (before measuring, place the jar or bottle in a pot of hot water or run hot tap water over it)
¼ cup honey, warmed (see above)

1 Have ready the cans or molds of your choice (see "Beautiful Steamer," above), well washed, dried, sprayed with cooking spray, and dusted with cornmeal. Also have ready some foil, the deep stockpot in which you'll be steaming, your trivet or equivalent (again, see "Beautiful Steamer") and one rubber band per steamer can. Put a large teakettle or pot full of water on to boil.

2 In a medium bowl, combine the whole wheat flour, cornmeal, baking powder, baking soda, and salt, stirring well. Add the raisins or dates. In a separate bowl, whisk together the buttermilk, molasses, and honey. Pour the dry mixture into the wet, stirring just enough to moisten well, and scrape the batter into the prepared cans, filling the cans about two-thirds full.

3 Cover the filled cans, using either a doubled-over square of foil sprayed with cooking spray, or brown grocery-bag paper. Puff the foil or paper a bit at the top to allow the bread room to rise above the can, and secure it around the edges of the can with a rubber band. Place the cans on a trivet, some wadded-up foil, or

VARIATION

Untraditional but awfully tasty: Add ½ cup toasted walnuts or black walnuts to the bread. The latter make it very Boston Mountains; our hillsides are covered with these native nut trees.

jar-rings in a deep stockpot, to raise them from the bottom of the pot. Check to make sure your pot is large enough so that the pot-cover will still fit tightly with the cans in place.

4 Pour the boiling water around the cans to a level about halfway up the cans. Turn the heat down to a low simmer, and cover the pot. Let the bread steam for 2 hours (for smaller can molds) to 3 hours (for coffee can–size molds), checking occasionally to add more water as needed. When done, the bread will have risen some, though not a lot, and will be firm to the touch through its foil or paper cover. Remove the cans from the pot and let the breads cool in the cans for about 1 hour before reversing out (the breads reverse out quite easily). Serve in thick slices, preferably with Old-Fashioned All-Day Baked Beans, Boston (Mountain)–Style (page 600). It is quite wonderful with butter, cream cheese or neufchâtel cheese, or Yogurt Cream Cheese (page 910).

Yeasted Breads

Let me be clear: My preference, almost always, is for a somewhat dense, grainy, substantial loaf of bread—one that truly could be the staff of life. This is not just a matter of health to me, but of taste, and I remain pretty steadfast. I just don't like most white breads much, even homemade.

I also prefer to hand-mix and hand-knead dough—a satisfying activity that makes me feel connected to life's rhythms and mystery, and that, to my mind, produces better bread. However, on this component of bread making I've become more flexible, though not without reluctance. Perhaps it's the e-mails from readers of my previous cookbooks telling me with great excitement about converting my conventionally prepared bread recipes to food-processor preparation. Perhaps it was the rotator cuff injury that took me out of good kneading form for a couple of months. Perhaps, most of all, it was the morning I walked into a television studio to do a cooking spot on an A.M. news show in Dallas and smelled, in the midst of that dark, cavernous chill, baking bread. It turned out that the camera crew, who arrived regularly at 4:00 A.M., had bought a bread-baking machine. Each of the crew—all fairly hurly-burly guys—took turns scouting recipes, procuring ingredients, and coming in to dump those ingredients into the machine's pan, so that they all had the baking scent to keep them going, as well as the knowledge that in a few hours' time, after the show was completed, there would be fresh bread.

Something about this struck me as moving. As a husky, dark-haired guy described the cinnamon-raisin bread he'd done a few days earlier, and eagerly asked me if the cookbook I was working on would have any bread machine recipes, my inner disputation of such appliances (as gimmicky short-changers no *real* cook would use) just washed away, to be replaced, instead, by respect. Our hungers, I thought, are universal.

So, reflecting these changes, here are some mostly whole-grain, wheat-based breads. You'll find one made by conventional kneading, one for the food processor, and one for the bread machine. A caveat about the last: Some of my food-snob disdain did creep back in. The machines are wonderful for mixing and kneading, they make clean-up a breeze, and they control the temperature for rising perfectly. But, but, but, I find that letting the machines bake the dough they've so handily prepared yields an inferior loaf, high-rising but too moist, and lacking in truly crusty crust. So, I use the machines (when I do) for everything but the actual baking; I remove the almost-finished dough from the machine's pan on its next-to-last rising, tuck it into a nonstick or oiled conventional pan, and bake it in a regular old oven.

Old-Fashioned Whole Wheat Bread with a Touch of Sorghum, Conventional Method

This basic, 100 percent whole wheat bread is straightforward and good. I like the special rounded character that sorghum syrup, that deeply Southern sweetener, gives here, but if you don't have it on hand, use molasses or honey. The bread has a fine texture and a firm crumb, and if you can wait until it has cooled, it slices nicely. **MAKES 2 LARGE LOAVES**

2 envelopes (2 scant tablespoons total) dry yeast
¼ cup lukewarm water, preferably spring or filtered
2 cups milk or soy milk, scalded and cooled to lukewarm
1 tablespoon oil
¼ cup sorghum syrup or molasses or honey
2½ teaspoons salt
4 cups whole wheat flour
Cooking spray

1 Place the yeast in a small bowl and pour the lukewarm water over it. Set aside for 10 minutes while it proofs (gets bubbly and shows you its stuff).

2 In a large bowl, combine the milk, oil, sorghum syrup, and salt. Pour in the proofed yeast.

3 Stir in the flour 1 cup at a time. When it's almost all added, turn the dough out onto a floured board. Let it sit for a

NOTE

FINDING BREADS GALORE

Locating the recipes for bread in this book requires a little adventuring. Why? There is not a bread chapter here per se. Rather, with seemingly-illogical-but-feels-right-to-me dragon-think, I chose to place individual breads where each seemed to fit best. Breads, after all, although the staff of life, have individual characters, and can play any number of roles in a meal, or a day's meals. Sometimes I placed a bread according to where and how it fit in a menu; for instance, crackerlike breads are with hors d'oeuvres (Chapter 2). More often I placed breads according to their main ingredients (thus, many breads are here in this chapter, since grain is what they are made of; cornbreads are in the section on corn, rye breads in the section on rye, and so on). This is admittedly a little idiosyncratic. To find other breads in this book, look at the index.

moment while you wash out the bread bowl, dry it thoroughly, and spritz it with cooking spray. Then return to the dough. Oil or spray your hands and knead the dough for about 5 minutes, adding a little more flour if required to make a dough that goes from sticky to elastic.

4 Place the dough in the prepared bowl, cover it loosely with a clean towel, and let it rise in a warm place for about 2 hours, or until doubled in bulk.

5 Turn the risen dough out onto the floured board and punch it down. Return it to the bowl, cover again, and let rise for a second time until almost doubled. This time the rise should be 1 hour to 1 hour and 15 minutes. Spray two 8-by-4-inch loaf pans with cooking spray.

6 Turn the dough back out onto the lightly floured board and divide it in two using a sharp knife. Give each half a couple of kneads, and shape into a loaf. Place the loaves in the prepared pans, cover loosely with clean towels, and let rise a third time until doubled in bulk. This rise should be 30 to 45 minutes.

7 About 20 minutes into the last rise, preheat the oven to 425°F.

8 When the loaves have completed their third rise, pop them in the oven and bake for 15 minutes. Lower the heat to 375°F, and bake for 45 to 55 minutes more, or until the loaves are a deep golden brown. Let cool in the pans for 10 minutes, then on a wire rack for 15 minutes, before slicing.

Sourdough Multigrain Loaf, Food-Processor Method

This pleasing multigrain loaf requires forethought . . . 2 to 3 days' worth. The do-ahead sourdough starter is the same one used in Old World–Style Sourdough Rye (page 575)—I like rye flour in a starter; it has muscle and oomph.

You'll have some starter left over from this recipe. It keeps in the refrigerator indefinitely if you feed it twice a week or so. You do that by removing it from the fridge, stirring in 1 cup unbleached all-purpose flour and ½ cup spring or filtered water, letting it stand at room temperature for a couple of hours, then re-refrigerating it. Use it for the rye bread mentioned above, or this bread; add a bit to any dough you wish to give a touch of sourdough soul to.

This bread earns its multigrain status by using unbleached and whole wheat flours along with rye, millet, and barley. The recipe moves really fast once the dough is in the food processor, so read it thoroughly before you start, and have all the ingredients at hand. **MAKES 1 LOAF**

THE FIRST STARTER

1 teaspoon dry yeast
¼ cup warm water, preferably spring or filtered
¼ cup rye flour, preferably medium-dark rye flour

THE SPONGE

1 tablespoon dry yeast
1 cup warm water, preferably spring or filtered
1 cup rye flour, preferably medium-dark rye

½ cup millet
2 cups unbleached all-purpose white flour
1 cup whole wheat flour, plus extra
⅓ cup barley flakes
2 teaspoons salt
¾ teaspoon dry yeast
2 tablespoons honey
1¼ cups lukewarm water, preferably spring or filtered
Cooking spray

1 Combine all the first starter ingredients in a small glass or pottery bowl. Mix well, cover with plastic wrap, and let ferment in a warm place (about 75°F) for 24 to 48 hours. After the starter has soured for the requisite time period, add all the sponge ingredients (yeast, water, and rye flour) to it and mix well. Cover loosely again and let stand for another 3 to 4 hours. It should be bubbly, tart-smelling, demonstrably active.

2 In a dry cast-iron skillet over medium heat, toast the millet for about 3 minutes, or until golden and fragrant. Remove from the heat and let cool.

3 Place the white and whole wheat flours, barley flakes, salt, yeast, and honey in a food processor. Pulse 3 or 4 times to blend. Then, with the machine off, add the toasted millet and ¾ cup of the starter, reserving the unused portion, covered and refrigerated, for another use.

4 Turn the food processor on and begin by pouring in 1 cup of the water; buzz for 15 seconds. Watch closely; you want to see the dough coming together and forming a ball, thwacking the sides of the work bowl and picking up most of the flour. If the dough seems too moist and is sticking to the sides of the bowl and the blade's shaft, add a tablespoon or so more wheat flour. If, on the other hand, the dough is dry and crumbly and resists forming a ball, add the rest of the water 1 tablespoon at a time until the dough holds together. All this is taking place with the machine on, for a total (including that initial 15 seconds) of

45 seconds. You should have a slightly sticky soft dough, a little moist, and noticeably warm to the touch.

5 Get out a large bowl, and lightly flour a kneading surface. Turn the dough out onto the surface, and bring it together—a shaggy, lightly floured ball of dough. Place in the ungreased bowl, and let rise, covered loosely with a kitchen towel, in a warm place, until doubled in bulk, 1½ to 2 hours.

6 Spray an 8-by-4-inch loaf pan with cooking spray, if not using nonstick, and reflour your kneading board well. Turn the risen dough out onto your kneading board. Pat it out into a loaf and place it in the prepared pan. Dust it with a little additional flour and cover it again with a towel. Let it rise a second time in a warm place, until it has again doubled, 1 to 1¼ hours this go-round.

7 About 20 minutes into the last rise, preheat the oven to 425°F.

8 When the loaf has completed the rise, pop it in the oven and bake for 20 minutes. Lower the heat to 375°F, and bake for 25 to 35 minutes more, or until the loaf is a deep golden brown. Let cool in the pans for 10 minutes, then on a wire rack for 15 minutes. If you want nice, even, unshaggy slices, the loaf should be completely cooled before you slice into it. However, a warm if shaggy slice of this with a sliver of butter might just be worth it.

Cornmeal-Oatmeal Whole Wheat Bread, Bread-Machine Method

Another multigrain bread, with an entirely different character than the previous. It is a little sweet, and begins with a sort of thin porridge of oatmeal and cornmeal. Rapidura, a delicious and less-refined sweetener made from granulated organic sugarcane juice, is ideal here, but if you don't have any on hand, regular old brown sugar will do. Expect a pleasantly even crumb and a great crust, too.

A glance at how many fewer steps are required here will tell you why time-pressed home bakers have fallen in love with the bread machine. But as I said earlier, I remove the loaf at the last minute and bake it in the oven. **MAKES 1 LOAF**

¾ cup water, preferably spring or filtered
¾ cup low-fat milk or plain soy milk
1 tablespoon butter or oil
⅓ cup cornmeal
⅓ cup rolled oats (regular cooking oatmeal)
1¾ cups unbleached white all-purpose flour
1 cup whole wheat flour
1½ teaspoons salt
¼ cup Rapidura or brown sugar
1 envelope (1 scant tablespoon) dry yeast
3 tablespoons flax seeds
Cooking spray

1 In a medium saucepan, combine the water, milk, and butter or oil and bring to a boil. Turn off the heat and whisk in the cornmeal and oatmeal. Don't worry if it's a bit lumpy. Let stand until lukewarm, 15 to 20 minutes.

2 Place the warm mixture in the bread machine's pan, along with all the remaining ingredients except the flax seeds and cooking spray. Program the machine for dough, and let 'er rip (that is, press Start). Ten minutes before the end of the first knead cycle (the instruction manual for your particular bread machine will tell you how long your kneading cycle is), add the flax seeds.

3 Spray an 8-by-4-inch loaf pan with cooking spray, if not using nonstick. When the dough has finished and machine has beeped, oil your hands and turn the dough out, pressing it down and shaping it into a loaf as you place it in the pan. Let the loaf rise a second time, covered loosely with a clean kitchen towel, until doubled in bulk, 40 to 50 minutes.

4 About 20 minutes into this rise, preheat the oven to 375°F. When the loaf has risen, place the pan in the oven. Bake for 20 minutes, then lower the heat to 350°F, and bake for 35 to 45 minutes more, or until the loaf is a deep golden brown. Let cool in the pan for 10 minutes, then on a wire rack for 15 minutes. For neat slices, let the loaf cool completely before cutting into it.

Amaranth Arrives

Tiny amaranth is one of the rediscovered ancient grains—newly hip, yet cultivated by the Incas and Aztecs a millennium ago. The smaller-than-poppyseed-size grains share some history, nutritional profile, and culinary properties with quinoa (see page 564), another old but newly popular South American grain. The two grains have similar flavors and a layered texture, soft but a little crunchy. Both are gluten-free, too, so those who are allergic to this component of wheat can eat amaranth with impunity. In addition to the expected fiber, calcium, phosphorus, and iron, amaranth, like quinoa, is high in lysine, a crucial amino acid that most other grains are low in. This larger-than-normal helping of lysine gives amaranth higher quality protein than any other grain except quinoa. This is why it's often used, in the form of flour, to enrich the nutritional profile of other grains, like natural foods store–brand cereal flakes and energy bars. Amaranth's high protein content may also be what gives it its filling, rich, stick-to-the-ribs quality; it will keep you going, energized and unhungry, for a surprisingly long time.

"An old-fashioned food is one you ate at home as a child; a 'new' food usually means one that someone somewhere else ate."

—Elizabeth Schneider

Although you'll often find amaranth flour in natural foods stores, and although whole-grain amaranth is readily available for purchase in any large natural foods store, you won't find many recipes for amaranth. This is because of its unique texture when cooked: It is one grain that does not, will not, and cannot get "fluffy," the texture so many Americans like. Amaranth is moist, the tiny grains are distinct but stick to each other in an almost caviarlike fashion. Since it is so different in texture and size from the grains we normally eat, it is a bit of an acquired taste; probably not the thing to spring on someone new to natural foods. But adventurous eaters, and those experienced with whole foods, will enjoy having amaranth in their grain repertoire. A good starting point may be to try it tossed with a more familiar cooked grain, such as rice.

Cooked amaranth makes a great breakfast cereal, and a good plain base, or mix-in, for any savory stew, either on its own or mixed with equal parts cooked brown rice or barley.

Many commercial natural foods brands of breakfast cereal flakes contain amaranth, both for its flavor and nutritional profile. Health Valley makes several particularly good flakes containing amaranth.

Like several other lesser-known grains, amaranth is at its best if quickly pan-toasted before being steamed. Beware—it pops like popcorn as it is toasted, so do this in a saucepan or other high-sided cooking pot.

Basic Amaranth

Here's one of amaranth's quirks—although amaranth grains are much tinier than quinoa grains, they take longer to cook. But pan-toast them first and not only will they cook swiftly, they will be the tastier for it. The taste is slightly sweet, with notes of corn and peanut, and a soupçon of appealing, faint bitterness. The texture is both moist and crunchy. **SERVES 4**

NOTE

Because of its wet consistency, amaranth may stick unless you use a nonstick pot and/or cooking spray.

1 cup amaranth
Cooking spray
1⅓ cups water, preferably spring or filtered
½ teaspoon salt
1 teaspoon butter or olive oil (optional)

1 Heat the amaranth in a dry, heavy skillet or wok over medium heat. Toast, stirring constantly, for 3½ to 4½ minutes, or until the grains start to develop a toasty smell and start popping.

2 In a nonstick saucepan, or one that has been sprayed with cooking spray, bring the water, salt, and butter or oil, if using, to a boil. Drop in the toasted amaranth. Stir once and let the water return to a boil, then lower the heat to a simmer, cover, and cook for 8 to 10 minutes. The water may not seem to be fully absorbed; the grain will look quite soupy on the top.

3 Turn off the heat. Leaving the pot covered, let the amaranth stand for 5 to 10 minutes. Lift the lid and stir. All of the water will have been absorbed, and you'll see that the grain is quite thick beneath the surface. Stirred, your amaranth will have something of the texture of a dry cream of wheat.

Amaranth-Bean Chili-Porridge

Here is a straightforward one-pot supper, homey and pleasing to those who like Southwestern flavors. Unlike your typical chili or stew, which is served over a cooked grain, in this one the amaranth is stirred right in, making use of its natural moist quality to make a thick, savory porridge. **SERVES 4**

NOTE

This is an update of the traditional and ancient methods of amaranth preparation.

1 can (14 ounces) diced Ro*Tel tomatoes and green chiles
1 can (26 ounces) pinto beans, well drained, or 2 cups cooked pinto beans, well drained
Cooking spray
1 cup amaranth, prepared as for Basic Amaranth (previous page)
1 bunch fresh cilantro leaves, chopped (about ¾ cup)
2 to 4 ounces (½ to 1 cup) grated sharp Cheddar or jack cheese (optional)

1 Combine the Ro*Tel, including any liquid, and pinto beans in a medium nonstick saucepan or one that has been sprayed with cooking spray. Bring to a boil, then turn down to a simmer.

2 Stir the cooked amaranth into the tomato-bean mixture. Heat through, stirring often. When the porridge is good and hot, stir in the cilantro. Remove from the heat.

3 Serve the porridge in soup bowls, each topped with a shower of shredded cheese, if using.

NOTE

Although a nut-butter finish is one of my favorite ways with grains for breakfast, it's exceptional here because amaranth has a bit of peanut flavor anyway.

Breakfast Amaranth

Pan-toasted, steamed amaranth cooked with milk or soy milk, with a bit of peanut butter stirred in at the end, makes a fine wintertime breakfast, sustaining and delicious. Serve hot, with brown sugar or maple syrup, sliced banana, and additional milk, soy milk, or vanilla soy milk. **SERVES 4**

1 cup amaranth
Cooking spray
1 cup water, preferably spring or filtered
½ teaspoon salt
⅓ cup low-fat milk, or soy milk or other nondairy milk of your choice
1 tablespoon natural, nonhydrogenated peanut butter

1 Heat the amaranth in a dry, heavy skillet or wok over medium heat. Toast, stirring constantly, for 3½ to 4½ minutes, or until the grains start to develop a toasty smell and start popping.

2 In a nonstick saucepan, or one that has been sprayed with cooking spray, bring the water and salt to a boil and drop in the toasted amaranth. Stir once and let the water return to a boil. Then lower the heat to a simmer, cover, and cook for about 5 minutes. Add the milk or soy milk, cover again, and cook for another 5 minutes.

3 Turn off the heat and add the peanut butter, dividing the spoonful into dabs. Cover the pot and let it stand for 5 to 10 minutes. Lift the lid and stir. Serve at once, with your favorite breakfast cereal fixings.

Bring the Barley

If you are new to whole-grain experimentation, barley—eaten by human beings since the Stone Age—is a good place to start. Cultivated in Egypt since at least 6000 B.C., barley grains were used as currency, measurement, medicine, beverage, sacred offering (grains were found in King Tut's tomb), and, of course, foodstuff. Some scholars believe that the bread Jesus multiplied in the miracle of the loaves and fishes was made of barley, a grain the Bible refers to as "the fruit of the Lord"; even today, Tibetan Buddhists use barley flour in their "prayer wheel" bread. But barley's background is not only spiritual, it's also lusty (it is used extensively in beer making) and sweet (sprouted barley is the source of a sugar called maltose, the basis for barley-sugar candies, malted milk, and a delicious, golden, intensely flavored syrup, available at natural foods stores, called barley-malt syrup).

For all its history, barley is au courant: In studies by the U.S. Department of Agriculture, two compounds in barley lowered cholesterol levels in animals by 40 percent, and, in a month-long study on human volunteers at the University of Montana, those with the highest levels of cholesterol cut LDL (the "bad" cholesterol) by 16 percent by eating increased amounts of barley. Another result, in a study conducted at the University of Wisconsin, is very interesting to those of us who like to eat or cook with eggs and have a hard time using only the whites for the sake of our health: Hens on a barley-rich diet laid eggs with 25 percent less cholesterol in the yolk. The scientists at the University of Wisconsin also pointed out that statistically, arteriosclerosis, hence coronary heart disease, is relatively rare among populations where barley is a regular part of the diet.

But no food is good unless it tastes and feels good, and barley does. Its texture is pleasing when cooked right: chewy yet tender, with distinct, cloven grains that give a little pop in the mouth. Its taste is benignly moderate, lacking much of the whole-grain "nuttiness" that many writers, including me, often ascribe to certain whole grains.

Barley guards its germ carefully, with not one but two husks, so it is always milled to remove these indigestible layers. Whole hulled barley has had only these hulls removed; hence it is the most nutritious barley. It is light brown in color, and easily found at natural foods stores. Exotic black barley, highly esteemed in Ethiopia, is also whole, and is (of course) a very dark purple-brown-black. It looks almost like tiny coffee beans before it's cooked, and it's gorgeous to serve, since it retains its glossy blackness when cooked. Both regular whole hulled and black barley can be cooked conventionally or in a pressure cooker (see following pages).

Pearl barley, unfortunately the kind most readily available at your average supermarket, is milled repeatedly—up to 6 times!—losing not just its husks but its germ and good bran layer in the process. However, there are degrees of pearling. "Scotch barley," or "pot barley," is slightly less pearled than some others. But remember, "pearled" means "refined." You can identify it because it's white.

Seek out the whole hulled variety. To complicate matters, whole hulled barley is sometimes sold as "hull-less barley for sprouting." But please don't give up: You will know it by its brown color when you find it. Don't buy unmilled barley, sometimes also sold for sprouting: It's easily recognized by the obviously inedible strawlike chaff attached.

But I may have saved the best form of barley for last: barley flakes. These are flattened ("rolled") slices of whole-grain hulled barley, and they cook in just 12 minutes, are extremely tasty, and widely available. You can buy flaked barley in bulk at natural foods stores or, most likely, packaged at your local supermarket. (One widely available, good brand is Mother's, a company owned by Quaker Oats.) Flaked barley has become one of my favorite in-a-hurry grains.

Barley is an amenable grain; it stands in nicely for cooked rice in many recipes, and combines beautifully with rice and cooked wheat or rye kernels in any pilaf or grain salad. For other recipes using cooked barley, please see Three-Grain Salad with Dried Cranberries and Grapefruit (page 109), Parsnip-Barley Burgers (page 831), Oven-Baked Three-Grain Casserole with Sun-Dried Tomatoes and Vegetables (page 476), and Stuffed Eggplant Halves with Zhoug, Spinach, and Barley (page 398).

VARIATION

Quicker to cook, and thus fuel-saving as well as time-saving, this does require planning ahead. Soak 1 cup whole hulled barley in 1 cup water overnight. Next day, cook as in the recipe, but using only 1½ cups water. After 15 to 20 minutes of cooking, the barley will be tender, though still a bit chewy (agreeably so), and will still have some liquid—the perfect hot-cereal breakfast consistency. At 20 to 25 minutes, it's done: All liquid is absorbed, and the fluffy, individual grains have good tender-chewy barley texture, ready for pilafs, salads, what-have-you.

Basic Barley, Stove-Top Method

Whole hulled barley shares with whole-grain wheat and rye kernels the distinction of being among the slowest-to-cook grains. Cooking them under pressure, below, is the speediest method, but if you don't mind waiting or are cooking a day ahead, this stove-top method works perfectly well. **MAKES ABOUT 3 CUPS; SERVES 4 TO 6 AS A COMPONENT**

Cooking spray
2½ cups water, preferably spring or filtered
¾ teaspoon salt
1 cup whole hulled barley, regular (light brown) or black

1 In a medium nonstick saucepan, or one that has been sprayed with cooking spray, bring the water and salt to a rapid boil over high heat.

2 Meanwhile, place the barley in a sieve and rinse well. Add the rinsed barley to the boiling water, and return it to a rapid boil.

3 Reduce the heat as low as you can (if your burners won't turn down very low without blowing out, you may wish to use a Flame Tamer over the burner). Cover the pot with a tight-fitting lid and cook for 65 minutes.

4 Let the pot sit for 10 minutes undisturbed. Then serve, or use in other dishes.

Basic Barley, Pressure-Cooker Method

Follow this method exactly and you will have perfect barley: light and fluffy, with no excess water and the perfect balance of tenderness and chewiness. In my opinion most cooking authorities advocate too high a proportion of water to barley. With a Flame Tamer, though, you can use less water and not risk the barley sticking to the bottom of the pot.

Barley is one of the grains with a tendency to foam, which can clog a pressure cooker; the oil keeps the foam down. **MAKES ABOUT 3 CUPS; SERVES 4 TO 6 AS A COMPONENT**

Cooking spray
2½ cups water, preferably spring or filtered
¾ teaspoon salt
1 cup whole hulled barley, regular (light brown) or black
1 teaspoon mild vegetable oil, such as corn, canola, or peanut

1 Spray a pressure-cooker pot with cooking spray. Add the water and salt and bring to a boil over high heat.

2 Meanwhile, place the barley in a sieve and rinse well. When the water is boiling hard, add the rinsed barley and the oil. Return it to a rapid boil.

3 Lock the lid down and bring to high pressure, then lift the pot from direct heat and slide a Flame Tamer over the burner. Set the cooker back down on it. Adjust the heat until the pressure is steady halfway between medium and high and cook for 40 minutes.

4 After cooking, allow the pot to sit for 10 minutes to naturally release the pressure. Unlock the lid and serve, or use in other dishes.

"The greatest dishes are very simple dishes."

—Auguste Escoffier

Basic Flaked Barley

I am most enamored of barley flakes, which are only very lightly pearled—they're the quickest, simplest way possible to get good, whole-grain barley. Try it once, and you'll find barley on your table once a week or so, as opposed to a mere couple of times a year. Besides being quick to cook and inherently tasty, they lend themselves to all manner of elaboration. **MAKES ABOUT 3 CUPS; SERVES 4 TO 6 AS A SIDE DISH**

2 cups water, preferably spring or filtered
¼ teaspoon salt
1 cup flaked barley

1 Bring the water and salt to a rapid boil in a medium saucepan.

2 Stir in the flaked barley. Bring back to a boil, then reduce the heat. Cover tightly and cook for 10 to 12 minutes, or until tender. There will still be a little liquid visible.

3 Remove from the heat. Let stand for 5 minutes, covered. The liquid will now be completely absorbed. Serve.

Gussied-up Basic Barleys

- ▲ *For Two-Tone Barley-Mushroom Pilaf, try tossing equal parts cooked black and brown whole hulled barley with a big handful of sautéed shiitake and common domestic mushrooms. Finish with 3 to 4 tablespoons finely minced parsley and a splash each of tamari soy sauce and vermouth. This is excellent with anything with a creamy sauce.*
- ▲ *Cooked whole hulled barley with a splash of tamari soy sauce, a sprinkle of nutritional yeast (see page 239), and a little grated Parmesan is Barley à la Old-Hippie Comfort Food.*
- ▲ *Dollop cooked whole hulled barley with rehydrated black or pinto bean flakes (see page 594), and a splash of any salsa or Chile Buzz (page 902), and tuck into a Southwest Barley Supper.*
- ▲ *Dollop cooked whole hulled barley or cooked barley flakes with a big spoonful of apple butter, a tiny jot of butter, and a sprinkle of brown sugar or a drizzle of barley-malt syrup. Serve with hot milk (dairy, soy, or almond) for a Sweet Barley Bowl—a comfort-food supper or breakfast par excellence.*

Simple and Savory Flaked Barley Pilaf with Sesame

Quick, healthful, and delicious, this is a simple grain pilaf. It could be made with any quick-cooking grain but is especially delightful with barley flakes. It's hard to think of a bean stew or stir-fry that wouldn't be perked up by an accompanying mound of this pilaf. The sesame seeds aren't strictly necessary, but add a great deal of flavor.

You'll need an 8- or 9-inch skillet with a tight-fitting lid to prepare this in. **MAKES ABOUT 3 CUPS; SERVES 4 TO 6 AS A SIDE DISH**

Cooking spray
2 teaspoons butter or olive oil
½ large onion, finely chopped
1 rib celery, finely chopped
1 carrot, finely chopped
2 cups plus 2 tablespoons water, preferably spring or filtered
1 teaspoon tamari or shoyu soy sauce
¼ teaspoon salt
1 cup flaked barley
1 tablespoon sesame seeds

1 In a nonstick skillet with a tight-fitting lid, or one that has been sprayed with cooking spray, heat the butter and oil over medium high heat. When hot, add the onion and turn down the heat to medium. Stir-fry for 1 to 2 minutes, then add the celery and carrot. Stir-fry for another 3 minutes.

2 Add the water, tamari, and salt and bring to a boil (this happens almost instantly). Add the flaked barley, stir once or twice, and bring back to a boil, then reduce the heat. Cover tightly and cook for 10 to 12 minutes, or until tender.

3 As the barley cooks, place the sesame seeds in a small, dry skillet over medium-high heat. Stirring the seeds or shaking the pan constantly, toast the sesame seeds for about 3 minutes, or until golden and toasty-smelling. Remove from the heat, transferring the seeds from the hot pan to a bowl so they don't continue to cook.

4 At the end of the barley cooking time, there will still be a little liquid visible. Remove the skillet from the heat and let stand for 5 minutes, covered. The liquid will now be completely absorbed. Sprinkle with the toasted sesame seeds and serve.

VARIATIONS

Cook double the barley called for here, and use the remainder to stuff red peppers (page 410). Or fix double the entire succotash recipe; eat it hot tonight, and serve it cold as a salad tomorrow or the day after, on a bed of spinach with some sliced garden tomatoes. You could pass some Cilantro Vinaigrette (page 94), too. Last but not least, you can heat the leftover succotash with 1 part vegetable stock and 1 part low-fat milk, perhaps with a couple of diced cooked potatoes thrown in. Season and serve it up.

Southwestern Succotash with Barley and Green Chiles

All it takes for grain and bean dishes to move from bland to captivating is artful, attentive seasoning. This perfectly delicious quartet proves the point: Classic succotash lima beans and corn are teamed with butternut squash and cooked barley. There's a Southwestern kick of cumin and green chile, mellowed by the sweetness of the squash. **SERVES 4 TO 6 AMPLY AS A MAIN COURSE**

- Cooking spray
- 1 teaspoon to 1 tablespoon butter or mild vegetable oil, such as corn, canola, or peanut
- 1 medium onion, chopped
- 2 teaspoons cumin seeds
- Large pinch of cayenne
- 1 medium butternut squash, peeled, seeded, and diced
- 2 cloves garlic, pressed
- ¼ cup peeled, chopped, roasted green chiles (see page 782), fresh or canned
- 1 package (10 ounces) frozen baby lima beans
- Salt and freshly ground black pepper to taste
- 1½ cups corn kernels, either frozen or fresh off the cob (2 to 3 ears)
- 2 cups cooked barley, either whole hulled or flaked
- 3 tablespoons finely minced parsley
- 3 tablespoons finely minced cilantro
- ⅓ cup Yogurt Sour Cream (page 910), Tofu Sour Cream (page 909), or reduced-fat sour cream (optional)

1. In a nonstick skillet, or one that has been sprayed with cooking spray, heat the butter or oil over medium heat. Add the onion and cumin seeds and sauté for about 5 minutes, or until the onion is softened and translucent. Stir in the cayenne, butternut squash, garlic, roasted green chiles, lima beans, and salt and pepper to taste.

2. Raise the heat to high to heat through, nice and hot, then lower to medium. Cover and let the vegetables steam for about 10 minutes, or until limas and squash are fairly tender.

3. Add the corn, and cook for 5 minutes more. Stir in the cooked barley, parsley, cilantro, and Yogurt Sour Cream, if using. (Or serve sour cream equivalent on the side.) Serve hot, at once, with a small sprinkle of grated sharp Cheddar on top, if you like.

Mushroom-Barley Ri-sort-of

Imagine the best mushroom-barley soup you ever had. Now imagine the best risotto you ever had. Now put them together. This is what happens when Italian comfort food meets Jewish comfort food with white-tablecloth flair.

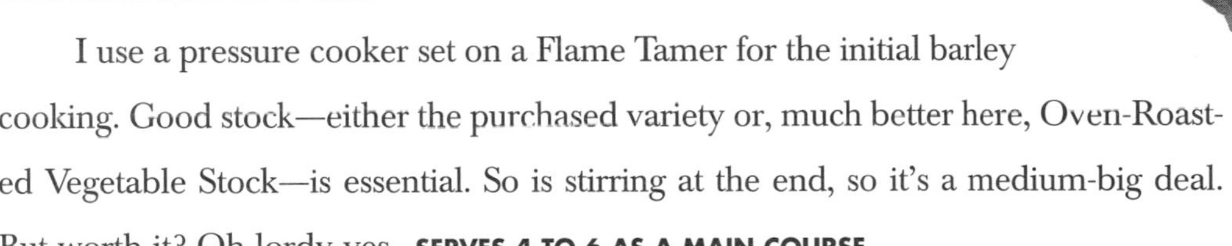

I use a pressure cooker set on a Flame Tamer for the initial barley cooking. Good stock—either the purchased variety or, much better here, Oven-Roasted Vegetable Stock—is essential. So is stirring at the end, so it's a medium-big deal. But worth it? Oh lordy yes. **SERVES 4 TO 6 AS A MAIN COURSE**

2½ cups Oven-Roasted Vegetable Stock (page 141) or good commercial stock
1 ounce dried porcini mushrooms
Cooking spray
1 tablespoon mild vegetable oil, such as corn, canola, or peanut
1 cup whole hulled barley
1 large onion, diced
½ pound shiitake mushrooms, finely diced
1 parsnip, peeled and finely diced
1 tablespoon chopped garlic (5 to 6 cloves)
1 cup white wine
1 teaspoon tomato paste
½ cup freshly grated Parmesan cheese, plus additional to pass at the table
1 tablespoon fresh thyme leaves
2 tablespoons minced Italian parsley
Salt and freshly ground black pepper to taste

1 Bring 1 cup of the stock to a boil in a small saucepan. Add the dried porcini, turn off the heat, and let soak for 1 hour, placing a plate on top of the mushrooms so they stay submerged.

2 Meanwhile, in a pressure cooker that has been sprayed with cooking spray, bring the remaining stock and 1 teaspoon of the oil to a hard boil over high heat. Place the barley in a sieve and rinse well. When the stock in the cooker is boiling hard, add the rinsed barley. Let it return to a hard boil. Lock the lid down and bring to high pressure, then lift the pot from direct heat and slide a Flame Tamer over the burner; immediately set the pressure cooker back down on it. Adjust the heat until the pressure is steady halfway between medium and high, and cook for 30 minutes.

3 As the porcini soak and the barley precook, heat the remaining 2 teaspoons oil in a nonstick skillet or one that has been sprayed with cooking spray. Add the onion and sauté over medium heat until softened, about 4 minutes. Add the shiitakes and parsnip and sauté for another 4 minutes. Lower the heat, add the garlic, and sauté for 3 more minutes. Add the wine and tomato paste and turn off the heat.

NOTE

A flat, disc-shaped heat diffuser about ¼ inch thick, a Flame Tamer—despite its dramatic name—is a handy, low-tech, inexpensive gadget available at hardware or housewares stores. You place it directly on the burner of your stove, turn on the flame, let the Flame Tamer preheat, and then place the pot or pressure cooker on it. Since it spreads the heat evenly, it ensures even cooking, without the hot spots that can cause scorching. I frequently use mine when cooking grains in the pressure cooker, or when making any slow-cooked dish with a thickened sauce, which is likely to stick (like certain stews).

4 Strain the mushroom-soaking liquid through a coffee filter into the skillet with the sauté. Carefully pick over the porcini, removing any twiggy pieces, and dice the mushrooms. Add the porcini to the mixture in the skillet, and turn the heat to low to rewarm.

5 When the barley is done, turn off the heat and allow the pressure to release naturally for 10 minutes. Unlock the lid, leaving the cooker uncovered. Place the cooker over medium heat. Add 1 large ladleful of the skillet mixture (liquid and solids), and stir into the barley. Stirring frequently, let the liquid cook off, about 3 minutes. Repeat, a ladleful at a time, 3 or 4 times, scraping in the last of the mushrooms and onions when you run out of liquid. By now the barley should be chewy-tender and just about done.

6 Stir in the Parmesan, herbs, and salt and pepper. Serve as soon as possible, with additional Parmesan at the table.

Buckwheat

Buckwheat, like amaranth and wild rice, is not a member of the cereal family, although it looks and cooks like it is, and its nutritional profile is similar. Buckwheat is actually in the rhubarb family, and its "grains" are technically fruit. These "grains" are called buckwheat groats, to distinguish them from buckwheat flour (known to most of us, deliciously, in pancakes) or buckwheat hulls (inedible, but a jim-dandy garden mulch and pillow filler). If toasted prior to cooking, buckwheat groats are usually called kasha (though things are slightly confused here, too, because some use that name for the untoasted groats, and in parts of Russia, any type of cooked grain is called kasha).

Buckwheat was brought to the United States by immigrants from Holland (who called it *bockweit*) and Germany (who called it *buchweizen*). Both these names translate as "beech-wheat": The triangular kernels resemble tiny beechnuts, but they seem nutritionally more like wheat. Naturally disease-resistant, buckwheat is rarely sprayed with pesticides, and, because it thrives on land too poor for other grain crops, it's rarely fed concentrated nonorganic fertilizers. Thus, you can count on it's being organic, or nearly so.

Well loved in Russia, buckwheat grows to maturity in a quick 10 to 12 weeks, and is tolerant of weather extremes. The same reasons for the Russians' fondness have ensured the plant's use throughout the world in many times (including the early Ozarks and New England) as a first crop on newly cleared land, and as an emergency crop, planted midsummer if another crop has failed.

Like all whole grains, buckwheat is high in carbohydrates and fiber, and contains a modest amount of protein. Although lower in the B-vitamin family than most, it is extraordinarily rich in potassium. It also contains a most interesting phytochemical, flavanol glycoside, known as rutin. Rutin, which works synergistically with vitamin C, was once much used to lower high blood pressure, but fell out of favor once faster-acting drugs were developed. Well, if high blood pressure ran in my family and I wished to avoid taking medication for it, or even if I were already doing so, I can tell you that buckwheat would be on my table a couple of times a week. Second, unlike wheat, rye, and many other grains, buckwheat has no gluten, so those who are intolerant of gluten can eat buckwheat with impunity. Third, it appears to offer special benefits to diabetics, because its sugars are absorbed very slowly, often improving glucose-tolerance levels in those with adult-onset diabetes. But here is one last reason to love buckwheat. It cooks in a *hurry*. Fifteen minutes! No pressure cooker! No fuss! Way to go, buckwheat!

It is also delicious, with a haunting, nutty flavor, like that of wild rice, but more intense. Traditional methods of using the whole groats include as filling for pierogi, knishes, or kreplach (see page 322) and in kasha varnishkes, which is seasoned toasted buckwheat groats cooked with bow-tie noodles (always bow-ties), a familiar Jewish dish. Yet another much-loved Russian use—a liberal scoop in the bottom of a bowl of red borscht (beet soup) or s'chee (sweet and sour cabbage soup).

Basic Buckwheat, Traditional Stove-Top Method

Traditionally, buckwheat groats are tossed with a beaten egg, then toasted in a hot skillet until dry. Supposedly this keeps the kernels from getting soggy while they cook. I don't find that this makes much difference in the finished flavor and texture, but I offer instructions for both methods. **MAKES ABOUT 3 CUPS; SERVES 4 TO 6 AS A COMPONENT**

Cooking spray
1 cup whole buckwheat groats
1 large egg
2 cups boiling water, preferably spring or filtered
½ to ¾ teaspoon salt

1 Place a nonstick skillet, or one that has been sprayed with cooking spray, over medium heat.

2 In a small bowl, combine the groats and egg, stirring together with a fork until well mixed. Turn the egg-coated groats out into the hot skillet, and cook, stirring, until the groats dry out and all grains have separated, about 3 minutes.

3 Pour in the boiling water, stirring, and add the salt. Reduce the heat to low, cover the skillet tightly, and cook, covered, for 15 minutes. Turn off the heat, let the groats stand for 5 to 10 minutes, then lift the lid, fluff, and serve.

Basic Buckwheat, Nontraditional Stove-Top Method

Not egg-coated, and thus even simpler and lower in fat than the above, this way of cooking buckwheat is also pleasing to vegans or those who are on low-cholesterol diets. **MAKES ABOUT 3 CUPS; SERVES 4 TO 6 AS A COMPONENT**

Cooking spray
1 cup whole buckwheat groats
2 cups boiling water, preferably spring or filtered
½ to ¾ teaspoon salt

1 Place a nonstick skillet, or one that has been sprayed with cooking spray, over medium heat. Add the groats and cook, stirring constantly, until they deepen slightly in color and give off a nice, toasty fragrance, about 3 minutes.

2 Pour in the boiling water, stirring, and add the salt. Reduce the heat to low, cover the skillet tightly, and cook, covered, for 15 minutes. Turn off the heat, let the groats stand for 5 to 10 minutes to absorb more water, then lift the lid, fluff the groats to separate them, and serve.

Buckwheat Pilaf with Cabbage and Herbs

The much-loved Russian grain combines beautifully with the much-loved Russian vegetable, cabbage. The herb finish adds freshness and flavor. Although we don't think of cilantro as Russian, it is common in the Georgian republic. And rosemary is another herb strong enough to stand up to buckwheat. Serve this pilaf topped with a healthy dollop of Tofu Sour Cream (page 909), and a big salad to start, or use it as a component in the next recipe. **SERVES 4 TO 6 AS AN ENTREE WITH ACCOMPANIMENTS**

Cooking spray
1½ cups whole buckwheat groats
1 teaspoon butter
2 teaspoons olive oil
½ large onion, finely diced
3 cups boiling water, preferably spring or filtered
1 tablespoon tamari or shoyu soy sauce
½ teaspoon salt
¼ head abbage, cored and thinly sliced
⅓ cup finely chopped fresh herbs (I prefer about 2 teaspoons minced rosemary, 2 tablespoons cilantro, and the remainder minced Italian parsley)

1 Place a nonstick skillet, or one that has been sprayed with cooking spray, over medium heat. Add the groats and cook, stirring constantly, until they deepen slightly in color and give off a nice, toasty fragrance, about 3 minutes. Pour the groats out of the skillet and set aside.

2 Allow the skillet to cool slightly, then return it to medium heat and add the butter and olive oil. When hot, add the onion and sauté, stirring, for 3 minutes, or until the onion is slightly softened. Return the toasted buckwheat to the pan and stir in the boiling water, tamari, and salt. Reduce the heat to low, cover the skillet tightly, and cook, covered, for 10 minutes.

3 Add the cabbage, sprinkling it atop the buckwheat. Do not stir. Cover the pan and cook for 5 minutes more.

4 Turn off the heat and sprinkle the groats with the herbs. Cover again and let stand for 5 to 10 minutes, then lift the lid, stir to combine, and serve.

Kasha Harvest Pilaf Platter with Winter Vegetables

This is a component plate: The buckwheat pilaf is surrounded by a ring of slow-roasted, diced winter vegetables with cooked chickpeas. It is quite beautiful, almost wreathlike in appearance, and delicious, too. Although any of the components would work on their own, put together they are the picture of healthful plant-based

WINTER SOLSTICE FEAST

Pumpkin-Tomato Bisque
(PAGE 181)

*

Kasha Harvest Pilaf Platter with Winter Vegetables

*

Gingerbread with Tofu-Cashew Crème
(PAGE 1062)

home cooking. To make it even showier, add cooked beets for a bright, deep-red bow on the wreath. Yet another delicious elaboration is to top the pilaf with a sprinkling of chopped toasted hazelnuts.

Start the vegetables roasting, and then, as they warm and perfume your kitchen, put together the pilaf. **SERVES 4 TO 6 AS A MAIN COURSE**

VEGETABLES

Cooking spray
2 large sweet potatoes, an intensely orange-red variety such as Garnet Red, peeled and cut into ½-inch dice
1 medium onion, cut into ½-inch dice
1 fist-sized potato, peeled or not as you prefer, cut into ½-inch dice
¼ head cauliflower, pulled into florets no bigger than ½ inch
1 red bell pepper, seeded and cut into large wedges
1 bay leaf
2 teaspoons black or brown mustard seeds
1 teaspoon celery seed
2 tablespoons olive oil
Salt and freshly ground black pepper to taste
1 teaspoon paprika
Dash of cayenne
2 cloves garlic, pressed
1 can (15 ounces) chickpeas, well drained

FOR ASSEMBLY

1 recipe Buckwheat Pilaf with Cabbage and Herbs (page 538)
2 to 3 warm cooked beets, diced (optional)
1½ tablespoons any homemade or commercial vinaigrette (optional)
Sprigs of fresh rosemary (optional)
¼ cup chopped toasted hazelnuts (optional)

1 Preheat the oven to 375°F.

2 Start the roasted vegetables: On the largest nonstick baking pan that will fit in your oven, or one that has been sprayed with cooking spray, toss together the sweet potatoes, onion, potato, cauliflower, red bell pepper, bay leaf, mustard seeds, and celery seeds, and drizzle with the oil. Season with salt, pepper, paprika, and cayenne and toss again.

3 Bake, uncovered, for about 40 minutes. Check the oven occasionally and shake the pan. All the vegetables should be a bit shriveled-looking; the potato and sweet potato should be cooked through and browned. (Meanwhile, make your pilaf.)

4 Remove the roasted vegetables from the oven and sprinkle them with the pressed garlic; toss again. Taste and adjust the seasonings. Add the chickpeas and toss well.

5 Assemble individual serving plates or a large platter as follows. Mound the buckwheat pilaf in the middle of the plate, leaving an empty ring around the edge for the vegetables. If using the beets, toss them with the vinaigrette and place a small pile of them on one part of the empty ring. Then scatter the diced roasted vegetables around the pilaf on the remaining empty portion of plate, and tuck the rosemary sprigs on either side of the beets. Sprinkle the hazelnuts over the buckwheat pilaf. Serve at once.

Tibetan Tukpa-Style Soba Noodles

Soba are Japanese noodles made wholly or partially of buckwheat flour. They have an addictive slithery texture and, of course, buckwheat's outspoken flavor. Soba's propensity to foam while cooking requires a unique method of noodle preparation, described in the box on the next page.

This very pleasing dish is loosely adapted from a traditional Tibetan dish, a soup frequently served as the evening meal, according to Betty Jung, author of *The Kopan Cookbook: Vegetarian Recipes from a Tibetan Monastery*. My version has less liquid, so it becomes a stewlike sauce. I've also added chunks of tofu and an optional sprinkling of cilantro at the end. The traditional noodle used in tukpa is a wheat-based egg noodle, but I think buckwheat's taste is perfect with the assertive spicings. As you'd expect, given its geographical placement, elements of both Indian/Nepalese and Chinese seasonings go into Tibetan cooking. **SERVES 4**

NOTE

The chile powder called for is pure powdered red chile pepper, which is not as hot as cayenne. If cayenne's all you have, cut the amount back to 1/4 teaspoon.

Cooking spray
1 tablespoon butter or ghee (see page 486)
1 medium red onion, chopped
1½ tablespoons peeled, finely minced ginger
6 to 8 cloves garlic, peeled and minced (about 1½ tablespoons)
1 teaspoon turmeric
1 teaspoon curry powder
1 teaspoon chile powder (or ¼ teaspoon cayenne)
1 teaspoon Garam Masala (page 902; optional but awfully good)
1 large tomato, diced (or 1¼ cup canned crushed tomatoes)
1 small potato, peeled and cut into ½-inch cubes
½ cup water, preferably spring or filtered
¼ pound fresh spinach leaves, well washed, stems removed, chopped
1 tablespoon tamari or shoyu soy sauce, or to taste
Salt and freshly ground black pepper to taste
1 pound conventional water-packed tofu, preferably reduced fat, cubed
1 pound soba noodles, cooked (see box on next page)
Cilantro leaves (optional)

1 Heat a large nonstick skillet with a tight-fitting lid, or one that has been sprayed with cooking spray, over medium heat. When hot, add the butter and onion.

VARIATION

Try substituting 1½ cups frozen peas for the spinach, adding the peas at the same point in the recipe. The peas' hint of sweetness is very, very nice here.

Sauté, stirring often, for 3 minutes, or until the onion starts to become translucent. Add the ginger and garlic and stir-fry for 1 minute. Add the turmeric, curry powder, chile powder, and Garam Masala and continue to stir-fry for another 30 seconds.

2 Add the tomato and potato and stir-fry for 1 minute more, then pour in the water and bring to a boil. Cover and simmer until the potato is barely done—just tender, but not mushy—8 to 10 minutes, lifting the lid and stirring occasionally.

3 Add the spinach, cover, and cook for 1 minute more, or until spinach wilts. Taste and season with tamari, salt, and plenty of pepper. Add the tofu.

4 Either stir the cooked soba into the vegetable mixture, or use the vegetable mixture as a sauce for the soba. Garnish, if you like, with a sprinkle of cilantro.

Soba Story

To prepare a 1-pound package of soba noodles, bring 2½ quarts water, preferably spring or filtered, to a rapid boil in a large pot over high heat. Have 2 to 3 cups cold water at hand. Add the soba to the boiling water, give a gentle stir or two, and lower the heat slightly. Almost immediately, foam will swell threateningly toward the top of the pot. Quick—pour in ½ to ¾ cup of the cold water, and the foam will subside. Allow the noodles to continue cooking, and whenever they threaten to foam and overflow, add another ½ cup cold water. Keep doing this until the noodles are cooked al dente, 7 to 9 minutes (start testing for doneness at 6 minutes). You'll probably need to repeat the cold water drill two or three times. Drain the cooked noodles, and rinse well with cold water to stop the cooking. Set aside.

Sweet and Sour Swedish-Style Rye-Buckwheat Bread

I have always preferred dark, toothy, grainy breads to soft, pale ones. Even a good crisp-crusted baguette made of white flour doesn't do it for me as much as a dark-hued, grainy loaf. A pal, Diane Wienerman, shared this predilection, and when we were housemates many years ago, we developed a whole-grain version of a faintly sweet Swedish rye bread, delicately flavored with orange. Some years after that I was preparing a Russian dinner, and in searching for the right bread I returned to this recipe. As I was making it I added some buckwheat—raw groats, not flour—to the dough. It was wonderful! Expect a heightened grainy flavor, dense texture, and grand crunch. Because the groats are so soft, neither extra water nor precooking is needed.

This bread is delicious as a base for cheese toasts (made with real dairy cheeses or soy cheeses, and especially gjetost, the peculiar and delicious Scandinavian cheese made from caramelized milk). It's also good as a sandwich, with conventional or tofu egg salad. Or serve it with a big bowl of borscht. **MAKES 2 LARGE OR 3 MEDIUM LOAVES**

2 tablespoons dry baking yeast
2 cups warm water, preferably spring or filtered
¼ cup honey or barley-malt syrup (see page 960)
1¼ cups buttermilk, yogurt, or soy yogurt
2 tablespoons butter (vegans may use margarine or corn or canola oil)
2 tablespoons cider vinegar
3 tablespoons blackstrap molasses
1 tablespoon caraway seeds
1½ tablespoons salt
Very finely grated rind of 1 orange
2¾ cups dark rye flour
1¼ cups unbleached white all-purpose flour
2 cups whole wheat flour
½ cup soy flour
1 cup buckwheat groats (not flour)
Additional white or whole wheat flour for kneading, up to 1¾ cups or so
Cooking spray

1 In a small bowl, dissolve the yeast in the warm water, adding the honey. Let stand until bubbly.

2 Meanwhile, in a small saucepan combine the buttermilk, butter, vinegar, molasses, caraway, and salt. Heat until quite warm; the butter will melt, and the mixture will curdle. Remove from the stove and let cool to lukewarm, then add the orange rind.

3 When the yeast is bubbly and the buttermilk mixture is lukewarm, combine the two in a large bowl and add the flours, 1 cup at a time, and the groats. Continue adding flour until the dough is of a kneadable consistency, bearing in mind that rye flour is always a bit sticky in the kneading. Oiling and/or flouring your hands helps, but basically you just get in there and do it, scraping your hands every few minutes. Turn the dough out onto a floured board and pause briefly to wash, dry, and spray or grease the dough bowl. Knead the dough for about 5 minutes, then place the dough in the bowl and let rise, covered loosely with a clean kitchen towel, in a warm place, for about 1 hour and 15 minutes, until not quite doubled in size.

4 Turn the dough out onto the floured board. Let it rest a minute or two while you arrange two large, or three medium nonstick loaf pans, or spray conventional ones with cooking spray. Knead the dough a few times and shape it into loaves. Place the loaves in the pans and let them rise a second time, loosely covered, in a warm place, for about 45 minutes. In the last 15 minutes of rising, preheat the oven to 450°F.

5 When ready to bake, lower the oven temperature to 350°F, open the oven door, and quickly throw a couple of ice cubes on the floor of the oven. This creates a steamy oven atmosphere, part of what gives this bread its special texture. Immediately put the pans in the oven.

6 Bake for 50 to 60 minutes, or until the crust has deepened in color. Turn the bread out of the pans and let cool on wire racks before slicing.

Mary's Famous Banana Buttermilk Buckwheat Pancakes

One of the few places Americans encounter buckwheat regularly is in pancakes. And among buckwheat pancakes, these are exceptional indeed. They're so good, in fact, that former innkeeper Mary Davies virtually built the reputation of Ten Inverness Way on them. So good that when she finally sold the California inn, a charming Craftsman-style cottage overlooking Tomales Bay, to Teri and Scott Mowery a few years back, guests insisted the pancakes stay on the menu.

Now Mary is a graduate at seminary, and Teri and Scott, who've known they wanted to be innkeepers ever since they met nearly a decade ago, garden, cook, and welcome inn guests with these pancakes.

The riper the banana, the better—it should be almost pouring out of its skin. And by the way, you can easily and deliciously add a fourth "b" to the banana-buttermilk-buckwheat combo: blueberries. Serve with butter and real maple syrup, of course.

SERVES 2 OR 3

VARIATION

Gently fold ¾ cup or so of fresh blueberries into the pancake batter, and cook as directed.

⅓ cup unbleached white all-purpose flour
⅓ cup whole wheat flour, preferably whole wheat pastry flour
⅓ cup buckwheat flour
2 teaspoons baking powder
½ teaspoon baking soda
¼ teaspoon salt
1 large egg
2 tablespoons mild vegetable oil, such as corn, canola, or peanut
1 cup buttermilk
1 very ripe banana, very well mashed
Cooking spray

1 In a medium bowl, thoroughly combine all three flours, the baking powder, baking soda, and salt. In a separate bowl, whisk together the egg, oil, buttermilk, and banana. Stir the wet ingredients into the dry, using a quick, light hand and mixing until just blended, about 20 seconds.

2 Heat a cast-iron griddle or heavy nonstick skillet over medium heat. When it's good and hot—almost smoking hot—give it a quick spritz of cooking spray (or, if you like, a quick light brush of oil with a pastry brush). Drop the pancake batter by ¼-cupfuls on the hot griddle, leaving adequate space between the pancakes for expansion. Flip the cakes when bubbles appear and pop on the top surface without filling back in with flowing batter. Allow about half as much time for side two to cook as for side one. You'll probably need to turn the heat down after the first batch, as the griddle itself will be holding heat.

3 Serve, preferably hot off the grill.

"Then [Pa] sat down, as they urged him, and lifting the blanket cake on the untouched pile, he slipped from under it a section of the stack of hot, syrupy pancakes. . . .

'You boys certainly live in the lap of luxury,' Pa remarked. The pancakes were no ordinary buckwheat pancakes. Almanzo followed his mother's pancake rule and the cakes were light as foam, soaked through with melted brown sugar."

—Laura Ingalls Wilder, *The Long Winter*

Make Mine Millet

Tiny round golden grains that look a bit like couscous, millet is very mild in flavor rather than intensely nutty, and so is ideal for whole-grain neophytes. Add to this the appeal of entirely different textures, depending on the cooking method, a respectable nutritional profile (plenty of phosphorus, B-vitamins, iron, and a large amount of the protein-building amino acid lysine), and the fact that it is relatively quick-cooking (about 20 minutes), and you have a winner. In fact, I've never found anyone not to like millet. What a pity, then, that most of the millet sold in the United States is in birdseed.

Assuming you're earthbound and prefer your millet cooked, there are a few simple provisos that ensure this amenable grain reaches perfection every time.

- ▲ Always buy millet at a natural foods store or market. It is possible to purchase millet at a feed and grain store or pet shop, but you want millet processed for human consumption, with the indigestible outer husk removed (don't worry, it still has its inner layer of bran).
- ▲ Always use fresh millet. There are some whole grains that can very happily sit in a jar for years and show no appreciable lack of flavor when cooked. Millet is not one of them. Buy millet in a vacuum-packed bag or, if in bulk, from a place that you know has a good turnover. (Don't be afraid to ask when it came in.) You don't need to refrigerate millet, nor do you have to cook it the minute you get home, but use it within, say, 2 or 3 months. Millet that hangs around for 8 months or a year can have a bitter flavor.
- ▲ Always rinse millet before cooking. Again, some grains seem to need this rinse to reach their full flavor potential. Just put your measure of millet in a fine-gauge mesh strainer and pour water (preferably spring or filtered) over it, swishing a couple of times. Let it drain thoroughly for a few minutes before starting the toasting process.
- ▲ Know how you plan to use the millet, so you can choose the appropriate cooking method. If you're cooking millet for a pilaf or as a plain grain to accompany some savory sauce, use the recipe for Basic Fluffy-Style Millet. If you want it for a cake or patty, or Millet Mash (page 551), make Basic Moist-Style Millet.
- ▲ Always toast millet in a dry skillet for a few minutes before cooking. There are a few quirky grains that do not come into their own unless they undergo this easy treatment. Toasting makes the difference here. Even if I'm using uncooked millet as an addition to bread, I toast it first. Directions for toasting are given in the two basic recipes.

Much-Loved Millet

Before rice, wheat, and corn became the grains dominating the world's tables, millet was a mainstay of the human diet, predating rice as the staple grain in China. Even now, this early grain gives sustenance to nearly a third of the world's population, mostly those inhabiting the hotter, arid parts of Africa and Asia. But as interest in both whole grains and authentic, indigenous foreign cuisines grows, millet—mild, pleasing, nutritious, versatile, and so quick to cook—may yet have another day. Those allergic to gluten also have reason to celebrate the small golden grain; like quinoa, rice, and corn, it is gluten-free.

Basic Fluffy-Style Millet

Use this millet any time you want a pleasingly mild bed of grain for a savory stew, sauté, stir-fry, or sauce. It's also the basis for Spanish Millet (see next page) and just about any other improvisational grain pilaf or mélange you might dream up. The resulting grain here is nice and fluffy, with little pleasing bits of crunch.

MAKES 3½ TO 3¾ CUPS

1 cup millet, well rinsed and very well drained
2 cups spring or filtered water, or vegetable stock (see page 139)
½ teaspoon sea salt

1 Over medium heat, in an ungreased cast-iron skillet, toast the millet, stirring frequently, until lightly fragrant but not browned, 2 to 3 minutes (if the millet is still very damp from rinsing, it might take 7 to 9 minutes). When it's reached the proper degree of toastiness it will also sort of skitter around the pan. Remove from the heat.

2 In a pot with a tight-fitting lid, bring the water or stock and salt to a boil. Stir in the toasted millet. Return to a boil, then turn down the heat to a simmer. Pop the lid on the pot and cook until the millet is tender and all liquid is absorbed, 18 to 22 minutes. Let stand, covered, for about 5 minutes, then fluff with a fork and serve.

Basic Moist-Style Millet

Use this millet when you need the tiny grains to stick together, as in Millet Mash with Cauliflower (page 551) or Outrageously Good Pan-Crisped Millet-Vegetable Cakes (page 825). Do not, under any circumstances, miss either of these captivating recipes. They will make a millet convert out of you forever. **MAKES ABOUT 4 CUPS**

1 cup millet, well rinsed and very well drained
3¼ cups spring or filtered water, or vegetable stock (see page 139)
½ teaspoon sea salt

Gussied-up Millet

Millet-Vegetable Pilaf: *Sauté sliced leek, diced celery, diced carrot, and shiitake mushrooms, and a couple of bay leaves in a little olive oil; deglaze the pan with a little vermouth if you have it and discard. Toss with cooked fluffy-style millet, seasoning with a little thyme.*

Millet Pilaf with Raisins and Cabbage: *Sauté sliced cabbage in a little oil; add cooked fluffy-style millet and steam until heated through. Serve as is, or add a few raisins and cashews and/or a splash of soy sauce, and/or stir in a few teaspoons of commercially available ginger-garlic paste.*

Citrus-Sparkled Millet-Nut Mélange: *Add the grated rind of 1 orange to the millet in its last 10 minutes of cooking. Chill the millet. When cold, toss in diced scallion, cucumber, and seeded orange pieces; a few toasted chopped almonds or hazelnuts; the juice of 2 oranges and a lemon, and a tiny bit of oil—preferably almond or hazelnut oil to intensify the nut flavor. A handful of dried blueberries, cranberries, or raisins and some minced parsley completes things. The oils and many add-ins can be ordered from King Arthur Flour: www.kingarthurflour.com*

Breakfast Bowl of Millet: *For one of the all-time great breakfast cereals, reheat cooked moist-style millet in a little milk (dairy or otherwise). When it's hot, stir in some almond butter—1 tablespoon for every 2½ cups or so cooked millet, adjusting proportions to taste. Serve hot, with sliced bananas and brown or maple sugar. Yum!*

1 Over medium heat, in an ungreased cast-iron skillet, toast the millet, stirring frequently, until lightly fragrant but not browned, 2 to 3 minutes (if the millet is still very damp from rinsing, it might take 7 to 9 minutes). When it's reached the proper degree of toastiness it will also sort of skitter around the pan. Remove from the heat.

2 In a pot with a tight-fitting lid, bring the water or stock and salt to a boil. Stir in the toasted millet. Return to a boil, then turn down the heat to a simmer. Pop the lid on the pot and cook until the millet is tender and all liquid is absorbed, 25 to 30 minutes. Let stand, covered, for about 5 minutes.

Spanish Millet

Unlike the Brazilian Rice (page 473), in which the rice is cooked with the spices and tomato, this savory and pleasing dish calls for plain precooked millet, into which various savory things—including tomato paste—are stirred. If you grew up in the '50s, this will remind you of the "Spanish Rice" of the era, which certainly wasn't Spanish but was very good. Millet is great with any dish containing corn. I like this recipe a lot with Simple Pot of Chicos and Nightfall Beans (page 454), or even just simple black beans. Serve whatever bean you choose side by side with this, dolloped with sour cream (or its low-fat or nondairy equivalent), sprig it with cilantro, and believe you me, no one will complain (except maybe the cook, who had hoped to have some left over for lunch). **SERVES 4 TO 6**

Cooking spray
2 teaspoons to 1 tablespoon olive oil
1 onion, sliced vertically into thin crescents
1 green bell pepper, diced
2 cloves garlic, pressed or finely diced
3 cups cooked Basic Fluffy-Style Millet (page 547)
Tabasco or similar hot sauce, to taste (optional)
3 tablespoons tomato paste

1 Heat a large nonstick skillet, or one that has been sprayed with cooking spray, over medium heat. Add the oil. Add the onion and sauté for 6 to 8 minutes, or until very soft and limp and slightly browned around the edges. Add the bell pepper and sauté for another 2 minutes. Add the garlic and sauté for 1 minute longer. Turn down the heat to very low.

2 Add the millet and cover the skillet tightly. Let warm over low heat for about 5 minutes. Lift the cover, sprinkle with Tabasco, if using, and incorporate the tomato paste into the millet, folding and stirring (it'll seem kind of clumpy at first, but then will combine nicely). Cover the skillet and let heat through a few minutes more. Serve hot, with any South-of-the-Border–accented beany stew, sauté, or sauce; as an accompaniment for enchiladas; or as is, with a fan of ripe avocado slices over the top.

Rose's Golden Millet "Gruel"

My friend Rose Agostini once helped me put together a brunch for a thousand people at the historic Decatur House in Washington, D.C., at the first presidential inauguration of former Dairy Hollow House guest Bill Clinton. I cooked; Rose decorated. She brought the tablecloths with her from Dallas, and buckets for the flowers, and her husband, Doug, who capered up and down ladders helping Ned hang quilts and bunches of herbs. This is what you want in a friend: loyalty, imagination, hard work (and big fun).

This Golden Millet "Gruel" (as Rose's daughter, Erica, affectionately calls this dish) is one of Rose's favorite at-home dishes. It wouldn't be Rose Food if it wasn't colorful, and here the scheme is yellow: pale gold millet, sun-yellow summer squash, deep golden curry powder. Tahini adds a rich, creamy depth of flavor.

Try this with a simple broccoli-tofu stir-fry. Or, for a slightly more elaborate, divine dinner, serve it with Rose's Cabbage Rose (page 721) and either Tempeh Tejas with a Sweet-Hot Jalapeño Glaze (page 643) or Stir-Fry of Tempeh and Green Beans with an Apricot-Mustard Glaze (page 646). **MAKES 3½ TO 3¾ CUPS**

1 cup millet, well rinsed and very well drained
1¾ cups spring or filtered water, or vegetable stock (see page 139)
½ teaspoon sea salt
1 tablespoon mild curry powder, or 1 to 2 teaspoons hot curry powder
2 to 3 golden summer squashes, trimmed, halved lengthwise, and sliced crosswise into ¼-inch half-circles
1 to 2 tablespoons tahini

1 Over medium heat, in an ungreased cast-iron skillet, toast the millet, stirring frequently, until lightly fragrant but not browned, 2 to 3 minutes (if the millet is still very damp from rinsing, it might take 7 to 9 minutes). When it gives off its toasty fragrance and skitters around the pan, remove it from the heat.

2 In a pot with a tight-fitting lid, bring the water or stock, salt, and curry powder to a boil. You may need to whisk the curry powder in so that it doesn't lump. Stir in the toasted millet. Return to a boil, then turn down the heat to a simmer. Pop the lid on the pot and cook until the millet is partially tender, about 10 minutes.

3 Lift the lid and add the yellow squash. Cover again and continue cooking until all liquid is absorbed and the squash is tender, 8 to 10 minutes more. Remove from the heat and drizzle the tahini over the mixture. Let the pot stand, covered, for about 5 minutes. Fluff with a fork, combining the squash and tahini with the millet, and serve.

Millet Mash with Cauliflower

This simple combination is astonishingly good—somewhat akin to a light, flavorful, fluffy mashed potato, yet with its own personality, and far more delicious than you could imagine from reading the recipe (which admittedly sounds peculiar). It is both vegetal and home-comfortingly starchy, but the mysterious and subtle toasty popcorn flavor of the millet is what takes it over the top. Another plus is that it takes almost no fat to get there—although I love from-scratch mashed potatoes, I think they take quite a bit of butter and neufchâtel and milk to reach swooningly good excellence.

If I knew who came up with the idea of mashing moist-style millet, I'd give them credit. The bright idea of mashing cauliflower into the millet, though, belongs, as far as I know, to natural foods chef Ron Pickarski, who gives a somewhat more complex version of this recipe in his book *Friendly Foods.*

This is sublime with a nice dark mushroom gravy spooned over it. **SERVES 4 TO 6**

2½ to 3 cups Basic Moist-Style Millet (page 547), warm or hot
½ large head cauliflower, broken into florets and steamed until quite tender, hot
1 teaspoon olive oil
Salt and loads of freshly ground black pepper to taste
Cooking spray

1. Combine all the ingredients, and either buzz in a food processor or mash with a potato masher until fairly smooth and creamy. (The processor will get it quite smooth; the potato masher will leave some texture. Both methods are good, but I prefer hand-mashing.)

2. If the mixture is fairly warm, serve. Otherwise, reheat it in a large nonstick skillet, or one that has been sprayed with cooking spray, over medium-low heat. Keep the skillet covered but lift the lid from time to time to stir, until the mixture is piping hot.

Full Moon Pumpkin Pilaf with Toasted Millet

VARIATION

Rinse a handful of frozen peas in a strainer under very hot water, just to thaw them. Toss them into the pilaf before fluffing the millet—very pretty.

Slightly sweet, rich from the coconut milk, this pale-orange-tinted millet—in which carrot juice is the secret ingredient—is nice with a Thai-influenced stir-fry, one that veers toward spicy or sweet (or both). Even with reduced-fat coconut milk, it is not a light dish, but it is worth it. **SERVES 4 TO 6**

- **2 cups millet, well rinsed and very well drained**
- **2¾ cups carrot juice**
- **1¼ cups reduced-fat coconut milk**
- **1 very small pie pumpkin or kabocha squash, or 1 medium butternut squash, peeled, seeded, and cut into ½-inch cubes (2 to 2½ cups)**
- **1 teaspoon salt**
- **1 stick cinnamon**

1 Over medium heat, in an ungreased cast-iron skillet, toast the millet, stirring frequently, until lightly fragrant but not browned, 2 to 3 minutes. Remove from the heat.

2 In a pot with a tight-fitting lid, bring the carrot juice and coconut milk to a boil. Drop in the pumpkin or squash, add the salt and cinnamon stick, and return to a boil. Stir in the toasted millet. Return to a boil, then turn down the heat to a simmer. Pop the lid on the pot and cook until the millet and squash are both tender and all liquid is absorbed, 15 to 20 minutes. Let the millet stand, uncovered, for 5 minutes, then fluff and serve.

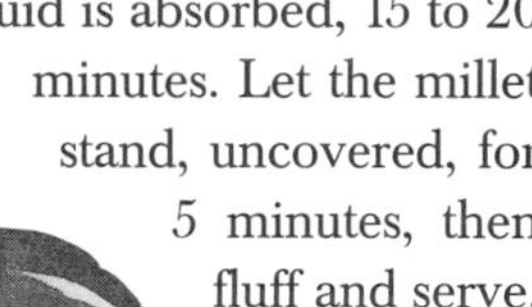

Devoted to Oats

All whole grains have in common a composition of starch, bran, and germ; although textures and flavors vary from grain to grain, all grains are rather plain if served unadorned (the very quality that makes them satisfying bases for full-flavored sauces and stews). But beyond this common ground, cooks and eaters venturing into whole-grain territory discover how idiosyncratic each grain variety is. Oats, the fourth most widely grown grain worldwide (after wheat, corn, and rice), have all these factors in common with other grains—especially individuality.

Consider this: Integral to the oat is a natural chemical that acts as a preservative. This gives oats, and foods made from oats, a resistance to spoilage and rancidity and thus a longer shelf life—all additive-free. What this means is that the whole oat, one of the slower-to-cook grains, can be processed to make a more quickly cooked cut-oat product (such as rolled oats, more commonly known as oatmeal, or Scotch oats) that keeps very well. So, while your basic supermarket corn or wheat product has been degerminated and refined, your basic supermarket oatmeal is the oat, the whole oat, and nothing but the oat.

A good thing, too: Oats are rich in seven B-vitamins, vitamin E, and nine minerals, the ever-needed calcium among them; it's higher in protein than corn or wheat, too. Oat bran, of course, is much touted for its cholesterol-lowering soluble fiber. Besides its healthful properties, soluble fiber gives the oat some interesting culinary traits: the uniquely oat ability to create a smooth, thick, almost creamy texture. This texture arises strictly from the fibers' solubility in liquid, and it is what makes oat "milk" by far the superior of the grain-based nondairy "milks" (like soy and rice) with a truly creamy, delicious mouthfeel. Based on this texture, several oat-based products have been developed as fat replacements; some of the large dairy companies are starting to add oat fiber to skim milk, because it tastes richer. This distinction enables oats to be used successfully in dishes like the "p'oatages" such as the "P'oatage" of Asparagus, White Wine, and Lemon (page 161)—creamy without a drop of dairy cream. Yes, yes, I know it's improbable—but have I led you astray so far?

Even if new oat-based foodstuffs are being invented as we speak, oats themselves are an old grain, originally treated by the ancients as a pesky weed with some medicinal uses, then coming into widespread use as a food for humans and animals around two thousand years ago. Although oats will grow almost anywhere (the colloquialism "sowing one's wild oats" is probably related to the plant's promiscuous ability to make itself at home in a variety of habitats), they do especially well in cooler climates. Hence their wide acceptance throughout the British Isles, especially, of course, Scotland (as Samuel Johnson's infamous dictionary entry of 1755 puts it: "OATS. A grain which in England is generally given to horses, but in Scotland supports the people").

Given all these available forms of oat, given the oat's tastiness, versatility, and healthfulness, it is downright discouraging to learn that less than 5 percent of all the oats grown worldwide are fed to people—the rest go to animals. Here are some ways to experience "h'oat" cuisine.

"I am one who eats his breakfast gazing at morning glories."

—Basho

Basic Whole-Grain Oats (Oat Groats)

Like most whole grains, oats are enclosed in an outer husk—actually, two. When oat kernels are processed for human consumption, they are cleaned, lightly toasted, then husked. It is in this state—almost entire and highly nutritious—that the brown, elongated kernels arrive at your local natural foods store, to be carried to your kitchen.

Basic cooked oats are softer than kamut or wheat berries, moister and less fluffy than millet and most rices. Their texture—a distinct "tooth" which surrounds a melting core, both soft and chewy—is probably most similar to barley. As such, cooked whole-grain oats make a great addition to any mixed grain salad or pilaf, as well as being good supporting players on their own. **SERVES 4 TO 6**

2 cups plus 2 tablespoons liquid (spring or filtered water, vegetable stock, see page 139, or milk)
1 teaspoon salt
1 cup whole-grain oats

Bring the liquid and salt to a boil. Drop in the oats, stir once or twice, and return to a boil. Immediately turn down the heat to a low simmer and cover. Cook, covered, for about 50 minutes, or until the liquid is absorbed and the oats are tender.

Oats It Is

Fluffier Whole Oats: *This method of oat-cooking is perfect for oats that are to be used in a grain salad. Follow the directions above, but cook for only 15 minutes. Then turn off the heat and let stand, covered, for about 50 minutes. I am grateful to Jane Brody for introducing me to this method in her* Good Food Book.

Pressure-Cooked Whole Oats: *Bring the liquid to a boil in a pressure cooker with salt and an additional ingredient—1 teaspoon mild vegetable oil, such as corn, canola, or peanut (the oil prevents foaming as the grains cook, which can cause the pressure valve to clog). Stir in the whole oats and lock the lid down. Cook under high pressure for 20 minutes, then allow the pressure to release naturally. Let stand for 5 minutes, unlock the lid, and serve.*

Steel-Cut or Scotch Oats for Breakfast Porridge

These are whole-grain oats that are cooked partially by steam, cut into small, coarse bits (by steel-bladed machinery), and dehydrated, which reduces their cooking time to 30 minutes. Because most steel-cut oats are imported from Ireland or Scotland, they are expensive as grains go—but devotees will have no other. Steel-cut oats make an exceptional breakfast cereal, with a pleasing, slightly granular texture quite unlike conventional oatmeal. (My Aunt Dot's longtime friend Jim Cherry eats steel-cut oats virtually every morning. Into his nineties, he played squash several times a week; he still practices law. What does that tell you about the regenerative power of this particular cereal?)

Although this recipe may make more than you'll eat at a single breakfast, you can't scale back the recipe successfully—because the cooking is so protracted, it's hard to cook in a small quantity. But never fear. Leftover porridge is an excellent addition to bread. And Jim Cherry makes a big batch at the start of the week, then reheats it as the days pass, cutting off a chunk of the cold solidified oatmeal and simmering it in a little boiling water. You can do likewise. **MAKES ABOUT 4 CUPS**

NOTE

I highly recommend using a heavy, good-quality nonstick pot to cook these in—or use the double-boiler or thermos methods that follow. Steel-cut oats are slow-cooking, and they want to stick near the end if your pot is too thin or distributes heat unevenly.

4 cups water, preferably spring or filtered
½ teaspoon salt
1 cup steel-cut oats

Bring the water to a boil with the salt in a large, heavy pot, preferably nonstick. Stir in the steel-cut oats and let the water return to a boil, then turn down to a very low simmer. Cook for about 30 minutes, stirring often, or until the porridge is thick and tender. Serve with any of the porridge fixings you like (see the box on page 557).

Double-boiler method: If time is not an issue, this is probably the most delicious way to cook these, and pretty close to foolproof. Cook the oats in the top pot of a double boiler, placed directly on the stove-top, stirring, for 5 to 8 minutes only, just until the porridge begins to thicken. Meanwhile, pour an inch of water into the bottom of the double boiler and bring it to a simmer. Transfer the pot with the oats to its upper position and cook, half-covered, for 40 to 45 minutes, stirring from time to time, until the oats are tender and the porridge is very thick.

Thermos method: The truly hassle-free way to have great hot cereal in the morning—provided you're a plan-ahead kind of person. Combine the oats, salt, and boiling water in a large thermos the night before. Close the thermos. Shake a few times. Next morning, open the thermos. Voila! Cooked steel-cuts.

Oatmeal, the Old-Fashioned Way

This is the oatmeal we all know and love—widely available, easily made, quickly cooked. It's manufactured by taking steamed whole oats, flattening them with a roller, and flaking them.

I have grown to like my oats creamier, so I start them off in cold water. If you prefer yours more distinct, just bring the water to a boil first before sprinkling in the oatmeal. Do not use "quick-cooking" oatmeal (which is merely even more flattened-out "regular" oatmeal; it loses texture in the process) or instant (which is tiny flakes of precooked, then dehydrated oatmeal to which you just add water—and which to me is flavorless and textureless—a poor excuse for the real thing). **SERVES 4**

4 cups liquid (spring or filtered water, milk, or part juice and part water)
2 cups rolled oats (regular cooking oatmeal)
½ teaspoon salt

1 In a heavy saucepan, preferably nonstick, combine the liquid, oats, and salt. Bring to a boil, reduce the heat, and cook, stirring occasionally. Although some recipes tell you to cover the pot, I never do.

2 Cook for 5 to 10 minutes, or until oatmeal reaches your preferred consistency.

Gussied-up Oatmeal

OATMEAL À LA HIPPIE: *I know how improbable this sounds, but in cold weather, particularly at stressful times, I get an overwhelming craving for this for days at a time. Up until now, I have only shared, I mean confessed, the recipe to a few trusted friends, because it's the kind of thing that could get you branded a nutcase in certain culinary circles. But let me tell you—everyone I've introduced to it loves it as much as I do.*

Here's what it is: Cooked oatmeal *(in water, nothing fancy), with a teeny chip of butter, a splash of tamari or shoyu soy sauce, a good sprinkle of nutritional yeast, and another of grated Parmesan.*

CAROLYN MORGAN'S GREAT PEANUT BUTTER OATMEAL: *In writing about several other breakfast cereal grains, I have mentioned the goodness of nut butter stirred in at the last. This was taught to me, in this manner, by the one and only Carolyn Morgan—wisecracking, irreverent, great mom to three boys, a former inn dairymaid and waitress, thin as a rail but with enough attitude to supply a herd of elephants.*

Cook the oatmeal in a mixture of half water, half apple juice. When it's almost done, stir in 2 tablespoons natural, nonhydrogenated peanut butter, pulled into small chunks. Serve, preferably with a sprinkling of real maple sugar or a judicious pour of maple syrup.

There are many tasty variations on this theme. Peanut butter also works deliciously with oatmeal cooked in half 2% milk and half water. Or, try other nut butter–juice combos: Natural, unsweetened apricot or peach nectar, mixed half and half with spring water, with a spoonful or two of almond butter, is food for earthy gods and goddesses. Or use pineapple juice and water as a cooking liquid, add cashew butter at the end, and serve hot with a topping of sliced bananas and a sprinkle of brown sugar.

CREAMY CAROLYN-STYLE PEANUT BUTTER OATMEAL: *Many tasty variations and enrichments can be rung on Carolyn's idea. Instead of fruit juice, for instance, try cooking the oatmeal in half water, half 2% milk or vanilla soy milk.*

SCHEHERAZADE'S ARABIAN-NIGHTS-IN-THE-MORNING OATMEAL: *Cook the oatmeal in equal parts spring or filtered water and unsweetened apricot juice. Instead of peanut butter, stir in any of the following: toasted tahini, toasted almond butter, or toasted pistachio nut butter. Instead of maple syrup, top with sliced medjool dates, and/or a dab of fruit-only apricot preserves.*

OATMEAL ALOHA: *Cook the oatmeal in equal parts spring or filtered water and unsweetened pineapple, or pineapple-coconut juice. Instead of peanut butter, stir in cashew butter at the end. The topping? Sliced bananas, perhaps diced fresh pineapple, a sprinkle of brown sugar.*

THE HOT CEREAL BAR: *If you need to make breakfast for a number of people inexpensively but well, try this trick, which I've seen employed at two of my favorite inns: The Swag, in Waynesboro, North Carolina, and The Inn at Brandywine Falls, in Sagamore, Ohio. Make a double or triple batch of any simple oatmeal and put the cooked oatmeal in a slow-cooker turned to low. Place the plugged-in cooker on an attractive sideboard, equipped with a ladle, bowls, and dishes of as many good topping things—each with its own spoon—as you can think of: dried fruits (diced dates, dried cranberries, blueberries, and raisins), sweet toppings (maple sugar or syrup, brown sugar, honey), dairy or quasi-dairy delights (yogurt, sour cream or sour half-and-half, little pitchers of milk and cream, butter, Tofu Sour Cream, page 909, soy milk), nut butters, sliced bananas, sliced fresh strawberries, diced fresh pears and/or apples, granola, chopped toasted nuts. Bountiful, fun, diverse, and easy on the cook (and her budget).*

OATMEAL PUDDING: *We don't usually think of oatmeal as dessert except in cookies or as a topping for crisps, but leftover cooked oatmeal can also replace the rice in any rice pudding, including the wild rice pudding on page 1057.*

VARIATION

SAVORY-STYLE ETHEREAL BUTTERMILK-OATMEAL PANCAKES ***are so good. It's amazing we don't use pancakes outside of breakfast more often in this country. Leave the pancake batter as is or add a tablespoon of finely minced Italian parsley. Then, as the oatmeal soaks, make a simple stir-fry of onions and carrots; maybe add broccoli. When the vegetables are done, stir in ¾ cup or so cooked or canned azuki or kidney beans. Cook the pancakes as directed, then serve with the savory vegetables ladled over or between the pancakes. What do you pass instead of maple syrup? Why, tamari or shoyu soy sauce, of course! Or maybe—just maybe—salsa, grated cheese, and yogurt, Yogurt Sour Cream (page 910), or Tofu Sour Cream (page 909).***

Ethereal Buttermilk-Oatmeal Pancakes

Oatmeal the porridge is everyday stuff. But *this* is oatmeal in a Sunday-morning guise, and quite heavenly. While one doesn't think of oatmeal or buckwheat as light, these featherweights nearly hover above the plate. They're fairly light fat-wise, too—no added oil, just two eggs—and they cook to perfection on a good-quality nonstick skillet; no need for oil or cooking spray to get a just-right, evenly browned cake every time. Much of the pancakes' ethereality rests on separating the egg white and folding it in, soufflé-style. Don't skip this step; accept that these do not lend themselves to a vegan variation.

Though delicate and airy, these cakes have tooth and substance; to paraphrase Gertrude Stein, there's a *there* there. This recipe makes a generous amount, but trust me, it'll all get eaten. The batter does keep in the refrigerator for a couple of days (and can be re-etherialized by folding in another stiffly beaten egg white or two), but it's best immediately after mixing.

Of course you can serve these in the time-honored breakfast manner, with butter and maple syrup and maybe sliced fresh strawberries, and they're also wonderful with mashed bananas or fresh blueberries folded into the batter—but why not try serving them some Sunday evening, savory-style (see variation), for a memorable supper?

MAKES 20 TO 22 PANCAKES; SERVES 4

2 to 2½ cups buttermilk
¾ cup rolled oats (regular cooking oatmeal)
¼ cup buckwheat flour
¼ cup whole wheat flour
½ cup unbleached white all-purpose flour
½ teaspoon salt
1 teaspoon baking powder
½ teaspoon baking soda
2 large eggs, separated
Sweet or savory accompaniments

1 In a medium bowl, pour 2 cups of the buttermilk over the oatmeal and let stand for 30 minutes. Stir in the buckwheat,

whole wheat, and white flours, along with the salt, baking powder, baking soda (put these through a sifter or strainer if they're at all lumpy), and egg yolks. If the batter seems very thick, add the remaining buttermilk, 1/4 cup at a time.

2 In a smaller bowl, preferably one with high sides, beat the egg whites until very stiff. Fold them gently into the batter with only as many strokes as necessary to combine.

3 Over medium-high heat, heat a nonstick skillet, or one that has been sprayed with cooking spray, then lower the heat to medium. Drop spoonfuls of batter in and cook until bubbles appear, 2 to 3 minutes (the top side will appear a little wetter than is typical for pancakes at this phase; don't worry). Flip the cakes over and cook for another 2 to 3 minutes.

4 Serve hot from the grill, accompanied by whatever pleases you.

Buttermilk-Oatmeal Whole Wheat Rolls with a Salt-Honey Glaze

The zing of buttermilk works magic with oats just as deliciously in rolls as it does in the previous pancakes. These make a perfect Sunday-dinner or Thanksgiving type of roll—a little rich, slightly fancy. They are nice and light, but still (thanks to the oatmeal and the whole wheat flour) have some satisfying tooth to them. The salty-sweet glaze, brushed on in the last few minutes of baking and then sprinkled with a bit of oatmeal, is addictive, and gives the oatmeal a rustic charm.

The buttermilk will curdle when you scald it, but this is to be expected and will in no way hurt these delicious rolls. If you should have leftovers—a virtually unknown occurrence—these are exquisite in Chocolate Bread Pudding Maurice (page 1059) or any of the savory bread puddings beginning on page 283. **MAKES 2 DOZEN ROLLS**

VARIATIONS

VEGAN "BUTTERMILK"-OATMEAL WHOLE WHEAT ROLLS WITH A SALT-HONEY GLAZE: *Omit the egg and make the following substitutions: Instead of honey, use Rapidura or rice syrup or barley-malt syrup; instead of butter, use canola oil or margarine; instead of buttermilk, use 1½ cups plain, unflavored soy milk plus 1 tablespoon lemon juice or cider vinegar (this supplies the tart tang buttermilk adds). For the glaze, omit the egg, and use rice syrup or barley-malt syrup plus margarine.*

SCALLIONED BUTTERMILK-OATMEAL WHOLE WHEAT ROLLS WITH A SALT-HONEY GLAZE: *A simple but amazingly good modification: Knead ¾ to 1 cup chopped scallions into the dough—this is 1 to 2 bunches scallions, trimmed, all the white and 3 inches of the green sliced.*

DOUGH

1 cup rolled oats (regular cooking oatmeal)
1¼ cups buttermilk
2 tablespoons plus 1 teaspoon honey
1 tablespoon butter
2 teaspoons salt
1 package (2½ tablespoons) dry yeast
½ cup warm water, preferably spring or filtered
1 large egg
3½ cups whole wheat flour (regular or bread flour, not pastry flour)
2½ to 3½ cups unbleached white all-purpose flour
Cooking spray

SWEET-SALTY GLAZE AND FINISH

1 tablespoon butter
2 tablespoons honey
1½ teaspoons salt
1 large egg, beaten
1 to 2 tablespoons rolled oats

1 Put the oatmeal in a large heatproof bowl. Bring the buttermilk to a boil in a small saucepan, then pour it over the oatmeal in the bowl. Stir in 2 tablespoons of the honey, the butter, and the salt. Let stand for 10 to 15 minutes, or until the mixture reaches room temperature.

2 Meanwhile, in a small bowl or glass measuring cup, dissolve the yeast in the warm water with the remaining teaspoon honey. Let stand for 5 minutes, or until bubbly. When the oatmeal mixture is no longer hot, beat in the egg, then stir in the yeast mixture, along with the whole wheat flour and 2½ cups of the unbleached flour, stirring until it begins to hold together and pull away from the sides of the bowl.

3 Dust your kneading surface well with some of the remaining unbleached flour and turn the dough out onto the floured area. Knead until the dough comes together, adding only enough of the flour to keep the dough from sticking. Let the dough rest for a few minutes while you wash out the dough bowl, dry it, and spritz it with cooking spray. Return to the dough, and continue kneading it for 5 to 8 minutes, or until it's springy, elastic, and doesn't want to stick to you or the kneading surface. Form it into a ball and place it in the bowl. Let rise, covered loosely with a clean kitchen towel, in a warm, nondrafty place, for about 1½ hours, or until doubled in bulk.

4 Punch down the risen dough (it will sigh), and turn it out onto the kneading surface. Let it rest for 5 minutes, then divide it into 24 even pieces. Have ready 2 nonstick, 9-inch square or round baking pans, or ones that have been sprayed with cooking spray. Roll each piece of dough into a nice ball and place it in the pans. Cover and let rise a second time, again until doubled—this time it will take 45 minutes to 1 hour. Toward the last 20 minutes of this second rising time, preheat the oven to 400°F.

5 When the rolls are ready they will have risen so that they are touching each other. Lower the temperature to 375°F and pop them in the oven. Bake for 12 to 15 minutes, or until the rolls are firm to the touch but not yet all the way done. They will have started to color a little bit here and there, but should still be relatively pale.

6 As the rolls bake, prepare the glaze: In a small saucepan, heat the butter, honey, and salt together. When the butter melts

and the honey has thinned, remove from the heat. Let cool for a few minutes, then whisk in the beaten egg.

7 Brush the glaze liberally over the partially baked rolls, then sprinkle with the oatmeal. Return the pans to the oven and bake for another 5 to 8 minutes, or until the rolls are deeply golden, and the oats of the topping are slightly toasted. Serve, preferably still warm from the oven.

Radical Departure Grown-up Granola

How fondly I remembered homemade granolas of my youth, but how high in fat and sugar they were. What could be done?

The method I came up with is a radical departure. The grains get a pretoasting, a light spritz of oil, and more toasting, followed by a modest bath of sweetness. The result: a low-fat, interesting granola in which the nutty, grainy taste comes through, enhanced but not overpowered by sweetness. Enough nuts, seeds, and coconut are left to make it satisfying; the oil is almost gone, and—surprise!—whole wheat breadcrumbs make an appearance. It's subtle, truly wonderful; granola for grown-ups. Like other homemade granolas, however, making it is labor-intensive, requiring stirring every 10 minutes or so. Expect it to take a while; count on giving it attention—not constant, but periodic.

I make this in a nonstick Circulon baking dish, 12 by 18 inches, and the times I give are based on this. If you have only smaller pans, you might divide the recipe in half, or play with the cooking times (the thicker the layer of grains, the longer it will take to cook) but you still have to stir at 10-minute intervals. If your pan is not nonstick, be sure to spray it with cooking spray before beginning. **MAKES ABOUT 3 QUARTS**

½ cup sesame seeds
5 cups rolled oats (regular cooking oatmeal)
½ cup shredded unsweetened coconut
1 cup whole wheat flour
½ cup wheat or oat bran
½ cup wheat germ
2 cups soft, coarse breadcrumbs, torn from whole wheat or oatmeal bread
1 to 2 cups nuts or seeds, coarsely chopped (I'd go for ½ cup almonds, and ½ cup raw cashews; or add some sunflower seeds)
Cooking spray (optional)
About 1 tablespoon canola or other mild vegetable oil from a sprayer
1 cup pure maple syrup
¼ cup honey
½ cup thawed, undiluted frozen apple juice concentrate
2 teaspoons pure vanilla extract
1 cup dried fruits (optional; I go for diced medjool dates)

1 Preheat the oven to 350°F. In a small, dry skillet, toast the sesame seeds over medium heat, stirring or shaking constantly, until they become fragrant, start to darken in color, and begin popping—3 to 5 minutes. Remove from the heat and pour into a food processor; pulse on and off repeatedly until seeds are broken up into a coarse powder.

2 In a large bowl, combine the ground seeds with the oats, coconut, whole wheat flour, bran, wheat germ, breadcrumbs, and nuts, tossing together well to mix. Sprinkle this over a large nonstick baking pan or one that has been sprayed with cooking spray. Use the largest pan that will fit in your oven; the larger the pan, the quicker the toasting.

3 Lower the oven temperature to 300°F. Bake for about 15 minutes. Remove from the oven, stir well, and bake for another 15 minutes. Spray with canola oil and stir well. Return to the oven for another 10 minutes. (Note: After the oil's been sprayed on, the mix will start to brown much more quickly.)

4 In a saucepan, combine the maple syrup, honey, concentrate, and vanilla. Heat over medium heat until the syrups thin. After the granola has baked for the last 10 minutes, drizzle this mixture over it, tossing well using two wooden spoons. The liquid will hiss as it hits the hot pan through the hot grains, and it will seem to clump and not be distributed evenly—don't worry, just keep tossing until it's reasonably well mixed.

5 Return to the oven, and bake for another 10 minutes. Check to see how brown it is, stirring well. You want it golden and toasty, but not too dark. It may need 10 or even 20 more minutes, or it may be ready to come out (much depends on the moisture content of the grains and bread, the accuracy of the oven, and whether the oven has hot spots).

6 Remove from the oven, stir in the optional dried fruit, and let cool completely before putting up in jars or tins. It gets crisper and crisper as it cools. This keeps nearly indefinitely if refrigerated—and if you don't eat it all up!

Pilaf of Oats with Ginger and Jalapeño

From considerations of oats in various breakfast items or baked goods, we move to one last use. The idea of an oatmeal pilaf may astonish; you will not believe how light and, yes, fluffy oatmeal can be when prepared as a pilaf. Toasting the rolled oat flakes before cooking, and using a much smaller amount of liquid than usual, makes all the difference.

But this concept tweaks accepted oatmeal beliefs in other ways, too, defying not just the texture but the soothingly bland taste. Here, instead, are wide-awake, bright flavors, mostly South Indian in origin: black mustard seeds, ginger, and green chile. The tomatoes cooked with the grain here are straight out of the Central American/Spanish rice mixtures we all know and love. The combination is astonishingly good—most palates will take to it at once, and return to it over and over.

Serve with a simple stir-fry of mushrooms and greens or broccoli, a little savory baked tofu added at the end, or with a not-too-elaborate curry, or with Dal (page 609). **SERVES 4**

1 cup rolled oats (regular cooking oatmeal)
Cooking spray
1 to 2½ teaspoons mild vegetable oil, such as corn, canola, or peanut
2 teaspoons black mustard seeds
1 onion, diced
1 jalapeño pepper, diced
1 tablespoon peeled, diced ginger
1 cup canned crushed tomatoes with garlic, with the juice
1½ cups water, preferably spring or filtered
1 teaspoon salt

1 Place the oats in a nonstick or ungreased skillet and toast them over medium heat, stirring constantly, for about 3 minutes, or until aromatic and slightly browned. Pour into a bowl and set aside, leaving the heat on.

2 If you aren't using nonstick cookware, spray the skillet with cooking spray. Add the oil to the skillet and heat. When it's hot, add the mustard seeds and heat for about 3 minutes, stirrring constantly, until they

pop. Add the onion and stir-fry for 2 minutes. Add the jalapeño and ginger and stir-fry for about 1 minute more. Then add the tomatoes, water, and salt.

3 Bring to a boil, then stir in the toasted oats. Reduce the heat to a simmer and cook, covered, until the oats have absorbed most of the liquid, about 10 minutes. Let the skillet stand, covered, for 10 minutes, then serve.

Ginger

Keenly Quinoa

Quinoa (pronounced KEEN-wah) is one of the ancient grains. The Incas might have been quite surprised to imagine the small staple seed they called "the mother grain" growing today in the Colorado Rockies and transported not just to natural foods stores but also to hip, pricy, restaurants such as . . . well, I could name names, but quinoa will be here long after restaurants have come and gone.

Quinoa is very tasty, with a unique flavor that has sweet corn notes combined with a wonderful texture—soft, but with bits of pleasing crunch, and an endearing shape like a white-edged star when cooked. It's extraordinarily quick-cooking as whole grains go, gluten-free, and possesses a dazzling nutritional profile.

Quinoa is higher in protein than any other grain—about 16.2 percent of the grain is made up of protein (millet has 9.9 percent, rice has 7.5, and wheat 1.4). Moreover, this is protein of an exceptionally high quality. It's high in the amino acids lysine, cystine, and methionine, which corn and the otherwise near-perfect soyfoods (soybeans, tempeh, tofu) are low in. Some vitamin C, some niacin, an impressive amount of B-6, a goodly portion of calcium, magnesium, and iron, a little fat, plus the much-needed fiber that all whole grains deliver, add up to a powerful package gift-wrapped in this tiny star-shaped seed. Perhaps it's this that makes it one of the most highly satisfying grains around. It takes a much larger portion of rice or pasta than quinoa to make me feel full.

As those of you who have gardened organically know, one of the first lines of defense is spraying vegetables with harmless compounds that are not to bugs' liking, such as garlic-and-hot-pepper spray or soapy water. Clever quinoa, in effect, doses itself with the latter in the form of self-emitted saponins, soaplike plant compounds that coat the grains and make the plant resistant to insect invasion—and hence, relatively easy to grow without pesticides. What the saponins mean to the cook, however, is that the grains must be thoroughly washed and rinsed in a sieve held under running water. Five or six rinses, with serious swishing each time, will remove the saponins. You can also partially submerge the sieve of quinoa in a larger bowl of cold water and "bounce" the quinoa up and down, as Lorna Sass says, changing the water several times, until it is completely clear.

Although quinoa is perfectly fine as a basic foundation for fancily sauced stews, stir-fries, and sautés, it has enough character that I often use it as a pilaf or marinated salad—something main-dishy. In that line, don't miss the Quinoa, Corn, and Buckwheat Noodle Salad (page 115).

Basic Quinoa

Unadorned but appealing. I love the tiny stars it makes. **SERVES 4**

1 cup quinoa
2 cups water, preferably spring or filtered
½ teaspoon salt

1 Place the quinoa in a fine-mesh sieve and rinse thoroughly several times, swishing the grains with your hand. Drain well.

2 Bring the water and salt to a boil in a saucepan and drop in the washed, drained quinoa. Stir once and let the water return to a boil. Lower the heat to a simmer, cover, and cook for 12 to 16 minutes, or until the water is absorbed and the individual grains have turned translucent, bordered by the white germ, making tiny little stars if you look closely.

3 Turn off the heat and let stand for a few minutes. Fluff and serve.

VARIATION

TOASTED QUINOA: ***Unlike millet, which positively requires pan-toasting to be at its best, quinoa's flavor is plenty good as is. Still, it does gain an extra dimension when pan-toasted. After washing and draining, place it in a dry cast-iron or nonstick skillet and toast, stirring frequently, over medium heat, until it is slightly more golden in color, more aromatic, and making a popping, crackling sound (about 3 minutes). Then proceed as for basic quinoa.***

Gussied-up Quinoa

- ▲ *Add a handful of frozen corn kernels, or fresh kernels, cut off the cob, in the last 3 minutes of cooking. Toss well and serve.*
- ▲ *Try the above, but add grated Cheddar, a little minced green chile or a touch of cayenne, and some minced cilantro. Serve with a simple dish of beans.*
- ▲ *Add a tablespoon of tahini and a teaspoon of toasted sesame oil to the quinoa pot in the last few minutes of cooking. Grill or broil some slices of fresh pineapple (brush 'em first with tamari, oil, and honey) and dice them when they come off the grill; toss into the sesame quinoa, along with a little diced savory baked tofu or tempeh. (Alternatively, and way easier if less tasty, use drained juice-packed canned pineapple chunks straight from the can.) Finish with a sprinkle of chopped cilantro or mint.*

VARIATION

THREE-GRAIN QUICK-COOK SIMPLE PILAF WITH PUMPKIN AND PUMPKIN SEEDS: ***Tamari-roasted pumpkin seeds are available at natural foods stores. Crisp, salty-savory, they are addictive, and high in essential fatty acids. They add a nice contrast to the pilaf, especially when it's embellished with onion and some of the sweet pumpkin itself. Heat a tablespoon of olive oil in a nonstick skillet or one that has been sprayed with cooking spray. Over medium heat, sauté 1 diced red onion until partially softened but not browned. Add about 1 cup diced, peeled pumpkin or butternut squash, and sauté for 1 minute more. Add the water for cooking the quinoa to the skillet and, when it boils, add the grains and cook, covered, as in the recipe. When the grains are done, sprinkle with tamari-roasted pumpkin seeds.***

Three-Grain Quick-Cook Simple Pilaf

Three whole grains cook together and are done in the same amount of time—15 minutes—giving the lie to the "But whole grains take too long cook" line. This is simple, intended as a rather plain accompaniment for your favorite gravied or sauced main dish. As with all grains or grain mixtures, though, you can always fancy it up by adding sautéed onions, mushrooms, and so on, or by cooking the grain in stock, or stock and tomato juice. You can substitute buckwheat for cracked wheat if you like, toasting it with the millet. **SERVES 6**

3 cups water, preferably spring or filtered
1 teaspoon salt
½ cup millet, toasted (see page 546)
½ cup quinoa, rinsed and toasted
½ cup cracked wheat

Bring the water to a boil with the salt. Stir in the toasted millet, quinoa, and cracked wheat. Return to a boil, then lower the heat to just barely simmering. Cover tightly and cook for 15 to 20 minutes, or until all the water has been absorbed. Let the grains stand for 5 to 10 minutes, covered, then fluff and serve.

Spice-Infused Quinoa

One of the simplest ways to get flavor into any grain is to cook it in a savory liquid. Here, whole spices are steeped in water or another liquid, then strained out; the resulting infusion is used to cook the quinoa. Optional fresh herbs can be tossed in at the last for further enhancement. Try this under any curry, or with a simple stir-fry of vegetables and tofu. **SERVES 4**

2½ cups water, preferably spring or filtered, or any mild homemade or commercial vegetable stock (see page 139)
½ teaspoon salt
2 bay leaves
5 black peppercorns
1 stick cinnamon, broken in two
2 pieces anise
5 whole cloves
2 cloves garlic, halved
1 cup quinoa
¼ cup finely minced Italian parsley (optional)
¼ cup finely minced fresh mint or cilantro (optional)

1 Bring the water and salt to a boil with all the dry spices and the garlic. Turn the heat down to a simmer and cook, uncovered, for about 30 minutes.

2 As the spices infuse, place the quinoa in a fine-mesh sieve and rinse thoroughly several times, swishing the grains with your hand. Drain well.

3 Strain the infusion and discard the spices and garlic. Measure the infusion. You'll need 2 cups. Add water if you need it, or, if you have a little extra liquid, add it to the sauce of whatever you plan on serving with the quinoa.

4 Bring the infusion back to a boil. Drop the washed, drained quinoa into it. Stir once, and let it return to a boil. Then lower the heat to a simmer, cover, and cook for 12 to 16 minutes, or until the liquid is absorbed and the individual grains have turned translucent, bordered by the white germ, making tiny little stars.

5 Turn off the heat and let stand for a few minutes. If desired, add the herbs. Fluff and serve.

Salad of Quinoa and Roasted Vegetables

An Incan grain meets mostly Mediterranean flavorings, with exceptionally pleasing results—scrumptious roasted garlic, the triple tang of red wine vinegar, tomato, and lemon juice, the sweet of charred red bell pepper—yum. You might think it'd be tabbouleh, but its character is unique. It's malleable, like most grain salads. **SERVES 6 TO 8**

NOTE

Though this makes a fairly large batch, it keeps for several days in the fridge, and it's nice to have on hand to nibble your way through in hot weather. It's also the perfect potluck dish.

VARIATIONS

Add crumbled feta cheese or drained, cooked chickpeas or cannellini beans if you want to make it more main-dishy; grill the vegetables instead of roasting them; add grilled corn, diced cucumber, or a handful of minced Italian parsley. Also, try the dressing with a spelt-barley combo, or rice, or even orzo pasta. Serve this salad on a bed of arugula, or any other greens with character, for a nice summer meal, adding an omelet if you like.

3 tablespoons olive oil
Cooking spray
1 head garlic, unpeeled, top third cut off to expose tops of cloves
1 zucchini, stem removed, cut lengthwise into 4 slices
1 eggplant
1½ cups quinoa
3 cups water, preferably spring or filtered
1 poblano chile, charred, peeled, seeded, and diced
1 red bell pepper, charred, peeled, seeded, and diced
½ cup pitted kalamata olives, chopped
2 plum tomatoes, peeled and seeded, 1 diced
½ teaspoon salt, or to taste
Freshly ground black pepper to taste
Juice of 1 lemon
1 tablespoon red-wine vinegar
Several fresh basil leaves
Several fresh rosemary needles

1 Preheat the oven to 375°F.

2 Put about 2 tablespoons of the oil in a food processor and set aside. Use a little of the remaining oil to rub the cut sides of the garlic and zucchini. Poke the eggplant all over with a fork, but leave whole. Place the garlic, zucchini, and eggplant on a nonstick baking sheet, or one that has been sprayed with cooking spray, and bake for 25 minutes. Remove the zucchini from the sheet and let the eggplant and garlic bake for another 25 minutes, or until the vegetables are very soft. Let the vegetables cool slightly.

3 As the vegetables bake, cook the quinoa in water as described in the basic recipe on page 565, preferably toasting the quinoa first. Place the warm quinoa in a bowl, and add the poblano, red bell pepper, and the olives. Add the diced tomato.

4 Add the whole tomato to the food processor with the oil. Squeeze the cloves of cooked garlic out of the papery skin of the bulb and into the food processor, adding salt, pepper, lemon juice, vinegar, basil, and rosemary. Buzz until smooth—this is your dressing.

5 Chop the cooked zucchini. Peel the eggplant and chop it into pieces, catching any liquid. Add the zucchini, eggplant, and any liquid from chopping to the cooked quinoa. Stir in the dressing. You may serve it warm, but it's even better when left to cool so that the flavors can blend—best the next day.

Incan Quinoa-Corn-Potato Ri-sort-of

A one-dish meal eaten in a bowl, this is a wholly imagined stew, based on the traditional Incan staple foods (quinoa, corn, and potatoes), combined with the traditional American creamy corn and potato chowder and a tiny kick of Southwestern flavors. It is thicker than a chowder, but has many of the same flavor notes and satisfactions. Naturally, I had to try it with Peruvian purple potatoes, just to play with the point—with their exotic coloration and faint sweetness, they are quite wonderful here. However, a combination of any white potato and a bit of sweet potato would also do well.

This is one of those intentionally wet grain preparations, the savory porridges, that sound improbable but really grow on a person. Serve with a crisp salad with vinaigrette, and you have a satisfying meal. **SERVES 4 TO 6**

Cooking spray
1 teaspoon butter (or, for vegans, mild vegetable oil or vegetable margarine)
1 large onion, diced
1 teaspoon cumin seeds
1 poblano chile, diced
3 cups vegetable stock (see page 139)
Salt
3 medium potatoes, preferably Peruvian purple potatoes, peeled and diced into ½-inch cubes
2 carrots, sliced into ¼-inch rounds
1 cup quinoa, thoroughly washed
1 cup corn, frozen whole-kernel or cut from 2 to 3 cobs
1 cup whole or low-fat milk, evaporated skim milk, or unflavored soy milk
Freshly ground black pepper to taste
Minced Italian parsley
Minced cilantro
Grated jack cheese (optional)
Sour half-and-half, Yogurt Sour Cream (page 910), or Tofu Sour Cream (page 909) (optional)
Tabasco or similar hot sauce, or cayenne (optional)

1 In a large nonstick soup pot, or one that has been sprayed with cooking spray, heat the butter over medium heat. Add the onion and cumin and sauté, stirring, for 3 to 4 minutes, or until the onion has softened somewhat. Add the poblano and sauté for 3 minutes more. Add the stock, and salt if the stock is unsalted (1 teaspoon, or to taste), and bring to a boil.

2 Drop in the potatoes, carrots, and quinoa. Let the stock return to a boil, stir well, then turn the heat down to a simmer. Cover the pot and simmer over low heat for 10 minutes. Lift the lid and drop in the corn. Cover and cook for 5 minutes more.

3 Turn off the heat. Pour in the milk, stir once, and let stand, covered, for 5 minutes. Spoon into bowls and top with parsley and cilantro. If you like, pass the grated cheese, sour half-and-half, and hot sauce at the table, allowing guests to modify their own dish.

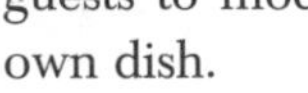

Southwestern Quinoa Tabbouleh

Southwestern flavors—always a natural with quinoa—are used in a tabbouleh-type quinoa preparation: a grainy, delicious main-dish salad. Take it for a picnic, maybe with some grilled-vegetable wraps, and you've got a very nice meal. Once again, I can't resist teaming corn with quinoa. **ABOUT 3¾ CUPS**

1 poblano chile
1 jalepeño pepper
2 ears corn, husked
2½ cups cooked Basic Quinoa (page 565)
1 can (16 ounces) black beans, very well drained and rinsed
2 tomatoes, chopped
Juice of 1 to 2 lemons
1 fist-sized jícama, peeled and diced
2 to 3 scallions, sliced, or ½ red onion, minced
2 to 3 tablespoons extra virgin olive oil
¾ cup finely chopped curly parsley
½ cup finely chopped cilantro
½ cup finely chopped mint
Salt and freshly ground black pepper to taste

1. Preheat the grill to high, then lower the heat to medium. Place the poblano and jalapeño on the grill and roast until the skins blacken, 5 to 7 minutes per side. At the same time, place the corn directly on the grill and grill until the kernels are just colored, 4 to 5 minutes per quarter-turn of the cob. Remove the peppers and corn from the grill. Let the peppers cool in a paper bag; let corn cool sitting out.

2. Place the cooked quinoa in a large bowl. Add the beans, tomatoes, juice of 1 lemon, the jícama, scallions, oil, and herbs.

3. Cut the grilled corn from the cobs and add it to the quinoa bowl. Peel the blackened skin from both peppers. Remove the seeds, fiber, and stems, and dice both peppers. Add the peppers to the quinoa bowl.

4. Toss the ingredients in the bowl together very well, and add salt (it will take a goodly amount) and pepper to taste. Add the juice of the second lemon if needed. Serve, chilled or at room temperature.

Reasons for Rye

"Well, the hardest work that ever I
done was plowin' in a field of rye
And the easiest work that ever I done
was eatin' chicken pie."

Vegetarians will want to reverse the claims made in a song recorded a few decades ago by Ry Cooder. That said, cooking rye does take a *little* work; the kernels of rye, like those of wheat, take a good long time to cook, though the process, as always, can be speeded up by presoaking or with the use of a pressure cooker. But rye is worth the wait. This self-assured grain holds its shape and texture beautifully in grain salads, and is great as a mixer or on its own in pilafs. And its nutritional content is not to be sneezed at.

Americans by far drink more rye—as whiskey—than they eat, but the grain, which grows well under conditions too cold and wet for most other grains, was at one time the main bread grain in Europe, especially northern Europe. The Swedes, Germans, and Russians, and the Jews of these places and many more are all famous for their rye breads, each of which has a distinctive flavor. I'm especially fond of the moist, dense, dark, grainy German rye breads, which are purchased packaged, and which keep very well; I also like the Swedish ryes, with their improbable hint of orange rind (see page 542)—delicious with that equally improbable caramelized Scandinavian cheese, gjetost. And of course, there's good old caraway-dotted Jewish rye (just made for tofu reubens; see page 869).

Rye resembles wheat in appearance; the brown grains are just a bit larger than those of converted rice. Rye also contains a bit of gluten (for more on gluten, see page 494). But rye's overall protein content is higher than that of wheat, as are its phosphorus, potassium, iron, and B-vitamin counts. Pleasantly chewy, with a delicious texture—the individual grains pop, caviarlike, in the mouth—rye's flavor, like many of the slower-cooking grains, is hearty, emphatic, like wheat with attitude. Food writer Elizabeth Schneider, who wrote a three-part article about grains in *Food Arts* magazine, calls rye "an assertive, spunky kernel with a grassy, beany flavor that begs for strong accompaniments and strong flavors." She makes the point that foods that are traditionally served with pumpernickel bread go well with the cooked grain: pickled and smoked foods, onions, cabbage, mustard, beets, raisins.

One extremely important proviso: For rye, ignore the always-cook-more-than-you'll-need suggestion I have made for grains and beans. Rye gets very hard if refrigerated after cooking. For this reason, don't use it in a dish to be served chilled.

King of Ryes

If the hankering for rye bread-baking takes you, as it does me periodically, you will want to know about King Arthur Flour, America's premier mill and mecca for home bakers. They've been in business since 1790 and do a brisk mail-order business, with one of the world's most irresistible catalogs—chatty, informative, and recipe-studded. King Arthur sells more varieties of rye flour than any other retailer: a light rye, a medium rye, a rye blend, and a pumpernickel flour. Call 800-827-6836 for a catalog, or visit their website at www.kingarthurflour.com.

VARIATION

Quicker to cook, thus fuel-saving as well as time-saving, this does require planning ahead. Soak 1 cup rye in 1 cup filtered or spring water overnight. Next day, cook as in the recipe, but use only 2 cups water. After 45 to 60 minutes of cooking, it will be tender, though still a bit chewy (agreeably so) and with some liquid—a perfect hot-cereal breakfast consistency. With another 20 to 25 minutes of cooking, it's done: all liquid absorbed, good tender-chewy texture, ready for whatever use you might have in mind.

Basic Rye, Stove-Top Method

Like whole-grain wheat, rye is among the slowest-to-cook grains. Cooking rye under pressure saves time and fuel, but if you don't mind waiting, this stove-top method works just fine. Some rye varieties take longer than others to cook, so keep an eye on things. Salt impedes the grains' water absorption, so add it at the tail end of cooking. **MAKES ABOUT 3 CUPS; SERVES 4 TO 6 AS A COMPONENT**

Cooking spray
3 cups water, preferably spring or filtered
1 cup whole-grain rye (often sold as rye berries)
¾ teaspoon salt

1 In a 4-quart nonstick saucepan, or one that has been sprayed with cooking spray, bring the water to a boil over high heat.

2 Meanwhile, place the rye in a sieve and rinse well. When the water in the pot's boiling hard, add the rye and let the water return to a hard boil.

3 Turn down the heat as low as you can (if your burners won't turn down way low without blowing out, you may wish to use a Flame Tamer over the burner; see page 535) and set a timer for 1 hour and 45 minutes.

4 When the timer goes off, check for doneness. The rye should still have texture, but be tender—some ryes take even longer, so cook more as needed. When tender, add the salt, and allow the pot to sit for 10 minutes undisturbed. Stir well to incorporate the salt, then serve as is, or use in other dishes.

Basic Rye, Pressure-Cooker Method

Follow this method exactly and you will have perfect rye—individual grains with that good bouncy "pop" to them, with little or no excess water (although this can vary according to the variety of rye) and the perfect balance of tenderness and chewiness. In my opinion most cooking authorities recommend too much water for cooking rye, but with a Flame Tamer you can use less and still avoid sticking. Also, rye has a tendency to foam, which can block the pressure-release mechanism; the oil keeps the foaming down. **MAKES ABOUT 3½ CUPS; SERVES 4 TO 6 AS A COMPONENT**

Cooking spray
3 cups water, preferably spring or filtered
1½ cups whole-grain rye (often sold as rye berries)
1 teaspoon mild vegetable oil, such as corn, canola, or peanut
¾ teaspoon salt

1 Spray a pressure-cooker pot with cooking spray. Add the water and bring to a boil over high heat.

2 Meanwhile, place the rye in a sieve and rinse well. When the water in the pot's boiling hard, add the rye and oil. Let it return to a hard boil.

3 Lock the lid down and bring to high pressure. Set a timer for 1 hour, then lift the pot from the direct heat and slide a Flame Tamer (see page 535) over the burner. Immediately set the pressure cooker back down on it. Adjust the heat until the pressure is steady halfway between medium and high.

4 When the timer goes off, let the pressure release naturally for 10 minutes. Unlock the lid, add the salt, stir well, and serve, or use in other dishes.

Gussied-Up Basic Ryes

▲ *For a three-grain combo that is truly addictive, start by soaking ¾ cup whole-grain rye in spring or filtered water overnight. Next day, combine ¾ cup long-grain brown rice and ½ cup black barley with the soaked rye. Drop this mixture into 4 cups boiling salted water in a pressure cooker. Lock the lid, raise the heat to high, transfer the cooker to a Flame Tamer (see page 535), and adjust the heat so the grains cook with pressure at the second ring for 28 minutes. Allow the pressure to release naturally. The flavors, colors, and contrasting tastes of these three grains are something else. A tiny nub of butter and a bit of grated Parmesan and this can stand up to many a fancier risotto, or serve it under a sauté of vegetables and mushrooms, or with almost any savory sauce.*

▲ *As with most cooked grains, you can't go wrong with a Simple Rye Pilaf: Sauté, in a little olive oil, some onion, celery, carrot, and—even though you probably think you don't like them—a teaspoon or so of caraway seeds. Toss this mixture, along with a splash of tamari, into the cooked rye. A little shredded cabbage or kale sautéed with the onion is excellent here too.*

▲ *Dollop cooked rye with plain, unsweetened yogurt, a tiny jot of butter, a sprinkle of brown sugar, a sprinkle of raisins, a touch of cinnamon, and a diced Gala apple. Serve with hot milk and you've got a Sweet Rye Breakfast Bowl.*

Winter Garden Full-Meal Rye-Barley Mélange

Root vegetables and hearty greens are boon companions to rye and barley. Here, turnips and chard combine deliciously with these cold-weather grains and edamame—soybeans (see page 626). You need the edamame that come shelled, out of the pod, for this recipe. I use cooked rye and barley here, but if you don't have any on hand, the two are easily combined and cooked in a pressure cooker (see previous page). Add a salad of bitter greens and you've got dinner. **SERVES 6**

2 large turnips, well washed, stems removed, diced
1 large sweet potato, peeled and diced
Cooking spray
1 tablespoon olive oil
1 large onion, chopped
2 ribs celery, chopped
1 teaspoon celery seed
1 red bell pepper, seeds and white fiber removed, diced
2 cloves garlic, minced
1 bag (12 ounces) frozen edamame (sometimes called sweet soybeans, or sweet beans)
½ cup dry white wine
2 cups cooked rye (see page 572)
2 cups cooked brown rice or barley
1 bunch chard, center ribs removed, sliced crosswise into thin ribbons
2 tablespoons minced fresh dill (optional)
Salt and freshly ground black pepper
Sour cream, reduced-fat sour cream, Yogurt Sour Cream (page 910), or Tofu Sour Cream (page 909)

1 Bring a medium saucepan of water to a boil and drop in the turnips. Blanch for 3 minutes, then drain well and rinse with cold water. Set aside. Repeat with the sweet potato.

2 In a large Dutch oven that has been sprayed with cooking spray, heat the oil over medium heat. Add the onion and sauté for 3 minutes, or until softened. Add the celery, celery seed, bell pepper, and garlic and stir-fry for another 3 minutes. Add the turnips, sweet potato, edamame, and wine; bring to a boil. Add the cooked grains and top with the chard. Cover and let steam until the greens wilt and the grains are piping hot, 4 to 5 minutes.

3 Season with the dill, salt, and pepper. Serve hot, with a dab of sour cream or equivalent atop each portion.

Old World–Style Sourdough Rye

Rye flour makes great bread for serious bread lovers—those who crave texture and toothsomeness and heft, who feel soft white bread doesn't cut it. Because rye is low in gluten, on which the structure of bread is built, the higher the percentage of rye to wheat flour, the heavier the bread. This deep, dark, sour rye—you begin the sourdough starter several days in advance—is satisfying; solid without being like a doorstop. Its substantiality makes it a good wintertime loaf; one bite and you'll see why all of northern Europe and Russia serves some form of this bread.

According to the folks at King Arthur Flour (see page 571), rye is often used in starters "because it instigates certain microbiological activity more quickly than wheat flour, and contains minerals that promote fermentation." **MAKES 2 MEDIUM-SIZE ROUND LOAVES**

THE FIRST STARTER

1 teaspoon dry yeast
¼ cup warm water, preferably spring or filtered
¼ cup rye flour, preferably medium-dark rye flour

THE SPONGE

1 tablespoon dry yeast
1 cup warm water, preferably spring or filtered
1 cup rye flour, preferably medium-dark rye flour

THE DOUGH

¾ cup warm water, preferably spring or filtered
1¼ teaspoons salt
1¼ cups rye flour, preferably a rye blend
¾ cup whole wheat bread (not pastry) flour
1 tablespoon gluten flour
About 1½ cups unbleached white all-purpose flour
Cooking spray
1 to 2 tablespoons cornmeal

1 Combine all of the first starter ingredients in a small glass or pottery bowl. Mix well, cover loosely with plastic wrap, and let ferment in a warm place (about 75°F) for 24 to 48 hours.

2 After the starter has soured for the requisite time period, add all the sponge ingredients to it and mix well. Cover and let stand for another 3 to 4 hours.

3 Transfer the sponge mixture to a large bowl and add all the remaining ingredients except the cooking spray and cornmeal in the order given, starting with just 1 cup of the unbleached white flour and adding more only if the dough is sticky. Mix well, working the flours in to make a dough. Turn the dough out onto a work surface floured with about ¼ cup of the remaining white flour. Let the dough stand for a few moments while you wash out the dough bowl, dry it thoroughly, and give it a spritz of cooking spray. Knead the dough for 6 to 7 minutes. (Alternatively, you may dump the dough in your bread machine—set on "manual" or "dough" and let it knead—I start out by hand-stirring 1 cup of the flour into the dough in the bowl, and adding another ¼ cup flour to the machine as it works). The dough, and it's a heavy one, will be very sticky at first, but will gradually grow elastic, smooth, and somewhat satiny-glossy. It will have a nice sourdough scent, too.

4 Place the kneaded dough in the prepared bowl, cover lightly with a clean kitchen towel, and let rise in a warm place for just 30 minutes. (This rise and the rises that follow are surprisingly quick because the yeast, having been fed and nurtured over these several days, is lively and raring to go.)

5 Divide the dough in half on a floured surface, kneading in just a touch more white flour if the dough is very sticky. Shape each portion into a round disc. Let the loaves rise on a cornmeal-sprinkled baking sheet in a warm place for another 20 minutes, covered wtih a clean towel.

6 Remove the discs from the baking sheet and gently reshape them, making oblong, somewhat oval loaves. Place these loaves back on the cornmeal-sprinkled baking sheet, cover loosely with a clean kitchen towel, and let rise in a warm place for the third and final time, 35 to 40 minutes. Preheat the oven to 450°F during the last 15 minutes of this rise.

7 When the rising time is completed, lower the oven temperature to 400°F. Carefully slash an elongated X into each loaf, throw a few ice cubes into the oven to create some steam (or mist the oven's interior with water), and quickly (before the steam disappears) slide the bread into the oven.

8 Bake for 40 to 50 minutes. If you like an extra-crisp crust, open the oven door a couple of times during cooking and spray the oven again (or toss in more ice cubes). Remove the loaves from the oven and let cool to at least warm, not hot, on a wire rack before cutting into them.

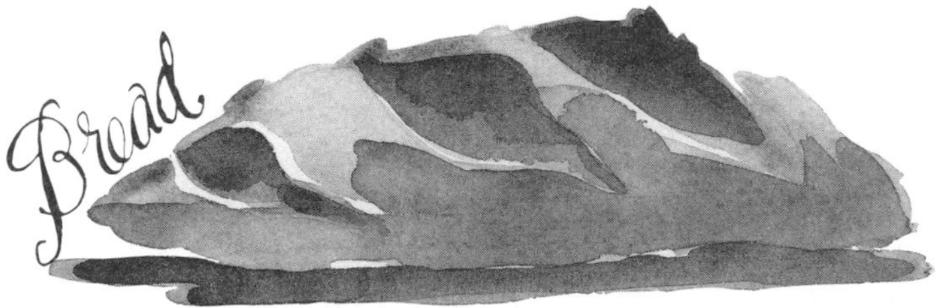

Stalking the Wild Rice

No grain has more storied romance to it than wild rice. Although corn, amaranth, and quinoa are also native to the Americas, wild rice is the only grain that is native specifically to North America. And it—not corn—is the grain with the most consistent association with American Indians of the Great Lakes region.

This is fitting, for although wild rice has been cultivated commercially since the 1950s, it has also been harvested for hundreds of years by the Ojibwe (formerly known as the Chippewa) and the Dakota, in northern Minnesota's lakes and rivers. And although the cultivated wild rice crop (some 4 to 6 million pounds a year, 80 percent of it grown in California) greatly exceeds the truly wild (a mere 1 million pounds yearly), the latter is still harvested the old way. In late summer and early fall, Ojibwe harvesters glide through the wetlands, two to a canoe, one poling, the other bending the ripe wild rice plants over the canoe and knocking the grains onto its floor with two long juniper sticks. A good day's effort yields a canoe's worth of rice. The grain—its Ojibwa name is *manomin,* or "good berry"—is then carefully hand-processed. (One particularly poetic step, in which someone wearing clean moccasins walks on the collected grain until the husks loosen, is called "dancing the rice.") Traditionally, women gathered the rice; today, both sexes do the harvesting.

While cultivated wild rice has made the once rare foodstuff inexpensive and widely available, the rarer hand-harvested rice can still be had by anyone willing to pay the premium price. Is it worth it? Yes, because the true wild rice, due to the Indian method of hand-processing, is fluffier and quicker to cook; and because the hand-harvesting draws rice from a variety of habitats, which is filled with a range of subtle taste differences. (Some wild rice aficionados, like wine lovers, have a rice they particularly love and can even identify by the lake or river in which it grew.) But additionally, its purchase helps support the protection of the ever dwindling wetlands, which are not only the sole environment in which natural wild rice can grow, but also are home to countless fish, amphibious creatures, and waterfowl.

Wild rice is technically a grass seed, not a true rice or even a grain at all, but its nutritional content and cooking method are so grainlike it is nearly always included with grains. Like most whole grains, it is high in carbohydrate, with some protein, and it's fiber-rich and packed with B-vitamins. Its greatest distinction nutritionally is its content of folacin, a B-vitamin; it has 35 milligrams in each ½-cup serving (brown rice, by way of contrast, has 6 milligrams). This essential nutrient is used by the body in the production of DNA and RNA.

The vast majority of wild rice is used in multigrain mixes, particularly rice mixes, where various lighter, shorter, rounder grains contrast beautifully in color and texture with the long, slender, delicate wild rice. Just a few grains can make all the difference in a mix—my friend Chou Chou's homemade rice mix, for example, uses only 1 or 2 tablespoons of wild rice to 1 cup of long-grain brown, and it's delicious and lovely to look at. But in Minnesota, wild rice's watery home turf, you can find the unadulterated grain, with its vibrantly nut-brown flavor, on many menus: as pilaf, unmixed with other grains; kneaded into bread or rolls; in soups; and in stuffing for fish or fowl or vegetables. At the famous Minneapolis vegetarian restaurant Café Brenda, you can enjoy wild rice, vegetable, and pecan croquettes served with wild mushroom cream sauce; you can even drink your wild rice in the form of microbrewed James Page Boundary Waters Wild Rice Lager Beer.

Wild rice is classified not only according to whether it is cultivated or the hand-harvested lake or river rice, but by various grades, which also determine price. Grades are based on length, and whether the grain is broken. The costliest is the extra-long, sometimes sold as giant: inch-long, elegantly thin needle-shaped grains. Medium-grade runs about half an inch in length, and will include some broken grains. Rice called "select" mostly is a shorter style. Broken wild rice is usually a bargain and is perfect for porridge-y preparations such as a Wild Rice and Mushroom "Ri-sort-of" (page 581).

Length of grain and method of processing also affect cooking time. This, like the amount of cooking water, is a matter of approximation. Most recipes advise cooking with extra water, then draining off the extra, but this is a waste of wild rice flavor and nutrients (unless the liquid is then used in a recipe). I offer a method and chart that should help you get around this.

Lastly, wild rice, like most foods with stand-up-and-take-charge flavors, finds allies in certain ingredients. To my taste, wild rice is at its best when partnered with mushrooms, nuts, and sherry, and, in the sweet line, dried fruits (particularly dried berries) and maple syrup. I return time and time again to combinations of these ingredients when I do the wild thing. See Wild Rice, Lentil, and Mushroom Soup (page 166) as well as the delectable Mushroom, Wild Rice and Lentil Timbale-Cake (page 304). Also, many of the grain salad recipes either contain wild rice or are great with a bit folded in.

Basic Wild Rice, Stove-Top Method

Wild rice should always be washed thoroughly before cooking. Also, doneness is determined by both mouth and eye. Start checking the rice at the shorter end of the time range given, tasting a few grains. They should be tender but not soft and mushy, and at least half the grains should have burst open, popcornlike, turning inside out into a curved shape (a phenomenon known as butterflying).

If, despite your best intentions, you end up with extra wild rice cooking water, don't throw it out. It can be used in recipes such as Wild Rice Bread with Maple, Blueberries, and Pecans (page 584). It also makes soulful soup stock for mushroom soup, some lentil or bean soups, and many creamy soups (but it's not right for others, such as vegetable soups where you want the individual vegetable's flavor to shine through). **SERVES 4**

1 cup wild rice
Water, preferably spring or filtered, measured according to the chart below
½ teaspoon salt

1 First, take a look at the rice and use the chart to approximate the cooking time and amount of water needed. Wash the rice, either by placing it in a strainer and rinsing it several times, or by putting it in a bowl, pouring cold water over it, swishing it back and forth for a few seconds with your hands, then draining it in a colander.

2 Bring the requisite amount of water to a boil with the salt. Add the wild rice and bring back to a boil, then lower the heat and cover. Simmer, covered, for the appropriate cooking time. Start checking the wild rice for doneness at the shorter time.

3 Ideally, all the water should be absorbed by the time the wild rice has achieved doneness. If the rice is not done and the water's gone, add more water—boiling water. If there's just a bit left, uncover the pot and let the rice cook for a few minutes longer, or until the excess has evaporated. If there's a lot of extra water, drain it and save it for another recipe.

4 When the rice is done and all the water is gone, turn off the heat and let the wild rice steam in the pot, covered, for about 10 minutes. Fluff and serve.

Cooking Wild Rice

TYPE OF WILD RICE	CONVENTIONAL STOVE-TOP METHOD			PRESSURE-COOKER METHOD		
	Water	**Rice**	**Cooking Time**	**Water**	**Rice**	**Cooking Time**
1-inch grains, black	3 cups	1 cup	60–70 minutes	2¾ cups	1 cup	22–25 minutes
1-inch grains, variegated	2¾ cups	1 cup	50–60 minutes	2⅔ cups	1 cup	19–22 minutes
½-inch grains, black	2½ cups	1 cup	45–55 minutes	2¼ cups	1 cup	18–21 minutes
½-inch grains, variegated	2 cups	1 cup	45–55 minutes	1¾ cups	1 cup	16–19 minutes

Note: *Finely broken wild rice requires a different cooking method; see Wild Rice Porridge, page 581.*
All hand-harvested, American Indian–processed rice cooks on the quicker end of the range, while the cultivated is slower to cook.

VARIATION

DOUBLE-BOILER METHOD: ***If time is not an issue, this is probably the most delicious and foolproof cooking method. In the top pot of a double boiler set directly on the burner, cook the wild rice, stirring, for 5 to 8 minutes only, just until the porridge begins to thicken. Meanwhile, heat an inch of water in the base pot until it reaches a simmer. When the rice begins to thicken, place the rice pot atop the water pot and cook, half-covered, for 40 to 45 minutes, stirring from time to time, until the wild rice is tender and the porridge is very thick. Remember to check the bottom pot at intervals and refill the water.***

THERMOS METHOD: ***The truly hassle-free way to have great hot cereal in the morning—if you can plan ahead. Combine the wild rice, salt, and boiling water in a large thermos the night before. Close the thermos. Shake a few times. Next morning, open the thermos—and there you have it.***

Basic Wild Rice, Pressure-Cooker Method

Please see the headnote of the previous recipe for advice on preparing wild rice. It's important to wash it thoroughly before you start cooking, and to recognize its unique signs of doneness to know when to stop. **SERVES 4**

1 cup wild rice
Water, preferably spring or filtered, measured according to chart on the previous page
½ teaspoon salt
Cooking spray

1. First, take a look at the rice and use the chart to approximate the cooking time and amount of water needed. Wash the rice, either by placing it in a strainer and rinsing it several times, or by putting it in a bowl, pouring cold water over it, swishing it back and forth for a few seconds with your hands, then draining it in a colander.

2. Bring the requisite amount of water to a boil with the salt in a pressure cooker that has been sprayed with cooking spray. Add the wild rice and bring back to a boil. Lock the lid down and bring up to high pressure, then lower the heat and allow the cooker to come to medium pressure. Cook for the length of time listed in the chart, then allow the pressure to release naturally. Start checking the wild rice for doneness at the shorter interval of time.

3. Ideally, all the water should be absorbed by the time the wild rice is done. If the rice is not done and the water's gone, add more water—boiling water. If it's really quite underdone, after adding the boiling water, relock the lid and bring back up to high pressure for 2 or 3 minutes, then allow the pressure to release naturally. If there's just a bit of water left, uncover the pressure cooker and let the rice cook for a few minutes longer, or until the excess has evaporated. If there's a great deal of extra water, drain it and save it for another recipe.

4. When the rice is done and all the water is gone, turn off the heat and let the wild rice steam, with the lid covering it but not locked down, for about 10 minutes. Fluff and serve.

Wild Rice Porridge

To those who love wild rice, there could hardly be a more satisfying breakfast cereal. When using it for this indulgent purpose, try tossing in a handful of dried cherries, blueberries, or cranberries in the last 5 minutes of cooking. Then serve with a thin pat of butter or a spoonful of Better (page 905) and a sprinkling of brown sugar or a pour of real maple syrup. However, if you plan on using some of the porridge as the base for Wild Rice and Mushroom Ri-sort-of (below), don't add the dried fruit.

I highly recommend using a heavy, good-quality nonstick pot for this—or follow the double-boiler or thermos method. Finely broken wild rice is slow-cooking, and it wants to stick near the end of cooking if your pot is thin or distributes heat unevenly. Like other coarsely or finely ground grains for porridges, broken wild rice is not suitable for preparation in a pressure cooker. **MAKES ABOUT 4 CUPS**

4 cups water, preferably spring or filtered
½ teaspoon salt
1 cup broken wild rice (it should be in little bits, pieces ranging from the size of a grain of sand to ⅛ inch), washed

Bring the water to a boil with the salt in a large, heavy pot, preferably nonstick. Stir in the wild rice bits and let the water return to a boil, then turn down to a very low simmer. Cook for about 30 minutes, stirring often, or until the porridge is thick and tender. Serve, with any porridge fixings you like.

Wild Rice and Mushroom Ri-sort-of

In texture, like a cross between polenta and risotto; in flavor, like nothing but its own sublime and swooningly good self. This was invented one night in my restaurant days as a last-minute addition to a component vegetable plate, and it is just so good—a comfort-food texture, a vibrantly full flavor, and an alluring presence on the plate. It is one of the few things I am willing to use a little heavy cream in, because it's worth it. **SERVES 4**

VARIATION

Add a little garlic after the mushrooms are soft, just before adding the wild rice, if you like. And grated nutmeg is always a hit where mushrooms and cream are concerned. But I prefer this fairly straightforward, since the flavors are already bold and forthright.

- 1 ounce dried porcini mushrooms
- ¾ cup vegetable stock (especially Oven-Roasted Vegetable Stock, page 141, but any good one will do), boiling
- Cooking spray
- 1 tablespoon butter
- 1 large onion, diced
- ½ pound shiitake mushrooms, stems removed, sliced
- 3 to 4 cups leftover Wild Rice Porridge (previous page)
- Salt and freshly ground black pepper to taste
- 2 tablespoons to ¼ cup heavy cream

1 Place the dried mushrooms in a small heatproof bowl. Pour the boiling stock over them and let steep for 30 minutes. Strain carefully through a coffee filter–lined fine-mesh sieve, reserving both the mushrooms and stock, but discarding the coffee filter with the grit or sand. Dice the mushrooms.

2 In a large heavy skillet that has been sprayed with cooking spray, heat the butter over medium heat. Add the onion and sauté, stirring, for about 7 minutes, or until the onion is very soft and starting to color. Add the shiitakes and stir-fry for 5 minutes, or until the mushrooms are limp.

3 Add the porridge, porcini soaking water, and diced porcini. Lower the heat slightly and cook, stirring frequently, until the porridge is piping hot and most of the liquid has been absorbed. The porridge should be very thick and fragrant; it will want to stick, but don't you let it. Taste for salt and pepper, adding a lot of the latter.

4 Just before serving, stir in the cream, starting with the lesser amount. Taste again. Serve ASAP.

"Among the trees they were continually cutting with their scythes the so-called 'birch mushrooms,' swollen fat in the succulent grass. But the old man bent down every time he came across a mushroom, picked it up and put it in his bosom. 'Another present for my old woman,' he said as he did so."

—**Leo Tolstoy,** *Anna Karenina*

Sherry-Splashed Double-Walnut Wild Rice Pilaf

Wild rice comes together with dried fruit, nuts, and a forebear of wheat in this recipe. This is almost a warm rice salad, and truly delectable, the crunch of the walnuts enhanced by the use of a bit of walnut oil at the end, which combines beautifully with the sweet nuttiness of the sherry. This goes very well with almost anything in a creamy sauce, especially a mushroom-tempeh dish; it's also a great potluck dish or part of a buffet. A pressure cooker makes relatively quick work of it. Serve hot, warm, or at room temperature. **SERVES 6**

Cooking spray
1 tablespoon mild vegetable oil, such as corn or canola
1 red onion, finely chopped
1¼ cups water, preferably spring or filtered
1 cup mild vegetable stock, commercial or homemade (see page 139)
½ cup cream sherry
½ cup long-grain wild rice
1 cup spelt, kamut, or barley (or a combination of all three)
1 teaspoon salt
½ cup unsweetened dried cranberries
½ cup chopped dried apricots
1 tablespoon walnut oil
3 tablespoons finely minced fresh sage (or 1 teaspoon dry leaf sage)
½ cup chopped toasted walnuts
¼ cup finely chopped Italian parsley

1 Spray a pressure-cooker pot with cooking spray and place it over medium heat. Add the oil and, when hot, sauté the onion for 3 minutes, or until softened. Add the water, stock, and sherry. Bring to a boil, then add the wild rice, spelt, kamut, or barley, and salt.

2 Lock the lid down and bring up to medium pressure. Lower the heat and maintain at medium pressure for 25 minutes. Turn off the heat and let the pressure release naturally.

3 Meanwhile, combine the dried cranberries, apricots, walnut oil, and sage in a bowl.

4 Unlock the pressure-cooker lid and drop the dried fruit mixture onto the grains. Don't stir yet. Relock the lid and allow the grains to steam for 5 minutes, then unlock the lid again. Add the walnuts and parsley. Toss well to combine, and serve hot or at room temperature.

NEW WORLD DINNER-AND-A-MOVIE OCTOBER SUPPER

The Salad
(PAGE 68)

*

Pumpkin-Tomato Bisque
(PAGE 181)

*

Wild Rice Bread with Maple, Blueberries, and Pecans

*

Honeyed Cranberry-Burgundy Poached Pears
(PAGE 993)

Wild Rice Bread with Maple, Blueberries, and Pecans

It was a revelation, one of those intensely life-is-good moments, the first time I tasted wild rice bread. Baked into crusty brown rolls, it was part of lunch for a group of culinary writers on a farm tour. Around us, the gently rounded hills of Sonoma County undulated, and we'd just walked through a grove of new olive trees, along with their passionate owner, gentleman farmer Ridgely Evers (who, before he started raising olives, developed a little software program you might have heard of: Quicken). Yet even under less idyllic circumstances, a first bite of master baker Peter Reinhart's wild rice bread would make anyone happy.

The recipe for his wonderful bread is in his thoughtful *Brother Juniper's Bread Book*; having been inspired by him, my bread went in a different direction. The result is a hauntingly delicious loaf, divine for breakfast, and even better for a fall supper with pumpkin soup. Be sure to cook the rice to extreme softness, since it gets firmer in the loaf.

I used ½-inch-long black wild rice for the cooked rice, and the timing given reflects this. Adjust cooking times according to the chart on page 579, based on the rice you have. Or, if you have cooked wild rice on hand, skip Step 1 altogether and simply use 1⅓ cups, very well cooked. Substitute one of the other suggested liquids for the wild rice cooking water.

For the wild rice flour, I recommend broken-up wild rice. If you make Yogurt Sour Cream (page 910), you may use the nice, tart whey you'll have on hand as the liquid; the pleasant acidity heightens the yeastiness of the bread. **MAKES FOUR 5-BY-2½-INCH MINIATURE LOAVES**

2 cups water, preferably spring or filtered
1¼ teaspoons salt
½ cup unbroken wild rice (to equal 1⅓ cups cooked)
⅓ cup wild rice, preferably broken (to be ground into a scant ⅓ cup flour)
1¼ cups warm liquid: the leftover wild rice cooking water plus water (spring or filtered) or buttermilk or leftover whey from Yogurt Sour Cream (page 910), as needed
1 package (1 scant tablespoon) dry yeast
½ cup maple syrup, at room temperature
2 tablespoons brown sugar or Rapidura
2 tablespoons mild vegetable oil, such as corn, canola, or peanut; or melted butter
1½ cups whole wheat flour (not pastry flour)
½ to ¾ cup dried blueberries, cranberries, currents, or raisins
¼ to ½ cup chopped toasted pecans or walnuts
Additional 3 tablespoons flour, either white or whole wheat
1½ to 2 cups unbleached white all-purpose flour
Cooking spray

1 Bring the water and 1 teaspoon of the salt to a boil in a small saucepan. Add the ½ cup wild rice, cover, lower the heat, and cook until the rice is very, very tender, 55 to 65 minutes. Remove from the heat. Drain the rice cooking liquid directly into a 4-cup glass measuring cup and set aside. Set the rice stand, uncovered, until it has cooled to just slightly warmer than room temperature.

2 Meanwhile, grind the remaining rice into flour using a blender or spice grinder: Just throw it in there and start buzzing. This will take about 1 (noisy) minute. You'll end up with fragrant, light brown flour, about the consistency of fine sand. Set aside.

3 After the rice has cooled, add additional liquid to the rice-cooking water in the measuring cup to equal 1¼ cups. Add the yeast and let stand until dissolved and bubbly, 5 to 7 minutes. Pour it into a medium bowl and stir in the maple syrup, brown sugar, oil, ¼ teaspoon salt, the wild rice flour, and whole wheat flour. Let stand, covered, in a warm place for 10 to 12 minutes.

4 In a separate, medium bowl, combine the cooked wild rice, the dried fruit, and nuts with the 3 tablespoons flour, and toss well.

5 After the wild rice–maple–whole wheat sponge has had its brief rest, transfer it to a large bowl and stir 1 cup of the unbleached white flour into it. When the flour is thoroughly mixed in, stir in the rice-nut-fruit mix. It will appear to be a large quantity of mix-ins, and the dough will be wet, but don't worry, the dough will incorporate it all beautifully.

6 Sprinkle your kneading surface well with ½ cup of the unbleached white flour.

Turn the dough out onto the surface and sprinkle some of the loose flour over it. Let the dough rest again for a couple of minutes while you wash the dough bowl, then dry it, then spritz it with cooking spray. Set aside. Now, flour your hands and start kneading. About 5 minutes should take the dough to smooth (other than the lumps of rice, nuts, and fruit, of course) and elastic. The dough will be a bit sticky. Place the dough in the bowl, cover loosely with a clean dish towel, and let rise in a warm place for 1 to 1¼ hours.

7 Reflour the kneading surface—you'll only need maybe ¼ cup flour this time—punch the dough down, and turn it out onto the floured surface. Give the dough a few kneads with floured hands. It'll be a bit sticky, but that's fine. Divide it and form into loaves. You can make 1 regular-size loaf or 2 medium-size ones, but I prefer to do this as several small loaves—it's a moist bread, and small loaves ensure that it gets done all the way through without being overdone on the crust. Spray the loaf pan(s) of choice with cooking spray and place the dough in them. Cover loosely and let rise in a warm place for 45 minutes.

8 A few minutes before the final rise is up, preheat the oven to 375°F. Bake the loaves for 15 minutes, then lower the heat to 350°F and bake for another 25 minutes or until deep brown and crusty. That's the timing for small loaves; larger ones will take 35 to 45 minutes after you lower the temperature. Let the bread cool on wire racks. Wait until the loaves are completely cool before slicing.

A Bountiful Bowl of Beans

Second only to grains, beans have been the chief and most lasting plant-based foodstuff for the human race throughout its history. Some researchers claim that fava beans, grown over four thousand years ago in Mesopotamia, are the world's oldest cultivated legume; others give this honor to lentils. By Biblical times, lentils were so well known and loved that they are mentioned in Genesis, in the famous verse where

Jacob cruelly deprives a hungry Esau of his birthright for a "pottage of lentiles." In ancient Rome, four leading families took their names from legumes: Lentullus (lentil), Piso (pea), Cicero (chickpea), Fabius (fava). Some beans were considered sacred and used as an offering to the god Apollo; in ancient Greece, besides being eaten, beans were used to cast votes, white "for," black "against."

But beans had an impact on other parts of the earth, too. Legumes have been part of the indigenous human diet in the Americas, where six-thousand-year-old beans have been found in caves near Ocampo, Mexico. New World beans include black beans, pintos, limas, and kidneys. China also has a venerable bean heritage, including soybeans, which date from about 2000 B.C., and mung beans. So does Africa, where the black-eyed pea originated.

Wrapped in shiny, vivid seed coats in every hue imaginable, solid or speckled, dappled or dotted, there are thousands of varieties of edible Leguminosae. We're talking about the familiar (lima beans, pinto beans, navy beans) but also the exotic (azuki, tongues of fire, Jacob's cattle, nightfall, butterscotch calypso, wren's egg, cranberry). You could eat a different variety of bean every day for over a year without duplication. Yet, within this abundant diversity are common traits. Each bean, no matter its variety, is the mature seed of a bean plant, containing within it the entire world needed to re-create itself.

This world is first, and most uniquely, protein. Of all the foods in the plant world, the protein content of legumes and products made from them (like tofu and tempeh) is the most concentrated source of plant-based protein. Six to eleven percent of beans' cooked weight is protein; ½ cup cooked beans, depending on variety, has about 8 grams (by contrast, an egg has 6 grams). The protein in beans is not only equal in quality to animal-based protein, it is in many ways *superior.* Bean protein has no cholesterol, it is low in fat, and it comes with a host of other benefits not found in animal-based protein.

Beans are extremely rich in the B vitamins (even though some are lost during the soaking and cooking process). They're high in iron, calcium, and phosphorus, and, of course, fiber—as a class of foodstuff, beans have more fiber than virtually anything except the bran in grains. Beans are rich in complex carbohydrates, too—the satisfying starch that gives them their creamy, stick-to-the-ribs, hearty quality.

Bean carbohydrate is no ordinary starch. *New York Times* writer Jane Brody calls bean carbs "nutritional wonders," pointing out that "On diets containing substantial amounts of beans, many adult-onset diabetics have been able to

Sipping after the Bean

Certain infusions are traditional stomach soothers. What better time to enjoy them than after a beany supper? Called carminatives, they relieve gas pains and aid digestion.

Available in tea bags at almost any supermarket is mint tea (either a mixed blend of mints, straight peppermint, or, my favorite, spearmint). Camomile is also a mild digestif.

More serious carminatives are fennel, anise, or cumin seeds. Allowing 1 teaspoon per cup of spring or filtered water, simmer the seeds in water over low heat for about 10 minutes, turn off the heat, and allow the seeds to steep as long as you like. Strain and drink while still a bit warm.

Ginger is another legendary stomach soother; substitute a few slices of fresh ginger for the seeds called for above, and follow the same directions.

Epazote, a Helpful Herb

Many herbs and spices are said to relieve beans', ahem, impolite side effects, summer savory, bay leaf, cumin, ginger, and cilantro among them. But the most famous is epazote (Chenopodium ambrosioides), *used throughout Mexico and Central America, which is reputed to be one of the most effective of such herbs. I first fell in love with this herb in New Mexico for its taste, clueless that it also had beneficial properties. I kept asking what the herbal-floral flavor was, and when a chef in Taos finally told me, I bought a huge sack of it, dried. It is sometimes called pazote, worm weed, wormseed, or Mexican tea. I have never tasted or purchased it fresh, but it's probably growing outside my window.*

According to Diana Kennedy, in The Cuisines of Mexico, *"It is a pungent herb with pointed serrated leaves" that she has found growing "in profusion" over many parts of the country, including New York City. She describes it as "very much an acquired taste, but after a while to cook black beans without it is unthinkable."*

reduce greatly or eliminate entirely their dependence on insulin and other medications to control blood sugar." Part of the probable reason for this is that we digest legumes very slowly . . . one of the very qualities that makes them so satisfying.

If all this isn't enough to make a bean convert of you, consider the results of a recent study conducted at Northern Arizona University, which reveals a "Mexican paradox" similar to the now-familiar French one. Although both these cultures have diets as high or higher in saturated fats than the American diet, their populations have far lower rates of heart disease. In France, the conundrum was chalked up to the *phenols* in red wine, which evidently break down LDL (the "bad") cholesterol. The Mexican diet is rich in a foodstuff containing a similar, related factor called *polyphenolics,* which has a like effect. What's it found in? You guessed it—beans, especially black beans and pintos.

Want some other reasons to become friendly with the legumes?

1 They're cheap. Major cheap. This is worth remembering when you're feeding a crowd.

2 They are one crop that actually *benefits* the soil, enriching it with nitrogen rather than depleting it during the growing process.

3 Beans are beautiful, soulful, and inspiring, not just in the eating but visually, sitting in glass jars on your kitchen shelf.

4 Beans are newly hip, especially the exotic varieties. You'll find beans somewhere on the menu of the most cutting-edge restaurants. Why? Because of the health concerns that are slowly reinventing what we eat in America, because of all of the reasons above, and last but not least because . . .

5 Beans are so good to eat.

Quiet Beans

The least "flatulating" legumes are said to be (in this order) lentils, split peas, azuki beans, mung beans, black-eyed peas, and anasazi beans. All of these beans are known to be lower in oligosaccharides, the sugars that ferment and cause gas to be released. In the low to middle range are probably the other nonhybridized heritage beans, such as teppary, calypso, nightfall, and so forth. Mid-range are chickpeas, black beans, and white beans. Higher still are limas and navy beans, with whole soybeans being the highest.

Bean Varieties

As we now know, there are hundreds of varieties of dry beans available, a handful of which can be found in every supermarket. Each has a slightly different flavor, texture, cooking time, culinary idiosyncrasy, and appearance. The following chart tells you something about the most popular ones. Before you get overwhelmed, know that beans are more alike than different. With the exception of the swift-cooking legumes (lentils, split peas, split chickpeas, black-eyed peas), the two delicate-skinned beans (large limas and black soybeans, which have salt added both before and during cooking, not after), and the tough-skinned fava (which must be peeled,

Name	Origins, Looks, Properties, Close Kin	Traditional Use	Cooking Time and Notes
Chickpeas a.k.a. garbanzo beans, cece, or cici; when split and skinned, channa dal; when ground into flour, besan	Middle East, Mediterranean. Round with a tiny ridge, golden-tan. Available dried, canned, and precooked then dehydrated. Rich in flavor, they keep their shape well when cooked. They're a bit grainier in texture, not quite as creamy as many beans. Chickpeas are excellent from the can. Besan is a great ingredient, adding richness and protein to eggless crêpes, as well as many Indian dishes.	In hummus, falafel, soups, and Moroccan tajines. In some North African and Near East countries, the skins are slipped off chickpeas after cooking. Channa dal are used in India in all kinds of curry, and besan is used in both India and Provence, where these cultures feast on pancakes made of the flour.	An extremely slow-cooking bean, they must be presoaked. Allow 2 to 3 hours conventional cooking or 35 minutes in a pressure cooker for presoaked beans. Channa dal cooks in 25 minutes without presoaking.
Fava beans a.k.a. broad beans	Middle East, Mediterranean. A large flat golden-tan bean, shaped like a large lima. Somewhat bland, they come alive with the seasonings of their region. Favas have one irritating idiosyncrasy: Their skins are extremely tough, and must be removed after soaking, but before cooking. They're usually sold dry, but may be found fresh in the spring. Dry favas are most often sold whole, but sometimes you can find dried split fava beans, prepeeled and partially precooked.	Favas are the central ingredient of ful medames, Egypt's national dish, a warm or room-temperature, much-garnished lemony salad.	Presoak dried favas overnight, then rub off the tough outer skins—they come off easily, but it's time consuming. Allow 40 to 50 minutes of conventional cooking time, 10 to 15 under pressure. Split prepeeled dried favas are time-savers, cooking conventionally in 20 minutes or less, but they don't hold their shape well.
Mung beans a.k.a. green gram in India and in Indian foods stores	Of Asian origin, they are green beans. They do not require presoaking, and cook quickly.	Mungs are the bean most commonly sprouted for the bean sprouts at your local market. And "green gram" is a staple South Indian supper dish, served with chapatis—the equivalent of beans and tortillas.	Unsoaked mungs cook to tenderness conventionally in about 40 minutes, or in a pressure cooker, again soakless, in just 10 to 12 minutes.

post soaking), all beans can be used interchangeably in basically the same ways; just check for doneness and watch cooking times. In other words, you could use lentils instead of black beans in your favorite black bean soup recipe, or substitute azuki beans for pintos in chili.

All cooking times below, unless otherwise stated, assume that beans have been soaked to full, though raw, hydration. *That means, remember, there's no pale dry spot in the center of a split-open bean after soaking. Soybeans and soybean products are covered separately (see page 625).*

Best Enjoyed In . . .	Where to Find Them	Bean Trivia
Salads, vegetable stir-fries, especially Mediterranean-accented ones. Hold their shape nicely in soups. Find them here in Thai Green Curry of Eggplant, Chickpeas, and Green Beans (page 200), Morroc'n'Roll Seven-Vegetable Seven-Spice Tagine with Couscous (page 506), Fresh Artichoke-Eggplant Lasagna with Lemon Sauce (page 365), and Masala Stuffed Eggplant (page 408). Use besan in Neo-Classic Crêpes (page 332), and Stuffed Eggplant "Fillets" Gujerati-Style (page 406).	Canned chickpeas are available at any supermarket. Dried are less widely found, but sometimes may be in the Mexican foods section. Natural foods markets also carry them. Channa dal and besan are available at Indian grocers, and sometimes natural foods markets. Roasted chickpeas as snacks are available at some natural foods and gourmet stores.	Max's Kansas City, the famous late-'60s, early-'70s hip haunt in New York's Union Square, beloved of Andy Warhol and friends, had a bowl of hard chickpea snacks on every table in lieu of peanuts or such.
Dishes flavored with olive oil, garlic, herbs, lemon, tahini. Try Ful Medames (page 605). The quicker-cooking favas are best used in soups where you want a savory, thick but indistinct beaniness, or in savory, hummus-like purees. Fresh favas are wonderful gently sautéed in a little butter with garlic, minced parsley, lots of lemon juice, salt and pepper.	Favas are available at some natural foods supermarkets and some gourmet markets; also in Arab markets. You might find them canned at the latter. Fresh favas may be available at farmers markets in the spring. Boil them in the pod for 10 minutes, shell them, then remove the tough skin from each individual bean and cook 5 to 10 minutes more.	Famous for being a Hannibal Lecter side dish, mentioned in *The Silence of the Lambs*. The reason favas are generally pureed is that, whether fresh or dry, those tough outer skins must be removed, which can make the tender bean inside fracture.
South Indian Green Gram (page 608), Jeanne Ramu's Three-Bean Mix (page 381)	Natural foods supermarkets, Asian groceries. Not available canned.	Mungs are so quick-cooking that they deserve a place in your cupboard for expediency's sake. Also, mungs are very easily digestible.

Name	Origins, Looks, Properties, Close Kin	Traditional Use	Cooking Time and Notes
Black-eyed peas a.k.a. black-eyes or cowpeas	Of ancient Indian origin, this creamy white bean dotted with a black spot quickly moved to Africa and remains very popular there. Black-eyes do not need presoaking. Available canned, and, in the spring, fresh, in the grocery aisle. Their texture is starchy-floury; their flavor earthy and a bit ashy, yet excellent. Divine with something spicy.	One of the best-loved beans in the American South, and certainly in the Ozarks, these are typically cooked with ham hocks, and served with slow-cooked greens and cornbread. The nontraditional vegetarian black-eye ways are every bit as good.	New-crop dried black-eyes cook on the stove-top, unsoaked, in as little as 35 to 45 minutes, though older ones might take up to 1¼ hours. Under pressure, allow 10 to 12 minutes—again, this is unsoaked. For fresh black-eyes, remove the pods, then simmer for 20 to 25 minutes.
Pigeon peas a.k.a. gondoles. Almost interchangeable with black-eyed peas, crowder peas, field peas, purple-hulls, and pink-eyed purple-hulls	Like black-eyes, these are all beans of Indian origin that migrated to Africa and thence the American South and the Caribbean. Most are a grayish tan, sometimes with a blush of pink. Because their skins are tougher than those of black-eyes, they do best with an overnight presoaking. Some are available canned.	While black-eyes and pigeon peas both traveled from India to Africa to the Americas via the slave trade, the latter wound up being popular in the Caribbean Islands.	Soaked pigeon peas cook on the stove-top in 35 to 45 minutes, though older ones might take up to 1¼ hours. Under pressure, allow soaked peas 10 to 12 minutes. If fresh, remove the pods, then simmer for 30 to 40 minutes.
Azuki or adzuki beans	These New World natives are small, round, and red. A black-hulled variety of azuki, split in two and skinned, is called urad dal and used in Indian cooking. Urad dal are sometimes also known as black gram or white lentils.	A favorite in macrobiotic cooking, these beans are often used in Asian cooking. If you've ever had the weird (to American) taste of very sweet red bean paste or red bean paste ice cream at a Japanese restaurant, this is the bean it's made from. Urad dal are used almost exclusively in Indian food.	Presoaked azukis take about 30 minutes to tenderize conventionally, or 4 to 5 minutes in a pressure cooker. Unsoaked will tenderize on the stove-top in 30 minutes, 5 to 8 minutes in a pressure cooker. In Indian cooking, urad dal are browned in oil and tossed in at the last minute in many dishes, adding nutlike crunch. Try the technique in White Coconut Chutney (page 924)—delicious.
Black beans a.k.a. turtle beans	New World natives, black, with a distinctive, rich, mellow flavor. Available dried, canned, dehydrated, and in a fermented salted Asian form, black beans are wholly versatile and delicious.	Black bean soup is both an American and Cuban classic—the former with a sherry finish, the latter with rice, green peppers and garlic, and olive oil. Asian salted black beans are used in hundreds of Chinese, Thai, and Vietnamese sauces.	Stove-top, presoaked black beans cook in 1 to 1½ hours; under pressure, if fully soaked, 6 to 10 minutes. Dehydrated black beans become a wonderful savory mass that tastes like refried but isn't, in about 8 minutes.

Best Enjoyed In . . .	Where to Find Them	Bean Trivia
Hillbilly Hummus (page 18), Dancin' John (page 619), Groundnut and Greens Palaver with Black-Eyes (page 211), Gingered East-West Three-Bean and Vegetable Stew (page 227), Ragout of Shiitake Mushrooms, Black-Eyed Peas, and Southern Greens (page 243). Simply cooked black-eyes come to life with a shot of Tabasco and one of vinegar, and a wedge of cornbread.	Available canned or dried at most supermarkets; occasionally available fresh and pre-podded in the produce aisle; or still in the pod at farmer's markets, generally in the South.	It is essential to eat black-eyed peas on New Year's Day, for good luck in the coming year.
Try any of the recipes given for black-eyed peas with any of these beans.	You'll usually find at least a few of these varieties, dried, at your local market, and maybe even some canned. Even more are available at Caribbean groceries. The numbers available increase at a natural foods store, and approach infinity when you order from Phipps (www.phippscountry.com). One can often find fresh purple-hulls in the late summer at Southern farmer's markets.	There really is a distinct purple tinge to purple-hulls' pod—but not to the beans themselves.
Quite good done with a sweet finish, try azukis in Old-Fashioned, All-Day Baked Beans, Boston (Mountain)–Style (page 600), Gingered East-West Three-Bean and Vegetable Stew (page 227), Casserole of Slow-Cooked Calypso Beans with Orange and Onion (page 601). There's also Brazilian Rice (page 473) or Spanish Millet (page 548) and Jeanne Ramu's Three-Bean Mix (page 381).	You'll find azukis dried in natural foods supermarkets. In recent years, one or two natural foods brands of canned azukis have also become available. Urad dal may be found in Indian markets, where they may be referred to as "black gram" (confusing because they are white—but they were black before they got hulled!). If you're not mixed up yet, get ready, because the Phipps web site offers them as "white lentils."	The leap to sweetness in the red bean paste used in several Asian desserts is not illogical—this bean has a natural sweetness.
Kachina's Chili (page 193) is a favorite. Instant black beans appear in the luscious Tomatoes Stuffed with Cornbread Dressing and Gravy (page 431), and Southwestern-Style Tomato Gravy (page 433).	Most supermarkets offer both dried and canned black beans, as do natural foods stores, which offer the dehydrated beans as well. Fermented black beans may be found in Asian foods markets, as well as the Asian foods section of larger supermarkets.	Black beans are my single favorite bean, and I crave the Cuban Black Bean Soup in *Dairy Hollow House Soup & Bread*. Black beans are also de rigeur in Feijoada (page 602) and many enchiladas and chilies.

Name	Origins, Looks, Properties, Close Kin	Traditional Use	Cooking Time and Notes
Great Northern and navy beans Indistinguishable from canellini beans, white kidneys	New World white beans: Great Northern a little larger, navy beans a little smaller. Available dried and canned. They are bland in flavor, exceptionally creamy in texture. An amiable all-purpose bean.	A classic bean for European and American soups, these are *the* bean for Boston baked beans. They are often dressed with olive oil, lemon or vinegar, and herbs, and served at room temperature as part of an appetizer plate in France, Italy, and the Near East.	Presoaked and conventionally cooked, these are done in 1 to 1½ hours; under pressure, allow presoaked 8 to 10 minutes.
Kidney beans	A beautiful burgundy red, these New World beans are, naturally, kidney shaped. They share with navy and Great Northerns a creamy-not-starchy texture; they share with azukis a touch of sweetness. They hold their shape well when cooked. Available canned or dried.	Classic in three-bean salads and many soups.	Allow 1¼ to 1¾ hours of conventional cooking time for presoaked kidney beans, or 10 to 12 minutes under pressure.
Lima beans and baby lima beans Large or baby butter beans, more likely to be called butter beans in the South and lima in the North.	This native of Peru is a flat disc shape with a shapely curve on one edge, neutral in flavor, more starchy than creamy in texture (although the babies are quite creamy) with a slight butteriness in flavor (hence their nickname). The large, as mentioned earlier, are the exception to the "don't salt till tender" rule—use salt in both soaking and cooking large limas, to strengthen their skins and help the beans hold together better when cooking.	A classic in succotash.	If cooking limas conventionally, allow 1¼ to 1½ hours for large presoaked-with-salt limas, 1½ to 1¾ for presoaked babies. (The babies take longer to cook because they are plumper.) A lima exception to the rule: Pressure cooking of large limas is advised *only* in kitchens with the "second generation"–type pressure cookers, not the old-fashioned "jiggle-tops," because the loose skins can more easily clog the vent. Atypically, add a teaspoon of oil to the new-generation cooker's pot to prevent possible clogging. Baby limas do not require presalting or added oil.
Pinto beans	A pretty, pinkish-red speckled New World bean, pintos are good just about any way you can do a bean. Creamy-textured and with more inherent flavor than most beans except black. Available dried, canned, and dehydrated.	The traditional Texas chili bean.	Stove-top, presoaked pinto beans cook in 1 to 1½ hours; under pressure, presoaked, 9 to 12 minutes. Dehydrated pintos become a wonderful savory mass that tastes refried but isn't, in about 8 minutes. Just pour boiling water over the dehydrated beans, as the package directs, and let 'em soak.

Best Enjoyed In . . .	Where to Find Them	Bean Trivia
Good with Greek and Mediterranean flavorings finished with sweetness or spice. You may find them here in Old-Fashioned, All-Day Baked Beans, Boston (Mountain)–Style (page 600), Tuscan Bean and Vegetable Stew (page 225), White Chili with Eggplant, Poblanos, and Posole (page 189), and Middle European–Style Stuffed Cabbage-Leaf Rolls (page 392). They work well in any marinated bean salad.	Available dry or canned in any supermarket or natural foods market.	These agreeable legumes are the variety used in the famous U.S. Senate Bean Soup.
Try kidney beans in any chili (pages 187–93) or with any Mexican/South American spicing, or seasoned Mediterranean-style. Try them in Chilaquiles Windflower (page 376). And don't—repeat, do not—miss Pumpkin and Bean Lasagna with Caramelized Garlic 367 (page 367). They work well in any marinated bean salad.	Available dry or canned in any supermarket or natural foods market.	Man walks into a store. "Do you have any kidley beans?" Shopkeeper: "I'm sorry, sir, do you perhaps mean kidney beans?" Man: "I said kidley, did'l I?"
Try limas, large or baby, in soups, with Southwestern flavors, or in Cholent (page 220). They're also nice in marinated bean salads, where their unusual shape gives visual interest.	Available dry or canned in any supermarket or natural foods market.	CD (MIDWAY INTO LONG, ENTHUSIASTIC BURST ABOUT FASCINATIONS OF BEAN WORLD RESEARCH): And limas . . . did you know they're natives of Peru, named after Lima-the-city? NED (DEADPAN): Really? I thought they were named after those British sailors, because they helped prevent scurvy. CD (QUARTER-BEAT LATER): No, you're thinking of navy beans.
They are great as stand-alones, especially seasoned with some spice, but also refried, stuffed in tortillas, and so on. Try them in CD's Neo-Traditional Red Chili (page 191) or Posole-Bean Soup-Stew with New World Vegetables (page 210). I also like them in minestrone, although they are not traditional in it.	Most supermarkets offer both dried and canned pinto beans, as do natural foods stores. The latter also offer the incredibly convenient and delicious dehydrated beans.	These are the first beans I grew to know and love, through my first husband, the proverbial long tall Texan. The first time he fixed his Yankee bride a pot of pintos, I was amazed at how good they were. I still eat them as he prepared them, with lots of jalapeños and scrambled eggs.

Bean Cookery, and the Streamlined Bean

Beans for the Speed Demon: Two Alternatives

CANNED BEANS: You want healthy? You want quick? You want beans? Open a can. Canned beans are one of the few shortcut foods that really are as wholesome as from-scratch, and taste *almost* as good.

There are three provisos to using canned beans:

1. Their packaging and the manufacture of that packaging wastes resources. Try to limit use of canned goods, especially when there are easy, environmentally sound alternatives, as with beans.

2. Herbs, spices, and flavorings cannot be cooked in, as the beans are already cooked. However, there are plenty of savory recipes in which the seasonings can be added to great effect.

3. You must be a label reader. Some canned bean varieties have animal products added to them, or may be excessively salty or sweet.

DEHYDRATED BEANS: These are a miracle product that should be in everyone's cupboard. Run, don't walk, to your natural foods store and buy several containers! Once you experience the 5-minute, one-pot, no-fat, absolutely delicious "refried" beans these enable you to make, there's no turning back. And wait'll you see the body and richness a few shakes of dehydrated beans will add to a vegetable soup—irresistible. Please note that this product produces mashed, not whole beans.

Basic Dried Bean Cooking Methods

To convert a dry, hard bean to a toothsome bowl of chili or dal, it is necessary to cook it. This is easy as rolling off a log, but time consuming to explain fully, so bear with me.

There are several options for bean cooking. Try different methods, and come up with what works best for you.

Whatever the method, the first step remains the same. Before cooking, sort the beans by picking through, sifting them with your fingers into a colander to remove any tiny rocks, pebbles, or pieces of straw. Then rinse well in cold filtered water. After rinsing, soak them, preferably in filtered water. Almost all slow-to-cook beans (that is, everything except lentils, split peas, azuki and mung beans, and black-eyed peas) do better when soaked. You do not strictly have to soak beans, but there are many reasons to do so. For one thing, they cook in up to a third less time. For another, soaking beans—if you discard the soaking water—reduces flatulence. You do lose some of the B vitamins by discarding the water (which is why in the past I have advocated cooking the beans in their soaking liquid), but if you avoid eating beans because of the discomfort, social or physical, that they cause you, well, you're not getting those B vitamins anyway. Draining the soaking water does not alter the protein content.

You'll know when the beans are adequately soaked, because they will be much inflated in appearance and, when you split one in half, you'll be able to see that it's fully hydrated, as it will be the

same color all the way through. If it's not fully hydrated, you'll see a paler dry spot at the center, and the beans need to soak longer.

Overnight soaking: This is the way I usually soak beans because I think it yields a nominally better product, evenly creamy.

Soak the picked-over, rinsed beans in enough filtered water to cover them by an inch or so, for 6 to 8 hours or overnight. They can soak at room temperature except in hot weather; in this case, refrigerate them.

The next morning, pour off any remaining soaking water, turn the beans out into a colander, and rinse them several times. Cook as desired.

Quick soak: Place the picked-over, rinsed beans in a medium-large pot, adding enough filtered water to cover them by an inch or so. Place the pot over high heat and bring to a hard boil. Cook the beans for 5 minutes. Turn the heat off, cover, and let stand for 1 hour. Pour off any remaining water, transfer the beans to a colander, and rinse them several times. Cook as desired.

Pressured quick soak: Place the picked-over, rinsed beans in a large pressure cooker. Add 3 cups filtered water for the first cup of dry beans and 2 cups water for each cup thereafter. Lock the lid in place and bring to high pressure. For smaller beans (azuki, navy, tepary), count to 10, turn off the heat, and let the pressure release naturally for 10 minutes before unlocking the lid. Give medium beans (black beans, kidneys) 1 to 2 minutes at high pressure, then let the pressure release naturally for 15 minutes before unlocking the lid. Allow 3 minutes at high pressure for extra-large beans (large limas) or hard beans (chickpeas), then let the pressure release naturally for 20 minutes before unlocking the lid. After the lid is removed, turn the beans out into a colander and rinse thoroughly. Cook as desired.

Pressure-cooking, without presoak: This is the fastest way to cook beans. Place rinsed beans in a pressure cooker, adding 1 teaspoon to 1 tablespoon oil per cup of dried beans (optional in "second generation" pressure cookers, but required in old-fashioned jiggle-tops to avoid clogging). Add the amount of water or stock called for in the specific recipe, or enough to cover beans by about 1½ inches, but don't fill the pot more than halfway full (these puppies expand). Lock the lid in place and cook under high pressure for 2 to 3 minutes (azukis, baby limas) to 10 to 14 minutes (favas, chickpeas). Allow the pressure to release naturally. Check for doneness, simmering conventionally if they are not quite done, or bringing back to high pressure for another minute or two if they are very underdone.

Hold the Salt

Almost never—except in the case of large limas and black soybeans—should you add salt to beans until after they are cooked and tender. The same goes for the addition of any acid ingredient (vinegar, lemon juice, even tomatoes). Salt and acid both toughen the skins of the beans.

Large limas and black soybeans are exceptions to this rule because they have unusually tender skins that tend to slip off while cooking, leaving a mushy-textured pot. Therefore, salt them before cooking. You can even salt the soaking water.

BASIC STOVE-TOP METHOD FOR SOAKED BEANS: Place drained, rinsed, soaked beans in a large, heavy nonstick pot, or one that has been sprayed with cooking spray. Cover with filtered or spring water, stock, or the liquid called for in the recipe, either in the measurement called for or enough to cover the beans by about 1 inch. Place over high heat and bring to a hard boil. Lower the heat to low and cover. Cook at a low simmer until done. Every so often—maybe every 30 to 45 minutes—check the beans and give them a stir. Add additional liquid as needed.

CROCKPOT METHOD FOR SOAKED BEANS: Combine soaked, rinsed beans with filtered or spring water or stock to cover in a crockpot set to high. Cook, covered, at high for 1 hour. Turn down to low and cook slowly till done—6 to 8 hours.

Pots of Beans

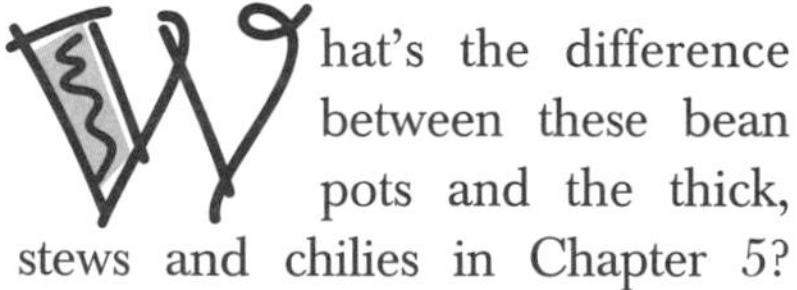

What's the difference between these bean pots and the thick, stews and chilies in Chapter 5? There's less liquid and fewer ingredients—no big chunks of potato, squash, or seitan, say. Like most of the recipes in that chapter, though, serve them with a salad and a starch and you've got a meal.

I usually cook beans by the overnight soak/stove-top method.

Buckaroo Beans

Forget bland and boring. These socko beans combine the method and a few of the seasonings of Boston-style slow-baked beans, with Southwestern flavors reminiscent of chili. Pinto or anasazi beans replace the white beans typically used in Boston-style baked beans. The smokiness once supplied by bacon is found in the canned chipotle in adobo (optional but very good) along with a sprinkle of vegetarian bacon bits. Unsweetend chocolate? It sounds strange . . . until you consider its presence in mole sauce. Coffee also sounds weird but adds a wonderful deep, dark richness.

Cornbread, or steamed or toasted corn or flour tortillas, are all perfectly delicious with this heady pot. Or try it with Smokin' Rice (page 472) or Brazilian Rice (page 473) for a double whammy. **SERVES 4 TO 6**

1 pound pinto, anasazi, or appaloosa beans, soaked (see pages 597–98)
2 bay leaves
Cooking spray
1 large onion, chopped
1 large green bell pepper, seeds and membrane removed, chopped
1 to 2 canned chipotle peppers, diced, with 1 to 2 teaspoons of their adobo sauce
1 ounce unsweetened chocolate, chopped
1 cup canned crushed tomatoes in puree
1 cup very strong coffee
3 tablespoons brown sugar
1 tablespoon chili powder
2 teaspoons dried oregano
2 teaspoons salt
1 teaspoon ground cumin
1 teaspoon dry mustard
Additional boiling water, coffee, or vegetable stock as needed
2 to 3 tablespoons vegetarian bacon bits (optional)
Accompaniments (optional): cornbread or tortillas, salsa, sour cream or Yogurt Sour Cream (page 910), diced raw onion, and grated Cheddar or jack cheese

1 Drain the beans well, rinse, and place in a large pot with fresh water to cover. Add the bay leaves and place over high heat. Bring to a boil; lower the heat and simmer until tender, about 40 minutes for anasazis, 1½ hours for pintos. Remove from the heat. Drain and reserve the cooking liquid.

2 Preheat the oven to 275°F.

3 Spray a bean pot or other deep, nonreactive casserole with cooking spray. Scatter the onion and green pepper over the bottom, then add the drained beans.

4 Whisk the chipotles and adobo sauce, unsweetened chocolate, crushed tomatoes, coffee, brown sugar, chile powder, oregano (crush the leaves between your fingers as you add it, to release the essential oils), salt, ground cumin, and dry mustard into the reserved bean cooking liquid. When well combined, pour over the beans. The liquid should just barely cover the beans; if it doesn't, add just enough boiling water, coffee, or vegetable stock to achieve this. Cover and bake for 6 hours, checking every once in a while to make sure the liquid level is maintained.

5 After the beans have baked for 6 hours, uncover. Stir to distribute the onion and green pepper throughout the beans. Return to the oven and bake, uncovered, for 50 minutes more. If using, stir in the bacon bits and bake for an additional 10 minutes. Serve, hot, with cornbread or torillas, and pass any desired accompaniments at the table.

NOTE

The 6-hour cooking may be done in a Crockpot set on low.

Old-Fashioned, All-Day, Baked Beans, Boston (Mountain)–Style

NOTE

The 6-hour cooking may also be done in a Crockpot set on low.

Raised on the East Coast, I grew up eating, at summer camp, boarding school, and occasionally at home, Boston baked beans, universally served with moist, steamed date-nut bread—Boston brown bread.

When I moved to the Ozarks in the '70s, I ate many a pot of beans and cornbread, but would occasionally get a hankering for the beans of my past. By this time I was a semivegetarian and had discovered that, although salt pork's flavor is distinctive, the fatty richness and "mouthful" it loaned the beans could be duplicated in any number of ways, peanut butter and tahini being two of the more interesting and surprisingly good ones. One day I added a few cubes of tofu to the nearly finished beans as a kind of visual joke. I found that tofu made perfect trompe l'oeil salt pork.

SERVES 4 TO 6

- **1 pound white beans (such as navy or Great Northern), soaked (see pages 597–98)**
- **Cooking spray or oil**
- **1 large onion, sliced**
- **⅓ cup brown sugar**
- **¼ cup molasses**
- **¼ cup tomato paste**
- **1 tablespoon golden miso**
- **1 tablespoon dry mustard**
- **1 teaspoon salt**
- **½ to 1 teaspoon freshly ground black pepper**
- **Pinch of ground cloves**
- **2 tablespoons butter, vegetable margarine, peanut butter, or tahini (optional)**
- **Boiling water or vegetable stock (see page 139)**
- **2 to 4 ounces firm tofu, cut up into large squares (optional)**

1 Drain the beans well, rinse, and place in a large pot with fresh water to cover by 1½ inches. Place over high heat and bring to a boil. Lower the heat and simmer until tender, about 1½ hours. Remove from the heat. Drain and reserve the cooking liquid.

2 Preheat the oven to 275°F.

3 Spray a bean pot or other deep, nonreactive casserole with cooking spray. Place the sliced onion in the bottom, then add the drained beans. Set aside.

4 Whisk the brown sugar, molasses, tomato paste, miso, dry mustard, salt, pepper, and ground cloves into the reserved bean cooking liquid. If using, stir in the butter. When well combined, pour over the beans. The liquid should just barely cover the beans; if it doesn't, add just enough boiling water or vegetable stock to achieve this. Cover and bake for 6 hours, checking every once in a while to make sure that the liquid level is maintained.

5 After the beans have baked for 6 hours, uncover. Stir to distribute the onion throughout the beans. If adding the tofu, scatter it over the top of the beans, pressing in lightly, but letting it show for the visual "salt pork" effect. Return to the oven and bake for 1 hour more. Serve hot, with steamed Boston brown bread (traditional) or cornbread (not traditional, but also wonderful). Some people like to offer ketchup or chile sauce (the sweet, almost relishy kind, not salsa) with this, or a sweet-tart relish like Cora Pinkley Call's Uncooked Ozark Relish (page 929).

Casserole of Slow-Cooked Calypso Beans with Orange and Onion

Spicy, sassy, and quite sweet, these have an Asian, teriyaki-ish twang to them, though there's no real reason why they should—no tamari, ginger, or the like. The heat comes from piquante-style ketchup; if you don't care for it, use ordinary ketchup or even tomato paste. On no account omit the black pepper—rather, be vigorous with it, as it balances the sweetness. I like this served with a slightly sweet bran or corn muffin. **SERVES 6 TO 8**

VARIATION

Without a slow cooker, slowly sauté the onion in the oil in a heavy Dutch oven sprayed with cooking spray. Then add all of the ingredients and bake, covered, at 325°F for 3 to 4 hours. If the beans seem too juicy, remove the cover for the last hour of baking.

1 pound (about 2½ cups) butterscotch calypso beans (or substitute navy, Great Northern, or yellow-eye beans), soaked (see pages 597–98)
2 tablespoons olive oil
2 large onions, chopped
1 tablespoon garlic, chopped, or 1 tablespoon Garlic Oil (page 898)
½ packed cup dark brown sugar
½ cup thawed frozen orange juice concentrate
½ cup spicy ketchup (such as Millina's Finest Organic Piquante Ketchup)
1½ teaspoons salt
Finely grated rind of 1 orange (optional)
Freshly ground black pepper to taste

1 Rinse the beans well and transfer to a heavy soup pot with fresh water to cover them by ½ to 1 inch. Place over high heat and bring to a boil. Lower the heat and simmer, half-covered, until tender, 45 minutes to 1¼ hours. Drain and reserve the cooking liquid.

2 As the beans cook, place the oil in a slow cooker or crockpot turned to high. Add the onions and, stirring occasionally, cook until very soft, 35 to 45 minutes. Turn the pot to low and add the garlic (or Garlic Oil). Cook for another 5 to 10 minutes.

3 To the slow cooker, add the brown sugar, orange juice concentrate, and spicy ketchup, stirring well to dissolve the sugar. Add the salt, along with the cooked beans, and stir well. Add just enough of the reserved cooking liquid to barely cover the beans and add the orange rind, if using, and stir again.

4 Cover the slow cooker and cook the beans on low for 3 to 4 hours, adding additional cooking liquid if needed. Stir in the black pepper and cook for 30 minutes more. Serve hot, with a big salad and corn or bran muffins.

Black Bean Feijoada

The national dish of Brazil, feijoada is a pot of black beans made savory by herbs, spices, a touch of orange, with lots of meat in various forms. I have omitted the meat in favor of various soysages, amplified the seasonings way up, and added some savory sautéed vegetables—with very satisfactory results. Chipotle chiles add a nice smoky flavor reminscent of the smoked meats. **SERVES 6 TO 8, WITH A RICE DISH**

2½ cups black beans, soaked (see pages 597–98)
2 bay leaves
1 onion, skin on, stuck with 4 cloves, plus 1 large onion, chopped
1 head garlic, skin on, plus 4 cloves garlic, pressed
1 canned chipotle chile with 1 teaspoon of the adobo sauce from the can
1 tablespoon dried oregano leaves
1 large white potato, cut into 1-inch cubes
1 large sweet potato, cut into 1-inch cubes
2 tablespoons tomato paste
2 tablespoons freshly grated orange rind
1 tablespoon miso
1 to 2 teaspoons salt
Cooking spray
8 commercially prepared vegetarian soysage links, ideally 4 Italian-style and 4 breakfast-style
2 to 3 tablespoons olive oil
2 carrots, diced
2 ribs celery, chopped
1 green bell pepper, stemmed, seeds and membrane removed, chopped
1 red bell pepper, stemmed, seeds and membrane removed, chopped
2 teaspoons ground cumin
2 teaspoons ground chili powder
¼ cup apple cider vinegar
Rice or Brazilian Rice (page 473)

1 Drain the beans and rinse well. Place the beans in a Dutch oven and add fresh water to cover. Add the bay leaves, clove-studded onion, whole head of garlic, chipotle, and oregano. Place over high heat and bring to a boil. Lower the heat to a nice low simmer and cook, covered, for about 1 hour, until partly done. Add the potato and sweet potato and simmer until the beans are just about done, about 30 minutes.

2 Scoop out and discard the onion. Scoop out and reserve the garlic. Set aside to cool.

3 Add the tomato paste, grated orange rind, miso, and salt to the beans.

4 Spray a skillet with cooking spray. Add the soysages and place over medium heat. Fry, turning occasionally, until brown on all sides, about 6 minutes. Remove the soysages from the skillet and let cool. When cool, slice soysages into 2-inch-long chunks. Set aside.

5 Heat the oil in the same skillet over medium heat. Add the chopped onion and sauté until limp and starting to color slightly, 6 to 7 minutes. Add the carrots and cook, stirring, for 3 minutes more. Lower the heat slightly and add the pressed garlic, celery, green pepper, red pepper, cumin, and chili powder. Cook, stirring, until the vegetables have lost their raw edge, about 8 minutes. Remove from the heat and set aside.

6 When the beans are done, stir in the seasoned vegetables. Also, squeeze the softened garlic out of the cooled garlic head and add to the beans.

7 Return the pot to high heat and bring to a boil. Lower the heat to a simmer and cook for 15 minutes. Add the soysage and stir in the vinegar. Serve hot (it doesn't hurt a bit to wait; it only gets better). Of course, you really must serve it over, or beside, rice.

LUSCIOUS LAMBADA

Beet and Orange Salad with Rainforest Vinaigrette
(PAGE 97)

*

Tempeh Picadillo Filling
(PAGE 359, STEPS 1 AND 2)
in red or yellow pepper halves
(SEE PAGE 410)

*

Black Bean Feijoada
(PREVIOUS PAGE)

*

Brazilian Rice
(PAGE 473)

*

Stir-fried kale, collard, beet, and turnip greens with garlic

*

Brazilian Salsa
(PAGE 914)

*

Pineapple Coconut Mousse-Custard
(PAGE 1053)
with sliced mango

COOK ONCE FOR 2 MEALS If you end up with leftovers of this, or any other chili or spicy bean stew, use them to fill Tamale Pie (page 449) or Cornbread Pie à la Hippie (page 451). Feijoada is so thick, however, that you'll probably need to thin it down a bit with some canned tomatoes and green chiles for these recipes.

Mediterranean-Style Bean Pot with Slow-Cooked Vegetables

Another savory pot of beans, good hot but even better lukewarm, to be served with a baguette or sourdough bread with olive oil and Bread Herbs for Dipping (page 904). This could be part of a table of mezze (see page 59), or brought to a potluck, or used to give heft to a dinner of grilled vegetables, or served over rice or barley or kamut. The Skordalia is an optional accompaniment, but it's so good you really ought to make it. **SERVES 6 TO 8**

1½ cups white beans (navy or Great Northern), soaked (see pages 597–98)
2 tablespoons olive oil
2 large onions, halved crosswise and very thinly sliced
7 to 10 cloves garlic, peeled and sliced
2 carrots, diced
2 ribs celery, diced
1 dried red chile, broken in half
2 bay leaves
½ pound green beans, rinsed, stems and tips removed, cut into 2-inch lengths
Salt and freshly ground black pepper
Yogurt Sour Cream (page 910) or Tofu Sour Cream (page 909) (optional)
Skordalia (page 939; optional)

1 Drain the white beans and rinse well. Place in a medium pot, cover with fresh water by about 1 inch, and place over high

heat. Bring to a boil and boil for 10 minutes. Drain and then return the beans to the pot. Again, add water to cover by about 1 inch and place over high heat. Bring to a boil, then lower the heat and cook, at a low simmer, for 50 minutes. Turn off the heat and let the beans sit for 30 minutes.

2 As the beans cook, place the oil in a Crockpot or slow cooker, with the heat on high. Add the onions, cover, and cook for 30 minutes. Turn the heat to low, lift the cover, and add the garlic, carrots, celery, and chile. Cover and cook for another 40 to 50 minutes, stirring a couple of times if you happen to think of it.

3 Drain and reserve the bean cooking liquid. Add the beans to the crockpot, along with 2 cups of the cooking liquid (if desired, save the rest for use in stock). Cover the pot and, leaving it on low, cook the beans for 1 hour.

4 Toward the end of the hour, bring a small saucepan of water to a boil over high heat. Add the green beans and blanch for 3 minutes. Drain the green beans and add them to the pot. Stir well and add salt and pepper to taste (expect to use plenty of both). Cover and cook for an additional 40 minutes. Turn off the heat and let the beans stand until lukewarm, 1 to 3 hours. Serve, warm or at room temperature, with the Yogurt Sour Cream and the Skordalia, if using, encouraging diners to dollop their beans with some of each.

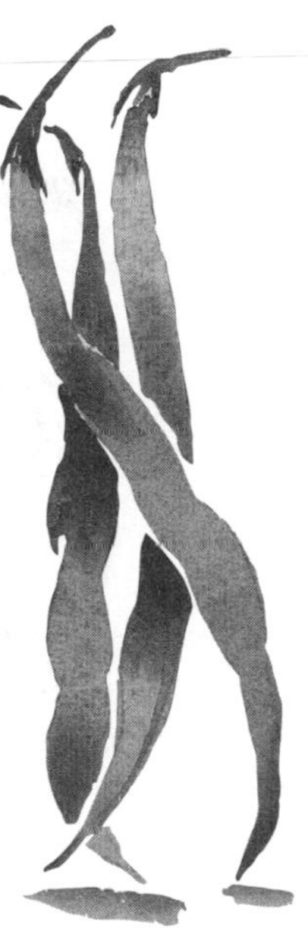

Ful Medames

Considered the national dish of Egypt, ful, pronounced "fool," is nothing more than a pot of savory beans, served up with simple condiments. It can be served hot, warm, or at room temperature, as a starter, a main course, or even at breakfast. That it is nutritious, refreshing, and highly delightful, like so much Middle Eastern fare, goes without saying. It's also quite simple to prepare.

The beans traditionally used are favas, which are available in several forms. I have most often found favas that look like a flat, buff-colored lima bean, but have also seen a small, more rounded variety and a large cracked type that comes skinned.

OVERLOOKING THE ARKANSAS RIVER, AT SUSAN & RICK'S

Salad of Local Greens and Basil Vinaigrette
(PAGE 71)

*

Sautéed polenta rounds

*

Gigi Hamilton's Really Hot, Really Delectable Mixed Beans with a Lot of Ginger

*

Parfait of layered mango sorbet and raspberry sorbet, with Amaretti and Cocoa-Stuffed Peaches
(PAGE 989)

*

After-Eight mints

*

Decaf coffee / mint tea

Ful can be used to mean fava beans generally, as well as this dish specifically. White beans (navy or Great Northern) or black-eyed peas can be substituted. As for the condiments, some quarter the eggs and mince the tomatoes (or vice versa); some add an onion to the beans as they cook, or serve with a crisp raw scallion; some sprinkle the eggs on top of the beans, with the parsley, paprika, and turmeric over the eggs. But the lemon and tomato are essential, and a little olive oil makes a mighty big difference. Serve, of course, with toasted pita bread wedges. **SERVES 4 TO 6**

BEANS

- 1½ cups dried fava or white beans, or black-eyed peas, well washed
- 2½ teaspoons ground cumin
- 6 cloves garlic, pressed
- Juice of 1 lemon
- ¼ cup finely minced parsley
- 3 tablespoons olive oil
- Salt and freshly ground black pepper to taste

CONDIMENTS AND GARNISHES

- Paprika
- Turmeric
- 3 red-ripe tomatoes, sliced
- 2 large hard-cooked eggs, finely chopped (preferably free-range, organic eggs)
- Olive oil in a small cruet
- Classic Tahini Sauce (page 953) in a small cruet (optional—an Israeli touch, and delicious; Egyptians offer just the olive oil)
- Lemon wedges
- Warmed pita breads, cut into wedges

1 If using fava or white beans, soak them overnight in water to cover, beginning early the night before. (Black-eyed peas do not need the overnight soak.) The next day, drain and rinse the beans. Peel off their skins by rubbing between your fingers. Place in a large heavy saucepan and cover with fresh water. Place over high heat and bring to a boil. Boil for 5 minutes, then lower the heat to a simmer. (Alternatively, turn the beans out into a crockpot turned to low, for continued slow cooking). Cover and simmer until the beans are nearly tender, adding water as needed to keep them barely covered. For new-crop black-eyed peas, this may be as little as 30 minutes; for favas, it may be 2 hours or—if from an older crop—as long as 4 hours.

2 When the beans are almost tender, add the ground cumin and continue cooking until tender. There should be not too much cooking liquid left. Remove the pan from heat. Add the garlic, lemon juice, and 2 tablespoons each of the parsley and oil. Stir to combine. Add salt and pepper to taste. Beans usually require more salt than a person would suppose. Transfer to a shallow bowl, wide enough so guests can easily dip from it.

Sprinkle with the remaining parsley, a small dusting of paprika, and an even smaller dusting of turmeric. Pass the tomatoes, eggs, olive oil and/or tahini, lemon wedges, and pita breads so each guest can doctor his own plate of ful.

Gigi Hamilton's Really Hot, Really Delectable Mixed Beans with a Lot of Ginger

Almost but not quite curried, this easy mixed-bean dish is hot enough to make you sit up and take notice, and so good you simply cannot stop eating it.

A spicy savory sauté with canned beans makes this quite quick and easy to do. You don't have to use both fresh chile and Ro*Tel; if you'd like it less hot but still kicky, omit the fresh chile. Note that the beans are drained of their liquid, which gives the finished dish lightness and makes the seasonings sparkle. **SERVES 6 TO 8 AMPLY**

NOTES

This makes a rather large batch, but it freezes well.

If you don't know about Ro*Tel, read all about it on page 190.

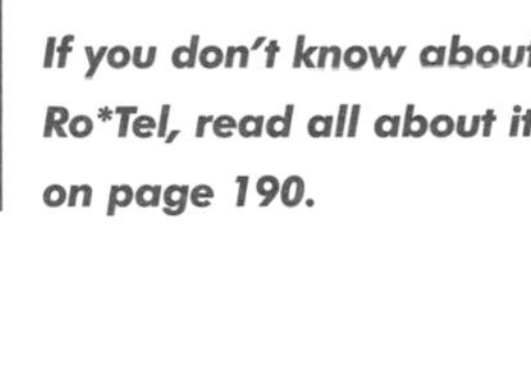

1 tablespoon olive oil
Cooking spray
2 large onions, chopped
5 cloves garlic, chopped
¼ cup loosely packed peeled, grated ginger (yes, ¼ cup!)
1 small hot chile (serrano or jalapeño), seeded or not, depending on your wish for heat, and diced (optional)
1 can (10 ounces) Ro*Tel diced tomatoes and green chiles
2 cans (30 ounces) white or navy beans, well drained
2 cans (30 ounces) kidney beans, well drained
1 can (15 ounces) black beans, well drained
1 can (15 ounces) chickpeas, well drained
1 can (15 ounces) white hominy, well drained
Stems from 1 bunch cilantro, chopped
Cilantro leaves (optional)

1. Heat the oil in a large nonstick Dutch oven, or one that has been sprayed with cooking spray, over medium heat. Add the onions and sauté for 4 minutes, then add the garlic and ginger, and, if using, the chile. Sauté for about 5 minutes more. Add the tomatoes and green chiles and cook, stirring often, until heated through.

2. Add the white, kidney, and black beans, along with the chickpeas and hominy. Bring to a boil. Lower the heat to a simmer, and simmer until the flavors have blended, about 20 minutes. Add the cilantro stems and cook for an additional 3 minutes.

3. Serve hot, accompanied by any cooked grain or bread, sprinkled with cilantro leaves, if desired.

Ginger

SWEET DREAMS SIMPLE SOUTH INDIAN SUPPER

South Indian Green Gram

*

Warmed chapatis (or whole wheat tortillas)

*

Salad of salted diced tomatoes and red onion

*

Small red banana

*

Warm milk, sweetened lightly with sugar

South Indian Green Gram

This is a pot of mung beans as served in South India, with coconut, spices, and tamarind (see page 90). *Green gram* is both the name of the legume and the finished dish. Though this sounds exotic, it has a surprisingly familiar flavor, almost more Texan than Indian. After the last time I left India, I thought I could be happy never eating it again for having had it so often, but now I get cravings for it regularly.

To split the chiles, cut them from tip to stem, but do not cut through the stem, so the chile still holds together. **SERVES 6 TO 8, ACCOMPANIED BY RICE OR WHOLE WHEAT CHAPATIS**

2 cups whole mung beans (green gram if you buy them at an Indian market), picked over and rinsed
6 cups water, preferably spring or filtered
1½ tablespoons ghee (see page 486), or mild vegetable oil
1 small red chile, such as a ripe serrano, halved (if no small fresh red chiles are available, use a dried red one)
1 tablespoon brown or black mustard seeds
6 to 8 green chiles, such as serannos, split as described in the headnote
1¾ cups reconstituted tamarind paste (see page 90)
1¼ teaspoons turmeric
½ cup dried, unsweetened coconut shreds
Plenty of salt to taste
Chopped cilantro (optional)

1 Combine the mung beans and water in a medium saucepan over high heat. Bring to a boil, then lower the heat to a simmer. Simmer, half-covered, until the beans are very softy and mushy, about 1¼ hours. Remove from the heat and set aside.

2 About 15 minutes before the beans are ready, heat the ghee in a small skillet over high heat. When it is sizzling hot, add the red chile and mustard seeds. When the seeds start to pop and the chile darkens, add the green chiles, tamarind paste, and turmeric. Lower the heat slightly and cook, stirring, for 3 minutes. Add the mixture to the cooked mung beans, along with the coconut and salt to taste—it'll need a lot. Return the bean mixture to a simmer and cook, stirring occasionally, until the flavors are well blended, 20 to 30 minutes more. Serve hot, with an optional sprinkle of cilantro, if desired.

Dal

Throughout the Indian subcontinent, a meal is not a meal without dal—a thick, spicy bean stew served over rice. This is an exceptional one. **SERVES 4 TO 6 AS AN ENTREE, WITH COOKED RICE**

Cooking spray
5 to 6 cups water, preferably spring or filtered
2 cups lentils (or split chickpeas), washed and picked over
1 bay leaf
3 tablespoons butter
1 large onion, chopped
1 tablespoon minced fresh ginger
1 tablespoon cumin seeds
1 tablespoon black mustard seeds (do not substitute yellow)
1½ teaspoons ground coriander
1½ teaspoons ground turmeric
Pinch of ground cloves
Pinch of cayenne, or to taste
Salt and freshly ground black pepper to taste
2 to 3 cups hot cooked rice

1 Spray a large heavy soup pot with cooking spray and add the water, lentils, and bay leaf. Place over high heat and bring to a boil. Lower the heat and cook at a low simmer, covered, until the lentils are very soft, about 1 hour.

2 While the lentils are cooking, melt the butter in a large skillet over medium heat. Add the onion and sauté until softened, about 3 minutes. Add the ginger and all of the spices. Lower the heat slightly and cook, stirring constantly, for 3 minutes. Scrape this spice mixture into the lentils and continue cooking until the lentils are very soft, thick, and saucelike. Season with salt and pepper. Serve hot over cooked rice, or let cool and reheat the next day (it will be even better).

Oh, Dal-ing

When an Indian cook goes to the market for beans, he or she may purchase gram or dal. *Gram refers to whole, unsplit beans;* dal, *to split, usually hulled, beans. But here it grows confusing, for dal, like couscous, is one of those food terms that mean both an ingredient and a dish commonly made from that ingredient. If you ask for dal in a restaurant, you'll get a highly seasoned dish, to be served as a sauce or stew over rice, or possibly as a soup. Ask for dal at your local Indian market, however, and you'll be pointed to a shelf of channa dal (split, hulled chickpeas), moong dal (split mung beans), thoor dal (similar to a yellow split pea), urad dal (split, hulled black azuki beans), and more.*

Quick-Cooking and Agreeable:

The little legumes—split peas, lentils, channa dal, and urad dal—are all versatile legumes, none of which requires presoaking; all cook in under an hour. Although you could pressure-cook them, I don't, since they're such a quick-fix anyway.

LENTILS *have a delicious, distinctive flavor, and are good cold or hot, in soups or as a sauce/stew to be served over grains, or mashed for various veggie burgers and loaves. They work quite well with a mixed palette of flavorings: Mediterranean, North African, Indian. I also make them sweet-sour on occasion. Stirred into a robustly seasoned tomato sauce, they lend a heartiness and mouthfeel not unlike a classic meaty Bolgonese sauce (see Tomato Sauce with Lentils, page 932); also good in Greek-Style Tomato Sauce with Lentils, (page 932).*

BROWN LENTILS, *raised in the American Northwest, are the brownish green, tiny discs commonly found in supermarkets or natural foods stores. They hold their own with strong, wintery flavors: wild rice, full-flavored mushrooms. They cook tender in 30 to 45 minutes.*

PARDINA (SPANISH) LENTILS, *about one-third the size of conventional lentils, hold their shape nicely when cooked. They have a slightly richer flavor than brown lentils, but they work well in similar pairings. They cook a bit more quickly, too.*

GREEN LENTILS, *slightly smaller, are imported from France and even more flavorful than the domestics. They also cook tender in 30 to 45 minutes.*

BLACK BELUGA LENTILS, *which, as far as I know, are available only through Indian Harvest, are captivating, tiny, round, black lentils that really do look like caviar. They cook in 20 to 30 minutes, have a nice nutty flavor, and offer a pleasant contrast when served with a pale cooked grain. Cooked separately and stirred in at the last, they are an excellent addition to risotti.*

RED LENTILS *are a stunning, vibrant coral orange before they're cooked. The hue mutes to a golden yellow with cooking—which is a mighty quick proposition. They cook up mushy in just minutes—no drawback, just something to*

The Little Legumes

work with. Try them instead of split peas in Sauce Mongole (page 933) or in Middle Eastern–Style Pilaf with Noodles and Red Lentils (page 483).

SPLIT PEAS *are a special variety of yellow or green peas grown specifically for drying. Usually sold split down the natural break in the center, they can also be purchased whole. Flavorful as a legume can be (at least, when tweaked with a little seasoning), split peas have the added benefits of being quick to cook and relatively low in gas-forming compounds.*

GREEN SPLIT PEAS *are probably the most familiar variety, as in oh-so-comforting split pea soup (there are three variations in my* Dairy Hollow House Soup & Bread, *all wonderful if I do say so myself). But because they cook up speedily and so very creamily, they can also be used in other surprising ways. The Quick Spinach–Split Pea Cakes (page 839) use instant split pea soup and are far more pleasing than they have any right to be. And Sauce Mongole (page 933) is lively, succulent, and very low in fat. Split peas do not need presoaking, and will cook to tenderness in as little as 30 to 40 minutes.*

YELLOW SPLIT PEAS *are used much more often in India than America, as the basis for soupy, spicy, pleasing dal, an all-purpose Indian dish of a thousand regional variations. Brighter in color, they seem to suggest bright, spicy flavorings—but, in truth, you can swap green for yellow or yellow for green in any recipe, Eastern or Western. Cooking time's the same.*

CHANNA DAL *(split, hulled chickpeas) are a blessing to the chickpea lovers among us who grow restive over the long, long cooking time of whole chickpeas. Channa dal cook in about 30 minutes, with no presoaking. You get good chickpea flavor with a split pea–like texture. This is ideal for soup, or dips, such as the famous hummus tahini, or as yet another alternative for Dal (page 609).*

URAD DAL *look like tiny white lentils, and they are sometimes sold as such. But they're actually split, hulled black azuki beans. Like channa dal, the best place to find this legume is at an Indian market, where they may be referred to as "black gram" (confusing because they are white). Urad dal are used almost exclusively in Indian food, where they are browned in oil and tossed in at the last minute to add a nutlike crunch and an elusive, delicious, mild, rather nutty flavor. Try the technique in White Coconut Chutney (page 924)—delicious.*

CASSOULET FOR COMPANY

Braised and Glazed Celery Française
(PAGE 733)

*

Salad of bitter greens, with Sharp Classic Vinaigrette with a Bite
(PAGE 72)

*

Vegetarian Cassoulet

*

Crusty peasant bread

*

Lemon Mousse-Custard
(PAGE 1052),
or poached pears and cookies

Vegetarian Cassoulet

Get ready for the absolute, hands-down best bean dish you have ever eaten. Plump, meltingly soft beans swim in their own rich sauce of bean liquid, tomato, herbs, aromatics, and olive oil, their texture at play with hearty sautéed soysage and vegetarian Canadian bacon, the whole baked under a crisply crumbed topping. Because traditional cassoulet is both meat-heavy and one of those dishes about which there is passionate opinion, I hesitated to call this garlicky dish by that hallowed name. But my touchstone in working out the recipe was indeed that famed French peasant classic, and this cassoulet can, definitively, hold its own against any other.

If you can get flageolets, by all means substitute them for navy beans. Also, read the recipe and ingredient list through before starting. For instance, ½ cup olive oil is called for, but it's used a tablespoon here and a tablespoon there throughout the recipe, while garlic is used at three different points, in three forms. Yes, this is a long and complex recipe—but it's far, far less time consuming than the meat versions. **SERVES 10 TO 12**

1 large bunch Italian parsley
3 sprigs thyme
2 sprigs oregano
Cooking spray
2½ cups navy beans, soaked (see pages 597–98)
1 whole onion, skin on, studded with 3 cloves, plus 2 large onions, chopped
1 head garlic, unpeeled, plus 5 cloves garlic, peeled and minced, plus 4 cloves garlic, peeled, whole
2 ribs celery
2¼ teaspoons salt
½ cup olive oil
1 package (10 ounces) breakfast-style vegetarian soysage
1 package (10 ounces) Italian-style vegetarian soysage
1 package (6 ounces) vegetarian Canadian bacon slices
3 carrots, scrubbed, sliced into ¼-inch rounds
1 can (28 ounces) chopped tomatoes
1 teaspoon honey or Rapidura
1 teaspoon dried chile flakes
½ teaspoon freshly ground black pepper
1 cup soft breadcrumbs

1 Tie 3 sprigs of the parsley, the thyme, and oregano together with kitchen twine. Set aside.

2 Spray a large heavy pot with cooking spray.

3 Drain the beans. Place the beans in the prepared pot. Add the herb bouquet and water (or vegetable stock) to cover by 1 inch. Stir and add the clove-studded onion, whole head garlic, and celery. Place over high heat and bring to a boil. Lower the heat to a simmer and cover. Simmer gently for 40 minutes. Uncover and add 2 teaspoons of the salt. Replace the lid and continue simmering for 30 to 45 minutes longer.

4 Spray a large skillet with cooking spray. Add 1 tablespoon of the oil and place over medium heat. Add both varieties of the soysage along with the vegetarian Canadian bacon and sear, turning as needed until all sides are golden brown, about 4 minutes. Remove the soysages and bacon from the pan and let cool. When cool enough to handle, quarter the bacon rounds and slice the soysage into ¾-inch pieces. Set aside.

5 Add 3 tablespoons of the remaining oil to the skillet. Place over medium heat and add the chopped onions. Sauté until beginning to soften, about 3 minutes. Add the carrots and sauté for another 4 minutes. Lower the heat slightly and add the minced garlic. Sauté for 1 minute, then add the tomatoes, honey, and chile flakes and cook for 10 minutes more.

6 Meanwhile, taste the beans. They should be just barely tender. If so, fish out and discard the clove-studded onion, the celery, and the herb bouquet. Also fish out the garlic, but don't throw it out—set it aside to cool.

7 Add the tomato mixture to the beans.

8 When the whole garlic has cooled sufficiently to handle, squeeze the garlic pulp into the beans and tomatoes, discarding the skin.

9 Preheat the oven to 300°F.

10 Spray a deep 9½-by-18-inch casserole with cooking spray. Set aside.

11 Combine 1 ladleful of the bean mixture with the whole garlic cloves, leaves from the remaining parsley, and 3 tablespoons of the remaining oil in a food processor. Buzz until smooth, then stir the puree into the beans and season with pepper. Taste the beans for seasoning, adding the remaining ¼ teaspoon salt, or more if needed.

12 Spoon half of the beans into the prepared casserole. Scatter the soysage and vegetarian Canadian bacon over the top. Spoon in the remaining beans.

13 Toss the breadcrumbs with the remaining tablespoon of oil. Pat the mixture over the top of the beans. Place the cassoulet in the preheated oven and bake until bubbling and aromatic, about 1½ hours. Remove from the oven and raise the temperature to broil. Place the cassoulet under the broiler until the crumb crust is a deep golden brown, 1 to 2 minutes. Serve hot, straight from the casserole.

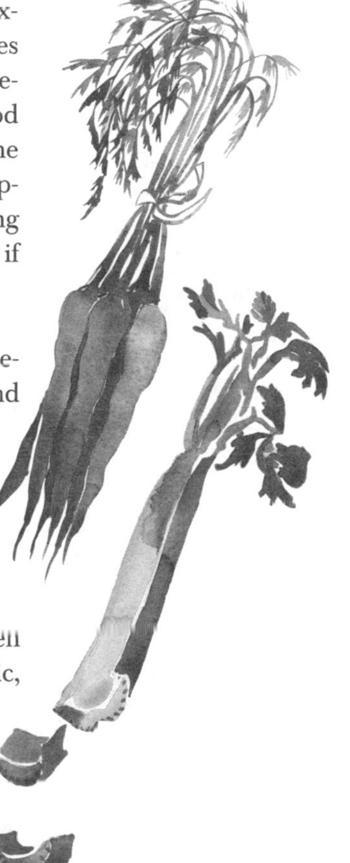

AN AMERICAN IN PARIS

The Salad
(PAGE 68)

*

Baguettes or other crisp-crusted French bread, preferably whole grain

*

French-Style Green Lentils

*

Jenelle's Tomatoes Rockefeller
(PAGE 430)

*

Apricot Mousse-Custard
(PAGE 1051)

French-Style Green Lentils

Lentilles du Puy—a.k.a. French or green lentils—are smaller and more flavorful than our common brown lentils. They also hold their shape well. Try them in this vegetarian version of the traditional French treatment, with tempeh bacon and olive oil standing in for the usual bacon. That and the extra ration of vegetables sautéed in the tempeh-flavored oil make for an exceptionally tasty dish.

The herbs are tied up in a piece of cheesecloth, called a bouquet garni, so they can steep in the cooking beans and then be retrieved without fishing through the whole bean pot. **SERVES 4 TO 6**

5 large sprigs Italian parsley
4 sprigs fresh thyme
2 bay leaves
1 teaspoon black peppercorns
2 large onions, halved, skin on
8 whole cloves
1 pound (about 2½ cups) French green lentils
¼ cup olive oil
1 package (6 ounces) smoked tempeh strips
4 leeks, white part only, split lengthwise, well washed, sliced
6 medium carrots, scrubbed, sliced into ¼-inch rounds
2 ribs celery, split lengthwise and sliced into ¼-inch pieces
4 to 6 cloves garlic, finely chopped
Salt and freshly ground black pepper

1 Make the bouquet garni by placing the parsley, thyme, bay leaves and peppercorns in a 6-inch cheesecloth square (you'll need to sort of fold the parsley branches). Pull the ends up to make a little bag and tie it closed with kitchen string.

2 Halve the onions lengthwise and stud each half with 2 cloves.

3 Place the lentils in a medium cooking pot with enough water to cover by 2 inches. Add the bouquet garni and clove-studded onion halves. Place over high heat and bring to a boil. Lower the heat to a simmer and simmer, uncovered, until the lentils are almost tender, about 20 minutes.

4 As the lentils cook, heat the oil in a heavy skillet over medium heat. When the oil is good and hot, add the tempeh strips and sear, turning once, until the tempeh is browned, 3 to 4 minutes on each side. Remove the tempeh from the skillet and let cool slightly. When cool, slice into

1-inch pieces. Set aside. Do not discard the oil.

5 Return the skillet and oil to medium heat. Add the leeks and sauté until softened but not colored, about 4 minutes. Add the carrots and celery and sauté until the vegetables have softened, 3 to 5 minutes. Add the garlic and cook for 30 seconds. Remove from the heat and set aside.

6 Back at the lentil pot. Using a pair of tongs, fish out and discard the clove-studded onion pieces and the bouquet garni. Stir the sautéed vegetables and any oil clinging to them into the lentils. Continue cooking the lentils until tender, another 10 to 15 minutes. Stir in the reserved tempeh. Add salt and pepper to taste and serve hot or at room temperature.

Beans Béchamel with a Kick

If you've ever enjoyed creamed chestnuts at a Thanksgiving dinner, you'll find this similar. To make it more of a main dish, I add sautéed onions and my eternal favorite, shiitake mushrooms, and for kick, I also throw in garlic and one finely diced serrano chile. Though its heat is tamed by the starch of the beans and the cream sauce, you still get a little chile buzz.

To my mind the perfect bean for this is the tiger-eye, available through Indian Harvest, but any individual bean or mixture would be good here. **SERVES 4**

2 teaspoons mild vegetable oil, such as corn, canola, or peanut
2 teaspoons butter
1 onion, sliced vertically into long crescents
¼ pound shiitake mushrooms, stems removed, thickly sliced
1 to 2 serrano chiles, minced (seeds and membrane removed or left in for extra heat)
2 tablespoons unbleached all-purpose flour
1½ cups milk (whole or low fat or evaporated skim; oat or rice milk—your choice)
2½ cups cooked or canned beans, preferably tiger-eye
1 tablespoon minced garlic, or Garlic Oil (page 898)
Salt and freshly ground black pepper
Finely chopped Italian parsley (optional)

1 Heat the oil and butter in a nonstick skillet over medium heat. When hot, add the onion and sauté until slightly softened, about 5 minutes. Add the mushrooms and chile (if you left the seeds and membrane in, the air may grow a bit incendiary, so stand back), and continue sautéing for 3 minutes.

2 Lower the heat slightly and sprinkle the flour over the onion mixture. Cook, stirring, for 5 minutes; then, very, very gradually, stir in the milk, smooshing the flour that's clinging to the mushrooms and onions into it (the flour will become incorporated only if you do this attentively).

3 Add the beans and garlic and simmer until heated through and the flavors have blended, about 3 minutes. Add salt and lots of black pepper. Serve hot, over any cooked grain, with a generous smattering of parsley, if desired.

Spice-Market Mélange of Chickpeas and Cauliflower

Is it a curry? Not quite. Is it Moroccan, Tunisian? You might think so from the seasonings, but you'd be wrong. Really, it's one of those "inspired by" dishes, a wondrous stew that's not really "from" anywhere except a hankering for something exotic and decidedly un-Christmasy. On a cold clear December Ozarks night, I had the vivid picture of bright red chiles drying on a tattered yellow straw mat under the too-hot South India sun in the back of my mind, and a cauliflower in the back of my fridge. Oh, and a can of chickpeas on the shelf. (The recipe didn't end up including chiles.)

You could make it more currylike by serving it over rice with yogurt and a sweet fruity chutney; you could make it more North African by serving it over steamed couscous. It would be good over a simple barley pilaf . . . even serve it over pasta. But Ned and I found it lavishly good with brown rice and a quick, sweet coleslaw. **SERVES 2 TO 4 (4 IF PART OF A COMPONENT MEAL)**

Cooking spray
2 teaspoons mild vegetable oil, such as corn, canola, or peanut
2 teaspoons black mustard seeds
½ teaspoon cumin seeds
½ onion, finely chopped
½ head cauliflower, cut into florets
2 teaspoons ground coriander
2 teaspoons paprika
1 teaspoon turmeric
½ teaspoon salt, plus more to taste
Pinch of ground cinnamon
Pinch of ground cloves
One can (15 ounces) chickpeas, with their liquid
½ cup canned crushed tomatoes in puree
1 tablespoon honey
Grated rind and juice of 1 small orange
Freshly ground black pepper
2 tablespoons coarsely chopped cilantro

1 Spray a wok with cooking spray, or use a deep nonstick skillet or nonstick wok and omit the cooking spray. Place the wok over medium heat until very hot. Add the oil, then the mustard seeds, and sauté until they start popping. (If the wok is hot enough, this could be almost instant; if not, it might take 1 to 3 minutes). Lower the heat slightly and add the cumin seeds and then the onion. Stir-fry until the onion is translucent, about 3 minutes. Add the cauliflower and stir-fry for another 2 minutes; stir in the coriander, paprika, turmeric, salt, cinnamon, and cloves. Stir-fry for 1 more minute. Cover and steam for 3 minutes.

2 Uncover the wok. Add the chickpeas and their liquid, tomatoes, and honey. Stir to combine, then add the grated orange rind and juice. Stir well and lower the heat. Simmer just to blend flavors, 5 to 10 minutes. Taste, and season with pepper and, if necessary, additional salt. Add the chopped cilantro, stir once, and serve hot, over or with the starch of your choice.

Bean Diversity

Modern agriculture rests heavily on few crops and few varieties. But the safety of our food supply depends on maintaining a diversity of plants—sometimes in ways that are not clear until we face a crisis of some sort.

Wild or lesser-known plants—including beans—enrich the gene pool. When wild plants are crossed with domesticated ones, resistance to diseases and pests, nutritional content, and yield are often improved. In the 1970s, a blight that had wiped out 15 percent of the U.S. corn crop was stopped in its tracks by the introduction of genetic material from wild Mexican corn species.

We cooks and consumers do our parts by purchasing organic foods, trying old-new varieties, and perhaps by growing seeds from bioconscious, heirloom-specializing companies, like Shepherd's Garden Seeds (www.shepherdseeds.com), or Seeds of Change (www.seedsofchange.com). Or participate in Seed Savers, a seed-exchange program based in Iowa (www.seedsavers.org). Or if we don't grow our own plants, by buying diverse kinds of beans and other kinds of foods from places like Phipps (www.phippscountry.com) or Indian Harvest (www.indianharvest.com).

Beans & Grains

Beans and grains together are a match made in heaven, yet about as earthy a combo as one could get. Throughout the world, and this book, you'll find them paired over and over again in one form or another—soups, sauces, tortillas, and so on. But I offer a few dishes in which they are cooked together in one pot, and the beans predominate slightly.

Jamaica Rice and "Peas," Veronica-Style

For about three formative years, my family had a Jamaican housekeeper named Veronica. I adored Veronica, who sashayed through the house with a lilt to her hips and a range of eyebrow-lifted expressions that could convey every shade of disbelief to disdain without a word. And then, when she did open her mouth! Bringing the color of the islands to three gray, cold East Coast winters, Veronica kept us all—from my parents to the dog, Cleo—in line. I always remember Veronica putting the dog's dish down, with that eyebrow raised, and calling, "Miss Clay-o! Miss Clay-o!" It is a cliché to call an island inflection musical, but so it was. Occasionally, she'd fix rice and peas (also called Jamaican coat of arms, so often is it eaten there): faintly sweet with the whisper of coconut milk, deliciously starchy, and (quite incidentally) vegetarian. From my first bite, I thought it was exotic, pleasing, and soothing. What she called "peas" were what we called kidney beans, and she stirred the dish as it cooked, releasing the starch and making a thick porridge-y mixture, as opposed to a fluffy one. She served rice and peas with long slices of crisp fried plaintain. I loved this meal.

Now, of course, grain and bean mixtures are staples of my diet, and I often think of Veronica when I make one and wonder where she is, and how her life turned after her brief sojourn at 29 Elm with the Zolotows. **SERVES 4 TO 6**

1 cup kidney beans, rinsed (see page 594)
1 can (14 ounces) reduced-fat unsweetened coconut milk
1 to 2 cloves garlic, pressed
1 bunch scallions, finely chopped
3 sprigs fresh thyme, or ½ teaspoon dried thyme
3 cups converted rice
Salt and freshly ground black pepper to taste
Boiling water, preferably spring or filtered

1 Drain the beans and rinse well. Combine the beans with the coconut milk in a medium saucepan over high heat. Add the garlic and bring to a boil. Lower the heat and simmer, half-covered, until the beans are tender but not mushy, about 1½ hours.

2 Add the scallions, thyme, rice, and plenty of salt and black pepper along with sufficient boiling water to cover the rice and beans by 1½ to 2 inches. Raise the heat and bring to a boil; stir once. Lower the heat and simmer, covered, lifting the lid once or twice to stir, until the rice is tender, 20 to 25 minutes. Serve hot.

Dancin' John: New South Black-Eyed Peas and Rice

In most of the world's cultures, there exist ritual good-luck dishes, to be consumed on the first day of the New Year. In the American South, the good-luck dish is black-eyed peas. (We once had December 31 inn guests who brought a can with them; when we delivered breakfast, they were eating their good-luck peas, cold, straight from the can). The usual preparation is Hoppin' John: black-eyed peas, rice, pepper, salt pork or ham hock, and onion.

VARIATION

RONNI-SPICED DANCIN' JOHN: *Ronni Lundy, one of my favorite "pan pals," in her generous-spirited book* **The Festive Table,** *selects traditional North African spices to add a fascinating savory note. Make the recipe above, but add the following spices when you add the carrots: 1 tablespoon cumin seeds, preferably crushed coarsely in a mortar and pestle; and 2 tablespoons peeled and minced ginger. Ronni doesn't use the carrot, celery, and bell peppers, but includes 4 cups chopped fresh tomatoes instead of tomato paste, and cayenne instead of the chipotle. She stirs cooked white or brown rice in at the end. When a dish is this good, inexpensive, homey, and healthy, why not have a couple of versions up your sleeve to bring warmth and light to gray days?*

"Where the name originated is a matter of dispute," writes Hoppin' John Martin Taylor, in *Hoppin' John's Lowcountry Cooking.* "Still, I believe the dish arrived here with the slaves, who numbered in the tens of thousands in Charleston and on the neighboring rice plantations of the 17th and 18th centuries."

Traditional Hoppin' John contained the fattiest of meats, ham hock, and never quite appealed to me even when I ate meat; it was a little plain for my taste. While Dancin' John is true to the spirit of the original pot, this version is more interesting. Chipotle chiles—essential here—add heat and a touch of the smoke ham hock usually lends. Garlic, tomato paste, miso (it lends something of the meat's saltiness and richness), a sauté of onions, carrots, and celery—you end up with a satisfying dish that is filled with layers of true flavor. **SERVES 8 TO 10 AS PART OF A MEAL; 6 TO 8 AS THE MAIN DISH**

2 cups black-eyed peas, picked over and rinsed
1 head garlic, unpeeled, plus 4 cloves garlic, pressed
2 bay leaves
4 cloves
1 onion, unpeeled, plus 1 onion, diced
1 canned chipotle chile
1 to 2 teaspoons salt, plus more to taste
2 to 3 tablespoons olive oil
2 carrots, diced
2 ribs celery, chopped
1 green bell pepper, seeds and membrane removed, chopped
1 red bell pepper, seeds and membrane removed, chopped
2 tablespoons tomato paste
1 tablespoon light miso
1 cup long-grain converted rice
Freshly ground black pepper
2 to 3 scallions, roots removed, white and 2 to 3 inches of the green chopped

1 Soak or quick-soak the black-eyed peas in water to cover by 2 inches. Drain and rinse well. Place the peas in a Dutch oven with enough water to barely cover. Add the whole head of garlic and the bay leaves. Stick the cloves into the whole onion and add that, too, along with the chipotle. Bring to a boil over high heat. Lower the heat to a simmer. Cover and simmer until almost tender, 40 minutes to 1½ hours. When the peas are tender, add the salt.

2 While the peas are cooking, heat the oil in a large skillet over medium heat. Add the diced onion and sauté until limp and starting to color slightly, 6 to 7 minutes. Add the carrots and cook, stirring, for 3 minutes more. Stir in the garlic, celery, green pepper, and red pepper and cook, stirring, for 3 minutes more. Remove from the heat and set aside.

3 When the black-eyed peas are almost tender, dig around with a slotted spoon and

remove and discard the clove-studded onion and the chipotle. Also scoop out the head of garlic but set it aside to cool.

4 Add 2 cups water to the peas and return to a boil over high heat. Stir in the tomato paste and miso. Add the rice and lower the heat to a simmer. Cover and simmer for 10 to 12 minutes. Uncover, but do not stir. Add the sautéed vegetable mixture and squeeze the pulp from the head of garlic directly into the pot. The vegetables and garlic will be sitting on top of the simmering stew. Make sure that there is still visible liquid; it should be soupy. If things look too dry, add ¼ to 1 cup additional boiling water.

Replace the lid and cook until both the black-eyed peas and rice are tender, 8 to 10 minutes. Turn off the heat and let sit, undisturbed, for 10 minutes. Stir gently to incorporate the sautéed vegetables. Season the dish with plenty of salt and black pepper. Serve hot, sprinkled with the scallions.

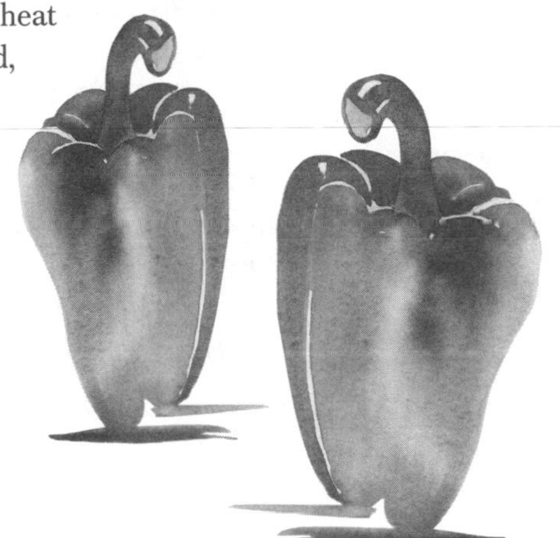

"Indian" Indian Kidney Beans

The European "discovery" of the Americas rested, you will remember, on its hunger for the spices of India. Alas, Christopher Columbus and his crew did not reach India, and the natives of the new world they found did not possess the cinnamon, cloves, nutmeg, black pepper, and other spices they sought. But the gifts (some might say plunder) of indigenous foodstuffs the Europeans brought back soon changed forever the nature of eating, all over the globe. It wasn't long before native American foods like chile peppers made their way to India and became so comfortable there that it's impossible to imagine that cuisine without them.

Here is a delectable dry curry—a spicy sauté with very little liquid to it—in which the original Indians and the American Indians are honored, proving that sometimes in this bad-old good-old world, confusion, colonialism, greed, a thirst for adventure, experimentation, and generosity can result not only in irretrievable loss but also in unforeseen gain. **SERVES 4 TO 6**

NOTE

If you serve this with whole wheat chapatis or tortillas, you will have world history and global culture right there on your plate (wheat being an ancient Mesopotamian grain). Add a dollop of yogurt, start with The Salad (page 68) dressed up with avocado and height-of-summer golden cherry tomatoes, and count yourself blessed to be part of this earthly feast.

- 1 cup kidney beans, rinsed and picked over
- Cooking spray
- 3 cups water, preferably spring or filtered
- 1 bay leaf
- 1 tablespoon plus 1 teaspoon Better (page 905)
- 1 large onion, chopped
- 1 green chile, such as Serrano, minced
- 1½ tablespoons minced, peeled fresh ginger
- 2 cloves garlic, pressed
- 1 tablespoon cumin seeds
- 1 teaspoon ground cumin
- 1 tablespoon black or brown mustard seeds (do not substitute yellow)
- 1½ teaspoons ground coriander
- 1½ teaspoons ground turmeric
- Pinch of cayenne
- Pinch of ground cloves
- 1 to 1½ teaspoons salt, or to taste
- 1 medium zucchini, cut in ¼-inch dice
- 1 cup diced cooked butternut squash (optional)
- Kernels from 3 ears fresh corn (about 1½ cups)
- 2 tablespoons chopped cilantro

1 Quick-soak the beans as described on page 597 and drain well. Spray a pressure cooker with cooking spray, and add the beans, water, and bay leaf. Lock the lid and bring to high pressure over medium-high heat. Lower the heat to maintain pressure, and cook for 12 minutes. Allow pressure to release naturally.

2 As the beans cook, prepare the spice sauté. Spray a large nonstick skillet with cooking spray, and place it over medium-high heat. Add the Better. When the Better has melted and is starting to sizzle, add the onion and sauté until softened, about 5 minutes. Add the green chile and ginger, lower heat to medium, and cook another 2 minutes. Lower heat further. Stir in the garlic and all the spices. Continue cooking, stirring constantly, another 3 minutes.

3 Open the lid of the pressure cooker. The kidney beans should be tender, but not mushy. Drain the liquid, reserving ½ cup. Discard the bay leaf.

4 Back at the skillet, add the reserved bean liquid, along with the salt, zucchini, butternut squash, if using, and corn. Raise the heat again to medium-high, and cook, stirring constantly, for 3 to 5 minutes, or until most of the liquid has evaporated. Lower the heat and stir in the kidney beans. Serve right away, hot, sprinkled with cilantro.

The Three Sisters

Beans and corn and squash—the American Indians called them the three sisters, and many tribes grew the three together, seeds of each in a mounded hill. The bean would climb the cornstalk, amiably wrapping its runners on the ascent. The squash would happily spread on the ground, forming a mat, which shaded the corn's roots, keeping them a little cooler. And while corn and squash take from the soil, the bean, which produces its own nitrogen, enriches it.

In addition to all this, corn, beans, and squash together make for good eating visually, taste-wise, and nutritionally. Each supplies what the other lacks: in color, in nutrients, in texture, and in flavor.

CHAPTER 10

Celebrating Soyfoods

As a soy-loving girl from way back I invite you to enter an ever-expanding universe of foods: not merely extraordinarily healthful, but delectable and diverse—great ingredients for a passionate cook. Whether you already enjoy soyfoods or are just tiptoeing cautiously toward exploration, you'll find many new ways to know and love them.

Anyone who has bought a cube of tofu, afloat in its plastic-entombed water bath, and left it sitting for 10 days in the fridge because they weren't sure what to do with it before finally throwing it out (a story I have heard countless times from would-be soy-cooks) is feeling dubious. To you, I would like to give special reassurance. To know soyfoods is, in most cases, to love them. But to "know" them requires know-*how.* I promise that by the time we leave this chapter you will know the specific properties and uses of soyfoods, and what they taste like. And with this knowledge a whole new world of cooking will open to you.

Throughout this book, this invitation to soy has been extended implicitly for every category. Here, though, we'll do it explicitly. We'll recap the health benefits of soy, briefly describe some of the hugely diverse numbers of soyfoods, and then jump into recipes.

The vast and diverse family of soyfoods encompasses dozens of ingredients all made from that single miraculous legume, the soybean. Some are ready to eat, such as commercially made lemon-marinated tempeh, and some are raw ingredients like soy flour. Tofu is just the beginning: There are various prepared, preseasoned tofus, tempeh and flavored tempehs, edamame, soysage, soy milk (including a really scrumptious egg-free soy-nog available commercially at Christmas), TVP (textured vegetable protein), soy cheeses, soy burgers, whole soybeans, and much more. The world of soyfoods is rapidly proliferating: there are now more than 250 American companies making and distributing various soyfoods. American sales of tofu and other soyfood products now top $1 billion a year, and nearly 100 million pounds of tofu are produced in America annually. There are tofu and soyfood consumer hotlines (1-800-TALK-SOY; 1-800-TOFU-NOW). There are tofu and soyfood web sites (www.talksoy.com; www.soyfoods.com).

To call a small, unprepossessing-looking legume known as soy "miraculous" is no exaggeration. Hundreds of well-documented scientific studies have proven the soybean's protective effect in helping prevent and lower the risk of many of humankind's most widespread and feared scourges, particularly heart disease and many cancers. Soybeans also stand up proudly in the treatment of other human woes (preventing or lessening hot flashes, curing chronic nosebleeds). None of this is far-out theory—it's solid science: On October 26, 1999, the FDA authorized the use of health claims about the role of soy protein in reducing the risk of coronary heart disease (CHD) on food labels, based on the agency's conclusion that foods containing soy protein, included in a diet low in saturated fat and cholesterol, may reduce the risk of CHD by lowering both the total and LDL blood cholesterol levels.

While soyfoods are just now finding their way to American tables, they have been on humankind's table for hundreds of years. Hundreds of millions of Asian people eat tofu, tempeh, and other soyfoods daily. This habitual soyfood-eating gave rise to some of the first compelling soy-demographics: Asian women have one-fifth the breast cancer rate of Western women—a profile that changes if they move to the West and begin to eat Western-style.

Let us begin our soyfoods odyssey by examining the legume from where it all begins: the soybean.

Innecdote

Ned and I were hard into the inn's busy season, and, in true shoemaker's-children-go-barefoot fashion, had let our own refrigerator get pretty bare. Now it was Sunday night, we were tired, didn't feel like going out. "Well," I said dubiously, "I can find something to put together, I guess, but there isn't much there. Tofu, some carrots, rice . . . sort of a silk-purse-from-a-sow's-ear kind of dinner."

"No," said Ned, "a silk purse from a soy's ear."

Whole Soybeans

The first reason soyfoods are so extraordinary, not only among beans but among all plant-based foods, is that they contain complete protein—all eight of the essential amino acids in good proportion to each other. Soy protein is equal in protein quality to that of beef, eggs, fowl, fish, or milk. The soybean's unique protein makeup is what makes possible all kinds of soy derivations, such as "soy milk." Made in Asia for centuries, soy milk is a creamy white liquid traditionally made from partially processed ground soybeans.

Beyond protein, soybeans and their products offer a panoply of additional benefits that make them, in many ways, superior to flesh-based foods, such as:

HEART-HEALTHY FATS: Although soybeans have considerably more fat than any other food-crop legume, they are lower in fat than many animal-based proteins, and their fat is cholesterol-free and mostly unsaturated. They contain the heart-beneficient Omega-3 fatty acids (also found in walnuts and many fish), which seem to work by reducing a blood-clotting prostaglandin produced in the body. When elevated, this prostaglandin tends to increase human risk of stroke and heart attack. Many studies indicate that replacing animal protein with soy protein in the diet causes serum cholesterol and triglyceride levels to drop in the blood. Beneficial effects are seen at levels of 25 to 50 grams of soy protein a day (4 ounces of firm tofu, an average serving, has about 10 grams; add some soy milk to your coffee and a serving of soysage at breakfast, and you're there).

Another fatty element of soybean oil that may prove to be heart healthy is lecithin, an antioxidant used in food manufacturing as an emulsifier and stabilizer. It tends to prevent sticking and limit spattering—for which reason you'll have discovered it used throughout this book, though you may not have noticed it; it's an ingredient in some cooking sprays.

PHYTOESTROGENS: Women in their forties and fifties face a tough choice: Estrogen offers demonstrated preventive benefits on osteoporosis, heart disease, possibly Alzheimer's, and a reduction of menopausal symptoms, but also increases (depending on family history and genetics) the risk of certain breast cancers, especially if the estrogen is taken long-term. The decision to take it or not is rarely straightforward.

Soybeans appear to offer a way around the dilemma. Two natural estrogen-like phytochemicals called isoflavones appear to confer synthetic estrogen's benefits (bone density, heart protection, reducing hot flashes) *without* increasing breast cancer risk. One of the two isoflavones, genistein, appears to actually *reduce* the risk of breast and other cancers, so markedly that the National Cancer Institute is investigating it as an anticancer drug. These same isoflavones, unique to soybeans, also appear to lower the risk for leukemia and cancers of the prostate, colon, lungs, and skin.

OTHER ANTICARCINOGENIC PHYTOCHEMICALS: In addition to phytoestrogens, soybeans contain compounds called protease inhibitors, which, according to Mark Messina, Ph.D., and Virginia Messina, R.D., authors of *The Simple Soybean and Your Health,* may inhibit cancers of the pancreas, mouth, and esophogus, in addition to kicking in to help fight the cancers already listed. This double-whammy cancer-fighting impact is further strengthened by three more soy-team players: phytates, saponins, and phenolic acids, all three of which help counteract the effects of free radicals, substances manufactured in our bodies that have a causal link with various cancers. Yet another soy component, phytosterols, have a protective effect on cancers of both the skin and colon.

OTHER MISCELLANEOUS BENEFITS: Various soy components have been demonstrated to reduce high blood pressure, prevent or control kidney disease, reduce gallstones, and lessen the frequency of chronic nosebleeds. And, like all beans, soybeans are rich in soluble fiber, which helps to stabilize blood sugar levels (essential for diabetics) as well as lower blood cholesterol levels.

SOY FAT: There is one caveat, nutritionally speaking, with soybeans. Compared to other beans, they are quite high in fat. The average bean's fat content is 5 percent; soybeans run at 38 percent. If you play the percentage game strictly by the numbers even tofu can look shocking—53 percent of its calories are derived from fat, and even reduced-fat varieties run at 38 percent of total calories. But tofu and soybeans are clearly great additions to anyone's diet.

In their natural forms, you have a choice of either black or yellow soybeans. Black soybeans are generally considered a bit tastier, but can be harder to find; they are also the bean used in Chinese black bean sauce or fermented Chinese black beans. Yellow soybeans are the variety used for tofu-, tempeh-, and soy milk–making.

Here is some information about available forms of soy:

Green Soybeans (Edamame)

Although edamame (ehd-a-MAH-may), also known as sweet beans, sweet soybeans, and green soybeans, have been eaten as a snack, appetizer, and side dish in Japan for centuries, they are relatively new to America. What a treat! They are fresh green soybeans, sometimes sold still in their green pods, sometimes already shelled, occasionally available fresh but more usually found in the freezer at natural foods markets, Asian food stores, and some large supermarkets.

Most Japanese restaurants offer them as an appetizer. An order brings a bowl of the deep green fuzzy-podded beans, steaming hot, usually lightly salted, along with a second empty bowl. Peel back the pod, pop the plump, sweet little green soybeans into your mouth, and discard the pods into the second bowl. Those Southerners who have enjoyed boiled peanuts will recognize a similar pleasure. Green soybeans are tender but not mushy, and give a slight pop in the mouth. At first taste you might think, "Good, but a little plain." But see if you can eat just one. Shelling them—as in shelling peanuts—is part of the experience.

Canned Soybeans

Available in natural foods stores and larger supermarkets, canned soybeans are cooked dried soybeans. They have their devotees too. My mother is one. She told me, "I have been blissful since I discovered canned soybeans!" She opens a can, transfers it to the fridge, and eats her way down, using a few tablespoons here and there in soups or casseroles or on salads. The bean stock in canned soybeans is slightly jelled rather than liquid, but it liquifies with heat.

Cooked Dried Soybeans

Most soybean cooks prepare the dry beans from scratch: time-consuming but economical. Because soybeans have plentiful amounts of oligosaccharides (see page 587), I highly recommend the *de-gassing soak* and *stove-top* method of cooking (page 595) to "deflate" them. Allow 2½ to 3 hours of cooking time after soaking—yes, you read that right. Follow any of the basic cooking methods in the bean chapter. If you pressure-cook, the time under high pressure using soaked beans will be a mere 12 to 14 minutes for the golden, a bit longer, say 20 to 22, for the black. In either case, quick-release the pressure after the cooking time is up. Since preparing soybeans is time-consuming, I highly recommend making a large batch and then freezing them in 1- to 2-cup quantities in zippered freezer bags. As with most beans, 1 cup dried soybeans yields a bit more than 2 cups cooked.

Though cooked dried soybeans won't knock your socks off tastewise—what bean will, without assistance?—there are plenty of delicious things you can do with them. I know—I spent the winter of 1970 eating my way through a 50-pound bag of soybeans on a rural collective populated by souls as intrepid, idealistic, young, and dumb as myself. Given this, I know you'll understand why it's difficult for me to be fair to the soybean in this form even today. Still, you won't be disappointed if you try cooked soybeans in Buckaroo Beans (page 598), in place of kidney or borlotti beans in any minestrone, or as the featured player in the dishes that follow.

Basic Fresh Edamame

If you are lucky enough to find fresh green soybeans in the pod that have never been frozen, this is how to prepare them to serve as a snack, starter, or part of a cocktail buffet. You might have to tell people what they are and how to peel them, but once they get the message, there are never leftovers. This amount would serve more if the beans were one of a number of starters. **SERVES 4**

8 to 10 cups water, preferably spring or filtered
1¼ pounds fresh green soybeans, in the pods
1½ teaspoons salt, plus more if desired

Place the water in a large pot and bring to a boil. Dump in the pods, along with the 1½ teaspoons salt. Return to a boil; then lower the heat to a slow boil and cook, uncovered, until tender, 12 to 15 minutes. Test one, rinsing it under cold water so you don't burn your fingers: The pod should peel off easily and the beans should be sweet and crisp-tender, not mushy-tender. Drain and serve, hot, in the pod, with additional salt for sprinkling (and an extra bowl for the emptied pods).

VARIATION

FROZEN EDAMAME IN THE POD: ***Follow directions for fresh edamane, but allow a little less cooking time; 6 to 8 minutes should do it. This may contradict the time given on the box or bag, but I've found that any longer makes the frozen ones get a little mushy.***

EDAMAME CHINOISE: ***To give a mild flavor and scent to the beans, add star anise to the boiling water.***

Basic Frozen Shelled Edamame

You can purchase bags of frozen shelled edamame. This basic cooked bean can be interchanged for any bean called for in bean or pasta salads, or for limas in succotash. It's also great in minestrone. Or stir-fry the cooked beans in a little olive oil with a handful of slivered spinach, a pressed clove of garlic or two, a shake of salt, and a grinding of black pepper. **SERVES ABOUT 4, DEPENDING ON HOW THE SHELLED BEANS WILL BE USED**

Place water—about five times as much volume as the beans—in a large pot and bring to a boil. Add the beans and lower the heat to a simmer. Cook until tender, 10 to 12 minutes. Drain well and rinse. The soybeans are now ready to give their all to any other dish.

Comforting Corn Chowder with Green Soybeans and Potatoes

The sweetness of green soybeans plays off the sweetness of corn very nicely in this soy-rich redo of a nourishing, classic corn chowder. It's warming and creamily comforting, despite the absence of any cream. Although, categorically, this ought to be in the soup section, I couldn't resist sliding it in here since it contains edamame, soy milk, and soy sauce. This would be even better with fresh corn cut off the cob, but chowders are such wintery foods I always wind up using frozen. Note that both corn and soybeans are added frozen.

The flavor of the soy milk used is all important, so be sure to read the notes on soy beverages, page 651. Try this with the Cornmeal Biscuits on page 513, or with a grilled cheese sandwich on whole grain bread. If you happened to use soy cheese, you could claim four soyfoods in a meal, most pleasurably. You can also stir in, at the last, a few strips of cooked smoked tempeh, or soy "bacon" bits, for a baconlike smoky flavor. **SERVES 6 TO 8**

1 tablespoon butter, margarine, or mild vegetable oil
Cooking spray
1 large onion, diced
1 carrot, diced
1 rib celery, diced
1 teaspoon celery seeds
1 bay leaf
3¼ cups vegetable stock (see page 139)
2 fist-sized potatoes (Yellow Finn, Yukon Gold, or American Beauty preferred), scrubbed but not peeled, cut into ½-inch dice
1 teaspoon salt
1½ cups frozen shelled green soybeans
1½ cups frozen corn
3 cups plain, unflavored soy milk (I prefer White Wave Plain Soy Silk)
1 tablespoon tamari or shoyu soy sauce
½ to 1 teaspoon Pickapeppa sauce
Few drops Tabasco or similar hot pepper sauce
1½ tablespoons cornstarch or arrowroot
Freshly ground black pepper
Minced scallion and/or parsley; crisp soy bacon bits, or sautéed tempeh strips, crumbled (optional)

1 Heat the butter (or margarine or oil) in a large Dutch oven that has been sprayed with cooking spray over medium-high heat. Add the onion and sauté until slightly softened, about 4 minutes. Add the carrot, celery, celery seeds, and bay leaf and sauté for 3 minutes more.

2 Add 3 cups of the vegetable stock along with the potatoes and salt. Bring to a boil; lower the heat to a simmer. Cook, half-covered, until the potatoes are not quite soft, about 10 minutes. Add the green soybeans and corn and return to a simmer. Simmer, half-covered, for another 10 minutes.

3 Add the soy milk, tamari, Pickapeppa, and Tabasco. Lower the heat slightly and let the chowder come to just under a boil.

4 Meanwhile, dissolve the cornstarch in the reserved ¼ cup stock, smushing to a lump-free liquid. Add a little of the soup liquid, stir well, and then stir the mixture into the pot, stirring until it thickens slightly. Pepper well, taste for other seasonings (salt, tamari, Pickapeppa), and serve at once, with diced scallions, minced parsley, and/or soy "bacon" bits or tempeh, if desired.

VARIATION

As you can probably tell, this is a totally "go with the flow" kind of recipe. Try adding a handful of pitted kalamata olives and/or (if you eat dairy) a little crumbled feta or finely diced mozzarella.

Summertime Pasta with Soybeans and Pesto

This is as simple as can be—just a quick summertime ziti that takes advantage of high-summer tomatoes and basil pesto but adds a little soybean protein to make a satisfying, quick dinner. **SERVES 4**

1 pound ziti
1 can (15 ounces) soybeans
3 red-ripe summer tomatoes, stems removed, chopped
1½ to 2½ tablespoons good pesto, homemade or commercial
Salt and freshly ground black pepper to taste
A little olive oil, pressed garlic, additional pesto (optional)

1 Cook the ziti in boiling water according to the package directions.

2 As the ziti cooks, run the can of soybeans under hot water to liquify the jelled bean-cooking liquid. Drain the soybeans well, reserving the broth for use in stock, if desired. Place the well-drained soybeans in a large bowl. Add the tomatoes and pesto, tossing well to combine.

3 When the ziti is ready, drain well and

immediately toss with the soybean mixture. Add salt and loads of pepper. If you like, add a bit of oil and some fresh-pressed garlic (these may or may not be necessary; it depends on your taste and the composition of your pesto). Or you might want a little more pesto. Toss again, and serve immediately.

Layered Wintertime Soybean Casserole

Fragrant, comforting, inspired by Italian dishes that layer good tomato sauce and cheese, this homey dish has many partisans. Serve with a crusty bread and a salad with a sharp vinaigrette, and you have a great meal. If you don't feel like making tomato sauce from scratch, buy a good commercial variety. You may also use canned soybeans and even commercial seasoned breadcrumbs. I prefer this with dairy cheese, but you may make it with soy cheese for those who are lactose-intolerant or vegan. **SERVES 4 TO 6**

Cooking spray
4 cups cooked dried yellow soybeans (about 2 cups before cooking), heated
1 recipe or 3½ cups Basic Wintertime Italian Tomato Sauce (page 931), heated
1 cup grated sharp Cheddar cheese, dairy or soy
¾ cup grated Parmesan cheese or nondairy soy-rice Parmesan-style cheese
1 cup Breadcrumb Topping Provençal (page 277)

1 Preheat the oven to 375°F.

2 Spray a deep ovenproof 1½- to 2-quart casserole with cooking spray. Spoon about one-third of the warm cooked soybeans into the casserole and top with one-third of the tomato sauce. Make a layer of one-third of each cheese. Repeat the layering twice more, beginning with the soy beans and finishing with the cheeses. Liberally sprinkle the top with the breadcrumb topping.

3 Tightly cover the casserole, either with foil or its own lid. Bake, covered, for 40 minutes. Uncover, raise the temperature to 450°F, and bake until the crumbs have crisped and browned nicely, and the beans are bubbling hot, about 15 minutes. Serve hot.

Corn-Soybean Potluck Special

A perfect potluck casserole; a substantial side dish; or, if you add the cheese, a light main dish. Corn and soybeans just taste good together. Pour the frozen corn kernels straight out of the bag; no need to precook them. If you wish, use canned soybeans to save time, and if time is really an issue, instead of using homemade Béchamel, go to the natural foods store and pick up a carton of Pacific Foods Organic Cream Sauce Base, which comes in both dairy and soy milk varieties and is quite delicious.

The optional cheese layer may be either dairy or soy. The minced parsley is also optional, but adds a very nice freshness. **SERVES 4 TO 6**

Cooking spray
3 cups cooked dried yellow soybeans (about 1½ cups before cooking), heated
1 cup frozen corn, rinsed under hot water to thaw
3½ cups Béchamel (page 945), dairy or soy, heated
6 ounces (1½ cups) grated Monterey Jack cheese, dairy or soy (optional)
¾ cup minced Italian parsley (optional)
½ cup crisp breadcrumbs
½ cup cornflakes, crumbled
1 tablespoon butter, margarine, or mild vegetable oil

1. Preheat the oven to 375°F.

2. Spray a deep ovenproof 1½- to 2-quart casserole with cooking spray.

3. Spoon about one-third of the warm cooked soybeans into the casserole and top with a layer of one-third of the corn, and then a layer of one-third of the Béchamel, and finally, if using, a layer of one-third of the cheese and one-half of the minced parsley. Repeat the layering, beginning with the soybeans, finishing with Béchamel or, if using, the cheese.

4. Combine the breadcrumbs and corn flakes and sprinkle the mixture evenly over the top of the casserole. Dot with butter or margarine, or drizzle with oil.

5. Tightly cover the casserole, either with foil or its own lid, and bake, covered, for 40 minutes. Uncover, raise the temperature to 450°F, and bake until the crumbs have crisped and browned nicely, and beans are bubbling hot, about 15 minutes. Serve hot.

Soybean Salad Sandwich Spread with Vegetables and Fresh Herbs

A lightly mayonnaise-dressed salad, loosely akin to a chicken or tuna salad, this is very satisfying with good summer tomatoes and leaf lettuce on whole grain toast, the grainier the better. You can take the fat count way down and up the soyfoods quota by substituting all or part homemade Tofu Mayonnaise for the conventional. You may omit the fresh herb called for but I am wild about the flavor of freshly minced dill here. If you want the salad to be even more reminiscent of chicken salad, use fresh tarragon. **MAKES ENOUGH TO FILL 4 SANDWICHES**

2 cups cooked soybeans, well drained (about 1 cup before cooking)
3 tablespoons very finely minced onion
1 rib celery, very finely minced
3 to 4 tablespoons mayonnaise, conventional or reduced fat, homemade or purchased, or all or part homemade Tofu Mayonnaise (page 906)
Salt and lots of freshly ground pepper
1 tablespoon or so of any chopped herb (optional)

1. Pulse/chop the soybeans in a food processor. You want them textured and broken up, not pureed. Transfer to a medium bowl.

2. Stir in the onion and celery and toss to combine. Add the mayonnaise, salt and pepper to taste, and the herb, if using. Mix well. Taste and adjust the seasonings if necessary. Use on sandwiches or to stuff tomatoes.

Tea Time

"Small teas provide good practice for 'hostessing'. Serving tea or orangeade to your mother's friends when they drop in for an afternoon visit will make you a smoother hostess in the future as well as pleasing your mother and her friends. Select a pleasant spot in the living room or sunporch. A small table covered with a cloth is all that is neccesary to hold the tea tray and plates of sandwiches . . ."

—*Family Meals and Hospitality* (1951 home economics textbook)

Milled Soybeans

Soy flour: *Soy flour is made from milled, ground preroasted soybeans, which become a rich-tasting, creamy-yellow powder, slightly sweet when finely ground. It is available natural (full fat) or defatted (the oils are removed during processing). You can generally replace between one-eighth and one-quarter of other flours in any bread, muffin, or pancake recipe and in most cookie and some cake recipes, with good success. Don't substitute more than that unless you are using a recipe specifically designed for soy flour use (see Sweet and Sour Swedish-Style Rye-Buckwheat Bread, page 542), since soy flour lacks gluten (see page 494). The difference a little soy flour makes is generally undetectable taste- or texture-wise but it does have extra nutritional benefits. You get those good soy*

isoflavones working for you; and you up the protein content of the baked good substantially (½ cup natural soy flour, for example, contains 16 grams of protein; defatted contains an astonishing 23½). If a white-flour, sugar-rich baked good supplies empty calories, a whole-grain product, amplified with a little soy, is the antithesis—every calorie is substantial, pulling its weight in substances that do magic things for your body and your health.

Soy grits: *Like soy flour, soy grits are ground toasted soybeans, except they are coarsely ground. Naturally, they are high in protein and their texture makes them a great grain-cooking partner. They take about 15 minutes to reach tenderness, so try mixing them with any grain that cooks in about that amount of time—millet, buckwheat, bulghur, some white rices. Measure 1 to 2 tablespoons soy grits into a cup measure, then fill the cup with the remaining grain of choice and cook as usual. In the case of millet and buckwheat, two grains I recommended toasting before cooking, simply measure your cup of grain, remove 2 tablespoons, toast the grain, and add the soy grits when you add the boiling liquid.*

Morning Glorious Muffins

Many American inns offer their guests a basket of morning glory muffins: a sweet, everything-but-the-kitchen-sink, cinnamon-scented confection of a muffin, studded with nuts, fresh and dried fruit, grated carrots, coconut, in a batter rich with eggs and lots of fat. They are delicious but carry little nutritional wallop for all those calories. I wanted to see if I could come up with a version just as pleasing, but more healthful. Here it is: wholesome, toothsome, and plenty glorious.

Try serving these warm, with neufchâtel reduced-fat cream cheese or soy cream cheese, either plain or beaten together with a little honey. **MAKES ABOUT 20**

VARIATION

Instead of the butter-oil combination given here, you could use ¼ cup Better (page 905). Vegans can use commercial egg-replacer.

Cooking spray (or paper muffin-cup liners)

DRY INGREDIENTS

1¾ cups whole wheat pastry flour
¼ cup full-fat soy flour
2 teaspoons baking soda
1½ teaspoons ground cinnamon, preferably Saigon
½ teaspoon salt
A few gratings of nutmeg

WET INGREDIENTS

2 egg whites
1 whole egg
⅔ cup Rapidura or brown sugar
½ cup soy milk, plain or vanilla
⅓ cup unsweetened applesauce
3 tablespoons mild vegetable oil, such as corn, canola, or peanut
1 tablespoon butter, melted
1 tablespoon lemon juice

MIX-INS

1½ cups canned unsweetened shredded pineapple, very well drained
1 cup grated carrots
½ cup raisins or chopped dates
¼ cup pecans or walnuts, toasted until fragrant, chopped
2 tablespoons flax seeds

3 tablespoons shredded dried coconut, sweetened or not as you prefer (optional)

1 Preheat the oven to 375°F.

2 Spray two 12-cup muffin tins well with cooking spray or line them with paper muffin-cup liners. Set aside.

3 Sift all of the dry ingredients together into a large bowl. Set aside.

4 Whisk all of the wet ingredients together in a medium bowl. Set aside.

5 In a third bowl, combine all of the mix-ins except the coconut, tossing to mix well. Sprinkle 1 tablespoon of the flour mixture over the mix-ins and stir to combine.

6 Pour the wet mixture into the dry and, using a wooden spoon, stir together using as few strokes as possible. The mixture should be shaggy and not fully combined, with spots of dry here and there. Add the mix-ins, combining with just a very few strokes.

7 Scoop the batter into the prepared muffin tins, filling each about two-thirds full. Top each muffin with a bit of the coconut, if using.

Bake until the muffins are firm, fragrant, a little browned on top and golden-brown on the bottom, 20 to 25 minutes. Remove from the oven and let cool on a wire rack for a minute or two before serving, still warm, in a calico-lined basket.

Powerballs

VARIATION

CHOCOLATE-COVERED POWERBALLS: ***Semisweet chocolate makes them like a peanut butter cup for grown-ups. Melt 8 ounces semisweet chocolate over simmering water. Line a baking sheet with waxed paper. Stick a toothpick into a Powerball, and, with a spoon at hand in case the Powerball drops off, swirl it into the warm chocolate. Dip half of each Powerball so that some of the filling shows or go for an all-the-way swirling. Quickly transfer the balls to the prepared sheet, and let cool until the chocolate has firmed.***

I am not big on confections and don't usually keep candy in the house. But every so often I get a hankering for something sweet, fast, and simple. When a blast of I-want-it-now force hits hard, my mainstay for years has been what I call Powerballs, a virtually instant sweet, that, while high in fat, packs quite a nutritional wallop. I used to make them with straight peanut butter but now I use a mixture of soynut and peanut butter. They are perfect with a crisp apple or a nice ripe pear. Powerballs taste a bit like the filling of a Reese's Peanut Butter Cup, but less salty, creamier, and not quite so teeth-on-edge sweet. Kids love them too, and, since they are uncooked, even very young children can help make them.

You will have to fool with the proportions of honey and milk powder: honeys differ, and unhydrogenated peanut and soynut butters have different amounts of oil. The mixture must be firm enough to hold its shape when rolled into balls.

MAKES ABOUT 18

½ cup soynut butter, at room temperature
½ cup natural, nonhydrogenated peanut butter
⅔ to 1 cup mild honey, such as clover
1½ teaspoons pure vanilla extract
1 cup to 1¼ cups instant powdered milk, dairy or soy

Using a wooden spoon, cream the soynut and peanut butters in a medium bowl. Beat in the honey, which will emulsify any remaining oil. Add the vanilla and stir in the powdered milk, adding as much as the mixture will smoothly incorporate. You want a smooth mixture firm enough to hold its shape when formed into balls. Roll into walnut-sized balls and serve.

Soynuts & Soynut Butter

SOYNUTS are yet another incarnation of the whole bean. They are a commercially available snack food much like peanuts, and are nothing more than whole soybeans, first soaked, then baked. They end up brown, crisp-crunchy, and quite good. They're rich enough so you'd think they were fried, but they aren't—it's the effect of the soybean's naturally high fat content. They are available at natural foods stores salted, unsalted, and in a variety of flavors, including chocolate-covered. Try adding them to a nut mix or a toasted cereal snack mix, or sub them for chopped peanuts, as a more healthful topping or ingredient in peanut-garnished Thai dishes, though they don't stay crisp for quite as long.

SOYNUT BUTTER is made from roasted soynuts that are ground and blended with soy or canola oil and salt, to make a spread that you use as you would peanut butter. It is slightly nutty in flavor, but not a dead ringer for peanut butter when used solo (use it 50/50 with peanut butter, or purchase a soynut-peanut butter spread combo). Soynut butter is firmer than peanut butter and, like it, contains 16 grams of fat in 2 tablespoons. But, in those same 2 tablespoons, the soynut butter has 8 grams of protein and isoflavones galore. It's available in natural foods stores.

Tempeh

Although the most common transformative magic soybeans make is turning into tofu, the legume can also, through careful alchemy, become a delectable cultured whole-soybean product known as tempeh, pronounced TEM-pay. Indonesian in origin and widely consumed there, it is much less well known in America than is tofu. It is as hearty as tofu is delicate; a healthful, versatile food with a stronger flavor and textural heft. Unlike tofu, tempeh is made from the whole bean, which gives it a nutritional edge. It's readily available in natural foods markets in many varieties.

To make tempeh, cracked, cooked whole soybeans are carefully cultured with a beneficent mold called *Rhizopus oligosporus,* in a process like those that turn milk to cheese or yogurt, or grapes to wine and vinegar. When the soybeans (sometimes mixed with grains, nuts, seeds, or flavorings) have been cultured long enough (about 24 hours), the *Rhizopus oligosporus* forms long white thread-like tissues called *mycellium,* which bind the legumes and grains into a firm, improbably delicious, solid cake. Just as yogurt renders milk more digestible because the culturing process itself partially "digests" some of the milk sugars and other compounds, so does the fermentation and culturing of soybeans transform some of their troublesome proteins, fats, and oligosaccharides (see page 587) into easier-to-assimilate forms.

What does tempeh taste like? I've always considered it both mushroomlike and reminiscent of veal. Its texture is much "meatier" than curdlike tofu. It is pleasingly solid, firm and chewy, not at all soft and bouncy like tofu, and not at all like individual beans. Tempeh's flavor is not beany, either. Bite into a piece of tempeh and you feel you are really getting something. Personally, I love tempeh, and have from the first time I tasted it.

In the United States, commercially available tempeh is often sold in 4-by-4-by-½-inch cakes. It is raw, ready to be cooked and used. Though the soybeans and grains are cooked before culturing, the rhizopus mold requires additional cooking. This is markedly different from tofu, which *can* be eaten straight from the fridge, though it's not advisable to do so with tofu purchased in bulk. This be-sure-to-cook-it caveat does not apply to tempeh purchased in ready-to-eat formulations, such as some frozen tempeh burgers and similar products.

Raw tempeh is highly versatile. After it is marinated—and tempeh is almost always marinated—it may be sautéed, grilled, baked, fried, steamed, added to sautés and casseroles, put in sandwiches, and the list goes on. Occasionally, it is ground or pulse/chopped raw in the processor, and used in burgers, fillings, or spreads.

Tempeh works out well with both assertive and delicate sauces. Tossed with pasta or grains, tempeh gives more textural contrast than does tofu. Another subjective difference: Many people perceive tofu as tasting "light," hence more summery, while tempeh seems "heavy" and wintery—though most tempeh is in fact lighter in fat grams.

Most American-made tempeh has a pebbled consistency, with visible golden-brown soybean pieces firmly held together by the white *mycellium* and a few slightly darker spots of gray or black. In

Tempeh

Tempeh has all the benefits of whole soybeans and none of their drawbacks, with a few extra pluses:

- *Because tempeh is made from the complete soybean, tempeh has much more fiber than tofu.*
- *Tempeh is often, but not always, a significant source of vitamin B_{12}, a nutrient in which vegetarians are sometimes deficient. Neither soybeans nor* Rhizopus oligosporus *are inherently high in B_{12}, but a benign bacteria, which often goes along for the ride, is—particularly in Indonesia, where tempeh is made at home, and the* Rhizopus oligosporus *is cultivated in wrappers of leaves, such as hibiscus leaves. The benign B_{12}–rich bacteria hitchhike with the* Rhizopus oligosporus *grown under these conditions. While this gives a healthful boost, it may mean that the tempeh was cultivated under sanitary conditions iffy to Americans. Most American tempeh, however, is made using an unadulterated, pharmaceutical-grade strain of* Rhizopus oligosporus; *meaning it's very sanitary but lacks B_{12}. A little label reading will tell you if the tempeh contains B_{12}.*
- *Because tempeh is so often combined with grains, the fat content of a tempeh dish can be dramatically lower than that of whole soybeans and tofu foods.*

Singapore, I tasted gorgeous Malaysian creamy-white beige tempeh with a surface as smooth as a baby's bottom; it was as fresh as could be, having just been unwrapped from the banana leaf in which it had been cultured—but I have never seen tempeh so delicate here.

Tempehs I Have Known

Fresh tempehs are raw and must be kept refrigerated or frozen. Like tofus, they are a high-protein food, and are as vulnerable to contamination as meat, eggs, and milk.

CLASSIC/TRADITIONAL, CONVENTIONAL, RAW, FRESH SOY TEMPEH

What It Is: Cakes of fresh, uncooked tempeh, made from soybeans and *Rhizopus oligosporos* mold only.

What It's Like: Depending on the brand and age of tempeh, mild to a little more assertive in flavor, with more "meatiness" than tofu; a bit like a cross between veal and very mild mushrooms. It is firm enough to easily be diced or sliced. Look for tempeh with visible golden-brown soybeans firmly held together in a white or creamy cake, with a few slightly darker spots of gray or black. The lighter the cake, the less far-along its fermentation, and the milder and sweeter the flavor.

Now, conversely, the more dark spots, the farther along the fermentation process is. A few dark spots are fine, and some prefer the stronger flavor they give tempeh. But if it's very spotty, or more gray-black than golden-beige, don't buy it; it's nearing the end of its life cycle. You should definitely discard any tempeh that is spotted in colors other than buff, brown, gray, white, and black, or if it has or develops an odor reminiscent of ammonia; this is spoiled tempeh. Don't worry; if you've got some you will know it.

How It's Sold and Packaged: Fresh tempeh is always kept refrigerated or frozen. Unlike tofu, it is not stored in water, nor (at least in America) is it sold in bulk. Most nationally available brands are sold in cakes about 4 inches square and ½ inch thick. However, some artisanal regional soyfood-makers form tempeh into cylinders or smaller, thicker squares.

How to Keep It: Fresh, raw tempeh has a relatively brief shelf life. Once purchased, vacuum-packed tempehs will keep, refrigerated, unopened, for a week or so. Once opened, use all of the tempeh within 3 days. Tempeh will keep, frozen, for 6 to 8 months. Freezing does not change the texture of tempeh, as it does tofu.

How to Use It: All raw tempehs can be used interchangeably. In general, the simplest thing to do is to marinate or splash tempeh with a seasoning liquid, then bake or sauté it. You can add cooked tempeh to other dishes or just spoon some sauce over it as the center of the plate attraction.

NEW-STYLE SOY-AND-MIXED-GRAIN TEMPEH, AND OTHER SOY-PLUS TEMPEHS

What They Are: Cakes of fresh, uncooked tempeh, made with various grains including but not limited to brown rice, wheat, quinoa, and amaranth. A particularly delicious and attractive tempeh combines soybeans with brown rice and a little wild rice for an interesting visual, textural, and flavor contrast. Sometimes the soybeans for tempeh are combined with more assertive ingredients such as peanuts or sesame seeds or shreds of the mild black seaweed known as hijiki. Additions to and adaptations of tempeh are areas in which New Age entrepreneurs are experimenting, so keep your eye out for new flavor combinations.

What They're Like: Adding grains does not, in most cases, change the characteristic flavor of tempeh. Even with the more

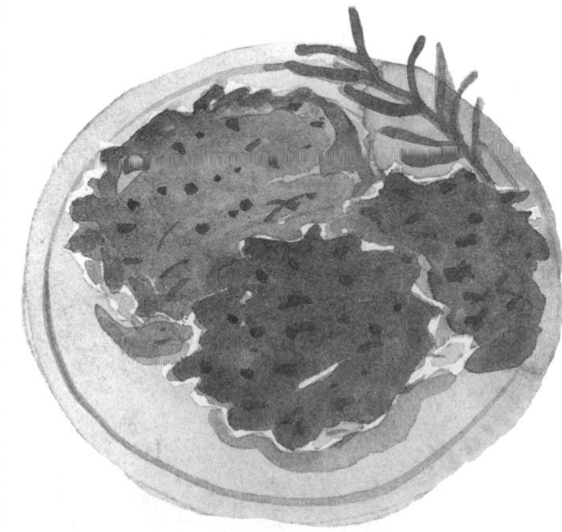

boldly flavored additions, I've noticed only minor flavor changes. It does alter it nutritionally, however, by lowering the fat content. In the case of tempeh with the sea-vegetable shreds, you also get their minerals and micronutrients.

How They're Sold and Packaged: As for fresh, raw tempeh (see previous page).

How to Keep Them: As for fresh, raw tempeh (see previous page).

How to Use Them: As for fresh, raw tempeh (see previous page).

Smoked tempeh "bacon"

What It Is: Strips of marinated, smoked tempeh with a smoky flavor somewhat reminiscent of bacon.

What It's Like: Remarkably baconlike in flavor, but not in texture. You can get a little closer to bacon if you fry the tempeh bacon-crisp in a good amount of oil (not that I would). I like the Fakin' Bac'n Smoky Tempeh Strips.

How It's Sold and Packaged: As for fresh, raw tempeh (see previous page).

How to Keep It: As for fresh, raw tempeh (page previous).

How to Use It: Unless you are wedded to crisp, brown the tempeh "bacon" in a nonstick skillet or one sprayed with cooking spray, turning once. Allow 2 to 3 minutes on each side to get the tempeh "bacon" nice and colored. Ned and I are very fond of tempeh "bacon," lettuce, and tomato sandwiches, with a little mayo (regular or tofu) and mustard on good whole grain toast. Also, try it at breakfast, in The "Jerry" Reuben (page 869), diced in casseroles, sauces, and stuffed vegetable fillings, or in The Wicked Weintz (page 871).

Prepared, cooked or partially cooked tempehs (perishable):

What They Are: Tasty convenience food for vegetarians, tempeh burgers or cakes are serving-size pieces of fresh tempeh that have been marinated, seasoned, and usually cooked or partially cooked (the package will tell you).

What They're Like: It depends completely on the brand and product. My favorite is White Wave's Lemon-Broil Tempeh, very lemony, made savory with garlic and tamari. However, new tempeh products in this category are coming out almost daily.

How They're Sold and Packaged: Packages generally offer two or three serving-size patties or cakes, and may be found in the refrigerator or freezer at your local natural foods market.

Like all convenience foods, you pay for the convenience. Prepared tempehs are more expensive than the plain raw ones, and generally higher in fat.

How to Keep Them: Keep frozen tempeh in the freezer; thaw in the fridge a day or two before you plan on using it. Once thawed, prepare it within 2 to 4 days.

How to Use Them: Throw any of these in a heated nonstick skillet, sauté till sizzling, and there you are. Tempeh burgers and Lemon-Broil Tempeh are primarily made for sandwiches, but they can also be diced for a stir-fry. If you're making an elaborate sauce, stick to plain tempehs; the pre-seasoned varieties conflict with some sauces. The lemon-sauced tempehs, though, are made in heaven with baked sweet pa match otatoes. Dice any sautéed lemon-sauced tempeh and combine it with diced baked sweet potatoes, sprouts, and diced fresh tomatoes. Roll it up in a whole wheat tortilla, burrito-style—too good.

Basic Oven-Baked Marinated Tempeh

Although the marinade sounds similiar to several of those given for tofu, it's just different enough that, when used on the completely different tempeh, you have a wholly distinct, and wholly delicious, dish. This is a base preparation. Use the baked tempeh as part of a component plate, sauced or unsauced, cut up as the filling for spring rolls with tempeh (page 315), added to a vegetable stir-fry, or as the centerpiece of a hearty sandwich.

Traditional Indonesian flavorings for such a marinade are salt water (in lieu of tamari or shoyu soy sauce), fresh pressed garlic, and dried coriander. **SERVES 3 TO 4 AS A MAIN COURSE, POSSIBLY MANY MORE IF FINISHED TEMPEH IS USED IN A STIR-FRY, SPRING ROLLS, PASTA DISH, OR CASSEROLE**

2 tablespoons tamari or shoyu soy sauce
1½ tablespoons vinegar (white, cider, balsamic, rice, red- or white-wine—whatever you have on hand or goes with the flavors of whatever your end-use recipe is)
1 teaspoon Pickapeppa (optional but good)
Any combination of the seasonings (see note; optional)
1 tempeh cake (8 ounces), cut in the size or shape appropriate to use
Cooking spray

1 Combine the tamari, vinegar, and Pickapeppa in a nonreactive dish and stir to combine. If using additional seasoning (see box), add it here. Add the tempeh. Marinate at room temperature, turning occasionally, for 20 minutes to 1 hour, or refrigerated for up to 2 days.

Seasoning Tempeh

The above is a basic recipe, designed to be compatible with almost any finished recipe. But the marinade can certainly be zapped up to good effect. Try any one to three of the following additions:

- *1 to 3 cloves garlic, pressed*
- *1 to 2 teaspoons peeled grated ginger*
- *¼ to ½ teaspoon freshly ground black pepper*
- *1 to 2 teaspoons honey*
- *1 teaspoon ground coriander*
- *1 to 2 teaspoons toasted sesame oil; ½ to 1 teaspoon Tabasco, sriracha, Chile Buzz (page 902) or other hot sauce;*
- *1 tablespoon ketchup or tomato paste*

2 Fifteen minutes before you are ready to cook the tempeh, preheat the oven to 375°F.

3 Place the marinated tempeh pieces on a nonstick baking sheet or one that has been sprayed with cooking spray, allowing plenty of air space between chunks. Bake for 12 to 15 minutes, then flip the pieces over and bake for another 10 minutes. Remove from the oven and use as desired.

Tempeh-tures Rising

Basic Oven-Baked Marinated Tempeh can take you in any number of directions with just a few tweaks. Here are my three favorite variations, two somewhat crispy and one extra-saturated in savory, garlicky flavor.

Basic Oven-Breaded Tempeh: *Follow the recipe for Basic Oven-Baked Marinated Tempeh through Step 1. Then make a breading of ½ cup nutritional yeast and ½ cup unbleached white all-purpose flour (or, if you like, the yeast plus ¼ cup unbleached white and ¼ cup cornmeal, or just the plain yeast). Add 1½ teaspoons paprika, and a little salt and freshly ground black pepper. Place the breading in a paper bag, add the tempeh a few pieces at a time, and shake like the dickens. Place the coated tempeh on a baking sheet and bake as for the basic recipe. (Leftover coating mix can be saved, refrigerated in a zippered freezer bag.)*

Basic Oven-Crisped Tempeh: *This is messy to make, and you'll think you're not doing it right because the egg coating will want to slither off, but for certain dishes the resulting crispness is worth it. Marinate the tempeh as in Step 1 of the above recipe. Then beat 1 egg together with 2 teaspoons water in a small bowl. Place 2 to 3 cups crisp breadcrumbs, cracker crumbs, or cornflake crumbs in a second bowl. Working with one piece of coated tempeh at a time, dip it into the egg, then the crumbs, pressing the crumbs in. Place each finished piece on the baking sheet, and bake as for the basic recipe, allowing 3 to 5 minutes longer per side.*

Ned's Rock 'Em Sock 'Em Marinated Tempeh Bake: *When Ned prepared breakfast at the inn, he would often make this assertive tempeh. It drew raves—not only from vegetarians, but even from guests who asked, "Say, what was that really good, kind of meaty, spicy thing at breakfast?"*

His marinade: ¼ cup each of tamari or shoyu soy sauce, frozen apple juice concentrate, spring or filtered water, and cider vinegar, plus 1½ tablespoons Garlic Oil (page 898). Grind in a lot of black pepper, whisk it well, and add 8 ounces tempeh, cut into ¾-inch-wide strips. Marinate overnight. Next morning, bake, but at 400°F.

Tempeh Tejas with a Sweet-Hot Jalapeño Glaze

This scrumptious dish might just be *the* way for you to introduce tempeh to a nonvegetarian. It's hard to imagine anyone not being delighted with it. I can tell you how good it is, how pretty on the plate, how divine the glaze—but you need to get cracking and make it for yourself. You won't be disappointed.

The glaze is faintly reminiscent of a Chinese sweet and sour sauce, but with more delicacy and a serious wallop of heat. The glaze and the sautéed pepper and onion components first made their appearance on pounded-out medallions of pork tenderloin at the inn's restaurant, after a bumper crop of jalapeños led us to making a bumper crop of quart jars of jalepeño jelly. One taste of the glaze and I knew it was too good to keep for the exclusive use of carnivores, so I began using it in tempeh recipes. **SERVES 6 TO 8, WITH RICE**

NOTES

For the best flavor, make sure that the jalapeño jelly you use is truly hot.

Remember, you need to marinate and bake the tempeh beforehand.

Splurge on a nice wine for the sauce, then serve the rest of the bottle with the finished dish.

1¼ cups low-tannin, fruity red wine, such as Beaujolais, Pinot Noir, or Dolcetto
1 tablespoon cornstarch
1 cup jalapeño jelly
1 to 2 tablespoons red wine vinegar
2 teaspoons mild vegetable oil, such as corn, canola, or peanut
Cooking spray (optional)
1 red onion, sliced vertically into thin crescents
2 red bell peppers, stemmed, seeded, and sliced vertically into strips
1 green bell pepper, stemmed, seeded, and sliced vertically into strips
1 jalapeño pepper, cut into small circles, with seeds (optional)
2 batches Basic Oven-Baked Marinated Tempeh (page 641), tempeh cakes halved the long way, then cut crosswise into strips about ¾ inch wide (marinated with red-wine vinegar, honey, and 2 teaspoons sriracha)

1 Measure out 2 tablespoons of the wine and place in a small dish. Whisk in the cornstarch and set aside.

2 Place the jalapeño jelly in a small saucepan over low heat. Cook, stirring occasionally, until it melts. When melted, add the remaining wine, along with the vinegar, and stir to blend. Cook at the lowest possible simmer as you finish the rest of the recipe.

3 Heat the oil in a nonstick skillet, or one that has been sprayed with cooking spray, over medium-high heat. Add the onion and stir-fry for 2 minutes. Add the red and green bell peppers and the jalapeño, if using, and cook just until seared, about 3 minutes. (The peppers should not be raw, but they should definitely still have some crunch, while the onions will have melted away to limpness.)

4 Lower the heat to medium and add the tempeh. Toss to blend and heat through.

5 Raise the heat under jalapeño-wine glaze and whisk in the reserved cornstarch mixture. The glaze should thicken and become clear almost immediately. Pour the glaze over the tempeh, tossing gently to combine. Serve at once, with rice or other cooked grain.

Double-Tempeh Stir-Fry with Yam, Apples, and Honey Mustard

Once again my penchant for the way sweet and hot play off tempeh is revealed in this hearty dish. Using both tempeh "bacon" and plain tempeh, it's nice in early winter when new-crop apples and garnet sweet potatoes are in. Pair it with a barley pilaf and a simply cooked green vegetable—steamed green beans or kale, for example. For a dressier meal, try my friend Jim Long's idea, and garnish each plate with a couple of slices of grilled fresh pineapple.

If you don't have commercial honey mustard on hand, use ⅓ cup regular Dijon-style mustard, with enough honey (roughly 2 tablespoons) added to equal ½ cup.

SERVES 4 TO 6

TEMPEH

- Cooking spray
- 1 package (6 ounces) smoked tempeh "bacon"
- 2 tablespoons mild vegetable oil, such as corn, canola, or peanut
- 2 packages tempeh (16 ounces total), cut into ½-inch dice
- 2 large sweet potatoes, peeled, cut into ½-inch dice
- ⅓ cup water, preferably spring or filtered, or apple juice or white wine

STIR-FRY SAUCE

- 2 teaspoons cornstarch
- 1 tablespoon balsamic vinegar
- ½ cup commercially made honey mustard
- 1 tablespoon Pickapeppa or vegetarian Worcestershire sauce
- 2 teaspoons freshly ground black pepper, or more to taste
- ¾ teaspoon salt, or more to taste

TO FINISH

- 1 large apple (Fuji, Braeburn, or Gala), unpeeled, cut into ½-inch cubes
- 3 scallions, roots removed, all the white and 4 inches of green sliced

1 Spray a large skillet with cooking spray and place it over medium-high heat. When the pan is hot, add the strips of smoked tempeh. Brown for 3 to 4 minutes, then turn and brown the second side. Remove the tempeh "bacon" from pan and set aside.

2 Leave the skillet on the heat and add the oil. When hot, add the diced tempeh and sauté, shaking the pan often, until some sides of the cubes are browned and some not, about 4 minutes. Add the sweet potatoes and sauté, shaking the pan, for another 2 minutes. Add the water (or juice or wine) and cover. Lower the heat slightly and steam until the sweet potatoes are barely tender, but not falling apart, 6 to 8 minutes.

3 Prepare the stir-fry sauce: Dissolve the cornstarch in the balsamic vinegar in a small bowl, smushing with your fingertips until smooth. Whisk in the mustard, Pickapeppa, 2 teaspoons pepper, and ¾ teaspoon salt. Set aside.

4 Chop the tempeh "bacon" into 1-inch-long pieces.

5 Uncover the skillet. Add the apple, raise the heat slightly, and sauté for 1 to 2 minutes more. (Use a spatula to gently turn as you stir-fry; you don't want the sweet potatoes to be mushy.) Again, raise the heat slightly and pour in the stir-fry sauce. Stir gently, and cook until the sauce is thick and clear. Stir in the scallions and the tempeh "bacon." Taste and adjust for salt and pepper. Serve hot, straight from the skillet.

VARIATION

THAI-INFLUENCED STIR-FRY OF TEMPEH AND GREEN BEANS WITH AN APRICOT-MUSTARD GLAZE: ***If you are a fan of serious kick with sweetness and Thai-style flavors, you'll love this. Add 1 teaspoon sriracha (hot pepper paste; or substitute Classic Harissa, page 921, or Tabasco), 1 teaspoon grated ginger, an additional teaspoon of tamari or shoyu soy sauce, and 3 cloves pressed garlic to the glaze. Just before the dish comes off the heat, toss in ½ cup coarsely chopped mint, Thai basil, or cilantro. And then, for the serious kicker, toss paper-thin rounds from 1 to 3 raw serrano chiles with seeds, over the final dish. Yowza!***

Stir-Fry of Tempeh and Green Beans with an Apricot-Mustard Glaze

This recipe combines Eastern technique with a Western saucing, piquantly pleasing and quickly put together. Sweet and hot, crisp and tender, this is a great company dish, though it does involve some last-minute fussing. As Stan Dean, a meat-eating friend who happily chowed down on it, once remarked approvingly, "Oh, it's *very* carnivorous." **SERVES 4 TO 6**

- 2 teaspoons mild vegetable oil, such as corn, canola, or peanut
- Cooking spray
- 1 onion, sliced vertically into thin crescents
- ½ pound green beans, preferably thin ones, trimmed, sliced diagonally into into ½-inch pieces
- 1 red bell pepper, stemmed, seeded, and sliced vertically into ½-inch-wide strips
- 1 cup fruit-only apricot jam
- ⅔ cup slightly sweet white wine
- 3 tablespoons Dijon mustard
- 2 teaspoons tamari or shoyu soy sauce
- 1 recipe Basic Oven-Baked Marinated Tempeh (page 641), each cake cut diagonally from corner to corner, making 4 triangles per cake (each about 2-by-2-by-3 inches)

1 Heat the oil in a large nonstick skillet or wok, or one that has been sprayed with cooking spray, over high heat. Add the onion and stir-fry until slightly softened, about 3 minutes. Add the green beans, lower the heat to medium, and continue stir-frying until the green beans are still crisp, but have begun to lose their rawness, 3 to 4 minutes. Add the red pepper and stir-fry for 2 minutes.

2 Quickly whisk the jam, wine, mustard, and tamari together. Pour the jam mixture over the vegetables. Toss in the cooked tempeh and stir gently to combine and heat through. Serve hot, with any kind of cooked grain as an accompaniment.

Tempeh "San Francisco Chicken Salad–Style"

Jan Brown and I offered up a wonderful fruited chicken salad recipe in the first Dairy Hollow House cookbook. This is an even better vegetarian version, energizing, and still very "ladies who lunch," though maybe rather New Age-y ladies.

Like all mayonnaise-y salads it's deceptive in its lightness. It feels light and low cal, but packs quite a caloric wallop. Remember this vis-à-vis the optional nuts: The cook in you will say, "Yes," the weight watcher, "No." But true prudence, far more courteous and moderate, should prevail: "Once in a while, crocodile."

Serve it on a bed of lettuce, scooped into a hollowed-out pineapple half or orange cup, with crisp crackers or warm whole wheat toast. Because it can be done ahead, it's a nice leave-in-the-fridge cold supper for those evenings when syncopated schedules mean no one in the family will really cross paths until bedtime. **SERVES 4 TO 6 AS A MAIN COURSE**

VARIATION

Grate the rind of the orange before sectioning it, and add the orange rind to the salad's dressing. Or add 1 to 2 teaspoons peeled, grated ginger to the dressing.

1 cup water, preferably spring or filtered
⅓ cup apple juice
3 tempeh cakes (8 ounces each)
10½ ounces (½ package) reduced-fat silken tofu
¼ cup Honeyed Red-Wine Vinaigrette (page 79)
2 ribs celery, chopped
2 oranges, peeled, sectioned, seeded, and coarsely chopped
2½ cups peeled, diced fresh pineapple
2 cups halved seedless green grapes
3 tablespoons finely minced red onion
Salt and freshly ground black pepper to taste

1. Place the water and apple juice in a large pot with a tight-fitting lid. Fit a steamer basket into the pot, making sure that it fits above the liquid. Cut each tempeh cake in half and place on the steamer. Cover and bring the liquid to a boil over high heat. Steam, tightly covered, about 15 to 20 minutes (check every so often to see if you need to add any more liquid, and to stir down any foam). Remove from the heat and let stand until the tempeh is cool enough to handle. Dice the tempeh into ½-inch chunks and set aside in a mixing bowl.

2. Buzz the silken tofu in a food processor along with the Honeyed Red-Wine

Vinaigrette. If it is not the consistency of mayonnaise, add a couple tablespoons of the apple juice remaining in the steaming pot. If it's too thin, add a little extra tofu.

Pour the dressing over the tempeh. Add the celery, oranges, pineapple, grapes, and onion. Season with salt and pepper to taste.

Tempeh au Poivre

This dish is as elegant, haute, and black pepper–laden as the steak preparation that inspired it.

The exact cut of the tempeh steaks will be determined by the shape of the tempeh you've purchased. You may simply quarter each cake, which gives you smaller but thicker pieces, or (my preference) cut each cake horizontally, and then in half—you get larger, thinner pieces, which crisp up nicely. Cracked peppercorns (not ground, not whole, but coarsely cracked) are commercially available. You can also crack them by placing them in a cloth or a plastic bag on a cutting board, bearing down with an iron skillet, and twisting.

Serve with mashed potatoes, Millet Mash (page 551), a brown rice–wild rice mix, or a grain pilaf—barley, brown rice, and wild rice are especially good here. Round the plate out with a simple, slightly sweet orange vegetable (Simple Sweet-Baked Winter Squash, page 807); sautéed carrots; or Carrots Vichy, page 731). Start the meal with marinated asparagus or a salad, or add some good garlicky broccoli rabe to the entree plate.

I prefer butter and oil, or Better (page 905), to straight oil here, but do as you like. For an even richer sauce, just before you take the dish off the heat, swirl in an extra teaspoon of butter. The better your vegetable stock, the better the sauce. **SERVES 4**

1 pound tempeh, cut into 8 large rectangles
3 tablespoons tamari or shoyu soy sauce
2 tablespoons red-wine vinegar
2 to 3 tablespoons coarsely cracked black peppercorns
Cooking spray
About 1 cup nutritional yeast (see page 239)
2 tablespoons Better (page 905) or 1 tablespoon butter plus 1 tablespoon olive oil
1 small red onion, finely diced
½ pound shiitake mushrooms, stems removed, sliced
5 cloves garlic, sliced
⅓ cup cognac or brandy
1 cup dry, full-bodied red wine
1 cup vegetable stock, the more flavorful the better (Oven-Roasted Vegetable Stock, page 141, is perfect here); or use aseptically packaged mushroom stock
Salt to taste

1 Place the tempeh in a flat, nonreactive dish. Drizzle with the tamari and vinegar, turning the tempeh so both sides get a splash. Add the peppercorns and press them into the tempeh with the heel of your hand (they will resist you). Turn the tempeh, and press pepper into the other side, to whatever extent you can. (Even if the peppercorns don't all stick, and they won't, you'll still get plenty of peppery good flavor, both in the tempeh and the finished dish.) Marinate the peppered tempeh, refrigerated, for 2 to 6 hours.

2 Thirty minutes before serving time, preheat the oven to 375°F.

3 Spray a baking sheet with cooking spray and set aside.

4 Place the nutritional yeast in a bag. Put the marinated tempeh, one piece at a time, along with any peppercorns affixed to it, into the bag. (Reserve any peppercorns left in the marinade dish.) Shake to coat. As it is coated, place the tempeh (there will be plenty of yeast left over), on the prepared baking sheet, allowing plenty of air space between chunks. Bake 12 to 15 minutes. Turn the cakes over and bake for another 10 minutes. Remove from the oven.

5 During the last 10 minutes of the tempeh baking time, organize the remaining ingredients by the stove, as the finishing must go quickly.

6 Heat the Better in a nonstick skillet, or one that has been sprayed with cooking spray, over medium-high heat. Add the onion and stir-fry for 3 minutes. Add the mushrooms and stir-fry for an additional 3 minutes. Add the garlic and stir-fry for 1 minute more.

7 Remove the tempeh from the oven and place it on top of the vegetables. Pour the cognac over the tempeh, heat for a couple of seconds, and, standing back, quickly set it alight with a match. When the flames die down (perhaps 20 seconds), lift the tempeh from the skillet and set it aside, keeping warm.

8 Add the red wine, stock, and any peppercorns left from the marinade to the skillet. Raise the heat as high as it will go and bring to a boil. Boil, stirring and scraping the pan often, until the sauce is reduced by half, 4 to 6 minutes. Taste and correct the seasonings, adding salt as necessary; return the tempeh to the skillet and cook to just heat through. Serve immediately.

VARIATION

Classic steak au poivre is done in either of two ways—more or less as above, or with a cream-mustard finish. To make a vegan version of the latter, once the sauce has reduced, lower the heat and stir in 3 to 4 tablespoons Tofu Sour Cream (page 909) and 1 teaspoon Dijon mustard. Heat through and serve at once.

Soy Many Other Choices . . .

Tofu and tempeh are just the start of the soybean's infinite transformative possibilities. You may drink your soy—as savory, brothy, salty miso; or as creamy, slightly sweet soymilk. Stew it, as TVP-filled chili; use it as a relish as with natto. Here are a few more of soy's forms.

Whole Bean Soy Foods

MISO: *A salty seasoning and condiment used in soups, sauces, dressings, spreads, glazes, and marinades. Please see a full explanation on page 173.*

NATTO *is a Japanese soyfood condiment made of whole fermented, cooked soybeans. The fermenting bacteria leaves the soybeans exceptionally high in several B-vitamins. The slippery dark brown beans are an acquired taste for most Westerners; their texture is viscous and stringy. In Asia, natto is traditionally served as a rice topping, or in miso soups; it's also sautéed with vegetables and used in dressings. Natto can be found in Asian (especially Japanese) groceries, and natural foods stores.*

From Soy Derivatives

OKARA *is basically fiber, the pulp left over when soy milk is made. Though it has much less protein than whole soybeans, the protein remaining is high-quality and rich in both fiber and isoflavones. Though less popular than tofu, okara has a long and honorable history of use in Asian cooking. It is often found as an ingredient in many commercially available soyfoods. Many regional soysage brands use okara, and you'll find okara burgers in the frozen-food sections of most natural foods markets.*

Soy Protein Isolates

One of the most common soy ingredients you'll find in everything from frozen dinners featuring soyfoods to protein mixes for smoothies to energy bars is something called soy protein isolates. It's the most highly refined soy protein food, having been removed from defatted flakes of soybeans, and ends up with a whopping 92 percent protein in a highly digestible form.

Textured Soy Protein

Almost every time I go to the natural foods market I see textured soy protein or flour (TSP or TSF) available in a new form. There are soft chewy nuggets of it, designed to mimic chicken or beef chunks; there are frozen and dehydrated equivalents; there are even seasoned ready-to-eat soy "jerkys." Most are made from textured soy flour, although some are derived from textured soy protein concentrates, spun soy fiber, or extruded defatted soy flour. TVP, textured vegetable protein, is a TSF copyrighted by Archer Daniels Midland. All these foods contain about 70 percent protein and most of the bean's fiber. Though they undoubtedly have their place in a vegetarian diet, I am among those who feel that they are so far from their original state that they kind of give me the all-overs. I would rather have real anything than ersatz anything—and the TSFs fall into the latter category to me. I have used TVP, though, for years, in chili and it's tasty in some brands of soysage. All these ingredients can be found in natural foods markets.

Soy Sauces

SOY SAUCE, *probably the first soy product most Americans experience, is a dark brown salty condiment made from fermented, processed soybeans. Shoyu, the most common soy sauce, is made from a blend of soy and wheat; tamari is made from soybeans alone. The two can be used interchangeably. Avoid soy sauces made with caramel coloring and other extraneous ingredients—they lack the deep mysterious richness that a tamari or shoyu will give. Reduced-salt versions are also available.*

TERIYAKI *and other cooking sauces are also widely available. Usually thicker than plain soy sauce, they include other ingredients: sugar, vinegar, ginger, chile, sesame seeds or oil, spices. I prefer to mix my own such concoctions, but prepared teriyaki is a convenience.*

Soy Milk & Soy Milk Products

SOY MILK: *The first time I tasted soy milk I turned up my nose. It was too "beany," and nothing like the cow's milk I knew. But traveling in Singapore I had truly fresh soy milk for the first time, and was amazed—sweet, pleasing, more creamy white than yellow, it was purely delicious.*

Since those early years of soy milk production, the technology has changed and the available varieties of soy milk have skyrocketed in number. You can now find plain, vanilla, chocolate, calcium-fortified, low- and full-fat varieties of soy milk in aseptic containers (nonrefrigerated and shelf stable), with much better flavor than that we had in the old days. You can now often find fresh soy milk in quart and half-gallon containers in the dairy case. My favorite variety is one called Soy Silk, made by White Wave from organic, non–genetically modified soybeans.

Soy milk cannot be frozen—its texture changes—but you can buy a powdered soy milk, which you reconstitute with water. I know several lactose-intolerant folks who travel with it.

SOY YOGURT: *If you can make soy milk, how about soy yogurt? Sure 'nuff—just as yogurt is cultured from cow's milk, soy yogurt is cultured from soy milk, and can be used in exactly the same way. I started out preferring cow's milk yogurt, but as soyfood expertise has grown, this product has vastly improved and comes in every imaginable variety; look for it in the dairy case at your natural foods store. From here, is it far to soy-based ice creams? Of course not. You'll find it right in there with all the other ice creams. A scoop of vanilla soy ice cream with fresh raspberries and a shot of Frangelico or homemade hot fudge sauce is a no-holds-barred treat.*

SOY CHEESES, *however, are a hard sell to me. Though there are dozens available, both in chunks and in single slices, "Cheddar-style," grated "Parmesan-type," and everything else, they just don't have a flavor and texture equal to the dairy varieties. This being said, I know that lactose-intolerant folks who go through a pound of assorted soy cheeses a weekend claim that, having gotten used to them, dairy cheeses taste weird. For them, and for vegans, soy cheese makes possible pizza and countless other cheese-topped foods.*

Tofu & Tofu Products

While there is certainly a place for cooked soybeans, on a day-to-day basis I use, and much prefer, soybeans transformed into tofu. As someone who has eaten tofu since girlhood, I have no doubt that to know, truly *know*, tofu, is to love it.

What Is Tofu? Soaked, raw soybeans are ground, cooked, pressed, and strained, creating a creamy white liquid, high in protein, that bears a resemblance to milk and is, in fact, called soy milk. (It is different from commercially available soy milks marketed as beverages.) As with conventional cheese-making, this soy milk is then coagulated into curds. After being drained of their free-flowing whey, the curds are placed in "settling boxes," cloth-lined perforated molds, the tops of which are weighted to press down on the tofu. This helps expel still more whey. After a total time of about 20 minutes, or until no more whey drips from the holes, the blocks, now tofu, are removed from the mold, rinsed, unwrapped, cut into squares, and cooled under water.

Tofu Recipes

Because tofu, as we've seen, is really many products, not one, there are dozens of directions to go in its preparation. What I've included here doesn't even begin to scratch the surface.

I've divided up the recipes here into three sections. *Basics* includes marinades, and guidelines for general tofu preparation. The *Eastern* recipes derive from those countries where tofu is a traditional foodstuff. Though not many recipes here are dot-every-i, cross-every-t traditional, all are strongly influenced by Asian flavors, ingredients, and techniques.

The *Western*-style recipes are more of a jump. Longtime vegetarians tend to adore things like barbecued tofu or "chicken-fried" tofu, reminiscent of but not dead ringers for once-loved meat dishes. Those who do eat meat may find them a bit puzzling at first. If you are new to tofu-world or are an occasional vegetarian who wishes to incorporate more soyfoods into your diet, you might be happiest starting with the Eastern-style recipes.

Know Your Tofus

To love tofu, you must understand that there are many different types, forms, and textures. **For good results, you must use the type of tofu appropriate to the specific recipe.** Here are several tofu types that await your exploration.

Fresh Perishable Tofus

Fresh tofus are those that must be kept refrigerated. They are as vulnerable to contamination as are meat, eggs, and milk.

Classic, Traditional Water-Packed Tofu

What It Is: Cakes of fresh white full-fat or reduced-fat tofu, available as firm or extra-firm.

What It's Like: It is slightly granular or curdlike, mild in flavor, with a delicate sweetness and a pleasing, slightly bouncy texture in the mouth. Classic, traditional tofu is firm enough to be diced and soft enough to be crumbled. If you cut open a cube of traditional tofu, it's a bit shaggy, with tiny pockmarks and crevasses, left from the drained whey. Its exterior is very lightly textured with the imprint of the cloth in which it was formed.

The "shaggy" quality of traditional tofu is what makes it perfect for marinades; it acts in a slightly spongelike manner, soaking up flavorful mixtures.

How It's Sold and Packaged: Delicate, fresh tofu is always kept refrigerated and stored in water to maintain its freshness. Traditionally, it was sold in bulk, the cubes floating in large tubs of water and scooped out with a skimmer or tongs. You'll still find it this way in ethnic markets, larger natural foods stores, or artisanal tofu shops (most large, and some medium-large, American cities have at least one). Lately, however, there have been questions concerning the possibility of contamination with salmonella or *E. coli* from bulk tofu. This is no problem if you cook it thoroughly, but if you occasionally eat it raw, straight from the fridge, you should purchase it packed in water and sealed, in the refrigerated section of a natural foods store or supermarket.

The supermarket brands, which are usually made by one of the large Asian companies, tend to be a little softer and less satisfactory than the natural foods brands. When I can get it, I always prefer really fresh, sweet artisanal tofu bought in bulk.

How to Keep It: Classic, traditional tofu has a relatively brief shelf life, whether bulk or preboxed. Bulk tofu must be put into a container of fresh cold water, preferably spring or filtered, the minute you get it home. Keep it covered, submerged in just enough water to cover and surround it. Change the water daily and it will keep for 5 days to a week. The tofus that come in individual plastic tubs maintain freshness unopened for a good while—perhaps 8 to 10 days. Once you open them, however, you must either use all the tofu in a single meal or keep the uncooked remainder in a container filled with water, which you change daily. At this point, the shelf life is about 5 days.

How will you know if your tofu is fresh? Fresh tofu smells "clean"—virtually odorless—and is white, gray-white, or creamy buff-white. Tofu that has turned smells noticeably off, may have yellowed, and when you touch it has a slimy texture.

Traditional tofu can also be frozen. Freezing changes the texture markedly in a way that some people adore, making it chewy, crumbly, and literally sponge-like—it will instantly soak up a marinade. There is a subculture of tofu-lovers who deliberately freeze tofu to achieve this texture. I am not one of them; in most recipes, I prefer the regular bouncy, not quite so chewy, texture. To freeze tofu, drain the water from it and press it, by placing it in a colander set on a plate. Place a saucer on top of the tofu with a can or something heavy to weight it down on the saucer. Let it sit, at room temperature, for about 30 minutes to squeeze extra moisture from it. Then, wrap the tofu in plastic wrap or place in a zippered freezer bag and place in the freezer. It keeps, frozen, for 4 to 6 months. Thaw overnight in the refrigerator, and squeeze the thawed tofu block by hand to wring out any remaining water. If using a marinade, drizzle it over the thawed tofu and watch it absorb like crazy.

How to Use It: Classic, traditional tofu, especially the firm kind, is ideal in stir-fries or sukiyaki; just dice it and toss it in at the last minute. It can also be marinated and baked (see page 670; this gives it a firm, chewy texture much prized among tofu aficionados). It is the perfect tofu for barbecued tofu (page 668), or, if firm, Kung Pao Tofu (page 662). It can also be breaded and sautéed, which gives it a crisp exterior. It can then be used to fill a sandwich or served with any number of wonderful sauces spooned over it. Crumbled, it fills CD's Famed Tofu Broccoli Enchiladas (page 340), stuffed shells (see page 326), and other good stuffed things. Another cross-cultural use is in curries, as the sweet mildness is great against assertive and spicy sauces.

When cooked in certain ways, classic tofu can be egglike, too. Scrambled Tofu (page 666), and Spinach and Wheatberry Tofu Quiche (page 263) exploit this similarity. They don't taste exactly like eggs, but they're eggish, and somehow satisfying in the same way, especially for vegans and others who don't or can't eat eggs.

Seasoned Tofus

Savory baked tofu

What It Is: Slices of fresh tofu are seasoned simply, rolled in nutritional yeast (see page 239), baked, and packaged for sale. Available in the refrigerated case at natural foods markets and some larger supermarkets.

What It's Like: It has a white interior, with a slightly gooey golden-brown exterior. With a firm, chewy texture and agreeable flavor, added to the fact that it's already prepared, it may be the tofu for those who are convinced they dislike tofu. Since you can use it as is, even eat it straight from the package, it is a highly convenient food.

How It's Sold and Packaged: No water. Savory baked tofu is sold 4 to 5 rectangles to a package, refrigerated, vacuum-packed in a small bag.

How to Keep It: Unopened, savory baked tofu will keep in the fridge for 10 days or so. Once the package is opened, transfer leftovers, wrapper and all, to a zippered freezer bag and they'll keep for another 5 days or so.

How to Use It: Sliced, savory baked tofu keeps its shape and texture well. Dice for a stir-fry or a stew, adding tofu at the last minute, or stir the cubes into your favorite pasta sauce or main-dish salad. This is the perfect tofu for The "Jerry" Reuben (page 869), or any sandwich in which a nonvegetarian might use sliced chicken or turkey.

Other seasoned baked tofus

What They Are: Slices of fresh tofu are seasoned with marinades and spicings from various cuisines, then baked and packaged. You'll see Thai-style tofu, Italian-style tofu, and others. Available in the refrigerated case at natural foods markets and some larger supermarkets. Again, check for regional brands.

Some smoked tofus are literally smoked in a smokehouse and some are marinated with flavorings and liquid smoke. Some are baked after being seasoned, others cooked solely by the smoke itself. The most widely available national brand is Tree of Life, which has a very smooth texture, a fairly strong flavor, and comes in thinnish slices. There are several excellent regional brands. A newcomer is Smoked Tofurkey, cold-cut–like slices with a texture close enough to real turkey to be off-putting to long-time vegetarians.

What It's Like: Though less versatile than savory baked tofu, most of the flavored tofus are a real find. Firm textured, flavored with characteristic seasonings, and already prepared, they are another good introductory tofu. They have an exterior that is usually browned and a little moist. They can be used as is, even eaten straight from the package with crackers for a snack. The smoked tofus have a more assertive flavor. Some people really enjoy them in sandwiches or diced and tossed with pasta.

How They're Sold and Packaged: Look ma, no water! These products are sold 4 to 5 pieces to a package, refrigerated, vacuum-packed in a small bag.

How to Keep Them: Unopened, seasoned tofus will keep in the fridge for 10 days or so. Once opened, transfer any leftovers, wrapper and all, to a zippered freezer bag, and they'll keep for another 5 days or so.

How to Use Them: Slices of seasoned baked tofu keep their shape and texture well. They may be diced for last-minute addition to a stir-fry or a stew or stirred into any pasta sauce or main-dish salad. I use Thai-style tofu, diced, in Quasi-Vietnamese Spring Rolls (page 314). They can be perfect in any sandwich in which a nonvegetarian might use sliced chicken or turkey.

The smoked is also good in The "Jerry" Reuben (page 869), or on a toasted bun with warm barbecue sauce. For me, the smokiness does not work in stir-fries.

Tofu dips

What They Are: Ready-made dips and spreads of pureed tofu, seasoned with herbs, garlic, and other flavors. Many use a great deal of oil.

What They're Like: Creamy and good, with flavors dependent upon the seasonings and local tastes. Few will notice any difference between them and conventional dips.

How They're Sold and Packaged: Usually in little plastic tubs. They are highly perishable, and should be kept refrigerated.

How to Keep Them: Use them within 3 to 4 days of purchase. Pour off any accumulated water or liquid that has come out of them before serving them.

How to Use Them: Anywhere and any way you'd use conventional nontofu dips—with raw vegetables, with chips, crackers, toasts, for artichoke leaf dipping. If you like a particular type, try tossing it with hot pasta and vegetables; it'll melt into a creamy sauce.

Homemade tofu dips, such as the ones in this book (pages 26–27), are just about as easy as purchasing ready-made ones, plus they're a lot cheaper, often lower in fat, and just as tasty, if not tastier. With a box of silken tofu, you can make most of them in under 3 minutes.

READY-GROUND TOFU

What It Is: A packaged tofu that is ground and flavored to resemble already-browned ground beef.

What It's Like: Of course it doesn't taste exactly like ground beef, but its texture, appearance, and (to some extent) flavor are close enough to give a vegetarian pause. Remember, it's already "browned" and crumbly—so you can't, say, form it into burgers. It's available plain (pretty tasteless), spicy (cumin-chile-ish), or with "savory garlic."

How It's Sold and Packaged: I've always found it in the freezer compartment at my natural foods store. It comes in 10-ounce vacuum-packed bags tucked into small boxes. Thaw overnight in the fridge, unless the package directions say otherwise. It keeps for 1 week, unopened, after thawing; once open, use within 3 to 4 days.

How to Use It: Try it in casseroles—particularly the '50s-era redux casseroles many of us remember with unaccountable fondness, like Nouveau Iowa Potato–Black Bean Pie (page 259) or Mulligan (page 675). It can also be stirred into chilies, spaghetti sauces, and the like. Although ready-ground has its purposes, it's an occasional ingredient rather than a daily dietary workhorse, as traditional, silken, and savory baked tofu are.

Dry or Packaged Tofus (Cupboard)

ASEPTICALLY PACKAGED SILKEN TOFU

What It Is: A specific variety of extremely smooth tofu that, due to its method of packaging, does not need refrigeration until opened. It is called kinugoshi tofu in Japan, where it is also available in fresh, perishable form.

What It's Like: The texture of silken tofu truly is silken in mouth feel—smooth, creamy, uniform. It has a semitranslucent, custardlike quality, quite unlike any other tofu. This smoothness means it is *never* an appropriate choice for marination—silken tofu just will not soak it up.

How It's Sold and Packaged: Silken tofu, in this country at least, is available almost exclusively aseptically packaged in cardboard boxes. It is available in soft, firm, and extra-firm varieties; also in regular or reduced fat. Many supermarkets keep it in the produce section next to the traditional tofu (which does need refrigeration).

Silken tofu is the most widely available tofu in America. It's a very good product, but its silken texture means it's best when used very specifically, in certain types of recipes (dips, sauces, many desserts) and not others (stir-fries, braises, stews).

How to Keep It: Silken tofu's shelf life, unrefrigerated, is 6 to 8 months; once opened, it must be kept refrigerated in a container or water, like traditional tofu. Change the water daily, and it will stay fresh for 3 to 4 days.

How to Use It: Although the firm and extra-firm silken tofus *can* be diced and added to stir-fries or dropped into clear soups, they are not nearly as good this way as the traditional, savory baked, or flavored tofus. But, in fact, I never use it this way. Instead, I try to emphasize its custardlike qualities in recipes that exploit its creaminess: purees for sauces, dips, mayos, and sour creams (see pages 26–27, 909 . . .). Use it in creamy soups in lieu of the cream; in smoothies instead of yogurt; or in desserts (see page 1062).

A combination of silken tofu and traditional works perfectly for some recipes, like Tofu-Filled "Cheese" Blintzes (page 336), or Lemon Glazed Tofu "Teasecake" (page 1009).

Other Miscellaneous Tofus

Lately tofu, not necessity, seems to be the mother of invention. Historically, soy-eating populations have come up with infinite ways to shape, season, and process tofu, creating foodstuffs that wholly belie their origins. A whole "mock" cuisine, developed by Chinese vegetarian Buddhists, approximates meat, fowl, and fish dishes, but is built around tofu and seitan. And contemporary New Age entrepreneurs are continuously developing new products. Recently, I saw herb-speckled tofu cubes with fresh basil and garlic stirred in during their manufacture—sort of a tofu Boursin.

Here are a few of the new tofu products I know about. Be prepared to discover, explore, and experiment with new sons and daughters of tofu as they emerge on the market.

Tofu burgers and sausages: *Countless veggie burgers and soy sausages are already on or are coming to market. One of my favorites is Boca Burger's Breakfast Patties. Some soy sausages are very breakfast sausage–like, dark, a bit chewy, crisp on the outside when oven-baked, and with a hint of sage. Lightlife Lean Italian Links are also terrific: pale, frankfurter-shaped, delicately seasoned in the style of sweet Italian sausage and very soft until sautéed. Once cooked they can be diced and added to tomato sauce, piled on a crisp baguette with sautéed onion and green pepper, or used in recipes such as Vegetarian Cassoulet (page 612).*

Deep-fried tofu *is a traditional Asian product, called agé. One sometimes sees agé, prefried and packaged, near water-packed tofus in the refrigerator case. Deep-frying triples tofu's calorie count, and the product is too greasy for my taste.*

Freeze-dried tofu *is one you'll likely run into only in dehydrated instant miso soup. The little squares puff up just as nicely as can be. Hint to the vegetarian traveler: Never be without instant miso soup on a plane—that way, when they fail to have your vegetarian meal (this happens at least 50 percent of the time) you still have nourishment.*

Tofu hot dogs *don't do it for me at all. But I do have friends who swear by them—or, at least, swear that their kids love them. I prefer soysage (see above).*

Yuba: *Far more delicious than tofu hot dogs are the mock meats made with dried bean curd wrappers, also known as yuba. They're made from the skin that forms on top of soy milk during processing, which is lifted and dried. I believe that this traditional Asian product will explode onto the American soy-scene soon because it is so versatile and delicious and has a long and honorable history as a meat alternative. It is the unique thin-chewy texture of yuba sheets, when layered with seasonings and shaped, stacked, cut, and prepared in certain ways, that gives such a convincingly "meaty" feeling to such dishes.*

What is a bean-curd "wrapper"? Go back to the idea of tofu being made from soy milk. I'm sure you've noticed the skin that forms on top as cow's milk is heated? Heat soy milk and a very similar skin forms. Yuba is that skin, commercially manufactured.

Those who live in areas with large Asian populations may be able to find it fresh (nama-yuba) or half-dried (namagawaki); smaller Asian food stores may carry dried (kanso-yuba). Occasionally frozen fresh yuba may also be found.

Six marinades for traditional water-packed tofu

Marinating tofu gives you a leg up on dozens of simple dishes and gives mild tofu some personality. Marinated tofus can be tossed into stir-fries, breaded and browned in the oven or skillet to be sauced, or tucked in a sandwich, or skewered and grilled. Always use *sliced, traditional-style, water-packed tofu* for marinating—never silken, which the marinade won't penetrate properly. I prefer firm or extra-firm, reduced-fat tofu for this purpose. If you want the flavor of the marinade to really saturate the tofu, and you like a chewy texture, freeze the tofu and then thaw it first.

The shape of the slices is dictated by how you want the finished dish to look, but you want lots of surface exposed, so the tofu can soak up the marinade. Usually I do large rectangles about 3 inches long by 2 inches wide and about ¼ to ½ inch thick, but this varies according to the shape of the tofu block and its firmness. This size, halved, makes a good shape for oven-baked tofu, sandwiches, barbecued tofu, or more elaborately sauced dishes. For stir-fries, I use 2-inch triangles or ¾-inch dice.

Since most marinades contain vinegar or other acids, do your marinating in a nonreactive pan or dish—glass or enamel-clad types are best.

Traditional Asian-Style Marinade for Tofu

This is the mother of all tofu marinades—what almost everyone starts out using. It's certainly not revolutionary (although you can give it your own twist with some of the optionals), but it is tasty and versatile, leaving you an already-seasoned tofu that can be used every which way. **MAKES ENOUGH TO MARINATE 12 TO 16 OUNCES TOFU**

- 3 cloves garlic, crushed
- 1 piece peeled ginger about the size of half your thumb, cut into several pieces
- 2 tablespoons to ¼ cup tamari or shoyu soy sauce
- 2 tablespoons mirin (Japanese rice wine) or dry sherry, or, if you prefer a sharper taste, rice vinegar
- 1 tablespoon honey, Rapidura, or brown sugar
- Any or all of the following: Several vigorous grinds of black pepper; Tabasco, sriracha, or other hot sauce to taste; 1 teaspoon toasted sesame oil, or to taste; 1 peeled and chopped fresh tomato; ¼ cup chopped onion; ¼ cup chopped scallions (optional)

Combine all of the ingredients in a food processor. Pulse/chop, then buzz, pausing to scrape down the sides of the work bowl as needed, until the mixture is almost smooth.

Pour over 12 to 14 ounces drained, sliced traditional water-packed tofu. Let soak for 40 minutes at room temperature, or cover and refrigerate overnight.

Smoky Onion-Garlic Marinade for Tofu

This 3-minute marinade could not be easier or more delicious. It's the base preparation for barbecued tofu (page 668), but a dish of tofu soaking in it has infinite possibilities. Dice and stir into scrambled eggs or vegetable sautés; toss with hot pasta or chilled salad greens, leftover cooked grain, diced tomato, and good dressing—impromptu, delicious, satisfying.

Because this marinade contains little oil, it is not suitable for grilling. **MAKES ENOUGH TO MARINATE 12 TO 16 OUNCES TOFU**

1 large onion, peeled and quartered
1 head garlic, peeled, cloves left whole (if you are in a rush, just use a couple of cloves)
¼ cup tamari or shoyu soy sauce
1 tablespoon mild vegetable oil, such as corn, canola, or peanut (optional)
2 tablespoons cider vinegar
2 to 4 drops liquid smoke

Combine all of the ingredients in a food processor. Pulse/chop, then buzz, pausing to scrape down the sides of the work bowl as needed. The consistency will be thin, with bits of ground onion in it.

Pour over 12 to 14 ounces drained, sliced traditional water-packed tofu. Let soak for 40 minutes at room temperature, or cover and refrigerate, turning occasionally, for up to 6 days. Tofu keeps much longer in this marinade than in others, because there is a larger amount.

Tandoori Tofu Marinade

As America's love of all foods ethnic explodes, you can now purchase curry pastes of all kinds, including Indian. Here is a marinade that takes advantage of commercially made tandoori marinade. **MAKES ENOUGH TO MARINATE 12 TO 16 OUNCES TOFU**

½ cup plain yogurt, regular or soy
⅓ cup commercially prepared tandoori marinade

Combine the yogurt and marinade, whisking well to blend.

Pour over 12 to 14 ounces drained, sliced traditional water-packed tofu. (If using for Southeast Asian Tofu Satay, page 663, cut into large cubes.) Let soak for 40 minutes at room temperature, or cover and refrigerate overnight.

Thai-Malaysian Curry-Ginger Marinade for Tofu

Bathe the plump cubes of tofu overnight in this marinade (along with vegetables for the satay on page 663). The flavors sock it to the simplicity of tofu. The ginger and peeled garlic need not be hand minced to the exact measurements I've specified; approximate the amount by eye, judging from the whole garlic cloves and larger pieces of ginger, and process with the other ingredients. **MAKES ENOUGH TO MARINATE 12 TO 16 OUNCES TOFU**

⅓ cup tamari or shoyu soy sauce
⅓ cup honey
¼ cup Dairy Hollow House Curry Spice Blend (page 901) or good commercial curry powder
3 tablespoons peeled, finely chopped or pureed garlic
3 tablespoons peeled, finely minced ginger
2 tablespoons vegetable oil
1 tablespoon rice vinegar
Pinch of cayenne or more to taste

Combine all of the ingredients in a food processor, buzzing until the ginger is finely chopped.

Pour the mixture over 12 to 14 ounces drained, sliced traditional water-packed tofu. Cut into large cubes if using for satay (see page 663). Let soak for 40 minutes at room temperature, or cover and refrigerate overnight.

Ginger

Western/Hippie-Style Marinade for Tofu

This is another tofu marinade that was once almost universal in some circles. It remains pleasing and useful. I'd call it "basic hippie home cooking" in style and flavor. You need it for Basic Skillet-Sautéed Tofu (page 667), a classic of this genre.

MAKES ENOUGH TO MARINATE 12 TO 16 OUNCES TOFU

2 tablespoons tamari or shoyu soy sauce
1 tablespoon cider vinegar
1 tablespoon Pickapeppa sauce
Several vigorous grinds of black pepper
Any or all of the following: Tabasco or similar hot sauce to taste, crushed garlic to taste; 1 teaspoon to 1 tablespoon bottled salsa (optional)

Whisk all the ingredients together in a small bowl.

Pour over 12 to 14 ounces drained, sliced traditional water-packed tofu. Let soak for 40 minutes or up to 8 hours at room temperature.

Traditional Asian-Style "Crisping" Marinade and Method for Oven-Baked Tofu

Originally developed for Kung Pao Tofu (page 662), this is a fine recipe in and of itself, just asking to be used in a sprightly stir-fry. The cornstarch makes magic when the tofu is baked, adding a slight, browned, crisp-chewy exterior that is very pleasing.

Please note that if making this for the Kung Pao Tofu, mirin, cornstarch, and garlic are also needed for the finishing sauce, so measure them out at the same time.

SERVES 4 TO 6, DEPENDING ON FINAL USE

3 cloves garlic, crushed
2 tablespoons mirin (Japanese rice wine) or dry sherry
2 tablespoons cornstarch
½ teaspoon salt
Several vigorous grinds of black pepper
2 packages (16 ounces total) firm- or hard-style reduced-fat conventional water-packed tofu, cut into fat strips about ½ inch by 1½ inches
Cooking spray

1 Up to 24 hours, but no less than 1 hour before you plan to cook the tofu, combine the garlic, mirin, cornstarch, salt, and pepper in a bowl, stirring well. Add the tofu and toss to coat. Let stand for at least 40 minutes at room temperature or refrigerate, covered, overnight.

2 Preheat the oven to 500°F.

3 Up to 2 hours before serving, spray a baking sheet with cooking spray. Lay the marinated tofu strips out on the baking sheet in a single layer. Bake the tofu until browned and lightly crisped on the bottom, 10 to 15 minutes, then flip them over and bake until golden brown, another 5 to 10 minutes. Remove the tofu from the baking sheet and use in Kung Pao Tofu, in any vegetable stir-fry, as a sandwich filling, or serve with brown rice and almost any savory sauce.

NOTES

Kung Pao Tofu requires advance prep. It helps if you're familiar with basic Chinese cooking, but if you're not, set up a mise en place tray (see page 107), and you will be rewarded by a great dish.

Warn diners to pick around chiles; they're in for flavor, not chewing (though my friend Sally Williams and I have been known to nibble them).

Kung Pao Tofu with Honey-Roasted Peanuts and Asparagus

Kung Pao is a Chinese restaurant classic that's as much-loved as it is high in fat: chunks of chicken or beef sautéed in a chile-spiced oil, with ginger, garlic, loads of peanuts. If, like me, you love the flavors but have said ix-nay to meat and/or all that oil, this dish will thrill you. Oven-crisped tofu replaces meat, less oil and fewer peanuts are used, and unexpected fresh asparagus lightens the dish. Traditionally the peanuts are fried; I stir in honey-roasted peanuts at the end. This is about the only time I use honey-roasted peanuts, which despite their name do not have honey in them and are not a natural food item—but they work here perfectly. The traditional flavors are the faint heat, sweetness, and ginger.

Ned, tasting this, once said, "Wow! This really puts the pow in Kung Pao!"

SERVES 4 TO 5, WITH RICE

- 1 recipe Traditional Asian-Style "Crisping" Marinade and Method for Oven-Baked Tofu (previous page)
- ⅔ cup Golden Stock (page 140)
- 3 tablespoons tamari or shoyu soy sauce
- 2 tablespoons mirin (Japanese rice wine) or dry sherry
- 1 tablespoon plus 1 teaspoon sugar, Rapidura, or honey
- 1 tablespoon plus 2 teaspoons cornstarch
- 1 tablespoon mild vegetable oil, preferably peanut
- 4 to 6 dried red chiles
- 2 tablespoons plus 1 teaspoon peeled, finely chopped ginger
- 2 teaspoons finely minced garlic (about 4 to 6 cloves)
- ½ pound fresh asparagus, tough part of stems snapped off, stems and tips cut on the diagonal into 1-inch lengths
- ½ cup water, preferably spring or filtered, or additional stock
- 1 bunch scallions, roots removed, white and 2 inches of green, white part split lengthwise, cut into ¾-inch lengths
- ⅓ cup honey-roasted peanuts
- Cooking spray

1 As the tofu bakes (see recipe, previous page), combine the stock, tamari, mirin, sugar, and cornstarch, smushing the cornstarch into the liquid with your fingertips to make a smooth sauce.

2 Prepare a mise en place tray, placing the sauce on it, along with all of the remaining ingredients and the baked tofu, each in its little bowl. Set the tray near the stove. Spray a wok or skillet, with a tight-fitting lid, with cooking spray and set it on the stove.

3 When ready to finish the dish, place the oil in the prepared wok or skillet over high heat. Let it get very, very hot—it will be fragrant and will get a sort of glazed, swirly look on top. Add the chiles and stir-fry for 1 minute. The chiles should darken. Working quickly, scoop the chiles out of the pan with a slotted spoon, leaving as much oil as possible. Reserve the chiles, in their bowl on the "mise" tray.

4 Add the ginger and garlic and stir-fry until they color slightly, 10 to 20 seconds. They may try to stick, but ignore that, just keep stirring. Add the asparagus and stir-fry for 10 seconds, then add the water and immediately pop a cover on the dish. Let steam over very high heat until the asparagus is crisp-tender and the water has almost evaporated, 3 to 5 minutes. Remove the lid, and let any remaining water boil off quickly. The minute the last bit of water has evaporated, toss in the scallions and stir-fry for 20 seconds. Give the sauce mixture a vigorous stir to blend the cornstarch and liquid, and pour it into the hot wok. Cook, stirring constantly, until the sauce becomes a clear, very thick glaze, about 30 seconds. Continue stirring for a few seconds more, adding the oven-crisped tofu and honey-roasted peanuts. Serve hot, ASAP, preferably over brown rice.

Southeast Asian Tofu Satay

The mixed colors threading a satay or shish-kebab skewer look irresistibly festive. So *don't* resist! The spirited curry-ginger-tamari marinade on page 659 zaps the tofu; pregrilling the marinade-touched eggplant, pepper, and pineapple extends the flavor range further still. For a variation, you may serve gado-gado sauce with it; but rest assured, it's quite good (and considerably lower in fat) as is.

SERVES 4 TO 6

1 recipe Thai-Malaysian Curry-Ginger Marinade for Tofu (page 659)
1 medium eggplant, stem end removed, skin left on, sliced crosswise about ⅛ inch thick, presoaked (see page 742) if bitter
1 green bell pepper, seeded and cored, cut into 2-inch squares
1 fresh pineapple, peeled, cored, and cut into 2-inch squares
¼ pound fresh shiitake mushrooms, stems removed
1 pint cherry tomatoes
Ribbons of basil and mint (optional)
Diced red bell peppers, (optional)

1 The night before you plan to serve the dish, place bamboo skewers in a tall jar of water to soak. Make the marinade and soak the tofu in it overnight.

2 Several hours before serving, lift the tofu from the marinade and set it aside. Reserve the marinade.

3 Place the sliced eggplant in the marinade for 15 minutes.

4 Preheat the grill.

5 Lift the eggplant slices from the marinade. Reserve the marinade. Place the eggplant on the grill. Immediately place the green peppers into the marinade. Grill the eggplant slices, turning once with tongs, just long enough to mark them with grill marks. Lift the green peppers from the marinade and grill them just until marked. Immediately place the pineapple into the marinade. As soon as the peppers come off the grill, grill the pineapple just until marked. Drop the shiitakes into what's left of the marinade, but do not grill them.

6 Up to 3 hours before serving, remove the wooden skewers from their soaking liquid. Alternately thread the marinated tofu, the grilled eggplant (fold each piece into thirds, fan-style), green pepper, pineapple, shiitakes, and cherry tomatoes onto each skewer.

7 Preheat the oven to 450°F.

8 Place the skewers on a large, deep, well-greased baking sheet with plenty of air space between them. Bake for 10 minutes. Remove from the oven and brush with any remaining marinade. Return to the oven until heated through, another 5 to 10 minutes. Serve hot, with a side of rice or any other grain, plain or pilaf'd, and, if desired, a ring of the mint and basil ribbons and diced red peppers edging the plate.

Skewered Tandoori Tofu with Eggplant

The Indian version of a satay. In India, this shish-kebab skewer is prepared with cubes of paneer, a firm, fresh cheese, rather than tofu, but it is easy, delicious, colorful, and healthful done this way. Serve this on a bed of brown or white basmati rice with a side of diced tomatoes, red onion, cucumbers, and plain yogurt, lightly salted. **SERVES 4 TO 6**

- **2 recipes Tandoori Tofu Marinade (page 659)**
- **12 to 16 ounces reduced-fat, firm, traditional-style tofu, drained**
- **1 medium eggplant, stem end removed, skin left on, sliced crosswise into ⅛-inch-thick slices, presoaked (see page 742) if bitter**
- **1 green bell pepper, seeded and cored, cut into 2-inch squares**
- **1 red or yellow bell pepper, seeded and cored, cut into 2-inch squares**
- **1 medium red onion, cut vertically into eighths**
- **¼ pound medium button mushrooms**
- **1 pint cherry tomatoes**
- **Ribbons of cilantro (optional)**
- **Diced red bell peppers (optional)**

1 The night before you plan to serve the dish, place bamboo skewers in a tall jar of water to soak. Make the double batch of the marinade and soak the tofu in it overnight.

2 Several hours before serving, lift the tofu from the marinade and set it aside. Reserve the marinade. Place the sliced eggplant in the marinade for about 15 minutes.

3 Preheat the grill.

4 Lift the eggplant slices from the marinade, reserving the marinade. There will not be much; let some of what's there adhere to the slices. Immediately place the peppers into the marinade. Grill the eggplant slices, turning once with tongs, just long enough to mark them with the grill. Lift the peppers from the marinade and grill them until just marked. Place the onion and mushrooms into what's left of the marinade, tossing to coat.

5 Up to 3 hours before serving, remove the wooden skewers from their soaking liquid. Alternately thread the marinated tofu, the grilled eggplant (fold each piece into thirds, fan-style), green pepper, red pepper, mushrooms, onions, and cherry tomatoes onto each skewer.

6 Preheat the oven to 450°F.

VARIATION

For another great Eastern way with tofu and tempeh, be sure to check out "A Spring Roll for All Seasons" (page 315).

SOYFUL SOULFUL SUNDAY BRUNCH

Fresh-squeezed orange juice

*

Blackberries, blueberries, raspberries, and sliced strawberries tossed with mango or papaya puree

*

Scrambled Tofu

*

Sautéed soysage

*

Morning Glorious Muffins (PAGE 634)

*

Hot coffee or ceylon tea (with soy milk for those who want it light)

7 Place the skewers on a large, deep, well-greased baking sheet with plenty of air space between them. Bake for 10 minutes. Remove from the oven and brush with any remaining marinade. Return to the oven until heated through, 5 to 10 minutes. Serve hot, with a side of rice or any other grain, plain or pilaf'd, and a ring of the cilantro ribbons and diced red peppers edging the plate, if you like.

Scrambled Tofu

Almost everybody who's eaten meatlessly has a scrambled tofu recipe; this is mine, and very good it is. It is both like and not like scrambled eggs; perhaps "somewhat reminiscent" would be accurate. Lots of sautéed vegetables, seasonings, and turmeric, for the yellow color, are its secrets. Serve with whole-grain toast and fresh fruit. Revise the vegetables, as taste, time, and what's on hand permit. Shiitakes, jalapeños, fresh spinach, ripe tomatoes cut into eighths—all these have occasionally found their way into my scrambled tofu. Sometimes I've served this rolled in toasted tortillas, sometimes with biscuits. Though oil is optional, the dish is much tastier when a bit is used.

A quickie way to do scrambled tofu, for all you I-don't-have-time-to-cook types, is to use NewMenu TofuMate Breakfast Scramble Seasoning Mix. **SERVES 4**

1 teaspoon to 1 tablespoon olive or vegetable oil (optional)
Cooking spray
1 onion, sliced
½ green or red bell pepper, cut into slivers (optional)
1 small handful button mushrooms, sliced (optional)
1 teaspoon turmeric
1 teaspoon paprika
2 to 3 cloves garlic, pressed (optional but very good)
1 package (12 to 16 ounces) traditional, water-packed tofu, preferably reduced fat, regular, firm, or extra-firm, crumbled into scrambled egg–sized clumps, well drained
Seasonings to taste: Tamari or shoyu soy sauce, salt and freshly ground black pepper, Pickapeppa, Tabasco, fresh minced herbs of any kind

1 Heat the oil, if using, in a nonstick skillet, or one that has been sprayed with cooking spray, over medium heat. Add the onion and sauté for 4 minutes. Add the pepper and, if using, the mushroom slices and sauté for another 3 minutes. Lower the heat slightly. Sprinkle with the turmeric and paprika, then add the garlic. Sauté for an additional minute.

2 Add the tofu, tossing to coat with the spices and to distribute the vegetables. Keep turning in the skillet until everything is nice and hot. Season as it suits you. Serve at once.

Basic Skillet-Sautéed Tofu

Tofu slices, splashed with seasoning, are breaded in nutritional yeast and sautéed. Hard not to nibble those little cubes as you're sautéing. Great as part of a component plate or served in lieu of sausage as a protein-packed side dish. Kids—at least those who've been raised with tofu—love it. (It's sort of the meatless equivalent of chicken fingers.) To fancy it up, serve with a cooked grain or a baked sweet potato, a pile of garlicky sautéed broc or green beans, and a mushroom, tomato, or roasted vegetable sauce. Like all such recipes it's a bit loosey-goosey. Season the breading mix (breadcrumbs or cornflake crumbs or cracker crumbs) as you like.

SERVES 4

1 package (12 to 16 ounces) traditional water packed tofu, preferably reduced fat, regular, firm, or extra-firm, sliced into pieces roughly 2½-by-1¼-by-½-inch, well drained
1 recipe Western/Hippie-Style Marinade for Tofu (page 660)
Cooking spray
About 1 cup nutritional yeast (see page 239)
¼ cup whole wheat or unbleached white all-purpose flour (optional)
Seasonings to taste: salt, freshly ground black pepper, paprika, maybe a little dried basil or sage
1 tablespoon to ½ cup any mild vegetable oil (optional)

1 Place the tofu in a flat dish and spoon the marinade over it. Toss well to coat. Let stand for a few minutes.

VARIATION

Though this makes it unvegan and raises the fat content, a little sharp Cheddar grated over this is very tasty indeed.

2 Generously spray a nonstick skillet with cooking spray. Place the skillet over medium heat until very hot.

3 As the skillet heats, combine, in a flattish dish, the nutritional yeast and flour and seasonings, if using, to make a tasty breading.

4 One at a time, dip the tofu slices into the yeast mixture, really pressing it on both sides. If you want the tofu to be really crisp and you don't care about fat content, go ahead and add the vegetable oil to the hot skillet, and let it heat just until it thins. Your heat should be a tad higher for frying in oil: medium-high, as opposed to a solid medium for pan-sautéing without added oil.

5 Place a few slices of the breaded tofu into the hot pan. If using oil, they will sizzle as you put them in and they must be turned the minute they start to look brown and crisp. Transfer oil-fried tofu slices to paper towels to drain. If using cooking spray only, place the tofu in the prepared hot skillet and cook for a few minutes. They should be golden with slightly darker speckles when you turn them. You may need to respray the pan a few times. Slow, steady cooking at medium heat will result in perfectly browned tofu.

6 Serve hot from the skillet with a splash of Tabasco, if desired.

"Terrible Delicious" Talk-of-the-Town Barbecued Tofu

Early one morning, in the wilds of nearly unpopulated Texas, Ned and I drove by a graying, sheet metal–roofed barbecue shack with a hand-lettered sign that said, "Terrible Delicious." Not a sign of habitation within miles, there it was, fragrant smoke curling up like a pig's tail. We didn't have to stop to know that its parking lot would be full later. Though it would offer nothing for vegetarians except maybe coleslaw, we sighed, with pleasure, at the sign and soul of the 'cue artist it revealed.

This less funky, untraditional version, is bliss for *non*-rib-eaters. It's a feed-large-groups-of-people-deliciously casual dish, well received by even the most skeptical.

The fat is optional. It helps the sauce brown and gives a requisite hint of greasy BBQ richness. Use just a tad of a solid fat, not an oil, for the right texture. Go withs? Texas toast (big fat slices of toasted bread; need I say that white is a classic?), a large bowl of potato salad, a large bowl of three-bean salad, baked beans, or slaw. Dessert? Watermelon. Much later on, when the fireflies are out and the kids have quit playing in the sprinklers, and someone has Sam Cooke on the CD player, maybe cookies or chocolate cake and good decaf. **SERVES 6 TO 8**

NOTE

This became the talk of Eureka Springs when I was asked to bring a vegetarian alternative to a fundraising dinner a few years back. The cause: a summer opera camp, Inspiration Point Fine Arts Colony. The featured entree: barbecued chicken. The alternative entree: this barbecued tofu. When the tofu upstaged the chicken—honestly, I think it would have been neck-and-neck except that the tofu's sauce was homemade and the chicken's out of a bottle—I got a lot of incredulousness ("This can't be tofu!") and tales of pitiful misadventures of one-time ventures into tofu-land. The next time I got my hair cut, the first words out of Eloise's mouth were, "Well! Your barbecued tofu certainly was the talk of the town out at Grassy Knoll yesterday!" After its appearance at the Inspiration Point Benefit, I gave the recipe out a lot. Years later, people still remember my barbecued tofu and ask for this recipe.

2 packages (12 to 16 ounces total) firm reduced-fat conventional tofu, sliced into ½-inch-thick pieces, either straight from the package or frozen then thawed, pressed for 15 minutes

1 recipe Smoky Onion-Garlic Marinade for Tofu (page 658)

SAUCE

2 cans (12 ounce total) tomato paste

3 to 4 fresh hot chiles, serrano or jalapeño, seeds and membranes removed for mildness or left in for extra heat

Grated rind and juice of 2 oranges

⅓ to ⅔ cup honey or brown sugar, or half of each

¼ cup cider vinegar

¼ cup Pickapeppa sauce

3 tablespoons tamari or shoyu soy sauce

1 teaspoon freshly ground black pepper

Salt to taste

2 drops liquid smoke (optional, omit if you will be preparing it in a smoker)

FOR BAKING

Cooking spray

1 tablespoon to ⅓ cup butter, margarine, or solid vegetable shortening (optional)

1 Place the tofu in a single layer in a nonreactive dish. Pour the Smoky Onion-Garlic Marinade for Tofu over the top. Let stand for at least 40 minutes at room temperature, or, better yet, overnight or for several days, covered and refrigerated.

2 While the tofu is marinating, make the barbecue sauce: Combine all of the ingredients in a food processor, blending to a thick, smooth sauce. Taste, adding more sugar, salt, vinegar, or heat as you wish. Place in a nonreactive container, cover, and refrigerate until ready to use.

3 If you are planning to smoke the barbecued tofu, soak wood chips when ready to barbecue it.

4 Preheat the grill to high or the oven to 500°F.

5 While the oven preheats, spray a large baking dish or 2 medium baking dishes large enough to hold the tofu in a single layer (slightly overlapped is okay, but not stacked) with cooking spray. Carefully lift the tofu from the marinade, letting some marinade cling to the pieces, and place it in the prepared baking dish. Reserve any leftover marinade.

Menu

DOWN HOME BRAND NEW MENU

Ronni's New Wave "Killed Lettuce Salad"
(PAGE 74)

*

Oven-Baked "Chicken-Fried" Tofu and Gravy

*

Steamed short-grain brown rice
(SEE PAGE 468)

*

Greek-Style Green Beans
(PAGE 689)

*

Vegan French-Style Gratin of Butternut Squash
(PAGE 289)

*

Cora Pinkley Call's Uncooked Ozark Relish
(PAGE 929)

*

Baked Sugarplum Apples with Lightened-up Pastry Cream and Almonds
(PAGE 970)

6 If using, add soaked wood chips to the grill.

7 Liberally brush the tofu with the barbecue sauce. If the sauce seems too thick, drizzle with a little marinade as well. Dot the tofu with the butter, if using. Cover the baking dish tightly with foil, being careful not to let the barbecue sauce come in contact with foil. (If there's any danger of that, add a layer of waxed paper between the tofu and foil.)

8 Reduce the oven temperature to 375°F or the grill to medium.

9 Bake or grill the tofu, tightly covered, until heated through, about 40 minutes. Uncover and bake or grill until the barbecue sauce has reduced and gotten dark and slightly crusty on top, 35 to 45 minutes. If you want extra crustiness—the favorite element, to many people—run the 'cue under the broiler, but watch closely; the sugar makes it burn quickly. Serve, hot or warm, with your favorite barbecue fixings.

COOK ONCE FOR 2 MEALS This same barbecue sauce is great for big portobello mushroom caps.

Oven-Baked "Chicken-Fried" Tofu and Gravy

No, it's not chicken. It's not even fried. And it's not for those new to meatless eating, who may consider it weird. But to vegetarians of long duration who still have an occasional hankering for the remembered flavors, this is amazingly satisfying. You've got the crunch, the tender inside, the hot, flavorful gravy . . . what you *don't* have is all that fat.

I dedicate this recipe, fondly, to my friend Shawn Bible, who once told me that she fried chicken *solely* to be able to eat chicken gravy over rice. I'm the first to admit that this recipe's natural and indeed near-mandatory complement, the Chicken-Style Gravy on page 949, *sounds* improbable, but brothers and sisters, one taste and you'll be a true believer. **SERVES 4 HARDCORE VEGETARIANS**

TOFU AND MARINADE

3 cloves garlic, pressed
2 tablespoons tamari or shoyu soy sauce
1 tablespoon nutritional yeast (see page 239)
1 teaspoon balsamic vinegar
½ teaspoon turmeric
1 to 2 dashes Tabasco or similar hot sauce
1 package (8 ounces) firm traditional water-packed tofu, preferably reduced fat, sliced the short way into rectangles ½ inch thick, well drained

BREADING

1 cup crisp, fine breadcrumbs
½ cup crushed Nutri-Grain or other no-sugar-added corn- or wheat flakes
¼ cup unbleached all-purpose white flour
¼ cup nutritional yeast (see page 239)
1 teaspoon paprika
½ teaspoon dried sage leaves, crumbled between your fingers
½ teaspoon dried thyme leaves
½ teaspoon dried basil leaves
Salt and plenty of freshly ground black pepper to taste
1½ teaspoons olive oil
Cooking spray or olive oil spray
1 egg, beaten (optional)
Chicken-Style Gravy (page 949)

1 Prepare the tofu: Combine the garlic, tamari, nutritional yeast, vinegar, turmeric, and Tabasco into a thin paste. Rub the marinade into the tofu. Cover and marinate, refrigerated, for at least 6 hours.

2 Make the breading: Combine the breadcrumbs, cornflakes, flour, nutritional yeast, paprika, sage, thyme, basil, and salt and pepper. Drizzle in the olive oil and toss together. Place the mixture in a large plastic bag.

3 Preheat the oven to 400°F.

4 Spray a baking sheet with cooking spray (or use a nonstick sheet). Set aside.

5 Beat the egg together with 2 tablespoons water and a little additional salt and pepper. Set aside.

6 One by one, drop the marinated tofu into the breading mixture. Shake the bag like crazy until the tofu is nicely coated with the crumbs. Dip the coated tofu into the egg; then again shake in the crumb mixture. (This is messy; you may have to assist with your fingertips, pressing the crumbs into any bald spots so the entire piece is well coated with two layers of crumb and one of egg.) Place the coated tofu on the prepared baking sheet. Repeat, until all of the tofu is coated. (Reserve leftover crumbs for another time, storing in a zippered plastic bag in the freezer.)

7 Very lightly spray the coated tofu with cooking or olive oil spray. Bake 10 to 12 minutes, turn over very gently (use tongs or a thin-bladed pancake turner), and bake for another 10 to 12 minutes. The tofu should be crisping up nicely; if it's not, run it under the broiler for a few moments. Serve the hot tofu at once, with rice or mashed potatoes and Chicken-Style Gravy.

VARIATIONS

This basic sauce can be turned into a Deep Brown Velvet Sauce by using a dark red or brown miso, such as hatcho or mugi. Try substituting cognac for the mirin, and consider sautéed mushrooms and sautéed red and green bell pepper strips instead of broccoli and potatoes. This is excellent over a pilaf of brown and wild rice, or in some kind of pastry shell. A Golden Sesame Sauce can easily be made by substituting sesame tahini for the peanut butter; in this case, add sautéed red bell pepper strips and carrot circles to the vegetable mix. And any of these variations take on a quite different and rather wonderful character with the addition of 2 to 3 teaspoons tomato paste and a tiny drizzle of honey.

Broccoli, Potatoes, and Tofu in Golden Peanut-Miso Velvet

When I felt peaky as a child, my mother would make things better with Chicken à la King—nursery comfort food of the '50s, dressed up elegantly: chunks of chicken in creamy white sauce, along with green peas and bright red canned pimentos, over crisp toast. Chunks of cooked potato and broccoli, and cubes of tofu cooked in a creamy, soothing golden sauce does the trick. Substitute any other cooked vegetables you like for the broccoli and potato. Truly useful and delicious stuff, you can dress it up or down, making it elegant or homey, and freeze it for the next rainy—or peaky—day. **SERVES 4, WITH GRAIN OR TOAST**

- 2 large cooked potatoes, peeled and diced
- 1 head broccoli, peeled stem and florets diced, steamed until barely crisp-tender
- 1 fresh tomato, diced
- 4 ounces savory baked tofu, diced
- Cooking spray
- 1 large onion, diced
- 2 cups vegetable stock (see page 139)
- 2 to 3 tablespoons sweet white miso
- 2 tablespoons smooth natural nonhydrogenated peanut butter
- 3 tablespoons nutritional yeast (see page 239)
- 3 tablespoons arrowroot
- 1 tablespoon mirin (Japanese rice wine) or sherry
- Salt (optional)
- Plenty of freshly ground black pepper
- Hot cooked rice or other grain, or toast

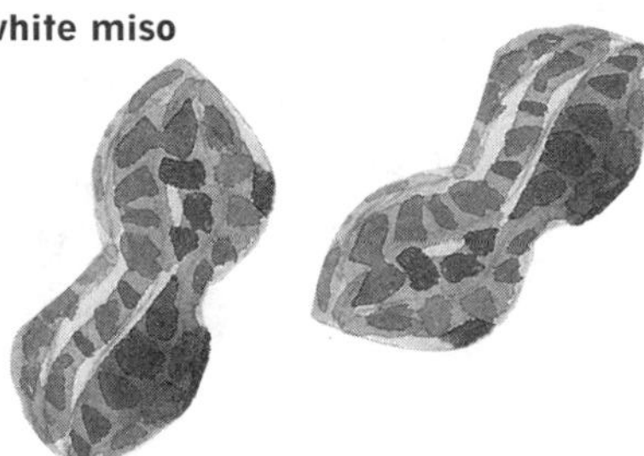

1 Combine the potatoes, broccoli, tomato, and tofu in a heatproof bowl and set aside. (If you're using leftover broccoli and potatoes, you might want to warm them with a quick steaming or stir-fry.)

2 Place a nonstick skillet, or one that has been sprayed with cooking spray, over medium heat. Add the onion and sauté until softened and translucent, about 5 minutes.

3 Pour 1¾ cups of the stock over the onion, reserving the remaining ¼ cup in a small bowl. Bring to a boil, then lower the heat to a simmer. Whisk in the miso and peanut butter and cook for a minute or two.

4 Meanwhile, whisk the nutritional yeast and arrowroot into the reserved stock until lump-free. Add the mirin and whisk into the simmering onion–peanut butter sauce. Cook, stirring, until the sauce is thick and smooth, 1 to 2 minutes. Taste for seasonings. You won't need much, if any, salt since the miso's so salty, but you will need a whole lot of pepper.

5 Pour the hot sauce over the vegetables and tofu. Serve immediately over hot cooked grain or toast.

COOK ONCE FOR 2 MEALS

Make a double recipe of the sauce and save it, refrigerated, for another day. Toss with cooked elbow macaroni, sautéed mushrooms, and fresh green peas; turn the combo out into a deep baking dish sprayed with cooking spray. Top with a mixture of herbed and garlicked whole-wheat breadcrumbs to which you've added a tiny bit of butter or olive oil. Bake at 350°F until the casserole is bubbly and the crumbs are starting to brown, about 40 minutes.

Smothered Tofu Country Captain

Hearty, spicy, colorful, totally satisfying chunks of savory baked tofu in a thick tomato and corn sauce: absolutely nonwimpy vegetarian food. A perfect winter dish, it's one of the happiest choices a host could make for entertaining—robust and pleasing to nonvegetarians, it can be made in advance and baked at the last.

SERVES 4 TO 6, OVER RICE, BARLEY, OR OTHER GRAIN

NOTE:

This is based on a classic Southern chicken dish called Country Captain, said to have originated in Savannah, Georgia, a busy seaport in colonial days. Supposedly, a sea captain sailing the spice routes gave a favorite recipe to a hospitable Savannah friend in thanks for his hospitality. But, oddly enough, Columbus Ohio, also claims the dish. In American Food, Evan Jones credits an unnamed North Carolina historian with a quote from General George S. Patton, who, on a whistle-stop through Columbus, sent word ahead, "If you can't give me a party and have Country Captain, put some in a tin bucket and bring it to the train."

- Cooking spray
- 1 to 2 tablespoons corn, canola, peanut, or other mild vegetable oil
- 1 onion, finely chopped
- 2 green bell peppers, cored and seeded, finely chopped
- ⅔ cup finely chopped Italian parsley
- 3 cups (or one 28-ounce can) diced tomatoes in puree
- ½ cup raisins (¼ cup each yellow and dark raisins, if you have them; otherwise, either one will do)
- 2½ teaspoons curry powder (see page 901)
- 1 teaspoon sweet paprika
- 3 to 4 gratings of nutmeg
- Salt and freshly ground black pepper to taste
- 2 cloves garlic, pressed
- 1 teaspoon honey
- ½ teaspoon Tabasco or similar hot sauce
- Kernels from 2 ears corn (about 1 heaping cup)
- 2 cups any good vegetable stock
- 1 tablespoon tomato paste
- 2 teaspoons cornstarch dissolved in 1 tablespoon water
- 16 ounces savory baked tofu
- Cooked rice, quinoa, millet, or other grain
- 2 tablespoons raw almonds, coarsely chopped and toasted (optional)

1. Preheat the oven to 400°F.

2. Heat a large nonstick Dutch oven, or one that has been sprayed with cooking spray, over medium heat. When hot, add the oil, then the onion. Sauté the onion until it starts to soften, about 4 minutes. Add the green peppers and continue sautéing until the peppers start to become limp and lose their rawness, 5 to 7 minutes.

3. Reserve 3 tablespoons of the parsley. Add the remainder to the skillet and sauté for an additional minute. Stir in the tomatoes and their puree, raisins, curry powder, paprika, nutmeg, salt, and pepper. When blended, add the garlic, honey, and Tabasco. Lower the heat to a gentle simmer and cook, stirring occasionally, for 20 minutes. Turn the heat off and stir in the corn, stock, and cornstarch mixture.

4. Transfer the mixture to an 11-by-14-inch nonstick baking dish or one that has been sprayed with cooking spray. Separate the pieces of baked tofu—there should be about 8—and push them down into the sauce. Tightly cover the baking dish (if using foil, cover first with waxed paper so that the tomatoes do not come in direct contact with the foil), and bake, covered, until quite hot, 30 to 35 minutes. Uncover and bake for an additional 10 minutes to reduce the sauce a little and make the top slightly dark and crusty. Serve hot from the oven, on warmed plates, spooning the sauce and 1 to 2 pieces of the tofu over the cooked grain on each plate. Garnish with a sprinkle of the reserved parsley and the toasted almonds, which, although optional, add a really desirable textural crunch.

Mulligan

This is tofu in a nonexotic, '50s homestyle mode: a tasty, homey casserole of Creole-style tomato sauce, mushrooms, cheese, and noodles. In this version, ground seasoned tofu takes the place of the traditional ground pork. The recipe has been freely adapted from Poker Hash Southern Style, Also Called Mulligan Hash, from one of my favorite old cookbooks, *The Gold Cook Book*, by Louis P. De Gouy. While I've reduced the fat considerably, it still has an amount of cheese that will alarm some. De Gouy says it's Southern, but I've never run into anything remotely like it in any part of the South. But my occasional assistant, Amber Alexander, whose Arkansas roots go back several generations, says her mother used to make a dish ("So similar it's scary," says Amber) using Ro*Tel tomatoes and green chiles, ground beef, noodles, and cheese. Whatever its origins, it makes an excellent, fairly quick family supper. **SERVES 4 TO 6**

VARIATIONS

VEGAN VARIATION: ***Simply omit the cheese or use a good soy cheese instead. Vegans will also need to substitute a nonegg pasta for the noodles.***

UPTOWN MULLIGAN: ***Festive, richer, and more caloric than the basic, this version is delicious. When the tomato sauce comes off the heat, add 4 to 6 ounces diced neufchâtel reduced-fat cream cheese, stirring until the cheese melts into the sauce. A handful of coarsely diced pimento-stuffed green olives is also a nice addition. Proceed as directed in the basic recipe.***

- 6 ounces wide egg noodles
- 1½ teaspoons olive oil
- 1 can (28 ounces) diced tomatoes in juice
- 1 cup vegetable stock, preferably roasted vegetable or other brown stock (see page 139), or 1 cup water with 1 tablespoon dissolved miso
- Cooking spray
- 2 onions, diced
- 3 ribs celery, diced
- 1 green bell pepper, diced
- 1 serrano chile, halved, seeded, and diced
- 1 teaspoon Pickapeppa sauce
- 1 teaspoon butter
- ½ pound mushrooms, wiped, stems chopped, caps sliced
- 1 package (10 ounces) prepared ready-ground tofu, preferably Hot and Spicy
- Salt and freshly ground black pepper to taste
- 5 ounces grated Cheddar cheese (or about ⅔ cup)
- 1 cup crisp breadcrumbs, or cracker crumbs

1 Bring a large pot of water to a boil. Add the noodles and cook, according to the package directions, until barely tender. Drain and toss them with ½ teaspoon of the olive oil. Set aside. Don't wash the pot. Put the tomatoes in it, along with the stock. Place over low heat to begin cooking.

2 Heat the remaining 1 teaspoon oil in a large nonstick skillet, or one that has been sprayed with cooking spray, over medium heat. Add the onions and sauté

until beginning to soften, about 4 minutes. Add the celery, green pepper, and serrano and sauté for another 5 minutes. Scrape the sauté into the tomatoes. Add the Pickapeppa sauce and continue cooking, stirring often, over low heat, 10 to 15 minutes. Don't wash that sauté skillet yet.

3 Preheat the oven to 350°F.

4 Now, back at the skillet, melt the butter over medium heat. Add the mushrooms and sauté until softened, 6 to 7 minutes. Add the cooked mushrooms, along with any juices in the pan, to the tomato sauce. Add the ground tofu, too. (Okay, now you can wash the skillet.) Last, toss in the noodles, and season liberally with salt and lots of pepper.

5 Combine the cheese and breadcrumbs in a small bowl and set aside.

6 Spray a 10-by-13-inch casserole with cooking spray. Turn the noodle mixture out into it, cover, and bake until very hot, 30 to 35 minutes. Remove the dish from the oven and raise the oven temperature to 425°F. Uncover and sprinkle the crumb-cheese mixture over the top. Return to the oven, uncovered, and bake until the crumbs brown and cheese is melting, 10 to 15 minutes.

COOK ONCE FOR 2 MEALS For a simple, basic tomato sauce, double the sauce, omitting the tofu. Use it on pasta or grains, over crêpes, in omelets, or mix it with an equal amount of cooked beans and serve with cornbread. Dilute with an equal amount of stock or water, add mixed vegetables, and you've got soup.

Sweet-Sour Skillet Soysage Supper

Family fare, this is a hearty and quickly put-together stew, made out of soysage. This recipe came about when Ned and I were an hour past dinnertime, ravenous. If you have some cooked grain on hand, dinner can be on the table in a trice. Even if you don't, cracked wheat cooks in 15 minutes, and its pleasant nuttiness works nicely here. **SERVES 4**

Cooking spray
6 to 8 ounces soysage, sliced into small rectangles about 1 inch long by ½ inch wide, and about ½ inch thick
1 teaspoon to 1 tablespoon mild vegetable oil, such as corn, canola, or peanut (optional)
1 onion, sliced vertically into thin crescents
2 carrots, sliced into angled rounds
¼ head savoy cabbage, sliced
1 can (14½ ounces) tomato fillets in juice
1 large potato, well scrubbed, very thinly sliced
2 teaspoons to 1 tablespoon umeboshi plum vinegar (see page 118) or lemon juice, or more to taste
1 tablespoon blackstrap molasses
1 tablespoon honey
1 tablespoon tamari or shoyu soy sauce
A couple of dashes of Tabasco or similar hot sauce (optional)
Salt and freshly ground black pepper
Cooked grain, such as cracked wheat
Tofu Sour Cream (page 909) or Yogurt Sour Cream (page 910) (optional)
Sprigs of fresh dill or minced Italian parsley (optional)

1 Gently brown the soysage in a nonstick skillet, or one that has been sprayed with cooking spray, with or without the optional oil, over medium heat, turning once. Remove the soysage from the skillet and set aside.

2 In the same skillet, sauté the onion in any remaining oil, until it begins to soften, about 4 minutes. Add the carrots and sauté for another 2 minutes. Add the sliced cabbage and sauté for 3 minutes. Add the tomatoes, potato, umeboshi plum vinegar, molasses, honey, tamari, and, if using, the Tabasco. Raise the heat and bring to a near boil. Immediately lower the heat to a simmer. Cover and barely simmer until the potato is done, 15 to 20 minutes. Season to taste with salt and pepper. You may also wish to adjust the sweet-sour balance by adding a little more vinegar or honey.

3 Just before serving, stir in the browned soysage. Serve, hot, over a warm cooked grain. If you wish, top each serving with a dollop of Tofu or Yogurt Sour Cream (or pass these at the table); a little sprig or sprinkling of herbs adds a nice fresh touch.

Soysage and Potatoes in Con Queso

Dairy products and soyfoods mix together in a captivating rich, creamy-spicy sauce reminiscent of that old-time Tex-Mex favorite, con queso. While the words literally mean "with cheese," con queso in border cuisine is essentially a

VARIATION

Stir some cooked green beans or sautéed onions and green peppers into the con queso-soysage-potato mix.

1950's–60's-era cheese sauce with enough Ro*Tel or similar canned tomato and green chile preparation stirred in to give it some heat. Just see how wonderful this old favorite is slightly lightened up, and served with soysage and potatoes. The consistency is like a thick, very chunky chowder; a creamy, main-dish stew with some kick.

Try this over Spanish Millet (page 548) or Brazilian Rice (page 473), with a side of black beans (use the instant dehydrated type, following package directions; they'll be ready by the time the main dish is). To start, a salad of mixed greens, yellow cherry tomatoes, avocado, and scallions with either of the Cilantro Vinaigrettes on page 94. Dessert? Fresh mango, with commercially made coconut sorbet. **SERVES 4 TO 6**

CON QUESO
2 bay leaves
½ onion, skin on
4 whole cloves
2 (3-inch) ribs celery, with leaves
Freshly grated nutmeg to taste
2½ cups 1% dairy milk or unflavored soy milk
4 teaspoons butter, Better (page 905), or vegetable oil or vegetable margarine
4 teaspoons unbleached all-purpose flour
2 tablespoons cornstarch
Pinch of cayenne (optional)
Salt and freshly ground black pepper to taste
1 cup grated sharp Cheddar

1 (14.5-ounce) can Ro*Tel or similar diced green tomatoes with chile
Cooking Spray
1 (14-ounce) package unformed soysage, like Gimme Lean Sausage-style by LightLife
4 fist-sized russet or Yukon Gold potatoes, scrubbed but not peeled, cut in 1 inch cubes and simmered until barely done
2 to 3 tablespoons finely minced cilantro (optional)

1 Make the con queso by following the directions for Béchamel Sauce (page 945), adding the cayenne, if using, when you add the salt and pepper, and stirring in the cheese at the end. You will have an extra-thick cheese sauce. Whisk the diced green tomatoes with chiles into it, and set aside, keeping it warm.

2 Spray a large nonstick skillet with cooking spray, and place it over medium heat. Meanwhile, slice the soysage into rounds about ½ inch thick and 2 inches in diameter. When the pan is hot, sauté the soysage rounds until golden brown, about 2 to 3 minutes per side. Remove from skillet.

3 Quarter each soysage patty, to make stew-sized pieces. Add the soysage and the cooked potatoes to the con queso sauce. Serve at once, hot, sprinkled with cilantro, if using.

Vegetable World

I believe in gardens. I miss the garden I once had, the gardening I once did. I miss the mornings when I'd wander, sometimes still in my bathrobe, mug of tea in hand, noting the exact progress of this stargazer lily bud, that blue lake pole bean vine moving up its support teepee.

Sometimes I'd find—to my horror, because I'd determined to discover all the golden crooknecks at 6 inches and no longer—a baseball bat–sized yellow squash hiding alligator-like beneath its bristly leaves. I'd pull a clump of Johnson grass that had broken through the mulch, snip a dead zinnia head, bruise a geranium leaf or rosemary sprig or tomato foliage and inhale deeply. The gracious principles behind these pleasures—that we should put back what we take out, that nourishing in return for being nourished is right and fitting—made time in my garden a small but powerful bulwark against much that is rude and wrong in our world.

Thomas Jefferson said, late in life, "I am an old man, but a young gardener." He knew that when we cultivate a garden, we cultivate ourselves and that little is more necessary or interesting than life—at least partly—with a garden. Whether we keep one ourselves or buy the products of others' gardens, we yearn for what Alvin Toffler called, in *Future Shock,* "enclaves"—places that reconnect us in our too-fast lives, to civility, stability, and a slowed-down cyclical past. Gardens, small, crafted places where plants for food and pleasure are coaxed from earth, are such enclaves.

Farmer's markets are also enclaves, nourishing body and senses, resting heart and soul. Indirectly, nongardeners too can receive the minimum requirement of wonder and pleasure. A plump sugar-snap pea, its sides rotund and bright; the first garden tomato, stem-end cracked and brown, smooth and heavy in the hand. A handful of dark green jalapeños, skins as sleek and elegant as a new Italian sports car. A double handful of succulent fresh shiitakes, dark outer surfaces patterned with crackled stars. A basket of tiny fuzzed green beans; marble-sized potatoes. A garden or a farmer's market is the boundary between the wild and the tame, the natural world and the built, the present and eternity.

Why Vegetable Families Matter to Human Cooks

"Freshness" is based on understanding how recently a vegetable left its home, and to what it might have been subjected between harvest and market. This takes at least a rudimentary understanding of how particular vegetables grow, and how they appear at peak ripeness.

Thus, the best cooks, even if they've never picked up a trowel, know how important a "garden variety" is in the kitchen. Almost all vegetables have relations, some botanical, some culinary, to other vegetables with whom they share certain characteristics: often nutritionally, sometimes in how they taste or smell, sometimes in texture. Of course, like us and our relatives, they also have individual quirks of personality. Still, if you know a particular vegetable's family background and what culinary properties that background endows, you will in most cases understand much about the other family members. You can easily make substitutions, play with recipes, and so on. So, while this chapter is arranged alphabetically, vegetable by vegetable, you'll also find a few vegetables within the alphabet organized by botanical family (such as the Cabbage Family, which includes cabbage, broccoli, broccoli rabe, cauliflower, Brussels sprouts, kohlrabi, and turnips) or culinary category (such as the Greens Gang, which includes all the lusty cooking greens, beets and kale and collards and so on, regardless of botanical category). But in cases where vegetables in one family have completely idiosyncratic cooking methods (eggplant, tomatoes, potatoes, and peppers are all part of the same family, but each is prepared very differently), they are listed separately, in alphabetical order.

So, whether you go to your local farmer's market or your own back yard, whether the patch of ground from which your dinner came was worked by your own hands or another's, you, too, can joyfully feed yourself and those you love, and believe in gardens.

Artichokes

My fondness for this idiosyncratic edible thistle knows no bounds. I go on buying sprees when artichokes first appear at the farmers' market each year. Here are the two recipes for which I am willing to go through the enormous hassle of cutting up raw artichokes to get whole, raw hearts. I've included directions within the recipe. California artichokes are available all year thanks to experimentation by growers with new methods and planting rotation, but the season peaks in early spring—March, April, and May; with a second, smaller peak in October. Springtime is when you'll likely find them at bargain prices, though.

Fresh Slow-Baked Artichoke Quarters with Minted Crumbs

Everything's essentially simple and straightforward once you get the artichokes dismembered. In fact, I suppose there are people who might taste the dish and think, "All *that* for *this*?" But to me, it's stratospheric: essence of artichoke, set off by a crisp, herbal crumb jacket. The mint makes a magic synergy. **SERVES 3 OR 4**

Water, preferably spring or filtered
2 lemons
6 artichokes, the larger the better
Cooking spray
3 cloves garlic, pressed
¼ cup very fine, soft breadcrumbs
¼ cup finely grated Parmesan
3 tablespoons minced fresh mint, preferably spearmint
1 tablespoon minced Italian parsley
½ teaspoon salt
Freshly ground black pepper to taste
1 tablespoon olive oil

1 Fill a medium bowl with water and juice the lemons into it. Set aside.

2 Using a sharp knife, cut off the top third of each artichoke. Break off (or snip with scissors) and discard the 1 to 3 rows of large, dark green leaves, and then smaller leaves at the base, until you begin to uncover slightly paler leaves. Cut each artichoke into quarters. With a very sharp paring knife, scoop out the hairy choke and cut away the spiky center leaves. Immediately drop the artichoke quarter into the lemon

NOTE

QUEEN OF "HEARTS"

The first annual Artichoke Festival was held in Castroville, California, in 1948, not to celebrate the harvest of the town's number one crop, but as a joint promotion. The festival was cooked up by two unlikely co-sponsors: a local jewelry store and Twentieth Century Fox, which was trying to publicize an emerging young starlet. The name of the first Artichoke Queen? Marilyn Monroe.

water, to minimize discoloring. Leave the artichoke quarters in the acidulated water until you're ready to cook them; they can be left for up to 5 hours.

3 Preheat the oven to 350°F.

4 Spray a large, shallow baking dish with cooking spray. Set aside.

5 Combine the garlic with the bread-crumbs, Parmesan, mint, parsley, salt, and pepper. Drizzle the oil over the top and toss to combine. Set aside.

6 Drain the artichokes and pat dry. Place in a single layer in the prepared baking dish. Sprinkle the crumb mixture over the heart and base of the leaves of each quarter. Bake until the artichokes are tender (though firmer than when steamed or boiled) and the crumbs are crisped, about 45 minutes. (Taste one, to make sure it's reached this point.) Serve hot or warm.

Shaved Artichoke "Carpaccio"

The one and only time I ate at the famed Berkeley restaurant Chez Panisse, a salad of raw artichoke, sliced paper thin and combined with equally thinly sliced fennel and lightly cooked fresh lima beans and a caress of vinaigrette, was on the menu. I'd never had raw artichoke, and it was a revelation. This "carpaccio" (the word originally referred to paper-thin slices of raw, air-dried beef but has come to be used for many types of very thinly sliced vegetable presentations) is even simpler: a little seasoning, of the very best quality, some lemon and some very fine olive oil are all the artichoke needs. This essence-of-spring dish may serve as a salad, an appetizer, or a side dish. You want artichokes that are very fresh (no browned spots on the leaves) and on the small-medium side; larger artichokes with be tougher and fibrous. And be sure your slicing knife is very sharp. **SERVES 4**

Water, preferably spring or filtered
3 lemons
3 to 4 very fresh medium-sized artichokes
2 tablespoons best-quality extra virgin olive oil
1 tablespoon finely minced Italian parsley
Salt, preferably fine sea salt, and freshly ground black pepper to taste

1 Fill a medium bowl with water and juice of 2 of the lemons into it. Set aside.

2 Using a sharp knife, cut off the top third of each artichoke. Break off (or snip with scissors) and discard the 1 to 3 rows of large, dark green leaves, and then smaller leaves at the base, until you begin to uncover slightly paler leaves. Cut each artichoke into quarters. With a very sharp paring knife, scoop out the hairy choke and cut away the spiky center leaves. Immediately drop the artichoke quarter into the lemon water, to minimize discoloring. Leave the artichoke quarters in the acidulated water until you're ready to dress them; they can be left for up to 5 hours.

3 Juice the remaining lemon into a medium bowl.

4 Just before serving, remove the quarters from the water, pat dry, and cut each in half widthwise. Slice each half lengthwise into thin-thin-thin paper-thin slices, immediately dropping them into the bowl containing the lemon juice. Toss well. Drizzle in the oil, sprinkle with the parsley, and add salt and pepper to taste. Toss well and serve at once.

VARIATION

I sometimes gild the lily by adding 1 small clove garlic, pressed, to the dressing. Further lily-gilding: If you have a block of excellent imported Parmesan, using a vegetable peeler shave curls of it over the artichoke.

Asparagus

A sign, spied early in May, propped up next to a basket of asparagus at our local Ozark Country Market, bragged, "None fresher except still growing in the garden!" Could anything but asparagus inspire such passionate and proud declarations?

Though asparagus is now in the market much of the year, every cook knows that spring is still asparagus's best, true time—when it's bold, crisp, a little sweet; when we crave its winter-defying greenness; when its vigorous spears have only just pushed through the still-raw, cold earth with a determination that tells you this old world is being renewed one more time. Take hope; take a bite.

Asparagus is fairly easy to grow, although, as a crop, it takes a couple of years to get really established. But almost everyone winds up shopping for it, because it comes up only a few spears at a time over a several-week period, yielding enough to nibble on in the garden or maybe throw into an omelet, but not adequate for a nice big splurgey spring-craving orgiastic asparagus feed. And one day, even the most diligent gardener misses a spear or two—only to find three-foot tall, feathery fronds of asparagus foliage, waving gracefully.

At the market, select spears of like diameter. *This is all-important.* Some prefer the delicate slender spears not much larger than a lead pencil; others the fatter, succulent spears. Each is a little different. Both have that gorgeous green essence-of-spring flavor, but the tinier spears are more tender and delicate; even if barely cooked, they almost melt in your mouth. The larger spears (excellent for grilling or roasting) are more fibrous, but that's by no means a drawback—because they're chewier, you wind up getting more of that asparagus taste from them. But, whichever you like, always select stalks of about the same width. A mixed-diameter bunch will cook unevenly.

Be sure the tips are compactly closed and free from any mushiness. As part of a component dinner with several other vegetables, or as a side dish, allow 6 to 8 medium to plump spears, or 10 to 15 skinny ones, per serving. This is about ⅓ to ½ pound untrimmed asparagus per person.

To prepare for cooking, snap the stalks near the base; the point at which the stalk snaps easily is the correct one, below it the spear is woody and tough. Next, give the stalks a swishing rinse in cold water. Personally, if I can get by without peeling a fruit or vegetable, I do so, and asparagus is no exception. If the stalks are as thin or thinner than a piece of chalk, there is, for me, no question of peeling; thicker, and you may consider it, since the skin gets a little tough. (Of course, "fiber-rich" is another way to express it.) I peel asparagus only if I have truly enormous stalks; just about as thick as a candle. Asparagus is peeled somewhat as carrots are. Holding the individual stalks, their tough ends already snapped, against a cutting board or other flat surface, tips facing you, begin each stroke of the vegetable peeler an inch or so below the tip. Work the peeler in long strokes away from you, revolving the spear as you peel. Peeling removes the small scales along the stalk as well as the theoretically tough skin—but as you can see, it runs into some time.

"To own a bit of ground, to scratch it with a hoe, to plant seeds, and watch the renewal of life—that is the commonest delight of the race, the most satisfactory thing. . . . However small it is on the surface, it is four thousand miles deep; and that is a very handsome property."

—**Charles Dudley Warner,** *My Summer in a Garden,* 1870

To many, the essence of asparagus is revealed when it is served crisp-tender, and so quick-cooking Chinese-style stir-fries are a natural. However, so is quick-blanching for hot and cold service, and so is asparagus done on the grill or baked. The dry heat of roasting brings out another asparagus dimension, intensifying and emphasizing the flavor, and adding a slightly chewy, pleasantly leathery quality. (I think that as long as it's not overcooked in water to "aspara-goo," there is hardly any wrong way to cook this vegetable. But overcooked asparagus is a sin. According to my late friend Sylvia Teague, the tyrannical emperor Tiberius, a great fan of the vegetable, used to instruct his executioner, "Dispatch him as quickly as it takes to cook asparagus."

Oven-Roasted Asparagus

It doesn't get any simpler—or much better. If you have experienced only steamed or stir-fried asparagus, you'll be amazed and pleased with the complete change in character this vegetable undergoes when roasted. This method is recommended for asparagus stalks 3/8 inch or thicker, but not thinner; thinner will just dry to a crisp, not the intended effect. **SERVES 4**

3 pounds asparagus, prepared for cooking (see opposite page)
1 tablespoon olive oil
Cooking spray (optional)
Salt

1 Preheat the oven to 475°F.

2 Toss the asparagus spears with the oil. If not using nonstick, spray a shallow baking tray with cooking spray. It must be large enough to hold the stalks in a single layer with plenty of air space around each one, so that the hot air can circulate and do its roasting magic. Place the asparagus in the preheated oven and set the timer for 10 minutes.

3 When the timer goes off, take the asparagus out and give it a shake. Look it over: When done, the stalks should be faintly shriveled, with the color deepened just a bit. At 10 minutes, they're probably not there yet, so return them to the oven for another 5 to 10 minutes, checking every few minutes.

Remove from the oven, salt lightly, and serve.

Stir-Fry of Asparagus with Black Bean–Ginger Sauce

Fresh, hot, simple, so good. A trip to an Asian market may well be necessary for the fermented black bean and garlic sauce, but sometimes larger supermarkets have it too.

Serve with rice, and perhaps a sweet and sour tofu. Or, dice fresh tofu into small cubes and toss it into the stir-fry at the last minute. **SERVES 3 OR 4**

2 pounds asparagus, tough ends broken off, cut diagonally into 1½-inch slices
2 tablespoons fermented black bean–garlic sauce
1 tablespoon peeled, minced ginger
Cooking spray (optional)
1½ teaspoons cornstarch
1 tablespoon water, preferably spring or filtered
1½ teaspoons mild vegetable oil such as corn, canola, or peanut
¾ cup Golden Stock (page 140) or other mild vegetable stock
1 tablespoon sherry
1½ teaspoons sugar
½ teaspoon tamari or shoyu soy sauce
½ teaspoon dried red pepper flakes
2 scallions, white and 3 inches of the green minced

1 Bring a large pot of water to a boil over high heat. Add the asparagus and boil until the color brightens, 1 to 2 minutes. Drain in a colander and immediately rinse under cold running water to stop the cooking. Set aside.

2 Combine the black bean sauce with the minced ginger in a small bowl. In a second small bowl, smush the cornstarch into the water. Set aside.

3 If not using nonstick, spray a wok with cooking spray and place it over medium-high heat. As it heats, put your mise en place in order (see page 107): the diluted cornstarch, the ginger–black bean mixture, the asparagus, the oil, and, in a glass measuring cup, the stock combined with the sherry, sugar and tamari.

4 When the wok is very hot, add the oil and the ginger–black bean mixture. Stir-fry for about 10 seconds—it will be immediately fragrant—then pour in the stock mixture. Bring to a boil. Add the asparagus and cook, stirring, for 1 minute. Add the red pepper flakes and then the scallions; stir until these ingredients are well blended. Immediately add the cornstarch paste and stir-fry until well glazed. Serve at once over rice or noodles.

". . . my greatest pleasure was the asparagus, bathed in ultramarine and pink and whose spears, delicately brushed in mauve and azure, fade imperceptibly to the base of the stalk—still soiled with the earth of their bed—through iridescences not of this world. It seemed to me these celestial nuances betrayed the delicious creatures that had amused themselves by becoming vegetables . . ."

—**Marcel Proust,** *Swann's Way*

Asparagus-Cheese Sauce with White Wine

There are plenty of innovative, delicious light pasta sauces in this book (she said immodestly), but this is *not* one of them. It's as close as I get to an alfredo, but I think it is far more fascinating. White wine, pureed asparagus, and wine-blanched asparagus tips all blend with the cream (which is not used in gratuitous amounts; just enough to smooth the sauce) and Cheddar cheese. It's rich, but not overkill, and a pure felicity of a combination. **MAKES ABOUT 4 CUPS**

½ cup water, preferably spring or filtered
½ cup dry white wine
2 pounds asparagus, prepared for cooking (see page 684)
2 tablespoons butter
2 tablespoons unbleached white all-purpose flour
2 cups milk
2 to 3 ounces (½ to ¾ cup) very finely grated sharp Cheddar cheese
Salt and freshly ground black pepper

1 Combine the water and wine in a medium saucepan. Bring to a boil and drop in the asparagus, cover, and cook until tender—not a second longer. Depending on the diameter of the asparagus, this could be anywhere from 3 to 6, even 7 minutes. When tender, immediately drain it, reserving the cooking liquid.

2 Lay the asparagus out on a cutting board, slice the tips off, then cut the stalks into ¾-inch pieces. Combine the tips and about one-third of the cut-up stalks and place in a bowl.

3 Combine the remaining stalk pieces in a food processor with the asparagus cooking liquid, and buzz until very smooth. (If you didn't peel the asparagus, the puree will have little stringy bits of fiber, which some may find objectionable. If so, you may pass the puree through a sieve to strain out the fibers.)

4 Melt the butter in a medium saucepan over medium heat. Whisk in the flour. Whisking constantly, cook for about 2 minutes, then gradually whisk in the milk. Cook until smooth and thick, about 5 minutes. Stir in the Cheddar and remove from the heat. You can do part of this as the asparagus cooks.

5 When ready to serve, add the reserved tips and stalk pieces and the asparagus puree to the cheese sauce. Place over medium heat, stirring constantly, until hot, about 2 minutes. Season to taste with salt and pepper. Serve hot.

VARIATION

Serve Asparagus-Cheese Sauce with White Wine over any pasta or grain, either as is, or with some stir-fried asparagus-plus-other-vegetables tossed in. Just to give you an idea of where you can go with this, consider Bow-Tie Pasta with a Stir-Fry of Asparagus, Red Pepper, and Onion, in Asparagus-Cheese Sauce, or Spinach Fettuccine with a Stir-Fry of Asparagus, Carrots, and Mushrooms, with Asparagus-Cheese Sauce. Either of these combos would make a wonderful brunch, rolled up in crêpes or an omelet.

The Bean Family

This generous family includes green beans, yellow beans, bean sprouts and peas and edible-pod peas (*Pisum*). Green soybeans, sometimes called edamame, are also family members, but I've treated them in the soy chapter. These podded delights—the word *legume* means "true pod"—when fresh and carefully prepared, are among the most succulent of vegetables.

Choose green beans that are smooth and even, consistently rounded or flat, depending on the variety. Also, pick up a bean and break it in two. It should snap, crisply, into two distinct pieces; if it bends limply, it is no longer fresh and will not be good eating. Another thing you can check by snapping is whether or not the bean has "strings"—threads of relatively tough fiber that edge the pods along the side seams. Many delicious beans and edible-pod peas do have strings, so it's not a drawback taste-wise, but it does mean extra prep time in removing them.

The pod is, of course, what we eat when we eat a green bean. The nomenclature is a bit confusing, because what we're actually eating is not a bean at all, but the seed case of the immature bean. Hence "green" bean—not only pertaining to color, but meaning youthful, not matured. The next stage of edible bean growth is what's usually called a shell bean, and is seldom seen these days unless you live in the country or shop in large metropolitan farmer's markets. A "shell" bean—this is the old country name—is a bean that has matured past the edible pod stage, but is itself edible. The pod is swollen and bumpy, and must be shucked off to get at the beans themselves. These can be cooked—for somewhat longer than you'd cook fresh green beans, but much more briefly than you'd cook dry beans . . . which are nothing more than these same beans with their moisture evaporated from them. Many beans, such as black-eyed peas or kidney beans, are edible and prized in all three stages: as green bean, shell bean, and dry bean.

The subject of cooking and eating dried and shell legumes is fully covered in Chapter 9, A Bountiful Bowl of Beans. Here, we are considering only the fresh bean, which is to say the succulent pod.

To prepare washed beans for cooking, you'll need to snip, pinch, or cut off and discard the stem end of the pods. Cut out any spoiled spots as well. If fresh, you need not remove the blossom end, unless the pods have "strings." Some will tell you that strings have been bred out of green beans; not true. Some varieties are indeed stringless, but some varieties that retain the string are

> *"The more you cook with grains, beans, and a large range of garden vegetables, the less obsessed you have to be with intricate nutritional battle plans."*
>
> —**Anne Mendelson,** *Gourmet* Magazine

exceptionally well flavored. So don't let the strings dissuade you; just snap off the stem end, pull down firmly; the string will curl back from the bean. Sometimes you can get both strings from the stem end; if you only get one, pinch off the blossom end and pull the string from the opposite side.

Beans are one vegetable that I don't find at their best when cooked crisp-tender. I believe that they should be tender, though never boiled to the falling-apart stage many of us may remember from school cafeterias. They must retain shape and have some texture, but I have really come to think that green beans are much tastier when not chewy or crisp at all. (Unless maybe in a salad, or if they are exceptionally slender and young.) If you eat crisp-tender green beans, you are missing their remarkable depth of flavor and texture.

Unless the green beans are little teeny-tiny skinny haricots verts, it is usually advisable to blanch them or presteam them in a collapsible steamer. In either case, they need to reach the point where their color deepens, and they no longer have their characteristic fuzz. This could be anywhere from 2 to 6 minutes, depending on the variety and thickness of the green beans. In certain recipes it may be desirable to take them slightly past this point.

Greek-Style Green Beans

This method of cooking—slowly sweating vegetables in a marmalade of garlic, tomato, and olive oil—is not only wondrous, but one of the top three or four ways of cooking any component vegetable.

Do it right, and the green beans will not be pretty. Use the larger amount of olive oil, and they'll be brown and caramelized and a little shriveled-looking; just this side, seemingly, of being burned. But wait until you taste them: melting and saturated with layers of flavor.

If you have Dragon Salt (page 900) on hand, substitute it for the other seasonings listed. And if you have Garlic Oil (page 898), omit the olive oil and garlic and instead use 1 tablespoon plus 1 teaspoon Garlic Oil. Having these two premade ingredients makes this quite simple to prepare. **SERVES 4 TO 6**

1½ pounds green beans, tips and stems removed
Cooking spray
2 teaspoons to 2 tablespoons olive oil
1 tablespoon finely chopped garlic
1 juicy, red-ripe tomato, chopped
Salt and freshly ground black pepper
½ to 1 teaspoon dried dill weed
A few dashes of cayenne

1 Bring a large pot of water to a brisk boil over high heat. Drop in the green beans and blanch for 4 minutes (if they're very skinny, a 2-minute blanch will do). Drain well, reserving the cooking water for use in soup stock.

2 Spray a heavy, 10- to 14-inch cast-iron skillet, one that has a tight-fitting lid, with cooking spray. Place over very low heat. Add the oil and garlic and the beans. Scatter the tomato over the beans.

3 Keeping the heat very low, and without stirring, cook, uncovered, for 5 minutes. Cover and cook for 30 minutes, again without stirring. Make sure that the heat is low enough to keep the mixture from burning. If you like, you can kind of push a few of the beans back to make sure the garlic on the bottom is merely cooking, very, very slowly with no trace of burning.

4 After 30 minutes, lift the lid. Stir gently, just kind of folding the green beans and tomatoes into each other. There may be excess liquid in the skillet. If so, raise the heat to high and cook, stirring occasionally, until there is no visible liquid, and the beans are dark, coated in a caramelized glaze of their own exuded juice, the tomatoes, and garlic.

5 Turn off the heat. Season with salt and pepper, sprinkle with dill and cayenne, and give a final stir. Serve hot.

Soulful and Simple Fresh Green Beans, White Beans, and Tomato Mélange

At midsummer, the green beans from our farmer's market are plump and succulent, and we can't get enough of them. I'm especially fond of pole beans, identified by their slightly flattened pod, and especially at the point that you can just start to see the bulges of the beans forming. To me, though not the most tender (until very well cooked), they are the best and most flavorful of green beans. I eat them plain, hot, cold; at room temperature Mediterranean-style with a little lemon, olive oil, salt, and pepper . . . and sometimes I make this quick combination. It's not a stir-fry, it's too thick to be called a sauce, and too simple and quickly done to be called a stew. Mélange it is, then, and it's just heavenly on a pile of steaming hot pasta or boiled or mashed potatoes. Start with a salad of bitter greens, pass a little grated Parmesan, and honey, you are *there*!

I use a pressure cooker, but steam or boil the green beans to get them tender if you like. **SERVES 4, WITH PASTA**

1 pound whole green beans, preferably older pole beans, stem ends removed
1 can (15½ ounces) navy beans, well drained (save liquid for stock)
¾ cup any good tomato sauce (commercially made, or Basic Wintertime Italian Tomato Sauce, page 931)
Cooked pasta, hot
Freshly grated Parmesan (optional)

1 Place the green beans on the steamer tray of a pressure cooker. Lock the lid down, and quickly bring the pressure up to the second ring. Cook for 1 minute, then turn off the heat and let the pressure release naturally.

2 Open the cooker. Drain any bean-cooking water, reserving it for stock if desired. Remove the steamer tray from the pot, leaving the beans—which will be gray-green and very tender. Gently stir in the navy beans and tomato sauce. Place over medium heat and bring to a simmer. Serve piping hot over pasta.

COOK ONCE FOR 2 MEALS Double this easy recipe. Use the mélange a day or two later as an omelet or crêpe filling.

VARIATIONS

Try diced shiitake or domestic mushrooms sautéed with the beans in place of the red pepper. Add a clove or two of minced garlic to the sauté, in any version. Substitute 1½ tablespoons basil for the tarragon, or 2 to 3 tablespoons minced Italian parsley, tossed in at the end. Use white wine instead of water in the steam-sauté phase.

Green Beans Moutarde with Grilled Red Peppers

These steam-blanched fresh green beans are sautéed, then tossed in a lively, tart mustard glaze sparked with citrus; red peppers add a visual exclamation point and a touch of sweet. They are crisp-tender, not soft-tender. Sprightly and appealing, this is an elegant combination: Serve with a simple baked marinated tempeh, shiitake mushrooms, and a big baked sweet potato, or perhaps a hunk of baked golden winter squash and a scoop of brown rice.

This recipe assumes you have teenaged green beans, about ¼ to ⅜ inch in diameter. If you have the skinny little haricots verts on hand, scale back the timing.

SERVES 4 TO 6

1 pound green beans, ends removed, cut diagonally into 1-inch pieces
Cooking spray
2 teaspoons butter
2 red peppers, charred, peeled, seeded, and chopped (see page 782)
About 2 tablespoons water, preferably spring or filtered
1 lime, lemon, or orange
2 tablespoons Dijon mustard
1 tablespoon finely minced tarragon
¼ teaspoon salt
Freshly ground black pepper to taste

1. Steam the green beans in a steamer until bright green and barely tender, 5 to 6 minutes. Alternatively, drop the green beans into a large pot of boiling water and blanch for 3 minutes. Drain well.

2. Melt the butter in a nonstick skillet or one that has been sprayed with cooking spray. Add the green beans and sauté for about 5 minutes. Add the red peppers and sauté for 1 minute. Add the 2 tablespoons water and cover. Let the beans steam in the butter and water for 4 to 6 minutes.

3. As the beans steam, grate about half the rind from the citrus fruit. Place it in a small bowl. Juice the fruit and measure 2 teaspoons juice into the bowl with the rind, reserving the remainder of the juice. Add the mustard, tarragon, salt, and pepper. Whisk until well blended.

4. Taste one of the beans; it should be tender but not mushy. If it's not there, sprinkle with water and steam just a bit longer. Add the mustard mixture and toss well to coat. Taste and adjust the seasoning, adding the additional citrus juice if necessary.

Bean Sprouts

Before a bean is a pod, a "shell" bean, or a dry bean, it is a sprout. These newly germinated infant beans are much prized in Asia, and they add greatly to any stir-fry or salad, with two provisos: They must be really fresh, and they must not be overcooked.

You'll find that most commercial bean sprouts are sprouted from mung or soybeans. In either case, select sprouts that are creamy white, crisp, and whole—avoid those that have turned brown, soft, and limp.

To prepare for cooking, fill a large bowl with cold water and dump in the bean sprouts. Swish the sprouts around, then tilt the bowl to one side. Lo and behold, the green mung bean husks and the broken sprouts will float to the top! Pick them off. Repeat a few times, then drain thoroughly.

For optimum crispness, make sure the wok is very, very hot before you put in the sprouts, and don't begin a sprout stir-fry until no more than 3 to 4 minutes before you plan on serving it.

Simplest Bean Sprout Stir-Fry

Quick, easily done—a wok full of unpretentious straight-up freshness to round out any Asian meal. The simple flavorings are not thickened. Serve with rice and one other more elaborate Asian stir-fry or Thai curry. Although many well-respected Chinese cooking authorities blanch bean sprouts before stir-frying them, this goes against everything I feel about the nature of bean sprouts. I finally tested this recipe both ways, side by side, and was vindicated when my tasters preferred the unblanched.

For a nice textural change, toss in a teaspoon or two of toasted sesame seeds at the end, either in lieu of or in addition to the sesame oil. **MAKES 4 TO 6 SMALL COMPONENT SERVINGS**

¾ teaspoon sugar
½ teaspoon salt
½ teaspoon tamari or shoyu soy sauce
½ teaspoon rice vinegar
½ teaspoon toasted sesame oil
Cooking spray
2½ teaspoons mild vegetable oil, preferably peanut
3 scallions, roots and wilted green parts removed, slivered lengthwise, then sliced into 1½-inch pieces
1 pound bean sprouts, washed and drained

1 Combine the sugar, salt, tamari, vinegar, and sesame oil in a small bowl. Set aside near the stove.

2 Spray a wok with cooking spray. Place over high heat until very hot. Immediately add the vegetable oil, and tilt the wok to coat with oil. Heat for another 15 seconds. Add the scallions, stir once or twice, and count to 10. Add the bean sprouts and the sugar mixture and, stirring and tossing, cook for 30 seconds more. Serve immediately.

Stir-Fry of Bean Sprouts, Shiitakes, and Red Peppers

Unlike most stir-fries, this is not done with soy sauce. Serve with a tofu-garnished Asian noodle dish, or rice and a stir-fry or Asian curry.

To smash the garlic, lay the garlic cloves on a cutting board, place the flat side of a knife blade on them, and whap!—hit the blade once with your fist. **MAKES 4 TO 6 SMALL COMPONENT SERVINGS**

1½ teaspoons cornstarch
3 tablespoons water, preferably spring or filtered
1 teaspoon salt
¾ teaspoon sugar
2 good grinds of black pepper
2½ teaspoons mild vegetable oil, preferably peanut
3 cloves garlic, lightly smashed
1 large scallion, roots and any wilted green parts removed, all the white and 3 inches of green thinly sliced
2 teaspoons peeled, finely diced ginger
5 or 6 shiitake mushrooms, stems removed, slivered
½ red bell pepper, seeds, stem, and membranes removed, thinly slivered
1 pound bean sprouts, washed and drained
1 teaspoon toasted sesame oil

1 Combine the cornstarch with the water in a small bowl and smush with your fingers until dissolved. Add the salt, sugar,

and pepper. Place one bowl on a mise en place tray (see page 107), along with the remaining ingredients.

2 Heat a wok over high heat until very hot. Add the vegetable oil, and tilt the wok to coat with oil. Heat for another 15 seconds. Add the garlic, scallion, and ginger, stir once or twice, and count to 10. Add the shiitakes and bell peppers and stir-fry over high heat for 30 seconds. Add the bean sprouts and the corn starch mixture and cook for 30 seconds more. Serve immediately.

Moo-Shu Vegetables

Traditionally, this Mandarin dish, an American Chinese restaurant standard, is made with shredded meat, chicken, or duck combined with stir-fried vegetables and scrambled eggs, wrapped in a rather dense, steamed hoisin-slathered pancake. I much prefer this lighter version, with its tofu-studded, full-flavored sprout-vegetable filling, and its delicious Neo-Classic Crêpe wrapping. If—and I realize that this is a big if—you have crêpes made or crêpe batter on hand, as well as commercially made hoisin sauce and black bean–garlic sauce, it is but 10 to 15 minutes' work to put together a dazzling, satisfying dinner. **SERVES 4 AS AN ENTREE**

- 2 teaspoons cornstarch
- ⅓ cup water, preferably spring or filtered, or vegetable stock (see page 139)
- 2½ teaspoons sugar, honey, or Rapidura
- 2 teaspoons fermented black bean–garlic sauce
- 1½ teaspoons toasted sesame oil
- Pinch of salt
- 2 good grinds of black pepper
- 2½ teaspoons mild vegetable oil, preferably peanut
- 3 cloves garlic, lightly smashed
- 2 teaspoons peeled, finely diced ginger
- 2 large scallions, roots and wilted green parts removed, all the white and 3 inches of green thinly sliced
- 1 carrot, well scrubbed, julienned
- 5 or 6 shiitake mushrooms, stems removed, slivered
- ½ pound bean sprouts, washed and drained
- 1 stalk bok choy, both stems and leaves, slivered
- 4 ounces conventional water-packed tofu, cut into ¼-inch dice
- 12 Neo-Classic Crêpes (page 332)
- About 3 tablespoons any good, commercially prepared hoisin sauce

VARIATIONS

For something closer to the original, scramble 2 well-beaten eggs in a very hot pan with a little peanut oil. Stir the scrambled eggs into the sautéed vegetable filling before wrapping it in the pancakes. You may do this instead of, or in addition to, the tofu.

Also, virtually any vegetables can step in or out here. Try a few diced water chestnuts, or slices of canned baby corn, or fresh spinach or celery or cabbage instead of bok choy.

1 Combine the cornstarch with the water in a small bowl and smush with your fingers until dissolved. Add the sugar, black bean–garlic sauce, ½ teaspoon of the sesame oil, salt, and pepper. Place the bowl close to the stove, along with the remaining ingredients.

2 Heat a wok over high heat until very hot. Add the vegetable oil and tilt the wok to coat with oil. Heat for another 15 seconds. Add the garlic and ginger, stir once or twice, and count to 10. Add the scallions and carrot and stir-fry to the count of 10. Add the shiitakes and stir-fry for another 15 seconds. Add the bean sprouts and bok choy and count to 20. Give the cornstarch mixture a quick stir and add it along with the tofu and remaining sesame oil. Stir-fry until all of the mixture is coated with the thickened sauce, 10 to 25 seconds more. Taste and adjust with more soy, sweetener, pepper, or whatever you like.

3 Immediately rush the hot stir-fry to the table. Generously coat half of each crêpe with hoisin sauce and scoop a portion of the vegetable mixture into the pancake. Fold and serve.

Peas

Peas *(Pisum),* also a member of the legume family, offer a whole other dimension of podded pleasure. Though good fresh peas are harder and harder to find, and few are willing or able to take the time to shell them, they're worth hunting down each spring; like asparagus, they're a seasonal rite of passage. To ensure just-picked-that-morning sweetness, choose well-rounded, bright green pods only at a farmer's market. Bend a pod; it should crisply snap open, not bend limply (this tells you how recently it was picked, and with peas, whose natural sugars swiftly turn to starch, this is essential). The pod should reveal light green peas within. Remember that time is of the essence: No matter how fresh they are when you buy them, the longer you wait to cook them the more disappointing they'll be. To prepare for cooking, sit yourself down with your peas in a bag, along with two bowls, one larger. Slit each pod open with your thumb-nail. Discard the pods into the larger bowl; place the shelled peas into the smaller.

Other than at the very start of spring, I rely on frozen peas. I only use them in things—both for their sweetness and bright polka-dot of color—but never as a side dish. Frozen peas do not need either cooking or thawing; just put some in a strainer, run hot tap water over them, and they're ready to enhance whatever dish calls out for them.

At the Market

"The nose and a fingernail, which should be left unlacquered, are sufficient tools for a trip to market. Are the peas fresh that are offered for sale? The greengrocer says yes; he will not be offended if a fingernail is dug into the pod. If sap appears in the wound the peas are fresh enough; if it does not appear then one does not want those peas because then one may be sure they left their parent vines many days before. . . . Vegetables cannot be good unless they are fresh; of course if they are [intentionally] dried vegetables, that is another matter, another flavour and a totally different cooking process."

—Henri Charpentier, *Those Rich and Great Ones, or Life à la Henri*

Edible-pod peas, however, are a different story. Sometimes called mange-touts (literally "eat-alls," in French), they can be either the Chinese classic snow pea, which is a flattened pod, or the sugar-snap—round and plumply rotund of pod, with the internal peas far more developed than in the snow peas. When purchasing either variety, bend the pea pod; it should snap crisply in two. To prepare for cooking, break off the stem end of the edible-pod pea, and pull sharply; a "string" down the side of the pod will unravel, curling. Pinch the other end of the pod and pull, removing the string that goes down the opposite side. Not all edible-pods have strings, but the majority do.

There is one other pea-perfect pleasure: pea shoots. They are the leaves, and a few inches of vine, of edible peas, and have the sweet verve of sugar-snaps along with a touch of conventional greens' soul. They cook practically instantly. At the market, seek out fresh, vibrant green pea shoots, ones that look like they're virtually still growing.

"I would stop at the table to see the peas which the kitchen girl had just shelled, all lined up and numbered like green marbles in a game."

—**Marcel Proust,** *Swann's Way*

Sugar-Glazed Peas with Radishes

A dish with the purest rush of spring, fresh peas are steam-blanched, quickly sautéed, glazed with a tiny bit of sugar, finished with a small handful of sliced radish, and rushed to the table. The radish is barely heated through; it retains both its slight pepperiness and crunch, and the color contrast is gorgeous. **SERVES 4**

1¼ pounds fresh young peas, shelled
Cooking spray
2 teaspoons butter
2 teaspoons sugar
4 young, fresh pink-skinned radishes, well washed, tops and roots removed, sliced crosswise
Pinch of salt

1 Place the peas in a steamer over boiling water until they are bright green, about 1 minute. Remove from the steamer basket and pat dry.

2 Spray a conventional skillet (not a nonstick, in this case) with cooking spray. Add the butter and place over medium heat.

When the butter has melted, toss in the peas and sugar. Cook, shaking the skillet constantly, until the sugar is no longer granular but has melted, and the peas are starting to stick, 2 to 3 minutes.

3 Quickly add the radishes and the slightest pinch of salt. Shake the peas and radishes for another 30 seconds. Serve immediately.

Gingered Stir-Fry of Snow-Peas and Carrots

That this is simple makes it no less delicious, especially compared to the carrots and peas you may have been forced to eat as a child. To turn this into an entree, simply toss in diced savory baked tofu and maybe some sliced water chestnuts (preferably fresh) just after you've added the stir-fry sauce.

Everything through Step 3 can be done in advance. **SERVES 4 TO 6**

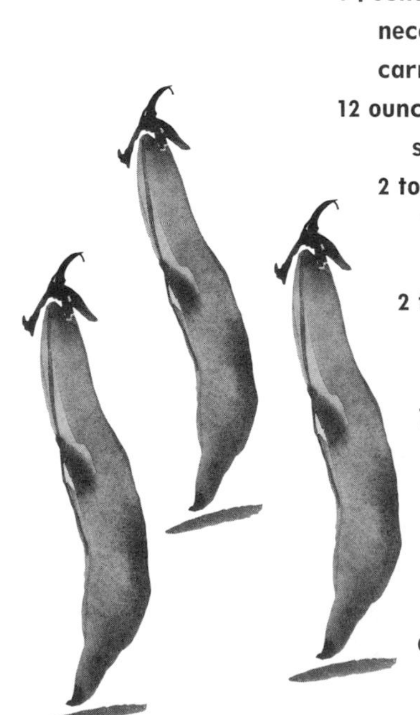

1 pound baby carrots, ends cut off if necessary (or use precut regular carrots in rounded 1-inch pieces)
12 ounces snow peas (or sugar snaps), strings removed
2 to 3 cloves garlic, peeled and finely minced (about 2½ teaspoons)
2 thumb-sized pieces fresh ginger, peeled and finely minced (about 2½ teaspoons)
1 tablespoon tamari or shoyu soy sauce
1 tablespoon rice vinegar
1 teaspoon brown sugar
2 drops Tabasco or similar hot pepper sauce
Cooking spray
1 teaspoon mild vegetable oil, such as corn, canola, or peanut
1 teaspoon toasted sesame oil

1 Bring a large pot of water to a boil over high heat. Add the carrots and blanch for as little as 1 minute if you have true narrow baby carrots, no fatter than a pencil; it will be 4 minutes if using mature carrots cut to look like babies.

2 Place the snow-peas in a colander. Drain the carrots over the snow peas (thereby blanching the snow peas at the same time), and refresh immediately and vigorously under cold running water, rinsing well. Blot the vegetables dry. Set aside.

3 Combine the garlic, ginger, tamari, vinegar, brown sugar, and Tabasco in a small bowl. Set aside.

4 When ready to eat, spray a conventional wok or skillet well with cooking spray. Add the oils and place over high heat. When very hot, add the blanched vegetables and stir-fry like crazy for 2 to 3 minutes. Add the garlic-ginger mixture and stir-fry until the sauce has largely evaporated and what's left is very fragrant, another 20 seconds. Serve immediately.

Stir-Fry of Fresh Pea Shoots

Pea shoots, also called pea greens, are simply wonderful, and should be eaten quickly, simply, and without fuss. The good old Asian standard stir-fry seasonings do the trick.

To turn this into a main dish, stir in some savory baked tofu at the end of their cooking period, and throw them on top of some cooked buckwheat or brown rice ramen noodles. Salutary. **SERVES 2**

Cooking spray (optional)
1 teaspoon mild vegetable oil, such as corn, canola, or peanut
2 cloves garlic, pressed
1 teaspoon peeled, very finely minced ginger
3 ounces fresh pea shoots
1½ teaspoons Thai Crystal (page 923) or 1 teaspoon sugar plus ½ teaspoon Tabasco or similar hot sauce
Dash of tamari or shoyu soy sauce
1 to 2 drops toasted sesame oil

1 In a nonstick skillet, or one that has been sprayed with cooking spray, heat the vegetable oil over medium-high heat. When the oil is quite hot, add the garlic and ginger and stir-fry for 10 seconds.

2 Add the pea shoots and continue stir-frying until they wilt, 45 to 60 seconds. Immediately remove from the heat and stir in the Thai Crystal, along with the tiniest bit of tamari and toasted sesame oil. Serve immediately.

Beets

The New World gave the Old tomatoes, potatoes and sweet potatoes, both chiles and sweet peppers, chocolate, squash, corn, as well as many varieties of squash and beans. The Old World gave the New . . . beets.

I love beets. It continually astonishes me that so many people only know them by the sodden, pickled-canned-or-out-of-a-jar varieties, beets of the salad bar type. Those sad-sack, limpid purple ovals, floating in a dark watery bath, are totally unrelated to the lively, densely flavored experience of true, fresh, real-life beets.

Fresh beets, like some of my favorite people, are both sweet and strong, tough and delicate. They are assertive, yet have a tender side. And they are *vivid*; probably the brightest members of the whole vegetable clan. And, to boot, beets have dual personalities: They are both root and leaf, each with its own characteristics. (See Greens Gang, page 755, for details on beet greens.)

The roots—usually round but occasionally cylindrical, with a long tapering "tail"—are sweet (in fact, some refined sugars are made from them). Their flesh is hearty, dense, and of a deep purple-pink, which turns a shocking fuschia when cooked (lately there are beautiful golden beets available too). Oddly, for all that intensity of color and flavor, the roots are not nutritional powerhouses: They have a little vitamin A, a little calcium, a respectable amount of iron and potassium. But the beet *greens,* that crowning of leaves (the outer of which are often large and a bit bedraggled, the inner of which are usually tightly furled, crisp, and fresh)—pack a nutritive wallop and are so delicious. Although they have been dealt with primarily in the Greens Gang, I have a few preparations combining greens and beets here. How could I resist? Not only do I deeply enjoy their flavor, but they are full of calcium (140 milligrams in a cup), iron (2.8 milligrams in same), potassium (480 milligrams), and an astonishing 7,400 IUs of vitamin A.

Beets, both the root and most of the leaves, should look sprightly and dewey fresh. The tails, for instance, should be fairly stiff; they should snap if you tried to break them. You don't want beets that are wrinkled or limp looking, though a few of the outer leaves might be. Whenever possible, buy beets with the tops intact.

Beets come in a range of sizes. Although small or baby beets (½ to ¾ inch in diameter) are often sweeter and fresher, this is not always the case. Medium beets, which range in size from ¾ inch to 2 inches, should, if fresh, also be nice and sweet. Sometimes the large ones—up to 3 inches and weighing ½ pound or so apiece—are very sweet too, again if fresh. But the larger beets sometimes have a slightly bitter, peppery cast, a bit turnip-y. Always try to purchase beets of like size, so they cook in the same amount of time. I allow 1 or 2 baby beets for a side plate, 3 or 4 if they're part of a component plate. If working with medium beets, think 1 per person for a side veggie plate, 2, maybe 3 for a component. Larger beets must be sliced, or cut into wedges; I usually cut wedges about 1 inch wide; 1 to 2 wedges for a side veggie plate, 3 to 5 wedges for a component.

Little, marble-sized beets are best when scrubbed well, and quickly steamed whole (with their teeny leaves intact). They are charming this way, and usually very sweet. I've also served them cold, marinated in Sharp Classic Vinaigrette with a Bite (page 72) or Jay McCarthy's Cascabel Dressing (page 89). For beets any larger than the babies, I highly recommend baking or pressure-cooking.

Basic Baked Beets

This simple recipe unlocks the door to gorgeous, firm beets, full of flavor and ready to be zapped in any number of appealing ways.

Because the beets are foil-wrapped, they are not really roasted; rather, they steam in their own juices, for intense, undiluted beetiness. Use this method if you don't have a pressure cooker, when it's cold enough that having the oven on for a while will be a comfort, when time is not an issue, and/or when you're using the oven to bake something else. **QUANTITY VARIABLE**

NOTE

The greens are removed prior to cooking; suggestions about how to cook them appear in the Greens Gang (page 755).

Whole fresh beets, all about the same size, greens removed but "tails" and about ¾ inch of the stem intact, very well scrubbed and dried
Mild vegetable oil, such as corn, canola, or peanut

1 Preheat the oven to 350°F.

2 Lightly coat each beet with oil. Individually wrap the oiled beets in sheets of foil.

3 Place the beets in a baking dish in the preheated oven.

4 Bake until done, testing with a fork (the fork should go in easily, but the beet should still offer a tiny bit of resistance). This could be as little as 35 minutes if beets are very small, up to 90 minutes if they are large.

5 Remove from the oven and let cool. When the beets are cool enough to handle, unwrap and, if desired, slip the skins off (they will come off easily). Cut large beets into eighths, medium into quarters or halves, or slice crosswise; small ones can be left whole. Refrigerate for later use or finish as directed in a specific recipe.

Basic Pressure-Cooked Beets

I have been baking beets for years. But this pressure-cooker method has its uses. Quickly, without heating up the whole kitchen or wasting fuel, you can have

Five Simple Beet Preparations

Prepare Basic Baked Beets for 4 to 6 people. Heat 1 teaspoon each butter and oil in a large nonstick skillet over medium heat. When the oils are sizzling hot, add the baked beets and toss them in the hot fat. Then, for:

FRESH GINGERED BEETS, *add 1 to 2 teaspoons peeled very finely diced ginger. Toss for about 30 seconds, then add 3 tablespoons brown sugar and 2 tablespoons water. Cook, stirring, until the water and brown sugar have bubbled into a glaze, about 30 seconds.*

BEETS WITH VANILLA, *a mind-blowing, perfumed way with beets that Joyce Goldstein once fed to me at her now, oh-so-sadly-defunct San Francisco restaurant, Square One. Add only 1 tablespoon each of water and granulated sugar, and a few drops of pure vanilla extract. Cook, stirring, until the water, sugar, and vanilla bubble into a glaze, about 30 seconds.*

CREAMY COUNTRY-STYLE SWEET-SOUR BEETS, *combine, in a small bowl, 1 tablespoon vinegar (cider, red wine, or raspberry vinegars each work nicely here) and 2 tablespoons brown sugar. Add ¼ teaspoon cornstarch, smooshing with your fingers. Stir in 2 to 3 tablespoons Yogurt Sour-Cream (page 910), Tofu Sour Cream (page 909), reduced-fat sour cream, or (what the heck) real sour cream, along with ¼ cup vegetable stock (see page 139). Toss the whole or wedged baked beets into the hot fat. When the beets are just heated, add the vinegar mixture and stir wildly, cooking just until the sauce has heated and thickened a tiny bit. Taste. If there is a raw cornstarch flavor, cook a bit longer. Season with salt and freshly ground black pepper.*

FRESH CURRIED BEETS, *instead of using butter, sauté the beets in 1 tablespoon mild vegetable oil, adding 2 tablespoons cider vinegar, 1 tablespoon each honey and Rapidura, and 2 teaspoons Dairy Hollow House Curry Spice Blend (page 901) Stir until heated through. Add salt to taste.*

TO MAKE GLAZED BEETS AND APPLES, *peel and julienne a Fuji or Braeburn or other firm, crisp apple. Sauté in 1 teaspoon each butter and oil for 2 minutes, then scoop out the sautéed apple pieces (they should be starting to soften, but still have some crispness). Add the baked beets to the pan along with 1 to 3 tablespoons frozen, thawed, undiluted apple juice concentrate and toss until the beets are heated through and most of liquid has boiled away. Return the apples to the pan, toss, and serve immediately.*

delicious, firm beets, ready to do your bidding in a thousand ways. Because very little water is involved, these retain an intense flavor. This is the ideal summer cooking method. When I come home from the farmer's market, I often scrub a few beets right off and pop them in the pressure cooker. By the time I've put away the rest of the produce, the beets are done: ready to be cooled, peeled, and fridged, for a salad, a *mezze* plate, or in any way that strikes my fancy. If they are particularly sweet and good I sometimes eat the slices just as they are, no dressing, no sauce, no anything. Remove the greens prior to cooking; suggestions for their use appear in the Greens Gang (page 755). **QUANTITY VARIABLE**

Water, preferably spring or filtered
Whole fresh beets, all about the same size, greens removed but "tails" and about ¾ inch of the stem intact, very well scrubbed and dried

1 Place ¼ inch or so of water in the bottom of a pressure cooker. Drop in the steaming disc. If you have a scale, weigh a single beet; otherwise just eye it and make your call: Is the beet large (5½ to 7 ounces), medium (4 to 5 ounces), or small (2 to 2½ ounces)? Place the beets in the cooker. Lock the lid down and bring the pressure to high over high heat. Cook under high pressure as follows: 18 to 21 minutes for large beets, 12 to 15 for medium, and 3 to 5 minutes for small. If you're not sure of the size, or if you like very firm beets, take a minute off these cooking times. Quick-release the pressure. Remove the lid and poke a beet with a fork. If it's not done enough, relock the lid and bring to pressure a second time, adjusting the cooking time according to the hardness of the beet and your taste.

2 Once you get used to the timing, do as I do and shorten it a bit, letting the pressure release naturally once you've turned off the heat. Remove the lid. Let cool. When the beets are cool enough to handle, slip off the skins, if desired (they will come off easily). Cut large beets into eighths, medium into quarters or halves, or slice into thick rounds. Small beets can be left whole. Refrigerate for later use, or finish as directed in a specific recipe.

Arugula

Scallioned Beets and Their Greens in Herbed Mustard Sauce

So savory and good, this makes an excellent vegetable supper all on its own with just a nice pile of brown rice. The colors just dance on the plate. By midsummer, you should be able to get good local beets . . . a few snippings of herbs from your garden, a little mustard—there you are. The vegan version with Tofu Sour Cream is exceptionally tasty too. **SERVES 4 TO 6**

1 teaspoon cornstarch
½ cup vegetable stock (see page 139)
3 tablespoons coarse-ground Dijon mustard
¼ cup Yogurt Sour Cream (page 910), Tofu Sour Cream (page 909), reduced-fat sour cream, or the real thing
2 teaspoons butter (or olive oil or vegetable margarine)
3 to 4 scallions, roots and wilted greens removed, finely diced
1 to 2 bunches (whatever came off the baked beets) beet greens, washed, stems finely diced, leaves stacked and sliced into ¼-inch ribbons
8 to 10 small-medium Basic Baked Beets (page 701), halved, or 4 to 5 large Basic Baked Beets, cut into wedges
2 to 4 cloves garlic, pressed
2 tablespoons minced Italian parsley
1 tablespoon minced basil
Salt and freshly ground black pepper to taste

1 Combine the cornstarch with 1 tablespoon of the stock in a small bowl. Smush together with your fingertips to dissolve the cornstarch, then whisk in the remaining stock, along with the mustard and Yogurt Sour Cream. Set aside.

2 Melt the butter in a large nonstick skillet over medium heat. Add the scallions and beet greens and sauté for 1 minute, then cover and cook for 3 minutes. Uncover and add the beets and garlic to the pan and toss until just heated through, about 1 minute.

3 Whisk the mustard mixture. Quickly stir it into the beets. Cook, stirring constantly, until the sauce is hot and thick, 1 minute at most. Stir in the parsley and basil. Taste. If there is a raw cornstarch taste, cook a minute longer. Season with salt and pepper. Serve immediatelty.

Brown Sugar–Glazed Beets with Fresh Kumquats

You couldn't ask for a more beautiful, surprising dish to add to a component entree than this. For years I'd made beets with brown sugar and orange juice. In the few minutes between cooking and plating them, I'd toss both halves of one of the oranges with the beets—not only to infuse them with extra flavor but just for my own pleasure, so visually energizing were the magenta beets next to the orange.

One day in late spring, back in the inn days, I was buying small organic beets up at Ozark Country Market, and saw a small basket filled with organic kumquats: tiny tart-sweet bright orange citrus fruits intended to be eaten peel and all (except seeds). I gazed at them and had a light-bulb-over-the-head moment. Kumquats and beets! Oh yes! Now guests would also get those exuberant colors. We got delighted comments and not a single beet or kumquat came back. Because kumquats are tarter than oranges, another dimension is added when you take a forkful that includes both kumquat and beet. **SERVES 4 TO 6**

6 to 8 fresh kumquats
2 teaspoons butter
12 to 14 small-medium Basic Baked Beets (page 701), halved, or 5 large Basic Baked Beets, cut into wedges
1 orange, halved
2 to 3 tablespoons brown sugar or honey

1 Cut the kumquats in half, carefully picking out all seeds. Then halve them again, so you have quarters. Place the kumquats in a small bowl. Set aside.

2 Melt the butter in a large nonstick skillet over medium heat. Add the beets and cook, stirring until warmed, about 1 minute. Squeeze the orange halves through a strainer right onto the beets. Add the brown sugar and cook, stirring, for 3 minutes.

3 Add the kumquats and toss until just heated through, about 1 minute. Serve at once.

Prairie Companion

I believe that not only my love of food, but my love of good writing about food, may have stemmed from my childhood reading of the Little House books by Laura Ingalls Wilder. The descriptions of food are so particular and mouthwatering, so delightful when some good-to-eat dish, whether a special item or a daily preparation, came in the direction of the observant little pioneer. And the sense of security when the attic was stocked with pumpkins and potatoes and dried vegetables and home-canned preserves and pickles was as palpable as the stark danger when natural disasters threatened the food supply. Laura Ingalls wrote, too, about a pioneer boy, Almanzo Wilder, who would grow up to become her husband. She describes a plate Almanzo's father ladled up for him one Sunday dinner. Besides being non-vegetarian and high fat (naturally enough, given the period, and the number of calories needed by a hard-working farm family, especially a growing boy), this dish would also have been pretty brown: chicken pie, gravy, baked beans, salt pork. Indeed, cold weather meals were mostly brown; fresh vegetables, other than keepers like potatoes, pumpkin, onions, and cabbages, just were not available. But one last item was served by "Father Wilder" before he handed the meal to his eager, hungry son: "At the edge of the plate he piled dark-red beet pickles." With their color and their sweet-tartness, they freshened the feast.

The Cabbage Family

Cabbage (Green and Red), Bok Choy, Broccoli and Broccoli Rabe, Brussels Sprouts, Cauliflower, Collards, Kale, Kohlrabi, Turnips, and Mustard Greens: all are members of the genus *cruciferae,* the distinguished and dignified-sounding Latin name for the cabbage family.

Serene cabbages, queen-like, dignified; pale green, full-blown roses. Tight white heads of cauliflower, beribboned with green leaves like a wrapped bride's bouquet. Elegant broccoli trees, tipped with thousands of tiny flower buds. Psychedelic red cabbage—wildly purple, really—cleaved to reveal a network of cream-colored veins emanating from a pale heart. With appearances so bewitching, and a

huge spectrum of tastes and textures, it would be greedy to expect any more. Yet the generous *brassicas* —botanically related to mustard—are improbable and generous fairy godmothers, for, in addition to beauty and deliciousness, they contain compounds—phytochemicals—called indole glusinolates, which have been linked to a lower incidence of digestive-system cancers. They appear to work, as studies done at the University of Minnesota Medical School first suggested, by changing the way our body responds when exposed to carcinogens. Even the National Cancer Institute now suggests eating brassicas on a regular basis.

The cabbage family has been much maligned, especially for its odor when cooked. But the fault is in the method, not the vegetables. The trick to bringing out the innate goodness of the members of the cabbage family is undercooking until crisp-tender, not soggy. (There are a few exceptions to the rule—but not many.) Here is a market-basket full of recipes to get you started. But please don't forget that brassicas turn up all over this book. I've indicated some special don't-miss recipes at the start of each vegetable.

Broccoli

Broccoli-bashing is popular among those who claim not to like vegetables, but I don't get it. It's a great favorite of mine; the one I spear out of stir-fries, routinely keep in the fridge, sauté a million different ways. When cooked right, broccoli's flavor is unique but never impertinent, with a satisfying texture. That flavor, plus its treelike form and energetic green, give vibrancy to otherwise pallid plates. In stir-fries and soups, over pasta, in stuffings, as a go-with for simple baked sweet potatoes—broccoli is often my vegetable of choice.

All this, and it's rich not only in those cancer-fighting phytochemicals, but also in vitamins C and A, potassium, and fiber, too.

Examine them closely. The tiny ball-like fragments of green are the flower heads in bud. On older broccoli, some of these buds will have started to open and yellow, which is not what you want. Go for green, compact flower heads. Check the stems; they should be relatively free of grayed cut marks along the side, where side stems were cut off. The smoother and firmer the stem, the better. Broccoli is available year round, but its peak season is late fall through early spring. Allow about 6 ounces per person as a side dish or component. Expect four generous accompaniment servings from a typical broccoli head.

To prepare for cooking, cut off the flowering head, including the stem up to where the individual branches meet the main stem. Do use any small leaves you find around the head, cutting them up and cooking them along with the other parts of the vegetable; they're extra-rich in nutrients, and very tasty. This head portion may be cut into florets, miniature trees, or whatever cut is called for in a specific recipe.

Remove the hard outer peel of the broccoli's stem. While you can peel it with a potato peeler, it is fiddly, time consuming work. Also, the tough portion can go fairly deep. I use a good kitchen knife and square off the stem, whacking down to take off the tough part, leaving me with a pale green more-or-less rectangular piece. This stem can be sliced crosswise into squares, julienned into long, thin strips, grated, or diced.

Quite often I'll blanch a cut-up head of broccoli ahead of time. Bring a large quantity of water (preferably filtered) to a boil, in your largest pot. You want enough so the water doesn't stop boiling when the broccoli, head cut into 1½-to 2-inch-tall trees, stems sliced an inch thick, is added. Give the broc a 30- to 120-second blanch (its green should intensify, but it should remain quite crisp), drain, and immediately rinse under cold running water. It is now ready for a quick stir-fry, in a nonstick or cooking-sprayed skillet with a smidgen of butter or olive oil. Salt, pepper, maybe a squeeze of lemon juice, and there you go. Alternatively, steam broccoli in a collapsible steamer (until the color intensifies, and it is still crisp-tender, 3 to 4 minutes) or stir-fry as part of a mix for pastas.

You can buy pre-cut broccoli in florets, as well as julienned, peeled broccoli stems. Both of these are good, quick options for the time-pressed, but *only* if they are cooked within a day, or two at most, of purchase as the minute they are cut open, they begin losing some of their goodness to air.

To see broccoli as a team player, check out CD's Famed Tofu Broccoli Enchiladas (page 340), and Broccoli, Potatoes, and Tofu in Golden Peanut-Miso Velvet (page 672).

Grilled Broccoli with Clary's Exquisitely Wicked Marinade

This comes from Clary at Eureka's Center Street South of the Border, where, as they say in resort towns, "the locals go." Most people know about grilled zucchini and eggplant, but few have experienced grilled broccoli. This version will blow you away! You can't imagine how it could taste so much like itself, yet be so different. I've left the marinade as she gave it to us, though at home we use less oil. You can also grill cauliflower, or a mixture of broccoli and cauliflower in this marinade. With rice, black beans, salsa, a little grated Cheddar, and some warmed tortillas, this is a feast.

If you have a gas grill, or if you're doing something else on the grill, you will find it simple and exquisitely good. The marinade should be made ahead of time.

SERVES 3 OR 4

10 cloves garlic, peeled
½ cup fresh pineapple juice
Juice of 2 limes
½ cup olive oil
2 tablespoons light rum
½ to 1 teaspoon adobo seasoning (a commercially available mixture found in the Hispanic foods section of your supermarket)
Salt and freshly ground black pepper to taste
1 head broccoli, cut into florets large enough not to slip through the grill bars (reserve stems for another purpose)

1 Combine the garlic and pineapple juice in a blender or the food processor, processing until the garlic is finely chopped. Add the lime juice, oil, rum, adobo, and salt and pepper and buzz to blend.

Pour this marinade into a bowl or zippered freezer bag and add the broccoli. Marinate, refrigerated, for 2 to 4 hours. Shake or turn the broccoli occasionally to distribute the marinade.

2 Preheat the grill to hot, then turn down to medium.

3 Place the broccoli pieces over indirect heat, and grill, covered, turning once halfway through, until the broccoli is crisp-tender and a little toasty in spots, 12 to 17 minutes. Serve at once.

Broccoli in Dijon Mustard Sauce

You would never guess, unless you drastically overcooked it, that broccoli is part of the mustard family. But drenched in this creamy low-fat sauce, you'll taste the affinity, light-handedly and amenably. Try this over pasta, whole wheat toast, brown rice, or any cooked grain. The sauce is also nice over a stir-fry of onions (cut into crescents, rather than diced), carrots, and broccoli, or leftover broccoli and potatoes. **SERVES 4 TO 6**

- ½ teaspoon olive oil
- ½ large onion, chopped
- 2½ cups low-fat milk
- 1 tablespoon plus 1 teaspoon cornstarch
- ¼ cup dry white wine (or stock or additional milk)
- 2 ounces neufchâtel reduced-fat cream cheese, softened to room temperature
- 2 cloves garlic, pressed
- 2 teaspoons Dijon mustard
- A few gratings of nutmeg
- Salt and freshly ground black pepper to taste
- 1 head broccoli, cut into florets, stem peeled and julienned, blanched (see page 707)

1. Heat the oil in a large nonstick skillet over medium heat. Add the onion and cook, stirring often, until translucent, 3 to 5 minutes. Add the milk and stir to combine.

2. Dissolve the cornstarch in the wine, smushing with your fingertips. When the milk is hot, whisk in the cornstarch mixture. As soon as the milk thickens, remove the skillet from the heat and whisk in the softened neufchâtel along with the garlic, mustard, nutmeg, salt, and plenty of pepper. Add the broccoli. Taste and, if necessary, adjust the seasonings.

3. Return the skillet to medium heat and cook, stirring, just until the mixture is piping hot. Serve immediately.

VARIATION

VEGAN VARIATION: ***Replace the milk with an equal amount of rice or plain soy milk. Omit the neufchâtel. Instead, buzz 4 ounces silken tofu in a food processor with 1 tablespoon cashew butter and the other seasonings. When the nondairy milk sauce is hot and thick, add it to the food processor and buzz until smooth. Pour the sauce over the broccoli and reheat briefly.***

Norma and Powell's Glorious Garlic and Walnut Sauce for Broccoli

This is an enormously delicious, gratifyingly indulgent sauce for almost any vegetable, but it's especially swoon-worthy spooned over tender, steamed broccoli. Invented by my friend Norma, and Powell, her longtime Barbados-born cook, it's comprised of chopped walnuts sautéed with butter or olive oil and a lot of garlic. It is for dishes like this—rich as all get-out and worth every bite—that I have sometimes described my cooking style as "fat-conscious, not fat-phobic," which leaves room for the occasional exception to the rule. Of course you could just have a *little* bit—but if so, you're made of stronger stuff than I.

It's important that the walnuts be chopped, but not too finely—they must retain some texture. And butter or olive oil? It depends what else you're serving with the meal. **SERVES 4**

About ¼ cup olive oil, butter, or Better (page 905)

3 to 5 large cloves garlic, peeled and very thinly sliced

⅓ cup walnuts, chopped to the size of large crumbs

1 Heat the oil (or butter) in a small skillet over medium-high heat. Add the garlic and cook, stirring constantly, until the garlic is deeply golden brown, but not burned. Assuming your oil is good and hot, this will be 30 seconds or less. Watch it carefully.

2 Add the walnuts and cook, stirring constantly, until the walnuts also brown just a little, and get infused with the garlicky oil, about more 2 minutes.

3 Pour the hot sauce over hot steamed broccoli, adding a little extra oil if needed.

Broccoli Rabe

Broccoli rabe is sometimes called broccoli raab or broccoli rape or or broccolini or, when young and tender and not yet matured to the flowering stage, rapini. Whatever you call it, it looks like it can't make up its mind. Are its small (pencil-width) stems and petite many-leafed flowering heads aspiring to scale up to full-size broccoli, or down to turnip greens? The truth is somewhere in between. This Mediterranean-native brassica, which dates from prehistoric times, is most likely the wild plant from which conventional broccoli was domesticated.

Broccoli rabe certainly tastes less tame than broccoli. It is perhaps the most tonic of the brassicas; thin stalks with leafy, addictively bitter-peppery greens and buds, often sautéed with garlic and olive oil, not infrequently appear in soups and stews, or ladled over pastas or good peasant bread. Because its flavor is so assertive, Italians frequently pair it with equally gutsy ingredients: garlic, red pepper flakes, and olives. However, sometimes its bitterness is played off something tender or sweet: creamily bland beans or meltingly soft caramelized onions.

You'll most likely find broccoli rabe in fall, winter, or early spring, as it's a cool-weather crop. Choose bunches with thin, vigorous-looking stems. The buds should be all green with no yellow flowers.

To prepare for cooking, trim and discard any thick, tough stalks, since they'll be woody. Although some peel the thinner stalks, I don't, preferring the crisper texture this gives the finished dish. Broccoli rabe is frequently a bit sandy, so swish it around in a sink or bowl full of warm water, rinse well with cold water, then drain it.

To precook or not to precook: Depending on how you like to work with broccoli rabe's intense flavors, you have two choices. You can either steam-wilt it directly in olive oil, tomato sauce, white wine, or broth, a method that allows its characteristic bitter-pepperiness to be present in full force. Or you can blanch it in salted water, then sauté it. This leaches out some of the bitterness (as well as some of the nutrients), and is the most common practice in Italy though often some of the cooking water is then added to the dish. Here are recipes showing each method.

Basic Garlic-Braised Broccoli Rabe

This is one of the classic preparation methods for broccoli rabe. If you see the vegetable offered as a side dish in an Italian restaurant, this is the way it'll be fixed. It's not blanched, retaining its bite as it is sauté-steamed slowly, cooking to true tenderness. Use this as a side dish with any red-sauced pasta and maybe some sautéed Italian-seasoned soysage). Do also try the fra diavolo—"in the style of the devil"—variation that follows.

You'll need a deep sauté pan, large enough to accommodate all of the rabe before it cooks down, with a tight-fitting lid. **SERVES 4**

1 to 2 tablespoons olive oil
2 cloves garlic, flattened with the side of a knife and coarsely chopped
1½ to 2 medium bunches broccoli rabe (about 1 pound), washed and trimmed
Salt to taste

1 Heat the oil in a large nonstick skillet over medium heat. Add the garlic and cook, stirring, until it starts to soften and become fragrant, but has not colored, 3 to 5 minutes.

VARIATION

BROCCOLI RABE FRA DIAVOLO: ***To dress this up most pleasingly, sauté a small dried red chile pepper—½ chile, if you're shy about things devilish—along with the garlic, and then, at the end, add a few tablespoons of niçoise olives, coarsely chopped. I am most happy to eat this tossed with hot pasta, a little raw pressed garlic, and the teeniest drizzle of olive oil.***

2 Between stirs of the garlic, give the broccoli rabe a good rinse under cold water, and then add it to the skillet, drops of water still sparkling on its leaves. Pop the lid on the skillet, and cook for about 5 minutes. Lift the lid, give a stir or two, and lower the heat to medium-low. Replace the lid, and cook until tender, another 15 to 20 minutes, lifting the lid occasionally to make sure that all the liquid has not evaporated. If it has, add a few tablespoons water.

3 Add salt to taste and serve.

COOK ONCE FOR 2 MEALS Fix a double recipe. Eat half of the rabe hot; refrigerate the rest. To serve, remove the cooked rabe from the fridge and bring it almost to room temperature—slightly chilled but not cold. Drizzle with a bit of olive oil, and squeeze the juice of half a lemon over it. Serve as a starter, part of a *mezze* plate, or in lieu of a salad.

Broccoli Rabe and Chickpea Peasant Supper

This is my own quick(er) take on an Italian dish, traditionally made of slow-cooked fava beans pureed with aromatics, then topped with a tangle of garlic-infused broccoli rabe. The smooth, sweet nuttiness of the beans is quietly awesome against the rabe's bitter-pepperiness, one of those earthy, ancient, Mediterranean-style dishes. It could be served any number of ways: room temperature, as part of a starter course; warm, on rounds of grilled or toasted bread or polenta to make crostini; hot, on pasta. Here, I use it as a sort of stew or sauce, so thick you eat it with a fork, over rustic bread, big rough slices honeycombed with holes to absorb the good flavors.

The rabe is precooked before being sautéed. This means that even though it still has bite, it is slightly tamed. **SERVES 4 TO 6**

3 tablespoons olive oil, plus additional
2 stalks celery with leaves, diced
1 carrot, scrubbed and diced
1 onion, chopped
1 bay leaf
2 cans (31 ounces total) chickpeas
Salt, preferably sea salt, to taste
Water, preferably spring or filtered
1½ to 2 medium bunches broccoli rabe (about 1 pound), washed and trimmed, chopped into 2½-inch pieces
2 cloves garlic, coarsely chopped
4 to 6 large slices porous country bread
Red chile flakes (optional)

1 Heat 1½ tablespoons oil in a large skillet over medium heat. Add the celery, carrot, and onion and sauté for 3 minutes. Add the bay leaf and sauté until the vegetables soften slightly but are not browned, about 5 additional minutes.

2 Drain the chickpeas, reserving the liquid. Add the bean liquid to the skillet and place the beans in a food processor. Lower the heat under the skillet to a simmer. Cover and cook for 15 minutes. Remove the bay leaf, and scrape the mixture into the food processor. Process until very smooth, pausing to scrape down the sides of the bowl. Add salt to taste, and, if desired, a little more olive oil. Keep the mixture warm.

3 Meanwhile, bring a 5-quart pot of water to a boil over high heat. Add 1½ tablespoons salt. Drop in the broccoli rabe. The water should not stop boiling—now you see why you needed so much!—and cook until tender, 5 to 6 minutes. Drain well.

4 Heat 1½ tablespoons oil in a skillet over medium-low heat. Add the garlic and slowly sauté it until it is soft and just starting to color, about 4 minutes. Add the broccoli rabe, tossing to coat. Turn off the heat.

5 Place a slice of bread on each of the dinner plates. Spoon the warm chickpea puree over each slice, spreading to cover the bread completely. Divide the broccoli rabe among the plates, a snaggle of greens atop each portion of beans and bread. Serve immediately. If desired, pass additional oil or dried red chile flakes at the table.

Pasta Sauced with Broccoli Rabe

I cannot resist including this unusual and captivating pasta–broccoli rabe dish, my vegetarian version of a recipe in Faith Willinger's *Red, White, and Greens.* I love the fact that the rabe is blanched, then the pasta is partially cooked in that same cooking water, which is then used to finish the sauce in which the pasta will finish cooking. Rabe to the nth degree!

The original offers the options of added salt pork or anchovy; I know traditionalists would say, "Just omit it, Crescent, and it'll be fine," and of course you can, and it is. But we like this at our house with a bit of sautéed tempeh "bacon"; the smoky-saltiness is a good flavor component. **SERVES 3 OR 4 AS AN ENTREE, 4 TO 6 AS A STARTER**

Water, preferably spring or filtered
3 tablespoons coarse sea salt, or 1½ tablespoons fine sea salt
1½ medium bunches (about 1 pound) broccoli rabe, trimmed and washed
3 tablespoons olive oil
4 slices tempeh "bacon" strips
3 cloves garlic, coarsely chopped
1 small fresh hot chile pepper, or dried red chile flakes to taste
1 pound penne, ditalini, or ziti (short, fat, tubular pasta)

1 Bring a 7-quart pot of water to a boil over high heat. Add the salt. Drop in the broccoli rabe and cook until tender, 5 to 6 minutes. Drain, reserving the cooking water. (Faith recommends just scooping the broccoli rabe out with a slotted spoon so the water stays in its original pot, but if you have a second big pot you can just put a colander over it and drain the rabe cooking water into it.) Rinse the cooked broccoli rabe in cold water and drain well.

2 Chop the broccoli rabe into bite-sized pieces. Set about two-thirds of the chopped broccoli rabe aside; puree the remainder (including any of the larger pieces of stem) in a food processor. Combine the puree with the reserved chopped broccoli rabe.

3 Heat 1 tablespoon of the oil in a large skillet over medium heat. When good and hot, add the tempeh strips. Cook until browned on one side, about 3 minutes; turn and fry the second side until brown, about 2 minutes. Remove the tempeh from the skillet and let cool. When cool, cut into ½-inch dice. Set aside.

4 Add the remaining oil to the skillet. Lower the heat slightly and add the garlic and chile. Slowly sauté until the garlic is soft and just starting to color, about 4 minutes. Add the greens—both pureed and chopped—tossing them in the oil and garlic for about 2 minutes. Remove from the heat and set aside.

5 Add 3 cups cold water to the rabe cooking water. Bring to a boil over high heat. Add the pasta and cook for about three-quarters of the time suggested on the package. Drain the pasta, reserving 2 cups of the cooking water.

6 Combine the cooked pasta and 1 cup of the cooking water with the broccoli rabe mixture in the pasta cooking pot. Place over high heat and bring to a boil. Lower the heat just a little and cook until the pasta is tender, adding additional cooking water, ¼ cup at a time, as needed to keep the pasta from drying out, another 3 to 5 minutes. An instant before you are ready to serve, add the reserved diced tempeh, and toss to combine. Serve immediately.

Brussels Sprouts

Brussels sprouts, available throughout the winter months, are adorable—tiny doll-sized cabbages—but often overcooked, served up sodden and sulfurous.

When purchasing, squeeze the sprouts. They should be firm and tightly balled, with few or no yellow leaves. One to 1½ pounds sprouts will yield 4 to 6 servings.

To prepare for cooking, cut off the stems close to the leaves. Pull off any loose or yellowed leaves, but detach as few leaves as possible when cutting away the stems. Cutting an X about ⅜ inch deep on the stem end of each sprout ensures even and quick cooking time; you can, however, halve the sprouts instead.

If precooking is desired, blanch, as for broccoli (see page 707) for 4 to 6 minutes; sprouts can also be used raw in many recipes.

Basic finishes can be as for broccoli (try Norma and Powell's Glorious Garlic and Walnut Sauce, page 709). Or stir-fry blanched sprouts in a nonstick pan with a smidgen of butter, with a handful of minced Italian parsley and, perhaps, with a little Garlic Oil tossed in before serving. Brussels sprouts are surprisingly good with a little lemon juice, grated orange zest, orange juice, a splash of tamari, and a tad of sugar and butter. Sear the citrused sprouts in a hot skillet sprayed with cooking spray, over medium-high heat until they start to stick. Serve piping hot.

Brussels Sprouts Noël, with Red Bell Peppers and Potato Sauce

This is a recipe, inspired by one in *Laurel's Kitchen,* that I return to time and again. It's "Noël" because its combines bright green and red, and its ingredients are in season just before and after the winter holidays. The sprouts are not blanched here, but the potato—mashed with the cooking liquid to make a savory sauce—is cooked beforehand. Nice on a component plate, with a big baked yam, some edamame (see page 626), and grilled or baked eggplant. **SERVES 4**

2⅓ cups vegetable stock (see page 139)
1 medium potato, peeled and cut into ½-inch dice
1 teaspoon vegetable oil
1 bay leaf
½ large onion, sliced vertically into thin crescents
1 red bell pepper, stemmed, seeded, and cut vertically into ½-inch strips
1½ pounds (about 6 cups) Brussels sprouts, prepared for cooking (see page 715)
Salt and freshly ground black pepper to taste
1 teaspoon butter, Better (page 905), or, for vegans, soy margarine (optional)

1 Place 2 cups of the stock in a small saucepan over high heat. Bring to a boil. Add the potato and cook until soft, about 10 minutes. While the potato cooks, proceed with the recipe.

2 Place the oil and bay leaf in a large nonstick sauté pan over medium heat. When hot, add the onion and sauté until soft and translucent, about 5 minutes. Add the bell pepper and sauté for 15 seconds. Add the Brussels sprouts and the remaining ⅓ cup stock. Pop a cover on the pan and steam until just tender, lifting occasionally to stir things around and check for doneness, 6 to 8 minutes.

3 Drain the potatoes, reserving the drained-off stock for another purpose (soup, sauce, grain- or bean-cooking water), if desired. Place the potatoes in a small bowl. Set aside.

4 Keeping the lid on the skillet, drain most of the liquid from the red pepper–Brussels sprout mixture into the potatoes. (The reason you are using this stock, rather than that in which the potatoes cooked, is that the skillet stock will have picked up some of the good flavor of the onion, red pepper, and sprouts, and will therefore underline these flavors in the sauce.) Mash the potatoes together with the stock, a little salt and pepper to taste, and the butter, if using.

5 Remove the bay leaf from the vegetables. Stir the mashed potato sauce into the vegetables and serve at once.

"Records indicate that Belgian markets had Brussels sprouts around 1213. They were grown in America in 1806, and to build up the market for the miniature cabbages, a New York produce manager interested the circus midget 'Tom Thumb' in the new vegetable, and for a time the sprouts were called 'Tom Thumb Cabbages.' Being a cool weather vegetable, the miniature cabbages mature in fall and seem to taste better after a touch of frost."

—**Louis P. De Gouy,** *The Gold Cook Book*

Cabbage, Savoy Cabbage, Red Cabbage, and Bok Choy

Certain plain-Jane, overlooked vegetables can—if you take them to the ball—turn into Cinderella. Such a vegetable is cabbage, red, green, or Savoy. With a stodgy reputation and an inexpensive price tag, oft-slighted cabbages are healthful, and can be easily coaxed into revealing their truly delicious nature. But freshness is everything. Even the most prosaic head of cabbage, if garden fresh and cooked attentively, is surprisingly sweet.

Purchase tight, firm heads, although a few wide-open outer leaves, attached at the base, are fine. The outer leaves of green cabbage should be a more intense gray-green; the inner, a pale Luna-moth green. What you don't want is yellow outer leaves, or an outer layer that is very pale—this indicates cabbage with so many leaves stripped away that it has obviously been around for ages, with the produce guys stripping off the outer leaves. A cabbage that is too old becomes harsh and vaguely mustardy in flavor and loses all the sweetness it once possessed. Red cabbage, which is actually more purple, should likewise come in tight, firm heads, and be free of yellowed outer leaves. Savoy cabbage, which has beautifully crumpled, wavy leaves, is very beautiful and a tad sweeter than ordinary green cabbage—look for a fresh, pale, crisp green, with no sign of wilting. Bok choy, or Chinese cabbage, is the cabbage with a split personality. It looks more like a tight cluster of fat white celery stalks with intensely green leaves topping and edging the white part. Look for bok choy that looks lively, not wilted.

One head of cabbage will yield 8 to 10 servings when cooked as a component; thus for home use I'll generally employ maybe half the cabbage in a stir-fry or other cooked dish, reserving the rest to use raw in salad or slaw.

Precut sliced cabbage, either plain or with shredded carrots and a little sliced red cabbage, is one of the newly available supermarket offerings. All precut vegetables should be used quickly, but sliced cabbage keeps much better than some other precuts, and really is handy for stir-fries and slaw. Speaking of which, the precut "stir-fry mixes" are usually mostly bok choy: they're overpriced, since bok choy is cheap, but they also keep pretty well.

To prepare green, red, or Savoy cabbage for cooking, the core is usually removed. You can do this the hard way by cutting around the core in a slanted, circular motion, and then easing out the cone-shaped wedge of core; or slice the cabbage in 4 large cuts around the core, thus boxing off the core, which you then discard, leaving you 4 large wedges of cabbage to slice for sautés or whatever. The latter is the much easier way to go.

To prepare bok choy for cooking, you can slice off the base, discard it, and then simply slice the leaves and ribs crosswise, to make strips to sauté. But one of its charms lies in exploiting its dual nature. Its leaves can be cut off at the stem and treated as one of the Greens Gang (page 755); and its white stalk diced and used in lieu of celery, which is frequently one of the more heavily insecticide-sprayed food crops.

I almost never blanch cabbage, since that is the quickest way to sulfur-smelliness with the exception of blanching whole leaves for Middle European–Style Stuffed Cabbage-Leaf Rolls (page 392). Cabbage recipes in other sections of the book that you might want to try out are Pumpkin Bean Lasagna with Caramelized Garlic (page 367), Crunch Salad (page 79), Cora Pinkley Call's Ozark "Sour Cream" Salad (page 85), Cascabel Salad of Grilled and Raw Vegetables (page 88), Cora Pinkley Call's Ozark-Style Stuffed Tomato Salad (page 91), Pineapple-Jícama Salad with Purple Cabbage and Baby Spinach (page 95), Orange, Grapefruit, and Avocado Salad with Jerusalem Artichokes (page 98), and "Hot Thai in the Old Town Tonight" Noodle-Tofu Salad (page 119).

Cabbage and Greens with Kidney Beans and Caramelized Garlic

This is a dazzling example of how the right ingredients and techniques can make the most down-home ingredients astronomically good. Greens, beans, and garlic together have long been my quick-fix preparation over pasta, but with the technique given for garlic-sautéed cabbage in Lynn Rosetto Kasper's *The Splendid Table,* my tried-and-true combo became splendid. Dicing the garlic into relatively large pieces and then slowly caramelizing it, creating a richly flavored sauté-oil as well as caramelized garlic, makes all the difference; the garlic ends up melting, pale gold, soft, and sweetened with its soul intact. This process takes about 8 minutes. Although requiring the addition of a little more olive oil than I customarily use, the extraordinary results are worth it. The olive oil adds its own inimitable flavor and also a waft of the garlic that has been slowly caramelized in it. This is why you really need at least a full tablespoon of olive oil (and two is better). **SERVES 4 TO 6**

½ head green cabbage, sliced into ribbons
1 to 2 tablespoons olive oil
5 to 7 cloves garlic, halved, any green core removed, cut into ¼-inch pieces (about 2 tablespoons)
2 bunches hearty greens (one bunch each of any two of the following: kale, collard, turnip, escarole, or mustard) washed, patted dry, and sliced into thin ribbons
2 cups cooked kidney beans, well drained
Salt and freshly ground black pepper to taste
8 to 12 slices "set-up" polenta, commercial or from scratch (page 442)
¼ to ⅔ cup freshly grated Parmesan cheese (optional)
⅓ pound ricotta salata (optional)

1 Steam the cabbage ribbons in a steamer over boiling water until just wilted, 1 to 2 minutes. Drain well and pat dry.

2 Heat the oil in a nonstick skillet over the lowest heat you can get without the flame blowing out. Add the garlic and

slowly and attentively cook, stirring quite often, until the garlic is an even pale golden, which will take about 8 minutes. Don't let it brown, or it will be bitter. Using a slotted spoon, remove the golden garlic from the pan and set it aside, leaving the oil in the pan.

3 Raise the heat to medium. When the oil is very hot, add the raw greens along with the cabbage and stir like heck, lowering the heat slightly. Cover the skillet to steam the greens just slightly, about 1 minute. Remove the cover and raise the heat a bit. Continue stir-frying until the greens are limp and some of the cabbage edges are starting to color, about 10 minutes. Remove from the heat. Add the beans and garlic and season with salt and pepper to taste. Serve over polenta with cheese.

Cabbage T'horin

In Kerala, the province in South India whose name means "Land of the Coconut Palms," almost everything contains coconut. Eaten almost daily at the large noon meal in Kerala, this mild dish brings out the natural sweetness of cabbage. T'horin is sometimes made from other vegetables, most notably green beans, but cabbage is the most popular base. Sometimes grated carrot is added with the mustard seeds, and of course freshly grated coconut—a lot of it—is used there. But it also works quite well with a lesser amount of the dried. Make sure that your knife is sharp and your cutting board (or food processor) is at the ready, for the cabbage must be finely chopped. As part of a component dinner, serve with rice and a simple salad of chopped tomatoes, onions, cucumber, salt, and a squeeze of lime. **SERVES 4 TO 6 AS A COMPONENT**

2 teaspoons mild vegetable oil, such as corn, canola, or peanut
1 onion, chopped
1 tablespoon black or brown mustard seeds
2 teaspoons sweet paprika
1 small head cabbage (about 1 pound), core removed, finely chopped into pieces no larger than ¼ inch on their longest side, preferably smaller
¼ teaspoon salt
2 to 3 tablespoons water, preferably spring or filtered
⅓ cup dry unsweetened coconut flakes (available at natural foods stores)

1 Heat the oil in a nonstick skillet over medium-high heat. Add the onion and sauté until softened, about 4 minutes. Add the mustard seeds and cook, shaking the pan often, until the mustard seeds begin to pop, about 3 minutes. Add the paprika and stir for 20 seconds.

2 Add the cabbage and stir well to combine and slightly sear the cabbage. After 20 seconds, add the salt, along with 2 tablespoons water, cover the skillet, lower the heat to medium-low, and cook, lifting the lid to stir now and then, and adding the extra tablespoon of water if needed, 6 to 8 minutes, until the cabbage is tender. (The dish should be dry—no liquid at all in the pan—though the cabbage will be moist.) Remove from the heat and stir in the coconut. Serve hot or at room temperature.

Braised Red Cabbage with Onions and Apples in Red Wine–Cranberry Sauce

A great German cabbage component dish, this is the best sweet and sour cabbage, tender and full of flavor, vividly colored, I have ever tasted—and I've had many versions. It will even blow away sworn red cabbage haters, most of whom were probably justified in their hatred since this poor brassica is usually subjected to mistreatment. It would seem inherently wintry—but is so pleasing I've made it during the summer and spring (try it with fresh asparagus and coarse yellow corn grits—yum). It's also excellent with potato dishes, and pleasing served with the Savory Indian Harvest Corn–Wild Rice Cakes (page 828) or Suppertime Vegetable Corn Pancakes (page 630).

Jellied cranberry sauce is the secret ingredient. The truly German version uses currant jelly, but it's harder to find and more expensive. **SERVES 6 TO 8**

1½ teaspoons butter
1 to 2 tart apples, such as Winesaps, peeled, cored, and chopped
1 small onion, chopped
1 tablespoon plus 1 teaspoon brown sugar or Rapidura
½ head red cabbage (about 1 pound), trimmed, cored, and thinly sliced
¼ cup red wine vinegar
¾ cup any good vegetable stock (Oven-Roasted Vegetable Stock, page 141, is especially good here)
¾ cup dry red wine, such as a northern Rhône
1 tablespoon plus 1 teaspoon unbleached white all-purpose flour
2 to 3 tablespoons jellied cranberry sauce
Salt and freshly ground black pepper to taste

1 Melt the butter in a large, deep skillet or Dutch oven over medium heat. Add the apples, onion, and brown sugar and sauté until the onions are fairly limp, about 5 minutes. Add the cabbage and sauté for another 5 minutes.

Add the vinegar and then ½ cup of the stock. Bring to a boil. Immediately lower the heat to a simmer. Cover and simmer until the cabbage is tender but still has a bit of crispness, 25 to 30 minutes. Uncover and add the wine. Raise the heat and bring to a boil.

2 In a small bowl, whisk the cranberry sauce and flour into the remaining ¼ cup stock. When the liquid is boiling, stir in the flour-stock mixture. Lower the heat slightly, and simmer, stirring often, for another 5 minutes. Season to taste with salt and pepper and serve.

Cabbage State

Although we think of red cabbage as a fundamentally German dish, it was also beloved of the Pennsylvania Dutch, who, despite their name, were originally from Germany. Soups, dumplings, pies and cakes, and doughnuts, and most especially pickles and preserves, were part of Pennsylvania Dutch tables, and an important meal (like a Sunday dinner) was said to virtually require the presence of "seven sweets and seven sours." Cabbage prepared as in this recipe, though unpickled, met the taste for both, and is said to have been a great favorite of President James Buchanan. Although known for his love of high-falutin' French cuisine, he could not turn his back on the homier dishes of his native Pennsylvania.

Rose's Cabbage Rose

From my friend Rose Agostini of Dallas, whose cooking is pared-down, healthful, and delicious. Her brilliant decorative sense, and bird-bright visual imagination—she decorates interiors and parties professionally, as well as her own stunning and much-photographed homes—comes out in her food. For instance, she'd serve this gorgeous red-purple cabbage with a side of bright orange sweet potatoes, perhaps simply baked. Add a veggie burger—one of those from Savory Cakes, Burgers & Patties (Chapter 12) with sliced tomato, and you have a dinner as colorful and tasty as it is good for you. Alternatively, serve with Rose's Golden Millet "Gruel" (page 549).

It may be served hot, cold, or at room temperature. Rose blanches the cabbage in boiling water, but I sometimes steam it—either way, it's quick. You want the cabbage a little crunchy, not overcooked.

Wondering why no salt? Remember, the umeboshi plum vinegar is not just sour but salty, too. **SERVES 4**

Water, preferably spring or filtered
1 head purple cabbage, halved, cored, halved again, and very thinly sliced into long thin strips
1 to 3 tablespoons extra virgin olive oil
1 to 3 tablespoons umeboshi plum vinegar (see page 118)

1 Bring a large pot of water to a boil over high heat. Drop in the cabbage and return the water to a boil. Boil until the cabbage is a bit limp, but still brightly colored and with a little crunch, 2 to 3 minutes. Drain well. If you plan to serve it cold, refresh the cabbage with cold water; otherwise, just put it in a bowl.

2 Starting with 1 tablespoon each of oil and vinegar, dress the cabbage. Toss and taste. Add additional oil and vinegar until it's to your liking. Serve hot, cold, or at room temperature.

Cauliflower

Bouquetlike cauliflower heads should be compact and snowy white or pale green, depending on variety. Choose smaller heads, which tend to be younger and tastier than the large, which incline toward sponginess. Look closely (to do so means avoiding prewrapped supermarket cauliflower; when possible, choose one at a farmer's market or a store with a good produce section)—Yu want lumpy white flower heads that are tightly formed, not granular. To prepare for cooking, cut the buds, with their individual branch of stem, off the core, discarding the core and any leaves. These are cauliflorets, which can be cut or broken into even smaller cauliflorets.

You can buy precut cauliflorets, either solo or teamed with broccoli. (Not my first choice, but better than nothing.) Cauliflower is relatively mild, and while I like it, I don't gravitate toward it nearly as much as I do to broccoli. I occasionally make Millet Mash with Cauliflower (page 551), which uses cauliflower's mildness to make a dish much like mashed potatoes. I also serve it at Thanksgiving with a classic Cheddar cheese–laden béchamel sauce too rich to even consider most of the time. I usually stir-fry it with more assertive and colorful vegetables as part of a mix for serving over pastas.

Thai Sweet-Garlicky Cauliflower with Red Pepper Strips

When cauliflower is quick-cooked with vibrant Thai seasonings, infused with flavor and sweetness and garlickiness, and treated to a touch of color, it is an entirely different vegetable from the sodden white stuff we may recall from childhood. This lively treatment is freely adapted from a Thai sweet and sour pork dish.

Turn this into an entree by adding 4 ounces diced commercial baked savory or Thai-style tofu at the last. This can also be done very nicely with half broccoli and half cauliflower. **SERVES 4 TO 6**

1 tablespoon mild vegetable oil, such as corn, canola, or peanut
1 tablespoon coarsely chopped garlic
½ medium cauliflower, cut into florets
2 tablespoons water, preferably spring or filtered
½ small onion, sliced vertically into crescents
½ red bell pepper, seeded and cut into long, thin strips
½ yellow bell pepper, seeded and cut into long, thin strips
3 tablespoons tamari or shoyu soy sauce
2 tablespoons sugar
Salt to taste

Heat the oil in wok or deep skillet over medium-high heat. When the oil is hot enough to immediately set a chunk of garlic sizzling, it's ready. Drop in all of the garlic and stir-fry until barely golden, about 15 seconds. Add the cauliflower. Add the water and cover. Steam for 30 seconds, then uncover and allow the water to evaporate without stirring. When the pan is almost dry and the cauliflower is tender, add the onion, bell pepper, tamari, and sugar. Toss to combine well. Taste, and, if necessary, add salt. Serve hot.

Kohlrabi

Kohlrabi looks sort of tuber-ish, but it grows above ground. In our restaurant days, one of our prep cooks used to call it "the vegetable from another planet," and would say things like, "Oh, look in the walk-in. Audrey got you some UVOs" (unidentified vegetable objects).

A different perspective is offered by Louis P. De Gouy, a passionate chef who wrote, in his 1947 *The Gold Cook Book,* "Kohlrabi, stepchild of the vegetable garden, can go to town as brilliantly as a Cinderella. Caught in tender youth [it is] bursting with flavory virtue." Kohlrabi's flavor is plain, mild, tasty but innocuous, and it looks unprepossessing on the plate. Still, because it's so rarely served, it's interesting once in a while—most people will be intrigued trying to guess what it is.

Kohlrabi has toughish pale green outer skin and a creamy white interior: round, about the size of a fist, with little ridges to which leaves may still be attached. Choose the smallest ones available; they'll be the youngest and most tender. You can probably count on 2 or 3 servings from each kohlrabi, unless they're really small.

To prepare for cooking, remove any leaves or upright stems. You may peel the globe, or simply leave it as is. Slice thinly and steam for 4 to 5 minutes. Toss with a tiny squib of butter, salt, and freshly ground black pepper or a bit of Garlic Oil (page 898) and some minced Italian parsley. Cooked in this manner, the skin can be tender enough to eat.

"Good cooking was a way of life and enjoyment. You did not save time but spent it recklessly, proudly, and with a full reward inside those four spotless walls."

—**Edward Harris Heth,** *The Wonderful World of Cooking*

Dairy Hollow House Kohlrabi Pudding

We always had at least one or two unusual items on the side vegetable plates that we sent out with entrees in the restaurant years. (I would have been disappointed had no inn guests asked, when I made the rounds of the dining room, "What did I eat on the vegetable plate?") One frequent member of the vegetable plate was some form of pudding or timbale, often made of kohlrabi.

The yield given is approximate. The 4 to 6 serving range means generous-sized portions, but if you're using a small square on a plate with other things, count on getting double the number of servings. In the larger size, this could be an entree. Serve it with a light tomato sauce, a baked yam, and a green salad to start, or serve it with a green stir-fry. When used as a component dish, skip the sauce.

SERVES 4 TO 6

Cooking spray
2 to 3 small kohlrabi, stem, root and ends trimmed, peeled and quartered
2 large eggs
4 ounces neufchâtel reduced-fat cream cheese, softened to room temperature
½ cup low-fat milk, buttermilk, yogurt, light sour cream, oat or rice milk, or, if feeling devil-may-care and you have it on hand, half-and-half or heavy cream
¼ cup cornstarch
1 teaspoon Pickapeppa sauce
1 teaspoon salt
3 or 4 gratings of nutmeg
Freshly ground black pepper to taste
¾ cup (6 ounces) finely grated Parmesan cheese

1 Preheat the oven to 375°F.

2 Spray a 9-inch square baking dish or six individual 6-ounce ramekins with cooking spray. Set aside.

3 Bring a large pot of water to a boil over high heat. Add the kohlrabi and cook until slightly softened, 3 to 5 minutes. Place in a food processor and puree. Measure out 3 cups of the puree, saving leftovers for another use (such as a chilled soup). Set the puree aside.

4 Place the eggs with the neufchâtel, milk, cornstarch, Pickapeppa, salt, nutmeg, and pepper in the food processor. Buzz until very smooth. Add the 3 cups puree and half of the Parmesan and buzz to incorporate. Taste and, if necessary season with more pepper.

5 Pour the pudding mixture into the prepared baking dish or into the individual ramekins. Place the dish or ramekins in a larger pan with hot water to come ½ inch up the sides of the dish or ramekins. Place the pan in the preheated oven and bake for 30 minutes.

6 Remove from the oven and sprinkle the remaining Parmesan over the top. Return to the oven and continue baking until the cheese is melted and golden and the pudding is firm, browned, and does not stick to your finger when you touch its surface, another 20 to 30 minutes. Serve, hot or warm, cut into squares or inverted out of the ramekins.

VARIATION

VEGAN KOHLRABI PUDDING: ***Substitute plain soy milk for dairy, soy cream cheese for neufchâtel, and rice parmesan-style cheese for dairy.***

Turnips

Let me say this upfront: I am not a turnip fan. To me, the mustardiness of the brassica family is seen in turnips in an unpleasing manner, though I've learned to love turnip greens (see the Greens Gang section, page 755), and, when really fresh, one can hardly deny the visual charm of these creamy white globes with a blush of magenta-rose. But I have found two turnip preparations I've learned, if not to love, to like—a good thing, since I happen to love a turnip-lover.

At the market, choose tiny, round baby turnips, not much bigger than a marble—with a diameter no larger than a quarter, and preferably with the stems still attached. Allow 1 to 4 baby turnips per person for a component dish. For larger turnips, seek out ones the size of a small fist, but make sure they're fresh and haven't been sitting around in cold storage for months. The optimum time to find really fresh turnips is the end of summer through fall at a farmer's market. You'll know them because the skin looks filled out and unwrinkled, and if you poke at 'em, they're hard, without any give. A surreptitious fingernail in the flesh will tell you much; if they're juicy and crisp, you've got a live one. Allow 2 to 3 servings from each of these larger turnips, unless you happen to be cooking for major turnip freaks.

Baby Turnips

Nothing could be simpler or cuter than these tiny turnips, still bedecked with tiny flaglike greens.

The turnipness is muted in the vegetable's youth, yet there is enough present to please those who savor the taste. A bunch in this case means 12 to 16 small turnips, ideally marble-sized but at least smaller than your average radish. **SERVES 4**

Water, preferably spring or filtered
Salt
1 bunch baby turnips, greens still attached, very well washed and scrubbed
Cooking spray
2 teaspoons butter
1 teaspoon honey
Freshly ground black pepper to taste

1 Bring a large pot of lightly salted water to a vigorous boil over high heat. Add the turnips and blanch for 3 to 4 minutes. Drain and rinse under cold running water. Pat dry.

2 Spray a small sauté pan with cooking spray and place it over medium heat. Add the butter. When the butter has melted and the pan is quite hot, add the turnips and toss them around. You want just enough butter to shine their pretty little skins. Add the honey with a touch of salt and a little pepper. Toss to coat. Serve hot, as a side vegetable or part of a component plate.

Jerry Stamps and Chou Chou's Collaborative Glazed Turnips

In every one of my Eureka Springs cookbooks, there has been at least one recipe from Jerry Stamps, for many years Carroll County's best-loved pharmacist and an all-around sweetheart; the kindest of men, with the most delightfully wicked laugh. I am happy to continue this tradition, though Jerry is gone from this earth now; I got this recipe from him many, many years back, when he and my friend Chou Chou hung out a lot together. **SERVES 4 TO 6 AS A COMPONENT**

6 to 8 fresh turnips, the size of a small fist, scrubbed, tops and tails removed, cut into chunks
Water, preferably spring or filtered
1 unsalted broth cube, crumbled, plus 1½ cups additional water, or 1 cup vegetable stock (see page 139)
2 teaspoons butter, or more to taste
1 to 2 teaspoons honey
½ teaspoon tamari or shoyu soy sauce
Dash or two of cayenne
Salt and freshly ground black pepper to taste

Place the turnips in a medium saucepan, and just barely cover with cold water. Bring to a boil over high heat, then immediately drain. Repeat, but instead of draining, add the broth cube and additional liquid, the butter, honey, tamari, cayenne, and salt and pepper. (My original notes say, "butter—'plenty of butter' says Jerry, 'I use a whole lot,' says Chou Chou.") Bring to a simmer and cook, uncovered, until the turnips are very tender, about 15 minutes. Serve with cornbread, "to sop up all that good juice," as Jerry said at the time.

Carrots

Red-orange, high in natural sugars, vitamin A, and beta-carotene, carrots—a member of the same botanical family as parsley (and, incidentally, Queen Anne's lace and hemlock), the Umbelliferae—are equally friendly to the stew-maker and the dieter. I more often use them in things than on their own, yet carrots also make a splendid component. At the inn, we used them in side vegetable plates, often in Roasty-Toasty Potatoes, Carrots, and Onions (page 790), but also frequently julienned, quick-blanched, and stir-fried with a sweet or aromatic finish. Carrots are often paired with something sweet, like maple syrup or apple cider, to point up their natural sweetness. They're very good this way—but a whole other dimension appears when they're given a piquant conclusion: a minced herb like dill or parsley, or the seasonings the Moroccans use in a grated carrot salad—cumin, paprika, and cayenne—spicy, surprising, and just remarkably good.

"The day is coming when a single carrot, freshly observed, will set off a revolution."

—Paul Cézanne

Carrots are one of the easier vegetables to find organically raised, and are almost always notably sweet. But conventionally grown carrots are now available in all kinds of precut shapes and sizes, much appreciated by the time-pressed. Sometimes you can buy carrots, organic or otherwise, with the fresh green tops still attached, but interestingly, the presence of tops seems to make no difference in the sweetness or freshness of the carrot. Of course you want the freshest carrot possible, but the only way to tell is to take a bite, behavior guaranteed not to endear you with the produce manager (and where do you wash it?). About the closest you can come is by touch. Take the carrot in both hands as if to snap it in two. If it bends, forget it. You want it to resist breaking—and if you did break it, it would be a chore to do so and the carrot would resist and then *snap* forcefully and firmly. If a carrot is so old that you can tell it by looking—it appears limp, wrinkled, or soft in spots—it's so far gone it deserves to be put in the compost pile.

To prepare for cooking, simply wash or scrub the carrots; peel them if required in a specific recipe or if the skin seems particularly tough. Remove the stem end. (Whole baby carrots never need peeling; their skin is always tender.) Cut into whatever shape the recipe requires.

I frequently blanch or steam carrots to not quite tender-crispness prior to finishing them with a bit of something good. This precooking can be done in advance, making the last-minute service practically instant. *Julienned carrots* need only a 3- to 4-minute steam, *sliced carrots or the 1-inch-long precuts* with rounded edges, 4 to 7 (see the delicious Gingered Stir-Fry of Snow Peas, and Carrots, page 698). *Whole carrots* for roasty-toasties (page 790) get a 4- to 6-minute blanch, but then they bake for a long, long time thereafter; if I were planning to merely sauté and glaze whole carrots post-steaming, I'd go for 10 minutes.

The second carrots come out of the steamer or blanching water, quickly drain them and douse them with cold water. Drain again, and set aside (refrigerated, if it's going to be longer than 30 minutes or so) until ready to finish. After such a quick blanch, there are countless carrot options.

Maple-Glazed Carrots

Simple, and pleasing with almost any entree, except those with a sweet sauce, this side dish is especially welcome in fall meals. **SERVES 4 TO 6 AS A COMPONENT**

1½ teaspoons butter, vegetable margarine, or mild vegetable oil, such as corn or canola
1 pound carrots, trimmed, scrubbed, julienned, and blanched (see opposite page)
3 tablespoons maple syrup
Pinch of salt

1 Place a large sauté pan over medium-high heat. Add the butter. When the butter is very hot, add the carrots.

2 Sauté until the carrots are hot and a few are coloring slightly, about 1 minute. Drizzle with the maple syrup and add a pinch of salt.

3 Cook, stirring constantly, until the syrup cooks down a bit and the carrots are coated in a sticky glaze, 2 to 3 minutes. Serve immediately.

Honey-Orange Glazed Carrots

Another sweet, quick, lovable carrot dish. This one has a bit of zing from the citrus. Whenever I made this (or Brown Sugar–Glazed Beets with Fresh Kumquats, page 704) in the restaurant, it always drew raves and recipe requests. Remember, citrus is an excellent note in many simple vegetable preparations.

SERVES 4 TO 6 AS A COMPONENT

1 orange
Cooking spray
1½ teaspoons butter, vegetable margarine, or mild vegetable oil, such as corn or canola
1 pound carrots, trimmed, scrubbed, julienned, and blanched (see opposite page)
2 tablespoons honey
Pinch of salt

VARIATION

Intensify the citrus flavor by adding 1 tablespoon orange marmalade along with the honey and juice.

1 Finely grate the rind of the orange. Scrape the grated rind into a cup. Juice the orange into the same cup, squeezing out every available drop of juice, but removing the seeds. Set aside.

2 Place a large sauté pan over medium-high heat. Add the butter. When the butter is very hot, add the carrots.

3 Sauté until the carrots are hot and a few are coloring slightly, about 1 minute. Drizzle with the honey. Add the juice-zest mixture and a pinch of salt.

4 Cook, stirring constantly, until the juice and honey have cooked down to a delicious glaze, about 3 minutes. Serve immediately.

Ginger-Glazed Carrots

VARIATION

After the glaze has formed, immediately before serving, toss in 1 tablespoon finely chopped cilantro.

These may just be my favorite of all sweet-glazed carrots, for they add the sass and sparkle of fresh ginger, with its exotic touch of heat. This was another one about which restaurant guests used to ask me, "And what *did* you put on those carrots? They were so good, but I couldn't quite guess . . ." Sometimes I make them with butter, and sometimes, to intensify the Asian flavors, sesame oil. The variation is wonderful too. **SERVES 4 TO 6 AS A COMPONENT**

1½ teaspoons butter, vegetable margarine, or toasted sesame oil
1 pound carrots, trimmed, scrubbed, julienned, and blanched (see page 728)
2 teaspoons peeled, minced fresh ginger
1 tablespoon honey
1 tablespoon brown sugar
2 teaspoons water, preferably spring or filtered
Pinch of salt (or a small splash of tamari or shoyu soy sauce)

1 Heat the butter in a nonstick skillet or large sauté pan over medium-high heat. When hot, add the carrots and ginger.

2 Sauté until the carrots are hot and a few are coloring slightly, about 1 minute. Add the honey, brown sugar, and water. Add a pinch of salt or a splash of tamari.

3 Cook, stirring constantly, until the honey and sugar cook down to a delicious glaze, about 3 minutes. Serve immediately.

Carrots Moutarde

The slightly spicy touch of ginger in the previous recipe is here replaced by the zing of mustard and a pinch of cayenne. This is nice with a French-inspired meal: green beans with vinaigrette for a salad starter, Vegetarian Cassoulet (page 612) or one of the gratins as an entree, French bread, of course, and apple tart for dessert.

SERVES 4 TO 6 AS A COMPONENT

VARIATION

HERBED CARROTS MOUTARDE are choice: omit the sugar, and throw in a tablespoon or so of minced fresh dill or parsley (or a combination of both) at the very end.

1 tablespoon Dijon mustard
2 teaspoons water, preferably spring or filtered
1 teaspoon brown sugar, Rapidura, or honey (optional)
Pinch of cayenne
1½ teaspoons butter, vegetable margarine, or mild vegetable oil, such as corn, canola, or peanut
1 pound carrots, trimmed, scrubbed, julienned, and blanched (see page 728)
Pinch of salt

1 Combine the mustard, water, brown sugar, and cayenne in a cup. Set aside.

2 Heat the butter in a nonstick skillet or large sauté pan over medium-high heat. When the butter is hot, add the carrots.

3 Sauté until the carrots are hot and a few are coloring slightly, about 1 minute. Spoon the mustard mixture over the carrots. Add a pinch of salt.

4 Cook, stirring constantly, until the liquid cooks down slightly to a smooth sauce, about 3 minutes. Serve immediately.

Carrots Vichy

I can no longer remember where I learned this classic carrot treatment, but I've been using it and countless variations for years. It's good, quick, simple, sprightly; the carrots taste wholly like themselves, undisguised with a sweet or savory glaze. This intensification takes place in part because the carrots are not preblanched; the water they are cooked in becomes part of the finished recipe. **SERVES 4 TO 6 AS A COMPONENT**

⅓ cup water, preferably spring or filtered
1½ teaspoons butter
1 pound carrots, trimmed, scrubbed, and julienned
1 scallion, roots removed, white and 4 inches of green very finely chopped
2 tablespoons minced Italian parsley
Pinch of salt
A light squeeze of lemon juice (optional)

1 Combine the water and butter in a medium saucepan with a tightly-fitting lid. Bring to a hard boil, drop in the carrots, cover tightly, and boil hard for 5 minutes.

2 Remove the lid and cook until all but maybe a teaspoon of liquid has boiled away. Quickly add the scallion, parsley, and salt and toss to combine. If using, add the lemon juice. Serve immediately.

Celery & Celery Root

A moment's attention to nomenclature: A bunch of celery is called a "stalk"; an individual piece of that celery, what you might logically call, looking at it, a stalk, is a "rib." I thought you should know. Further: Celery "hearts" are the paler green, tender celery ribs at the inner core of the stalk. Okay, we've got that straightened out.

Celery is a carrot relative. And like carrots, celery's one of those kitchen commonplaces that finds its way into our hearts less as soloist than as a team player. In fact, the sauté of diced onion, carrot, and celery used to lay a sauce foundation is so basic to the French that it is known by its own designation: *mirepoix*. But not many Americans enjoy celery cooked as a side vegetable, probably because they've usually had it overcooked. But try the celery recipes that follow—one French in origin, and one Italian, and you may be amazed at how responsive these pale green ribs are to proper treatment. The Italians, especially, know how to make use of one of the most flavorful parts of celery, the bright green leaves, which they call *sedano*.

Celery is also a vegetable with a split personality: The leaf-tipped stalks, which we commonly know, and the less-frequently seen (in America, at least) celery root, sometimes called celeriac, a different variety of celery, grown solely for its root. I love the knobby, ugly-looking root, which keeps its treasures so well hidden. Celery root, with its mild celery taste, ivory color, crunchy texture when raw and creamy when cooked, is outstanding.

Always try very hard to locate organic celery. According to the Environmental Working Group, conventionally grown celery is one of the 10 most heavily sprayed vegetables we eat. An organic celery stalk usually weighs about 1 pound, 6 ounces; the nonorganic tend to be larger, 1½ to 1¾ pounds, and tougher. In either case, look for a tightly shaped stalk, heavy for its size, and upstanding. You want no ribs curling back, no yellowed leaves, no bruised, cracked, or trimmed-out places. Celery is available year round. You're most likely to find celery roots in the fall and early winter. Small to medium-sized roots, the size of a child's fist, are the best for cooking whole. Avoid those that are tennis ball–sized or larger unless you are grating them for use raw or peeling and cooking. As always, avoid any with soft spots, bruises or wrinkles—knobby yes, wrinkled no.

To cook celery stalks, start by slicing off the hard base of the stalk. Discard the base, then separate the ribs and rinse them well under cold running water, for they may be sandy, particularly toward the base and inner ribs. For celery root, some recipes will require peeling the knobby brown skin; others will not. Whichever, always wash your celery root well, and scrub it clean. Remove any little whiskery fibers and rootlets. Then prepare as directed in a specific recipe.

Braised and Glazed Celery Française

A delicate bouquet of celery, braised in water, finished with a touch of citrus, butter, and sugar, makes an amazingly fresh-tasting dish. Try this as part of a winter dinner: a good beany soup to start, like the January Out-of-the-Cupboard Lima Bean and Sun-Dried Tomato Soup (page 180), a rugged salad with some bitter greens and a gutsy vinaigrette, and then this, served alongside Roasty-Toasty Potatoes, Carrots, and Onions (page 790). A feast! A great winter vegetable dish that surprises people who think they don't like celery. **SERVES 4 TO 6 AS AN ACCOMPANIMENT**

NOTE

You will need the tender celery hearts for this dish to be at its best. Save the outer ribs and the leaves for another preparation. Don't be reluctant to use water rather than vegetable stock—the dish will still come out perfect.

Cooking spray
1½ pounds celery hearts, washed, trimmed, and cut diagonally into thirds (pieces 3 to 4 inches long)
½ cup water, preferably spring or filtered
2 teaspoons butter
½ teaspoon salt, or to taste
1 lemon
1 tablespoon honey or Rapidura
1 tablespoon finely minced Italian parsley

1 Spray a casserole, with a very tight-fitting cover, with cooking spray. Place the celery in it and add the water, 1 teaspoon of the butter, and the salt. Place over high heat and bring to a boil. Cover and lower the heat to a simmer; cook until tender, 20 to 25 minutes.

2 As the celery simmers, finely grate about half of the rind from the lemon.

Place the rind in a small bowl, and squeeze in the juice of the lemon through a strainer.

3 When the celery is tender but not mushy, using a slotted spoon, lift it from the liquid and set it aside. Return the liquid to a hard boil. Add the honey and the remaining 1 teaspoon butter and boil, uncovered, until the liquid reduces down to a syrupy ⅓ to ½ cup. Return the celery to the pan. Cook for another minute or two to reheat. Add the reserved lemon juice–rind mixture and the parsley and serve immediately.

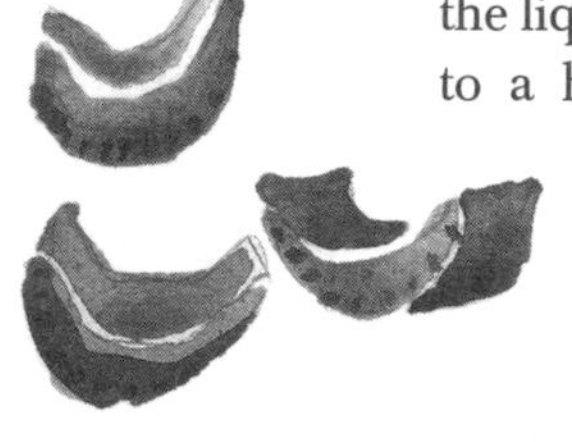

Italian Braised Celery, Tomato, and Garlic

The Italian ways with vegetables are many and marvelous. Often served as a separate course, the simpler Italian vegetable dishes work equally well as accompaniments. Done ahead of time, chilled, and brought to room temperature, this *sedano rifatto* is a fine starter. Served hot—with an optional sprinkling of Parmesan—it is a pleasing accompaniment to many carbohydrate-based meals. Try it alongside a garlic-oil-and-parsleyed pasta, with a chunk of sweet winter squash, or a big pile of mashed potatoes. **SERVES 4 TO 6 AS A COMPONENT DISH**

1 pound celery, leaves included, washed, trimmed, sliced diagonally into ¾-inch lengths
Water, preferably spring or filtered
Salt
1 tablespoon olive oil
5 cloves garlic, finely chopped
1 medium tomato, peeled, seeded, and chopped
½ to 1 teaspoon honey (optional)
2 tablespoons finely minced Italian parsley
Parmesan cheese (optional)

1 Place the celery on a vegetable steamer set up in a medium-sized pot with a tight-fitting lid over boiling salted water and steam until tender, about 7 minutes. Drain the celery, reserving the steaming water. Rinse the celery quickly in cold water, drain well, and pat dry.

2 Heat the oil in a skillet over medium heat. Add the garlic and cook, stirring often, until fragrant but not yet colored, about 1 minute. Add the celery and stir-fry

for 1 minute, then add 3 tablespoons of the steaming water and the tomato. Raise the heat slightly and cook, stirring constantly, until most of the liquid has evaporated. Season with salt to taste and perhaps a bit of honey.

3 If serving hot, remove from the heat and stir in the parsley. Toss well and transfer to a serving dish. Top with the Parmesan, if using. If serving cold, let cool to room temperature, then stir in the parsley and refrigerate. Serve at room temperature.

COOK ONCE FOR 2 MEALS Tapenade made with celery is delicious. Double the recipe, serving half as prepared. Process the remaining half with ½ cup each pitted green and black olives. Serve as a topping for bruschetta (pages 34–35).

Roasted Celery Root

Did you know you can roast a whole celery root, just as you would a potato or sweet potato? Yes, indeed you can. Roasting is so simple and satisfying, it's good to find yet another vegetable that thrives with this treatment. Get this going in the oven along with some Roasty-Toasty Potatoes, Carrots, and Onions (page 790) for a tasty late-fall supper. **SERVES 4 AS A COMPONENT**

2 medium celery roots, whole, very well washed and scrubbed, skin left on
Mild vegetable oil, such as corn, canola, or peanut
Butter, salt, freshly ground black pepper, grainy Dijon mustard, and tamari or shoyu soy sauce (optional)

1 Preheat the oven to 350°F.

2 Coat the celery roots lightly with oil. Place them in a baking dish, leaving plenty of air space around them. Bake, uncovered, until tender. This should be about 1 hour, but poke the roots with a fork after about 35 minutes, just to see how they're doing: You want tender but not soft.

3 Remove from the oven and split lengthwise. Serve hot. Your lucky diners, once they know what they're eating, may choose to mash a little butter into their baked celery root, along with any of the other additions. Butter, a few drops of tamari, and a bit of mustard, all mashed in, suit me fine, thank you.

Corn

Fresh corn is the vegetal essence of high-summer, the-living's-easy-and-the-cotton-is-high, casual hands-on, hands-in eating. Grilled, steamed, buttered, chile-buttered, even raw—yellow- or white-kerneled, or that charming two-color blend sometimes called butter-and-sugar corn—no one turns down sweet summer corn.

The nature of fresh corn has changed dramatically in the last ten or twelve years. It is now possible—although out of tune in terms of eating harmoniously with the seasons—to eat fresh sweet corn that is not at all bad while the snow drifts pile up around the house and the wind wails.

Now, probably everyone over the age of ten who grew up in a home where fresh vegetables were served knows the old rule of thumb: Ideally, you should put the pot of water on to boil before you go out to pick the corn. (I remember actually doing this with Miss Kay, our next-door neighbor and the first vegetable gardener I knew. What a revelation that first bite was!) There was sound reasoning behind this, in the old days: The sugars in corn begin, almost immediately, to convert to carbohydrate after picking. Sound reasoning no longer: Corn has been bioengineered. While I question such practices on principle, and decry most of them, it's hard in this case, as an eater and cook, to argue with the results.

First off, corn has been bred for ever increasing sweetness—in addition to what we used to call "sweet," which had 5 to 10 percent sugar, we now have "sugar-enhanced" at 15 to 18 percent and "supersweet," which, at 25 to 30 percent sugar, certainly lives up to its name.

But this is only part of how corn has changed. The second, and I think more important factor, is this: These new varieties are also being bred to retard the sugar-to-starch conversion process. Some varieties, according to Betty Fussell, America's culinary corn authority, can stay sweet *two weeks* after picking. "That is why," Betty writes, in

Crazy for Corn, one of two books she's written on the subject, "you are now getting fresh corn grown in Florida and shipped nationwide all winter long. . . . Winter sweet corn does not have the creaminess of seasonal summer corn freshly picked . . . but fresh winter corn is a good alternative to either frozen or canned corn."

When it comes to what you should look for when buying corn, the first rule is always, always buy corn in the husk, never those sad, nude cobs, embalmed on their non-biodegradable bier of styrofoam and shrouded with plastic film. The green husks keep the kernels fresh. While it is true that husks may hide

A Little Corny

Our family friend, Jim Cherry, doted on corn, and feasted on it each summer at my Aunt Dot's Vermont farm, before he and she returned to New York shortly after Labor Day. One fall, Jim drove out to their favorite farm stand for one last splurge of corn. The market-owner remarked that that was it until next year. "Then I suppose," said Jim, gesturing to the fields behind the stand, "that those are . . . the last rows of summer."

the end of an ear that is not entirely filled out with kernels, or a little soft or funky, it's also true that you can easily cut off the end of any cob. Husks should be a pale but vibrant green, fresh-looking as opposed to dried-out—though of course the silk will be brown at the top.

To prepare for cooking, at least in the ways that I do it, strip back that husk and remove it and the silk. For raw, grilled, or steamed corn, that's it. But oftentimes you need to strip the kernels from the cob for a recipe. The kernels come off cooked corn far more easily and less messily than they do raw, but raw are required for more recipes. I suggest holding the cob, raw or cooked, upright in a shallow pan large enough to give you room to bear down when cutting. Cut straight down, using a small, sharp paring knife. This minimizes the corn flying all over the kitchen. (A bowl especially minimizes it, but makes cutting down difficult.) After the kernels are removed, run the knife down the cob one more time to get any residual corn liquid.

Raw Corn

The new corn varieties are so sweet and tender that they truly don't need cooking at all. They can be eaten straight off the cob, or the kernels cut off and sprinkled on a spinach or mâche salad, along with a garden tomato and a sesame vinaigrette dressing. Perfect summer lunch.

I wouldn't serve raw corn on the cob to people I didn't know well. However, back when we used to serve corn cut off the cobs at the restaurant, there would be some mild contention among Freddie (René) Maese, our prep chef, Ned, and me as to who would get to finish off the little bits of corn still left on the cob. (After we'd finished them, the cobs would go to the compost bin, where the raccoons and possums and woodchucks no doubt would argue over them. A cob after a raccoon has gnawed it is really bare. Everybody loves corn.)

Grilled Corn

Grilled corn may be the only thing better than raw, and in the course of writing this book, my intrepid tasters and I sampled every known method of corn-grilling. Hands down, the favorite way was corn done *directly* on the grill. No nonsense about presoaking or keeping it in the husk or pulling back the husk, soaking, replacing the husk, and then grilling. It is not only the tastiest method, it is simplest, in contrast to what most authorities suggest. The sugar in the corn caramelizes slightly, bringing the sweetness up another notch. To me it's so pleasing it really doesn't need butter, although I always put some out for the die-hards, along with a few other add-ons.

On Juhu Beach in Bombay, corn is grilled just this way. Then it's salted, given a squeeze of fresh lime and a sprinkle of cayenne, and you eat it just like that, happily burning your mouth and fingers as the tide rolls in. **ALLOW 1 OR 2 EARS PER PERSON**

1 or 2 ears corn per person, shucked
Any or all of the following optional condiments: butter, Honey-Jalapeño Butter (recipe follows), Dragon Salt (page 900), sea salt, pepper, lime halves

1 Preheat the grill to high, then turn it down to medium.

2 Place the corn over indirect heat or low direct heat and grill, covered, for 3 to 5 minutes. Rotate the ears and grill for another 3 to 5 minutes. The yellow of the corn should intensify slightly, and there should be lots of golden-brown scorched spots. The texture will be a little tougher and chewier than raw or boiled corn, but that is part of its charm. Serve immediately.

Honey-Jalapeño Butter

Flavored butters are largely a thing of my past, but I make Honey-Jalapeño Butter at least once a summer, usually if I am having people over for an off-the-grill dinner or am bringing a load of grilled corn to a potluck. You'll probably have some left over; it keeps well in the fridge and is very special on biscuits.

Leaving the jalapeño seeds in and adding the cayenne makes for a very hot, spicy butter, just the way I like it. For a somewhat tamer butter, remove the seeds and membranes of the roasted jalapeños and omit the cayenne. **MAKES 1 CUP**

VARIATION

I am a cilantro-loving gal and would happily add half a bunch of it to this butter—both leaves and stems, washed—but my husband feels this would be a desecration of good grilled corn. If you have cilantro-accord in your house, go for it.

2 fresh jalapeño chiles
2 sticks (1 cup) butter, at room temperature
2 to 4 tablespoons honey
¼ teaspoon cayenne (optional)

1 Preheat the grill.

2 While firing up the grill for the corn, char the jalapeños until blackened on all sides, turning occasionally, 5 to 8 minutes total grill time. Remove the jalapeños from the grill and wrap them in a paper towel to sweat until they're cool enough to handle, just a few minutes.

3 Remove the blackened jalapeño skin. I suggest slipping your hands into two plastic bags to do this, to avoid getting jalapeño juice on your fingers. Keep the bags on and remove the stems from the jalapeños, and, if you wish, remove the seeds.

4 Put the jalapeños in a food processor with the butter, honey, and cayenne. Buzz until smooth. Taste, adding more honey or cayenne, if desired.

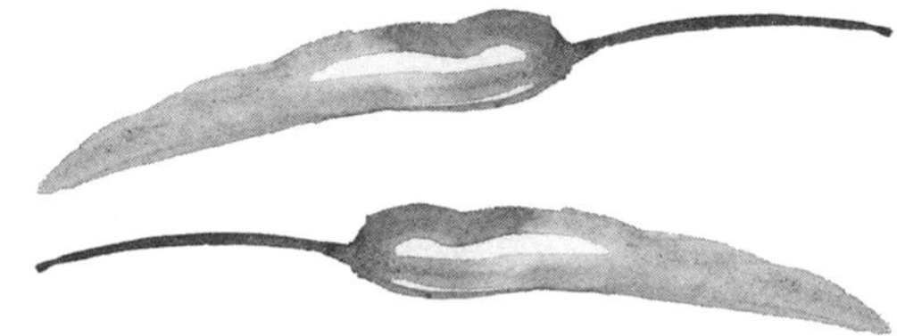

Boiled Corn

As mentioned earlier, today's corn really doesn't require cooking at all. But a quick dip in boiling water is not a bad thing: It intensifies the yellow of the corn, and softens it slightly. **ALLOW 1 OR 2 EARS PER PERSON**

1 or 2 ears corn per person, shucked
Any or all of the following optional condiments: butter, Honey-Jalapeño Butter (opposite), Dragon Salt (page 900), sea salt, pepper, lime halves

Bring a really large pot of *unsalted* water (large enough so that it won't really stop boiling, just sort of pause momentarily, when you drop the husked corn in) to a boil over high heat. Add the corn and cook for no more than 45 seconds. Serve hot, with accompaniments. I feel boiled corn needs butter in a way grilled corn doesn't, so encourage guests to try everything you've got out.

Suppertime Vegetable-Corn Pancakes

Not fritters, not thin crépes with a corn filling, but pancakes, real pancakes, thick, done in a skillet, savory and packed with vegetables. They're healthful, delicious, utterly satisfying, and quick to whip up—just made for impromptu summertime dinners (you know, the kind where you glance at the clock, and good heavens! It's 9:30 P.M. and you still haven't eaten!) and for using up odds and ends in the refrigerator.

The only unusual ingredient called for is chickpea flour (besan), which is available at Indian groceries. I have fallen in love with this seemingly exotic flour. It adds a distinctive hearty texture, has a rich but mild, slightly nutty, appealing flavor, and amps up the protein content in dishes in which it's used. It keeps for a good long time on the shelf, too. You can replace the besan with one of the other flours if you must, but I highly recommend using it.

Almost any combination of fresh or leftover vegetables is good in this. **SERVES 4**

VARIATIONS

BUTTERMILK VEGETABLE PANCAKES WITH CORN FOR SUPPER: ***Omit the soy milk and vinegar, substituting 2 cups buttermilk or 1¾ cups plain yogurt and ¼ cup filtered water.***

VEGAN VEGETABLE PANCAKES WITH CORN FOR SUPPER: ***Omit the egg. In a food processor, blend 1 cup soy milk with 3 ounces silken tofu and 1 teaspoon cornstarch until smooth. Combine with the remaining liquid ingredients and proceed.***

- 2 large eggs (or 1 egg and 2 egg whites)
- 1⅞ cups (2 cups minus 2 tablespoons) low-fat soy milk
- 2 tablespoons cider vinegar
- 2 teaspoons canola oil
- ¾ cup whole wheat pastry flour
- ¼ cup cornmeal, preferably stone-ground yellow cornmeal
- ¼ cup buckwheat flour
- ¾ teaspoon salt
- ¼ cup chickpea flour (besan)
- 2 teaspoons baking soda
- Kernels cut from 2 ears corn (raw, or leftover cooked; either is fine)
- 2 scallions, roots and wilted greens removed, white plus 3 inches of green, thinly sliced
- 1 medium carrot, grated
- ½ to ¾ cup additional finely chopped vegetable of your choice (optional; see box below)
- Cooking spray
- Tamari or shoyu soy sauce, butter, plain cooked beans (optional)

1 Combine the eggs with the soy milk, vinegar, and oil in a small bowl, whisking to combine. Set aside.

2 In a separate medium-large bowl, combine the whole wheat pastry flour, cornmeal, buckwheat flour, and salt. Sift in the chickpea flour and baking soda (they tend to lump slightly). Stir to combine.

3 In a small bowl, combine the corn, scallions, and carrot with the optional additional vegetable. Sprinkle with 1 tablespoon of the flour mixture, and toss to coat.

4 Spray a large nonstick skillet very lightly with cooking spray. Place over medium-high heat. As the skillet heats, quickly stir the dry ingredients into the wet, whisking to make sure the mixture is well combined. The dry ingredients should be just moistened, but a few lumps won't hurt anything. With a few quick strokes, stir in

Pancake Possibilities

Here are some choices for optional or additional vegetables for these pancakes. Some are cooked, some raw, but whatever you choose, make sure they're well drained or blotted dry. Try:

- ▲ *1 small zucchini cut into teeny-tiny—less than ¼-inch—dice*
- ▲ *¾ cup finely diced cooked green beans*
- ▲ *¾ cup grated raw green beans (the food processor's grater attachment does a good job)*
- ▲ *¾ cup steamed chopped broccoli or cauliflower florets*
- ▲ *½ cup cooked spinach, kale, or other green, squeezed very dry*

the vegetable mixture. Drop ladlefuls of the vegetable pancake mixture onto the hot skillet, lowering the heat a little as needed to let the pancakes slowly cook. Cook until the bottom is golden (the top side will have visible bubbles and be dry-looking around the edges), 2 to 3 minutes, then flip and cook the second side. Re-spray the skillet as needed. Serve hot, with any or all of the optional accompaniments.

Eggplant

Eggplant, a member of the Solanaceae or nightshade family, is native to India. There it is known as *brinjals,* but India is also where its odd English name originates, since most Indian eggplants are small, white, and egg-shaped. And I once read that in one of the Arab countries, where eggplant is much esteemed (and individual female achievements perhaps less so), every bride was expected to bring to her marriage, along with her virginity, at least one hundred methods of preparing eggplant. Leaving aside its value as a predictor of marital fitness, as well as the question of egalitarianism (if she must have chastity and eggplant wisdom, why not he? What if they each brought fifty ways of preparing it?), this piece of apocrypha does point out how various, and addictively succulent, are the ways of eggplant cookery.

A lot of these ways are vegetarian, for eggplant has long had a reputation as a meat substitute. Perhaps this is because when the sensuous eggplant, at least the larger varieties, is sliced, then baked, grilled, or breaded and fried, it bears a striking resemblance to a fish fillet; or perhaps because its delicate flesh is receptive to many preparations traditionally used with meat dishes. But it could simply be that eggplant, prepared with care, is so very delicious and its pale subtle-ivory flesh so uniquely creamy. It must be these reasons, not nutritional ones, for, being low in protein, eggplant is *not* an apt meat alternative. Unlike many vegetables, it's also not a nutritional all-star, though it has plenty of fiber, a decent amount of potassium, and some folic acid. Eat eggplant, then, for pleasure.

You may find small or large eggplants with a deep burgundy-purple, pale lavender, pale green, green striped, or white exterior. But since the most common and predictably located eggplants are still the large, dark purple type, those are what I've used in recipes unless otherwise noted. Do experiment with the others as you find them. In all cases, choose eggplants that are free of blemishes, bruises, or soft spots, with tight, unwrinkled, glossy skins. The texture should be firm but buoyant; press the eggplant with your thumb—it should give and then spring back. Examine where the hairy stem joins the skin. There should be a segment of the vine still attached. Note the juncture closely. Each point of the stem should still be firmly attached to the vegetable, not curled back. On a really straight-from-the-garden eggplant this hairy stem may be quite prickly; it may even stick you when touched.

Also, lift the eggplants in your hand. If you notice a difference in weight between two eggplants of the same size, pick the lighter. Overly mature eggplants are heavier than younger; the elders have more fully developed seeds, and are more likely to be bitter.

To prepare for cooking, and to know the ultimate creamy pleasures of eggplant, you must deal with the question of bitterness. Many recipes (including mine) advise you to soak cut-up eggplant in salted water—1 tablespoon salt to 3 quarts water—for about 20 minutes. Because the eggplant is light and floats, you're also advised to weigh it down with a plate to keep it submerged. After soaking, the eggplant should be drained and blotted dry before cooking. All this is said to be necessary to "draw out any bitterness." Is it?

Yes and no. Some eggplants *are* bitter. The best way to ensure that yours aren't is to pick them carefully. However, even with the most careful selection, once in a while you will get a bitter, or slightly bitter, eggplant. The only way to be absolutely certain—and hence, to answer the soak-or-not-to-soak question—is to nibble a bit of the raw eggplant and taste it. If it's even slightly bitter, soak away. Soaking also makes eggplant cook up more tenderly. However, it does add a step to the prep, and also leaches out some water-soluble nutritional elements. But if, when you nibble a bit of the raw flesh, you find that the eggplant is very bitter, throw it out, because no amount of soaking, and no delicious sauce or stuffing, will make it palatable.

I give quite a bit of eggplant info, especially on cutting eggplants, in the section on stuffed vegetables (see page 385). Take a cruise over there for ideas, then come back here for more.

The Nightshade Family

Of all the vegetable families, none is more sinister, appealing, or idiosyncratic than the nightshades of the Solanum *genus. Only mushrooms come close, and for similar reasons: Certain outré members of both families are associated with death, madness, and hallucination. The placid potato is related botanically to the poisonous deadly nightshade, the addictive tobacco, and the psychotropic datura. Yet* Solanum *genus also includes the innocent petunia and the beneficial, lycopene-rich tomato.*

The edible nightshades are a group of gifted but eccentric members. Each one—eggplant, peppers, potatoes, tomatoes—has a distinct personality. Unlike the cucurbits (squash) or the brassicas (cabbage), where most modes of preparation are basically interchangeable between members, an eggplant requires a wholly different approach from a chile pepper, and a chile pepper from a tomato or potato.

But the fascinating thing is—again like certain families of eccentrics—the solanums often work well together because of their very differences, creating some of our most favored culinary unities: chiles and tomatoes make salsa; bell peppers and tomatoes make pasta sauce. Eggplant is served with tomato in eggplant parmigiana, with tomato and peppers in ratatouille, caponata, and G'vetch (page 749).

Although there is some controversy about edible nightshades—some claim that cutting out all members of this family eases arthritis—these vegetables are among the essentials for vegetarian cooks: There's nothing else like them. Eggplant's shape and texture make it a natural starting point for many entrees—no one could consider it at all meatlike, and yet . . . where would we be without comforting potatoes, adaptable, agreeable? Tomatoes, like peppers and eggplant, provide a tasty edible carriage for stuffings (see page 385), and our sauce palette would be drabber without them. Bell peppers add sweetness and brightness, as vivid to the eye as to taste. And chiles—well, chiles are a world unto themselves.

Oven-Roasted Jerk Eggplant

I first heard about jerk, the spice-rubbed equivalent of Jamaican barbecue, long after becoming a vegetarian. I felt deprived—while I could taste it mentally, I wanted to experience it, though not on chicken or goat. The late Sylvia Teague, one of my primary recipe testers and the possessor of one of the most discerning, imaginative, and vocal vegetarian palates I have known, was in no way an eggplant fan. When she, like everyone else who sampled this, licked her chops, I knew we had scored.

The eggplant needs to marinate for at least several hours, preferably overnight; factor this into time estimates. Serve as part of a Jamaican dinner (see the menu on page 348). **SERVES 4**

2 whole eggplants, stems removed, sliced vertically into 10 to 12 "fillets" (discard skinny end pieces that are mostly skin)
1½ to 2 cups Jamaican Wet-Jerk Marinade (recipe follows)
1 cup crisp, fine breadcrumbs
½ cup crushed Nutri-Grain or other no-sugar-added corn- or wheat flake cereal
¼ cup unbleached white all-purpose flour
¼ cup nutritional yeast (see page 239)
1 teaspoon paprika
A touch of salt and freshly ground black pepper
1½ teaspoons vegetable oil
2 large eggs, beaten, or, for vegans, ⅓ cup plain full-fat soy milk (optional)
Cooking spray or olive oil spray

1 Place the eggplant in cold salted water, weighting them down so they stay submerged. Soak for 30 to 45 minutes. Drain well, rinse, and pat dry.

2 Rub the Jamaican Wet-Jerk Marinade into the cut sides of the eggplant, making sure every surface is well coated. Place the jerk-rubbed eggplant in a nonreactive container with a cover or in zippered freezer bags. Refrigerate for at least 4 hours, preferably overnight.

3 Preheat the oven to 450°F. At the same time, place a baking sheet in the oven.

4 Remove the jerk-marinated eggplant from the refrigerator and let it come to room temperature.

5 Combine the breadcrumbs, cereal flakes, flour, nutritional yeast, paprika, and salt and pepper in a large, shallow dish. Stir in the vegetable oil.

6 In a separate bowl, combine the beaten eggs and ¼ cup water, preferably spring or filtered (vegans, use rice or soy milk, omitting the eggs and water). Set aside.

7 Line a tray with waxed paper. Working with one eggplant slice at a time, dip the eggplant into the crumb mixture, then into the egg mixture (or soy milk), then back into the crumbs. At this point the eggplant slices will be rather huge and bristly with crumbs. (This is a somewhat messy process, especially when it comes to the egg-then-redip phase; you may have to assist with your fingertips, pressing the crumbs into any bald spots so the entire piece is coated with two layers of crumb and one of egg.) Place the crumbed piece on the prepared tray. Repeat the breading until all of the eggplant is coated.

8 Lower the oven temperature to 375°F.

9 Remove the hot baking sheet from the oven. Quickly but thoroughly spray it with cooking spray or oil (or give it a swipe with a paper-towel dipped in vegetable oil). Place the coated eggplant on the hot baking sheet. Bake until somewhat browned, 30 to 40 minutes. Remove the baking sheet from the oven and carefully turn the slices. Return to the oven and bake until crisp and golden, about another 25 minutes. Serve hot, preferably with Jamaican Rice and "Peas," Veronica-Style (page 618).

Jamaican Wet-Jerk Marinade

This recipe specifies that many of the spices be freshly ground. It's more delicious done that way, but the dish will be fine if you use preground spices (as long as they're reasonably fresh). I say this because for many of us, grinding all those spices is too labor intensive; however, if you have a spice mill or coffee grinder that you use specifically for that purpose, it's no big deal. If you don't have a spice mill, it means hard work with the old mortar and pestle. In the tough-to-grind category, I'd put allspice berries, cinnamon, and coriander. However . . . nutmeg's soft, nutlike kernel is easily ground on a nutmeg grater, or even the finest side of a conventional grater. And black pepper—do it in your peppermill. Freshly grinding these two will add something special to the jerk. **MAKES 3 TO 4 CUPS**

2 bunches scallions (15 to 20) roots and any wilted green parts removed
½ cup loosely packed thyme, any tough stems removed
2 to 3 Scotch bonnet or habanero chiles, stemmed and quartered
5 to 7 cloves garlic, peeled and chopped
¼ cup peeled, finely minced ginger
¼ cup mild vegetable oil, such as corn, canola, or peanut
1 tablespoon freshly ground allspice
1 tablespoon freshly ground black pepper
1 tablespoon freshly ground coriander seeds
1 teaspoon freshly grated nutmeg
1 teaspoon freshly ground cinnamon
2 teaspoons salt
Juice of 1 lemon or lime

Place the scallions and thyme in a food processor, then add the chiles, garlic, ginger, and oil. Pulse/chop a few times. Add the allspice, pepper, coriander seeds, nutmeg, and cinnamon, as well as the salt and lemon or lime juice. Buzz, scraping down the sides of the work bowl several times, until you have a compact, chunky paste. Use as directed in a specific recipe, or store, covered and refrigerated, for up to 5 days.

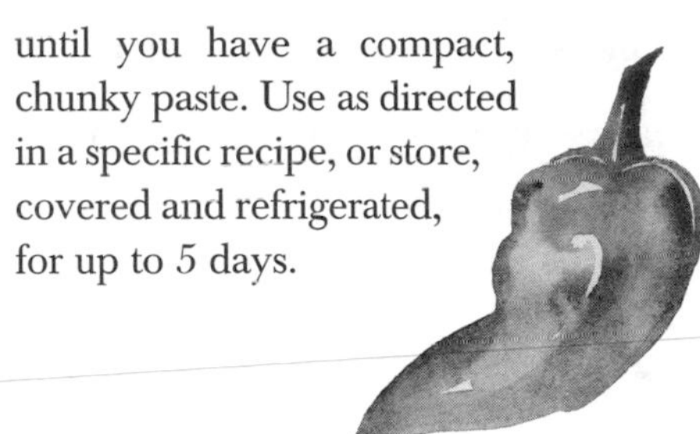

Sweet-Sour Glazed Eggplant Panchphoran

Panch is the Sanskrit word for "five"; our beverage punch, which originally had five ingredients, derives from it. Panchphoran is a Bengali seasoning of equal parts of five spices: cumin, fennel, fenugreek, mustard, and kalongi seeds. If you have an Indian market nearby, you may be able to purchase it ready-mixed; if not, go to a natural foods store or any market that carries bulk spices. Purchase ¼ ounce of each seed. Kalongi, also called *kalonji, nigella,* onion seed, or in Arabic markets, *siyah daneh,* are tiny black seeds, and the only one that may be difficult to find. Although they're a delicious addition, this eggplant is also divine without them. One other exotic here is reconstituted tamarind. To make it, see page 90. It adds both tartness and richness to the dish . . . but you can substitute lemon juice for a thinner, but quite successful, adaptation.

The original version called for precooking the eggplant in oil. By grilling instead, the dish is lightened considerably and tastes even better. A gas grill makes grilling a simple, no-big-deal affair. But if you don't have a grill, or have only a charcoal type, you can use your broiler instead, cooking the eggplant to the same point of almost-tenderness and then proceeding with the recipe. Or you may also use a stove-top "grill," a ridged oiled or nonstick pan, oiling the eggplant slightly first.

Serve with rice, Dal (page 609), and any tomato-sauced curry, and you will have a feast. **SERVES 6 TO 8**

2 medium-large eggplants, peeled, cut crosswise into ½-inch-thick rounds, soaked in salt water for 30 minutes if needed to remove bitterness (see page 742)
Cooking spray
1½ tablespoons sesame seeds
1 tablespoon mild vegetable oil, such as corn, canola, or peanut
1 teaspoon cumin seeds
1 teaspoon fennel seeds
1 teaspoon fenugreek seeds
1 teaspoon black or brown mustard seeds
1 teaspoon kalongi seeds
1 medium onion, sliced
1 tablespoon water, preferably spring or filtered
2 tablespoons reconstituted tamarind (see page 90), or fresh lemon juice
2½ tablespoons sugar, honey, or Rapidura
Pinch of cayenne

1 Preheat the grill to high, then lower the heat to medium.

2 If you have soaked the eggplant, rinse it and pat it dry; otherwise just proceed with the recipe. Lightly coat the eggplant on both sides with cooking spray, and place directly on the grill. Grill until the eggplant slices are marked and almost tender, about 5 minutes on each side. Remove from the grill and let cool slightly. Cut into large pieces and set aside.

3 Place the sesame seeds in a dry nonstick skillet over medium heat. Toast until they turn golden and fragrant, 3 to 4 minutes. Immediately remove from the hot pan to a small dish. Set aside.

4 Add the oil to the hot skillet and immediately add the cumin, fennel, fenugreek, mustard seeds, and kalongi. The seeds will immediately begin popping. Let sizzle for about 10 seconds, then add the onion. Sauté until the onion starts to get limp, about 5 minutes. Add the eggplant and stir-fry for 1 minute. Add the water, cover, and steam for 1 minute.

5 Uncover and add the tamarind (or lemon juice), sugar, and cayenne. Cook, stirring constantly, for about 1 minute; it will want to stick, so keep stirring.

6 Add the toasted sesame seeds. Stir-fry for 30 seconds more and serve.

Eggplant Fans

A world away from India, I was taught to make this dish in Paris, by Miriam Cendrars, daughter of the French poet Blaise Cendrars, and herself his biographer and a distinguished editor. The preparation is traditionally Provençal, best made in summer and early fall, when tomatoes are red ripe, and fresh herbs easily found.

Like many dishes from this part of the world, this is best served slightly warm or at room temperature, but not hot or cold. The liquid that comes out of the vegetables as they cook is delicious drizzled over any accompanying grain or pasta.

SERVES 4 TO 6

Cooking spray
2 tablespoons olive oil
1½ teaspoons tamari or shoyu soy sauce
¾ teaspoon ground coriander seeds
½ teaspoon salt
Freshly ground black pepper to taste
6 cloves garlic, very thinly sliced
2 large onions, halved horizontally, then sliced paper-thin (a food processor can be used)
2 teaspoons olive oil, plus more to taste
2 large eggplants
3 large garden-ripe tomatoes, a little on the firm side, sliced in half vertically, then crosswise into ⅓-inch-thick pieces
8 to 10 small sprigs fresh thyme, oregano, or savory (or a combination)
8 to 10 whole basil leaves
4 bay leaves (fresh, if possible)

1 Preheat the oven to 450°F.

2 Spray a large ceramic, enamel-clad, or glass gratin dish with cooking spray.

3 Combine all but 1 teaspoon of the oil, the tamari, ground coriander seeds, salt, and pepper in a small bowl. Set the seasoning liquid aside.

4 Combine the garlic and onions, tossing together with the remaining teaspoon oil. Place half the onion mixture in the prepared dish. Set aside.

5 Cut off the stem end of the eggplant, as well as a small slice off the dimpled blossom end. Cut the eggplant in half lengthwise, each with a curved skin side and a flat cut side. With the flat side down, starting from the blossom end, slice each half lengthwise into ½-inch-thick oval-shaped pieces, stopping about 1 inch short of the stem end, so the slices remain attached. On an average eggplant, you'll get 3, maybe 4 slices in each half, the end slice being smaller and curved.

6 Rub the fleshy parts of the eggplant with the seasoning liquid. Slide 2 or 3 tomato slices, and a sprig or leaf of each of

the herbs, between the eggplant slices. Not every layer of eggplant has to get every herb.

7 Place the stuffed eggplant fans on the onion bed in the gratin dish. Tuck the remaining onions around the fans. If desired, drizzle with additional oil. Tightly cover the dish with foil. Lower the oven temperature to 350°F.

8 Bake for about 50 minutes, then uncover and bake until the eggplants are meltingly tender and slightly shriveled-looking on top, another 15 to 20 minutes. Turn off the oven and leave the dish in the oven for another 20 minutes or so. Remove from the oven and serve warm, as is, or refrigerate and bring to room temperature for later use.

Basil

COOK ONCE FOR 2 MEALS Make a double recipe. Serve the fans warm, one night, with a grain dish or pasta. A day or two later, take the second batch, and carefully slide a thin slice of mozzarella or a bit of feta or ricotta salata into each fan-slit. Serve at room temperature on a bed of arugula, with good European-style crisp-crusted bread.

Grilled Eggplant with Sweet Asian Glaze

The flavors of citrus, mirin, and miso are magical together, and what they do to a simple slice of grilled eggplant is beyond belief. The glaze keeps well, so you can make one eggplant now, and save the rest for a week or so until you just can't *stand* it and have to have that tasty eggplant again! This recipe is adapted from a dish served at Cafe Brenda, a Minneapolis vegetarian restaurant. **SERVES 4 TO 6**

- Cooking spray
- 2 to 3 large eggplants, stem removed, sliced lengthwise into large ½-inch-thick ovals, soaked in salt water if bitter (see page 742)
- 2 to 4 teaspoons mild vegetable oil, such as corn, canola, or peanut
- 1 orange
- 1 thumb-sized piece ginger, peeled and minced
- ¼ cup mirin (Japanese rice wine) or dry sherry
- ¼ cup golden or white miso
- 1 tablespoon honey
- 1 teaspoon tamari or shoyu soy sauce

1 Clean and then spray the grill with cooking spray. Preheat the grill to high, then lower the heat to medium.

2 Lightly brush the cut sides of the eggplants with the oil. Place on the grill, cover, and grill until the eggplants are medium-tender and grill-marked on one side, 8 to 10 minutes. Using tongs, carefully turn the eggplant slices and grill until very tender, another 8 to 10 minutes.

3 Meanwhile, grate the rind from about half of the orange and place it in a small bowl. Cut the orange in half and squeeze the juice in over the rind, removing the seeds. Stir in the ginger, mirin, miso, honey, and tamari to make a thin paste. Very lightly brush the grilled eggplant with the orange glaze. Turning with tongs, brush the second side more heavily. Cover the grill and cook until the eggplant is very tender and the under side is deep golden brown, but not burned, 2 to 4 more minutes. Serve immediately.

COOK ONCE FOR 2 MEALS This dish is also lovely cold, the next day, eaten as a kind of salad. I also use the slices on Asian Pizza (page 274). So go ahead and make extra; you'll be glad you did.

G'vetch: Russian Eggplant and Vegetable Stew

Dill-scented, both hearty and subtle in flavor, this braised vegetable stew is the Russian equivalent of ratatouille. It can be served warm, cold, or at room temperature, but it is rarely, if ever, served hot. In its traditional form, this dish is virtually braised in olive oil. Here is a lighter, more delicate approach; the vegetables start out being roasted in a much-reduced amount of oil, then are finished by stewing on the stove-top. Anya von Bremzen and John Welchman, in *Please to the Table,* suggest making G'vetch a day ahead of time to achieve the fullest flavor. The first day it's very good, the second day, excellent, the third or fourth—outstanding, not to be missed. The dill grows more pronounced but never overwhelming, and the olive oil states its presence without the hyperbole of the original recipe. **SERVES 8 TO 10**

NOTE

This can be served at room temperature as part of an appetizer spread. Called zakusky, the Russian version of the Middle Eastern mezze are the embodiment of irresistible, welcoming hospitality. G'vetch also adds infinite charm to a component dinner.

4 medium potatoes, peeled and cut into ½-inch cubes
2 carrots, peeled, quartered lengthwise, and cut into 1-inch lengths
1 eggplant, cut into 1-inch cubes
2 tablespoons olive oil
Cooking spray
1 large onion, finely chopped
2 ribs celery, finely chopped
1 to 2 Italian frying peppers (also called banana or Hungarian wax; yellow or pale green, mild to slightly hot), seeded and cut into half-rings
½ pound green beans, stems and tips removed, sliced into 1-inch lengths
3 cloves garlic, sliced, plus 1½ teaspoons minced garlic
6 to 8 tomatoes, peeled, seeded, and chopped, or 1 can (15 ounces) chopped tomatoes in juice
Leaves from 4 large sprigs thyme
2 bay leaves
3 tablespoons coarsely chopped dill
2 tablespoons coarsely chopped Italian parsley
About 4 cups Golden Stock (page 140) or other mild but flavorful vegetable stock
10 to 15 (3-inch) okra pods, stems removed
1 zucchini, cut into ½-inch dice
1 teaspoon salt
½ teaspoon freshly ground black pepper
1 can (15 ounces) navy beans or chickpeas, well-drained (or 2 cups cooked beans)
2 tablespoons tomato paste
1 tablespoon red-wine vinegar
2 teaspoons sugar, honey, or Rapidura

Thyme

1 Preheat the oven to 375°F.

2 Combine the potatoes, carrots, and eggplant in a large bowl and toss with 1 tablespoon of the oil. Spray your largest baking sheet with cooking spray. Scatter the potatoes, carrots, and eggplant over it in a single layer. Bake until just starting to soften and turn a little golden brown—you don't want the vegetable pieces too brown or dried out, about 15 minutes.

3 In a nonstick Dutch oven, or one that has been sprayed with cooking spray, heat the remaining tablespoon oil, add the onion, and sauté until the onion is soft and translucent, about 5 minutes. Add the celery and peppers and sauté for another 3 minutes. Add the green beans and the sliced garlic and sauté for an additional minute. Add the roasted vegetables, along with the tomatoes, thyme, bay leaves, dill, and parsley. Stir well and add enough stock to just barely cover the vegetables. Bring to a boil, then lower the heat to medium, and cook at a steady simmer for 10 minutes. Lower the heat as low as it will go and cook, covered, at an almost-simmer for 45 minutes.

4 Uncover and add the okra, zucchini, salt, and pepper. Cover and simmer for another 30 minutes. Stir in the navy beans, tomato paste, vinegar, sugar, and minced garlic. Cook for an additional 5 minutes. Remove from the heat. Let cool, then refrigerate, covered, overnight.

5 The next day, fish out the bay leaf, and taste to correct the seasonings. More salt or pepper? A little additional vinegar or sugar? Rewarm slightly before serving.

COOK ONCE FOR 2 MEALS This makes a large batch of G'vetch. In its room-temperature mode, serve it as part of an hors d'oeuvres spread, with extra olive oil for drizzling. Or, turn it into a casserole: Layer with cooked lasagne noodles and ricotta, top with grated mozzarella and Parmesan, and bake until bubbly, for off-the-cuff vegetable lasagne. Try it heated, with any larger chunks diced a bit, and rolled up in Neo-Classic Crêpes (page 332), or an omelet (page 884).

Best of all, try a Russian Garden Sandwich, an improvisation that had Amber, my ever faithful recipe-testing assistant, and me groaning with delight. Toast a large whole wheat tortilla in a skillet. Turn it, and generously sprinkle half with feta cheese crumbles. Pile over the cheese as much room-temperature G'vetch as you can fit. Fold the unfilled half over the filling and slide the whole thing off onto a plate.

Fennel

Fennel, a member of the same family as celery and Queen Anne's lace, is an anise-flavored vegetable much loved by the Italians. In fact, it was virtually impossible to find in America until it was planted in the home gardens of Italian immigrants. Since after World War II, it has slowly and steadily gained popularity, and now the odds are good that you can find it in any good supermarket with a well stocked produce section.

It is delicious eaten thinly sliced, raw, on an antipasto platter. But that's only the beginning of how to enjoy this intriguing anise/licorice-flavored bulb.

There are two fennel soups in *Dairy Hollow House Soup & Bread*; both win wows and satisfaction. Also scoot over to Gratin of Fresh Fennel and Artichokes with Feta (page 286); intriguing, elegant, full of energetic flavors, yet in a creamy sauce.

Fennel is very tasty grilled, though it tends to fall apart (the bulbs are built somewhat like a tight celery; rings wrapped around a core) and you inevitably lose some when you flip it over; hence these days I usually stir-fry it at fairly high heat.

Choose the firm, smaller bulbs over the larger ones, always with the stalks and feathery greenery still attached. Allow one-half to three-quarters of a bulb per person.

To prepare for cooking, cut off the stalks and all that feathery foliage (save a little of the latter, though, to garnish and intensify the finished fennel dish). Cut a thin slice off the base of the bulb, and remove any outside ribs that appear tough. Slice the trimmed fennel bulb crosswise into pieces about ½ inch thick (or vertically if you plan to grill them), and you're ready to go.

Skillet-Seared Fennel

I like fennel still crisp and crunchy, but seared along the edges. Some people blanch or steam-blanch it first for a more tender effect, but for me, it would lose some of its charm. This, though simple, is unusual enough that anyone I've fed it to seemed to view it as exotic. **SERVES 4 TO 6**

1 tablespoon olive oil
3 bulbs fennel, prepared for cooking (see previous page), in round slices
2 teaspoons tamari or shoyu soy sauce
1 teaspoon Pickapeppa sauce
Salt if needed, and freshly ground black pepper to taste
A few finely minced fennel fronds (1 to 2 teaspoons)

Heat a nonstick skillet over high heat. Add the oil. When very hot, add the fennel; it should sizzle as it goes in. Lower the heat slightly and cook, stirring almost constantly, until the fennel starts to get just a little limp, 4 to 6 minutes. Drizzle with the tamari and Pickapeppa, and stir-fry for 2 to 3 minutes more. Sprinkle with salt, if it needs it, and pepper. Garnish with fennel fronds and serve immediately.

The Queen Anne's Lace Family

Hemlock is majestic: a graceful evergreen tree with horizontally spreading limbs, gently drooping branches, and exceptionally fine, soft, feathery needles. It doesn't look in the least edible, though, and it's not: As you might remember, Socrates died by drinking a cup of hemlock tea.

Yet strange to say, hemlock is related botanically to carrots and celery. Those feathery needles, mimicked in carrot fronds, give the relationship away. You see that foliage again in the ferny green foliage on crisp, licorice-y fennel, another relative. And though you don't usually purchase it with fronds attached, if you did you'd also see this ferny foliage on parsnips. The family resemblance is also visible, if you look for it, in parsley, cilantro, caraway, chervil, and anise. And all of these are related to delicate Queen Anne's lace, which grows wild up and down Dairy Hollow, and indeed throughout much of America east of the Rockies, from June through September . . . and whose white explosions give delicacy and drama to almost any flower arrangement. Were you to have such a bouquet on your table the same night you, say, grilled a bulb or two of fennel, or served a carrot soup, you would have the pleasure of being in on a family secret.

Parsley

Garlic

When I view the giant, nutmeg-scented pink and burgundy freckled lily that has bloomed in the Dairy Hollow garden all these years, its lovely fragrance wafting clear across the road each July, it is hard to believe it is a relative of the food I am perhaps more passionate about that any other: garlic. But so it is.

We think of garlic as the ultimate Mediterranean seasoning; indeed it has been used in that region since the Stone Age. It was prized by ancient Egyptians, Greeks, and Romans not only for its culinary properties, but because it was believed to strengthen and harden soldiers, slaves, gladiators—anyone who labored and needed sheer physicality. Today, with the study of the ever expanding world of phytochemicals and their unique properties, we can start to understand why this might be so. Garlic contains a powerful compound called alliin, which converts in an enzymatic reaction to allicin, which in turn has been cited in various studies as an antibiotic, an anticoagulant (helping to lower blood pressure), an antiparasitic, and, when eaten raw, a decongestant. But what is this to the sheer joy that garlic's powerful, in-your-face flavor gives countless dishes, in countless world cuisines?

Choose tightly formed, firm heads of garlic. The cloves should fill out their skins, not rattle in them (a sure sign of a dried-out garlic clove). Both the bluish-lavender–skinned and white-skinned varieties are good (and both hold ivory-white cloves of garlic within), but elephant garlic (which is not a true garlic but a member of the leek family), with its giant and easily peeled cloves, is a disappointment to the true garlic lover; it lacks the full punch of the real thing. Store garlic at room temperature, in a wire basket (to permit good air circulation); never refrigerate it. And don't even think about buying preminced garlic; vinegar or other preservatives must be added to it, and they change its flavor radically.

To prepare for cooking, separate as many cloves of garlic as you need from the head, lay them sideways on a cutting board, and give them a sharp *whap* with the flat side of a large knife. The thin peel is then much more easily removed. If the butt end of the garlic appears hard, slice it off. And though a bit of green at the tip doesn't matter, if there is a noticeable green sprout poking out, you may wish to slice the clove lengthwise down the middle, and remove the green part; it can be bitter when cooked.

Garlic junkies should be sure to make The One, the Only, the Greatest Garlic Spaghetti (page 864).

Double Garlicked Stir-Fry with White Beans, for Ravioli

This mixture of stove-top caramelized garlic combined with Roasted Garlic puree, mixed with stir-fried red pepper strips, broccoli rabe, and white beans is sublime tossed with any good-quality commercial ravioli, tortelli-

ni, or other stuffed pasta. I am especially fond of the excellent fresh-frozen ravioli made by Putney Pasta, nationally available at both natural foods markets and gourmet stores, and made just a few miles from my family's summer place in Vermont. This combination is nothing less than marvelous on their black-pepper ravioli stuffed with wild mushrooms, or their butternut squash ravioli. **SERVES 4**

VARIATIONS

Almost any green vegetable substitutes admirably for broccoli rabe. Tender juliènne of raw zucchini sautées nicely with the red pepper. A handful of fresh green peas is tonic, as is asparagus, cut in thin diagonal strips and sautéed with the pepper. Another good option: Toss the stir fry with Basic Oven-Baked Marinated Tempeh (page 641) and fettucine or bowtie pasta. Lastly, for a finish with the feeling of a sauce rather than a stir-fry, simply buzz the Roasted Garlic and cooked beans in a food processor till smooth. Use as is over any pasta, or toss with the stir-fry.

1 bunch (about 12 ounces) broccoli rabe
Cooking spray
1½ tablespoons olive oil
8 cloves garlic, peeled, sliced crosswise into ½-inch circles
1 package (9 ounces) good-quality frozen or fresh commercial ravioli
1 red pepper, stemmed, seeded, and cut into thin lengthwise strips
1 recipe Roasted Garlic puree (see page 899)
1 cup cooked (or canned) navy or cannellini beans, well drained
Salt and freshly ground black pepper
Minced flat-leaf parsley (optional)
Freshly grated Parmesan cheese (optional)

1 Bring a large pot of water to a boil. Drop in the broccoli rabe and blanch for 2 minutes. Drain, refresh immediately under cold running water, and drain well again.

2 In a nonstick skillet, or one that has been sprayed with cooking spray, heat about half the olive oil over medium heat. When the oil is hot, lower heat as far as it will go, and add the sliced garlic, stirring frequently for about 8 minutes, or until it turns an even golden-brown. Remove both the garlic and any residual oil, and set aside.

3 As the garlic caramelizes, bring a large pot of water to a boil and cook the ravioli according to package directions.

4 Add the remaining olive oil to the skillet, and, over medium-high heat, stir-fry the red pepper strips for 1 to 2 minutes, or until they are barely starting to brown at the edges. Add the blanched broccoli rabe, and stir-fry another 2 minutes or so. Remove the skillet from the heat, and stir in the roasted garlic, beans, and reserved caramelized garlic.

5 Toss with the cooked and drained ravioli, salt and pepper liberally, and, if desired, sprinkle with a shower of fresh minced parsley. Serve hot, immediately, passing Parmesan at the table, if desired.

Greens Gang

Greens. To know them is to love them, although if you didn't grow up with them, it might take a couple tries to fully know them. They are arranged here not as a botanical entity, but because, like a club or gang, they have an affinity of shared interests.

Greens are edible leaves, heartier and larger in personality than most lettuces, hence eaten cooked (sometimes baby greens are eaten as salad, though). Sometimes the leaves are grown solely for themselves: chard, spinach (the tenderest of the lot), kale, mustard greens (a brassica, but cooked like a green), collard greens. Sometimes, useful greens yield a second crop, an edible root produced below, with that headdress of greens above, such as beet greens and turnip greens. Most are cultivated, but there are many, many edible wild greens: lamb's quarter, plantain leaf (not related to the cooking banana of the same name much used in the Caribbean), purslane, even the leaves of wild violets. But when you're at the market, select what looks freshest and best. Need I say that the greens should be sprightly, never limp or wilted? Always remember to get way more than you think you need; a huge stack of greens cooks down to a tiny bit; specifically, 1 pound of raw greens, equaling about 3 quarts when sliced and prepped, yields only 1 to 2 cups cooked greens at the most, the yield varying slightly according the water content of specific leaves. Twelve ounces of prewashed, bagged spinach might make a salad for two; cooked, it's barely a single portion. I'd allow ½ pound greens, minimum, per serving. Alas, at least as far as we spinach-lovers are concerned, spinach makes the top-ten list of most heavily insecticide-sprayed vegetables. Unless you can buy certified organic spinach, you might consider substituting other greens most of the time. (Such a shame.)

Each green has its own character—some, like collards or kale, are fairly tough and require quite a long cooking time; others, like young spinach, are tender as can be. Most fall in between. Some have a decidedly bitter twang to them, like collards and kale; in mustard greens the twang is a bit hot. But believe me when I say that if you give them a chance, these greens, too, will be cherished by you. Chard, the beauty queen of the greens patch, has a faint lemony flavor; beet greens are delicious, their sweetness highlighted by a tonic touch of bitter. Although I adore arugula's peppery bite raw, to me it's disappointing as a cooked green, and I never use it that way, although many people do. It's a good idea, as you get to know greens, to try cooking each individually to get a sense of these differences. But they are also wonderful in combination . . . a mess of greens. And, in these parts at least, they are some of the easier vegetables to acquire organically.

To prepare greens for cooking, wash them thoroughly, picking over to remove any wilted, rotten, or yellowed leaves. Bulk spinach is sometimes extremely muddy and sandy and may require several washings and swishings to really come clean—part of the allure of the prewashed. Some batches of some varieties of greens may have a few tiny worms hidden in the crevices, particularly if they're organic. Just pick them off.

Some greens have a tough center rib, the toughest part being at the base and the lower few inches of rib. You may wish to cut the ribs out, and either discard them or finely dice them. If you do the latter, and keep them separate from the leaves, you can give the diced ribs a headstart on cooking so they'll be tender at the same time.

In any case, most recipes will ask you to stack, then slice the washed leaves crosswise.

Basic greens-cooking can go in many directions. You can precook the tougher greens by blanching them in a large pot of boiling water until they soften slightly, which has the advantage of removing some of the stronger flavor from the more assertive greens. But I hate to do this, myself, because these guys are such nutritional powerhouses, and you lose both nutritional value and those strong flavors, which I have grown to love. Much better, if you want to cook the greens to a fairly melting softness, is to incorporate the liquid as part of the dish, as in Parky's Southern Braised Kale with Sweet Potatoes (page 758).

You can steam greens in a collapsible steamer basket set over hot water, in a large pot with a tight-fitting lid. A batch of greens won't all fit in a single steamer basket, but jam the cover on; they'll almost instantly wilt, and then you can add more until you've got them all softened enough to fit. Steaming time for tender but not overcooked greens varies from 2 minutes (for tender spinach) to 5 to 10 minutes (for rugged, never-say-die kale).

Steam-sautéing is probably my favorite greens-cooking method. You start out sautéing as many cut greens as you can reasonably fit and still shove them around in a little oil in a deep nonstick skillet. Put the cover on after they start wilting (20 seconds to 1 minute), and steam until the greens are quite wilted, about 2 minutes. Uncover, add more greens, shove things around with a spatula, and cover again. This is fast, and tasty; you can get all kinds of good things in there with the greens as you sauté: Garlic, spices, and so on, and just a little oil, Better (page 905), or butter make a big difference. The total steam-sauté time varies from 1 minute or less to 10 to 12 minutes. Two quick-fix steam-sautés:

- ▲ Steam-sauté 1 to 1½ pounds fresh spinach in a nonstick skillet with 1 teaspoon butter and 2 minced cloves garlic. When done, toss with 1 to 2 tablespoons reduced-fat sour cream and the same amount of Parmesan. Add salt, loads of freshly ground black pepper, a little nutmeg. Mmm!
- ▲ Steam-sauté 1 to 1½ pounds beet greens with 1 teaspoon vegetable oil, tossed with small wedges of cooked beet and 1 to 2 tablespoons reduced-fat sour cream or Tofu Sour Cream (page 909). (This turns a brilliant pink.)

Here's what greens give you, besides satisfying flavor, texture, and color: Vitamins A, C, E. Loads of iron. Calcium. Potassium. Beta-carotene. And just 60 to 70 calories *a pound*. Need I say more—or less?

New South Stir-Fry of Hearty Greens with Garlic

The South rises again in these delectable stir-fried greens, a far piece from the slow, slow, slow-cooked greens with a chunk of salt pork that are part and parcel of much Southern cuisine, but that never much appealed to me even when I did eat meat. Here, the great flavor, color, and nutritional value of the greens stay intact, a bit of hot pepper is added, and the garlic is caramelized. It's important to wash your greens well, remove any tough ribs, stack the leaves, and cut across the grain into delicate, ¼-inch-wide strips. **SERVES 4**

3 bunches (about 2 pounds) hearty greens, any combination of kale, collards, turnip, escarole, or mustard, washed and sliced into thin ribbons
1 to 2 tablespoons olive oil
5 to 7 cloves garlic, halved, any green shoot in the middle removed, cut into ¼-inch pieces
About 1 dried red chile pepper, broken into a few pieces but not crushed or crumbled
Salt and freshly ground black pepper to taste
Lemon wedges or vinegar (optional)

1 Steam the greens in a steamer basket placed over boiling water until just wilted, about 30 seconds, jamming them in to fit. Drain the greens well. (If desired, drink any liquid remaining in the steamer pot; incredibly tonic, and rich in iron, especially important for vegetarians.) Blot dry.

2 Heat the oil in a nonstick skillet over the lowest heat you can get without the flame blowing out. Add the garlic and red pepper and slowly cook, stirring frequently, until the garlic is an even pale golden color. This will take about 8 minutes. Do not let the garlic brown. Using a slotted spoon, remove the garlic and chile pieces. Set them aside, leaving the oil in the pan.

3 Turn the heat under the skillet to medium. When the oil is hot, add the greens and stir like heck, lowering the heat slightly. Cover for 1 minute to steam just slightly. Uncover and raise the heat a bit. Stir-fry until all the greens are limp, and starting to go from bright to dark green, 5 to 6 minutes. (They will continue to reduce greatly in volume.) Remove from the heat and season with salt and black pepper. Stir in the garlic and chile. Serve at once, with lemon wedges or vinegar passed at table, if desired. You can also serve with cornbread, tossed into pasta, over rice with Dancin' John (page 619), or Oven-Baked "Chicken-Fried" Tofu and Gravy (page 670); it's perfect as part of a Southern dinner.

Parky's Southern Braised Kale with Sweet Potatoes

From John Parkhurst, known affectionately around Eureka Springs as Parky, comes this braise with the vigorous zing of both citrus and a splash of vinegar, gentled with sweet potato. It's an agreeable alliance, somewhat like a stew. It's best eaten in a bowl, with cornbread or over brown rice. These flavors soften the kale's slight bitterness so nicely. **SERVES 4**

3 large sweet potatoes, scrubbed
1 tablespoon mild vegetable oil, such as corn, canola, or peanut
Cooking spray (optional)
1 red bell pepper, diced
½ onion, diced
1 to 2 jalapeño peppers, minced (seeds and membranes removed for mildness or left in for extra heat)
2 pounds kale, washed, tough ribs removed, leaves stacked and coarsely chopped (you may substitute any hearty green or combination of greens)
⅓ cup Golden Stock (page 140) or any mild vegetable stock
1 orange
1 to 2 tablespoons balsamic vinegar
2 medium tomatoes, chopped
Salt and freshly ground black pepper to taste

1 Bring a large pot of water to a boil over high heat. Add the sweet potatoes, lower the heat, and simmer until just tender, about 25 minutes (alternatively, you may pressure-cook them for 6 minutes). When the potatoes are done, rinse under cold running water, peel them, and cut into thick slices.

2 Heat the oil in nonstick Dutch oven or very deep skillet, or one that has been sprayed with cooking spray, over medium-high heat. Add the red bell pepper, onion, and jalapeño. Sauté for 5 minutes.

3 Add the kale. It will begin to wilt and grow more intensely green immediately. Top with the sliced sweet potato. Pour the stock over the dish, cover, and braise until the kale is cooked but still bright green, 4 to 5 minutes.

4 Grate the rind of the orange; squeeze its juice into a cup. When the kale is done, uncover and

add about 1 teaspoon of the grated rind, about 3 tablespoons of the juice, 1 tablespoon of the vinegar, the tomatoes, and salt and pepper. Taste and, if necessary, adjust with extra orange zest and juice, vinegar, and salt and pepper. Serve hot.

Swiss Chard with Raisins, Olives, and Onions

Greens and dried fruit are a beloved combination, common in North Africa, Sicily, and parts of the Caucasus as far back as medieval times. Sometimes black or green olives are added, sometimes curry spices (turmeric, coriander), sometimes enormous amounts of olive oil, sometimes pine nuts or feta cheese, and sometimes the whole is stuffed in a crust. This simple version uses Swiss chard, with its faint lemony undernote, but any green will do.

This is excellent with almost any grain dish or pilaf. **SERVES 4**

2 teaspoons olive oil
1 medium onion, chopped
1 bunch (1½ to 2 pounds) Swiss chard, well washed, tough ribs removed and finely chopped, leaves stacked and cut crosswise into ½-inch slices
1 to 2 tablespoons water, preferably spring or filtered, or mild vegetable stock (see page 139)
¼ cup raisins, preferably golden
¼ cup green pimento-stuffed olives, sliced crosswise into thirds
Salt (just a little, if any) and freshly ground black pepper to taste

1 Heat the oil in nonstick Dutch oven or very deep skillet over medium heat. Add the onion and sauté for 3 minutes, then add the chard stems and sauté for another 3 to 4 minutes, by which point both the stems and onions should be softened.

2 Add the chard leaves and sauté for 1 minute. Add the water (or stock). Stir in the raisins and olives. Cover, lower the heat, and steam for about 4 minutes. The liquid should be mostly evaporated; if not, raise the heat and cook for just a bit longer. Taste and, if necessary, add salt and pepper. Serve hot.

NOTE

If possible, purchase pimento-stuffed olives in bulk or in jars; canned olives can have a metallic taste and sodden texture.

Mr. Panseer's North Indian–Style Spinach

Soulful, elemental, primitive . . . these are traditional folk greens from North India, where they have been eaten this way since time out of mind. Intensely delicious, they are cooked to melting softness with ginger, garlic, and chile, and traditionally served with *makki ki roti,* a cornbread reminiscent of a cross between tortillas and chapati. **SERVES 4**

- **1 tablespoon clarified butter or mild vegetable oil**
- **1 onion, finely diced**
- **1 to 2 green chiles, such as serranos, diced (seeds and membranes removed for mildness or left in for extra heat)**
- **1 tablespoon peeled, minced ginger**
- **1 tablespoon finely diced garlic**
- **2 pounds fresh spinach, stems included, picked over, very well washed, coarsely chopped**
- **2 tablespoons water, preferably spring or filtered**
- **1 teaspoon salt**
- **½ teaspoon freshly ground black pepper**
- **Rice, chapatis, whole wheat or corn tortillas, or cornbread**

1. Heat 2 teaspoons of the clarified butter (or oil) in a large nonstick skillet with a tight-fitting lid. Add the onion and cook until the onions are starting to become translucent, about 2 minutes. Lower the heat slightly. Add half of the chiles and half of the ginger and sauté for 2 minutes. Add the garlic and sauté for 1 minute. Set the remaining ginger and chiles aside.

2. Begin heaping in the washed spinach, with the water still clinging to it. Jam in as much as you can, and cover the pan. As the spinach cooks down, add another batch. Keep going until you've added all the spinach.

3. Add the water, salt, and pepper. Cover and cook, very slowly, over extremely low heat, until the spinach is entirely soft and velvety, at least 1 hour.

4. Just before the spinach is ready, heat the remaining clarified butter (or oil) in a small nonstick skillet. Over medium high heat, cook the remaining ginger and chiles together until sizzling hot, about 45 seconds. Stir into the cooked spinach and serve at once. Serve with the rice or bread of your choice.

CD's Country Spinach

I have been making this combination for so long I've forgotten who taught it to me. Although I've cut the fat back considerably from the good old bad old days, it's still very, very good. Some people stem the spinach and either discard the stems (sacrilege!) or eat them separately, as another vegetable dish the next day, but I just throw 'em in with the leaves. **SERVES 4**

2 teaspoons butter
6 or 7 small mushrooms, sliced
3 scallions, roots and any wilted green parts removed, diced
2 cloves garlic, pressed
2 pounds fresh spinach, well washed and chopped
3 tablespoons reduced-fat sour cream or Yogurt Sour Cream (page 910)
3 tablespoons freshly grated Parmesan cheese
Salt and freshly ground black pepper
Freshly grated nutmeg

1 Melt the butter in a nonstick skillet over medium heat. Add the mushrooms and sauté for 5 minutes. Add the scallions and sauté for another 3 minutes. Add the garlic and stir well.

2 Add as much spinach as the skillet will hold. Cover, steam to reduce the bulk of the spinach, continually adding more until all of the spinach has been wilted down. Uncover and sauté, stirring, until most or all of the liquid has evaporated and the spinach is greatly reduced but still very green, about 10 minutes. Stir in the sour cream and Parmesan. Season to taste with salt, pepper, and nutmeg. Serve immediately.

Jan Brown's Greens Lebanese

This is a slightly revised version of the way my dear friend Jan fixed greens back when we did our first cookbook together. Add the lemon a little at a time, but don't be afraid to make it lemony. This is excellent served with Polenta,

Parmesan and Roasted Garlic Pudding (page 301), or with Middle-Eastern-Style Pilaf with Noodles and Red Lentils (page 483). **SERVES 4**

2 teaspoons butter
2 teaspoons olive oil
1 large onion, sliced vertically into thin crescents
4 cloves garlic
2 pounds fresh greens, well washed and chopped
1 lemon, halved
Salt and freshly ground black pepper to taste
¼ cup finely minced basil leaves

1 Combine the butter and olive oil in a nonstick skillet over medium heat. Add the onion and sauté for 5 minutes. Add half of the garlic and sauté for another minute.

2 Add as many of the greens as the skillet will hold. Cover and steam to reduce the bulk of the greens, continually adding more until all the greens have been wilted down. Uncover and sauté until most or all of the liquid has evaporated. Cover and continue cooking until tender (this might be almost no time if you used a tender green like spinach, or it might be 10 to 12 minutes if you used collard, kale, or turnip greens). The greens should be totally wilted and tender, but still very green, with a bit of texture.

3 Squeeze half of the lemon over the greens, add the remaining garlic, and the salt and pepper, along with the basil. Toss again and cook just until the basil wilts, 20 or 30 seconds. Have a bite, and, if needed, add the juice of the second lemon half and/or additional salt and pepper. Serve immediately.

Essence of Greens Tart with Fresh Herbs

If greens are the predominating flavor you want, this is the tart for you. With just enough binding to hold it together, this is little more than good old greens, sparked with fresh herbs, in a substantial, relatively low-fat crust. Be sure to use a mix for the second pound of greens—using only peppery arugula or watercress would be too much, but combined with a milder companion, like chard, it is most tonic. **SERVES 6**

Swiss Chard

1 pound fresh spinach, stems removed, washed
Water, preferably spring or filtered
1½ teaspoons salt, plus more to taste
1 pound assorted miscellaneous greens (kale, collards, turnip, arugula, watercress), washed, stems removed
Cooking spray
1 tablespoon olive oil
1 large onion, chopped
2 cloves garlic, minced
1 tablespoon cornstarch
2 scallions, roots and any wilted green parts removed, coarsely chopped
1 large egg
4 ounces silken tofu (about one-third of a 12.3-ounce box)
⅓ cup chopped assorted fresh herb leaves, such as basil, cilantro, dill, Texas Tarragon (see page 37), a little rosemary, thyme, oregano
5 or 6 gratings of nutmeg
5 or 6 good grinds of black pepper
1 Savory Sesame-Oatmeal Pie Crust (page 991), partially prebaked
¾ cup freshly grated Parmesan cheese (optional)

1 Place the spinach in a steamer basket over boiling water until it has wilted and is deep green. Remove from the heat, rinse quickly in cold water, and drain well. Using your hands, squeeze the spinach over a small bowl, reserving the liquid. Place half of the spinach in a food processor. Using a sharp knife, chop the remaining spinach medium-fine and set aside.

2 Add 1½ teaspoons salt to a large pot of water. Bring to a boil over high heat. Drop in the raw greens, and cook until fairly tender, 5 to 6 minutes. Remove from the heat, rinse quickly under cold running water, and drain well. Using your hands, squeeze the greens over the same bowl holding the spinach liquid, reserving the liquid (there should be about 1 cup total). Place half of the greens in the food processor with the spinach. Using a sharp knife, chop the remaining greens medium-fine. Add the chopped greens to the chopped spinach and set aside.

3 Preheat the oven to 350°F.

4 Heat the oil in a nonstick skillet. Add the onion and sauté until the onion is quite limp and starting to brown, 7 to 8 minutes. Add the garlic and sauté for another minute. Scoop out about half of the sautéed mixture and add to the coarsely chopped greens. Leave the skillet on the heat.

5 Dissolve the cornstarch in the greens liquid, squishing the cornstarch in with your fingers, pour the cornstarch into the hot skillet with the remaining onions, and stir with a wooden spoon to combine. It will almost instantly thicken into more of a clump than a sauce. Remove from the heat and add to the food processor mixture, along with the scallions, egg, tofu, herbs, nutmeg, and salt and pepper to taste. Buzz until quite smooth. Combine the pureed mixture with the chopped greens. Scrape this mixture into the pie crust.

6 Bake until the filling is smooth and firm on the surface, 30 to 35 minutes. Sprinkle the Parmesan, if using, over the top of the tart and bake until the cheese melts and is golden, another 20 to 25 minutes. Remove from the heat. Blot the surface of the tart with a paper towel to absorb any excess oil from the cheese. Let stand for 5 to 10 minutes, then cut and serve.

Jerusalem Artichokes

These small, knobby-looking tubers have nothing to do with either Jerusalem or artichokes. A hybrid variation allows them to form beneath sunflowers, giving rise to the other name by which they're sometimes known—sunchokes. Somewhat resembling ginger root in appearance, they have a thin, golden-brown edible skin (which is good, as they're too knobby to peel), over an ivory flesh. The flesh has a split personality: Uncooked, it is sweet and crisp, much like fresh water chestnuts; cooked, it turns soft and somewhat potatolike. Usually available only in the fall, they are an idiosyncratic delicacy, to enjoy a few weeks each year.

The recipes that follow explore the cooked version. Get to know the raw in Orange, Grapefruit, and Avocado Salad with Jerusalem Artichokes (page 98). Or substitute half diced raw Jerusalem artichokes for celery in your favorite Waldorf salad recipe.

Choose firm Jerusalem artichokes, with no soft spots or bruises. *To prepare for cooking* or eating raw, wash well under cold running water. To remove bits of dirt or sand that may be hiding in their crevices, spread any particularly close-together knobs on the tuber, and rinse well.

Basic Steam-Sautéed Jerusalem Artichokes

Try these once absolutely straightforward, to experience their earthy, sweet goodness. Then doll them up in one of the ways that follow. **SERVES 4 TO 6 AS AN ACCOMPANIMENT**

1½ pounds Jerusalem artichokes, well scrubbed, unpeeled, cut into ¼-inch-thick slices
1½ teaspoons butter, preferably Browned Butter (page 1024), or mild vegetable oil, such as corn, canola, or peanut
Salt to taste

1 Steam the Jerusalem artichokes in a collapsible steamer basket set above boiling water until slightly softened but not yet tender, 6 to 8 minutes. Remove the artichokes from the steamer and give them a quick run under cold water to stop the cooking.

2 Heat the butter in a nonstick skillet over medium-high heat. When hot, add the steamed Jerusalem artichokes and stir-fry until they are starting to brown, very hot and tender but not mushy (keep testing, so you'll know when you've reached the right point), 3 to 5 minutes. Season with salt to taste and serve.

Jazzed-Up Jerusalems

DOUBLE-SUNFLOWER SUNCHOKES: *As the Jerusalem artichokes steam, toast, stirring constantly, 1 to 2 tablespoons sunflower seeds in a hot, dry skillet over medium heat, until the seeds darken slightly in color and give off a fragrance, about 3 minutes. Remove the seeds from the skillet and set aside. Add to the Jerusalem artichokes, toss a few times, and serve.*

JERUSALEM ARTICHOKES WITH SOUR CREAM: *The tartness of a soured dairy product against the sweetness of the choke is quite magical. Just add 1 to 2 tablespoons sour cream, sour half-and-half, Yogurt Sour Cream (page 910), or Tofu Sour Cream (page 909), in the last few seconds of the stir-fry. Add some freshly ground black pepper and serve.*

CITRUS-SPLASHED JERUSALEM ARTICHOKES: *Like beets, Jerusalem artichokes respond to citrus in a big way. Very finely grate the rind of an orange, then halve the orange and squeeze its juice. Combine the juice, grated rind, and 2 to 3 tablespoons honey or brown sugar. Pour over the Jerusalem artichokes as you stir-fry them, cooking until they are nicely glazed. Serve hot.*

Roasty-Toasty Jerusalem Artichokes

A variation of one of the Dairy Hollow classic vegetable preparations, this method is perfect for the elemental, from-the-earth quality of these good little tubers. Be sure to use a shallow pan large enough to hold the sunchokes in a single layer with plenty of air space, so they can roast evenly. A too-small pan will have the vegetables lying on top of each other, while a too-deep pan will throw the evaporating water back down, preventing the all-important shrivelly roastiness.

SERVES 4 TO 6

2 pounds Jerusalem artichokes, very well scrubbed, whole
Cooking spray
2 teaspoons mild vegetable oil, such as corn, canola, or peanut
1 tablespoon tamari or shoyu soy sauce, plus additional to taste

1. Preheat the oven to 400°F.

2. If not using nonstick, spray a baking dish (large enough to hold the Jerusalem artichokes comfortably in a single layer) with cooking spray.

3. Place the Jerusalem artichokes in the prepared baking dish. Add the oil, tossing to coat and rubbing it in a bit with your hands. Bake for about 30 minutes, then drizzle with the tamari and toss again. Bake until the Jerusalem artichokes are golden brown and soft but not mushy, about 20 minutes longer. Serve straight from the oven.

Mushrooms

Mushrooms are not vegetables but edible fungi, simple plants that lack chlorophyll, roots, leaves, and botanical stems. They cannot draw food from light, the magic trick of all other forms of vegetable life; they live, rather, on the dead tissue of other plants. If this sounds creepy, especially when many mushrooms are deadly poisons and others are hallucinogens, it also adds to the strange allure of those fungi that are deliciously edible, particularly the more exotic ones. Equally mysterious are their cousins, yeasts and molds; if some are lethal, others raise bread, turn juice to wine, make cheese of milk, heal infections. Tonic or treacherous, mushrooms also perform their part in soil renewal by helping to decompose organic matter.

The range of edible fungi now available—especially if you live in a metropolitan area—is staggering. I love the intensely flavored porcini or cèpes (though here we only get them dried). Morels, which we now find at the farmer's market in the spring, are delicate yet woodsy; great in a mixed-mushroom sauté and omelets, they also seem to be made to serve with that other springtime delicacy, asparagus. Also at the farmer's market every so often are beautiful apricot-colored chanterelles, mild, earthy, pleasing. Wild puffballs are mostly airy texture melting to ethereal tenderness. The domestic mushroom is a reliable standby, and the portobello—which is the more mature and flavorful self of the cremini, or common brown mushroom—makes for a dramatic presentation. Enokis, cute as can be, are essentially tasteless; but lobster mushrooms, oyster mushrooms, black trumpets, and especially matsutake (also called hen- or chicken-of-the-woods) each have a definite personality.

But, for me, the shiitake tops the list. I feel fortunate to live in an area where they are grown, and are consequently inexpensive. I have been cooking with them for years, and still find them satisfying every time and every way that I prepare them. In America shiitakes are relative newcomers, but they have been highly prized for centuries in Japan and China, where they are carefully graded. (Top grades, dehydrated and of a uniform size, are so esteemed that they are sold, carefully wrapped, to be given as gifts.) The best grade is that which the Japanese call *donko*. This is not a varietal name, and sometimes you won't find it at all. But look at the top side of shiitake caps. If they're a smooth, moist, uniform reddish brown, the growing conditions were a bit wet, and they'll be good, but not great. If they're a slightly lighter brown and drier, they'll be better. But *donko shiitakes*, due to perfect growing conditions, have concentrated flavor and an unspongy, firm texture: supreme mushrooms. *Donko shiitakes* are easy to pick out, because their caps have a distinctive webbing of cracks across them. As if incomparable flavor and texture weren't reason enough to fall for the shiitake, it also contains among the most intriguing of phytochemicals, *lentinan*, cited in dozens of studies in various scientific journals as a potent anticarcinogen. For all these reasons—but primarily the culinary ones—you will find shiitakes in dozens of recipes throughout this book. They are not just my favorite mushroom, but one of my all-time favorite ingredients.

No matter what type of mushroom you purchase, make sure it is not bruised, or spotted with dampness. Also, avoid mushrooms that appear shriveled, especially at the base of the stem.

To prepare for cooking, cut off any tough spots (this might be the entire stem or just the base), saving the trimmings as a particularly valuable addition to stock. For years it has been a part of culinary wisdom that mushrooms should be wiped with a towel, not wetted with water, but culinary chemist Harold McGee debunked this myth by measuring

the water content before and after, and if a rinse is okay with him, it's okay with me. Shiitakes and some other exotics require fairly careful picking over, as they are grown in oak logs, so there might be little chips of bark here and there in the gills. By the way, new evidence suggests that the common *Agaricus,* or button mushroom, the most widely grown domestic, must be cooked to be safe. Although frequently eaten raw in spinach salads and the like, these mushrooms do contain potent toxins that are inactivated by even a brief cooking. Another piece of the mushroom mystery.

How should you fix mushrooms? Anytime I want to easily spiff up a component plate, my first thought is Oven-Roasted Shiitake Mushrooms with Garlic and Coarse Salt (page 48), a dish as simple to make as it is swooningly delicious. But stuffed mushrooms, such as Stuffed Deviled Mushrooms with Basil and Garlic (page 50), or mushrooms in a savory sauce, such as Mushrooms Diablo (page 51), also make the simplest rice-beans-greens component plate something to write home about. Polenta Lasagna with Mushrooms Béchamel (page 374) is a main course to please any mushroom-lover, as are piroshki stuffed with the dense, dark Mushroom Filling à la Eva (page 354). Creamy Gratin of Exotic Mushrooms and Potatoes (page 282), which uses dried exotics, is heavenly, not to be missed. But for the true essence-of-mushroom main dish, try Mushroom, Wild Rice, and Lentil Timbale-Cake (page 304) with Mushroom-Miso-Mustard Gravy (page 952)—good past reckoning.

As you will see in my recipes, mushrooms are natural with garlic, or, for that matter, any of the alliums: onions, shallots, leeks, scallions. Less fortunate is the edible fungi's deep affinity for butter or olive oil: They soak it up like a sponge, and cutting back the oil doesn't usually work, because most varieties then exude so much moisture they become soggy. If you find some exotics to try, you can hardly go wrong (from a culinary, not nutritional, point of view) slicing and sizzling them with butter and garlic. This way you can get acquainted with the individual characteristics. If you want to go whole hog in this direction, a splash of cream and a little white wine or brandy is supreme—great on pasta. But I would reserve such treatment only for once in a blue moon.

The grill may be the perfect compromise in much mushroom cookery; you have to use some oil to prevent the mushrooms from sticking, but you can get by with less, and the dry heat benefits the watery nature of most mushrooms.

Basic Mushroom Sauté with Garlic

Whether as part of a component plate, an accompaniment to a center-of-the-plate entree, or scooped over pasta, earthy or elegant, this mushroom dish will fit in. Using a nonstick pan greatly decreases the amount of oil or butter needed. Choose the type of fat according to whatever other dishes you are serving, and use more if you like (standard versions use up to 5 tablespoons; way too much for my taste, but maybe not yours). This is an excellent recipe for really understanding the flavor of a particular type of mushroom, so if you come upon, say, gorgeous hen-of-the-woods or chanterelles for the first time, splurge and try them this way. On the other hand, this recipe also works superbly as a mixed sauté, using mostly the inexpensive regular button mushrooms, with just a few exotics thrown in.

Use your largest skillet—the mushrooms must have plenty of space as they sauté.

SERVES 4 AS AN ACCOMPANIMENT OR COMPONENT

1 tablespoon butter, Better (page 905), or olive oil (or a combination)
1¼ pounds mushrooms, one variety or a combination of several, cleaned and sliced or quartered
2 large cloves garlic, minced
Salt and freshly ground black pepper

1 Melt the butter in a large nonstick skillet over high heat. When the skillet is very

hot, add the mushrooms and quickly sauté. They'll want to soak up every bit of fat you're using, so you must move quickly to distribute it.

Lower the heat to medium-high and continue sautéing. Depending on the varieties you're using, the mushrooms may exude juice, but don't worry; keep sautéing and eventually the liquid will evaporate, its essence reabsorbed by the mushrooms, which will also start to color slightly. This will take 5 to 7 minutes.

2 Add the garlic and sauté for another 30 seconds or so. Season with salt to taste and several grindings of black pepper and serve immediately.

More Mushrooms

Mushroom Sauté, French-Style: *Use butter or Better (page 905), and at the very end, toss in 1 to 2 tablespoons finely minced curly parsley and 1 tablespoon white wine or the juice of ½ lemon.*

Mushroom Sauté, Greek-Style: *Use olive oil. When you add the garlic, toss in ¼ teaspoon dried Greek oregano (or 1 tablespoon finely minced fresh) and ¼ teaspoon dried mint (or 1 tablespoon finely minced fresh Italian parsley), as well as the juice of ½ lemon.*

Mushroom Sauté, Italian-Style: *Use olive oil. Add an extra clove of garlic and, with it, 1½ teaspoons each minced fresh parsley, Italian oregano, and fresh mint. Another option: Add 1 teaspoon tomato paste.*

Mushroom Sauté, Russian-Style: *Use butter or Better (page 905). Cut the garlic back to 1 clove. When you add it, add 2 teaspoons finely minced fresh dill. Just at the moment the mushrooms come off the heat, add 1 to 2 tablespoons sour cream, Yogurt Sour Cream (page 910), sour half-and-half, or Tofu Sour Cream (page 909). Toss well and serve. Try this as part of a component dinner with a rice pilaf, baked beets, and mashed butternut squash.*

Simple Grilled Portobellos

An excellent this-couldn't-get-much-simpler preparation. What do you do with a giant grilled portobello? Make a sandwich of it between slices of good bread (with anything from sliced cheese, tomato, and onion on a whole-grain bun, to a whole pile of other grilled vegetables on a garlic-mayo–spread baguette). Or just plunk it down as an impressive player on a component plate. Or treat it as a centerpiece, as you would a steak—place it in the middle of the plate, perhaps with a big stack of grilled onions atop it. **ALLOW 1 LARGE PORTOBELLO PER PERSON**

1 portobello mushroom—the largest you can find—per serving
Olive oil or cooking spray
Salt to taste

1 Preheat the grill to high, then lower the heat to medium. (Alternatively, using the stove-top, preheat a nonstick skillet or ridged pan to very hot.)

2 Using a pastry brush, lightly coat both sides of the mushroom with oil. Alternatively, give each side a quick spray of oil or cooking spray.

3 Place the oiled mushroom on the grill over indirect heat, or right into the hot skillet, gill side down. Grill until softened and seared, 3 to 4 minutes. Turn gill side up, and grill for 3 to 4 minutes. The mushroom should be tender and hot all the way through. Remove from the grill (or pan), salt lightly, and serve.

Ned's Marsala-Marinated Portobello Grill

NOTE

Essential to preparing this is an outdoor grill, or a heavy-gauge non-stick ridged grill.

In our household, come suppertime, I usually cook and Ned washes dishes, an exchange that leaves us both grateful. But every so often—if I'm harried or in general need of nurturing, he'll cook *and* wash dishes. When Ned cooks, his dishes are always interesting, and usually so good I find myself wondering if I have done him a disservice by being the food preparer most of the time. (But then I wash the dishes a few times, and say to myself, "Nah.")

This Ned-invention is sweet, salty, and peppery, just packed with flavor that explodes in the mouth, and pretty durn quick. **SERVES 2 TO 4 AS A COMPONENT**

⅓ cup Marsala
1 tablespoon honey
1 tablespoon tamari or shoyu soy sauce
1 to 2 teaspoons olive oil
½ to 1 teaspoon hot sauce, such as Choulula Mexican Hot Sauce
½ teaspoon freshly ground black pepper, or more to taste
6 ounces portobello mushrooms, sliced crosswise into ¼-inch-thick strips

1 Combine the Marsala, honey, tamari,

oil, hot sauce, and black pepper in a small nonreactive bowl. Mix well, then add the sliced portabello mushroom. Marinate for 20 to 30 minutes, tossing every so often.

2 Preheat the grill to high (alternatively, heat a ridged, nonstick grill pan over medium-high heat). When the grill is hot, using a pair of tongs, lift the mushroom strips from the marinade, shaking off any excess. Carefully place the strips on the grill (over indirect heat), one by one. Grill just long enough so they get a good, grill-marked sear, 3 to 5 minutes. Turn and grill the other side until heated through, 2 to 4 minutes. Serve at once.

COOK ONCE FOR 2 MEALS Make a double recipe of these divine mushrooms. Use the first half, hot from the grill, for Ronni's New Wave "Killed Lettuce Salad" (page 74) with Ned's Marsala-Marinated Portobello Grill (page 770). Reserve the remaining half and serve the next day, cold as a side dish or reheated and used as a sandwich filling with arugula, slivered purple cabbage, and, if dairy is not a problem, paper-thin slices of smoked provolone cheese on a good crusty, crisp halved baguette.

VARIATION

This is also an excellent treatment with shiitakes, though, being a drier mushroom, they sear more quickly.

Ned's Frizzled Shiitakes

Another of Ned's ways with mushrooms, this takes the time-honored combo of mushrooms and garlic, but adds a new element: crispness. This is achieved without frying or breading—just tossing the mushrooms with a little flour and broiling. Watch closely—they burn in a heartbeat.

Although this great preparation can be served as an accompaniment, its crispness makes it an excellent topping. Scatter it over steamed cauliflower or broccoli; slit open a hot baked potato and pile it on; use it to top a gratin or pasta, or in lieu of crisp breadcrumbs on a mushroom-filled crêpe. **SERVES 4 TO 6**

¾ pound shiitake mushrooms, cleaned, stems removed, sliced into ¼-inch strips
4 large cloves garlic, pressed
1 tablespoon olive oil
½ teaspoon salt
Several vigorous grindings of black pepper
2 tablespoons unbleached white all-purpose flour
Cooking spray

1 Preheat the broiler.

2 Combine the mushrooms, garlic, oil, salt, and pepper with the flour, tossing well to distribute evenly.

3 Generously spray a large, shallow baking dish with cooking spray, and scatter the mushrooms in it. Although the mushrooms will tend to clump, push them around a little to make a single layer.

4 Broil for about 3 minutes. Pull the dish out and shake the mushrooms around. Broil for another 3 minutes; repeat the pull-out and shake maneuver. Note how hot the mushrooms are and if they're beginning to color. You will probably need to repeat the 3-minute pull-and-shake routine two more times, for a total of 15 minutes, until the mushrooms are very hot and somewhat limp, but golden, and with crisp crumbs of the flour-oil-garlic mixture. Serve, hot, immediately.

Mushroom and Tempeh Stroganoff

NOTE

Although I've called for regular domestic button mushrooms here, feel free to substitute shiitakes for part of the mushrooms.

This is one of my workhorse vegetarian entrees, one I have been making various versions of for as long as I can remember. This is possibly because beef stroganoff was one of my mother's standby party dishes when I was growing up. My current renditions are not only vegetarian, they're much lower in fat, and often vegan. I have turned it into a stir-fry of mushrooms, onions, and green peppers, with chunks of baked tempeh, and a nutmeg-scented sour cream sauce. Sometimes I add broccoli; sometimes I serve it over barley, rice pilaf, or pasta. Whenever I make it for my mother, she comments on how much she likes it—much better, she says, than the real thing that inspired it.

I opt for the butter-oil combination and sour half-and-half or low-fat sour cream. However, the oil–Tofu Sour Cream version, which will make vegans and the lactose-intolerant very happy, is not bad at all. **SERVES 4 TO 6 AS AN ENTREE**

Cooking spray
1 tablespoon butter or olive oil, or ½ tablespoon of each
1 large onion, sliced vertically into crescents
1 green bell pepper, stemmed, seeded, membranes removed, sliced vertically into strips
1 red bell pepper, stemmed, seeded, membranes removed, sliced vertically into strips
¾ pound domestic button mushrooms, cleaned and sliced
3 cloves garlic, minced
¾ cup rich, dark stock (preferably the dark Oven-Roasted Vegetable Stock with mushrooms, page 141, or Imagine Foods Mushroom Broth)
2 teaspoons cornstarch
8 to 10 gratings of nutmeg
1½ teaspoons Pickapeppa sauce (or vegetarian Worcestershire sauce)
½ teaspoon salt
Several vigorous grindings of black pepper
¾ cup sour cream, sour half-and-half, low-fat sour cream, Yogurt Sour Cream (page 910), or Tofu Sour Cream (page 909)
1 recipe Basic Oven-Baked Marinated Tempeh (page 641)

1 Place a large nonstick skillet, or one that has been sprayed with cooking spray, over medium-high heat. Add the butter. When it is good and hot, add the onion. Cook, stirring often, until the onion is limp and just starting to brown, 7 to 8 minutes. Add the bell peppers and mushrooms, and stir-fry until the peppers begin to soften, about 4 more minutes. Lower the heat to medium. Add the garlic and stir-fry for 1 minute more.

2 Raise the heat to high and add ½ cup of the stock. Dissolve the cornstarch in the remaining stock and stir in the nutmeg, Pickapeppa, salt, and pepper—a lot of pepper. Add to the skillet, stirring constantly. Immediately add the sour cream and the tempeh. Cook, stirring constantly, until heated through, perhaps 30 seconds. Remove from the heat, taste, and, if necessary, adjust the seasonings—it will probably require additional black pepper, maybe more salt and nutmeg, too. Serve immediately.

VARIATION

A bit of crisp-tender, steamed or stir-fried broccoli is good in this. I occasionally use a Russian-style seasoning with the addition of a teaspoon or so of prepared mustard to the sour cream mix. For a really tasty, simpler version, instead of making Basic Oven-Baked Marinated Tempeh, sauté one of the ready-made seasoned tempehs, such as lemon-broiled. Or use diced tofu in lieu of tempeh.

On Stroganoff

Stroganoff has a couple of mysteries associated with it. Sometimes it's spelled with one f, sometimes with two, sometimes with a v. Adding to this confusion: which actual Stroganoff was it named after? Food writer Anya von Bremzen, in Please to the Table: The Russian Cookbook, *hypothesizes that it was either Pavel Stroganoff, who lived in the late nineteenth century, or the earlier Alexander Stroganoff, a contemporary of Catherine the Great. She tips the likelihood to Pavel, who was famed for the luxurious ostentation of his banquets, though she personally prefers Alexander, "a great patron of the arts without whose generosity Russia's passage into true enlightenment would have been difficult." But to me, a child of the '50s, the larger Stroganoff mystery is this: Why, at the height of the Cold War, was America's number-one fancy dish Beef Stroganoff? Perhaps it is as the Russian anarchist Peter Kropotkin once remarked: "If you want to know the people of a nation, I am sure you can judge a great deal more about them from their cooking and eating traditions . . . than from the words and actions of their public officials."*

Okra

If the South loves okra—and it does—okra also loves the South. *Abelmoschus esculentus,* to call the spined edible pod by its Latin name, adores hot, sunny weather, and humidity doesn't faze it in the least. Long, long after the spinach and cilantro have bolted and the tomatoes are looking worse for wear, okra grows proudly, forthrightly, even show-offly. Not only is the okra plant tall—5 to 6 feet—it has the most gorgeous, splashy yellow blossoms, easily 2 inches across, with a deep red-burgundy center. If you've ever traveled to the tropics, you'll immediately recognize those flowers; they look exactly like hibiscus blossoms, because okra is a member of the hibiscus genus, as you might have guessed from its Latin name. They also resemble hollyhocks, another family member.

But okra blossoms are nothing compared to the lusty oddity of okra pods. For the pods—unlike squashes on the vine, or tomatoes, or peppers, or anything, anything but itself—the okra pods come out in all defiance of gravity (and, perhaps, decency), pointing their tips straight up in the air.

These pods, sometimes called ladies' fingers, are the edible part of the okra. The second half of the plant's Latin name, *esculentus,* means "succulent." They are succulent indeed. The mucilaginous interior texture that some find objectionable is, in the hands of a good cook who understands the plant, part of that succulence that can be used to advantage in a gumbo, or downplayed to non-existence in fried okra. Only boiled okra—and no one who had the slightest respect for this vegetable would *ever* boil it—is "slimy," the pejorative word that those who haven't experienced its sublimity sometimes oh-so-wrongly use.

Frying is a time-honored Southern approach, and gumbo another. Pickling "seems to have surfaced about 40 years ago and rocketed to prominence," according to Southern food authority John Egerton, who says that he was unable to find a recipe for it in any cookbook predating World War II. But there is no doubt that the South has taken this vegetable (of African, almost certainly Ethiopian, origin, brought to America by the slaves) to its heart.

Whether you live in the South and already know okra, or are a Yankee or Californian or from Wisconsin or some place that is more or less okra-ignorant, you have good eating ahead.

Although you may find weather-beaten okra any time of year, imported from who-knows-where, the best time to find good okra is in the highest, hottest arch of midsummer. Good, tender, young pods are short—no more than 2½ to 3 inches in length—and fancifully ridged, a sort of rounded triangular cone capped by a sprightly stem at one end and a sharp tip at the other. Choose those that are solid green—though some varieties are striking reddish purple and turn green as the pod cooks. But it should have that bursting, proud look of freshness to it, and be free of any darkening, the sure sign of okra that is past its prime. Pick up a pod and bend it; it should resist, bending only slightly. Don't be put off by its slightly bristly feel, or the touch of fuzziness; these are lost entirely in the cooking.

To prepare for cooking, just rinse it. For the recipes here, leave the pods whole. But if you want to fry your okra, that's another story. John Egerton's *Southern Food* or Ronni Lundy's *Shuck Beans, Stack Cakes, and Honest Fried Chicken* can both tell you how.

Greek-Style Smothered Okra

Here is the third slow-cooked, Greek-style vegetable I make, the other two being green beans and summer squash. It's good with summer squash, but with okra or green beans this method is nothing less than superlative. I urge you to try it. If you are, as I used to be, an always-cook-only-to-crisp-tender person, this may open your eyes to a whole new approach to vegetables. For further understanding of this synergistic, lovely combo, please see pages 689 and 799. **SERVES 4 TO 6**

CICADA-SONG SUPPER IN AUGUST

Cilantro Chile'd Hot Potatoes
(PAGE 787)

*

Simple Sweet-Baked Winter Squash
(PAGE 807)

*

Greek-Style Smothered Okra

*

Scallioned Beets and Their Greens in Herbed Mustard Sauce
(PAGE 703)

*

Ronni's Skillet-Sizzled Kentucky Cornbread Buttermilk
(PAGE 452)

*

Plum Crisp
(PAGE 978)

Cooking spray
1 tablespoon chopped garlic (or omit garlic and olive oil and use 1 tablespoon plus 1 teaspoon Garlic Oil, page 898)
2 teaspoons to 1 tablespoon olive oil
1½ pounds 2- to 3-inch-long very fresh okra pods, washed well, but not cut open in any way
1 large, juicy, deep-ripe summer tomato, chopped
Salt and freshly ground black pepper to taste
A few dashes of cayenne
½ to 1 teaspoon dry dill weed

1 Spray a heavy, 10- to 14-inch cast-iron skillet, one that has a tight-fitting cover, with cooking spray. Place over very low heat. Add the garlic, oil, and okra. (In contrast to most sautés, the okra is added when neither pan, nor oil, nor garlic is yet hot.) Scatter the tomato over the okra.

Cook, uncovered, for 10 minutes. Do not stir. Cover and cook for 30 minutes more. Do not stir, but make sure the heat is low enough so nothing burns. If you like, you can kind of push a few of the pods back to make sure the garlic on the bottom is not burning, but merely cooking, very, very slowly.

2 Uncover. Stir cautiously, just a few times—the okra should be quite tender, soft and sort of golden-brown. While stirring, you want to break it up as little as possible; rather, just recombine the ingredients, though it is likely that a few pods will split if they have not already done so.

3 Turn off the heat. Season with salt and pepper to taste. Sprinkle with cayenne and dill, stir one more time, and serve. Serve the whole pods. Eaters can either cut off the stems at the top of the pods themselves (with a fork and knife), or pick them up by the stems and nibble their way down, or even eat the stems—firmer, of course, than the tender pod, but edible and tasty.

Grilled Marinated Okra Three Ways

Although I have been an okra fan for years, this is my latest and most favorite way to cook it. Grilled okra? Oh yes indeedy; it is, as they say, so good you'd slap your mama for the last bite. You place the pods on a soaked wooden skewer—not lengthwise, not crosswise, but on an angle—that way you can get a lot of them on each skewer, and they're securely affixed enough to be easily flippable. After they're skewered, choose one of the three quick marinades, and pour it over the okra. You'll notice that all the marinades include a fresh tomato; my belief that okra and tomatoes are a match made in heaven is unshakable. You'll also notice that the marinades are distinctly salty; grilled okra requires salt.

There's something very alligatory-looking about the pods on the stick. Besides being scrumptious, they're fun to eat. Serve them as part of a grilled dinner, keying the marinade to the rest of the meal. Serve the Mediterranean marinated okra with a rice or barley pilaf and an assortment of *mezze*-type dishes (baba ganouj, olives, sliced tomatoes, and so on); serve the South-of-the-border marinade version with Black Bean Feijoada (page 602) and Brazilian Rice (page 473); serve the Indian (a truly sublime mixture) with Dal (page 609), yogurt, basmati rice, and Katherine's Paneer in Tomato Masala (page 198). **SERVES 3 OR 4**

1 pound 2- to 3-inch-long okra pods
Marinade (your choice of any of the three that follow)

1. About 1 hour prior to beginning the recipe, soak six to eight 9-inch wooden skewers in cold water. (I usually put them in a glass of water, leave them, then reverse them, so that both ends get a soak.)

2. Holding an okra pod at a 45-degree angle to the soaked skewer, push the okra down onto the skewers, pod by pod and skewer by skewer. The pods should be close together, and all facing the same direction. You should end up with 7 or 8 pods per skewer. Place the skewers on a shallow baking tray.

3 Pour the marinade of choice over the pods. They will not be swimming in marinade; it will be necessary to divide the marinade between all of the skewers, rubbing it a bit to distribute it equally. Marinate for 1 to 2 hours at room temperature, or up to 6 hours refrigerated.

4 Preheat the grill to high, then lower the heat to medium.

5 Place the skewered okra on the preheated grill and cook over indirect heat until the first side is grill-marked, 3 to 4 minutes. Turn the skewers and grill the second side for 3 minutes. Serve immediately.

Three Marinades for Grilled Okra

Place all of the ingredients in the food processor and buzz until smooth, pausing to scrape down the sides of the bowl:

Mediterranean: 6 to 8 large leaves fresh basil; 2 cloves garlic, peeled and quartered; 1 large tomato, peeled, seeded, and chopped; 2 tablespoons olive oil; 1 tablespoon balsamic vinegar; and 2 teaspoons salt.

South of the Border: 2 cloves garlic, peeled and quartered; 1 large tomato, peeled, seeded, and chopped; ½ bunch cilantro leaves; juice of 1 lemon; 2 tablespoons olive oil; 2 teaspoons adobo sauce; ¼ canned chipotle pepper in adobo; and 2 teaspoons salt.

Indian: 2 cloves garlic, peeled and quartered; 1 large tomato, peeled, seeded, and chopped; ⅓ cup chopped cilantro leaves; juice of 1 lime; 2 tablespoons sesame or peanut oil; 2 teaspoons salt; 1½ teaspoons peeled, chopped ginger; 1 teaspoon ground cumin; 1 teaspoon ground turmeric; and ¼ teaspoon ground cayenne.

I'm Okra, You're Okra

Onkra is adored in the South. This story gives you an idea of how much. One summer not long after I'd arrived in Eureka, there was a bumper crop of okra. A man named Ken actually threw an okra party. This was easily twenty-five years ago, and there were probably fifteen or twenty of us at his house, standing around the kitchen as he cheerfully fried the cornmeal-breaded okra slices, letting them drain on brown paper grocery bags, while we took turns slicing, standing around the kitchen, eating paper plate after paper plateful, talking, gossiping, and catching up, while outside, just beyond the screened porch, the cicadas and tree frogs and crickets made their loud, dedicated midsummer proclamations.

Phyllis McGinley once wrote that cities "offer a vast and solacing anonymity or an equally vast and solacing gregariousness. But one needs a neighbor on whom to practice compassion." Yes, and with whom to eat okra on a hot summer night.

Parsnips

Why won't more people try these scrumptious roots? True, their name sounds Dickensian, and they look like a vampire-drained carrot. But give these unprepossessing white roots a chance, and you'll be a parsnip fan forever. They are sweet, with an underlying faint parsley flavor. Their taste and appearance tell the story of their family tree—they're relatives of both carrots and parsley, as well as hemlock.

Although I most often use parsnips in soups and stews, the colonials used them in dessert pies as we use pumpkins. Nearly every nineteenth and early twentieth-century American cookbook has a recipe for parsnip cake or patty. This is what convinced me to fool with the recipe below.

Choose the most slender parsnips you can find, avoiding any that are bruised or shriveled. All parsnips, like carrots, taper from a root end point to a wider stem end; look for parsnips no wider than 1 inch; any larger and you risk a tough, woody core. Avoid parsnips that are coated in heavy, protective wax, or the cut-up parsnips sometimes marketed in packets of "vegetables for soup." Both of these tend to be past their prime.

To prepare for cooking, give parsnips a good scrub under cold running water. Cut off the stem end. Halve, lengthwise, and, using a paring knife, remove any woody core (it will be several shades darker). If for some reason the only available parsnips are wax-coated and you have to use one, be aware we're talking real wax, not a waxy shine such as that sometimes sprayed on peppers. This looks as if the poor vegetables were dipped into melted white candle wax, and it must actually be peeled off and discarded.

Sweet Parsnip Nubbins

These scrumptious little cakes, which have a sweet, comforting custardiness to them, were one of my favorite discoveries in working on this book. Before I tested these, I figured they'd need some kind of sauce to dress them up. Absolutely not. And while I'm sure a vegan variation could be done, I am so pleased with them I don't want to mess with the recipe. Try these cunning nubbins with a mixed grain dish and a stir-fry of broccoli; start the meal with a tomato-based soup. **MAKES 12 SMALL CAKES; SERVES 4**

1 teaspoon salt
2 pounds (about 16) parsnips, scrubbed, peeled, and quartered lengthwise, woody cores removed
2 large eggs, beaten
⅓ cup unbleached white all-purpose flour
2 tablespoons honey
6 to 8 gratings of nutmeg
Freshly ground black pepper to taste
About 1 cup fine, soft breadcrumbs
1½ tablespoons melted butter

1 Bring a large pot of water to a boil over high heat. Add ½ teaspoon of the salt. Drop the prepared parsnips into the boiling salted water and cook until tender, 8 to 10 minutes. Drain well (reserve the water to use as the base for stock). Alternatively, you may steam (8 to 10 minutes) or pressure-cook (2 to 3 minutes) parsnips until tender.

2 Place the parsnips in a bowl and, while hot, mash in the eggs, flour, and honey. Season with nutmeg, the remaining ½ teaspoon salt, and the pepper. When nicely mashed, cover and refrigerate until chilled, about 1 hour.

3 Preheat the oven to 375°F.

4 Shape the chilled parsnip mixture into twelve 2- to 3-inch-wide, ½-inch-thick patties.

5 Place the breadcrumbs in a shallow dish. Press each patty into the breadcrumbs, pressing in the breadcrumbs to coat evenly. Place the patties on a nonstick baking sheet. Using a pastry brush, lightly coat each patty with a tiny bit of the melted butter. Reserve a little butter for later use.

6 Bake until golden on top, about 25 minutes. Turn the patties over and brush with the remaining butter. Bake for another 10 minutes. Serve hot.

Peppers

Nothing is more sculpturally pleasing than the curved planes of a bell pepper, no palette more vivid than its colors: bright red or gold, seemingly lit from within, gleaming intense green and deep chocolate purple-brown. Add the dark shiny black-green of the sweet-hot, heart-shaped poblanos, the plump green bullets of fresh jalapeños, the arrowlike green serranos, the tiny red chiles sharp as a bird's beak, the squat but deadly hot habaneros . . . so elegant a profusion of sweet and hot beauty did the New World spread to the Old. Oddly enough, all peppers are members of the nightshade family, along with eggplant, potatoes, and tomatoes, although you have to look hard for the family resemblance. There are, however, countless dishes in which these vegetables collaborate congenially (probably melding more smoothly than most human relatives).

Peppers are virtually calorie-free, but packed with vitamins. The green and yellow bell peppers have more vitamin A; the reds, more vitamin C. The hot peppers are rich in phytochemicals, some just now being researched—no doubt those of us who are "chile heads" will soon have new reasons to justify our craving for heat.

Choose peppers that are unblemished, firm-skinned, smooth and unwrinkled, and that seem to almost burst with freshness. Check around the stem to make sure there's no sign of softening or mold. But the most important tip is this: Bell peppers are one vegetable that should be purchased certified organic, or not purchased at all, especially in the winter months. I know those bright, sweet peppers glow in the produce aisle on dark November days . . . but alas, according to the Environmental Working Group and many in the organic growing community, bell peppers are among the most heavily pesticide-sprayed crops, especially in the winter months, when they're imported from Mexico and South America, where there are fewer controls on pesticide use than here. Oddly, chile peppers are not so sprayed, so you can indulge to your heart's content.

I buy local peppers by the half bushel a couple of times each summer. I char a grillful, and take time to peel, seed, and freeze them, red and green and yellow separately. All winter long I am so glad I did this—frozen, thawed, and grilled are just about indistinguishable from fresh. Slightly less satisfactory, but acceptable for most dishes, is to freeze raw green peppers. Simply dice the raw green peppers, tossing them with a paper towel to dry slightly, and freeze in a single layer on a baking sheet or tray. When solid, transfer the frozen pepper dice into small zippered freezer bags (small because you only need a small quantity at any given time), and freeze for future use.

To prepare for cooking, first rinse them well, then . . . well, what happens next depends on the pepper.

For bell peppers, hold them upright and slide the knife down in four or five cuts, in essence cutting around the stem, the white fibrous core (which sometimes has tiny embryonic interior peppers attached, which are also discarded), and most of the seeds. This 1-2-3 method leaves 4 or 5 large pepper wedges, plus a smaller squared piece at the base. Brush or pick off any seeds clinging to the wedges. Lay each wedge of pepper, skin side down, on the cutting board, and, with a sharp paring knife, working parallel to the pepper, cut away any visible interior pale membrane of pepper flesh. Finally, cut the peppers as directed in the specific recipe: into strips, small slivers, large wedges, or the teeny-tiny dice known to us as "confetti" (this is primarily a garnish; a scattering of confetti of red, yellow, and green bell pepper edging a finished dinner plate is mighty pretty).

For poblano peppers, do the same thing, except that, because of the pepper's flattened heart-shape (as opposed to the blocky shape of the bells), you can't stand them upright to cut into wedges; you must lay them flat on their sides, and work parallel to both pepper and cutting board. Then proceed as above. (It bears mentioning here that a poblano is the fresh version of this heart-shaped sweet-hot pepper with a faintly chocolate-y undernote; an ancho is the same chile, dried.)

Hot chile peppers, in numberless variety, hold much of their heat concentrated in their seeds and membranes. So make the call according to personal preference. How hot do you want the finished dish to be? Hot to very, very, very hot? If the latter, leave them in (and invite me to supper). But to some Americans, blazingly hot food may be cruel and unusual punishment. If you are of that ilk, remove them.

There are countless hot pepper shapes and sizes, with heat ranging from warm to incendiary. And the very same variety of pepper can differ in heat, pepper to pepper and by season. As the weather heats up, so do the peppers. Year after year I notice that jalapeños available in winter and early spring at the market are relatively mild. By mid-July, they will take the top of your head off.

To prepare chiles, cover your hands by sliding them into plastic bags from the grocery store—much easier to work with than rubber gloves. You may also want to use a special cutting board, one you devote solely to garlic and hot peppers—the essential oils in the chile will saturate the board, giving whatever you cut on it a strong hint of hot. Slice the stem end from the chile. If removing the seeds and membranes, slit the pepper and, with a knife tip, pick out the seeds and cut out any membranes. Dice or cut as directed in the specific recipe. If you've decided to go for the heat, just dice or cut up the chile, seeds and membrane and all.

Even if you wore bags on your hands, be sure—especially when working with super-hots, like habaneros—to wash your hands very, very well, at least several times afterwards. Avoid touching your eyes, taking out contact lenses, or touching other tender body parts for some time after working with chiles.

How to use peppers: I almost always use bell peppers as an ingredient (usually diced and sautéed, with onion, garlic, celery or bok choy, or whatever). They are also great carriers for stuffing (see page 385). And every so often I get a sudden yen for the vegetarian equivalent of sausage and sautéed pepper and onion heros like I used to eat on the streets of New York, a recipe for which is given here.

Veggie Sausage, Pepper, and Onion Heros

I used to avoid soyfoods that masqueraded as meat. But in recent years, hip food companies and new methods of soy manufacturing have changed that. I must say, I love the nationally available Lightlife Lean Italian Links, a pale, soy-based sausage deliciously seasoned with the haunting fennel-anise and other herbs and spices I remember fondly from real Italian sausage. They are naturally, and desirably, way less fatty than the real thing. **SERVES 2 OR 3**

Cooking spray
1 package (11.2 ounces) Lightlife Lean Italian Links
2 teaspoons olive oil, plus more if desired
1 large onion, sliced vertically into crescents
2 green bell peppers, stemmed, seeds and membranes removed, cut vertically into slivers
1 baguette or other crisp-crusted long French or Italian bread, ideally whole grain

1 Spray a skillet with cooking spray. Place over medium-high heat and when it's good and hot, lay the sausage links in the skillet, leaving space between them. Lower the heat to medium and cook until golden brown on the side touching the pan, about 2 minutes; give a quarter-turn and sauté the next side. Continue until the links are golden on all sides. Remove from the skillet and set the links aside.

2 Add the oil to the skillet and raise the heat slightly. Add the onion and cook, stirring often until softened and just starting to brown, 7 to 8 minutes. Add the bell peppers (and, if you wish, a little extra oil) and continue frying until the peppers soften, another 5 to 6 minutes.

3 Slice the cooked sausage lengthwise, then crosswise on a diagonal, into thick slices. Slice the baguette lengthwise, and then crosswise into 2 or 3 pieces large enough for sandwiches. If desired, drizzle a little extra oil on the cut sides of the bread.

4 Return the cut sausage to the pan and quickly toss with the peppers and onion. Scoop the mixture onto the baguette, close the sandwich, and serve.

VARIATION

MARINATED PEPPERS FOR MEZZE: ***For every 4 or 5 prepared peppers, cut in strips, add 1 to 2 finely minced cloves of garlic, a drizzle of extra virgin olive oil, a small pinch of coarse salt, and the juice of ½ to 1 lemon. These will keep a little longer—3 to 4 days, refrigerated.***

Roasted or Charred Bell Peppers

Simple, but a bit picky to make (literally—you have to pick the charred skin from the roasted peppers, which can take a bit of time), roasting red or yellow bell peppers transforms their crisp, sweet, delicious flesh into silken smoothness with a seductive whisper of smoke. Roasted peppers are the basis for Roasted Red Pepper Soup (page 144), Voluptuous Roasted Red Pepper Spread (page 17), fabulous on The Relish Tray Redefined (page 53), and great on many sandwiches. Use the same method to roast poblanos, or green peppers, or even jalapeños, each of which have their own distinct characteristics. (Always wear plastic gloves when handling the hotter peppers.)

Roast as many peppers as you have. Sliced, seeded, and stored in zippered bags, they freeze like a dream for up to six months and will brighten some winter day for you. I allow one large pepper for four people when part of a mezze plate. **QUANTITY VARIABLE**

Whole red or yellow bell peppers, preferably large ones, or hot peppers of choice

1 Decide which of three heat methods you'd like to use: stove top (gas stove required), broiler, or grill. Have a pair of long-handled tongs nearby. For stove top, simply turn on the burner to full flame, and balance whole peppers on the metal grate above the flame, 3 or 4 peppers per burner, so that one side of each pepper is in contact with the flame. For the broiler method, arrange whole peppers on a sheet of aluminum foil, and place within 3 inches of direct broiler heat. For grill, preheat the grill to hot, then lay the whole peppers on the grill next to, but not right on, the high-heat area.

2 For all methods: Watch closely, tongs at the ready. When the portion of pepper skin closest to the heat becomes black—literally charred and bubbling—use the tongs to rotate the pepper. Repeat until as much of the pepper as possible is blackened.

3 When fully charred, immediately place the piping hot peppers into a paper bag or a bowl tightly covered with plastic wrap—the idea is to trap the steam generated by the peppers, which will loosen the skin.

4 Let the peppers steam until cool enough to handle—15 to 25 minutes, no longer. Then remove and discard the skin, stem and seed the peppers, and add the roasted pepper flesh to any number of dishes.

Potatoes

Time was, a single lump in a pile of mashed potatoes was proof sufficient of a cook's mediocrity and slovenliness. But today, when instant mashed potatoes are the unhappy norm in much home cooking, a lump is the badge of the real thing, a clear demonstration of the potato's provenance—from ground to sink to pot to mashing bowl, with no stop in whatever machinery is used to commercially divorce the potato from its soul. That, and their inherent and deeply soothing comfortable deliciousness, is why real mashed potatoes are in with chefs. Add to this the fact that they blend willingly with all kinds of things, from mushrooms to garlic to herbs to wasabi.

So let us take our lumps with the potato, the single starchy member of the mysterious nightshade family. The humble potato has traveled from its native Andes to be welcomed in kitchens from Ireland to India to Idaho. In fact, China produces more potatoes than any country in the world.

At the market, you'll find what may at first seem an almost bewildering variety of potatoes, and it is true that each type has its own personality. Yet all potatoes fall into one of three categories: boiling, baking, and all-purpose. What differentiates these categories? Moisture and starch content. These qualities are dependent on the quirks of individual varieties and the age of the potatoes. It's worth getting to know your potato categories and varieties a little, to ensure you'll get the result you want. Here is a brief potato primer.

Baking potatoes are low-moisture, high-starch potatoes perfect for baking, but their versatility does not end there. Their flesh is relatively dry, with a fluffy, almost flaky texture described (unappealingly, I think) as "mealy." Surprisingly, they're also perfect for mashing. What they are *not* good for is any dish where you want cooked potatoes in distinct pieces; such as in a potato salad or stew. Common baking potatoes include the ubiquitous dark brown ovoid Idaho, and the knobby russets (note that russets are brown, not red). Russet Burbank and Lemhi Russet are two heritage baking varieties that are extra-flavorful. Baking potatoes have slightly thicker, heartier skins than the other two types.

Boiling potatoes contain low starch and high moisture. There are many more varieties of boilers than bakers, but they can be easily discerned because their skin is thin and smooth; they're usually referred to as "waxy." For boiling, you want a potato whose cubes or slices remain discrete, as for salad or soups or stews. Cook them in liquid (ironically, you should never actually boil them, but use a slightly lower heat for optimum results). Or roast them—they come out as small, well-browned, often crisp-skinned little darlings (see Roasty-Toasty Potatoes, Carrots, and Onions, page 790). Now, just to confuse things, it happens that all varieties of potatoes, *when young,* fall into this category, because until they grow to maturity, their sugars do not all convert to starch—these are the small and succulent, slightly sweet potatoes called "new potatoes," usually easily available in spring. If you can rub the skin off easily with your fingertips, it is "new."

However, some varieties of potatoes do retain their youthful low starch–high moisture allure into maturity. Boilers include the beautiful White Rose (oblong, light brown, thin-skinned); the Anoka (thin brown skin and a white interior), Butterfinger (delicious golden yellow flesh, finger-shaped) and Russian Banana (also finger-shaped). One eccentrically lovely boiler, All Red, is red clear through; another, Rose Finn Apple, is a smaller potato of a knuckly, finger shape, boasting a thin red skin covering a creamy yellow flesh—a delicious, milder version of Yukon Gold's buttery flavor. French fingerling is another favorite, creamy and buttery—our farmer's market potato experts, Lee and Louise McCoy of Highlander Farm, say they hardly ever put anything but salt on this white potato with sprightly red skin.

All-purpose potatoes attempt a happy medium: medium starch, medium moisture, okay for baking or boiling, flesh somewhere between waxy and mealy. Their skin is a bit heavier than that of boiling potatoes, but not as thick as that of Idahos or russets. Yukon Golds are the current favorite of the potato-loving world, with a decidedly yellow and buttery-tasting flesh (some claim they use less butter on Yukons; others claim they like Yukons because they're so good with butter). The otherworldly looking blue and purple potatoes—All Blue and Purple Peruvian (I think the latter is superior; creamier, with a touch of sweetness) fall into this category. So do Red Golds—bright golden yellow flesh under a red skin. Yellow Finn is an

Ozark Potatoes

"'We don't have to dig our 'taters. We just cut the ends off the rows and they roll out.'

'My 'taters got so big, travelers reported the hills was Indian mounds and conservationists and perfessers brought in crews to excavate 'em.'

With countless stories like [these], Ozarkers entertained each other with the vast contrast between hard reality and the Edenic ease so fertile in the imagination. [They knew] how difficult it can be to get a living in the Ozarks and the long odds—I won't say impossibility—that strangers will ever readily understand Ozarks life."

—Donald R. Holliday,
"What Is Work For?" *OzarksWatch*, 1996

all-purpose variety that has taken the potato-eating world by storm in recent years for its yellow color and somewhat buttery flavor. Other all-purpose kinds include the Corolla (smooth brown skin, yellow flesh) and the Castille—light buff skin, very bright white flesh.

Whatever varieties you choose, seek out organic potatoes; according to a farmer friend, "If you saw the amount of chemicals that go into growing the average potato, you'd never eat one again." Organic or not, you want potatoes that are smooth and free of soft spots, wrinkles, and cracks, with few or no sprouts. Pass over potatoes with a greenish cast to their skin. Store potatoes unwashed, out of direct sunlight.

Potatoes can exhibit the dangerous side of their kinship with the nightshade family: They contain solanine, a poison, in minute quantities. But if exposed to sunlight, the potato develops a greenish cast—which means that the solanine content has skyrocketed, to possibly dangerous levels. Peel any potatoes that look green. According to food chemist Shirley Corriher, all the solanine is located just under the skin; peeling about 1/16 inch deep removes all toxicity. Other solanine-rich parts are any sprouts or eyes, which should also be removed.

To prepare for cooking: I prefer to eat a potato with its skin, which is a large part of its visual and textural appeal, and its salt-of-the-earth, close-to-the-ground pleasure. Skin or no, however, remove all eyes (the miniscule starts of sprouts) from potatoes before cooking them, using the tip of a knife or the rounded end of a potato peeler to gouge out the eye, going about 1/4 inch below and around it. If a potato must be peeled, try using one of the clever, ergonomically designed peelers by Oxo; their thick plastic handles fit the hand and they glide smoothly. To prevent oxidation (the darkening that takes place when most cut fruit or vegetables are exposed to air), drop each potato, as it's peeled, into a bowl of cold water to which you've added a tiny spritz of lemon juice.

You'll find another great crop of potato recipes in the gratin section, pages 435 to 586.

Basic "Boiled" Potatoes

You should always cook potatoes—even those called boiling potatoes—in water that has not yet come to a boil. Dropping potatoes into water at a hard boil makes the potato starch break down unevenly, often leaving you with potatoes that may be mushy on the outside and underdone on the inside, or soggy clear through.

Of the basic potato cooking methods, I prefer pressure-cooking first, steaming second. But I opt for this method when the potatoes are to be mashed.

You may wish to save potato cooking water. It's good in breads (and especially nice instead of plain water in the starter for sourdoughs). Some also enjoy potato water as part of the liquid in mashed potatoes. **SERVES 4**

Water, preferably spring or filtered
2½ teaspoons salt
5 to 6 medium potatoes (1½ to 1¾ pounds) scrubbed, eyes removed, peeled or not as you prefer, and left whole, sliced, quartered, or chunked, depending on recipe

1 Bring a large pot of water—at least 3 quarts—to a boil. Add the salt, then lower the heat to just below a simmer.

2 Drop in the potatoes and cook, uncovered, until done, testing for tenderness with the tip of a knife. Whole medium potatoes will be done in about 30 minutes, large chunks around 20, slices about 15.

3 Drain well, reserving the potato water if desired. Rinse the potatoes under cold running water before proceeding to use them in a specific recipe.

Basic Steamed Potatoes

Lee and Louise McCoy, whose many varieties of organic potatoes have achieved cult status at the farmer's market in Fayetteville, Arkansas, almost always steam their potatoes. Why? "Because they don't soak up a lot of water," says Louise. "And the skins don't peel off. Also, they keep their shape better in salads." She especially likes steaming for the small succulent fingerlings and new potatoes. "I'm sure steaming saves nutrients, too, but of course if you cooked potatoes in water and used the potato water, you'd be okay."

How does she eat the steamed potatoes? "Basically butter, salt, and pepper is fine with me. I like to eat stuff that's fresh pretty simply." Me too—though for new potatoes I always add a shower of fresh, very finely minced parsley. **SERVES 4**

Water, preferably spring or filtered
5 to 6 medium potatoes, or 12 to 14 small new or fingerling-type potatoes (1½ to 1¾ pounds), scrubbed, eyes removed, peeled or not as you prefer, and left whole, sliced, quartered, or chunked, depending on recipe

1 Place a collapsible metal steamer basket in a medium saucepan with a tight-fitting lid, adding water to come just below the basket. Bring to a hard boil.

2 Place the potatoes on the basket and pop on the lid. Steam, covered, until done,

testing for tenderness with the tip of a knife. Whole medium potatoes will be done in about 25 minutes, large chunks in 15 to 20, slices in 10 to 15, whole fingerlings in about 15. Check occasionally to make sure the water has not boiled away, adding additional water if needed.

3 Drain well, reserving any potato steaming water if desired. Rinse potatoes well with cold water before proceeding to use them in a specific recipe.

Cilantro Chile'd Hot Potatoes

These are one of my favorite quick, interesting, no-hassle component plate potatoes, especially in midsummer. This, some bright orange butternut squash or beets, done with a touch of sweet, and some quickly sautéed broccoli or greens with garlic, make a wholly satisfying vegetable dinner. I use a combination of Peruvian Purple and white potatoes when I can get both, but straight white or gold are fine too.

Since I always keep a batch of Chile Buzz (page 902) on hand, this really is *fast.* Oh yes.

This very simple recipe will also teach you the basic way to pressure-cook potatoes. **SERVES 4 TO 6**

Water, preferably spring or filtered
4 to 5 small to medium-sized boiling or all-purpose potatoes (1 to 1¼ pounds), scrubbed and halved
¾ pound Peruvian Purple potatoes, scrubbed and halved
1 tablespoon coarsely chopped cilantro
2 teaspoons butter
Salt to taste
Chile Buzz (page 902) to taste

1 Set up the pressure cooker using the steamer tray and add about ¼ inch water. Place the potatoes on the tray. Cover and bring the pressure to high over high heat. Adjust the heat so that the potatoes continue cooking under high pressure for 10 to 12 minutes.

2 Release the pressure. Transfer the potatoes to a large bowl. Toss with the cilantro, butter, and salt and Chile Buzz to taste. Serve immediately.

Basic Mashed Potatoes

How long has it been since you've had real, made-from-scratch mashed potatoes? They are superb, a simple, satisfying comfort food. To be at what I consider their best, they must be almost smooth, with just a few lumps, and prepared with a little more beaten-in fat and richer dairy products than one would want to consume on a daily basis. However, a very decent vegan mashed potato is also possible (see the box on the opposite page).

Liquid should always be hot or warm when added to the hot potatoes. The potatoes you use must be bakers and must be hand-mashed or you end up with a gluey mess. I also like chunks of peel in my mashed potatoes; I peel about half the potatoes before cooking.

"What," asks a perplexed, meat-eating friend who loves fried chicken and gravy with potatoes, "do vegetarians *put* on mashed potatoes?" Although there are many possibilities, I must say a rich shiitake mushroom sauce like Mushroom-Miso-Mustard Gravy (page 952) certainly does it for me. And the New Mexico–Style Green Chile Sauce (page 942) over simple mashed potatoes is superb, as is the Chicken-Style Gravy (page 949). **SERVES 4 TO 6**

Water, preferably spring or filtered
About 1 tablespoon salt, plus additonal to taste
5 to 6 medium russet- or Idaho-type baking potatoes (about 1½ to 1¾ pounds), scrubbed, eyes removed, half of them peeled, half with skin on, cut into ½ inch slices
1½ cups any of the following liquids, or a combination thereof: heavy cream, half-and-half, low-fat milk, buttermilk, potato cooking water
2 tablespoons butter
One or two of the following optional enrichments: 3 ounces neufchâtel reduced-fat cream cheese, ¼ cup sour cream, sour half-and-half, low-fat sour cream, or Yogurt Sour Cream (page 910)
Freshly ground black pepper to taste

1 Bring 2 quarts water and 2 teaspoons of the salt to a boil over high heat. Lower the heat to just below a simmer. Drop in the potatoes and cook, uncovered, until they are almost but not quite done, about 30 minutes. The tip of a knife will enter

Do the Mashed Potato with Me

Among the numberless changes that can be rung on mashed potatoes, here are a few favorites:

Vegan Mashed Potatoes: *Substitute olive oil for the butter and use ½ to 1 cup homemade Tofu Sour Cream (page 909) in the mash, along with ½ to 1 cup unflavored full-fat soy milk. Olive oil in mashed potatoes is quite different from butter, but it is voluptuous and good, and the Tofu Sour Cream further intensifies this richness.*

Mashed Potatoes Lamont: *Lamont Richie, co-owner of Rock Cottage Gardens, an inn here in Eureka, often cooks potatoes for mashing with a vegetable bouillion cube or two in the water to amp up flavor. Particularly nice when making Vegan Mashed Potatoes.*

Double-Garlicked Mashed Potatoes: *Heavenly! The mashed potatoes are studded with bits of caramelized garlic, then zapped with fresh, raw garlic. Make the caramelized garlic described in step 2 of Cabbage and Greens with Kidney Beans and Caramelized Garlic (page 718). Make whichever variation of mashed potatoes you like, adding 1 tablespoon each of olive oil and butter (vegans can go for all oil), and add 2 pressed cloves of raw garlic to the mash. When the potatoes are fluffily mashed, stir in the caramelized garlic.*

Smashed Potatoes with Apples and Onions: *This is an incredibly appealing combination. Sweet and savory bounce off each other nicely. While cooking the potatoes, make an apple-onion sauté as directed below, with the following ingredients: 1 tablespoon butter; 2 medium well-flavored apples, such as Braeburns, peeled, cored, and sliced into eighths; 1 large onion, chopped; 2 teaspoons sugar; a few gratings of nutmeg; and 1 lemon, halved. Spray a skillet with cooking spray. Add the butter and melt over medium heat. Then add the apples and onion. Sauté until the onion is soft and the apples have started to soften, 5 to 6 minutes. Add the sugar and nutmeg, and squeeze in the lemon juice through a strainer to catch the seeds. Sauté for an additional minute; then lower the heat as low as it'll go, cover, and cook for another 10 minutes. When the potatoes have been mashed, stir in this sauté.*

Mashed or Smashed Potatoes with Bitter Greens: *Steamed, steam-sautéed, or sautéed-with-garlic greens are natural companions for mashed or smashed (intentionally lumpy) potatoes. Serve such greens alongside the potatoes, or stir them right in. This is close kin to colcannon, one of many favorite Irish potato recipes. Steam half a head of shredded green cabbage until limp but not overcooked. Stir it into the mashed potatoes along with 1 bunch finely chopped scallions. You may use the scallions raw (my preferred way) or lightly sautéed in a little extra butter (Ned's choice).*

Mashed or Smashed Potatoes with Wasabi: *To one batch of mashed or smashed potatoes, stir in 1 heaping teaspoon wasabi paste (prepared from wasabi powder according to the package directions). If this isn't open-your-sinuses-and-make-you-jump-up-and-down enough, for your taste buds add more until it's right You can also stir 1 bunch of finely chopped raw scallions and 1 to 2 teaspoons toasted sesame oil into the wasabi'd mashed potatoes. It sounds confusingly fusioned, but I assure you, it is excellent with a stir-fry.*

Blue Moon Mashed or Smashed Potatoes: *To one batch mashed or smashed potatoes enriched with neufchâtel and sour cream, and mashed with buttermilk, add crumbled gorgonzola or Maytag blue cheese. Start with 4 ounces and work up until it's as blue cheesy as you like it. (Leave some small chunks of cheese; don't mash it completely smooth.) Pile into an oiled ovenproof dish with a little bit of butter and run under the broiler until the top is golden brown.*

without resistance, but the potato won't feel fully soft at this point.

2 Drain well, reserving the cooking water if desired. Rinse the potatoes well under cold running water. If immediately making the mashed potatoes, return them to the cooking pot. If prepping them in advance, cover and refrigerate them.

3 Add warm water to the cooled potatoes just to cover and bring them to a boil over high heat. Lower the heat to a simmer and cook until you can mash them easily into the side of the pot with a fork; about 7 minutes. Drain, reserving the cooking water if you like.

4 Meanwhile, unless using buttermilk, heat whatever liquid you've chosen in a medium saucepan over medium heat. Keep warm. (If using buttermilk, do not heat it. Use half of one of the other liquids, as well, heat almost to a simmer, and combine with the buttermilk just before adding the liquid to the hot potatoes.)

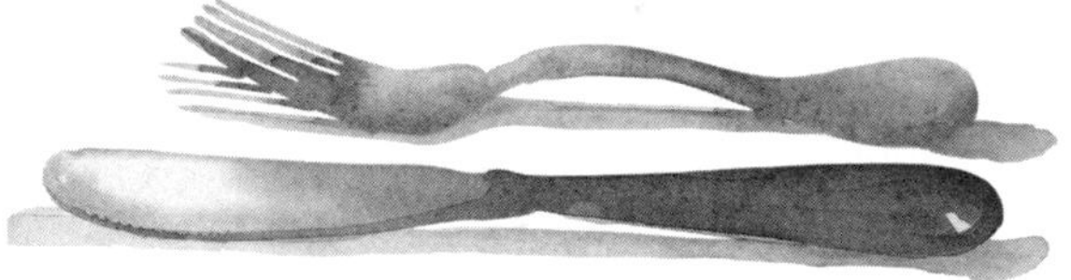

5 When ready to mash, bring the liquid to a boil. Add the butter, enrichment(s), and hot liquid to the potatoes. Mash with a hand masher until the potatoes are fluffy and have just a few lumps, and, of course, the pieces of peel. Add the remaining 1 teaspoon salt, plus more to taste, and pepper to taste.

COOK ONCE FOR 2 MEALS Spread any leftovers in a cooking-sprayed shallow gratin dish (you don't want the mixture thicker than an inch, or it won't heat through properly). Dot the top with a teaspoon or two, max, of butter. Bake in a preheated 425°F oven until the peaks are nicely browned, 20 to 25 minutes. Or, for a pleasing casserole that's supper in itself, try adding 1 to 2 cups well-drained sauerkraut to the mashed potatoes. Heap into a nonstick baking dish or one that has been sprayed with cooking spray. Top with a little grated Jarlsberg cheese, and bake at 375°F until the top is browned and the casserole is heated through. This is delicious with plain mashed potatoes or the apple-onion or garlic variation. Do the same—absent the sauerkraut—for the greens-enriched potatoes, or colcannon.

Roasty-Toasty Potatoes, Carrots, and Onions

These potatoes were the single most requested vegetable recipe at the inn, where our waiter, John Mitchell, used to describe them to guests as possessing "campfire elegance." They have something of the slightly crisped, caramelized browning of little potatoes baked alongside roast beef—except, of course, they're vegetarian. They taste elemental and like the essence of themselves; like our cornbread, I've eaten them hundreds of times and never fail to be satisfied. The carrots should look fairly dark in spots and a bit shriveled; unprepossessing, but wait'll you taste them.

The only trick you need to know to make perfect roasty-toasties is to allow them plenty of air space. This means you need a pan large enough so the vegetables are in a single layer, but not too deep. A deep pan will throw back the evaporating water, preventing the all-important roastiness.

There are many ways roasty-toasties can lend their simple brilliance to other dishes, so always make more than you need. **SERVES 4 TO 6**

Cooking spray
Water, preferably spring or filtered
2 pounds boiling or all-purpose potatoes (about 8 small but not tiny potatoes), scrubbed, eyes removed
1 pound carrots (about 6 medium), washed and scrubbed, unpeeled, stem end left on
2 large onions, quartered, peel left on
1 tablespoon mild vegetable oil, such as corn, peanut, or canola
1 to 2 tablespoons tamari or shoyu soy sauce, plus more to taste

1 Preheat the oven to 375°F.

2 Spray a baking dish or dishes—you need baking space large enough to accommodate all the vegetables so they're in a single layer—with cooking spray. Set aside.

3 Bring 2 large pots of water to a boil over high heat.

4 Drop the potatoes into one pot of boiling water and blanch for 6 to 8 minutes. Drain well, and rinse under cold running water.

5 Place the carrots in the second pot of water and cook for 4 minutes for long, skinny carrots; 5 to 6 minutes for fatter carrots. Drain well.

6 Place the potatoes and carrots in the prepared baking dish with the onion quarters (raw, skin still on). Toss the vegetables with the oil, rubbing it into the vegetables a bit with your hands. Bake for about 30 minutes, then drizzle with the tamari and toss again. Continue baking until the potatoes and carrots are soft—you should be able to pierce them easily with a fork at their thickest point—and quite browned here and there, especially on the sides that have touched the pan. This will take 45 to 55 minutes total. Remove from the oven and serve at once. These agreeable vegetables also don't mind staying in a warm place for 30 minutes or so—even an hour—if need be before serving.

NOTES

Roasties do not really need to be baked at 375°F. You could bake them at 350°F for 1 hour, 325°F for 1½ hours—and you'd still get good roasty-toasties. They work with whatever else you have going in the oven.

If ever there was a vegetable preparation made for déjà food, roasty-toasties are it. Leftover roasty potatoes are great in an omelet or frittata; leftover carrots turn into Roasted Carrot Spread with Fresh Ginger and Curry (page 15), which in turn is both superlative dip and head start on the best curried lentil soup you'll ever eat. All three combined give you a jump on Oven-Roasted Vegetable Stock (page 141), the richest vegetarian stock I know.

Not only that, but everyone will want seconds or thirds of these vegetables.

VARIATIONS

OVEN-BROWNED SPUDLETS WITH ONIONS AND GARLIC: ***When you uncover the potatoes, add 1 onion, coarsely chopped, and 3 cloves garlic, finely chopped. Stir them in and bake for that last 15 minutes, not forgetting those all-important 5-minute shakings.***

OVEN-BROWNED SPUDLETS WITH ONIONS, GARLIC, AND SHIITAKES: ***The traditional German recipe from which this is adapted browns the potatoes in the rendered fat of smoked bacon and leaves the little dice of bacon in the dish. Vegetarians can get a reminiscent effect by upping the butter to 1 tablespoon and adding about ⅓ cup diced shiitake mushroom caps with the potatoes. Cook them throughout, both on the stove and in the oven. Then, add the onions and garlic as above, in the last 15 minutes of uncovered baking time.***

Oven-Browned Spudlets

One can't have too many ways to prepare the sweet new potatoes of spring. I usually just throw them in near-boiling water or steam them, toss with a tiny squib of melted butter, salt, and a lot of finely minced Italian parsley or a little rosemary, but these give herb-buttered spuds a major run for the money.

SERVES 2 TO 4

Cooking spray
1 tablespoon butter
1½ pounds new potatoes, as small as possible (ideally no larger than pecans or Brussels sprouts), well scrubbed, whole, dried off after scrubbing
About ½ teaspoon fresh rosemary needles, finely chopped
Salt and freshly ground black pepper, to taste

1. Preheat the oven to 400°F.

2. Spray an ovenproof skillet with cooking spray. Place over medium heat. Add the butter. When it's melted, add the potatoes and cook, shaking them around from time to time, for 5 minutes.

3. Remove from the heat and cover tightly. Bake for 15 minutes if you've been lucky enough to get really tiny marble-sized potatoes, 20 minutes for medium (ping-pong ball–sized), and 30 minutes for larger (small egg–sized).

4. Uncover and add the rosemary, salt, and pepper. Shake vigorously to combine, then return the skillet to the oven, uncovered. Bake for another 15 minutes, removing the pan from the oven and shaking hard every 5 minutes. Serve at once.

Ned's Fiery Oven French-Bakes

Addictive is the word for these spicy, Cajun-style French fries that aren't fried but baked. Tamari or shoyu eliminates the need for salt, a *lot* of Tabasco adds major kick (you can adjust to your own taste-thermometer). Try these for supper with any of the burgers or cakes, especially The Very Best Tofu Cakes (page 832), or an omelet or scramble. No matter how many of these you make, you'll wish there'd been more. If you do scale up the recipe, cut back on the oil a bit. Use 2½ teaspoons Garlic Oil (page 898), if you have it on hand, instead of the garlic called for (in this case, also cut olive oil back slightly). **SERVES 2**

Cooking spray (optional)
3 to 4 medium-large red- and/or white-skinned boiling potatoes, washed, eyes removed, peel left on, sliced into ¼-inch-wide French fry strips
4 to 5 cloves garlic, pressed
2 teaspoons olive oil (use only ½ to 1 teaspoon if also using Garlic Oil)
2 tablespoons tamari or shoyu soy sauce, or to taste
1 to 3 teaspoons Tabasco sauce, or to taste
2 tablespoons rice wine or other unseasoned vinegar
6 to 8 grinds of black pepper

1 Preheat the oven to 375°F. Place the rack on the highest position in the oven.

2 Spray a baking sheet with cooking spray. Set aside.

3 Place the potatoes in a bowl. Add the garlic and oil, tossing until the potatoes are well coated with the oil. Sprinkle with the tamari, Tabasco, and vinegar and toss again to evenly distribute the seasonings.

4 Transfer the potatoes to the prepared baking sheet, spreading them out so that they are in a single layer. Grind on the pepper.

5 Bake, removing from the oven to shake and turn the potatoes about every 10 minutes, for 25 to 30 minutes. Test for doneness, and continue to bake them until they're browned, cooked through, and starting to crisp up on the skinny ends. Serve hot.

Tuscan-Style Potato-Chickpea Skillet Stew

Home fries go to Tuscany. Slowly, slowly cooked until browned on the outside, tender within, red-tinted because of a bit of tomato (indistinguishable

NOTE

Traditional Tuscan versions of this dish call for double or triple the olive oil, and omit the greens and beans. But 2 tablespoons is enough to get sublime results, especially if you use a good nonstick pan. Also, with a nonstick you can keep the heat very low, and cook for an additional 20 to 30 minutes, adding water and giving an occasional stir, with results that are astonishingly good.

at the end), and flavored with sage, these potatoes have a subtle, irresistible charm that grows with each bite. Chickpeas and hearty greens round out the flavor and nutritional profile, and, as with many potato dishes, a poached egg on top is a match made in heaven. Though not very juicy, it's also good scattered over pasta, with a little freshly shaved Parmesan cheese. Fresh sage is essential. Even though it seems like a lot of sage, the perfuming is very subtle in the finished dish, because the leaves remain whole and are picked out at the end. If the sage you are using seems very strong, start with the lesser amount.

The spritz of lemon juice at the end finishes the dish to a T. **SERVES 4 TO 6**

2 tablespoons olive oil
Cooking spray
4 cloves garlic, chopped
7 fresh sage leaves, 4 whole, 3 minced
1 fresh tomato, peeled, seeded, and diced
1 tablespoon tomato paste
2½ pounds potatoes, peeled and cut into 1-inch chunks
Salt and freshly ground black pepper to taste
2 tablespoons to ¼ cup water, preferably spring or filtered
1 bunch kale or chard, well washed, sliced crosswise into ½-inch strips, or broccoli rabe, sliced into 1-inch pieces
1 can (15 ounces) chickpeas, well drained
Lemons, quartered

1 Heat the oil in a very large nonstick skillet, or one that has been sprayed with cooking spray, over medium heat. Add the garlic, reduce the heat to low, and cook, stirring often, for 5 minutes. Add the whole sage leaves and cook for another 5 minutes. The garlic should color only slightly. Add the tomato and tomato paste and cook for an additional 3 minutes. Raise the heat slightly.

2 Rinse the potatoes well under cold running water. Place them in the skillet with some water still clinging to them. Turn the potatoes several times to coat them in the tomato-oil-sage mixture. Season to taste with salt and pepper and cook, covered, for 10 minutes. Uncover and add 2 tablespoons of the water, stir, cover, and cook for another 5 minutes.

3 Uncover and pick out the whole sage leaves. Add the greens and stir well. Cover and cook for another 5 minutes. Uncover, stir well, and add the chickpeas and the minced sage. Stir again, cover, and lower the heat as low as it will go. Cook until the potatoes are meltingly tender and the stew is hot, 20 to 25 minutes. Watch closely so that the potatoes don't stick or burn, stirring in an extra tablespoon or so of water as necessary. Remove from the heat and serve immediately. Pass lemon quarters at the table for those who'd like a salutary spritz of citrus.

Hungarian Potatoes Paprikash

A great example of the mysterious synergy the nightshade family members—in this case potatoes, peppers, and tomatoes—have when cooked together. I have enjoyed preparing this for almost twenty years, but many changes have been rung over the years. To cut down on the butter, I bake the dish in the oven during the scorch-prone period. After my friend Barbara Metzger returned from a visit to Hungary and reported that the paprikash dishes that she had tasted had a good ol' hot pepper kick, I turned up the heat. I add a smidge of sugar, as I do when cooking tomatoes, which are otherwise too acidic for my taste. **SERVES 4 TO 6**

Cooking spray
2 teaspoons butter (or, for vegans, mild vegetable oil or margarine)
1 large onion, diced
2 to 3 long, pale green peppers (Italian frying, Hungarian wax, or banana peppers—if not available, substitute 1 large green bell pepper), seeded and diced
5 to 6 medium potatoes (about 1½ pounds), sliced ¼ inch thick (they are traditionally peeled; peel or not as you prefer)
1 cup diced, peeled, seeded tomatoes or diced canned tomatoes with juice
½ teaspoon brown sugar
1½ teaspoons sweet Hungarian paprika
Dash of hot Hungarian paprika or cayenne
Salt and freshly ground black pepper to taste

1 Preheat the oven to 400°F.

2 Spray a cast-iron skillet or other ovenproof skillet with cooking spray. Place the skillet over medium heat and melt the butter. Then add the onion and sauté until soft and golden, with edges beginning to brown, about 9 minutes.

3 Add the peppers and sauté for another 2 minutes. Add the potatoes and toss everything to combine. Cover tightly and bake until the potatoes are fork-tender, 15 to 20 minutes. Remove the skillet from the oven.

4 Uncover and add the tomatoes, brown sugar, sweet paprika, hot paprika, and salt and pepper. Place on the stove-top over medium heat. Cook, stirring often, for 10 minutes. Serve hot.

The Squash Family

The squash family is generous—*and* generative. The cucurbit family has thousands of members—not only edible squash, but decorative gourds and other ornamentals, melons of all kinds, cucumbers. And some of these babies get *big*. Consider the way-larger-than-a-bushel-basket jack-o'-lanterns we see each Halloween, and, in the summer, zeppelinlike watermelons and overgrown zucchini.

But this abundance of cucurbit flesh goes beyond volume. Cucurbits aren't just large, there are lots of them—not only in the family, but on any given plant. They are numerous and explosive. When you think cucurbit, think productive. One hill of zucchini could feed a family of four for a summer; three hills, a neighborhood (oh, you've noticed those paper sacks of summer golden crooknecks deposited on your doorstep, too, have you?). And leave a respectable 6- to 8-inch summer squash on its vine a day or two too long, and it can turn into a monster—a giant's club, a baseball bat, a boa constrictor.

Still, in a world that is often ungenerous, you have to admire something about a vegetable that just doesn't know when to stop.

Summer Squashes

ZUCCHINI, GLOBE ZUCCHINI, YELLOW, PATTYPANS, AND CHAYOTE: Summer squashes shine in preparations that add character to their moist, mild, sometimes spongy flesh. Ideally, you should have a number of ways to do that up your sleeve, given how much summer squash you are likely to have, and how bored you'll be if you don't get imaginative.

Even if you don't have a garden, or friends with a garden, come midsummer at the farmer's market, baskets and boxes overflow with scalloped pattypans, green and yellow, and large and small and infant zucchini, oblong and round, and golden-yellow squash. Late summer brings chayote (a.k.a. mirliton). These displays could intimidate, but just as well inspire. And at summer's peak, if you have to pay for these at all, it won't be much. Be picky and get the best. Select burstingly fresh squash, free of any soft spots or wrinkles or spoilage: cylindrical summer squash and zukes that are plump, glossy-skinned, very firm, and on the small side—no longer than 7 inches—unless you intend to stuff them (see page 415) or use them decoratively. In the case of the round pattypan squashes, also sometimes called cymlings, search out those that are 4 inches or less in diameter (as cookbook writer Bert Greene has said, "no wider in circumference than an English muffin").

To prepare for cooking, wash them and trim off the stem and blossom ends. Slice or dice as directed in a specific recipe. Of the summer squashes, chayote is idiosyncratic. Pale green, pear-shaped, light of flesh, with one large seed in the center, it requires unique prep. Whole chayote is cooked in boiling water until barely fork-tender (8 to 10 minutes), or steamed for 8 to 10 minutes, or pressure-cooked for about 1 minute. After cooking, cut it in half and discard the large seed at the center. Chayote is usually stuffed (see page 415), but after this blanching they can be peeled, cut up, and prepared as you would any summer squash. Try them in the

Dairy Hollow House Summer Squash Pudding (page 296).

Treat summer squash wisely and you'll be pleased at their goodness. If they held themselves aloof, only making a brief appearance for a week or two, or were priced like truffles or artichokes, perhaps we might use them with more delicacy and thoughtfulness.

Quickly steam squash to tenderness, drain very well, and:

- ▲ Toss with a little bit of butter, salt, freshly ground black pepper, and a handful of minced Italian parsley.
- ▲ Do the same, but hold the butter and use olive oil and a pressed clove (or 2, or 3) of garlic.
- ▲ Do the same, omit the garlic, and add a peeled, diced, seeded tomato and a tablespoon of your favorite pesto.
- ▲ Amend any of the above by tossing, hot, with a couple of tablespoons of finely crumbled feta cheese, and a serious sprinkle of fresh chopped herbs: some dill, basil, oregano, and a little tarragon if you have it, plus salt and pepper.
- ▲ Follow the recipe for Eggplant Fans (page 747), using zucchini. This is a do-ahead vegetable, and its attractiveness, individual serving sizes, and the fact that it can be served hot, warm, or at room temperature, all suggest it for a special-occasion component.

A number of detailed squash-centered recipes follow, but let me steer you toward some in other parts of this book: Sorrel-Scented Kugel-Gratin of Greens, Potatoes, and Zucchini (page 280), Spinach or Zucchini Featherbeds (page 283), Posole-Bean Soup-Stew with New World Vegetables (page 210), Deep December Ragoût of Seitan, Shiitakes, and Winter Vegetables (page 218), G'vetch (page 749), Dairy Hollow House Summer Squash Pudding (page 296), and Tuscan Bean and Vegetable Stew (page 225), as well as all the stuffed squashes (pages 415–22).

Grilled Summer Squash

As simple (if you have a gas grill, or if you're doing something else on the grill) as it is good, and vice versa. This is an excellent use of the superabundance of squash that seems to come everyone's way by midsummer. **SERVES 4 TO 6**

NOTE

This basic marinade of oil, tamari, and seasonings goes well with many vegetables.

1 tablespoon olive oil
1 teaspoon tamari or shoyu soy sauce
Any of the following, if desired:
freshly ground black pepper, 1 teaspoon Pickapeppa sauce, 1 teaspoon Thai Crystal (page 923), 1 tablespoon Lemon, Basil and Sun-Dried Tomato Pesto (page 918)

6 zucchini or other cylindrical summer squash, stems removed, sliced lengthwise into ⅓-inch ovals, 3 or 4 ovals plus 2 small, thin skin-edged side pieces per squash

1 Preheat the grill to high, then turn down to medium.

2 As the grill preheats, combine the oil, tamari, and one of the optional seasonings in a small bowl, whisking well. Using a pastry brush, lightly coat the zucchini slices with the mixture, brushing all but the thin end pieces (those that have the outer skin on one side) on both sides. Brush the end pieces on the flesh side only.

3 Place the zucchini on the preheated grill. Cover and grill over indirect heat, turning once halfway through, or until vegetables are somewhat softened and grill-marked, but not completely soft, 12 to 17 minutes. Serve at once, as part of a component plate.

VARIATION

SYRIAN SWEET-SOUR SUMMER SQUASH WITH MINT, ***adapted from a very sprightly recipe in Faye Levy's*** **International Vegetable Cookbook,** ***which she says she learned from a Syrian friend. Omit the poblano, corn, and dill. After the 3-minute squash-searing, add the following: 3 tablespoons water; 1 pressed clove garlic; 1 tablespoon lemon juice; 2 teaspoons sugar; 1 teaspoon crumbled dry mint (a spearmint tea bag is the simplest way to get it); and salt and pepper to taste. Cover; steam until tender. Add a few drops more fresh lemon juice,***

Summer Squash with Corn, Dill, and Peppers

A simple steam/stir-fry, in which height-of-summer stuff, mostly of New World origin, combines felicitously. Dill, instead of the cumin you might expect with poblano peppers, is a nice touch. **SERVES 4 TO 6**

1 to 2 teaspoons olive oil
Cooking spray
1 small onion, diced
1 poblano pepper, seeded and diced
3 to 4 (6- to 7-inch) zucchini or summer golden crooknecks, stem and blossom ends removed, sliced into ½-inch rounds; or pattypans, cut into wedges
Kernels from 2 or 3 ears corn (about 1½ cups corn kernels; use frozen if needed)
1 teaspoon to 1 tablespoon finely snipped fresh dill
Salt and freshly ground black pepper to taste

Heat the oil in a nonstick skillet, or one that has been sprayed with cooking spray, over medium heat. When nice and hot, add the onion, and sauté for 3 minutes. Add the poblano, and sauté for 4 minutes. Add the zucchini and corn and raise the heat to medium-high. Sauté to sear the vegetables for about 3 minutes. Lower the heat slightly, cover, and steam until the zucchini are crisp-tender, 3 to 5 minutes. Stir in the dill and season with salt and pepper to taste. Serve hot.

Greek-Style Summer Squash

I used to be an always-cook-only-to-crisp-tender person where vegetables were concerned, but Roasty-Toasty Potatoes, Carrots, and Onions (page 790) and this method of cooking—which I also use for okra (page 775) and green beans (page 689, the ultimate)—have changed my perspective. Now I like some vegetables with tooth and some meltingly soft—it depends on the vegetable, and the cook's skill and intent.

This squash is cooked until it's falling-apart tender, but not watery-wet. The cooking medium is essentially a garlic-tomato marmalade. Every bite is imbued with flavor—garlicky, a little hot, and oh so good. While it has nominally more olive oil than will please some, know that it was cut down from similar traditional Greek recipes that—I kid you not—use ½ to ¾ cup! The tablespoon or so here will give you flavor, but not drown you in a sea of oil. If I use this on a component plate or side dish of vegetables, I usually make sure I have some other crisp-tender vegetables for contrast; I'm quite happy with a salad, a big mound of this, and brown rice (or pasta or mashed potatoes). **SERVES 4 TO 6**

NOTES

When making Greek-Style Summer Squash, I use the smaller amount of oil called for at home, the larger when cooking professionally. Also, if you have Dragon Salt (page 900) on hand, omit all the seasonings called for and use Dragon Salt instead.

Cooking spray
2 teaspoons to 1 tablespoon olive oil (2 tablespoons if you're feeling devil-may-care)
1 tablespoon chopped garlic (or omit garlic and olive oil and use 1 tablespoon plus 1 teaspoon Garlic Oil, page 898)
6 (6-inch) summer squash, stem and blossom ends removed, sliced about ⅜ inch thick
1 Roma or other Italian plum tomato, chopped
Salt and freshly ground black pepper
A few dashes of cayenne
½ to 1 teaspoon dried dill weed

1 Spray a heavy, 10- to 14-inch cast-iron skillet with a tight-fitting lid with cooking spray. Place over very low heat. Add the oil and garlic, then the squash. Scatter the tomato over the squash. Cook, uncovered, for 10 minutes. Do not stir. Cover and cook for 30 minutes more. Do not stir, but make sure that the heat is low enough so nothing is burning. If you like, you can kind of push a few of the squash back to make sure the garlic on the bottom is not burning, but merely cooking very, very

slowly. Some of the squash circles will be browned on one side, which is good.

2 After 30 minutes, uncover and stir cautiously, just a few times. The squash should be quite tender, and you don't want to break it up, just gently recombine the ingredients. It is likely, unless your skillet is very large, that there will be a lot of liquid in the skillet. If so, blast the heat *way* up, and, stirring occasionally, cook until the liquid is evaporated and the squash is almost like a chunky puree. Turn off the heat. Season with salt and pepper to taste, sprinkle with cayenne, and stir in the dill. Serve immediately.

Deviled Summer Squash Casserole

A very pleasant component casserole of steamed squash in a creamy tomato sauce with a little kick. Quite hearty, it's almost a main dish. I find it very satisfying as part of a vegetable dinner (try it with steamed green beans, new potatoes, and cornbread). Since this calls for cooked squash, steam it ahead of time. Better yet, cook more than you need for dinner one night, and save the leftovers for this. **SERVES 4 TO 6**

VARIATION

VEGAN VARIATION: ***Omit the neufchâtel. Buzz the following in the food processor along with the other sauce ingredients: 4 ounces silken tofu, 1½ tablespoons tahini, 2 teaspoons mellow white miso, and an extra teaspoon of cornstarch. Omit the grated Cheddar, or use a soy cheese instead.***

- 2 teaspoons mild vegetable oil, such as corn, canola, or peanut
- Cooking spray (optional)
- 1 large onion, diced
- 1 serrano or jalapeño pepper, seeded and finely diced
- 1½ cups sliced shiitake mushroom caps (save the stems for stock)
- 2 large tomatoes, preferably dead-ripe summer tomatoes, quartered, stem ends removed (or 1½ cups canned tomatoes)
- 3 ounces grated Cheddar cheese (optional)
- 3 ounces neufchâtel reduced-fat cream cheese, softened
- 2 cloves garlic, quartered
- 1½ teaspoons Pickapeppa sauce
- 2 teaspoons cornstarch or arrowroot
- 4 cups assorted blanched, steamed-until-just-tender sliced summer squashes, any one kind or a mixture, well drained
- Freshly ground black pepper to taste
- ½ teaspoon salt
- ½ cup fine, soft whole wheat breadcrumbs

1 Preheat the oven to 375°F.

2 Place the squash in a large bowl and set aside.

3 Heat 1 teaspoon of the oil in a nonstick skillet, or one that has been sprayed with cooking spray, over medium heat. When hot, add the onion and sauté for 3 minutes. Add the serrano and shiitakes and sauté for another 5 minutes.

4 Place the tomatoes, Cheddar cheese (if using), neufchâtel, garlic, Pickapeppa, cornstarch, salt and pepper in a food processor and buzz until smooth. Scrape into the bowl with the squash. Add the onion mixture and stir to combine.

5 Spray a shallow 8-inch square baking dish with cooking spray. Scrape the squash mixture into it and top with the breadcrumbs. Drizzle with the remaining 1 teaspoon oil. Bake until heated through and the crumbs are slightly crisp, 30 to 35 minutes. Serve hot.

Calabacitas

Festive though it sounds, *calabacitas* is Spanish for, simply, "squash"—zucchini squash. But when you see calabacitas on a menu in Texas or New Mexico, or in a Southwestern cookbook, rest assured that you will not get plain old zucchini. Usually the squash is cut into a small, neat dice, then quickly sautéed with a couple of aromatics and a few other vegetables. The results are quick, fresh, and perky. Calabacitas is a great starting point for many dishes—a crêpe or enchilada filling, a casserole entree (see Calabacitas Cobbler with Cornmeal Biscuit Crust, page 254)—but it also makes a nice side dish just as it is. **SERVES 4 TO 6**

2 teaspoons mild vegetable oil, such as corn, canola, or peanut
Cooking spray (optional)
1 onion, diced
1 finely minced serrano or jalapeño pepper, with or without seeds and membranes, depending on how hot you'd like it (optional)
½ teaspoon cumin seeds
1 tablespoon water or vegetable stock (see page 139)
½ to 1 small butternut squash, peeled and cut into ¼-inch dice (optional)
3 to 6 small zucchini, stems removed, cut into ¼-inch dice (use the larger amount of zucchini if you are not including the butternut squash)
¼ teaspoon salt, or to taste

1 Heat the oil in a nonstick skillet, or one that has been sprayed with cooking spray, over medium heat. Add the onion and sauté until the onion is starting to give off an aroma, about 2 minutes. Add the serrano and cumin seeds, and sauté until the onion is beginning to soften, another 2 to 4 minutes.

2 Add the butternut squash and water or stock. Cover and steam until the squash is starting to soften, 4 to 8 minutes. Uncover, raise the heat slightly, and add the zucchini. Sauté, stirring often, until the zucchini is crisp-tender, about 5 minutes. Season with salt to taste and serve hot.

COOK ONCE FOR 2 MEALS Do two skillets' worth of basic calabacitas. Serve one as is, as an accompaniment or part of a component plate. Add corn or beans to the remainder (see particulars below) and fold into hot tortillas, with or without cheese and salsa. Or, stuff vegetables with the mixture. Or, try Calabacitas Cobbler with Cornmeal Biscuit Crust (page 254) or Quick Calabacitas Corn-Bean Stew (opposite).

A Collection of Calabacitas

Calabacitas con Elote: *Add the kernels from 3 to 6 ears corn along with the zucchini. The corn can be added to the recipe above, or substituted for the butternut squash. A very nice stuffing for tomato or pepper halves, especially with chiles added.*

Calabacitas con Frijoles: *To any of the completed variations, add 1 can (15 ounces) black beans, very well drained, stirred in at the last minute. A superb filling for enchiladas or crêpes.*

Calabacitas con Crema: *Dice 2 to 4 ounces neufchâtel reduced-fat cream cheese, and stir it into the finished calabacitas, along with 2 teaspoons tomato paste. Again, a top-notch filling for enchiladas or crêpes.*

Creamy Lima'd Calabacitas à la Lady Bird: *Lady Bird Johnson's Texas roots showed in a lima bean casserole said to be a family favorite. I make it with calabacitas: a very fine preparation. First, cook one 10-ounce package frozen baby lima beans according to package directions. Drain them and set aside. Begin Calabacitas, doubling the oil, and substituting ½ teaspoon chili powder for the cumin seed. Omit butternut squash. Sauté ½ pound sliced mushrooms with the zucchini, and, after 3 minutes, sprinkle the vegetables with 3 teaspoons unbleached white flour. Stir a moment, then gradually stir in 1½ cups warmed lowfat milk. Let cook until thickened, 3 to 4 minutes, then stir in reserved limas and about ⅓ cup (4 ounces) grated sharp Cheddar cheese.*

Quick Calabacitas Corn-Bean Stew

If you were smart and cooked a double portion, your Saturday or Sunday calabacitas could be yielding you this practically instant supper on Monday or Tuesday. If you've learned to always cook more rice or grain than you need, you probably have the perfect satisfying starch to pile it onto.

But, to me, "instant" means nothing unless the results are really good. This is—satisfying, spicy, wholesome, fragrant . . . *and* quick. You'll want seconds.

SERVES 4 TO 6

1 can (10 ounces) diced tomatoes with green chiles
About 3 cups leftover Calabacitas (opposite), preferably with corn and black beans added (see the box on the opposite page)
Cooking spray (optional)
1 tablespoon cornstarch
Salt and freshly ground black pepper to taste
Tabasco or similar hot pepper sauce to taste
Cooked rice or other grain, warmed (optional)
Freshly grated sharp Cheddar cheese (optional)

1 Reserving the liquid, drain the can of tomatoes and green chiles, mixing the solids with the leftover calabacitas and placing the liquid in a small bowl. Transfer the calabacitas mixture to a nonstick skillet or one that has been sprayed with cooking spray. Place over medium heat and cook, stirring from time to time, until bubbling.

2 As the calabacitas heats, add the cornstarch to the tomato–green chile liquid, smushing it in with your fingers until it is smooth and free of lumps.

3 When the calabacitas mixture is bubbling hot, add the cornstarch-tomato liquid, stirring until the mixture thickens and a clear sauce has formed (this should be almost immediate; if it's not, the calabacitas wasn't hot enough when you added the cornstarch). Remove from the heat. Season to taste with salt, pepper, and Tabasco. Serve hot, over cooked rice or other grain, topped with a sprinkle of Cheddar cheese, if desired.

Winter Squashes

ACORN, BUTTERNUT, DELICATA, GODIVA, HUBBARD, PUMPKIN, SPAGHETTI, TABLE QUEEN, TURBAN: Winter squashes are not nearly so vigorous as their summer kin. But what they lack in numbers, they make up in nutritional bounty. Summer squashes, pale of flesh, supply mostly fiber, water (they are 95 percent water, in fact!), and a modest amount of vitamin C (of course, their calories are also negligible). But the winter squashes, starchy, sweet, with intensely orange flesh and hearty texture, are probably the nourishment bargains of the vegetable universe. Most winter varieties (including butternut, one of the sweetest and most versatile) are rich in beta-carotene, one of the nutrients that's recently received much favorable press (the reason it may be a prophylactic against tumor growth, the current thinking goes, is its boosting of white blood cell activity). Winter squash have plenty of fiber, plenty of vitamin A (which goes hand in hand with beta-carotene), a good helping of vitamin C—but still just 80 to 110 calories a cup.

Best of all, winter squash are *so* good, but not nearly as widely known as they deserve to be. If you haven't yet discovered them, one bite could change that—it did for me. That bite was of pureed butternut squash, at a now-defunct restaurant in Little Rock called Jacques and Suzanne's. It was voluptuous and deep with flavor and the vividest gold on the plate. I've been butternutting ever since.

Besides the recipes that follow, look to the following recipes for artful winter squash ideas: Vegan French-Style Gratin of Butternut Squash (page 289), Timbale of Butternut Squash Pudding with Caramelized Onions (page 294), Brown Tepary Bean, Seitan, and Ancho Chili Stew (page 187), West Indian Rundown, (page 206), Posole-Bean Soup-Stew with New World Vegetables (page 210), Mélange of Braised Winter Vegetables with Savory Tofu (page 223), and New World Succotash Stew (page 248).

You'll find winter squashes at their best from fall through midwinter. They should feel heavy for their size, and their skin should be uniformly hard, free of any soft spots (but expect a sort of hard wartiness on certain varieties). Spaghetti squash, an anomaly, are best when pale yellow rather than bright, and larger—about football-size—rather than smaller (younger spaghetti squash may not have fully formed the distinctive strands that give them their name). Winter squashes bought in the late winter and spring are liable to be old, hence drier and less sweet; winter squash bought in early to midsummer are liable to be young and a bit watery; purchase winter squash from late summer until almost winter's end.

Be aware that the appropriate cooking method for winter squash varies. Here are some general guidelines. If the squash is to be baked and served in its hard shell, with diners scooping out the flesh, then you'll need to slice off its top

Eat Your Vegetables

In recent years we've heard a lot about beta-carotene, the substance that gives sweet potatoes and butternut squash their vivid orange, kale and chard their bright green, and is the underlying rationale beneath your parents telling you that if you ate your carrots you'd be able to see in the dark. Beta-carotene used to be thought of merely as provitamin A, a substance that, if eaten, the body would convert to vitamin A. But now beta-carotene is recognized as an antioxidant, a substance said to protect the body against dangerous free radicals, which (though a grown-up '60s person can hardly write the name with a straight face) are highly unstable molecules that attack other molecules, doing damage to the body on a cellular level, and implicated in hastening many degenerative diseases.

(a fairly major deal sometimes, as some squash shells are really hard, and some squashes are enormous; make sure your knife is razor sharp before you start). You may also need to cut a thin slice off the squash's bottom so it can stand without wobbling. Scoop out and discard the seeds, along with any fibrous membranes attaching them to the rest of the squash. (If the seeds are particularly plump and you're particularly frugal, remove all fiber and roast the seeds with a spritz of tamari at 350°F for about 30 minutes. Crack open and eat the tender, nutty kernel within, spitting out the tough outer wrapping.)

Sometimes a prepped squash is blanched, sometimes not; the recipe will direct you. In some recipes, you are directed to peel and cut up the squash raw after seeding it. In others, you may be asked to peel after cooking. Peeling a butternut is picky, pain-in-the-neck work. But the results are worth it. One of my very favorite treatments of winter squash is still the first I experienced: Chef Paul Bash's butternut squash puree: Steam chunks of butternut squash until tender. When cool enough to handle, using a sharp paring knife and your fingers, peel off as much of the buff-colored skin as you can, leaving the orange flesh behind. Some prefer to simply scoop the soft flesh off the skin with a big spoon, no knife needed. Throw the flesh in a food processor with a dash or two of salt, perhaps a teaspoon of butter, and buzz until smooth. If it's not decidedly sweet, you might add a teaspoon of sugar or maple syrup. Reheat and serve.

Eccentric spaghetti squash demands its own quirky mode of precooking and preparation. This notably peculiar edible squash is hard-shelled, pale yellow, and occasionally mottled with a speckling of grainy buff warts. Spaghetti squash is cooked until a fork can pierce the outer shell without much difficulty. If boiling, cook them whole, after poking several times with a fork; if you use any other method, halve them before cooking. Times for cooking spaghetti squash are as follows: steaming, 30 to 40 minutes (it will take a large steamer); boiling, the same amount of time; pressure-cooking, 10 to 12 minutes. The first and last methods are the most satisfactory; boiling tends to make the squash a little soggy. When cool, cut the squash in half. Scoop out the seeds in the center, and then, either by hand or with a large metal spoon, scrape out the flesh. A little around the edges will be solid, but the bulk breaks into yellow strands, like fine spaghetti. The flavor of the strands is more summer squash than winter, but the texture is absolutely unique . . . tender, crisp, each strand distinct. I probably fix spaghetti squash twice a year, and each time I think, "Why don't I make this more often?" Toss cooked spaghetti squash with any of the following: Basic Wintertime Italian Tomato Sauce (page 931), with or without a dusting of Parmesan; pesto, commercial or homemade (page 918), sautéed mushrooms and a scatter of peas; Creole-Style Tomato Sauce (page 932), a little butter, Parmesan, and a lot of just-ground black pepper; Salsa Poblano Blanca y Verde (page 947). Spaghetti Squash Sonora (page 808) is delicious and really more of a main dish than a component; you won't need much by way of accompaniment to make a satisfying meal of it.

> *". . . when we laughed round the corn heap with hearts all in tune our chair a broad pumpkin our lantern the moon"*
>
> **—John Greenleaf Whittier,** 1844

SUMMER'S END SUPPER

Salad of mixed bitter greens and end-of-summer tomatoes, with Sharp Classic Vinaigrette
(PAGE 72)

*

September Sauté of Winter and Summer Squash

*

Brown basmati rice
(SEE PAGE 463)

*

Roasty-Toasty Potatoes, Carrots, and Onions
(PAGE 790)

*

Sautéed pears with raisins and ginger, in Neo-Classic Crêpes
(PAGE 332),
with vanilla frozen yogurt or Soy Delicious

September Sauté of Winter and Summer Squash

This excellent side dish is made to go alongside anything tomato-y: say, a tomato-sauce-and-pasta dish or a tomato-and-bean casserole. You could add garlic (but you probably have it in the tomato-y dish). You could add red and yellow bell pepper cubes (sauté them with the zucchini, and maybe some tofu and a shot of tamari, and that, over quinoa or rice or fettucine, would be dinner in itself, not rather than accompaniment or component). **SERVES 4**

1 medium butternut squash, peeled, seeded, and cut into ½-inch dice
Cooking spray (optional)
1 teaspoon butter
1 teaspoon olive oil
1 medium zucchini, sliced lengthwise then cut into ¼-inch half-circles
¼ teaspoon salt
¼ teaspoon sugar
2 tablespoons finely minced Italian parsley

1 Place the butternut squash in a steamer basket over boiling water and steam until it is almost-to-just-barely tender, but still maintaining its shape, about 7 minutes.

2 Heat the butter and oil together in a nonstick skillet or wok, or one that has been sprayed with cooking spray, over medium heat. Add the zucchini and toss it around with a wooden spoon for about 30 seconds. Cover and steam for 30 seconds. Uncover and stir-fry until the zucchini is losing its raw look, becoming translucent, and very slightly browned on an edge here and there, 4 to 6 minutes more. Add the steamed squash, along with the salt and sugar, and stir-fry for 1 to 2 minutes more—just to finish any last edge of rawness, combine the ingredients, and heat through. Remove from the heat, toss in the parsley, and serve.

Simple Sweet-Baked Winter Squash

This recipe is the surest thing to make with a winter squash whose varietal characteristics you are not sure of: an intriguing find at the market, perhaps, but one where the produce manager may not even have a clue as to the name, let alone the mode of preparation. While particular varieties may be larger or smaller, moister or drier, they're all (except spaghetti squash) good with this treatment.

The sweetest and most richly flavored of the varieties I'm familiar with are butternut and kabocha (a dead heat for great flavor), baby pumpkins, turban, sweet dumpling and delicata, hubbard, buttercup, golden nugget, acorn, calabaza.

QUANTITY VARIABLE

Winter squash, unpeeled, cut into large curved chunks roughly 3 inches square, or individual whole baby pumpkins or acorn squash, allowing 1 chunk or whole small squash per person
Cooking spray
Butter (or, for vegans, vegetable margarine)
Tamari or shoyu soy sauce
Maple syrup, honey, brown sugar, or Rapidura
Salt and freshly ground black pepper to taste
Paprika to taste
1 or 2 oranges, halved (optional)

1 Preheat the oven to 400°F.

2 Do whatever you need to by way of prep on the squashes: Scoop out seeds, whack tops off baby pumpkins or acorns, and so on (see pages 804–805).

3 Spray a shallow baking dish large enough to accommodate all the squash pieces with cooking spray. Add the squash. Place about ¼ teaspoon butter in the hollow of each squash, followed by a teaspoon of tamari, 1 to 2 teaspoons sweetener, and salt, pepper, and paprika to taste. If you like, squeeze a little orange juice over the squash. Cover tightly with foil.

4 Bake until fork tender (the thinner the flesh of the squash, the more quickly it bakes), 35 to 50 minutes. Raise the heat to 500°F, and uncover the squash. Continue baking until slightly browned, 10 to 12 minutes. Serve immediately, nice and hot. If you like, you can mash the seasonings into the flesh a little before serving, but I usually just suggest this to guests at the table.

VARIATIONS

SIMPLE SWEET-HOT BAKED SQUASH ***has its ardent fans, me among them, but it's not for everyone. Simply add a sprinkle of cayenne to the squash before baking.***

SIMPLE SWEET PRESSURED WINTER SQUASH: ***This is even easier for those who know and love their pressure cookers. It's also far quicker, and uses less cooking fuel. Remove the seeds from the winter squash. Cut into large serving-size chunks. Cook under high pressure for 10 to 15 minutes—this yields an extremely tender squash. Spoon it out of the cooker directly onto the dinner plates, adding a tiny chip of butter and a healthy scoop or drizzle of whatever sweetener you like. Instruct diners to mash the sweetener into their squash.***

VARIATION

VEGAN VARIATION: ***Use the New Mexico–Style Green Chile Sauce or the vegan variation of Salsa Poblano Blanca y Verde and omit the grated cheese. Instead, use some nondairy soy cheese, and top the dish with fine, soft breadcrumbs, lightly drizzled with a little oil. Bake as directed.***

Spaghetti Squash Sonora

Strands of well-seasoned spaghetti squash, tossed with your choice of two very flavorful sauces, sandwich a generous bean filling. This casserole may be messy to serve, but one taste and no one will care in the least. Now, which of the two sauces should you make? The slightly creamy Salsa Poblano Blanca y Verde is a bit elegant, very good—but you must be a cilantro-lover. New Mexico–Style Green Chile Sauce is quite a bit spicier, more rugged, rough and tumble.

Serve with rice or warmed tortillas and a salad with a sweet cilantro dressing, tomatoes, and avocado slices, and you've got a fine dinner. Leftovers heated up in a tortilla make a great lunch the next day. **SERVES 4 TO 6 AS AN ENTREE**

- 1 package (8¾ ounces) dehydrated pinto bean flakes, such as Taste Adventure brand
- 2½ cups boiling water, preferably spring or filtered
- ½ large spaghetti squash, cooked as described on page 805, cooled, seeds removed, pulled into strands
- 3 cloves garlic, minced
- 1½ teaspoons olive oil
- ¼ teaspoon salt
- Plenty of freshly ground black pepper
- 2 to 3 cups Salsa Poblano Blanca y Verde (page 947) or New Mexico–Style Green Chile Sauce (page 942)
- 4 ounces freshly grated sharp Cheddar cheese

1. Preheat the oven to 400°F.

2. Place the dehydrated pintos in a heatproof bowl and pour the boiling water over them. Let stand for 5 minutes, stir well, and set aside.

3. As the beans rehydrate, combine the spaghetti squash with the garlic, oil, salt, and pepper—lots of the latter. Set aside.

4. Reheat the Salsa Poblano Blanca y Verde or New Mexico–Style Green Chile Sauce in a small saucepan over low heat.

5. Pat half of the squash mixture into a shallow 9-by-11-inch baking dish. Spoon half of the sauce onto the squash, then add spoonfuls of the beans, patting down with your hands (it will be blobby, and that's okay). Pat the remaining squash on the bean layer, then spoon on the remaining sauce. Top with the cheese.

6. Bake until the casserole is good and hot and the cheese is nicely melted, 20 to 25 minutes. Serve hot.

Sweet Potatoes & Yams

If asparagus is the first vegetal reward of spring, and red-ripe, dead-ripe tomatoes and local corn bracket high summer, then sweet potatoes and/or yams are both the herald and the prize of fall and winter. Whatever you call them, these bright tubers add sweetness, savor, and sustenance to the short gray days of November and the holiday table. One of their magical oddities is that they undergo a conversion process contrary to old-fashioned corn. The natural sugar in corn (at least until the recent bio-engineered varieties) begins almost immediately to convert to starch after picking. Sweet potatoes behave entirely differently. As time passes after they're harvested, the starch actually converts to sugar! Hence commercially raised sweet potatoes are almost always "cured"—kept in a climate-controlled, hot, humid environment for a week or so after harvest—to speed up this natural alchemy. How kind of nature to provide us with this sweet golden-orange succulence at the very moment we might be homesick for a brighter season.

If eating yams or sweet potatoes is a matter of deep satisfaction, understanding their nomenclature is one of frustration. Yams and sweet potatoes are—botanically speaking—two different vegetables entirely, from different families. They look very similar, and moreover are so often mislabeled that it's hard to know which you're getting. Fortunately, since even when *not* mislabeled, they're cooked similarly, it doesn't much matter about trying to tell them apart.

The sweet potato, *Ipomoea batatas,* is a member of the morning glory family (which is why the heart-shaped leaves that vine up when you grow one in a jar of water on your windowsill may look familiar). A New World vegetable, the sweet potato was initially a much greater success in Europe than the white potato. As time went on, sweet potatoes traveled the world, becoming popular in India, China, Japan, and the Pacific islands.

True yams—*Dioscorea bulbifera,* not mislabeled sweet potatoes—are technically not a root at all, but a rhizome, like ginger, or iris, and are rarely seen in this country, other than at the occasional Caribbean or Hispanic market. Oddly, like their strange bedfellows garlic and onion, true yams are in the lily family. They are native to both the Old World and the New, but are especially widely grown and used throughout Africa, where almost 6 million acres are planted in yams, and 90 percent of the world's yam cultivation takes place. In the right environment—hot, humid, tropical—true yams can grow as long as 8 feet and weigh close to 100 pounds. I've never seen any that big, but in South India (where the climate certainly meets the profile) I've seen some that were probably 30- or 40-pounders.

Most likely the naming mix-up began when slaves, who had lived on the true yams in their homelands, "called them by the African word 'to

Royal Sweet Potato

Henry VIII, king of England from 1509 to 1547, was a big (in both senses) sweet potato fan. He first tasted sweet potatoes when he received them as part of the dowry of his first wife, the Spanish Catherine of Aragon, and often consumed up to two dozen at a meal, usually turned into sweet potato pies. When he divorced her, he lost his source of sweet potatoes.

Of course, a king has his ways. Henry managed to get his own sweet potato plants, but they failed to thrive in the cool, moist English summer. Could his disappointment at being thus deprived have led to his repeated remarriage, a total of six times?

eat,'" says Bert Greene, in *Greene on Greens.* This word is *nyami* in Senegalese, which became *njam* in Gullah, the African-American language dialect spoken to this day by slave descendants on the coastal islands off Georgia. "The appellation," says Greene, "obviously stuck." So, unfortunately, did the confusion.

Visually, get a fix on which is which as follows: yams are more elongated, almost cylindrical, with a few sinuous curves tapering to a skinny tip. Sweet potatoes are plumper, more a rounded oval, and they reach their tips more abruptly.

But all this has little to do with what you'll usually find at the market, which is two varieties of sweet potato, and how they will be labeled. One is what growers call "dry," and this is the type usually labeled a sweet potato. Its flesh is paler by far; pale gold, pale yellow, almost white, sometimes a pale creamy yellow patterned with a faint purplish veining; its outer skin is more brown-yellow than red-orange. These are by far the least satisfactory of the sweets, because they are indeed drier of flesh; also less sweet, and sometimes rather fibrous. Avoid them.

Instead, go for the "moist" sweet potatoes. These (this is where it gets complicated) are usually, though wrongly, labeled "yams"—which evidently some marketing guy thought sounded more appealing than sweet potatoes. These have darker, more energetically red-orange skins, and bright, intensely colored, almost Day-Glo interiors.

When you dig through the sweet potato (or "yam") bin, here's what you should look for: plumped-out, smooth-skinned sweets, unwrinkled, unbruised, unblemished, and not sprouting (unless you want one to start, as the Victorians did, for a houseplant). Avoid those with shriveled ends or soft spots; even if the latter are excised, they can adversely affect the flavor of the whole root.

To prepare for cooking, decide how you want to fix your sweets. What's your pleasure—baked or boiled or steamed or grilled? Other than scrubbing, there's not really any "preparation" as such.

Basic Baked Sweet Potato

In the sweet potato world, baked is simplest, and, with a really good sweet potato, hard to beat. Although I've listed their baking temperature as 400°F, they are equally happy to bake at 300°F for a longer time, or 375°F, or at whatever heat the oven is on for something else—just throw a couple of sweets in along with it. (The smell of baking sweet potatoes and baked apples, going at one time, is intoxicatingly pure fall and early winter to me.)

Baked sweets are wonderful with butter and tamari . . . but the big surprise is how good these are split, with hot chili ladled over them. Try Steven's Spicy Black Bean Soysage Stew (page 216) or CD's Chili Mole (page 193): a great lunch or supper on a snowy day. The spicy/sweet conjunction is *very* nice. Try a baked sweet with Dragon Salt (page 900), too.

I always bake extra sweets, because they get sweeter after an overnight sojourn in the fridge (stored in their jackets), and, to my taste, are good cold, reheated, or mashed—in fact, I prefer using baked sweets to boiled or steamed for mashed sweet potatoes. Cookbook author Lorna Sass is so fond of leftover cooked sweet potatoes that she has confessed, in print, to frequently carrying one with her, wrapped, in her purse! **QUANTITY VARIABLE**

1 large sweet potato per person, well scrubbed
Cooking spray (optional)

1 Preheat the oven to 400°F.

2 Poke each sweet potato several times with a fork. Place the sweets on a piece of heavy-duty foil (opened, not enclosing them) or a baking dish that has been sprayed with cooking spray. Do not bake them directly on the rack, as you would white potatoes, because with all their natural sugar, sweet potatoes exude a syrupy juice as they bake—one that you neither want to smell burning on the oven floor during baking, nor clean up afterwards. Bake until done, testing with a fork, which should go in easily. Rounder, fatter sweets take longer to bake than narrower ones; baking time could be anywhere from 45 minutes to 1 hour and 15 minutes (for a very large, rounded sweet potato). Be sure it's really all the way tender; slightly underdone sweets can be disappointing.

COOK ONCE FOR 2 MEALS I always bake several more sweets than I need. I cut the leftovers up into soup, use them in the delectable recipe that follows, mash them as the topping for Jazzman's Pie (page 257), or use them to add a golden glow and moist, hard-to-define sweetness to the dough for rolls or biscuits.

Innecdote

The baked sweet potatoes were exceptionally deep red, very sweet Red Garnets. I had simply baked them, one for Ned, and one for me. I have forgotten what made that particular fall day such a long, hard one, but we were both exhausted. At last, it was dinnertime. The table off the porch was set for two, the phone wasn't ringing, the Scrabble set was out for a game later, and the kitchen was filled with the scent of the baking sweet potatoes.

Too tired to speak just yet, we each picked up a knife, slit the papery skin into the dense, fragrant steaming flesh. We each slipped in a spoonful of Better, added a modest splash of tamari, picked up a fork. We mashed in the melting Better, took forkfuls. We blew. We tasted.

Perfection.

We looked at each other in shared food-rapture. We chewed and swallowed.

"Oh," I said to Ned, at last capable of speech. "Oh, yum."

"No," he replied, and said, emphatically and with sincerity, "Yam."

Simply Boiled Sweet Potatoes

Another very simple method, fine for sweets to be mashed. I always leave them in their jackets, removing the skins later if at all, but you can peel them before cooking if you wish. Although boiling is quicker than baking, it is less satisfactory because you lose some of the good flavor, as well as nutrients, to the water, and the sweets are soggier. **SERVES 4 TO 6**

Water, preferably spring or filtered
3 to 4 large sweet potatoes, well-scrubbed, peeled or not, as you prefer

Bring a large pot of water to a boil over high heat. Drop in the sweet potatoes, lower the heat to a simmer, and cook until tender, 20 to 30 minutes.

Sweets by Steam

When I make sweet potatoes on top of the stove, I more often steam or pressure-cook than boil. Again, peel or not as you prefer. If I'm steaming, I'll generally slice them about ¼ inch thick and steam, tightly covered, in a collapsible metal steamer basket over boiling water until tender, 10 to 15 minutes. Pressure-cooking is even faster, and, to my mind, yields a better result than boiling, because so little water is used and the cooking process is so quick. Leave the skin on and quarter the scrubbed sweet potatoes lengthwise. Cook under high pressure for 6 to 8 minutes. Release the steam, remove the potatoes, and peel the skin (it will come off easily). This is also a good method for sweets that will be mashed.

Grilled Sweet Potatoes

Addictive; intensely wonderful. Please note that grilled sweet potato slices are used in East-West Lasagne (page 372), a wonderful dish. Leftovers are good on salad, too, especially with Cilantro Vinaigrette (page 94). **SERVES 4 TO 6**

4 to 6 sweet potatoes, well-scrubbed, peel on, sliced into long ovals

1 recipe Clary's Exquisitely Wicked Marinade (page 707) or the simple marinade for Grilled Summer Squash (page 797)

1 Preheat the grill to high, then lower the heat to medium.

2 Using a pastry brush, lightly coat the sweet potatoes with the marinade and grill over indirect heat, covered, until grill-marked, about 10 minutes. Carefully turn, and grill on the second side for 8 to 10 minutes.

COOK ONCE FOR 2 MEALS Make a great big batch of grilled sweets, eat your fill of them hot from the grill, and save the rest to go into East-West Lasagna. Reheat the sweets in the oven before enfolding them in the lasagna.

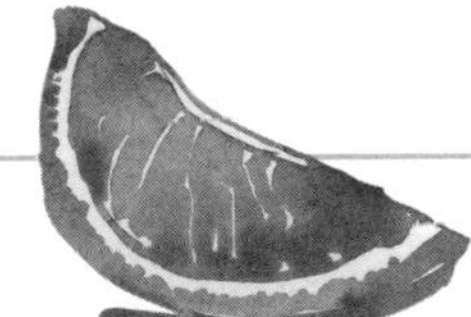

Sweet Potatoes with Grand Marnier, in Orange Cups

These are the knockout sweet potatoes that we served at the inn every Thanksgiving for almost two decades. And though the inn is now closed, I will be serving these for every Thanksgiving, anywhere, forever. Yes, they're one of *those* dishes. I hesitate to confess this, but they are my favorite thing on the whole Thanksgiving menu, and I know little moderation where they are concerned.

I like to make them in the orange cups, but you can forgo this bit of frou-frou if you wish. You will have more sweet potato mixture than orange cups. Bake the extra on the side, in a small, oiled baking dish, for second helpings. Or, if you're the plan-ahead type, save the shells of orange halves that have been juiced and freeze them, tucked into one another, in large zippered freezer bags. Thaw before filling with the sweet potato mixture. **SERVES 4 TO 6**

NOTE

GIVING THANKS

Although the particularly American celebration called Thanksgiving reputedly dates back to 1621, the roots of harvest festivals stretch back in time as long as humankind has cultivated and reaped from the earth. The Jews celebrate the Feast of the Tabernacles; the ancient Greeks fêted and feasted in honor of Demeter, the harvest goddess, as the ancient Romans did Ceres, the goddess of grain (this Roman festival was called Cerealia). But in America, Abraham Lincoln was the first to make it official, asking that the last Thursday of November be set apart "as a day of thanksgiving and praise to our beneficent Father who dwelleth in the heavens . . . and should be solemnly, reverently, and gratefully acknowledged as with one heart and voice by the whole American people."

4 or 5 oranges (if you are not making the orange cups, 2 oranges will do)
6 large, deep-red sweet potatoes, preferably the "moist" type often marketed as yams, baked, peeled while hot
2 tablespoons butter
⅓ cup brown sugar
½ teaspoon salt
4 to 5 tablespoons Grand Marnier, Napoleon, or other orange liqueur
Cooking spray

1 Grate the rind from 2 of the oranges. Set it aside.

2 Halve the oranges and juice them. Set the juice aside. If you plan to serve the sweets in orange cups, save the 4 to 6 juiced half-shells with skin intact, setting them aside too.

3 Begin whipping the hot sweet potatoes with a hand-held or stationary electric mixer. Beat in 1 tablespoon of the butter, along with about half the brown sugar and the salt. Beat in half the orange rind, 2 tablespoons of the Grand Marnier, and about ½ cup of the orange juice. Taste for seasoning and texture. You want a mixture that is not as thick as mashed potatoes—just a bit softer—and is decidedly orange-y. Continue adding zest and juice until you taste perfection. If you want them richer, well, you know what to do: Add more butter.

4 If you're placing the mixture in orange cups, spray the wells of a muffin tin as well as a small baking dish with cooking spray. Set the orange cups in the sprayed wells of the muffin tin and fill each one with as much of the sweet potato mixture as it can hold (you'll have more filling than will fit in this number of cups). Place the remaining sweet potato mixture in the small baking dish (or in extra, thawed orange cups, if you've saved them). This can be done in advance and stored, refrigerated, until an hour or so before serving.

5 About 1 hour before serving, preheat the oven to 375°F. Make a small indentation with the tip of a teaspoon in each filled orange cup and dot the mixture in the casserole dish with several indentations. Sprinkle the remaining Grand Marnier over the sweet potatoes. Add a teeny-tiny chip of the remaining butter to each indentation, and follow with a good solid sprinkle of the remaining brown sugar.

6 Place in a preheated oven and bake, 40 to 50 minutes for refrigerated sweet potatoes, 30 to 40 minutes if they're at room temperature or warm. The sweet potatoes should be hot all the way through, and the tops nice and golden brown, with little crunchy spots. If they have not reached this point by the end of the allotted cooking time, raise the oven temperature to 500°F and bake for 8 to 12 minutes longer.

Tomatoes

Tomatoes, in the same mysterious deadly nightshade family as potatoes, eggplant, and peppers, *used* to be considered poisonous. They *used* to be called love apples. Now they're just *used!* Nothing is better than a red-ripe tomato, sun-warmed in the garden and eaten out of hand, its dense, sweet-acid flesh dripping juice.

By contrast, it's discouraging to try to even tell you what to do at the market because it seems like every year, in the effort to breed tomatoes that will ship and hold up, the tomatoes grow poorer and poorer. The newest trick—as if pallid shades and mushy interiors weren't bad enough—is a tough skin, truly horrible; chewing a piece is like chewing plastic wrap. Every so often, a really good supermarket will surprise you, however, and have memorable tomatoes: Several times, in metropolitan areas, I've found Israeli tomatoes, the size of a small egg and still on the stem; they cost the earth, but they were the real thing, lush and full-flavored.

As a rule, organic tomatoes are much better than those "shippers" at the mega-chains—they could almost be a different vegetable. The other notable exception here is farmer's markets at midsummer: almost always a good bet, unless climate conditions have been off in a particular year. In late fall, you can often find green tomatoes, picked just in time to beat an incoming frost, at a good price. Buy them, by all means. The book and movie notwithstanding, fried green tomatoes are truly a treat, and you can get by with very little oil using my method (page 820). Just as good—maybe better—is Ronni's Great Green Tomato Casserole (page 821). Also, be sure to try Fabulous Green Tomato Mincemeat-less Pie Filling (page 1025).

No matter what market you head off to in your tomato quest, look for tomatoes that are heavy in the hand, deeply colored, and—most important—give off a heady tomato fragrance. A few brown crackled lines at the top can also be a good sign. Don't get them out of the refrigerator case . . . tomatoes must, must, *must* be kept at room temperature; bad changes occur when a tomato is chilled; there's decided loss of flavor and the texture grows cottony.

If I get desperate enough at midwinter, I, too, will use a mediocre fresh tomato in a sandwich or something. But in general, and certainly for most cooking purposes, good canned tomatoes are far superior to blah fresh ones.

To prepare for cooking . . . well, it all depends on what kind of cooking you're doing. I like to avoid the old peeled-and-seeded routine, but sometimes it does make a difference in the dish (this points up the fact that, mostly, tomatoes are used as an ingredient in other dishes); do, however, see Jenelle's Tomatoes Rockefeller (page 430), Southern Tomato Pudding (page 292), and the stuffed tomatoes on pages 430 to 434. If you have to peel and seed, there are several ways to go.

The "Grate" Paula Wolfert Method is ideal for when you're making just one tomato, and the finished texture doesn't much matter—you end up with a kind of chunky fresh tomato puree. Here's how: Halve the tomatoes, and using your fingertip, poke out and discard the seeds (or squeeze lightly, if you don't mind losing some juice). Grate the tomato, cut side in, on the coarse side of the grater, discarding the skin and using the grated pulp).

The Picky Perfection Method: With a firm, not-too juicy tomato, notably an Italian plum tomato, cut a shallow X at the stem end (just deep enough to pierce the skin), and, starting there, peel off the skin with a vegetable peeler. Then halve the tomato lengthwise and, with your fingertip, scoop out and discard any seeds or squeeze lightly. Peeling is considerably trickier with a red-ripe summer tomato, but can usually be done using a sharp peeler. (This is Marcella Hazan's preferred method. She reminds people to saw back and forth with the peeler as they go; it's much easier that way.)

The Expedient, Not-So-Bad Method: Though this sounds more complex, it's actually easier and most useful if you're in a hurry, or need several tomatoes peeled and seeded. Bring a large pot of water to a boil and drop in a few tomatoes at a time. Blanch for 20 to 30 seconds, remove, immediately placing in a bowl of ice water or under cold running tap water. When cool, peel away the skin with a sharp paring knife. Halve the tomatoes and, using your fingertip, remove and discard the seeds. The only disadvantage to this method is that even the briefest dip in boiling water gives a cooked quality to the layer of tomato flesh just under the skin, though the inside still has that pleasing rawness.

Slow-Baked Caramelized Tomatoes

This is one of those magic techniques everyone should know about, yielding a fresh tomato with some of the intensity of sun-drieds. Although slow to cook, the prep time is zip, and there's nothing to this simple method, transformative even for mediocre tomatoes. Although it's best with straight-from-the-garden summer tomatoes, it so concentrates the tomato flavor that it can do pretty durn well with even cottony midwinter offerings. **SERVES 4**

4 large tomatoes, halved (or proportionally more small tomatoes)
3 cloves garlic, minced (not pressed)
1½ tablespoons olive oil
½ teaspoon freshly ground black pepper
¼ teaspoon salt
1 teaspoon balsamic vinegar (optional)

1 Preheat the oven to 300°F.

2 Place the tomatoes, cut side up, in a nonstick baking dish large enough to accommodate the tomato halves in a single layer with plenty of air space around each one. Bake for 1½ hours.

3 Combine the garlic, oil, salt, pepper, and, if using, the vinegar.

4 Remove the dish from the oven and, using a pastry brush, lightly coat the tomatoes with the garlic mixture.

5 Return the dish to the oven and continue to bake until very soft and caramelized, almost collapsed, another 1½ to 2 hours. Using a slotted spoon, carefully remove the tomatoes from the baking dish. There will probably be a little dark, exuded, essence-of-tomato in the baking dish, which you should divide among all the tomatoes.

COOK ONCE FOR 2 MEALS Bake a double or triple batch of these and, if you don't eat them all, you have the basis for a dandy Pasta with Oven-Roasted Tomatoes: Cut up the leftovers, toss them with plenty of good hot rotini, a handful of minced Italian parsley, a tablespoon or so of olive oil, salt and plenty of fresh ground pepper, maybe a squeeze of pressed garlic—and there you have it. No one would complain if you add minced fresh basil, too.

How Sweet It Is: Caramelization

Caramelization is technically a very simple culinary process: Sugar is heated until it liquefies and browns, changing color from pale golden to deep brown. But beneath this simple process lies an infinity of uses, applications, facts, and indeed chemical processes themselves.

Consider what happens to the bite of a white onion, as it is slowly, slowly sautéed; it grows browner, and sweeter—the slower the sauté, the deeper the brown and the sweeter the taste. For a delicious experience of caramelization, make Roasty-Toasty Potatoes, Carrots, and Onions (page 790). The vegetables are treated with salty tamari, which draws out the liquid, which in turn pulls the vegetables' sugars to the surface—they grow brown and wrinkled looking and sweet. The Greek-style vegetables in this chapter—green beans, page 689; squash, page 799; and okra, page 775—all owe their marvelous transformation to the slow caramelization of not only the vegetables' inherent sugars but that of the garlic and tomato. Garlic is a vegetable that's like onion to nth degree as caramelization transfigures it: Its compounds go from strong, feisty, in your face, and delicious to extraordinarily sweet and silky (see the recipe for Cabbage and Greens with Kidney Beans and Caramelized Garlic, on page 718). And then there are the wonderful tomatoes above; dark, a little evil-looking, they hardly appear as if they would be a taste revelation. But, like so many vegetables transformed via this process, they are. Sweet indeed.

Caramelized tomatoes, by the way, are not strictly contemporary. There's a presidential precedent. Herbert Hoover, elected in 1928 as our thirty-first president, lived from 1874 to 1964. The family's cook was Mary Rattley, highly esteemed among White House guests. "Her inventiveness at concocting new specialties won her quite a reputation," Poppy Cannon and Patricia Brooks note in The Presidents' Cookbook. *Mary was pretty stingy with handing out her recipes: ". . . lucky guests who tasted one rarely learned how these delectable dishes were made." One exception was Maryland Caramel Tomatoes. Nothing like the recipe that follows, it simply consists of firm tomatoes, stem end cut off, a small indentation made with a spoon, and in that indentation, a teaspoon of butter and a teaspoon of sugar. The tomatoes were baked, at an unspecified given temperature, for an unspecified length of time, or until "cooked but not squashed." Plus ça change.*

Herb-Frizzled Cherry Tomatoes

When I can get lots of summer-ripe cherry tomatoes—tiny ones, preferably no larger than a marble, and preferably of different colors—this is how I treat them for a quick, delectable component. The tomatoes barely get heated through; they're warmed, rather than cooked. **SERVES 4**

Cooking spray
2 teaspoons butter (or olive oil, though I prefer butter here)
1 pound assorted tiny cherry tomatoes: red, yellow, both round and pear-shaped
Salt and freshly ground black pepper to taste
Pinch of sugar (optional)
1 to 2 tablespoons finely minced fresh herb: dill is my personal fave here, but basil is classic, rosemary and thyme are also good, and minced Italian parsley lets the tomatoes' taste shine

1 Heat the butter in a nonstick skillet, to the point of fragrance over medium-high heat (it will want to burn, so watch it carefully).

2 Add the tomatoes and vigorously shake the pan back and forth. Keep shaking frequently and cook until the tomatoes are hot and a few are starting to crack at the edges, about 3 minutes. Quickly add the salt and pepper, and, if using, the sugar. Toss in the herb. Shake the pan for 30 seconds and serve immediately.

Parsley

Green Tomatoes

Green tomatoes have an entirely different character than the red-ripe tomatoes, and a delicious, distinctive character it is: tarter, firmer, more acidic. It's difficult, if you're a home gardener, to convince yourself that it's worth foregoing the pleasure of ripe tomatoes by taking the tomato while it's still youthfully verdant—but it is, at least sometimes. If you can't bring yourself to pluck a tomato in the green of its youth, the first frost will bring you plenty, either from your own garden or that of friends, or at a farmer's market in late fall. So treat yourself to fried green tomatoes, Yankee-style (breaded in flour, caramelized during browning, finished with cream or its substitute) or Southern-style (dipped in buttermilk and cornmeal). But my dear and highly esteemed Louisville pan-pal and culinary writer, Ronni Lundy, introduced me to an even simpler way of enjoying green tomatoes that, as she says in her cornucopia-like book *Shuck Beans, Stack Cakes, and Honest Fried Chicken,* "has the same flavorful whang, but none of the drawbacks of frying. Not only is it gentler to the heart and digestive system, but it's fairly muss free." Fried green tomatoes are traditionally served at breakfast, but I like them for supper, as I do Ronni's fine casserole.

Also, don't miss Fabulous Green Tomato Mincemeat-less Pie Filling (page 1025): vegetarian, and out-of-this-world good—a zillion times more delicious than any store-bought mincemeat.

Yankee-Style Fried Green Tomatoes

Traditionally, green tomatoes are fried in a truly frightening amount of oil or bacon fat, but you can get a crisp crusty coat with almost none—*if* you have a good-quality nonstick pan. The "gravy" is optional, but good: The creaminess against the acidity is a piquant contrast. In their original incarnation, such tomatoes usually got a pour of heavy cream. **SERVES 4**

VARIATION

VEGAN VARIATION: ***Simply omit the gravy, or make it using rice or unflavored soy milk.***

1 teaspoon cornstarch
½ cup low-fat milk
1 drop Pickapeppa sauce
About 1 cup unbleached white all-purpose flour
Salt and freshly ground black pepper to taste
Cooking spray
1 teaspoon butter
1 teaspoon mild vegetable oil, such as corn, canola, or peanut
4 large (or 6 to 8 small) firm green tomatoes, rinsed, stem end plus a thin slice of the bottom cut off, sliced into 1/2-inch-thick rounds
1 tablespoon dark brown sugar

1 Place the cornstarch in a small bowl and, using your fingers, smush in about 1 tablespoon of the milk. When smooth, add the remainder of the milk and the Pickapeppa. Set aside.

2 Place the flour in a shallow pan and season it with salt and pepper.

3 Spray a nonstick skillet with cooking spray, and put it over medium heat. Add half of the butter and half of the oil.

4 As the butter and oil heat, begin dredging the sliced tomatoes in the seasoned flour.

VARIATION

SOUTHERN-STYLE FRIED GREEN TOMATOES, VEGAN VARIATION: ***Use vegan buttermilk (a scant ½ cup plain soymilk mixed with 1 tablespoon lemon juice) instead of dairy buttermilk.***

SOMEWHAT TRADITIONAL VARIATION: ***Usually some of the fat left in the pan is used to make gravy, full of savor from the little bits of crunchy goodness left from the tomatoes. Here you don't have the fat left. So you can either make the cornstarch milk gravy in the previous Yankee version or melt an extra tablespoon of butter in the pan in which the tomatoes were cooked. Stir in 2 tablespoons unbleached white flour and cook, stirring, until the flour is slightly colored, 1 to 2 minutes. Gradually whisk in 1 cup low-fat milk and cook, stirring constantly, for 3 to 4 minutes. Season with salt and pepper and pour over the tomatoes.***

5 When the skillet is good and hot, carefully add the tomato slices, and put a tiny sprinkle of brown sugar on each one. Fry until nicely browned on the bottom, about 6 minutes.

6 Add the remaining butter and oil to the pan. Very gently, turn the tomatoes over. Sprinkle the remaining brown sugar on the already browned side and fry until the second side is nicely browned, 3 to 4 minutes. Transfer to a platter.

7 Give the cornstarch mixture a vigorous stir and, whisking like the dickens, pour it into the hot skillet. Cook, whisking, until it thickens (just about instantly). Add a little salt and pepper to taste, then spoon a little of it over each of the tomato slices and serve immediately.

Southern-Style Fried Green Tomatoes

Cornmeal instead of flour, and the dairy product of choice is buttermilk—the tomatoes get dipped in it as part of the breading process, which makes this slightly messier. But oh so good! I really love tomatoes fried both ways, and try to have each version once every fall.

Both this recipe and the previous one show how nothing much can, in the hands of talented home and country cooks, turn into some stupendously fine eating. **SERVES 4**

About 1 cup fine yellow cornmeal
Salt and freshly ground black pepper to taste
About ½ cup buttermilk
Cooking spray
1 teaspoon butter
1 teaspoon mild vegetable oil, such as corn, canola, or peanut
4 large (or 6 to 8 small) firm green tomatoes, rinsed, stem end plus a thin slice off the bottom cut off, sliced into ½-inch-thick rounds

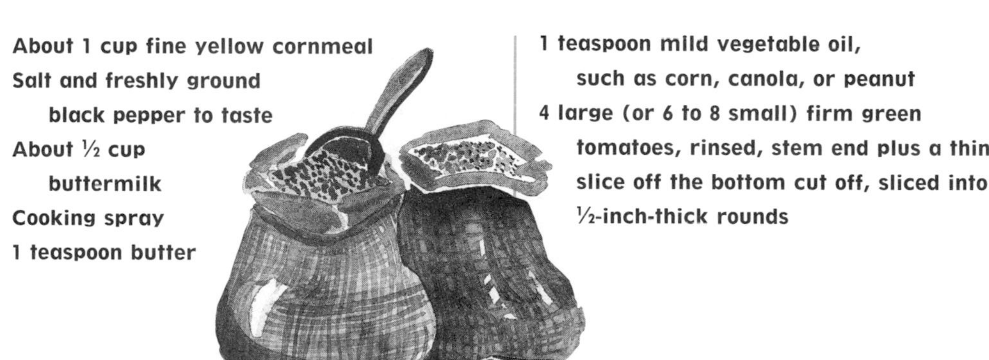

1 Place the cornmeal in a shallow pan, and season it with salt and pepper. Go a little heavy on both.

2 Place the buttermilk in another shallow pan.

3 Spray a nonstick skillet with cooking spray, and place it over medium heat. Add half of the butter and half of the oil.

4 As the butter and oil heat, begin dredging the sliced tomatoes: first in the buttermilk, then in the seasoned cornmeal.

5 When the skillet is good and hot, carefully add the tomato slices. Fry until nicely browned on the bottom, about 6 minutes.

6 Add the remaining butter and oil to the pan. Very gently, turn the tomatoes over. Fry until nicely browned on both sides, 3 to 4 minutes. Serve immediately.

Green Gloating

"Ma and Laura picked the tomatoes. The vines were wilted down, soft and black, so they picked even the smallest green tomatoes. There were enough ripe tomatoes to make almost a gallon of preserves.

'What are you going to do with the green ones?' Laura asked, and Ma answered, 'Wait and see.'

She washed them carefully without peeling them. She sliced them and cooked them with salt, pepper, vinegar, and spices.

'That's almost two quarts of green tomato pickle. Even if it's only our first garden on the sod and nothing could grow well, these pickles will be a treat with baked beans this winter,' Ma gloated."

—Laura Ingalls Wilder, The Long Winter

Ronni's Great Green Tomato Casserole

One last green tomato recipe, simply too good, too unusual, and too easy to leave out. It comes from my friend Ronni Lundy. The only change I make at home is to use my beloved Ak-Mak crackers for the crumbs, rather than the soda crackers Ronni calls for. At times, I've also used dried breadcrumbs, and my friend Jo Fraterigo has used Ritz crackers—all successful. This is something like a cross between a very simple gratin, a bread pudding, and stuffing—crisp crumbs on top, the elusive and delicious, slightly acid green tomatoes underneath, their tartness gently pointed up by the buttermilk. Serve on a component plate with a big pile of Oven-Roasted

Shiitake Mushrooms with Garlic and Coarse Salt (page 48), and a sauté of broccoli rabe, and you have a wonderful fall supper. **SERVES 4 TO 6**

Cooking spray
5 medium green tomatoes, some just starting to ripen to pinkishness, rinsed, stem ends removed, cut into ¼-inch dice
1 onion, very finely diced
¾ cup Ak-Mak cracker crumbs
1 tablespoon melted butter
Salt and plenty of freshly ground black pepper to taste
½ cup buttermilk

1 Preheat the oven to 325°F.

2 Spray a 2-quart casserole with cooking spray.

3 Combine the tomatoes, onion, and cracker crumbs with the butter and salt and pepper to taste. Stir in the buttermilk. Transfer to the prepared dish. Bake for 45 minutes. If the top hasn't browned, place under the broiler for a minute or two. Serve hot.

CHAPTER 12

Savory Cakes, Burgers & Patties

Round as moons, cunning little discs, perfect to take to hand; small savory fritters, cakes, and patties have long fascinated humankind. From falafel, the much-loved Middle Eastern fried chickpea patty, to the venerable hamburger, how we do love them—though we usually dollop them with sauce, relish, salad, or all three, and pack them in the pocket of a pita or between slices of bread.

Dozens of perfectly wonderful small cakes are meatless; the challenge in them lies in decreasing their fat content, since many of them owe their charm to a crispness brought about by frying; a caloric bath in hot oil that I try to avoid. Baking often works instead of frying—a sojourn in a hot nonstick skillet can also sometimes do the trick. Less problematic but still requiring attention is how to make these cakes egg free. Eggs serve a valuable function as binders because they start out liquid, turn solid during cooking, and add a kind of rich, satisfying neutral flavor that nothing else quite matches. I do use them in many cases, but vegans and those on low-cholesterol diets will also find plenty of good alternatives here.

One point essential to loving these treats is to let them be themselves: unique, distinctive, paralleling but not duplicating the meat experience.

I have arranged these "baby cakes" according to their most prominent ingredient: grain, tofu, nuts, or vegetables/legumes.

Grain Cakes

The idea of a cake or burger built on rice, millet, or another grain might be off-putting initially: We're used to thinking of the patty as supplying the protein, and the idea of a grain-based burger on an also grain-based bun sounds odd. Yet most who eat little or no meat grow quite fond of grain burgers in various permutations—and the addition of nut or seed butters (most frequently tahini), an egg, legumes, cheese, or other dairy products makes them higher in protein than one would expect.

One of the cakes here, the Indian Harvest cake, is really more of a thick, savory pancake than a burger. But it's delicious, substantial, and an excellent late-night supper.

Risotto Cakes

As mentioned in the section on risotti (pages 486–92), one of the best uses for a nonstick pan is in making little cakes of crisp-crusted leftover risotto with no added fat. They are remarkably good, and I always make extra risotto for just this reason. I try to save it for lunch or dinner following a risotto night, but I must confess I usually wind up having them for breakfast.

Shape leftover risotto into palm-size patties. Heat a dry nonstick skillet to fairly hot. Add the risotto patties and lower the heat to medium-low. Let cook, without turning or disturbing, until undersides have formed a nice brown crust, 6 to 8 minutes. Flip and brown the second side (4 to 6 minutes) and serve at once.

Outrageously Good Pan-Crisped Millet-Vegetable Cakes

In my view, millet is *the* grain for grain burgers. Wholly different from anything commercially available, gorgeous, and quite delicious, these are my favorite grain-based cakes. When I first developed the recipe, my husband literally closed his eyes and moaned with pleasure: love at first bite.

Imagine the audacious flavorings of hummus made subtle, then added to the gently flavored millet, in a cake comfortingly soft within, slightly crisped without. Perhaps best of all, these are a truly stunning visual. They are definitely and decidedly *pink,* thanks to some grated beet. The color gets even better as they cook: The part of the cake in direct contact with the pan turns a kind of golden orange, but the pink interior is retained. Every time I make these I have the feeling this millet mixture would be a great stuffing for portobellos done in the oven, though I haven't tried this yet. It holds together much better than most grain burger mixtures. Any of you vegans with a touch of the romantic as well as the outrageous in your soul might consider making these in heart shapes for Valentine's Day. **MAKES 6 LARGE CAKES**

1 small or ⅓ large raw beet
1 carrot
[illegible] cups Basic Moist-Style Millet (page 574)
½ cup canned baby butter beans or navy beans, rinsed and very well drained
2 tablespoons tahini
3 to 5 cloves garlic, peeled and split
Juice of 1 lemon
1 tablespoon tamari or shoyu soy sauce
Salt and freshly ground black pepper to taste
Cooking spray
Accompaniments (see note that follows)

1 Using the grater blade of a food processor, grate the beet and carrot. Transfer the vegetables into a large bowl containing the millet. Set aside.

NOTE

OF MILLET-CAKES & NEW HOME-BODIED PLEASURES

I enjoyed my first millet-cake—actually, a bite of Ned's—in Fayetteville, Arkansas, at the Village Epicurean, a small natural foods, mostly vegan deli, opened for lunch on weekdays. The atmosphere was cozy, unpretentious, friendly; the food ever-changing, eclectic, fresh, exceptionally good. The bite of Ned's millet-burger was downright inspiring: crunchy outside, tender within, savory throughout, and very satisfying when fitted out with all the good bun stuff. I discussed it at length with Kathryn Laurrain, the sweet-natured proprietress, lovely and lanky as a flower-stalk, and a truly gifted natural foods chef. Her version inspired this millet burger: quite different, but just as delicious.

VARIATION

Substitute leftover, cooked-until-very-tender oatmeal for all or part of the millet.

2 Without washing the processor, replace the grater blade with the S blade. Add the beans, tahini, garlic, lemon juice, and tamari. Process until very smooth. Work this mixture into the millet, using your hands. Taste and add salt, pepper, and perhaps more tamari, until the mixture is to your liking.

3 Shape the mixture into patties 3½ to 4 inches wide, and about 1½ inches thick. (You can make these larger than most veggie burgers because the millet mixture coheres so well.)

4 Spray a large skillet, preferably nonstick, with cooking spray, and heat it over medium-high heat. Let it get good and hot, then add the millet cakes and lower the heat to low-medium. Let the cakes cook fairly slowly, 8 to 9 minutes, before gently flipping them. (Isn't that color fabulous?) Let cook on the second side for about 6 minutes.

Accompaniments

This burger lends itself to an amazing array of finishes. Of course, you can do the bun-lettuce-tomato thing, but I think these are better served un-bunned when hot (save the bun for the cold leftovers and brown-bag them). Try the millet cakes as the prettiest possible piece of a component dinner, accompanied by steamed or stir-fried beet greens (you have them on hand from the beet in the recipe, right?) and a kabocha squash with maple syrup or brown sugar. Enjoy their soothing subtlety or zap them with some Thai Crystal (page 923) and serve alongside a vibrant stir-fry of gingered asparagus and red pepper strips. And for a mixed metaphor that has no reason to be so wonderful, but is, use them for a Reuben sandwich on toasted rye bread: a fat millet cake with sauerkraut, sliced tomato, mayonnaise with a dab of ketchup stirred in, and a thin slice of Swiss or Jarlsberg melted over the top.

Sweet Onion Inn's Mountain Patties

This is my version of the good, grainy, solid burgers from a vegan inn just outside Hancock, Vermont, smack-dab in the middle of the state that is the cradle of classic country inns, and right between the ski resorts of Killington and

Sugarbush. The unpretentious six-room Sweet Onion Inn is surrounded by old apple trees and new herb gardens, and the inn's farmhouse, where guests stay, was built in the 1820s. But the Sweet Onion became an inn only in September 1994. That's when Ron Heatley, a former natural foods store owner from Michigan, opened the inn with his wife, Kathy. "Every morning now," says Ron, "I wake up and ask myself what good thing I did to deserve to live in such a spectacular area." Ron used to teach in-store cooking classes, and now makes the inn's breakfasts and dinners.

Ron generally serves these patties with mushroom gravy (try the Mushroom-Miso-Mustard Gravy, page 952) and likes to start the meal with a soup of fresh corn blended with tomato, onion, garlic, and herbs. He uses whole wheat pastry flour in his patties; I prefer the texture of patties made with gluten flour. I also like to substitute a red bell pepper for the green, or to use some of each. **MAKES 6 TO 8 PATTIES**

2 tablespoons olive oil
1 large onion, diced
1 rib celery, with leaves, diced
1 carrot, diced
1 green or red bell pepper, stems, seeds, and ribs removed, diced
6 cloves garlic, pressed
½ teaspoon dried basil or 1 tablespoon finely minced fresh basil
½ teaspoon dried oregano or 1 tablespoon finely minced fresh oregano
1 tablespoon tamari or shoyu soy sauce
3 cups cooked brown rice, preferably short grain
¼ cup tahini
½ cup gluten flour
Salt and freshly ground pepper to taste
Cooking spray

1 Preheat the oven to 350°F.

2 Heat the olive oil in a skillet. When the pan is hot, add the onion, and sauté over medium heat for about 4 minutes. Add the celery, carrot, and green pepper, and sauté for another 5 minutes. Add garlic. Sauté 2 minutes more, and remove from heat.

3 In a large bowl, combine the sautéed mixture with all the remaining ingredients, stirring well to combine. Taste for seasonings. Consistency will be soft.

4 Scoop the mixture with a ½-cup measure and form 3-inch patties, about 1¼ inches high, directly on a nonstick baking sheet or one that has been sprayed with cooking spray. Smooth the tops slightly. Leave ½ inch space between the patties; they spread slightly. Bake for 25 to 30 minutes, or until firm and slightly browned.

Savory Indian Harvest Corn–Wild Rice Cakes

VARIATION

QUICKER SAVORY INDIAN HARVEST CORN–WILD RICE CAKES: *Omit the olive oil, onion, garlic, and cilantro, which lets you skip the sautéing step and a lot of chopping. You end up with a tasty, more neutral-flavored cake—one you could even enjoy with maple syrup. And if you have the cooked grains already on hand, this is a very quick fix.*

Called Indian Harvest not only because the cake features two native American grains, one of which is still hand-gathered by American Indians, but because the recipe is a reduced-fat, dairy-free version of one from one of my favorite mail-order grain sources, Indian Harvest. This is actually less a burger than a substantial, savory pancake studded with grains. It is an excellent supper dish, soothing yet faintly exotic. If you're feeling devil-may-care about fat content, heat ¼ inch of oil in the skillet, get it hot, and fry the cakes in it for a crisp, frittery texture.

Although you can hold these, uncovered, on a foil-lined baking sheet in a 250°F oven for a few minutes, they are best hot off the grill, so to speak. You can go in any number of directions in serving them, all good: Use them as one element on a component vegetable plate; serve them with mushroom sauce, such as Mushroom-Miso-Mustard Gravy (page 952); try them with Arkansalsa (page 913), Pamela Jones's Absolutely Incredible Roasted Vegetable Salsa (page 915), Western-Style Blueberry Chutney (page 927), or Cora Pinkley Call's Uncooked Ozark Relish (page 929).

MAKES 12 LARGE CAKES OR 24 SMALL ONES, SERVES 4 TO 6

1 tablespoon olive oil
1 large onion, diced
1 tablespoon finely chopped garlic
¾ cup corn kernels, fresh (from about 2 ears corn) or thawed frozen kernels
2 tablespoons finely minced cilantro
2½ cups cooked wild rice

BATTER
3 ounces silken tofu, preferably reduced fat
⅔ cup rice milk or low-fat dairy milk
1 large egg
1 cup unbleached all-purpose flour
¼ cup whole wheat pastry flour
1 teaspoon salt
¼ teaspoon freshly ground black pepper
1 teaspoon baking powder

Cooking spray

1 Heat the oil in a large skillet over medium-high heat. Add the onion and

sauté for 5 to 6 minutes, or until softened, translucent, and just starting to brown. Lower the heat to medium. Add the garlic and sauté for 1 minute longer.

2 Scrape the sauté into a medium bowl. Add the corn kernels, cilantro, and rice and toss well. Set aside.

3 Combine all the batter ingredients in a food processor and buzz until smooth, pausing to scrape the sides a couple of times. Pour the batter over the rice-corn mixture and stir well.

4 Heat a nonstick griddle or skillet, or one sprayed with cooking spray, good and hot over medium heat. Scoop up about 2 tablespoons of the batter and drop it onto the grill. Pat it out gently and carefully with your hand to form a cake 3 to 4 inches in diameter and ⅜ to ½ inch thick—or make smaller cakes, if you wish. (If you got the skillet hot enough, the batter will sizzle as it goes in.) Repeat until the skillet is full.

5 Let the cakes cook slowly over medium heat; you can't hurry the process. After 2 to 3 minutes, when the cakes are brown underneath and dry-looking on top, carefully flip the cakes over and let brown for 1 to 2 minutes more. Serve as soon as possible, accompanied by any salsa or relish, or just plain tamari or shoyu soy sauce.

Herb Garden Grain-Lentil Cakes

A mild and tasty vegetable-grain-legume burger, vegan, high in unrefined carbs, and rich in protein (from the sunflower or sesame seeds, lentils, and chickpea flour) as well. The only fat comes from 2 teaspoons of oil and the seeds. These are good plain and even better dressed up. I served them once at a dinner party with Quick Hot Asian Ketchup (page 923) and Fresh Ginger and Pear Relish (page 930), and everyone raved, to the extent of begging for doggie bags.

Though the recipe looks lengthy, everything comes together quickly. Essentially, you make the sauté, then buzz everything in the food processor. **MAKES 12 CAKES**

NOTE

It's a formidable temptation not to get so busy as one ages that important but inessential personal pleasures fall away. For me, one such early casualty was my devoted tending of a small but bountiful flower, vegetable, and herb garden.

Being the all or nothing type, for many years I had no garden at all, just the pang. But about five years ago, as I relinquished the idea of becoming a gardener again any time soon, I began buying a few large pots of fresh herbs a year. All summer these sit on the limestone front steps off my porch. My globe basil is particularly glossy and sassy this year. I always have it, and holy basil, and lemon thyme, rosemary, Texas tarragon (see page 37), a mint, and occasionally lemon verbena or lemon grass. I cannot tell you how deep the pleasure is from just these few fresh herbs—how satisfying snipping here and there is, the joy even in glancing at them as I go up and down.

2 teaspoons mild vegetable oil, such as corn, canola, or peanut
1 onion, chopped
2 ribs celery with leaves, finely minced
2 carrots, grated
1 tomato, peeled, seeded, and chopped
¼ cup sunflower seeds
6 to 8 cloves garlic
2 slices soft whole wheat bread, pulled into pieces
8 to 10 large leaves fresh basil
Leaves from 2 stems fresh thyme
Leaves from 4 or 5 stems Italian parsley
Leaves from 1 stem fresh oregano or marjoram
5 tablespoons water, preferably spring or filtered, or as needed
A few drops Tabasco or similar hot sauce
⅓ cup chickpea flour
1 tablespoon cornstarch
1½ cups cooked barley or brown rice or a combination of both
3 cups cooked lentils, tender but not mushy, well drained
1 tablespoon tamari or shoyu soy sauce
Salt and freshly ground black pepper to taste
Cooking spray

1 Preheat the oven to 375°F.

2 Heat the oil in a nonstick skillet, or a conventional skillet sprayed with cooking spray, over medium heat. Add the onion and sauté for 5 minutes, or until softened and translucent. Add the celery and carrots and sauté for 6 minutes longer, stirring, until the vegetables are softened. Add the tomato and raise the heat. Cook for another 6 minutes, or until most of the tomato liquid has evaporated.

3 As the vegetables sauté, pulse the sunflower seeds in a food processor until a chunky powder is formed. Turn out into a bowl. Without washing the processor, add the garlic, bread, basil, thyme, parsley, and oregano or marjoram and process until the herbs and garlic are finely chopped. Add water as needed to form a thick paste, then add Tabasco to taste. Add the chickpea flour and cornstarch and buzz until a thick batter, almost a paste, is formed. Add this batter to the pulsed sunflower seeds, add the barley and lentils, and stir well.

4 When the vegetable sauté is done, scrape it into the bowl with the lentil mixture. Add the tamari to the skillet and scrape any browned bits from the bottom, then pour the liquid into the bowl. Stir to combine. Season to taste with salt and pepper.

5 Shape the mixture into 12 patties, each about 3 inches wide and ¾ to 1 inch thick, and place on a nonstick cookie sheet or one that has been sprayed with cooking spray. Bake for 12 to 15 minutes, then remove the sheet from the oven, flip the burgers, and bake on the second side for 10 to 12 minutes, or until burgers are firm and browned.

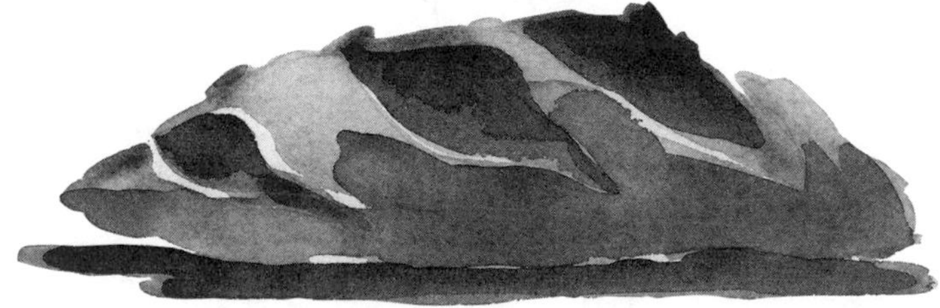

Parsnip-Barley Burgers

I'll be the first to admit that these cakes sound improbable, but sweet parsnip, chewy-tender whole hulled barley, and artful seasonings add up to a very pleasing burger. Potato and potato starch serve as the binder. The combination of flavors was inspired in part by a recipe for Parsnip and Barley Stew in *The Second Seasonal Political Palate,* by the Bloodroot Collective. These make a hearty addition to a component dinner. **MAKES ABOUT 15 SMALL CAKES, SERVES 5 OR 6**

½ pound parsnips, peeled, stems and any woody cores removed, cut into ½-inch pieces
½ pound russet potatoes, peeled and diced into ½-inch cubes
1 tablespoon plus 1 teaspoon tamari or shoyu soy sauce
Salt and freshly ground black pepper to taste
Several vigorous gratings of nutmeg
Leaves from 2 stems fresh thyme
Leaves from 4 or 5 stems Italian parsley
Leaves from 1 stem fresh oregano or marjoram
⅓ cup potato starch
¼ cup tahini
1 teaspoon mild vegetable oil, such as corn, canola, or peanut
1 onion, chopped
1 tablespoon chopped garlic
2½ cups cooked whole hulled barley
6 to 8 cloves garlic
Cooking spray

1 Bring a large pot of water to a boil with ½ teaspoon salt and drop in the parsnips and potatoes. Cook until both are tender, 8 to 10 minutes. Drain well Alternatively, steam or pressure cook the parsnips and potatoes until tender.

2 Mash the parsnips and potatoes while still hot, with the tamari, salt, pepper, and nutmeg. Stir in the thyme, parsley, oregano or marjoram, and potato starch, then add the tahini, blending well. Set aside.

3 Heat the oil in a nonstick or conventional skillet over medium heat and sauté the onion for 5 minutes, or until softened and translucent. Add the garlic, lower the heat, and sauté for 10 minutes longer, stirring.

4 Add the sautéed onion and garlic to the mashed parsnip mixture. Stir in the cooked barley. Cover and refrigerate for at least 1 hour.

5 Preheat the oven to 375°F. Shape the chilled parsnip-barley mixture into 12 to 15 patties, each 3 inches wide and ½ inch thick. Place the patties on a nonstick baking sheet or one that has been sprayed with cooking spray. Bake for about 25 minutes, or until golden on top. Flip the patties and bake for 10 minutes longer. Serve hot.

A VEGETABLE FEASTING PLATE

Golden Days of Summer Corn Soup
(PAGE 163)

*

The Salad
(PAGE 68)

*

Parsnip-Barley Burgers

*

Fresh garden tomato slices with ribboned basil

*

Butternut squash puree
(PAGE 805)

*

Brown Sugar–Glazed Beets with Fresh Kumquats
(PAGE 704)

*

Chocolate-Orange Biscotti
(PAGE 1034)

*

Ginger Sorbet
(PAGE 1045)

Tofu & Tempeh Cakes

Soyfoods, discussed in detail in Chapter 10, make great burgers—substantial, high in protein, and a bit chewy. The first tofu burger here, which is vegan, is my current favorite; the second, which calls for an egg, was for many years a standby in our household and I love it still.

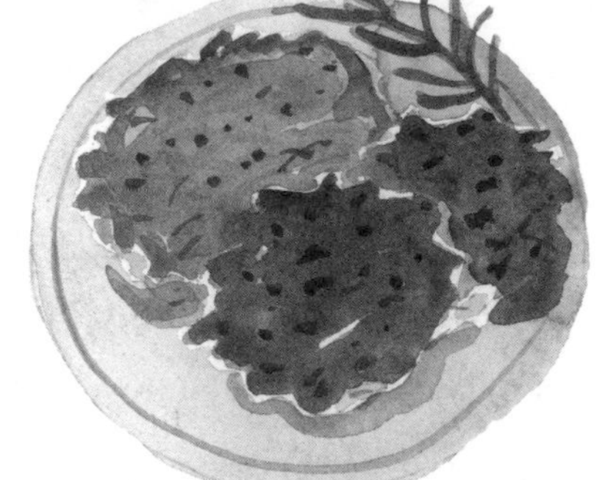

The Very Best Tofu Cakes

What makes these tofu cakes the very best? They are deeply flavorful, brown, and chewy, as perfect in a sandwich with all the fixings as they are served hot with a nice sauce over them—Sauce Soubise (page 946), say, or Mushroom-Miso-Mustard Gravy (page 952), or Vegan Sesame Velouté (page 950). Make them large for buns, small or medium if they're to be sauced.

The unique savor of tofu cakes comes from an artful array of seasonings (good old garlic and miso, friendly basil, a bit of muscle from tomato paste), but the magical chewiness comes from *freezing* the tofu (traditional water-packed style, not silken) prior to use. This changes it from tender to chewy, a transformation that this preparation sets off very well.

Please note that these cakes are vegan and relatively low fat. They're also quite quick to put together: Everything goes in the food processor and that's that. **MAKES 4 LARGE, 6 MEDIUM, OR 8 SMALL CAKES; SERVES 4**

- 1 pound firm conventional tofu, preferably reduced fat, drained and frozen for 24 hours, then thawed
- ⅔ cup crisp whole-grain breadcrumbs
- 1 tablespoon water, preferably spring or filtered, or vegetable stock
- 2 to 3 cloves garlic
- 1 tablespoon plus 1 teaspoon tamari or shoyu soy sauce
- 2 teaspoons golden or white miso, preferably chickpea-rice miso
- 2 tablespoons almond butter or tahini
- 1 tablespoon tomato paste
- 1 tablespoon cornstarch or 2 teaspoons arrowroot
- 1 teaspoon honey, sugar, or Rapidura
- Leaves from 3 sprigs fresh basil, coarsely chopped (optional)
- 3 or 4 sprigs Italian parsley, coarsely chopped (optional)
- A few tablespoons water, preferably spring or filtered
- Salt and freshly ground black pepper to taste
- Cooking spray

1 Preheat the oven to 400°F.

2 Using your hands, squeeze out any residual water from the thawed tofu. Pull it into small pieces. Set about three-quarters of the tofu aside; place the remaining quarter in a food processor.

3 Add the breadcrumbs, water, garlic, tamari, miso, almond butter, tomato paste, cornstarch, honey, and basil and parsley, if using. Buzz, pausing to scrape down the sides, until a very thick paste is formed. You may need to add water to get this consistency; if so, add it a tablespoon at a time.

4 Turn the paste out of the processor bowl and add to the shredded tofu, stirring well. You will have a mixture that is moist but not wet, and firm enough to shape into patties. Season to taste with salt and pepper.

5 Form 4 large, 6 medium, or 8 small cakes and place them on a nonstick baking sheet or one that has been sprayed with cooking spray. Bake for 20 to 25 minutes, or until firm and a little dry on top, and golden brown underneath. Carefully flip the patties, and return them to the oven for 8 to 10 minutes more. Serve hot with a sauce as an entrée (accompanied by a fresh green vegetable and a simply cooked grain) or in a sandwich or as a burger.

COOK ONCE FOR 2 MEALS You can double this recipe and try the cakes several of the ways described above. These keep well, refrigerated, for several days.

VARIATION

Sauté 1 small or ½ large onion, finely chopped, along with a handful of chopped mushrooms (shiitake or regular old buttons) in the smallest amount of butter or olive oil you can get by with. When soft, add these to the bowl containing the crumbled thawed tofu at the end of Step 2, then continue as directed. A little grated nutmeg is good when adding mushrooms to the mix.

Curried Tofu Cakes

The page with Tofu Patties in my old, first-edition, jacket-long-lost copy of *Laurel's Kitchen* is spotted, notated, and flour-speckled, so loved, used, and

NOTE

ALAS, POOR TOFU

Tofu, that much maligned soybean cake, has been a favorite of mine since childhood. I have cherished memories of my father taking me to tatami-matted Japanese restaurants in New York before and after matinées. On these occasions, the meal always included tofu, thus it seemed a special delicacy to me, exotic and representative of grown-up adventures.

played-with was the basic recipe. My version differs only slightly from that one, but since the recipe was incomprehensibly left out of the revised edition, honor compels me to give this light, curried, simple cake a second life. It keeps well in the fridge and makes an excellent cold sandwich. Better, I think, cold than hot.

MAKES 8 TO 10 CAKES

2 teaspoons olive oil
1 small onion, diced
1 rib celery, diced
⅓ green bell pepper, seeds and ribs removed, diced
1 carrot, diced
1 (20-ounce) package firm conventional tofu, preferably reduced fat
1 large egg
2 cloves garlic, halved
2 tablespoons whole wheat flour
2 to 3 tablespoons chopped Italian parsley (optional)
½ teaspoon salt
1 tablespoon tamari or shoyu soy sauce
1 teaspoon Pickapeppa sauce
2 teaspoons best-quality curry powder or red, green, or yellow curry paste
Cooking spray
Hamburger fixings, such as buns, sliced tomatoes and onion, lettuce leaves, mayonnaise or Tofu Mayonnaise (page 906), and ketchup

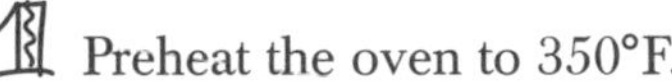

1 Preheat the oven to 350°F.

2 Heat the oil over medium heat in a nonstick or conventional skillet. Add the onion and sauté for 5 minutes, or until softened and translucent. Add the celery, green bell pepper, and carrot and sauté for 6 minutes more, stirring, until the vegetables soften.

3 As the vegetables sauté, puree the tofu with the egg, garlic, flour, parsley, if using, salt, tamari, Pickapeppa sauce, and curry powder in a food processor until a thick paste is formed, pausing to scrape the sides of the bowl. When the vegetable sauté is done, scrape it, too, into the food processor. Pulse/chop a few times, just to blend.

4 Shape the mixture into 8 to 10 1-inch-thick, 3-inch-round patties and place them on a nonstick baking sheet or one that has been sprayed with cooking spray. Bake for 12 to 15 minutes, remove the sheet from the oven, flip the burgers, and bake on the second side for 10 to 12 minutes, or until the burgers are firm and browned.

5 Serve, hot or cold, on buns with tomatoes and all that other good stuff you know and love.

Jalapeño-Glazed Tempeh Burgers

Rich, substantial tempeh makes a nice, solid, tasty burger, here given exuberance by a last-minute brush with a jalapeño jelly glaze. For a good chewy texture, half the tempeh is ground in the food processor with various savory seasonings and the other half is finely chopped and combined with sautéed diced vegetables. **MAKES 8 LARGE PATTIES**

MARINADE

2 tablespoons frozen apple juice concentrate, thawed
2 teaspoons Pickapeppa sauce
1 tablespoon tamari or shoyu soy sauce
1 tablespoon cider vinegar
Plenty of freshly ground black pepper

Two 8-ounce packages soy-rice tempeh, each tempeh cake quartered
2 cloves garlic
1 tablespoon cornstarch
1 teaspoon salt
⅔ cup crisp breadcrumbs
1 tablespoon mild vegetable oil
1 large onion, diced
1 small potato, peeled and finely diced
2 medium carrots, diced
1 fresh jalepeño, stem, seeds, and ribs removed, finely diced
Cooking spray

GLAZE

½ cup jalepeño jelly
1 tablespoons natural foods store ketchup or tomato paste
2 teaspoons tamari or shoyu soy sauce

1. Combine all the marinade ingredients in a mug, cup, or small bowl.

2. Place the tempeh in a small bowl and pour the marinade over it. Let marinate for at least 1 hour, preferably overnight.

3. Lift the tempeh from the marinade, putting any leftover marinade liquid in a food processor for later use. Put the tempeh in a collapsible steamer in a medium pot. Add enough water to steam the tempeh, cover the pot, and bring to a boil. Steam the tempeh for 5 minutes, then remove from the heat. Discard the steaming water.

4. Add half the tempeh to the marinade already in the processor. Add the garlic, cornstarch, and salt. Pulse, then buzz to a smooth, thick paste, pausing several times to scrape the sides of the bowl.

5. Dice, but not too fine, the remaining tempeh, and place it in a large bowl. Add the breadcrumbs and the mixture from the processor and set aside.

6 Heat 1 teaspoon of the oil in a skillet. Add the onion and sauté over medium heat for 4 minutes. Add the potato, raise the heat just a little, and sauté for 4 minutes more. Add the carrots and sauté for 1 minute. Lower the heat slightly, cover, and let steam for 4 minutes. Add the jalepeño and give it a last 1-minute sauté. Remove from the heat and add the contents of the skillet to the bowl. Stir well to combine.

7 Preheat the oven to 400°F.

8 Form the tempeh mixture into 8 patties, 3 to 4 inches wide and ½ inch thick, and place on a nonstick baking sheet or one that has been sprayed with cooking spray. Bake for 20 to 25 minutes, or until firm. Remove the sheet from the oven and flip the patties over to bake for 8 minutes on the second side.

9 As the burgers bake, combine the glaze ingredients in a small saucepan. Cook over medium heat, stirring, until the jelly dissolves and the ingredients are well combined.

10 When the burgers are baked, remove the sheet from the oven and turn the oven heat to broil. Brush the burgers well with the glaze. Broil them quickly, keeping a close eye on them, just until the glaze browns slightly, probably 1 to 3 minutes, depending on how close to the flame your broiler rack is.

Tofu-Seitan "Meatballs" for Spaghetti and . . .

NOTE

The optional anise or fennel seeds give a hint of flavor reminiscent of sweet Italian sausage.

In a world that has been pasta primavera'd to death, it's easy to forget how satisfying plain old spaghetti with a good red sauce can be. But for non–meat-eaters, something can be missing in this American-Italian dish—the meatballs, with their visual, textural, and taste contrast, and the protein.

This vegetarian parallel universe will not, nor is it intended to, fool anyone. These meatballs are not a dead ringer for beef or pork meatballs. Yet they do provide, and deliciously, the contrast and the protein. Simple and quickly made, these are excellent scattered over a big plate of steaming spaghetti, with a ladleful of your favorite red sauce. **SERVES 4**

- 1 (12- to 14-ounce) package traditional water-packed tofu, preferably reduced fat, well drained
- ½ package (about 4 ounces) traditional-style seitan, drained and quickly rinsed
- 4 cloves garlic
- ½ cup crisp breadcrumbs, preferably whole grain
- 1 large egg
- 2 to 3 tablespoons finely minced Italian parsley
- 2 tablespoons nutritional yeast (see page 239)
- 1 teaspoon anise seeds (optional)
- Salt and freshly ground black pepper to taste
- Cooking spray

1 Preheat the oven to 400°F.

2 Combine all the ingredients except the cooking spray in a food processor. Pulse, then buzz to form a smooth, thick mixture, pausing to scrape the sides of the bowl. Taste for seasonings (bearing in mind that the mixture is a little bland, and it's supposed to be—the tomato sauce gives a major kick).

3 On a nonstick baking sheet, or one that has been sprayed with cooking spray, use 2 spoons to make small ballish patties.

4 Bake for 15 to 20 minutes, or until the balls are firm, hot, and slightly browned.

Parsley

Nut Burgers

Like almost everyone in a certain subset in Eureka, we once loved the dense and heavy little pan-fried nut cakes served at Brenda & Lana's, a long-defunct Eureka hangout. They came with a toasted bun, mayo, lettuce, tomato, onion: good but a caloric wipeout (and we always wondered but followed a don't-ask-don't-tell policy, were they in fact fried on the same dripping-with-fat grill as the regular old hamburgers?).

Here is a less nutty, but still very tasty, version of same, fat considerably reduced. It is quite pleasing on a picnic or as a once-in-a-while treat for lunch. Very stick-to-the-ribs; rich but not the sink-a-battleship rich of old-time versions with equal parts nuts and rice. You can also use the burger mix, unbaked, as a stuffed vegetable filling; it's particularly good baked in large portobello mushroom caps (see vegan variation).

While these don't contain tofu or other soy products, they are filled with protein, so I always think of them as being related. **MAKES 8 THIN, SMALL BURGERS**

VARIATION

VEGAN VARIATION: ***Omit the egg. Substitute a second tablespoon of cornstarch dissolved in an extra tablespoon of broth.***

2 tablespoons sesame seeds, toasted
2 tablespoons pumpkin or sunflower seeds
¼ cup nuts, such as pecans, almonds, walnuts, or cashews, or any combination, toasted
2 cups cooked brown rice
1 tablespoon cornstarch
2 tablespoons vegetable broth
4 slices whole wheat bread, pulled into coarse crumbs
1 large egg
½ cup mushroom stems, raw, rough ends trimmed off
1½ cups cooked broccoli, well drained
2 cloves garlic, peeled and quartered
1½ teaspoons tamari or shoyu soy sauce
1 teaspoon Pickapeppa sauce
Salt and freshly ground black pepper to taste
Cooking spray
Hamburger fixings, such as buns, sliced tomatoes and onion, lettuce leaves, mayonnaise or Tofu Mayonnaise (page 906), and ketchup

1 Preheat the oven to 375°F.

2 Combine the sesame seeds, pumpkin or sunflower seeds, and nuts in a food processor. Pulse/chop until ground to a coarse-textured powder (do not overprocess, or you'll end up with nut butter—not what you want here). Transfer the mixture to a large bowl and add the cooked brown rice. Toss the rice and powdered nut-seed mixture together; set aside. With your fingers, smush the cornstarch into the broth and set it aside, too.

3 Combine the breadcrumbs, egg, mushroom stems, broccoli, garlic, tamari, Pickapeppa, salt, and pepper in the food processor, then add the dissolved cornstarch. Pulse/chop, then process to make a thick, slightly gloppy liquid paste, pausing to scrape down the sides. Turn this paste out into the bowl with the brown rice mixture. Combine, working the mixtures together with your hands. The consistency should be thick but fairly sticky and wet. (You won't believe it'll turn out at this point, but it will.) Taste, adding salt and pepper as needed.

4 Form into 8 small, fairly thin (½ inch or so) patties and place them on a nonstick baking sheet or one that has been sprayed with cooking spray. Bake for 15 to 20 minutes, or until slightly brown and firmed up (and much drier). Remove from the oven, flip the patties, and bake for another 10 to 15 minutes. Serve, hot, with your favorite hamburger fixings.

Romaine

Vegetable & Legume Cakes

Almost all cakes and croquettes contain at least one or two vegetables in some form—a savory sautéed onion, diced carrots, celery, green or hot peppers, for instance—but in these cakes, vegetables and beans (along with something to hold them together) are the featured players. Lighter than grain- or nut-based cakes, but featuring protein-rich beans and luscious vegetables, these taste combinations are pleasing, unusual, and healthful. In miniaturized versions, they work as starters too; try them as stuffings in small mushroom caps, hollowed cherry tomatoes, or grilled poblano pepper halves.

Quick Spinach–Split Pea Cakes

These are delightful burgers: firm-textured, mild, and pleasing, with a base of spinach and split peas, reminiscent of a nonspicy falafel. They are simple and they satisfy, especially when put on a nice bun with a good tomato and dressing. A nice herby-garlicky tofu mayo (see page 906) or Tofu Sour Cream (page 909) is perfect here. If your children grew up on McDonald's, they might not be converts, but vegetarian-raised kids are wild about these cakes. Ten minutes to mix 'em, ten to fix 'em. Eat them hot tonight, cold in the lunchbox tomorrow.

If you didn't remember to thaw the spinach and you have a microwave, you could do your thawing in it while the split pea mix rehydrates. **MAKES 12 CAKES, SERVES 3 OR 4**

VARIATION

VEGAN SPINACH CAKES: ***Omit the egg. Add 1 tablespoon chickpea flour (also called besan) to the split pea soup and use an additional 2 tablespoons water.***

1 (5-ounce) package dehydrated split pea soup, such as Taste Adventure Low Fat Split Pea Soup, California Style
1½ cups boiling water, preferably spring or filtered
4 full-size Ak-Mak cracker sheets, the large sheets scored into four individual crackers
1 (10-ounce) package frozen chopped spinach, thawed and squeezed dry
1 large egg
Cooking spray

1 Place the split pea mix in a food processor, and pour the boiling water over it. Let stand for 3 minutes.

2 Add the Ak-Maks, crumbling them coarsely into the split pea mixture. Add the egg and buzz, pausing to scrape the sides of the processor, to make a fairly smooth, well-combined, thick mixture. Add the spinach, pulsing to combine. Spray your hands with cooking spray and form the mixture into 12 to 15 patties, 2 to 3 inches in diameter and about ½ inch thick. (The mixture will be sticky, but don't let that bother you.)

3 Heat a nonstick skillet, or one that has been sprayed with cooking spray, over medium heat. When the pan is hot, add four of the cakes. Cook for 2 minutes, or until slightly browned, then flip them over and cook for another 1 to 2 minutes. Repeat with the remaining cakes.

NOTES

POINTER 1: ***Since this recipe will not work with a soaked and salted (de-bittered) eggplant, nibble a bit of the eggplant raw to make sure it's sweetly mild, not bitter. If you've got a bitter one, de-bitter it (see page 742) and use it in some other recipe.***

POINTER 2: ***When grilling the finished burgers, remember: slow and steady. Don't flip them too soon, or they'll stick.***

Twice-Grilled Eggplant Cakes

These full-flavored, meaty (no other word describes them quite so accurately) cakes of eggplant had their starting point in the recipe for Bogey's Burgers from *The Sensuous Vegetarian Barbecue,* by Vicki Rae Chelf and Dominique Biscotti.

The cakes are dark and rich (belying their relatively low fat content), and the texture is slightly crunchy outside, soft inside. Their flavor is indefinable. You might think, "Mushroom? Mushroom and beef?" Although one could serve them with toasted bun, lettuce, and tomato, their flavor and texture are best experienced without being blanketed. Use them as one item on a special component plate. **MAKES 8 CAKES, SERVES 4 TO 8**

- 2 large eggplants, sliced crosswise into ½-inch rounds
- 3 tablespoons olive oil (impossible to get by with less here, alas)
- 3 tablespoons tamari or shoyu soy sauce
- 3 to 5 large cloves garlic, peeled and halved
- 2 small end-pieces of commercially made whole wheat bread or one center-loaf slice, torn into pieces
- 1 tablespoon cashew butter
- 1 teaspoon Pickapeppa sauce
- Freshly ground black pepper to taste
- 1½ cups dry (unreconstituted) textured vegetable protein (see page 650)
- ¾ teaspoon liquid smoke
- Ketchup or Quick Hot Asian Ketchup (page 923)

1 Preheat a grill to hot, then turn down the heat to medium. Set 1 tablespoon of the oil aside for later use and brush each eggplant slice on both sides with just a little of the remaining 2 tablespoons oil. Place the slices on the preheated grill, and grill slowly over indirect heat until the slices are grill-marked on their undersides, 5 to 10 minutes. Turn with tongs and grill on the other side. The eggplant slices should be well marked with grill lines on both sides and tender and yielding to the touch. When they've reached this point, remove from the grill and transfer to a food processor. Lower the grill heat to low.

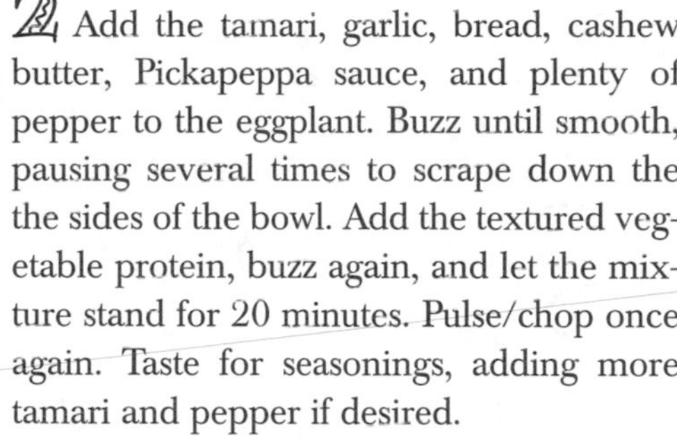

2 Add the tamari, garlic, bread, cashew butter, Pickapeppa sauce, and plenty of pepper to the eggplant. Buzz until smooth, pausing several times to scrape down the the sides of the bowl. Add the textured vegetable protein, buzz again, and let the mixture stand for 20 minutes. Pulse/chop once again. Taste for seasonings, adding more tamari and pepper if desired.

3 Form the mixture into 8 patties 3 inches in diameter and about ¾ inch thick. Make the patty edges as straight up and down as possible, instead of tapering them out; this will help the cakes cook through more evenly.

4 Combine the remaining oil with the liquid smoke in a cup measure, whisking the liquid smoke into the oil with a fork to emulsify. Brush a little of this mixture on 1 side of each cake and place the cakes, oiled side down, on the grill. Brush the top side with the remaining oil mixture. Grill slowly for 5 to 10 minutes, or until the top appears a little dried out. Slide a long-handled, thin-bladed spatula gently beneath one of the burgers; if it has cooked long enough, it should release fairly easily, sticking only minimally to the grill bars. The cake should be grill-marked, too. Flip and grill on the second side for another 5 to 10 minutes. The cake will come off easily. Serve at once, hot off the grill, or use cold in sandwiches the next day, with a little ketchup or Asian ketchup, as one would an old-fashioned meatloaf sandwich.

COOK ONCE FOR 2 MEALS Grill a double batch of these. Serve one round hot off the grill; use the second, cold, as a sandwich filling.

VARIATIONS

OVEN-BAKED, ONCE-GRILLED EGGPLANT CAKES: ***Instead of grilling the finished cakes, admittedly a slightly tricky maneuver, you may prefer to bake the cakes on a baking sheet in a preheated 375°F oven for 25 to 30 minutes, flipping once halfway through.***

GIANT EGGPLANT-STUFFED PORTOBELLO CAPS: ***Instead of forming patties, mold the mixture into the cap of medium-large portobello mushrooms, pressing down and smoothing the top over. Brush the exterior of the mushroom with a little tamari and oil and bake at 375°F. These stuffed mushroom caps are a show-stopping, center-of-the-plate entrée.***

Neo-Traditional Falafel

Baked, not fried. They're best right out of the oven, when they have some nice exterior crispness, but believe me, you wouldn't say no to them for lunch the next day, even after a night in the fridge! Canned chickpeas make fairly quick work of things. The spicing is very nice here; complex, in that flavors begin one way and build through several layers, leaving you with a slight, pleasant, after-burn of heat. **MAKES 20 TO 25 SMALL CAKES; SERVES 5 OR 6 WITH FIXINGS**

FALAFEL

¼ cup bulghur or cracked wheat
½ cup water, preferably spring or filtered
1 (15- or 16-ounce) can chickpeas, well drained
2 cloves garlic
1 large egg
¼ to ½ teaspoon salt
½ teaspoon cumin
¼ teaspoon freshly ground black pepper
¼ teaspoon ground turmeric
¼ teaspoon ground coriander
Pinch of cayenne
2 tablespoons finely chopped Italian parsley leaves
⅓ cup crisp breadcrumbs
Cooking spray

ACCOMPANIMENTS

Tahini Dressing (recipe follows)
Kibbutz Salad (recipe follows)
Toasted pita breads or mini pitas, preferably whole wheat

1 Soak the bulghur or cracked wheat. If using bulghur, simply warm the water, pour it over the bulghur, and let soak for 20 minutes. For cracked wheat, a coarser whole grain, bring the water to a boil, stir in the cracked wheat, and let soak for 1 hour (or even overnight). Most or all of the water will be absorbed; drain off any water that is left.

2 Place half of the chickpeas in a medium bowl and mash slightly with a potato-masher or your knuckles; they should still have texture. Add the soaked bulghur or cracked wheat.

3 Place the other half of the chickpeas in a food processor with the garlic, egg, salt, cumin, pepper, turmeric, coriander, and cayenne. Process until smooth, pausing several times to scrape down the sides of the bowl. Add the parsley and breadcrumbs and pulse/chop a few times.

4 Combine the processor mixture with the mashed chickpeas in the bowl. Taste, and season the mixture to your liking,

amping up any of the spices, salt, or pepper. Refrigerate the mixture for 30 minutes, or as long as overnight, so it can firm up.

5 Preheat the oven to 350°F.

6 Remove the falafel mix from the fridge, and shape it into flattened discs, 20 to 25 small ones or 10 to 12 larger ones. Place them on a nonstick baking sheet, or one that has been well sprayed with cooking spray, and bake for 25 minutes. Remove from the oven, flip the cakes, and bake for 5 minutes on the other side, or until golden brown.

7 Serve with a drizzle of Tahini Dressing, a good scoop of Kibbutz Salad, and some shredded romaine lettuce, all tucked into a toasted whole wheat pita bread or mini pita.

Tahini Dressing

This recipe follows the traditional flavorings, but the fat is somewhat reduced, with silken tofu making up for the texture lost with the tahini cut-back. Make sure you use a good, tasty, *toasted* tahini (sesame butter), not raw; if your tahini's not good, the sauce won't be either. This is still pretty high-fat; be judicious in your dribbling.

⅓ cup tahini
½ cup cold water, preferably spring or filtered
1 to 2 ounces reduced-fat silken tofu
Juice of 1 to 2 lemons
3 to 4 cloves garlic
Salt and freshly ground black pepper to taste
Dash cayenne

Combine all the ingredients in a food processor and buzz until smooth.

Kibbutz Salad

All through the Middle East, folks are happy to eat this simple, incredibly restorative salad, not only with falafel but with virtually anything, anytime, anywhere. I've even been served it at breakfast, at a Philadelphia coffee shop called the Maccabean—owned by Moroccan Jews who immigrated to America.

2 to 3 fresh tomatoes, preferably densely red-ripe ones, diced
2 small cucumbers, preferably unwaxed, diced
3 scallions, thinly sliced
5 to 7 radishes, thinly sliced
½ teaspoon salt
Freshly ground black pepper to taste
Juice of 1 lemon
1 to 2 teaspoons extra virgin olive oil

Combine all the ingredients and toss well. Cook's bonus: Pour the accumulated liquid into a teacup and drink it. Beautifully refreshing on a hot day.

NOTE

OPEN SESAME

Sesame seeds are as tiny as their history is long—their use is recorded as far away and long ago as Assyria, 3,000 B.C. The seed, a bit sweet with an exceptionally savory and distinctive, fragrant nuttiness when toasted, grows widely throughout Asia, Africa, the Middle East, and India. Each of these parts of the world has its own ways with sesame, which comes to us in 3 basic forms—whole seed, ground seed (the rich, peanut butter-esque paste called tahini), and sesame oil, which is pressed from the seeds, either before or after those seeds have been toasted.

Like all high-oil seeds and nuts, sesame seeds go rancid quickly. Store them in an airtight container at coolish room temperature for 2 or 3 months, or refrigerate or freeze them up to 6 or 7 months.

New South Falafel

Can the concept of falafel—spicy-savory bean fritters, tucked in a local breadstuff with a splash of sauce and something relishy—translate to the culinary favorites of the American South? It can and does in these great little nubbiny fritters. To go the whole nine yards, you'll need some of Cora Pinkley Call's Uncooked Ozark Relish to replace the Kibbutz Salad served with the Neo-Traditional Falafel on the previous pages, and a batch of Cornmeal Biscuits instead of pita. The Tahini Dressing is transmuted to a peanut butter sauce, and it, too, is dynamite. The fritters themselves are made with black-eyed peas and a touch of spinach or other greens, seasoned with mint and cayenne—so good, especially when fully dolled up. I know it seems like a lot of fussing, but it's worth it.

The rice called for should be extremely tender, not in the least al dente. Short-grain rice, which cooks up soft and sticky, is best here. **SERVES 5 TO 6 WITH FIXINGS**

½ cup cooked brown or white rice, preferably short grain
¼ onion, finely diced
1 (15- or 16-ounce) can black-eyed peas, very well drained
½ package (5 ounces) frozen chopped spinach, turnip greens, or collards, thawed and all possible moisture squeezed out or 1 cup cooked fresh greens, very well drained, finely chopped
1 tablespoon cornstarch
2 cloves garlic
Leaves from 3 or 4 stems fresh mint
1 large egg
½ teaspoon salt
¼ teaspoon freshly ground black pepper
2 teaspoons finely minced fresh sage leaves
⅛ to ½ teaspoon cayenne
2 tablespoons (loosely packed) minced Italian parsley leaves
½ to ¾ cup crisp breadcrumbs, preferably cornbread crumbs
Cooking spray

ACCOMPANIMENTS
Cornmeal Biscuits (page 513)
New South Peanut Sauce (recipe follows)
Cora Pinkley Call's Uncooked Ozark Relish (page 929)
Ozark New South Falafel Salad (recipe follows)

1 Place the rice, onion, and half of the black-eyed peas in a medium bowl. Using a potato masher, mash well, but not to a paste; the peas should still have texture. Stir in the chopped spinach.

2 Place the other half of the black-eyed peas in a food processor. Add the cornstarch, garlic, mint, egg, salt, pepper, sage, and cayenne. Process until smooth, pausing several times to scrape down the sides of the bowl. Add the parsley and breadcrumbs and pulse/chop a few times.

3 Combine this mixture with the mashed black-eyed pea mixture in the bowl. Taste and season to your liking, amping up any of the spices, salt, or pepper. Refrigerate the mixture for 30 minutes, or as long as overnight, so it can firm up.

4 Preheat the oven to 350°F. Remove the mix from the fridge and shape into flattened discs, 25 to 30 small ones or 12 to 16 larger ones. Place them on a nonstick baking sheet, or one that has been well sprayed with cooking spray, and bake for 25 minutes. Flip the falafels over and bake for 5 minutes more, or until brown.

5 Serve on split biscuits, drizzled with peanut sauce and a little scoop of Ozark Relish or Ozark Falafel Salad. Eat as soon as assembled; in fact, it's best to lay out all the fixings and let people serve themselves.

New South Peanut Sauce

Not at all like Indonesian peanut sauces.

¼ cup natural-style peanut butter
½ cup cold water, preferably spring or filtered
1 to 2 ounces reduced-fat silken tofu
Juice of 1 to 2 lemons
2 cloves garlic
Salt and freshly ground black pepper to taste
Dash cayenne

Combine all the ingredients in a food processor and buzz until smooth.

Ozark New South Falafel Salad

2 fresh tomatoes, preferably densely red-ripe ones
1 small cucumber, preferably unwaxed, diced
3 scallions, thinly sliced
5 to 7 radishes, thinly sliced
1 thick slice cabbage, slivered into fine slices
1 to 2 tablespoons commercially prepared or homemade salsa
1 tablespoon honey
½ teaspoon salt
Freshly ground black pepper to taste
Juice of 1 lemon
1 teaspoon extra virgin olive oil

Combine all the ingredients in a large bowl and toss to combine.

NOTE

Relatively small bean cakes—3 to 3½ inches in diameter and ¼ to ½ inch thick—are perfect as an hors d'oeuvre or as a player on a component plate. If using the cakes as a starter, allow 1 or 2 per person; if using them as part of a component plate, allow 2 or 3 per person. If using them as a center-of-the-plate entree, make them larger, 4 to 5 inches in diameter and ½ inch thick, and allow 3 per person. If you plan to use them as a burger on a bun with trimmings, make them much thicker; ¾ to 1 inch thick.

Pan-browning bean cakes, like making pancakes, is a 2- or 3-at-a-time job. Either serve them as they come off the stove, or keep them warm in a 200°F oven until all have been made and you are ready to serve. Be aware, however, that they do not keep much longer than 20 minutes, or they'll start drying out.

Black Bean Cakes

Here is one of the simplest of bean cakes, easily made and easily dressed up. After all, they're just cooked beans of any sort (leftover, canned, or reconstituted dehydrated beans) pureed with some form of binder, then cooked.

Within these parameters, there are options galore. Highly season the bean puree or leave it on the plain side and instead act out with the topping. Drizzle with a ribbon of sour cream, yogurt, or Tofu Sour Cream, and they look elegant and taste even better, especially with a good salsa. Or make plumper patties and serve them on toasted whole wheat buns with mustard or mayo. One of the nicest dress-ups I've run into comes from Cynthia Pedregon, who uses a creamy soup with green chiles as a sauce for the dear little things. *This is exquisite.* You would bet your bottom dollar that it's thick with cream and butter, but it isn't. (See my version on page 947.) **MAKES 9 OR 10 BEAN CAKES**

- 2 cups dehydrated black bean flakes, such as Taste Adventures (seasoning omitted)
- 2 cups boiling water, preferably spring or filtered
- 1 large egg, beaten
- 1 slice whole wheat bread, torn into pieces, or 3 tablespoons uncooked rolled oats
- 1 tablespoon mild vegetable oil, such as corn, canola, or peanut

ACCOMPANIMENTS

Pamela Jones's Absolutely Incredible Roasted Vegetable Salsa (page 915)
Yogurt Sour Cream (page 910)
Salsa Poblano Blanca y Verde (page 947)
Arkansalsa (page 913)
Tofu Sour Cream (page 909)

1 Place the dehydrated bean flakes in a heatproof bowl. Pour the boiling water over them, stir, and let stand for 5 minutes.

2 Transfer the beans to a food processor. Add the egg and bread and process until smooth, pulsing and scraping the sides of the bowl as needed.

3 Heat a nonstick skillet over medium-high heat. Brush lightly with the merest bit

of oil. Drop rounds of the bean mixture onto it, patting out the top with the heel of your hand or a plastic spatula until the cakes are 3 to 3½ inches in diameter and ¼ to ½ inch thick. Lower the heat to medium and let the cakes cook, uncovered, until they get brown and slightly crisp underneath, 3 to 5 minutes. Turn and cook for another 1 to 2 minutes.

4 Serve immediately with any of the accompaniments. (If you put the yogurt or tofu sour cream in a squeeze-bottle, you can drizzle fine lines across the cakes, making for a pretty, if fussy, presentation.) If you like, the cooked cakes can be kept warm on a baking sheet in a 200°F oven for 10 to 20 minutes until ready to serve, though they're best straight from the pan.

Lentil Croquettes

For most of our years as innkeepers, these croquettes, served with shiitake mushroom gravy and accompanied by a small stuffed pumpkin and other fixings, were the entree we offered vegetarians at Dairy Hollow Thanksgivings. Though rather plain as savory cakes go, the deep, dark colors and flavors are autumnal and satisfying. Sure, most guests chose turkey, but vegetarians were ecstatic about these. In fact, one of my sources of residual Innkeeper Guilt is the nice thank-you note I got from two such, begging me for the recipe. I am not territorial about recipes and had no problem—or wouldn't have, if I'd ever measured what I did. They actually called the front desk *twice* to ask again (Guilt! Guilt!) but by the time I had measured, and written, a year had gone by. I sent the recipe, groveling and apologetic. Alas, they had moved, forwarding service expired. If you two are out there reading this, I hope you will accept my apologies.

At the inn I always used to fry these, but I am very pleased with this nonfried version. These are slightly tricky to work with because the batter is soft and messy. Just persevere: They come out delicious. I prefer this with 2 eggs—one in the batter, one as part of the breading mix—but it is possible to make it vegan, too. **MAKES ABOUT 20 SMALL CROQUETTES, SERVES 4 OR 5**

CROQUETTE BATTER

1¼ cups lentils
3¾ cups water, preferably spring or filtered
2 bay leaves
½ cup uncooked oatmeal
3 cloves garlic, peeled and quartered
1 large egg
2 tablespoons cornstarch
1 teaspoon dried basil
¼ teaspoon Tabasco or similar hot sauce
Salt and freshly ground black pepper to taste

FOR SHAPING AND BAKING

1 cup crisp, fine breadcrumbs
½ cup crushed Nutri-Grain or other no-sugar-added corn- or wheat flakes
¼ cup unbleached all-purpose flour
1 tablespoon nutritional yeast (see page 239)
1 teaspoon paprika
½ teaspoon dried leaf sage, crumbled
Salt and plenty of freshly ground black pepper
½ teaspoon dried thyme
1½ teaspoons olive oil
1 large egg (optional)
Cooking spray or olive oil spray

1 Combine the lentils, water, and bay leaves in a medium pot. Bring to a boil, turn down to a simmer, and cook, half-covered, until tender, 35 to 45 minutes. Cool, then drain off any excess liquid and set aside.

2 When ready to complete the croquette batter, combine the lentils with all the other batter ingredients in a food processor. Buzz until the garlic is pureed and a soft, somewhat goopy paste is formed. Let the batter rest, covered and refrigerated, for at least 4 hours, or up to 2 days.

3 When ready to bake the croquettes, preheat the oven to 400°F. Set up a breading station: Combine the breadcrumbs and cornflake crumbs in a bowl. In a second bowl, make a seasoned flour by combining the flour, nutritional yeast, paprika, sage, salt and black pepper, thyme, and olive oil and tossing together well. In a third bowl, beat the egg, if using, with a tablespoon of water. Place the bowl of croquette mixture next to all this, along with a nonstick baking sheet or one that has been sprayed with cooking spray.

4 Using 2 large spoons, form a slightly flattened fat oval 3 to 4 inches long and ½ inch thick. Drop it into the seasoned flour. Sprinkle the top of the oval of batter with more flour and lift it out of the flour with your fingers. Dip the batter oval into the egg, which will coat it, though it will resist in spots. Drop the egg-coated ball into the crumbs, and, with your fingers, roll it around. When coated with this second jacket of crumbs, place on the baking sheet. Repeat with the rest of the batter.

5 Spray the crumbed croquettes very lightly with olive oil (if you have some in a spray bottle) or cooking spray. Bake for 15 to 20 minutes, turn very gently using a thin-bladed spatula, and bake for another 10 to 12 minutes. The crumb coating should be crisping up nicely; if it's not, run the croquttes under the broiler for a few moments.

6 Serve hot, as soon as possible, with a sauce such as Mushroom-Miso-Mustard Gravy (page 952). Leftovers can be served in buns, with all the fixings.

CHAPTER 13

Quick Fix

All of us sometimes (and some of us always) want and need good healthy food—fast. My mother said to me, “Oh, Quick and Easy, the one I need.” Paula Martin, former Dairy Hollow House bookkeeper, said, “Oh, Quick and Easy, the one I need.” And every time my friend Phyllis Jones tastes something of mine she likes, she says, “Oh, so good. But how long does it take to make?” Here are the best recipes, ingredients, and strategies I know for fixing good, quick, simple, healthy dishes.

Quick Strategies

There are three basic tools that make the preparation of good, quick, healthy food possible. They are:

- ▲ Planning and learning to cook and shop in an organized way
- ▲ Knowledgeable and time-saving use of ingredients, including the best-quality convenience foods
- ▲ Quick, easy recipes

Cooking and Shopping

More than thirty years ago I read something in a now-forgotten time management handbook that stayed with me all these years: The more time is taken in planning a project, the less time is needed to execute it. Planning, to me, means making sure you have options available, in the form of raw and cooked ingredients, so that on any given night you can fix something good, andquickly, if you want or need to. While lists are essential, detailed meal planning leaves no room for the unexpected—anything from having to work late to the market being out of some key ingredient or having another ingredient on sale or looking especially appealing. How does my kind of planning work? Here are some specific planning and cooking strategies.

USE LEFTOVERS: When you cook, intentionally make déjà food, a.k.a. leftovers, whenever possible. Never ever fix just one cup of beans or rice. The rice that will go underneath tonight's curry could be the basis for a rice salad at lunch tomorrow; the last little bits the foundation for grain burgers the next day. The beans could be, to quote the old saw about Mexico City weather forecasts, "hot today, chili tamale." Why cook a few stalks of broccoli when you could just as easily fix a whole head, and then use the leftovers to fill an omelet, puree as the base for soup, cut up into salad or for a casserole? Some leftover soups easily transmute to sauce, and vice versa. Homemade tomato sauce has a hundred uses, and keeps nicely in the fridge for at least five days, and in the freezer indefinitely. When making time-consuming casserole dishes, such as lasagna, make a second batch and freeze it.

This kind of planning is more a state of mind than a sit-down-with-a-list kind of planning. Because I so strongly believe in this hopscotching of meals, there are Cook Once for Several Meals tips throughout this book, at the end of various recipes. Having good déjà food on hand lets you be certain of good quick meals.

MAKE *MISE EN PLACE* A WAY OF LIFE: Mise en place, a French term, means "put in place." In the kitchen it means that you have a tray or section of a counter where you put out all your ingredients, measured and prepared up to the point of cooking. Without a *mise,* you end up with a messy kitchen, find you've left out the cumin, and feel frazzled because your working environment is frazzled. The simple act of *mise* makes preparing any recipe smoother and more relaxed.

BUNDLE LIKE WITH LIKE: There are countless applications to this simple organizational tactic.

- ▲ **Bundle like with like on a shopping list.** Make your own shopping list form, on the computer or by hand, and then copy it. It'll take a couple of attempts to get it down right, so don't copy it until you've used it a few times. Think about what you get where

and organize your list accordingly. For example, I buy things at a supermarket, a natural foods store, and a farmer's market, with occasional forays to an Asian or Hispanic market. Within the supermarket, there are some sections I visit often (produce) and some never (meat). Bundling like with like on my form allows me one pass through each section, for a relatively quick in and out, instead of an aimless, glazed wander, crisscrossing the store in frustration. Headings on our home shopping list run something like this:

Supermarket:

Dairy	Produce
Frozen	Canned
Dry	Household

Natural foods market:

Produce	Refrigerated
Frozen	Bulk
Herbs	Personal Care
Bottled or Canned	Supplements

When you bundle like with like on your list, you can bundle like with like as you move through space, store to store, section to section. Planning equals a lot of time saved in action. Our minds move more swiftly than our bodies.

- ▲ **Bundle like with like when cooking.** If you know you'll be making a soup, an entree, and a side dish, and they each call for an onion, cut three onions at the same time, not one. And if all the onions are to be sautéed in olive oil, do them all at once, in one skillet, and then divide them. Won't you feel pleased—all those skillets you won't have to wash, those trips from onion bin to stove you won't have to make?

- ▲ **Bundle like with like for time and tasks.** Set aside the occasional do-ahead day, or

A Quick Caveat

When you add "quick" to "truly delicious" and "healthful," you're asking an awful lot of a recipe, and there is often a trade-off. It's easy to do, quick, and truly delicious if you don't try too hard for healthful (and every so often it just might be worth it to be devil-may-care and cavalierly add a couple of tablespoons of butter or cream). It's also not impossible to pull off quick and healthful—if you're willing to accept good instead of truly delicious. I feel this way about pasta with vegetables, sometimes frozen ones, cooked in the water with the pasta. These dishes are quick as can be; they use one pot for cooking, a colander for draining, and the plate you eat from. And they're healthful. Are they truly delicious? No. But they're good and they're satisfying, and while I'd hesitate to feed them to guests and would be unhappy to pay for them at a restaurant, they please me enough for their other virtues that I'll eat them maybe even a couple of times a week, during flat-out busy, pedal-to-the-metal times. Still, if I want truly delicious, I don't boil the vegetables, and I don't use frozen: The vegetables are fresh and they are stir-fried, meaning both extra time and extra cleanup, though not necessarily much of either.

While I believe such recipes will always have their place and can be done with savvy, flair, and vitality, the real recipe and strategy has to be this: Take time out, open up some breathing room and space in your life, for activities that nourish not just body but heart and soul. Cooking well, healthfully, and thoughtfully is but the tiniest part of this, and it can be done—even when you find time is running short.

afternoon, or several hours to build up a savings account of fully or partially prepared food. While this doesn't work for everybody, it's an amazingly powerful way to provide for yourself and your family. Many people like to use Sunday afternoon for this time, possibly because it gives them a secure feeling going into the week knowing that they have a nicely stocked fridge and freezer. I'd encourage you to at least occasionally do not only basics but one or two exotics—a dressing or condiment, a pesto or salsa—for something inspiring to spiff up those staples and keep you out of a rut.

Don't worry if this looks overwhelming, or if you just can't cope with taking a prep day or afternoon even once a year. There are still strategies available to you.

Time-Saving Tricks

Weekly:

- ▲ If prewashed, top-quality, super-fresh salad green mix isn't available, wash one to three different salad greens, say, a head of romaine, a head of butter lettuce, and a bunch of arugula. After rinsing the greens, spin then pat them dry and store whole leaves in a bowl, greens layered between paper towels. At last! Easy salads! Also, fresh leaves for sandwiches.
- ▲ Chop several onions; store in zippered plastic bags. This takes care of the first step of most sautés. Though onions are better chopped right before you use them, a precut onion is better than none at all.
- ▲ Cook 2 or 3 cups of any whole grain; try brown rice one week, quinoa another, wheat or kamut berries another, millet, or barley for use under any stir-fry or curry or soup. Grains can also be reheated with seasonings for a quick pilaf or used to make grain cakes.
- ▲ Cook a pound of beans, split peas, or lentils at once. Use for soup; stir into sautéed onions and peppers to fill a tortilla; puree with garlic and tomato and herbs for a quick pasta sauce; make a hummuslike sandwich spread; scoop over a baked potato and top with salsa and grated cheese; or reheat and serve with a cooked grain and a green salad.
- ▲ If you're an egg eater, some weeks hard-cook half a dozen eggs for eating out of hand or dicing for a salad or sandwich.
- ▲ Cut up fresh vegetables for sautéing, or eating raw, or adding to salad, or combining with cooked beans and vegetable stock to make soup, or tossing into the pasta water to cook with the pasta, or steaming and mashing with the inside of a baked potato then topping with cheese, or filling an omelet or crêpe.
- ▲ Grate fresh cheeses ahead. Put into small zippered plastic bags and freeze. Grated cheese finishes a quick pasta; transforms a tortilla into a quesadilla; makes every new vegetarian's standby, the grilled cheese sandwich; tops a baked potato; fills an omelet.

Every couple of weeks:

- ▲ Soak a pound of tempeh or tofu in varying marinades; it can be left in the marinade (it will keep all week as you use it) or baked on prep day (cooked, it will keep for only 2 or 3 days, however). Use it in sandwiches, cut it up and add it to stir-fries or casseroles, sprinkle on salads, use as part of a crêpe filling, add a quick sauce and serve as is.
- ▲ Prepare grain, vegetable, or tofu cakes or patties, hot for dinner, cold in sandwiches, reheated and served with Quick Hot Asian Ketchup (see page 923) or another sauce.
- ▲ Prepare a vinaigrette (try different kinds: fresh basil in summer, Quick Hot Asian-style for

spring, and so on) and alternate with a creamy tofu mayonnaise to pour over salad greens, or toss with pasta and vegetables for a pasta salad. Use the vinaigrette as a dip base, spread on a sandwich, even toss with hot pasta and vegetables as a kind of a sauce. The vinaigrettes, even with fresh herbs, will keep for several weeks, due to the preservative effects of vinegar; the tofu-based dressings keep for 2 or 3 days.

- ▲ Make a large pot of soup (eat it hot; sometimes, eat it cold; use leftovers to sauce grain or pasta).
- ▲ Roast several heads of garlic for Roasted Garlic puree (see page 899) or make Garlic Oil (page 898). Garlic Oil keeps for about a month, though it's at its best the first 2 weeks; Roasted Garlic puree, if kept in an airtight container, keeps for a week in the refrigerator.
- ▲ Make a batch of Roasty-Toasty Potatoes, Carrots, and Onions (page 790), or roasted beets.
- ▲ Make a tofu crème or biscotti or some other fat-sparing and healthful but satisfying dessert.
- ▲ Precook some shell or corkscrew pasta, or commercially made fresh tortellini for pasta salad or to toss into hot stir-fried vegetables for lunch.

MONTHLY, OR AS NEEDED:

- ▲ Make one or two batches of Dark Stock and/or Golden Stock (pages 140). Let cool to room temperature and divide it into 1-cup portions, ladling them into sturdy zippered plastic bags, and freeze.
- ▲ Make a batch of Better (page 905).
- ▲ Make a double batch of one big-deal casserole, such as lasagna. Eat one during the week after making it and freeze the other.
- ▲ Make a batch of sweet breads; freeze. Use as a breakfast treat or dessert.
- ▲ Make a batch or two of turnovers; freeze two-thirds of them; leave the remainder for eating during the week.
- ▲ Make a batch of crêpe batter (the Neo-Classic Crêpe, page 332, is healthful, easy, and versatile).

EVERY COUPLE OF MONTHS:

- ▲ Make a sorbet (sure, you can purchase them, but your own are so much better, and they're really remarkably simple).
- ▲ If you are a serious sweet eater or live with one, make plain layers of any simple chocolate and/or vanilla cake and freeze them. They can be quickly thawed and dolled up and are great for a friend who didn't tell you it was her birthday until the last moment or for a child who suffered a disappointment and needs unscheduled cheering.

SEASONALLY:

- ▲ Make pickles or preserves. Though not quick, it's nice to make one or two batches of something special each year to keep you in tune with the seasons. Use them to perk up sandwiches and other meals.
- ▲ Make pestos and herb pastes and freeze them to have on hand for pastas and grains.
- ▲ Buy red, yellow, green, and ancho peppers by the dozen when they are in season, inexpensive, and, ideally, organic. Char, peel, and seed them. Freeze them, cut up or pureed. They thaw like a dream—you'd think they just came off the grill—and add year-round freshness and exuberance to salads, sandwiches, and sauces. Toss them into dressings or over pasta or grain, or add to a stir-fry.

The Quick-Fix Pantry List

Ideally, you want to keep your pantry stocked at all times with dry, canned, and frozen ingredients that can quickly be turned into a meal, as well as assorted fresh ingredients. And happily, with each year, the choices for the healthy, organic, vegetarian, or whole foods consumer grow more numerous and better. No doubt more and more healthful newcomers will come to market. Keep checking.

The foods that follow are not intended as a complete pantry list, just my top choices for quick-fix staples. Keep these on hand, do an occasional prep day, and you'll eat well and easily.

Dry

PASTA: *fettuccine, spaghetti, bow-ties, shells, both imported Italian and natural foods store brands, both regular durum wheat pasta and seasoned pasta (wild mushroom and lemon-pepper are two where the flavor really does come through) as well as natural foods whole-grain types: whole wheat, corn, buckwheat soba, jerusalem artichoke, kamut, spelt, and quinoa pastas. And don't forget whole-grain ramen noodles. For those with wheat or gluten intolerance, there are wheat-free varieties available.*

DEHYDRATED INSTANT BEAN FLAKES *(see page 594): Pintos and black beans and instant split pea soup are four-star: truly quick (5 minutes), delicious (as good as freshly cooked, mashed beans), versatile, healthful, and not well known yet.*

ASEPTICALLY PACKAGED SILKEN TOFU *(see page 655): I use silken tofu in dozens of recipes, usually dips, sauces, and desserts. Tofu keeps indefinitely in this form.*

QUICK-COOKING GRAINS: *millet, buckwheat (kasha), quinoa, popcorn, and couscous (not a grain, but it looks and feels like one) and whole wheat couscous. Popcorn makes a great garnish for soup, and some people eat it in a bowl of milk, like cereal.*

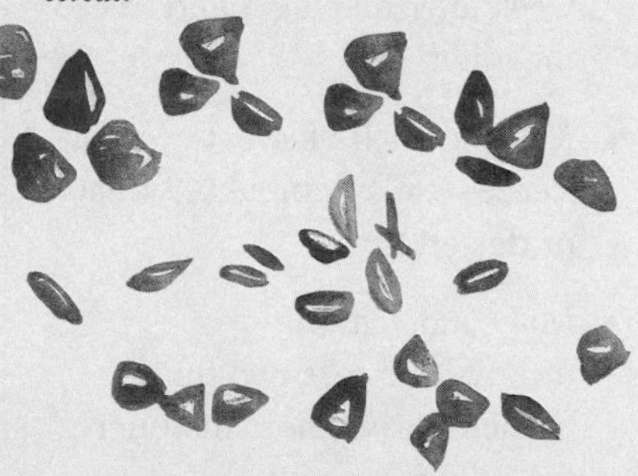

POLENTA IN A TUBE: *This ready-made polenta comes in a 1½-pound tube and does not need refrigeration until it is opened. I hate to say this, being the from-scratcher that I am, but sliced and sautéed, it is identical to homemade polenta. It's made with a fine-grain organic yellow meal and is available plain and in several flavored varieties. Simply slice, sauté, and serve as undergirding for almost any vegetable, in almost any kind of sauce. Those who can't or don't eat wheat will be especially thrilled.*

ASIAN RICE PAPER WRAPPERS: *Soak them for 30 seconds and they're ready to be filled and rolled. It doesn't get easier. Almost anything tastes good in a rice paper wrapper.*

CHICKPEA FLOUR *(garbanzo bean flour, also called besan): A remarkable, versatile ingredient, it can be used to make an incredible egg-free crêpe batter. It can also firm up grain burgers and take the place of egg as a binder in many recipes. You can even make hummus out of it (follow the recipe on the box). Purchase it at a natural foods store or Indian grocery store.*

INSTANT TABBOULEH: *I'm a tabbouleh-from-scratch person from way back, but I have to tell you this is good! It's virtually instant to make, though it needs to sit for an hour or so after being mixed.*

INSTANT SOUPS: *When traveling in non–vegetarian-friendly parts, I carry along a small stash of meatless instant soups, so I've tried 'em all. Most are strictly desperation measures. Try several until you find one you like. Miso or bean-based ones are tastiest.*

Canned or Bottled

Assorted canned beans: *black beans, kidney beans, white beans, chickpeas, and so on.*

Canned tomato products: *tomato paste, tomatoes with basil and garlic, fire-roasted tomatoes, and tomatoes with green chiles.*

Unsweetened, reduced-fat coconut milk.

Bottled or packaged curry pastes: *green, red, and/or Massaman. If you like hot stuff or exotica, you'll be thrilled with these.*

Good bottled spaghetti sauce: *Check the label; many are low-fat, but you have to check; some contain Parmesan cheese, which makes them problematic for vegans.*

Aseptically packaged vegetable stock.

Salsa: *In addition to homemade and hot sauces, a bottle of good salsa is nice to have around.*

Nut butters: *Peanut butter, tahini, cashew butter, soynut butter. High in fat, yes, but nutrition-rich. Always buy nonhydrogenated and refrigerate after opening.*

Fresh

Greens: *salad greens, spinach, and mesclun are available prewashed. Throw on some dressing or a squeeze of lemon juice or splash of herbal vinegar.*

Packaged, precut vegetables: *Try a couple of different ones each week. Shredded broccoli stems, stir-fry mixes (typically a blend of napa cabbage, bok choy, broccoli, carrots, and snow peas), coleslaw mix (shredded carrots, cabbage, and red cabbage), and broccoli and cauliflorets make stir-fries practically instant. Throw out any little seasoning packages that come with them.*

Breads: *Whole wheat and corn tortillas, whole wheat pita breads, Boboli crusts.*

Eggs: *Omelets. Scrambled eggs. Breakfast food for dinner. Though eggs have gotten a lot of bad press and few of us eat as many as we once did, they were not so long ago the quick "light" supper of choice. Well, they're still a great fallback (assuming that you're not vegan). If you are extremely cholesterol conscious, try one of the egg whites-only products, such as Egg-Beaters.*

Refrigerated tofus of all kinds: *This includes water-packed traditional tofu, preferably reduced fat. Preseasoned tofus also have a place; so, to some, do soy- and seitan-based luncheon meat alternatives. Some of these products are ready to eat, right from the package, in sandwiches and stir-fries. Almost as quick are the sauté-and-serve soysages. Baconlike strips of smoked tempeh are delish.*

Frozen

Frozen tamales: *Available in the frozen foods section of some natural foods stores, these are just about as good as homemade. I pressure-cook or steam them.*

Broiled tempeh: *Available in the frozen foods section of natural foods stores, this can be quickly sautéed for a very satisfying sandwich or just served, post-sauté, with a pile of cooked grain or pasta*

Vegetarian burgers.

Frozen vegetables and frozen vegetable-rice mixes: *Superior natural foods brands are now proliferating. You can't beat these mixtures as a basis for those we-must-eat-and-we-must-eat-now nights.*

Pastas

Pasta is the first refuge of the too-busy, but you already knew that, right? There are times when, much as we hate to admit it, we wind up eating pasta two, three, even four nights a week. To me, this, like a suspicious mole, is an early warning signal—Danger: Too busy. Here are a number of super-quick pasta fixes, all good and satisfying. Since these quick-fix pasta dishes frequently wind up being one-dish meals, I allow very large portions: 8 ounces of dry pasta to serve two or three, but if appetites are more delicate than this and you have leftovers, eat them the next day, cold on greens as a salad or quickly sautéed in a nonstick skillet to reheat.

About half of these are vegan. Few call for eggs. I've tried to be moderate where fat is concerned, but if you want fast, you cut corners—and fat is the easiest way, tastewise, to make up for corner-cutting.

All these quick-fix pastas begin the same way, and all are done by the time the pasta has cooked: Take 8 ounces of dry pasta, throw it in a large pot of fiercely boiling salted water, and cook until done. Meanwhile place in a bowl any one of the following:

▲ ½ to 1 cup large- or small-curd cottage cheese, 2 teaspoons butter, and salt and freshly ground black pepper to taste. Pasta of choice: broad egg noodles or fettuccine (this is classic Jewish comfort food).

▲ ½ to ¾ cup of any of the dips based on silken tofu, listed under A Palette of Sour Cream–Style Dips (page 26). They can be done with Yogurt Sour Cream, but the silken tofu's far quicker. I sometimes gild the lily by adding a diced tomato or two and tossing the whole thing together, for texture, visual contrast, and thinning-down of the "cream" sauce. Pasta of choice: fettuccine or fresh tortellini.

▲ Freshly grated Parmesan cheese, a teaspoon of olive oil or butter, and loads of freshly ground black pepper; dried red chiles, crushed, are optional. Nondairy folks can try this with soy Parmesan-type flakes. Pasta of choice: fettuccine.

▲ 1 to 2 tablespoons homemade or commercially made pesto, a small handful of oil-cured olives, 1 can well-drained chickpeas, and salt and freshly ground black pepper to taste. Pasta of choice: small shells (the chickpeas manage to cozy into the shells).

▲ 1 to 3 tablespoons commercial or homemade Olivada (olive spread with garlic; page 24), 2 to 3 ounces coarsely crumbled feta cheese, 1 large diced tomato or a handful of small cherry tomatoes, and salt and freshly ground black pepper to taste. Pasta of choice: bow-ties, ziti, rigatoni, or rotelli (corkscrews).

▲ 1 tablespoon tomato paste; 1 tablespoon olive oil; 3 tablespoons commercial or homemade pesto, traditional or otherwise; lots of freshly ground black pepper; and some Parmesan. Pasta of choice: bow-ties.

▲ 1 to 3 tablespoons curry paste (Thai red, green, Massaman, or Indian); 2 to 3 tablespoons dry-roasted peanuts, and half a package savory baked tofu, diced. Pasta of choice: spaghetti.

- ▲ 3 to 4 cloves garlic, pressed, with salt and freshly cracked black pepper; 1 teaspoon to 1 tablespoon olive oil; and a big handful of finely chopped Italian parsley. Pasta of choice: fettuccine or spaghetti.
- ▲ Finely grated zest and juice of 1 lemon; 3 to 4 cloves garlic, pressed, or 1 teaspoon Garlic Oil (page 898), or 1 tablespoon Roasted Garlic puree (see page 899); salt and freshly ground black pepper; 1 teaspoon to 1 tablespoon olive oil; and a big handful of finely chopped Italian parsley. Pasta of choice: fettuccine or spaghetti.
- ▲ 1 small jar marinated artichoke hearts plus 1 tablespoon marinade; finely grated zest of 1 lemon; 2 to 3 cloves garlic, pressed, with salt and freshly ground black pepper; a big handful of finely chopped Italian parsley; and 1 large diced tomato. Pasta of choice: ziti or rigatoni.
- ▲ 1 orange, peeled, seeded, and diced; ½ large red onion, diced; 8 to 10 oil-cured olives; a good handful of minced Italian parsley and/or cilantro; 1 teaspoon to 1 tablespoon olive oil; a tiny bit of cayenne. Pasta of choice: small shells or orecchiette.
- ▲ 2 tablespoons toasted walnuts, finely chopped; 3 tablespoons sugar; and 1 teaspoon to 1 tablespoon melted butter, preferably Browned Butter (page 1024). (Believe it or not, this is a classic Austrian dish, and quite nice for a late, quick, comfort-food kind of supper.) Pasta of choice: broad egg noodles.

Here is a slightly different approach to super-fast pasta. Take 8 ounces of pasta, throw it into a large pot of fiercely boiling water, cook till not quite al dente, and pour in about a third to half of a 1-pound loose-pack package of any of the following frozen vegetables.

- ▲ "California mix" (broccoli, cauliflower, green beans, and red pepper).
- ▲ "Creole vegetable mix" (corn kernels, lima beans, red peppers, and okra).
- ▲ Any unsauced frozen vegetable mix that strikes your fancy.

The water will stop boiling as you add the vegetables, then quickly (almost immediately if you're using a very large pot) return to a boil. Continue cooking until the pasta is done and the vegetables are done but still bright. Drain well and toss with any of the following (and some can be combined to good effect):

- ▲ A squib of butter or olive oil.
- ▲ Freshly grated Parmesan cheese (nutritional yeast for vegans or nondairy eaters).
- ▲ Salt and freshly ground black pepper.
- ▲ Dried crushed chiles.

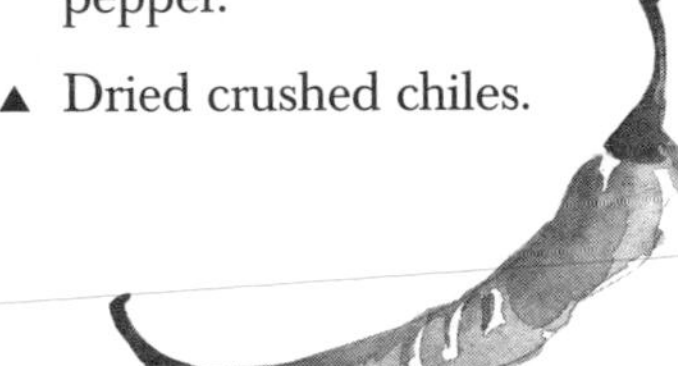

- ▲ If using the Creole vegetable mix, or any mix that has corn in it, add a cup or so of cooked beans, 2 tablespoons salsa, and sprinkle a little grated Cheddar over each portion. Add minced cilantro if you have it.

Now, if you're feeling slightly ambitious, willing to add 5 to 8 minutes' time and to sully a cutting board, knife, and skillet in addition to the pot, colander, and bowl, on the next pages are a number of more detailed but still very quick pasta and vegetable stir-fries.

* * *

PLEASING PASTA PRESTO

Aseptically packaged cream of tomato soup (doctored with cayenne; dolloped with sour cream)

*

Small shell pasta with pesto, olives, and chickpeas

*

Lemon sorbet splashed with Grand Marnier

Pasta with Hearty Greens and Beans

Speedy, hearty, healthful. Eat this pasta just as it is or serve it with a little grated Parmesan cheese or soy Parmesan-style cheese. **SERVES 2 OR 3**

VARIATION

Instead of the beans, cook 2 fist-size potatoes, preferably red-skinned, scrubbed and diced into ½-inch cubes, and add them to the pasta at the end.

8 ounces fettucine or buckwheat ramen
1 large bunch kale, chard, turnip, or collard greens, washed, any tough center ribs removed, sliced crosswise
2 teaspoons to 1 tablespoon olive oil
Cooking spray
1 can (15.5-ounces) cannellini, navy, or other white beans, rinsed and very well drained
3 cloves garlic, pressed, or 1 teaspoon Garlic Oil (page 898), or 1 tablespoon Roasted Garlic puree (see page 899)
Salt and freshly ground black pepper
½ lemon (optional)
Dried chiles (optional)

1 Start the fettuccine, if using, in vigorously boiling water.

2 Heat the oil over medium-high heat in a nonstick skillet or one that has been sprayed with cooking spray. Stir the greens in the oil for 2 minutes, cover, and let them steam for 2 to 3 minutes, until tender but not overdone (time varies according to age and variety of greens). If you are using buckwheat ramen, start them as the greens cook.

3 Place the beans, garlic, a bit of salt, and a lot of pepper in a bowl. Add the greens and pasta when they are done and toss. Add a squeeze of lemon juice, if you like. Pass dried chiles for guests to crush over their plates of pasta.

Pasta with Pumpkin

One of the best pastas I ever had at a restaurant was this, simple as can be, a special-of-the-day at Positano, a now-defunct New York spot. The only time-consuming bit is peeling the uncooked pumpkin. If you can purchase a fresh pasta, it's excellent here; just start it cooking later in the process. **SERVES 2**

8 ounces fettuccine, dried or fresh
1 wedge (about 1½ pounds) eating pumpkin (see page 804) or any sweet orange-fleshed squash, sliced into long, ⅓-inch-thick pieces
2 teaspoons to 1 tablespoon olive oil, plus additional for serving
Cooking spray
3 cloves garlic, pressed
Salt and freshly ground black pepper
Freshly grated Parmesan or soy Parmesan-type cheese

1 Start the fettuccine in vigorously boiling water.

2 As the pasta cooks, heat the oil in a nonstick skillet or one that has been sprayed with cooking spray. You'll want a skillet with a tight-fitting lid. Add the pumpkin or squash and sauté over medium-high heat for 3 minutes. Cover tightly and steam over medium-low heat, stirring every now and again. Add the garlic and stir-fry for 30 seconds or so longer.

3 When the pumpkin is tender around the edges but still has a bit of bite to it, transfer it to a bowl and toss with the cooked fettuccine. Season. Serve at once, hot, with Parmesan cheese, more olive oil to drizzle, and lots of pepper.

VARIATION

PASTA WITH BROCCOLI: ***Use broccoli florets, either cut up by you or precut, instead of pumpkin. Or, if you prefer, use precut julienned broccoli stems. Serve at once, hot, with Parmesan cheese, nutritional yeast (see page 239), more olive oil to drizzle, and crushed hot red chile peppers. Pasta of choice: rotelli, or quinoa spaghetti.***

Pasta à la Chinoise

Look, Ma, no cutting! Quick, very fresh-tasting, good. You can make it even faster by cutting out the tamari, sweetener, hot sauce, and sesame, and instead using a few tablespoons of your favorite commercial stir-fry sauce. A heaping teaspoon of garlic-ginger paste, usually found in the produce section at the supermarket, hurled in with the stir-fry, is a great flavor booster. **SERVES 2 OR 3**

8 ounces thin whole wheat spaghetti
2 teaspoons to 1 tablespoon mild vegetable oil, preferably peanut
Cooking spray
1 package (8 ounces) fresh, precut vegetable stir-fry mix
4 to 8 ounces diced tofu, any kind except silken (optional)
1 tablespoon tamari or shoyu soy sauce
1 teaspoon sugar, honey, or Rapidura
1 teaspoon sriracha or similar hot chile paste or sauce
A few drops of toasted sesame oil

VARIATION

THAI-ISH PASTA: ***Add 1 teaspoon red, green, or yellow curry paste to the stir-fry.***

1 Start the spaghetti in vigorously boiling water.

2 As it cooks, heat the vegetable oil over medium-high heat in a nonstick skillet or wok or one that has been sprayed with cooking spray. Add the stir-fry mix and sauté for 3 minutes. Add the tamari, sugar, sriracha, and sesame oil and continue stir-frying until done, 2 to 3 minutes more, depending on the size of the vegetables. You may also throw in some diced tofu at this time.

3 Drain the cooked pasta and toss it with the stir-fry or serve the stir-fry over it.

Tortellini with Mushrooms and Peas

This is a very good combination, respectably company-worthy. You might use small ravioli instead of tortellini, and the filling might be anything from butternut squash or spinach-feta to herb-accented tofu to a national-brand vegetable ravioli you can find in the refrigerator case with the fresh pastas at almost any supermarket.

I like a combo of butter and olive oil in the sauté, but you could use one or the other in the interest of speed. Also, the mushrooms can be purchased presliced. You can easily forgo the minced parsley (the only fussy part). **SERVES 2 OR 3**

1 package (8 to 12 ounces) stuffed pasta
1½ teaspoons butter or Better (page 905)
1½ teaspoons olive oil
Cooking spray
12 ounces mushrooms, sliced
3 cloves garlic, minced
1 cup frozen peas
Salt and freshly ground black pepper to taste
½ cup minced Italian parsley (optional)
Parmesan and/or soy Parmesan-style flakes (optional)

1 Start the pasta in vigorously boiling water, cooking according to package directions.

2 Heat the butter and oil over medium-high heat in a nonstick skillet or one that has been sprayed with cooking spray. Add the mushrooms and sauté for 5 to 8 minutes, stirring often, until they start to brown slightly (this is easier with the larger amounts of oil and butter). If they appear to be exuding juice but not browning, raise the heat. When they're almost done, add the garlic and sauté for 1 minute more.

3 Pour the frozen peas directly from the freezer bag into a colander. Drain the pasta over them (this will cook the peas just enough). Transfer the peas and pasta to a warmed serving bowl and toss with the sautéed mushrooms and garlic. Add salt and pepper to taste and toss again. Serve at once with the parsley and/or Parmesan, if desired.

Speedy and Delicious-Beyond-Belief Pasta Salad

The name says it all. The even speedier way: Use leftover cooked pasta from the night before. With leftover pasta, this is on the table in under five minutes.

SERVES 3 OR 4

8 ounces ziti or shells, cooked, drained, and rinsed
½ package (8 ounces) shredded precut coleslaw mix
2 to 3 tablespoons commercial sesame-garlic sass dressing (available in the refrigerator case at natural foods stores), or to taste
4 ounces savory baked tofu, diced
Freshly ground black pepper to taste
1 teaspoon tamari or shoyu soy sauce (optional)

Place the cooked pasta in a bowl and toss with all remaining ingredients, including the tamari if desired.

VARIATIONS

Any hearty green might step in for the broccoli, and if I have the time and the herbs, I like to toss in a good handful of minced Italian parsley or fresh basil in season. A scoop of commercial or homemade pesto, such as Sylvia's Lemon and Basil Pesto (page 918) is also good. Sometimes I add the grated zest and juice of a lemon, too, and often I leave out the feta (I always pass Parmesan though). I have also been known to add drained beans—chickpeas are best here—during the final toss. And if you have grilled eggplant, cut it into strips and toss it in.

These variations might or might not take the dish out of the Quick-Fix category; it depends on how well you've prepped your kitchen.

Pasta Sol

Slightly more complex than the Speedy and Delicious-Beyond-Belief Pasta Salad, but nothing fancy. Just bright, sunshiny colors, nice heat from the chiles, sit-up-and-take-notice Mediterranean flavors. I really love this kind of mix, and have served it to drop-in company. Feel free to adapt according to what you have on hand. I've sometimes tossed in a few bottled marinated artichoke hearts, halved, at the end. This is a quick fix—the stir-fry can be done by the time the pasta's finished cooking—but only if you have all the stuff on hand and know your way around a cutting board and a sharp knife pretty intimately. If you don't, add 10 minutes or so of prep time.

Because you'll be frying chiles, if you don't have a vent hood you may very likely find yourself coughing on chile fumes some as this cooks.

Warn your guests about the olive pits and the chiles. Neither are to be eaten. Or, time permitting, pit the olives and fish out the chiles. **SERVES 2 TO 4**

8 ounces fettuccine
1 tablespoon olive oil
Cooking spray
1 onion, preferably red, cut vertically into thin crescents
3 to 5 dried red chiles
1 red bell pepper, stem and seeds removed, cut into ¼-inch strips
About 1 cup peeled and diced butternut squash
1 small head broccoli, cut into florets, or 8 ounces precut broccoli florets
4 to 5 cloves garlic, pressed, or 1½ teaspoons Garlic Oil (page 898), or 1½ tablespoons Roasted Garlic puree (see page 899)
2 to 3 ounces crumbled feta cheese or ricotta salata (optional)
½ cup kalamata or oil-cured black olives
Salt and freshly ground black pepper to taste
Freshly grated Parmesan cheese or soy Parmesan-style flakes (optional)

1 Bring a large pot of salted water to a boil and drop in the pasta.

2 As the water for pasta heats, heat the oil over medium-high heat in a nonstick skillet or one that has been sprayed with cooking spray. Add the onion and red chiles and sauté for 4 minutes. Add the red bell pepper and sauté for 2 minutes more. Lower the heat to medium, add the squash, and sauté for 2 minutes, then cover tightly and steam over medium-low heat for 2 minutes more. Stir well and add the broccoli. Sauté, uncovered, for 2 minutes, pop the cover back on just to steam for about 1 minute.

3 Place the garlic in a warmed serving bowl with the feta cheese, if using, and the olives. Drain the pasta, add it to the bowl, along with the stir-fry, and toss well. Salt lightly, pepper vigorously, and serve at once, hot, passing Parmesan cheese, if desired, at the table.

Shocking Pasta

I'd place this on the All-Time Hit Parade of great pastas, though I know it's not for everyone. I first had it with Richard Mintz, a former guest of ours who had worked on the Little Rock–based presidential campaign of another former guest of ours. When that former guest did in fact become president in 1993, both Richard and B.C. moved to Washington, and Richard headed up the press office for the inaugural team. When I arrived on a book tour, Richard insisted on taking me out to dinner.

Richard took me to an Italian restaurant called I Matti. (No reservation. No trouble getting a table, though a free one didn't appear to exist when we walked in. Waitstaff and maitre d' were highly solicitous.) And I was delighted with the garlicky, shocking pink beet sauce I Matti served over bow-tie pasta. I'm sure their version was fancier, but I've made this simple one ever since and enjoyed it.

Please note: This is quick-fix *only* if you have cooked beets (see page 701) on hand. Otherwise, forget it. Well, don't forget it. It's still quick in terms of prep time, it just takes a while for the beets to bake. **SERVES 3 OR 4**

8 ounces bow-tie pasta
3 to 4 medium beets, cooked or roasted (see page 701), warm, skins slipped off, quartered
4 to 5 cloves garlic, pressed, or 1½ teaspoons Garlic Oil (page 898), or 1½ tablespoons Roasted Garlic puree (see page 899)
1 to 2 tablespoons olive oil
Salt and freshly ground black pepper to taste
Freshly grated Parmesan or soy Parmesan-style flakes (optional)

1 Bring a large pot of salted water to a boil and drop in the pasta. Cook until done.

2 As the pasta cooks, place the beets in a food processor with the garlic, oil, salt, and pepper. Buzz until smooth, pausing a couple of times to scrape down the sides of the work bowl.

3 Drain the pasta and toss it with the beet puree. Serve immediately, hot, passing the Parmesan cheese, if using, at the table.

The One, the Only, the Greatest Garlic Spaghetti

I have saved my very favorite, all-time great, quick pasta dish for last—the recipe I wish to have chipped on my tombstone as my greatest contribution to human happiness. This vegetarian, very, very garlicky version of spaghetti à la carbonara is one I created many years ago, long before we were fat-phobic and warned off raw eggs to boot. It remains a great recipe, though I now eat it twice a year instead of twice a week and have toned down the butter a tad. Yes, both egg and garlic are intentionally raw: When the hot pasta hits the garlic paste, the butter melts, the egg cooks just a tiny bit, the cheese melts, and the garlic aroma makes you levitate. Although I believe in offering dairy- and egg-free versions of many dishes, this one does not translate to vegan or low fat, so don't try. Don't wuss out on the amount of garlic, either, or you'll miss out on one of the very best dishes known to woman or man.

It is appropriate, given Garlic Spaghetti's truly in-your-face character, its raw, audacious, easy wonderfulness from the first inhalation, that it seems to know no boundaries or categories. Since it appeared in Jan Brown and my *Dairy Hollow House Cookbook,* small cults of Garlic Spaghetti lovers have gathered around the country: I hear of Garlic Spaghetti parties in Nashville, L.A., Phoenix, Boston, and San Francisco. I have myself spread its fame by giving the recipe verbally to taxi drivers, flight attendants, talk show hosts, and hotel maids on my travels. Perhaps most amazing of all, this recipe inspired an extraordinary fine-art quilt, titled *Garlic Spaghetti,* made by artist Nancy Halpern of Natick, Massachusetts (the recipe was one of her favorites, too). The quilt—a gorgeous affair, with a voluptuously curled, scaled green dragon, whose flames are heating a pot of water, from which issue whorls of steam while spaghetti flies like wizard's pick-up sticks through a lavender garlic-imaged atmosphere—was part of a group show toured by the Smithsonian. The exhibit, "Women of Taste: A Collaboration Celebrating Quilt Artists and Chefs," traveled all over America. **SERVES 2 OR 3**

NOTE

This recipe contains an egg that does cook some on contact with the hot pasta, but maybe not enough for all eaters. Because of the risk of salmonella from undercooked eggs, if you are cooking for children, the elderly, or someone with a compromised immune system, always make sure your eggs are thoroughly cooked.

8 ounces spaghetti or fettuccine
1 raw large egg, preferably free-range
7 to 8 cloves garlic, peeled
3 to 4 tablespoons butter, softened
¼ to ⅓ cup freshly grated Parmesan cheese
1 teaspoon dried basil
Salt and freshly ground black pepper
Crushed red pepper (optional)
Vegetarian bacon bits (optional)

1 Bring a large pot of water to a vigorous boil. Drop in the pasta.

2 As the pasta cooks, gently warm either the bowl from which you'll serve the pasta or individual plates.

3 Combine the egg, garlic, butter, Parmesan, basil, a little salt, and a lot of pepper in a food processor. Buzz, pausing to scrape down the sides, until a thick paste is formed.

4 When the pasta is done, drain it, but do not rinse. Quickly transfer it to a bowl (the warmed serving bowl, if you wish) and dollop it with the garlic paste. Toss like wild, adding a little more pepper and maybe a dash or two more salt. By now the garlic aroma should be driving you crazy, so . . .

5 Sit down and eat, serving the dish ASAP on the warmed plates, passing the red pepper, veggie bacon bits, and, if you like, additional Parmesan and a peppermill. Swoon.

Frozen Rice and Vegetable Stir-Fry

Pasta water taking too long to boil? Forget to leave time for the vegetables? No access to a good whole-foods store for a one-bag full-meal dinner? Well, it happens. Try a bag of regular supermarket frozen rice and vegetable stir-fry instead of pasta as the basis for your quick cooking adventures. Each bag feeds 2 to 4 people as an entree, depending on how much other stuff you add to it.

Here are a few directions to travel with it. Each starts the same way. The chart opposite elaborates on your options as far as oil, type of seasonings, and which protein foods you may add in.

2 teaspoons to 1 tablespoon oil (see chart)
Cooking spray
1 bag (1 pound) frozen unsauced rice and vegetable stir-fry mix
Seasonings and spices (see chart)
2 tablespoons water, preferably spring or filtered
Add-ins (see chart)
Garnishes and condiments (see chart)

1. Heat your chosen oil over medium-high heat in a 10-inch nonstick skillet or one that has been sprayed with cooking spray. Add the bag of frozen vegetable and rice mix and sauté it for about 1 minute, or until clumps break up and the rice starts to grow translucent. Add seasonings and water, cover, and let the rice steam for 1 minute.

2. Stir in your chosen add-ins. Continue cooking until everything is nice and hot. Serve, fast, with as many of your chosen garnishes as you wish, or with none.

Mix & Match Flavors

Options	Asian	Southwestern	Mediterranean
OILS	Peanut, or peanut and a few drops toasted sesame	Corn or canola	Olive
SEASONINGS	1 to 2 tablespoons green curry paste, either homemade (see page 901), or commercial; 1 to 2 tablespoons honey; tamari to taste	1 teaspoon chili powder; 3 tablespoons commercial hot sauce or salsa; 1 teaspoon Garlic Oil (page 898) or 2 pressed cloves garlic; or omit everything but salsa and use 3 tablespoons Pesto Santo Tomas (page 920)	Use ¼ cup white wine instead of water as liquid, along with 1½ teaspoons tomato paste, plus 3 cloves minced garlic (or 1 tablespoon pesto).
ADD-INS	4 to 8 ounces tofu, commercially made Thai-style or savory baked	1 can (16 ounces) black beans, well drained	1 can (16 ounces) chickpeas or kidney beans, well drained
GARNISHES	Chopped roasted peanuts or raw cashews; minced scallions; finely chopped fresh mint, Thai basil, or cilantro	Grated Cheddar or jack cheese or soy cheese equivalent; finely chopped fresh cilantro; chopped fresh tomato and onion; pickled jalapeño peppers	⅓ cup finely minced Italian parsley; ⅓ cup finely minced fresh basil; grated Parmesan or provolone or equivalent soy cheese

Breads & Tortillas

Sandwiches

The next quick fix begins in a familiar place: the sandwich. Take something savory, put it between slices of bread, and you're on it. From there, it's just a short hop to the venerable cheese toast, high in fat, yet loved by many: bread with cheese, run under the broiler till melted, embellished before or after. There are a couple of other great, classic, almost embarrassingly easy and homey bread fixes here too, like milk toasts. And from bread, it's a natural progression to tortillas, in which almost anything can be rolled.

Here are some simple sandwich ideas you may not have thought of. Before we start: Attention! Have you incorporated prep day into your wild life yet? If so, you could have a homemade grain, bean, or vegetable patty nestled right in there between those two slices of bread. If not, make do with store-bought.

Bread & Milk

Bread and milk? You mean, like milk toast? Most people who have never had it recoil. Too simple; too much of the nursery to it; too bland; it sounds horrible if you've never had it; *milquetoast* is the word for a spineless husband; and so on. I've heard such comments often, so I keep my secret predilection for the occasional bowl of milk toast quiet.

But in this stressed-out, we-have-no-time world, it may be the moment for a revival of this dish, the epitome of comfort and made in the blink of an eye.

If you've had milk toast, you know how soothing and seductive its simplicity can be. And if bread in a bowl, with milk poured over it (or buttermilk, for its tart tang), sounds disingenuous, think of it this way: It's the precursor to French toast and bread pudding, cousin to cereal and milk, second cousin to pudding or custard, and a distant but traceable relation to such milk-and-pasta comfort foods as macaroni and cheese. If you have known comfort and satisfaction from these, give milk toast a try when you're feeling like a whipped dog. It doesn't get much simpler, or (at times) much better. Of course you should be wearing fuzzy slippers and a long bathrobe, and it should be cold and rainy, and if you imagine yourself long-suffering and friendless, so much the better, in terms of the improvement such dishes can bring.

Tortillas

Man (and woman) cannot live by bread alone. But add tortillas, and something congenial to put in them, and you've made a good start—at least on the physical side. It's no wonder wraps have taken the lunch counter world by storm. I always have a package of whole wheat tortillas in my refrigerator. They go so fast—and so well with beans, with eggs, with roasted veggies, with spreads, with just about anything, really.

The "Jerry" Reuben

A Reuben sandwich without corned beef? Radical! The basic idea is from the Pita Hut, a now long-gone but still-missed Eureka Springs sandwich spot where we used to eat this on benches out under an umbrella-like ginkgo tree. Jane Fishman, one of its proprietors, now lives in Savannah; we miss her still. But the other Pita Hut chef-owner, Billie King, moved back to Eureka Springs, after a long stint in Key West, to cofound the local newspaper, *The Lovely County Citizen*. Hooray!

If you don't eat dairy products, substitute Swiss-style soy cheese. **MAKES 2**

- **1 tablespoon Tofu Mayonnaise (page 906) or other mayonnaise**
- **1 teaspoon ketchup**
- **¼ teaspoon honey (optional)**
- **1½ teaspoons sweet pickle relish (optional)**
- **2 large, thin slices Jarlsberg or Emmental cheese**
- **4 slices best-quality rye bread**
- **8 ounces Basic Skillet-Sautéed Tofu (page 667) or commercially made savory baked tofu**
- **1 to 1¼ cups good-quality preservative-free sauerkraut from a jar (not a can), well drained, heated**
- **1 large tomato, preferably red-ripe, sliced**
- **2 paper-thin slices red onion**

1 Combine the mayo, ketchup, and honey and sweet pickle relish, if using, and set aside. This is an impromptu Russian dressing.

2 Place the sliced cheese on 2 of the pieces of bread, covering them, and place under the broiler to broil until starting to melt.

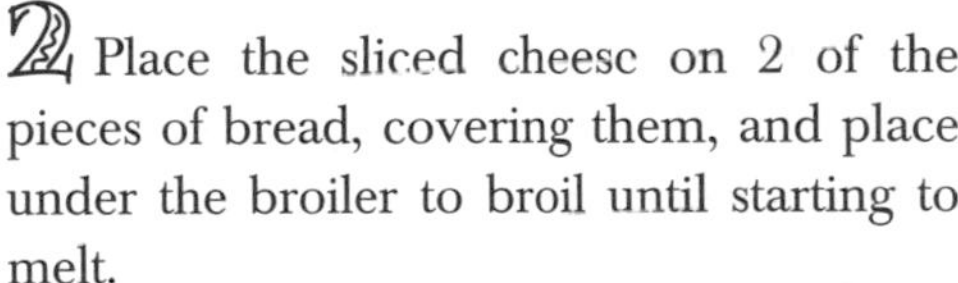

3 Meanwhile, spread the remaining slices of bread with the Russian dressing. Then layer on, in this order: the tofu, a big handful of sauerkraut (squeeze it dry before placing it on the sandwich), tomato, and onion.

4 When the cheese-topped bread comes out of the broiler, top the sandwich with it, cut in half, and serve.

VARIATION

You can substitute a toasted commercial veggie burger, or sautéed soy bacon, for the tofu. And in the lily-gilding department: After assembling the sandwich smear the outside of each bread slice very lightly with ⅛ to ¼ teaspoon melted butter or Better (page 905) and brown slowly in a cast-iron skillet that has been sprayed with cooking spray.

Sandwiches I Have Loved

Old favorites revisited

▲ *Peanut butter with Medjool dates, bananas, and honey, on whole wheat pita (this is about a million times tastier than it sounds).*

▲ *Smoked tempeh, sautéed or grilled, with lettuce, tomato, and a dab of tofu mayonnaise, on toasted oatmeal or cracked wheat bread.*

▲ *Ned's Dagwood: a slather of softened neufchâtel cheese on top of toasted cracked wheat bread, studded with thinly sliced pimento-stuffed green olives, covered with paper-thin slices of onion, thicker slices of tomato, sliced grilled soysage, thinly sliced Cheddar cheese, thinly sliced Jarlsberg or soy cheese, alfalfa seed sprouts, thinly sliced cucumber, and a light spread of Dijon mustard on the top slice of toast.*

▲ *Any vegetarian burger or cake, purchased or homemade, with all the ol' burger fixings (lettuce, tomato, red onion, pickle, tofu mayo or mustard) on a toasted whole wheat sesame bun.*

▲ *Grilled Cheddar, Jarlsberg, or provolone cheese, done on good whole wheat bread, with the merest little bit of real butter spread on the outer sides, grilled slowly in a cast-iron skillet that has been sprayed with cooking spray.*

▲ *Egg salad, or tofu salad, done with Tofu Mayonnaise (page 906), a big slice of tomato, and romaine lettuce on a toasted whole-grain English muffin.*

▲ *Curried egg or curried tofu salad with Western-Style Blueberry Chutney (page 927) on toasted oatmeal bread.*

▲ *Too-No-Fish Sandwich: 1 can chickpeas, drained well, coarsely mashed, mixed with Tofu Mayonnaise (page 906), minced celery and red onion, lots of freshly ground black pepper, a few drops of lemon juice, and a little fresh minced tarragon, with sliced tomato and limestone lettuce, on toasted seven-grain bread.*

Nouveau sensations between the bread

▲ *Goat cheese on a split baguette with a bit of Olivada (page 24), topped with sliced tomato and arugula, inside top of the baguette sprinkled with vinegar and minced fresh herbs.*

▲ *Split baguette spread with Garlic-Feta Cream (page 38), topped with grilled red pepper, slivered red onion, grilled eggplant, and romaine lettuce.*

▲ *Whole portobello mushroom, brushed with tamari and olive oil, grilled, and served hot with its juices on a toasted whole wheat bun, with fresh spinach and sliced yellow tomatoes.*

▲ *Commercially made lemon broiled tempeh with sautéed onions and mushrooms, grilled and served as a hot sandwich on toasted sourdough bread.*

▲ *Veggie salad pocket: shredded carrots tossed with a few sliced raw mushrooms, a little diced onion, shredded romaine, a sprinkle of lemon juice, 1 ounce grated sharp Cheddar cheese, and 1/4 perfectly ripe avocado, diced, in a toasted whole wheat pita bread.*

▲ *Ned's Grilled Tofu: a slab of firm tofu, dipped in tamari and Pickapeppa sauce with a splash of vinegar, rolled in nutritional yeast (see page 239), then seared in a hot nonstick skillet, or one that has been sprayed with cooking spray, with sliced ripe tomato, red leaf lettuce, and Tofu Mayonnaise (page 906), on a kaiser roll.*

- ▲ *Ozark Tempeh Plus: a slab of Basic Oven-Baked Marinated Tempeh (page 641), with well-drained Cora Pinkley Call's Uncooked Ozark Relish (page 929), sliced tomato, and Tofu Mayonnaise (page 906), on toasted sourdough.*

- ▲ *Spinach, tomato, and paper-thin Jarlsberg cheese on moist German-style dense whole-grain rye bread with well-drained Cora Pinkley Call's Uncooked Ozark Relish (page 929), and a smear of coarse mustard.*

- ▲ *Artichoke Pockets: marinated artichoke hearts, drained and diced; crumbled feta cheese; julienned raw carrot; minced red onion; sliced tomato; and fresh spinach in a toasted whole wheat pita.*

- ▲ *Sweetheart Sandwich: ricotta cream with a bit of grated orange zest and fruit-only apricot jam on toasted challah bread.*

- ▲ *Neufchâtel cheese on toasted cinnamon-raisin bread, with grated carrot, thinly sliced peeled Granny Smith apple or ripe Bosc pear, and a drizzle of honey.*

- ▲ *Green and Blue on Brown: neufchâtel cheese, crumbled blue cheese, fresh spinach, and thinly sliced red onion on moist German-style dense whole-grain rye bread.*

- ▲ *Paul Wank's Talk-of-the-Town Special Lemon Sandwiches: More of a tea sandwich, this unusual combo is peculiarly addictive. It was through tracking down the bearer of this wonderful recipe to some function or other that I officially met Paul, a former Louisiana State University librarian who retired here. His sandwich: simply paper-thin slices of seeded lemon, zest and all (cut the lemons on the thinnest blade of your food processor), on thin-sliced best-quality white sandwich bread, with homemade mayonnaise or Tofu Mayonnaise (page 906).*

- ▲ *Ned's Low-Class Egg Sandwich: 2 or 3 eggs scrambled in butter with julienned scallions and ketchup, on thin-sliced best-quality untoasted white sandwich bread (Ned's advice: "Preferably eaten alone, out of wife's view").*

- ▲ *Olive-pesto spread: 2 parts Olivada (page 24) mixed with 1 part Lemon, Basil, and Sun-Dried Tomato Pesto (page 918) and 3 parts neufchâtel or ricotta, with arugula or mesclun on a small hard roll.*

- ▲ *The Wicked Weintz: from my friend Steven Weintz. Sautéed tempeh bacon, feta, lettuce, tomato, and roasted red pepper on toasted multi-grain bread smeared with black olive paste.*

- ▲ *Kristine Kidd's Secret Sensation: when you get a sandwich recipe from the food editor of* Bon Appetit, *believe it, it's good no matter how it sounds at first. On dense, grainy, toasted bread, slather a best quality non-hydrogenated peanut butter and top with thick slices of garden-ripe, height-of-summer tomatoes.*

- ▲ *Ken's Country Synergy Sandwich: thick sliced garden tomatoes and thick slices of sweet Vidalia onion on toasted whole-grain bread. Put plenty of mayonnaise on the tomato side of the bread and a good squidge of yellow, unfancy bullpark mustard on the onion side. Salt lightly with coarse sea salt; add a vigorous grind of black pepper. Mmm-mmm-mmm!*

Southern-Style Cornbread and Milk

Southern-style milk toasts are, of course, made from cornbread. This means they are not truly quick-fix unless you have cornbread on hand, since you can't buy good cornbread (it's a quick bread and its glory is evanescent). But let's just assume that you have a couple of plain, not gussied-up, slices. (If you make cornbread regularly, you might plan to stash a few pieces in a zippered plastic bag in the freezer for just such an occasion.)

Stale cornbread is fine; in fact, some say, preferred. It can also be toasted first. And you'll want to have ready your favorite soup spoon. These things matter. I would

Milk Toast for Grown-ups

Cinnamon Milk Toast: *If you can get good grainy slice-it-yourself cinnamon-raisin bread, try it in Northern-Style Milk Toast. Very pleasing.*

Sweet-Spiced Milk Toast: *This is from Marion Cunningham's beautiful, gently wrought* The Breakfast Book, *a volume with something of the quality of haiku. It is prepared as above, but with a tablespoon of sugar and a little grating of fresh nutmeg added to the milk when you take it off the stove. (Marion also adds a tablespoon of butter at that point, but I prefer less, applied directly to the toast before pouring on the milk.)*

Baked Milk Toast: *This is also from Marion Cunningham. She gives a recipe for two, but since this is a dish that to me is solo food, I do it for one, in a smaller baking dish. Preheat the oven to 350°F, take 2 slices of buttered bread ("preferably homemade and cut ¾ inch thick," says Marion), and lay it in an oiled baking dish or one that has been sprayed with cooking spray. Pour a cup of cold milk over the bread, cover, and bake for 30 minutes. "Sometimes," she says, "a light sprinkle of granulated sugar is just right on milk toast." I agree, but I would choose Demerara or granulated maple sugar.*

Silk Nog Milk Toast: *There are many dishes I happily use soy milk in, but milk toast is not usually one of them, except during the month of December, when rich-tasting, sweet, nutmeggy Silk Nog (Soy Silk's vegan version of eggnog) is available at the natural foods store. A whole-grain toast with a pour of warm Silk Nog is like an unfussy bread pudding.*

a thousand times rather eat soup or cereal or milk toast with a soup spoon that has a round bowl rather than an oval one; just fits the mouth better. They don't make them much anymore; that person you saw browsing through the tag-ends of mismatched silver utensils at the flea market last weekend might have been me.

Sweet milk, by the way, does not mean sweetened with sugar, it means "regular" milk, as opposed to buttermilk or clabbered (soured) milk. When talking about cornbread and milk, the word *milk* is always qualified as sweet or otherwise. Also, if you're accustomed to low-fat milk, use that; otherwise it will taste too rich to you. If you're accustomed to whole, use that; otherwise it will taste poor. **SERVES 1**

1 or 2 wedges cornbread, such as Ronni Lundy's (page 452) or Dairy Hollow House (page 451)
1½ to 1¾ cups sweet milk, whole or low fat, preferably organic

1 If desired, split the cornbread wedge and toast it lightly.

2 If you'd like the milk warmed (though in Southern milk toasts, people generally use cold), heat it almost to a simmer, then remove from the heat.

3 Crumble your piece of cornbread into a bowl. Pour the milk over the crumbled cornbread and eat, in the warmest place in your kitchen, with your spoon.

VARIATION

SUMMERTIME VERSION: ***Crumble the cornbread into a tall glass. Pour cold sweet milk or buttermilk over it, and eat with a long-handled iced-tea spoon, nibbling on a washed scallion (roots removed) between bites. Sounds surpassingly strange if you didn't grow up with it, but there is nothing more refreshing.***

Northern-Style Milk Toast

Northern-style milk toasts are made with sliced bread, not crumbled but left in a whole, toasted slice. The milk is always warmed, never cold.

My own choice would be a good challah bread or a not-too-heavy but firm-textured oatmeal or whole-grain bread. A home-baked bread is best (as if you're likely to have that on hand, given that we're talking about quick fixes here), but a good bakery bread will also do just fine. Just don't use a spongy supermarket-type bread. If possible, use unsliced bread, so you can cut thickish slices from the loaf yourself. **SERVES 1**

2 thick slices bread
About 2 teaspoons butter
1½ to 2 cups sweet milk, whole or low fat, preferably organic

1 Toast the bread, and butter it lightly, very lightly.

2 Heat some milk in a small saucepan. Two cups will be more than you need, but you could go ahead and heat 2 cups, because that way you can pour on more milk if it turns out you would like more.

3 Place the buttered, toasted bread in a soup bowl. Get your favorite spoon ready. As soon as the milk has just barely reached the boiling point, take it off the stove and pour enough over the toast to cover it. Put a plate atop the soup bowl to hold in the heat, and wait for 5 minutes.

4 Then eat it, hot, with a spoon and a sense of deep delight.

Tofu Green Chile Wraps

Green chile is a flavor that always makes my palate very happy. Wrapped in a warm whole wheat tortilla and combined with creamy silken tofu, it's irresistible. **MAKES 6**

VARIATION

This is also excellent with a canned chipotle in adobo instead of green chiles.

6 whole wheat tortillas
1 box (12.3 ounces) silken tofu
2 or 3 tablespoons canned green chiles
2 cloves garlic
4 sprigs cilantro
½ teaspoon olive oil
Salt and freshly ground black pepper
Chopped tomatoes, avocados, chopped onion or scallions, and mesclun
Salsa (optional)

1 Over medium heat, warm the tortillas in a dry skillet. The first side can get very slightly browned, but when you flip the tortillas over, do it just long enough to warm the second side. Keep the tortillas warm.

2 As the tortillas warm, buzz the tofu in a food processor with the green chiles, garlic, cilantro, oil, salt, and pepper, pausing to scrape down the sides of the work bowl.

3 As soon as the tortillas come off the pan, quickly and liberally spread each tortilla with a little of the green chile mixture, top with chopped tomatoes, chopped onion, shredded lettuce or mesclun mix, and maybe a splash of bottled salsa. Roll or fold.

Con Queso Veggie Wraps

This makes use of more life-in-the-fast-lane veggie tricks—stir-fry a frozen vegetable stir-fry mix or (even better) a bag of commercially cut fresh vegetables. The recipe does, however, require two skillets—one for warming the tortillas, the other for cooking the filling. **MAKES 4 TO 6 WRAPS**

NOTE

TO WARM TORTILLAS

▲ ***SKILLET HEATING:*** ***Heat a dry skillet over medium heat. Add a tortilla. When the first side is warmed and slightly brown, 30 to 45 seconds, turn it and warm the second side just long enough to be pliable, 10 to 15 seconds. Remove from the skillet. Keep warm by stacking on a plate, covered with a towel.***

▲ **OVEN-HEATING:** ***good for large quantities. The tortillas don't brown, but they do become soft and pliable. Preheat the oven to 400°F. Stack 5 or 6 tortillas one on top of the other, and place inside a sturdy brown paper sack. Lightly dampen a clean dishtowel, fold it, and place it in the bag with the tortillas. Place the whole thing in the oven for 6 to 8 minutes. (The damp towel creates steam within the closed bag.)***

Cooking spray
1 teaspoon olive oil
½ bag (1 pound) frozen vegetable stir-fry mix, or 1 bag (8 ounces) fresh precut vegetables for stir-fry
4 to 6 whole wheat tortillas, warmed (preferably skillet method)

ANY TWO OR THREE OF THE FOLLOWING (OPTIONAL)
4 ounces neufchâtel cheese or commercially made soy cream cheese–style product
Commercially made black bean dip
Commercially made salsa

1 Heat a skillet that has been sprayed with cooking spray over medium-high heat. Add the oil.

2 Pour the stir-fry vegetable mix, frozen or fresh, into the hot skillet. Over medium-high heat, sauté the vegetables for a minute or 2, stirring often, then cover for about 30 seconds. Remove the cover and continue stir-frying until the frozen vegetables are hot and the fresh are tender-crisp.

3 As you're stir-frying, begin to prepare the heated tortillas: Spread a tiny bit of neufchâtel cheese and/or black bean dip on the hot tortillas, top with a good scoop of stir-fry, and dress with salsa. Dig in!

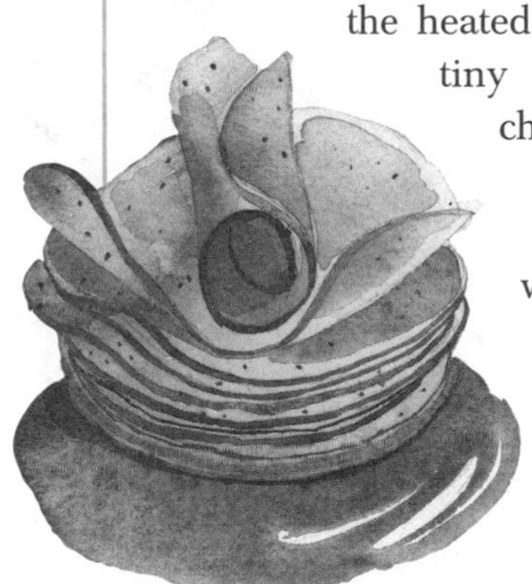

Huevos Wraps

The Earl of Sandwich meets whatever anonymous but blessed ranch-hand cook first came up with huevos rancheros. Simple, truly speedy, satisfying; also easy to modify with whatever scrambled-egg additions you have on hand.

If you like, heat up some Southwestern-spiced tomato sauce or commercially made enchilada or green chile sauce, and spoon it over the finished wrap. This is one you have to eat with a fork. **MAKES 2**

2 or 3 large eggs or 1 whole egg and 3 or 4 egg whites
1 tablespoon milk or unflavored soy milk
Salt and freshly ground black pepper to taste
Cooking spray
2 or 3 whole wheat tortillas, heated

ADDITIONS (OPTIONAL)
A few ounces firm tofu, crumbled
¼ to ½ cup leftover cooked vegetables or potatoes
1 to 2 ounces grated sharp Cheddar cheese or soy cheese equivalent
Commercially made green chile sauce or commercially made salsa
2 whole wheat tortillas, heated

1 Beat together the eggs, milk, salt, and pepper in a small bowl.

2 Heat a nonstick skillet, or one that has been sprayed with cooking spray, over medium heat. When it's hot, add the eggs and scramble, stirring in any of the optional additions as you scramble and adding a big splash of green chile sauce toward the end. Don't overcook the eggs.

3 Whomp those eggs into those tortillas and you've got you a good breakfast, lunch, or supper.

Wrap Party

The tortilla itself matters. Give me whole wheat every time. They taste good, have a nice texture, and give you more nutritional wallop. Here are a number of simple tortilla wraps that please me regularly.

GREEK WRAPS: *Can't go wrong with the Mykonos omelet (page 885) wrapped in a tortilla. Or try a modest smear of some commercially made kalamata olive paste, a little mesclun, a diced fresh tomato, a sprinkle of feta, a dusting of dried oregano.*

BEAN WRAPS: *Put 1 cup's worth of instant dehydrated pinto or black beans, made according to the directions on the packet, or use a good commercially made bean dip, on half a tortilla. If you like, add a little grated cheese. Fold the unfilled half of the tortilla over this, and serve, with bottled salsa.*

SALAD WRAPS: *Heat the tortilla in a skillet until brown on one side and flip just long enough to warm on the second side. Remove from the skillet, fill with mesclun, a splash of commercial or homemade dressing, and a little diced savory baked tofu.*

MOCK BLINTZ WRAPS: *Spread a tortilla with a little neufchâtel cheese and/or a line of low-fat cottage cheese and top that with fruit-only preserves, the variety of your choice. Roll it up.*

Quick-Cooking Grains

Those grains that cook in 15 minutes or less are bulgur, millet, buckwheat (kasha), quinoa, and popcorn. Couscous—not a grain per se but a tiny pasta—is also listed here, since most people think of it as a grain and its texture is that of a cooked grain. Most of these are taken up in the grains chapter, so please check for recipes there, too. But I did want to touch on two here: popcorn and couscous.

POPCORN: May I recommend that you try Popcorn à la Hippie at your earliest convenience? It's freshly popped popcorn tossed with a few dashes of tamari or shoyu soy sauce, nutritional yeast (see page 239), and, if desired, grated American-style Parmesan cheese (meaning out of the green shake-it container, not the good Italian stuff). This will make a nutritional yeast convert out of the most stalwart opponent. A squib of butter is, of course, incredibly good on this. There's also Spicy Popcorn à la Hippie: Add curry powder and cayenne but no Parmesan. Excellent. Strangely irresistible, in fact.

COUSCOUS: What is generally understood as couscous in America is a pasta of refined, partially cooked semolina flour.

Paula Wolfert, who brought couscous to the attention of Americans in her book *Couscous and Other Good Food from Morocco,* advocates the traditional method, which yields a glorious product, but it's a big deal: You wash the couscous, dry it, steam it, dry it again, steam it again. Time-consuming. Few of us are willing or able to do this on a regular basis. Yet if you've had the real thing, steamed to fluffy, delicate perfection, it's hard to go back. So I understand why Wolfert decries instant couscous. Still, many time-pressed vegetarians rely on quick-cooked couscous and love it.

My own solution? A middle-ground method for making couscous. It's not as instant as the recipe on the box, but it still comes in at under 10 minutes and uses only one cooking vessel. You start the couscous on top of the stove and finish it quickly in the oven.

Grains under Pressure

I want to remind you, again, how a pressure cooker joins the need for speed with the slower-cooking grains and whole grains. I'm begging, I'm groveling here: If you're dedicated to quick, healthy eating, please consider investing in one. It will change your kitchen life. The new generation of cookers are safe, simple, and unscary. A grain that takes an hour to cook conventionally can be done to perfection in 20 minutes. I can tell you firsthand that that 40-minute savings makes a real difference in how often you fix whole grains.

The only pressure-cooker alternative, for the time-pressed, is the cook-more-than-you-need-in-advance technique described on page 850.

Without one or both of these strategies, there won't be time in your busy life for all those healthful, varied slow-cooking grains, each with its distinct taste, shape, and texture, each delivering unique contributions nutritionally. You need those straight unadulterated whole grains, which taste as good as they are good for you.

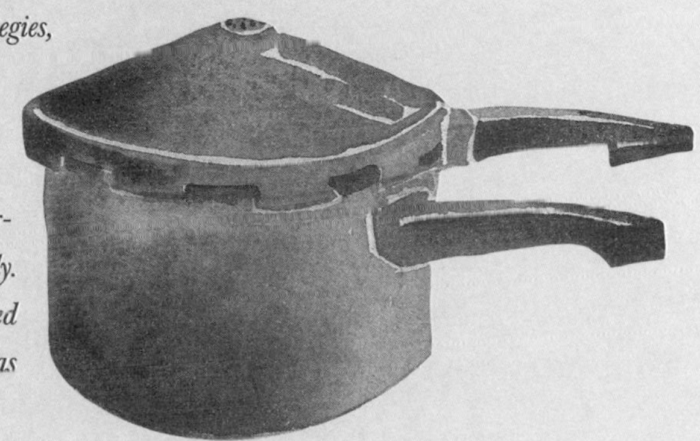

VARIATIONS

Simple variations on this recipe, like any basic grain recipe, are many. Try butter or toasted sesame oil instead of olive oil. Cook in vegetable stock, tomato juice, or a mixture of carrot and tomato juice instead of water.

COUSCOUS CASABLANCA: ***Add a pinch of cinnamon and a few finely minced apricots to the cooking water.***

MARILYN HARRIS'S SPICED COUSCOUS: ***Add ¼ teaspoon each freshly ground black pepper and allspice, and ⅛ teaspoon mace.***

Marilyn's Quick and Easy Couscous

This technique was developed by food writer Marilyn Harris, who allowed her friend Bert Greene to use it in *The Grains Cookbook.* This is a low-fat version for basic, plain couscous. The recipes that follow turn it into a main-dish meal. **SERVES 4 AS A SIDE DISH**

- 1 teaspoon olive oil
- Cooking spray
- 1½ cups instant couscous
- 2 cups water, preferably spring or filtered
- ½ teaspoon salt

1 Preheat the oven to 375°F, and make sure it's up to temperature before beginning the recipe.

2 Heat the oil over medium-low heat in a nonstick ovenproof skillet or one that has been sprayed with cooking spray. Add the couscous and cook, stirring, for 2 minutes. Add the water and salt, and cook, tossing gently with 2 forks, until all the liquid has been absorbed, about 2 minutes.

3 Cover tightly, transfer to the hot oven, and bake for 5 minutes.

Golden Curried Cabbage, Chickpeas, and Couscous

A dollop of yogurt or Tofu Sour Cream (page 909) is good with this simple skillet dish. Add sliced garden tomatoes and bottled chutney for a fast supper. I like hot stuff, so I use the larger amount of curry paste; those who are hesitant in the heat department should use less. A sprinkle of fresh cilantro makes this even better. **SERVES 3 OR 4 AS AN ENTREE**

1 teaspoon mild vegetable oil, such as corn, canola, or peanut
Cooking spray
½ package (16 ounces) precut shredded coleslaw vegetable mix (cabbage, carrot, and red cabbage), or 3 to 4 cups shredded cabbage
2 teaspoons to 2 tablespoons commercially made Thai Massaman curry paste
1½ cups instant couscous
2¼ cups water, preferably spring or filtered, or vegetable stock (see page 139)
⅓ cup raisins, preferably golden
½ teaspoon salt
1 can (15 ounces) chickpeas, drained

1 Preheat the oven to 375°F and make sure it's up to temperature before you begin the recipe.

2 Heat the oil over medium-high heat in a large nonstick ovenproof skillet or one that has been sprayed with cooking spray. Add the coleslaw vegetable mix and sauté, stirring, for about 3 minutes, or until the cabbage begins to wilt. Stir in the curry paste and cook for 1 minute more.

3 Lower the heat slightly, add the couscous, and continue to cook, stirring, for 2 minutes. Add the water or stock to the couscous and quickly bring to a boil. Add the raisins and salt. Cook, tossing gently with 2 forks, until the couscous has absorbed the liquid, about 2 minutes. Stir in the chickpeas.

4 Cover tightly, transfer to the oven, and bake for 5 minutes. Remove from the oven and let stand for 5 minutes more. Serve.

Sweet and Sour Pineapple-Tofu Couscous

Don't worry about the length of the ingredient list: This is still a quickie, and mighty tasty—kind of like a vegetable-y Spanish rice but with Chinese sweet-sour flavors. You'll find yourself going back for seconds.

The first seven ingredients (straight from the cupboard) are combined for cooking liquid, and from there on it's one-two-three, well within the allotted time. I've made use of commercial ginger-garlic paste. It livens things up without extra chopping. **SERVES 3 OR 4 AS AN ENTREE**

"For everything you have missed you have gained something else; and for everything you gain, you lose something. Every evil has its good; every sweet its sour."

—**Ralph Waldo Emerson,** *Compensation*

Juice from 1 (15-ounce) can pineapple chunks, chunks reserved
2 tablespoons tomato paste
2 tablespoons sugar
2 tablespoons rice vinegar
2 tablespoons tamari or shoyu soy sauce
½ teaspoon ginger
⅛ teaspoon salt
Water, preferably spring or filtered, or vegetable stock, as needed
2 teaspoons mild vegetable oil, such as corn, canola, or peanut
Cooking spray
1 package (8 ounces) precut fresh vegetables for stir-fry
2 teaspoons commercially made ginger-garlic paste
1½ cups instant couscous
1 package (8 ounces) savory baked tofu, cut into bite-size pieces

1 Preheat the oven to 375°F, and make sure it's up to temperature before beginning the recipe.

2 Pour the pineapple juice into a glass measuring cup, add the tomato paste, sugar, vinegar, tamari, dry ginger, salt, and water or stock as needed to equal 2¼ cups. Stir well with a fork to dissolve the tomato paste, and set aside.

3 Heat the oil over medium-high heat in a large nonstick ovenproof skillet or one that has been sprayed with cooking spray. Add the stir-fry vegetable mixture and sauté, stirring, for about 3 minutes, or until the vegetables begin to soften. Stir in the ginger-garlic paste and cook for 1 minute more.

4 Lower the heat. Add the couscous and continue to cook, stirring, for 2 minutes. Pour in the pineapple juice mixture and bring to a boil. Cook, tossing gently with 2 forks, until the couscous has absorbed the liquid, about 2 minutes. Stir in the pineapple chunks and diced tofu.

5 Cover tightly, transfer to the hot oven, and bake for 5 minutes. Remove from the oven and let stand for 5 minutes. Fluff well with a fork and serve.

Spinach, Feta, and Tomato Couscous Skillet Supper

These classic flavors of the Middle East are simple but quite pleasing. If you have some fresh dill on hand, snip a little into it at the end. Vegans may omit the feta cheese and add 1 cup well-drained chickpeas with the tomato. **SERVES 3 OR 4 AS AN ENTREE**

1½ teaspoons olive oil
Cooking spray
1 onion, peeled and sliced vertically into thin crescents
3 cloves garlic, pressed
1 package (12 ounces) prewashed fresh spinach
1½ cups instant couscous
2 cups water, preferably spring or filtered, or vegetable stock (see page 139)
¼ teaspoon salt or 1 teaspoon Dragon Salt (page 900)
Freshly ground black pepper
1 tomato, chopped
2 to 4 ounces feta cheese, crumbled into large chunks
1 to 2 lemons, halved (optional)

1 Preheat the oven to 375°F, and make sure it's up to temperature before beginning the recipe.

2 Heat the oil over medium-high heat in a large nonstick ovenproof skillet or one that has been sprayed with cooking spray. Add the onion and sauté, stirring, for about 4 minutes, or until it starts to become translucent. Lower the heat slightly and add the garlic. Stir for 30 seconds more. Add the spinach, stems and all, and toss with the onion and garlic insofar as it's possible (it will seem bulky), then cover and steam for 3 minutes, or until the spinach has wilted.

3 Add the couscous and continue to cook, stirring, for 2 minutes. Add the water or stock and quickly bring to a boil, adding the salt and a lot of black pepper. Cook, tossing gently with 2 forks, until the couscous has absorbed the liquid, about 2 minutes. Stir in the tomato.

4 Cover tightly, transfer to the hot oven, and bake for 5 minutes. Remove from the oven, sprinkle with the feta, and let stand, covered, for 5 minutes. If using lemon, squeeze the juice over the skillet. Fluff gently and serve.

QUICK-FIX DINNER AT THE OASIS

Commercially made hummus

*

Toasted whole wheat pita

*

Salad of sliced oranges, sliced purple onions, and olives

*

Spinach, Feta, and Tomato Couscous Skillet Supper

*

Commercially made baklava or Medjool dates and whole almonds

Eggs

Thus far in this chapter, we have played variations on a single theme: the rapid and congenial pairing of a carbohydrate (pasta, frozen rice, bread, tortillas, popcorn, couscous) with vegetables, beans, cheese, tofu, or some savory, artfully seasoned combination. Now we move to a new theme. Instead of the carb being the sun around which the planets of the meal revolve, protein takes over—in the form of the egg. Once called nature's most perfect food, certainly stylistically perfect in its discreet and pristine private oval, the egg was for years the first thing many people thought of for a quick, light, late supper. Though *light* is not the first word that comes to mind when we consider eggs, they *feel* that way—light in the stomach, easily digested, almost primally satisfying, and, of course, quick. For all we have been encouraged to, most of us are still reluctant to give up the egg. Nothing quite replaces the egg in the range of culinary magic tricks it can perform, tasks it can do, and recipes to which it is integral. And there's nothing faster, easier, and with so much possibility for satisfaction as the egg. My own take, unless I am cooking for someone who is vegan or reducing dietary cholesterol, is to eat eggs in moderation and only if they are free-range eggs.

> *"Eggs constitute a complete food. They give immeasurable strength and health to the American people."*
>
> —**Louis P. De Gouy,** *The Gold Cook Book*

What does free-range mean? That the chickens producing the eggs live a somewhat natural life: They range, as opposed to being caged, and keep regular hours—ranging by day busily doing chicken things, sleeping by night. Their food is possibly organic, but at least unadulterated, not full of hormones and selective nutrients to induce greater egg production at the cost of the quality of both the eggs and the hen's lifestyle. By contrast, caged hens live their lives inside of chicken-houses, the lights stay on twenty-four hours a day, and their feed is geared strictly toward their laying more eggs. Preliminary studies have shown free-range eggs to be lower in cholesterol than factory farm-produced eggs and less likely to be contaminated with salmonella. Best of all, from a culinary standpoint, free-range eggs taste perceptibly better. Are they more nutritious? Your own observation can tell you that the shells of free-range eggs are thicker; they may take two or three or four hard whacks to break because they're richer in calcium. And compare the yolk of a free-range egg with a cage egg: bright yellow with beta-carotene as opposed to pallid and anemic, sitting up strong and dome-shaped, not spreading. It's a no-brainer as to which is more nutrient rich.

Some say that the only bad part of the egg is the yolk. Many cholesterol-conscious eaters enjoy the whites and throw away the yolks. Or they use one whole egg with three whites. I understand the rationale behind it, but there is in me enough of a whole-foods bias that this makes me wince. Can it not be that there are as yet undiscovered micro-nutrients in the yolk that somehow balance out factors in the white, as is the case in whole, versus partial, grains?

Something that just rises up in me protests the egg white omelet: Perhaps it's the consumer in me and many years of living on a freelancer's budget (discard those perfectly good yolks?) as well as being a passionate cook.

What follows are a few of my favorite quick-fix egg dishes, which I make at regular intervals from free-range eggs. However often you choose them, I'm sure they will please you.

From the Coop

One April day I passed down the alley our pals the Douglasses share with their neighbors, potters Steve Beecham and Gary Egan. Gary and Steve keep a few pet chickens within their fenced Ozark-Chinoise garden—in keeping with the garden's theme, the hens, affectionately known as "the girls," are Asian Black Rose-Combs. And there, in Bill and Irene's mailbox, its flap open, sat a bowl of eggs, a gift from Gary and Steve, with a note saying, "From the girls!"

About Omelets

Good-quality, heavy-gauge nonstick cookware is perfect for omelets. A heavy, smooth-surfaced nonstick 8-inch skillet makes using any butter at all strictly optional, though I like to use about ⅛ to ¼ teaspoon butter or Better (page 905) for omelets.

Omelet Bases: My longtime home-cooked omelet secret is to go heavy on the filling, light on the egg. I have become so accustomed to this that when I eat an omelet at a restaurant I wind up picking out all the filling and eating maybe a third of the egg.

CD's Omelet Base: When I make omelets for myself, I use a base of 1 egg, 2 teaspoons to 1 tablespoon low-fat milk or plain soy milk (a larger egg gets the full tablespoon), and 2 teaspoons dry instant non-fat powdered milk (this is my secret ingredient), plus seasoning, whipped up with a fork. This results in an omelet wrapping that is somewhere between decidedly eggy and a little crêpe-y, a wrapping that is light, pleasing, and, to me, perfect, because I like to load up on filling. It rolls, or folds, fairly neatly, provided your pan temperature was hot enough when the eggs went in.

Classic Omelet Base: If you prefer the traditional envelope of large, thick coagulated egg, go with 2 eggs, 1 tablespoon milk, and seasonings.

Reduced-Cholesterol Omelet Base: If you, or someone you are cooking for, is of the school of omelet composition that says egg yolks are villainous, combine 1 whole egg and 2 egg whites, 2 teaspoons milk or plain soy milk, and seasonings.

Omelet Technique: Here is the precise, spelled-out omelet-making technique, using my preferred omelet base, but it works just as well with the other formulas, too. The basic recipe is followed by a number of fillings that will please you greatly. Some couldn't be more instant or quick-fix; others rely on having amenable leftovers around.

VARIATION

To make CD's Basic Omelet for Two, just double the ingredients and make one thicker omelet (which is easier to roll, by the way). Roll it, cut it in half, and serve half to each person. Or just repeat, making the 1-egg omelet twice. A happy medium for yolk-phobic omelet lovers: For two, use 1 whole egg, 3 whites, and double the remaining ingredients. If this seems skimpy to you, remember my basic philosophy: Load up on fillings, easy on the egg wrapping.

CD's Basic At-Home Light Omelet for One

As described above, this is my choice for an omelet that marries nutritional sanity, excellent flavor, and a delicate, not-quite-traditional flavor, the better to encase various fillings. It's very simple to do, and it would be simple to show you if we were together in my kitchen. But we're not, so here are *very* detailed instructions. It will take you longer to read them than to actually make the omelet, scout's honor. **SERVES 1**

1 large egg, preferably free-range
2 to 3 teaspoons low-fat milk, depending on the size of the egg
2 teaspoons dry instant non-fat powdered milk
Salt and freshly ground black pepper to taste
Seasonings and fillings (suggestions follow)
¼ teaspoon butter or Better (page 905) (optional)

1 Place a 6- to 7½-inch nonstick skillet or omelet pan over medium-low heat. Warm a serving plate slightly, if feasible (by, for example, placing it in an oven that has been preheated briefly to 350°F, then turned off).

2 In a teacup or small bowl, use a fork to beat together the egg, milk, powdered milk, and salt and pepper. Have your filling ready and at hand as well as a spatula that's safe to use on nonstick.

3 Raise the heat under the skillet to medium-high and add the butter. The butter is going to tell you when the precise moment to put the eggs in the pan has arrived, but you have to watch and listen. First it will melt, then it will bubble and there will be a clearly audible sizzle. Then, the butter will stop sizzling and the bubbles will die down a bit. *This is the perfect moment to add the beaten egg mixture.* Do so. The egg mixture will sizzle as it goes in, and almost immediately begin to cook at its outside edges and underneath.

4 When you see this happening, move your spatula to this most done-looking edge. Holding the handle of the skillet with your nondominant hand (left hand, if you are right-handed), simultaneously slide the spatula in underneath the omelet where it's started to cook, and, with your left hand, tip the skillet away from you to draw any runny mix down toward the edge you've lifted up. Repeat, lifting the omelet edge in another part, and tilting

Omelet Fillings

Fillings are limited only by your imagination and refrigerator contents. Leftovers can provide great inspiration. Try using leftover:

- ▲ *Roasty-Toasty Potatoes (page 790).*
- ▲ *Steamed vegetables or greens (leftover steamed spinach with sautéed mushrooms and a few gratings of Jarlsberg cheese).*
- ▲ *Tofu-based sour cream-style dips (page 26).*
- ▲ *Sautéed shiitake mushrooms or Oven-Roasted Shiitake Mushrooms with Garlic and Coarse Salt (page 48).*
- ▲ *Eggplant-Lentil Caponata (page 390).*
- ▲ *Paper-thin apple slices, sautéed until pliable, with diced Brie or Camembert.*

Another good bet is any good homemade or commercial pesto or salsa, with or without a little cheese or soy cheese. It doesn't take a lot of cheese to add flavor; just a few crumbles of feta or chèvre, or gratings of Parmesan or Cheddar, will do. And just a few tablespoons of almost any sauce or gravy make an exceptional omelet filling when combined with a few tablespoons of crisp breadcrumbs and snippings of any fresh herbs you have (a great idea picked up from the first Political Palate *cookbook, where it is called Omelette Grand-mère).*

There's also what I call the Mykonos omelet, with bright fresh Greek flavors for a lesiurely breakfast or quick supper. Fill the omelet with 1 tablespoon crumbled feta cheese, ½ small tomato, diced, a little snipped fresh dill, and diced scallion or onion; scatter 3 or 4 kalamata olives, pitted and diced, on top. Even quicker: these same components scrambled with an egg or two. Serve with a toasted whole wheat pita or a thick slice of crisp-crusted rustic whole-grain bread.

Lastly, consider a quicker-than-quick dessert omelet: sweet but not too sweet; a nice Sunday supper. Simply fill the omelet with a few dabs of your favorite jam (raspberry's nice, so's apricot). Roll, giving a light dusting of confectioner's sugar, with or without a touch of cinnamon. Another tasty sweet omelet is filled with diced ripe but not overripe banana, cinnamon, and a touch of brown sugar. You may add tofu or conventional or reduced-fat sour cream to any of these fillings, or a dab of cottage cheese, too.

the skillet in that direction. With a 1-egg omelet this happens pretty quickly.

5 Place the desired filling either in a line down the middle of the pan parallel to the handle (if you wish to roll the omelet) or in a half circle on the half farthest from the handle (if you wish to simply fold it; the latter allows a greater quantity of filling).

6 Lifting and tipping the pan with the nondominant hand and using the spatula in your dominant hand, edge along the outside of the omelet with the spatula, holding the pan at an angle over the warmed serving plate and either rolling or folding, nudging the omelet along onto the plate. Since this is a thinner omelet than usual and composed of slightly different ingredients, its browning pattern will be a bit different from the typical omelet, and it may break in places until you get the hang of it. But it will still be pretty (especially post garnishing) and taste good.

TABLE FOR ONE

Salad of prewashed mesclun mix with herbs, with a splash of extra virgin olive oil and fresh lemon, salt and freshly ground black pepper

*

Omelet California

*

Seven-grain toast with Better (PAGE 905)

*

Perfectly ripe peach, Red Haven variety if available

*

2 squares bittersweet chocolate

Omelet California

Another excellent omelet. Pair it with freshly squeezed orange juice, raisin-bread toast or Cornmeal-Oatmeal Blueberry Bread (page 447), steaming hot coffee or tea, maybe some soysage, and you'll find that this omelet has Festive Sunday Brunch written all over it. Or have it with a glass of Chablis, for a terrific quick-fix supper that says, "I know how to treat myself right." **SERVES 1**

1 CD's Basic At-Home Light Omelet for One, or one of the other omelet bases (page 854)
About 1 tablespoon grated Monterey Jack cheese
1 teaspoon nutritional yeast (see page 239)
½ small tomato, diced
1 scallion, sliced, or 1 teaspoon minced red onion
¼ avocado, peeled and pitted, sliced lengthwise

1 Prepare the omelet through Step 4 as directed on page 884.

2 Scatter the omelet with all the remaining ingredients, roll or fold, and serve.

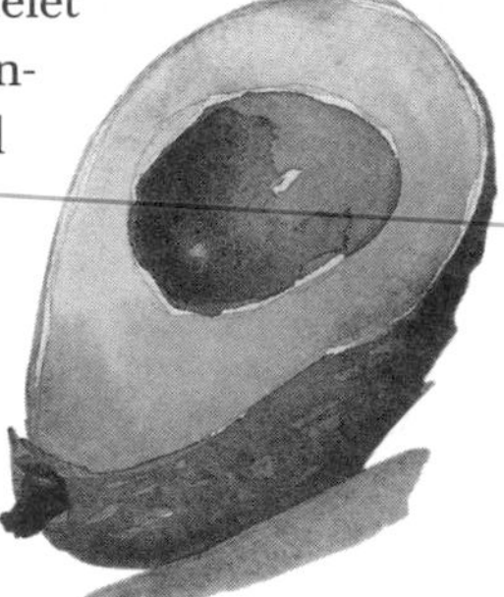

To Market Omelet

Not the voluptuous farmer's markets of high summer, but a browse at the local gourmet shop or fancy food aisle will yield the tidbits here. If you are not a sun-dried tomato fan (many like them, but their flavor is a little overstated and pushy for me), try some diced, commercially bottled roasted red peppers. Quick fixes like this are reason enough to keep an interestingly stocked pantry. **SERVES 1**

- CD's Basic At-Home Light Omelet for One, or one of the other omelet bases (page 884)
- About 1½ tablespoons crumbled goat cheese
- 1 teaspoon nutritional yeast (see page 239)
- ½ small tomato, diced, or 1½ teaspoons diced sun-dried tomatoes
- 1 or 2 marinated artichoke hearts, coarsely chopped
- Scissored fresh basil or Italian parsley (optional)
- Freshly ground black pepper
- 1 scallion, sliced, or 1 teaspoon minced red onion

1 Prepare the omelet through Step 4 as directed on page 884.

2 Scatter the omelet with all the remaining ingredients, roll or fold, and serve.

Farmer's Omelet

The heartiest of the lot, this is quick-fix only if you have some leftover cooked potatoes in the fridge. Very enjoyable. When the clock isn't ticking, sauté the onion and peppers in a little oil or butter before adding them. If you're able to serve this with cornbread or corn muffins, you'll find its pleasing rusticity enhanced.

SERVES 1

- CD's Basic At-Home Light Omelet for One, or one of the other omelet bases (page 884)
- About 1½ tablespoons grated extra-sharp Cheddar
- 1½ teaspoons diced onion
- 1½ teaspoons diced red or green bell pepper, or both
- 1 small cooked potato, diced and warmed
- Dash of Pickapeppa sauce

1 Prepare the omelet through Step 4 as directed on page 884.

2 Scatter the omelet with all remaining ingredients, roll or fold, and serve.

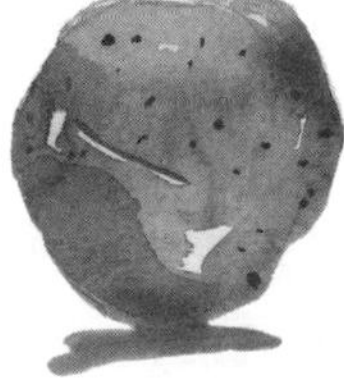

VARIATION

Omit the pepper; substitute scallion for the onion, and add a few tablespoons of spinach, either leftover steamed spinach or fresh baby leaves. Or, in summer, add slices of rich, red garden or farmstand tomatoes.

San Antonio Omelet

VARIATION

SANTA FE OMELET: ***Omit the avocado, tomato, and onion. Use a couple of tablespoons of New Mexico–Style Green Chile Sauce (page 942) or commercially made green chile sauce. Substitute well-drained canned black beans for the pintos. Serve with grilled whole wheat tortillas.***

Hot does it for me every time. I combine these flavors often, in scrambles or with grains. The eggs are even better served with Sweet Harvest Applesauce Breakfast Bundt Cake (page 1015) or cinnamon toast. Garnish with a sprig of cilantro, a dollop of Yogurt Sour Cream, (page 910), reduced-fat sour cream, or Tofu Sour Cream (page 909), maybe more avocado, and your favorite salsa. **SERVES 1**

CD's Basic At-Home Light Omelet for One, or one of the other omelet bases (page 884)
About 1½ tablespoons grated Monterey Jack cheese
¼ avocado, peeled and pitted, sliced lengthwise
1½ teaspoons diced onion
1 teaspoon minced cilantro, or more to taste
½ fresh tomato, chopped
About 2 tablespoons cooked or canned pinto beans, drained and warmed
Dash of adobo sauce (from canned chipotle chiles)

1 Prepare the omelet through Step 4 as directed on page 884.

2 Scatter the omelet with all the remaining ingredients, roll or fold, and serve.

Scrambled Eggs

These are even simpler, obviously; no rolling or folding. With good nonstick skillets, it's possible to make these with no added butter at all, but a little Better (page 905) does enrich them. What liquid do you scramble your eggs with? Milk or plain soy milk gives a creamy custardiness, water makes it eggier, but carbonated water gives a surprising lightness. I even know a couple who use beer as the scrambling liquid. Oddly enough, it's tasty—the eggs taste like themselves, yet with indefinable body and flavor. Holding back a little of the liquid egg mixture, then adding it at the end adds a pleasing fluffy moistness to the eggs. Try it and see if you don't like the difference this simple fillip makes. **SERVES 2**

3 large eggs, preferably free-range
⅓ cup milk, plain soy milk, water, preferably spring or filtered, carbonated water, or beer
1 teaspoon butter or Better (page 905; optional)
Salt and freshly ground black pepper to taste
Seasonings and add-ins (suggestions follow)

1 Put a small nonstick skillet on over medium-low heat.

2 Combine the eggs with about two-thirds of the liquid of choice in a small bowl and whisk them with a fork for 10 or 20 seconds, or until all is combined but not uniform (reserve the last tablespoon or two of liquid).

3 Raise the heat under the skillet a tiny bit. Add the butter, if using, and when it has melted, sizzled, and ceased to sizzle or when pan is good and hot, pour in the eggs. Scrape the eggs slowly but constantly, using a spatula and a pushing motion, then a stir, then a push, to combine cooked egg with uncooked egg.

4 When the eggs are about halfway done, add salt, plenty of pepper, and seasonings and add-ins. When almost done, add the remaining liquid. Remove from the heat when they're still a tad underdone; they'll continue cooking off the heat.

Add-Ins for Scrambles

First, look at the omelet fillings. Most of the filling components can be stirred into the scramble. I particularly like the mixture used in the Mykonos omelet; to me, dill plus eggs plus feta has a synergistic magic.

But here's one that we do only scrambled; in fact, we used to serve it an the inn as French Scrambled Eggs: Add about 1 tablespoon neufchâtel cheese, scooped into small bits, and a thinly sliced scallion or two—so fresh and good.

Another way, much loved by children, is to scramble some well-drained, best-quality cottage cheese into the eggs and serve with a dollop of jam on the side.

Eggs in Hell

Eggs poached in good tomato sauce! What could be more revolutionary, tastier, quicker?

For at least the first decade of my cooking life—before our culture demonized eggs, cheese, and fat in general—this was one of my all-time favorite quick fall-back dishes: showy, off-beat, both familiar and exotic, extraordinarily good. I never served it to anyone who didn't love it, and I delighted in it every time. Scrumptious over pasta or toasted Italian bread, for brunch, lunch, or dinner. Now I make it maybe once every two or three years, and each time I do I'm reminded of how very good it is.

"When one buys eggs one must take them on faith, but with most other things faith is unnecessary."

—Henri Charpentier, *Those Rich and Great Ones, or Life à la Henri*

I developed my original recipe—a slightly more time-consuming version is in the *Dairy Hollow House Cookbook*—from M. F. K. Fisher's in *With Bold Knife and Fork;* she found its predecessor in Irma Goodrich Mazza's charming *Herbs for the Kitchen,* now long out of print. **SERVES 4 TO 6**

2½ cups Basic Wintertime Italian Tomato Sauce (page 931) or any very tasty spaghetti sauce with a relatively low fat content
6 to 8 large eggs, preferably free-range
1 to 3 ounces freshly grated cheese, such as Parmesan, Cheddar, mozzarella, or Monterey Jack
8 French or Italian bread rounds, toasted, or cooked fettuccine, for serving
Minced Italian parsley (optional)

1 Heat the tomato sauce in a 10½-inch nonstick skillet until bubbly hot. Using a spoon, pull back the sauce a bit to make an indentation and break one of the eggs into it. Repeat until all the eggs are nestled in. The level of the tomato sauce will rise and half cover all the eggs, but you can help things along by spooning a bit of sauce over them.

2 With the heat at medium-low, cover the skillet tightly and let the eggs poach, keeping an eye on them. I like them with the whites cooked but still tender and the yolks still a bit runny. (I'm supposed to warn you here about salmonella in undercooked eggs. Okay, you're warned. See my notes on this on page 864.) This takes about 8 minutes, and some eggs may be a bit more done than others, depending on your burner. About halfway through, lift the lid and sprinkle the eggs with the cheese. Re-cover.

3 Set up plates with 1 or 2 pieces of toast, or a mound of pasta. Scoop an egg onto each toast; divide the tomato sauce among all the portions, spooning it over the eggs and bread or pasta. Of course you can doll this up with minced parsley if you like. Serve immediately.

Pasta & Eggs

What happens when you combine two quickies, leftover pasta and eggs? As with the milk toasts, something much more wonderfully synergistic than you'd think possible. And quick, too. These recipes alone are reason enough to cook more pasta than you need, but when you drop in pasta salads, reheated pasta under stir-frics, pasta casseroles—well, you see why this kind of cooking ahead saves you time and gives you turn-around room.

Parky's Pasta Frittata

I've long made frittatas—thick Italian omelets that start on the stove and finish in the oven—and long made pasta. I've even made pasta omelets, or pancakes. But it was not until John and Marge Parkhurst's July, 1996, edition of the *Pepper Mill* newsletter (see page 111) arrived that I considered trying pasta in frittata. Yum! Here is my version, drawn from theirs. **SERVES 2 OR 3 AS A SUPPER ENTREE**

1 tablespoon olive oil
½ large onion, thinly sliced
2 to 3 cloves garlic, pressed, or ½ to 1 teaspoon Garlic Oil (page 898)
4 large eggs, preferably free-range, beaten
1 ounce Parmesan cheese, freshly grated
1 to 2 cups leftover cooked pasta, such as leftover orzo or riso from Parky's Pepper Mill Pasta Salad à l'Italia (page 111)
2 to 3 teaspoons dried leaf herbs, such as oregano, basil, rosemary, and thyme, or a combination, or 2 tablespoons finely minced fresh herbs
Salt and freshly ground black pepper to taste
2 to 3 Roma or plum tomatoes, chopped
12 kalamata or oil-cured olives, pitted and halved

1 Preheat the broiler.

2 Heat the oil over medium heat in a nonstick ovenproof 8- to 9-inch pan. Add the onion and sauté for 3 minutes, then lower the heat slightly and add the garlic, sautéing for 2 minutes more.

3 Preheat the broiler. Combine the eggs, Parmesan, pasta, herbs, and salt and pepper and whisk well. Set aside.

4 Add the tomatoes and olives to the pan, and raise the heat. When everything is very hot, quickly pour in the eggs and turn the heat down to medium-low. Cook until the bottom of the eggs and edges of the frittata are becoming firm but the center and surface are still definitely liquid.

5 Quickly transfer the skillet to the broiler and broil until the top is lightly browned, 2 to 3 minutes. Remove from the broiler, loosen the edges of the fritatta, and turn out onto a serving plate. Serve, immediately, cut into wedges like a pie.

Dairy Hollow Broccoli-Potato Frittata

We used to make this rustic, hearty breakfast frittata at the inn, and it was always very well received. This is a quick one only if you have leftover broccoli and potatoes on hand. It can be dolled up, stripped down, improvised on indefinitely. The big trick with frittatas is to get them done through, but not overdone or rubbery. You want them firm but tender, so note that they do continue to cook a bit when removed from the heat. A larger skillet, hence a thinner frittata than is traditional, will help, as will making them a few times and getting a feel for how things work with your particular stove. **SERVES 3 OR 4**

"Small cheer and great welcome makes a merry feast."

—**William Shakespeare,** *The Comedy of Errors*

Cooking spray
4 large eggs, preferably free-range, beaten
¼ cup milk or reduced-fat sour cream
¼ cup freshly grated Parmesan cheese
3 small red potatoes, cooked and sliced into ¼-inch rounds
1 large spear cooked broccoli, florets cut off, stalk julienned
Salt and freshly ground black pepper to taste
2 teaspoons olive oil
½ cup grated Provolone, or a combination of mozarella and Cheddar cheese
About ¼ cup Breadcrumb Topping Provençal (page 277; optional)

1 Preheat the broiler.

2 Combine the eggs, milk or sour cream, and Parmesan and whisk well. Stir in the potatoes, broccoli, salt, and lots of pepper. Set aside.

3 Heat the oil over medium heat in a nonstick ovenproof 8- to 9-inch pan.

4 When the pan is hot, add the egg mixture and turn the heat down to medium-low. Cook until the bottom of the eggs and edges of the frittata are becoming firm but the center and surface are still definitely liquid. Sprinkle on the grated cheese, then the breadcrumbs.

5 Quickly transfer the skillet to the broiler and broil until the top is lightly browned, 2 to 3 minutes. Remove from the broiler, loosen the edges of the frittata, and turn out onto a serving plate. Serve, immediately, cut into wedges like a pie.

Spaghetti Pancake

The minute I saw the recipe for spaghetti pancake in Jane Brody's *Good Food Book,* I knew I would love it. Of course, I also love to tinker, so I have added a few flourishes of my own (Garlic Oil, anyone?). Jane Brody's recipe will serve four. Not mine! Mine serves two, and the one that didn't serve it is likely to ask hopefully, "Is there any more?" knowing full well there isn't.

Whenever I cook pasta, some of the leftovers are allocated for this great breakfast, lunch, or supper dish. (This recipe also works well with offbeat grain pastas, such as corn, buckwheat, or quinoa pasta.) To get a nice golden-brown cake, don't be in too much of a rush to flip it over. The waiting, as the old Tom Petty and the Heartbreakers song says, is the hardest part. **SERVES 2 OR 3**

1 large egg white, preferably free-range
1 whole large egg, preferably free-range
1 teaspoon Garlic Oil (page 898)
2 tablespoons milk
4 cups cooked spaghetti
¼ cup freshly grated Parmesan cheese
Salt and freshly ground black pepper to taste
Pinch of cayenne
1 teaspoon butter
Cooking spray
Crushed red pepper (optional)

1 In a medium bowl, whisk together the egg white and egg. Add the Garlic Oil and milk and, lastly, stir in the pasta. The egg mixture will not come anywhere near covering the pasta; just stir and toss to coat well. Stir in the Parmesan and season with salt, lots of pepper, and cayenne.

2 Melt the butter over medium heat in a 10- to 12-inch nonstick skillet or one that has been sprayed with cooking spray. When the butter has sizzled and then become silent, pour in the egg-spaghetti mixture, all at once.

3 Cook over medium-low heat for about 10 minutes, or until the bottom of the cake is golden brown. Using the edge of your spatula—a plastic one if you're using nonstick—cut the pancake in half down the middle, or in quarters, and carefully flip each one. Let brown. Serve, immediately, hot, with the crushed red pepper, if desired.

Quick Miscellany

Here are a few quickies that defy categorization, pulled from other corners of this book on the basis of their speedy preparation. These, with Garlic Spaghetti, may well be the gems of this chapter. "There is," as Francis Bacon wrote, "no excellent beauty that hath not some strangeness in the proportion." In these two recipes you will find both strangeness and excellence.

Mother-of-Invention Quick Quasi-Thai Stew

Iced in at Moonshine Cottage, my writing studio, on a January night of bone-chilling cold, Ned and I had considerably less stuff on hand by way of fresh or even frozen ingredients than is usual for us, because we were about to leave on our annual off-season trip. While admittedly what our rummage through the pantry turned up is more exotic than most folks probably keep on hand, we were delighted and surprised to (1) find anything at all, and (2) unearth such an intriguing, lemony, haunting blend of flavors.

The sauce is tart but made velvety with coconut milk and tinted the palest possible pink from the purple cabbage. Ned and I both felt it was something of an off-the-cuff miracle. Its tanginess would probably be excessive were it not balanced out by rice. You can cook Thai jasmine rice in 15 minutes, Uncle Ben's in 20, brown rice under pressure in 22. If all else fails, serve over pasta. **SERVES 3 OR 4**

NOTE

This recipe calls for a commercially made product: A Taste of Thai tangy coconut ginger soup mix. Each package of the soup contains two envelopes. You'll use just one in this recipe.

- **1 can (14 ounces) reduced-fat coconut milk**
- **1 envelope A Taste of Thai tangy coconut ginger soup mix**
- **1 or 2 large spears broccoli, cut into florets, stems peeled and diced**
- **¼ head red cabbage, coarsely shredded**
- **4 to 6 shiitake mushrooms, stems removed and caps sliced**
- **4 ounces commercially made savory baked tofu, finely diced**

1 Heat the coconut milk to a boil in a large skillet, then reduce the heat to a simmer. Whisk in the envelope of soup mix.

2 Add the broccoli, cabbage, mushrooms, and tofu. Stir well and simmer, uncovered, for 2 minutes. Cover. Reduce the heat slightly and simmer, covered, just till vegetables are crisp-tender, 2 to 4 minutes. Serve hot.

"Pot Roast" of Seitan, Aunt Gloria–Style

This is fast and seriously good. Weird as it sounds, try it once and you'll come back to it. Children are thrilled with it too. It's virtually instant to put together, but does need to simmer for 15 minutes. If you get really crunched, forgo sautéing the onion.

"YOU MUST HAVE SPENT HOURS OVER THE STOVE" DINNER

The Salad
(PAGE 68)

*

Creamy portobello mushroom soup (aseptically packaged, natural foods store brand zapped with a shot of sherry and a grating of nutmeg)

*

"Pot Roast" of Seitan Aunt Gloria–Style

*

Sautéed potato pancakes, commercially made (frozen)

*

Chocolate ice cream or Soy Delicious, with a good commercial bittersweet hot fudge sauce and thawed frozen rasperries

Now to the recipe's provenance. I'll bet my Aunt Gloria—my father's sister—is going to be astonished that I still have the recipe for the meatballs with the totally bizarre but inexplicably delicious cranberry-and-tomato sauce that she gave me back in 1969, and that that self-same recipe has been converted, to surface again almost thirty years later with seitan. You end up with a sweet-sour sauce, given attitude by the horseradish. It's still a wildly improbable combination, still easy, still infinitely better than it has any right to be.

Serve over pasta or any cooked grain or with mashed potatoes. **SERVES 3 OR 4**

Cooking spray
2 teaspoons mild vegetable oil, such as corn, canola, or peanut
1 large onion, thinly sliced
1½ cups tomato sauce, commercial or homemade, such as Basic Wintertime Italian Tomato Sauce (page 931)
1 can (16 ounces) jellied cranberry sauce
1 tablespoon prepared horseradish
1 teaspoon dry mustard
3 tablespoons red wine vinegar
¼ cup Oven-Roasted Vegetable Stock (page 141), or commercial mushroom stock, or 1 tablespoon tamari or shoyu soy sauce plus 3 tablespoons red wine
16 ounces (2 packages) traditional-style seitan, well drained and sliced about ⅜ inch thick

1. Heat a large nonstick Dutch oven or one that has been sprayed with cooking spray. When hot, add the oil and onion and sauté over medium heat for about 5 minutes, or until the onion starts to soften.

2. Add the tomato sauce, cranberry sauce, horseradish, dry mustard, vinegar, and stock. Raise the heat and bring the sauce to a hard boil. Lower the heat to medium and simmer, uncovered, stirring occasionally, for about 15 minutes.

3. Add the seitan. Lower the heat to a simmer and cook, covered, for 15 minutes more. Serve hot, or refrigerate overnight, reheat, and serve the next day.

Sauces, Salsas & Seasonings

What's sauce for the goose may well be sauce for the gander. But when one eats little or no goose or gander, a sauce—or salsa, relish, seasoning paste, or dip—is for almost anything. Such finishes add countless shades to the flavor palette of a meatless diet. We're talking the gravy for your mashed potatoes, the salsa for your burrito. We're talking deep, dark mushroom sauce to give elegance and mystery to the plainest grains. We're talking about taking that skillet of simple sautéed vegetables on a trip around the world, with a ticket to Thailand, Italy, or India, and many other stops as well, written strictly by sauce. We're talking silken, seductive tahini, a magic carpet ride to the Middle East in a mouthful.

Sauces and other savory finishings get a bad rap in some circles, often deemed high fat or fussy. Certainly they can be, but they can just as easily be light to moderate in fat content, and simply made. Some of the most irresistible sauces are the essence of simplicity and healthfulness: Salsa verde is just raw vegetables and herbs tossed in a food processor, but how good it is! I have offered you a few high-fat sauces here for occasional indulgence, though the fat is usually from nuts or coconut milk, not cream. On the whole, I've stayed away from those.

You will, however, find a world of different sauce foundations, deeply flavored and colored. There are sauces based on vegetables from classic tomato, to vivid beet, to roasted vegetables, sauces based on stocks, dairy and grain milks, herbs, and even a few surprises, like legumes and lemons. Besides sauces, you'll find salsas galore, a few sweet-savory chutneys, and various seasoning pastes that might be called starts rather than finishes.

So—let's take a gander.

Starts, Salts & Seasonings

Garlic Oil

Invest twenty minutes in making a batch of this oil, and your food will taste better, be more quickly prepared, and be easier to clean up after, for at least a month or so. Yes, you can buy pureed garlic, but it usually has vinegar added as a preservative and its volatile oils have begun to oxidize, changing its flavor.

Garlic oil is simply peeled garlic cloves pureed in olive oil and kept under refrigeration. You can make it thin or you can make it pastelike. But there must be enough oil so that the garlic bits are completely covered in oil; otherwise, with exposure to air, the flavor changes and you lose freshness. I use garlic oil almost every time minced or pressed garlic is called for in a recipe—it saves my cleaning a garlic press and a cutting board hundreds of times a year. I add it toward the end of a preliminary sauté of onions and aromatics, just long enough to swizzle it around a bit before adding the liquid. But I also sometimes stir it into soups in the last few minutes of cooking if the flavor doesn't seem to be quite right, and it makes doing Greek-style vegetables (pages 689, 775, 799) a dream. The two places I don't use it are in Asian food, in which olive oil is not the fat traditionally used and hence sounds an off note, and in making The Salad (page 68), in which absolutely fresh-from-the-press garlic is required. I suggest doubling this recipe if you are a garlic-loving cook. **MAKES ABOUT 1 CUP**

NOTE

Refrigeration is a must whenever the Garlic Oil is not in use. Don't leave it out at room temperature for more than a few minutes under any circumstances.

1 cup garlic cloves, peeled
1 cup extra virgin olive oil

1 Combine the garlic and olive oil in a food processor. Buzz until a paste is formed, pausing to scrape down the sides of the workbowl with a rubber spatula and adding as much oil as needed, either directly into the bowl or through the feeder tube. Turn out into a clean jar and refrigerate immediately. It will solidify under refrigeration.

2 To use, just scoop out as much of the soft paste as is called for. Garlic Oil is at its best within a week of being made, but I have used it for as long as a month.

Roasted Garlic

Garlic sweetens and becomes mild as it cooks. Although I usually prefer using it raw and lusty, sometimes this tamed-down version is just what I want in sauces, adding a subtle sweetness with a savor that creeps up on you. Roasted garlic is also good squeezed right out of the skin onto crusty bread slices.

MAKES ½ TO ⅔ CUP ROASTED GARLIC CLOVES

VARIATION

ROASTED GARLIC PUREE: ***Squeeze the cooked cloves out of the 10 heads of roasted garlic. Assuming the cloves are cooked through to complete and melting tenderness, you can mash them to a semismooth paste with a fork. Or, if they are a bit firmer, puree them in a food processor or a mini-processor (the latter is preferred, since we are talking small quantities here). Ten medium heads of roasted garlic yield about 1¼ cups puree.***

10 heads garlic, pointy ends sliced off so tops of cloves are barely exposed
1 tablespoon olive oil
Cooking spray
1 cup vegetable stock

1 Preheat the oven to 325°F.

2 Rub the garlic heads with the oil. Place them in a nonstick 13-by-9-inch baking dish, or one that has been sprayed with cooking spray, and pour in the stock.

3 Roast slowly until the garlic is very soft, 60 to 75 minutes. Let cool slightly.

4 Serve warm, in the skin, for guests to squeeze out their own, or squeeze out the bulbs yourself to make Roasted Garlic puree. (Save any leftover stock in the pan for another use; it's extra-flavorful for sauces or soups.)

Dragon Salt

Some years ago at the inn we used a hot but nicely herbal seasoning salt from New Orleans. The packaging—a round yellow tube with bright aquatic drawings—made it resemble a canister of fish food, but I loved it anyway, even though I wasn't wild about the granulated garlic it included. I am mad for garlic, but with drying and granulating, it loses the best of its soul, leaving only the worst of its flesh.

I used the seasoning salt for a while on almost anything—pasta, vegetables, egg dishes of all kinds. When it became unavailable, I began making my own, which a member of the inn's kitchen staff christened Dragon Salt. I love the homemade version even more, because it has all the good herbal flavors and heat, but no granulated garlic.

When using Dragon Salt, I often put a little Garlic Oil (page 898) in the same dish. If you have both the oil and this salt on hand, you can make Greek-Style Summer Squash or green beans (pages 799 and 689) very easily. **MAKES ABOUT 1½ CUPS**

- ⅓ cup salt, preferably sea salt
- ⅓ cup medium-coarsely ground fresh black pepper
- ¼ cup ground cayenne
- ¼ cup dried dillweed
- 2 tablespoons sweet Hungarian paprika
- 1 tablespoon dried basil leaves
- 1 tablespoon celery seeds

1 Combine all the ingredients and toss gently. Stand back as you toss; tossing the cayenne can be cough-producing.

2 Transfer to a jar with a tight-fitting lid. This keeps indefinitely, though it begins to lose potency after a year or so.

Dairy Hollow House Curry Spice Blend

This recipe may necessitate a trip to the spice store, but it is oh so very much better than commercial curry powder. Sweet, hot, filled with flavors that subtly burst on the tongue like fireworks, this seasoning once earned the Inn a rave in *Gourmet*. **MAKES 1 GENEROUS CUP**

- ⅓ cup coarsely ground black fresh pepper
- ¼ cup ground cumin
- 3 tablespoons dry mustard
- 3 tablespoons best-quality curry powder
- 1½ tablespoons ground cardamom
- 1½ tablespoons ground coriander
- 1 tablespoon ground mace
- 1 tablespoon freshly grated nutmeg
- 1 tablespoon ground cinnamon
- 1 tablespoon ground cloves
- 1½ teaspoons cayenne

Combine all the ingredients and store in a tightly covered jar. If stored in a dark, cool place, this blend will keep for about a year with no diminution of flavor. Use this mix anywhere curry powder is called for.

NOTE

Canela is the variety of cinnamon used in Mexico; it is softer and more flavorful than what we usually get. It grinds more easily, too.

Garam Masala

A toasted spice mixture—different from curry powder—garam masala is generally stirred into curries at the end for a final complex layering of flavor. You can add a bit of garam masala at the very last to almost any curry, whether or not the recipe calls for it, with good results. Though there are as many variations as there are cooks, garam masalas are not hot (a curry's chiles are added in a separate step), and they never contain turmeric. You can buy garam masala ready-made at Indian markets, but most curry-heads wind up making their own sooner or later. This is a good blend.

A spice grinder can be a dedicated mini-processor, a hand-cranked small old-fashioned coffee grinder, a hand-cranked spice grinder, or a mortar and pestle.

MAKES A GENEROUS ½ CUP

- ¼ cup coriander seeds
- 3 tablespoons cumin seeds
- 2 tablespoons cardamom seeds
- 3 tablespoons black peppercorns
- 2 sticks cinnamon, preferably canela
- 4 bay leaves
- 1 teaspoon whole cloves
- 1 whole nutmeg

Combine all the spices except the nutmeg in a dry, heavy skillet. Toast over medium heat, stirring constantly, for about 3 minutes, or until fragrant and slightly browned. Remove from the heat and scrape into a bowl to stop the cooking process. Grate about ⅓ of the nutmeg directly onto the toasted spices. Transfer the mixture to a spice grinder and pulverize to a fine powder. Store, tightly covered, for up to 8 months.

Chile Buzz

Nirvana for lovers of serious heat. I can't tell you what a lift this gives a midwinter plate of scrambled eggs or tofu wrapped up in a whole wheat tortilla, or a plate of rice and black beans. It's not for the weak of palate, though. Buzz doesn't need refrigeration, because the vinegar and salt preserve it (though of course if you want to refrigerate it, you may). My preferred type of storage jar for the Buzz is an old peanut butter jar—a glass jar with a tight-fitting yellow plastic lid. Metal lids and rings don't work here; if the Buzz were to come into prolonged contact with such a lid, it would corrode the metal. **QUANTITY VARIABLE**

3 parts assorted hot chiles, stemmed
1 part garlic cloves, peeled
Salt
Cider vinegar, red wine vinegar, sherry vinegar, or white wine vinegar, as needed

Put the chiles into a food processor and pulse/chop, standing away from the chile fumes. Add the garlic and about 1 teaspoon salt for every 1½ cups of the mixture. Add enough vinegar to half-cover the chiles and garlic. Pulse to a salsa-like puree. Pour into a clean jar, cover, and keep at room temperature. Keeps indefinitely.

Wendy's Sherried Ginger–Gingered Sherry

As well as sharing her revised (and wonderful) version of my pumpkin-apple soup with curry and cream (see Wendy's Pumpkin-Apple Soup with Curry and Coconut Milk, page 152), Wendy Schatz, a *Soup & Bread* reader from Bethesda, Maryland, wrote me the following: "I store leftover fresh ginger cut into coins in dry sherry."

This is a *great* tip. It means that you will never again have those little nubs of left-over ginger that mold or dry out before you have a chance to use them. The sherry (I prefer sweet sherry) and ginger are fabulous flavoring agents; the ginger can be diced and used in lieu of fresh ginger in almost any recipe. **QUANTITY VARIABLE**

FULL-MOON CHRISTMAS EVE DINNER

Antipasto Platter: Mediterranean Cornucopia of Olives (PAGE 44)
Marinated Beets (SEE PAGE 702)
Marinated Vegetable Antipasti (PAGE 46)
Sliced provolone

*

Homemade French bread, Bread Herbs for Dipping (PAGE 904), **olive oil**

*

Polenta Lasagna (PAGE 374) **and Jenelle's Tomatoes Rockefeller** (PAGE 430)

*

Double-Density Chocolate-Walnut-Espresso Torte (PAGE 1003)

*

Vanilla frozen yogurt, gelato, or Soy Delicious; Persimmon Sorbet (PAGE 1046)

*

Hazelnut Biscotti (PAGE 1037), **organic Costa Rican decaf**

Fresh ginger, peeled and cut into rounds
Good—but not tip-top-quality—sweet sherry

Place the ginger in a clean jar and pour the sherry over it. Refrigerate until the ginger sinks, adding pieces of ginger as you have them. As long as there is more sherry than ginger, this will keep, refrigerated, virtually indefinitely.

Bread Herbs for Dipping

Many restaurants now bring olive oil to the table, in place of or in addition to butter, for bread. To my taste this only works well with gutsy, crisp-crusted bread and very, very good olive oil. But it works even better when a second item is also provided—a mixture of dried herbs, hot peppers, salt, and pepper—a simple trick that too few restaurants offer. Here's what you do: Pour a little puddle of olive oil on your bread plate, and place a spoonful of the herb mixture (I like *a lot*) beside the oil. Take your crusty bread, just barely dip it into the oil, then plunge it into the herbs. Eat.

The dryness of the herbs is essential. All the herbs should be dried leaf herbs—not ground, not fresh. Assuming the herbs were fairly recently dried when you mixed the dip, it will keep its potency nicely for nine months to a year. **MAKES ABOUT 2 CUPS**

½ cup dried whole oregano leaves
½ cup dried whole thyme leaves
½ cup dried basil leaves
¼ to ½ cup crushed red pepper

FOR SERVING
Medium-coarse or kosher salt
Black pepper in a pepper mill
Bread, preferably a rustic Italian, French, or other European-style bread, sliced, warmed slightly if desired
Extra virgin olive oil in a cruet

1 Combine all the herbs and the red pepper and toss well.

2 When ready to serve, either place in a dish for guests to serve themselves or pile 2 to 3 teaspoons on a corner of each bread plate. Sprinkle the herbs lightly with salt, then grind black pepper liberally over them. Dip the bread in the oil, then the herbs.

Basics

Some basics we all know—mayonnaise, for instance, or sour cream. But here you'll find both made with tofu. If you are not a tofu fan already, this may be your conversion experience. Though these concoctions are old friends of longtime natural-foods aficionados and vegetarians, those new to these dishes may be skeptical—until the first taste. Make sure you use the smooth, moist variety of tofu known as "silken" (see page 655) for these recipes.

In addition to the tofu mayos and a couple of other alternative-style creams, a few simple splashes (fast and great for perking up vegetables, fat-free style) appear here, as does Salt of the Earth Breadspread (page 911).

Better

Better than *what?* This mixture of butter and oil is better than straight butter for almost everything except some baking: It's just as delicious as butter, but more healthful, easier to spread, and better for sautéing because its smoking point is higher than that of plain butter. It's better than margarine, more healthful than many of the trans-fatty-acid- or hydrogenated-fat-containing brands on the market, and certainly much tastier than any of them. And it's better than oil for many kinds of toast: Sure, the olive oil and herb thing is great, but do you really want it at Sunday brunch, or on cinnamon-raisin toast?

I vary the oils I use with the butter, alternating any of the three exceptionally buttery, mild-tasting oils listed in the ingredients list, or combining them. Although they're not the ones that have received the most press for healthfulness, I tend to think that's just because they're more obscure (and a little more expensive). You may call this unscientific, but remember, the greater the variety of foods you eat, the better your chance of ingesting still-unidentified health-benefiting phytochemicals and other good-for-you components.

Quickly made in a food processor, a batch of this concoction lasts about two and a half months. I divide it among three or four ramekins, refrigerating one and freezing the others. Get into the habit of making Better, and you'll never scrape hard butter onto your toast again: This isn't just a health thing, it's a pleasure thing.

I prefer salted butter, but you could also use unsalted and/or omit the bit of salt I add. **MAKES 4½ CUPS**

1 pound salted butter, preferably organic, at room temperature
2½ cups macadamia nut, almond, or avocado oil, or a combination
1¾ teaspoons fine sea salt, or more to taste

1 Combine the softened butter with the oils and salt in a food processor and buzz until smooth, scraping the sides of the processor occasionally.

2 Transfer the mixture into a small and presentable container as well as a storage container or two. Serve, from fridge to table, in its presentable container. Thaw and use the remainder as needed.

Tofu Mayonnaise

VARIATION

STREAMLINED VERSION: ***Omit the olive oil, mustard, and lemon juice.***

Not only is tofu mayo much lower in fat than traditional mayonnaise, not only is it easier to put together (three minutes, max), not only will it make vegan diners very happy, but it is just plain delicious—fresh tasting and lemony, smooth and creamy, without the richness of classic mayo or the fakeness of low-fat ersatz mayo. I promise you will love this. Use it as the basis for any dip for which you'd ordinarily use mayo or sour cream.

Umeboshi plum paste may sound like a strange ingredient, but it just *makes* this recipe. I used to make it without the umeboshi; you certainly can do so, and it will be good, but somehow the umeboshi sets it off to a T. Add this to your list of things to buy at the natural foods market. **MAKES ABOUT 2 CUPS**

1 (10½-ounce) box silken tofu, preferably soft, reduced fat
1 tablespoon extra virgin olive oil
½ to 1 heaping teaspoon Dijon mustard
Juice of 1 lemon
1 heaping teaspoon umeboshi plum paste (see page 118)
½ to 1 teaspoon salt
Several grinds of black pepper

1 Combine all the ingredients in a food processor and buzz until very smooth. Taste and adjust the seasonings.

2 Transfer to a storage container or jar. Use immediately or refrigerate. This will keep for up to 4 days, thickening and releasing water slightly over time. Drain off any water that accumulates.

All-American-Style Tofu Mayonnaise

I prefer the plain tofu mayo, but some prefer the slight sweetness in this one. It is astonishingly good, with a creamy texture distinct from but definitely akin to traditional mayonnaise. **MAKES ABOUT 2 CUPS**

1 (10½-ounce) box silken tofu, preferably soft, reduced fat
1 tablespoon white or cider vinegar
2 teaspoons sugar, honey, or rice syrup
1 teaspoon salt
Several grinds of black pepper
1 teaspoon Dijon mustard
2 to 3 tablespoons mild vegetable oil, such as corn, canola, or peanut

1 Combine all the ingredients in a food processor and buzz until very smooth. Taste and adjust seasonings.

2 Transfer to a storage container or jar. Use immediately or refrigerate. This will keep for up to 4 days, thickening and releasing water slightly over time. Drain off any water that accumulates.

Tofu Mayos

Tofu mayonnaises can be used in many ways, from spreading on sandwiches or veggie burgers to serving as the base for an artichoke dipping sauce. They are vegan, they are healthful, they are delicious. A little can also be buzzed into a vinaigrette-type dressing to make it creamy.

Tofu mayonnaise keeps for several days under refrigeration. A bit of water—1 or 2 teaspoons—releases from the mayo as it sits, tending to make it thicker. Pour off the water or stir it back in before using the mayo, depending on thickness desired.

Herbed Tofu Mayonnaise

Another winning variation on a theme. A fine dip for simple crudités, too. I like to use a mixture of different varieties of basil—a tablespoon or so each of variegated lemon basil, Thai basil, curly basil, and globe basil. I also sometimes throw in a charred, peeled, stemmed, and seeded red or yellow bell pepperor a poblano or two. **MAKES ABOUT 2 CUPS**

VARIATION

To make a really lovely and interesting salad dressing or sauce, use ½ cup basil and ½ cup cilantro leaves and omit the other herbs. Add ¼ cup extra virgin olive oil and plenty of freshly ground black pepper.

- 1 recipe Tofu Mayonnaise (page 906) or All-American-Style Tofu Mayonnaise (page 907)
- 2 cloves garlic or squeezed-out cloves of 1 head Roasted Garlic (page 899)
- ¼ cup basil leaves
- 2 teaspoons rosemary leaves
- 2 sprigs tarragon or Mexican marigold (see page 37), leaves stripped from the stems (2 teaspoons to 1 scant tablespoon loosely packed leaves)
- ¼ to ⅓ cup Italian parsley leaves
- Salt and freshly ground black pepper to taste

1 Combine all the ingredients in a food processor and buzz until very smooth. Taste and adjust the seasonings.

2 Transfer to a storage container or jar. Use immediately or refrigerate. This will keep for up to 4 days, thickening and releasing water slightly over time. Drain off any water that accumulates.

MYO Sauce

MYO means Make Your Own. Simple as that. This sauce is proof that vegetarian dishes can have at least a touch of the funky charm of a New Orleans oyster bar. I have known people to eat this with boiled potatoes, chicken-fried tofu, tempeh, and vegetarian patties of all types. Kids adore it, though they tend to forego the horseradish and Tabasco. **QUANTITY VARIABLE**

Tofu Mayonnaise (page 906) and/or regular mayonnaise
Ketchup, homemade (see page 923), from the natural foods store, or good ol' Heinz
Cocktail sauce
Fresh lemon wedges
Tabasco sauce
Prepared horseradish
Pickapeppa sauce
Zhoug (page 919)

Set all the ingredients on the table. Supply a small dish for each person, so each can mix up his or her own ideal dipping sauce.

Tofu Sour Cream

It's not that Tofu Sour Cream tastes like dairy sour cream, it's that it's sour cream in a parallel universe—a thousand times more delicious and authentic in the mouth than those repellent non-fat "sour creams" (a product one feels compelled to put quotation marks around). It's hard to believe how good Tofu Sour Cream is. Use it virtually anywhere you'd use conventional or yogurt sour cream: in dips, dolloped on Mexican dishes, in baked goods, or sweetened and served over fruit. Vegans get very happy with this as an option; nonvegans love it too. The umeboshi plum paste, which is salty and sour yet has the tiniest trace of bitter and sweet to it, is optional, but to me it is the magic ingredient. Silken tofu gives a voluptuous creaminess. **MAKES ABOUT 1¾ CUPS**

1 (10½-ounce) box silken tofu, preferably soft, reduced fat
1 teaspoon umeboshi plum paste (see page 118)
½ teaspoon salt
2 tablespoons extra virgin olive oil, mild vegetable oil, tahini, or cashew butter
1½ tablespoons sugar, honey, Rapidura, or rice syrup, or to taste (optional)

1 Combine all the ingredients in a food processor and buzz until very smooth. Taste and adjust the seasonings.

2 Transfer to a storage container or jar. Use immediately or refrigerate. This will keep for up to 4 days, thickening and releasing water slightly over time. Drain off any water that accumulates.

NOTE

Use olive oil if you intend this for a savory use, such as with Mexican food, or soup, or as a dip for vegetables, toasts, or crisps; use any of the other oils if you plan to use it for a dessert or sweet dish. Add the sweetener then as well. You could add a drop of vanilla or almond extract, too.

Chipotle con Crema

Serve a dollop of this with enchiladas, tamales, black bean cakes, or plain beans and rice. A feast! You may make the sauce chunky by simply stirring in the diced adobo, or smooth by following the method below. If you want to fancy it up, make it extra-smooth by removing the seeds from the chipotles and adding a tablespoon or so more adobo sauce so the sauce can be easily squeezed from a squeeze bottle to make bright lines of color and flavor on the plate. **MAKES 1½ CUPS**

1¼ cups Tofu Sour Cream (page 909), dairy sour cream, low-fat dairy sour cream, Yogurt Sour Cream, or crème fraîche
2 medium canned chipotle peppers in adobo sauce
2 tablespoons adobo sauce

In a food processor, blend the Tofu Sour Cream with the chipotles and adobo, buzzing until smooth. Pause to scrape down the sides of the work bowl, and buzz again. This will keep for 4 or 5 days in the fridge.

VARIATION

YOGURT CREAM CHEESE: ***After the yogurt has reached sour cream consistency, stir in a tiny bit of salt, gather the edges of the cheesecloth up around the yogurt, and bind it at the top, tying it shut with a rubber band, twist-tie, or piece of string. Suspend this ball somewhere where its drips can be caught—on a hook above a bowl, or from the faucet above the sink. Let the yogurt hang overnight, or perhaps a little longer. Unwrap it—it will hold its shape and the cheesecloth will unfurl from it easily—and use just about anywhere you'd use cream cheese. 1 quart yogurt yields 1¼ to 1½ cups.***

Yogurt Sour Cream

Is it as high in fat as it tastes? "No whey!" Instead, this is a concentrated yogurt that can be used almost everywhere you'd use sour cream. Once you have it on hand, you will wonder how you did without it, and why no one ever told you about this. For a tangier yogurt sour cream, do the dripping at room temperature. **MAKES ABOUT 2½ CUPS**

1 quart plain fat-free yogurt

Line a colander with 2 layers of cheesecloth, set the colander over a baking dish to catch the water as it's released, and dump the yogurt into the colander. Cover with plastic wrap, refrigerate, and let the yogurt drip until it's of sour cream consistency, 3 to 4 hours. Turn the yogurt out of the cheesecloth-lined colander into a storage container, and use the concentrated yogurt instead of sour cream. This will keep, covered and refrigerated, for about 1 week.

Salt of the Earth Breadspread

A salty, savory, piquant spread that I first tasted on crackers at a tiny health food store in New England almost thirty years ago. It's not at all butterlike in flavor, nor is it low-fat, but it is delicious, even haunting, in its own way. It's also cholesterol free and vegan and incorporates one of the traditional soy foods. Different varieties of miso give different colors and flavors to it. **MAKES 2 CUPS**

1 cup miso, any variety
1 cup tahini

Combine the miso and tahini in a food processor and buzz until smooth, thick, and thoroughly integrated. Serve in lieu of butter or olive oil as a spread for bread. Keep the spread refrigerated and bring it to room temperature before serving. Under refrigeration, this will keep indefinitely (the salty miso acts as a preservative).

VARIATIONS

Use almond, peanut, or cashew butter instead of tahini.

SALT-AND-SWEET OF THE EARTH BREADSPREAD: ***Roast some seeded, very sweet orange squash, a butternut or kabocha, say, or even a sweet potato. Scoop the flesh into the food processor with the other ingredients and buzz until smooth. This keeps for about 10 days in the refrigerator.***

Simple Splashes for Veggies

I am almost embarrassed to list these, yet all the time people say, "But if you don't use butter, what do you do?" These splashes are a little plain-jane for company but are standbys for family suppers. Just splish-splash 'em over whatever needs livening up, including pasta or grains.

FAT FREE:

- *A squeeze of fresh lemon*
- *A drop of tamari or shoyu soy sauce*
- *Lemon juice and tamari or shoyu soy sauce together*
- *Lemon juice, tamari or shoyu soy sauce, and a little freshly grated peeled ginger or ginger juice*
- *Vinegar: herbal, fruited, garlic, with a base of red or white wine, balsamic, cider, etc.*
- *Vinegar and tamari or shoyu soy sauce*
- *Thai Crystal (page 923)*
- *Lemon juice, tamari or shoyu soy sauce, Thai Crystal, and a bit of grated ginger*

NOT SO FAT FREE:

- *Garlic Oil (page 898)*
- *Toasted sesame oil*
- *Extra virgin olive oil*

Salsas

Salsas are not just for Southwestern foods. They embolden all paler dishes with their brilliant tones. They're good with pastas, with eggs, on baked potatoes, stirred into a sauce at the end to add a little soulful spark, and in salad dressings. Perhaps you've heard that, nearly a decade ago, salsa sales in America beat those of ketchup. Salsa devotees were not surprised. The real question is how did we live and eat before salsa exhilarated our meals?

Basic Fresh Summer Salsa, Pico de Gallo–Style

NOTE

My friend Emily Kaitz and her friend Marilyn Cain actually wrote a song about pico de gallo ***(see page 916).***

This is the best possible version of your basic Tex-Mex salsa—also called salsa cruda or salsa fresca—fresher than fresh, raw and red, and anything *but* basic. While you could throw it all in the blender, I think much of the charm of this salsa lies in carefully hand chopping its ingredients. I encourage you to do so. At the inn, we served a variation of this with featherbed eggs (see page 283), but it's great with any egg dish, and, of course, anything in the beans-and-rice and tortillas line.

The Spanish name *pico de gallo* means "beak of the rooster." There are many explanations for this name: that the chiles originally used were smaller ones shaped like a bird's beak; that the repeated dipping motion you make when eating this resembles a rooster pecking at grain; that the chopping you do resembles the rooster's pecking; that the pieces end up minced as fine as chicken feed. No matter which, if any, are true, you will like this. **MAKES ABOUT 2 CUPS**

Salsa, Salsa, Salsa . . .

All these salsas, except for the Smoked or Grilled Salsa, are best eaten pronto. The Basic Fresh Summer Salsa lends itself to countless variations with just a few added ingredients. Try some of these:

▲ **ARKANSALSA:** *Add 1 cup well-drained cooked or canned black-eyed peas or black beans to the salsa and toss well.*

▲ **ARKANSALSA WITH CORN:** *Use green or red peppers. Add corn kernels, cut from 2 or 3 ears, to the Arkansalsa and toss well.*

▲ **FRUITED SALSA:** *Substitute ½ peeled crisp apple, finely diced, for the bell pepper. Use fresh diced orange (peel, pith, and s eeds removed) instead of, or in addition to, the tomato.*

▲ **CHIPOTLE SALSA:** *Substitute 1 to 2 canned chipotles in adobo, diced, for the fresh jalapeño called for here, and cut the amount of tomato back to 1 small tomato. Trickle in a bit of adobo sauce, too. This is one hot salsa, but oh so good.*

▲ **SMOKED OR GRILLED SALSA:** *Smoking or grilling tomatoes, peppers, or other components of salsa adds the inimitable complexity only fire-kissed foods have. Smoke or grill any of the vegetables on your grill or in your smoker. When cool enough to handle, peel, stem, and seed them. The flavor of this salsa is even better the next day.*

▲ **WINTERTIME SALSA:** *During the colder, grayer months of the year, when supermarket bell peppers tend to be watery and the tomatoes worse, you can still get some brightness by omitting both of these ingredients. Instead, buzz a cup or so of good-quality canned tomatoes—you can even find canned organic fire-roasted diced tomatoes these days—in a food processor with 4 or 5 cloves of garlic, 2 tablespoons tomato paste, ⅔ cup chopped cilantro, ⅔ cup chopped Italian parsley, the chiles, salt, and lemon. When this is pureed, stir in the finely diced onion. This is more or less the salsa from the first* Dairy Hollow House Cookbook, *and one we often served at the inn with featherbed eggs (see page 283); I still love it.*

1 onion, finely diced
1 to 2 jalapeño peppers or green chiles, stemmed, about half the seeds and ribs removed, diced
½ yellow, green, or red bell pepper, stemmed, seeds and ribs removed, finely diced
1 large fresh tomato, diced, or 2 small Roma or plum tomatoes for less juicy salsa
⅔ cup chopped cilantro
1 teaspoon salt
1 lemon or lime, halved

1. Combine all the ingredients except the lemon or lime in a medium bowl and toss together.

2. Squeeze the lemon or lime into the salsa mixture through a strainer. Stir, taste, and correct the seasoning. Although the salsa will keep for a day or even two, refrigerated, it's at its best when eaten right away.

Chou Chou's Simple "Yer Cheating Heart" Salsa

My longtime Eureka pal Chou Chou appreciates good food, especially Tex-Mex, but bristles at having to spend too much time or money on it. Her quick fixes are excellent and always use time spent in the kitchen economically; that is, they cheat the clock. Here is one such primo shortcut. **MAKES ABOUT 1 QUART**

1 quart inexpensive, commercially made bottled salsa
1 bunch coarsely chopped cilantro leaves (about 1½ cups, loosely packed)
1 or 2 chipotle peppers in adobo sauce
2 teaspoons adobo sauce, or to taste

1 Combine all the ingredients in a food processor and pulse, then buzz, to make a slightly textured puree.

2 Transfer to a bottle and serve immediately or refrigerate. This keeps for about 1 week in the refrigerator.

Brazilian Salsa

Surely, surely this can't be the real thing—I mean, Tabasco Sauce is from Avery Island, Louisiana, not Rio, right?—but this relishy salsa is really, *really* addictively good (that is, if you are a devotee of comestibles hot, hotter, hottest). I can't remember where I first came across the recipe; it was ten or twelve years ago, when I was searching for items to balance our Brazilian Tasting Plate for Vegetarians back in the inn days. The Brazilian pedigree is probably false, but the original formula contained the same ingredients as in Tabasco: hot peppers and vinegar and salt, to which were added onions and oil. Then, I think, some enterprising American said, "Hey! Why not use Tabasco and simplify all this?" I only regret that I cannot credit that master- or mistressmind. Try this salsa with Black Bean Feijoada (page 602), but keep it on hand to brighten anything and make it interesting. It keeps indefinitely in the fridge. **MAKES ABOUT 1 CUP**

1 large red onion, thinly sliced crosswise
½ cup Tabasco sauce
1 teaspoon salt
1 tablespoon olive oil
2 tablespoons cider vinegar

Combine all the ingredients in a small bowl. And—that's it! Use immediately or let stand for up to a week; the vinegar keeps everything nice and fresh.

Pamela Jones's Absolutely Incredible Roasted Vegetable Salsa

The superlatives apply. Oh boy, do they. This is salsa to the nth degree: Roasting the vegetables is the source of the magic. Making this is a fairly big production, as salsas go. That is why this salsa makes a mega-size batch; you will want extra on hand. It keeps, refrigerated, for about a week, but I prefer to divide it among several 2-cup containers and freeze it. I make it in the summer, when fresh, local, organic peppers of countless varieties are available. Opening a thawed container on a bleak February day is luxury indeed.

Plan a trip to the produce section or farmer's market to make Pam's sauce. Each of the chiles called for—ancho or serrano chiles, Hungarian wax and jalapeño peppers—add their own personality and layers of flavor and heat to this sauce. And yes, it is hot. But so good. **MAKES ABOUT 1 QUART**

VARIATION

Char the peppers on the stove-top (see page 782) while the other vegetables roast, let them cool, then peel and seed them. This makes the peeling easier, and you get a nice charred flavor that helps boost the roasted flavor of the vegetables.

Cooking spray
12 Roma or plum tomatoes, halved
12 tomatillos, 2½ to 3 inches in diameter, husked and halved
1 large onion, quartered
1 head garlic, separated into cloves, unpeeled
5 serrano chiles, left whole
5 ancho or poblano chiles, left whole
4 hot Hungarian wax peppers (sometimes called hot banana peppers), left whole
4 jalapeño peppers, left whole
1 to 3 tablespoons olive oil, or more if needed
½ cup loosely packed cilantro leaves
1 teaspoon salt, or to taste
1 teaspoon cumin seeds, toasted (optional)

1 Preheat the oven to 400°F. Have ready three 12-by-15-inch baking sheets, either nonstick or ones that have been sprayed with cooking spray.

2 Combine the tomatoes, tomatillos, onion, garlic, chiles, and peppers in a large bowl. Toss with 1 tablespoon oil, or enough to gloss them, adding up to 2 tablespoons more if needed. Place the oiled vegetables on the prepared baking sheet, leaving air space around each vegetable.

3 Bake for about 40 minutes, or until the skins of the peppers are blistered and the garlic is soft.

4 Let the vegetables cool until you can handle the peppers. Peel them, stem them, and remove as many of the seeds and ribs as you wish. (Pamela removes them all, but I leave some, because I like stuff that is seriously hot.)

5 Place the peppers, tomatoes, tomatillos, and onion in a food processor. Squeeze the garlic cloves out of their skins directly into the processor. Buzz until smooth. Add the cilantro, salt, and cumin seed, if using, and buzz again. This salsa keeps for about a week in the fridge, but I suggest dividing it up into portions and freezing most of it in several smaller containers. It freezes well for up to 4 months.

COOK ONCE FOR 7 MEALS Use this to top enchiladas (see pages 340–45), on scrambled eggs or in omelets, on scrambled tofu, with chips, or with beans.

Pico de Gallo

Pico de gallo, you ought to give it a try-o
Even if you're from Ohio, it'll get you by-o
Don't get it in your eye-o, unless you want to cry-o
So come on don't be shy-o, eat some pico de gallo

It's got jalapeños, I reckon y'all have seen those
They're kinda hot for gringos, and probably flamingos
Just add some tomatillos, onions and cilantro
lime juice and tomatoes, you'll have pico de gallo
It was Cinco de Mayo, and I was down on the bayou
With my friend Venus de Milo, we were watching Hawaii Five-O
She wanted some French fry-o, or maybe apple pie-o,
But I said why-o why-o, when you got pico de gallo

—**Emily Kaitz and Marilyn Cain,** *Pico de Gallo,* © Pinglegobber Music

Mediterranean Rim Salsa

You could serve this bright, fresh, herbal blend of flavors and textures as a salsa, as a salad, as an appetizer, with toasted pita bread. It is the kind of food I like best: clear, simple, singing with flavor, good hot or cold.

All the herbs called for should be stripped from the tough, woody portions of the stem. You can increase or decrease amounts of particular herbs according to taste. You may also add a second jalapeño or other chile (I would), extra garlic (I would), or substitute green olives for the black (I would sometimes). **MAKES ABOUT 1 QUART**

1 medium cucumber, peeled if waxed, seeded, cut into ¼-inch dice
1 large ripe tomato, diced
1 onion, finely diced
1 fresh jalapeño pepper or green chile, stemmed, about half the seeds and ribs removed, finely diced
1 yellow or red bell pepper, charred, peeled, seeded, and diced
1 cup cilantro leaves, chopped
1 cup mint leaves, preferably spearmint, chopped
1 cup Italian parsley leaves, chopped
⅔ cup fresh basil leaves, chopped
⅔ cup fresh dill, chopped
2 cloves garlic, pressed
Freshly ground black pepper to taste
2 tablespoons extra virgin olive oil
½ cup pitted kalamata or dried olives, diced
1 to 2 lemons, halved
Salt to taste

1 Combine all the ingredients except the lemons and salt in a medium nonreactive bowl. Toss well to combine.

2 Add the juice of ½ lemon, squeezed through a strainer to catch the seeds. Toss the mixture again and taste for seasonings. (Salt may not be needed, since the olives are salty.) Add, as needed, the juice of the second, or a third or a fourth lemon half—whatever it takes to get it just right. Let stand at room temperature for at least 20 minutes before serving to let the flavors blend.

VARIATION

Add 1 to 2 teaspoons ground cumin, toasted in a hot dry skillet for about 3 minutes, or until fragrant.

Pestos & Seasoning Pastes

More colors to add to your seasoning palette. I never have all of these pestos and other seasoning pastes in my fridge at one time—but I'd never be without at least one or two. If you are convinced that you don't have time to make these, find yourself some brands you like from a good takeout place, gourmet shop, or natural foods market, and keep them in your fridge. See also Jamaican Wet-Jerk Marinade (page 744) and Green Curry Paste (page 202).

VARIATION

LEMON, BASIL, AND SUN-DRIED TOMATO PESTO

Use 2 tablespoons pine nuts, 6 cloves garlic, ½ cup sun-dried tomatoes, snipped into shreds, 3 cups basil, ¾ cup parsley, and 2 to 4 tablespoons lemon juice along with the olive oil, cheese, and salt. Delicious on pasta or grilled eggplant.

Sylvia's Lemon and Basil Pesto

By now I'm sure they know how to make pesto even on Mars. Still, you'll find some surprising pleasures in this version. Sylvia Teague was my much-loved sometime assistant—a great, original, and very thoughtful cook. This lemony pesto developed as she gradually cut back the fat in the classic, and began looking for other ways to boost the flavor. To tweak the lemony flavor even more, try using some lemon basil, if you can get it. An assortment of basil varieties—there are many, from Thai to lemon to French to purple frilled—adds extra interest and depth to pesto, but I do especially like the lemon here. If you are a major lemon enthusiast, go even further with a bit of grated lemon zest.

You may reduce the amount of nuts or seeds and of olive oil if you are watching your fat intake. If you are vegan, simply omit the Parmesan altogether, or use soy or rice Parmesan-style cheese. **MAKES ABOUT 1½ CUPS**

Basil

½ cup pine nuts, walnuts, or sunflower seeds
4 cloves garlic, halved
3 cups loosely packed fresi basil leaves
¾ cup loosely packed Italian parsley leaves
¼ cup freshly squeezed lemon juice, or to taste
3 tablespoons extra virgin olive oil
½ cup freshly grated Parmesan cheese (optional)
Salt to taste

1 Place the nuts or seeds and the garlic in a food processor and pulse to finely chop. Add the basil and parsley, about half the lemon juice, and the oil. Pulse or buzz to reach your preferred consistency (mine is a little chunky, not all the way pureed). Scrape down the processor sides once or twice.

2 Transfer the pesto to a small bowl and stir in the Parmesan, if using, and salt (perhaps a bit more salt than you think it needs, as this is a seasoning paste). Add the remaining lemon juice if you like. Serve at once, store in the fridge for up to 1 week, or freeze for up to 4 months.

VARIATION

HABANERO PESTO: ***The brainchild of Dr. John Dosser, who grows all his own basil in his Oklahoma City garden. Buzz 1 head garlic, the cloves peeled and any hard stem bits removed, in a food processor until finely chopped, then add 4 to 6 packed cups basil leaves. Buzz until a paste is formed, then add 2 fresh habanero chiles, stems, seeds, and ribs removed. Add ⅓ cup very finest quality extra virgin olive oil, about ⅓ cup freshly grated Parmesan cheese, 2 tablespoons pine nuts, and about ¾ cup toasted sunflower seeds. Buzz again just to incorporate. You should have a medium-grained paste. Serve with any kind of bread, pasta, or rice. If you want more assertive habanero heat, why, simply add another chile.***

Zhoug

This Lebanese-Yemenite Jewish condiment—somewhere between pesto, salsa, table sauce, and very spicy relish—shows another (non-Mexican) side of the exhilarating combo of cilantro, cumin, and hot pepper. These ingredients take on a very different character when used as they have been since time out of mind in India, parts of the Middle East, North Africa, and the Caucasus.

Zhoug, a paste of raw pureed herbs and seasonings, a little like the purees of coriander or mint we may know from Indian restaurants, is searingly hot, complex in flavor, and extremely toothsome. Parsley, cumin, black pepper, and olive oil join the cilantro and green chile and what a difference a few ingredients make. Suddenly a new breeze blows in, ruffling the kitchen curtains.

I learned about zhoug from the exceptionally interesting semivegetarian *Yemenite Cookbook,* by Zion Levi and Hani Agabria. They promise it will "give fire to your blood and improve the well-being of your body." Zhoug certainly does deliver on the fire part! Like Thai Crystal (page 923), it's one of those things I like to have in the refrigerator all the time. Just a little bit gives a whole new slant to a stir-fry or to cream cheese or yogurt for a dip; it can also be tossed with pasta or whisked into scrambled eggs or tofu.

Other than the stems being removed from the green chiles in zhoug, they are left whole—which means it's hot, since the bulk of the chiles' incendiary oils are found in the seeds and ribs. If you want to wuss out, you could split open each of the chiles and remove the seeds and ribs. But if you were a wimp you probably wouldn't be making this recipe in the first place, would you? No, I thought not. **MAKES ABOUT 2½ CUPS**

10 ounces small green chiles, stemmed
1 cup Italian parsley leaves, coarsely chopped
1 cup cilantro leaves and stems, coarsely chopped
8 medium cloves garlic, peeled
1 teaspoon freshly ground black pepper
1 teaspoon salt
1 teaspoon ground cumin
2 tablespoons extra virgin olive oil

1 Puree the chiles by pulse/chopping, then buzzing them, in a food processor. You should end up with 1 cup of green chile puree. Add all the remaining ingredients and, again, buzz like crazy, until everything is fairly smooth and thick. Expect the air to get sort of incendiary with all those chile oils being released. Go outside and cough, blow your nose. It's worth it.

2 Transfer to a glass jar, cover, and store, refrigerated. According to the authors of *The Yemenite Cookbook,* "it will remain fresh for many months." But it's never lasted that long for us: When we make it, it's gone in a week.

NOTE

Chile lovers know that New Mexico–grown green chiles have an incomparable flavor. But even if you can't get them, you'll have good luck with supermarket chiles if you select Anaheims, Chimayos, or Big Jims, the varieties grown in New Mexico.

Pesto Santo Tomas

They do some remarkable things with green chiles in northern New Mexico, which inspired this recipe. It is named for an old, pristine adobe church in Las Trampas, a little town Ned and I drove through on the high road from Santa Fe to Taos as the late-afternoon sun burnished the hillsides and, later, the moon rose over the *arroyos.* This was maybe seventeen years ago, and if I never get back there again, I still have the vision of that church to carry with me.

Toasting the nuts may seem fussy, but it intensifies their flavor (and ultimately the pesto). This is pure heaven tossed with just-cooked fresh tortellini or ravioli (ricotta or squash), or slathered on quesadillas. Of all the pestos given here, this is my current absolute favorite. Also, you must be a cilantro-lover to take joy in this. I am and I do.

Unlike most pestos, this is vegan. **MAKES ABOUT 1½ CUPS**

⅓ cup pine nuts
4 poblano chiles, charred, peeled, stemmed, and seeded
4 New Mexico–style green chiles, charred, peeled, stemmed, and seeded
5 to 6 cloves garlic, halved
2 to 2½ cups loosely packed cilantro leaves
¼ cup extra virgin olive oil or any mild vegetable oil
1 teaspoon salt, or to taste

1 Heat a dry, small, heavy skillet over medium heat. Add the pine nuts and lightly toast them, shaking or stirring frequently, for about 3 minutes, or until golden. Remove from the heat.

2 Combine the pine nuts with all the remaining ingredients in a food processor and buzz to a very thick paste. Transfer to a storage container. This will keep for about 1 week, refrigerated.

Classic Harissa

The real hot pepper paste, inspired by food writer Paula Wolfert. **MAKES ABOUT 1⅓ CUPS**

1 ounce whole dried red chile peppers (about 1⅓ cups)
1 clove garlic
1 teaspoon salt
1 teaspoon olive oil

1 Soak the hot peppers in hot water for 2 hours.

2 Drain the peppers and dice fine, then pound in a mortar and pestle with garlic and salt until a coarse paste is formed. Store, refrigerated, in a small jar, with olive oil drizzled on the surface of the paste. It will keep for 2 weeks.

NOTE

Harissa becomes a key part of Seven-Vegetable Seven-Spice Tagine with Couscous (page 506), a dish fit for pashas and houris.

Quick Harissa Paste

Not authentic, but good for anyone who doesn't have a mortar and pestle, or time to pound. This is another of those quick, hot finishes that adds dimension to so many dishes. **MAKES ABOUT 3 TABLESPOONS**

2 tablespoons cayenne pepper
2 cloves garlic, pressed
1 teaspoon salt
1 to 2 teaspoons olive oil

Cream the above ingredients together in a small bowl. Sotre in a small jar, with olive oil drizzled on the surface of the paste. Store, refrigerated, for up to 2 weeks.

Condiments, Ketchups, Chutneys & Pickles

The same guidelines I mentioned at the beginning of the pesto section apply here: While not strictly necessary, these go-withs—which lean toward sweet-sour accompaniments rather than seasonings—add color to cuisine. This may be why, although not every cooking culture widely uses seasoning pastes, virtually every nation in the world uses at least some of these with at least some dishes. Even the British, not exactly known for exciting food (although that's changing), eat mint jelly with roast lamb. And how they took to the chutneys of colonized India!

Again, if you lack time or inclination to make these from scratch, find some commercial brands you like and keep them in your pantry.

Quick Hot Asian Ketchup

It doesn't get faster than this combination of two ready-made Asian condiments: rich, sweet hoisin sauce, with a base of fermented soybeans, and sriracha sauce, a delectable take-your-head-off hot paste of chiles and garlic with just a bit of salt, sugar, and vinegar. This combination is quite wonderful with Crisp Lettuce Tempeh "Spring Rolls" (page 38), or with any vegetable or grain burger or patty. If it's too hot for you, use more hoisin next time or stir in a bit of honey or tomato paste. **QUANTITY VARIABLE**

Hoisin sauce
Sriracha sauce

Combine equal parts of hoisin and sriracha. This keeps in the fridge in a small jar virtually indefinitely.

Thai Crystal

Known to us as Thai Crystal, this condiment is actually called *Nahm Jeem Gratiem,* which translates, according to my friend Nancie McDermott, as sweet-hot garlic sauce. That translation sums it up but doesn't do it justice. Make it once, and you will never, ever let your refrigerator be without a jar. Crystal clear (hence its name) other than the little red pepper flakes that float in it, hot as the dickens, and fat free, its sweet-sour heat is incredibly addictive. There are few savory dishes it won't perk up big-time. Have at it.

Child's play to make (other than peeling and mincing all that garlic), Thai Crystal is the best of classic, basic Thai food.

And if you really can't deal with garlic peeling, buy the commercially peeled and minced garlic. It's not as good as fresh, but since vinegar is added, it works here. **MAKES ABOUT 1⅓ CUPS**

2 cups sugar
1 cup water, preferably spring or filtered
½ cup white or rice vinegar
About ¼ cup minced garlic (about 40 cloves) or commercial minced garlic
2 teaspoons salt
2 tablespoons crushed red pepper

1 Combine the sugar, water, vinegar, garlic, and salt in a medium-sized heavy saucepan and bring to a rolling boil over medium heat. Stir to dissolve the sugar and salt and reduce the heat to low. Simmer until the liquid reduces to a light syrup, about 20 minutes.

2 Stir in the red pepper. Let cool to room temperature. Transfer to a clean jar. It keeps indefinitely in the refrigerator. Shake well before using.

NOTE

Curry leaf has nothing to do with curry powder. It is a fresh green leaf with a distinctive herbal-lemony-floral taste. You'll need two sprigs' worth for this recipe. You may be able to buy them fresh at an Indian market. (Get the channa dal there, also, as well as the coconut oil.) If you can't get curry leaves, omit them, or use a few fresh bay leaves or perhaps kaffir lime leaves (quite different, but either one adds the green note).

White Coconut Chutney

Chutneys as we know them in America are sweet preserves combining fresh and dried fruit with savory and sweet spices, onions (usually), and just a bit of heat, like Major Grey's (remember when a bottle of it on your shelf was a hallmark of exoticism?). Such chutneys are delicious, but they're more British Raj than truly Indian. Indian chutneys are more like salsas. The sweetened hot mint or coriander dip you often get with the appetizer at Indian restaurants is North Indian. This is the South Indian version. Try it with the potato topping for Masala Bruschetta (page 34).

I learned to make this in a kitchen in Kerala, India, where the first step to preparing it was to go outside and get a few coconut husks to start the fire with. **MAKES ABOUT 3 CUPS**

FOOD PROCESSOR MIXTURE

Grated meat of 1 fresh coconut (about 1¼ to 1¾ cups)
5 fresh green chiles, stemmed
1 thumb-size piece ginger, peeled and sliced
1 small tomato, stem end removed, quartered
2 shallots, peeled and halved
2 cups water, preferably spring or filtered
10 to 12 small curry leaves
1¼ teaspoons salt, or to taste

STIR-FRY MIXTURE

1 tablespoon coconut oil
4 shallots, peeled and sliced
1 to 2 dried whole red chiles, broken in half
1¼ teaspoons black mustard seeds
1 teaspoon channa dal or urad dal (see page 610)
1 sprig fresh curry leaves (about 10 leaves, left on the sprig)

1 Combine the coconut, chiles, ginger, tomato, shallots, and 1 cup of the water in a food processor. Buzz until a medium-thick paste is formed, stopping to scrape down the sides of the work bowl once with a spatula. The finished mixture will have a grainy texture.

2 Transfer the mixture to a bowl and add the remaining 1 cup water, the curry leaves, and salt. Set aside.

3 To make the stir-fry, heat the coconut oil in a small wok or round-bottomed pan over medium to high heat until the oil is very hot, almost smoking. Add the shallots and stir-fry quickly, for about 15 seconds. Add the red chiles (which should turn black almost immediately) and stir-fry for 10 seconds more, then add the black mustard seeds, channa dal or urad dal, and the curry leaves, still on the stem. Stir-fry for 15 seconds more—the mustard seeds will pop—and pour in the coconut-chile paste.

4 Reduce the heat slightly and cook just until heated through. Remove from the heat. Serve warm or at room temperature. Although you can refrigerate any leftovers for a couple of days, this chutney is really at its best freshly made.

VARIATION

RED COCONUT CHUTNEY: ***Omit the green chiles from the processor mixture, replacing them with 1 to 2 tablespoons ground dried red chiles (not chili powder, but straight powder of whole red chiles).***

Pineapple or Mango Pachadi

This fresh fruit curry was one of my very favorites when I lived in South India. It was a welcome, sweetly cooling contrast to the fiery hot dishes being served and to the big mound of Kerala rice (huge, puffy grains, with reddish brown veins, unlike any rice I've encountered elsewhere). Pachadi wasn't served daily, so I was always happy to see it. Sweet it may be, but a *little* heat does sneak in, and it wouldn't be Kerala cooking without coconut (the literal translation of that state's name is "land of the coconut palms"). You can call pachadi a salad or a raita, a condiment, or a curry, but no matter what, you'll call it delicious.

If you can't find curry leaves, substitute bay leaves or kaffir lime leaves, or omit them. Try the pachadi with rice or Katherine's Ghee Rice with Cashews and Melting Onions (page 485) and dal (see page 609) for a true feast. **SERVES 6 TO 8**

2 cups water, preferably spring or filtered, more if using dried coconut
¼ teaspoon salt
2½ cups peeled and diced ripe pineapple or peeled and pitted mango
2 curry leaves or bay leaves (optional)
¾ cup ground fresh coconut meat or unsweetened dried coconut flakes
1 serrano chile, stemmed
2¼ teaspoons brown or black mustard seeds
⅛ teaspoon ground cumin
1 teaspoon mild vegetable oil, such as corn, canola, or peanut
2 dried red chiles
¼ cup plain yogurt

1 Heat 2 cups water in a saucepan with the salt. Drop in the diced pineapple or mango and curry or bay leaves. Simmer for about 15 minutes.

2 Meanwhile, combine the fresh coconut (or dried coconut plus 2 tablespoons water), serrano, ¼ teaspoon of the mustard seeds, and the ground cumin in a food processor or blender. Pulse, scraping down the sides, to make a thick paste. Set aside.

3 Heat the oil in a small, heavy wok or skillet. When hot, add the remaining mustard seeds and the dried red chiles. Stir, watching closely, until the mustard seeds begin to pop. Remove from the heat.

4 Combine the cooked fruit and its cooking liquid with the coconut paste, the mustard seed mixture, and the yogurt. Remove the red chiles and curry or bay leaves and discard. Serve the pachadi warm or at room temperature.

VARIATION

CANNED PINEAPPLE PACHADI: ***Use canned pineapple in its own juice instead of fresh pineapple.***

TOMATO PACHADI: ***Substitute 2½ cups diced canned tomatoes with their juice for the pineapple. Though untraditional, this is also exceptionally good.***

Western-Style Blueberry Chutney

Blueberries are one of the Ozarks' most widely and successfully grown organic crops, and a trip to a pick-'em-yourself blueberry farms is a late-June, early-July ritual. It is blissful to be out there under the sun, among the large, shiny-leaved bushes hung with the misted blues.

I have been making this preserve from blueberries for years. At the inn, game hen glazed with blueberry chutney was an ever-popular entree, but for vegetarian consumption I'd always do blueberry chutney–glazed tempeh with an herbed rice and wild rice pilaf.

If you are familiar with canning, you can put up this chutney, hot, in hot, clean jars with sealing lids—no water processing needed, since the vinegar, sugar, and salt preserve it nicely. But even without being sealed, it keeps under refrigeration for months. **MAKES ABOUT 2½ QUARTS**

Cooking spray (optional)
2 quarts fresh blueberries
2 cups raisins or dried blueberries
2 onions, diced
1 green bell pepper, stemmed, cored, and diced
2 fresh jalapeño peppers, stemmed and diced
2 tablespoons peeled and minced ginger
2 teaspoons ground cinnamon
1 teaspoon ground cloves
1 (12-ounce) can unsweetened frozen apple juice concentrate, thawed
2 cups vinegar, preferably blueberry or raspberry vinegar, but a good apple cider vinegar will do
4 cloves garlic, pressed
1 tablespoon salt
1¾ cups honey or Rapidura, or 1¾ cups packed brown sugar

1 In a large, heavy-bottomed, nonreactive nonstick pot, or one that has been sprayed with cooking spray, combine all the ingredients and bring to a boil. Reduce the heat to a simmer. Let simmer, stirring often, until the mixture is thick and somewhat dark in color, 35 to 45 minutes.

2 Put the chutney up, hot, in hot jars, or let cool to room temperature and store in the refrigerator.

Kimchee

The irresistible, tongue-tingling, hot-sour-salty-sweet Korean pickle is one of the world's great condiments. You can easily buy it at most Asian markets and even in some supermarkets, but some brands have fish sauce or dried fish added. Besides, it's fun to make it from scratch once in a while. Every Korean family's kimchee is different, so feel free to adjust the recipe to make yours more or less spicy, gingery, or sweet. **MAKES ABOUT 1½ QUARTS**

1 head napa cabbage, outer leaves and base discarded, separated into leaves
2 large carrots, coarsely grated
⅔ cup kosher salt
2 heads garlic, cloves separated and peeled
3 tablespoons peeled and coarsely chopped ginger
Juice of 4 lemons
1 tablespoon sriracha or other hot pepper paste, or more to taste
½ cup sugar, Rapidura, or honey

1 Spread out a layer of cabbage leaves in a large, nonreactive bowl. Scatter some carrots over the cabbage, then some of the salt. Spread out another layer of cabbage leaves, add another scattering of carrot, and sprinkle again with salt. Continue until all cabbage leaves, carrots, and salt are used up. A layer of cabbage leaves should be the top layer. Place a plate or platter on top of the salted cabbage, and weight the plate with an iron skillet. Let the salted cabbage sit at room temperature overnight.

2 The next day, transfer the cabbage and carrots to a colander and rinse thoroughly to get rid of excess salt. Drain well, then blot dry on paper towels. Stack the leaves, along with the grated carrots clinging to them, and slice, crosswise, into ¼- to ½-inch ribbons.

3 Combine the julienned cabbage with all the remaining ingredients and toss well. Let the flavors develop for at least 1 hour, but preferably several days, covered, in the refrigerator. Store in a nonreactive container; a mason jar is just fine as long as the metal lid is not in direct contact with the pickle.

Cora Pinkley Call's Uncooked Ozark Relish

This is the best American-style relish I have ever had. Period, end of story. It's what pickle relish ought to be, but never, ever is. It will perk up almost any sandwich or meal it's served with. Cora, may she rest in peace, was a Eureka Springs native who in 1950 wrote *From My Ozark Cupboard*, in which she said of the relish, "Super . . . DEE-licious!" Her descendent, June Westphal, still lives here and is a devoted town historian.

This is Cora's recipe almost exactly, other than my cutting back the sugar just a bit (heaven knows, it's plenty sweet as is). Oh, and of course she didn't have a food processor; she no doubt put the onions through a food grinder. **MAKES 4 QUARTS**

NOTE

The relish is not quite uncooked, since you do seal it in a boiling-water bath. If you're not up to it, just put the relish in jars and keep it refrigerated. Because of the vinegar, sugar, and salt, all natural preservatives, it will keep indefinitely.

4 large onions, peeled and cut into eighths
4 green bell peppers, stemmed, seeded, and finely chopped
4 red bell peppers, stemmed, seeded, and finely chopped
½ cabbage, core removed, cut into thin ribbons
2 red or green chiles, stemmed and finely chopped
2 tablespoons salt
1 quart cider vinegar
3½ cups sugar
1 tablespoon mixed pickling spices
¼ cup yellow mustard seeds

1 Place the onions in a food processor and pulse/chop at first, then buzz until the onions are a slushy, pungent paste. Turn the paste out into a large nonreactive bowl, and add the green and red peppers, the cabbage, and the chiles. Add the salt. Let stand, covered, overnight.

2 The next morning, drain off and discard the liquid that has accumulated in the bowl. Add the vinegar, sugar, pickling spices, and mustard seeds. Mix well.

3 Transfer the uncooked relish into hot jars, leaving ½ inch of head room. Cover, screwing on the lids. Lower the jars into a hot-water bath for 15 minutes to seal.

Fresh Ginger and Pear Relish

This is another great relish, somewhat like a chutney, an impromptu rendering from some years back when I was given a huge bounty of hard cooking pears from an old tree on Ruth Eichor's farm, farther down in Dairy Hollow. Most Thanksgivings during our inn years, this would find its way to the restaurant's Relish Tray Redefined (page 53).

"A pot of boiling syrup scents the air with cloves and cinnamon. They are making preserves."

—**Ellen Douglas,** *Can't Quit You, Baby*

While I prefer putting up a few relishes, chutneys, jams, and the like each year the old-fashioned way, in hot sealed jars (which, when cool, can sit smugly on the shelf, jewel-like and waiting); such condiments can be stored safely in the refrigerator for months. **MAKES 3½ TO 4 QUARTS**

12 to 15 pears, unpeeled, cored, chopped into ½-inch pieces
5 onions, finely chopped
3 cups packed dark brown sugar
2½ cups vinegar
3 green bell peppers, stemmed, seeded, and finely chopped
2 red bell peppers, stemmed, seeded, and finely chopped
5 green serrano chiles or jalapeño peppers, stemmed, seeds and ribs removed if desired, finely chopped
1 tablespoon celery seeds
1 tablespoon black mustard seeds
2 tablespoons salt
3 tablespoons finely minced peeled ginger
2 sticks cinnamon

1 Combine all the ingredients except the cinnamon sticks in a large nonreactive pot, preferably nonstick. Bring to a boil, turn down the heat to a simmer, and let simmer, stirring often, for 30 to 40 minutes, or until thickened.

2 Meanwhile, heat quart canning jars, either in boiling water or in a hot oven. Place a cinnamon stick in the bottom of each hot jar (¼ stick if you are doing pints). Ladle the pear relish, hot, into the hot jars and seal at once.

Vegetable- or Fruit-Based Sauces

Long before *low-fat* became the most overused nutritional term of the last century, Americans were eating, and loving, Italian red sauce, which is, of course, tomato based.

But tomatoes are not the only vegetable to base a sauce on. Widen your horizons, invite the whole garden—the chiles and beets and squashes, and even some fruits—into your kitchen. Your pastas, grain dishes, casseroles, and happy diners will all love you for it. It's a matter not only of flavor but also health-giving phytochemicals. Not to discount flavor: From red and green enchilada sauces that make your mouth mambo to tart Lemon Sauce à la Grecque, you'll add many of these to your permanent repertoire.

Basic Wintertime Italian Tomato Sauce

If I had a dollar for every cup of this good basic sauce and its numerous variations that I have made in my three-some decades of serious cooking, I would be a wealthy woman. And I am wealthy—in the many dinners I have shared with Ned, friends and family, guests at the inn, year in and year out—often while eating a dish prepared with this sauce.

An excellent tomato sauce is a must-have. This one is good, basic, and vital to almost any cook's repertoire for dozens, maybe hundreds, of recipes. And it is the starting point for countless variations.

NOTE

If possible, let this sauce age, refrigerated, for 6 to 8 hours or overnight; it just gets better and better. Reheat and remove the bay leaf before serving.

By the way, it's a myth that long cooking brings out herbal flavors; cooking a sauce for too long at too high a heat can actually remove taste. **MAKES ABOUT 3½ CUPS**

2 tablespoons olive oil
Cooking spray (optional)
1 large onion, chopped
1 to 4 medium cloves garlic, pressed
1 (28-ounce) can tomatoes in juice
1 to 2 tablespoons tomato paste
1 teaspoon honey, or to taste
1 bay leaf, broken in half
1 to 2 teaspoons dried basil
1 to 2 teaspoons dried oregano
¼ teaspoon dried rosemary
1¼ teaspoons dried thyme
Salt and freshly ground black pepper to taste

. . . and More Sauce

Basic Wintertime Italian Tomato Sauce is the first step of the journey of a thousand sauces. Now that you've begun, travel onward with these lush variations.

▲ **RED SAUCE FIORI:** *Use the larger amount of oil, and sauté 1 diced carrot and 1 stalk celery with the onion. With the tomatoes, add ¼ cup raisins. With the herbs, add 1 to 2 teaspoons anise seed and ½ teaspoon red pepper flakes.*

▲ **GREEK-STYLE TOMATO SAUCE:** *Add ¼ cup hearty red wine, with an additional 2 teaspoons honey. Use the lesser amount of all the herbs except the oregano and add the secret ingredient: ¼ teaspoon cinnamon. Because you've used additional liquid, allow additional cooking time.*

▲ **TOMATO SAUCE WITH ROASTED EGGPLANT:** *Cut 1 large eggplant (peeled or not, as you prefer) into large cubes, salt and drain it if necessary (see page 742), toss with a tiny bit of olive oil, and roast, uncovered, at 375°F, until slightly browned, about 30 minutes. Stir the roasted eggplant into any of the other tomato sauces when they're done.*

▲ **TOMATO SAUCE WITH EXOTIC OR DOMESTIC MUSHROOMS:** *Sauté 2 cups sliced button mushrooms in olive oil, either with the onions as they sauté or separately, and add them at the last minute. But for a real treat, stir in a handful of Oven-Roasted Shiitakes with Garlic and Coarse Salt (page 48), thickly sliced, in the last few minutes of cooking.*

▲ **TOMATO SAUCE WITH LENTILS:** *Add 1½ to 2½ cups cooked (but not overcooked) lentils to the basic sauce.*

▲ **GREEK-STYLE TOMATO SAUCE WITH LENTILS:** *Add 1½ to 2½ cups cooked (but not overcooked) lentils to the Greek variation. Use in hearty Greek casserole dishes.*

▲ **VEGETARIAN BOLOGNESE:** *Stir a 10-ounce box of thawed ground tofu into the basic sauce or the Red Sauce Fiori (far left) when almost done.*

▲ **CREOLE-STYLE TOMATO SAUCE:** *Sauté 1 green bell pepper, diced, 3 scallions, diced, and 2 stalks celery, diced, with the onion. Add ½ to 1 teaspoon Tabasco or similar hot sauce, a pinch of allspice, 1 tablespoon Pickapeppa sauce, and 1 teaspoon thyme.*

1 Heat the olive oil in a large nonstick skillet, or a cast-iron skillet that has been sprayed with cooking spray, over medium heat. Add the onion and cook, stirring, for 5 to 7 minutes, until limp and translucent and just starting to brown around the edges. Stir in the garlic, cook 1 minute more, taking care not to let it stick, then add the tomatoes, tomato paste, and honey. Turn down the heat to a low simmer.

2 Add the bay leaf, then add the basil, oregano, rosemary, and thyme, crushing each between your fingers to release essential oils. Add pepper at this point—plenty. Raise heat to almost a boil, turn it down to a simmer, and cook the sauce for about 20 minutes, until thick.

3 At this point, taste for acidity, saltiness, and herb flavors. If too acid, add a little more honey. The sauce probably needs some salt now, but maybe not too much, given that canned tomatoes are salted and that such sauces are often incorporated into dishes that include cheese. If it's not herbal enough for you, add additional pinches of herbs (in this case you'll need to let the sauce stand for at least half an hour, longer if possible, to let the herbal flavors develop).

NOTE

I've called for 2 tablespoons olive oil here; ¼ cup or more is traditional. But by using cooking spray or olive-oil spray or a nonstick skillet, you can get by with much less and still end up with a delicious sauce.

Sauce Mongole

Potage Mongole, which has nothing to do with Mongolia, is a soup that combines split peas and tomatoes. This pale green concoction calls for a lightened-up cream sauce with instant split peas and savory seasonings to make a smooth, astonishingly good, faintly exotic sauce that will liven up the simplest stir-fry or grain dish. After you've sauced whatever you're serving with this, sprinkle it with a bit of minced parsley or cilantro. It makes the pale and unusual green of the sauce look more intentional.

Although I have listed the vegan version as a variation, the dairy-free recipe is the zone I first came up with, when a close friend developed a milk allergy but craved creamy things. This had him swooning, and it's the version I make most often. **MAKES A GENEROUS 2 CUPS**

VARIATION

Vegans should use vegetable oil or vegetable margarine, plain soy milk, and soy Parmesan-style cheese.

Cooking spray
1 tablespoon butter, Better (page 905), or vegetable oil or vegetable magarine
1 tablespoon unbleached all-purpose flour
1½ cups low-fat milk, dairy or soy
⅔ cup dry instant vegetarian split pea soup mix, unreconstituted
3 to 4 tablespoons freshly grated Parmesan cheese
½ teaspoon dry mustard
1 teaspoon white, golden, or sweet miso, not dark miso (see page 173)
Salt and freshly ground black pepper to taste

1 Melt the butter in a nonstick saucepan, or one that has been sprayed with cooking spray, over medium heat. Whisk in the flour and cook, stirring often, until the flour and fat are slightly colored, a golden ivory, 3 to 4 minutes. Add the milk gradually, whisking it in, and let cook until the milk is hot and the sauce is slightly thickened.

2 Whisk in the dry pea soup mix, Parmesan, dry mustard, miso, and salt and pepper (I like a lot here). Turn off the heat and let the sauce stand for about 5 minutes, then serve.

Asian Red Sauce

I am very pleased with this reinterpretation of red sauce, which shows how changing the seasonings utterly changes the character of a dish. I invented this for the stacked East-West Lasagna (page 372), but it's very good on a variety of vegetables, Basic Oven-Baked Marinated Tempeh (page 641), or any of the milder cooked grains. Stirred into simple cooked beans, it makes them very special. **MAKES ABOUT 3½ CUPS**

VARIATION

ASIAN GOLD: ***Use 3 cups peeled and finely chopped fresh pineapple (or canned crushed pineapple) instead of tomatoes, or 2 cups pineapple and 1 cup tomatoes. Improbable but lovely, this sauce is excellent over buckwheat soba noodles and tofu.***

2 teaspoons mild vegetable oil, such as corn, canola, or peanut
1 teaspoon toasted sesame oil
Cooking spray
1 large onion, chopped
1 carrot, chopped
1 heaping tablespoon coarsely chopped unpeeled ginger
3 medium cloves garlic, pressed
3 cups diced tomatoes or 1 (28-ounce) can tomatoes in juice
2 to 3 stalks lemon grass, cut into 3-inch lengths and pounded
2 tablespoons honey, sugar, or Rapidura
2 tablespoons dry sherry or mirin
1 teaspoon tamari or shoyu soy sauce
Sriracha or other similar hot pepper paste (optional)
Salt to taste

1 Heat the vegetable oil and sesame oil in a nonstick skillet, or a large cast-iron

Raising Tomatoes in the Ozarks

"Tomato seeds were traditionally planted on the second day of April, which was also school meeting and election day. [The] perfect place to plant tomato seeds was in ground where a brush pile had been burned [because the] fire killed the weed seeds, allowing the fragile plants to emerge without competition. If necessary, farmers would protect the seedlings from frost on a cold night by covering them with paper. . . . Transplanting . . . began six weeks after planting the seeds when the sun had warmed the . . . steep, rocky hillsides. . . .

Farmers prayed for rain in early summer. . . . A farmer, trailing his mule which was hitched to a cultivator, trod up and down each row, slowly shifting the soil and uprooting the weeds. The first green knobs set by the first of July . . . and the pinkish-orange tomatoes developed by mid-August. Harvest lasted until the cool weather of autumn. . . ."

—Robert McGill,
"Red Gold Ozark Tomatoes,"
in OzarksWatch, 1996

skillet that has been sprayed with cooking spray. Add the onion and carrot and cook over medium-high heat, stirring, for 5 to 7 minutes, or until the onion is limp and translucent and just starting to brown around the edges. Reduce the heat slightly and stir in the ginger and garlic. Cook, stirring, for 1 minute more.

2 Add the tomatoes, lemon grass, honey, sherry, and tamari. Raise the heat to quickly cook the tomatoes and draw out, then evaporate, their juices. Simmer for 10 to 15 minutes, stirring often. Remove from the heat and let cool slightly. If a hot sauce is desired, add up to 1 tablespoon sriracha, or to taste.

3 Puree the sauce in a food processor, then push through a strainer to remove bits of ginger fiber and tomato skin. Taste for seasonings, adding tamari, honey, sherry, or salt as needed.

Cupboard Enchilada Sauce

You want simple? You got simple! It doesn't get easier than this, unless you buy ready-made enchilada sauce. This has a much fresher, sassier taste, even though it uses canned tomatoes. You can use it to top any enchilada. I use it often on CD's Famed Tofu-Broccoli Enchiladas (page 340). **MAKES ABOUT 3 CUPS**

½ onion
1 (14-ounce) can whole tomatoes in juice
3 cloves garlic
3 to 4 tablespoons commercial hot salsa
1 red bell pepper, charred, peeled, stemmed, and seeded (optional)
1 teaspoon salt

Combine all the ingredients in a food processor and buzz until smooth. That's it!

NOTE

The larger amount of olive oil called for, and then some, is traditional for these sorts of sauces, but by using cooking spray or a nonstick skillet, you can use less oil and still end up with a delicious sauce.

"Macro-Red" Sauce

Periodically I have been called upon to cook for people who avoid eating vegetables in the nightshade family—tomatoes, potatoes, eggplant, and peppers—because these vegetables contain the compound solanine, said to be deleterious to arthritis and joint diseases. For people who follow such a regimen, this alternative red sauce, versions of which have kicked around macrobiotic circles for years, is a godsend, serving deliciously in any recipe where conventional tomato sauce is called for. With traditional seasonings, and beet plus butternut squash standing in for tomatoes, this fine sauce is not just a substitute, but something wonderful in its own right. Mild, a tad sweet, and a vibrant red just a tone or two purpler than the orange-red of conventional tomato sauce, it's entirely pleasing—and it freezes well too.

Two pounds of carrots, stem ends cut off, well scrubbed or peeled, can be substituted for the more-difficult-to-peel butternut squash. I prefer the butternut, but both are good.

This is one place where you want a mild, less-assertive vegetable stock, not a dark-roasted or mushroomy one. **MAKES ABOUT 4½ CUPS**

About 3 cups mild vegetable stock (page 139)
2 pounds (1 medium) butternut squash, peeled, seeded, and cut into large chunks
2 small beets, scrubbed, halved or quartered
1 teaspoon to 3 tablespoons olive oil
Cooking spray
1 large onion, chopped
4 cloves garlic, pressed
1½ teaspoons honey, or to taste
2 tablespoon red wine vinegar
1 bay leaf, broken in half
1 to 2 teaspoons dried basil
1 to 2 teaspoons dried oregano
¼ teaspoon dried rosemary
¼ teaspoon dried thyme
Salt and freshly ground black pepper to taste

1 Place about 2 cups of the vegetable stock in the bottom of a Dutch oven. Place a vegetable steamer in it and add the squash and beets. Cover tightly and steam until the vegetables are tender, 25 to 30 minutes, adding more stock as needed. Let cool slightly. Peel the beets.

2 Puree the squash and beets in a food processor, buzzing until smooth, adding stock as needed to achieve the consistency of tomato puree. Set aside.

3 Heat the olive oil in a nonstick skillet, or a large cast-iron skillet that has been sprayed with cooking spray, over medium-high heat. Add the onion and cook, stirring, for 5 to 7 minutes, until limp and translucent and just starting to brown around the edges. Stir in the garlic and cook for 1 minute more, taking care not to let it stick, then add the squash and beet puree, the honey, and vinegar. Reduce the heat to a low simmer.

4 Add the bay leaf. Add the basil, oregano, rosemary, and thyme, crushing between your fingers to release the essential oils. Add freshly ground pepper at this point—plenty. Let simmer until the mixture is thick and has the consistency of a sauce.

5 Taste for acidity, saltiness, and herb flavors. If not acid enough, add a little more vinegar. It probably needs some salt now too. If it's not herbal enough for you, add additional pinches of herb (in this case you'll need to let the sauce stand for at least half an hour, longer if possible, to let the herbal flavors develop). If possible, let this sauce age, refrigerated, for 6 to 8 hours or overnight; it gets better and better. Reheat and remove the bay leaf before serving.

NOTE

Agreeable butternut squash, sweet and with the smoothest of textures when pureed, not only steps in for tomatoes, as in Macro-Red, but for pumpkin (it makes a better-than-pumpkin pumpkin pie filling) and, if grated raw, for carrots in carrot cake. Its creaminess allows it, when pureed, to serve as a base for voluptuous creamless bisques that you'd swear were dairy-rich. For more uses, see Chapter 6.

Jan Hazard's Rich Roasted Vegetable Sauce

This voluptuous sauce is adapted from a fine recipe of Jan Turner Hazard's, onetime food editor of *Ladies Home Journal.* The first time I met Jan was in a step aerobics class in San Francisco.

At our second, more intentional meeting, I complimented her on this sauce, which she had just run in the magazine, though made with chicken broth. Here is my vegetarian version. In it, the plush oranges and reds of tomatoes, butternut squash, and carrots are roasted to intensify their flavors, then pureed with vegetable broth—either a mild or a heartier stock works well here, though I prefer the latter.

It's hard to imagine a pasta that wouldn't be happy with this. Also try it over any milder stuffed vegetables, or crêpes, in omelets, in lasagne, with good-quality ravioli or tortellini, or as a refreshing change anywhere you'd use red sauce. Any leftovers are great stirred into a mixed stir-fry. **MAKES ABOUT 1½ QUARTS**

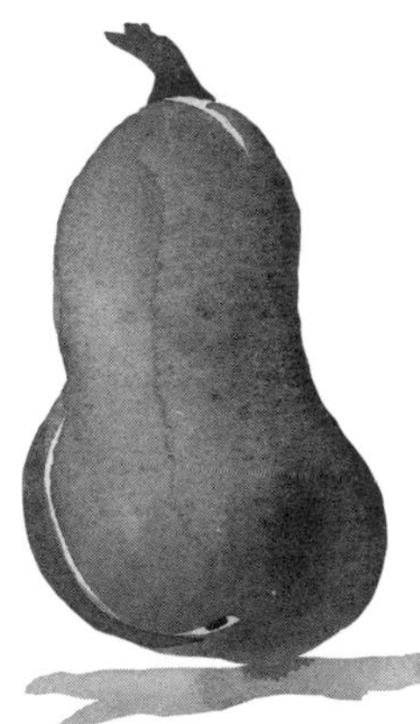

Cooking spray
2 pounds (about 16) Roma or plum tomatoes, halved lengthwise
3 red bell peppers, stemmed, seeded, and halved lengthwise
1 medium (2 pounds) butternut squash, unpeeled, seeded and cut into 2-inch chunks
1 head garlic, pointed end cut off straight across to expose cloves
3 medium onions, unpeeled, quartered
2 carrots, tops removed, cut into 2-inch chunks
1¼ cups vegetable stock (page 139)
1 tablespoon balsamic vinegar
1½ teaspoons salt, or to taste
Freshly ground black pepper to taste
1 tablespoon extra virgin olive oil
2 teaspoons finely chopped garlic (about 4 cloves) or thickish Garlic Oil (page 898)
Shredded fresh basil for garnish (optional)

1 Preheat the oven to 425°F. Spray 2 large baking sheets with sides at least ½ inch high, but no higher than 1½ inches, with cooking spray.

2 Place the tomatoes and peppers, cut side down, on the pans; tuck the squash, whole garlic head, onions, and carrots

among them. Spray the vegetables lightly with cooking spray. Bake for 1 hour, or until the vegetables soften and start to color, switching upper and lower pans in the oven halfway through. Let the vegetables cool until you can handle them.

3 Slip the skins off the tomatoes and place the tomatoes in a large bowl. Scoop the squash from its peel and the onions from their skins and add the squash and onions to the tomatoes. Squeeze the garlic cloves from the papery skin directly into the bowl, discarding the skin. Remove the peel from the peppers, cutting off their stems and discarding the seeds, and place them, too, in the bowl.

4 In two batches, puree the roasted vegetables in a food processor with the stock. Season with the vinegar, salt, and pepper.

5 Heat the oil in a large, deep skillet or Dutch oven over medium heat. Add the chopped garlic and stir-fry for 30 to 40 seconds, until the garlic just barely starts to turn golden. Immediately stir in the roasted vegetable puree and heat through. Serve with a sprinkle of basil, if desired.

Skordalia

Used as a sauce, dip, or condiment, skordalia is a garlicky Greek dressing given substance by the addition of potatoes.

It's traditional to mash the garlic to a paste with salt by hand with a mortar and pestle; traditional, also, to hand-mash the potatoes and drizzle the olive oil. You do get a fluffier, more delicate product that way, true. But the beater shortcut is only slightly less wonderful, and considerably easier. Don't just throw it all in the food processor or blender, though; it leaves the potatoes gluey. **MAKES ABOUT 1¼ CUPS**

½ pound potatoes, peeled
8 cloves garlic, peeled, halved, any visible green shoot removed
½ teaspoon salt
½ cup good, fruity olive oil, placed in a spouted cup measure
2 to 4 tablespoons lemon juice or red wine vinegar, to taste
1 to 1½ tablespoons water, preferably spring or filtered (optional)

Bring a small saucepan of salted water to a boil over high heat. Add the potatoes and bring to a simmer. Lower the heat and simmer until tender but not mushy, about 15 minutes. Drain well and transfer to a nonreactive bowl or the bowl of a standing mixer. Using a potato masher or electric mixer, beat until smooth, fluffy, and free of lumps.

Beat in the garlic (you can crush it right from the press into the bowl) and salt. With the motor running, or stirring like crazy with a wooden spoon, very gradually drip in the oil, alternating it with the lemon juice or vinegar. Beat until the mixture is very smooth. If it's too thick for your liking, beat in a little water.

Roasted Red Pepper Sauce with Fresh Pineapple Mint

Pineapple mint is a variegated green-and-white mint with a decided pineapple flavor note. Of course, you could use spearmint or any other mint, but the pineapple has a magic synergy with the emphatic flavor of charred red bell peppers. Slightly sweet, with a touch of heat and fruitiness, the sauce is just made for Middle Eastern and Greek or other Mediterranean flavors. Try this over pasta or grains, or with a stuffed vegetable, such as Stuffed Summer Suns: Pattypans Baked with Ricotta-Corn Filling (page 419), with or inside omelets, or stirred into a sauté of mushrooms and scooped on top of polenta or risotto. Charring and peeling the peppers is a labor of love: not difficult, but time consuming. I frequently use the grill to char them if I'm doing any more than two or three. Peppers vary tremendously in weight; the 3 pounds called for here might be as few as 5 large ones, as many as 8 or 10 small. **MAKES ABOUT 1½ QUARTS**

Cooking spray
3 tablespoons extra virgin olive oil
6 to 8 cloves garlic, halved
2 onions, coarsely chopped
3 pounds red bell peppers, charred, peeled, stemmed, seeded, and coarsely chopped
1 cup vegetable stock (page 139)
¾ cup loosely packed mint leaves, preferably pineapple mint
1⅛ teaspoons cayenne
1 tablespoon honey, brown sugar, or Rapidura
Salt and freshly ground black pepper to taste

1 Place a deep nonstick skillet or a conventional skillet over medium heat. Add the oil and garlic and sauté, stirring, for about 2 minutes, until the garlic just barely starts to turn golden. Remove the garlic with a slotted spoon and set aside.

2 Add the onions to the pan and sauté, stirring often, until they are quite soft and browning around the edges, 8 to 10 minutes. Add the red peppers and stock. Return the garlic to the pan and bring the sauce to a boil. Reduce the heat to a simmer and cook, uncovered, until all the vegetables are very soft, 15 to 20 minutes.

3 In two batches, buzz the skillet contents in a food processor with the mint, pausing to scrape down the sides of the work bowl. Add the cayenne, honey, and salt and pepper to taste. Either let the sauce rest, refrigerated, overnight to blend and intensify the flavors, or reheat right away and serve.

Lemon Sauce à la Grecque

Great over any green vegetable; just a little drizzle of this tart, creamy sauce can make the simplest grain and steamed or stir-fried vegetable supper sprightly and pleasing. It's reminiscent of avgolemono, the classic custard-smooth, egg yolk–thickened Greek sauce, but there's nary an egg to be found here. And, in the simpler variation that follows, if you use canned or on-hand stock, it's a quick fix—under 12 minutes. **MAKES ABOUT 1 QUART**

1½ teaspoons olive oil
Cooking spray
1 onion, chopped
1 tablespoon coarsely chopped garlic (5 to 6 cloves)
2 ribs celery, coarsely chopped
2 carrots, coarsely chopped
½ cup dry white wine
1 tablespoon tomato paste
3 cups mild vegetable stock (page 139)
Salt and freshly ground black pepper
2 lemons
1 tablespoon butter, Better (page 905), or additional olive oil
1 tablespoon plus 1 teaspoon unbleached all-purpose flour

1 Heat the olive oil in a nonstick soup pot, or one that has been sprayed with cooking spray, over medium heat. Add the

VARIATION

SIMPLER LEMON SAUCE À LA GRECQUE: ***Omit the olive oil, onion, carrot, and celery; use just a mixture of stock, wine, and tomato paste for the liquid. You need simmer for only 10 minutes in this case. Add the juice and zest of the lemons and thicken as described. Instead of butter, stir in 1 tablespoon of one of the commercially made roasted garlic olive oils at the end. When making this for the Fresh Artichoke-Eggplant Lasagna with Lemon Sauce (page 365), use only 1 lemon, and cut the stock to 1½ cups. Use olive oil for the roux, leaving the proportions the same, to make a thicker sauce.***

onion and sauté until it starts to soften, about 5 minutes. Reduce the heat slightly and add the garlic, celery, and carrots. Continue sautéing, stirring often, for 2 minutes more.

2 Add the wine, tomato paste, and the stock and bring to a boil, then reduce the heat. Add salt and pepper to taste and simmer, half covered, until the vegetables are very soft, about 40 minutes. Strain the liquid through a sieve, pressing down on the solids to extract as much liquid as possible. Discard the solids. Keep the sauce warm.

3 As the stock simmers, grate the zests of the lemons, then halve the lemons and squeeze the juice, discarding the seeds.

4 Melt the butter in a nonstick, nonreactive skillet or one that has been sprayed with cooking spray. Add the flour, whisking. Cook for about 2 minutes, then slowly whisk in the reserved enriched stock and the lemon juice and zest. Cook for 1 minute, whisking; it's then ready for use. This will keep, refrigerated, for at least 5 days, sometimes longer.

VARIATION

NEW MEXICO–STYLE GREEN CHILE STEW: ***Add 1 to 2 diced potatoes and 1 thinly sliced carrot after you add the chiles to the roux. Simmer, stirring, until the potatoes are done. Add a cup or so of cooked black beans. Serve hot with grated sharp jack or Cheddar on top. Drained posole or fresh corn can be substituted for the potato.***

New Mexico–Style Green Chile Sauce

In that whole vibrant panoply of New World flavors—Southwestern and Central American, Mexican, and Tex-Mex—the seasonings of New Mexico stand out. Unique and true, their heart and soul is the distinctive New Mexican green chile, both the pepper and the sauce made from it, which is also called green chile.

New Mexican green chile peppers are about 3 to 4 inches long; they are a medium-hot chile of the type known as California chile. Soil conditions, rainfall, and felicity give New Mexican green chiles a complexity of flavor not found elsewhere. This flavor is deepened when they are dried.

Try this sauce over any enchilada or beans-and-rice supper, or over an omelet. Actually, it's sublime with eggs in any form or with scrambled tofu, and wickedly pleasing with potaotes, too. Or try the stew variation. Hot? Definitely, but not incendiary. Addictive? Definitely. **MAKES 2½ TO 3 CUPS**

VARIATION

NEW MEXICO–STYLE FRESH GREEN CHILE SAUCE:* *Take 2 to 2¼ pounds mixed fresh green chiles, at least half of the mix Anaheim. Char, stem, and chop them to yield 3 cups; remove the seeds and ribs if you like less heat. Simmer the chiles and 1½ cups of the water for 15 to 25 minutes, until slightly thickened. Then, make the recipe as directed, but add only 1½ cups water to the roux, and stir in the cooked fresh green chiles instead of dried. Then cook for 15 to 20 minutes.

2 tablespoons olive oil, or any mild vegetable oil, such as corn, canola, or peanut
1 small onion, diced
4 to 6 cloves garlic, diced
3 tablespoons unbleached all-purpose flour
4 cups water, preferably spring or filtered, heated to almost a boil
1 cup (about 1½ ounces) dried New Mexico green chiles, large chunks crumbled into smaller pieces
½ to 1 teaspoon dried oregano or marjoram
½ to 1 teaspoon salt, or to taste

1 Heat the oil in a large, deep skillet, preferably nonstick, over medium heat. Add the onion and sauté for 5 minutes. Add the garlic and sauté for 1 minute more, then sprinkle with the flour.

2 Reduce the heat slightly and, stirring almost constantly, cook until the flour starts to color, 5 to 7 minutes. Then start whisking in the water, a little at a time. When all the water has been added and the mixture is smooth, raise the heat and cook until slightly thickened, 3 to 5 minutes longer. Add the chiles, oregano or marjoram, and salt.

3 Let simmer over medium-low heat, uncovered, stirring occasionally, until the chiles are rehydrated, the sauce thickened slightly, and the kitchen aromatic. This takes about 45 minutes. Remove from the heat and serve at once or let it rest for a while. This sauce freezes very well and keeps for 2 or 3 days in the fridge.

Chile to Go

When you start cooking with chiles, especially with dried New Mexico chiles, you will become addicted and, if you are like me, have to import the chiles regularly. I call The Chile Shop (505-983-6080; thechileshop.com), a mail-order and retail shop in Santa Fe, which has been owned and run by the redoubtable Su-Anne Armstrong since 1983. If you have a chile question, she has a chile answer. Su-Anne, who never cooks anything the same way twice, says she sometimes uses olive oil in her green chile, and sometimes vegetable oil, but no longer stock for the liquid, just pure water. "I used to use stock," she says, "but I've gone back to water. The simpler, the better. You really taste the green chile then. Go very, very easy on the oregano, too." But, Louisiana-born gal that she is, she's not above browning the roux, "just a little." She also rehydrates the chiles in the sauce, a technique used here.

Tomatillo Salsa Verde

Simple and incredibly good with chips, on enchiladas, with breakfast eggs and tortillas, with rice and beans, ad infinitum. This got the Ned seal of approval in a big way. Make this once and it will become part of your standard repertoire, at least if you love Southwestern food as much as we do. Try it in Chilaquiles Verde with Pinto Beans and Potatoes (page 378) or in lieu of any other enchilada sauce, or just with beans and rice. **MAKES ABOUT 3 CUPS**

- **1½ pounds fresh tomatillos, husks removed**
- **½ large onion, quartered**
- **½ cup cilantro leaves and stems, coarsely chopped**
- **2 cloves garlic**
- **1 to 2 fresh serrano chiles or jalapeño peppers, stemmed**
- **1 teaspoon salt**

Combine all the ingredients in a food processor. Buzz until smooth. That's it—finito! Now is that fast or what?

Tomatillos

What makes Salsa Verde verde? The tomatillo. It looks like a green tomato but is actually a botanical relative of the kiwi fruit and ground cherry. It's small, round, and light green and comes gift wrapped in an easily removed papery husk. You don't even peel it, just pull off the husk and you're done.

Tomatillos have a mild tart flavor, a little sweet, with notes of both citrus and underripe tomato. You used to be able to find tomatillos only in Hispanic markets, but now most supermarkets carry them, to the delight of salsa lovers of all ethnicities.

The recipes I've given assume tomatillos about 2½ inches in diameter; if yours are smaller or larger, adjust the recipe accordingly, bearing in mind that salsas are anything but fussy.

Looking for a sprightly, not the same-old, same-old tomato sauce? Check out Tomatoes Stuffed with Cornbread Dressing and Gravy (page 431) and Southwestern-Style Tomato Gravy (page 433). Tomato gravy is much and rightly loved in parts of the Deep South—one taste and you'll see why. On biscuits or breadstuffs or grains of any type, it's hard to beat.

Dairy-Based Sauces

It's easy to make cream sauces if you don't scruple to use fat (especially butter), and dairy products. But many of us do scruple. There is good news, though: It's just as easy to make creamy sauces with a reduced fat content, using low-fat dairy milk or some types of plain (unflavored) soy milk. And the really good news is, they are very tasty. In fact, once you kick the habit of Alfredo-esque sauces, such embellishments begin to taste not only heavy but dull. By contrast, these lighter concoctions spark and sparkle. See also the Creamed Spinach Sauce (page 306).

Béchamel Sauce

Béchamel, named for a seventeenth-century French courtier named Louis de Béchamel, is one of the so-called mother sauces of French cuisine. This is your classic white sauce, gentle and agreeable, ready not only to sauce but to bind or to serve as a starting point for countless dishes. My béchamel matches classic béchamel sauce in its ability to get along, and in its flavor and texture, but it has a lighter fat profile. Make it with unflavored soy milk, and it becomes even more healthful and very pleasing. **MAKES ABOUT 1¼ CUPS**

NOTE

Most béchamels begin with simmering a few aromatics in the milk to make the sauce more flavorful, but you can skip this if the dish will contain highly seasoned ingredients.

Béchamel is usually made on the thick side, since it's the easiest thing in the world to thin the completed sauce with a little additional milk, soy milk, or other savory liquid.

- 1 bay leaf
- ¼ onion, skin on
- 2 whole cloves
- 1 (3-inch) rib celery, with leaves
- Freshly grated nutmeg
- 1¼ cups 1% dairy milk or unflavored soy milk, such as plain Soy Silk
- 2 teaspoons butter, Better (page 905), or vegetable oil or vegetable margarine
- Cooking spray
- 2 teaspoons unbleached all-purpose flour
- 1½ teaspoons cornstarch
- Salt and freshly ground black pepper to taste

More Sauce Satisfactions

Béchamel begs for invention, theme, and variation. Next time you're feeling saucey, try one of these versions. From cheese-enriched (dairy or vegan) to herbal or oniony, you'll find something to suit your palate.

▲ **Vegetarian Velouté:** *Substitute vegetable stock for the soy milk. This makes a lustrous sauce, ivory, golden, or brown, depending on the stock.*

▲ **Mornay Sauce:** *After the sauce is hot and thickened, add ¼ cup finely grated cheese (about 1 ounce). It can be one kind of cheese, or a combination: straight extra-sharp Cheddar, or 2 tablespoons each Parmesan and Jarlsberg, or whatever you fancy. Vegans or the lactose intolerant may substitute soy-, rice-, or nut-based cheese (or try the next variation given). I always season my cheese sauces with about ½ teaspoon dry mustard, a drop of Tabasco or a fleck of ground cayenne, and a drop of Pickapeppa sauce or vegetarian Worcestershire sauce.*

▲ **Vegan Mornay:** *For those who don't eat dairy and find that soy cheeses don't cut it, this is as close to the orange Cheddar cheese sauce your childhood macaroni and cheese had as you can get. It is surprisingly good—to my taste, better than a Mornay made with soy cheeses. As the soy milk infuses, combine, in a food processor, 1 canned red pimiento pepper (or 1 red bell pepper, charred, peeled, stemmed, and seeded) and 3 tablespoons raw cashews. When the béchamel is done, transfer it to the food processor and buzz it with the other ingredients until smooth. Stop the machine, scrape down the sides, and sprinkle with 3 tablespoons nutritional yeast (see page 239). Buzz again, scrape one more time, and there you have it. Season, if desired, as for the regular Mornay (see above).*

▲ **Sauce Moutarde:** *Add 2 tablespoons Dijon mustard, smooth or grainy style, to the basic béchamel.*

▲ **Tangy and Delicious Béchamel:** *Omit the aromatics and instead heat and thicken only ½ cup milk or soymilk. Substitute a good unflavored yogurt, soy yogurt, or plain kefir for the remaining ¾ cup milk. Dissolve the cornstarch in a little of it, then stir the slurry into the remainder of the yogurt. When the sauce is hot and thickened, stir in the yogurt mixture with the heat on medium. Heat, whisking often, until the sauce is smooth and thick, but don't boil, and then take it off the heat once the desired thickness has been achieved. Too much cooking will make the sauce separate. Add a few scallions and some chopped cilantro, if desired.*

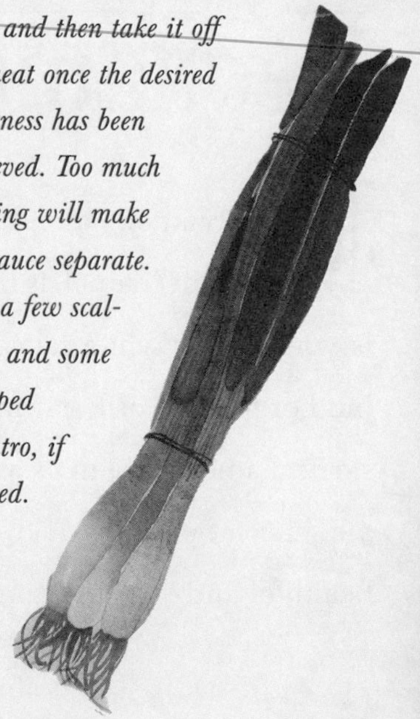

▲ **Sauce Soubise:** *Stir 2 to 3 very slowly sautéed onions into béchamel or velouté. Add a drop of tamari.*

1 Affix the bay leaf to the onion, using the cloves as tacks. Place this embellished onion with the celery top and a few scrapings of nutmeg in a medium saucepan, preferably nonstick. Pour all but 2 tablespoons of the dairy or soy milk over the vegetables and bring to a simmer over medium heat. Reduce the heat to low and simmer very, very gently for 15 minutes.

2 Meanwhile, toward the end of the simmering time, melt the butter over medium-low heat in a medium nonstick skillet or one that has been sprayed with cooking spray. Stir in the flour and cook, uncovered, stirring often, until the flour is slightly golden colored and aromatic but not darkened, 2 to 3 minutes. This is the roux.

3 Between stirs of the roux, dissolve the cornstarch in the reserved 2 tablespoons milk or soy milk.

4 Pour the warm infused milk through a strainer into the skillet containing the roux, whisking the roux into the heated milk so the sauce is lump free. Bring the sauce to a simmer and let it cook, whisking often, until it is the consistency of a very thin sauce or cream soup, about 6 minutes. Raise the heat slightly.

5 Whisk the cornstarch-milk mixture, to re-amalgamate the starch and milk, and stir this into the hot, thickened milk mixture, whisking. The sauce should quickly grow quite a bit thicker. Remove from the heat. Add salt and pepper to taste. Use immediately, or cool to room temperature and refrigerate for later use. (After refrigerating, reheat quickly; extended reheating will cause the cornstarch to lose its thickening power, making your sauce thinner in consistency.)

BE MY VALENTINE BRUNCH

Magic Grapefruit
(PAGE 984)

*

Sautéed smoked tempeh strips

*

Poached eggs and steamed broccoli on toasted whole wheat English muffins, sauced with Mornay Sauce with Cheddar
(OPPOSITE PAGE)

*

Chai tea

Salsa Poblano Blanca y Verde

Poblano peppers, also called anchos, are dark green, with a slightly flattened heart shape, and they are one of the most magical of the capsicum family—medium hot, but with a gentle, sneak-up-on-you heat, and a distinct sweetness. Charring them, over the stove-top burner or on the grill, brings out everything that's good.

This creamy, slightly chunky, utterly addictive sauce is pale green flecked with a deeper green. The poblanos team up with fresh cilantro to sublime effect

VARIATION

GREEN CHILE TWO-CORN CHOWDER: ***Add an extra ½ cup stock to the finished sauce, along with 1 diced cooked potato, 1 cup corn kernels (frozen or cut from the cob), and 1 cup drained canned posole. Heat through, topping with grated Cheddar. Heartily, spicily, creamily delicious.***

over enchiladas, crêpes, and bean cakes, and in dozens of other recipes. The sauce is adapted from a recipe from Cynthia Pedregon of the Peach Tree Tea Room in Fredericksburg, Texas; she adds more stock and purees the whole thing. At the Peach Tree, this is served as a soup, but Cynthia also uses it as a sauce over her bean cakes. Although I'm in love with the fresh grilled poblanos, Cynthia's trick of using canned green chiles makes a good quick variation.

A little evaporated skim or soy milk mellows the heat of the peppers and brings out their sweetness. You can easily make this vegan or lactose free. And you won't believe how low-fat this is! **MAKES A GENEROUS 3½ CUPS**

1½ teaspoons butter, Better (page 905), or vegetable oil or vegetable margarine
Cooking spray
1 onion, chopped
2 cloves garlic, minced
1 carrot, chopped
2 cups vegetable stock, preferably Golden Stock (page 140)
1¼ cups evaporated skim milk or unflavored soy milk, such as plain Soy Silk
¼ cup unbleached all-purpose flour
4 fresh poblano peppers, charred, peeled, stemmed, and seeded
½ cup fresh cilantro leaves
Salt and freshly ground black pepper to taste

1 Melt the butter over medium heat in a medium nonstick saucepan or one that has been sprayed with cooking spray. Add the onion and sauté, stirring, until it is softened, about 4 minutes. Add the garlic and carrot and sauté for 3 minutes more. Add the stock and bring to a boil. Turn the heat down to a simmer and cook, half covered, until the vegetables are very tender, about 25 minutes.

2 Meanwhile, put the evaporated skim milk or soy milk and the flour in a food processor and buzz to smoothness. Add the roasted poblanos and the cilantro and pulse/chop until the peppers are chopped and the mixture is chunky, scraping the sides of the work bowl as needed.

3 When the vegetables are done, scoop out a ladleful of the hot broth. Add to the processor and buzz again. Pour the processor mixture into the simmering stock and vegetables, and whisk the devil out of it. Raise the heat slightly and cook, whisking often, until the sauce is creamy and thickened. Add salt and pepper to taste. Remove from the heat.

Stock-Based Sauces

Here are some more ways to use the great flavors of stocks (pages 139–41) to create sauces that will make even the simplest dinner both pleasing and interesting. Enjoy any of these over rice, pasta, potatoes, or biscuits, or use them to sauce the filling for pot pies, or shepherd's pies, as described in Deep Dish, Chapter 6.

Chicken-Style Gravy

The ingredients of this gravy sound improbable, but "delicious" doesn't even come close to how good the finished dish is. As someone who used to work for us—I think it was E-Rae—would remark of something particularly tasty, "You'd stomp your momma for the last bite."

I would say that this gravy is a dead ringer for the real thing, except that (1) it is its *own* real thing, and (2) it may be even better than the original. It makes the already-pretty-darn-good Oven-Baked Chicken-Fried Tofu (page 670) really excellent, and it's amazing over baked sweet potatoes. When you have a smidgen left over, try my secret trick: Hide it in the fridge, and the next day, happily, very happily, spread it, cold, on toast, especially Sourdough Multigrain Loaf (page 522). This is the kind of thing a person hesitates to confess in print because it makes her come across as a bit of a fruitcake, but there you are.

MAKES ABOUT 4 CUPS

VARIATION

SOUTHERN-STYLE "GIBLET" GRAVY: ***After thickening the gravy, stir in 1 tablespoon very finely minced onion, 1 tablespoon very finely minced celery, and 1 hard-boiled egg (optional), diced. Simmer over very low heat. You may also add a few shiitake mushroom stems, if you have any on hand. Slice them crosswise into thin circles—very giblety indeed.***

4 cups full-flavored vegetable stock
1 whole head garlic, unpeeled
1 carrot, halved
1 onion, coarsely chopped
1 bay leaf
½ teaspoon coarsely cracked black peppercorns
¼ cup nutritional yeast (see page 239)
½ teaspoon paprika
2 tablespoons butter or margarine or olive oil
2 tablespoons unbleached all-purpose flour
Salt and freshly ground black pepper to taste

1 Combine the stock, garlic, carrot, onion, bay leaf, and cracked peppercorns in a medium saucepan. Bring to a boil over high heat, reduce the heat to a low simmer, and simmer, partially covered, for 45 minutes. Pour the stock through a strainer, reserving the stock and the whole cooked garlic. Discard the carrot, onion, and bay leaf.

2 When the garlic is cool enough to handle, squeeze the soft garlic cloves out of their skins directly into the strained stock. Whisk in the nutritional yeast and paprika and reheat over low heat.

3 Melt the butter over medium-low heat in a skillet and cook it gently for 2 to 3 minutes. Whisk in the flour and cook, stirring almost constantly, until the flour paste browns slightly, 3 to 4 minutes. Gradually whisk in the hot strained stock. Simmer gently until very hot and slightly thickened, about 12 minutes. If you want a thicker gravy, cook it just a little longer. Season with salt and pepper.

COOK ONCE FOR 2 MEALS You can double this recipe for gravy and save half as the basis for Wild Rice, Lentil, and Mushroom Soup (page 166).

Vegan Sesame Velouté

No meat, no dairy, no lack of flavor. A lovely sauce, rich (courtesy of the tahini) and voluptuous, this velouté makes a simple meal of grains and steamed vegetables something special. **MAKES ABOUT 2¼ CUPS**

2 cups full-flavored vegetable stock (page 139)
1 clove garlic, pressed
2 tablespoons tahini
1 tablespoon cornstarch or 1 scant tablespoon arrowroot
1 tablespoon tamari or shoyu soy sauce
3 tablespoons nutritional yeast (page 239)
¼ cup oat or soy milk
Salt, freshly ground black pepper, paprika, and/or a little dried sage to taste

1 Place 1¾ cups of the stock and the garlic in a small saucepan and bring to a boil over medium heat. Reduce the heat slightly and whisk in the tahini.

2 Combine the cornstarch and tamari in a small bowl. Using your fingers, mash them together to form a smooth paste, gradually adding the reserved ¼ cup stock.

3 Whisk the cornstarch-stock paste, the nutritional yeast, and the oat or soy milk into the hot stock. Cook, whisking often, until the sauce is hot and thick, about 1½ minutes. Remove from the heat and season with salt, pepper, paprika, and sage.

Mushroom Sauce Veronese

This Italian-style mushroom sauce, different from the preceding, is caressed with Marsala and more subtly flavored, more straight-mushroom. Although regular domestic button mushrooms are fine here, feel free to throw in a few shiitakes, a portobello, a little dried-and-rehydrated porcini—whatever you have on hand. Try this sauce over pasta or mashed potatoes; toss it with mashed tofu and leftover vegetables; use it to fill crêpes, spooning some sauce over the tops of the crêpes.

MAKES ABOUT 2½ CUPS

- 1 teaspoon butter or Better (page 905)
- 1 teaspoon olive oil
- Cooking spray
- ½ onion, chopped
- 2 cloves garlic, minced
- 2 tablespoons minced parsley
- 2 tablespoons unbleached all-purpose flour
- ½ pound mushrooms, cleaned and sliced
- 3 tablespoons Marsala or sweet vermouth
- ⅔ cup vegetable stock (page 139)
- Salt and freshly ground black pepper, to taste

1 Heat the butter and olive oil together over medium heat in a nonstick skillet or one that has been sprayed with cooking spray. Add the onion and cook, stirring occasionally, for 4 to 6 minutes, or until the onion is starting to color. Add the garlic and parsley and sauté for 2 to 3 minutes more.

2 Sprinkle the sauté with the flour, add the mushrooms, stir well, and add the Marsala. Gradually stir in the stock. Bring to a boil, turn down the heat to a simmer, and cook, stirring occasionally, for about 10 minutes. Season with salt and pepper and serve.

Mushroom-Miso-Mustard Gravy

White wine, Dijon, miso, good vegetable stock—the flavors in this are incredibly good and fly in the face of anyone who thinks that something vegetarian and low-fat cannot be intensely delicious. Instead of the fat-intense roux technique that is typical of gravy making, the thickeners are buzzed in the food processor with some of the liquid. This sauce is a must with the Mushroom, Wild Rice, and Lentil Timbale-Cake (page 304), but countless entrees and entree plates would be sparked by it—basic baked tempeh or tofu, for instance, with a grain side dish and some steamed broccoli.

If you are making the sauce to go with the timbale, you'll have the mushroom caps called for in the recipe on hand. **MAKES ABOUT 4 CUPS**

1 teaspoon butter or Better (page 905)
1 teaspoon olive oil
Cooking spray
¼ medium onion, finely chopped
2 cups sliced mushroom caps (about ⅓ pound)
3¼ cups vegetable stock (page 139)
¾ cup dry white wine
2 cloves garlic, peeled and quartered
¼ cup unbleached all-purpose flour
1 tablespoon golden miso (sweet white miso)
1 tablespoon dark miso (traditional red miso)
3 tablespoons nutritional yeast (see page 239)
1 teaspoon Dijon mustard
Salt and freshly ground black pepper, to taste

1 Melt the butter and olive oil together in a large skillet, well sprayed with cooking spray, over medium heat for about 1 minute. Add the onion and sauté, stirring often, for about 4 minutes, or until the onion begins to soften. Raise the heat slightly and add the mushroom caps. Continue cooking, stirring often, for 5 to 6 minutes more.

2 Pour the vegetable stock into a medium saucepan or Dutch oven, preferably nonstick, and warm over medium-low heat.

3 Pour the wine into a food processor and add the garlic, flour, golden miso, dark miso, nutritional yeast, and mustard. Buzz together to form a paste.

4 Whisk the paste into the warmed, but not hot, vegetable stock. Gently bring to a boil, then reduce to a simmer. Take a ladleful of this liquid and swirl it into the sautéed mushroom mixture, stirring well to scrape up any little flavorful bits from the bottom of the skillet. Add the mushrooms, onions, and liquid to the pot with the stock, scraping the sauté pan clean.

5 Reduce the heat to very low and let the sauce simmer very gently, stirring occasionally, for about 30 minutes. Correct the seasonings with salt (you'll need little, if any, since miso is salty) and a lot of pepper. Serve hot, ladled over whatever good thing you are serving.

Classic Tahini Sauce

This is old-school, pre–fat-conscious vegetarian cooking. But if you want a sauce that is indulgent and rich, with deeply interesting flavors, it can't be beat. Reserve it for every once in a while. A little goes a long way—a tablespoon can do beautiful things when tossed with a huge mound of steamed vegetables, so it's not *quite* as unconscionable as it might seem. **MAKES ABOUT 1 CUP**

VARIATION

SPICED TAHINI SAUCE: ***Add ½ teaspoon ground cumin, toasted in a skillet until fragrant, a dash of cayenne, and plenty of freshly ground black pepper.***

½ cup tahini
½ cup freshly squeezed lemon juice (3 to 4 lemons)
2 to 3 cloves garlic, pressed
½ teaspoon salt
About ½ cup water, preferably spring or filtered

VARIATIONS

THICK, CREAMY NEW WAVE TAHINI SAUCE: ***Use 1/3 cup toasted tahini, and just 1/4 cup water. Add 1 (10½-ounce) box reduced-fat firm silken tofu. Buzz until smooth, adding additional garlic and lemon to taste. Heat and serve.***

GOLDEN TEMPLE TAHINI DRESSING: ***Combine 1 cup toasted tahini, ½ cup mild vegetable oil (corn, canola, or peanut), 1/4 cup tamari or shoyu soy sauce, 1/3 cup lemon juice, ½ of a 10½-ounce box reduced-fat firm silken tofu, 1 chopped celery rib, and 1 seeded and chopped green bell pepper, and buzz in a food processor. When well incorporated, add about ½ cup water, a little at a time, until the dressing is of the consistency you like.***

1 Combine the tahini, lemon juice, garlic, and salt in a food processor. Buzz until very smooth and thick, then, with the machine running, drizzle in the water a little at a time to make a smooth, creamy sauce, as thin or as thick as you like.

2 Heat the sauce in a medium saucepan until good and hot, but don't let it boil. Serve immediately.

Rich and Righteous Miso-Tahini Stir-Fry Sauce

Mix this up in a small saucepan while you quickly stir-fry onions, red pepper strips, and broccoli. Toss some tofu or baked or steamed tempeh into the stir-fry and then pour this simple but luscious concoction over it. Or spoon it over a big mound of brown rice. A bit rich for everyday, but so fast and so good you'll be glad you have it in your repertoire. Peanut butter can substitute for the tahini, and the optional seasonings make variations easy. **MAKES A SCANT ¾ CUP**

1½ tablespoons toasted tahini
1½ tablespoons red miso
1½ tablespoons honey or Rapidura
1½ teaspoons finely chopped peeled ginger
½ cup water, preferably spring or filtered
Any of the following (optional):
  zest and juice of 1 orange, a couple of cloves pressed garlic, 2 teaspoons commercial ginger-garlic paste, or a few drops toasted sesame oil

Combine all the ingredients in a small saucepan and bring to a boil, whisking out the lumps of miso and tahini. Cook at a simmer for a minute or so, until it thickens slightly and smooths out. Serve hot over grains, veggies, pasta, whatever pleases you. Leftovers keep for several days, refrigerated.

CHAPTER 15

Just Desserts

Nobody really *needs* dessert. Dessert serves pleasure, not necessity, pleasure belonging both to the cook and those eating her or his offerings. I've seen friends, family, guests at the restaurant, writers at the Colony, take a spoonful of dessert—a bite of voluptuous chocolate bread pudding, or icy-sweet-hot ginger sorbet, or creamy, tart mousse redolent with fresh lemon, or a hundred other desserts—seen them take that bite, close their eyes, and just *stop,* the better to savor the sensations. Since I've also often been the one making and serving the dessert, I know it's sweet no matter what side of the equation you are on.

Do desserts have a place in a healthful diet? Sure. Sugar and fat have been demonized, and there are legitimate health concerns with their overconsumption . . . but what of desserts that are calorie-sane and nourishment-rich? And doesn't once-in-a-while indulgence have its place in anyone's diet? How much does the "No, I really *shouldn't*" sensibility affect our overall capacity for saying yes to pleasure? Is it not possible to just plain old enjoy dessert?

Over the years I've become the following: vegetarian, middle-aged, devoted to working out, an ex-restaurateur. My once-rampant sweet tooth has moderated itself to a degree; better yet, I've made peace with it. Six years of working long, late night hours at the inn with total access to all the butter- and cream-rich desserts, chocolate and other indulgences, all from scratch, all to my personal liking, lessened the allure of the forbidden. On restaurant nights, I might have a single bite of pecan pie at the end of a long shift. (Although I really still craved—I mean *craved*—our ginger sorbet.)

These days, unless I'm traveling, and experiencing what local chefs have to offer, I eat a luscious, high-fat dessert maybe once a month, if that. I've included a few of my favorites in this category. These are the feel-good desserts that were top favorites at our restaurant, the ones that guests requested over and over, described in embarrassing superlatives, asked for doggie bags and the recipe to take home, or sometimes even seconds (and bear in mind, our portions on "firsts" were anything but skimpy). Our Honeyed Browned-Butter Pecan Pie, our Double-Density Chocolate-Walnut Espresso Torte (known to us in-house as "Double-D"), our beloved Chocolate Bread Pudding Maurice are irresistible at times: dream desserts. There is no nutritional defense or apology for them. But when looking for rich, knockout desserts, I believe you can't find any better. And I hope you enjoy them, absolutely guilt-free, on those occasions when nothing but serious indulgence will do.

"Let us sit down soon to eat with all those who haven't eaten, let us spread great tablecloths, put salt in the lakes of the world, set up planetary bakeries, and a plate like the moon itself from which we will all eat."

—**Pablo Neruda,** *The Great Tablecloth*

Does this mean forgoing dessert the rest of the time? *Au contraire.* I still enjoy sweets and often make a little something for Ned and myself and any friends at home. But the daily choices pull their weight nutritionally. Fresh fruit, whether plain or as compote or cup, and sorbets are classic, calorie-sane, low-fat choices, rich in phytochemicals and so very good. But there is also a very pleasant middle ground, where you want something with a little more indulgence-quotient but without the ultra-caloric, fat-gram wallop. I offer many such alternatives that I hope you will love. The Lemon Mousse-Custard, one of the four or five all-time best recipes I've developed, is tofu-based, no eggs, no cream, and divine. I've also included other, homier classic desserts that are nominally reduced-fat (or inherently low-fat) but delicious: fruit cobblers and crunches, biscotti, some goofy trompe l'oeil dessert nachos, even a few cakes.

Will you join me for dessert? It would be my pleasure.

How Sweet It Is

Almost all sweeteners (save those artificially created) are concentrated sources of calories and little else. What sets them apart from one another? Though nutritionists usually say "sugar is sugar is sugar," different sweeteners are distinguished by flavor, texture, cooking properties, in some cases phytochemicals or other micronutrients, plus the speed at which an individual's body metabolizes them. This last is dependent on two things: the particular biochemical makeup of the sweetener, and the body and timing of the individual eating it.

Most of our common sweeteners are simple sugars (mono or di-saccharides; made up of single or double chain molecules). Such sugars include white, brown, raw, and turbinado sugars, honey, maple syrup, Rapidura, and molasses. They are quickly absorbed into the bloodstream, causing the frequently alluded-to "sugar rush–sugar crash." More gradually metabolized sweeteners are composed of complex sugars (poly-saccharides or multi-branched molecular chains). Derived from malted or fermented grains, like barley or rice, they break down slowly in the body, providing steadier energy.

Where does the individual metabolism, and the question of timing, come in? In determining how sensitive to sugar a particular system is, one must factor in not only the type of sugar, but when the person involved last ate. If one hasn't eaten breakfast and then crashes at midday, grows ravenous for sweets, gratifies the hunger with a chocolate bar, and crashes again, it's a very different matter from eating a sweet after a balanced dinner.

It is best to incorporate desserts (mostly more healthful ones, but occasionally the go-for-it densely sugary ones) into a way of eating that is *healthful as a whole.* Avoid daily ingestion of sugar's "empty calories" . . . but know they do no great harm if your diet is a healthful one.

Oh, Honey

Honey—flower nectar transmogrified by bees into a gloriously thick, sweet syrup in a range of ambered hues—is a fabled ingredient. Its origins are romantic, and among primitive peoples it was not only a rare find but about the only source of concentrated sweetener available. Mentioned repeatedly in the Old Testament, it's been used in pastries since ancient times. Mead, a beer based on fermented honey, was served by the Babylonians at weddings, supposedly giving rise to the post-marriage period (originally marked as a twenty-eight–day moon cycle) as a "honeymoon," while ancient Egyptians included honey in the marriage contract (husbands had to agree to supply their new wives with thirty-two pounds of honey per year).

Honey has also been an element of countless folk medicine cures for centuries. Although nutritionists frequently have stated that it is metabolized by the body identically to sugar, honey die-hards say "Yes, but—" and enumerate its other health-giving properties. Lately, it seems they have some reason to do so: Research done at the University of Illinois shows that honey is rich in certain antioxidants, those healthful micronutrients, while researchers in New Zealand have turned up impressive data on honey's antibiotic and wound-healing properties.

Natural, unrefined honey is known as "raw," though it has been heated very slightly so that it can be strained more easily to remove the comb. Raw honey contains a few other micronutrients: bee pollen, propolis (probably the antibiotic element), minute quantities of proteins and enzymes. (Please note that raw honey should not be fed to children under eighteen months; their digestive tracts and immune systems are not yet developed enough to handle the bacteria that are sometimes present in raw honey.)

Whatever may show up eventually in the lab, honey's lasting place in the kitchen is assured. It is about 25 to 50 percent sweeter than sugar, and it is not just neutrally sweet, like sugar, but full of flavor, character, and individual variation in taste and texture, based on the flowers at which the honey-making bees supped and how long it has been in the jar.

Its lack of neutrality and its inconsistency can be a drawback when cooking, especially baking, with honey; nonetheless, it can be done by following a few simple guidelines:

- Since honey is sweeter than sugar, for every cup of sugar called for, substitute ⅔ cup honey.
- Since honey is liquid and sugar is solid, for every cup of honey used, decrease the other liquid in the recipe by ¼ cup.
- Cakes spiced with ginger, cinnamon, or nutmeg stand up to and moderate honey's distinctive flavor.
- Since honey caramelizes more swiftly than sugar, reduce oven temperatures by 25 degrees.
- Honey is slightly acidic; when using in a recipe that is leavened by baking powder, for a lighter product with a better rise add ¼ teaspoon baking soda per cup of honey. (If the recipe already contains baking soda, you need not do this.)
- All honey (with the idiosyncratic exception of tupelo) crystallizes in time. To reliquefy it, place the opened honey jar in a pan of hot water and warm over low heat.
- When measuring sticky honey, first spray the inside of the measuring cup with cooking spray, or measure the oil or butter called for in the recipe in the measuring cup before the honey, so that every last drop will pour out smoothly.

Consider the strength, character, and flavor of a particular honey to decide whether it will go well in a given recipe.

- Honeys that are light in color tend to be mildest in flavor. Those that are a light, pale gold color such as clover, alfalfa, tupelo, and most blends labeled just "honey," are in this category. These milder honeys are generally best for cooking. Exception to the rule: basswood honey, which, though pale, has a medium-strong flavor.
- Deeper brown honeys tend to have stronger flavors; you will either love or hate them. I adore most buckwheat honey, arguably the most muscular in flavor, particularly on pancakes. Orange blossom honey, midway between light and dark honey, has the faintest aroma of orange blossoms and is sublime on hot buttered cornbread.
- One honey I dislike is eucalyptus, which retains a cough-drop-like menthol quality. Not good for cooking, in my view.
- Greece is known for exceptional honeys. Greek fino, or forest, honey is truly food for the gods. And so are Greek pine and thyme honeys.
- Manuka honey from New Zealand is also divine: floral, rich, and complex.

What a Sap: Maple Syrup & Maple Sugar

This intoxicatingly delicious sweetener is second only to honey in terms of romance; the latter, drawn by bees from flowers; the former, from certain kinds of maple trees (usually sugar maples) by humans. American Indians were drawing out the sap and boiling it down, in much the same process that we use today, when the Europeans arrived. Walk my Aunt Dot's farm in Saxtons River, Vermont, and you can see the tubes affixed to the trees year round, in preparation for the spring's sugaring.

It takes forty years for a sugar maple tree to grow large enough to tap, and the tapping must be done at just the right moment: after winter has done its worst, but before spring is in full spate. Then, and only then, is the sap flowing. This in-between thawing season lasts only about a month, six weeks at most, and it takes about 5½ days for a tree to give enough sap —forty gallons—to yield a single gallon of maple syrup once the mildly sweet sap has been boiled down. A few drops of butter, oil, or cream are added to the sap during the boiling process to reduce foaming. Amazingly enough, tapping does the tree no harm.

Once it has been opened, maple syrup should be refrigerated. Of course, using it on pancakes —especially buckwheat pancakes —is a joy, but you may also bake with it. I love Maple-Oatmeal Cookies (page 1028) and Vermont-Style Browned-Butter Maple-Walnut Pie (page 1024). Wow!

When revising a recipe that calls for white sugar, follow the general guidelines given for cooking with honey, except, because maple syrup is a bit thinner than honey:

- ▲ substitute ⅔ cup maple syrup for each cup of white sugar;
- ▲ reduce any other liquid called for in the recipe by ⅓ cup for each cup of sugar the original recipe called for.

If you really nose around for it and don't mind paying a premium, you can also purchase granulated maple sugar. I buy about one quart a year, specifically for Magic Grapefruit (page 984), but you can also bake with it, substituting it for sugar cup for cup. I order mine from Butternut Mountain Farm, in Johnson, Vermont (800-828-2376), or Black Horse Farm, in Mason, New Hampshire (800 221-1720; sales@blackhorsefarm.com).

Sugar, Rapidura & Other Sweeteners

White sugar, refined from pressed sugarcane, leaves two separate products: strongly flavored molasses (which contains the B-vitamins, iron, and other nutritional elements the sugarcane plant offers in addition to its sugars) and white sugar (sweet, neutral, dry, consistent, and bereft of much except calories). Brown sugar, which may look less refined, is actually just white sugar with a trace of molasses added back in for color or flavor. Both conventional brown and white sugar raise the blood sugar level quickly, which has led people and businesses preferring natural foods to search for alternatives.

- ▲ Rapidura is one of my favorite sweeteners, which was originally trademarked as Sucanat (a contraction of "Sugar Cane Natural") from organically grown sugar. Rapidura combines sugar and quite a bit of molasses to produce a delicious, dry, granular sweetening product. It is just about as versatile to cook with as white sugar, but retains many of the vitamins, minerals and trace elements of the sugarcane plant. While its deep reddish brown crystals are larger than those of white sugar, it can easily be substituted for white sugar, cup for cup. Although you'd expect from its color that it would be very strongly flavored, it is mild and agreeable. It's still sugar, but far less refined than white sugar, so it is generally metabolized more smoothly. You can buy it in bulk or in 1- to 5-pound bags at natural foods markets.
- ▲ Blackstrap molasses is the end product of the sugar making process—what's left after most of the sugar has been refined. It contains all the good stuff removed from the sugar: most of the original plant's vitamins, minerals, and trace elements (iron, potassium, calcium, and magnesium). Probably the most nutritious of all sweeteners, its strong flavor limits its use. In fact, it is best used as

a flavoring agent—it's wonderful in gingerbread, gingersnaps, and molasses cookies—rather than as a sweetener. Most recipes using it call for sugar as well, to moderate its taste, which, unadulterated, has a bitter, dominant whang.

▲ Barbados molasses has nothing to do with the Caribbean island. Rather, it is another type of molasses. A byproduct of the early stages of sugar refining, it is lighter and sweeter than blackstrap. It can be a good choice when you want the molasses flavor, but not its potency. But you do run into the cooking conundrum of liquid-for-solid sugar-replacement.

▲ Rice syrup is half as sweet as sugar or honey, and many people who have trouble with those sweeteners find they can tolerate this mild, thick, golden brown syrup far better. When made from brown rice, the syrup can take two to three hours to be digested, resulting in a steadied blood sugar level and an even supply of energy. It is usually produced by culturing brown rice with a minute amount of natural fungal enzymes, which break down the starches. The liquid is drained off and cooked to a thick syrupy consistency. It can be substituted for sugar using the rules for honey (see page 958), but bear in mind that the finished product will be much less sweet. Also, you should add an extra ¼ teaspoon leavener per cup of syrup, since the enzyme tends to break down the rising agent. (A nonenzyme brown rice syrup is the artisanal Genmai Syrup, made by Suzanne's Specialties.) Like honey, brown rice syrup will crystallize in time. Simply place the opened jar of crystallized rice syrup in a saucepan of hot water, and simmer gently until it reliquefies, about 10 minutes.

Rice syrup's flavor is mild and agreeable; not quite as neutral as sugar, but less dominant than honey, or certainly molasses. Drizzle it into any sauce calling for sugar, honey, or Rapidura; try it as a delicious bread spread mixed in equal parts with peanut butter, almond butter, or tahini; enjoy it as a sweetener in rice pudding. It's also pleasing on pancakes. I've developed one dessert specifically for those who are devoted to rice syrup, the Almond Blond Brownies (page 1029).

▲ Barley malt is made like rice syrup, by fermenting grain with benign bacteria that convert the barley starch into a combination of simple and complex sugars. Much darker in color than rice syrup, it's also more strongly flavored; similar to molasses. You can substitute it for sugar using the guidelines given for honey. Because of its dominant flavor, I recommend it for spice cakes, or in recipes where just a bit of sweetener is required. It's also nice in strong sauces and stews that need a touch of sweet; chili, say, or in a red wine–based sauce.

▲ Concentrated fruit juices, like frozen thawed apple juice concentrate, sound good in principle. Yet they contain very little of the nutrients present in fresh fruit and none of the fiber that balances blood sugar. These sweeteners bear little resemblance to the fruit from which they are derived. When I use them, I do so because they work particularly well in a given recipe, not because they're healthful.

A sugar note for vegans or animal rights–oriented vegetarians:

Several brands of white cane sugar use a filter of highly purified carbon to remove color and trap any impurities as part of the refining process. This carbon, known as bone char, is made from purified beef bones. According to extensive research done by the Vegetarian Research Group (VRG), Domino, Savannah Foods, California and Hawaiian Sugar all use bone char filters in the manufacture of brown, white, and confectioners' sugar. None of the bone char passes into the sugar, but the sugar does pass through it, as water does through a water filter.

This is not an issue with sugar derived from beets, rather than cane, nor do all sugar cane refineries use bone char. Refined Sugar, manufacturer of Jack Frost Sugar, uses granular carbon instead of bone char; so does Florida Crystal sugar. Also, turbinado sugar, sometimes sold as sugar in the raw, the light brown sugar with granules larger than those of white sugar, is made without char.

Fruit Desserts:
From Orchard, Vine & Bramble-bush

"Plants, being rooted to their particular spots, must enlist the aid of mobile agents in nature to disperse their offspring, the seeds," food scientist Harold McGee explains. We, albeit unknowingly, are among those agents. Fruit is the snare by which the plant induces us to do its bidding and scatter its seed. "Ripening, that sudden transformation of a fruit's color, flavor, and texture, takes place only when the seeds are ready to be dispersed," he says. So, when we lift a ripe, in-season peach at the market, feel the curve of its fuzzed globe heavy in our hand, inhale its perfumed scent, bag up a pound to take home—when we do this, we are gloriously taking part in the same cycle of life that bees, squirrels, bats, and all other creatures do.

If, as McGee concludes, fruit "is both the final confection of the meal, and the formal invitation to dine," it is natural, then, that the starting point for thinking about dessert is fruit.

Mostly we crave, rightly or wrongly, embellishment and elaboration before we get excited about fruit. So we sugar fruit, splash it with liqueur, macerate it with citrus zest or mint, dollop it with cream, freeze it, combine it with other fruits, at the very least cut it up and arrange it. And these are the simple preparations! We put it beneath or on top of or between cakes or shortcakes or crunchy mixtures; we wrap it in crêpes or pastry, caramelize it, serve it over ice cream, and layer it with cake crumbs, custard, jam, and whipped cream and call it a "trifle"! In the process, as in so many processes where innocence is balanced by knowledge or sophistication, we both lose and gain. Didn't this happen to Eve once, and wasn't an apple involved?

But with fruit, we can still have it both ways. There are many fruits and four seasons. We can enjoy the crisp perfection of a plain Newtown Pippin apple throughout the fall; the homey pleasure of a crunchy brown-sugary streusel-topped apple crisp, and the stunning elaboration of a cinnamon'd, pastry-wrapped apple, baked and syruped and studded with black peppercorns and served with real vanilla-bean ice cream.

Our foods, like our lives, are most delicious when they are both simple and elaborated, each pointing up the pleasures of the other.

This section begins with simple fruit compotes and medleys, then moves on to other desserts—some lighter, some heavy on the indulgence factor—fruit by individual fruit.

Fruit Cups & Compotes

If you think fruit cups are boring and don't really count as dessert, let me help you rethink that assumption here and now. You may perhaps be going back to the canned, sugar-syruped fruit cocktails of your youth (and the school cafeteria), or you may have had one too many versions of not-good simply cut-up fresh fruit. While the latter is fine if the fruit itself is at its best, too often the combinations are done without giving thought to their synergy, and, more important, without tasting the individual elements before throwing them in—I'm thinking of the big appetizing-looking but so-disappointing bowl of cut fruit on a hotel breakfast buffet, for instance, where every strawberry turns out to be mushy, every melon cube flavorless.

And there you have the first rule of fruit for dessert—make sure the fruit is as close to the peak of ripeness as possible. That usually means going for local and in-season when you can. A dense and tender strawberry, spurting with bright red juice, grown in the field outside the farm-stand where it was picked an hour or two earlier, is an entirely different experience from the one that is larger, firmer, with a paler and more fibrous interior, the better to withstand shipment. Obviously, there are exceptions to the local-and-in-season rule, otherwise most people in America would never eat a pineapple, orange, or banana. But buy fruit attentively, with some awareness of what's in season.

Besides choosing the absolute best raw ingredients, there's the matter of minor-to-major jazzing up to yield big-time results. First, note that fruit "cups" are usually raw, cut-up fruit combinations while compotes generally involve at least one cooked fruit, a sweet spice, and a poaching bath in wine. Either can be served as is or dressed up: Biscotti are always excellent with poached fruit desserts; an alternative is a scoop of icy lemon sorbet, or a scoop of your favorite creamy frozen vanilla confection—say, ice cream or yogurt.

Warm Compote of Cranberries, Apples, and Bananas

Just made to go with a scoop of vanilla ice cream, frozen yogurt, or soy ice cream, this compote is also gratifying with any plain cake—try Miss Kay's Orange Sponge Cake (page 1013). The gingered variation is very good, too. Although the bananas are optional, when barely poached, they reveal a surprising new side to their character; they also broaden the cranberries' horizons so that their assertive goodness shines through. **SERVES 6 TO 8 AS AN ACCOMPANIMENT**

1 package (12 ounces) fresh cranberries, picked over to remove any that are dried out or rotted
3 tart, firm apples, peeled, cored, and cut into ¾-inch chunks
¼ cup brown sugar, Rapidura, rice syrup, or honey, or to taste
2 cups frozen apple juice concentrate, thawed
2 bananas, firm but ripe, sliced

Combine the cranberries, apples, and brown sugar in a medium nonstick, nonreactive saucepan. Add the concentrate and place over high heat. Bring to a boil, then lower the heat and simmer, stirring occasionally, until the cranberries open and the apples are tender, about 10 minutes. Add the bananas and cook for another 2 minutes. Remove from the heat and serve immediately.

VARIATION

Add 1 tablespoon peeled, minced fresh ginger when adding the bananas.

Fall Compote of Apples, Oranges, and Raspberries with Red Wine

This full-flavored mélange is plush with the brilliance of the Ozarks' fall colors: October apples and autumn-crop raspberries, the first of the winter oranges, all subtly underlined by a red-wine syrup. The fruits are elegantly arranged on the plates, not jumbled together.

The Orange Biscotti on page 1036 go nicely here, giving you something to dip into your decaf—or the red-wine syrup—as you linger over the table and talk. **SERVES 6**

3 oranges
2 cups dry red wine
¼ cup honey
¼ cup frozen apple juice concentrate, thawed
One 3-inch stick cinnamon
2 to 3 large, crisp fall apples, peeled, cored, and sliced into eighths
¼ cup raspberry jam, preferably all-fruit, no sugar added
1 box (6 ounces) red raspberries
1 box (6 ounces) yellow raspberries (optional)

VARIATION

***No-Fuss Last-Minute Variation:* Dice the apples into large bite-sized chunks (which means they'll take less time to poach). Cut the oranges into bite-size pieces. Combine the poached apples, oranges, and syrup in the serving bowl and refrigerate. Just before serving, scatter the raspberries on top.**

1 Grate the rind from 1 of the oranges. Set aside. Carefully peel all 3 oranges, removing all of the white pith. Cut crosswise into ½-inch slices. Place in a shallow bowl and set aside.

2 Combine the red wine, honey, concentrate, cinnamon stick, and orange rind in a large nonreactive skillet over high heat. Bring to a boil, immediately lower the heat, and simmer for 3 minutes. Carefully drop in the apples and poach until translucent, infused with red, tender but not mushy, and easily pierced with a fork. A really firm apple, such as an Arkansas Black, may take as long as 20 to 25 minutes; a Golden Delicious will be done in far less time. Using a slotted spoon, carefully lift the apples from wine and set aside aside. Let cool slightly, then cover and refrigerate.

3 Add the jam to the simmering red mixture. Raise the heat to medium, and simmer until the liquid is reduced by half and is syrupy, 7 to 8 minutes. Remove from the heat and let cool slightly.

4 Strain the still-warm syrup over the reserved orange slices. Cover and refrigerate.

5 When ready to serve, pool a little of the syrup on each of 6 of your prettiest simple dessert plates. Overlap a few orange wheels on each plate, and divide the poached apple pieces among the plates. Scatter the raspberries over the plates. Pass any remaining syrup at the table.

Compote of Golden Fruits in Orange Syrup

Sunlight in a bowl; bright, big, romantic flavors in every bite. If you have a footed glass bowl that you rarely use, this is the time to drag it out. Hazelnut Biscotti (page 1037) are very nice accompanying this; so is Miss Kay's Orange Sponge Cake (page 1013). **SERVES 4**

1 cup orange bay-leaf syrup (see page 985)
4 large pieces crystallized ginger, cut into slivers
½ cup dried whole apricots, halved horizontally
2 oranges, peeled, seeded, and cut into half-sections
1 perfectly ripe mango, peeled, seeded, and diced
2 bananas, ripe but not soft, peeled, halved lengthwise then across (do not cut them until just before serving)
Needlethreads (page 986; optional)

1 Combine the orange bay-leaf syrup with the crystallized ginger in a medium nonreactive saucepan over high heat. Bring to a hard boil. Drop in the apricots and immediately turn off the heat. Allow the apricots to macerate in the syrup until the syrup has come to room temperature. Toss in the oranges and the mango. Store, covered and refrigerated, until serving time.

2 When ready to serve, place a banana quarter on opposite sides of each of 4 dessert plates. Place the apricot-orange compote between the bananas, dividing it equally among the plates. Drizzle some of the syrup over the bananas. If desired, sprinkle each portion with a few Needlethreads, and serve.

Compote of Poached Bananas and Star Fruit with Dried Cherries

Who could imagine how very wonderful bananas are when poached? Star fruit also takes on an admirable new character, moderating its sometimes excess tartness. American Spoon Foods, a premium mail-order company (800-222-5886), sells what are, hands down, the best dried cherries on the market, tart or sweet varieties with no sugar added. **SERVES 6 TO 8**

4 ripe but firm bananas
½ lemon
2¾ cups semidry white wine, such as a Riesling
1 vanilla bean, split lengthwise
¼ cup frozen apple juice concentrate, thawed
⅓ to ½ cup packed brown sugar
½ cup dried cherries (or dried cranberries or dried blueberries)
3 star fruit, cut crosswise into ½-inch slices, any visible hard seeds removed
Whipped cream, Yogurt Sour Cream (page 910), Ricotta Crème (page 1061), Tofu-Cashew Crème (page 1062), or vanilla frozen yogurt (optional)

1 Peel the bananas, then slice them first in half, lengthwise, then crosswise, to make 4 curved quarters per banana. Squeeze the juice of the ½ lemon into a medium bowl. Add the bananas and enough water to barely cover. Set aside.

2 Combine the wine, vanilla bean, and concentrate in a nonreactive skillet over high heat. Add brown sugar to taste, and bring to a boil. Lower the heat and simmer, covered, for 3 minutes. Add the dried cherries, cover, and simmer for another 3 minutes. Add the star fruit and simmer, covered, for 5 minutes.

3 Remove the bananas from the acidulated water and add them to the skillet. Depending on the size of your skillet, you may need to add a bit of extra wine to ensure that the fruit is covered. Simmer, covered, until the bananas are almost translucent, 3 to 5 more minutes. Remove from the heat and serve slightly warm, as is or with any of the optional creamy dollops.

Fresh Pineapple–Frangelico Coupe

This is light, refreshing, straightforward, with a bit of pizzazz and sparkle: perfect after just about any rich entree. The raspberry-pineapple combination is superb, kin to the classic Southern ambrosia, but a bit more soigné. Hazelnut biscotti, homemade or purchased, are a nice complement, since Frangelico has a hazelnut base. **SERVES 6 TO 8**

1 fresh pineapple, peeled, eyes and core removed, cut into 1-inch cubes
2 oranges, peeled and sectioned
¼ cup Frangelico
2 tablespoons confectioners' sugar
1 bag (12 ounces) frozen raspberries
2 tablespoons finely chopped toasted hazelnuts (optional)
2 tablespoons Needlethreads (page 986; optional)

1 Up to 4 hours before serving, combine the pineapple, oranges, Frangelico, and confectioners' sugar. Toss to blend well. Cover and refrigerate.

2 Ten minutes or so before serving, toss in the still-frozen raspberries. (They will thaw slightly on contact with the liqueur and fruit, but remain a bit frozen, which keeps them from becoming mushy and adds a nice little bite.)

3 If desired, garnish each serving with a sprinkle of toasted hazelnuts and Needlethreads and serve with biscotti.

Fruit by Fruit

Walk with me now, fruit by fruit, through the orchard, the garden, the berry patch, and into the kitchen. Bite the ripest peach out of hand, leaning forward off the edge of the porch so the juice doesn't drip down your chin, peel the fresh mango and eat it plain and over the sink for the same reason. And after selecting strawberries and cantaloupe by their aroma, when you get truly fragrant ones rush them home and eat them as they are, at room temperature. Let me remind you about crisp October apples, which spit juice when your teeth sink into their resistant flesh, and handfuls of fresh local blueberries in June. And imagine what it is, in spring, to have the wild black-cap raspberries appear, as we do here, brambling up and down the clay-and-gravel and dirt roads you travel all year, pale green leaves and stickery arching branches, a fresh crop appearing each time it rains over a month or so from mid-June to mid-July. . . .

We may eat plain fruit out of hand for a snack, after lunch, or if dieting. But plain, unadulterated fruit is somehow too chaste, too pure, to be truly dessert to most of us. Elaboration can come, sometimes, in the experience of gathering I have just described (of course the fruit itself is more full-flavored, too), but mostly, with store-bought fruit, it takes an additional step of preparation to become the meal's crowning, conclusive confection.

But, as I mentioned before, with fruit we can have it both ways. Our lives, like our desserts, can be, should be, and must be, at times, both cooked and raw.

Apples

Dedicated farmers have patiently brought back once all-but-lost apple varieties. In addition to the ubiquitous Red and Golden Delicious and McIntosh, and the occasional Jonathans and Romes, we now commonly have Granny Smiths, Fujis, Galas, Braeburns. And in their season, we have dozens of others, the very names of which give off old-fashioned romance: Macoun and

Empire, Cox's Orange Pippin, Spitzenberg (said to be Thomas Jefferson's favorite variety), Lady, Mutsu, Gravenstein, Akane, Sheepnose, Roxbury Russet. One of our local best is Arkansas Black, a very dark red, hard-crisp apple with a slightly yellow flesh, and quite fragrant.

Each variety has its best use. Two notes on two commonly available apples: although the Granny Smith, when fresh and unwaxed, is a superb eating apple, it is not good for baking; the apples stay firm and don't break down into that pleasant, barely textured smoothness vital in pies or baked apples. A good Golden Delicious, on the other hand, while undistinguished as an eating apple, bakes up beautifully, achieving nuances of flavor and a creamily melting texture.

I think apple pies, applesauces, and the like are superior when made with a variety of apples. My favorite pie or strudel apples would be a combination of Golden Delicious, Braeburn, Macoun, Ida Red, Gravenstein, Wealthy, and Winesap or Stayman Winesap. But even two from this list make a filling special.

Deep-Dish Apple Strudel

Strudels are fillings rolled up in pastry. To engineer this rolling requires a large percentage of pastry to filling, and the pastry requires a large percentage of fat. Even filo pastry, fat-free in itself and used by almost everyone in strudel making (except perhaps German and Hungarian grandmothers), turns to an unpleasant floury paste if it is not brushed with enough butter before baking. What's enough? Well, to me, having made lots of fat-reduction experiments with filo, 2½ teaspoons to 1 tablespoon melted butter per sheet of filo is the minimum. Sorry, but there it is.

Actually, I'm not *that* sorry. Because with this recipe, which uses only 3 sheets of filo and hence 3 tablespoons butter, each portion adds up to only ¾ teaspoon of butterfat. Toasted walnuts add crunch, and just a few additional fat grams. These are generous portions, too, not little wussy ones; at 3 by 3½ inches, this is *dessert,* not a tease.

The way this all works is more filling, less pastry. The apple taste is intensified with raisins, spices, sweetness; less pastry is used, but with enough butter to make it truly what pastry is meant to be. **MAKES 12 SERVINGS**

2 cups frozen apple juice concentrate, thawed
1 cup water, preferably spring or filtered
8 cups peeled, sliced apples, preferably of several different varieties (15 to 20 apples)
¼ cup raisins or currants
3 tablespoons unbleached white all-purpose flour
1 tablespoon sugar, or slightly more to taste
¼ teaspoon ground cinnamon
A few gratings of nutmeg
Juice of ½ to 1 lemon (optional)
Cooking spray (optional)
2 tablespoons chopped toasted walnuts
2 tablespoons fine graham cracker crumbs
3 tablespoons butter, melted
3 sheets filo dough
Confectioners' sugar

1 Preheat the oven to 375°F.

2 Combine the concentrate and the water in a large saucepan. Place a steamer basket into the saucepan but do not allow it to touch the liquid. Place the saucepan over medium-high heat and add the apple slices to the steamer. Steam for 3 to 4 minutes, until slightly softened. (You'll probably have to do this in two batches.) Transfer the steamed apples to a large bowl.

3 Remove the steamer basket from the saucepan and raise the heat. Bring to a boil and, watching closely, boil the liquid down until it's reduced to ½ cup. (Don't turn your back on it for a minute, as the liquid will burn in the worst way.)

4 Pour the reduced liquid over the apples and let cool slightly. Once cool, drain off all the excess liquid (reserve it for another purpose; it's great as pancake syrup, or to poach bananas in).

5 Toss the apples with the raisins, flour, 1 tablespoon sugar, cinnamon, and nutmeg. Taste. If you think the apples need additional sugar, add it, a tablespoon at a time. If the apples are lacking in flavor, add the lemon juice. Set this mixture aside.

6 If not using nonstick, spray a 9-by-13-inch baking dish with cooking spray. Spoon the apple mixture into the dish. Set aside.

7 Combine the walnuts and graham cracker crumbs in a small dish. Place on the counter, along with a dish with the melted butter, and a pastry brush if you've got one, or a teaspoon if you don't. Prepare to work with the filo (see page 311 if you don't know the drill).

8 Drape 1 sheet of the filo over the top of the apples so that the filo sheet overhangs on 2 sides of the pan by about 5 inches. Working quickly, brush or drizzle slightly less than 1 tablespoon of the melted butter over the filo sheet. Sprinkle with a little less than half of the walnut–graham cracker crumb mixture. Quickly fold up one short edge of the overhang, then the long edge, and quickly give them a butter-brush and a crumb-sprinkle. This means that two edges of the dessert now have a double layer of filo, and one corner, where the folded-over portions overlap, has four layers. Repeat with the remaining 2 sheets of filo, alternating the sides of the pan where you fold the overhangs. End with a buttered but not crumbed layer of filo.

9 Using a sharp knife, gently and lightly score the filo dough into 12 pieces, each

VARIATION

Try Deep-Dish Plum Strudel, with 8 cups sliced plums, 5 tablespoons flour, no raisins. Or Pear Strudel (add 1 to 3 teaspoons peeled, finely minced ginger, substitute minced dates for raisins). Or Peach Strudel (5 tablespoons flour, plus a drop of almond extract; dried cherries). Raves every time, every fruit. Berries are too wet to work here; the filo comes out soggy.

approximately 3 by 3¼ inches (you don't need to worry about cutting down through the apples, just the pastry). Because the pan is quite full and the apple liquid may bubble over, set the baking dish on a nonstick cookie sheet to catch any drips, then pop it into the oven and bake until the filo is golden brown, 35 to 45 minutes. Remove from the oven. If possible, serve when still a little warm. When plated, lightly dust each portion with sifted confectioners' sugar.

Baked Sugarplum Apples with Lightened-up Pastry Cream and Almonds

Baked apples go out in evening dress and a stretch limo. This luscious dessert, quite company-worthy, was inspired by the recipe for Mele con Crema Pasticerra from *Cooking from an Italian Garden,* by Paola Scaraveli and Jon Cohen. Although fairly labor-intensive as baked apples go, one bite will convince you that every moment was time well spent.

Make the Lightened-up Pastry Cream before starting the apples. Although you need a crisp, tart apple, avoid Granny Smiths; they do not soften properly. **SERVES 6**

6 medium-large flavorful, firm, tart baking apples (such as Gravensteins, Macouns, Northern Spies, or Winesaps)
Juice of 1 lemon
3 tablespoons sugar
Cooking spray (optional)
¼ cup sherry or Marsala
¼ cup frozen apple juice concentrate, thawed
¼ cup water, preferably spring or filtered
3 tablespoons sugar, divided
¼ cup almonds, toasted, then coarsely chopped
½ cup currants
1 tablespoon cognac
1 recipe Lightened-up Pastry Cream (recipe follows)

1 Preheat the oven to 350°F.

2 Cut the tops of the apples off about ⅓ to ½ inch down from the stem. Reserve the tops. Rub the cut side of each top with a little of the lemon juice and set the tops aside. Using a melon-baller, serrated grapefruit spoon, or apple-corer, reach down into the center of each apple and scoop out and discard all traces of the core. Scoop out and reserve a little of the apple pulp, leaving a good-sized center cavity. When scooping, be careful not to pierce the bottom of the apples, as they are about to become little edible ramekins, and you don't want them to leak. Rub the remainder of the lemon juice over all the cut apple surfaces. Using about 2 tablespoons of the sugar, sprinkle the interior of each apple.

3 If not using nonstick, spray a 9-by-13-inch baking dish with cooking spray. Combine the sherry with the concentrate and water. Pour this mixture in the bottom of the baking dish. Set aside.

4 Finely chop the reserved apple pulp and combine it with the almonds, currants, and cognac. Stir in the Lightened-up Pastry Cream and mix well. Stuff each apple cavity about three-quarters full with this mixture (it puffs up a bit as it bakes), and cover with the apple top. Place the stuffed apples in the prepared baking dish. Sprinkle the remaining tablespoon of sugar over the top.

Bake, uncovered, for 50 to 60 minutes, until the apples are very tender when pierced with the point of a small, sharp knife. Serve with a little of the pan juices poured over the top. If you wish to gild the lily, serve with biscotti or any nice crisp cookie.

COOK ONCE FOR 2 MEALS This recipe will leave you with a little extra filling: eat it for breakfast; use it to fill crêpes; toss it with a peeled, sectioned orange or two and a sliced banana and serve it for dessert.

Lightened-up Pastry Cream

How satisfying it is when you fool with a recipe and succeed in reducing the fat without minimizing the flavor! This pastry cream can be used in dozens of desserts.

1½ cups low-fat milk, dairy or soy
1 large egg yolk
½ cup sugar or Rapidura
⅓ cup unbleached white all-purpose flour
1 tablespoon cornstarch
Grated rind of 1 lemon
1 teaspoon pure vanilla extract

1 Slowly heat 1 cup of the milk in a heavy-duty saucepan or skillet over medium-low heat.

2 Combine the egg yolk, sugar, flour, and cornstarch with the remaining milk in a food processor. Buzz until smooth. Whisk into the warmed milk. Raise the heat ever so slightly and cook, stirring constantly, until the pastry cream is thick and smooth, about 3 minutes.

3 Remove from the heat. Stir in the lemon rind and vanilla. Let cool for a few minutes before using. Or cover and refrigerate until ready to use.

VARIATION

Try this with peach halves, mounding the stuffing in the center, substituting dried cherries for the currants, and cutting the baking time by 15 to 20 minutes. Almonds, cherries, and peaches are in the same botanical family, so you can imagine the taste affinities you get going here.

Autumn Cobbler

A fall multifruit cornucopia, this simple biscuit-topped cobbler is homey and welcoming. Golden Delicious apples melt down in a very satisfying way, but Macouns, if you can get them, have more personality. **SERVES 6 TO 8**

FILLING

Cooking spray (optional)
7 to 8 Golden Delicious, Macoun, or other good baking apples, peeled, cored, and thinly sliced
¾ cup dried cranberries
3 tablespoons honey
3 tablespoons Rapidura or brown sugar
¼ cup frozen apple juice concentrate, thawed
¼ cup unbleached white all-purpose flour

BISCUIT TOPPING

1 cup unbleached white all-purpose flour
1 tablespoon sugar
1¼ teaspoons baking powder
½ teaspoon baking soda
¼ teaspoon ground cinnamon, preferably Saigon
¼ teaspoon salt
1 tablespoon chilled butter, or Browned Butter (page 1024)
1½ teaspoons mild vegetable oil, such as corn, canola, or peanut
½ cup plus 1 to 2 tablespoons buttermilk or vegan buttermilk (½ cup soy milk with 1 teaspoon lemon juice)
1 teaspoon pure vanilla extract

1 Preheat the oven to 400°F.

2 If not using nonstick, spray an 8½-by-11½-inch baking dish with cooking spray.

3 Combine the apples and cranberries in a mixing bowl. Stir in the honey and Rapidura. Toss in the ¼ cup flour. Add the concentrate and stir to blend well. Transfer the mixture to the prepared baking dish and place the dish in the oven while you prepare the topping.

4 To make the topping, sift the flour, sugar, baking powder, baking soda, cinnamon, and salt into a medium bowl. Cut the chilled butter into small pieces and scatter over the flour mixture. Drizzle in the oil and, using two knives or a pastry cutter, quickly cut the fats into the dry ingredients. Add the buttermilk and vanilla. Stir just until blended. Remove the baking dish from the oven. Drop the dough by rounded tablespoonfuls onto the hot fruit. Return to the oven and bake until the topping is golden and the fruit juices have thickened, 20 to 25 minutes. Serve warm.

Bananas

Bananas are sweetest when they are fully ripe, even what might appear to be overripe: fully yellow, and with a moderate speckling of brown. More excessively speckled, they are often available at giveaway prices. You should grab a big ol' sack of such bargain bananas and take them home for Spice Islands Banana-Date-Walnut Bread (page 517), Old-Fashioned Banana-Almond Layer Cake (page 1017), or simply to peel and freeze for smoothies. Frozen bananas in smoothies add a delicious chill and thickening power, along with their sweet mild flavor—especially lovely in buttermilk- or yogurt based smoothies. And don't miss New South B & B White Chocolate–Banana Cream Pie in a Pecan Crust (page 1020), when the yen for total indulgence overtakes you.

Banana lovers will rejoice in the small (4 to 5 inches, usually) red bananas that are now available. They are markedly sweeter than the large yellow ones, and have a creamy, almost custard-like texture. Sliced and topped with yogurt, Yogurt Sour Cream (page 910), Tofu-Cashew Crème (page 1062), or any of the other dessert creams (see pages 1061–63), or reduced-fat sour cream, and a sprinkle of brown sugar, they make a fine simple dessert.

Baked Bananas

A simple but surprisingly good homey dessert, much loved by children. The bananas must be very ripe, without a tinge of green, yet not to the point of being mushy. **SERVES 4**

4 ripe bananas, unpeeled
Butter or Better (page 905)
Brown sugar, Rapidura, or granulated maple sugar

1 Preheat the oven to 350°F.

2 Place the whole bananas, with peel on, directly on the rack in the preheated oven, just as you would place baking potatoes. Bake until the peel blackens and the flesh is very soft, 22 to 27 minutes. Remove the bananas from the oven and place on individual dessert plates. Slit each banana lengthwise; its filling will be very soft. Serve with a dab of butter and a touch of sweetener.

Bramble Berries: Blackberries, Raspberries

When June comes, like Emily Dickinson, inebriate of air am I. Leafed-out trees hide most hillside dwellings, so almost every home becomes a secret treehouse. The warm, scented days are rarely hot (at least, not usually until the end of the month); still, we begin anticipating swims at Beaver Lake, and try to get in one last float before the King's River dries too much for summer canoe trips. And the woods (of what orchard enthusiast Guy Ames calls the Ozarks' "deciduous rainforest") are suddenly madly abloom with intoxicatingly fragrant wild roses and honeysuckle.

Since wild berries are sometimes relatively few in number, I developed a dessert back in the restaurant's earliest days to show off an assortment. It always drew raves. Not only did it turn out to be visually pleasing—a brown basket of a praline pastry that shattered at the tap of a fork, containing ice cream, assorted fresh berries, and a splash of liqueur—it was as delicious as it was pretty.

Tulipe Pralinée Baskets with Seasonal Fresh Berries and Ice Cream

Gild the lily, if you like, with hot fudge sauce (see page 1063), but it is unnecessary. The delicate praline cookie cups come out of the oven soft; let them firm slightly before you drape them over a soup bowl to take their shape. They should only be made on a sunny, clear day; humidity quickly makes them chewy, not crisp. The crispness is essential for the basket to hold its shape, and it also offers contrasting texture (creamy ice cream and soft berries).

"Long about knee-deep in June
'Bout the time strawberries melt
On the vine."

—James Whitcomb Riley

The ice cream can be a homemade (or not) vanilla, a vanilla reduced-fat soy-based ice cream, or the hauntingly good Jay's Buttermilk Ice Cream (page 1043).

SERVES 6

Tulipe Pralinée Baskets

The batter takes but a moment's work. The only part that requires special attention is the draping. This batter spreads like crazy, so bake only two cookies on a sheet. Using two baking sheets will speed the process considerably.

MAKES 6 LARGE BASKETS

½ cup butter
⅔ cup light brown sugar
½ cup light corn syrup
1 cup unbleached white all-purpose flour
1 tablespoon plus 1 teaspoon unsweetened cocoa powder
⅓ cup rolled oats (regular cooking oatmeal)
½ teaspoon pure vanilla extract
Cooking spray

1 Preheat the oven to 375°F.

2 Combine the butter, brown sugar, and corn syrup in a medium saucepan over medium heat. Bring to a boil and immediately remove from the heat.

3 As the sugar mixture is coming to a boil, combine the flour and cocoa in a medium bowl. When the sugar mixture boils, pour the syrup over the flour-cocoa combination, stirring constantly as you pour. Stir in the oats and vanilla.

4 If not using nonstick, spray 2 baking sheets with cooking spray. Drop a tablespoon of batter per cookie onto the prepared sheets, making just two cookies per sheet. Push the sticky batter from the spoon with your fingers, placing the 2 cookies as far from each other as possible. The batter will spread and become almost paper-thin, to something like quadruple in size as it bakes.

Bake for 5 to 6 minutes (watch them closely). The cookies should be bubbly in the middle, and appear underdone. Remove the baking sheet from the oven to a counter to cool for 1 minute.

5 While the first sheet is cooling, place the second sheet of cookies into the oven to bake.

6 Invert 4 soup bowls on the counter.

7 Ease a long, thin-bladed spatula under each baked cookie, which by now, though still a bit floppy, should be firm enough to lift carefully from the cookie sheet. Drape one cookie over each inverted bowl. It will immediately embrace the bowl, and begin hardening into the coveted basket shape. (If the center is still very gooey, the cookies need to be baked a tad longer. It can take a few cookies to get the whole procedure down.)

8 Allow the cookie sheet to cool slightly before reusing it. Continue baking and making baskets until all of the batter has been used.

NOTE

This recipe will leave you with a bit more batter than necessary to make the 6 tulipe baskets. This is so you can make mistakes. With extra batter, you can also dollop teaspoonsful of the batter to create thin lace cookies roughly 2 inches in diameter, which can then be drizzled with a little semisweet chocolate: a very nice holiday cookie.

VARIATIONS

A drizzle of The Very Best Hot Fudge Sauce (page 1063) will embellish each scoop of ice cream before the berries are scattered. Or, for a lighter direction, one that really points up the freshness and delicacy of the berries, substitute lemon or ginger sorbet for the ice cream.

9 As the cookie baskets cool and hold their shape, remove from the bowls and gently place them, right side up, on a tray. They're very fragile at this point. Keep them out of harm's way until serving time.

Seasonal Fresh Berries

3½ cups assorted fresh, seasonal, small whole berries, gently rinsed and picked over to remove any leaves, as wide a variety as possible: raspberries, black raspberries, yellow raspberries, blueberries, mulberries, blackberries, wineberries

1 cup larger berries, sliced or quartered, or large pitted fresh cherries

½ cup Frangelico, amaretto, or your favorite liqueur

Combine the berries and liqueur in a small nonreactive bowl up to 1 hour before serving.

Assembling the Baskets

6 tulipe baskets, prepared as above

1 quart ice cream, or alternative choice

Seasonal Fresh Berries, prepared as above

Mint sprigs (optional)

Place each basket, open side up, on an individual dessert plate.

Place a scoop or two of ice cream in each basket and scatter the top with berries. Drizzle a bit of any macerating liqueur over all. If desired, garnish with fresh mint. Serve at once.

"My wife Martha was walking through the blackberries and she overheard two women talking. She heard one say to the other, 'As soon as we finish picking the blackberries, we'll have to come through and pick some of these red raspberries.' Martha stepped in and tried to explain to them that blackberries are red when they're green."

—**Earnie Bohner,** proprietor,
Persimmon Hill Farms, Lampe, Missouri

Blueberries

In the Ozarks, June is the month of berries. The delicate flavor explosions known as wild black raspberries can be found along any hedgerow. By month's end, along the hillside road by one local banker's home, garnet red wineberries, in surprising fuzzy brown cases, begin opening. Dizzyingly complex in flavor, jewel-like in color, they peak at the Fourth of July, as do the large, bittersweet wild blackberries arching on their prickly brambles. But most of all, June is blueberry time. Signs for you-pick-'em blueberries begin appearing at mid-month. Picking blueberries under the hot sun, bees buzzing, the bushes covered with the mist-dusted mysterious midnight-blue berries, always makes me glad I am alive.

Blueberries may also help *keep* you alive. They contain some of the most powerful and potentially anticarcinogenic antioxidants, and are high in potassium and vitamin C, and are said to be as effective as cranberries in reducing urinary tract infections. Don't miss the recipe for Western-Style Blueberry Chutney (page 927). This can serve as a not-too-sweet dessert, and is delicious with a scoop of vanilla ice cream, frozen yogurt, or Soy Delicious.

Blueberry Crisp

I make simple, homey, and superlative crisps in at least twenty different ways, but the fresh blueberry version is unsurpassed. June would not be June without one huge bowl of this, with vanilla ice cream. Much loved by inn and writers' colony guests, too. **SERVES 6 TO 8 AMPLY**

Cooking spray
8 cups fresh blueberries, rinsed and picked over
¼ cup honey
¼ cup unbleached white all-purpose flour
¼ cup butter, softened
⅔ cup brown sugar
1 teaspoon pure vanilla extract
1 cup rolled oats (regular cooking oatmeal)
½ cup whole wheat flour
⅛ teaspoon ground cinnamon
2 tablespoons to ¼ cup walnuts or pecans, chopped after measuring (optional)

1 Preheat the oven to 375°F.

Grapes

There are those who are enamored of a grape pie or crisp, made as for blueberry crisp, using 8 cups halved, seeded purple grapes, or tiny seedless champagne grapes, pulled from the stem. Less sweetener is required, since grapes are sweeter, and about 2 teaspoons more flour, since they are juicier.

Yet if the grapes are at their pinnacle, they are best eaten either out of hand, or perhaps with some soft creamy cheese like Brie or Saint André and a plain or slightly sweet cracker. Or try Icy Grapes à la Charlotte, my mother's simple summer treat: washed seedless green grapes, stripped from the stem and frozen on a tray, then bagged. That's it. Just toss a frozen grape in your mouth on a hot day and let the miniature self-made grape sorbet melt in your mouth, cooling and flavor-packed.

VARIATION

Plum crisps are plum delicious. Substitute 1¾ to 2 pounds any variety, or better yet, mixed varieties, of red and purple plums, pitted and sliced but not peeled, for the blueberries. You should have about 5 cups all told. Follow the recipe otherwise as given. The late Richard Sax, cookbook writer and dessert maven par excellence, was an aficionado of warm plum desserts, and used to recommend adding a few sliced plums to any berry or nectarine crisp "just to deepen the flavor."

2 Spray an 11-by-14-inch baking dish with cooking spray. Set aside.

3 Toss the blueberries, honey, and white flour together in a medium bowl; then, put your hand in and squeeze one fistful of blueberries to release the juices. Toss again. Place the blueberry mixture in the prepared baking dish.

4 Combine butter and brown sugar in a food processor, first pulsing to blend, then buzzing to combine, pausing to scrape down the sides of the bowl. Add the vanilla. Add the oatmeal and pulse, pausing to scrape the sides of the bowl, until the oats are slightly chopped but not completely powdered.

5 Transfer to a bowl. Add the whole-wheat flour and cinnamon, blending with a spoon to make a crumbly mixture. Stir in the nuts, if using.

6 Scatter the crumbly mixture over the blueberries. Bake until the blueberry juices are thickened and bubbling and the topping is crisp and brown, 35 to 40 minutes.

Warm Blueberry Crêpes

During the peak of blueberry season, these are perfection, not just for dessert but for breakfast or brunch. Special enough to serve company; simple enough for family. If you use Soy Delicious or one of the tofu-based dessert crèmes, this heavenly dish is unobtrusively vegan.

I like my filling on the slightly runny side; if you'd like it more pudding-y, add an extra tablespoon each of cornstarch and water to the paste. **SERVES 4**

". . . for me there is an excitement of adventure in preparing such a thing as an order of Crêpes Suzette and then watching after a lovely lady has had her first taste, to see her smile and know that actually what I compounded was not Crêpes Suzette but a later stage in its transmogrification, a happy human being."

—**Henri Charpentier,** *Those Rich & Great Ones, or Life à la Henri*

Sauciest Blueberry Filling

This warm blueberry filling can also be used as a sauce; think warm-blueberry sundaes . . . think warm blueberry sauce over French toast. Mmmm. Or use it to make Emergency Summer Birthday Cake, *invented by me and the late Sylvia Teague at Dairy Hollow's restaurant when a guest told us, last minute, that it was his wife's birthday and asked if we could do a cake. Take a layer of plain white or yellow cake (preferably homemade; we kept two in the freezer for just such occasions, but you could also use a purchased one, or a purchased pound cake). Slice horizontally, making two thin layers. If using a loaf-shaped cake, such as a pound cake, make two or three slices, creating three or four thin layers. Spoon blueberry mixture between the layers. Cover the whole thing with whipped cream and serve ASAP, with one tall, skinny birthday candle, as needed.*

8 Neo-Classic Crêpes (page 332)
6 cups fresh blueberries, rinsed and picked over
About ¼ cup honey, Rapidura, or sugar, or more to taste
3 tablespoons cornstarch
3 tablespoons water, preferably spring or filtered
1 drop almond extract
½ lemon (optional)
Confectioners' sugar (optional)
Your choice of dessert crèmes (pages 1061–63), ice cream, or Soy Delicious

1. Preheat the oven to 300°F.

2. Wrap the crêpes in aluminum foil and place them in the oven to warm for a few minutes.

3. Place the blueberries in a nonstick saucepan. Plunge your hand in and mash a couple of handfuls of the berries to release their juices. Add the honey and place over medium heat. Raise the heat to medium-high and cook, stirring often, until the berries come to a boil.

4. Dissolve the cornstarch in the water, smushing it with your fingers until smooth. Add the almond extract.

5. When the blueberries are boiling, quickly stir in the cornstarch mixture. The berry filling should quickly thicken and become clear; remove from the heat as soon as it does. Taste the berries, adding more honey if needed, or a spritz of lemon juice if the berries need a little perking up.

Remove the crêpes from the oven and unwrap them. Spoon an equal portion of the filling into each crêpe. Roll each one up, and place on each of 4 dessert plates. Sift a small amount of confectioners' sugar over the crêpes, and serve, still warm, with a creamy dessert sauce or ice cream on the side.

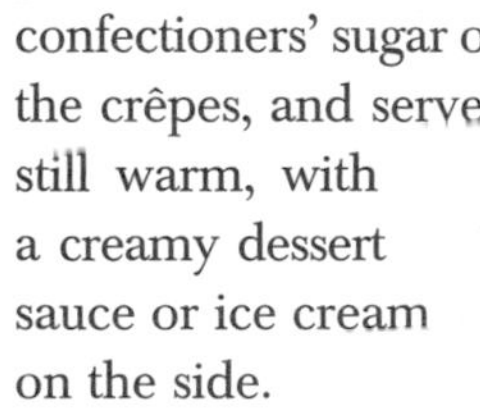

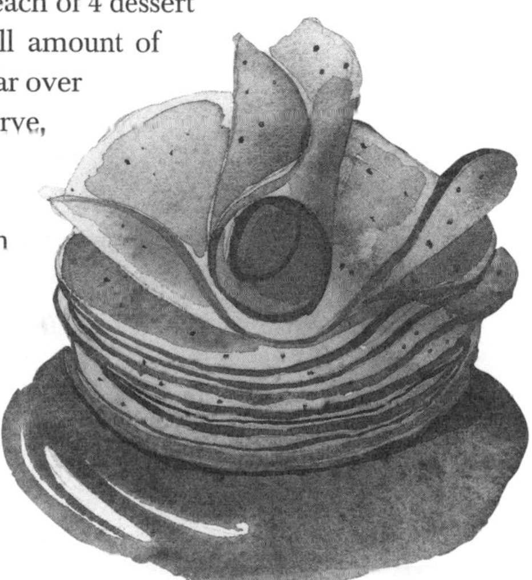

Cherries

One of my personal peak moments of Ozark experiences was a visit years back to Dharma Farma, an organic farmstead down six slow, bumpy miles of rutted road. There, in perfect stillness broken only by our voices, the buzzing of bees, and the songs of darting birds, we walked a hilltop orchard: some fifteen hundred fruit trees. Magness pears, Gala, Liberty, and Arkansas Black apples, and cherry trees. The cherry trees were covered with fruit, and because the sun was shining, each red cherry appeared translucent and aglow as if from within, among the dense green leaves. We stopped and ate, there in the sun.

Cherry season—which lasts only about eight weeks starting in early June—is so short that I believe these sweet, romantic fruits should be enjoyed mostly out of hand.

Place a well-washed bowlful, still on the stem, on the table. The yellow-blushed-with-pink Rainier cherries are exceptionally sweet and juicy, almost the size of small plums. And if you can get fresh sour pie cherries, they are a revelation raw. If you do find them, make a fresh cherry crisp. Use the recipe for Blueberry Crisp (page 977), substituting halved, pitted sour cherries and a little more sweetener.

VARIATION

CHERRY-PEACH CRISP: ***This combination is slightly easier than a straight cherry crisp because it requires less pitting. Follow the recipe for Blueberry Crisp (page 977), substituting for the blueberries a combination of 6 cups peeled, sliced, fresh peaches and 2 cups halved, pitted sweet red cherries.***

Cherried Yogurt, Black Forest–Style

Black Forest cakes are deep dark chocolate with a tart cherry filling. This is a quick chocolate-cherry indulgence I make for myself from time to time. The combination might sound bizarre, but I'll tell you, I eat every bite and lick the bowl. The secret is really good ingredients. Both the dried cherries and hickory nuts, should you use them, are available from American Spoon Foods. **SERVES 1 AMPLY**

⅔ cup plain Brown Cow (all-natural) yogurt, preferably full-fat
About 1 tablespoon unsweetened cocoa powder, or to taste
About 2½ teaspoons brown sugar, or to taste
1 drop pure vanilla extract (optional)
6 to 8 fresh sweet cherries, rinsed, stemmed, pitted, halved or quartered
1 heaping tablespoon unsweetened dried tart cherries
1½ teaspoons coarsely chopped almonds, walnuts, or hickory nuts

Combine the yogurt, cocoa, brown sugar, and, if using, the vanilla. Taste, adding more cocoa or sugar if needed. Stir in the remaining ingredients, sit down, eat, and be as pleased as the cat that ate the canary.

Cranberries

An underutilized winter fruit whose many possible uses are often overlooked, cranberries are almost penalized by being venerated as a sauce or jelly to accompany the Thanksgiving feast. I like them in a chutney, such as the Western-Style Blueberry Chutney (page 927), but with considerably more sweetener added, since cranberries are oh so tart, and with diced dried apricots replacing the raisins (dried apricots and cranberries have an almost voodoo-strong affinity). They're also good simply cooked and sweetened, spooned warm over ice cream, soy ice cream, frozen yogurt, or with a plain cookie—biscotti (pages 1034–37), Chocolate Slice Cookies (page 1039)—or cake, like Miss Kay's Orange Sponge Cake (page 1013).

Fresh Cranberry–Dried Apricot Crisp

Tucked under a blanket of streusel crumbs, which bake to a golden, fragrant crispness, tart cranberries could hardly be better: juicy, sweet-sharp, bright. The apricots add a touch of summer remembered. As with the blueberry version, I prepare the fruit right in the baking dish, and I advise making a double or triple batch of topping—it keeps beautifully for several weeks if refrigerated in a zippered freezer bag. I use honey as the sweetener with blueberries, but to my taste sugar works best with the cranberries.

Try to find sulfite-free dried apricots, which are available in most natural foods markets. They are darker and more leathery, but far more flavorful. A brief soak in boiling water plumps them to full tenderness.

I like using all or mostly whole wheat pastry flour; its nutty taste and solid texture taste right to me with crisps. However, you can use all unbleached white flour or half of each if you prefer. **SERVES 8**

FRUIT FILLING

1½ cups dried apricots, preferably sulfite-free
1½ cups boiling water, preferably spring or filtered
Cooking spray
2 quarts fresh cranberries (about 1½ pounds), picked over and rinsed
1½ cups sugar, or to taste
⅓ cup unbleached white all-purpose flour

FOR CRISP TOPPING:

¾ cup rolled oats (regular cooking oatmeal)
½ cup whole wheat pastry flour
¼ cup unbleached white all-purpose flour
¾ cup dark brown sugar, or Rapidura
1 teaspoon ground cinnamon, preferably Saigon or canela
½ cup butter, softened to room temperature, or Better (page 905)
1 teaspoon pure vanilla extract
½ cup toasted walnuts, optional

"I knew the sheltered valley . . . where the apricots had ripened on the south wall every year; I learnt the names of dogs and ducks and horses, and the smells of seasons . . . of sweet clouded wine drunk foaming off the press . . . of the tree that bore three-hundred weight of plums and the swinging fall of rye before the scythe. I learnt the terms of beekeeping; I learnt of clean straw, oats, and clover, of winter honey, walnuts and March wool. . . ."

—**Sybille Bedford,** *A Legacy*

FOR SERVING (OPTIONAL)

Vanilla ice cream, commercial or homemade (see Jay's Buttermilk Ice Cream, page 1043), dairy or soy, or Burnt Sugar Ice Cream (page 1044)

1 Place the apricots in a heatproof bowl and pour the boiling water over them to cover. Set aside to soak until the apricots are tender and have absorbed most of the water, 1 to 2 hours. Coarsely chop the apricots and set aside.

2 Preheat the oven to 375°F. Spray an 8-by-12-inch baking dish or a 12-inch gratin dish with cooking spray.

3 Place the cranberries in the prepared baking dish. Add the apricots, along with any residual soaking liquid, as well as the white sugar. Sprinkle with the ⅓ cup white flour. With one hand, grab a large handful of cranberries and squeeze to release the juices. Return the "squoze" berries to the dish, and toss all together. Taste. You may need more sugar, but probably not. Pat the berries into an even layer. Set aside.

4 To make the topping, combine the oats with the flours in a large bowl. Add the brown sugar and cinnamon, and then the butter. Using your fingers, crumble the butter into the dry mixture (or pulse the mixture in a food processor; just be careful not to overprocess it). Drizzle in the vanilla and add the nuts, if using; toss again.

5 Scatter the topping over the fruit. Bake until golden brown and firm, with little springs of bright garnet cranberry juice bubbling up here and there, 45 to 55 minutes. Let cool slightly. Serve warm, with ice cream, if you wish.

Figs

Seed-filled and sweet, moist and heavy, large, swollen tear-drops of succulence, fresh figs are to me among the most sensual of fruits, and almost unbearably delicious. Whenever you can get them fresh, they should be eaten out of hand. Choose figs that are soft to the touch, yielding with the slightest pressure of a finger, and eat them very soon. They will have a slight fuzz to them. (If you purchase underripe figs, never fear—just leave them uncovered at room temperature for a day or two and they will reach the point of perfection.)

Figs are perfect as is; don't spoil them by cooking them. However, served raw with a slice of the Garlic-Feta Cream (page 38) they are an unparalleled and beautifully simple starter. And this same idea carries over to dessert, with a minor change.

Fresh Figs with Ricotta Salata

Any variety of ripe fig will do here, the more flavorful the better. For ricotta salata, however, try to find the imported Italian cheese. Though I have never met a ricotta salata I didn't like—it's a pressed, firm, sliceable ricotta—the Italian varieties are both sweet and salty, perfection here. **SERVES 4 TO 6**

6 ounces ricotta salata
12 to 15 ripe figs, rinsed, stems snipped off

1 Slice the cheese into thin oblong lozenges, about 1¼ inch long by ½ inch wide by ⅛ inch thick.

2 Slice each fig almost but not quite in half, from the stem end down toward, but not through, the wider base. Insert a slice of the cheese between the still-joined halves of each fig and lightly press together. Place on a platter and serve, at room temperature, within an hour.

Grapefruit

Most people think of grapefruit as breakfast, but the following is a simple and outstanding dessert. I know a Texas girl who spoke not a word of French and, on the first night of her first trip to Paris, dined at the fanciest restaurant she and her husband had been able to find. She'd decided to knock herself out at dessert, figuring *Well, anything'll be fabulous, it's a French dessert.* She just picked the most elegant-sounding menu item, *pamplemousse.* She had in mind pampering-plus-mousse, and pictured a mile-high frozen soufléed mousse in a little ramekin . . . but out came half a grapefruit.

Grapefruit has a peculiar enzyme that enhances the ability of the liver to metabolize certain medications. If you take any prescription drugs, especially heart medications, antianxiety drugs, or sleeping pills, please promise me you'll be sure to ask the pharmacist about its interaction with grapefruit and avoid taking medication within 8 hours of drinking or eating grapefruit.

Magic Grapefruit

When ruby-red grapefruits are in season, I have grapefruit fixed this way three meals a day. When I first put this together I pretty much went on a grapefruit binge.

This is simplicity itself, and has no right to be as good as it is—what logical reason is there for tropical, sun-raised grapefruit to sing in combination with northern maple sugar? But it is a flat-out irresistible combination. **SERVES 2**

1 perfectly ripe, juicy grapefruit, preferably ruby red, halved and sectioned
2 heaping teaspoons pure granulated maple sugar

Place grapefruits in serving dishes. Top each with half the maple sugar and enjoy!

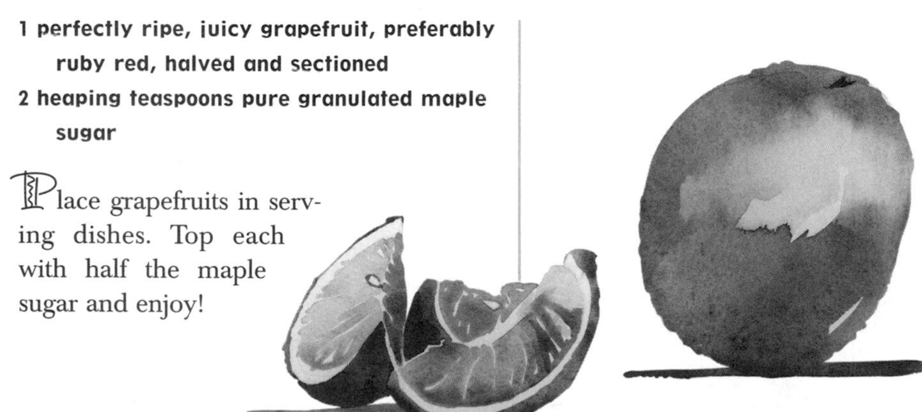

Melons

A sweet melon is so good; an underripe one such a disappointment. The one reliable way to pick a melon is with your nose: press the stem end of the melon and inhale. If there is no perfumed fragrance, put the melon back.

Here are a few quick notes on what to do with a perfectly ripe wedge of melon:

- ▲ Serve cantaloupe with a scoop of cottage cheese, frozen yogurt, ginger sorbet, or chocolate ice cream (the last combination is my mother's favorite). Or, try the Cantaloupe-Campari Sorbet (page 1048).
- ▲ Watermelon seeds are not only edible but delicious and good for you (high in protein, said to be good for the urinary tract). They are not roasted and shelled like pumpkin seeds, but edible as they are—crunch them up with every bite. I can't even remember who taught me this, although I've been cheerfully crunching away on them for years.
- ▲ Serve honeydew in a green-fruit cup—diced, with peeled diced kiwis, halved green seedless grapes, and finely minced spearmint. Extreme refreshment.
- ▲ Nibble a wedge of fresh, ripe, crisp watermelon with a wedge of feta; an Israeli combination.

"It was not a Southern watermelon that Eve took; we know it because she repented."

—Mark Twain

Oranges

A bowl or hanging basket of oranges is in my kitchen mid-November through early March. Vitamin C, in a form as round as, and even more bright in color than, the summer sun, oranges brighten winter visually, health-wise, and in every juicy bite. The California navels and the mysterious-looking blood oranges are my favorites.

But I have also become enamored with kumquats in recent years. See if a whole sweet-tart, faintly bitter kumquat popped into your mouth, seeds spit out, doesn't make your toes curl with delight. . . . It does mine.

Oranges in Bay-Leaf Syrup

Sublime and simple. I've poached oranges every so often for as long as I've been cooking, but it was only from the very likable cookbook *Sweets for Saints and Sinners,* by Janice Feuer, that I learned the magical trick of adding bay leaves to the poaching syrup. This adds a flavor that can only be called haunting. Janice Feuer also added whole cloves and allspice to the poaching liquid; you could do this, or toss in

NOTE

Save extra syrup for use in Compote of Golden Fruits in Orange Syrup (see page 964).

a cinnamon stick or a slice of fresh ginger—but mostly I use unalloyed bay and orange. A delicious end to any rich meal.

Start this early in the day you intend to serve it, or even a couple of days ahead of time; the oranges don't poach as much as marinate, absorbing that elusive, almost floral, sweet syrup. Try one of the oranges before you begin poaching—you want it to be a perfectly juicy, flavorful eating orange. **SERVES 4 TO 6**

2 cups water, preferably spring or filtered
1 cup sugar
3 large bay leaves
4 medium-large, or 6 small-medium, juicy eating oranges, peeled, white pith removed
Needlethreads (see box; optional)

1 Combine the water and sugar in a heavy saucepan. Cook, stirring constantly, over low heat, slowly dissolving the sugar in the water. After the sugar has dissolved, raise the heat and bring the syrup to a boil. Boil for 5 minutes. Lower the heat to a bare simmer and add the bay leaves (and any of the other spice additions mentioned in the headnote). Simmer, uncovered, for 1 hour.

2 Add the oranges to the syrup and bring to a simmer. Simmer for 5 minutes, constantly spooning syrup over the oranges. Using a slotted spoon, lift the oranges from the syrup, placing them in a heatproof bowl. Set aside.

3 Raise the heat under the syrup, bringing it back to a boil, then immediately remove from the heat and pour over the oranges. Let cool to room temperature, then cover and refrigerate.

4 Marinate, refrigerated, at least overnight, but preferably for 2 to 3 days. Shake the bowl every once in a while to turn the fruit. Serve, cold, with syrup spooned over the oranges and a garnish of Needlethreads, if you wish. This is one dessert that really requires a knife and fork.

Needlethreads

"Needlethreads" are Janice Feuer's name for paper-thin julienned slivers of poached, not candied, orange and lemon rind, which are, as she says, perfect as a garnish for any citrus dessert. Like all recipes using citrus peel, organic fruits, the peels of which are not treated with waxes and fumigants, are much preferred.

To make them, using a vegetable peeler, remove just the very thin colored portion of the rind from 1 orange, as well as 1 lemon. Using a very sharp knife, cut the pieces of rind the long way into strips that are as thin as you can possibly make them—about 1/64 inch wide, says Janice. Bring a cup of water, preferably spring or filtered, to a boil and drop in the strips. Boil hard for 1 minute, then strain, discarding the liquid and keeping the strips. Blot the strips with a towel, then set them out on a plate to dry before using.

Italian Caramelized Oranges

Years back, on a trip to London, jet-lagged, I stirred myself enough to walk half a block to a nice, not-too-fancy but white-tablecloth Italian restaurant. After a simple tonic salad of bitter greens and pasta, the waiter pointed to the pastry cart. There, in a crystal bowl were a dozen spheres afloat in golden syrup. "Perhaps some *aranci caramelizzati,* signorina?" he suggested. Caramelized oranges? I acquiesced. The dish was perfect: sweet, light, explosively juicy, scattered with delicate bits of blanched peel. Some years later, I came across the following in Elizabeth David's *Italian Food,* written in 1954, updated in 1987: "Caramel oranges have long become a cliché of London Italian restaurants." *Cliché?* Harumph. Well, I loved 'em, they were new to me, so there you go.

Simple, pleasing, refreshing, these work beautifully after almost any spicy, faintly exotic meal: Indian, Middle Eastern, even Spanish. Note: The oranges themselves must be full-flavored and juicy for this to be transcendent. If you can, make them 1 to 3 days ahead of time. The longer they soak in the syrup, the better. **SERVES 4 TO 6**

4 medium-large or 6 small-medium oranges, peeled, white pith removed, sliced crosswise into ½-inch wheels or left whole
1 cup sugar
¼ cup water, preferably spring or filtered
1 tablespoon corn syrup
1 teaspoon fresh-squeezed lemon juice
¼ cup fresh-squeezed orange juice
Grated rind of 1 orange
1 to 2 tablespoons Grand Marnier, Orange Napoleon, or Cointreau (optional)
Needlethreads (opposite; optional)

1 Place the oranges in a heatproof bowl. Set aside.

2 Combine the sugar, water, corn syrup, and lemon juice in a medium-sized, heavy saucepan, *not* a nonstick. Place over medium heat and cook, stirring often, until the sugar is dissolved. Raise the heat and bring to a boil. Boil without stirring until the syrup is a beautiful pale golden-amber shade. The timing will vary from 8 to 12 minutes.

3 Immediately, but carefully and standing back a bit, stir in the orange juice (if you pour it in down the side of the saucepan, rather than in the middle, there'll be less boiling up Sturm und Drang) and the grated rind. The caramel will harden. Cook, stirring, until it is again liquid, about 3 minutes.

4 Remove from the heat and immediately pour the hot syrup over the oranges. Let cool to room temperature. Once cool, add the liqueur, if using. Cover and refrigerate at least overnight, but preferably for 2 to 3 days. Shake the bowl every once in a while to turn the fruit in the syrup. Serve cold, with the syrup spooned over the oranges and a garnish of Needlethreads, if desired.

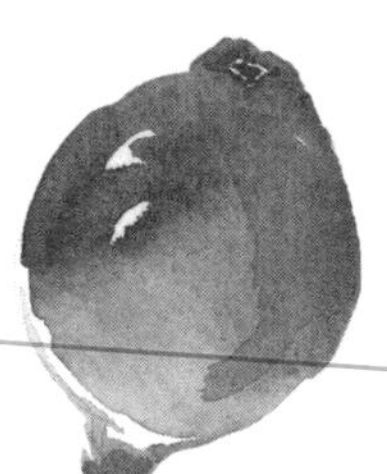

Citrus Compote with Poached Lemon, Bay Laurel, and Grand Marnier

I cannot resist including one more truly lovely poached orange dish. This a compote that combines grapefruit and lemon with the orange, with a hint of Grand Marnier. It's a great finale to a heavy or fancy meal, and can be made 1 to 2 days in advance. During the inn days, we often used it as the breakfast fruit during the winter months.

Catch the juices of the oranges and grapefruit as they're being cut to add to the marinating liquid. **SERVES 8 TO 10**

Water, preferably spring or filtered
1 lemon, peel on, halved horizontally, then sliced paper-thin and seeded
½ cup sugar
Grated rind of 2 oranges
3 bay leaves
4 oranges, peeled (use the 2 oranges whose rinds were grated), sectioned, seeded, cut into ½-inch pieces
3 grapefruits, preferably pink, peeled, seeded, sectioned, and cut into ½-inch pieces
1 to 2 tablespoons Grand Marnier, or more to taste

1 Bring a small pot of water to a boil over high heat. Drop in the lemon, and blanch for 1 minute. Remove from the heat and drain well.

2 Combine ¾ cup water and the sugar in a medium saucepan over high heat. Bring to a boil, stirring to dissolve the sugar. Add the blanched lemon slices, the orange rind, and bay leaves and bring to a simmer. Lower the heat and simmer for 10 minutes. Remove from the heat and let the syrup cool slightly.

3 Combine the orange and grapefruit pieces, plus any saved juices, in a bowl, preferably a glass one. Pour the warm syrup over the fruit. Add the Grand Marnier and stir. Cover and refrigerate overnight or up to 2 days.

4 When ready to serve, discard the bay leaves. Serve the compote in glass bowls.

Peaches

With their cleavage shape, pink-red blush-tinged interior, and fuzzy skins, peaches rival figs for sexuality. Select peaches that are fragrant, and yield just a little to the pressure of your thumb. The July Red Haven variety is exceptionally sweet. And what more description do we need for the succulent heirloom peach called Nipples of Venus?

Check out the Peach Pie in a Sesame-Oatmeal Crust (page 990), Cherry-Peach Crisp (page 980), and also the lovely peach variation for Baked Sugarplum Apples with Lightened-up Pastry Cream and Almonds (page 970). Or try these simple but indulgent stuffed peaches.

Amaretti- and Cocoa-Stuffed Peaches

Use this no-cook peach dessert when you'd like something special but unfussy to end a meal. You need to make these 24 hours in advance so the peach juice gets a chance to soak into the filling. Amaretti cookies—crisp, almond-rich, sprinkled with coarse sugar—come wrapped in twists of paper, two cookies to a wrapper. Since peaches are in the same family as almonds, the flavors, amped up with a little amaretto, are sublime. One of the dessert crèmes lends a nice finish. Garnish with a few fresh raspberries and a mint sprig if you like.

If you object to the fuzzy skin remaining on the peach, peel them by lowering the peaches into a pot of boiling water for a few seconds, lifting them out with a slotted spoon, refreshing quickly in cold water, and peeling with a small sharp knife. To me, though, the rawness of the peach is part of the pleasure. **SERVES 8**

4 very juicy, perfectly ripe large summer peaches, halved and pitted
8 teaspoons unsweetened cocoa powder
4 teaspoons confectioners' sugar or Rapidura
About 2 tablespoons amaretto liqueur
8 amaretti cookies
One of the dessert crèmes (pages 1061–63)

1 Place the peaches, cut side up, in a dish.

2 Place 1 teaspoon cocoa powder and ½ teaspoon confectioners' sugar in the center of each peach cavity. Drizzle a little amaretto into each cavity. Then, press an amaretti cookie, curved side down, into each cavity.

3 Tightly cover with plastic wrap and refrigerate for at least 24 hours.

4 Serve, a half peach per serving, on chilled dessert plates. The dessert crème may either be passed at the table or spooned onto each plate. Since the peaches are not cooked, you may need a fork and knife, as well as a spoon, to navigate this dessert.

Peach Pie in an Oatmeal-Almond Crust

This is divine with fresh height-of-summer peaches. Finely chopped almonds replace sesame seeds in the crust, and you can add additional almonds to the streusel. Cinnamon is optional; I actually prefer the recipe without it, so the peach flavor shines through. When I want a little spice here, I prefer a touch of lemony-sweet cardamom. **MAKES ONE 9-INCH PIE; SERVES 6 TO 8**

STREUSEL TOPPING

- ½ cup rolled oats (regular cooking oatmeal)
- ½ cup brown sugar
- ½ cup whole wheat pastry flour
- ¼ cup butter, softened
- ¼ cup chopped toasted almonds (optional)
- ½ teaspoon cinnamon or ¼ teaspoon ground cardamom (optional)

FILLING

- 8 cups peaches, peeled, pitted, and sliced (about 15 medium peaches)
- ⅓ cup brown sugar or Rapidura
- 2 tablespoons honey
- 1 tablespoon water, preferably spring or filtered
- 1 tablespoon cornstarch
- 1 drop almond extract
- 1 Sweet Sesame-Oatmeal Pie Crust, with 2 tablespoons finely chopped toasted almonds substituted for the sesame seeds, partially prebaked (recipe follows)

1 Preheat the oven to 400°F.

2 To make the streusel topping, combine the oats, brown sugar, flour, butter and, if using, the almonds and cinnamon, in a food processor. Pulse to make a crumbly mixture. Set aside.

3 Combine the peaches, brown sugar, honey, and water in a nonstick saucepan. Cover tightly and bring to a boil over medium-high heat. Lower the heat to medium and simmer until the peaches begin to soften, 5 to 6 minutes.

4 Using a ladle, scoop out 2 tablespoons or so of the liquid the peaches will have started to exude. Place it in a saucer and let it cool slightly, then smush the cornstarch into the peach juice with your fingers. Stir the cornstarch mixture into the peaches, and cook until thickened, a moment or two. Remove from the heat and add the almond extract. Let cool to lukewarm.

5 Transfer the filling to the partially prebaked crust. Sprinkle the streusel topping over the filling. Bake for 15 minutes. Lower the heat to 350°F, and bake for another 30 to 40 minutes, until the topping is golden brown, crisp, and firm.

"The ripest peach is highest on the tree." —James Whitcomb Riley

Sweet Sesame-Oatmeal Pie Crust

Many people go into raptures over flaky pie crusts, but I am not one of them. I prefer something more . . . soulful. Where is the flavor in a traditional crust? As for texture . . . well, yeah, a crust should be crisp (to provide a contrast to the pie's filling), but what's so great about multiple flaky layers? I'm just talking personal taste here, mind you, leaving aside health matters. And yet, can we leave them aside, knowing the fat it takes to make a crust flaky? I much prefer a toothy crisp crust, with real flavor and texture and interest. Fortunately, this is easily achievable with oil and many whole-grain flours.

VARIATIONS

SAVORY SESAME-OATMEAL PIE CRUST: *Omit the sugar. Substitute 3 tablespoons freshly grated Parmesan cheese, and cut back the oil to 2 tablespoons. Or, for vegans, add 3 tablespoons wheat germ or oat bran, keeping the oil proportions as given.*

DOUBLE-SESAME-OATMEAL PIE CRUST: *For all you sesame fans, this jazzed-up, amped-up version is great. Just use toasted sesame oil for 1 tablespoon of the oil. Quite nice with a pumpkin or banana pie.*

This—slightly sweet, sparked with sesame and oats, a bit reminiscent of oatmeal cookies—is one of my favorites. I particularly love it with Rhubarb-Custard Tart (page 1002). A version for savory pies is here, too.

MAKES 1 9-INCH PIE CRUST

Cooking spray
1 tablespoon sesame seeds
¾ cups rolled oats (regular cooking oatmeal)
½ cup whole wheat pastry flour
¼ cup unbleached white all-purpose flour
3 tablespoons Rapidura or brown sugar
1 teaspoon baking powder
⅛ teaspoon salt
3 tablespoons mild vegetable oil, such as corn, canola, or peanut
3 to 4 tablespoons water, preferably spring or filtered

1 Preheat the oven according to the filling recipe you are using.

2 Spray a 9-inch pie pan with cooking spray.

3 Combine the sesame seeds and oats in a dry cast-iron skillet over medium-high heat. Toast, stirring constantly, until they give off a fragrance, 4 to 6 minutes. The sesame seeds will begin popping, and the oats will turn a deeper brown, with some of them decidedly golden and toasted. Remove from the heat and transfer to a food processor. Buzz until finely ground, then transfer to a bowl.

4 Stir in the whole wheat and white flours, Rapidura, baking powder, and salt. Toss well, then drizzle in the oil. Work it in with your fingers until the mixture is crumbly. Add the water, a tablespoon at a time, stirring with a fork until the dough just comes together. Knead the dough 7 to 10 times. Form it into a flattened disc. Place the disc between two sheets of waxed paper. Roll it out to a circle about 12 inches in diameter. Transfer the circle to the prepared pie pan, peeling off the waxed paper. Press the crust down evenly, repairing any tears; make an even edge with your fingers. Bake in one of the following ways:

- For a crust that is baked with the filling, follow the specific filling recipe.
- For a crust that is to be prebaked, line the crust with foil and weigh it down with beans, rice, or pie weights. Bake at 375°F until the crust is firm to the touch, 8 to 12 minutes. Remove the foil and weights and bake until the crust is golden, another 6 to 9 minutes.
- For a crust that is to be partially prebaked (as in the Rhubarb-Custard Tart, page 1002), line the crust with foil and weigh it down with beans, rice, or pie weights. Bake at 375°F until the crust is firm to the touch, 8 to 12 minutes. Remove the foil and weights. Fill the pie with filling and bake according to the specific recipe's directions.

"Still, blue, very still—and the warmth lay gently across the ladies' shoulders like a blessing. A bee got into the carriage. In the Valee du Loup the almonds were out among the peach trees, the young slim peach trees, rows and rows of the pink and white, all over the hillside."

—**Sybille Bedford,** *A Legacy*

Pears

A perfectly ripe pear is second only to grapes for eating out of hand with cheese and crackers. Try the thinnest of slices of Roquefort or Stilton with a ripe pear, a wedge of oozing Camembert or Brie, a shaving of buttery Jarlsberg—delicious, and somehow both chaste and indulgent. Pear and ginger are also a time-honored combination; a bowl of ripe Boscs or Anjous with a tiny bowl of crystallized ginger to pass around, and maybe a few simple purchased cookies make a sophisticated, pleasing, low-hassle dessert.

Pears, even meltingly ripe ones, have a slight grittiness of texture. This is not objectionable in the least when a pear is in its raw state; merely part of its personality. But it is a little off-putting in a pastry, which is why I steer clear of these.

Honeyed Cranberry-Burgundy Poached Pears

Served frequently both at the inn (as part of breakfast, or as dessert when guests desired a low-calorie offering) and the Colony (as dessert, with Tofu-Cashew Crème), these are lovely, vivid in both taste and color, sensuous in shape. You can use all Burgundy, all cranberry juice, or a combination. I prefer the latter. Purchase pears a little firmer than you'd normally eat them, but not rock hard. When cooked, the consistency should be meltingly smooth; you should be able to cut them with a spoon. Serve with a sauceboat of any dessert crème on the side. **SERVES 8**

NOTE

To dress them up, cut each pear half from the base up to but not through the stem end, in a series of very thin slices, connected at the top. Puddle a little of the gem-like red syrup on individual serving plates, and fan the sliced pear out and over it.

3 to 4 cups Burgundy wine or cranberry juice, or a mix of 2 cups each
1 stick cinnamon
4 pears, Anjou, Bartlett, or Bosc, unpeeled, halved vertically, and cored
About ¼ cup honey
Any dessert crème (pages 1061–63; optional)

1 Pour the wine and/or cranberry juice into a large nonreactive skillet. It should fill the skillet about halfway. Add the cinnamon stick. Place over high heat and bring the liquid to a simmer.

2 Carefully lay the pear halves in the liquid, cut side down. The liquid should cover the pears by about three-quarters. Simmer for 6 to 8 minutes. Gently flip the pears over (using tongs is easiest); continue simmering for a few minutes.

3 The pears should be tender when pierced with a toothpick, but not falling apart. When they have reached this point, scoop them from the liquid, and place them in a medium dish.

4 Add the ¼ cup honey to the liquid remaining in the skillet and raise the heat. Watching carefully, cook the juices down to a medium-thin syrup. Keep a close eye on this, as the syrup burns easily.

5 Let the syrup cool slightly, and remove and discard the cinnamon stick. Pour the cooled syrup over the pears, cover the dish tightly with plastic wrap, and refrigerate overnight or up to 3 days. Serve chilled, plain or with Tofu-Cashew Crème or other dessert crème on the side.

Stuffed Ginger–Black Pepper Baked Pears

NOTE

For the gingersnaps called for here, use any that are crisp, non-chewy—grocery store varieties will do nicely.

Homey in appearance, these are a great casual, kitchen table–style dessert. Use as you would baked apples. Ginger and pears are made for each other, and the pepper adds even more snap. Choose firm, almost-ripe, round rather than elongated pears. Core them by cutting a tunnel from the top through the bottom, using either an apple-corer or a sharp paring knife. Serve warm with ice cream, regular or soy. **SERVES 6**

Cooking spray
¾ cup gingersnap crumbs
1 tablespoon brown sugar
2 teaspoons butter, Better (page 905), or Browned Butter (page 1024)
1 teaspoon finely grated lemon rind
6 dried apricots
6 round pears, cored but left in one piece
1½ cups frozen apple juice or white grape juice concentrate, thawed
5 or 6 (¼- by 1-inch) slices ginger, unpeeled
1 tablespoon whole black peppercorns

1 Preheat the oven to 350°F.

2 Spray a small baking dish with cooking spray.

3 Combine the gingersnap crumbs, brown sugar, butter, and lemon rind. Set aside.

4 Push an apricot down into the hole through each pear, plugging the at the bottom. Evenly divide the crumb mixture

between the cored pears, stuffing it on top of the apricot. Arrange the pears in the prepared baking dish.

5 Pour the concentrate over the pears and scatter the ginger and peppercorns over all.

6 Bake, basting occasionally, until the pears are tender enough to be pierced easily with a toothpick, 55 to 65 minutes. Serve warm with a drizzle of the syrup in which they were baked, straining out the peppercorns and ginger slices.

Plums

In the Ozarks, we have a tiny semi-wild pink plum, not much larger than a cherry, sweet and delicious, that I've only heard called a "hog plum." They are ripe in mid-June. But if you can't raid your friend Chou Chou's garden or the old homesite on Pivot Rock Road as I can, never fear—almost all plums are succulent if ripe, though some varieties and some years' harvests are sweeter than others.

Plums cook up very successfully. Try substituting them for the blueberries in Blueberry Crisp (page 977), or in Western-Style Blueberry Chutney (page 927). Adjust the sweetener according to the sweetness of the plums.

Like cherries, perfectly ripe plums are one of the best dessert fruits eaten right out of hand. And like many fruits, they are also delicious with cheese.

Roasted Plums

Use the late-summer Italian prune plums for this; they are freestone, leaving you nice-looking halves. Thawed frozen grape juice concentrate, rather than the apple juice I normally use, is employed here, boosting the already deep color. Cardamom adds a floral-exotic lemony fragrance and flavor.

These are delicious as is, for a simple, healthful dessert, or can accompany the Lemon Mousse-Custard (page 1052) or Neo-Zialetti cookies (page 1038) for something a little dressier. **SERVES 4**

Cooking spray
8 Italian prune plums, halved and pitted
½ cup frozen grape juice concentrate, thawed
¼ cup water, preferably spring or filtered
3 whole cardamom pods
2 teaspoons butter or Better (page 905)
1 teaspoon pure vanilla extract

1 Preheat the oven to 350°F.

2 Spray a shallow baking dish with cooking spray.

3 Place the plums, cut side down, in the prepared dish. Set aside.

4 Combine the concentrate and the water with the cardamom, butter, and vanilla in a small saucepan and cook over medium heat just until the butter melts. Immediately pour or spoon the syrup over the plums.

5 Bake, basting with the liquid a few times during baking, for 30 to 40 minutes. The plums should be soft, but not mushy. Remove from the oven and remove and discard the cardamom pods. Serve warm, allowing 4 overlapped plum halves per person and dividing the baking liquid among the servings, spooning it over the plums.

Stuffed Plums with Port

NOTE

For the blue cheese, my first choices would be a run-off between American-made Maytag Blue and British Cheshire; Michelle recommends Castello Blue or Oregon Blue.

Good fresh fruit, good cheese, and walnuts are a classic ending to a great meal, a finish both simple and urbane. This take combines all three and adds the novelty of melting the cheese slightly. The styling is inspired by a version in Michele Anna Jordan's *A Cook's Tour of Sonoma County,* which uses apples, more complex spicing, and sugar. **SERVES 4 TO 8**

Cooking spray
1¾ cups port
½ cup frozen apple juice concentrate
1-inch piece stick cinnamon
4 Italian plums, halved and pitted
4 ounces any superior blue-veined cheese
8 perfect walnut halves, toasted
2 to 3 tablespoons coarsely chopped toasted walnuts (optional)

1 Preheat the oven to 325°F.

2 Spray a shallow baking dish with cooking spray.

3 Combine the port wine, concentrate, and cinnamon stick in a large nonreactive skillet over medium-high heat. Bring to a boil, then lower the heat to a simmer. Add the plums, cut side down, and gently simmer until the plums are not quite tender, 4 to 6 minutes. Remove from the heat. Using a slotted spoon, transfer the plums to the prepared baking dish, placing them cavity side up. Add 2 to 3 tablespoons of the poaching liquid to the dish as well.

4 Divide the cheese into 8 even slices and place one in the cavity of each plum.

Tightly cover the baking dish with foil and bake until the plums are soft and tender, but not mushy, about 20 minutes. Uncover, and raise the oven temperature to 375°F. Bake for 5 additional minutes.

5 While the plums are baking, return the poaching liquid to high heat and boil until it is reduced to a syrupy consistency.

6 Place a pool of the reduced poaching liquid on each of 4 dessert plates. Place 2 to 4 halves on each plate, and press a toasted walnut half into the center of each. If desired, scatter with the chopped walnuts.

Port-Poached Plums

Select Italian prune plums for their ease of pit removal. This is another fine light dessert that can be dressed up in all of the ways listed in the previous recipe. I find that a small amount of cinnamon enhances, rather than overshadows, the plums, but if you prefer an unspiced, purer plum flavor, by all means omit it. Port adds a depth and sophistication to the poaching liquid that is quite special. **SERVES 4**

NOTE

Instead of using lemon rind in the poaching liquid, try serving this with a scattering of Needlethreads (page 986).

¾ cup port
½ cup frozen apple juice concentrate, thawed
1-inch piece stick cinnamon
8 Italian prune plums, halved and pitted
Grated rind of 1 lemon

1 Combine the port, concentrate, and cinnamon stick in a large nonreactive skillet over medium heat. Bring to a boil, then lower the heat to a simmer. Add the plums, cut side down, and let simmer gently for 12 to 18 minutes, until the plums are tender but not mushy.

2 With a slotted spoon, remove the plums from the liquid and set aside. Remove and discard the cinnamon stick. Add the lemon rind and raise the heat under the poaching liquid. Boil down quickly until slightly syrupy. Keep a close watch on this—depending on the juiciness of the plums, this could take 2 minutes or as long as 6. Remove from the heat and let come to room temperature.

3 Allow 4 overlapped plum halves per person, spoon some of the poaching liquid over the plums, and serve at room temperature.

Blueberry-Plum Streusel Tart in a Sesame-Oatmeal Crust

How handy that the seasons for sweet red Santa Rosa plums and blueberries coincide. You can make it with all plums, however, if you prefer, or with several varieties of plums combined. This sweetheart of a pie is plenty indulgent, but far more healthful than those with a traditional crust. **MAKES 1 9-INCH PIE; SERVES 6**

STREUSEL TOPPING

½ cup rolled oats (regular cooking oatmeal)
½ cup whole wheat pastry flour
½ cup brown sugar
¼ cup butter, softened
½ teaspoon ground cinnamon

FILLING

5 cups sliced plums (about 12 medium plums, preferably Santa Rosas, washed, unpeeled, sliced)
⅓ cup brown sugar or Rapidura
2 tablespoons honey
1 tablespoon water, preferably spring or filtered
1 pint fresh blueberries, rinsed and picked over
1 tablespoon cornstarch

1 Sweet Sesame-Oatmeal Pie Crust, partially prebaked (page 991)

1 Preheat the oven to 400°F.

2 Combine the oats, flour, the ½ cup brown sugar, butter, and cinnamon in a food processor. Pulse to make a crumbly streusel. Set aside.

3 Combine the plums, the ⅓ cup brown sugar, the honey, and water in a nonstick pot. Cover tightly and bring to a boil. Lower the heat to medium and let simmer until the plums begin to soften, about 5 minutes.

4 Scoop out about ½ cup of the blueberries, and place them in a small bowl. Squeeze them in your hand to make a rough paste. Stir in the cornstarch, then stir the mixture into the hot plums; cook until thickened, just a moment or two. Remove from the heat and stir in the remaining blueberries. Let cool to luke warm.

5 Transfer the filling to the partially prebaked crust. Sprinkle the streusel topping over the filling. Bake for 15 minutes. Lower the heat to 350°F, and bake until the topping is crisp, golden brown, and firm, 30 to 40 minutes.

Persimmons

I am inordinately fond of the wild American native persimmon, *Diospyros virginiana,* but for those whose lifestyles or locations make the pure grace of wandering and persimmon-gathering impossible, markets now offer several cultivated persimmons. Natives of China and very popular in Japan (where they've been raised for more than thirteen hundred years), these persimmons are now grown on parts of every continent except Antarctica.

Persimmons grow in hedgerows and weedy patches and are easily identifiable. A temperate-zone member of the ebony family, they are found from Connecticut to Florida and west to Oklahoma. Their fruits are small, round, and, when ripe, orange with a misty purple cast to them. The fruits are "puckery" (alum-rich) until soft and ripe, but then—oh my!—they are stunningly sensual, a fruit right out of the Song of Solomon. At this point, just around frost (late October–early November), they are very sweet, somewhat like a ripe date, but with an elusive, delicate flavor. They are beautiful and easily spotted—smallish trees, with simple, leafless branches, hung with bright fruit as if hung with Christmas balls or tiny lanterns.

There are two main cultivated varieties, each distinct from the other and from the wild variety. They have a cross-shaped calyx (stem) at the top, and the whole fruit, except for the seed and calyx and the seeds in some varieties, is edible.

The nonastringent fuyu persimmons have a flattened shape and are slightly more yellow-orange; they're notable because they don't have to be dead-soft to be eaten, and they're seedless. Fully ripened on the tree, they can be eaten when firm, even crisp, without a trace of puckeriness. Their firmness also means they can be chopped for use in fruit salads, garnishes, even salsas.

Hachiya, the other generally available type of persimmon, looks almost like large, bright acorns, heart-shaped with a point at the tip; they are a more vivid red-orange. Some Hachiyas can have seeds. Like their wild American cousins, Hachiyas are astringent until they are very, very soft (however, you need not choose one that is already soft; hachiyas will continue to ripen on your countertop). Extremely sweet (a bit more so than Fuyus), Hachiyas are ideal for recipes calling for persimmon puree, and for a virtually instant, intensely flavored persimmon sorbet. They also make a sunset-colored smoothie that is out of this world and rarely requires any additional sweetening. Try persimmon puree stirred into maple syrup and spoon it over whole-grain or oatmeal pancakes—breakfast heaven, served with some sautéed soysage on the side.

Peak harvest for cultivated persimmons runs from October to December, with the Fuyus coming in first and the Hachiyas about three weeks later.

Jewels of the Autumn Fruit Cup

This particular and unusual selection of fruits gives knockout colors and spectacular flavor to a fruit salad. For a more formal effect, don't mix everything together, but slice each fruit except the pomegranate and arrange it on a platter, scattering the pomegranate seeds and drizzling the Hachiya puree over the top. To make the puree, simply buzz a couple of Hachiya persimmons in a blender. But you can skip the puree if it seems too fussy. If particularly ripe pineapples, mangoes, or papayas are available, by all means, add them. This salad can be made up to a couple of hours in advance, if stored covered and refrigerated. **SERVES 6**

2 Fuyu persimmons, calyx removed, cut into ½-inch pieces
2 kiwi fruit, peeled, quartered lengthwise, cut into ½-inch slices
2 blood oranges, peeled and sectioned
1 ruby-red grapefruit, peeled and sectioned
1 Asian pear, peel on, cut into ⅓-inch cubes
½ pound green seedless grapes, halved
½ cup Hachiya persimmon puree
1 pomegranate, halved, seeds scooped out of white fiber

1 Combine the Fuyu persimmons, kiwi, blood oranges, grapefruit, pear, grapes, and persimmon puree in a serving bowl, tossing well to combine.

2 Sprinkle the pomegranate seeds over the top and serve.

Land of Milk and Honey Persimmon-Citrus Pie

Rich, wonderfully full flavored, and as easy as can be, this no-bake pie has a cheesecakelike filling. A classic prebaked graham cracker crust makes it simpler to put together. Allow a couple of hours in the fridge for it to set up. Vegans can substitute an equivalent amount of soy cream cheese for the neufchâtel; if you're feeling devil-may-care calorically, fold a cup of sweetened whipped cream into the filling. Garnish with additional sliced persimmon and a sprig of mint.

I love this with La Vigne's remarkable kumquat preserves (see box), but you may also use bitter orange marmalade. **SERVES 6 TO 8**

2 packages (16 ounces total) neufchâtel reduced-fat cream cheese, softened to room temperature
½ cup kumquat preserves, or orange marmalade
2 tablespoons honey
½ teaspoon orange extract
4 Fuyu persimmons (about 1 pound), calyx removed
1 9-inch crust from Chocolate Dream Pie (page 1022), prebaked and cooled

1 Combine the softened neufchâtel, 3 tablespoons of the preserves, the honey, and orange extract in a food processor. Process until well combined.

2 Dice 1 of the persimmons finely and set aside. Transfer the neufchâtel mixture to the crust, carefully spreading it out evenly. Place in the refrigerator to chill for at least 2 hours.

3 Up to 4 hours before serving, cut the remaining persimmons lengthwise into ¼-inch-thick wedges. Lay the slices, just barely touching or slightly overlapping, concentrically on top of the filling.

4 Place the remaining preserves in a small saucepan over medium heat. Heat, stirring constantly, until melted. Gently drizzle or brush the melted preserves over the sliced persimmons. Refrigerate for at least another 30 minutes before serving.

Grove Grooving

I once had the pleasure of wandering over the lush, intensely gardened acres of La Vigne/Beck's Grove, an organic orchard in Fallbrook, California. There, more than fifteen varieties of fruit are grown by Helene Beck and her husband, Robert. Avocado and persimmon groves alternate with a dozen varieties of citruses, including kumquats and blood oranges. The landscape is almost poetically lovely, scented with lime blossoms and filled with flower beds, a row of cypress trees punctuating the terrain like exclamation marks. The produce is as heavenly as the land on which it was grown, and the conserves, sauces, and purees Helene makes from them are extraordinary, including a persimmon-chipotle grilling sauce. Visit the web site, at www.lavignefruits.com, where you can also buy persimmon puree, an excellent alternative when fresh persimmons are out of season.

Rhubarb

Rhubarb is another purely seasonal taste. The evening I make a dinner for Ned and myself that starts with local asparagus and ends with rhubarb, I know spring has truly arrived. Improbable though it looks—like reddish-pink celery stalks—and tart though it is without major sweetening, its fragrant, almost floral flavor is simply unlike anything else, intense yet delicate, much like spring itself. Strawberries are a classic pairing with rhubarb in a two-crust pie, but I like my custard version even better.

Rhubarb-Custard Tart

Finish a spring feast with this fine, rustic offering, and you will know that the new season has well and tryly arrived. **MAKES 1 PIE; SERVES 6**

VARIATION

VEGAN VARIATION:
Use this combo for the custard mix: 6 ounces (½ package) silken tofu; 2 tablespoons soy milk; 1 tablespoon sugar or Rapidura; 2 teaspoons cashew butter; 2 teaspoons cornstarch; 1 teaspoon pure vanilla extract. Bake the pie a little longer, 25 to 30 minutes.

1 pound rhubarb, all leaves removed, cut into ½-inch slices
½ cup brown sugar or Rapidura
1 large egg
4 ounces neufchâtel reduced-fat cream cheese
⅓ cup cottage cheese or ricotta
1 tablespoon sugar
1 teaspoon pure vanilla extract
1 Sweet Sesame-Oatmeal Pie Crust, partially prebaked (page 991)

1. Preheat the oven to 375°F.

2. Combine the rhubarb and brown sugar in a small nonreactive saucepan over medium-high heat. Cover and cook until the rhubarb starts to exude juice, about 4 minutes. Uncover, lower the heat slightly, and stir a few times. Simmer until the rhubarb has softened but is still in distinct pieces, 3 to 4 minutes more. Remove from the heat and let cool.

3. Meanwhile, buzz the egg, neufchâtel, cottage cheese, sugar, and vanilla in a food processor.

4. Using a slotted spoon, lift the rhubarb from the saucepan, allowing any excess juice to remain in the pan. Scatter the drained rhubarb over the partially baked crust. Pour the egg mixture over the rhubarb.

5. Bake the tart until the custard sets and colors, 18 to 22 minutes.

6. If there's just a little juice remaining in the rhubarb cooking pot, do nothing. If you have more than a few tablespoons, place over high heat and boil down to equal no more than 1 to 2 tablespoons.

7. When the tart is set, remove from the oven and place it on a wire rack. Spoon the rhubarb syrup over the top. Let cool for 20 minutes, then serve, still warm.

Cakes

More than any other type of dessert, cakes spell festivity. They are the archetypal celebration sweet: round as the sun, tiered for weddings and layered for birthdays; complex—sandwiched with fillings of one kind, icings of another, sometimes piled with decoration. Yet they can also be down-home and simple: a coffee cake or the simplest of gingerbreads brought to the teacher's lounge or neighborhood potluck, perhaps served out of its own pan. There is also a magical alchemy that takes place between the batter and finished cake. As I described it in a children's poem: *You put it in wet / It comes out cake / That is why / I like to bake.*

Here are some of my favorite cakes, plain and fancy, simple and elaborate, some healthful, some decadent to the nth degree. (Cakes in which fruit is a predominant ingredient can be found earlier in this chapter, under the particular fruit.) I hope you'll enjoy mixing, baking, sniffing them as they transmute fragrantly, icing them, and serving them to happy people whom you adore.

Double-Density Chocolate-Walnut Espresso Torte

This and Chocolate Bread Pudding Maurice (page 1059) are the richest, most serious chocolate desserts I make. It's chocolate for grown-ups: a no-kidding, bittersweet, intense chocolate experience, with a faint touch of coffee. In inn days we made it with the cold-filtered coffee concentrate we used, but the instant freeze-dried crystals are fine too. It's a one-layer, intentionally dense cake; please note that there's no baking powder or soda. It's also fairly simple: if you can make brownies, you can make this. And it bears repeating: Do not over-bake this cake. **SERVES 10 TO 12**

Cooking spray
8 ounces best-quality unsweetened chocolate, chopped
1 cup butter
4 tablespoons boiling water, preferably spring or filtered
1½ tablespoons instant coffee or decaffeinated coffee crystals
5 large eggs
3 cups sugar
2 teaspoons pure vanilla extract
¼ teaspoon salt
1½ cups unbleached white all-purpose flour
1 recipe Creole Chocolate-Espresso Icing (recipe follows)
2 cups toasted walnuts, chopped

1 Preheat the oven to 375°F.

2 Generously spray a 10-inch round cake pan, preferably one with fairly deep sides, with cooking spray. Do not substitute a pie tin or any round pan with slanted sides; don't use a glass pan.

3 Combine the chocolate and butter in a heavy saucepan. Place over very low heat and cook, stirring constantly, until melted and blended. Remove from the heat and set aside to cool slightly.

4 Combine the boiling water with the coffee crystals in a small heatproof bowl. Stir until the crystals are dissolved. Set aside.

5 Place the eggs, sugar, vanilla, and salt in the bowl of an electric mixer. Beat on high speed until light, fluffy, and nearly doubled in bulk, at least 8 minutes. (A hand-held mixer takes a little longer than a stand mixer.)

6 Add the coffee mixture, and the slightly cooled chocolate-butter mixture. Beat until the ingredients are combined.

7 Remove the bowl from the mixer and, using a wooden spoon, beat in the flour by hand.

8 Transfer the batter to the prepared pan. Bake until the surface is dull and the edges of the cake have started to pull away

Bittersweet Chocolate Torte Ibarra

Mexico's combinations with chocolate are brilliant, unique, complex: ground almonds, canela cinnamon, and distinctive Mexican vanilla. I developed this excellent, even richer cake to take advantage of these complex flavors. It has become my favorite chocolate torte.

Coarsely chop 2 cups whole almonds into chunks in a food processor, and toast them at 350°F for about 8 minutes, or until fragrant and lightly browned. Return them to the food processor and pulse again until they are ground to a coarse powder. Set aside.

Follow the recipe for Double-Density Chocolate-Walnut Espresso Torte, but omit the walnuts, as well as the coffee, in both cake and glaze. Substitute pure Mexican vanilla, available at any Hispanic grocery, for the conventional vanilla extract. Reduce the flour to 1 cup. Add, with the flour, ½ teaspoon canela cinnamon (available in Hispanic groceries, and sometimes in supermarket spice sections), and ½ cup of the toasted almond powder. Bake the cake, and make the icing, as directed. Press the remaining toasted almond powder onto the top and sides of the frosted torte.

from the pan, about 35 minutes. It will still look a little underdone in the middle; ignore this. Do *not* overbake this cake; moistness is essential.

9 Remove the cake from the oven and set aside in the pan for 10 minutes. Run a knife around the edge of the pan and turn the cake out onto a wire rack. Cool completely. When cool, cover with the icing; press the walnuts into the top and sides of the cake. Serve at room temperature.

Creole Chocolate-Espresso Icing

Though it is simplicity itself to make, in flavor and texture this is the most sophisticated and divine icing you will ever taste. Very bittersweet—again, adult chocolate, not kid stuff. Once you discover this you might not make any other chocolate icing, ever. **MAKES ENOUGH FOR 1 TORTE**

12 ounces semisweet chocolate (either chocolate chips, or chopped squares)
1 cup sour cream, or whole milk, or plain yogurt
½ teaspoon pure vanilla extract
1½ to 2 tablespoons instant coffee or decaffeinated coffee crystals
4 tablespoons boiling water, preferably spring or filtered

1 Place the chocolate in the top half of a double boiler. Heat over hot water, stirring often, until melted.

2 Remove from the heat and stir in the sour cream, vanilla, and instant coffee dissolved in the boiling water. Using a wooden spoon, beat until smooth and glossy. Let cool, stirring occasionally, for about 5 minutes. Using a spatula, spread over cooled cake as directed.

Alice Medrich's Chocolate-Pecan-Bourbon Cake

One more very wonderful chocolate cake I am happy to share with you is from my "pan-pal" Alice Medrich, who developed it for *American Health* magazine in 1996. Alice's cookbooks *Chocolate and the Art of Low-Fat Desserts* and *Cocolat* are classics in the field. This is not "killer" like the previous tortes, but still a pleasure of the first order. A slice of this, a scoop of soy ice cream or frozen yogurt, and fresh raspberries or cherries or lightly thickened, lightly sweetened canned tart pie cherries, and a dessert-lover couldn't be happier. **MAKES 1 CAKE; SERVES 8**

Cooking spray
¼ cup pecans
2 tablespoons unbleached white all-purpose flour
½ cup unsweetened Dutch-process cocoa powder
1 cup sugar
3 ounces bittersweet or semisweet chocolate, finely chopped
½ cup boiling water, preferably spring or filtered
2 large egg yolks
1 tablespoon bourbon
4 large egg whites, room temperature
¼ teaspoon cream of tartar
Confectioners' sugar (optional)

1 Position the oven rack in the bottom third of the oven. Preheat the oven to 375°F.

2 Spray the bottom and sides of an 8- or 9-by-2½-inch springform pan with cooking spray. Set aside.

3 In a food processor, buzz the pecans and the flour until the mixture has the texture of fine meal. Set aside.

4 Combine the cocoa with ¾ cup of the sugar and the chocolate in a large heatproof bowl. Add the boiling water, whisking until the chocolate melts. Whisk in the egg yolks and bourbon. Set aside.

5 Combine the egg whites and cream of tartar in a medium bowl. Using an electric mixer, beat at medium speed until soft peaks form. Add the remaining ¼ cup sugar a little at a time, continuing to beat at high speed until the mixture is stiff and glossy.

6 Whisk the flour-pecan mixture into the chocolate mixture; fold about one-quarter of the egg whites into the chocolate. When incorporated, fold in the remaining egg whites, and scrape the batter into the prepared pan.

7 Bake for 30 to 35 minutes, until the cake has risen, the top is dry, and a toothpick inserted in the middle comes out with, as Alice says, only "a few moist crumbs clinging to it." Transfer the cake to a wire rack to cool. Don't be distressed when it sinks and the top crust cracks here and there. To serve, run a knife around the edge of the cake, unhook the springform hinge, and remove the sides. Leaving the cake on the base of the springform, transfer it to a serving plate. Sift confectioners' sugar over the top, if desired, and serve.

Orange-Scented Chocolate-Apricot Swirl Cake

Not a solid chocolate cake, this is light, quick, and calorie-sane. Try it after a simple Italian dinner, or in lieu of coffeecake. I developed it using a light olive oil Bertolli had just put on the market, to see if it really could work in desserts. It did, wonderfully. Any mild-tasting oil will work.

Buttermilk gives an especially tender crumb, compensating for the reduced fat. Apricot and chocolate, with the touch of orange here, is a dream flavor combination.

MAKES ONE CAKE; SERVES 6 TO 8

⅓ cup plus 2 teaspoons light olive oil
⅔ cup sugar
1 large egg plus 2 large egg whites
¾ teaspoon pure vanilla extract
Finely grated rind of 1 orange
1 cup plus 2 tablespoons sifted unbleached white all-purpose flour
1 teaspoon baking powder
½ teaspoon baking soda
¾ cup low-fat buttermilk
2 tablespoons unsweetened cocoa powder
3 tablespoons semisweet chocolate chips
½ cup fruit-only apricot jam or preserves
3 tablespoons finely chopped toasted pecans
1 ounce semisweet chocolate

1 Preheat the oven to 375°F.

2 Using 2 teaspoons of the oil, generously coat a 10-inch round cake pan. Set aside.

3 Pour the remaining ⅓ cup oil into the bowl of a standing mixer. Add the sugar and turn the mixer to low. Beat for 1 minute, then raise the speed to high. Add the egg and the egg whites, vanilla, and orange rind. Beat for 2 minutes.

4 Sift together the flour, baking powder, and baking soda.

5 Turn the mixer speed to very low, and alternately beat in the flour mixture with all but 1 tablespoon buttermilk. Beat just until the batter is blended.

6 Make the chocolate cake batter by combining ½ cup of the batter with the reserved 1 tablespoon buttermilk. When smooth, stir in the cocoa, then the chocolate chips.

7 Pour about half of the remaining vanilla cake batter into the prepared pan. Drop

the chocolate batter, by spoonfuls, atop the vanilla, marbling lightly with a knife. Drop spoonfuls of the apricot jam over the marbled cake, being careful not to let the jam touch the sides of the pan. Spoon the remaining vanilla batter over the jam, spreading to the pan edges. Top with the pecans.

8 Bake until the cake is golden and fragrant, and has pulled away from the pan edges, 30 to 35 minutes. Remove from the oven and let cool in the pan for 10 minutes. Run a knife around the edge of the cake to loosen it and then reverse it out onto a wire rack. Let cool for 10 minutes, then reverse again so that the pecans are on top. Cool completely, then transfer to a serving plate.

9 Place the semisweet chocolate in a small pan over very low heat. Melt, stirring constantly. Drizzle over the top of the cake and serve.

Dr. Feelgood's Chocolate Cake

This is one of those improbable-sounding recipes that periodically recur in community cookbooks and family magazines, often under names like "Wacky Cake" or "One-Bowl Chocolate Cake." It *is* sort of wacky—with a combination of ingredients that have no business being as good as they are—and it is easily done in a single bowl, in ten minutes or less. It is a classic in its way, and endures because it's one of the best moist, chocolatey cakes. I use it as a base for Black Forest cake and other more elaborate cakes. It is also, unbelievably, vegan, and without saturated fat.

MAKES TWO 9-INCH CAKE ROUNDS OR ONE 9-BY-13-INCH CAKE

Cooking spray
2 cups plus 2 tablespoons sugar
⅔ cup unsweetened cocoa powder American-style (not Dutch-process)
3 cups unbleached white all-purpose flour
2 teaspoons baking soda
1 teaspoon salt
2 cups water, preferably spring or filtered
½ cup mild vegetable oil, such as corn or canola
2 tablespoons cider vinegar, white vinegar, or fresh-squeezed lemon juice
1 tablespoon pure vanilla extract

1 Preheat the oven to 350°F.

2 Generously spray 2 9-inch round cake pans or 1 9-by-13-inch cake pan with cooking spray. Combine 2 tablespoons of the sugar and 2 tablespoons of the cocoa and place in the sprayed pans, knocking the pans around to coat well. Knock out any excess. Set the pans aside.

3 Sift the flour, the remaining sugar and cocoa, soda, and salt together into a large bowl.

4 Combine the water, oil, vinegar, and vanilla in a 4-cup glass measuring cup. Stir well. Pour the water mixture into the cocoa-flour mixture, whisking vigorously for a couple of minutes, until smooth and free of lumps.

5 Pour the batter into the prepared pans, and whack the pans on the counter a couple of times to release any air bubbles.

6 Place in the preheated oven and bake until the edges of the cake have pulled away from pan sides slightly and the cake tests clean with a toothpick, 25 to 30 minutes.

Lemon-Glazed Tofu Teasecake

Next to chocolate cakes, cheesecakes were the most frequently requested dessert cakes at the inn. If you have a cheesecake recipe you'd like to lighten up, try using neufchâtel or a Yogurt Sour Cream (page 910) dripped for twenty-four hours to replace all of the cream cheese. You'll get an immediate fat reduction, and no one will notice the difference.

Tofu cheesecake is another story. Although tofu cheesecakes have had a cult following for at least twenty-five years, Teasecake, the perfect name, was invented, as far as I know, by Susan Jane Cheney in her captivating *Breadtime Stories.* But whatever you call it, most serious vegetarian bakers have at least one such recipe.

These confections are incredibly good when updated with new products. Thanks to the advent of silken tofu, raw cashew butter (instead of tahini), and flavor notes, lemon especially, they really work. They get even better made ahead and chilled—for me they're best the next day. **MAKES ONE 8½-INCH CAKE; SERVES 6 TO 8**

CRUST

Cooking spray
⅓ cup graham cracker crumbs
⅓ cup ground Grape-Nuts cereal
2 teaspoons brown or maple sugar
2 teaspoons butter, preferably Browned Butter (page 1024), or vegetable margarine

FILLING

Four boxes (10½ ounces each) silken tofu, preferably reduced fat, firm or extra firm
¾ cup plus 1 tablespoon sugar or maple sugar (not syrup)
½ cup plus 2 tablespoons cashew butter
¼ cup cornstarch
Juice and grated rind of 1½ lemons
1 teaspoon pure vanilla extract
¾ teaspoon almond extract
¼ teaspoon salt

LEMON GLAZE

½ cup sugar
1 tablespoon plus 2 teaspoons cornstarch
1 cup water, preferably spring or filtered
Grated rind and juice of 2 lemons
Pinch of salt

1 Preheat the oven to 400°F.

2 Spray the bottom and sides of an 8½-inch springform pan with cooking spray. Set aside.

3 Combine all of the remaining crust ingredients in a small bowl. Work with your fingertips until the mixture is crumbly. Press into the bottom of the prepared pan.

4 Bake until slightly browned, 4 to 6 minutes. Remove from the oven and let cool. Lower the oven temperature to 350°F.

5 Make the filling: Combine the tofu, sugar, cashew butter, and cornstarch in a food processor. Add the lemon juice and rind, vanilla, almond extract, and salt, blending until smooth, pausing to scrape down the sides of the bowl.

6 Scrape the filling into the prepared crust. Using a spatula, smooth the top. Bake until set, pale golden, and slightly risen, 55 to 60 minutes. Turn off the oven and let the cake sit in the oven for 10 minutes.

7 Remove, place on a wire rack, and let cool to room temperature. Don't worry if the surface is cracked; sometimes it happens. When cool, run a knife around the edge of the Teasecake and unhinge the springform. Transfer to a serving platter.

8 Make the glaze: Combine the sugar and cornstarch in a small bowl and whisk in enough of the water to make a smooth, thin paste. Whisk in the lemon juice and rind and the salt. When blended, pour into a small, nonreactive saucepan and place

over medium heat. Cook, stirring, until the mixture comes to a boil, at which point it will turn thick and clear. Remove from the heat and let cool slightly. Pour over the cake. Chill, if possible, for 2 to 3 hours or overnight, before serving.

The Good Old-Fashioned, New-Fashioned Jelly Roll

A good old-fashioned simple jelly-roll cake belongs in every home baker's repertoire. It's the base for hundreds of variations, some very homey, some show-offy, some do-ahead to have in the freezer for treats. My version is low-fat (only what's in the egg yolks) and dairy-free, with a delicate texture, ethereal, and amenable to many changes. It's a satisfying conclusion to a special meal, yet the simplest meal becomes special with its addition.

Although simple to make, there is a fairly long spell of beating, and the eggs must be at room temperature. A standing mixer is easier, for the sugar is added a little at a time, but it's certainly doable with a hand-held.

I prefer a double-insulated jelly-roll pan. **MAKES ONE JELLY-ROLL CAKE; SERVES 6 TO 8**

Cooking spray
¾ cup plus 1 tablespoon sugar
¾ cup plus 1 tablespoon sifted unbleached white all-purpose flour
1 heaping tablespoon cornstarch
¾ teaspoon baking powder
¼ teaspoon salt
4 large eggs, at room temperature
1½ teaspoons pure vanilla extract
¼ cup confectioners' sugar
½ to 1 cup filling of your choice (see box on next page)

1 Preheat the oven to 400°F.

2 Generously spray a 11-by-15-by-1-inch jelly-roll pan with cooking spray, then line it with a long strip of waxed paper, extending the paper by about 1½ inches beyond the short ends of the pan.

Spray the waxed paper with cooking spray, then sprinkle 1 tablespoon each of the sugar and flour over the waxed paper. Knock out the excess. Set the pan aside.

3 Sift the remaining flour, the cornstarch, baking powder, and salt together twice. Set aside.

4 Place the eggs in the bowl of an electric mixer and beat the eggs until lemon-colored and thick, about 3 minutes. Lower the mixer speed and add the remaining sugar, a tablespoon or two at a time. When all the sugar has been added, return the speed to high and beat for exactly 8 minutes. The eggs and sugar will triple in volume, becoming light and creamy. Lower the speed, and beat in the vanilla.

5 Remove the bowl from the mixer. Pour the sifted flour-cornstarch mixture over the eggs and sugar, and, using a spatula, gently fold the flour into the eggs, turning and folding and turning and folding, until the mixtures are incorporated completely, but on no account overmixed.

6 Pour the batter into the prepared pan, spreading it evenly and completely with the spatula. It must cover the entire pan.

7 Bake until the cake is golden, the edges are just starting to pull away from the sides of the pan, and the cake springs back when lightly touched at the center with an inquiring fingertip, 12 to 14 minutes. Don't overbake the cake or it will be dry and tough.

Jelly Rollin' Along

Simple Jelly Roll: *Spread with a good tart, flavorful jelly or jam. Garnish with an orange slice and a mint leaf, or a piece of the fresh fruit. If desired, pass any of the dessert creams (pages 1061–63), ice cream, whipped cream, yogurt, light sour cream, or soy ice cream, at the table.*

Almond-Apricot Roll: *A super variation. Add ½ teaspoon almond extract to the batter. Sprinkle ½ cup toasted, slivered almonds over the waxed paper, spreading the batter over that. Fill with apricot jam, or a mixture of dried apricots soaked in apple juice until tender, then pureed with a little sugar, honey or maple syrup. If desired, pass any of the dessert creams (pages 1061–63), ice cream, whipped cream, yogurt, light sour cream, or soy ice cream, at the table.*

Lemon Jelly Roll: *Hands down my favorite, since I am a big proponent of lemon desserts anyway. Prepare the cake using ¼ teaspoon vanilla extract and ¾ teaspoon lemon extract. As the cake bakes, make the Lemon Mousse-Custard (page 1052), but use an extra ½ teaspoon powdered agar. Let it set while the cake cools, then fill, reroll, and refrigerate.*

Ice Cream Roll: *Fill with slightly softened ice cream, frozen yogurt, or soy ice cream. This seems messy and improbable, but it all comes together nicely once you pop it back in the freezer. Take it out of the freezer 10 minutes before serving, and it can easily be sliced. This has the great virtue of being able to do-ahead by several days. It's excellent for summer, served with mixed berries and, if you wish, a drizzle of The Very Best Hot Fudge Sauce (page 1063).*

8 While the cake is baking, spread a clean dish towel out on the kitchen counter, and sift the confectioners' sugar evenly over the towel.

9 When the cake is done, turn it out onto the prepared towel. Gently lift off the pan (if the cake wants to stick, hold the waxed paper ends and gently tug, which will ease the release). Grasp one of the overhanging waxed paper ends and pull the paper from the cake. Swiftly, while the cake is still hot, roll the cake up from its short side, rolling the sugar-covered towel up with it. Leave it rolled for about 10 minutes.

10 Carefully unroll the cake, spread with the filling of your choice, and reroll (without the towel, of course). Place the rolled cake, seam side down, on a small cutting board (if you intend to serve it in slices from the kitchen) or serving plate (if you intend to offer it whole, and then serve it at the table). Let cool completely; serve at room temperature, garnished if desired (see the box on the opposite page), or refrigerate and serve chilled.

If your filling allows, this can be frozen, well wrapped, for up to 1 month.

Miss Kay's Orange Sponge Cake

This simple, delicious cake is the first I ever made, with Miss Kay, my first outside-the-family culinary mentor (see page 325). It is a bit exacting, so I have given precise directions that I urge you to follow closely.

With 4 or 5 eggs in the batter, egg quality makes a difference. If you use free-range country eggs, the cake will be tastier and more golden. For this reason I tend to make this cake in the early spring, when the chickens go on a natural egg-laying jag. If you don't live somewhere where you're likely to see a hand-lettered sign that reads EGGS FOR SALE, buy 'em at a natural foods store.

VARIATIONS

TWO-CITRUS SPONGE CAKE ***was another Miss Kay variation; she'd add the grated rind of 1 lemon with the orange, as well as 1 teaspoon lemon juice to the orange juice.***

CRUNCHY-TOPPED SUGARED SPONGE CAKE: ***Very nice if you're not filling or rolling the cake, but serving it with just fresh fruit. All you do is sprinkle the top of the cake, before baking, with 1½ tablespoons turbinado sugar.***

CHOCOLATE SPONGE CAKE, ***cloud-light and exceedingly low in fat for a chocolate cake, requires only that you substitute 6 tablespoons sifted Dutch-process cocoa powder for an equal amount of the flour.***

It is important to *sift the flour before measuring,* then *spoon* (do not scoop) the sifted flour into a measuring cup. Don't tap the cup down; this defeats the purpose of sifting, which is to aerate the flour. Level off the cup with the flat side of a knife. I know all of this sounds fussy; but following these directions exactly makes all the difference.

I usually make this as a roll cake, so that is why I am giving that version first. The more classic sponge cake treatment—in an angel food pan—follows. **MAKES ONE JELLY-ROLL CAKE; SERVES 6 TO 8**

2 to 3 oranges
¼ cup cornstarch
1½ cup sifted unbleached white all-purpose flour
⅛ teaspoon salt
1 teaspoon baking powder
1¼ cups granulated sugar
¼ teaspoon cream of tartar
Confectioners' sugar
5 large, or 4 extra-large eggs, at room temperature, separated
½ to 1 cup filling of your choice (see box on page 1012; optional)

1 Preheat the oven to 350°F.

2 Line an 11-by-15-inch jelly-roll pan, with sides about ¾ to 1 inch high, preferably doubly insulated, with parchment paper. The paper should extend 2 inches over the short sides of the pan. Do not grease the pan or paper. Set aside.

3 Also set up a stand mixer, and set a mise en place tray (see page 107) next to it.

4 Grate the rind from 1 of the oranges and set it in a little dish on the "mise" tray. Cut the orange in half, and squeeze the juice. You'll need ½ cup freshly squeezed juice. (Juice the second and third oranges if you need to.) Place the juice in a bowl on the "mise" tray.

5 Place the cornstarch in a bowl. Using a 1-cup dry (not liquid) measuring cup, and a ½-cup dry measuring cup, gently spoon in the sifted flour until both 1- and ½-cup measures are full. Level them with the flat edge of a knife. Turn out into the bowl with the cornstarch, and add the salt and baking powder, blending these into the flour-cornstarch mixture with a few turns of a wire whisk. Set this on your "mise" tray.

6 Place the granulated sugar, cream of tartar, and confectioners' sugar on the "mise" tray.

7 Place the egg whites in the bowl of a stand mixer. Begin whipping the egg whites and, when they are foamy, add the cream of tartar. Continue whipping until soft peaks form. Sprinkle 1 tablespoon of the granulated sugar over the egg whites and continue beating until the egg whites are stiff. Turn the egg whites out of the mixing bowl into a clean, dry bowl. Don't wash the beaters or the mixing bowl.

8 Place the egg yolks in the mixing bowl along with the orange rind and the

remaining granulated sugar. Beat, on high, until thick, lemon colored, and about tripled in volume, about 5 minutes.

9 Sprinkle about one-third of the flour mixture, along with about 2 tablespoons of the orange juice, over the yolk mixture. Gently fold in, using a rubber spatula. Repeat, sprinkling and folding, until all the flour and orange juice have been incorporated.

10 Fold in the egg white mixture. When blended, pour the batter into the prepared pan. Bake until the cake is golden, slightly more so around the edges, dry looking on top, and tests clean with a toothpick, 20 to 25 minutes.

11 Remove from the oven and let cool completely in the pan. The top of the cake will be sticky. Dust liberally with confectioners' sugar, and lay a sheet of waxed paper over it. Run a knife around the edges, and turn the cooled cake out (the waxed paper is now on the bottom). Carefully peel off the parchment paper. Trim about ⅛ inch from all around the cake. The edges are slightly crisp, so removing them will make rolling easier—and give you something to nibble as a reward for all this travail. Sprinkle the surface with confectioners' sugar. Top with waxed paper, followed by a clean towel.

12 Roll the cake up jelly-roll fashion, rolling the towel and waxed paper up along with it. It may want to crack or fall apart, but don't worry, everything will come out right. Tightly cover with plastic wrap and let set, rolled, for up to 24 hours. At any time during this period, you can unroll the cake, remove the towel and paper, spread the filling on, and reroll without fear.

Miss Kay's Tube Style

Filling and flavoring variations are infinite. But first, let me give you the classic, much easier, non jelly-roll sponge cake in a tube pan. First off, use an ungreased 10-inch tube pan to bake in, rather than a jelly roll pan. Bake at 325°F, not 350°F, for about an hour, not 20 minutes. And, to cool the cake without bearing down on its delicate top, you'll need to suspend the pan upside down while it cools, by perching it on a bottle (the bottle neck goes through the hole in the center of the pan). When the cake is thoroughly cool, go around the edges with a knife to loosen it, then turn it out. To cut slices without crushing the delicate crumb, use two forks (not a knife) to pull the cake apart, slice by delicate slice.

Sweet Harvest Applesauce Breakfast Bundt Cake

The particular inn where I first had this cake, in a small coastal southeastern city, is closed now, but the memory of its gorgeous breakfast lingers. The crown jewel: a variation of this tall, dark, sweet bundt cake—bread, dusted generously with confectioners' sugar. I told Mrs. Innkeeper how good it was while nibbling a tiny scrap, knowing the usual fat content of sweet bread. She thanked me, adding offhandedly, "You know, it's very low in fat, too." At that point I took another piece—and took notes as she dictated the recipe. It makes use of a trick much called on in fat-reduced baking: Replace most of the fat with fruit puree, which works particularly well with prunes and apples, since both are high in pectin, a natural jelling agent. If one allows these flavors full rein—instead of trying to, say, make a chocolate cake and hide the prune puree in it—the results can be gratifying. Especially so here, where apple is paired with its classic partners—cinnamon and other sweet spices. It's even better if you use whole wheat pastry flour. If you don't have a bundt pan, use loaf pans.

Try this with Ricotta Crème, Tofu-Cashew Crème, conventional or vegan crème anglaise, frozen yogurt, or ice cream; something smooth, creamy, and mild to play off its opulent spiciness (see the section on crèmes, page 1061, or frozen desserts, page 1043). As a breakfast cake, try it with ricotta topped with apple butter.

Of the denser fruit-noted cakes, this is my favorite after Cornmeal-Oatmeal Blueberry Bread (page 447). On no account omit the dusting of confectioners' sugar; it is essential. The cake is even better the day after it's made. **MAKES ONE 9-INCH BUNDT CAKE; SERVES 12**

Cooking spray
1½ cups unbleached white all-purpose flour or whole wheat pastry flour, plus a little additional for the pan
1¼ teaspoons baking powder
¼ teaspoon baking soda
1 teaspoon ground cinnamon, preferably Saigon
8 to 10 good vigorous gratings of nutmeg
Dash of ground cloves
Dash of ground allspice
½ cup raisins
2 to 4 tablespoons walnuts, toasted and chopped (optional)
½ cup white sugar
½ cup brown sugar
1 large egg
1¼ cups applesauce
¼ cup mild vegetable oil, such as corn, canola, or peanut
1 teaspoon pure vanilla extract
Confectioners' sugar

1 Preheat the oven to 350°F.

2 Decide on the pan: a 9-inch bundt cake pan, an 8-by-4-inch loaf pan, or three 5-by-2-inch loaf pans. Spray the selected pan(s) thoroughly with cooking spray. Dust each pan with a little flour, knock out the excess, and set aside.

3 Combine the flour, baking powder, baking soda, cinnamon, nutmeg, cloves, and allspice (if the baking powder and baking soda appear at all lumpy, sift them in, but the other dry ingredients do not have to be sifted). Reserve 1 tablespoon of the flour mixture and place it in a small bowl along with the raisins and, if using, the walnuts. Toss this mixture well, and set both bowls aside.

4 Combine the sugars with the egg, applesauce, oil, and vanilla and, using a wooden spoon, beat the flour mixture together with the applesauce mixture. Stir in the raisins and walnuts and spoon the batter into the prepared pan.

5 Bake until the cake tests clean with a toothpick; the top will still appear a little glossy and feel sticky-tacky to the touch—30 to 35 minutes for the large loaf or bundt cake pan, and 20 to 25 for the small. Remove from the oven and let cool in the pan(s) on a wire rack for about 10 minutes. Run a knife around the inner edges of the pan(s), and invert onto the rack with a sharp rap. Let cool completely, then either tightly cover with plastic wrap for storage in the refrigerator or freezer or place on a serving plate, dust with a generous drift of confectioners' sugar, and serve.

Old-Fashioned Banana-Almond Layer Cake

The favorite cake of my friend Steve Colvin, who requested it for birthdays. After trying many banana cakes, I feel confident in saying that this is the ultimate. And while it is a terrific birthday cake, it's also nice after a simple vegetable soup and salad dinner, say. Its starting point was a fine recipe from Marilyn Moore's *The Wooden Spoon Dessert Book*. Half of the shortening has been replaced by butter, pointing up the banana flavor; cinnamon has been reduced for a barely-there hint of spice, and I've added almonds—to me, bananas and almonds are soul mates. Almond extract flavors both the buttercream and cake; toasted almonds stud the exterior, and, best of all, a thin layer of almond paste and buttercream is sandwiched inside. The whole is dazzling, in a very homey, afternoon-at-Grandma's way. The cake layers, unassembled, freeze superbly, too.

There is no way this is light or low fat. If you are avoiding trans-fatty acids, omit the shortening. Omit the butter, too, and substitute ½ cup Better (page 905) for both. Better does not have to be softened; it'll give you buttery flavor and a nominally more healthful fat profile.

Almond paste really puts this cake over the top. It may be purchased at specialty foods stores or from catalogs like King Arthur Flour, or in the baking sections of some supermarkets. You can either purchase it or make your own; Rose Levy Beranbaum's recipe in *The Cake Bible* is excellent. **SERVES 8 TO 10**

Cooking spray
2 cups plus 1 tablespoon, unbleached white all-purpose flour
1½ cups plus 1 tablespoon sugar
¾ teaspoon baking powder
¾ teaspoon baking soda
½ teaspoon salt
¼ teaspoon ground cinnamon
¼ teaspoon freshly grated nutmeg
¼ cup butter, softened to room temperature
¼ cup vegetable shortening
2 large eggs
1 teaspoon almond extract
1 cup pureed very ripe bananas (about 2 large)
¼ cup buttermilk
Almond Cream-Cheese Icing (recipe follows)
8 ounces almond paste, at room temperature
Confectioners' sugar
About 1½ cups slivered almonds, toasted

1 Preheat the oven to 350°F.

2 Spray two 9-inch round cake pans with cooking spray.

3 Combine 1 tablespoon of the flour and 1 tablespoon of the sugar in a small bowl. Sprinkle the sugar-flour mixture over the sprayed cake pans, knocking out any excess. Set the pans aside.

4 Sift together the remaining flour, the baking powder, baking soda, salt, cinnamon, and nutmeg. Set aside.

5 Cream the butter and shortening together with the remaining sugar, beating until fully incorporated, smooth, and fluffy, about 3 minutes. Beat the eggs in one at a time. Add the almond extract, then the puréed bananas.

6 Using a wooden spoon, stir half of the flour mixture into the banana mixture.

When the flour is well incorporated stir in the buttermilk. Stir until smooth, then stir in the remaining flour mixture.

7 Turn the batter out into the prepared pans and bake until the cakes are fragrant, golden brown, test done with a toothpick, and have pulled away from the pan edges slightly, about 30 minutes. Remove from the oven. Let cool in the pans for 10 minutes, then run a knife around the edges of the pans. Invert the cakes onto wire racks to cool completely. (As the cake cools, you'll have plenty of time to make the icing.)

8 Knead the almond paste slightly to soften it. Then, on a flat surface sprinkled with confectioners' sugar, roll out the almond paste to a smooth round, 9 inches in diameter and a ¼ inch or so thick. You may not get this exactly—don't worry. Lay one layer of the cake on a serving plate (or a 10-inch cardboard cake round) and lay the rolled-out almond paste over it as best you can, patching any holes as needed. Completely cover the top of this cake layer, and trim off any overhanging paste with kitchen shears.

9 Spread a little of the Almond Cream-Cheese Icing over the almond paste, and top it with the second cake layer.

10 Ice the entire cake with a generous smoothing of Almond Cream-Cheese Icing. Refrigerate for 30 minutes or so, just long enough for the icing to firm up. Finally, press almond slivers into the sides of the cake, leaving the top plain. If some almonds fall off, don't worry—just press 'em back in. If you've placed the cake on a cardboard round, lift the cake, round and all, onto a serving plate. If not, just let it rest where it is, on the serving plate, in slightly messy but undeniable glory.

Almond Cream-Cheese Icing

A variation of the much-loved icing often found on carrot cakes.

6 ounces cream cheese or neufchâtel reduced-fat cream cheese, softened
3 tablespoons butter
About 1 tablespoon milk or heavy cream
3½ to 4 cups sifted confectioners' sugar
1 teaspoon almond extract

Cream the cream cheese, butter, and 1 tablespoon milk until smooth and fluffy. Beat in the confectioners' sugar, adding more sugar or milk as needed to make a spreadable mixture. This is a soft icing that firms up when refrigerated. In warm weather, refrigerate the frosted cakes until 1 hour before serving.

"Milk in the batter! Milk in the batter! We bake cake and nothing's the matter!"

—Maurice Sendak, *In the Night Kitchen*

Pies

Here I've included two super-rich, much-loved pies from the inn days, New South B & B White Chocolate–Banana Cream Pie in a Pecan Crust and Honeyed Browned-Butter Pecan Pie. They are world class, within their class: once-in-a-while, big-time indulgence. It's hard for me to feel at ease with the amount and type of fat (much and saturated) required to make a classic flaky pie crust, let alone the fillings of such. . . . I lean much more toward fruit-heavy desserts where the "crust" is a topping, be it an oatmeal and brown sugar crisp or a biscuit-y cobbler. When only a fruit pie will do, the choice is just to roll on and enjoy a classic crust. But after all these years as a more-or-less natural foods eater, my personal taste runs alternatively, to crisp rather than flaky, grainy and toothsome rather than shattering with a fork. Could a nonfruit pie contain equal measures of indulgence plus reasonable healthfulness—and be vegan to boot? *And* easy to make? Um-hmmm. Enter the Chocolate Dream Pie. You will thank me for this one.

I've also included in this section one very special personal favorite pie filling, the Fabulous Green Tomato Mincemeat-less Pie Filling. It is old-fashioned, and it's perfection in the mince category. I put up a few jars annually for vegetarian Thanksgiving pies; if you are not the home-canning type, divide it into 3- to 4- cup portions in zippered freezer bags and freeze until November.

New South B & B White Chocolate–Banana Cream Pie in a Pecan Crust

To what ecstatic heights can this old truck-stop favorite be raised! A crust with a few pecans, a filling in which white chocolate melds custard and banana, caressed by the addition of B & B liqueur . . . what can I say but *wow.* (Of *course* that's real whipped cream on top.) Make this on the morning of the day you intend to serve it. It takes time to set up in the fridge, but if it sits too long, the bananas discolor and the filling gets a bit runny.

If you want to simplify preparation, use a prebaked, commercially made pie shell. **MAKES ONE 9-INCH PIE; SERVES 8**

PECAN PIE CRUST

1⅓ cups unbleached white all-purpose, flour
3 tablespoons very finely chopped toasted pecans
2 tablespoons sugar
½ teaspoon salt
⅓ cup vegetable shortening
2 tablespoons plus 2 teaspoons butter, slightly softened
3 to 4 tablespoons ice water, preferably spring or filtered

B & B WHITE CHOCOLATE–BANANA CREAM PIE FILLING

3¼ cups milk
6 large egg yolks
1⅓ cups sugar
½ cup unbleached white all-purpose flour
⅓ cup cornstarch
4 ounces white chocolate, coarsely chopped
2 ripe bananas, peeled and sliced
¼ cup B & B liqueur
½ teaspoon pure vanilla extract

GARNISH

1 cup heavy cream, whipped
Semisweet chocolate curls (optional)
Fresh mint leaves
1 banana, peeled and sliced on the diagonal

1. Preheat the oven to 450°F.

2. Make the crust: Combine the flour, pecans, sugar, and salt. Cut in the shortening and butter. Drizzle in the ice water, a tablespoon at a time, stirring until the dough comes together. Chill for 15 minutes.

3. Roll the crust out on a lightly floured board to a circle about 11 inches in diameter. Fit into a 9-inch pie pan, prick the bottom of the crust with a fork, and crimp the edges. Line the shell with foil, fill with pie weights or beans, and bake for 6 minutes. Remove the foil and weights and bake for another 5 minutes. Turn off the oven, leaving the crust in the oven until it is uniformly golden brown, another 3 to 5 minutes. Let cool completely before filling.

4. Place 3 cups of the milk in a medium-large, heavy-bottom saucepan over medium heat. Whisk the remaining ¼ cup milk together with the egg yolks, sugar, flour, and cornstarch until smooth and thoroughly combined.

5. When the milk is scalding hot, ladle out 1 cup of it and whisk it into the yolk-sugar mixture. Whisk the yolk-sugar mixture into the hot milk, whisking thoroughly until the mixture begins to thicken and bubble. Switch to a wooden spoon, and, stirring constantly, cook for 1 minute. Remove the custard from the heat. Taste to make sure there is no starchy taste (if so, cook for a few seconds longer).

6. Place the white chocolate, the 2 sliced bananas, the B & B, and vanilla in a food processor. Pour the hot custard over these ingredients and buzz for about 40 seconds, or just until the bananas and white chocolate are thoroughly incorporated.

7 Pour into the cooled crust until the filling is even with the upper edge. There will be extra filling; place the extra filling in a small bowl, and refrigerate the filled pie and the extra filling for 15 minutes. Remove the pie and filling from the refrigerator and spoon the extra filling, which will have partially set up, onto the middle of the pie, mounding it up toward the center (this gives the "mile-high pie" effect). Refrigerate for at least 1 hour to chill thoroughly. Top with whipped cream and, if desired, chocolate curls. Serve, garnished with a sprig of fresh mint and an oval slice of banana.

Chocolate Dream Pie

Indulgence is not just for the dairy- and egg-eaters of the world. This easier-to-make pie is vegan. Most cookbooks using tofu have some variation of a chocolate tofu dessert; this is mine, and it is very, very good. Using melted chocolate as well as cocoa, plus the richness of cashew butter, makes the difference. If the only chocolate pies you know are old-fashioned chocolate custard or super-rich French silk, it might take your palate a taste or two to adjust.

Vegans will want to use dairy-free natural chocolates. **MAKES ONE 9-INCH PIE; SERVES 6 TO 8**

CRUST

Cooking spray or oil (optional)
½ cup graham cracker crumbs
½ cup crushed Nutri-Grain or other no-sugar-added corn- or wheat flakes
2 tablespoons unbleached white all-purpose flour
2 tablespoons brown sugar
½ teaspoon salt
1 tablespoon melted butter or Better (page 905), or mild vegetable oil, such as corn, canola, or peanut
2 to 3 tablespoons water, preferably spring or filtered

FILLING

1 ounce unsweetened chocolate, chopped
1 ounce semisweet chocolate, chopped
¾ cup Rapidura
2 packages (21 ounces total) silken tofu, firm or extra firm
2 tablespoons cashew butter
⅓ cup unsweetened cocoa powder
1 teaspoon pure vanilla extract

VARIATIONS

CHOCOLATE-ORANGE DREAM PIE: ***Cut the vanilla back to ¼ teaspoon, and add the grated rind and the juice of 1 orange. Combining orange with the chocolate is a neat trick; the flavors complement each other very nicely, and dispense with the teeny remnant of tofu-ness that anyone accustomed to the other variety of chocolate cream pie might discern.***

CHOCOLATE-ORANGE DREAM MOUSSE ***is made by putting the same mixture into cups.***

FOR SERVING (OPTIONAL)
Tofu-Cashew Crème (page 1062)
Fresh raspberries (you may substitute other fresh fruit in season, such as strawberries or sliced oranges, with or without a sprig of mint)

1 Preheat the oven to 425°F.

2 If not using a nonstick pan, spray an 8- to 9-inch pie pan with cooking spray, or oil it.

3 Combine the graham cracker and cereal crumbs, flour, brown sugar, and salt. Add the melted butter and 2 tablespoons of the water. Add the remaining water only if needed to make a consistency that can be pressed into the pan. Using your fingers, press the mixture into the prepared pan to cover the bottom and sides evenly. Bake for 10 minutes. Remove from the oven and set aside to cool.

4 Melt the chocolates in the top half of a double boiler over hot water.

5 Place the Rapidura in a food processor along with the tofu and cashew butter. Buzz until smooth, stopping to scrape down the sides of the bowl. Add the melted chocolates, cocoa, and vanilla. Process until very smooth.

6 Pour the chocolate mixture into the cooled pie crust. Place in the refrigerator and chill for at least 4 hours. Serve, chilled, with the Tofu-Cashew Crème and fresh raspberries, if desired.

Honeyed Browned-Butter Pecan Pie

What makes my rendition of this Southern classic dessert, more confection than pie, soooo good? Browning the butter? The touch of honey? Make it and see, and do try the variation that follows.

Pecan is the nut everyone loves in nut pies, but I urge you to expand your horizons. Almonds are divine, and, to my taste, somehow Christmas-y. But hazelnuts may just be the ultimate. So ultimate that when I entered my hazelnut version of this in a contest sponsored by the Hazelnut Board, I won the grand prize! **SERVES 8**

NOTE

The center of the pie will still seem a bit liquid when it's removed from the oven; it sets up further as it cools, so let it cool completely.

VARIATION

VERMONT-STYLE BROWNED-BUTTER MAPLE-WALNUT PIE ***combines maple pies from my girlhood summers in Vermont with the browned-butter technique. Follow the recipe, but cut the corn syrup to ¼ cup and omit the honey. Add ¾ cup Grade B (or Grade A dark amber) maple syrup. Substitute 1 cup granulated pure maple sugar (see page 958) for the sugar, and use walnuts, or, if you can get them, butternuts —the common name for white walnuts, an Eastern variety—for the pecans.***

½ cup butter
3 large eggs
1 cup sugar
¾ cup light corn syrup
¼ cup honey
1 teaspoon pure vanilla extract
⅛ teaspoon salt
1 cup chopped pecans, almonds, or hazelnuts
One 9-inch pie crust, unbaked
1 cup heavy cream, whipped (optional)

1 Preheat the oven to 425°F.

2 Place the butter in a saucepan over low to medium heat and cook, watching closely but not stirring, until golden brown, 5 to 8 minutes. Do not burn. Pour browned butter into a bowl and set aside.

3 Blend the eggs, sugar, corn syrup, honey, vanilla, and salt in a food processor until smooth. Add the browned butter and blend. Add the pecans and process with just a few quick on-off pulses.

4 Pour the mixture into the pie crust. Bake for 12 minutes; lower the heat to 325°F and bake for another 40 minutes. Remove from the oven and set on a wire rack to cool. Serve at room temperature, with a dollop of whipped cream, if desired, on each slice.

"What Bennett and his brothers loved best . . . was Florida's karo pecan pie. Her pecan pie had big chunks of pecans, often taken right from their own pecan tree. The filling was soft and gooey and sweet, but not too sweet. . . . Bennett's mother closed her eyes while she was eating. . . . Bennett and his brothers kept their eyes open and ate as fast they could, so they might get seconds."

—Alan Lightman, *Good Benito*

Browned Butter

Want more flavor from less butter? Brown the butter first. It makes it so much more flavorful and fragrant. This is a trick I used in the pre–fat-conscious days as a taste-intensifier, but it's especially handy when you're trying to cut back on butter. With browned butter, you can truly have your cake—or pie or cookie—and eat it too.

Here's the method. Make as much as you want, but no less than ½ cup, because it's nearly impossible to do less without burning it. If you're a dedicated low-fat baker, why not make a pound at a time? Refrigerated, it keeps quite a while, and that way you'll have it ready, should the low-fat big-flavor dessert urge strike.

Browned Butter is used satisfyingly in a number of dessert recipes in this book, including Neo-Zialetti, Ozark-Style Cornmeal Cookies with Lemon and Raisins (page 1038).

Unsalted butter

1 Melt the butter in a medium- to medium-large saucepan over medium heat. Lower the heat so that the butter stays at a steady simmer. Cook, uncovered, stirring

often and watching closely, for 5 to 8 minutes. First the butter will foam, then the foam will subside and the butter will gradually turn a nice deep golden—almost but not quite a brown, despite its being called browned butter. You want to keep the milky sediment on the bottom from burning.

2 The instant "golden" has been achieved, remove the saucepan from the heat. Stir for 30 seconds or so to prevent further cooking, then set aside to cool to lukewarm. Transfer to a container with a tight lid and store, refrigerated, for up to 3 weeks, or frozen for up to 4 months.

Fabulous Green Tomato Mincemeat-less Pie Filling

Mincemeat pie fillings are a combination of fresh and dried fruits, seasoned and sweetened and vinegared, dating back to Elizabethan times. This version, of course, has not a whisper of meat. It was given to me way back when by a friendly, much older neighbor-lady when I first moved to the Ozarks. Like all natives who came up through hard times, she was frugal ("Use it up, wear it out, make it do, or do without," was one of the maxims I heard in those days), but wrung pleasure from her economies. This exquisite filling is one such example. It uses up green tomatoes, which might otherwise go wasted, and combines them with many other ingredients that at first blush might sound incongruous but blend perfectly. If you are a mincemeat lover, you'll find this the ultimate version. In those pre–food processor days, we put the orange and raisins through a food grinder.

Use an organic orange here, whose peel has not been treated with fumigants and waxes, because you will be using the entire rind. Also, this should be cooked in an enamel-clad pot, or a brand-new, never-scratched, heavy stainless-steel pot because the large amount of vinegar will react with iron, aluminum, or scratched stainless steel. Besides using this as a pie filling, it's excellent served warm over ice cream or soy ice cream, rolled into crêpes, or layered with vanilla pudding or custard as an essence-of-fall parfait. **MAKES ABOUT 4 QUARTS**

1 orange, quartered, all seeds picked out
1 pound raisins
1 cup cider vinegar
2½ quarts chopped, cored apples, peeled or not as you prefer (Northern Spies, Stayman Winesaps, and Macouns are good varieties here, but use what you have)
2½ quarts chopped, stemmed green tomatoes
1 pound pitted prunes, halved
1 pound brown sugar
½ cup dark (not blackstrap) molasses or sorghum syrup
1 tablespoon ground cinnamon
1 teaspoon ground cloves
½ teaspoon ground allspice
½ teaspoon freshly grated nutmeg
½ teaspoon salt
½ teaspoon ground ginger

1 Combine the orange with half of the raisins and the vinegar in a food processor. Process to a chunky, even texture, somewhere between paste and puree, scraping down the sides of the bowl a couple of times. Transfer to a large nonreactive pot. Add the remaining whole raisins.

2 Add all of the remaining ingredients, and bring to a boil over high heat, stirring often. Lower the heat to a simmer and cook, stirring often (due to the sugar, the mixture will want to stick), until good and thick, and the kitchen is fragrant. The apples and tomatoes should be soft, but still distinguishable; 30 to 40 minutes of simmering should do it.

3 If canning, place the hot mincemeat into sterilized jars. Seal. Or let cool, and transfer to zippered freezer bags in 3-cup portions (one pie's worth of filling) and freeze. Look forward to Thanksgiving!

Cookies

If fruit desserts celebrate the changing seasons and are the best choice for both daily and soigné occasions, and if cakes mark celebratory rituals, cookies are somewhere in between. Both homey and special, they are a sweet down-to-earth "I love you," round or square or elaborately shaped, hand-sized, to be tucked into a lunchbox or passed around on a plate or nibbled with coffee or tea in late afternoon.

I saw, firsthand, the power of cookies to soothe, please, and welcome in Dairy Hollow House days. Guests would melt at the sight of a plate of huge, Triple-Caress Mocha–Chocolate Chip Cookies, one per guest, awaiting them in their rooms at check-in (along with hot apple cider in cold weather, or a pitcher of Iced Herbal Cooler, page 380, in warm weather). Every day, they'd return to their rooms to find a different variety of cookie, comfortingly waiting on its white plate, plastic wrap pulled tightly over the dish. When guests stayed for five or six days, it sometimes became a challenge to come up with different cookie varieties that weren't too labor-intensive, but we managed. Always, however, the stay would start with chocolate and end with oatmeal, and I got asked for these two recipes constantly.

To provide the defining cookie experience, cookies, with three exceptions, require a high fat content. The exceptions: a few special-ly developed recipes like Pecan-Cinnamon Parchment Triangles, and Excellently Reasonable Brownies plus meringues and biscotti. Meringues are egg-white based and crisp: no added fat, very sweet; people love 'em or hate 'em. As for biscotti: remember, real Italian biscotti are hard cookies, designed to be dipped into wine or coffee, not the softer, butterier variation we Americans have grown accustomed to.

Dairy Hollow House Oatmeal Cookies

In the inn days, as they checked out, each guest was given a bag containing one very large oatmeal cookie, to eat on the way home. Their astonishment and joy in receiving these was always gratifying.

I have given directions for making both huge and normal-sized cookies. They have the perfect balance between crispness and chewiness. I got bored making them

VARIATION

THE CAN'T-LEAVE-WELL-ENOUGH-ALONE ORANGE-ALMOND OATMEAL COOKIE: ***This reinvention of the classic oatmeal cookie makes an excellent tea cookie, and is also good for holiday nibbling or giving. I suggest making these in the small size. Omit cinnamon, substituting 2 teaspoons freshly grated orange rind. Cut vanilla back to ¾ teaspoon, and add ½ teaspoon almond extract. Substitute finely chopped dried apricots for raisins, and chopped almonds for walnuts or pecans. To me, this combination is the ne plus ultra of oatmeal cookies.***

over the years, but wouldn't have dared to change them. The variation to the left is what I started serving at home and to friends.

This makes a *huge* batch. Please note that the dough can be frozen in scooped balls, then very successfully baked straight from the freezer. **MAKES ABOUT 21 VERY LARGE COOKIES OR ABOUT 72 2-INCH COOKIES**

1½ cups white sugar
1½ packed cups dark brown sugar
¾ cup butter, softened
¾ cup vegetable shortening
3 large eggs
1½ teaspoons pure vanilla extract
4½ cups rolled oats (regular cooking oatmeal)
3 cups unbleached white all-purpose flour
1½ teaspoons baking soda
1½ teaspoons ground cinnamon
¾ teaspoon baking powder
¾ teaspoon salt
1½ cups raisins
1½ cups chopped walnuts or pecans
Cooking spray

1 Preheat the oven to 375°F.

2 In a large bowl, cream the sugars, butter, and shortening together. Beat in the eggs, one at a time. When blended, stir in the vanilla.

3 In a second large bowl, combine the oats, flour, baking soda, cinnamon, baking powder, and salt, tossing well to combine. Stir all but 1 cup of the oatmeal mixture into the creamed mixture.

4 Toss the remaining 1 cup oatmeal mixture with the raisins and nuts.

5 Spray a cookie sheet with cooking spray. Using a large ice cream scoop, scoop the dough onto the cookie sheet, leaving at least 3 inches between each cookie. (You can only do 2 or 3 of the large cookies at a time.) Bake until light brown, bearing in mind that these are best when underbaked, so they're slightly chewy, 8 to 10 minutes. Using a spatula, immediately remove from the cookie sheets, placing them on wire racks to cool. (For conventionally sized cookies, scoop by rounded teaspoonfuls, with 1½ inches between cookies, and bake for 6 to 8 minutes.)

Maple-Oatmeal Cookies

Subtle and truly wonderful, these are the most grown-up oatmeal cookies you will find; utterly different from the previous. They are very simple and plain-looking, but quite addictive. Use the grade-B maple syrup as specified; it makes a difference. Grade A is lighter in color and more subtle; I much prefer the darker, more maple-y grade B. **MAKES 3 TO 4 DOZEN COOKIES**

Cooking spray
½ cup butter, softened to room temperature
¾ cup grade-B maple syrup
1 teaspoon vanilla
1½ cup whole wheat pastry flour
1 teaspoon baking soda
¼ teaspoon salt
2 cups rolled oats (regular cooking oatmeal)

1 Preheat the oven to 325°F.

2 Spray a double-insulated cookie sheet (or two) with cooking spray. Set aside.

3 Using an electric mixer, cream the butter. Gradually beat in the maple syrup, about ¼ cup at a time. Add the vanilla. Set aside.

4 Place the flour in a medium bowl. Sift the baking soda and salt into the flour. Add the oats and toss well to combine.

5 Combine the two mixtures together with a wooden spoon, stirring until all of ingredients are well incorporated; don't overbeat. Drop the batter by rounded teaspoonsful onto the prepared cookie sheets, leaving about 2 inches between cookies.

6 Bake until the cookies are firm, about 15 minutes. Remove from the oven and let cool on the cookie sheets for a few minutes, then remove them to a wire rack to cool.

VARIATION

VEGAN MAPLE-OATMEAL COOKIES: ***Just substitute vegetable margarine for butter.***

Almond Blond Brownies

Blond brownies (a.k.a. butterscotch brownies, a.k.a. blondies) as commonly made, are quick, chewy, delicious, deadly sweet and rich. This is a more healthful, still satisfying equivalent, equally quick, chewy, and good. Those who don't eat one thing or another but still like to eat well will be pleased: it is egg- and dairy-free and calls for rice syrup and barley-malt syrup. Plus, it's low in fat and what fat there is comes from oil and the almonds. A little more "health-foody" than most of the desserts I make, but believe me, with a bowl of vanilla soy ice cream, nobody is going to turn it down, and those with dietary restrictions will cheer.

Pulse/chop the almonds to a medium-fine consistency in a food processor before you begin. **MAKES 9 BLOND BROWNIES**

Cooking spray
1¼ cups, plus 1 tablespoon whole wheat pastry flour, sifted
1¼ teaspoons baking powder
⅛ teaspoon salt
⅓ cup barley-malt syrup
¼ cup brown rice syrup
2 tablespoons mild vegetable oil, such as corn, canola, or peanut
1 teaspoon pure vanilla extract
½ teaspoon almond extract
¼ cup soy milk
½ cup whole almonds, chopped medium-fine

1 Preheat the oven to 325°F.

2 Spray one 9-inch square pan with cooking spray and dust it with 1 tablespoon of the flour, knocking out the excess. Set aside.

3 Sift together the sifted flour, baking powder, and salt into a medium bowl. Set aside.

4 Whisk together the barley-malt syrup, brown rice syrup, oil, vanilla, and almond extract in a medium bowl. Gradually stir in half of the flour mixture. Using a hand-held mixer set on low, beat in half of the soy milk until incorporated. Add the remaining flour and soy milk and continue beating until the batter is thick and smooth. Stir in the almonds.

5 Scrape the batter into the prepared pan and bake until golden at the edges, or until the center of the cake springs back to the touch, 18 to 20 minutes. Remove from the oven and allow the brownies to cool in the pan, undisturbed, for about 10 minutes, then gently invert onto a platter. Let cool completely before cutting.

Excellently Reasonable Brownies

You might think you wouldn't want any brownie that could be called reasonable, but I love these. For a luncheon dessert that doesn't leave you logy with excess fat and sugar, these, reduced in fat from the classic but still deeply chocolate, fit the bill admirably. You can dress them up by serving them warm, with a scoop of coffee soy ice cream. They freeze well, and are good straight from the freezer; I sometimes make a batch, cut them up, and freeze them just to have something—well, reasonable—for those late-night chocolate joneses. The starting point for this recipe was the even more reasonable Michael's Fudge Brownies from Alice Medrich's *Chocolate and the Art of Low-Fat Desserts*. And if you want to make my version even less reasonable, just stir in ½ cup toasted pecans or walnuts.

Using Browned Butter heightens the flavor the brownies pull from a mere 5 tablespoons; but they are delicious made with straight butter or even Better. And if you like a mocha taste, add 1 teaspoon instant coffee crystals dissolved in 1 teaspoon hot water, as Alice does.

Now if you want a truly *un*reasonable brownie, decadent in the extreme, head over to the Double-Density Chocolate-Walnut Espresso Torte (page 1005), and just make it, minus frosting, in a square pan. **MAKES 16 SMALL BROWNIES**

Cooking spray
5 tablespoons Browned Butter (page 1024), Better (page 905), or butter
1½ ounces unsweetened chocolate, chopped
1 cup sifted unbleached white all-purpose flour
½ cup plus 1½ teaspoons unsweetened Dutch-process cocoa powder
¼ teaspoon salt
¼ teaspoon baking powder
1¼ cups sugar
1 large egg
2 large egg whites
1½ teaspoons pure vanilla extract
2 tablespoons semi-sweet chocolate chips

1 Preheat the oven to 350°F.

2 Spray an 8-inch square pan with cooking spray.

3 Melt together the Browned Butter and the chopped unsweetened chocolate in a medium saucepan over very low heat.

4 As the chocolate melts, thoroughly whisk together the flour, cocoa, salt, and baking powder.

5 Remove the butter-chocolate mixture from the heat and stir in the sugar (it will be grainy and unpromising-looking). Stir in the egg, egg whites, and vanilla and beat until well combined.

6 Scrape the chocolate mixture into the flour mixture and, using a wooden spoon, beat until completely blended, but no more (overbeating will toughen the brownies). Stir in the chocolate chips.

7 Transfer the mixture to the prepared pan, spreading it evenly. Bake until the top has dried a little, but it's still a little gooey in the center when toothpicked, 20 to 25 minutes. Let cool before cutting.

NOTE

You might think the rolling and cutting is a big hassle, but it's much easier than rolling conventional butter-cookie dough. This dough is sturdy, not fragile: In fact, you have to kind of beat it up. And turning the cookies over? I still say it's easier than conventional butter cookies. Look, do you want a low-fat, low-sugar cookie that is really good? Just do it! This makes a large batch, but these keep well in an airtight container and, addictive as they are, will not last long.

Pecan-Cinnamon Parchment Triangles

These are mysteriously wonderful, addictive, not-too-sweet cookies that achieve the impossible: they are both crisp and low fat. I am truly proud of my achievement. I have to thank the *King Arthur Baking Sheet Newsletter* for introducing me to a cracker called Parchment Bread; cooking teacher and culinary colleague Vicki J. Caparulo, for introducing them to it; Amber Alexander, who rolled out countless batches in search of perfection; and Linda Rodriguez, who gave the magic suggestion of a dusting of confectioners' sugar—obvious only in retrospect—that took the dough, finally, from cracker to cookie. **MAKES ABOUT 128 COOKIES**

1¾ cups unbleached white all-purpose flour
1 cup semolina flour
¼ cup whole wheat flour
⅓ cup sugar
1½ teaspoons cinnamon, preferably Saigon
¼ teaspoon salt
1 cup plus 1 tablespoon warm water, preferably spring or filtered
2 teaspoons pure vanilla extract
About ½ cup pecans
Confectioners' sugar (optional)

1 Preheat the oven to 450°F at least 30 minutes before baking the cookies. A very hot oven is essential.

2 Spray a baking sheet, preferably double-insulated, with cooking spray. Set aside.

3 If using a bread machine, combine the flours with the sugar, cinnamon, and salt in it. Add the water and vanilla and program for Dough. Let the machine knead until the dough just comes together to make a rough mass; immediately remove from the machine and go to the next step. Or, if making the dough by hand, combine the dry ingredients, then add the liquids a little at a time, kneading until a stiff dough has formed.

4 Turn the dough onto a lightly floured surface and give a few good hand-kneads to bring the dough together. Divide the dough into 16 pieces, shaping each piece into a small ball. Dust with flour, and set aside on a plate. Let the balls rest, covered, for 10 minutes to "relax" the dough and make it easier to roll out.

5 While the dough relaxes, place the pecans, if using, in a food processor and pulse/chop to make a medium-fine meal of the pecans—not quite, but almost, a powder.

6 Working with one ball at a time, keeping the remaining balls covered, reflour the ball and, if using, sprinkle it with about ½ teaspoon or so of the pecan meal, and vigorously roll it out. Flip the dough over and, if using, sprinkle the second side with pecans and roll again. Continue turning, rolling, flouring as needed (you won't need additional pecans, though) until you have a large, irregularly shaped disc, thin enough to see your hand through (that would be about 1⁄16 inch thick, if you cared to measure it). Again, this requires vigorous, hard rolling—nothing delicate about it. You're almost beating the dough with the rolling pin.

7 Cut the disc into 8 to 10 pie-wedge–style triangles. (This is virtually instant if you use a pizza wheel for cutting: zap, zap, zap, you're done.) Place the cookies on the prepared baking sheet. The cookies should not touch, but can be quite close together; they won't spread. Depending on the size of your baking sheets, you'll be able to bake 2, maybe 3 or 4 of your balls of dough at a time.

8 Bake in the preheated oven until the cookies start to bubble and turn light brown around the edges, 3 to 6 minutes. Remove from the oven and, using tongs, flip each cookie. Continue to bake until golden, baking 2 to 4 minutes more. Watch carefully, as they burn easily after turning. Remove from the oven and let cool on the sheets.

9 Continue rolling out each ball, turning, flouring, pecaning, cutting into cookies, and baking, until all the dough has been used.

10 The cookies may be served conventionally, placed on a nice plate and dusted lightly with confectioners' sugar (most of which will, however, snow-fall off them), or used in the following recipe.

VARIATION

VEGAN VARIATION: ***Substitute 4 ounces silken tofu for the neufchâtel, and add 2 teaspoons cashew butter.***

Dessert Nachos

Tee Fi Faux Fun—this is a silly but adorable dessert. The cinnamon-pecan triangles resemble corn chips; the irresistible lemon cream dip is the sour cream element; and the fruit salsa completes the illusion. **SERVES 8 TO 10**

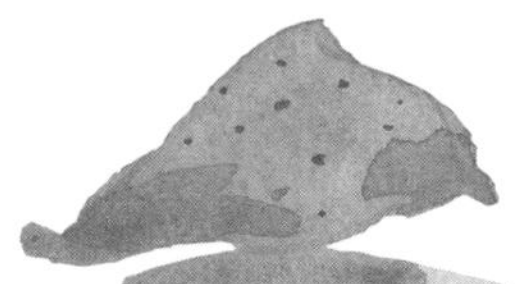

½ cup sugar
3 tablespoons cornstarch
½ cup water, preferably spring or filtered
Juice of 3 lemons
Grated rind of 1 lemon
Pinch of salt
4 ounces neufchâtel reduced-fat cream cheese, softened
Pecan-Cinnamon Parchment Triangles (page 1032)
Fruit Salsa (recipe follows)

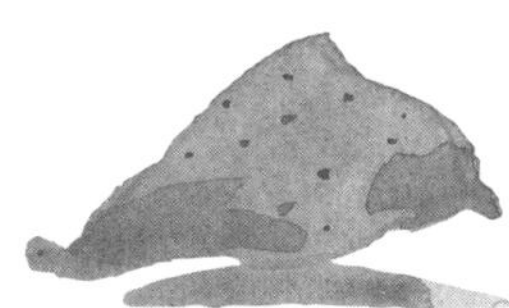

1 Combine the sugar and cornstarch in a small bowl, with just enough water to make a smooth, thin paste. Whisk to combine. Whisk in the lemon juice, lemon rind, and salt. When well combined, pour into a small nonreactive saucepan.

2 Place over medium heat and cook, stirring, until the glaze comes to a boil, at which point it will turn thick and clear. Remove from the heat and let cool slightly. Place in a food processor together with the neufchâtel. Process to blend. Serve with Pecan-Cinnamon Parchment Triangles and Fruit Salsa.

Fruit Salsa

This sprightly fruit salsa—spicy or not, sparked with mint—completes the faux nachos visually and deliciously. Add any fresh seasonal fruits you like; diced fresh mango, papaya, or pitted ripe cherries are all special additions. **MAKES ABOUT 2 CUPS**

1 crisp apple, such as Gala or Fuji, unpeeled, cored, and finely diced
1 navel orange, peeled and seeded, and finely diced
1 slice fresh pineapple, peeled, cored, and finely diced
1 small handful fresh strawberries, finely diced
Juice of 1 lime
1 tablespoon honey
1 tablespoon fresh mint leaves, minced
½ jalapeño chile, finely diced (optional)

Combine all ingredients in a small bowl and serve alongside Dessert Nachos.

Chocolate-Orange Biscotti

These days, almost any good-sized market offers an excellent selection of commercial biscotti. But these, and the recipes that follow, are something special, besides being much lower in fat. Cornmeal adds a grainy crunch that is irresistible.

MAKES 2½ DOZEN COOKIES

NOTE

Homemade biscotti always look a little more ragged than their commercial counterparts, but they always taste better.

Cooking spray
⅔ cup sugar
3 tablespoons butter, softened to room temperature
Grated rind of 2 oranges
2 large egg whites
1 large egg
1 teaspoon pure vanilla extract
1½ cups unbleached white all-purpose flour
½ cup unsweetened cocoa powder
2 tablespoons cornstarch
2 tablespoons cornmeal
1½ teaspoons baking powder
½ teaspoon baking soda
⅛ teaspoon salt

1 Preheat the oven to 350°F.

2 Spray a baking sheet with cooking spray. Set aside.

3 Using an electric mixer, beat the sugar and butter until well combined. With the mixer on low, beat in the orange rind, egg whites, whole egg, and vanilla.

4 In a separate bowl, combine the flour, cocoa, cornstarch, cornmeal, baking powder, baking soda, and salt. Using a wooden spoon, beat the dry ingredients into the egg mixture.

5 Divide the dough in half and place on the prepared baking sheet.

6 Spray your hands with cooking spray and pat the dough into two 8-by-3-inch loaves. The dough will be sticky and resist shaping a bit, but you can get it in order once your hands are well sprayed.

7 Bake until the rolls are firm to the touch, 20 to 30 minutes. Remove from the oven and let cool on the baking sheet for 10 minutes. Do not turn the oven off. Transfer the loaves to a cutting board and, using a serrated knife, cut on an angle into ½-inch-thick oblong slices.

8 Place wire racks on the baking sheet, then lay the sliced biscotti on the racks and return to the oven until the cookies are crisp and dry, 18 to 22 minutes. Remove from the oven and let cool completely. Store in an airtight container.

Orange Biscotti

A straight-up citrus twist. Yummy with lemon sorbet; heavenly with the Italian Caramelized Oranges (page 987) or the Oranges in Bay-Leaf Syrup (page 985). Or try it with a smear of neufchâtel cheese and a slather of marmalade or kumquat preserves. **MAKES 2½ DOZEN COOKIES**

Cooking spray
2 large eggs
2 large egg whites
½ cup confectioners' sugar
⅔ cup Rapidura or brown sugar
2 tablespoons mild vegetable oil, such as corn, canola, or peanut
1½ teaspoons orange extract
2¾ cups unbleached white all-purpose flour, plus an additional 2 tablespoons
¼ cup stoneground yellow cornmeal
3 tablespoons cornstarch
1 teaspoon baking powder
½ teaspoon baking soda
¼ teaspoon salt
Grated rind of 3 oranges

1 Preheat the oven to 350°F.

2 If not using nonstick, spray a baking sheet with cooking spray. Set aside.

3 Whisk the eggs and egg whites together with the confectioners' sugar and Rapidura, oil, and orange extract.

4 Into a separate bowl, sift the 2¾ cups flour, the cornmeal, cornstarch, baking powder, baking soda, and salt. Then sift the dry ingredients into the egg mixture. Stir well to combine. Stir in the orange rind. You want a sturdy yet moldable dough, a little soft. If you're not there, add the additional 2 tablespoons flour a tablespoon at a time.

5 Divide the dough in half, and place the two pieces on the prepared baking sheet. Spray your hands with cooking spray and then pat the dough into two 8-by-3-inch loaves—the dough will be sticky and resist shaping a bit, but you can get it in order once your hands are well sprayed.

6 Bake until the loaves are firm to the touch, 20 to 30 minutes. Remove from the oven and let cool on the baking sheet for 10 minutes. Do not turn the oven off. Transfer the loaves to a cutting board and, using a serrated knife, cut on an angle into ½-inch-thick oblong slices.

7 Place a wire rack on the baking sheet, then lay the sliced biscotti on the rack and return to the oven until the cookies are crisp and dry, 18 to 22 minutes. Remove from the oven and let cool completely. Store in an airtight container.

Hazelnut Biscotti

If you are a hazelnut lover as I am, for sheer once-in-a-while pleasure you can't beat these served with a premium Italian hazelnut gelato drizzled with a little Frangelico. Follow with a dark European roast decaf, and another biscotti for dunking.

MAKES 2½ DOZEN COOKIES

2 large eggs
½ cup confectioners' sugar
⅔ cup brown sugar
2 tablespoons mild vegetable oil, such as corn, canola, or peanut
2 teaspoons hazelnut extract (available from King Arthur Flour)
1 teaspoon pure vanilla extract
3 tablespoons cornstarch
¼ cup stoneground yellow cornmeal
2¾ cups unbleached white all-purpose flour, plus an additional 2 tablespoons
¼ teaspoon salt
1 teaspoon baking powder
½ teaspoon baking soda
½ cup hazelnuts, toasted, papery brown skins rubbed off as much as possible, and coarsely chopped
Cooking spray

GLAZE

1 ounce semisweet chocolate
¼ cup unsweetened cocoa powder
¼ cup confectioner's sugar
1 tablespoon honey
3 tablespoons plus ½ teaspoon Frangelico
½ teaspoon hazelnut extract

1 Preheat the oven to 350°F.

2 In a large bowl, whisk together the eggs, confectioners' and brown sugars, vegetable oil, and hazelnut extract.

3 In a separate bowl, combine the cornstarch, cornmeal, 2¾ cups flour, salt, baking powder, and baking soda.

4 Sift the dry mixture into the egg mixture and stir well to combine. Stir in the hazelnuts. You want a sturdy, yet moldable dough, a little soft. If you're not there, add the additional 2 tablespoons of flour, a tablespoon at a time.

5 Divide the dough in half. On a nonstick baking sheet, or one that has been sprayed with cooking spray, with oiled hands, pat the dough into two 8- by 3-inch loaves.

6 Bake 20 to 30 minutes, or until the loaves are firm to the touch. Remove from the oven and let cool on the baking sheet 10 minutes. Transfer loaves to a cutting board, and, using a serrated knife, cut the loaves on a diagonal widthwise into slices about ½ inch thick.

NOTE

King Arthur Flour has a wonderful mail-order catalog that every serious baker should receive. Find it on the web at www.kingarthurflour.com or call (800) 827-6836.

7 Place a wire rack on the baking sheet, then lay the biscotti slices on the rack and return to the oven for another 18 to 22 minutes, or until the cookies are crisp and dry. Let cool completely, then glaze.

8 Make the glaze: Combine all glaze ingredients in a small heatproof bowl. Place the bowl over hot water and heat, stirring constantly, until the glaze is runny. Drizzle it over the cooled biscotti. In order to maintain runny drizzling consistency, you may have to reheat the glaze. When the glaze has firmed on the biscotti, you may store them in an airtight container or zippered storage bags.

NOTE

These unprepossessing-looking cookies, with several layers of crunch—from the cornmeal, from the sugar topping, and from the crisp edges—are perfect with espresso or good hot decaf; with fresh fruit or any of the poached fruits or compotes; or with sorbet (especially lemon).

Neo-Zialetti Ozark-Style Cornmeal Cookies with Lemon and Raisins

I love these not-too-sweet homey cookies, rather adult in flavor: a reduced-fat version of an Italian classic that's long been a favorite of mine. This is not a cookie about which you say "Wow" on the first bite; rather, it subtly sneaks up on you, and all of a sudden you discover that you cannot stop eating them—or, worse, that you *have* eaten all of them. **MAKES ABOUT 3 DOZEN**

½ cup golden raisins
2 tablespoons brandy
Cooking spray
¼ cup chilled Browned Butter (page 1024)
½ cup plus a few additional tablespoons sugar
1 large egg
1½ cups unbleached white all-purpose flour
¾ cup fine-ground yellow cornmeal
¼ teaspoon salt
A little less than ½ cup low-fat milk
1¾ teaspoons grated lemon rind

1 Place raisins in a small bowl and pour brandy over them. Soak until plump, at least 1 hour.

2 Spray a baking sheet with cooking spray. Set aside.

3 Preheat the oven to 375°F.

4 Cream the browned butter and the ½ cup sugar together in a small bowl. Stir in the egg.

5 In a separate bowl, combine the flour and cornmeal with the salt. Cut in the butter mixture.

6 Drain the raisins well, catching the soaking liquid in a cup measure. Set both liquid and raisins aside.

7 Add enough milk to the brandy to equal ½ cup liquid. Stir the brandied milk and lemon rind into the flour mixture. Stir in the raisins.

8 Drop by teaspoonfuls onto the prepared cookie sheet. Flatten each cookie with the bottom of a glass dipped in the additional sugar. Bake until lightly browned around the edges, 12 to 15 minutes. Transfer to wire racks to cool.

Chocolate Slice Cookies

A basic chocolate cookie, crisp on the outside, slightly cakey-chewey at the center, plain but sophisticated. This is the perfect go-with cookie. Excellent with Lemon Mousse-Custard (page 1052), any ice cream, or frozen yogurt.

A food processor makes quick work of this, but you could merely whisk the flour mixture together, and use a mixer for the butter-egg component. **MAKES 3 TO 4 DOZEN COOKIES**

2 cups unbleached white all-purpose flour
1 cup plus 2 tablespoons Dutch-process cocoa powder
¾ cup brown sugar
¾ cup white sugar
½ teaspoon baking soda
¼ teaspoon salt
⅔ cup Browned Butter (page 1024), Better (page 905), or butter
2 large eggs
1¾ teaspoons pure vanilla extract
Cooking spray

1 Lay two 12-inch-long strips of plastic wrap on a table.

2 Place the flour, cocoa, sugars, baking soda, and salt in a food processor and pulse to blend. Transfer to a mixing bowl.

3 Place the Browned Butter, eggs, and vanilla in the food processor. Buzz until smooth, pausing to scrape down the sides of the bowl.

4 Pour the egg mixture into the flour-cocoa mixture. Using your hands, gently but thoroughly incorporate the wet into the dry. You'll think it won't come together—that it'll be too dry—but it will. Once the dough is amalgamated, divide the dough in half. Shape into two logs, placing one on each strip of plastic wrap. The traditional cookie log for slicing is round, but I prefer a square look. Tightly wrap each log in the plastic wrap and smooth it out against the table or countertop, turn and do it again to make four even sides.

5 Refrigerate the wrapped logs for at least 1 hour, or up to 3 days. Alternatively, give them a second wrapping and pop them in the freezer; providentially, the frozen dough keeps nicely for up to 2½ months.

6 When ready to bake, preheat the oven to 350°F.

7 Spray 2 baking sheets, preferably double insulated, with cooking spray.

8 Remove the dough from the fridge and, while it is still cold, slice it no more than ¼ inch thick. Don't worry about the end slices; they are the cook's kitchen treat. Place the cookies ½ inch apart on the prepared sheets.

9 Bake for 12 to 14 minutes. Remove from the oven and let cool on the baking sheet for 20 to 30 seconds. Using a thin-bladed spatula, carefully lift them to a wire rack. Let cool completely. Store in an airtight container.

Chocolate Meringue Kisses

Essentially egg whites, sugar, and flavorings, light as a lover's sigh and very sweet, it's no wonder these low-fat cookies are often called "kisses." You can fold in all kinds of delicious optionals at the end—bittersweet chocolate chips, finely chopped toasted walnuts or hazelnuts, diced medjool dates—but they are also quite good plain. Half an ounce of chocolate or a full ounce? Unsweetened or bittersweet? It's your call—the recipe works within this range. Me, I'd probably go for ½ ounce each unsweetened and bittersweet.

If stored in an airtight container they'll keep for a couple of days; if frozen, a couple of weeks—unless Ned gets into them.

Meringues are best made on a crisp, dry, nonhumid day. Also, note the slow, long baking time at very low heat. Lastly, remember that the beaters, bowl, and all things touching the egg whites must be absolutely free of any residual oils, otherwise the meringues will not achieve full volume. Use a metal bowl; sometimes even well-washed plastic can retain trace amounts of fat. For the same reason, when you separate your eggs, you must be positive there is no trace of yolk in the whites.

NOTE

You can put the batter through a pastry tube, but I usually just dollop it with a teaspoon, using a second teaspoon to scrape.

MAKES ABOUT 2½ DOZEN

Cooking spray
2 tablespoons cornstarch
¼ cup unsweetened cocoa (American style, such as Hershey's, not Dutch-process)
½ cup confectioners' sugar
½ to 1 ounce unsweetened or bittersweet chocolate, finely grated (or ground to a powder in the food processor)
3 large egg whites, at room temperature
A dash of salt
⅔ cup sugar
1 teaspoon vanilla

1 Preheat oven to 350°F. Line several baking sheets with either parchment paper or wax paper that has been sprayed with cooking spray. Set aside.

2 Sift together the cornstarch, cocoa, and confectioners' sugar. Stir in the finely grated chocolate. Set aside.

3 In a very clean high-sided metal mixing bowl, begin beating the egg whites with the mixer set on medium. Beat the whites until foamy. Then add the salt and set the mixer speed as high as it will go. Beat just until the egg whites begin to form soft peaks.

4 Lower the oven temperature to 250°F.

5 Now, back at the egg whites, start adding the granulated sugar a little at a time (say 2 tablespoons or so), continuing to beat the mixture at a high speed. A beautiful transformation will take place as the sugar is incorporated: In about 3 minutes, the mixture will be glossy, smooth, and very thick. Beat in the vanilla.

6 By hand, using a rubber spatula, fold in the cocoa-chocolate mixture. You want it well-incorporated, but be a little delicate in your folding, and don't overmix, or you'll slightly deflate those beautiful whites you've just beaten air into.

7 Spoon, or pipe, the mixture into kisses about 1¼ inches in diameter. They can be dolloped quite close together on the sheet; they don't spread much, if at all, during baking.

8 Bake the kisses on the oven's center rack for 18 to 20 minutes, or until firm on the outside but slightly soft inside. Remove from the oven and let cool on the sheet before carefully peeling the cookies from the paper.

Triple-Caress Mocha Chocolate Chip Cookies

Another cookie from the inn days. These were the ones waiting in the guests' rooms, and boy did we get raves and recipe requests. As well we should have: Any chocolate lover can scan the ingredients and see why. Especially when made large (as we used to do), these really have an unconscionable amount of fat and calories; but you know, sometimes you just have to be unconscionable. **MAKES ABOUT 33 SMALL COOKIES OR 15 LARGE COOKIES**

Cooking spray
4 ounces semisweet chocolate, chopped
¼ cup butter
¼ cup vegetable shortening
2 large eggs
¾ cup brown sugar
¾ cup white sugar
1½ tablespoons instant decaf coffee crystals
1½ tablespoons boiling water, preferably spring or filtered
1½ teaspoons pure vanilla extract
2 cups unbleached white all-purpose flour
⅓ cup unsweetened American-style (not Dutch process) cocoa powder
½ teaspoon baking powder
¼ teaspoon salt
8 ounces fine-quality semisweet chocolate chips
6 to 8 ounces pecans or walnuts, toasted and chopped

1 Preheat the oven to 350°F.

2 Spray 2 double-insulated baking sheets with cooking spray. Set aside.

3 Combine the semisweet chocolate with the butter and shortening in a small saucepan. Place over medium-low heat and cook, stirring occasionally, until all ingredients are uniformly melted. Remove from the heat, stir until smooth, and let cool to room temperature.

4 Using an electric mixer, beat the eggs and both sugars at medium-high speed for 5 minutes.

5 Place the coffee crystals in a small heatproof bowl and pour in the boiling water, stirring to dissolve. Stir in the vanilla. Add the decaf mixture, along with the melted chocolate mixture, to the egg mixture. Beat for 2 minutes.

6 In a separate bowl, combine the flour, unsweetened cocoa, baking powder, and salt. Whisk to blend.

7 Remove the bowl from the mixer and, using a wooden spoon, stir in the dry ingredients. When well blended, stir in the chocolate chips and the nuts, if using.

8 To make ordinary-size cookies (about 3 inches in diameter), drop batter by the rounded teaspoonful, about 2 inches apart, onto the prepared baking sheets. To make very large cookies, 6 to 8 inches in diameter, scoop batter with a 2½-inch ice cream scoop (⅜ cup capacity). You can get 2 or 3 of the large cookies on a sheet. (There is no need to "splat" the cookies out with your hand; they will spread while baking.) Bake small cookies for about 10 minutes; large ones will take about 20 minutes. Remove from the oven and let cool on the sheets for 1 minute, then transfer to wire racks to finish cooling.

Ice Creams & Sorbets

I love all kinds of frozen desserts, but none more than sorbets. A good homemade sorbet calls my name as not even the densest chocolate dessert can. The chill, the refreshment, the sharp sparkle of lemon or bite of ginger combined with icy sweetness has a regenerative effect: It seems to revive the whole system. A homemade sorbet is entirely different from the purchased variety, which is usually too sweet and smooth for my taste.

Ice cream used to be irresistible to me, particularly homemade, and out of sentimental feeling I have included two recipes here.

To those who have never done it, making ice cream or sorbet usually seems like an impossibly big deal. But get an electric ice cream freezer, plug 'er in and let 'er rip—you'll discover it is far easier to make delicious frozen desserts than the proverbial pie.

Jay's Buttermilk Ice Cream

Jay Herring, of Fayetteville, Arkansas, is the founder of (though no longer involved with) Little Rock's renowned Mama's Manna bakery. This unique ice cream was passed down through generations of her father's family. It is not vanilla, although it has vanilla in it. It is not sorbet or even "light," since it does contain 2 cups of heavy cream. But with no egg yolks and the mystery ingredient—2 full quarts of buttermilk—it's a lot lighter than conventional ice cream, and it is refreshing.

Buttermilk, you ask? This gives it its haunting flavor, a bit tart and lemony—just delicious. "In the days of my grandfather, this lusciously sweet-tart ice cream was beaten by hand in wooden bowls," Jay recalls. "An ice cream freezer does the job now, but the dessert's South Mississippi roots still imbue every creamy spoonful." Assuming you have an ice cream machine, the recipe could not be simpler.

Though perfect for summer, its refreshment quotient makes it worth remembering at holiday time. **MAKES ABOUT 2½ QUARTS**

2 quarts buttermilk
2 cups heavy cream
2 cups sugar
2 tablespoons pure vanilla extract

1 Combine all of the ingredients in a large bowl, stirring until the sugar dissolves.

2 Place the mixture in an ice-cream maker and freeze according to the manufacturer's directions. When the ice cream is done, transfer to a freezer container with a tight-fitting lid. Let the ice cream rest in the freezer for 3 to 4 hours to firm up slightly before serving.

Burnt Sugar Ice Cream

This delectable, very old-fashioned recipe is for a true "frozen custard" ice cream flavored with caramelized sugar. It dates from the pre-cholesterol days, when it was a springtime–summertime delicacy—the cows were still "fresh" (giving milk) from spring calving, and the chickens were laying like crazy. Burnt sugar was common in the Ozarks and ingeniously used in cakes and icings. When you have fewer ingredients, you coax more out of them: Sugar was cheaper than vanilla, lemon, and chocolate—and caramelizing it gave a whole new taste. **MAKES ABOUT 2 QUARTS**

3 cups whole milk
2¼ cups sugar
1 teaspoon corn syrup (optional)
6 large egg yolks (preferably from bright-yolked free-range eggs)
Pinch of salt
1 quart heavy cream
2 tablespoons pure vanilla extract

1 Heat the milk in a large saucepan over low heat. Do not allow it to boil.

2 Place 1 cup of the sugar in an ungreased, heavy iron skillet over medium heat, stirring until the sugar dissolves. Raise the heat to a full boil. If there are any lumps that resist dissolving, add the corn syrup. Cook, without stirring, until it's a golden brown color, but not burned—7 to 10 minutes. Timing varies, so keep a close eye on it, swirling the pan occasionally. Remove from the heat when the color is right.

3 Place the egg yolks in a medium bowl and whisk them until very light. Set aside.

4 Carefully pour the melted sugar into the hot milk, along with the remaining 1¼ cups sugar. Whisk thoroughly, until the sugar is dissolved and the milk takes on a little color from the caramel.

5 Ladle a cup or so of the hot milk-sugar mixture into the bowl with the beaten egg yolks, and whisk well. Stirring, add the beaten yolks and the salt to the sugared milk. Place over low-medium heat and cook until the mixture thickens, about 3 minutes. Use a spoon to troll gently along the bottom of the pot so that any of the quicker-thickening portions get incorporated into the whole, the better to thicken evenly.

6 Remove the saucepan from the heat. Transfer the custard into a container with a tightly-fitting lid. Cover and refrigerate for a few hours or until well chilled. This is the custard base for your ice cream.

7 When ready to make the ice cream, stir 2 cups of the cream and the vanilla into the chilled custard. Whip the remaining cream, and fold it into the custard.

8 Place in an ice-cream maker and freeze according to the manufacturer's directions. When the ice cream is done, transfer it to a freezer container with a tight-fitting lid. Let the ice cream rest in the freezer for 3 to 4 hours to firm up slightly before serving.

Ginger Sorbet

This is *the* sorbet—my very favorite and in my view one of the three or four best recipes in this book. Ginger sorbet is one of those wake-up-in-the-middle-of-the-night-craving-it things. Perfection in hot weather, no doubt tonic because of the ginger's health-giving properties, it is also most soothing to a sore throat, or perfect after any hearty, spicy, or complex meal.

I have never seen commercial ginger sorbet—if you want to experience it, you'll have to make it. Fortunately, assuming you have an ice-cream maker, this is simple. Timing note: Allow 24 hours for the ginger to steep in the syrup as it cools.

MAKES ABOUT 1¾ QUARTS

3 cups water, preferably spring or filtered
1½ cups sugar
2-inch piece fresh ginger, minced (unnecessary to peel)
¾ cup fresh-squeezed lemon juice

1 Combine the water and sugar in a medium nonreactive saucepan over high heat. Bring to a boil. Lower the heat and simmer for 5 minutes. Remove from the heat and add the ginger. Let cool, then cover and refrigerate for 24 hours.

2 Strain the syrup, pressing down on the ginger to extract as much flavor as possible. Discard the ginger. Combine the syrup with the lemon juice, place in an ice-cream maker, and freeze according to the manufacturer's directions. When the sorbet is done, transfer it to a freezer container with a tight-fitting lid. Let it rest in the freezer for 3 to 4 hours to firm up slightly before serving.

Persimmon Sorbet

This, the simplest and most intensely flavored sorbet you are ever likely to eat, is made possible by the use of soft-ripe Hachiya persimmons, which have an extremely high natural sugar content. Its color is as vivid as its flavor. Be ready to eat it the second you've prepared it; the texture will be soft. Serve in footed, chilled glass dishes if you have them. A slice of pound cake is a nice, but wholly unnecessary, accompaniment. **SERVES 4**

4 dead-ripe, jelly-soft Hachiya persimmons, calyx and any seeds removed
Juice of 1 orange, or about ½ cup white grape juice

1 Lay a piece of waxed paper on a baking sheet small enough to fit into your freezer.

2 Place the serving dishes you will be using in the freezer.

3 Cut the persimmons into large chunks (they will almost be falling apart) and place the chunks on the prepared sheet. Place in the freezer until solid, about 1 hour.

4 Immediately before serving, transfer the frozen fruit to a food processor, adding as little juice as is needed to pulse/chop then puree the persimmons. Scoop the frozen puree into the chilled dishes and serve at once.

Buttermilk-Lemon Sorbet with Cardamom and Rose Water

There's a divine and very rich buttermilk ice cream on page 1043; this is something wholly different and exotic. With its flavors of the Indian subcontinent, it is pure pleasure after an Indian dinner. **SERVES 6**

10 cardamom pods
1½ cups sugar
1 cup water, preferably spring or filtered
5 cups buttermilk
1¼ cup fresh-squeezed lemon juice
1 tablespoon finely grated lemon rind
2 teaspoons rose water
Dash of salt

1 Combine the cardamom and sugar with the water in a medium saucepan over medium-high heat. Bring to a boil; then lower the heat slightly and boil for 5 minutes. Remove from the heat and let stand until cooled to room temperature. Strain the syrup, discarding the cardamom pods.

2 Combine the syrup with the buttermilk, lemon rind, lemon juice, rose water, and salt. Place in an ice-cream maker and freeze according to the manufacturer's directions. When the ice cream is done, transfer it to a freezer container with a tight-fitting lid. Let it rest in the freezer for 3 to 4 hours to firm up slightly before serving.

Cantaloupe-Campari Sorbet

When cantaloupes are ripe and inexpensive, exuding fragrance at the farmer's market, that is the time to make this romantic, sunrise-blush-colored sorbet, deeply refreshing. Since cantaloupes vary in size, it is difficult to say precisely how many are needed to make the puree—about 2 large or 4 small. Prepare the puree by removing the rind and all the seeds, cutting the fruit in large chunks, and pureeing in a food processor. **MAKES ABOUT 2 QUARTS**

4 cups cantaloupe puree
2 cups sugar
3 cups water, preferably spring or filtered
¾ cup Campari
½ cup fresh-squeezed lemon juice

1 Combine the cantaloupe puree and sugar in a medium bowl. Refrigerate, stirring occasionally, for 2 hours to dissolve the sugar.

2 Add the water, Campari, and lemon juice to the chilled cantaloupe mixture, stirring well to combine. Place in the freezer until quite cold, about 1 hour.

3 Transfer to an ice-cream maker and freeze according to the manufacturer's directions. When the ice cream is done, transfer it to a freezer container with a tight-fitting lid. Let it rest in the freezer for 3 to 4 hours to firm up slightly before serving.

Sangria Sorbet

Using alcohol in large quantities in a sorbet is tricky, as alcohol doesn't freeze well. But because I think few things are more refreshing than a good fruity sangria, I fooled around with the recipe to get the proportions right for freezing. Try this after Mexican, Spanish, or spicier Mediterranean food. **MAKES ABOUT 1¼ QUARTS**

1¾ cups fruity red wine, such as an inexpensive Burgundy
1 cup plus 2 tablespoons sugar
Finely grated rind of 2 oranges
Finely grated rind of 2 lemons
¾ cup water, preferably spring or filtered
1¾ cups fresh-squeezed, unstrained orange juice (that is, pulp included, but not seeds)
1 cup fresh-squeezed, unstrained grapefruit juice
⅓ cup fresh-squeezed, unstrained lemon juice

1 Combine the wine with the sugar in a medium nonreactive saucepan over medium heat. Cook, stirring, until sugar dissolves, about 5 minutes. Drop in the grated orange and lemon rind, then add the water. Bring to a simmer and cook at a gentle simmer for 6 minutes. Remove from the heat. Let cool to room temperature.

2 Stir in the water and the fresh orange, grapefruit, and lemon juices. Place in an ice-cream maker and freeze according to the manufacturer's directions. When the ice cream is done, transfer it to a freezer container with a tight-fitting lid. Let it rest in the freezer for 3 to 4 hours to firm up slightly before serving.

Five-Fruit Summer Sherbet

As you may have guessed, I am a big fan of citrus-flavored sorbets. In this sherbet the flavor spangles with lemon and orange and glistens with strawberries, fresh pineapple, and ripe banana, all smoothed out with a little milk, dairy or non. The nons can be rice or coconut milk; soy milk freezes unpredictably. Rice milk is good; coconut is even better, but higher in fat. **MAKES ABOUT 2 QUARTS**

1 to 2 oranges
1 to 2 lemons
1 ripe banana, peeled and sliced
½ fresh, ripe pineapple, peeled, eyes removed, cored, and finely chopped
1½ cups red-ripe strawberries, hulled
¼ cup fresh-squeezed pineapple juice, or unsweetened canned or bottled pineapple juice
4 cups rice milk, dairy milk, or canned unsweetened reduced-fat coconut milk
1¾ cups sugar
Dash of salt

1 Grate enough rind from 1 orange and 1 lemon so that you end up with 1 teaspoon each. Set aside.

2 Cut the citrus fruits in half and squeeze enough juice to yield ¼ cup lemon juice and ¼ cup orange juice. You probably won't need the second orange and lemon.

3 Place the juice and rind in a medium bowl with the banana, pineapple, strawberries, and pineapple juice and mash together with a potato masher (alternatively, pulse/chop in a food processor). You want a definitely chunky, textured puree. Add the milk, sugar, and salt and stir to combine. Place in an ice-cream maker and freeze according to the manufacturer's directions. When the sherbet is done, transfer it to a freezer container with a tight-fitting lid. Let it rest in the freezer for 3 to 4 hours to firm up slightly before serving.

Mousses, Custards & Puddings

Mousse—French for "froth" or "foam"—is usually that most contradictory of desserts: It "feels" light, but is anything but. Its airy, ethereal texture belies the serious fat and calorie wallop, since the frothiness usually comes from whipped cream, folded into a base, usually a custard. Custard also is no lightweight: egg yolks, maybe cream, along with the flavoring (fruit puree or chocolate, generally).

I used to consider traditional mousses and custards pleasures of the highest order. But as my tastes changed they quit tasting so good. I began wondering if I could come up with a dessert that had some of that combination of light and lush, with the lovely intense flavor of the mousse of yesteryear yet without that fattiness that had grown so much less pleasing to me.

Enter a new mousse . . . well, part mousse, part custard, a little pudding-ish . . . a dessert category that doesn't really have a name. Its consistency is somewhat like that of the old "Bavarian creams" (custard-based mousses with whipped egg whites folded in, set with gelatin) . . . but really, its character is its own. It is based on the tofu, fruit, and agar desserts pioneered by the women of Bloodroot, a feminist vegetarian restaurant in Bridgeport, Connecticut. My proportions, method, and ingredients are a bit different, but the lineage is clear.

You will be astonished at how very delicious these mousses are, and how much of the delicacy of the originals they retain. Yet they are relatively healthful, and you can feed them with impunity to vegans or those who are watching their saturated fat intake. The richness these mousses have is imparted by the use of raw cashew butter, a product available at any natural foods market. It has a sweet butteriness that is subtle and gives the perfect textural note. It's delicious, and while it is a fat, it is largely the good-for-you unsaturated type. Do not substitute toasted or roasted cashew butter—roasting nuts always amplifies their flavor, and here you need the gentle, bland, nonassertive face, where the particular flavor of the mousse, not the cashews, comes forward.

Apricot Mousse-Custard

By using dried apricots *and* canned apricots, intense, pure apricot flavor comes through. Though not airy, this dessert is quite light in texture. Served with a crisp cookie, like the Maple-Oatmeal Cookies or Chocolate Slice Cookies (pages 1028 and 1039), this is a special-occasion, seriously indulgent dessert. This recipe uses maple sugar, not syrup, but you can substitute brown sugar.

Please note that the dried apricots must be soaked overnight. **SERVES 6**

½ cup dried apricots
2 cans (32 ounces total) apricots packed in juice, not syrup
About ¼ cup water, preferably spring or filtered
2 tablespoons cornstarch
1 teaspoon agar powder (see page 127)
1 cup granulated maple sugar (see page 959) or brown sugar
1 package (10½ ounces) silken tofu
3 tablespoons raw cashew butter
⅛ teaspoon salt

1 Place the dried apricots in a small bowl. Open 1 can of the apricots and strain the juice over the dried apricots. Cover and soak for about 12 hours, or until soft. (Reserve the open can of apricots in the refrigerator.)

2 Drain the juice from the second can of apricots into a liquid measuring cup. Place the apricots into a food processor along with the reserved apricots. Drain the liquid from the dried apricots into the liquid measuring cup. Place the soaked apricots in the food processor. You should have about 2 cups apricot juice in the measuring cup. Add water as needed to bring the total amount to 2¼ cups liquid. Pour all but ½ cup of this juice into a small saucepan. Set aside.

3 Add the cornstarch and agar to the liquid remaining in the measuring cup, smushing it in with your fingertips or whisking until dissolved. Let the mixture sit for 2 minutes.

4 Add the maple sugar to the juice in the saucepan. Place over medium heat and bring to a boil.

5 Whisk in the cornstarch-agar mixture. It should turn cloudy as you add it, then almost immediately become clear and thick. Turn down the heat to medium-low, stirring, and simmer for 1 minute. Remove from the heat.

6 To the food processor, add the tofu, cashew butter, and salt. Buzz to make a very thick, fairly smooth

mixture, pausing to scrape down the sides of the bowl. Add the thickened apricot juice, and buzz to blend.

7 Pour the mousse into 6 custard cups or ramekins and refrigerate until chilled and set, about 2 hours. Serve in cups or invert onto dessert plates.

Lemon Mousse-Custard

The pale color gives no hint as to its intense, rich, wondrous, luscious, creamy lemoniness. Better than lemon curd, better than lemon meringue pie filling—one of my four or five very favorite recipes developed for this book. Start squeezing those fresh lemons now.

The tofu adds creaminess, and there's a bit more cashew butter than I use in most of these mousse-custards, to give the tart-taming mellow richness that eggs typically impart. But the final result defies the ingredients: You just can't believe how good this is. **SERVES 8**

¾ cup fresh-squeezed lemon juice
3 tablespoons cornstarch
2 teaspoons agar powder (see page 127)
1¾ cups plus 2 tablespoons sugar
1¾ cups water, preferably spring or filtered
1 package (10½ ounces) silken tofu
1 tablespoon plus 2 teaspoons grated lemon rind
3 tablespoons raw cashew butter
8 paper-thin slices of lemon, 8 raspberries (optional), 8 mint leaves (optional)

1 Place ½ cup of the lemon juice in a small bowl. Whisk in the cornstarch and the agar and let stand for 2 minutes.

2 Combine the remaining juice with the sugar and water in a medium saucepan over high heat. Bring to a boil and add the cornstarch-agar mixture. It should turn cloudy as you add it, then almost immediately become clear and thick. Turn down the heat to medium-low, and simmer, stirring, for 1 minute. Remove from the heat.

3 Place the tofu, lemon rind, and cashew butter in a processor. Begin buzzing to make a thick, smooth mixture, pausing to scrape down the sides of the bowl. Add the thickened lemon juice mixture and buzz to combine.

4 Pour the mousse into 8 custard cups or ramekins and refrigerate until chilled and set, about 2 hours. You may invert the mousses onto dessert plates, or serve them in their cups. If desired, garnish each serving with a lemon slice, raspberry, and mint leaf.

Pineapple Coconut Mousse-Custard

Serve this with a nice, crisp, gingery cookie following a dinner of Caribbean or Indian or South American food. **SERVES 8**

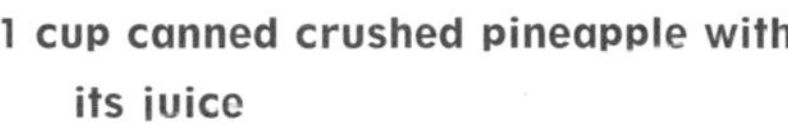

1 cup canned crushed pineapple with its juice
Cooking spray
3 tablespoons cornstarch
2 teaspoons agar powder (see page 127)
1 cup plus 2 tablespoons sugar
1 can (14 ounces) reduced-fat coconut milk
1 package (10½ ounces) silken tofu
3 tablespoons dark rum
1 tablespoon raw cashew butter

1 Puree the pineapple with its juice in a food processor. You should have about ¾ cup puree.

2 Spray 8 custard cups or ramekins with cooking spray. Set aside.

3 Place ½ cup of the pineapple puree in a small bowl and whisk in the cornstarch and agar. Let stand for 2 minutes.

4 Combine the remaining puree with the sugar and coconut milk in a small saucepan over medium-high heat. Bring to a boil and add the cornstarch-agar mixture. It should almost immediately become clear and thick. Lower the heat to medium-low and simmer, stirring, for 1 minute. Remove from the heat.

5 To the food processor, add the tofu, rum, and cashew butter. Buzz to make a thick, smooth mixture, pausing to scrape down the sides of the bowl. Add the coconut milk mixture to the food processor and buzz until smooth.

6 Pour the mousse into the prepared custard cups or ramekins and refrigerate until chilled and set, about 2 hours. Serve in the cups or ramekins, or inverted onto dessert plates.

NOTE

Fresh pineapple won't work in this recipe for two reasons. First, you need the juice that the canned pineapple is packed in, and second, the enzymes of raw, fresh pineapple prevent the agar from setting.

Coconut Crème Caramel Mousse-Custard

VARIATION

CAFÉ CON LECHE MOUSSE CUSTARD: ***Omit the coconut milk, substituting an equal amount of soy milk. Substitute a concentrate of 1 tablespoon instant coffee or decaf crystals, dissolved in 2 tablespoons boiling water, for the rum.***

It is possible to have an egg-free, dairy-free flan/crème caramel that is truly luscious, thanks to the richness of coconut milk. I keep the custard low fat, but the caramel is made in the classic way.

Please note: To get these to invert with all the caramel sauce intact, you *must* make them in advance. Let the finished mousse-custards sit in their ramekins in the refrigerator for at least 24 hours, preferably 48, before serving. **SERVES 8**

1⅔ cups sugar
⅓ cup cold water, preferably spring or filtered
¾ milk, low-fat dairy or soy
3 tablespoons cornstarch
1½ teaspoons agar powder (see page 127)
1 can (14 ounces) reduced-fat unsweetened coconut milk
1 package (10½ ounces) silken tofu
3 teaspoons pure vanilla extract
2 tablespoons dark rum
Dash of salt

1 Combine 1 cup of the sugar and the water in a heavy saucepan or skillet over medium heat, wiping down the sides of the pan with a wet pastry brush to avoid the formation of sugar crystals, and cook until the syrup is at a full boil. Boil, without stirring, until the syrup is a medium-dark golden/amber color, 8 to 10 minutes. Have ready a larger pan (or sink) with an inch or two of cold water. At the moment the sugar syrup reaches perfect caramelization, immediately place the pan in the cold water, so that the bottom is immersed, to stop the cooking. Count to 10, remove the pan from the water, and carefully pour the caramel into 8 custard cups or ramekins, swirling and tilting each cup to cover the bottom with caramel. Set aside.

2 Place ½ cup of the milk in a small bowl. Whisk in the cornstarch and the agar. Let stand for 2 minutes.

3 Combine the remaining milk and the remaining sugar with the coconut milk in a small saucepan over medium heat. Bring to a boil and add the cornstarch-agar mixture. It should then almost immediately become clear and thick. Lower the heat to medium-low and simmer, stirring, for 1 minute. Remove from the heat.

4 Place the tofu, vanilla, rum, cashew butter, and salt in a food processor. Buzz to make a thick, smooth mixture, pausing to scrape down the sides of the bowl. Pour the cooked coconut milk mixture into the food

processor and buzz until smooth, pausing to scrape the sides of the bowl.

5 Pour the mousse over the caramel in the 8 custard cups or ramekins and refrigerate until well chilled and the caramel has softened. To get the full, caramel-dripping effect, leave the custards in the refrigerator long enough for the caramel to soften, at least 24 (preferably 48) hours.

6 When ready to serve, run a knife around the edge of the custards and invert them onto serving plates.

Pumpkin Mousse-Custard

This is a lovely autumnal dessert. If you are willing to forgo pie for Thanksgiving, it's a great finish. **SERVES 8**

1½ tablespoons cornstarch
1 teaspoon agar powder (see page 127)
1¾ cup evaporated skim milk or soy milk, plain or vanilla
1 cup brown sugar or Rapidura (if using vanilla soy milk, use 2 tablespoons less sugar)
1 package (10½ ounces) silken tofu
2 tablespoons raw cashew butter
1 teaspoon vanilla
1 teaspoon ground cinnamon
5 gratings of nutmeg
1 cup canned unsweetened pumpkin
1 to 2 tablespoons diced crystallized ginger

1 Whisk the cornstarch and agar into ⅛ cup of the evaporated milk in a small bowl. Let stand for 2 minutes.

2 Combine the remaining evaporated milk with the brown sugar in a small saucepan over medium-high heat. Bring to a bowl and add the cornstarch-agar mixture. The milk should turn cloudy as you do this, then almost immediately become clear and thick. Lower the heat to medium-low and let simmer, stirring, for 1 minute. Remove from heat.

3 Put the tofu, cashew butter, vanilla, cinnamon, and nutmeg in a food processor and puree. Add the pumpkin. Buzz to make a thick, smooth mixture, pausing to scrape down the sides of the bowl. Add the milk mixture and buzz to blend. Add the ginger and pulse just to combine.

4 Pour the mousse into 8 custard cups or ramekins and refrigerate until chilled and set, about 1 hour. Serve chilled.

VARIATION

SAFFRON'D VEGAN CRÈME ANGLAISE: ***The color of Vegan Crème Anglaise is what diverges most decisively from the classic. Without all those golden egg yolks, the crème is white. Hence the development of this saffron variation. Saffron, the stamen of a special variety of crocus, is usually imported from Spain. It tints foods with a lovely golden hue and adds a delicate floral taste.***

Soak ½ teaspoon saffron threads with the cornstarch, agar, and milk called for in Step 1. Then continue the recipe as given. The golden color will not emerge in all fullness until after the sauce has been processed and refrigerated. Again, shake well before serving.

Vanilla-Bean Crème Anglaise, Vegan-Style

Custard desserts have always been among my favorites, for they combine sensuality with comfort. When my dear one-of-a-kind spouse said to me dreamily one night, "Ooooh, your skin feels just like vanilla custard!" I took it as the high praise he intended.

The recipe that follows is not traditional, but very good and a boon to those who are "dyslactic," vegan, or cholesterol-watching. Soothing, seductive, and sweet, it is, like regular crème anglaise, an excellent foil for spicy or fruity desserts. The texture is very close to that of an egg-rich crème anglaise, but, the flavor is different and quite delicious. **MAKES ABOUT 2½ CUPS**

2 teaspoons cornstarch
¼ teaspoon agar powder (see page 127)
2 cups soy milk
1 vanilla bean, split lengthwise
3 tablespoons white or brown sugar, or Rapidura, depending on your intended use
Pinch of salt
3 ounces silken tofu
1 tablespoon raw cashew butter

1 Combine the cornstarch and agar with ¼ cup of the soy milk in a small bowl. Let stand for 2 minutes.

2 Place the remaining soy milk in a small saucepan over medium heat. Add the vanilla bean, sugar, and salt and bring to a simmer. Add the cornstarch mixture to the soy milk. The soy milk should turn cloudy as you do this, then almost immediately become clear and thick. Lower the heat to medium-low and simmer, stirring, for 1 minute. Remove from the heat. Let cool slightly.

3 Lift the vanilla beans from the thickened milk, and scrape the seeds back into the soy milk mixture; discard the pods.

4 Place the tofu and cashew butter in a food processor, and pulse a few times. Add about ½ cup of the soy milk mixture. Buzz until thick and smooth, pausing to scrape down the sides of the bowl. Add the remaining soy milk mixture, and buzz to blend. When smooth, transfer the crème to a container with a lid. Cover and refrigerate until ready to serve. Shake well before serving.

Wild-Rice Pudding with Maple Syrup and Dried Cherries

Enamored of the wild rice–maple–cherry flavor combination, I had to try it in a pudding. See if you don't agree that rice pudding is reborn—delicious, and somehow both elegant and earthy; quite irresistible. It requires having cooked brown and wild rice on hand. **SERVES 4 TO 6**

Cooking spray
½ cup dried tart cherries
3 tablespoons sweet sherry
1½ cups cooked short-grain brown rice
1 cup cooked wild rice
1 quart (4 cups) milk
Pinch of salt
⅓ cup maple syrup, preferably dark
2 tablespoons brown sugar or Rapidura
1¼ teaspoons pure vanilla extract
⅓ cup heavy cream
¼ teaspoon or so freshly grated nutmeg, or ground cinnamon, preferably Saigon

1 Spray an 8-inch square glass baking dish with cooking spray.

2 Combine the dried cherries and sherry in a small bowl. Set aside to soak.

3 Combine the brown and wild rices with the milk and salt in a large, heavy nonstick pot. Bring to a boil, then immediately lower the heat to medium-low. Simmer, uncovered, stirring often, until the mixture thickens, about 30 minutes. Stir in the maple syrup and brown sugar. Continue simmering, stirring often, until the mixture is thick, another 15 to 20 minutes.

4 During the last 10 minutes of cooking time, preheat the oven to 350°F.

5 Remove the rice mixture from the heat. Stir in the vanilla and the cherries and sherry. Turn the rice into the prepared dish, smoothing the top. Carefully drizzle the cream over the rice, covering the top as much as possible, then dust with just a bit of the nutmeg or cinnamon, or a hint of both.

6 Bake until the top is browned and bubbly, 30 to 35 minutes. Remove it from the oven and let cool on a wire rack. Serve at just a bit warmer than room temperature. You can also refrigerate this dish for an hour or so to chill it slightly.

VARIATION

VEGAN VARIATION: ***Not a dead ringer for the original, but excellent in its own right. Follow the recipe, but substitute plain or vanilla soy milk or oat milk for the dairy milk. Omit the cream. Instead, buzz the following in a food processor: 1 box (12.3 ounces) reduced-fat firm silken tofu, 1 to 2 tablespoons raw cashew butter, 2 teaspoons cornstarch, ¼ cup Rapidura, and 1 teaspoon pure vanilla extract. Spread this mixture over the rice pudding once it's in the baking dish, and sprinkle lightly with the spices. Bake a bit longer, 40 to 50 minutes, or until the tofu custard topping is browned and firm.***

Sweet Polenta Pudding

Primitive and satisfying, somewhat in the line of a bread pudding, this is pure comfort. Though this is technically a dessert, I sometimes enjoy it as a wintertime supper. Have the leftovers with a dollop of vanilla yogurt, or warmed milk (dairy or soy) for breakfast. This dish finds its origins in a description in *The Splendid Table,* by Lynn Rosetto Kasper, who explains that a slow-baked polenta with milk was a one-dish supper for families in the Italian province of Emilia-Romagna. Her depiction of the layered dish (ricotta, raisins, walnuts or almonds, cinnamon, honey-drizzled, butter-dotted) was so lush I had to create a recipe! Here it is. **SERVES 6 TO 8**

Cooking spray
About ½ recipe polenta, any method (pages 441–46), "set up" and sliced into pieces about ¼ inch thick (but more or less is fine)
1 large egg
2 cups ricotta
2 tablespoons brown sugar
1 teaspoon pure vanilla extract
½ teaspoon cinnamon
⅓ to ½ cup honey
⅔ cup raisins
¼ cup chopped toasted walnuts
1 tablespoon butter

1 Preheat the oven to 300°F.

2 Spray a 9-by-13-inch baking dish with cooking spray. Fit half of the polenta slices together to make a thin layer on the bottom of the baking dish. It's okay if there are spaces between the polenta pieces.

3 Place the egg, ricotta, brown sugar, vanilla, and cinnamon in a food processor and process to blend. Spread this over the polenta layer, and drizzle the top with half of the honey. Sprinkle with the raisins and walnuts, then top with the remaining polenta. Cover with foil and bake for 1 hour.

4 Remove the dish from the oven. Raise the oven temperature to 400°F. Uncover the casserole. Drizzle the remaining honey on top of the dish. Dot with the butter. Return the dish to the oven and bake, uncovered, until bubbly and golden brown, 10 to 15 minutes. If after 15 minutes the top is not golden, run it under the broiler for a few seconds. Serve warm, or chilled the next day.

VARIATIONS

This is a happily adaptable recipe. Try these:

▲ Cook the polenta in milk instead of water.

▲ Add a layer of peeled, cored, thinly sliced apples (steam the apples for 2 minutes to soften slightly before adding them) on top of the ricotta layer.

▲ Substitute diced dried apricots or cherries for the raisins.

▲ Add grated nutmeg and a shot of brandy to the ricotta mixture.

SWEET POLENTA PUDDING, VEGAN-STYLE: ***Instead of the ricotta filling, buzz the following in a food processor: 1 package (10½ ounces) low-fat medium-firm silken tofu and 2 tablespoons raw cashews until smooth. Add 1 tablespoon cornstarch, a dash of salt, and the same amount of brown sugar, vanilla, and cinnamon as in the recipe. If you are cooking for vegans of the no-honey-eating school, substitute barley-malt syrup, maple syrup, or rice syrup. Substitute olive oil for the butter.***

Chocolate Bread Pudding Maurice

This is a special recipe on a number of scores. It is as rich as possible, a delicate, satiny-smooth, very chocolate-y custard in which small saturated pieces of bread—homemade is best—float, half-dissolved. The whole is set off to perfection by the tang and hue of raspberry sauce. This was frequently on the inn menu, and the recipe was requested whenever it was.

It is named for my late father, the irreplaceable, irrepressible Maurice Zolotow. He adored this dessert. When we made it at the inn, we used to serve it on a large plate, first writing "Maurice Z" in raspberry sauce on the plate, then scooping on the chocolate bread pudding in one corner. Waitstaff, buzzing in, would call, "I need two Maurices . . ." Adoring my father as I did, to hear his name in this fashion was a pleasure tinged with the sharp knowledge that all we love we must lose, that we are all here on loan—sweet and bitter as the chocolate.

This makes a huge pan's worth, so make it for a party. *And don't under any circumstances overbake it.* It should be quite wet when it comes out of the oven; it sets as it cools. A good bread is part of the allure. Homemade rolls or European-style unsweetened whole grain loaves work well. **SERVES 12 TO 18**

Cooking spray
2¾ cups large crumbs of good bread, sufficient to cover the pan ½ inch deep
2 cups heavy cream
1⅓ cups half-and-half or whole milk
5 ounces semi-sweet chocolate, coarsely chopped
5 ounces unsweetened chocolate, coarsely chopped
1⅔ cups sugar
5 large eggs
3 large egg yolks
1 tablespoon pure vanilla extract
Raspberry Sauce (page 1064)
Lightly sweetened whipped cream
Fresh fruit (strawberries, raspberries, kiwi fruit slices, star fruit slices, fresh orange twists), and mint leaves or sprigs

1 Spray an 11-by-14-by-2-inch pan with cooking spray. Spread the bread crumbs evenly over the bottom of the pan. You want a layer about ½ inch deep. Set aside.

2 Scald the cream and half-and-half in a heavy-bottom saucepan over medium heat. Add the chopped chocolates and whisk until the chocolate is melted. Remove from the heat.

3 Place the sugar, eggs, egg yolks, and vanilla in a food processor; buzz to blend. Add about half of the chocolate mixture and buzz until smooth and well combined. Whisk this mixture back into the saucepan until very well combined.

4 Pour the hot mixture over the bread crumbs. Let sit, covered, at room temperature for 1 hour.

5 Toward the end of the hour, preheat the oven to 325°F. Set the pan with the pudding in a larger pan of very hot water (read how to use a bain marie on page 275), and place it in the preheated oven. Bake until the top is dark and glossy, about 35 minutes. Do not overbake; it should be fairly liquidy—the first time you make it, you will be dubious that it'll set up. Remove the pans from the oven and let the pudding cool slowly, at room temperature, then refrigerate. It will set to the consistency of a soft, custardlike pudding as it cools; don't expect the bricklike masses you may have known in the past as bread puddings. This is scooped with a spoon, not cut in squares with a spatula.

6 To serve it the way we used to, use a dinner plate, not a dessert plate, with a plain white center. Write the name "Maurice Z" with Raspberry Sauce placed in a squeeze-bottle (or, ladle a little pool of Raspberry Sauce.) Scoop a serving of chocolate bread pudding—not too big, it's really rich—to the side. Top with a dollop (or pipe on) some whipped cream. Garnish with fresh fruit and a mint leaf.

Irrepressible Maurice

Maurice Zolotow, my father, looked a little like one of the comedians at the beginning of Broadway Danny Rose. *Although he was erudite and given to quoting from Proust, James Joyce, and T. S. Eliot, he was also wholly keyed into pop culture. He was Marilyn Monroe's first biographer, and a photograph of him with John Wayne (another of his subjects) and Ann-Margret is on my wall. At the time of his death he was working on a memoir called* Famous People Who Have Known Me. *He continually tore out and sent me clippings and magazine articles he felt I must read, immediately, relevant parts circled in red.*

But a different Maurice—calm, a little reverent, proud—came out when I fed him. He adored sweets, in particular this bread pudding. The first time I served it to him, he took off his glasses so he could peer at it closely (he was nearsighted). He inhaled it. He took a spoonful, closed his eyes. Swallowed. Opened his eyes. "Wow," he said (probably the sole one-word sentence he ever spoke to me). Another bite. Then, gazing up at me with his large pale blue eyes, he said, "Cres, on a scale of 1 to 10, I give this dessert a 5,000."

Sauces & Toppings

Cookies or sorbets are simple dress-ups for plain-Jane fruit desserts. Another option is something creamy.

"Something creamy" is classically whipped cream or custard. You know the pros and cons of real whipped cream. (Luscious but high in fat.) Custard, while it must contain at least one whole egg to be worthy of its name, is quite easily made in a reduced-fat and even nondairy version (see page 971) that is, to my taste, genuinely better than the traditional crème anglaise. Of course you could just use plain yogurt—but that's a bit humdrum and says "breakfast," not "dessert." Yogurt sour cream with a side of brown sugar, though? Now you're talking.

Here are three other dessert creams to dollop on top of or pass with all manner of fresh fruits. They are neither ascetically lean nor gratuitously high fat. Two are even nondairy.

Of course, the sauce world expands beyond the creamy. Fruit purees add sparkle and color, and the very best of these is raspberry. And where would the chorus line of sauces be without The Very Best Hot Fudge Sauce kicking up its heels?

Ricotta Crème

The most mainstream of these three creams, this is just as delicious as can be—something of a cross between cheesecake, whipped cream, and crème anglaise. Everyone loves it. It can be served instead of "pouring cream," and will never fail to satisfy. And it couldn't be easier, more agreeable, or less demanding.

MAKES ABOUT 1½ CUPS

1½ cups part-skim ricotta, the fresher the better
¼ cup Yogurt Sour Cream (page 910) or plain yogurt or reduced-fat sour cream
2 tablespoons neufchâtel reduced-fat cream cheese
1 teaspoon pure vanilla extract
2 tablespoons brown sugar
Pinch of ground cinnamon or freshly grated nutmeg (optional)

Combine all the ingredients in a food processor and process until smooth. Store, covered and refrigerated, for 2 to 3 days.

Tofu-Cashew Crème

If we had vegan guests staying at the inn for several days, one of their likely breakfasts would be an enormous plate of fresh and dried fruit and nuts, surrounding a glass cup of this creamy concoction. It can be used as topping or dip. Some vegans do not eat honey or sugar, and for them maple sugar or Rapidura are ideal choices. Or the added sweetener can be omitted and a couple of soft, pitted Medjool dates can be buzzed in. This is best made a few hours ahead of time, so the flavors have a chance to blend, but it's fine made on the spot. **MAKES ABOUT 1½ CUPS**

8 ounces conventional water-packed soft tofu (not firm, not silken)
2 tablespoons raw cashews
1 to 2 tablespoons maple sugar, Rapidura, brown sugar, or honey
1 teaspoon pure vanilla extract
Pinch of ground cinnamon and/or freshly grated nutmeg (optional)

Combine all of the ingredients in a food processor. Buzz until smooth, pausing to scrape down the sides of the bowl. Store, covered and refrigerated, for 2 to 3 days.

Maple-Vanilla Tofu Whipped Cream

This is a great, versatile mix for those who do not eat dairy or are watching their saturated-fat intake, used just about anywhere you'd use whipped cream. Where the previous tofu cream has a dip- or spreadlike texture, this is more like pudding.

1 box (10½ ounces) silken tofu, preferably reduced-fat
⅓ cup maple syrup
3 tablespoons cashew butter
2 teaspoons pure vanilla extract
2 teaspoons fresh-squeezed lemon juice
1 cup vanilla soy milk, such as Soy Silk
1 tablespoon plus 1 teaspoon cornstarch or arrowroot
½ teaspoon agar powder (see page 127)
Dash of salt

1 Combine the tofu, maple syrup, cashew butter, vanilla, and lemon juice in a food processor. Buzz, pausing to scrape down the sides of the bowl, until smooth.

2 Place ½ cup of the soy milk in a small bowl and add the cornstarch or arrowroot and agar. Smush to mix and let stand for 2 minutes.

3 Place the remaining ½ cup soy milk in a very small saucepan over high heat. Bring to a boil and quickly whisk in the soy milk–agar mixture. Whisk like crazy until very thick and clear. Immediately remove from the heat, and scrape into the tofu mixture. Buzz until smooth. Transfer to a bowl. Cover and refrigerate for at least 1 hour, until well chilled. This keeps, refrigerated, for 1 to 2 days.

The Very Best Hot Fudge Sauce

Use the best chocolate you can find. Of course, "best" is a personal matter. Valrhona is a classic, but I am awfully impressed by Scharffen Berger (www.scharffenberger.com), a California-based company, and Chocolove, a Belgian chocolate made from both African and Caribbean cocoa beans. Best of all may be Rapunzel, a delicious chocolate made from organic cocoa beans. It's found in both natural and specialty foods stores. Ideally, you want a chocolate with a 60 to 70 percent cacao content, whose only ingredients are cocoa liquor, sugar, cocoa butter, lecithin, and maybe vanilla.

Try hot fudge in the Tulipe Pralinée Baskets (page 975) when you make them with only a single fruit, like strawberries or raspberries. It's too dominant to let the

flavors of the individual berries shine through. But a good hot fudge belongs in most everyone's arsenal, in the very-occasional-treat file. **MAKES ABOUT 3 CUPS**

1 cup evaporated milk, Soy Silk, or, if you feel like going hog wild, light cream
4 ounces unsweetened chocolate, coarsely chopped
2 ounces semisweet chocolate, coarsely chopped
2 cups sugar
¼ cup corn syrup
2 tablespoons butter or Better (page 000)
¼ teaspoon salt
2½ teaspoons pure vanilla extract (or 2 tablespoons of your favorite liqueur, such as Frangelico, amaretto, or even crème de menthe or kirschwasser)

1 Combine the evaporated milk with the chocolates, sugar, corn syrup, butter, and salt in the top half of a double boiler set over simmering water. Cook, uncovered, giving an occasional stir, until the chocolates have melted. This should take about 5 minutes. Give the sauce a thorough stirring, and let it cook, undisturbed, until it has thickened slightly and is nice and smooth, about 10 minutes. Remove from the heat and let stand for 5 minutes. Stir in the vanilla.

2 You may serve the sauce hot from the pot; however, it's even better if you place it in a small, very clean container with a tight-fitting lid and let it meld in the refrigerator at least overnight. Reheat over hot water when ready to use. The sauce will keep, covered and refrigerated, up to 4 months—but only if you forget it's there.

VARIATION

NATURAL FOODS, DAIRY-FREE HOT FUDGE: ***Use Soy Silk instead of evaporated milk or cream; use Tropical Source or Rapunzel brand chocolate. Substitute Rapidura for sugar, and honey or rice syrup for corn syrup. Because Rapidura, honey, and rice syrup all have flavor, their use makes an interesting and unusual fudge sauce, with a bit of a floral and brown-sugary note.***

Raspberry Sauce

The simplest, prettiest, most flavorful zing for countless desserts, especially Chocoate Bread Pudding Maurice (page 1059), and cheese blintzes (page 335).

One bag (1 pound) frozen unsweetened raspberries, thawed
2 tablespoons sugar, or to taste

1 Puree the raspberries in a food processor. Push the berries through a strainer to remove any seeds. Add sugar to taste, whisking to combine the sugar and berries.

2 Using a funnel, pour the sauce into a 1½-cup plastic squeeze bottle, the type with a cone-shaped twist lid, the tip of which you've cut off, leaving a small opening through which you can pool the sauce, or write with it.

Thoughtful Vegetarian's Bookshelf

I write about vegetarian cuisine primarily as a passionate cook and eater. Others approach the field from the points of view of health, nutrition, environmentalism, and significant social and economic questions about how what is on our individual plates affects the health and well-being of our planet and all who dwell here. Hence this bookshelf. This list is a starting point. As you discover the cornucopia of plant-based foods and the transformational wonder of cooking them, you will doubtless be led to seek further.

Vegetarian Nutrition

THE NEW LAUREL'S KITCHEN: A HANDBOOK FOR VEGETARIAN COOKERY AND NUTRITION *by Laurel Robertson, Carol Flinders, Brian Ruppenthal (Ten Speed Press, 1986).* A classic. Stellar nutrition section. Components of a meatless diet (vitamins, minerals, proteins, etc.) are discussed individually, then integrated. Detailed tables are included. Well organized, thorough, it is wholesome, strict on limiting sweets, and excellently teaches the principles of satisfying, healthful vegetarian meal planning. Family oriented; less apropos for the time-pressed or single.

EATING WELL FOR OPTIMUM HEALTH: THE ESSENTIAL GUIDE TO BRINGING HEALTH AND PLEASURE BACK TO EATING *by Dr. Andrew Weil (Quill, 2001).* Semivegetarian (it includes fish), this clear, thoughtful, holistic book is from the director of the Program in Integrative Medicine at the University of Arizona. Weil understands that eating should be pleasurable, healthful, sociable, and that food choices are part of one's identity. Besides nutrition, he tackles organics, phytochemicals, and weight loss, and offers a comprehensive appendix with dietary recommendations for dozens of specific health problems, all in a tone that's clear, well reasoned, good-humored. On the web at:
www.drweil.com.

BEING VEGETARIAN FOR DUMMIES *by Suzanne Havala (Wiley, 2001).* One of the best new books on meatless nutrition, filled with information not only about home cooking, but also transitional diets, food choices at restaurants or while traveling, handling holidays, etc. The solid, well-organized content has a lighthearted, easy-to-understand spin, Dummies-style. Suzanne Havala, a registered dietician and vegetarian herself, knows her stuff and is wholly sympathetic to the new or semi-vegetarian.

LOMA LINDA VEGETARIAN HEALTH & NUTRITION NEWSLETTER. Helpful, up-to-the-minute nutritional news. Editor Patricia Johnston, Ph.D., is dean of the School of Public Health at Loma Linda University and a professor of nutrition; senior editors Mark and Virginia Messina, both Ph.D.s, are renowned authorities on soyfoods; he is a former program director in the Diet and Cancer Branch of the National Cancer Institute. Subscribe or check out recent articles on the web at:
www.llu.edu/llu/vegetarian/

DR. DEAN ORNISH'S PROGRAM FOR REVERSING HEART DISEASE: THE ONLY SYSTEM SCIENTIFICALLY PROVEN TO REVERSE HEART DISEASE WITHOUT DRUGS OR SURGERY *(Random House, 1990).* Holistic, both solidly scientific and heartfelt, Dean Ornish's approach offers a very low-fat vegetarian diet as a means of literally reversing heart disease. The book is compelling and well written, and I particularly like that he talks about factors beyond the strictly dietary–like "opening your heart" (to your own feelings, to other people, to your higher self).

Environment, Economics, Ethics

MAD COWBOY: PLAIN TRUTH FROM THE CATTLE RANCHER WHO WON'T EAT MEAT *by Howard F. Lyman with Glen Merzer (Scribners, 1998).* A fourth-generation dairy farmer and cattle rancher who grew up on a dairy farm in Montana, Lyman ran a feedlot operation for twenty years. His close-up overview of present-day cattle-raising practices and their effects on both individual and environmental health is harrowing: His epiphany and subsequent vegetarianism seem inevitable. This book was excerpted by Self magazine. On the web at: www.madcowboy.com

The Food Revolution: How Your Diet Can Help Save Your Life and Our World *by John Robbins, with an introduction by Dean Ornish, M.D. (Conari, 2001).* The author, an ex–Baskin-Robbins heir, makes many of the same cases that *Diet for a Small Planet* does, with an evangelism some find passionate and others a turn-off. He discusses how what's on your plate impacts environmental issues (like global warming), world hunger, individual health, animal rights, and genetically modified foods. As with *Fast Food Nation,* you may learn some details you'd rather not have known about factory-farming practices, hormone and antibiotic use in animal feed, etc. Robbins does conclude with a call for hope, and the book is well written, if at times strident and sentimental.

Diet for a Small Planet *(20th Anniversary Edition) by Frances Moore Lappé and Anna Lappé (Ballantine, 1992).* For many people, this book began it all, connecting the dots between meat-filled plates and a hungry world. It revolutionized vegetarian thinking by pointing out that protein is "shrunk" when twenty-plus pounds of feed that could be eaten directly by humans is, instead, eaten by livestock to yield adressed weight of a pound of animal flesh. On the web at: www.dietforasmallplanet.com

Hope's Edge: The Next Diet for a Small Planet *by Frances Moore Lappé and Anna Lappé (J. P. Tarcher, 2002).* Published thirty years after the original (above), this expands on its tenets, looking at new concerns, including genetically engineered foods and obesity-related health issues. The mother-daughter team offers hope, showing how individual food choices affect the world's economy and environment as well as personal health. Also included: profiles of food producers and others committed to sustainable agriculture, eco-friendly social change, and ending world hunger. On the web at: www.dietforasmallplanet.com

Fast Food Nation: The Dark Side of the All-American Meal *by Eric Schlosser (Houghton Mifflin, 2001).* Schlosser, a journalist, wrote this bestselling exposé of the many-tentacled monster fast food chains created by bringing assembly-line principles to commercial kitchens. He shows how such practices devastate diet and health, environment, economy, workforce, even education and school systems. Schlosser's investigative work is brave, readable, horrifying, and superbly well researched.

Goodbye, and Hello

My life (culinary, literary, teaching, and otherwise) is, like all human lives, a work in progress. Mine is at the moment perhaps more transitional than usual, due to the events I referred to in the introduction: Ned's death truly shifted the tectonic plates of my world. If you'd like to keep up with me, please visit my web site, www.dragonwagon.com.

And if you have questions about this book, or would like more recipes as I develop them, or would like to share favorites of your own, please come on over to www.passionatevegetarian.com.

One of Ned's and my last cocreative acts was founding the Writers' Colony at Dairy Hollow (www.writerscolony.org) at the site of what had been our inn, Dairy Hollow House. Although I am no longer associated day-to-day with the colony—it is run by a board of directors and staff—I encourage writers and readers to make contact with this generous-spirited nonprofit organization, which nurtures the fundamental processes of creativity.

Thank you for being part of this book and, though I may not know you, part of my life. We are all so different, and so utterly alike: Do we need further introduction in this world of famine and feast, loss and love, courage, the struggle for self-mastery, and tiny, irrational, vital hope? I think not. I think we have already met.

Respectfully,

Crescent Dragonwagon

Index

"Bacon," smoked tempeh, 640

C

F

G

M

P

Sabbath suppers, 221

T

U

V

W